HANDBOOK OF RESEARCH METHODS IN SOCIAL AND PERSONALITY PSYCHOLOGY

This indispensable sourcebook covers conceptual and practical issues in research design, methods of research, and statistical approaches in social and personality psychology. The chapters provide state-of-the-art treatment of various methods, written by key experts in the field.

The primary purpose of the Handbook is to provide readable yet comprehensive chapters on the full range of methods and tools used by researchers in social and personality psychology. In addition, it will alert researchers to methodological possibilities they may not have thought of. Innovative research methods work best when they allow researchers to ask theoretically driven questions that could not have been asked previously, thereby enhancing the quality and depth of their empirical knowledge base.

With the help of this comprehensive text, both new and established social psychologists will learn about appropriate uses of each method and the opportunities they provide for expanding knowledge. The *Handbook of Research Methods in Social and Personality Psychology* will be invaluable to graduate students and established researchers alike.

Harry T. Reis is Professor of Psychology in the Department of Clinical and Social Sciences, University of Rochester. He is author of *Interpersonal Influence* (with Wheeler, Deci, and Zuckerman) and editor of *Naturalistic Approaches to Studying Social Interaction*.

Charles M. Judd is Professor of Psychology at the University of Colorado at Boulder. He is author of *Data Analysis: A Model Comparison Approach* (with McClelland) and *Research Methods in Social Relations* (with Smith and Kidder).

HANDBOOK OF RESEARCH METHODS IN SOCIAL AND PERSONALITY PSYCHOLOGY

Edited by

HARRY T. REIS
University of Rochester

CHARLES M. JUDD
University of Colorado at Boulder

CAMBRIDGE
UNIVERSITY PRESS

PUBLISHED BY THE PRESS SYNDICATE OF THE UNIVERSITY OF CAMBRIDGE
The Pitt Building, Trumpington Street, Cambridge, United Kingdom

CAMBRIDGE UNIVERSITY PRESS
The Edinburgh Building, Cambridge CB2 2RU, UK   http://www.cup.cam.ac.uk
40 West 20th Street, New York, NY 10011-4211, USA   http://www.cup.org
10 Stamford Road, Oakleigh, Melbourne 3166, Australia
Ruiz de Alarcón 13, 28014 Madrid, Spain

© Cambridge University Press 2000

First published 2000

Printed in the United States of America

Typeface Meridien 9.25/11.5 pt.   *System* LaTeX 2_ε [TB]

A catalog record for this book is available from the British Library.

Library of Congress Cataloging in Publication Data
Handbook of research methods in social and personality psychology /
   edited by Harry T. Reis, Charles M. Judd.
          p.   cm.
   ISBN 0-521-55128-5
      1. Social psychology–Research–Methodology.   2. Personality–
Research–Methodology.   I. Reis, Harry T.   II. Judd, Charles M.
   HM1019.H36   2000
   302′.07′2 – dc21   99-16937
                                                                          CIP

ISBN 0 521 55128 5 hardback
ISBN 0 521 55903 0 paperback

This Handbook is dedicated to three individuals who have had a profound effect on research methods and data analysis in social and personality psychology:

Robert Abelson
Donald Campbell
Jacob Cohen

For showing us how to do research properly and why it matters.

Contents

Contributors

Joel Aronoff, Department of Psychology, Michigan State University

Roger Bakeman, Department of Psychology, Georgia State University

John A. Bargh, Department of Psychology, New York University

Kim Bartholomew, Department of Psychology, Simon Fraser University

Victoria Benet-Martinez, Department of Psychology, University of Michigan

Jeremy C. Biesanz, Center for Developmental Science, University of North Carolina

Jim Blascovich, Department of Psychology, University of California, Santa Barbara

Marilynn B. Brewer, Department of Psychology, Ohio State University

Tanya L. Chartrand, Department of Psychology, Ohio State University

Linda M. Collins, The Methodology Center and Department of Human Development and Family Studies, Pennsylvania State University

Alice H. Eagly, Department of Psychology, Northwestern University

Leandre R. Fabrigar, Department of Psychology, Queen's University

Shelly L. Gable, Department of Clinical and Social Sciences in Psychology, University of Rochester

Reid Hastie, Department of Psychology, University of Colorado at Boulder

Antonia J. Z. Henderson, Department of Psychology, Simon Fraser University

Oliver P. John, Department of Psychology, University of California, Berkeley

Blair T. Johnson, Department of Psychology, University of Connecticut

Charles M. Judd, Department of Psychology, University of Colorado at Boulder

Deborah A. Kashy, Department of Psychology, Texas A&M University

David A. Kenny, Department of Psychology, University of Connecticut

Norbert L. Kerr, Department of Psychology, Michigan State University

Jon A. Krosnick, Department of Psychology, Ohio State University

Paul J. Lavrikas, Department of Journalism and Communication, Ohio State University

James E. Marcia, Department of Psychology, Simon Fraser University

Gary H. McClelland, Department of Psychology, University of Colorado at Boulder

Lawrence A. Messé, Department of Psychology, Michigan State University

Steven C. Pitts, Department of Psychology, Arizona State University

Harry T. Reis, Department of Clinical and Social Sciences in Psychology, University of Rochester

Aline G. Sayer, The Methodology Center and Department of Human Development and Family Studies, Pennsylvania State University

Charles P. Smith, Department of Psychology, City University of New York, Graduate School

Eliot R. Smith, Department of Psychology, Purdue University

Garold Stasser, Department of Psychology, Miami University

Penny S. Visser, Department of Psychology, Princeton University

Duane T. Wegener, Department of Psychology, Purdue University

Stephen G. West, Department of Psychology, Arizona State University

Introduction

HARRY T. REIS AND CHARLES M. JUDD

It is no accident, we believe, that many of the most influential methodologists in the behavioral sciences happen to identify themselves as social–personality psychologists. Throughout the methodological literature in psychology, citations to Robert Abelson, Donald Campbell, Thomas Cook, Donald Fiske, David Kenny, and Robert Rosenthal, to name just a few, are ubiquitous. The reason we believe that this is not an accident is that social–personality psychologists have set for themselves a particularly challenging methodological task. Their domain of inquiry concerns all of social behavior, from intergroup relations and large-scale social conflict to dyadic interaction and close relationships. They study individual judgments, cognitions, and affects about social phenomena as well as the evolution of social norms and interdependent behaviors at the level of societies. Most recently, entire cultures, and the belief systems associated with them, have become a major area of interest. And, in the tradition of Kurt Lewin, social–personality psychologists are firmly committed to a rigorous empirical approach to whatever they study. They are convinced that a strong and reciprocal relationship between theory and evidence is fundamental to the acquisition of knowledge: that data demand good theories and that theories demand quality data.

As a result, social–personality psychologists have developed and made use of an extensive array of methodological tools. Although the field is sometimes criticized for an overreliance on laboratory experimentation, in fact the diversity of methodological approaches represented in the leading journals is impressive. From surveys to simulations, from laboratory experiments to daily event recordings, from response latency and physiological measures to think-aloud protocols, and from the internet and palmtop computers to paper-and-pencil reports, the diversity of research designs and procedures, measurement methods, and analytic strategies that social psychologists employ is, in our view, extraordinary.

Our goal in putting together this Handbook was to provide a series of state-of-the-art presentations spanning both traditional and innovative methods that have moved and continue to move the discipline forward. The product, we believe, documents the incredible wealth of methodological tools that social–personality psychologists have at their disposal. Intentionally, we sought to include chapters that might strike some readers as a bit unusual in a book devoted to research methods. Certainly, some of these topics would not have been included in a book of this sort 20, or perhaps even 10, years ago. So, for example, chapters by Hastie and Stasser on simulation, Collins on studying growth and change, McClelland on transformations and outliers, Bargh and Chartrand on cognitive mediation, Reis and Gable on daily experience methods, and Blascovich on psychophysiological measures are a far cry from the traditional chapters on design, measurement, and analysis that one might routinely expect in a research methods textbook. Several statistics chapters are included because we believe that new developments in statistical methodology make it possible to extract valuable insights about social psychological phenomena from data collected with diverse methods in many different settings.

But then, it was not our goal to provide yet another research methods textbook cataloguing standard procedures and principles. Many excellent textbooks serving this function are already available. Although this Handbook might well be used as a textbook, our goal was more ambitious than teaching the field's traditional core. Rather, we sought to demonstrate and highlight the tremendous methodological richness and innovativeness to be found in social psychological research, and additionally, to provide social–personality psychologists with resources for expanding the methodological diversity employed in their research.

Such innovation is central to the legacy we have inherited from the field's founders. Social–personality psychologists value their reputation as both rigorous and clever methodologists; indeed, among the behavioral sciences, social psychologists are notorious for their exacting methodological standards and for the pinpoint precision with which the fit of evidence to theory is scrutinized. These practices reflect two considerations: the growth of a cumulative literature, which allows researchers to ask ever-finer questions about phenomena and their mediators and moderators, and the availability of new technologies capable of providing information not even imagined a generation or two ago. For example, researchers rarely investigated questions of mediation in the 1960s. With the advent of computerized tests of cognitive mediation, sophisticated measures of physiological mediation, and covariance structure methods for evaluating mediational models, these questions have become commonplace. A guiding principle in preparing this volume was that theoretical and methodological questions are not independent. Theory leads us to choose and extend existing methods and search for new tools; methods get us thinking about new ways to test and refine our constructs.

One of Donald Campbell's seminal and lasting contributions is the notion that validity is achieved only through triangulation, by using a variety of methodological approaches and procedures. In its original formulation, this argument primarily addressed the validity and reliability of measurement: through multiple diverse indicators one could eliminate both random and systematic measurement errors and arrive at more accurate appraisals of underlying constructs (e.g., Campbell & Fiske, 1959). We, as researchers, were taught that such a multifaceted measurement approach ought to be employed in each and every study that we conducted.

The discipline is coming to realize that this sort of triangulation is fundamental not simply in measurement but in all aspects of methodology. In this sense, then, it is fitting that the first chapter in this Handbook, by one of Donald Cambell's students, Marilynn Brewer, sets the tone for the entire volume. Brewer argues that only through the use of multifaceted research strategies, adopted not only within individual studies but also, and much more important, across an entire program of research, that research validity in its broadest sense is achieved. All the diversity that is represented in this volume, and the diversity of methods and approaches yet to be developed, is essential if social–personality research is to produce valid findings, defining validity in its most comprehensive sense: that our conclusions and theories ultimately provide accurate understandings of the social world that we inhabit.

Putting together this volume has inspired in us great pride in social–personality psychology's commitment to methodological rigor and innovation, as well as in the methodological richness of contemporary social psychology. Our hope is that this volume will similarly inspire both new and established researchers alike to broaden and enhance their methodological practices. Additionally, we hope the volume will serve as a stimulus for yet unknown approaches and procedures that further contribute to the validity of the research we conduct. Our legacy as social–personality psychologists mandates that we continue to capitalize on methodological and technological innovations in the service of evermore informative and useful theories and knowledge.

REFERENCE

Campbell, D. T., & Fiske, D. W. (1959). Convergent and discriminant validation by the multitrait-multimethod matrix. *Psychological Bulletin, 56*, 81–105.

PART ONE

DESIGN AND INFERENCE CONSIDERATIONS

CHAPTER ONE

Research Design and Issues of Validity

MARILYNN B. BREWER

Validity refers to "the best available approximation to the truth or falsity of *propositions*" (Cook & Campbell, 1979, p. 37; italics added). In this sense, we cannot speak of the validity or invalidity of research per se. Rather, it is the statements, inferences, or conclusions we wish to draw from the results of empirical research that can be subject to validation. Of course, the way that a research study is designed and conducted has a great deal to do with the validity of the conclusions that can be drawn from the results, but validity must be evaluated in light of the *purposes* for which the research was undertaken in the first place.

RESEARCH PURPOSE AND TYPES OF VALIDITY

There are any number of ways in which the various objectives of research can be classified, but for present purposes the goals of empirical research in social psychology can be differentiated into three broad categories: demonstration, causation, and explanation.

Research undertaken for the purpose of *demonstration* is conducted in order to establish empirically the existence of a phenomenon or relationship. Much demonstration research is intended to be descriptive of the state of the world, including the frequency of occurrence of specified events across time or space (e.g., distribution of forms of cancer, variations in crime rates, probability of intervention in emergency situations, participation in collective demonstrations, etc.) and the assessment of the degree of relationship between specified states or conditions (e.g., the correlation between cigarette smoking and lung cancer, the relationship between ambient temperature and violent crime, the correlation between economic prosperity and collective protest, etc.). Although most descriptive research is conducted in field settings with the purpose of assessing phenomena as they occur "naturally," some demonstration studies are also undertaken in the controlled setting of the psychological laboratory. Studies of gender differences or personality types are often conducted in lab settings. Further, many of the classic studies in social psychological research – including Sherif's (1935) studies of formation of arbitrary group norms, Asch's (1956) original conformity studies, Milgram's (1963) study of obedience to authority, and Tajfel's (1970) initial studies of ingroup favoritism – were essentially demonstrations of social psychological phenomena in the laboratory.

Although establishing that the presence or absence of one event is correlated with the presence or absence of another is often of interest in its own right, most of the time scientists are interested in whether such covariation reflects a causal relationship between the two events. Thus, much research is undertaken not simply to demonstrate that a relationship exists but to establish a cause–effect linkage between specific variables (i.e., testing linkages of the form, if X then Y). For this purpose we are using the concept of causation in the utilitarian sense (Collingwood, 1940; Cook & Campbell, 1979; Gasking, 1955; Mackie, 1974). In this sense, the search for cause–effect relationships is for the purpose of identifying agents that can be controlled or manipulated in order to bring about changes in outcome. In other words, research on causation (cf. West, Biesanz, & Pitts, this volume, Ch. 3) is intended to demonstrate that interventions that produce change in one state of the world will produce subsequent changes in the outcome of interest. For this purpose, the goal of research is to establish causal connections, not to explain how or why they occur (Cook & Shadish, 1994).

When research has the purpose of establishing causal relationships in this sense, the purported causal factor is generally referred to as the "independent variable" and the outcome or effect as the "dependent variable." In fact, the use of these terms in describing a study is effectively a statement of purpose. However, there are important differences across types of research in the meaning of "independent variable" – differences that have to do with how variation in the purported causal variable is produced. When the state of the independent variable is manipulated by interventions under the control of the researcher, we have research that can be defined as an experiment or "quasi-experiment" (Campbell & Stanley, 1963, 1966). In correlational field studies, by contrast, the so-called "independent variable" is not manipulated or controlled but instead variations are assessed as they occur naturally for purposes of establishing the relationship between such variations and subsequent variations in the outcome variable of interest. In such cases, causal inference is usually predicated on temporal precedence, establishing that variations in the purported cause precede variations in the purported effect. Such temporal precedence is a necessary but not sufficient basis for inferring causation. In studies of this type, the independent variable(s) might better be labeled "predictor" variables. As we shall see, the validity of causal inferences can be significantly influenced by differences in how the independent variable is defined and varied.

As a goal of research, utilitarian causation is sufficient for most applied and action research purposes. Knowing that a reliable cause–effect relationship between X and Y exists is a critical step in designing interventions that can bring about desired changes in the outcome, Y. For utilitarian purposes, what "works" is what counts, irrespective of why it works. For basic, theory-testing research purposes, however, knowing that a cause–effect relationship exists is not sufficient. The purpose of this type of research is *explanation*, or establishing the intervening processes that mediate the linkage between variations in X and Y. This reflects the "essentialist" conceptualization of causation to which most scholars now subscribe (Cook & Campbell, 1979). Research undertaken for the purpose of explanation has the goal of determining not only whether causation exists but why and under what conditions.

Although there are many legitimate questions about validity that can be raised in connection with conclusions drawn from demonstration research, the fact is that most of the controversies that arise over validity issues in the social psychological literature revolve around inferences about causation and explanation. It was specifically in connection with research intended to establish cause–effect relationships that Campbell introduced the now-classic distinction between internal validity and external validity (Campbell, 1957; Campbell & Stanley, 1963, 1966).

Internal validity, in Campbell's terms, refers to the truth value that can be assigned to the conclusion that a cause–effect relationship between an independent variable and a dependent variable has been established within the context of the particular research setting. The question here is whether changes in the dependent measure were produced by variations in the independent variable (manipulation, in the case of an experiment) in the sense that the change would not have occurred without that variation. *External validity*, in Campbell's original terminology, referred to the generalizability of the causal finding, that is, whether it can be concluded that the same cause–effect relationship would be obtained across different subjects, settings, and methods.

In a later elaboration of validity theory, Cook and Campbell (1979) differentiated the concept of external validity further. The term *construct validity* was introduced to refer to the extent to which a causal relationship could be generalized from the particular methods and operations of a specific study to the theoretical constructs and processes they were meant to represent. The term external validity was reserved to refer to the generalizability of findings to target populations of persons and settings. It is this tripartite distinction – internal, external, and construct validity – that will provide the basis for organizing the discussion of validity issues in the remainder of this chapter.

INTERNAL VALIDITY: THE THIRD VARIABLE PROBLEM

As stated above, the essence of internal validity is establishing that variation in an effect (dependent variable) has been produced by changes in level or intensity of the independent variable and not by some other causal force (or forces).[1] In notational form, we are interested in the proposition:

$$X \rightarrow Y.$$

Threats to the validity of this proposition come from any plausible claim that the obtained variations in the outcome variable (Y) were actually produced by some third factor which happened to be correlated with the

---

[1] This does not mean that the independent variable under investigation is assumed to be the only cause of the outcome, but rather that this variable has a causal influence independent of any other causal forces.

variations in level of X. Again in notational terms, the alternative proposition is

$$C \rightarrow Y$$
$$\updownarrow$$
$$X.$$

In this case, the relationship between X and C (the "hidden" third factor) is not a causal one. However, because X and C are correlated, causes of the variation in Y could be misattributed to X when they were actually produced by C. This pattern is referred to as a *spurious* correlation between X and Y.

It is this third-variable causation pattern that is, in part, responsible for the well-known dictum that "correlation does not prove causation." Two variables can be correlated with each other because both are correlates of a third factor, even when there is no direct or indirect causal relationship between the first two. Consider, for example, the results of a hypothetical study of weather conditions and psychological mood. Let's say that the researcher finds that the incidence of depression and suicide is greater on rainy days than on sunny days. Before we could conclude from this relationship that rain causes depression we would have to take into account the fact that there are a number of other weather-related factors that are correlated with the presence or absence of rain – including atmospheric pressure and gray skies – any of which could plausibly be the true causal factor. In this case, the conclusion that rain causes depressed mood would have low internal validity in that we cannot assign it a high truth value with any confidence.

In social psychological research, many potentially problematic "third variables" are those associated with self-selection. If a researcher is concerned with the effects of some environmental variable or treatment (such as interracial contact or presentation of a persuasive message), causal inference is undermined if exposure to different levels of the treatment variable is correlated with differences among people in personality or aptitudes. If persons choose for themselves what experiences they will be exposed to, there may be a relationship between the experience (treatment) and the outcome variable (e.g., persons who engage in intergroup contact are less prejudiced; individuals who listen to a Democratic campaign speech are more likely to vote Democratic). However, we cannot tell whether the outcome was influenced by the treatment or whether it would have occurred because of the correlated individual differences even in the absence of the treatment experience.

Hidden causes are not the only way that unintended third variables can influence the validity of cause–effect inferences. Sometimes causal relationships can be either augmented or blocked by the presence or absence of factors that serve as *moderator variables* (Baron & Kenny, 1986). To take another weather-related illustration, consider the causal relationship between exposure to sun and sunburn. Although there is a well-established cause–effect link here, it can be moderated by a number of factors. For instance, the relationship is much stronger for fair-skinned individuals than for dark-skinned persons. Thus, fair skin is a moderator variable that enhances the causal relationship between sun exposure and burning. However, this does not mean that the sun–sunburn relationship is spurious. The moderator variable (skin pigmentation) does not cause the effect in the absence of the independent variable (sun exposure).

Other moderator variables can reduce or block a causal sequence. For instance, the use of effective suntan lotions literally "blocks" (or at least retards) the causal link between the sun's ultraviolet rays and burning. Thus, a researcher who assesses the correlation between sun exposure and sunburn among a sample of fair-skinned people who never venture outdoors without a thick coat of 30 SPF sunblock would be ill-advised to conclude that the absence of correlation implied the absence of causation.

Like Baron and Kenny (1986), I think it is important here to distinguish between third variables that serve as *moderators* (as the illustration above) and those that serve as *mediators* of a cause–effect relationship (cf. Judd, this volume, Ch. 14). Moderator relationships can be represented notationally as follows:

$$C$$
$$\downarrow$$
$$X \rightarrow Y.$$

The causal link is actually between X and Y, but the observed relationship between these two variables is qualified by levels of variable C, which either enhances or blocks the causal process.

A mediational relation, on the other hand, is represented as follows:

$$X \rightarrow C \rightarrow Y.$$

In this case, the presence of C is necessary to complete the causal process that links X and Y. In effect, varying X causes variations in C, which in turn causes changes in Y. To return to our weather example, the effect of rain on depression may be mediated by social factors. Rain causes people to stay indoors or to hide behind big umbrellas, hence reducing social contact. Social isolation may, in turn, produce depression. However, rain may not be the only cause of social isolation. In this case, rain as an independent variable is a sufficient, but not necessary, cause in its link to depression. To demonstrate that X causes Y only if C occurs does not invalidate the claim that X and Y have a causal relationship; it only explicates the causal chain involved.

In order to establish unequivocally the causal relationship between two variables, variation in the causal factor has to be produced or observed under conditions that are isolated from third factors that may produce a spurious correlation. These third variables must be either held constant or uncorrelated with variations in X. This is the essence of the logic of good experimental design. In addition to control over variation in the independent variable, random assignment of subjects to different levels of the manipulated factor serves to rule out many potential third-variable threats to causal inference. Without random assignment, manipulating the independent variable is not sufficient to achieve the internal validity of a true experiment. This does not mean that correlational or quasi-experimental studies in field settings can never lead to justified causal inferences. However, many potential threats to the internal validity of such inferences have to be ruled out one by one, whereas random assignment rules out whole classes of potential spurious causal variables in one operation (cf. West et al., this volume, Ch. 3).

By way of caveat, it should be noted that even true experimental design does not always guarantee internal validity. Ill-conceived or poorly executed experimental studies can introduce many potential third-variable artifacts that undermine causal inference. A fuller treatment of the relationship between the design and conduct of laboratory experiments and internal validity is provided in the following chapter (Smith, this volume, Ch. 2).

FROM CONSTRUCT TO OPERATION AND BACK AGAIN

For many applied research purposes it is sufficient to know that a specific intervention (e.g., passage of a particular gun control law) produces a specific outcome (e.g., reduction in violent crime). Most social psychological research, however, is inspired not by such specific action-oriented questions but by general theories about the interrelationships among cognition, affect, and social behavior. Theories are stated in terms of abstract concepts and hypothetical constructs that cannot be directly observed or measured. In order to be subject to empirical testing, theoretical constructs must be "translated" from the abstract to the more concrete, from concepts to operations that can be observed and replicated.

Most social psychological researchers accept the philosophy that the specific operations and measures employed in a given research study are only partial "representations" of the theoretical constructs of interest – and imperfect representations at that. Hence, the conduct of theory-testing research has a cyclical nature of the form

$$\text{Construct}_1 - \text{Operations} - \text{Construct}_2,$$

where the first link refers to the stage of translating initial theoretical concepts into empirically testable hypotheses and specific operations, and the second link refers to the process of inference from empirical results back to the level of theoretical concepts, which then become the starting point for the next cycle of research.[2] Construct validity refers to inferences made at both stages of research linking concepts to operations. At the front end, we can ask how valid are the specific operations and measures used in a research project as representations or manifestations of the theoretical constructs to be tested; in other words, how good is the logic of translation from concept to operation? At the last stage, inference goes in the other direction (from empirical operations to hypothetical constructs and processes), and the question becomes how justified is the researcher in drawing conclusions from the concrete findings to the level of theory.

The validity issues that mark the initial, operationalization stage of research have been represented as in Figure 1.1 by Rakover (1981). LH-1 refers to the inferential link between the operational definition of the independent variable in an experiment and the corresponding causal concept at the theoretical level. LH-2 refers to the analogous link between the hypothetical effect and the actual response measure assessed in an experiment. (To this system I would add an LH-3 referring to the linkage between direct and indirect assessment of mediating variables and the hypothetical mediational processes, because measures of process are now common in social psychological research.)

Rakover claimed that both links are problematic in social psychological research because there are no standardized operations that correspond closely to our

---

[2] Because abstract definitions and theory are rarely unaffected by the process and outcomes of empirical research, we assume here that Construct_1 and Construct_2 are not necessarily conceptually equivalent.

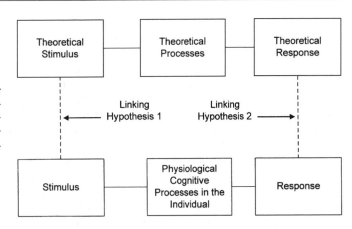

Figure 1.1. Constructs and Operations. From Rakover (1981). Social psychology theory and falsification. *Personality and Social Psychology Bulletin, 7*, p. 125. Copyright SAGE Publications, Inc. and Society for Personality and Social Psychology. Reprinted with permission.

hypothetical constructs, and the inferential steps between concept and operation are often quite remote. The LH-1 and LH-2 links represent little more than "intuited causal relationships" (Rakover, 1981, p. 125). More specifically he identified four major difficulties in connecting theory and data: the stimulus and response validity problems and the "unknown range of stimulus variation" and "unknown range of measurement" problems. The stimulus and response validity problems are the standard construct validity questions of whether the stimulus variations and response measures of the empirical research actually reflect variation in the corresponding theoretical states (cf. John & Benet-Martinez, this volume, Ch. 13). The unknown range problems refer to the failure to specify precisely what levels of the independent variable are expected to be causally significant, and over what range of outcomes. Because of these problems, it is difficult to determine whether a failure to confirm a predicted causal or explanatory relationship represents a failure of theory or a failure of operation. The hypothesized relationship could be true at the conceptual level but go undemonstrated because operations were unrepresentative or failed to capture the effective range within which the causal process operates.

Causes and Confounds

Criticisms of construct validity often revolve around the meaning of the independent variable as operationalized (the LH-1 link in Rakover's, 1981, model). Even when the causal efficacy of the independent variable is not in question, there can be questions about the conceptual causal process that is actually operating to produce the observed effect.

In any research study, the operations that are meant to represent a particular causal construct can be construed in multiple ways. Any particular operation (manipulation of the independent variable) may be associated with variation in more than one hypothetical state, any one of which may be the "true" causal variable. This is what experimentalists are often referring to when they talk about "confounding" the independent variable; something about the independent variable is causing the outcome of interest, but it is not clear what.

For instance, a researcher may be interested in the effects of social isolation on susceptibility to influence. An independent variable is designed to produce variations in feelings of social isolation (e.g., waiting in a room with others present, waiting alone for a short time, waiting alone for an extended period of time), but these experimental conditions may also be producing variations in other subjective states, such as fear of the unknown or cognitive rumination. Any causal effects of this "treatment" may be attributable to social deprivation (as intended by the researcher), but could also be due to these other factors that are confounded with isolation in this particular operation.

This type of confounding should be distinguished from threats to internal validity because they are inherent in the independent variable itself. The causal effect (in the utilitarian sense) of the treatment is not threatened in this case, but the validity of the explanation of the effect is in question. Internal validity is threatened when the independent variable covaries with other variables that are correlated with but separate from (or extraneous to) the treatment itself. Self-selection, for example, undermines internal validity because individual personality differences have effects that are independent of any effects associated with variations in the intended independent variable. Construct confounds, on the other hand, are causal factors that are intrinsic rather than extrinsic to the independent variable as operationalized.

Potential threats to internal validity can be evaluated or ruled out by examining whether the variations in the independent variable are inadvertently correlated with variations in extraneous variables. Threats to construct validity cannot be so readily disentangled. Nonetheless, there are ways of planning and designing research operations so that the number of potentially confounding factors associated with the independent variable can be reduced.

Many potential confounds arise from the general "reactivity" of social psychological research (Cook & Campbell, 1979) that exists because such research involves social interaction, and subjects are usually aware that they are participants in a research study. Reactivity effects include "demand characteristics" (Orne, 1962), "experimenter expectancies" (Rosenthal, 1966), and "evaluation apprehension" (Rosenberg, 1969). All of these effects derive from the fact that alert, aware participants are actively seeking cues in the research setting to inform them of what they are expected to do or what they should do in order to present themselves in a favorable light. Different levels of the independent variable may contain different cues that influence participants' guesses about what the research study is really about or what constitutes a proper response. When experimental treatments and demand characteristics are confounded in this way, the construct validity of the independent variable is compromised.

We can use the concept of demand characteristics to illustrate the difference between methodological *confounds* (which affect construct validity) and methodological *artifacts* (which are threats to internal validity). Demand characteristics confound the conceptual interpretation of the causal effect of an independent variable when the cues are inherent in the experimental manipulations themselves. To take an example from classic dissonance research, the amount of money participants are offered to write a counterattitudinal essay is intended to manipulate the presence of high or low external justification for engaging in an attitude-discrepant behavior. However, offering a participant as much as $20 for the favor requested by the experimenter may also carry extraneous cues to the participant that convey the idea that the requested behavior must be either unpleasant or immoral to be worth paying so much. In this case, the "message" is implicit in the independent variable itself; $20 carries a different cue or message than an offer of $5 or $1. As a consequence, when participants show less attitude change under the high payment condition than under the low payment condition, we cannot be sure whether this is due to the external justification provided by the money

offered (the theoretical construct of interest) or to the demand characteristic inherent in the manipulation itself.

Contrast the above example with another case illustration in which demand characteristics are created by experimenter expectancy effects. Because the researcher may be biased or predisposed to elicit different responses in different experimental conditions, he or she may deliver the experimental instructions in ways that vary systematically across treatment conditions. For instance, the $20 offer may be delivered in a different tone of voice or with different nonverbal cues than the $5 condition. Such experimental behaviors are extraneous to the independent variable itself, but if they are correlated with the differences in instructional conditions, they are procedural artifacts that threaten the internal validity of any causal interpretations of the effects of the independent variable. This is an illustration of how poor procedural controls can undermine the internal validity of even a true experiment with random assignment to treatment conditions.

Construct Validity and Conceptual Replications

Apart from methodological confounds, research operations are subject to multiple theoretical interpretations. Many interesting controversies in the social psychological literature have been fueled by disagreements over the correct theoretical interpretation of a particular phenomenon. Such debates require conceptual replication of the phenomenon, using different operations that are intended to represent the same causal construct.

Consider, for example, the classic study by Aronson and Mills (1959), in which cognitive dissonance was induced by having female participants read aloud some embarassing, obscene passages in the guise of an "initiation" test for admission to a discussion group. The intended conceptual independent variable here was a state of dissonance associated with inconsistency between the participant's behavior (going through high embarassment in order to join the group) and any negative perceptions of the group. But when participants recite a list of obscene words and then listen to a boring group discussion, one cannot be sure that this represents an empirical realization of the intended conceptual variable and nothing else. The complex social situation used by Aronson and Mills has many potential interpretations, including the possibility that reading obscene materials generated a state of sexual arousal that carried over to reactions to the group discussion. If that were the case, it could be that transfer of arousal, rather than dissonance accounted for attraction to the group.

A conceptual replication of the initiation experiment by Gerard and Mathewson (1966) was undertaken to rule out this alternative interpretation. Their experiment was constructed so as to differ from the Aronson and Mills (1959) study in many respects. For example, Gerard and Mathewson used electric shocks instead of the reading of obscene words as their empirical realization of severe initiation (and the dissonance it produced), the shocks were justified as a test of "emotionality" rather than as a test of embarrassment, and the group discussion that participants listened to was about cheating rather than sex. Thus sexual arousal was eliminated as a concomitant of the experimental operationalization of the independent variable. The results confirmed the original findings: People who underwent painful electric shocks in order to become members of a dull group found that group to be more attractive than did people who underwent mild shocks. Such a confirmation of the basic initiation effect under quite different experimental operations supported the contention that it was cognitive dissonance produced by a severe initiation, and not some other conceptual variable, that was responsible for the results in the original experiment. A considerable amount of research in social psychology has been motivated by similar controversies over the valid interpretation of results obtained with complex experimental procedures. Designing conceptual replications to assess threats to construct validity of the causal variable is both challenging and important to the theoretical development of our field.

Multiple Operations: Convergent and Discriminant Validity

These early dissonance experiments illustrate a general principle underlying the idea of construct validity as originally defined by Cook and Campbell (1979). According to Cook and Campbell, the most serious threat to construct validity of any program of research comes from a "mono-operation bias," that is, the tendency to use only a single operation or measure to represent a particular theoretical construct. Because any one operation invariably underrepresents the construct of interest, and embodies potentially irrelevant constructs as well, the conceptual interpretation of single operations can always be challenged. It takes conceptual replication across multiple different operationalizations of the same construct to establish construct validity.

Ideally, multiple operations will allow for testing both convergent and discriminant validity of the construct being studied (Cook & Campbell, 1979). *Convergent* validity is established when different operations representing the same underlying theoretical construct produce essentially the same results (as in the Gerard and Mathewson, 1966, experiment described previously). Equally important, however, is establishing that operations that represent the construct of interest show the predicted effect, whereas other operations which do not reflect the theoretical construct do not have similar effects. If Gerard and Mathewson had demonstrated that dissonance aroused by tolerating electric shock had produced attraction to the discussion group, whereas sexual arousal alone (without dissonance) did not produce attraction, they would have gone further in establishing that the dissonance explanation had discriminant validity. That is, dissonance arousal would have been demonstrated to produce effects that differentiate it from other types of arousal.

Measures of dependent variables can also be subjected to the tests of convergent and discriminant validity. In order to establish measurement construct validity, it is necessary to demonstrate that a particular measure correlates positively with different ways of measuring the same construct and does not correlate as strongly with other measures that use similar methods but are intended to assess a different construct. This is the logic behind the use of the "multitrait multimethod matrix" to establish construct validity of psychological instruments (Campbell & Fiske, 1959; John & Benet-Martinez, this volume, Ch. 13). The multitrait–multimethod procedure involves measuring more than one theoretical construct using more than one method for each construct. If a measure has construct validity, two different measures of the same trait should be more highly related than two different traits assessed by the same method. At a broader level, this logic can be generalized to testing the theoretical framework within which a construct is embedded. Theoretical validity is established when measured constructs prove to be related to theoretically relevant variables and not to theoretically irrelevant ones. Ultimately, then, construct validity is equivalent to theoretical validity.

Causal Processes and Mediational Analyses

Some theoretical debates do not revolve around conceptual interpretation of the operations themselves but are about the intervening processes that mediate the link between the causal variable and its effects. To return to Figure 1.1, these debates over theoretical processes cannot be resolved by examining the construct validity of the independent variable (LH-1) or the dependent variable (LH-2) alone. Theoretical controversies at this level require operations that tap into the intervening physiological, cognitive, and affective processes themselves.

The long-standing debate between alternative explanations of the counterattitudinal advocacy effect derived from dissonance theory and self-perception theory provides a case in point (Greenwald, 1975). In this controversy, the validity of the basic empirical finding and the research operations were not in doubt. Theorists on both sides acknowledged that a causal relationship exists between the presence or absence of external incentives (e.g., monetary payment) and the resulting consistency between behavior and expressed attitudes. What was at issue was the nature of the mediating processes that underlie the relationship between induced behaviors and subsequent attitudes. Self-perceptions theorists held that the effect was mediated by cognitive, self-attribution processes, whereas the dissonance theory explanation rested on motivational processes. As in many cases in social psychological research, the efforts to establish construct validity helped to refine and clarify the theory itself.

Years of attempts to resolve the debate through "critical experiments" were of no avail (Greenwald, 1975). In each case, the same experimental operations could be interpreted as consistent with either theoretical construct. It wasn't until a clever experiment was designed to assess directly the mediating role of motivational arousal that the deadlock was effectively broken. Zanna and Cooper (1974) used a mediational design to demonstrate that the presence of arousal was necessary to produce the attitude change effect and that when the motivational effects of arousal were blocked (through misattribution), attitude change following counterattitudinal behavior did not occur. These findings regarding process were more consistent with the dissonance interpretation of the phenomenon than with the self-perception interpretation, although they established that both motivational and cognitive processes were essential mediating factors.

THE MANY FACES OF EXTERNAL VALIDITY

Construct validity represents one form of generalizing from the observed results of an empirical study to conclusions that go beyond the results themselves. Another form of generalizability has to do with the empirical replicability of the phenomenon under study. External validity refers to the question of whether an effect (and its underlying processes) that has been demonstrated in one research setting would be obtained in other settings, with different research participants and different research procedures.

Actually, external validity is not a single construct but represents a whole set of questions about generalizability, each with somewhat different implications for the interpretation and extension of research findings. The sections that follow discuss three of the most important forms of external validity – robustness, ecological validity, and relevance. Each of these raises somewhat different questions about where, when, and to whom the results of a particular research study can be generalized.

Robustness: Can it Be Replicated?

The robustness issue refers to whether a particular finding is replicable across a variety of settings, persons, and historical contexts. In its most narrow sense, the question is whether an effect obtained in one laboratory can be exactly replicated in another laboratory with different researchers. More broadly, the question is whether the general effect holds up in the face of wide variations in subject populations and settings. Some findings appear to be very fragile, obtainable only under highly controlled conditions in a specific context; other findings prove to hold up despite significant variations in conditions under which they are tested.

Technically, robustness would be demonstrated if a particular research study were conducted with a random sample of participants from a broadly defined population in a random sampling of settings. This approach to external validity implies that the researcher must have theoretically defined the populations and settings to which the effect of interest is to be generalized and then must develop a complete listing of the populations and settings from which a sample is drawn. Such designs, however, are usually impractical and not cost-effective. More often, this form of generalizability is established by repeated replications in systematically sampled settings and types of research participants. For instance, a finding initially demonstrated in a social psychology laboratory with college students from an eastern college in the United States may later be replicated with high school students in the Midwest and among members of a community organization in New England. Such replication strategies are not only more practical but they also have potential advantages for theory-testing purposes. If findings do not replicate in systematically selected cases, we sometimes gain clues as to what factors may be important moderators of the effect in question (Petty & Cacioppo, 1996).

Generalizability across multiple populations and settings should be distinguished from generalizability to a particular population. A phenomenon that is robust in the sense that it holds up for the population at large may not be obtained for a specific subpopulation or in a particular context. If the question of generalizability is specific to a particular target population (say, from college students to the elderly), then replication must be undertaken within that population and not through random sampling.

Generalizability from one subject population or research setting to others is probably the most frequently raised issue of external validity for experimental studies conducted in laboratory settings. Sears (1986) provided what is probably the most cogent arguments about the limitations of laboratory experimentation with college student participants. A review of research articles published in the major social psychology journals in 1985 revealed that 74% were conducted with undergraduate student participants, and 78% were conducted in a laboratory setting. According to Sears, this restriction of populations and settings means that social psychology has a "narrow data base" on which to draw conclusions about human nature and social behavior.

It is important to point out here that Sears (1986) was not claiming that college students or psychology laboratories are any less generalizable to the world at large than any other specific type of persons or settings. Just because an effect has been demonstrated in a particular field setting rather than a lab does not automatically render it more externally valid. What Sears was criticizing is the overrepresentation of a specific type of subject and setting across a large number of studies, all of which then share the same limitations on external validity.

Before we can conclude, however, that the oversampling of college student participants actually limits the external validity of our findings and interpretations, we have to specify in what ways undergraduate students differ from other populations and how these differences might alter the effects we observe. Drawing on research in cognitive and social development, Sears (1986) suggested that there are several distinguishing characteristics of college students that may be relevant to social psychological findings. Compared with the general population, undergraduates are likely to have stronger cognitive skills, less well-formulated or crystallized attitudes and self-concepts, and less stable group identities – differences that are likely to be exacerbated when studies are conducted in academic laboratories with academic-like tasks. Do these differences make a difference? Sears contended that because

of these characteristics of our subject population and setting, results of our research may exaggerate the magnitude of effects of situational influences and cognitive processes on social attitudes and behavior.

To argue that characteristics of the setting or subject population qualify the conclusions that can be drawn about cause–effect relationships is, in effect, to hypothesize that the cause interacts with (i.e., is moderated by) the characteristics of the population or context to produce the effect in question. To translate Sears's (1986) arguments into these terms, he is postulating that manipulations of the type of influence used interact with participant characteristics to determine amount of attitude change. For instance, the magnitude of the effect of influence attempts that rely on cognitive elaboration would be expected to differ depending on whether the effect is tested with college students or with older, nonstudent populations. In this case, age is expected to moderate the causal effect of treatments that require cognitive elaboration.

External validity is related to settings as well as to participant populations. The external validity of a finding is challenged if the relationship between independent and dependent variables is altered when essentially the same research procedures are conducted in a different laboratory or field setting or under the influence of different experimenter characteristics. For example, Milgram's (1963) initial studies of obedience were conducted in a research laboratory at Yale University, but used participants recruited from the community of New Haven. Even though these experiments were conducted with a nonstudent sample, a legitimate question is the extent to which his findings would generalize to other settings. Because participants were drawn from outside the university and because many had no previous experience with college, the prestige and respect associated with a research laboratory at Yale may have made the participants more susceptible to the demands for compliance that the experiment entailed than they would have been in other settings.

To address this issue, Milgram undertook a replication of his experiment in a very different physical setting. By moving the research operation to a "seedy" office in the industrial town of Bridgeport, Connecticut and adopting a fictitious identity as a psychological research firm, Milgram hoped to minimize the reputational factors inherent in the Yale setting. In comparison with data obtained in the original study, the Bridgeport replication resulted in slightly lower but still dramatic rates of compliance to the experimenter. Thus, setting could be identified as a contributing but not crucial factor to the basic findings of the research.

Cook and Campbell (1979) made it clear that questions of external validity, or generalizability, are implicitly questions about interactions between the independent variable (treatment) and contextual variables such as subject selection, history, and research setting. In other words, the quest for external validity is essentially a search for moderators that limit or qualify the cause–effect relationship under investigation. As the Milgram experiments illustrate, once one has identified what the potential moderators are, the robustness of an effect can be tested empirically by varying those factors systematically and determining whether the effect is or is not altered.

Ecological Validity: Is It Representative?

The question of whether an effect holds up across a wide variety of people or settings is somewhat different than asking whether the effect is representative of what happens in everyday life. This is the essence of *ecological validity* – whether an effect has been demonstrated to occur under conditions that are typical for the population at large. The concept of ecological validity derives from Brunswik's (1956) advocacy of "representative design," in which research is conducted with probabilistic samplings of subjects and situations.

Representativeness is not the same as robustness. Generalizability in the robustness sense asks whether an effect can occur across different settings and people; ecological validity asks whether it does occur in the world as is. In the Brunswikian sense, findings obtained with atypical populations (e.g., college students) in atypical settings (e.g., the laboratory) never have ecological validity until they are demonstrated to occur naturally in more representative circumstances.

Many researchers (e.g., Berkowitz & Donnerstein, 1982; Mook, 1983; Petty & Cacioppo, 1996) take issue with the idea that the purpose of most research is to demonstrate that events actually do occur in a particular population. Testing a causal hypothesis requires demonstrating only that manipulating the cause can alter the effect. Even most applied researchers are more interested in questions of what interventions could change outcomes rather than what does happen under existing conditions. Thus, for most social psychologists, ecological validity is too restrictive a conceptualization of generalizability for research that is designed to test causal hypotheses. Ecological validity is, however, crucial for research that is undertaken for descriptive or demonstration purposes.

Further, the setting in which a causal principle is demonstrated does not necessarily have to physically resemble the settings in which that principle operates in real life for the demonstration to be valid. As Aronson, Wilson, and Brewer (1998) put it, most social psychology researchers are aiming for "psychological realism," rather than "mundane realism," in their experiments. *Mundane realism* refers to the extent to which the research setting and operations resemble events in normal, everyday life. *Psychological realism* is the extent to which the psychological processes that occur in an experiment are the same as psychological processes that occur in everyday life. An experimental setting may have little mundane realism but still capture processes that are highly representative of those that underlie events in the real world.

Relevance: Does It Matter?

In a sense, the question of ecological validity is also a question of relevance – is the finding related to events or phenomena that actually occur in the real world? However, relevance also has a broader meaning of whether findings are potentially useful or applicable to solving problems or improving quality of life. Again, relevance in this latter sense does not necessarily depend on the physical resemblance between the research setting in which an effect is demonstrated and the setting in which it is ultimately applied. Perceptual research on eye–hand coordination conducted in tightly controlled, artificial laboratory settings has proved valuable to the design of instrument panels in airplanes even though the laboratory didn't look anything like a cockpit.

Relevance is the ultimate form of generalization, and differences among research studies in attention to relevance is primarily a matter of degree rather than of kind. All social psychological research is motivated ultimately by a desire to understand real and meaningful social behavior. But the connections between basic research findings and application are often indirect and cumulative rather than immediate. Relevance is a matter of social process, that is, the process of how research results are transmitted and used rather than what the research results are (Brewer, 1997).

Is External Validity Important?

External validity, like other validity issues, must be evaluated with respect to the purposes for which research is being conducted. When the research agenda is essentially descriptive, ecological validity may be essential. When the purpose is utilitarian, robustness of an effect is particularly critical. The fragility and non-generalizability of a finding may be a fatal flaw if one's goal is to design an intervention to solve some applied problem. On the other hand, it may not be so critical if the purpose of the research is testing explanatory theory, in which case construct validity is more important than other forms of external validity.

In the field of physics, for example, many phenomena can only be demonstrated empirically in a vacuum or with the aid of supercolliders. Nonetheless, the findings from these methods are often considered extremely important for understanding basic principles and ultimate application of the science. Mook (1983) argued compellingly that the importance of external validity has been exaggerated in the psychological sciences. Most experimental research, he contended, is not intended to generalize directly from the artificial setting of the laboratory to "real life," but to test predictions based on theory. He drew an important distinction between "generality of findings" and "generality of conclusions" and held that the latter purpose does not require that the conditions of testing resemble those of real life. It is the understanding of the processes themselves, not the specific findings, which has external validity.

In effect, Mook (1983) argued that construct validity is more important than other forms of external validity when we are conducting theory-testing research. Nonetheless, the need for conceptual replication to establish construct validity requires a degree of robustness across research operations and settings that is very similar to the requirements for establishing external validity. The kind of systematic, programmatic research that accompanies the search for external validity inevitably contributes to the refinement and elaboration of theory as well.

OPTIMIZING TYPES OF VALIDITY

Among research methodologists, controversies have ensued about the relative importance of different validity concerns, ever since Campbell and Stanley (1963) took the position that internal validity is the sine qua non of experimental research and takes precedence over questions of external validity (e.g., Cook & Shadish, 1994; Cronbach, 1982). The debate includes discussions of whether there are necessary trade-offs among the various aspects of validity or whether it is possible to demand that research maximize internal, external, and construct validity simultaneously.

It is possible to conduct a single research study with the goal of maximizing internal validity. Questions of

external validity and construct validity, however, can rarely be addressed within the context of a single research design and require systematic, programmatic research studies that address a particular question across different operations and research settings. Thus, it is patently unfair to expect that any particular piece of research have high internal, external, and construct validity all at the same time. It is more appropriate to require that programs of research be designed in a way that addresses all types of validity issues (see also Smith, this volume, Ch. 2).

In order to design such a research program it is important to recognize the ways in which efforts to maximize one form of validity may reduce or jeopardize other types, hence the need for a diversity of methods as represented throughout this volume. By understanding such trade-offs, we can plan research projects in which the strengths and weaknesses of different studies are complementary. Thus, this chapter will close with a brief discussion of some of these important complementarities.

Setting: Lab Versus Field

It is a common assumption that laboratory research achieves high internal validity at the expense of external validity, whereas research conducted in natural field settings is associated with greater external validity albeit at the cost of more threats to internal validity. There is some basis for this implied association between research setting and types of validity. The laboratory does often permit a degree of control of the causal variable that maximizes internal validity to an extent that is difficult to achieve in "noisy" real-world contexts. And to the extent that natural settings reduce the reactivity that is characteristic of laboratory-based research, one threat to external validity is reduced.

It is hoped, however, that the earlier discussion of the different types of validity has made it clear that there is no invariable association between the setting in which research is conducted and its degree of internal, external, or construct validity. Tightly controlled experimental interventions can be introduced in field settings (and, conversely, laboratory studies can be poorly controlled). Most important, conducting research in a naturalistic context does not by itself confer external validity. Any specific context has limited generalizability. Even if the setting has been chosen to be highly representative or typical of naturally occurring situations, ecological validity is suspect if the research introduces conditions into that setting that do not occur spontaneously.

Establishing either construct validity or external validity requires that the conclusions drawn from research hold up across variation in context. Thus, it is the complementarity of field and lab as research settings that contributes to validity, not the characteristics of either setting alone. One good illustration of the use of selected field sites in conjunction with laboratory research comes from the literature on mood and altruism. A variety of mood-induction manipulations have been developed in laboratory settings, such as having participants read affectively positive or negative passages (e.g., Aderman, 1972). After the mood state induction, participants are given an opportunity to exhibit generosity by donating money or helping an experimental accomplice. Results generally show that positive mood induction elevates helping behavior but depressed mood inhibits helping.

Despite multiple replications of this effect in different laboratories with different investigators, the validity of these findings has been challenged both because of the artificiality of the setting in which altruism is assessed and because of the potential demand characteristics associated with the rather unusual mood-induction experience. To counter these criticisms, researchers in the area took advantage of a natural mood-induction situation based on the emotional impact of selected motion pictures (Underwood et al., 1977).

After some pilot research, in which ratings were obtained from moviegoers, a double feature consisting of *Lady Sings the Blues* and *The Sterile Cuckoo* was selected for its negative-affect-inducing qualities, and two other double features were selected to serve as neutral control conditions. A commonly occurring event – solicitation of donations to a nationally known charity with collection boxes set up outside the movie theater lobby – was chosen as the vehicle for a measure of the dependent variable of generosity.

Having located such naturally occurring variants of the laboratory mood-induction operation and altruism measure, the major design problem encountered by the researchers was that of participant self-selection to the alternative movie conditions. Although random assignment of volunteer moviegoers was a logical possibility, the procedures involved in utilizing that strategy would have created many of the elements of artificiality and reactivity that the field setting was selected to avoid. Therefore, the investigators decided to live with the phenomenon of self-selection and to alter the research design to take its effect into consideration. For this purpose, the timing of collection of donations to charity at the various theaters was randomly alternated

across different nights so that it would occur either while most people were entering the theater (before seeing the movies) or leaving (after seeing both features). The rate of donations given by arriving moviegoers could then be a check on preexisting differences between the two populations apart from the mood induction. Fortunately, there proved to be no differences in initial donation rates as a function of type of movie, whereas post-movie donations differed significantly in the direction of lowered contribution rates following the sad movies. This pattern of results, then, preserved the logic of random assignment (initial equivalence between experimental conditions) despite the considerable deviation from ideal procedures for participant assignment.

Two points should be emphasized with respect to this illustration of field research. First, the field version of the basic research paradigm was not – and could not be – simply a "transplanted" replication of the laboratory operations. The researchers had considerably less control in the field setting. They could not control the implementation of the stimulus conditions or extraneous sources of variation. On any one night a host of irrelevant events may have occurred during the course of the movies (e.g., a breakdown of projectors or a disturbance in the audience) that could have interfered with the mood manipulation. The researchers were not only helpless to prevent such events but would not have been aware of them if they did take place. In addition, as already mentioned, in the field setting the experimenters were unable to assign participants randomly to conditions and had to rely on luck to establish initial equivalence between groups.

Second, the results of the field experiment as a single isolated study would have been difficult to interpret without the context of conceptually related laboratory experiments. This difficulty is partly due to the ambiguities introduced by the alterations in design and partly to the constraints on measurement inherent in the field situation where manipulation checks, for example, are not possible. The convergence of results in the two settings greatly enhances our confidence in the findings from both sets of operations.

Isolation Versus Construct Validity

Laboratory experiments are inherently artificial in the sense that causal variables are isolated from their normal contextual variation. This isolation and control is the essence of testing causal hypotheses with a high degree of internal validity. It has been pointed out repeatedly in this chapter that isolation does not necessarily jeopardize external validity if the experimental situation has psychological realism, that is, if the causal processes being represented in the lab setting are the same as those that operate in nonlaboratory contexts.

It is this matter of whether the process is the "same" when the context is altered that constitutes the stickiest issue of validity. Greenwood (1982) called this the problem of "the artificiality of alteration," the problem that arises whenever bringing a variable into the laboratory changes its nature. Greenwood argued that this alteration is particularly problematic for social psychology because social psychological phenomena are inherently relational or context-dependent and hence do not retain their identity when isolated from other psychological processes. He takes this as a fatal criticism of laboratory research methods in social psychology, but the truth is that it applies to any context in which a phenomenon is observed as psychological experiences are never exactly the same from one time or place to another.

The issue here is one of the level of abstraction at which constructs or principles are defined. Consider, for example, the construct of "threat to self-esteem." No one would seriously deny that being informed that one had failed a test of creative problem-solving would have more impact on self-esteem of a Harvard undergraduate than it would on a 50-year-old mineworker. Thus, if we were interested in the effects of lowered self-esteem on aggression, we might have to use different techniques to lower self-esteem in the two populations. Threats to self-esteem based on challenges to one's academic self-concept are certainly different in many ways from challenges that threaten one's sense of group belonging or of physical stamina. But if each of these, in their appropriate context, proves to have an impact on anger or aggressiveness, then we have gained confidence in a general principle that threats to areas of self-esteem that are important or central to one's sense of identity increase aggression.

This, then, is the ultimate challenge for valid theory-building in social psychology. Our theoretical constructs must be abstract enough to generalize across a range of contexts and specific manifestations, yet precise enough to permit testing at an empirical level. Each empirical demonstration is inevitably limited to a specific context and subject to multiple interpretations. But each time a theoretical proposition is tested in a new setting or with new operations, a contribution is made to the overall picture. Validity is never the achievement of a single research project but the product of cumulative theory-testing and application.

REFERENCES

Aderman, D. (1972). Elation, depression, and helping behavior. *Journal of Personality and Social Psychology, 24,* 91–101.

Aronson, E., & Mills, J. (1959). The effect of severity of initiation on liking for a group. *Journal of Abnormal and Social Psychology, 59,* 177–181.

Aronson, E., Wilson, T., & Brewer, M. B. (1998). Experimentation in social psychology. In D. Gilbert, S. Fiske, & G. Lindzey (Eds.), *The handbook of social psychology* (4th ed., Vol. 1, pp. 99–142). Boston: McGraw-Hill.

Asch, S. E. (1956). Studies of independence and conformity: A minority of one against a unanimous majority. *Psychological Monographs, 70* (9, Whole No. 416).

Baron, R. M., & Kenny, D. A. (1986). The moderator–mediator variable distinction in social psychological research: Conceptual, strategic, and statistical considerations. *Journal of Personality and Social Psychology, 51,* 1173–1182.

Berkowitz, L., & Donnerstein, E. (1982). External validity is more than skin deep: Some answers to criticisms of laboratory experiments. *American Psychologist, 37,* 245–257.

Brewer, M. B. (1997). The social psychology of intergroup relations: Can research inform practice? *Journal of Social Issues, 53*(1), 197–211.

Brunswik, E. (1956). *Perception and the representative design of psychological experiments* (2nd ed.). Berkeley, CA: University of California Press.

Campbell, D. T. (1957). Factors relevant to the validity of experiments in social settings. *Psychological Bulletin, 54,* 297–312.

Campbell, D. T., & Fiske, D. W. (1959). Convergent and discriminant validation by the multitrait-multimethod matrix. *Psychological Bulletin, 56,* 81–105.

Campbell, D. T., & Stanley, J. C. (1963). Experimental and quasi-experimental designs for research on teaching. In N. Gage (Ed.), *Handbook of research on teaching* (pp. 171–246). Chicago: Rand-McNally.

Campbell, D. T., & Stanley, J. C. (1966). *Experimental and quasi-experimental designs for research.* Chicago: Rand-McNally.

Collingwood, R. G. (1940). *An essay on metaphysics.* Oxford, England: Clarendon.

Cook, T. D., & Campbell, D. T. (1979). *Quasi-experimentation: Design and analysis issues for field settings.* Chicago: Rand-McNally.

Cook, T. D., & Shadish, W. R. (1994). Social experiments: Some developments over the past fifteen years. *Annual Review of Psychology, 45,* 545–580.

Cronbach, L. J. (1982). *Designing evaluations of educational and social programs.* San Francisco: Jossey-Bass.

Gasking, D. (1955). Causation and recipes. *Mind, 64,* 479–487.

Gerard, H. B., & Mathewson, G. C. (1966). The effects of severity of initiation on liking for a group: A replication. *Journal of Experimental Social Psychology, 2,* 278–287.

Greenwald, A. G. (1975). On the inconclusivenes of "crucial" cognitive tests of dissonance versus self-perception theories. *Journal of Experimental Social Psychology, 11*, 490–499.

Greenwood, J. D. (1982). On the relation between laboratory experiments and social behaviour: Causal explanation and generalization. *Journal for the Theory of Social Behaviour, 12*, 225–250.

Mackie, J. L. (1974). *The cement of the universe.* Oxford, England: Oxford University Press.

Milgram, S. (1963). Behavioral study of obedience. *Journal of Abnormal and Social Psychology, 67*, 371–378.

Mook, D. G. (1983). In defense of external invalidity. *American Psychologist, 38*, 379–387.

Orne, M. (1962). On the social psychology of the psychological experiment. *American Psychologist, 17*, 776–783.

Petty, R. E., & Cacioppo, J. T. (1996). Addressing disturbing and disturbed consumer behavior: Is it necessary to change the way we conduct behavioral science? *Journal of Marketing Research, 33*, 1–8.

Rakover, S. S. (1981). Social psychology theory and falsification. *Personality and Social Psychology Bulletin, 7*, 123–130.

Rosenberg, M. J. (1969). The conditions and consequences of evaluation apprehension. In R. Rosenthal & R. Rosnow (Eds.), *Artifact in behavioral research* (pp. 279–349). New York: Academic Press.

Rosenthal, R. (1966). *Experimenter effects in behavioral research.* New York: Appleton-Century-Crofts.

Sears, D. O. (1986). College sophomores in the laboratory: Influence of a narrow data base on social psychology's view of human nature. *Journal of Personality and Social Psychology, 51*, 515–530.

Sherif, M. (1935). A study of some social factors in perception. *Archives of Psychology, 27*(187), 1–60.

Tajfel, H. (1970). Experiments in intergroup discrimination. *Scientific American, 223*(2), 96–102.

Underwood, B., Berenson, J., Berenson, R., Cheng, K., Wilson, D., Kulik, J., Moore, B., & Wenzel, G. (1977). Attention, negative affect, and altruism: An ecological validation. *Personality and Social Psychology Bulletin, 3*, 54–58.

Zanna, M., & Cooper, J. (1974). Dissonance and the pill: An attribution approach to studying the arousal properties of dissonance. *Journal of Personality and Social Psychology, 29*, 703–709.

CHAPTER TWO

Research Design

ELIOT R. SMITH

Research design is the systematic planning of research to permit valid conclusions. It involves, for example, the specification of the population to be studied, the treatments to be administered, and the dependent variables to be measured – all guided by the theoretical conceptions underlying the research. Research design most fundamentally affects the internal validity of research, that is, the ability to draw sound conclusions about what actually causes any observed differences in a dependent measure. However, design also has implications for other forms of validity (Cook & Campbell, 1979). Statistical conclusion validity is affected by such design-related issues as the number of participants used in a study and the way they are allocated to conditions. Construct validity, the ability to link research operationalizations to their intended theoretical constructs, is affected by many aspects of design, such as freedom from confounding. External validity or generalizability is affected by the way other design factors besides those of key theoretical interest are held constant or allowed to vary. This chapter points out the implications of design for all of these forms of validity, as they become relevant. See Brewer (this volume, Ch. 1) for more on the types of validity and their interrelationships.

FOCUS OF THIS CHAPTER

Research design is inextricably linked to data analysis. An appropriate design can ensure that the substantive and statistical assumptions for the data analysis, such as

Thanks to Howard Weiss as well as the editors for helpful comments on earlier versions of this chapter. Preparation of the chapter was supported by a Research Career Development Award K02 MH01178 from the National Institutes of Mental Health.

the assumptions that permit strong causal inferences, are met. This chapter focuses on design and Judd's chapter 14 on analysis, but at a number of points in this chapter brief references will be made to important analytic issues. The presentation here is largely nonmathematical. Treatments of the mathematical principles underlying design can be found in Kirk (1968), Keppel (1982), Winer (1971), and other sources. This chapter follows the lead of Campbell and Stanley (1963), Cook and Campbell (1979), and Abelson (1995) in emphasizing logic rather than equations. Also, this chapter downplays the "nuts and bolts" aspects of research procedures, such as how to construct a plausible cover story and how to administer a manipulation to participants. Extensive discussions are available in Judd, Smith, and Kidder (1991, chapter 8) and in Aronson, Ellsworth, Carlsmith, and Gonzales (1990).

Research designs can be divided into three fundamental categories. An *experimental design* involves a manipulation of at least one independent variable, along with random assignment of participants to conditions. Levels of a manipulated factor are often termed "treatments." A *quasi-experimental design* involves manipulation without randomization, for example the assignment of two preexisting groups to different treatments. A *nonexperimental or passive observational design* (sometimes confusingly termed "correlational") includes neither manipulation nor random assignment. This chapter focuses almost exclusively on experimental design, for two main reasons. The most obvious reason is the heavy predominance of experimental designs in social psychology today. The other is the increasing recognition of the advantages of experimental design, even among researchers who study the effects of social interventions in field settings. Cook and Shadish (1994) wrote that "the last decade has witnessed a powerful

Level 1				Level 2			
Participant 1	Participant 2	Participant 3	Participant 4	Participant 5	Participant 6	Participant 7	Participant 8
X_{11}	X_{12}	X_{13}	X_{14}	X_{25}	X_{26}	X_{27}	X_{28}

Figure 2.1a. A between-participants factor defines groups of participants exposed to different levels. X_{ij} is an observation from participant j in condition i.

shift in scientific opinion toward randomized field experiments and away from quasi-experiments or non-experiments. Indeed, Campbell and Boruch (1975) regret the influence Campbell's earlier work had in justifying quasi-experiments where randomized experiments might have been possible" (p. 557).

In social psychology, the units that are studied are usually individual people and in this chapter they are called "participants." However, the reader will keep in mind that the units could equally well be couples, groups, etc. And the laboratory is usually assumed as the research setting; again, this emphasis simply reflects the predominance of research within social psychology today. Useful discussions of field research (with an emphasis on the practical issues of conducting experimental research outside the lab) can be found in West et al.'s chapter 3 and in Cook and Shadish (1994).

INDEPENDENT VARIABLES (FACTORS)

In an experimental design there are always at least two *factors* or *independent variables*, variables that are considered to influence the dependent variable response. There is a factor corresponding to participants (or whatever other units are randomized) and at least one other factor as well. A factor may be *between participants*, which means that distinct groups of participants are

Figure 2.1b. A within-participants factor exposes each participant to multiple levels of the factor. Participants randomly assigned to Group 1 encounter level 1 then level 2; participants in Group 2 receive the opposite order.

exposed to the different levels of the factor (see Figure 2.1a). If the participants are randomly assigned to these groups, then the design can be considered an experiment. In this case differences between groups on the dependent variable cannot readily be attributed to alternative causal influences like differences in the composition of the groups and are most reasonably attributed to the treatment itself. Alternatively, a factor may be *within participants*, meaning that each participant is exposed to more than one level of the factor. In this case the order of exposure is what is randomly assigned in an experimental design. As Figure 2.1b shows, participants are randomly allocated to groups that receive the levels of the factor in different orders. If order is not randomly assigned, alternative causes like history or maturation could be responsible for systematic differences between measurements taken at different times.

In the following section, we first discuss a series of questions that must be answered regarding each individual factor in a design. Most obviously, how should the levels of the factor be chosen? Then we consider the possible ways that multiple factors included in a single experiment may be interrelated.

Fixed or Random Factor?

DEFINITIONS. The levels of a factor can be considered to be fixed or random. With a *fixed* factor, the levels used in a study are selected for their intrinsic theoretical or practical interest. Any conclusions resulting from the research apply only to those levels. So for example, in a study of effects of gender stereotypes on participants' evaluations of essays supposedly written by another student, the relevant levels of essay-writer's gender would be male or female. In a study of the effects of group discussion on decision making, the participants'

		First Observation	Second Observation
Group 1	Participant 1	X_{11}	X_{21}
	Participant 2	X_{12}	X_{22}
	Participant 3	X_{13}	X_{23}
Group 2	Participant 4	X_{24}	X_{14}
	Participant 5	X_{25}	X_{15}
	Participant 6	X_{26}	X_{16}

decisions would be measured before or after a group discussion. With a fixed factor, one wants to use the observations from the sample of participants in each condition to estimate the mean of a hypothetical population of participants exposed to that condition, and then to test hypotheses concerning differences among condition means.

With a *random* factor, in contrast, the research interest goes beyond the particular levels of the factor included in a study. Instead, the hypotheses of interest involve a population of conditions or levels of the factor, and the sample of levels used in the experiment is assumed to be representative of the population. The most obvious example of a random factor is the participants factor in a typical experiment. Nobody is intrinsically interested in the particular results (e.g., condition means) produced by the specific participants who participated in a given experiment. Instead, we take a test of statistical significance applied to those results as indicating that we can safely generalize beyond the studied participants, to other "generally similar" participants.

PARTICIPANTS AND OTHER RANDOM FACTORS. It is instructive to consider the way researchers typically treat the participant factor, as a basis for handling other types of random factors. Suppose we wish to investigate the effects of mild versus severe consequences of an accident on people's attributions of responsibility. Scenarios could be written involving various types of accidents (e.g., an auto accident, a kitchen fire), with the severity of the consequences varied. Different participants would read each scenario and make ratings of responsibility for the accident. Suppose that the results show that – across all the types of accidents tested – significantly more responsibility is attributed when consequences are more severe. What would that result mean? The answer hinges on the treatment of the "scenario" or "accident type" factor. If the factor is considered to be fixed, then the result can be said to hold for these specific accident scenarios only. The profoundly unsatisfying nature of this limited generality can be easily seen from the typical absence of any reference to it in authors' discussions of the implications of their research results. If the factor is considered to be random, however, we are given warrant to take the result as holding for the population of accident types similar to those that were tested. This is, roughly, the same type of generalization we expect (and routinely make) across participants.

Note that for neither participants nor other factors (e.g., types of accidents) is formal random sampling necessary for the treatment of the statistical factor as random. Formal random sampling, as used in survey research, offers statistical assurance that results from a sample can be generalized back to the parent population, plus or minus the practical problems of actually attaining a perfect response rate, etc. But in actual research practice we do not randomly sample our participants from among the university's undergraduate students. For one thing, the license to declare that our results generalize statistically to the Midwestern University student body as a whole (instead of just to those introductory psychology students who enrolled in our study) adds nothing to the interest value of the result and would be purchased at a very high cost. Instead, we rely on independent replications of major results as the chief assurance of their generality across participants.

If we apply these considerations about participant sampling to other factors across whose levels we wish to generalize, two lessons are clear. First, formal random sampling is not a necessary precondition for treating a factor as random. The researcher may write stories about diverse types of accidents rather than sampling from some universe of accident types, even if such a thing existed. In general, we construct and select experimental materials to be (subjectively) particularly good examples of the domain under investigation, rather than typical or representative examples. But such selection is not inconsistent with considering the factor as random. Second, when research is replicated, different levels of the factor should be selected (just as different participants would be used), as the most effective way to demonstrate the generalizability of the results across such levels. I will return to this issue shortly. The significant point is that when participants or any other factor is considered to be random, the generalization is to participants or levels of the factor that are similar to those used in the study. Random sampling from a precisely defined population is not necessary to consider a factor as random.

DECIDING ON THE TREATMENT OF A FACTOR. When a factor (such as accident type in an attribution study, or the topic of persuasive messages in an attitude change study) could be treated as either random or fixed, how can the researcher decide which to use? As a guideline, consider how one would ideally replicate the study. If one would leave the levels of the factor the same, the factor is fixed; if one would use other levels that are similar to (not identical with) those used earlier, it is random. Certainly a replication would use new participants, so the participants factor is invariably considered random. Ideally, if researchers recognized that topics and similar factors are arbitrary and conceptually unimportant contexts across which generalizability is desired, they would select new topics in a replication study, which corresponds to treatment of the factor as random. In actual practice, existing persuasive messages, accident scenarios, and similar materials are often reused in replications on the grounds that they are known to "work" (as well as because copying them involves less effort than constructing new materials). However, this practice is dangerous. For example, early research on the "risky shift" was based on an observation that with certain types of decision problems, group discussion led participants to move toward riskier choices (Bem, Wallach, & Kogan, 1965; see Brown, 1986). Researchers consistently used the same set of problems, which "worked" in the sense of replicating the conventional result. Yet even the original set of problems included a few that tended to reverse (produce conservative shifts after discussion). Only when a broader sampling of the domain of possible decision problems was undertaken could it be recognized that the shift to risk was specific to particular problems. The whole phenomenon could then be reconceptualized much more generally (and fruitfully) as group polarization (Myers & Lamm, 1976).

As Abelson (1995, p. 145) pointed out, a given factor frequently has both fixed and random aspects. His example was a study of the effects of persuasive communications from expert versus nonexpert sources, with messages on several different topics. From one viewpoint, topics could be considered a random factor; the researchers presumably wish their findings to be generalizable across all kinds of controversial topics. From another viewpoint, specific topics could be considered fixed (and in fact particular topics, such as the institution of comprehensive exams for college seniors, have become fixtures of the research literature on persuasion) but the particular messages giving arguments on those topics could be random. That is, a researcher wishing to replicate the initial study could (a) reuse the original materials without change, (b) write new essays on the same topics, or (c) write essays on a completely new set of topics. The original factor is actually topic-plus-essay, and it is possible to see it as a mixture of fixed and random characteristics. Still, the way the factor is treated in the data analysis constrains the degree of generalization that is appropriate for the research results.

POWER WITH RANDOM FACTORS. The greater generalizability that is possible for a factor treated as random obviously must come at a cost. Consider at an intuitive level that generalization for a fixed factor involves treating the experimental observations as samples that yield evidence concerning the true population means in the given conditions. Generalization for a random factor involves the same inferential leap (sample values to population means for the conditions included in the study) plus another step, treating the factor levels in the study as a sample from a larger population of levels whose overall mean is to be estimated. The latter must involve less power, often drastically less (see Abelson, 1995, pp. 139–140). The main implication for researchers who wish to use random factors in their designs is to use many levels. Power depends on the number of levels of any random factor, including items (e.g., stories) as well as participants. Typical research practice, strongly influenced by tradition rather than rational analysis (Cohen, 1990), involves the use of many participants (perhaps 60–120 in a typical social psychological experiment) but a much smaller number of levels of other factors – often just 2–4. In the case of a fixed factor, this may be fine, depending on the specific hypothesis being tested. But in the case of a random factor, such as stimulus replications, the use of only a few levels of the factor may lead to very low levels of power. Fortunately, it may well be easier and less costly to double or quadruple the number of levels of such a factor than to multiply the number of participants by the same factor.

Consider the factor "experimenter sex" as an example. This seems on its face like a fixed factor, but the individual experimenters who instantiate the levels of sex are best treated as random. Most researchers realize that if they just have John and Joan serve as experimenters it is impossible to draw conclusions about effects of experimenter sex, for it is confounded with all of John and Joan's other personal characteristics. What many may fail to realize is that using two or three experimenters of each sex is almost as weak; an analysis that treats experimenter-within-sex as random will have fatally low power. Considerably greater power will result with 10 to 15 experimenters of each sex, even with the same total number of participants divided up among experimenters.

This is a chapter on design rather than analysis, so I only mention that proper analysis of studies involving more than one random factor (e.g., participants and a materials factor) typically requires the use of quasi-F ratios (rather than standard F tests). Using standard F tests, or simply summing across levels of a random factor to produce the dependent variables for analysis, can produce massive bias; see Santa, Miller, and Shaw (1979). Detailed treatments of these analytic issues can be found in standard analysis of variance texts or in Kenny, Kashy, and Bolger (1998).

Extremity of Levels

In writing accident scenarios with mild and severe consequences, perhaps one drafts a story in which a driver carelessly leaves a car on a hill without setting the parking brake, and the car rolls down the hill. The result could be either minor scrapes and dents for the car or severe injuries to a passerby who is struck by the car. But the manipulation could be larger: no damage whatsoever versus killing three people or even hitting a gas pipeline and setting off an explosion that kills and injures dozens. In other situations a researcher might need to manipulate levels of the communicator's physical attractiveness or expertise or the strength of the arguments used in a study of persuasion. How can one decide about the appropriate levels of extremity for manipulations in research?

MATCHING NATURALLY OCCURRING TREATMENTS. One approach to answering this question, termed "ecological design" (Brunswik, 1955), emphasizes constructing manipulations that match those found in everyday life. Stories involving severe accidents might be sampled from newspaper reports, for example – although a thoughtful researcher might realize that the newspaper reports themselves are far from representative of the population of accidents that actually occur. For manipulations of many theoretically specified constructs it is not clear how to apply the principle of ecological design. Should one select communicators whose physical attractiveness falls one standard deviation above and below the mean on some scale of rated attractiveness in a given population?

One advantage of ecological design is that an experiment might yield useful information about the size of a given treatment effect, so that one can judge whether it is practically important or meaningful. Another claimed advantage of using ecologically representative manipulations is an improved ability to generalize experimental results to nonexperimental settings. This idea has a certain intuitive appeal. However, consider the distinction made by Aronson et al. (1990) between *mundane realism* (a match on superficial features between an experimental manipulation and some aspect of everyday life) and *experimental realism* (the impact and meaningfulness of a manipulation for the subjects). In these terms the call of ecological design is for high levels of mundane realism. However, it is not clear why mundane realism should be the most important

desideratum for research design. As Brewer (this volume, Ch. 1) argues, construct validity is much more closely linked to experimental than to mundane realism. And construct validity is the chief concern with respect to the generalizability of theory-testing research (see also Mook, 1983).

POWERFUL MANIPULATIONS. On the other side, the potential advantage of strong (even unrealistically strong) manipulations is statistical power. As long as they do not provoke ethical problems or excite suspicion or ridicule, factors can often be manipulated powerfully in the laboratory. Thus a researcher might try to write extremely strong and extremely weak arguments and choose photos of extraordinarily attractive and unattractive individuals to manipulate the characteristics of the communicator. Strong manipulations, when they are possible, will lead to larger effect sizes (increasing the mean differences among conditions without increasing the error variance that serves as the denominator of the effect size estimate) and more statistical power. It is important to recognize, though, that research manipulations are not invariably more powerful than conditions found in everyday life. Effects of situations such as life-threatening illness, the death of a close relative, or watching thousands of murders and violent assaults on television over the course of many years are important to study, but must be studied as they naturally occur for they cannot be reproduced as manipulations.

SCALING EFFECT SIZES BY MANIPULATION SIZES. Abelson (1995, pp. 47–52) introduced the notion of *causal efficacy*, a scaled measure of effect size defined as the difference between conditions on the dependent variable divided by the difference between conditions on the independent variable. For example, if participants practice a task for different numbers of trials in different conditions, the effect of practice might be expressed in terms like percent increase in accuracy per trial of practice. Of course, only a small number of typical social psychological manipulations (e.g., number of persuasive arguments, trials of practice, number of people in audience) are points on a quantitative scale. In other cases, Abelson suggested that a rating of the conceptual independent variable in each condition, which is usually assessed in any case as a manipulation check, can be used as the denominator for the causal efficacy estimate. In a persuasion study we might calculate difference in amount of attitude change divided by difference in rated strength of arguments to compare two conditions. Like an unstandardized regression coefficient, which it conceptually resembles, this measure of causal efficacy is unaffected by the extremity of the manipulation's range. That is, though a larger range always produces greater statistical power, causal efficacy estimates should be comparable across studies with larger and smaller ranges of manipulation.

Widespread use of this ratio in interpreting results might be helpful. For example, it might help researchers avoid the elementary error of designing a study manipulating two variables X and Y, finding a larger effect of X (perhaps no significant effect of Y at all), and declaring that X is a more powerful influence than Y on the dependent variable. The fallacy is obvious: Because the extremity of manipulation is ordinarily an arbitrary choice, the researcher might have obtained different results simply by manipulating X less strongly and Y more strongly. The causal efficacy estimates for X and Y are not affected by this arbitrary choice. (They will not be directly comparable, though, unless the factors X and Y have identical scales.)

Number of Levels

How many levels of a given factor should be used? First, as already noted, if a factor is treated as random the number of levels effectively becomes the "N" that heavily influences statistical power. For example, there may be many stories, scenarios, or videotapes (vehicles for a given manipulation) that serve as replications. In this situation the more levels, the better.

Another common case is a factor that represents an ordered continuum (more or less severe damage from an accident, strong or weak arguments, stereotype-consistent or stereotype-inconsistent behaviors). The typical research design uses just "high" and "low" levels of such a factor, an approach that maximizes simplicity and statistical power to detect a hypothesized linear effect (McClelland, 1997). However, it can be argued that using more than two levels spaced along the continuum can yield unexpected findings – such as a nonlinear or even nonmonotonic effect of the variable – that may be conceptually important. The cost is reduced efficiency for detecting the linear effect. For example, McClelland (1997) showed that relative to using just the extreme ends of the continuum (with half of the participants in each group), dividing the participants into three equally spaced groups gives an efficiency of .67, and five equally spaced groups just .50. The total number of participants would have to be boosted by 50% or 100%, respectively, to compensate for this loss of efficiency. Perhaps few researchers would accept this trade-off if they realized the magnitude of its cost, in

situations where the linear effect is of key interest and the possibility of a nonlinear effect is only considered as an afterthought.

Sometimes researchers make the mistake of dichotomizing continuously measured variables (such as pretests or personality or attitude scores) to fit the overall analysis into a rigid analysis of variance (ANOVA) framework. It is well-known that dichotomizing a continuous variable throws away valid variance and reduces power. Still, some researchers argue that if they obtain significant effects of the dichotomized variable despite the acknowledged loss of power there is no harm done. Recent work by Maxwell and Delaney (1993) showed, however, that this approach can lead to bias, even making another factor in the design appear to have a significant effect when in reality it does not; the issue is discussed further by Judd (this volume, Ch. 14). There is no good reason to commit this sin in the first place; widely available analysis programs, such as SAS PROC GLM, are flexible enough to use measured continuous variables as well as classification variables (e.g., manipulated factors) in a single analysis.

RELATIONS AMONG FACTORS

Multiple factors in a design can be crossed, nested, or confounded. *Crossed* factors include each level of one factor in combination with each level of the other (e.g., strong and weak arguments are each delivered by an attractive and an unattractive communicator, in a total of four different conditions). *Nested* factors involve multiple levels of a subsidiary factor that occur uniquely within a given level of a more encompassing factor (e.g., several individual experimenters nested within experimenter sex). Figure 2.1a shows an example, with participants nested within levels. *Confounded* factors are two or more conceptually distinct variables that covary perfectly so their effects cannot be empirically disentangled (e.g., individual experimenters and experimenter sex when there are only one male and one female experimenter).

Reasons for Using Between-Participants Versus Within-Participants Factors

One important aspect of a design is whether the factor representing participants (or other units of study, such as groups, couples, etc.) is crossed by or nested within other factors. A between-participants design is one in which participants are nested within all other factors; that is, a distinct group of participants is exposed to the condition created by each combination of the other design factors. A within-participants design has one or more factors crossed by participants, so that each participant is measured under more than one condition. A *mixed* design has both between-participants and within-participants factors.

The reasons for preferring to manipulate a factor within or between participants generally boil down to power versus the possibility of bias. Power is often greater for a within-participants manipulation. This is because with many types of dependent variables, differences among participants are by far the largest source of variance. Such differences inflate the error term for testing effects of between-participants factors, but are irrelevant for within-participants comparisons. Sometimes this advantage is stated as "each subject serves as his or her own control" in a within-participants design.

However, within-participants designs allow for several types of bias. *Carryover effects* occur when a participant's response in a given condition depends on conditions that participant experienced previously within the experiment. This could occur, for example, if previous stimuli serve as an anchor or context for the participants judgments and reactions to the next stimulus. Likewise, previous conditions could create fatigue, prime specific cognitive representations, or influence participants' mood. Fortunately, carryover effects can be detected in the data analysis as differences in responses when conditions are administered to participants in different sequences.

In addition, participants in a within-participants design see more than one condition and are thus in a better position to guess at the experimental hypotheses. The resulting *demand characteristics* (Orne, 1962) are an important potential source of bias, as participants start wondering "what are they getting at here" or "what am I supposed to do in this experiment" rather than simply performing the task. For example, a participant who is asked to evaluate the credentials of several "job candidates" may notice that some are men and others are women and leap to the conclusion that the study concerns gender stereotyping and discrimination. It is virtually impossible that this participants responses to the stimulus persons could remain unaffected by this thought. A participant who evaluates only one candidate is less likely to draw the same conclusion, though the possibility obviously still remains.

Sometimes researchers informally apply an additional consideration, whether the factor of interest or its conceptual relatives occurs "between or within participants" outside the laboratory (cf. Brunswik, 1955). For example, an investigator who is interested in people's reactions to different types of advertisements for consumer products or political candidates could in principle use a between- or within-participants design, weighing power versus potential carryover biases. But he or she might well conclude that in everyday life, people often encounter many ads for competing products or candidates in quick succession and that the experimental design might as well match that reality.

Reasons for Crossing Factors: I. Testing Theoretically Predicted Interactions (Construct Validity)

Perhaps the most important reason for including crossed factors in an experimental design is to test a predicted interaction. Suppose one has a finding, for example that people can better recall expectation-inconsistent than expectation-consistent information about a person (Hastie & Kumar, 1979). If a theoretical explanation holds that the effect depends on effortful cognitive processing, one might then predict that people who (as a measured individual difference) enjoy thinking hard might show the effect more strongly than other people. Or one might predict that people under time pressure would not be able to engage in sufficient thought to show the effect, compared with people who have as much time as they need. Such interaction predictions have been tested and support the validity of the theoretical explanation. In general, theories that predict more details of a data pattern (such as a specific interaction pattern rather than a simple main effect) gain more in credibility when their predictions are confirmed. This use of interactions in a design improves construct validity. In social psychology, history and tradition seem to give special honor to nonobvious predictions of all kinds, but particularly interaction predictions (Abelson, 1995, p. 113).

DEMONSTRATING THEORETICALLY PREDICTED DISSOCIATIONS. Theoretical predictions of null effects can be important. For example, if a particular judgmental bias is thought be be automatic and uncontrollable, one might predict that it will be unaffected by participants' motivation to be accurate (manipulated, say, by offering a substantial financial reward for accuracy). Such predictions in general should not be tested standing alone, but in a larger design in which the predictions take the form of an interaction. To illustrate, suppose that one predicts that variable X does not cause Y. If one simply manipulates X and measures Y, a finding of no effect is virtually meaningless; too many alternative explanations (including a weak manipulation of X

or an insufficient N resulting in low power) are available. The problems are greatly lessened if one can show in the same study that X affects Z while not affecting Y (a pattern termed a single dissociation, conceptually equivalent to an interaction of the X manipulation by measure [Y vs. Z]). Still, however, one alternative explanation remains open – that the Y measure is insensitive or highly resistant to change for theoretically irrelevant reasons. If nothing could affect Y, the theoretical import of the finding that X in particular does not affect Y is minimal. The answer to this interpretive ambiguity is the full *double dissociation* design: Manipulate both X and an additional variable W and demonstrate that X affects Z (and not Y) while W affects Y (and not Z). The logic of convergent and discriminant validity, as applied in this form, is necessary to permit meaningful interpretations of the obtained null effects (see Dunn & Kirsner, 1988, for a related argument).

INTERPRETING INTERACTIONS VERSUS CONDITION MEANS. One interpretive issue involving interactions will be briefly mentioned here, though it receives more complete coverage in Judd's chapter 14 on analysis. Should interpretation focus on the interaction effect per se, or on the simple effects? For example, in a 2×2 design (say, Participant Sex $\times$ Treatment/Control), should one focus on interpreting the effects of treatment separately within each sex, or interpret the interaction effect itself? This issue has aroused some controversy (e.g., Abelson, 1996; Petty, Fabrigar, Wegener, & Priester, 1996; Rosnow & Rosenthal, 1995, 1996). The key is to understand that the interaction effect is precisely a test of the difference between the two simple effects. The direction and significance of each of the simple effects is a separate question. For instance, a significant interaction is consistent with a pattern in which one main effect is near zero and the other positive, or one main effect is negative and the other positive, or even with neither main effect differing significantly from zero. In most research situations, the hypothesis tested by the interaction – that the two simple effects differ – is the hypothesis of interest, and researchers should beware of formulating and testing hypotheses (such as predicting that one simple effect is positive and the other zero) that involve not only the interaction but also the direction and relative magnitude of overall main effects in the design.

POWER FOR INTERACTIONS. In an experimental design with equal numbers of participants assigned to the cells, tests of interactions have the same power as tests of main effects. This can easily be seen in a 2×2 design because interactions and main effects can be viewed as different 1-*df* contrasts on the four condition means treated as a one-way design. However, when one or more factors are measured rather than manipulated, statistical power for testing interactions can be lower, sometimes by an order of magnitude, than power for testing main effects in the same study. First, if the design includes few cases that have extreme values on both of the crossed factors, power for testing the interaction can be devastatingly low (McClelland & Judd, 1993). Of course, this may be the case for variables that are personality scores or other more or less normally distributed measurements, but not if the two crossed factors are experimentally manipulated. Second, low power for tests of interactions can result from measurement unreliability. If the two factors that enter into the interaction are imperfectly measured, it is well-known that tests of their effects lose power – and tests of their interaction lose even more (Busemeyer & Jones, 1983; Jaccard & Wan, 1995). Again, experimentally manipulated factors (which generally have no measurement error) do not suffer from this problem. But outside of the planned experiment context, in a field study or in an experiment that includes one or more measured independent variables, low power for interactions is a serious threat to a researcher who is theoretically interested in interaction effects.

TRANSFORMATIONS COMPLICATE INTERPRETATIONS. Another issue concerning interactions is that with ordinal interactions (those that do not involve crossover patterns), transformations of the dependent variable can create or remove interactions. Unless the applicability of transformations can be ruled out on a theoretical basis, claims about the presence or absence of an interaction are weak. That is, unless a researcher can defend the idea that a log, square-root, square, or some other transformation cannot meaningfully be applied to the response scale, he or she is in a poor position to argue that an ordinal interaction is present or absent in the data. As an example, several studies have drawn theoretical conclusions based on findings suggesting that long-term (chronic accessibility) and temporary (priming) sources of accessibility of mental constructs do or do not interact (e.g., Bargh, Bond, Lombardi & Tota, 1986). But the data patterns never show crossovers, and so conclusions as to the additivity or interactivity of these sources of accessibility are weak at best. No argument against the application of transformations is likely to be convincing. The level of activation of an unobservable mental representation (presumably the construct of true theoretical interest) has an effect through two steps, neither obviously linear: Activation affects the probability or intensity of use of the mental representation to encode a given stimulus, which in turn affects an overt rating scale response when the participant is asked to make judgments about the stimulus. In cases like this, in which the assumption of linearity of the construct–response scale relationship is indefensible, an argument can be made for applying whatever standard data transformation makes the results of a body of studies simplest – for example, main effects without interactions (Abelson, 1995, pp. 117–118).

Reasons for Crossing Factors: II. Reducing Error Variance (Statistical Conclusion Validity)

Besides increasing construct validity by testing specific theoretical predictions, researchers may have other reasons for including crossed factors in a design. A second reason is related to statistical conclusion validity: Added factors can reduce error variance and therefore increase the statistical power of a design to detect an effect of interest. Consider that variables affecting a particular dependent measure can be held constant, allowed to vary unsystematically, or varied systematically. For instance, if the researcher is interested in the effect of strong versus weak persuasive arguments on attitudes concerning a controversial social issue, he or she may attempt to hold constant participants' motivation to read the persuasive message carefully (by instilling a high level of motivation in all participants). Differences in the amount of participants' knowledge about the issue may be allowed to vary unsystematically. And participant factors such as gender, or situational factors such as the time of day, may be systematically varied and recorded so that their potential effects on the dependent variable can be assessed.

COVARIATES AND POWER. Relative to allowing an influential variable to vary freely, either holding it constant or statistically controlling for its effect will decrease the amount of residual error variance in the dependent variable. In turn this increases the statistical power of the study to detect effects of other independent variables of interest. Factors that are included in an experiment specifically for this purpose, because they represent theoretically irrelevant sources of variance that are known to have strong effects, are termed covariates (if they are continuous measured variables) or blocking factors (if they are categorical). For example, a pretest attitude score, if available, could be used

as a covariate. The choice between treating a variable as a covariate and using it to create blocks should be based on the degree of correlation between the covariate and the dependent variable; higher levels of correlation give an advantage in statistical power to the covariate treatment and lower levels to blocking (Feldt, 1958).

ANALYSES WITH COVARIATES. In the results of such a study, a main effect of a covariate or blocking factor is usually expected but of little theoretical interest. Interactions between the factor of conceptual interest and the covariate or blocking factor, however, may be theoretically important. For example, a given message may be found to have a larger persuasive effect on participants with one initial attitude position rather than another. Such interactions have implications for the generality of the treatment effect and are discussed more fully later in this chapter. Treatment-by-covariate interactions are not considered in the traditional analysis of covariance framework, but can be tested without difficulty in a general linear model framework (Cohen, 1968; e.g., SAS PROC GLM).

Covariates may be measured once per participant or once per observation in a within-participant design. To illustrate, imagine a study in which participants make repeated ratings of their overall impression of a social group, as they encounter information about more and more individual group members. In this design, "number of group members encountered" is a within-participants independent variable. If the researcher can obtain participants' scores on a personality measure, such as authoritarianism, which is expected to influence ratings of out-groups, this variable might be used as a covariate (with a single score per participant). If it is believed that participants' mood might also affect the positivity of their ratings of the group, an assessment of momentary mood might be taken at the same time each rating is made, and used as a within-participants covariate. Either of these types of covariate might not only have a main effect on the dependent variable, but might interact with the experimental factor. For instance, effects of increased exposure to the out-group might lead to more positive ratings among participants in positive moods. Judd and McClelland (1989, pp. 473–491) discussed analysis of such designs.

An important conceptual point regarding the use of covariates is the time of their measurement and their conceptual status as control variables or mediators. Ordinarily, covariates (or blocking factors) used purely to control error variance are measured before the treatment is applied. If treatments are randomly assigned, this means that the covariate and the treatment factors are expected to be independent. However, what if the covariate is measured after the treatment is administered? In this case the treatment might affect the covariate as well as the dependent variable, and controlling for the covariate would mean that the treatment effect would not be properly estimated. However, this exact design is used when one considers the covariate as a potential mediator of the treatment effect on the dependent variable, a situation that is discussed later (Judd & Kenny, 1981, pp. 59–60).

Because this chapter focuses on experimental design, it is assumed here that the main factor of interest (such as strong versus weak arguments in the example) is randomly assigned and manipulated. In this context, the use of covariates serves to increase power but is not necessary to correct for initial differences between the groups of participants exposed to the different treatments. Indeed, because of random assignment such differences are not expected to exist. In a nonexperimental design often termed the nonequivalent control group design, levels of a treatment are administered to intact or self-selected groups that differ in unknown ways. In this case, covariates serve (more or less unsatisfactorily) to adjust for some of the differences between the treatment groups. This design raises many difficult issues; see discussions by Cook and Campbell (1979) and West et al.'s chapter 3 in this volume.

Reasons for Crossing Factors: III. Establishing Generality of an Effect (External Validity)

A third reason for including crossed factors in a design is related to external validity: the desire to establish the generality of a given effect across multiple levels of another factor. Once again, recall that the three ways of handling a potential influence on a dependent measure are to hold it constant, allow it to vary unsystematically, or vary it systematically (manipulate or measure it). We noted earlier that holding constant and varying systematically were preferable from the viewpoint of statistical conclusion validity. Now it turns out that varying unsystematically and varying systematically are preferable from the viewpoint of external validity. Abelson's (1995) Seventh Law is "You can't see the dust if you don't move the couch" (p. 155).

VARYING A FACTOR UNSYSTEMATICALLY. Let us consider three ways of allowing variation in a contextual factor, one that might influence a dependent variable but whose effects are not of primary theoretical interest. First, allowing the factor to vary unsystematically (as compared with holding it constant) offers the advantage of establishing at least a minimal level of generalizability of the experimental effect of interest. For example, if an experiment calls for a confederate to interact with participants and administer a manipulation, using five different confederates (as opposed to just one) can show at least that the result holds averaged across the unsystematic influences of the confederates' personal characteristics (see Cook & Campbell, 1979, pp. 71–73). However, one cannot say for certain that the effect holds at each level of the unsystematically varied factor.

VARYING A FACTOR SYSTEMATICALLY. Second, systematically varying the contextual factor (e.g., using "confederate" as a design factor crossed with condition and analyzing for its effects) offers potential advantages. To the extent that contexts have lawful effects on the dependent variable, this approach, compared with unsystematic variation, will reduce error variance and increase power (see above). And the analysis can potentially establish that the effect of interest holds at each level of the contextual factor (not just averaged across levels, as in the previous approach). The drawback is that the contextual factor probably should be considered as random, as discussed earlier, with important implications for the power of the research.

The ideal pattern of results is an effect of the theoretically important factor, but no interactions of that factor with the contextual variables (such as confederate). Abelson (1995, pp. 108–113, 142–143) discussed issues involved in interpreting such interactions, particularly the differences between qualitative and quantitative interactions. He introduced three useful and novel terms: a *tick* is a specific, articulated finding, such as a reliable difference between two means; a *but* is a qualification on a tick; and a *blob* is an undifferentiated and therefore meaningless "finding" (e.g., a significant multi-df F-test). Examples may illustrate the use of these terms. "Compared to the control condition, Treatment X improved performance on Task Y" or "... on all tasks" is a tick. "Compared to the control condition, Treatment X improved performance on Task Y but not on Tasks Z or W" – a quantitative (noncrossover) interaction – is a tick and a but. "Treatment significantly interacted with Task" is a blob. "Treatment X improved performance on Task Y but decreased performance on Task Z," a crossover interaction, is two ticks – really two findings rather than a single finding with a qualification. And "Treatment X improved performance to the degree that subjects expected success on the task" could be an insightful and parsimonious redescription of the two-tick result as a single tick (Zajonc, 1965, is a classic example). Abelson's introduction of these terms leads to a useful metric for assessing the merit of alternative descriptions of results: Never use blobs, minimize ticks (in the interests of parsimony), and minimize buts (in the interests of generality).

VARYING A FACTOR ACROSS STUDIES. A third approach is to hold a given variable constant in a particular study and rely on variation of contexts across studies to establish generalizability of an effect of interest. This approach may be taken either within a given investigator's lab (e.g., use one confederate in one study and a different confederate in a similar study conducted the next semester) or across labs. Replication across labs is obviously the most feasible approach to varying several potentially important types of contexts that might influence a research result, such as the participant population, type of equipment used, specific implementation of treatments, and so on. Replications across different studies, whether in one or many labs or other settings, can be summarized with the technique of meta-analysis (Johnson & Eagly, this volume, Ch. 19).

In recent years, authorities chiefly interested in the analysis of social interventions in natural settings (Cook & Shadish, 1994) and those concerned with the generality of theoretical conclusions from laboratory-based research (e.g., Abelson, 1995; Hedges & Olkin, 1985) have converged on a recommendation to take this third approach: Replicate in separate studies and meta-analyze to establish generality. Cook and Shadish (1994) noted that

Interest has shifted away from exploring interactions within individual experiments and toward reviewing the results of many related experiments that are heterogeneous in the times, populations, settings, and treatment and outcome variants examined. Such reviews promise to identify more of the causal contingencies implied by [the philosopher] Mackie's fallibilist, probabilistic theory of causation; and they speak to the more general concern with causal generalization that emerged in the 1980s and 1990s. (p. 548)

Abelson (1995) noted that a narrow focus on generalization from a single study is misplaced, given that "In practice, real research investigations usually involve multiple studies conducted as part of an ongoing conceptual elaboration of a particular topic. This permits a richer variety of possible assertions about outcomes" (p. 38).

ADDITIONAL CONSIDERATIONS. There are several other considerations involving replication. First, the emphasis here is on what has sometimes been called conceptual replication rather than exact replication. In a *conceptual replication*, the researcher looks for new ways to manipulate or measure the conceptual variables of interest, rather than striving to reproduce exactly all the procedures of the original study. Exact replications are rarely carried out in social psychology; the most important exceptions are when a study is being criticized. For example, conducting an exact replication study seems to be necessary when a new researcher believes the original results are simply a product of Type I error, or when he or she wishes to demonstrate that some confounding factor produced the results of the original study and that removal of the confound will change the results. Outside of these limited circumstances, replications ordinarily involve some variation rather than precise following of a recipe, and they often involve the addition of extra conditions or measures in an effort to explore the limits of an effect as well as incorporating the conditions of the original study.

Second, researchers frequently overestimate the likelihood of a replication being successful. After all, the original study demonstrated the effect, so shouldn't a similar study be able to also? However, Greenwald, Gonzalez, Harris, and Guthrie (1993) showed that if an original study produced a significant effect at the .05 level, the chance of obtaining significance in an exact, independent replication using the same N is quite low. Only if the first study produced $p < .005$ does the replication have a power level of .80 to detect the effect at the .05 level! This is an instance of researchers' general overoptimism about power levels and their consequent tendency to run low-powered studies, which has frequently been noted and decried (Cohen, 1962, 1990).

Nonindependence of Observations in Within-Participants Designs

In any design in which multiple measurements are taken per participant (or other unit, such as couple or group), the observations must be assumed to be nonindependent. For example, evaluations of multiple stimulus persons given by a single participant will probably be positively correlated, as a result of the participant's expectations about people in general, tendencies to use particular ranges of the response scale, etc. In other situations, such as in a study measuring the amount of talking time by leaders versus other members in a problem-solving group, the variables are likely to be negatively correlated: the more talking by one person, the less by others. In fact, hidden sources of nonindependence may be present and contaminate observations even when a design is intended to focus on individual participants. For example, if several participants at a time are seated in a room to fill out individual questionnaires, they may influence each other (perhaps by muttering comments about the questions or their answers), or situational factors (such as an uncomfortably warm room or an audible disturbance in the hallway outside) may have common influences on all participants in a group.

If nonindependence between observations is ignored in the data analysis, bias will result. Judd and McClelland (1989, p. 425) described the direction of bias in different situations. When participants (or groups, or other units that produce multiple observations) are nested within conditions, a positive correlation produces a "liberal" bias (F statistics too large) and a negative correlation produces a "conservative" bias (F statistics too small). When participants are crossed with conditions, the opposite pattern emerges. Thus, nonindependence of observations can result in an increased likelihood of either Type I or Type II errors depending on the specific circumstances. The bias can be large in realistic circumstances (Kenny & Judd, 1986).

As a result, the data analysis must take account of nonindependence. Two approaches are widely used, repeated-measures ANOVA and multivariate ANOVA (MANOVA). The latter is more general in that it does not require certain statistical assumptions about the covariances of the errors, which repeated-measures ANOVA requires and which are often problematic in practice. Kenny (1985, pp. 491–492) gave a clear description of an alternative approach, involving coding within-participants contrasts for effects of interest, that may be helpful in understanding how a true MANOVA works.

Nonindependence raises the question of what is the "unit" in a given study. One basic principle is that in an experimental design the units of analysis must always be the same units that were randomly assigned. So if students within classrooms were randomly assigned to different treatments one would analyze students (with classrooms used as a blocking variable); if intact classrooms were assigned to treatments one would analyze classrooms. However, the unit of measurement may or may not be the same as the unit of assignment and analysis. For example, observations of teacher behavior would be a variable measured at the classroom level, whereas attitudes or achievement test scores may be measured on individual students and aggregated to form classroom-level dependent variables.

Researchers studying dyads or groups frequently face unit-of-analysis issues. In many studies groups are assigned to conditions (e.g., time pressure or no time pressure), so groups also constitute the units of analysis. The problem is that the analysis will be low powered because of the small number of groups relative to individual participants. Where the dependent measures are actually assessed at the group level (e.g., group decision, degree of inequality in talking time) then this problem has no solution. But if the actual measures are at the individual level (e.g., satisfaction with the group's decision) one can analyze participants nested within groups nested within conditions. If analysis shows that the participants within groups and groups within conditions mean squares are roughly equal, one can pool them to form an error term for testing the conditions effect with greater power (see Judd & Kenny, 1981, p. 178).

Counterbalancing and Latin Square Designs

COUNTERBALANCING. Suppose that one wishes, for theoretical reasons, to investigate the effect of a prior expectation about a person on recall of the person's behavior. One could tell participants that a fictitious character, call him "John," is an honest fellow and then expose them to a list of some of his honest and dishonest behaviors (randomly ordered). Hastie and Kumar (1979) performed a study like this and found superior recall for the expectation-inconsistent behaviors. However, there is a problem with this design as described. Because honest and dishonest behaviors necessarily differ in content, one set might be more unusual, more distinctive, more concrete, more imageable, or different in some other way that affects memorability. We would be unable to tell whether it is inconsistency with expectations or some uncontrolled factor of this nature that led to the superior memory.

There are two possible approaches to this type of confounding. One could attempt to have judges prerate all the stimuli (here, the behaviors) for concreteness, distinctiveness, imageability, and so on, and then select sets of honest and dishonest behaviors that are exactly equated on all these factors. But this approach, besides being incredibly cumbersome, is ultimately doomed to failure: However long the list of factors that can be rated and equated, it can never be guaranteed to include all that might affect the items' memorability. Hastie and Kumar (1979) chose an alternative approach that is both simpler and more effective. They employed a *counterbalanced* design, in which the same behaviors served as expectation-consistent stimuli for some participants and expectation-inconsistent ones for others. That is, different groups of participants (randomly assigned) initially learned that John was honest or that John was dishonest. Then the same list of behaviors was administered to all participants. This approach uses the logic of design to ensure that all factors affecting the memorability of a behavior – even those that the researchers are unaware of – are equated between consistent and inconsistent behaviors, across the entire experiment.

As another example, suppose a researcher wishes to compare people's ability to decode nonverbal cues from a friend versus a stranger. If participants are just asked to come to the study bringing a friend to use as one target, and a research assistant or videotape clip (etc.) is used as the stranger target, the particular characteristics of participants' friends (e.g., their sex) may influence their scores. A solution to this problem is as follows (Kenny, 1985, p. 491). Pair participants randomly, calling the members of each pair A and B. Each reports to the lab with a friend; then A's friend serves as the stranger target for B and vice versa. In this way, across the entire study the personal characteristics of the "friend" and "stranger" targets will be exactly equivalent. A similar logic is involved if a researcher wishes to construct written stimulus materials that are specifically tuned for each participant, using words or constructs that that participant employs frequently (termed "chronically accessible") and also words or constructs that are employed less frequently (e.g., Higgins, King, & Mavin, 1982). Again, a solution is pairing participants and using A's chronically accessible words as the less accessible words for B, and vice versa. Across the entire experiment this design guarantees that the distribution of characteristics of accessible and less accessible words are the same.

Note that pairing participants in these ways potentially creates nonindependence within each pair of participants, requiring that pairs be treated as units in the analysis. For example, the characteristics of A's friend or A's accessible words influence both A's and B's responses in the study. In addition, one important consideration is whether there is some clear basis for assigning the members of each pair to the "A" and "B" roles in the analysis. A study of dyadic interaction, for example, may pair a male with a female or a parent with a child in each dyad, or may bring together pairs of male participants. In the latter case, with nothing in particular to differentiate the participants, results can

be affected by the way they are assigned to roles in the analysis; see Griffin and Gonzalez (1995).

LATIN SQUARE DESIGNS. Counterbalancing frequently makes use of a type of design termed a Latin square. Figure 2.1b shows the simplest instance of this design, with two groups of participants who receive two levels of the treatment, in a counterbalanced order. Group 1 receives level 1 then level 2, and Group 2 receives level 2 then level 1. Analysis of such a design (see any ANOVA textbook or Judd & McClelland, 1989, pp. 456–472) can separate order effects from treatment effects. Note one important qualification, however: Treatment is completely confounded with the Group × Order interaction. Thus, treatment effects can be interpreted only if it is assumed that this interaction is absent. In an experimental design, where participants are randomly assigned to groups, this assumption poses no problem. There is no reason why two randomly constructed groups of participants should differ in the effect of order on their responses. Nevertheless, in principle this interaction is confounded with treatment; similarly, Group × Treatment is confounded with order. The Treatment × Order interaction (confounded with group) is the one to examine for the presence of any carryover effects (e.g., effects of a treatment that differ depending on whether it was the first, second, etc. treatment encountered by a participant).

The same principle can be further generalized to the situation where factors other than order are associated with different treatments. In many studies, a treatment is embedded in some type of stimulus that serves as a vehicle (e.g., a photo manipulation of physical attractiveness embedded in a folder of information about a target person, a manipulation of source expertise embedded in a persuasive message about some topic). For reasons of power it is often desirable to use within-participants designs with such materials, but a given participant can see each stimulus in only one condition. It would be nonsensical for a participant to see different photos paired with the same person information, or the same message attributed to both an expert and nonexpert source. Again, a Latin square design is the solution.

Kenny and Smith (1980) presented methods for constructing and analyzing appropriately counterbalanced designs, where the rows are groups of participants and columns are groups of stimuli, and treatments are assigned to particular cells of the design. An example (Smith & Miller, 1979) is an attribution study in which 32 sentences describing simple behaviors were used as stimuli. Each behavior was paired with additional consistency, consensus, and distinctiveness information (in a $2 \times 2 \times 2$ design) that was expected to influence attributions concerning the cause of the behavior. In the design as implemented, each participant responded to each of the 32 behaviors, 4 in each cell of the $2 \times 2 \times 2$. In such a design, it is important to randomly assign stimuli to the stimulus groups (8 groups in this case), just as it is important to assign participants randomly to participant groups as in Figure 2.1b above. Also, in this design the Latin square is used to control for the effects of particular stimuli that make up the columns of the Latin square. Order is not statistically controlled and must be handled in some other way (Smith & Miller randomized order of presentation separately for each participant). Finally, Kenny and Smith (1980) emphasized that the stimulus factor (e.g., the 32 behaviors) is properly considered as random. As Santa et al. (1979) have demonstrated, simply summing over stimuli to form a dependent measure for each condition, or mistakenly treating the stimuli factor as fixed, can give rise to upward-biased F-tests. This is because variation due to items or stimuli would be confounded with variation due to conditions. This error frequently occurs in the literature.

OTHER FORMS OF INTENTIONAL CONFOUNDING. Latin squares involve the confounding of effects (e.g., treatment with Group $\times$ Order effects). Other designs can be constructed that involve intentional confounding, which keep the required numbers of participants down. Suppose a researcher wishes to implement a 2^8 design but is limited to 128 participants, only half as many as the cells of the full design. With a type of design termed a "fractional factorial," this study can be done. But some confounding of effects is inevitable. The key is to observe that in such a scenario, high-order interactions (e.g., five-way or higher) are not likely to be theoretically predicted and are probably going to be uninterpretable even if found. By giving up the ability to look at these relatively uninteresting effects, the researcher can focus on the main effects and lower-order interactions of chief interest. One can arrange matters so that it is the high-order interactions that are confounded with main effects. Winer (1971, pp. 240–260) discussed the implementation of such designs.

Nested Factors

In addition to being crossed or confounded, factors may be nested. We have already discussed the issues involved in the most common cases of nesting, where the inner (nested) factor is random (e.g.,

participants within experimental conditions, individual experimenters within experimenter sex). Rarely, a nonrandom nested factor is used, such as a manipulation of specific occupations within occupational status ([low status] janitor, secretary; [high status] manager, physician) in a study of occupational stereotypes. In a case like this the researcher may be interested in the specific effects of each level of the nested variable (occupation in the example) and also in comparing the larger categories (low vs. high status). However, this situation need not be conceptualized as two nested factors and in fact usually is not; an equally effective alternative approach is to regard occupation as the only design factor and to perform planned comparisons to examine effects of status.

DEPENDENT VARIABLES

Issues involving the treatment of one or more dependent measures in a study are also part of experimental design, and these choices can influence power, internal validity, construct validity, and external validity.

To Pretest or Not to Pretest?

Pretesting participants with a measure identical or related to the dependent variable can increase power. As discussed above, the pretest can be used as a covariate or to set up a blocking factor with blocks composed of participants with similar pretest scores. The increase of power depends on the covariate's within-groups correlation with the dependent variable. If that correlation is r, the experiment's error variance decreases by approximately a factor of $1 - r^2$ in either a randomized-blocks or covariance design (Kirk, 1968, p. 486). If a covariate with a correlation of .70 is available, its use would cut error variance roughly in half, then, doubling all F statistics.

Yet pretesting is not common in social psychological experiments. Why not? Some obvious reasons include the popularity of types of studies in which pretests hardly make sense, such as social cognition studies in which the dependent variables are various measures of participants' judgments concerning specific stimulus materials. Participants cannot be asked to make judgments of the materials before the study begins. Likewise, in within-participants designs where variation between participants does not enter into the error term, pretesting is of little use. But even in attitude-change research, in which a pretest measure of the target attitude could be administered before the persuasion manipulation, pretests are often not used. The main reason is a concern about biases caused by exposure to the pretest (Cook & Campbell, 1979). Participants who have completed a pretest measure of some attitude or other construct may respond differently to a relevant manipulation than unpretested participants, weakening the generalizability of research conclusions. If the possibility of pretest sensitization can be eliminated at the cost of a modest decrease of power (which can be overcome by using a larger N), perhaps pretesting is best avoided.

Another approach to avoiding pretest sensitization is to administer a pretest in a separate session, completely unconnected with the main experiment in the participants' minds. For example, in a mass pretesting session at the beginning of an academic term, members of the participant pool may fill out numerous measures. Among these may be pretests for experiments in which they may participate later in the term. This type of procedure should greatly reduce or eliminate the possibility that participants will respond differently in the main experiment than they would have without the relevant pretest.

The Solomon Four-Group Design, which is essentially a Pretest/No Pretest × Treatment/Control 2 × 2, can be used to examine whether pretest sensitization effects exist in any given instance (Campbell & Stanley, 1963). But this design is rarely employed in practice, for if researchers suspect the possibility of pretest sensitization they usually prefer to avoid it rather than to study it.

Selection of Items for Dependent Measure

One important issue regarding the selection of items or stimuli of any sort in the construction of a dependent measure has strong parallels with an issue discussed earlier, the treatment of "contextual" factors that are not of primary theoretical interest (such as different types of accident scenarios that serve as vehicles for a manipulation of accident severity). In fact, "items" could be considered a within-participant factor. But the issue is reviewed here because conceptually it has to do with the nature of a dependent measure. As in the case discussed earlier, there are several possible choices a researcher might make. In the following, an "item" could be a question on a pencil-and-paper questionnaire, a stimulus that participants make judgments about, etc.

USE ONE ITEM. A researcher may use a single item, presumably selected on the basis of pretesting as "the best." This is similar to holding constant a contextual factor as described earlier, such as using only a single experimental confederate. This approach has the advantage of minimizing the participant's time and effort, but it has very important disadvantages as well. It may lead to low reliability, for the resulting measure has only a single item. More important, holding any factor constant leaves the extent of the generality of the findings uncertain.

SUM ACROSS MULTIPLE ITEMS. Most frequently, researchers employ several items and sum (or average) them to form the dependent variable for analysis. This is by far the most common approach when a questionnaire includes multiple items that have the same scale (e.g., a 1–7 Likert response scale). This approach corresponds to unsystematically varying a contextual factor, such as using several confederates but not treating confederate as a factor in the data analysis. This approach permits a modicum of confidence about the generality of a result, which can be demonstrated to hold across a set of items (though not necessarily for each individual item). This approach also gains power by the use of multiple items. Bush, Hess, and Wolford (1993) described alternative ways to combine multiple measurements within participants, some that appear to have considerably higher power than simply taking a sum or mean of the raw observations. Even if the sum or mean is preferred for reasons of conceptual simplicity, researchers may wish to standardize each item separately (e.g., to zero mean and unit variance) before combining them, to avoid overweighting items with larger variances.

TREAT ITEMS AS A FACTOR. A researcher may use several items and treat "item" as a within-participants factor in the analysis. Again, each item should have the same scale (either in raw form or after standardization). This approach corresponds to systematically varying a contextual factor, such as using several confederates and analyzing for their effects. Compared with the use of a single item, this approach gains power by the use of multiple items. It also permits good confidence about the generality of a result if it can be demonstrated to hold across items.

There is a catch, however. It seems fairly clear that in this context "items" should be treated as a random rather than fixed factor (the same argument was made earlier about confederates or similar contextual factors). This means that a large number of items needs to be used before the appropriate statistical tests will have adequate power to show that the effect of interest generalizes to the general population of items that are similar to those used in the study. (It is worth reminding the reader that, as noted earlier, a random factor need not involve explicit random sampling from a population – for instance, participants is invariably considered a random factor though social psychologists rarely perform formal random sampling of participants.) Using a large number of items is essential if studies are to yield conclusions that can be expected to generalize across items (stories, photos, behavior sentences, etc.) rather than holding only for those used in a given study (Abelson, 1995; Kenny & Smith, 1980). Remember the moral of the "risky shift" research: An effect that can be repeatedly obtained with a given set of items (decision problems) may embarrassingly fail to hold when the overall domain of items is sampled more broadly.

And there is another catch – or what seems to be one. Treating items as an explicit factor in the design (whether fixed or random) allows for the detection of Treatment × Items interactions. These interactions often raise questions that researchers would rather not face, for they point to inadequacies in our theories! Yet noting such effects is essential for learning about the limitations of our theories and can even spur fundamental theoretical advances. Consider that the "risky shift" phenomenon, when it was found to reverse with new types of decision problems, was felicitously reconceptualized as "group polarization" (Myers & Lamm, 1976). Positive effects of an audience on performance of some tasks and negative effects on other tasks gave rise to Zajonc's (1965) model of drive strength and social facilitation. Findings that the strength of persuasive arguments did not affect attitude change equally for all topics played a role in the development of the elaboration likelihood model of persuasion (Petty & Cacioppo, 1979). In all these cases the trick, as Abelson (1995, pp. 144–148) explained, is to take a Treatment × Contexts or Treatment × Items interaction and come up with a creative and insightful theoretical account of the nature of the differences across contexts or items that causes the treatment to behave differently. Such an account, if it passes tests in further studies specifically designed for the purpose, necessarily integrates more data than the earlier theories that predicted general main effects of treatment across all items or contexts.

ANALYZE EACH ITEM SEPARATELY. Occasionally a researcher may choose to analyze multiple dependent variables separately. Conceptually, two different situations must be distinguished (see Abelson, 1995, pp. 128–129). If the multiple dependent variables are regarded as alternative measures of the same construct yet produce different results it is not clear what to make

of that. Perhaps a minor deviation in results for one measure is simply due to measurement error or other chance factors. Certainly one would not want to place any importance on the fact that a given effect reached $p < .05$ for one measure but only $p = .06$ for another. Perhaps in this situation one should avoid analyzing the different items separately but rather analyze with items as a factor and consider a deviation to be meaningful (a "but" in Abelson's terms, a qualification on an overall pattern of results) only if the items factor significantly interacts with one of the experimental factors. If several such interactions emerge, clearly the original assumption that the items all reflect a common underlying construct needs to be rethought.

If different dependent measures are considered to reflect distinct constructs, then analyzing them independently (rather than combining them into a single index prior to analysis) is a reasonable approach. Parallel results might be described with a phrase like "not only"; for example, "The effect of treatment was found held not only for the attitude measure but also for behavioral intentions." In Abelson's terms this is two ticks (two discrete findings) rather than a tick and a but (a limitation or qualification on a finding).

USE A STRUCTURAL EQUATION MODEL. When measures of multiple conceptual variables are included in a study and the researcher has hypotheses concerning their causal and mediational interrelationships, the data can be considered in a multiple-group structural equation framework. For example, a design might have a 2 × 2 with a manipulated factor (say treatment vs. control) and a measured independent variable (such as participant sex) and dependent measures of attitude, behavioral intention, and behavior. The researcher might hypothesize that the independent variables will affect the dependent variables in particular ways, and also that the dependent variables have specified causal paths among themselves. Further discussion of this approach to conceptualizing and analyzing an experimental design will be given below.

USE MANOVAS. For completeness, let us consider one more potential approach to the analysis of multiple dependent measures: MANOVAs. At least if the overall multivariate analysis is not followed up with specific univariate tests, the MANOVA approach in this situation is deeply unsatisfactory (Abelson, 1995, p. 128). The reason is that simply declaring that a multivariate F was significant tells nothing about the actual dependent variable that was analyzed – it only indicates that some empirically derived linear combination of the items significantly differentiated the groups. Outside of a purely exploratory context, this finding tells the researcher nothing with any theoretical content. For more details, see Judd (this volume, Ch. 14).

An exception to this generalization is that, according to Cole, Maxwell, Arvey, and Salas (1993), MANOVA is appropriate for the analysis of causal indicators, a set of observed variables that are regarded as causes (rather than effects) of the conceptual dependent variable. An example is variables reflecting the presence or absence of several diseases or disabling conditions that might be combined into a measure of overall health status. Two distinctions separate the case of causal indicators from the much more common situation in which the observed indicators, like responses to a number of questionnaire items, are regarded as caused by the underlying construct of interest. (a) The causal indicators actually cause the dependent variable (e.g., a worsening of arthritis causes reduced health status, although a change in one attitude item would not cause a change in an overall attitude); and (b) there is no special reason to expect cause indicators to be correlated (e.g., someone with worse arthritis will not necessarily have worse asthma as well, although multiple indicators of an attitude should be correlated). The use of causal indicators (and therefore this application of MANOVA) appears to be rare in social psychology.

ADDITIONAL CONSIDERATIONS REGARDING DESIGN

Power

LOW POWER OF TYPICAL DESIGNS. The design-related advice that receives probably the most lip service and the least frequent implementation is advice to consider the power of a study. Cohen (1962) found that published studies in social psychology had a median power to detect a "medium-sized" effect of only .46. This means that even before the typical study began, and even if the researchers were clever enough to be testing a hypothesis that actually was true and had a medium-sized effect, the study had less than an even chance of finding a significant result. Despite much attention to the issue in the intervening years, more recent surveys of published studies have found virtually identical results (Cohen, 1990, p. 1311). And, of course, it is a certainty that the population of all studies has a much lower average power than the subset of studies that are published. Because Cohen (1988) has provided researchers with easily accessible ways to evaluate the power of a planned or already-conducted study, researchers have little excuse for wasting effort by conducting low-powered studies.

Consider the plight of a researcher who develops an interesting hypothesis, tries three times to test it in low-powered studies obtaining nonsignificant results, and gives up in discouragement when a single study with the same total N (or a meta-analysis of the three studies) might have found a significant effect. Principled advice to this researcher would have been to conduct a power analysis before running the first study (using related results in the literature as guidelines to the expected effect size) to determine how large a study to run. At least, after the first small study yielded nonsignificant results a power analysis would be in order, using the actual effect size estimate from that study.

POWER IS NOT THE ONLY CONSIDERATION. However, in the real world of research, other considerations may temper this advice. For a novel and untested hypothesis, the researcher might not wish to devote the resources to a single adequately powered study (or might not have those resources in the first place), so it might be rational to place a relatively small bet and hope for a favorable outcome despite long odds. (We hope that tenure doesn't hang on the outcome, or if it does, that the researcher is placing many independent bets.) Also, a researcher might learn things from a small initial study – despite the nonsignificance of the hoped-for main result – that would allow the refinement of the procedure, measures, or manipulations for succeeding studies. Some might argue that a researcher who incrementally modifies the details of a paradigm over several unsuccessful studies and finally "gets it to work" has learned a lot about the parameters of his or her effect (though assessment of the value of this knowledge must take into account the fact that it will almost always remain as local "lab lore" rather than being shared widely with the research community through publication).

A rejoinder to this plausible claim might be that if you run several studies each with a power of .30 or so to detect a real effect, one will eventually pop up as significant by chance alone, even if the procedural variations that are being tested make no real difference. The pattern of results would then convey no actual information about the supposed benefits of the variations, so the "lab lore" about what works and what doesn't would be purely illusory. The point of this example is not to say that power analysis is unimportant, but to say that decisions about how to spend available resources (particularly participant hours and the associated costs of testing participants, such as research assistant time) are among the most difficult faced by any researcher, and power is only one of the relevant considerations.

WAYS TO INCREASE POWER. Besides the number of participants, other design features that can contribute to statistical power include the choice of within-participant rather than between-participants designs and the use of covariates or blocking factors, reliable measures of dependent variables, powerful and consistent implementations of treatments, and focused one-df tests of key hypotheses (rather than multi-df omnibus F-tests). All of these issues have been mentioned earlier in this chapter.

One additional consideration is less frequently recognized: the use of optimal design, or the allocation of a fixed number of participants across conditions in a way that maximizes power. McClelland (1997) gives a concise treatment of the issues. Here is an example based on McClelland's discussion. A researcher may wish to test three conditions consisting of a control (C) and two experimental treatments (E1 and E2). For example, in an attitude change study an unadorned version of a persuasive message may serve as the control, and the message plus two different heuristic cues (such as an attractive source and an expert source) may be used in the experimental conditions. The researcher (knowing Rosenthal and Rosnow's advice, 1985, to avoid multi-df omnibus F-tests) plans to analyze the data with two single-df hypotheses: (a) comparing E1 and E2 together against C to see if any heuristic cue aids persuasion, and (b) comparing E1 against E2 (ignoring C) to see which heuristic cue performs better. McClelland showed that no allocation of participants across the three conditions can be optimal for both of these hypotheses simultaneously. If the first contrast is of crucial importance, then half the participants should be allocated to the C condition and one quarter to each of the others for maximal power (but then the efficiency for the second contrast is only .5). On the other hand, if the second contrast is of central importance, all the participants should be divided between E1 and E2 for maximal power, meaning that the first contrast cannot even be tested. An equal-N division (one third to each condition) gives higher relative efficiency to the first contrast than to the second. If the two questions are equally important, allocation of $\frac{1}{4}$ of the participants to C and $\frac{3}{8}$ to E1 and E2 provides equal efficiency for the two questions. This type of example (testing two conditions against a common control and against each other) is a common one but the principles it illustrates are even more general. The efficiency of a design with a fixed number of participants is affected by the way the participants are allocated to conditions, and the allocation that gives maximal power depends on the specific hypotheses to be tested.

Unequal Ns

Cell sizes in a design may be unequal when the design reflects a sample from an underlying population in which different categories have unequal sizes (e.g., male and female liberal arts and engineering majors). Or they may be unequal even when an investigator was attempting to produce equal cell sizes for a design involving one or more manipulated factors – as a result of procedural mistakes, equipment failures, and the fuzziness of randomization. Neither of these situations is a major problem. Both can be analyzed with readily available programs that use the general linear model approach, though one must be wary of the different assumptions used by different programs. The issues involved in analysis will be discussed in other chapters in this handbook. Also, modestly unequal cell sizes do not hurt power very much. For example, McClelland and Judd (1993) demonstrated that in a 2×2 design, even when half of the observations fall into one cell with the remainder spread out equally across the other three, efficiency for detecting an interaction effect is 80% of what it would be with exactly equal Ns.

For experimental design, the moral of this story is not to obsess about having exactly equal Ns. Even when researchers set out to have exactly 20 participants per cell, equipment failures and the like may mean that the actual cell Ns fall between 17 and 20. But this does not create substantial data-analytic or interpretive problems, and certainly one possible remedy (discarding data to bring every cell down to the size of the smallest) is a cure worse than the disease.

Confounds and Artifacts

There are several types of confounds that the randomization used in an experimental design cannot altogether rule out. These are best regarded as issues of construct validity rather than internal validity (Cook & Campbell, 1979). In no case is there a question of whether the experimental treatment as manipulated causes the observed effects – the question is whether it has its effects through the theoretically postulated mechanism or in some other, conceptually less interesting way. Among the potential confounds in an experiment are the following.

DEMAND CHARACTERISTICS AND EXPERIMENTER BIAS. Participants' reactions to their perceptions (correct or incorrect) of the purpose of the research may influence their responses. Standard precautions against demands include the use of a coherent and believable cover story, which can at least ensure that all participants hold the same views of the purpose of the experiment rather than varying in their perceptions (perhaps in a way that is correlated with conditions). Some researchers apparently believe that if participants cannot correctly guess the research hypotheses, demands could not influence their behavior. This belief is mistaken, for even incorrect guesses may well influence participants' behavior as they attempt to be good participants by confirming what they consider to be the hypotheses (or bad ones by disconfirming them).

Another precaution is to keep experimenters, confederates, and others who have contact with participants unaware of each participant's condition insofar as possible. This means that unconscious biases cannot cause the experimenters to treat participants in subtly different ways in different conditions, which might artifactually lead to confirmation of the experimental hypotheses. What is sometimes regarded as an alternative – keeping these individuals unaware of the experimental hypotheses – offers no real protection against biases that vary by condition (for the experimenters will come up with their own, possibly misguided, ideas about the research hypotheses).

DIFFERENTIAL TREATMENT-RELATED ATTRITION. If participants drop out from the experiment whether by physically leaving or by failing to follow instructions, giving nonsensical answers, etc., it may falsely produce differences between conditions. The only real solution is to have no attrition. It is commonly assumed that if attrition rates are relatively equal across conditions there is no problem, but this is incorrect; in one condition the 5% highest self-monitors (or most motivated participants, or whatever) may become frustrated and drop out, whereas in another condition it may be the 5% lowest self-monitors (least motivated, etc.) who leave. The remaining subpopulations are not equivalent (despite having been randomly assigned at an earlier point) and hence may respond differently on the dependent measure. Demonstrations of no pretest or background differences between participants who quit and those who stay may provide some reassurance. Differences between participant groups caused by differential treatment-related attrition would be caused by the independent variable as operationalized, but not

for the theoretically expected reason (it represents a problem with construct rather than internal validity as defined by Cook & Campbell, 1979).

BIASES DUE TO SOCIAL COMPARISONS AMONG CONDITIONS. Cook and Campbell (1979, pp. 56–58) listed "compensatory rivalry or resentful demoralization" as potential issues when participants see treatments as differentially desirable. Participants may react to their perceptions of their good or bad outcomes by trying harder or slacking off, potentially producing differences on the dependent variable of interest. In many social psychological studies, effects of different conditions on participants' mood represents another related potential confound. Mood may be influenced by many types of common manipulations and is known to affect a wide range of judgments and behaviors. For this reason, experimenters often assess participants' mood and perform analyses designed to show that mood was not affected, or at least (when used as a covariate) that it cannot explain the effects obtained on the main dependent variable.

Other related issues are discussed by Abelson (1995, pp. 189–197). The entire issue of preventing potential confounds and artifacts in experiments is a large one (see Aronson et al., 1990; Judd et al., 1991; Miller, 1972; Rosenthal & Rosnow, 1969).

Designs for Studying Mediation

Experimental designs can be set up to test hypotheses about the mediation of causal relationships (Baron & Kenny, 1986; Brewer, this volume, Ch. 1). That is, the question is not just whether X causes Z, but whether X causes Y which in turn causes Z. Such a design involves multiple dependent variables regarded as indicators of two or more causally interrelated constructs, including the ultimate dependent variable(s) and one or more putative mediators.

The most flexible analytic approach to such a model involves using LISREL (Joreskog & Sorbom, 1991) or a related program to set up a measurement model (describing the relationships of the observed variables to their underlying unobserved constructs) and a causal model linking the unobserved variables. Of course, no measurement model would be used if there is only a single indicator for each theoretical construct. If mediation is expected as described above, one can manipulate X and measure Y and Z (possibly with multiple indicators for each). There is no need to estimate several separate regression equations and make specific comparisons as described by Baron and Kenny (1986);

instead, simply estimate the entire hypothesized model including causal paths from X to Y, X to Z, and Y to Z. The mediation hypothesis is supported if the causal paths from X to Y and from Y to Z are both statistically reliable. The direct path from X to Z may be found significant or not. If it is nonsignificant, whereas the X–Z relationship in a so-called reduced-form model that omits the Y variable is significant, then Y is a full mediator of the X–Z effect. More often the direct path remains significant when Y is included in the model, corresponding to the theoretical claim that Y is a mediator (rather than *the* mediator) of the X–Z relationship. Note, however, that the best evidence for mediation requires showing not only that the obtained data are consistent with the mediation model (using the analytic approach just outlined) but also that other models are either theoretically implausible or inconsistent with the data. Seldom, if ever, is only a single causal model consistent with a given set of data, so a fit between model and data is only a first step, not the last, in concluding that the model is valid.

The same causal-modeling analytic approach can handle multiple participant groups (i.e., independent groups of participants defined by measured variables or manipulations) as an extension. For example, suppose a manipulated variable creates two conditions and both male and female participants are tested in a 2×2 design. Multiple measures of two constructs, an attitude and a behavioral intention, are taken. A researcher might hypothesize that the manipulation will affect attitudes differently for male and female participants, but that the attitude to behavioral intention path as well as the measurement models will be the same for all participants. A multiple-groups LISREL analysis can be set up to reflect precisely these assumptions. The researcher can define male and female participants as two groups, set up a causal model with the manipulation as an exogenous variable, and test any parameter or combination of model parameters for equivalence between the groups (Cole et al., 1993; Rock, Werts, & Flaugher, 1978). For example, one could test the equivalence of measurement, then test for the fit of a model with common causal paths for both groups, then test for the hypothesized group difference in a single parameter. This approach is superior to one obvious alternative, analyzing the male and female participants independently, in that (a) it allows focused tests of specific hypothesized differences between the groups, and (b) it uses all the data from both groups to estimate parameters that are common. This is a chapter on design rather than analysis so further details are not provided

here (see Cole et al., 1993, for an introduction). The major point is that modern analytic techniques such as multiple-group LISREL modeling permit the conceptualization and implementation of designs that test simple mediational hypotheses (or even more complex causal structures) as well as hypotheses about differences in measurement or structural parameters across groups of participants.

CONCLUDING COMMENTS

Design is basic to all research, in social psychology as well as in other scientific fields. Yet in some ways classic treatments of design seem less than perfectly applicable to current practice in social psychology and therefore offer incomplete guidance to a researcher struggling to make the best decisions about his or her work. Some of the ways in which this is true have been hinted at earlier (e.g., in the discussion of power analysis) but two related points will be made explicit now.

The background for both of these points is the observation that principles of research design were developed originally in the context of agricultural research and have been elaborated particularly by Donald Campbell and his coworkers as they thought about evaluations of educational innovations and large-scale social interventions (e.g., Campbell & Stanley, 1963; Cook & Campbell, 1979). In all these areas, the key research question is ordinarily, "Does a given treatment have an effect?" and the goal is usually to answer the question with a single study. After all, a study may cost millions and take years (or at least an entire growing season!) to conduct. Implicitly, these assumptions have been imported into social psychology by what researchers learn about design. Yet neither really applies to our field. Given this reality, what extensions in our thinking about research design are called for?

First, social psychologists today are interested in mediational questions – questions of how X causes Y – as often, if not more often, than questions about whether X causes Y (see Brewer, Ch. 1). Some earlier discussions (e.g., Baron & Kenny, 1986) as well as this chapter describe ways to assess mediation within the context of a research design. Yet more development is needed in this area. For example, current treatments of power analysis focus on power to detect an effect but are less directly applicable to the issue of power to detect a mediational path. And current thinking about generalizability does not address issues of the generalizability of a mediational finding (as opposed to a simple causal effect).

Second and even more important, in social psychology today the most important "unit" of research is not the individual study. As Abelson (1995, p. 38) stated in a remark already quoted in this chapter, in social psychology "real research investigations usually involve multiple studies conducted as part of an ongoing conceptual elaboration of a particular topic." Let us term this unit, a series of conceptually related studies, a "research program." A program is most often associated with a given investigator and his or her group of collaborators, but may include work from several distinct laboratories. The research program is not conveniently handled by the classic concepts of research design (power, generalizability, etc.), which focus on an individual study. Nor is it well-captured by the new meta-analysis movement (e.g., Hedges & Olkin, 1985), which focuses on drawing empirical conclusions from large numbers of heterogeneous studies on a given issue. The program is larger than an individual study but too small a body of research for meta-analysis.

However, the research program is arguably the unit that is most important in the advancement of social psychology as a field. There are several reasons for this. As Brewer (Ch. 1) notes, a single study can be almost definitively assumed to have good internal validity (based on its use of experimental design), but the broader forms of validity, construct and external, almost always emerge only from a series of interrelated studies that can compensate for each others' weaknesses. In addition, the conceptual replications that are inherent to a research program, besides strengthening construct and external validity, bring conceptual structure to a series of studies. Programmatically related studies almost necessarily focus on theoretical questions and build on one another, rather than addressing superficially interesting but atheoretical questions in scattershot fashion. Perhaps for these reasons, isolated studies that are not part of a program seem to have relatively little scientific impact. Finally, the program is clearly the unit that is most relevant to the individual scientist trying to make decisions about how to conduct his or her ongoing research.

To illustrate such decisions, imagine that a researcher is designing a study intended to test a certain primary theoretical hypothesis that predicts a particular effect. In the tentative design, another potential effect, if found, would be somewhat interesting but ambiguous: It might reflect theoretically interesting processes or a relatively mundane artifact. An additional condition could be included in the design to disambiguate this possible finding by ruling out the artifactual explanation – at the cost of doubling the size of the design. Should this condition be used or not? This question is not answerable by reference only to the standard principles of research design. Though many courses of action would be defensible, one reasonable approach would be to omit the extra condition and focus the initial study on the effect of primary interest. If the secondary effect is not found in that study, well and good. If it does appear, a follow-up could be conducted with the extra condition included to evaluate the reason for the effect. The number of participants required for these two studies would be the same as for the extended version of the initial study only, and a two-study package is probably a better bet for publication in any case.

Decisions at this level, the level of the research program, really are a matter of strategy rather than tactics. This scenario illustrates one principle that I tentatively propose as a strategic maxim: More, smaller studies are often better than fewer, larger ones. One fundamental reason is that in a research program the primary questions of theoretical interest evolve over time. One large study may give a definitive answer to the question that one had 2 years ago (when that study was designed), but several smaller studies in the same amount of time will often lead to different questions. Conceptual advancement in research is measured as much by evolution in the questions that are asked as by the answers that are obtained. A second reason is that a series of relatively small studies is more likely to involve variation in nonessential factors (settings, measurement techniques, etc.) and therefore is likely to be stronger in construct and external validity, compared with a single massive study. This is particularly true if the studies are methodologically diverse rather than being variants on a single narrow paradigm.

A research program has all the same goals as an individual study – maximum power, minimum cost, ability to rule out confounds, ability to generalize – and involves additional principles as well, such as Abelson's MAGIC criteria for the persuasiveness of data-based arguments (1995, pp. 12–13 and Ch. 8), including "interestingness." However, principles at this level have not yet been clearly codified so that they can be explicitly taught to apprentice researchers. Perhaps, just as Campbell's influential conceptualization of the forms of validity grew out of the context of massive studies evaluating large-scale social and educational interventions, an expanded treatment of research design that takes account of the research program level as well as the individual study may arise from the context of today's programmatic, mediationally focused research in social psychology.

REFERENCES

Abelson, R. P. (1995). *Statistics as principled argument*. Hillsdale, NJ: Erlbaum.

Abelson, R. P. (1996). Vulnerability of contrast tests to simpler interpretations: An addendum to Rosnow and Rosenthal. *Psychological Science, 7,* 242–246.

Aronson, E., Ellsworth, P. C., Carlsmith, J. M., & Gonzales, M. H. (1990). *Methods of research in social psychology* (2nd ed.). New York: McGraw-Hill.

Bargh, J. A., Bond, R. N., Lombardi, W. J., & Tota, M. E. (1986). The additive nature of chronic and temporary sources of construct accessibility. *Journal of Personality and Social Psychology, 50,* 869–878.

Baron, R. M., & Kenny, D. A. (1986). The mediator–moderator variable distinction in social psychological research: Conceptual, strategic, and statistical considerations. *Journal of Personality and Social Psychology, 51,* 1173–1182.

Bem, D. J., Wallach, M. A., & Kogan, N. (1965). Group decision making under risk of aversive consequences. *Journal of Personality and Social Psychology, 1,* 453–460.

Brown, R. (1986). *Social psychology* (2nd ed.). New York: Free Press.

Brunswik, E. (1955). *Perception and the representative design of psychological experiments* (2nd ed.). Berkeley: University of California Press.

Busemeyer, J. R., & Jones, L. E. (1983). Analysis of multiplicative combination rules when the causal variables are measured with error. *Psychological Bulletin, 93,* 549–562.

Bush, L. K., Hess, U., & Wolford, G. (1993). Transformations for within-subject designs: A Monte Carlo investigation. *Psychological Bulletin, 113,* 566–579.

Campbell, D. T., & Boruch, R. F. (1975). Making the case for randomized assignment to treatments by considering the alternatives: Six ways in which quasi-experimental evaluations tend to underestimate effects. In C. A. Bennett & A. A. Lumsdaine (Eds.), *Evaluation and experience: Some critical issues in assessing social programs* (pp. 195–296). New York: Academic Press.

Campbell, D. T., & Stanley, J. C. (1963). *Experimental and quasi-experimental designs for research*. Chicago: Rand McNally.

Cohen, J. (1962). The statistical power of abnormal-social psychological research: A review. *Journal of Abnormal and Social Psychology, 65,* 145–153.

Cohen, J. (1968). Multiple regression as a general data-analytic system. *Psychological Bulletin, 70,* 426–443.

Cohen, J. (1988). *Statistical power analysis for the behavioral sciences* (2nd ed.). Hillsdale, NJ: Erlbaum.

Cohen, J. (1990). Things, I have learned (so far). *American Psychologist, 45,* 1304–1312.

Cole, D. A., Maxwell, S. E., Arvey, R., & Salas, E. (1993). Multivariate group comparisons of variable systems: MANOVA and structural equation modeling. *Psychological Bulletin, 114,* 174–184.

Cook, T. D., & Campbell, D. T. (1979). *Quasi-experimentation*. Chicago: Rand McNally.

Cook, T. D., & Shadish, W. R. (1994). Social experiments: Some developments over the past fifteen years. *Annual Review of Psychology, 45,* 545–580.

Dunn, J. C., & Kirsner, K. (1988). Discovering functionally independent mental processes: The principle of reversed association. *Psychological Review, 95,* 91–101.

Feldt, L. S. (1958). A comparison of the precision of three experimental designs employing a concomitant variable. *Psychometrika, 23,* 335–354.

Greenwald, A. G., Gonzalez, R., Harris, R. J., & Guthrie, D. (1993). *Using p values and effect sizes to evaluate novel findings: Significance versus replicability and demonstrability*. Unpublished manuscript, University of Washington.

Griffin, D., & Gonzalez, R. (1995). Correlational analysis of dyad-level data in the exchangeable case. *Psychological Bulletin, 118,* 430–439.

Hastie, R., & Kumar, P. A. (1979). Person memory: Personality traits as organizing principles in memory for behaviors. *Journal of Personality and Social Psychology, 37,* 25–38.

Hedges, L. V., & Olkin, I. (1985). *Statistical methods for meta-analysis*. New York: Academic Press.

Higgins, E. T., King, G. A., & Mavin, G. H. (1982). Individual construct accessibility and subjective impressions and recall. *Journal of Personality and Social Psychology, 43,* 35–47.

Jaccard, J., & Wan, C. K. (1995). Measurement error in the analysis of interaction effects between continuous predictors using multiple regression: Multiple indicator and structural equation approaches. *Psychological Bulletin, 117,* 348–357.

Jöreskog, K. G., & Sörbom, D. (1991). *LISREL 7: A guide to the program and applications* (2nd ed.). Chicago: SPSS.

Judd, C. M., & Kenny, D. A. (1981). *Estimating the effects of social interventions*. Cambridge, England: Cambridge University Press.

Judd, C. M., & McClelland, G. H. (1989). *Data analysis: A model-comparison approach*. San Diego, CA: Harcourt Brace Jovanovich.

Judd, C. M., Smith, E. R., & Kidder, L. H. (1991). *Research methods in social relations* (6th ed.). Fort Worth, TX: Holt, Rinehart, & Winston.

Kenny, D. A. (1985). Quantitative methods for social psychology. In G. Lindzey & E. Aronson (Eds.), *Handbook of social psychology* (3rd ed., Vol. 1, pp. 487–508). New York: Random House.

Kenny, D. A., & Judd, C. M. (1986). Consequences of violating the independence assumption in analysis of variance. *Psychological Bulletin, 99,* 422–431.

Kenny, D. A., Kashy, D. A., & Bolger, N. (1998). Data analysis in social psychology. In D. Gilbert, S. T. Fiske, & G. Lindzey (Eds.), *Handbook of social psychology* (4th ed., Vol. 1, pp. 233–265). New York: McGraw-Hill.

Kenny, D. A., & Smith, E. R. (1980). A note on the analysis of designs in which subjects receive each stimulus only once. *Journal of Experimental Social Psychology, 16,* 497–507.

Keppel, G. (1982). *Design and analysis: A researcher's handbook* (2nd ed.). Englewood Cliffs, NJ: Prentice-Hall.

Kirk, R. E. (1968). *Experimental design: Procedures for the behavioral sciences.* Belmont, CA: Brooks/Cole.

Maxwell, S. E., & Delaney, H. D. (1993). Bivariate median splits and spurious statistical significance. *Psychological Bulletin, 113,* 181–190.

McClelland, G. H. (1947). Optimal design in psychological research. *Psychological Methods, 2,* 3–19.

McClelland, G. H., & Judd, C. M. (1993). Statistical difficulties of detecting interactions and moderator effects. *Psychological Bulletin, 114,* 376–390.

Miller, A. G. (1972). *The social psychology of psychological research.* New York: Free Press.

Mook, D. G. (1983). In defense of external invalidity. *American Psychologist, 38,* 379–388.

Myers, D. G., & Lamm, H. (1976). The group polarization phenomenon. *Psychological Bulletin, 83,* 602–627.

Orne, M. (1962). On the social psychology of the psychological experiment. *American Psychologist, 17,* 776–783.

Petty, R. E., & Cacioppo, J. T. (1979). Issue involvement can increase or decrease persuasion by enhancing message-relevant cognitive responses. *Journal of Personality and Social Psychology, 41,* 847–855.

Petty, R. E., Fabrigar, L. R., Wegener, D. T., & Priester, J. R. (1996). Understanding data when interactions are present or hypothesized. *Psychological Science, 7,* 247–252.

Rock, D. A., Werts, C., & Flaugher, R. L. (1978). The use of analysis of covariance structures for comparing the psychometric properties of the multiple variables across populations. *Multivariate Behavioral Research, 13,* 403–418.

Rosenthal, R., & Rosnow, R. L. (Eds.). (1969). *Artifact in behavioral research.* New York: Academic Press.

Rosenthal, R., & Rosnow, R. L. (1985). *Contrast analysis: Focused comparisons in the analysis of variance.* Cambridge, England: Cambridge University Press.

Rosnow, R. L., & Rosenthal, R. (1995). "Some things you learn aren't so": Cohen's paradox, Asch's paradigm, and the interpretation of interaction. *Psychological Science, 6,* 3–9.

Rosnow, R. L., & Rosenthal, R. (1996). Contrasts and interactions redux: Five easy pieces. *Psychological Science, 7,* 253–257.

Santa, J. L., Miller, J. J., & Shaw, M. L. (1979). Using quasi *F* to prevent alpha inflation due to stimulus variation. *Psychological Bulletin, 86,* 37–46.

Smith, E. R., & Miller, F. D. (1979). Attributional information processing: A response time model of causal subtraction. *Journal of Personality and Social Psychology, 37,* 1723–1731.

Winer, B. J. (1971). *Statistical principles in experimental design* (2nd ed.). New York: McGraw-Hill.

Zajonc, R. B. (1965). Social facilitation. *Science, 149,* (Whole No. 3681), 269–274.

CHAPTER THREE

Causal Inference and Generalization in Field Settings
Experimental and Quasi-Experimental Designs

STEPHEN G. WEST, JEREMY C. BIESANZ, AND STEVEN C. PITTS

The purpose of this chapter is to introduce researchers in social psychology to designs that permit relatively strong causal inferences in the field. We begin the chapter by considering some basic issues in inferring causality, drawing on work by Rubin and his associates (Holland, 1986, 1988; Rubin, 1974, 1978) in statistics and by Campbell and his associates (Campbell, 1957; Campbell & Stanley, 1966; Cook, 1993; Cook & Campbell, 1979; Shadish, Cook, & Campbell, in press) in psychology. Rubin's approach emphasized formal statistical criteria for inference; Campbell's approach emphasized concepts from philosophy of science and the practical issues confronting social researchers. These approaches are then applied to provide insights on a variety of difficult issues that arise in randomized experiments when they are conducted in the field. In addition, Cook's (1993) new perspective on the generalization of causal effects is also discussed. We then turn to consideration of three classes of quasi-experimental designs – the regression discontinuity design, the interrupted time series design, and the nonequivalent control group design – that can sometimes provide a relatively strong basis for causal inference. The application of the Rubin and the Campbell frameworks helps identify strengths and weaknesses

of each design. Methods of strengthening each design type with respect to causal inference and generalization of causal effects are also considered.

The emphasis on designs for field research in the present chapter contrasts sharply with recent practice in basic social psychology in which the modal research design consists of a randomized experiment, conducted in the laboratory, lasting no more than 1 hour, and using undergraduate students as the participants (West, Newsom, & Fenaughty, 1992). This practice has clear strengths that are articulated in other chapters in this handbook. At the same time, the recent extraordinary level of dominance of this practice potentially limits the generalization of social psychological findings in important ways. At earlier points in the history of the field, it was far easier to find examples of basic social psychological hypotheses that were tested in both laboratory and field settings (see Bickman & Henchy, 1972; Swingle, 1973, for collections of examples); currently, the majority of research conducted by social psychologists in field settings is applied in nature. The earlier interplay between laboratory and field research often provided a more convincing basis for generalization of causal effects found in basic social psychological investigations. We suggest that perhaps at least some of the current widespread perception that many articles in our leading journals "just aren't that interesting anymore" (Reis & Stiller, 1992, p. 470; see also Funder, 1992) may be occasioned by the limited contexts in which social psychological phenomena are studied and the distance of present research paradigms from the real world.

The current modal laboratory research paradigm is particularly good at establishing internal validity, that is, the treatment caused the observed response. However, as complications are introduced into the

Stephen G. West was partially supported by NIMH Grant P50-MN39246 during the writing of this chapter. We thank Tom Belin, Tom Cook, Bill Graziano, Chick Judd, Chip Reichardt, Harry Reis, Will Shadish, and the graduate students of the Fall 1997 Psychology 555 class (experimental and quasi-experimental designs in research) at Arizona State University for their comments and suggestions on an earlier version of this chapter. Correspondence should be directed to Stephen G. West, Department of Psychology, Arizona State University, Tempe, AZ 85287-1104 (e-mail: sgwest@asu.edu).

laboratory setting, establishing internal validity becomes more tenuous. Experiments conducted over repeated sessions involve attrition; requests for participants to bring peers or parents to the laboratory are not always fulfilled. Basic and applied social psychological research conducted in field settings may further magnify these potential issues. Consequently, researchers must increase their focus on articulating those threats to internal validity, which Campbell (1957) termed "plausible rival hypotheses," that may be problematic in their specific research context. A central theme of this chapter is the identification of major classes of plausible rival hypotheses associated with each of the design types and the use of specific design and analysis strategies that can help rule them out. And, as we will indicate, many of these strategies also turn out to have potential implications for traditional laboratory experiments as well.

A FRAMEWORK FOR CAUSAL INFERENCE IN EXPERIMENTS AND QUASI-EXPERIMENTS

Over the past two decades, Donald Rubin and his colleagues in statistics (Angrist, Imbens, & Rubin, 1996; Holland, 1986, 1988; Imbens & Rubin, 1997; Rosenbaum & Rubin, 1983, 1984; Rubin, 1974, 1978, 1986) have developed a very useful framework for understanding the causal effects of treatments. This framework has come to be known as the Rubin Causal Model (RCM). The use of the RCM is particularly helpful in identifying strengths and limitations of many of the experimental and quasi-experimental designs in which the independent variable is manipulated and posttest measures are collected at only one point in time following the treatment.

Consider the simple case of two treatments whose effects the researcher wishes to compare. For example, the researcher may wish to compare a severe frustration (treatment condition) and a mild frustration (comparison condition) in the level of aggressive responses they produce (see Berkowitz, 1993). Or, the researcher may wish to compare a 10-week smoking prevention program (treatment condition) and a no program group (comparison condition) on attitudes toward smoking among teenagers (see Flay, 1986).

Rubin begins with a consideration of the hypothetical ideal conditions under which a causal effect could be observed. He defines the causal effect as the difference between what would have happened to the participant under the treatment condition and what *would* have happened to the same participant under the control condition under identical circumstances. That is,

the causal effect is defined as:

$$Y_t(u) - Y_c(u).$$

Here, t refers to the treatment condition, c refers to the comparison condition (often a control group), Y is the observed response (dependent measure), and u is the unit (in psychology, typically a specific participant) on which we observe the effects of the two treatments.

Rubin's definition leads to a clear theoretical statement of what a causal effect is, but it also implies a fundamental problem. "It is impossible to observe the value of $Y_t(u)$ and $Y_c(u)$ on the same unit and, therefore, it is impossible to *observe* the effect of t on u" (Holland, 1986, p. 947, italics in original). We cannot expose a preteenage boy to the 10-week smoking prevention program, measure his attitudes toward smoking, then return the child to the beginning of the school year, expose him to the comparison (control) program and remeasure his attitudes toward smoking. Because of this fundamental problem of causal inference, we will not be able to observe causality directly. However, by making specific assumptions, we can develop research designs that permit us to infer causality. The certainty of the causal inference will depend strongly on the viability of the assumptions that we make. Three design approaches that address the fundamental problem of causal inference are available, which may be employed alone or in combination. After briefly presenting the first two design approaches, we focus on the third approach, randomization, because it is most often used in basic and applied social psychology.

Design Approaches to the Fundamental Problem of Causal Inference

WITHIN-SUBJECT DESIGNS. In within-subject designs, participants are exposed to treatment (i) and their responses are measured, following which they are exposed to treatment (ii) and their responses are measured. Within-subject designs make two strong assumptions. First is *temporal stability*, which means that the response does not depend on the time the treatment is delivered. Many factors such as normal human development, historical events, fatigue, or even daily or monthly cycles (see Cook & Campbell, 1979, chapter 2) can affect participants' responses. Second is *causal transience*, which means that the effects of each treatment and each measurement of the response do not persist over time. For example, in a study of the effects of a high-stress and a low-stress film clip on increases in blood pressure, the researcher would need to make the strong assumptions that exposure to the initial film clip did not affect the perception of the second clip, the participant had fully returned to her baseline level for all bodily systems (i.e., not only blood pressure, but also physiological, motivational, and cognitive systems), and that the initial blood pressure measurement did not affect subsequent blood pressure measurements (e.g., changes in blood pressure readings from the participant's anticipation of the unpleasant constriction from the inflation of the blood pressure cuff). For studies of physical devices, such as the performance of engines under varying treatment conditions, the assumptions of temporal stability and causal transience will often be reasonable. For studies of social psychological phenomena, these assumptions will often be more problematic. Greenwald (1976), Erlebacher (1977), Rosenthal and Rubin (1980), Judd and Kenny (1981), and Keren (1993) presented fuller discussions of issues in within-subject designs.[1]

UNIT HOMOGENEITY. If experimental units can be assumed to be identical in all respects, then it makes no difference which unit receives the treatment. That is, $Y_t(u_1) = Y_t(u_2)$ and $Y_c(u_1) = Y_c(u_2)$, where u_1 and u_2 represent two different units (participants). In this case, $Y_t(u_1) - Y_c(u_2)$ [or $Y_t(u_2) - Y_c(u_1)$] will provide an accurate estimate of the causal effect. Again, this assumption of unit homogeneity is often made in the physical sciences and engineering, but it will almost never be reasonable in social psychology. Even monozygotic (identical) twins who are known to share identical genes can easily differ in knowledge, motivation, mood, or other participant-related factors that may affect their responses to treatment.

RANDOMIZATION. Randomization is used to equate approximately the treatment and control groups at pretest, prior to any treatment delivery. In randomization, participants are assigned to treatment conditions using a method that gives every participant an equal

chance of being assigned to the treatment and control conditions.[2] Common randomization methods include flipping a coin (e.g., heads = treatment; tails = control), drawing a number out of a hat (e.g., 1 = treatment; 2 = control), or using a computer to generate random numbers identifying treatment and control group assignments. Although randomization is normally straightforward in the laboratory, some field research settings present very difficult randomization problems. For example, in health care settings participants often arrive when they become ill; facilities to deliver the experimental treatment, the control treatment, or both may or may not be available at that time. A wide variety of different methods reviewed by Boruch (1997) and Shadish et al. (in press) have been developed to address complex randomization problems.

Following random assignment to treatment conditions, each participant then receives the treatment condition (e.g., experimental treatment vs. comparison [control] treatment) to which he or she was assigned. Then, the responses of each participant are measured after the receipt of the treatment condition. These procedures are characteristic of the basic randomized experiment used in both laboratory and field settings in social psychology.

Random assignment means that the variable representing the treatment condition (treatment vs. control) can be expected on average to be independent of any measured or unmeasured variable prior to treatment. This outcome is reflected in two closely related ways.

1. At pretest, prior to any treatment delivery, the mean levels in the treatment and control groups will, on average, be equal for any measured or unmeasured variable. More formally, the expected values for the two groups (Group 1 and Group 2) will be equal, $E(\bar{Y}_1) = E(\bar{Y}_2)$, for any variable Y. At pretest, the demographic characteristics, the attitudes, the motivations, the personality traits, the abilities, as well as any other participant attributes can, on average,

---

[1] A hybrid approach that combines elements of the within-subject design and randomization approaches has been traditionally used in some areas of experimental psychology. In the simplest version of such a design, half of the participants are randomly assigned to receive treatment (i) and then treatment (ii), whereas the other half of the participants are randomly assigned to receive treatment (ii) and then treatment (i). Such designs make the typically untestable assumption that there are no interactions between treatment condition and order of presentation or treatment condition and trial. This assumption will be met when there is no causal transience. Statistical presentations of the assumptions and analysis of such counterbalanced and Latin Square designs can be found in Winer (1971) and Kirk (1995).

[2] In fact, the probability of being assigned to the treatment and control conditions may differ. For example, the probability of assignment to the treatment group might be .25 and the probability of assignment to the control group might be .75 for each participant. Unequal allocation of participants to treatment and control groups is normally used when the cost or difficulty in implementing one of the treatment conditions is substantially greater than for the other. We will assume equal allocation of participants to treatment and control groups here. Given usual statistical assumptions underlying hypothesis testing, this equal allocation strategy maximizes the power of the test of the null hypothesis.

be expected to be equal in the treatment and control groups.

2. The treatment variable (hereafter referred to as t for treatment and c for comparison) will, on average, be unrelated to any measured or unmeasured participant variable prior to treatment. One implication of this is that the correlation of the treatment variable and any participant variable measured prior to treatment delivery will, on average, be 0.

These two outcomes allow the RCM to provide a new definition of the causal effect that is appropriate for randomized experiments. The estimate of the causal effect is now defined as:

$$\bar{Y}_t - \bar{Y}_c.$$

Three observations are in order. First, the comparison must now shift to the *average* response for the group of participants receiving the experimental treatment compared with the *average* response for the group of participants receiving the control treatment. Causal inferences may no longer be made about individual participants. Second, the two outcomes are expectations: They are what occurs "on average." Exact equivalence of the pretest means of variables and exact independence of the treatment and pretest measures of participant variables does *not* occur routinely in practice. With simple randomization, exact pretest equivalence and exact independence of the treatment and background variables occur only if randomization is applied to a very large ($n \to \infty$) population or the results are averaged across a very large number (all possible) of different randomizations of the same sample. In any given real sample, there is no guarantee that pretest means will *not* differ on important variables, in which case the estimate of the causal effect, $\bar{Y}_t - \bar{Y}_c$, will be too low or too high. Randomization replaces definitive statements about causal effects with probabilistic statements based on sampling theory. Third, for causal inference we need to assume that neither the randomization process itself nor participants' potential awareness of other participants' treatment conditions influence the participants' responses. This assumption, known as the stable-unit-treatment-value assumption is considered in more detail following the presentation of an illustrative example to help make some of these ideas concrete.

Illustrative Example: Randomization and Rubin's Causal Model

In Table 3.1 we present an example data set that we will use throughout this section of the chapter. There

TABLE 3.1. Illustration: Estimating the Causal Effect – Ideal Case

Participant	a_1	a_2	a_3	Y_c	Y_t
1	0	1	0	1	1.5
2	1	0	0	2	2.5
3	1	0	1	2	2.5
4	1	0	0	2	2.5
5	0	0	0	2	2.5
6	0	1	0	3	3.5
7	1	1	0	3	3.5
8	1	0	1	3	3.5
9	0	1	1	3	3.5
10	0	1	0	3	3.5
11	0	1	1	3	3.5
12	1	0	0	4	4.5
13	0	0	1	4	4.5
14	0	1	1	4	4.5
15	1	1	1	4	4.5
16	0	0	1	5	5.5
17	1	1	1	1	1.5
18	1	1	0	2	2.5
19	0	0	0	2	2.5
20	1	0	1	2	2.5
21	1	1	0	2	2.5
22	0	1	0	3	3.5
23	1	1	1	3	3.5
24	1	1	1	3	3.5
25	0	0	1	3	3.5
26	0	0	0	3	3.5
27	1	1	1	3	3.5
28	1	0	0	4	4.5
29	1	0	0	4	4.5
30	0	0	1	4	4.5
31	0	0	1	4	4.5
32	0	0	0	5	5.5

Note: The column labeled Y_c contains the true response of each participant in the control condition. The column labeled Y_t contains the true response of each participant in the treatment condition. a_1, a_2, and a_3 represent three different random assignments of 16 participants to the control group and 16 participants to the treatment group. In each random assignment, 0 means the participant was assigned to the control group and 1 means the participant was assigned to the treatment group. The mean of all 32 participants under the control condition is 3.0, the mean of all 32 participants under the treatment condition is 3.5, and the standard deviation of each condition is 1.0. The distribution within each group is approximately normal. The causal effect for each participant is 0.5, corresponding to a moderate effect size.

are 32 participants. The example is constructed based on Rubin's ideal case: The response of each participant is observed under both the control (Y_c column) and treatment (Y_t column) conditions. The causal effect, $Y_t - Y_c$, has a constant size of 0.5 for each participant. The mean in the control group is 3.0, the mean in the treatment group is 3.5, and the standard deviation for the example is 1.0. The distributions within each group are roughly normal. Note that in this example the standardized measure of effect size is $d = \frac{\mu_t - \mu_c}{\sigma} = 0.50$. This standardized effect size is described by Cohen (1988) as moderate, and he believes it represents a typical effect size found in the behavioral sciences. By way of comparison, some recent meta-analyses have found mean effect sizes of $d = 0.54$ for the effect of alcohol on aggression (Ito, Miller, & Pollock, 1996), $d = 0.34$ for the effect of prevention programs on improved mental health outcomes for children (Durlak & Wells, 1997), and $d = .59$ for the relation between confidence and accuracy in studies of eyewitness identification (Sporer, Penrod, Read, & Cutler, 1995).

Also presented in Table 3.1 are three columns labeled a_1, a_2, and a_3. These represent three different actual random assignments of the 32 participants. In each case, 16 participants are assigned to the control condition, and 16 participants are assigned to the treatment condition. In general, there are $\binom{2n}{n}$ different possible random assignments, where n is the number of participants in each treatment group (Cochran & Cox, 1957). In the present example, there are $\binom{32}{16} = \frac{32!}{16!16!} = \frac{32 \times 31 \times 30 \times \cdots \times 2 \times 1}{(16 \times 15 \times 14 \times \cdots \times 2 \times 1)(16 \times 15 \times 14 \times \cdots \times 2 \times 1)}$ combinations or over 600 million different possible random assignments.

The result of random assignment is that we will be able to observe only one of the two responses for each participant. Table 3.2 illustrates this result for randomization a_1. We see that for Participant 1, the response is observed under the control condition, but not the treatment condition; for Participant 2, the response is observed under the treatment, but not the control condition; and so on. The black squares represent the unobserved response for each participant.

In Table 3.3, we show the calculations of the causal effect for each of the three randomizations, a_1, a_2, and a_3. The example is constructed so that the true standard deviation ($\sigma = 1$) is known for both the treatment and control conditions for the full set of 32 participants in this ideal case, so we can use the z-test, rather than the more typical t-test, for two independent groups. The true causal effect of treatment in the population is 0.50. However, note that the estimates of the causal effect in the three samples are 0.0, -0.125, and 0.875. We can

TABLE 3.2. Illustration: Estimating the Causal Effect – Randomized Experiment (a_1)

Participant	a_1	Y_c	Y_t
1	0	1	■
2	1	■	2.5
3	1	■	2.5
4	1	■	2.5
5	0	2	■
6	0	3	■
7	1	■	3.5
8	1	■	3.5
9	0	3	■
10	0	3	■
11	0	3	■
12	1	■	4.5
13	0	4	■
14	0	4	■
15	1	■	4.5
16	0	5	■
17	1	■	1.5
18	1	■	2.5
19	0	2	■
20	1	■	2.5
21	1	■	2.5
22	0	3	■
23	1	■	3.5
24	1	■	3.5
25	0	3	■
26	0	3	■
27	1	■	3.5
28	1	■	4.5
29	1	■	4.5
30	0	4	■
31	0	4	■
32	0	5	■

Note. The column labeled Y_c contains the true response of each participant in the control condition. The column labeled Y_t contains the true response of each participant in the treatment condition. a_1 represents the random assignment of 16 participants to the control group and 16 participants to the treatment group. ■ means response was not observed.

construct 95% confidence intervals (CI) around these estimates by applying the formula:

$$\text{CI} = (\bar{Y}_t - \bar{Y}_c) \pm (1.96)(SE),$$

where SE is the standard error, which is equal to $\sqrt{\sigma^2(\frac{1}{n_t} + \frac{1}{n_c})}$. For randomization 1, CI $= 0.0 \pm (1.96)$

TABLE 3.3.

Random assignment: a_1

$$\bar{Y}_c = \frac{\sum Y_c}{n_c} = \frac{1+2+3+3+\cdots+4+4+5}{16} = \frac{52}{16} = 3.25$$

$$\bar{Y}_t = \frac{\sum Y_t}{n_t} = \frac{2.5+2.5+2.5+3.5+\cdots+3.5+4.5+4.5}{16} = \frac{52}{16} = 3.25$$

Estimate of causal effect: $\bar{Y}_t - \bar{Y}_c = 0.0$

$$z = \frac{\bar{Y}_t - \bar{Y}_c}{\sqrt{\sigma^2\left(\frac{1}{n_t}+\frac{1}{n_c}\right)}} = \frac{0}{\sqrt{1\left(\frac{1}{16}+\frac{1}{16}\right)}} = 0$$

Random assignment: a_2

$$\bar{Y}_c = \frac{\sum Y_c}{n_c} = \frac{2+2+2+3+\cdots+4+4+5}{16} = \frac{53}{16} = 3.3125$$

$$\bar{Y}_t = \frac{\sum Y_t}{n_t} = \frac{1.5+2.5+3.5+3.5+\cdots+3.5+3.5+3.5}{16} = \frac{51}{16} = 3.1875$$

Estimate of causal effect: $\bar{Y}_t - \bar{Y}_c = -0.125$

$$z = \frac{\bar{Y}_t - \bar{Y}_c}{\sqrt{\sigma^2\left(\frac{1}{n_t}+\frac{1}{n_c}\right)}} = \frac{-0.125}{\sqrt{1\left(\frac{1}{16}+\frac{1}{16}\right)}} = -0.35$$

Random assignment: a_3

$$\bar{Y}_c = \frac{\sum Y_c}{n_c} = \frac{1+2+2+2+\cdots+4+4+5}{16} = \frac{45}{16} = 2.8125$$

$$\bar{Y}_t = \frac{\sum Y_t}{n_t} = \frac{2.5+3.5+3.5+3.5+\cdots+3.5+4.5+4.5}{16} = \frac{59}{16} = 3.6875$$

Estimate of causal effect: $\bar{Y}_t - \bar{Y}_c = 0.875$

$$z = \frac{\bar{Y}_t - \bar{Y}_c}{\sqrt{\sigma^2\left(\frac{1}{n_t}+\frac{1}{n_c}\right)}} = \frac{0.875}{\sqrt{1\left(\frac{1}{16}+\frac{1}{16}\right)}} = 2.47$$

(.354) $= -.69$ to $+.69$; for randomization 2, CI $= -.82$ to $+.57$; for randomization 3, CI $= .18$ to 1.57. None of these estimates represent really extreme values: Each of the 95% confidence intervals include the true causal effect of 0.50.

Also included in Table 3.3 are the traditional statistical tests of the significance for the null hypothesis that the true causal effect is 0. Two of these three significance tests fail to reject the null hypothesis at the traditionally accepted $p < .05$ value. Figure 3.1 presents the distribution of estimates of the causal effect that we would get if each of the over 600 million randomizations were performed, and we computed the causal effect $\bar{Y}_t - \bar{Y}_c$ for each randomization. Half of the estimates are less than 0.5 and about 8% are less than 0, surprisingly suggesting that the treatment might have

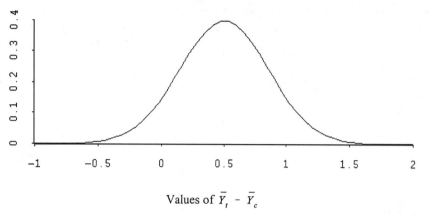

Values of $\bar{Y}_t - \bar{Y}_c$

Figure 3.1. Distribution of $\bar{Y}_t - \bar{Y}_c$.

Note. The mean of the sampling distribution is 0.5. The standard deviation of the sampling distribution is 0.354. $\bar{Y}_t - \bar{Y}_c$ must exceed $1.96 * 0.354 = 0.69$ to reject the null hypothesis of no difference between $\mu_t - \mu_c$ in the population. The experimenter will correctly reject the null hypothesis about 30% of the time.

had a negative effect on the response.[3] Only about 30% of the estimates (i.e., those > 0.69) would lead to correct rejection of the null hypothesis of no causal effect. Indeed, had we been in the more usual situation and used a *t*-test rather than *z*-test because we did not know the population standard deviation, this value would have been slightly lower, about 28%. This value is known as the *statistical power* of the test, the probability of rejecting the null hypothesis when it is false. We consider the issue of statistical power in more detail later in the chapter.

According to the traditional null hypothesis significance testing view,[4] if the null hypothesis can be

rejected as being unlikely (typically $p < .05$), then we can conclude that an effect of the treatment exists. $\bar{Y}_t - \bar{Y}_c$ provides an unbiased estimate of the causal effect of the treatment. Once again, this estimate is accurate on average; however, there is no guarantee that the estimate will be accurate in any specific experiment – the value may be too high or too low. These considerations highlight the value of replications and meta-analyses (see e.g., Hedges & Olkin, 1985; Hunter & Schmidt, 1990; Johnson & Eagly, this volume, Ch. 19) in establishing more accurate and more certain estimates of causal effects.

FIELD EXPERIMENTS

Both basic and applied social psychological experiments may be carried out in field settings. The defining characteristics of the field experiment closely follow those of the laboratory experiment in social psychology (Aronson, Wilson, & Brewer, 1998; Smith, this volume Ch. 12) – random assignment, manipulation of the treatment conditions, and measurement of the dependent variable. However, additional issues arise because of differences between the field and laboratory

---

[3] Researchers typically only see the causal effect estimate from their own single experiment. They have worked hard designing the experiment, recruiting and running the participants, and analyzing the data and consequently have great confidence in the results of their single experiment. When another researcher fails to find the same result, it is easy to attribute his lack of findings to methodological problems (the "crap research" hypothesis; Hunter, 1996). However, Hunter argued that meta-analyses of several research areas have suggested that methodological quality accounts for relatively little of the variability in the causal effects. Rather, simple sampling variability of the type illustrated here appears to be the main source of the variability in estimates of causal effects (Hunter, 1996).

[4] At the time of this writing, intense reconsideration of hypothesis testing procedures is taking place among methodologists (see Harlow, Mulaik, & Steiger, 1997; Wilkinson, L. and

the Task Force on Statistical Inference, 1999). Our belief is that traditional null hypothesis testing procedures will likely be revised or replaced by an alternative procedure during the next few years. One major alternative is that researchers will be asked to report confidence intervals for all effect estimates. Confidence intervals that do not include 0 lead to the same conclusions as null hypothesis significance tests with respect to ruling out chance as a plausible interpretation of the results. But, confidence intervals also provide information about the size of the treatment. Standardized and unstandardized measures of the size of treatment effects are likely to become increasingly important in many areas of psychology in the future (Cohen, Cohen, Aiken, & West, in press).

contexts. Below we first briefly present two simplified examples of field experiments, then identify some of the new issues that arise as well as possible solutions for those issues.

Illustrations of Field Experiments

Some field experiments test hypotheses derived from basic social psychological theory. For example, Cialdini, Reno, and Kallgren (1990) conducted a series of field experiments to examine the impact of norms on littering. In one study on the impact of descriptive norms (what most others do), solitary dormitory residents retrieving their mail (which contained a flier) were confronted with an environment containing either no litter, a single conspicuous piece of litter, or many pieces of litter. More residents in the heavily littered environment condition discarded the flier than in the other two conditions. However, fewer residents in the single piece of litter condition littered than in the clean environment condition. Cialdini et al. argued that the single piece of litter invoked the descriptive norm against littering.

Other field experiments test hypotheses from applied social psychology. For example, Evans et al. (1981) evaluated the effectiveness of a program to deter smoking among junior high school students in Houston. The program built on social psychological theory and research (e.g., Bandura, 1977; McGuire, 1964). The program included three major components: (a) social pressures created by peers, family, and the media to smoke; (b) the immediate negative physiological effects of smoking; and (c) methods of resisting pressures to smoke. The program was intended to be of 3 years duration. Entire schools were assigned to program (treatment) and no treatment (control) conditions. Although the great majority of students participated, informed consent requirements resulted in a sample of self-selected volunteers. Complex methodological issues arose in this experiment: How to assign the small number of units (schools) to treatment conditions, how to analyze data from students in the treatment condition who received from 1 to 3 years of the program because of school transfers, and how to address the loss of participants at the posttest measurement. At the end of the 3-year experiment, students in the smoking prevention program reported lower intentions to start smoking and lower rates of cigarette smoking than did control students. A number of experiments evaluating other smoking prevention programs derived from Evans et al.'s original work have shown generally positive results in preventing or delaying the onset of smoking in preteenagers (Flay, 1986).

Problems of Randomized Experiments and Their Remedies

THE STABLE-UNIT-TREATMENT-VALUE-ASSUMPTION (SUTVA). Randomization yields unbiased estimates of the causal effect given that the SUTVA is met. SUTVA has two parts. First, the assignment mechanism, here randomization, should not affect the participants' response to the experimental or control treatment. Although we normally consider randomization to be an inert process with respect to the participant's response, consider the following thought experiment. A student volunteers for an exciting new graduate training program in which she is handsomely funded each summer of her graduate career to work with a different professor of her choice in her speciality area at any university in the United States. She is informed that she has been chosen for this program on the basis of (i) her extraordinary merit, or (ii) random assignment. Would the participant's response (e.g., measured achievement in research) to the same program be identical in each case? At least some social psychological theorizing (e.g., Weiner, 1974) would predict that a student who believed good luck was responsible for her program participation might show lower achievement than the same student who believed her own high levels of ability and effort were responsible for her program participation.

Second, the response of the participant should not be affected by the treatments other units receive. Knowledge of other treatments may change the participants' level of motivation, particularly for those in the control group, a problem Higginbotham, West, and Forsyth (1988) termed "atypical reactions of control participants." For example, participants assigned to the control group in a randomized experiment of a promising new treatment for a serious disease may give up their normal health-maintaining activities, leading to poorer outcomes in the control group than normal (resentful demoralization). Alternatively, participants assigned to a well-liked standard (comparison) program may try harder if the existence of the standard program may be in jeopardy as a result of a positive outcome for a new, experimental program (compensatory rivalry). Such atypical responses of control participants can lead to overestimates or underestimates of causal effects, respectively. The participant's response can also be affected in other ways when the response involves a comparative evaluation. For example, the causal effect of a job training program relative to a no training control group may be overestimated in a small community if most of the limited pool of available jobs are then taken by trainees, so that there are few, if any, of the usual number of possible positions available for control group members.

Researchers have developed a variety of strategies to increase the likelihood that SUTVA is met, of which the following three are the most commonly used.

1. If participants are not aware of the random assignment and are only aware of the nature of the experimental condition in which they participate, the likelihood that SUTVA will be met is greatly increased. Such conditions can typically be achieved in laboratory settings[5] and some field settings. In particular, geographical or temporal isolation of the participants in the treatment and control conditions can often help minimize these problems in field settings. However, a caution is in order here: Informed consent procedures sometimes mandate informing participants that they will be randomly assigned to one of several treatment conditions whose nature is outlined in the consent form. Such procedures may potentially lead to violations of SUTVA.

2. Successful masking (blinding) procedures in which the participants (and ideally the experimenter as well) are kept unaware of their treatment condition also increase the likelihood that SUTVA will be satisfied. Such procedures are commonly used in drug research in which participants are not informed whether they are receiving an active drug or an inert placebo. However, masking procedures often cannot be successfully applied in real world experiments. For example, consider an experiment (Mallar & Thornton, 1978) in which released prisoners are given transitional financial aid for 6 months (treatment) or no financial aid, and the researchers recorded whether they return to jail for property crimes during the following year. Keeping released

prisoners unaware that they have received financial assistance would eliminate any positive effects this treatment could be expected to have. Further, treatment masking is not always successful: Participants sometimes see through even the best masking procedures on the basis of outcomes they experience early in the experiment (Meier, 1991). Even in the most carefully conducted drug trials, participants sometimes can identify the medication they have been assigned based on factors such as its taste, early positive effects, and early side effects. Participants who have strong positive (or negative) expectations about the effects of that drug may then show increased positive (or negative) responses to the drug.

3. The specific treatments do not represent outcomes or opportunities that are important to participants. Participants assigned to a 6-person simulated jury in a laboratory experiment are unlikely to change their responses on the basis of their knowledge that other participants have been assigned to a 12-person simulated jury. In contrast, released prisoners in the control condition may well be angered or demoralized if they learn that other former prisoners in the treatment condition receive 6 months of transitional aid to cover basic living expenses. An alternative strategy is to offer control (comparison) participants an equally attractive program that is not expected to affect the response. Bryan, Aiken and West (1996) presented an example of this design, comparing the effectiveness of an STD-(sexually transmitted disease) prevention program with an equally attractive stress-reduction comparison program. The stress-reduction comparison program did not include any content that focused on increasing condom use and was thus not expected to influence the response of interest, condom use.

BREAKDOWN OF RANDOMIZATION. For the randomized experiment to yield an unbiased estimate of the causal effect, $\bar{Y}_t - \bar{Y}_c$, random assignment of participants to treatment and comparison conditions must, in fact, be properly carried out. Studies of large-scale randomized field experiments, particularly those conducted at multiple sites, suggest that full or partial breakdowns of randomization occur with some frequency (Boruch, McSweeny, & Soderstrom, 1978; Conner, 1977). Problems tend to occur more frequently when the individuals responsible for delivering the treatment, such as school or medical personnel, are allowed to carry out the assignment of participants to treatment conditions and when monitoring of the

---

[5] SUTVA may be violated in laboratory experiments through prior communication of information about the experiment among potential participants. The little research to date (e.g., Aronson, 1966) suggests that this may be a minor problem, at least among unacquainted participants, given adequate debriefing following the experiment. Potentially more problematic, but little researched, is the prevalence and effects of communication through informal social networks of acquaintances who may seek information prior to signing up for a particular experiment.

maintenance of the treatment assignment is poor. For example, Kopans (1994) reviewed the large recent Canadian experiment on the effectiveness of mammography screening for reducing deaths from breast cancer. He presented data suggesting that women in the mammography group had a substantially higher cancer risk *at pretest* than women in the no mammography screening group. It seems likely that some of the physicians involved in the trial saw to it that their patients with family histories of breast cancer or prior episodes of breast-related disease were assigned to the screening group.

One way to address this problem is through careful monitoring of the randomization process as well as careful monitoring of the treatment(s) each participant actually receives following randomization (Braucht & Reichardt, 1993). For example, students (or their parents) in school-based experiments are sometimes able to agitate successfully to change from a control to a treatment class during the randomization process itself or during the school year following randomization. Careful monitoring can help minimize this problem and can also allow formal assessment of the magnitude of the problem. If there is a systematic movement of children between treatment conditions (e.g., the brighter children are moved to the treatment group), the estimate of the causal effect of treatment will potentially be biased. Attempts to correct for such bias need to be undertaken.

An alternative strategy to minimize breakdowns of randomization is to use units that are temporally or geographically isolated in the experiment. For example, randomization breakdowns in school-based experiments, particularly those which occur postassignment, are far more likely when different treatments are given to different classrooms (low isolation of units) than when different treatments are given to different schools (high isolation of units).

GROUP ADMINISTRATION OF TREATMENT. Often in field research interventions are offered to groups of participants. For example, Evans et al. (1981) delivered their smoking prevention intervention to intact school classrooms; Aiken, West, Woodward, Reno, and Reynolds (1994) delivered a program encouraging compliance with American Cancer Society guidelines for regular screening mammograms to women's groups in the community; and Vinokur, Price, and Caplan (1991) recruited unemployed individuals to participate in a job-seeking skills training program that was delivered in a group format. Group administration of treatments, whether in the laboratory or the field, leads to statistical and conceptual issues that need to be considered.

When treatments are delivered to groups, the entire group is assigned to either the treatment or control condition. Thus, randomization occurs at the level of the group and not the individual participant. The statistical outcome of this procedure is that the responses of the members of each treatment group may no longer be independent. As an illustration, consider the Evans et al. (1981) smoking prevention experiment. The responses of 2 children randomly chosen from a single classroom would be expected to be more similar than the responses of 2 children randomly chosen from different classrooms (Kashy & Kenny, this volume, Ch. 17). Although nonindependence has no impact on the causal effect estimate, $\bar{Y}_t - \bar{Y}_c$, it does lead to estimates of the standard error of this effect that are typically too small.[6] The magnitude of this problem increases as the amount of dependence (measured by the intraclass correlation) and the size of groups to which treatment is delivered increase. For example, Barcikowski (1981) showed that, even with relatively low levels of dependency in groups (intraclass correlation = .05), when groups were of a size typical of grade school classroom studies ($n = 25$ per class), the Type 1 error rate (rejecting the null hypothesis when in fact it is true) was in fact .19 rather than the stated value of .05.

Following Fisher (1935), researchers traditionally "solved" this problem by aggregating their data to the level of the group (e.g., average response of each classroom). The unit of analysis should match the unit of assignment – "analyze them as you've randomized them" (Fisher, as cited in Boruch, 1997, p. 195). However, this solution is often not fully satisfactory because such analyses can be generalized only to a population of groups, not to a population of individuals, which is typically the researcher's interest. Over the past decade, new statistical procedures termed "hierarchical linear (random coefficient, multilevel) models" have been developed. These models simultaneously provide an estimate of the causal effect at the group level as well as individual level analyses that appropriately correct standard errors for the degree of nonindependence within groups. Introductions to these models are presented in Bryk and Raudenbush (1992), Hedecker, Gibbons, and Flay, (1994), and Kreft and DeLeeuw (1998).

---

[6] In randomized field experiments, participants are nearly always more similar within than between groups. In other situations involving within-subject designs or other forms of dependency, the direction of bias may change (see Kenny & Judd, 1986).

Given the proper use of hierarchical linear models to analyze the data, the random assignment of groups to treatments (when participants are also randomly assigned to the individual groups) rules out traditional sources of confounding, known as ecological bias, associated with aggregation of units (Greenland & Morgenstern, 1989; Robinson, 1950). However, a conceptual issue remains. Rubin's causal model emphasizes that causal effects represent the comparison of one well-articulated treatment with another well-articulated treatment. In comparisons among treatments delivered to individuals in group settings, the articulation of the treatment becomes murkier as treatment now includes the other individuals in the setting and all of the activities of members within the group. Cronbach (1976) and Burstein (1980) discussed many of the issues and opportunities associated with multilevel designs, although their recommendations of analytic strategies have been superseded by the hierarchical linear modeling approaches noted previously. Draper (1995), Holland (1989), Burstein (1985), and Burstein, Kim, and Delandshire (1989) considered many of the inferential issues associated with hierarchical linear modeling.

TREATMENT NONCOMPLIANCE. When participants are randomly assigned to treatment and control conditions in field experiments, not all participants may actually get the treatment. A portion of the participants randomly assigned to programs designed to increase exercise, improve nutrition, or improve job-seeking skills simply do not show up for program sessions, and so do not receive the treatment. These participants are referred to as treatment noncompliers. Practical methods exist for minimizing this problem, notably making the program attractive to participants, removing barriers to program attendance (e.g., providing transportation or child care), giving participants incentives for program attendance, and only including those participants who are willing to participate in both the treatment and control programs in the randomization (Cook & Campbell, 1979). Despite these efforts, some participants assigned to treatment condition never receive any treatment. We assume in this section that the researcher was able to measure the dependent variable on all participants, including those who do not receive treatment.

Three statistical approaches have been taken in response to this problem. The first, known as the *intention to treat* analysis (Lee, Ellenberg, Hirtz, & Nelson, 1991) is to compare the mean response of all participants assigned to the treatment condition (regardless of whether they received treatment) with the mean response of all participants assigned to the control condition. This analysis typically yields conservative estimates of the causal effect and requires no assumptions beyond those required for the randomized experiment. The second is to throw out all participants assigned to the treatment group who do not in fact receive treatment. Such a comparison will yield a biased estimate of the causal effect (with the direction of bias being unknown) unless the stringent assumption can be made that the participants who drop out of the treatment condition represent a random sample of the participants in that condition.[7] The third, known as the complier average causal effect (CACE), uses ideas from econometrics and missing data theory (Little & Rubin, 1987) to create an unbiased estimate of the treatment effect for participants who actually receive the treatment (Angrist et al., 1996; Little & Yau, 1998; see also Bloom, 1984). Both the first and the third approaches produce meaningful estimates of treatment effects; however they answer different questions (see West & Sagarin, 2000). The intention to treat analysis estimates the causal effect in the entire sample, whereas CACE estimates the causal effect only for those participants who actually receive the treatment.

To understand these three approaches, let us consider the data presented in Table 3.4. Table 3.4 uses the same data as Table 3.1 with some added features. First, in assignment 4 (a_4) Participants 1–16 who are assigned to the control group are assumed to be perfectly matched with Participants 17–32 who are assigned to the treatment group. In this assignment, Participant 1 is identical to Participant 17, Participant 2 is identical to Participant 18, and so on, so that we do not need to consider the effects of sampling error. Second, we have indicated a systematic pattern of noncompliance. In column c_1, participants with the lowest scores prior to treatment do not comply with the treatment. These participants are termed "never takers" in Angrist et al.'s (1996) model.

The use of the RCM, which emphasizes the comparison of the same unit receiving the treatment and the control conditions, highlights an easily overlooked point. Participants 1–5 in the control group are identical to the never takers in the treatment group (Participants 17–21) in Table 3.4. They are participants who would

---

[7] The approach of throwing out participants has been the standard procedure in laboratory experiments in social psychology when technical problems arise or when participants are suspicious or uncooperative. The possibility that this procedure introduces potential bias should always be considered.

TABLE 3.4. Illustration of Effects of Treatment Noncompliance

Participant	a_4	c_1	Y_c	Y_t
1	0	0	1*	1.5
2	0	0	2*	2.5
3	0	0	2*	2.5
4	0	0	2*	2.5
5	0	0	2*	2.5
6	0	1	3*	3.5
7	0	1	3*	3.5
8	0	1	3*	3.5
9	0	1	3*	3.5
10	0	1	3*	3.5
11	0	1	3*	3.5
12	0	1	4*	4.5
13	0	1	4*	4.5
14	0	1	4*	4.5
15	0	1	4*	4.5
16	0	1	5*	5.5
17	1	0	1*	1.5
18	1	0	2*	2.5
19	1	0	2*	2.5
20	1	0	2*	2.5
21	1	0	2*	2.5
22	1	1	3	3.5*
23	1	1	3	3.5*
24	1	1	3	3.5*
25	1	1	3	3.5*
26	1	1	3	3.5*
27	1	1	3	3.5*
28	1	1	4	4.5*
29	1	1	4	4.5*
30	1	1	4	4.5*
31	1	1	4	4.5*
32	1	1	5	5.5*

Note. The column labeled Y_c contains the true response of each participant in the control condition. The column labeled Y_t contains the true response of each participant in the treatment condition. a_4 represents the assignment of the first 16 participants to the control group and the second 16 participants to the treatment group. $c_1 = 1$ means participant follows the treatment or control condition as assigned. $c_1 = 0$ means participant is a never taker and does not comply when in the treatment condition. The starred value of Y is the value actually observed for each participant. As before, the true causal effect, $Y_t - Y_c$, is 0.5.

if they were given the opportunity. As will be illustrated below, the failure to consider this group of participants potentially yields biased estimates of treatment effects.

Applying these three statistical approaches to the present example, the intention to treat analysis compares the observed data (indicated with an asterisk in Table 3.4) for participants assigned to the treatment with the observed data for participants assigned to the control group. The mean for the control group is as before, $\bar{Y}_c = 3.0$. However, in the treatment group Participants 17–21 did not comply and thus received no benefit from treatment. Consequently, the treatment group mean is correspondingly reduced, $\bar{Y}_t = 3.344$. The causal effect estimate, $\bar{Y}_t - Y_c$, is 0.344 – more than a 30% reduction in the effect size from the true value for compliers of 0.50.

Following the second approach, Participants 17–21 are eliminated from the analysis and the mean for the treatment group is $\sum_{i=22}^{i=32} Y_i/11 = 4.045$. Thus, the causal effect estimate is $\bar{Y}_t - \bar{Y}_c = 4.045 - 3.000 = 1.045$, which in this case is considerably larger than the true value of 0.5. Finally, using the CACE approach (Little & Yau, 1998), we eliminate the never takers from both the treatment and control groups. We find that

$$\bar{Y}_t = \frac{\sum_{i=22}^{i=32} Y_i}{11} = 4.045, \quad \bar{Y}_c = \frac{\sum_{i=6}^{i=16} Y_i}{11} = 3.545,$$

so that the estimate of the causal effect, $\bar{Y}_t - \bar{Y}_c$, is 0.5, which is equal to the true effect for compliers.

The conceptual problem with CACE is that we cannot identify which participants in the control group would comply if they were in the treatment group. However, given a randomized experiment and SUTVA, an unbiased estimate of CACE can be calculated. In the simplest case (Bloom, 1984), in which we assume the treatment effect is constant for all participants, the causal effect estimate, $\bar{Y}_t - \bar{Y}_c$, from the intention to treat analysis (.344) can be adjusted by the inverse of the proportion of compliers in the treatment group $(11/16)^{-1}$. In the present example, this effect can be calculated as CACE = (.344)(16/11) = 0.5. Angrist et al. (1996) and Little and Yau (1998) provided more advanced statistical discussions of the CACE approach. Vinokur, Price, and Caplan (1991) provided an empirical illustration.

The CACE approach makes several assumptions. For field experiments in social psychology, the most important of the assumptions is that the response of a never taker participant who does not comply with the treatment will be identical to the response of the same

not have complied with the treatment if they had been assigned to the treatment group. All standard analyses that throw out noncompliers fail to take into account this group of participants who would fail to comply participant in the control group. This assumption implies that the treatment received by noncompliers in the treatment group must be identical to the treatment received by participants in the control group. It will only be met in designs in which the control group represents "no treatment" or in which the control group represents a base treatment (t_{base}, which everyone receives) to which one or more additional components are added in the treatment group ($t_{base} + t_{additional}$; the constructive research strategy; see West & Aiken, 1997). Designs in which an alternative treatment is used as the comparison group will violate this assumption.

The assumption will also be violated in experiments in which participants partially comply with treatment (e.g., they attend 5 of 20 required treatment sessions). Attempts to adjust intention to treat causal effect estimates based on careful measures of degree of compliance of participants in *both* the treatment and control groups have thus far not been fully satisfactory. They require either an excellent model of the determinants of compliance in both the treatment and control groups or the use of a successful double-masking (blinding) procedure, in which neither the participant nor the experimenter is aware of the participant's treatment condition. Holland (1988) presented an extensive discussion of this problem in terms of the RCM. Efron and Feldman (1991) presented one of the best of the current procedures for addressing partial treatment compliance. The discussions following both the Holland and the Efron and Feldman articles clearly articulate the complex issues and limitations associated with the use of such procedures.

PARTICIPANT LOSS AT POSTTEST MEASUREMENT.

The approaches for addressing treatment noncompliance just discussed assumed that posttest measurements were available for all participants regardless of whether they complied. A second problem that occurs in many randomized field experiments is that some participants in both the treatment and comparison groups cannot be remeasured at posttest. This problem, known as participant *attrition*, is a major potential source of bias in the estimation of causal effects.

Attrition can often be minimized by careful attention during the planning of the experiment. Securing the addresses and telephone numbers of the participants, their close friends or relatives, and their employer or school greatly aids in locating dropouts (attriting participants). Keeping in touch with both treatment and control participants through periodic mailings or telephone calls and providing incentives for continued participation can also help minimize participant loss. A considerable body of specialized techniques for tracking, locating, and contacting participants now exists in many research areas (Ribisl, Walton, Mowbray, Luke, Davidson, & Bootsmiller, 1996). Nonetheless, even given the use of careful procedures, attrition still typically does occur. For example, Biglan et al. (1991), in their review of longitudinal studies of substance abuse prevention, reported attrition rates ranging from 5% to 66% (mean = approximately 25%). Furthermore, dropouts typically report greater substance use at the initial measurement. Such findings suggest that estimates of treatment effects on the outcomes of interest may be biased if attrition is not addressed.

Researchers have some ability to estimate the likely effects of attrition on their results – but only if pretest measures that are expected to be related to the response measures of interest have been collected. Jurs and Glass (1971; see also Cook & Campbell, 1979) have outlined a two-step strategy to detect possible bias introduced by differential attrition between the treatment and comparison groups.

1. The first step is to compare the percentage of participants who drop out in the treatment and comparison groups. If these values differ, then the differential attrition (participant loss) rates may be interpreted as a treatment effect. However, the interpretation of all measured response variables becomes more problematic (see Sackett & Gent, 1979).

2. The second step is to conduct a series of 2 (treatment group: t vs. c) $\times$ 2 (completer vs. attriter) ANOVAs on each of the pretest measures. The goal is to identify all possible background characteristics (e.g., attitudes, behaviors, personality, demographics) on which participants may differ. A main effect for treatment group indicates a possible failure of the randomization to properly equate the groups prior to treatment. A main effect for attriter versus completer indicates that the characteristics of the attriters (dropouts) differ from those of the completers, suggesting that the findings of the experiment cannot be generalized to the full population of interest (external validity threat). Of most concern, a Treatment Group $\times$ Attrition Status interaction indicates that the characteristics of participants who dropped out differed in the treatment and control conditions, indicating potential bias in the estimate of the causal effect (internal validity threat). When problems of differential attrition are identified, researchers should explore possible adjustments of the treatment effect through missing data imputation techniques (Little & Rubin, 1987; Little & Schenker, 1995), through attempts to understand

and model the effects of attrition on the response (e.g., Arbuckle, 1996; Muthén, Kaplan, & Hollis, 1987), or through attempts to estimate reasonable maximum and minimum values that bracket the treatment effect (Shadish, Hu, Glaser, Knonacki, & Wong, 1998; West & Sagarin, 2000). Comparison of alternative adjustments that make different assumptions to see if they yield similar results is particularly worthwhile.

There are two major problems in the use of the Jurs and Glass (1971) technique just outlined. First, differential attrition may be related to participant characteristics that were not measured at pretest. If these unobserved characteristics differ between the treatment and control groups and are related to the responses of interest, the causal effect estimate may be misleading. For example, it is possible that attriters from smoking prevention programs may have peers or parents who smoke and who put pressure on them to drop out of the program. In contrast, children in the control group with parents or peers who smoke would not experience similar pressure and would be less likely to drop out. If measures of peer and parent smoking are not collected at pretest, this potential source of differential attrition could not be detected. Second, the Jurs and Glass technique uses statistical hypothesis tests to identify variables that are related or unrelated to attrition status. Concluding that a variable is unrelated to attrition status requires the researcher to accept the null hypothesis that there is no Treatment × Attrition Status interaction. In fact, some of the individual pretest variables, or combinations of these pretest variables, may represent important sources of differential attrition even though the statistical test fails to reach conventional levels of significance. Some researchers (e.g., Hansen, Collins, Malotte, Johnson, & Fielding, 1985) have called for using less conservative levels of significance (e.g., $\alpha = .25$) for all tests so that the corresponding Type II error rates will be reduced. Others (Tebes, Snow, & Arthur, 1992) have proposed choosing the Type I error rate (α) based on an expected or calculated effect size so that the ratio of Type II to Type I errors will approximate the ratio of 4:1 (viz. $\beta = .20$; $\alpha = .05$) recommended by Cohen (1988). The bottom line is that rejection of the null hypothesis is used as a method of screening potentially important from unimportant sources of differential attrition. The basic goal is to identify all potential sources of differential attrition that should be retained for further investigation. Even if a large number of tests are performed, they should not be corrected for alpha inflation (experimentwise error rate). Such correction defeats the basic goal of the procedure.

OTHER ISSUES IN EXPERIMENTS

Statistical Power

For a randomized trial to be worth doing, it must have adequate statistical power to detect differences between the treatment and control conditions. Yet, existing reviews of the statistical power of tests in major psychology journals, including the *Journal of Personality and Social Psychology* (e.g., Rossi, 1990), have suggested that many researchers continue to conduct statistical tests with inadequate power. Following Cohen (1988), differences between the treatment and control groups of .80, .50, and .20 standard deviation units, (d), are defined as large, moderate, and small effect sizes, and .80 is defined as adequate statistical power. In a randomized experiment with an equal number of participants in the treatment and control groups, 52 total participants ($n = 26$ per condition) would be needed to detect a large effect, 126 participants would be needed to detect a moderate effect, and 786 participants would be required to detect a small effect at alpha $= .05$ and power $= .80$. Our earlier example illustrated this issue: With 32 total participants, we were able to detect a moderate effect size ($d = 0.5$) only about 30% of the time. Given an estimate of the likely effect size based either on prior research in the area (especially estimates from meta-analyses) or on a normative basis (e.g., $d = .50$ following Cohen, 1988), statistical power can now be easily computed in advance of conducting an experiment with user-friendly software (e.g., Borenstein, Cohen, & Rothstein, 1997).

In the design of experiments, several methods can be used to increase power. These methods are extensively discussed in Higginbotham, West, and Forsyth (1988, chapter 2); Hansen and Collins (1994); Lipsey (1997); and Dennis, Lennox, and Williams (1997). The most obvious method is to increase the sample size. However, practical issues such as cost, available resources, or the limited availability of certain special participant populations (e.g., bereaved children; intensive care nurses) often restrict this option, even in large metropolitan areas. Other methods include using stronger treatments, maintaining the integrity of the treatment implementation, using more reliable measures, maximizing participant uniformity, minimizing participant attrition, and adding covariates measured at pretest that are related to the dependent variable. Also of interest are a variety of rarely used techniques that equate participants on one or more covariates that are known to be important predictors of the response prior to random assignment to treatment and control conditions. Such procedures are particularly valuable when only a small number of units are available for randomization.

Equating participants at pretest on a single variable is straightforward. Typically, participants are simply ranked on the background variable and then grouped into pairs (the 2 highest, the next 2 highest, and so on, down to the 2 lowest scores on the pretest measure). Then, 1 participant from each pair is randomly assigned to the treatment and the other to the control condition. A matched-pairs t-test is used to compare the response of the treatment and control groups. If the basis for matching participants is highly related to the response variable, these procedures can lead to large increases in statistical power. For example, Student (1931, the nom de plume of W. S. Gosset, a statistician at the Guinness brewing company) critiqued the Lanarkshire milk experiment, an early experiment comparing the gains in height and weight of 5,000 children given pasteurized milk with those of 5,000 children given raw milk. He noted that identifying 50 pairs of identical twins and then randomly assigning 1 twin from each pair to the pasteurized milk condition and 1 twin to the raw milk condition would yield the same statistical power as the original experiment with 10,000 children.

With several variables, these procedures become more complex. To illustrate one method of matching on several variables, imagine that the 32 participants in our earlier example had been measured on several important background variables at pretest. We noted earlier that there were over 600 million different possible randomizations of the 32 participants into two equal groups ($n_1 = n_2 = 16$). We could have a computer program generate a large number (e.g., 1,500) of different randomizations. A multivariate measure (e.g., Hotelling's T^2) of the difference between the two groups on the pretest measures would be calculated for each of the 1,500 randomizations. We could then rank order the randomizations according to their success in equating the treatment and control groups on the pretest measures on the basis of the multivariate measure. We would then randomly select one of the best randomizations (e.g., from the 50 with the lowest value of the Hotelling's T^2) to use in our experiment. Such procedures assure that our two groups are well-equated at pretest, minimizing sampling error to the extent the pretest measures are related to the response.[8]

---

[8] Analysis of covariance or blocking on the pretest score can also be used to increase statistical power. These techniques

Generalization of Causal Relationships

Our presentation of the RCM has focused primarily on what Cook and Campbell (1979) have termed *internal validity*: Something about the particular treatment caused the specific observed response in this particular experiment. The RCM is focused on the estimation of the causal effect; it is largely mute as to what the active causal agent(s) of the treatment might be or how one might go about determining them. Campbell (1986) also emphasized the limited causal understanding provided by internal validity, even suggesting that internal validity be relabeled as "local molar (pragmatic, atheoretical) causal validity" (p. 69).

In contrast, social psychological researchers are rarely interested in limiting their causal statements to a specific treatment implementation, delivered in a specific setting, to a specific sample of participants, and assessed with a specific measure. Methodologists (Campbell, 1957; Campbell & Stanley, 1966; Cook, 1993; Cook & Campbell, 1979; Cronbach, 1982; Shadish et al., in press; see also Brewer, this volume, Ch. 1) have articulated principles for understanding and generalizing the causal effect obtained in a single experiment. Cronbach (1982) developed a model with a focus on generalization with respect to four dimensions: units (typically participants), treatments, observations (measures or responses), and settings. He labeled the specific values of these dimensions that characterize a specific experiment as (lower case) **u**nits, **t**reatments, **o**bservations, and **s**ettings (utos). He labeled the target values of the dimensions that characterize the classes to which the results of the experiment can be generalized as (upper case) **U**nits, **T**reatments, **O**bservations, and **S**ettings (UTOS). In Cook and Campbell's (1979, chapter 2) analysis of validity, generalization to Treatments and Observations represent two dimensions of the issue of construct validity, and generalization to Units and Settings (and Times) represent the dimensions of the issue of external validity. Cronbach (1982) also described another type of generalization, utos to U*T*O*S*. Here, the researcher desires to generalize to new populations of Units, Treatments, Observations, and Settings (U*T*O*S*) that were not studied in the original experiment.

---

are more sensitive to violations of assumptions (e.g., curvilinear relationship between pretest measure and response) than matching and generally perform less well in small samples. Maxwell and Delaney (1990, chapter 9) presented a thorough discussion and comparison of matching and blocking techniques in experiments.

Figure 3.2. The formal statistical model for generalization.

Note. The purpose of step B is to provide unbiased estimates of the causal effect of the treatment. The purpose of step A is to permit generalization of the results obtained in the sample to a defined population of participants.

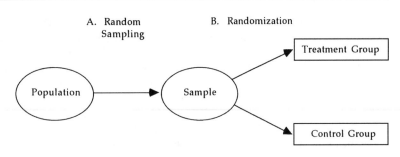

Let us apply the Cronbach model to the Evans et al. (1981) experiment described earlier. In this experiment, the units were children in specific school classrooms in Houston, the treatment was this specific implementation of the social influences smoking prevention program, the observations were children's reports of smoking, and the setting was the classroom. The UTOS to which Evans et al. presumably wished to generalize were all school children of specific ages, the social influences smoking prevention program, cigarette smoking, and school classrooms. As an applied experiment, the goal is to generalize to specific participant populations and to a specific school setting. The treatment is also conceptually quite circumscribed as is the observation of interest, smoking.

Strategies for Generalization

STATISTICAL STRATEGY: RANDOM SAMPLING. The only formal statistical basis for generalization is through the use of random sampling from well-defined populations. Surveys using national probability samples assess the attitudes of representative samples of adults; other surveys may assess the attitudes of a more focused sample, such as hospital nurses in a section of Denver. In each case, a defined population is enumerated from which a random sample is collected, yielding estimates of the attitudes of the population that are accurate to within a specified level of sampling error.[9]

Figure 3.2 presents the randomized experiment in the context of this formal sampling model. Stage A

represents random sampling from a defined population; the purpose of this stage is to assure generalization to a defined population of Units (participants) as is discussed below. Stage B represents random assignment of the units in the sample to treatment and control conditions; as discussed previously, the purpose is to achieve unbiased estimates of the causal effect in the sample. The combination of Stages A and B formally permits generalization of an unbiased causal effect of the specific treatment conditions, studied in the context of a specific experimental setting, using the specific dependent measures to the full population of Units (participants). Note that generalization to Treatments, Observations, and Settings is not formally addressed by this model.

This formal sampling model is routinely recommended by statisticians and epidemiologists (e.g., Draper, 1995; Kish, 1987) as the ideal model for experimental research. Unfortunately, it is extraordinarily difficult to implement in practice. With respect to Units (participant populations), many cannot be precisely enumerated (e.g., children whose parents are alcoholics; Chassin, Barrera, Bech, & Kossak-Fuller, 1992). Even when the researcher can precisely enumerate the participant population (e.g., using official court records to enumerate recently divorced individuals), there is no guarantee that such participants can actually be located. Further, even if they are located, participants may refuse to be randomized or refuse to participate in a particular experiment, despite being offered large incentives for their participation.

A few recent experiments have approximated the ideal model of statisticians despite the difficulties. Randomized experiments have been conducted within national or local probability surveys (e.g., investigating question context; Schwarz & Hippler, 1995). Randomized experiments have compared treatment versus control programs using random samples of specific populations of individuals in the community (e.g., job seekers selected from state unemployment lines;

---

[9] Social psychologists interested in basic research have traditionally focused primarily on whether theoretically predicted effects exist. However, recent criticisms of traditional null hypothesis significance testing (e.g., Cohen, 1994; Harlow, Mulaik, & Steiger, 1997) and the increased prominence of meta-analysis have greatly increased the focus of both basic and applied psychologists on the size of treatment effects. This shift in focus is likely to lead to a stronger focus on issues of generalization in basic as well as in applied research in the future.

Vinokur et al., 1991; Wolchik et al., in press). Such experiments routinely include heroic efforts to study nonparticipants in the experiment in order to understand the probable limits, if any, on the generalization of their findings to the full participant population of interest. Nonetheless, even such extraordinary efforts only address the generalization of units; they only take us from u to U. When our interest turns to the generalization of findings to a class (or population) of Treatments, Observations, and Settings, we almost never have any strong basis for defining a population of interest. In short, in nearly all basic and applied social psychological research we have to turn to extra-statistical methods of enhancing causal generalization.

EXTRA-STATISTICAL APPROACHES: COOK'S FIVE PRINCIPLES. Cook (1993) synthesized earlier ideas about causal generalization and articulated five general principles. These principles may be applied to strengthen causal generalization with respect to Units, Treatments, Observations, and Settings.

PROXIMAL SIMILARITY. The specific units, treatments, observations, and settings should include most of the components of the construct or population, particularly those that are judged to be prototypical. A researcher wishing to generalize to a population of nurses (e.g., in metropolitan Denver) should choose nurses from this area in his sample. The sample should include the various modal types of nurses (e.g., LPN, RN). To generalize to settings, the modal settings in which nurses work (e.g., hospital, home-care) should be identified, and nurses should be sampled from each. With respect to constructs, the researcher should design a treatment and either design or select a measurement instrument that includes most of the important components specified by the theory.

HETEROGENEOUS IRRELEVANCIES. The units, treatments, observations, and settings we use in our experiments are specific instances chosen to represent the population or the construct. They will typically underrepresent certain features of the target Units, Treatments, Observations, and Settings. They will typically also include other extraneous features that are not part of the target of generalization. For example, nearly all research on attitudes uses paper-and-pencil measurement techniques, yet paper-and-pencil measurement is not part of the definition of attitudes (see Sears, 1986, and Houts, Cook, & Shadish, 1986, for other examples of these issues). Following the principle of heterogenous irrelevancies calls for the use of multiple instances in our research that are heterogenous with respect to aspects of units, treatments, observations, and settings that are theoretically expected to be irrelevant to the treatment–outcome relationship. To the degree that the results of the experiment are consistent across different types of Units, different manipulations of the independent variable (Treatments), different measures of the dependent variable (Observations), and different types of Settings, the researcher can conclude that generalization of the findings is not limited.

DISCRIMINANT VALIDITY. Basic social psychological theory and theories of programs (Lipsey, 1993; West & Aiken, 1997) have specified the processes through which a treatment is expected to have an effect on the outcome. These theories identify specific Treatment constructs (causal agents) that are supposed to affect specific Observation constructs (dependent variables). For example, the specific Treatment of frustration, defined as the blockage of an ongoing goal-directed behavior, is hypothesized to lead to increases in aggression. Other similar treatments that do not involve goal blockage, such as completing an exciting task, should not produce aggression. Similarly, given the focus of the hypothesis on the construct of aggression, the researcher should be able to show that frustration does not lead to other emotion-related responses, such as depression or euphoria. To the extent that the causal agent of the Treatment (here, frustration) is shown to match the hypothesized construct and the class of Observations (here, aggression) affected by the Treatment matches those specified by the theory, claims for understanding the causal relationship are strengthened. This same approach can be taken to Units and Settings when hypotheses identify specific classes of units or settings over which the causal effect will generalize.

CAUSAL EXPLANATION. To the extent that we can support a causal explanation of our findings and rule out competing explanations, the likelihood of generalization is increased. The causal explanation distinguishes the active from the inert components of our treatment package and provides an understanding of the processes underlying our phenomenon of interest. These features permit us to specify which components need to be included in any new experimental context. This principle has long been at the heart of basic experimental work in social psychology with its focus on the articulation and ruling out of competing theoretical explanations. More recently, both basic and applied social psychologists have used mediational analysis (Baron &

Kenny, 1986; MacKinnon, 1994; West & Aiken, 1997) as a means of probing whether their favored theoretical explanation is consistent with the data. To the extent that the data support the favored theoretical explanation, it can provide strong guidance for the design, implementation, and evaluation of future programs. However, mediational analysis does not automatically rule out other competing explanations for the observed effects. To the extent that these alternative causal explanations (a) are plausible and (b) make different predictions when new units (participants), new treatments, new observations, or new settings are studied, generalization of the findings of an experiment will potentially be limited.

EMPIRICAL INTERPOLATION AND EXTRAPOLATION. For ease of presentation, this chapter has focused on the comparison of two treatment conditions, typically treatment versus control (or comparison) groups. Although experiments are conducted in social psychology with more than two levels of each separate treatment variable, such experiments are not common, particularly in applied social research. In general, a high dose of the treatment (e.g., a smoking prevention program carried out over 3 years; Evans et al., 1981) is compared with a no treatment (or minimal treatment) control group. This practice yields an estimate of the causal effect that is limited to the specific implementations of treatment and control groups used in the experiment.

Occasionally, parametric experiments or dose-response (response surface) experiments involving one or more dimensions (Box & Draper, 1987; Smith, this volume, Ch. 2; West, Aiken, & Todd, 1993) can be conducted. Such experiments help establish the functional form of the relationship between the strength of each treatment variable and the outcome of interest. Once the functional form of the dose-response curve (or response surface) is known, causal effects for the comparison of any pair of treatment conditions can be estimated through interpolation.

In the absence of such dose-response curves, caution must be exercised in generalizing the magnitude of causal effects very far beyond the specific levels of the treatment and control groups implemented in a particular experiment. The functional form of dose-response relationships may be nonlinear. Complications like threshold effects, the creation of new processes (e.g., psychological reactance if an influence attempt becomes too strong), and the influence of interactions with other background variables become increasingly likely as the gap between the treatments studied and those to which the researcher wishes to generalize increases. To the extent we are extrapolating beyond the range of units, treatments, observations, or settings used in previous research, our generalization of estimates of treatment effects become increasingly untrustworthy.

SUMMARY. Traditional social psychological perspectives on generalization (e.g., Aronson et al., 1998; Berkowitz & Donnerstein, 1982) have relied nearly exclusively on the single principle of causal explanation, making interpolation and extrapolation of causal effects difficult in the absence of a formal specification of the Units, Treatments, Observations, and Settings addressed by the theory. Cook's five principles add other criteria beyond causal explanation that help identify when generalization of the causal effects to the UTOS of interest is possible.[10] Cook (1993) and Shadish et al. (in press) also noted that these same five principles can also be applied to meta-analyses of entire research literatures.

QUASI-EXPERIMENTAL DESIGNS

The randomized experiment is nearly always the design of choice for testing causal hypotheses about the effects of a treatment. In many real-world contexts, however, randomization may be precluded by ethical, legal, practical (logistic), or policy concerns. In such cases, it is frequently possible to develop alternative quasi-experimental designs that share many of the strengths of the randomized experiment in reaching

---

[10] Some social psychologists concerned primarily with basic research argue that constancy of the direction of the causal effect is all that is needed for successful generalization. Taking a position based on traditional null hypothesis significance testing, they argue that whether the effect of a treatment is large, moderate, small, or even tiny in magnitude makes little difference so long as it is in the predicted direction (but see Greenwald, Pratkanis, Leippe, & Baumgardner, 1986; Reichardt & Gollob, 1997). On the other hand, some influential social psychological theorists (e.g., McGuire, 1983) have emphasized the contextual nature of social phenomena and much of the basic research conducted in social psychology during the past four decades has emphasized the finding of predicted interaction effects, ideally of a disordinal or crossover form. In contrast, in many areas of applied research, the magnitude of effects is currently viewed as more important. For example, an expensive job training program that led to a consistent mean increase of $100 per year in the participants' annual salary would be deemed to be ineffective, no matter how consistently the effect was obtained or how tiny the associated p-value of the statistical test (e.g., $p < .00001$).

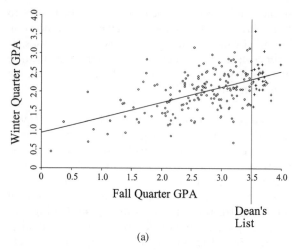

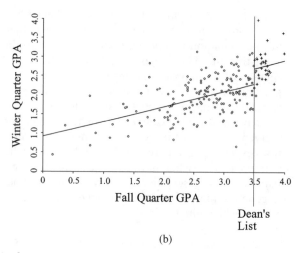

Dean's
List

(a)

Dean's
List

(b)

valid estimates of the causal effect of a treatment (Cook & Campbell, 1979; Reichardt & Mark, 1997). Each of these designs involves manipulation of the independent variable by the experimenter or other entities, pretest and posttest measurement, and design or statistical controls that attempt to address plausible threats to internal validity.

Regression Discontinuity Design

One of the strongest alternatives to the randomized experiment is the regression discontinuity design. The regression discontinuity design can be used when treatments are assigned on the basis of a quantitative measure, often a measure of need or merit. Following Reichardt and Mark (1997), we term this measure the *quantitative assignment variable*. For example, at some universities, entering freshmen who have a verbal scholastic aptitude test (SAT) score below a specified value (e.g., 380) are assigned to take a remedial English course, whereas freshman who have a score above this value are assigned to a regular English class (Aiken, West, Schwalm, Carroll, & Hsuing, 1998). The outcome of interest is the students' performance on a test of writing skill. Similarly, children who reach their sixth birthday by December 31 of the school year are assigned to begin first grade, whereas younger children do not begin school (Cahan & Davis, 1987). The outcome of interest is the children's level of performance on verbal and math tests taken the following Spring. Union members are laid off from work on the basis of their number of years of seniority. Mark and Mellor (1991) compared the degree of hindsight bias (retrospective judgments of the perceived likelihood of layoffs) among laid-off workers (< 20 years seniority) and workers who survived layoffs (20 or more years of seniority). The central feature of each of these examples

is that participants are assigned to treatment or control conditions solely on the basis of whether they exceed or are below a cutpoint on the quantitative assignment variable and that an outcome hypothesized to be affected by the treatment is measured following treatment. This assignment rule meets the objections of those critics of randomized experiments who believe that potentially beneficial treatments should not be withheld from the neediest (or most deserving) participants.

To understand the strengths and weaknesses of this design, let us review a classic regression discontinuity study by Seaver and Quarton (1976) in some detail. Seaver and Quarton were interested in testing the hypothesis that social recognition for achievement leads to higher levels of subsequent achievement. A random sample of undergraduate students who completed the Fall and Winter quarters in a large university constituted the participants. As at many universities, those students who received a Fall quarter grade point average (GPA) of 3.5 or greater were given formal recognition by being placed on the Dean's list, whereas students who did not attain this GPA were not given any special recognition. The grades for all students were recorded at the end of the Winter quarter as a measure of subsequent achievement. Seaver and Quarton estimated that the awarding of Dean's list led to a 0.17-point increase in the students' GPA, the equivalent of a full grade higher in one 3 hour course during the next term.

To understand how the regression discontinuity design works, it is useful to consider several possible outcomes patterned generally after those of the Seaver and Quarton (1976) study. Each of the outcomes presented in Figure 3.3 is based on simulated data from 200 students, with about 17% of the students having Fall quarter GPAs of 3.5 or better (Dean's list).

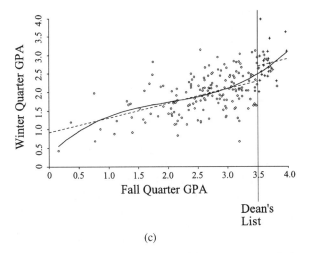

(c)

(d)

Figure 3.3 illustrates four possible outcomes of the study, of which outcomes (A) and (B) are important in the present context.

Outcome (A) illustrates a case in which the treatment, Dean's list, has no effect on Winter quarter GPA. Note that we have a single regression line that characterizes the full range of the data. The slope of the regression line indicates only that there is a strong positive relationship (correlation) between Fall quarter and Winter quarter GPA. In contrast, outcome (B) illustrates the general pattern of results found by Seaver and Quarton (1976). Here, the same regression line as in outcome (A) holds for students who have Fall GPAs below 3.5. However, for those students who have GPAs of 3.5 or above and are awarded Dean's list, the regression line is now elevated. At the cutpoint of 3.5 for Dean's list, we see that the difference in the levels (intercepts) of the two regression lines changes by 0.17, which represents Seaver and Quarton's estimate of the treatment effect. This discontinuity in the two regression lines can potentially be interpreted as a treatment effect.

Statistically, the treatment effect is estimated through the use of the following regression equation:

$$Y = b_0 + b_1 X + b_2 T + e. \qquad (1)$$

In this equation, Y is the outcome variable, here Winter quarter GPA; X is the quantitative assignment variable, here Fall quarter GPA; and T is a dummy code which has a value of 1 if the participant receives the treatment, here the social recognition of Dean's list, and a value of 0 if the participant does not receive treatment. Each of the bs is a regression coefficient that may be estimated by any standard statistical package (e.g., SPSS; SAS). The regression coefficients are most easily interpretable if the data are rescaled so that X has a value

Figure 3.3. Illustration of possible outcomes in the regression discontinuity design.
(A) No effect of treatment.
(B) Positive effect of treatment.
(C) Curvilinear functional form.
(D) Nonparallel regression lines in treatment and control groups.

Note. In each panel, the relationship between students' Fall quarter and Winter quarter GPAs is indicated. The fit of a line represents the fit of a Fall GPA cutoff for Dean's List. ○ represents Control student; + represents a student on Dean's list. In Panel (A), representing no treatment effect of Dean's list, a single regression line fits the data for both the Dean's list and Control students. In Panel (B), the vertical distance between the regression lines for the Dean's list and for the Control students (the discontinuity) represents the treatment effect. In Panel (C), the solid line represents the fit of a curvilinear relationship between students' Fall and Winter quarter GPAs; the dotted line represents the treatment effect that would result if this relationship were specified as being linear. In Panel (D), the slope of the regression line for the Dean's list students is steeper than the slope of the regression line for the Control students (Treatment × Pretest interaction).

of 0 at the cutpoint (i.e., $X = \text{GPA}_{\text{Fall}} - 3.5$). In this case, b_0 is the predicted value of Winter quarter GPA for participants at the cutpoint (3.5) who are in the control group (non-Dean's list), b_1 is the slope of the regression line (i.e., the predicted amount of increase in the Winter quarter GPA corresponding to a 1-point increase in the Fall quarter GPA), and b_2 represents the treatment effect. The test of b_2 informs us whether being on the Dean's list led to a significant increase in GPA the following quarter. Finally, e is the residual (error in prediction). Readers wishing a more thorough presentation of the statistical procedures should see Aiken and West (1991, chapter 7); Cohen and Cohen (1983); Reichardt, Trochim, and Cappelleri (1995); or Trochim (1984).

The ideas behind the regression discontinuity design are straightforward, but the design is counterintuitive because it explicitly violates a usual canon of research: The treatment and control groups should be as equivalent as possible at pretest. Instead, this design takes advantage of the known rule for assignment to treatment (Dean's list: Fall GPA $\geq$ 3.5) and control groups (no recognition: Fall GPA < 3.5). A statistical adjustment is performed that permits comparison of the levels in the two groups at the same value on the quantitative assignment variable[11] (GPA = 3.5). The estimate of the treatment effect is now conditioned on the participant's Fall GPA.

STATISTICAL ASSUMPTIONS OF THE REGRESSION DISCONTINUITY DESIGN. Because of its strong reliance on statistical adjustment to yield proper estimates of treatment effects, the regression discontinuity design requires two statistical assumptions in addition to those required for the randomized experiment. The ability to check these assumptions will be much greater in studies with large sample sizes, in which the cutpoint is not too extreme.

CORRECT SPECIFICATION OF FUNCTIONAL FORM. Researchers in social psychology rarely have strong a priori theoretical or empirical bases for specifying the form of the relationship between two variables. Consequently, we normally assume that the form of the relationship between the two variables is linear, as was done in the regression equation (Equation 1). To the degree that the form of the relationship between Fall quarter and Winter quarter GPA in our example is not well approximated by a straight line, the estimate of the treatment effect based on Equation 1 may be biased. For example, Cook and Campbell (1979, p. 140) presented data suggesting that a single curvilinear relationship without a treatment effect could fit the Seaver and Quarton (1976) data equally as well as the more typical linear regression equation (Equation 1). (Figure 3.3, Panel C illustrates this issue.) Consequently, it is important for researchers to examine the robustness of the results as the functional form of the

relationship between the quantitative assignment and outcome variables is varied.

Two simple probes of the functional form may be performed. First, scatterplots of the relationship between the quantitative assignment variable and (a) the outcome measure and (b) the residuals should be carefully examined. As is usual in regression analysis, evidence of outliers, nonconstant variance of the residuals across the range of X, and nonnormality of the residuals suggest potential problems in the specification of the regression model (see R. D. Cook & Weisberg, 1994; McClelland, this volume, Ch. 15). Of particular importance in the context of the regression discontinuity design is the existence of systematic positive or negative residuals from the regression line near the cutpoint, suggesting a potentially major problem in the estimation of the treatment effect. This examination is greatly facilitated by the use of modern graphical techniques, such as the fitting of lowess curves (Cleveland, 1993) separately to the treatment and the control groups. Lowess curves are "non-parametric" curves that may be used to describe the functional form of the relationship in the sample. Second, the regression equation may be estimated using a nonlinear functional form. Following Trochim (1984) and Reichardt et al. (1995), higher order polynomial terms (e.g., X^2) are typically added to the regression equation and tested for significance. Alternatively, the data may be transformed to achieve linearity (Daniel & Wood, 1980), or other parametric or nonparametric regression equations suggested by the lowess curve may be estimated (Daniel & Wood, 1980; Hastie & Tibshirani, 1990). To the extent that similar estimates of the treatment effect are found, or the alternative specifications of the model fit the data less well than Equation (1), the possibility that a misspecified functional form accounts for the results can be minimized.

NO TREATMENT $\times$ PRETEST INTERACTION. Researchers normally make the assumption that the regression lines will be parallel in the treatment and control groups. However, this need not be the case, as is depicted in Figure 3.3, Panel D. In this example, there is no discontinuity in the regression line at the cutpoint of 3.5, but the slope of the regression line is slightly steeper above this value. This example illustrates one form of a Treatment $\times$ Pretest quantitative assignment variable interaction that may occur.

Treatment $\times$ Pretest interactions represent another variant of misspecification. Once again, they may be detected from careful examination of scatterplots and plots of residuals. If a Treatment $\times$ Pretest interaction

[11] In terms of RCM, the expected value of the treatment group is compared with the expected value of the control group, conditioned on the specific value of the quantitative assignment variable at the cutpoint (Rubin, 1977). If the quantitative assignment variable is the sole basis on which participants are given the experimental versus comparison treatments, then this difference provides an unbiased estimate of the treatment effect.

is suspected, a new term, XT, representing the interaction may be added to Equation (1), resulting in Equation (2):

$$Y = b_0 + b_1 X + b_2 T + b_3 XT + e. \tag{2}$$

Once again, the b_2 coefficient estimates the treatment effect, and the b_3 coefficient provides information about the magnitude of the difference in the slopes in the treatment and control groups. Note that X must be rescaled so that it has a value of 0 at the cutpoint if b_2 is to be easily interpretable (Aiken & West, 1991).

When significant changes in slope are detected, researchers need to be cautious in their interpretation of the results. If there is no discontinuity between the two regression lines (i.e., no treatment main effect), differences in slope are not usually interpretable. The alternative explanation that there is no treatment effect, but rather a nonlinear relationship between the quantitative assignment variable and the outcome variable cannot be easily ruled out. However, when there is a substantial discontinuity between the two regression lines at the cutpoint, such an alternative explanation becomes considerably less plausible, and the treatment effect can be directly interpreted at the cutpoint (Trochim, Cappelleri, & Reichardt, 1991). As with any interaction, the estimate of the treatment effect is conditional: It would be different at any other potential cutpoint. Statistically, treatment effects at other cutpoints are easily estimated by rescaling the value of X to be 0 at the new cutpoint and examining the new b_2 effect; however, extrapolation of estimates of treatment effects to other cutpoints makes two strong assumptions (Cochran, 1957). First, the regression model is a close approximation of the "true" regression model in the population. Second, the same true regression model holds for all values of the quantitative assignment variable. Thus, extrapolation yields treatment effect estimates that are less precise and less credible than the estimates at the actual cutpoint on the quantitative assignment variable.

SELECTION ISSUES IN THE REGRESSION DISCONTINUITY DESIGN. The regression discontinuity design assumes that participants are assigned to treatment and control groups solely on the basis of the cutoff score on the quantitative assignment variable. Any other influences that affect assignment represent a potentially serious misspecification of the model. Paralleling our earlier review of the randomized experiment, breakdowns in treatment assignment give rise to the possibility that there may be important differences in the people participating in the treatment and control groups after statistical adjustment for the quantitative assignment variable, even in the absence of treatment. We term such influences participant selection issues; they can arise in the regression discontinuity design in at least 3 ways.

1. If the population to which a desirable (or undesirable) treatment is being offered is aware of the cutpoint, participants may decide to enroll in the study based in part on their perception of the likelihood that they will receive the treatment. Meier (1985) reported that the Salk polio vaccine was tested in some states using a simple version of the regression discontinuity design in which the child's age was the assignment variable. However, many parents knew that children in a specified age range would receive the experimental polio vaccine. Gilbert, Light, and Mosteller (1975) documented how refusals of parents of children in this age range to permit their children to participate in the study led to a large bias in the estimates of the effectiveness of the vaccine.

2. Practitioners may "adjust" the scores of individuals who are just below (or above) the cutpoints so that these individuals may receive a desired treatment, a problem Campbell (1969) termed "fuzzy assignment rules." Teachers may give their favorite students better grades so these students receive academic honors; welfare workers may understate a family's income so that a child may receive special medical or educational treatment. Those in charge of treatment allocation may also take into account other unquantified factors, such as letters of recommendation or interviews with the candidates.

3. Following the pretest, participants may drop out of the treatment and control groups. In such cases, participant characteristics that may not have been measured at pretest, such as their interest in the topic area of the study, may determine in part whether they complete the study. As in the randomized experiment, the estimate of the treatment effect will be biased to the extent that attrition is substantial, the characteristics of attriters and completers differ in the treatment and control conditions, and these characteristics are related to the measured outcome variable.

Many of the remedies for selection issues in the regression discontinuity design are extensions of those used in the randomized experiment. In terms of design approaches, not announcing the cutpoint until after participants have been assigned to conditions masks (blinds) the assignment rule from both participants and personnel in the institutional setting and thereby helps minimize the first two selection issues. Trochim and Cappelleri (1992) have suggested that the assignment rule used in the regression discontinuity design addresses the third selection issue because it is more sensible to participants; however, little evidence exists with which to evaluate their claim of reduced attrition. A variety of simple (e.g., dropping participants within a narrow range around the cutpoint; Mohr, 1988) and complex econometric approaches have attempted to provide more adequate adjustments when fuzzy assignment appears to have taken place (see Trochim, 1984, for a review). Statistical work on issues related to other selection issues is less well-developed. However, many of the statistical techniques suggested for the problems of treatment noncompliance and attrition in the randomized experiment can potentially be extended to the regression discontinuity design. These approaches make the strong assumptions that the quantitative assignment variable provides the only basis for treatment assignment and that the functional form of the relationship between the quantitative assignment variable and the outcome variable has been correctly specified.

OTHER ISSUES

STATISTICAL POWER. The regression discontinuity design will typically have considerably lower power than the randomized experiment, with the degree to which power is reduced being dependent on the extremity of the cutpoints and the magnitude of the correlation between the quantitative assignment variable and the posttest (Cappelleri, 1990; Cappelleri, Darlington, & Trochim, 1994). Goldberger (1972) estimated that, in properly specified models in which the quantitative assignment variable and the posttest had bivariate normal distributions and a relatively strong correlation, 2.75 times as many participants would be required using the regression discontinuity design to achieve the same level of statistical power as in the randomized experiment. The lesson is clear: Researchers planning regression discontinuity designs will need to use relatively large sample sizes, both to provide a test of the treatment that has adequate statistical power and to probe the statistical assumptions underlying the test.

CAUSAL GENERALIZATION. Drawing on Cook's (1993) five principles of causal generalization discussed earlier, we see that generalization of results using the regression discontinuity design is limited relative to the randomized experiment by the use of one cutpoint.

Ideally, generalization of the treatment effects should be restricted to values that are close to the original cutpoint. Often this will be sufficient: Regression discontinuity designs are typically conducted with the populations and in the settings of interest and are thus high in external validity. The cutpoints used are also often those for which there are supporting data (e.g., cutoffs for clinical levels of high blood pressure) or strong historical tradition for their use (e.g., Dean's List = 3.5 GPA). Thus, this limitation is often an issue more in theory than in practice because of the restricted range of generalization that is sought.

SUMMARY. The regression discontinuity design provides an excellent approach when participants are assigned to conditions on the basis of a quantitative measure. As Marcantonio and Cook (1994) noted, the regression discontinuity design is one of two quasi-experimental designs that stand out "because of the high quality of causal inference they often engender" (p. 134). When its assumptions are met, it rules out most of the threats to internal validity and has good external validity for much applied work. On the negative side, it is considerably lower in power than the randomized experiment. The central concerns of the design focused around a number of selection-related issues and the correct specification of the functional form. More complex variants of the regression discontinuity design can be implemented: Multiple pretest measures may be used to assign participants to treatment, multiple treatments may be delivered with multiple cutpoints, multiple pretest measures may be used as additional covariates, and multiple outcome variables may be collected (see Judd & Kenny, 1981; Shadish, et al., in press; Trochim, 1984). In addition, the regression discontinuity design can be supplemented with a randomized tie-breaking experiment around the cutpoint to provide even stronger inferences (Rubin, 1977; Shadish, et al., in press; see Aiken et al., 1998, for an empirical illustration of combining these designs).

Interrupted Time Series Design

The interrupted time series design is the second of the two quasi-experimental designs that Marcantonio and Cook (1994) highlighted as engendering a high quality of causal inference. In the basic interrupted time series design, measurements of the outcome variable are collected at equally spaced intervals (e.g., daily; yearly) over a long period of time. An intervention is implemented at a specific point in time; the intervention is expected to affect the outcome variable measured in the series. Time series analysis permits the researcher to identify changes in the level and slope of the series that occur as a result of the intervention.[12] In terms of the RCM, the expected value of the treatment group is compared with the expected value of the control group, conditioned on the specific point in time at which the treatment is introduced. If (a) time is assumed to be a good proxy for the actual rule upon which treatment and control conditions are assigned (Judd & Kenny, 1981) and (b) the correct functional form of the relationship between time and the outcome variable is specified, then controlling for time will lead to an unbiased estimate of the treatment effect. If time is not an adequate proxy, then estimates of the magnitude of the treatment effect may be biased.

Interrupted time series designs have typically been utilized in two different research settings. First, time series designs provide an excellent method of conducting naturalistic studies of the effects of a change in law or a social innovation. To cite two examples, West, Hepworth, McCall, and Reich (1989) used this design to test whether the introduction of a law requiring a 24-hour mandatory jail term for driving under the influence of alcohol led to a subsequent decrease in fatal traffic accidents. Hennigan et al. (1982) used this design to test the hypothesis that the introduction of television broadcasting in U.S. cities in the late 1940s and early 1950s would lead to subsequent increases in crime rates, particularly violent crime rates. Second, time series designs may be used to test the effects of interventions in single-subject designs. This approach has primarily been followed by experimental psychologists in the Skinnerian tradition and clinical researchers who wish to make causal inferences at the level of the individual participant (Crosbie, 1993; Franklin, Allison, & Gorman, 1996; Horne, Yang, & Ware, 1982; Sidman, 1960). For example, Gregson (1987) used time series methods to understand individual differences in the pattern of response to treatment in 9 participants with chronic headaches. These participants reported the intensity and duration of their headaches on a daily basis over an extended period of time. In each of these examples, the treatment in this design was assigned a priori on the basis

of time (or after a fixed number of observations[13]), and possible treatment effects may be inferred from a change in the level of the behavior that has occurred between the baseline and treatment periods.

Figure 3.4 illustrates some of the different types of effects that can be detected using interrupted time series designs. In Panel A, there is no effect of the intervention. In Panel B, the intervention leads to a dramatic decrease in the level of occurrence of the behavior. In Panel C, the intervention leads to an immediate effect of the intervention, followed by a slow decay of the treatment effect over time. Finally, in Panel D, there is a permanent change in both the level and the slope of the series following the intervention. Each of the results depicted in Panels B–D are potentially interpretable as treatment effects, given appropriate statistical analyses and attention to potential threats to internal validity.

From consideration of Figures 3.3 and 3.4, readers may have detected a strong similarity between the regression discontinuity design and the interrupted time series design. In both designs, treatment is assigned beginning at some specific point represented on the X-axis. Any alternative explanations of the results need to provide an account of why the level, slope, or both of the series change at that specific point. Note, however, that there is one major conceptual difference between the two designs: In the interrupted time series design, participants are assigned to the treatment or control group on the basis of time; in the regression discontinuity design, participants are assigned to the treatment or control group on the basis of their score on the quantitative assignment variable. As we show below, this change from pretest scores to time on the X-axis greatly complicates the statistical analysis and leads to a different set of potential threats to internal validity.

AN OVERVIEW OF STATISTICAL ANALYSES. To illustrate time series analysis, consider a classic study by McSweeny (1978). McSweeny was interested in the effects of the introduction of a monetary charge for calls to directory assistance. He obtained the monthly records of the number of calls made to Cincinnati Bell directory assistance for the period 1962 to 1976. Beginning in March 1974, and announced with considerable publicity, Cincinnati Bell began charging 20 cents

---

[12] Although less often hypothesized by social psychologists, changes in the variance of the series or in cyclical patterns in the series following an intervention can also be detected. Larsen (1989) has discussed some ways in which cyclical patterns of variables such as mood and activity levels may be important in human social behavior.

[13] Franklin et al. (1996) discussed some of the inferential problems that occur when other assignment rules (e.g., the participant's level of responding reaches asymptote) are used to determine when treatments are introduced or withdrawn.

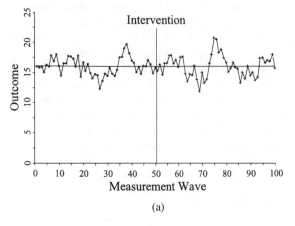

(a)

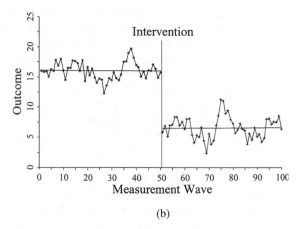

(b)

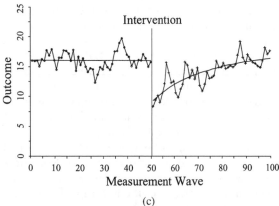

(c)

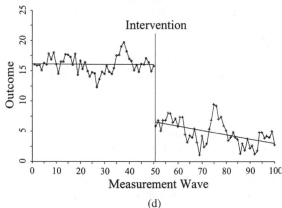

(d)

Figure 3.4. Illustration of possible outcomes in the interrupted time series design (A) No effect of intervention. (B) Intervention decreases the level of the outcome variable. (C) Intervention produces an immediate drop in level followed by a slow return to the baseline level of the series. (D) Intervention produces both an immediate drop in the level and a change in the slope of the series.

Note. The same outcome is assessed at each wave of measurement of the study. The vertical line indicates the point at which intervention is introduced (between measurements 50 and 51).

for each directory assistance call. As can be seen in Figure 3.5, the number of calls made to this service generally increased up to the point of the intervention (20-cent charge). At this point, the number of calls made to this service showed a large drop, then began increasing again at about the same rate as before.

The basic regression equation used in time series analysis closely parallels Equation 1, the equation used to estimate the treatment effect in the basic regression discontinuity design. To test the effect of the introduction of the charge for directory assistance, the following

regression equation would be used:

$$Y = b_0 + b_1 T + b_2 Z + e. \tag{3}$$

Here, Y is the number of calls made to directory assistance each month (outcome variable), T is the month in the series, and Z is the intervention effect, again dummy coded with 1 representing treatment (20-cent charge) and 0 no treatment control (no charge). Once again, the bs are regression coefficients, with b_0 representing the intercept (the predicted value of Y when T and $Z = 0$) and b_1 the slope of the regression line, and with b_2 representing the treatment effect (the change in the level of the series at the point of the intervention). For purposes of interpretability, T is typically rescaled so that it has a value of 0 at the point of implementation of the treatment.[14]

Although this equation appears to be nearly identical to Equation 1, the use of time rather than the

---

[14] Using this rescaling, b_0 always gives the predicted value for the control series at the point of the intervention. In more complex models, such rescaling can be particularly important.

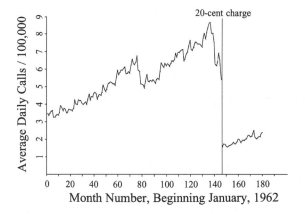

Figure 3.5. Intervention effect: Introduction of a charge for directory assistance.

Note. The series represents the average daily number of calls to directory assistance per 100,000 total calls. The vertical line indicates the point (the beginning of month 147 of the series) when the charge for directory assistance was introduced. The effect of this charge is shown by the large vertical drop in the level of the series at the point of intervention.

pretest score introduces major complications into the statistical analysis. In the analysis of time series data, three statistical problems must be adequately addressed or the regression equation will be misspecified. First, any long-term linear or curvilinear trends over time must be properly represented. In the present example, the long-term linear increase over time in the series is represented by the $b_1 T$ term in Equation 3. Second, time series data, particularly those in which the data are collected on a hourly, daily, or monthly basis, frequently contain cycles. For example, people's moods often change according to a regular weekly cycle, with particularly large differences being found between the weekend and weekdays. Again, these cycles must be detected, and terms representing the cycles must be added to the regression equation to avoid misspecification (see West & Hepworth, 1991). Finally, when data are collected over time, adjacent observations are often more similar than observations that are further removed in time. For example, the prediction of today's weather from the previous day's weather is, on average, far better than the prediction of today's weather from the weather 7 days ago. This problem, known as serial dependency, implies that the residuals (the *e*s) in Equation 3 will not be independent (Judd & Kenny, 1981; West & Hepworth, 1991). Failure to properly specify the long-term trends, the cycles, or both in the model may lead to model misspecifications and consequently to bias in the estimate of the treatment effect.

Failure to adequately represent the serial dependency leads to incorrect standard errors and consequently to incorrect significance tests and confidence intervals (Box, Jenkins, & Reinsel, 1994; Chatfield, 1996; Judd & Kenny, 1981).

Time series analysis offers a variety of graphical displays and statistical tests that are useful in the detection of trends, cycles, and serial dependency. Time series techniques are most accurate in large samples where the number of time points is 100 or more, although even in large samples there can be problems in correctly identifying the pattern of serial dependency (Velicer & Harrop, 1983). In smaller samples, there is a high likelihood that several models will adequately fit the data, and the possibility exists that each of these models may be associated with a substantially different estimate of the treatment effect (see Velicer & Colby, 1997). This result occurs because time series analysis requires a series of preliminary tests to determine whether the model is correctly specified; these preliminary tests require large numbers of observations to distinguish sharply between different possible models. Among the techniques that may be used to identify potential problems with time series models are graphical techniques for visualizing trends and cycles (see Cleveland, 1993) and plots of specialized statistics (e.g., spectral density plots; autocorrelograms) to detect cycles and serial dependency. McCleary and Hay (1980), Judd and Kenny (1981, chapter 7), West and Hepworth (1991), and Velicer and Colby (1997) presented good introductions to the ideas of time series analysis. Chatfield (1996), Box, Jenkins, and Reinsel (1994), and Velicer and Mac-Donald (1984) presented more in-depth treatments of the traditional and newer statistical procedures for the identification and testing of time series models.

THREATS TO INTERNAL VALIDITY. As in the regression discontinuity design, for threats to internal validity to be plausible, they must offer an explanation of why a change in the level, slope, or both of the series occurred at the point of the intervention (Shadish et al., in press). Three generic classes of explanations that are potential threats to the internal validity of the design can be identified; however, the plausibility of each of these threats will depend on the specific research context.

As an illustration, consider the example of a new smoking prevention program implemented at the beginning of a school year. Based on school records, the total number of students who are cited by school personnel for smoking each month on school grounds for 5 years prior to and 5 years after the beginning of the intervention provide the data for the time series.

HISTORY. Some other event that could also be expected to decrease smoking may occur at about the same time that the smoking prevention program is initially implemented. For example, the community may remove cigarette machines or institute fines for selling cigarettes to minors, making access to cigarettes more difficult.

SELECTION. The population of the students in the school may change in the direction of having a greater proportion of nonsmokers. Parents who support the prevention efforts may hear about the planned intervention and make efforts to enroll their children in the school, whereas parents who support smokers' rights may transfer their children to other districts.

INSTRUMENTATION. Aspects of the record-keeping procedures may change, leading to decreased reports of smoking. Students caught smoking may no longer be written up for their first offense or decreased staff may be available for monitoring of the school's grounds.

Once again, these threats are only plausible if they occur at about the point of the intervention. For example, if the community were to remove cigarette machines 3 years after the implementation of the smoking prevention program, this action would not provide an alternative explanation of a drop in the number of students who are cited for smoking at the point of implementation of the program. Many of these threats are less plausible in time series designs using single participants, in which the experimenter has considerable control over the procedures than in less controlled, naturalistic designs testing the effects of new laws, programs, or new innovations on a population of participants.

DESIGN ENHANCEMENTS. The three potential threats to internal validity can be made less plausible through the addition of one or more design enhancements to the basic time series design. We consider three design enhancements that can often be used both in naturalistic tests of policy and single subject designs.

NO TREATMENT CONTROL SERIES. Comparable data may be available from another similar unit that did not receive treatment during the same time period. Recall that West et al. (1989) studied the effect of a new state law in Arizona that mandated a 24-hour jail term for drivers convicted of driving while intoxicated. They showed that this law led to an immediate 50% decrease in traffic fatalities in the city of Phoenix; however, the magnitude of this decrease declined over time following the intervention. In an attempt to rule out possible historical effects (e.g., unusually good weather; change in speed limit) coinciding with the implementation of the new law, West et al. also analyzed the traffic fatalities from a city (El Paso) in a nearby state that did not introduce a similar drunk driving law during the period of the study. The results showed no comparable change in traffic fatalities in El Paso at the same point in time (July 1982) when the law went into effect in Arizona. Ideally, the control series should be as similar as possible to the treatment series and similar data should be available for the same time period.

OTHER CONTROL SERIES. Sometimes data are available from another series that would not be expected to be influenced by the treatment, but which would be expected to be impacted by many of the same nontreatment influences as the treatment series of interest. Reichardt and Mark (1997) illustrated examples of such control series using data collected on the same participants in different settings or using different measures that are not expected to be affected by the treatment. Often such a series can be constructed by disaggregating a series into units in which little, if any, impact is expected versus units in which a large impact of the intervention is expected. In a classic study, Ross, Campbell, and Glass (1970; see also Glass, 1988) studied the introduction of a new intervention to decrease drunk driving in Great Britain. British police were equipped with breathalysers and were empowered to suspend the drivers license of anyone who was driving while intoxicated. Ross et al. divided the data into weekend evenings when the amount of alcohol use is normally high and weekday mornings when alcohol use is normally low. Consistent with their predictions, the implementation of the breathalyser program led to a large decrease in fatalities in the weekend evening hours, followed by a slow return to baseline. However, the implementation of the program did not lead to a detectable decrease during the weekday morning hours. The comparison of the two series helps rule out effects due to history and changes in instrumentation that should affect both series equally. Selection is an implausible threat in this case because it is unlikely that a country would experience appreciable in or out migration or changes in the population of drivers that were associated with a traffic safety campaign against drunk driving.

SWITCHING REPLICATIONS. In some cases, the same intervention may be implemented in more than one locale at different times. Time series analyses of the data from the different locales would be expected to show similar effects occurring at the point of intervention in each locale. For example, West et al. (1989) found that California implemented a law mandating a 24-hour jail term for driving under the influence of alcohol 6 months before the similar law was implemented in Arizona. Analysis of highway fatality data from San Diego showed a similar effect to that which occurred 6 months later in Phoenix – an immediate 50% reduction in highway fatalities followed by a slow decrease in the magnitude of the effect over time. The replication of the effect at a different point in time helps rule out other possible explanations associated with history (e.g., weather) and changes in instrumentation.

COMBINING DESIGN ENHANCEMENTS. As should be evident, multiple design features can be combined in a single study to strengthen further the causal inferences that may be made. For example, West et al. (1989) combined all three of the previously discussed design features in their studies of the effects of drunk driving laws. Ross et al. (1970) added a number of other control series to their basic time series design, together with a number of other design and measurement features that were designed to address specific threats to internal validity. When the researcher has control over treatment delivery, the design can be further strengthened by introducing and removing treatments following an a priori schedule. In well-designed time series designs, inferences can sometimes be made with a certainty approaching that of a randomized experiment.

DELAYED EFFECTS. Time series designs provide a relatively strong basis for causal inferences when the intervention produces immediate effects, but the strength of the causal inference may be weakened considerably when treatment effects are delayed – unless the length of delay in the effect is predicted ahead of time. As an illustration, consider again our example of the school-based smoking prevention program. Suppose that a gradual decrease in the number of students cited for smoking on school grounds began 1 year following the implementation of the program. Under such circumstances, it would be difficult to attribute these changes in the level and slope of the series to the prevention program.

True delayed effects normally occur in one of two ways. First, new policies often do not go abruptly into effect on the specific starting date of the intervention.

New programs often require time for personnel to be trained before they fully go into effect; new innovations often require time to diffuse through society. Inferences from time series may be strengthened by collecting supplementary data that assess the extent of implementation of the intervention over time. Using such data to model a gradual implementation process can strengthen causal inferences and increase the power of the statistical tests in time series analyses. Hennigan et al. (1982) used data on the proportion of households with television sets following the beginning of television broadcasts to strengthen their potential causal inferences about the effects of television on crime rates. In addition, they observed that the pattern of increase in burglaries was nearly identical following the beginning of broadcasting in some American cities in 1948 and others in 1952 in their switching replication design.

Second, some interventions affect processes whose outcomes will only be evident months or years later. To cite two examples, a birth control intervention would be expected to affect birth rates about 9 months later. A nationwide school-based smoking prevention program would be expected to show effects on lung cancer rates beginning about 35 years after the intervention as the participants matured into the age range when lung cancer first begins to become manifest. In both cases theory provides a strong basis for expecting the effect to occur at a specified time lag or over a specified distribution of time lags following the intervention. In the absence of strong theory, similar strong causal inferences cannot be made. As previously noted, a decrease in school citations for smoking 1 year following the introduction of a smoking prevention program cannot be interpreted confidently as a program effect.

STATISTICAL POWER. Two issues of statistical power commonly arise in time series analysis. First, researchers often evaluate the effects of an intervention shortly after an intervention has been implemented, giving rise to a series with many preintervention, but few postintervention observations. Given a series with a fixed number of time points, the statistical power of the analysis to detect treatment effects is greatest when the intervention occurs at the middle rather than one of the ends of the series. Second, the existence of serial dependency has complex effects on calculations of statistical power. Within the preintervention series and within the postintervention series, to the degree that observations are not independent, each observation in effect counts less than 1, thus increasing the total number of observations needed to achieve a specified level of statistical power. On the other hand, the use of the same participant or same population of participants throughout the series reduces the variability of the series relative to one in which different participants are sampled at each time point. The statistical power of a given time series analysis is determined in large part by the trade-off between these two effects in the specific research context.

CONCLUSION. Interrupted time series designs provide a strong quasi-experimental approach when interventions are introduced at a specific point in time so that time may be used as a proxy for the true model of treatment assignment. Such designs provide a strong basis for the evaluation of the effects of changes in social policy or new innovations that are implemented at a specific point in time. The basic time series design often allows researchers to credibly rule out several threats to internal validity: Any alternative explanation, to be plausible, must account for why the change in the series occurred at a particular point in time. Design enhancements, including the use of various control series, switching replications, and the introduction and removal of treatments, can further strengthen the causal inferences that may be made (see also Barlow & Hersen, 1984; Kratochwill & Levin, 1992). Given their ability to rule out alternative explanations through both design features and statistical adjustment, interrupted time series designs represent one of the strongest alternatives to the randomized experiment.

Nonequivalent Control Group Design

The most commonly used quasi-experimental alternative to the randomized experiment is the nonequivalent control group design. In this design, a group of participants is given a treatment, or a "natural event" occurs to the group. A second (comparison) group that does not receive the treatment is also identified. Both groups of participants are measured both before and after the treatment. Randomization is not used to determine the treatment group assignment; rather the process through which participants end up in the treatment and comparison groups is not fully known and is therefore difficult to model statistically. To cite three examples, Lehman, Lampert, and Nisbett (1988) compared the level of statistical reasoning of advanced graduate students in psychology, which emphasizes training in statistics, with that of advanced graduate students in other disciplines (e.g., chemistry) that have substantially lower training emphasis in statistics.

Coleman, Hoffer, and Kilgore (1982) and Murname, Newstead, and Olson (1985) compared the academic achievements of students who attended private schools with those who attended public schools. And, Martin, Annan, and Forst (1993) compared the subsequent arrest rates of individuals who were convicted of drunk driving and who were sentenced by one of two judges. One judge sentenced virtually all persons to a 2-day jail term, whereas the other (comparison) judge sentenced virtually all persons to non-jail alternatives (e.g., monetary fines, community service). In each example, measures of the important outcome-related variables of interest were collected in the treatment and control groups both prior to and following the intervention. The outcomes in the treatment and control group at posttest were compared after attempting to remove any differences between the groups that were observed at pretest.

The nonequivalent control group design appears to provide a straightforward way of investigating the causal effect of a treatment when randomization is not possible. However, direct (unadjusted) comparison of the treatment and control group means is only legitimate when a strong assumption is met: The treatment and control groups must be equivalent in terms of all important background characteristics at pretest. This assumption requires that both the mean pretest levels of the treatment and control groups are the same and that the rate of maturation (growth or decline) in the two groups is the same in the absence of treatment. Given random assignment to treatment and control groups, this assumption is normally met because the treatment group assignment is expected, on average, to be independent of all participant background characteristics. However, in the nonequivalent control group design, the treatment and the control groups must be presumed to be nonequivalent at pretest; researchers must also presume that measured (or unmeasured) participant characteristics at pretest will be related to treatment assignment. Following Rosenbaum (1995), we refer to variables assessed at pretest (or other background variables measured prior to treatment) as *covariates* and variables not assessed at pretest as *hidden variables*. Ruling out the possibility that the two groups may differ prior to treatment in terms of either measured covariates or hidden variables is the central task facing the researcher using this design. Major disputes have occurred in the literature over the "true effectiveness" of treatments (e.g., the Head Start program) that have been evaluated using this design. Researchers may legitimately retain considerable uncertainty as to whether preexisting differences between the treatment and control groups on covariates and hidden variables have been adequately ruled out as potential explanations for observed differences on the outcome variable (e.g., see Barnow, 1973; Bentler & Woodward, 1978; Cicarelli, Cooper, & Granger, 1969; Magidson, 1977 for diverse analyses and reanalyses of the data from the original Head Start study). Because of this problem, researchers are well advised to add other design features (presented later in this section) to the basic nonequivalent control group design in order to reach more convincing causal inferences.

STRATEGIES FOR EQUATING GROUPS. From the standpoint of the RCM, the goal of the researcher using the nonequivalent control group design parallels that of the regression discontinuity design: The researcher must adequately model the mechanism by which participants were assigned to the treatment and control groups. When this goal is accomplished, the treatment effect estimate will be an unbiased estimate of the treatment effect in the population (Rosenbaum, 1984; Rosenbaum & Rubin, 1984). As in the regression discontinuity design, the estimate of the treatment effect is conditioned on the participant background variables that are related to treatment assignment.

As noted previously, the central problem in the nonequivalent control group design is that units (participants) are not assigned to the treatment and control groups according to any known rule. Researchers must use whatever information they have available to identify pretest or other background variables (e.g., socioeconomic status, prior educational or medical history) with which to model the process of selection into the treatment and control groups. The critical background variables are those that are related to both (a) selection into the two treatment groups and (b) the outcome variable in the population. Pretest variables that are only related to either (a) or (b) but not both do not bias treatment effect estimates (Berk, 1988).

Researchers use these pretest and background variables in an attempt to adjust statistically for differences between the two groups that existed prior to treatment. Several assumptions must be made in order for these statistical adjustment techniques to produce unbiased estimates of the causal effect. These include

1. All important covariates have been identified; there are no hidden variables.
2. Each of the covariates has been measured with perfect reliability, or statistical procedures (e.g., structural equation modeling) have properly adjusted for unreliability in the covariates.

3. The functional form (e.g., linear) of the relationship between the pretest variables and the outcome variable has been correctly specified.
4. The pretest maturation rates do not differ in the treatment and control groups or proper adjustments for differences in the pretest maturation rates have been successfully undertaken. In the basic nonequivalent control group design, such differences in maturation rates can be indicated by Group × Pretest interactions or unequal variances in the treatment and control groups at pretest or posttest.

When each of these assumptions is met, the nonequivalent control group design has in effect been made equivalent to the regression discontinuity design. The estimate of the treatment effect conditioned on the statistical model that properly adjusts for selection into the treatment and control groups will lead to an unbiased estimate of the causal effect in the population. All other covariates and hidden variables will then be unrelated to treatment condition, a condition that has been termed *strong ignorability* (Holland, 1986; Rosenbaum, 1984; Rosenbaum &Rubin, 1984). In practice, however, meeting these assumptions and thereby achieving strong ignorability is both extraordinarily difficult and fraught with uncertainty. Consequently, researchers cannot be confident in practice that their estimates of the treatment effect using the nonequivalent control group design are unbiased.

SELECTING COVARIATES. Statisticians and methodologists have considered a variety of possible methods of identifying important covariates that should be included in statistical models that attempt to adjust for pretest differences and achieve strong ignorability. Reichardt, Minton, and Schellenger (1986) suggested considering both (a) those variables that are theoretically expected to be related to selection into the treatment and control groups and (b) those variables that are known from the literature to be related to the outcome variables. Cochran (1965) and Rosenbaum (1995) have both suggested conducting exploratory analyses of all variables measured at pretest. Based on simulation work, Cochran suggested retaining any covariate for further consideration for which the t-value for the difference between the treatment and control groups was greater than 1.5 at pretest (see also Canner, 1984, 1991). This technique can be supplemented by a reexamination of the excluded covariates once the selection model has been developed to detect any remaining covariates that are not adequately equated in the treatment and control groups (Rosenbaum, 1995).

Note that the pretest measure of the outcome variable of interest has a special status in the nonequivalent control group design. Reichardt (1979) and Rosenbaum (1995) have both noted that the best method of reducing sensitivity to unmeasured variables is to identify covariates that are (a) unaffected (i.e., not caused) by the treatment, but are (b) strongly related to the outcome variable. The pretest score on the outcome of interest, particularly when there is a short time lag between pretest and posttest, normally meets these requirements.

STATISTICAL ADJUSTMENT TECHNIQUES. A variety of statistical techniques can be used to analyze the data from the nonequivalent control group design. The techniques do not always produce the same result; they use different statistical procedures and consequently have different strengths and weaknesses. For example, only the second technique considered below, analysis of covariance with correction for unreliability, addresses the issue of measurement error. Nonetheless, each statistical technique has the same goal: To attempt to achieve strong ignorability by providing a statistical adjustment that properly removes prestest differences between the treatment and control groups.

ANALYSIS OF COVARIANCE. Analysis of covariance adjusts the posttest score for the *measured* pretest scores. Typically, adjustment is made only for the linear effect of the pretest scores on the posttest scores. No adjustment is made for variables that are not included in the analysis nor is the proper adjustment made for variables that are measured with error. When one covariate is used, unreliability will result in too little adjustment for the initial differences between treatment groups. When more than one covariate is used and one or more of the variables is less than perfectly measured, the outcome is less clear: Typically, unreliability results in too little adjustment, but proper adjustment, or even overadjustment, may occur in some cases. In a specific study, the estimate of the treatment effect may be too large, too small, or even just right.

ANALYSIS OF COVARIANCE WITH CORRECTION FOR UNRELIABILITY. In this procedure, an attempt is made to adjust the treatment effect based on an estimate of what the pretest scores would have been if they had been measured without error (Huitema, 1980). This adjustment is now typically performed using structural equation modeling programs such as EQS (Bentler, 1995)

or LISREL (Jöreskog & Sörbom, 1993). In one variant of this procedure, each measured covariate is specified to be the result of an unmeasured true score and an error of measurement. The variance of the error of measurement is normally set equal to the product of the variance of the variable $\times (1-$ reliability of the measure), i.e., $\sigma^2[1 - \rho_{XX}]$; see Bollen, 1989. The test-retest correlation for a relatively brief time interval is normally preferred as the estimate of ρ_{XX}, although other measures of reliability may be preferred in some situations[15] (Campbell & Boruch, 1975; Campbell & Erlbacher, 1970; Linn & Werts, 1973). The outcome variable is then regressed on the true scores of each pretest variable and a dummy coded variable representing the treatment. The estimate then represents the effect of the treatment adjusted for the differences among the covariates at pretest, corrected for the measure of unreliability. A second important method of correcting for unreliability uses multiple measures of each pretest construct rather than a single measure that is adjusted with an estimate of unreliability. Using structural equation modeling, the multiple measures are used to provide a theoretically error-free estimate of each latent construct assessed at pretest. The difference between the latent means on the outcome variable in the treatment and control groups is compared after adjustment for the latent construct(s) represented by the covariates (Sörbom, 1979). Aiken, Stein, and Bentler (1994) illustrated the application of this approach to the nonequivalent control group design in their comparison of the effectiveness of two drug treatment programs.

GAIN SCORE ANALYSIS. Kenny (1975; see also Huitema, 1980; Judd & Kenny, 1981) has proposed an alternative approach to the analysis of the nonequivalent control group design. In this approach, the pretest and posttest scores are first transformed so that the pretest and posttest variances are equated. This transformation is most easily accomplished by separate standardizations of the pretest and posttest data using the pretest mean and standard deviation (see Huitema, 1980, chapter 15 for details). The mean gain in the treatment group is then compared with the mean gain in the control group to provide an estimate of the treatment effect. This approach provides good estimates of the treatment effect when it can be assumed that the natural pattern of growth in the absence of treatment is linear and constant in the two groups or is of a fan

---

[15] Cook and Reichardt (1976) and Judd and Kenny (1981) have suggested conducting sensitivity analyses using several plausible estimates of the reliability to bracket the true effect.

spread pattern, in which the growth is linear, but occurs at a higher rate for participants having higher scores at pretest. Many other forms of growth (or decline) may not be not well modeled by this procedure.

ECONOMETRIC SELECTION MODELS. A variety of selection models originally developed in econometrics have been applied to the nonequivalent control group design (e.g., Barnow, Cain, & Goldberger, 1980; Heckman, 1979, 1989, 1990; Muthén & Jöreskog, 1983). In these models, two separate regression equations are estimated. The first (selection) equation uses measured variables to predict the assignment of the participant to the treatment versus the control group and yields a probability for each participant of assignment to the treatment group. The second equation uses this selection probability, the treatment actually received by the participant, and other measured covariates to estimate the treatment effect. In practice, both equations are estimated simultaneously.

Selection models can be shown to provide highly accurate estimates of treatment effects when their assumptions are met. These models presume that highly reliable measures of all variables related to selection are included in the equation and that the sample size is relatively large. More critical, the results of these models are highly sensitive to violations of several additional statistical assumptions (e.g., the inclusion of a measured variable that affects selection, but is independent of the outcome measure) that must be made for proper estimation. Simulation studies by Stolzenberg and Relles (1990) and Virdin (1993) showed that selection models produced much poorer estimates than simpler techniques, such as analysis of covariance and gain score analysis when these assumptions are violated (see also Imbens & Rubin, 1994). Lalonde (1986) showed large discrepancies between causal effect estimates obtained from randomized experiments and econometric selection models.

MATCHING: TRADITIONAL AND MODERN PROCEDURES. In the simplest form of matching that is traditionally considered, each case in the treatment group is paired with a single case in the control group using a single measured covariate. To illustrate, consider a simplified example comparing two small school classrooms ($n_A = 12$; $n_B = 13$), one of which is to be given a new instructional treatment and one of which is to be given standard instruction (control group). Table 3.5 presents hypothetical data for this illustration in which the pretest (e.g., IQ) data have been ordered from low to high within each group. We note

that adequate matches are available for 10 pairs of students. On the positive side, the mean difference on the pretest for the 10 matched pairs is considerably smaller ($\bar{X}_A - \bar{X}_B = 0.1$) than for the full, unmatched classes ($\bar{X}_A - \bar{X}_B = 11$). On the negative side, adequate matches are not available for all participants. The participants with the two highest and three lowest pretest scores must be dropped from the analysis; consequently, generalization to the full population of students will be limited.

The strategy of matching as an approach to equating the treatment and control groups at pretest in the nonequivalent control group design has been viewed differently by social psychologists and statisticians. Social psychological methodologists (e.g., Crano & Brewer, 1986; Judd, Smith, & Kidder, 1991) have focused on simple, traditional matching procedures, often arguing that matching is an especially flawed method of equating groups. They point to (a) the practical difficulty of finding good matches, particularly when the two groups must be matched on multiple covariates; (b) the frequent necessity of dropping participants from the analysis (illustrated in Table 3.5) because adequate matches cannot be found; and (c) the problem of regression to the mean, which we consider below.

Regression to the mean (see also Brewer, this volume, Ch. 1; Campbell & Kenny, 1999, Ch. 4) may occur under any one of three conditions. (a) Different measures are used to match participants at pretest (e.g., IQ) and to assess the outcome of the treatment at posttest (e.g., reading achievement scores). (b) The measures used to match participants do not have perfect internal consistency (see John & Benet-Martinez, this volume, Ch. 13). (c) The test–retest correlations between the pretest and posttest measure are less than 1.0. When disparate groups (e.g., children attending a public vs. a private school) are compared in nonequivalent control group designs, these groups are selected from two populations that may have different means on the covariates (e.g., the private school children may have a higher IQ and family income). Under these conditions, more children who are below the mean of their school on the measured covariate (e.g., IQ) will be systematically selected from the advantaged private school group, whereas more children who are above the mean of their school on the measured covariate will be systematically selected for matching from the disadvantaged public school group. In the case of matching on the basis of a single measured covariate, the combination of unreliability and systematic selection leads to the result that matching will underadjust for the initial

TABLE 3.5. Illustration of Simple Matching of Two Classrooms on Pretest IQ Scores

Pair	Classroom A	Classroom B
	150	
	130	
1	125	128
2	120	119
3	118	119
4	117	116
5	115	116
6	110	112
7	108	106
8	103	102
9	100	99
10	99	97
		92
		85
		80

Note. Scores are ordered within classes and represent the pretest IQ measures of the students. Pairs of students on the same line represent matched pairs. Two students in Classroom A and three students in Classroom B have no matched pair and are thrown out of the design. The mean IQ for all 12 students in Classroom A is 116; the mean IQ for all 13 students in Classroom B is 105. For the 10 matched pairs, the mean IQ is 111.5 in Classroom A and 111.4 in Classroom B.

true differences between the means of the two groups on the matching variable. This is exactly the same problem we noted earlier with using analysis of covariance (without correction for unreliability) to adjust for initial differences between groups.

Statisticians have been more enthusiastic about the possibilities of matching and have developed techniques that can overcome several of the limitations noted above. Of special importance is Rosenbaum and Rubin's (1983, 1984) development of the concept of matching on the propensity score (see Rubin & Thomas, 1996). As in econometric selection models, the propensity score takes seriously the idea of attempting to develop a model of selection into the treatment and control groups. In this approach, a logistic regression equation is developed in which all of the available covariates are used to predict group assignment (treatment vs. control). For example, Rosenbaum and Rubin (1984) began with 74 available covariates in

their comparison of the effectiveness of two treatments for heart disease in a study of 1,500 patients. Based on this equation, they estimated a propensity score for each participant that represents the probability that the specific participant would be assigned to the treatment group, given these background variables. These propensity scores are then used as the basis for matching participants in the treatment and control groups.

Rosenbaum and Rubin (1983, 1984) have shown that matching on propensity scores minimizes pretest differences between the treatment and control groups across the full set of measured variables. Rosenbaum (1986) also pointed out that matching adjusts for any functional form of relationship between the propensity score and the outcome measure, whereas the typical analysis of covariance only adjusts for linear relationships. Many of the earlier problems in finding adequate matches in the treatment and control groups can also be reduced through the use of modern computer search algorithms that identify the optimal pairing of participants[16] (Rosenbaum, 1995). Further, if matching on propensity scores is supplemented with other analyses, a variety of other potential issues can be probed (see Rosenbaum, 1986, 1987, 1995; Rubin & Thomas, 1996). The two following sets of supplementary analyses are of particular interest.

1. Although matching on propensity scores optimally balances the treatment and control groups across the set of covariates, it may not optimally match the two groups on variables of particular theoretical or empirical importance (e.g., the pretest measure of the outcome variable of interest). The treatment and control groups on each of the covariates may be compared using *t*-tests. If a researcher believes that certain covariates are especially critical and they do not appear to be well equated, the researcher may also perform analysis of covariance (or analysis of covariance with correction for unreliability to address issues of measurement error) to provide more precise adjustment for the effects of baseline differences in these specific variables.

2. A number of sensitivity analyses have been developed for matched group designs. These sensitivity analyses give an indication of the magnitude of bias

---

[16] The failure to find adequate matches highlights the limitations of generalization of the findings. Model-based statistical adjustments such as analysis of covariance imply that generalization across the full theoretical range of the covariate is possible. However, in regions where there are sparse data in one of the groups, such model-based generalization can represent a risky extrapolation of the findings (Cochran, 1957; see also Cook, 1993).

due to hidden variables that would be necessary to eliminate the treatment effect. As a simple example, Rosenbaum (1987) suggested calculating the standardized effect size d for the covariate (not including the pretest) that shows the largest (unadjusted) difference at pretest – this estimate is used as a rough estimate of the magnitude of an important hidden variable. The correlation of the pretest and the posttest on the outcome variable of interest (ρ_{12}) is taken as the estimate of the maximum possible value of the relationship of the hidden variable with the outcome variable of interest. The product $d\rho_{12}$ is then used as a reasonable estimate of the amount that an important hidden variable not assessed at pretest could potentially reduce the estimate of the causal effect. If the difference between the treatment and control groups on the outcome variable can be reduced by this (or even a larger) amount and still attain statistical significance, then the estimate of the causal effect is taken as an indication that the treatment effect is likely to be robust to the effects of hidden variables. Rosenbaum (1991a, 1991b, 1994, 1995) also developed procedures for conducting sensitivity analyses using matched designs for cases involving a dichotomous outcome variable and for cases involving multiple continuous outcome variables. He has also developed procedures based on rank statistics that are less dependent on assuming that a specific statistical model (e.g., linear regression) is correct.[17]

In summary, the use of propensity scores overcomes many of the objections that were directed at earlier and simpler versions of matching. Particularly when supplemented by additional analyses to address specific issues (quality of matching on key covariates; unreliability on these key variables) and sensitivity analyses to address the likely impact of hidden variables, matching on the propensity score often provides distinct advantages over the sole use of statistical adjustment techniques. Belin et al. (1995) and Rosenbaum (1986) presented empirical illustrations of how the use of propensity scores combined with careful supplementary analyses can strengthen the conclusions that can be reached from the nonequivalent control group design. Recent meta-analytic studies in several areas of

applied research have also provided an optimistic assessment of the success of careful matching procedures: These studies found no detectable difference in either the mean or variance of estimates of standardized treatment effects from randomized experiments and matched group designs (Heinsman & Shadish, 1996; Shadish & Ragsdale, 1996). Nonetheless, a strong caveat remains: The fundamental condition of strong ignorability that is necessary for the causal interpretation of treatment effects in the nonequivalent control group design can be probed, but never definitively established. Thus, there is always a degree of uncertainty associated with estimates of causal effects on the basis of this design.

THREATS TO INTERNAL VALIDITY. In terms of Campbell's approach, the basic nonequivalent control group design is particularly susceptible to four threats to internal validity (Cook & Campbell, 1979). The strength of the design is that the inclusion of the control group rules out basic threats, such as maturation, that occur equally in the treatment and control groups. The weakness of the basic design is that it does not rule out cases in which these threats operate differently in the treatment and control groups.

MATURATION. The treatment and control groups may differ in the rate at which the participants are growing or declining on the outcome variable prior to treatment. To illustrate, consider a nonequivalent control group design in which the Evans et al. (1981) smoking prevention program is given to all students in a suburban high school, whereas students in an inner city high school receive a control program unrelated to smoking. An example of the threat of differential maturation would occur if the number of cigarettes smoked per day in an urban high school was increasing at a faster rate than in the suburban high school in the absence of intervention.

HISTORY. Some other event may occur to one of the two groups, but not the other, that may be expected to affect the outcome variable. For example, the media in the suburban site might independently start a series pointing out the dangers of teenage smoking. Alternatively, lower cost generic or contraband cigarettes might become available in the urban, but not in the suburban area.

STATISTICAL REGRESSION. Participants may be selected for the treatment or control group based on an unreliable or temporally instable measured variable.

---

[17] Rosenbaum (1986, 1987, 1995) also provided illustrations of a third type of supplementary analysis. He showed how the combination of propensity score matching and substantive theory in an area can be used to make predictions that provide checks on the assumption of strong ignorability. Because his examples depend on theory in substantive areas other than social psychology, they will not be discussed here.

Participants selected for the study in the inner city school may have on average been temporarily smoking fewer than their normal number of cigarettes per week (e.g., if several of the participants had just recovered from colds), whereas participants in the suburban school may have on average been smoking their normal number of cigarettes per day. Upon remeasurement, participants in each group would tend to report their typical level of smoking.

INSTRUMENTATION. Some aspect of the measuring instrument may change from pretest to posttest in only one of the two groups. This threat can take many forms, which can be manifested in such problems as differences in the factor structures (see Pitts, West, & Tein, 1996), the reliability of the scale, or the interval properties on the scale itself between the two groups (e.g., ceiling or floor effects). Local changes in record keeping practices or in the sensitivity of the measures can also produce this threat.

SUMMARY. In the example given above, the smoking prevention program was expected to reduce the number of cigarettes that were smoked by the average student. Given that the suburban high school was assigned to receive the smoking prevention program, any observed treatment effect is confounded with the specific forms of the threats of maturation, history, regression, and instrumentation presented above. Any observed difference between the means of the treatment and control group means may be due to the causal effect of treatment, the specific threats to internal validity, or both. However, note that if the smoking prevention intervention had been assigned to the inner city instead of the suburban school, none of the specific forms of threats to internal validity illustrated above would provide a plausible alternative explanation of the effects of the program. In this second case, the threats to internal validity bias the estimates of the causal effect, but in a direction opposite from that expected for true effects of the program. These specific threats may lead to estimates of the causal effect of treatment that are too low, thus lowering the statistical power of the test. However, these threats do not call the existence of the causal effect into question.

DESIGN ENHANCEMENTS. The basic nonequivalent control groups design may be strengthened by adding design and analysis components that specifically address the plausible threats to validity. The ideas here build on previous discussions of design enhancements for addressing threats to internal validity in other quasi-experimental designs. Reynolds and West (1987) presented extensive examples of the use of several of these techniques in the evaluation of the effectiveness of a sales campaign.

MULTIPLE CONTROL GROUPS. Typically, no control group can be identified that is comparable to the treatment group on all factors that could affect the outcome of the study. It is often possible, however, to identify multiple imperfect control groups, each of which can address some of the threats to validity. For example, Roos, Roos, and Henteleff (1978) compared the pre- and postoperation health of tonsillectomy patients with (a) a nonoperated control group matched on age and medical diagnosis and (b) nonoperated siblings who were within 5 years of the patient's age. The first control group roughly equates the medical history of the treatment participant; the second control group roughly equates the genetic predisposition, environment, and family influences of the treatment participant. Obtaining similar estimates of the causal effects across each of the comparison groups can help minimize the plausibility of alternative explanations of the obtained results. Rosenbaum (1987; see also associated discussion papers) discussed several methods of using the data from carefully chosen multiple control groups to reduce the likelihood that hidden variables may be responsible for the results.

NONEQUIVALENT DEPENDENT VARIABLES. Sometimes data can be collected on additional dependent variables or in different contexts on the same group of participants. Ideally, the measures selected should be conceptually related to the outcome variable of interest and should be affected by the same threats to internal validity as the primary dependent variable. However, the researcher would *not* expect these measures to be affected by the treatment. To illustrate, Roos et al. (1978) compared the tonsillectomy group and two control groups on their primary outcome variable, health insurance claims for respiratory illness, which they expected to decrease only in the treatment group. They also compared health insurance claims for other nonrespiratory illness that would not be expected to decrease following treatment. To the extent that the hypothesized pattern of results is obtained on the primary outcome variable, but not on the nonequivalent dependent variables, the interpretation of the results as a causal effect is strengthened.

MULTIPLE PRETESTS OVER TIME. The addition of multiple pretests on the same variable over time to the nonequivalent control group design can help rule out threats associated with differential rates of maturation or regression to the mean in the two groups. In this design, the multiple pretests are used to estimate the rates of maturation in the two groups prior to treatment. These estimates can then be used to adjust the treatment effect under the assumption that the pattern of maturation within each group would not change during the study. For example, Reynolds and West (1987) used data from sales in treatment and comparison stores prior to the introduction of a sales campaign in treatment stores to adjust for potential (maturational) trends in sales levels. Recent applications of hierarchical linear models to repeated measures data (Bryk & Raudenbush, 1992; Willett & Sayers, 1994) have provided a number of promising and flexible models of adjusting the treatment effect based on information about each participant's growth rate and the mean growth rates within the treatment and control groups (see Pitts, 1999, for a detailed development of possible models).

PATTERN OF RESULTS. As we briefly noted previously, not all threats to internal validity are plausible given certain patterns of results. Cook and Campbell (1979) noted that the four threats to validity may increase or decrease in plausibility depending on the specific area of research and the pattern of results that is obtained. For example, cases of differential rates of maturation almost never involve cases in which only one group is growing or the two groups are growing in opposite directions; rather, they involve differential rates of either growth or decline in the two groups. Similarly, regression to the mean involves a disadvantaged group improving or an advantaged group declining on remeasurement relative to another selected group. It is implausible to expect that regression to the mean would lead a previously disadvantaged group to surpass a previously advantaged group.

Figure 3.6 draws on these ideas and helps identify the likely threats to internal validity that would be associated with several different possible outcome patterns. For example, applying the previous reasoning to the examples, outcomes B and E suggest that differential rates of maturation should be carefully considered as a potential threat to the internal validity of the results. In contrast, differential rates of maturation is a less likely threat given outcomes A, C, or particularly D.

Using the guidelines presented by Figure 3.6, researchers can identify those threats to internal validity that deserve special attention given the specific pattern of results obtained in their study. For example, if we consider outcome D, the threats of differential maturation rates, instrumentation, and regression are unlikely, leaving differences in history in the two groups

as the threat to the internal validity toward which researchers should focus their attention. If examination of careful documentation of other possible influences on the treatment and control groups failed to identify plausible historical influences that differed in the two groups, the researchers could reach at least a tentative conclusion that their treatment led to a causal effect.

OTHER ISSUES

STATISTICAL POWER. As noted previously, to the extent the condition of strong ignorability can be approached, the nonequivalent control group design theoretically becomes increasingly similar to the regression discontinuity design. Because in practice researchers cannot convincingly establish that the assumptions necessary for strong ignorability have been met, multiple analyses must often be conducted to probe assumptions and to rule out plausible threats to validity. Methodologists frequently suggest that researchers attempt to bracket the estimate of the treatment effect, sometimes reporting the mean (or median), largest, and smallest effect sizes across diverse analyses (see Reichardt & Gollob, 1997, for a discussion). This strategy increases the certainty of our causal inference to the extent that all of the analyses yield similar estimates of the treatment effect. However, this strategy also implies that if we wish to show that the bracket does not include a treatment effect of 0, our estimate of statistical power must be based on the statistical model that can be expected to lead to the greatest attenuation of the magnitude of the treatment effect. As a result, the power of the statistical tests in the nonequivalent control group design can be expected to be lower than for a randomized experiment.

CAUSAL GENERALIZATION. Nonequivalent control group designs are normally conducted with the units and settings of interest and are thus typically relatively high in external validity. Randomization can and should be implemented more frequently than it has been (Cook & Campbell, 1979; Rosenbaum, 1986; Shadish et al., in press), but many potential participants and organizational contexts will not accept this assignment procedure. Consequently, the nonequivalent control group design, ideally including the design enhancements discussed previously, is sometimes the only feasible option. For example, it would be difficult to get public and private schools to accept random assignment of students; furthermore, not all students (or their families) would be willing to participate in such an assignment process. Even if a random assignment process could be implemented, it is likely that the

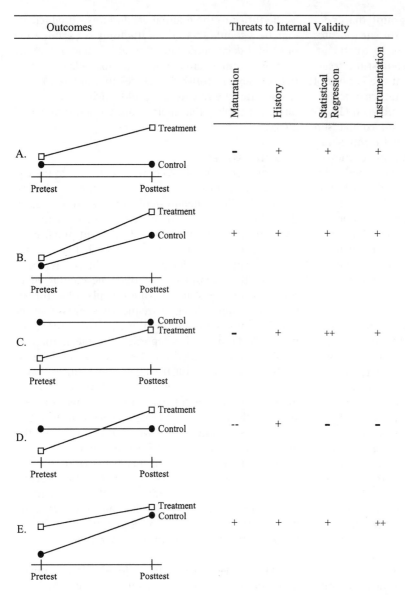

Figure 3.6. Interpretable outcomes associated with the nonequivalent control group design.

Note. ++ indicates a highly likely threat to the design when this outcome occurs. + indicates a likely threat to the design when this outcome occurs. –– indicates a less likely threat to the design when this outcome occurs. – indicates a very unlikely threat to the design when this outcome occurs.

Adapted from S. G. West, Beyond the laboratory experiment, chapter in P. Karoly (Ed.), *Measurement strategies in health psychology*, p. 227. Reprinted by permission of John Wiley and Sons.

participating families and schools would be highly atypical of the population of units and settings to which the researchers intend to generalize their results (West & Sagarin, 2000). In addition, treatments and observations in nonequivalent control group designs are often more similar to those that will be implemented in actual settings, further enhancing causal generalization to the UTOS of interest. The ability to generalize causal effects to the UTOS of interest is one of the primary strengths of the nonequivalent control group design; the inability to make precise statements about the magnitude (and sometimes direction) of causal effects is its primary weakness.

CONCLUSION. The basic nonequivalent control group design provides the least satisfactory of the three quasi-experimental alternatives to the randomized experiment we have considered. Such designs have traditionally been viewed as "very weak, easily misinterpreted, and difficult to analyze" (Huitema, 1980, p. 352). From the perspective of the RCM, there is always some uncertainty as to whether the conditions of strong ignorability and SUTVA have been met. From the perspective of Cook and Campbell (1979) and Shadish et al. (in press), the four threats of differential maturation rates, history, statistical regression, and instrumentation in the two groups represent the primary threats to internal validity that must be ruled out. The internal validity of the design can potentially be enhanced by the inclusion of design features that address specific threats to internal validity, such as multiple control groups, nonequivalent dependent measures, and multiple pretests over time, (Reynolds & West, 1987). Data may sometimes be collected that permit the researcher either to adequately model the selection process or match groups on propensity scores. The use of multiple statistical adjustment procedures that have different assumptions, but which converge on similar estimates of the causal effect can also produce increased confidence in the results. In general, strong treatment effects that can be shown through sensitivity analyses to be robust to the potential influence of hidden variables coupled with careful consideration of the remaining threats to internal validity can sometimes overcome most of the limitations of this design.

SOME FINAL OBSERVATIONS

This chapter has provided an introduction to experimental and quasi-experimental designs that are useful in field settings. In contrast to the laboratory research methods, in which social psychologists have traditionally been trained, modern field research methodology reflects the more complex and less certain real-world settings in which it has been applied. As we have seen, even the randomized experiment may not definitively rule out all threats to internal validity – problems such as attrition, treatment noncompliance, and atypical responses of control groups occur with some regularity. Weaker quasi-experimental designs, such as the nonequivalent control group design, rule out a far smaller set of the threats to internal validity. Consequently, social psychologists working in field settings must carefully articulate the threats to internal validity and use specific procedures in an attempt to minimize the likelihood that a specific threat to internal validity could account for the results. These procedures include adding specific design features (e.g., multiple control groups), additional measurements (e.g., time series data), and statistical adjustments (see also Reichardt & Mark, 1997). The use of these procedures can in some cases produce strong designs whose internal validity approaches that of a randomized experiment. In other cases, one or more threats to internal validity will remain plausible despite the investigator's best efforts.

Because of the complexity and uncertainty associated with research conducted in the field, it is important for researchers to acknowledge publicly the known limitations of their findings and to make their data available for analysis by other researchers (Cook, 1983; Houts et al., 1986; Sechrest, West, Phillips, Redner, & Yeaton, 1979). Public criticism of research provides an important mechanism through which biases and threats to internal validity can be identified and their likely effects, if any, on the results of the study can be assessed. Additional studies, with different strengths and weaknesses, can then be conducted to help bracket the true causal effect. Although considerable uncertainty may be associated with the results of any single study, a consistent finding in the research literature can greatly increase confidence in the robustness of the causal effect (Shadish et al., in press).

Reflecting recent practice, the majority of the research examples discussed in this chapter have been applied in nature. The development of the methods discussed in this chapter has provided a strong basis for applied social psychologists to make causal inferences about the effects of treatment programs delivered in the settings of interest in the field. At the same time, social psychologists interested in basic research are beginning to develop new areas of substantive interest. Among these areas are the influence of culture (e.g., collectivist vs. individualist), major life stressors, long-term relationships, and new aspects of the self (e.g., generativity). Methodological issues that arise in these areas, such as selection of participants into conditions, attrition, and growth or decline over time require that researchers consider many of the specific design, measurement, and statistical techniques developed to address these problems. Interest in problems such as coping with the stress of physical illness often require that researchers collect data in settings outside the laboratory. And interest in problems like long-term relationships and generativity will often require that researchers study relevant samples of participants over extended time periods. These substantive developments suggest that the traditional modal study in social psychology identified in West et al.'s (1992) review – a randomized experiment, conducted in the laboratory, lasting no more than 1 hour, and using undergraduate students as participants – may no longer represent the design of choice in many of these emerging research areas. These substantive developments call for new variants of the laboratory experiment that incorporate some of the features of modern field experiments and quasi-experiments discussed in this chapter. These developments also may portend a possible return to modern improved versions of research methods more commonly used in some previous eras in the history of social psychology – experiments, quasi-experiments, and other studies testing basic social psychological principles in field contexts. Such potential developments would help social psychology broaden the Units, Treatments, Observations, and Settings represented in its research base, providing a stronger basis for causal generalization. They would supplement the demonstrated strengths and complement the weaknesses of traditional laboratory experiments. Such designs hold the promise of a more balanced mix of methodological approaches to basic issues in social psychology, in which researchers could make legitimate claims for both the internal validity and the causal generalization of their effects.

REFERENCES

Aiken, L. S., Stein, J. A., & Bentler, P. M. (1994). Structural equation analyses of clinical subpopulation differences and comparative treatment outcomes: Characterizing the daily lives of drug addicts. *Journal of Consulting and Clinical Psychology, 62,* 488–499.

Aiken, L. S., & West, S. G. (1991). *Multiple regression: Testing and interpreting interactions.* Newbury Park, CA: Sage.

Aiken, L. S., West, S. G., Schwalm, D. E., Carroll, J. L., & Hsiung, S. (1998). Comparison of a randomized and two quasi-experimental designs in a single outcome evaluation: Efficacy of a university-level remedial writing program. *Evaluation Review, 22,* 207–244.

Aiken, L. S., West, S. G., Woodward, C. K., Reno, R. R., & Reynolds, K. D. (1994). Increasing screening mammography in asymptomatic women: Evaluation of a second generation, theory-based program. *Health Psychology, 13,* 526–538.

Angrist, J. D., Imbens, G. W., & Rubin, D. B. (1996). Identification of causal effects using instrumental variables (with commentary). *Journal of the American Statistical Association, 91,* 444–472.

Arbuckle, J. L. (1996). Full information estimation in the presence of incomplete data. In G. A. Marcoulides & R. E. Schumacker (Eds.), *Advanced structural equation modeling: Issues and techniques* (pp. 243–278). Mahwah, NJ: Erlbaum.

Aronson, E. (1966). Avoidance of inter-subject communication. *Psychological Reports, 19,* 238.

Aronson, E., Wilson, T. D., & Brewer (1998). Experimentation in social psychology. In D. T. Gilbert, S. T. Fiske, & G. Lindzey (Eds.), *Handbook of social psychology* (4th ed., Vol. 1, pp. 99–142). Boston: McGraw-Hill.

Bandura, A. (1977). *Social learning theory.* Englewood Cliffs, NJ: Prentice Hall.

Barcikowski, R. S. (1981). Statistical power with group mean as the unit of analysis. *Journal of Educational Statistics, 6,* 267–285.

Barlow, D. H., & Hersen, M. (1984). *Single case experimental designs: Strategies for studying behavior change* (2nd ed.). New York: Pergamon.

Barnow, L. S. (1973). The effects of Head Start and socioeconomic status on cognitive development of disadvantaged students (Doctoral dissertation, University of Wisconsin, Madison, 1974). *Dissertation Abstracts International, 34,* 6191A.

Barnow, L. S., Cain, G. G., & Goldberger, A. S. (1980). Issues in the analysis of selection bias. In E. S. Stromsdorfer & G. Farkas (Eds.), *Evaluation studies review annual* (Vol. 5, pp. 43–59). Beverly Hills, CA: Sage.

Baron, R. M., & Kenny, D. A. (1986). The moderator–mediator distinction in social psychological research: Conceptual, strategic and statistical considerations. *Journal of Personality and Social Psychology, 51,* 1173–1182.

Belin, T. R., Elashoff, R. M., Leung, K.-M., Nisenbaum, R., Bastani, R., Nasseri, K., & Maxwell, A. (1995). Combining information from multiple sources in the analysis of a non-equivalent control group design. In C. Gatsonis, J. S. Hodges, R. E. Kass, & N. D. Singpurwalla (Eds.), *Case studies in Bayesian statistics* (Vol. 2, pp. 241–260). New York: Springer-Verlag.

Bentler, P. M. (1995). *EQS structural equations program manual.* Encino, CA: Multivariate Software, Inc.

Bentler, P. M., & Woodward, J. A. (1978). A Head Start re-evaluation: Positive effects are not yet demonstrable. *Evaluation Quarterly, 2,* 493–510.

Berk, R. A. (1988). Causal inference for sociological data. In N. J. Smeltzer (Ed.), *Handbook of sociology* (pp. 155–172). Newbury Park, CA: Sage.

Berkowitz, L. (1993). *Aggression: Its causes, consequences, and control.* New York: McGraw-Hill.

Berkowitz, L., & Donnerstein, E. (1982). External validity is more than skin deep. *American Psychologist, 37,* 245–257.

Bickman, L., & Henchy, T. (Eds.). (1972). *Beyond the laboratory: Field research in social psychology.* New York: McGraw-Hill.

Biglan, A., Hood, D., Borzovsky, P., Ochs, L., Ary, D., & Black, C. (1991). Subject attrition in prevention research. In C. G. Luekefeld & W. Bukoski (Eds.), *Drug abuse prevention intervention research: Methodological issues* (pp. 213–234). Washington, DC: NIDA Research Monograph # 107.

Bloom, H. S. (1984). Accounting for no-shows in experimental evaluation designs. *Evaluation Review, 8,* 225–246.

Bollen, K. A. (1989). *Structural equations with latent variables.* New York: Wiley.

Borenstein, M., Cohen, J., & Rothstein, H. (1997). *Confidence intervals, effect size, and power* [Computer program]. Mahwah, NJ: Erlbaum.

Boruch, R. F. (1997). *Randomized experiments for planning and evaluation.* Thousand Oaks, CA: Sage.

Boruch, R. F., McSweeny, A. J., & Soderstrom, E. J. (1978). Randomized field experiments for program planning, development, and evaluation. *Evaluation Quarterly, 2,* 655–695.

Box, G. E. P., & Draper, N. R. (1987). *Empirical model building and response surfaces.* New York: Wiley.

Box, G. E. P., Jenkins, G. M., & Reinsel, G. C. (1994). *Time series analysis: Forecasting and control* (3rd ed.). San Francisco: Holden-Day.

Braucht, G. N., & Reichardt, C. S. (1993). A computerized approach to trickle-process, random assignment. *Evaluation Review, 17,* 79–90.

Bryan, A. D., Aiken, L. S., & West, S. G. (1996). Increasing condom use: Evaluation of a theory-based intervention to prevent sexually transmitted disease in young women. *Health Psychology, 15,* 371–382.

Bryk, A. S., & Raudenbush, S. W. (1992). *Hierarchical linear models: Applications and data analysis methods.* Newbury Park, CA: Sage.

Burstein, L. (1980). The analysis of multilevel data in educational research and evaluation. In D. Berliner (Ed.), *Review of research in education* (Vol. 8, pp. 158–223). Washington, DC: American Educational Research Association.

Burstein, L. (1985). Units of analysis. In *International encyclopedia of education* (pp. 5368–5375). Oxford, England: Pergamon.

Burstein, L., Kim, K.-S., & Delandshire, G. (1989). Multilevel investigations of systematically varying slopes: Issues, alternatives, and consequences. In R. D. Bock (Ed.), *Multilevel analysis of educational data* (pp. 233–276). San Diego, CA: Academic Press.

Cahan, S., & Davis, D. (1987). A between-grade-levels approach to the investigation of the absolute effects of schooling on achievement. *American Educational Research Journal, 24,* 1–12.

Campbell, D. T. (1957). Factors relevant to the validity of experiments in social settings. *Psychological Bulletin, 54,* 297–312.

Campbell, D. T. (1969). Reforms as experiments. *American Psychologist, 24 ,* 409–429.

Campbell, D. T. (1986). Relabeling internal and external validity for applied social scientists. In W. M. K. Trochim (Ed.), *Advances in quasi-experimental design and analysis* (Vol. 31, pp. 67–78). San Francisco: Jossey-Bass.

Campbell, D. T., & Boruch, R. F. (1975). Making the case for randomized assignment by considering the alternatives: Six ways in which quasi-experimental evaluations tend to underestimate effects. In C. A. Bennett & A. A. Lumsdaine (Eds.), *Evaluation and experience: Some critical issues in assessing social programs* (pp. 195–296). New York: Academic Press.

Campbell, D. T., & Erlbacher, A. (1970). How regression artifacts in quasi-experimental evaluations can mistakenly make compensatory education look harmful. In J. Hellmuth (Ed.), *Compensatory education: A national debate. Volume. 3: Disadvantaged child* (pp. 185–225). New York: Brunner/Mazel.

Campbell, D. T., & Kenny, D. A. (1999). *A primer on regression artifacts.* New York: Guilford.

Campbell, D. T., & Stanley, J. C. (1966). *Experimental and quasi-experimental designs for research.* Chicago: Rand McNally.

Canner, P. (1984). How much data should be collected in a clinical trial? *Statistics in Medicine, 3,* 423–432.

Canner, P. (1991). Covariate adjustment of treatment effects in clinical trials. *Controlled Clinical Trials, 12,* 359–366.

Cappelleri, J. C. (1990, October). *Power analysis of regression-discontinuity designs.* Paper presented at the annual meeting of the American Evaluation Association, Washington, DC.

Cappelleri, J. C., Darlington, R. B., & Trochim, W. M. K. (1994). Power analysis of cutoff-based randomized clinical trials. *Evaluation Review, 18,* 141–152.

Chassin, L., Barrera, M., Jr., Bech, K., & Kossak-Fuller, J. (1992). Recruiting a community sample of adolescent children of alcoholics: A comparison of three subject sources. *Journal of Studies on Alcohol, 53,* 316–319.

Chatfield, C. (1996). *The analysis of time series: An introduction* (5th ed.). London: Chapman & Hall.

Cialdini, R. B., Reno, R. R., & Kallgren, C. A. (1990). A focus theory of normative conduct: Recycling the concept of norms to reduce littering in public places. *Journal of Personality and Social Psychology, 58,* 1015–1026.

Cicarelli, V. G., Cooper, W. H., & Granger, R. L. (1969). *The impact of Head Start: An evaluation of the effects of Head Start on children's cognitive and affective development.* Athens, OH: Ohio University and Westinghouse Learning Corporation.

Cleveland, W. S. (1993). *Visualizing data.* Summit, NJ: Hobart Press.

Cochran, W. G. (1957). Analysis of covariance: Its nature and uses. *Biometrics, 13,* 261–281.

Cochran, W. G. (1965). The planning of observational studies of human populations (with discussion). *Journal of the Royal Statistical Society, Series A, 128,* 134–155.

Cochran, W. G., & Cox, G. M. (1957). *Experimental designs* (6th ed.). New York: Wiley.

Cohen, J. (1988). *Statistical power analysis for the behavioral sciences* (2nd ed.). Hillsdale, NJ: Erlbaum.

Cohen, J. (1994). The earth is round, $p < .05$. *American Psychologist, 49,* 997–1003.

Cohen, J., & Cohen, P. (1983). *Applied multiple regression/correlation analysis for the behavioral sciences* (2nd ed.). Hillsdale, NJ: Erlbaum.

Cohen, P., Cohen, J., Aiken, L. S., & West, S. G. (in press). The problem of units and the circumstance for POMP. *Multivariate Behavioral Research.*

Coleman, J., Hoffer, T., & Kilgore, S. (1982). Cognitive outcomes in public and private schools. *Sociology of Education, 55,* 65–76.

Conner, R. F. (1977). Selecting a control group: An analysis of the randomization process in twelve social reform programs. *Evaluation Quarterly, 1,* 195–244.

Cook, R. D., & Weisberg, S. (1994). *An introduction to regression graphics.* New York: Wiley.

Cook, T. D. (1983). Quasi-experimentation: Its ontology, epistemology, and methodology. In G. Morgan (Ed.), *Beyond method: Strategies for social research*. Beverly Hills, CA: Sage.

Cook, T. D. (1993). A quasi-sampling theory of the generalization of causal relationships. In L. B. Sechrest & A. G. Scott (Eds.). *New directions for program evaluation*, (Number 57, 39–81). San Francisco: Jossey-Bass.

Cook, T. D., & Campbell, D. T. (1979). *Quasi-experimentation: Design and analysis issues for field settings*. Boston: Houghton-Mifflin.

Cook, T. D., & Reichardt, C. S. (1976). Statistical analysis of data from the nonequivalent control group design: A guide to some current literature. *Evaluation, 3*, 136–138.

Crano, W. D., & Brewer, M. B. (1986). *Principles and methods of social research* (2nd ed.). Boston: Allyn & Bacon.

Cronbach, L. J. (1976). *Research on classrooms and schools: Formulation of questions, design, and analysis*. Occasional Paper, Stanford Evaluation Consortium, Stanford, CA.

Cronbach, L. J. (1982). *Designing evaluations of social and educational programs*. San Francisco: Jossey-Bass.

Crosbie, J. (1993). Interrupted time-series analysis with brief single-subject data. *Journal of Consulting and Clinical Psychology, 61*, 966–974.

Daniel, C., & Wood, F. S. (1980). *Fitting equations to data* (2nd ed.). New York: Wiley.

Dennis, M. L., Lennox, R. D., & Williams, R. (1997). Practical power analysis. In K. Bryant, M. Windle, & S. G. West (Eds.), *The Science of prevention: Methodological advances from alcohol and substance abuse research* (pp. 367–404). Washington, DC: American Psychological Association.

Draper, D. (1995). Inference and hierarchical modeling in the social sciences. *Journal of Educational and Behavioral Statistics, 20*, 115–147.

Durlak, J. A., & Wells, A. M. (1997). Primary prevention mental health programs for children and adolescents: A meta-analytic review. *American Journal of Community Psychology, 25*, 115–152.

Efron, B., & Feldman, D. (1991). Compliance as an explanatory variable in clinical trials (with discussion). *Journal of the American Statistical Association, 86*, 9–26.

Erlebacher, A. (1977). Design and analysis of experiments contrasting the within- and between-subjects manipulation of the independent variable. *Psychological Bulletin, 84*, 212–219.

Evans, R. I., Rozelle, R. M., Maxwell, S. E., Raines, B. E., Dill, C. A., Guthrie, T. J., Henderson, A. H., & Hill, P. C. (1981). Social modeling films to deter smoking in adolescents: Results of a three-year field investigation. *Journal of Applied Psychology, 66*, 399–414.

Fisher, R. A. (1935). *The design of experiments*. London: Oliver & Boyd.

Flay, B. R. (1986). Psychosocial approaches to smoking prevention: A review of findings. *Health Psychology, 4*, 449–488.

Franklin, R. D., Allison, D. B., & Gorman, B. S. (Eds.). (1996). *Design and analysis of single case research*. Mahwah, NJ: Erlbaum.

Funder, D. C. (1992). Psychology from the other side of the line: Editorial processes and publication trends at *JPSP*. *Personality and Social Psychology Bulletin, 18*, 493–497.

Gilbert, J. P., Light, R. J., & Mosteller, F. (1975). Assessing social innovations: An empirical base for policy. In C. A. Bennett & A. A. Lumsdaine (Eds.), *Evaluation and experiment: Some critical issues in assessing social programs.* (pp. 39–193) New York: Academic Press.

Glass, G. V. (1988). Quasi-experiments: The case of interrupted time series. In R. M. Jaeger (Ed.), *Complementary methods for research in education* (pp. 445–464). Washington, DC: American Educational Research Association.

Goldberger, A. S. (1972, April). *Selection bias in evaluating treatment effects: Some formal illustrations* (Discussion paper 123–72). Madison: University of Wisconsin, Institute for Research on Poverty.

Greenland, S., & Morgenstern, H. (1989). Ecological bias, confounding, and effect modification. *International Journal of Epidemiology, 18*, 269–274.

Greenwald, A. G. (1976). Within-subjects design: To use or not to use. *Psychological Bulletin, 83*, 314–320.

Greenwald, A. G., Pratkanis, A. R., Leippe, M. R., & Baumgardner, M. H. (1986). Under what conditions does theory obstruct research progress? *Psychological Review, 93*, 216–229.

Gregson, R. A. (1987). The time-series analysis of self-reported headache symptoms. *Behavior Change, 4*(2), 6–13.

Hansen, W. B., & Collins, L. M. (1994). Seven ways to increase power without increasing N. In L. M. Collins & L. A. Seitz (Eds.), *Advances in data analysis for prevention intervention research* (pp. 184–195). Rockville, MD: NIDA Research Monograph 142. NIH Publication No. 94-3599.

Hansen, W. B., Collins, L. M., Malotte, C. K, Johnson, C. A., & Fielding, J. E. (1985). Attrition in prevention research. *Journal of Behavioral Medicine, 8*, 261–275.

Harlow, L. L., Mulaik, S. A., & Steiger, J. H. (Eds.).(1997). *What if there were no significance tests?* Mahwah, NJ: Erlbaum.

Hastie, T. J., & Tibshirani, R. J. (1990). *Generalized additive models*. New York: Chapman & Hall.

Heckman, J. J. (1979). Sample bias as a specification error. *Econometrica, 46*, 153–162.

Heckman, J. J. (1989). Causal inference and nonrandom samples. *Journal of Educational Statistics, 14*, 159–168.

Heckman, J. J. (1990). Varieties of selection bias. *American Economic Review, 80*, 313–318.

Hedecker, D., Gibbons, R. D., & Flay, B. R. (1994). Random effects regression models for clustered data with an example from smoking prevention research. *Journal of Consulting and Clinical Psychology, 62*, 757–765.

Hedges, L. V., & Olkin, I. (1985). *Statistical methods for meta-analysis*. Orlando, FL: Academic Press.

Heinsman, D. T., & Shadish, W. R. (1996). Assignment methods in experimentation: When do nonrandomized experiments approximate answers from randomized experiments. *Psychological Methods, 1*, 154–169.

Hennigan, K. M., del Rosario, M. L., Heath, L., Cook, T. D., Wharton, J. L., & Calder, B. J. (1982). Impact of the introduction of television on crime in the United States: Empirical findings and theoretical implications. *Journal of Personality and Social Psychology, 42*, 461–477.

Higginbotham, H. N., West, S. G., & Forsyth, D. R. (1988). *Psychotherapy and behavior change: Social, cultural, and methodological perspectives*. New York: Pergamon.

Holland, P. W. (1986). Statistics and causal inference (with discussion). *Journal of the American Statistical Association, 81*, 945–970.

Holland, P. W. (1988). Causal inference, path analysis, and recursive structural equation models (with discussion). In C. Clogg (Ed.), *Sociological methodology 1988* (pp. 449–493). Washington, DC: American Sociological Association.

Holland, P. W. (1989). Discussion of Aitkin's and Longford's papers. In R. D. Bock (Ed.), *Multilevel analysis of educational data* (pp. 311–317). San Diego, CA: Academic.

Horne, G. P., Yang, M. C. K., & Ware, W. B. (1982). Time series analysis for single subject designs. *Psychological Bulletin, 91*, 178–189.

Houts, A. C., Cook, T. D., & Shadish, W. R. (1986). The person-situation debate: A critical multiplist perspective. *Journal of Personality, 54*, 52–105.

Huitema, B. E. (1980). *The analysis of covariance and alternatives*. New York: Wiley.

Hunter, J. E. (1996, August). Needed: A ban on the significance test. In P. E. Shrout (chair), Symposium. Significance tests – should they be banned from APA journals. American Psychological Association, Toronto, Ontario, Canada.

Hunter, J. E., & Schmidt, F. L. (1990). *Methods of meta-analysis: Correcting error and bias in research findings*. Newbury Park, CA: Sage.

Imbens, G. W., & Rubin, D. B. (1994). *On the fragility of instrumental variables estimators*. Discussion paper # 1675, unpublished manuscript, Harvard University, Institute of Economic Research.

Imbens, G. W., & Rubin, D. B. (1997). Bayesian inference for causal effects in randomized experiments with noncompliance. *Annals of Statistics , 25*, 305–327.

Ito, T. A., Miller, N., & Pollock, V. E. (1996). Alcohol and aggression: A meta-analysis on the moderating effects of inhibitory cues, triggering events, and self-focused attention. *Psychological Bulletin, 120*, 60–82.

Jöreskog, K. G., & Sörbom, D. (1993). *Lisrel 8: User's reference guide*. Chicago: Scientific Software.

Judd, C. M., & Kenny, D. A. (1981). *Estimating the effects of social interventions*. New York: Cambridge University Press.

Judd, C. M., Smith, E. R., & Kidder, L. H. (1991). *Research methods in social relations* (6th ed.). Fort Worth, TX: Harcourt Brace Jovanovich.

Jurs, S. G., & Glass, G. V. (1971). The effect of experimental mortality on the internal and external validity of the randomized comparative experiment. *Journal of Experimental Education, 40*, 62–66.

Kenny, D. A. (1975). A quasi-experimental approach to assessing treatment effects in the nonequivalent control group design. *Psychological Bulletin, 82*, 345–362.

Kenny, D. A., & Judd, C. M. (1986). The consequences of violating the independence assumption in analysis of variance. *Psychological Bulletin, 82*, 345–362.

Keren, G. (1993). Between-or within-subjects design: A methodological dilemma. In G. Keren & C. Lewis (Eds.), *A handbook for data analysis in the behavioral sciences: Methodological issues* (pp. 257–272). Hillsdale, NJ: Erlbaum.

Kirk, R. E. (1995). *Experimental design: Procedures for the behavioral sciences* (3rd ed.). Pacific Grove, CA: Brook/Cole.

Kish, L. (1987). *Statistical designs for research*. New York: Wiley.

Kopans, D. B. (1994). Screening for breast cancer and mortality reduction among women 40–49 years of age. *Cancer, 74* (Suppl), 311–322.

Kratochwill, T. R., & Levin, J. R. (Eds.). (1992). *Single-case research design and analysis: New directions for psychology and education*. Hillsdale, NJ: Erlbaum.

Kreft, I. G. G., & de Leeuw, J. (1998). *Introducing multilevel modeling*. London: Sage.

Lalonde, R. (1986). Evaluating the econometric evaluations of training programs. *American Economic Review, 76*, 604–620.

Larsen, R. J. (1989). A process approach to personality psychology: Utilizing time as a facet of data. In D. M. Buss & N. Cantor (Eds.), *Personality psychology: Recent trends and emerging directions* (pp. 177–193). New York: Springer-Verlag.

Lee, Y., Ellenberg, J., Hirtz, D., & Nelson, K. (1991). Analysis of clinical trials by treatment actually received: Is it really an option? *Statistics in Medicine, 10*, 1595–1605.

Lehman, D. R., Lempert, R. O., & Nisbett, R. E. (1988). The effects of graduate training on reasoning: Formal discipline and thinking about everyday events. *American Psychologist, 43*, 431–442.

Linn, R. L., & Werts, C. E. (1973). Errors of inference due to errors of movement. *Educational and Psychological Measurement, 33*, 531–545.

Lipsey, M. W. (1993). Theory as method: Small theories of treatments. In L. B. Sechrest & A. G. Scott (Eds.), *New directions in program evaluation*. (Number 57, pp. 5–38). San Francisco: Jossey-Bass.

Lipsey, M. W. (1997). Design sensitivity: Statistical power for applied experimental research. In L. Bickman & D. Rog (Eds.), *Handbook of applied social research methods* (pp. 39–68). Thousand Oaks, CA: Sage.

Little, R. J. A., & Rubin, D. B. (1987). *Statistical analysis with missing data*. New York: Wiley.

Little, R. J. A., & Schenker, N. (1995). Missing data. In G. Arminger, C. C. Clogg, & M. E. Sobel (Eds.), *Handbook of statistical modeling for the social and behavioral sciences* (pp. 39–76). New York: Plenum.

Little, R. J., & Yau, L. H. Y (1998). Statistical techniques for analyzing data from preventive trials: Treatment of no-shows using Rubin's causal model. *Psychological Methods, 3*, 147–159.

MacKinnon, D. P. (1994). Analysis of mediating variables in prevention and intervention research. In A. Cezares & L. Beatty (Eds.), *Scientific methods for prevention intervention research*. Rockville, MD: National Institute on Drug Abuse.

Magidson, J. (1977). Toward a causal modeling approach to adjusting for pre-existing differences in the nonequivalent group situation: A general alternative to ANCOVA. *Evaluation Quarterly, 1*, 399–420.

Mallar, C. D., & Thornton, C. V. D. (1978). Transitional aid for released prisoners: Evidence from the life experiment. In T. D. Cook, M. L. Del Rosario, K. M. Hennigan, M. M. Mark, & W. M. K. Trochim (Eds.), *Evaluation studies review annual* (Vol. 3, pp. 498–517). Beverly Hills, CA: Sage.

Marcantonio, R. J., & Cook, T. D. (1994). Convincing quasi-experiments: The interrupted time series and regression-discontinuity designs. In J. S. Wholey, H. P. Hatry, & K. E. Newcomer (Eds.), *Handbook of practical program evaluation* (pp. 133–254). San Francisco: Jossey-Bass.

Mark, M. M., & Mellor, S. (1991). Effect of self-relevance of an event on hindsight bias: The foreseeability of a layoff. *Journal of Applied Psychology, 76*, 569–577.

Martin, S. E., Annan, S., & Forst, B. (1993). The special deterrent effects of a jail sanction on first-time drunk drivers: A quasi-experimental study. *Accident Analysis and Prevention, 25*, 561–568.

Maxwell, S. E., & Delaney, H. D. (1990). *Designing experiments and analyzing data: A model comparison perspective*. Pacific Grove, CA: Brooks/Cole.

McCleary, R., & Hay, R. A. (1980). *Applied time series analysis*. Beverly Hills, CA: Sage.

McGuire, W. J. (1964). Inducing resistance to persuasion: Some contemporary approaches. In L. Berkowitz (Ed.), *Advances in experimental social psychology* (Vol. 1, pp. 192–229). New York: Academic Press.

McGuire, W. J. (1983). A contextualist theory of knowledge: Its implications for innovation and research in psychological research. In L. Berkowitz (Ed.), *Advances in experimental social psychology* (Vol. 16, pp 1–47). New York: Academic Press.

McSweeny, A. J. (1978). The effects of response cost on the behavior of a million persons. *Journal of Applied Behavior Analysis, 11*, 47–51.

Meier, P. (1985). The biggest public health experiment ever: The 1954 field trial of the Salk polio vaccine. In J. M. Tanur, F. Mosteller, W. H. Kruskal, R. F. Link, R. S. Pieters, & G. R. Rising (Eds.), *Statistics: A guide to the unknown* (2nd Ed.) (pp. 3–15). Monterey, CA: Wadsworth & Brooks/Cole.

Meier, P. (1991). Comment. *Journal of the American Statistical Association, 86*, 19–22.

Mohr, L. B. (1988). *Impact analysis for program evaluation*. New York: Basic Books.

Murname, R. J., Newstead, S., & Olson, F. J. (1985). Comparing public and private schools: The puzzling role of selectivity bias. *Journal of Business and Economic Statistics, 3*, 23–35.

Muthén, B., & Jöreskog, K. G. (1983). Selectivity problems in quasi-experimental studies. *Evaluation Review, 7*, 139–174.

Muthén, B., Kaplan, M., & Hollis, M. (1987). On structural equation modeling with data that are not missing completely at random. *Psychometrika, 52*, 431–462.

Pitts, S. C. (1999). *The use of latent growth models to estimate treatment effects in longitudinal experiments*. Unpublished doctoral dissertation, Arizona State University.

Pitts, S. C., West, S. G., & Tein, J.-Y. (1996). Longitudinal measurement models in evaluation research: Examining stability and change. *Evaluation and Program Planning, 19*, 333–350.

Reichardt, C. S. (1979). The statistical analysis of data from nonequivalent group designs. In T. D. Cook and D. T. Campbell, *Quasi-experimentation: Design and analysis issues for field settings* (pp. 147–205). Boston: Houghton-Mifflin.

Reichardt, C. S., & Gollob, H. F. (1997). When confidence intervals should be used instead of statistical tests, and vice versa. In L. L. Harlow, S. A. Mulaik, & J. H. Steiger (Eds.), *What if there were no significance tests?* (pp. 259–284). Mahwah, NJ: Erlbaum.

Reichardt, C. S., & Mark, M. M. (1997). Quasi-experimentation. In L. Bickman & D. Rog (Eds.), *Handbook of applied social research methods* (pp. 193–228). Thousand Oaks, CA: Sage.

Reichardt, C. S., Minton, B. A., & Schellenger, J. D. (1986). *The analysis of covariance (ANCOVA) and the assessment of treatment effects*. Unpublished manuscript, University of Denver.

Reichardt, C. S., Trochim, W. M. K., & Cappelleri, J. C. (1995). Reports of the death of regression-discontinuity analysis are greatly exaggerated. *Evaluation Review, 19*, 39–63.

Reis, H. T., & Stiller, J. (1992). Publication trends in *JPSP*: A three-decade review. *Personality and Social Psychology Bulletin, 18*, 465–472.

Reynolds, K. D., & West, S. G. (1987). A multiplist strategy for strengthening nonequivalent control group designs. *Evaluation Review, 11*, 691–714.

Ribisl, K. M., Watlon, M. A., Mowbray, C. T., Luke, D. A., Davidson, W. A., & Bootsmiller, B. J. (1996). Minimizing participant attrition in panel studies through the use of effective retention and tracking strategies: Review and recommendations. *Evaluation and Program Planning, 19*, 1–25.

Robinson, W. S. (1950). Ecological correlations and the behavior of individuals. *American Sociological Review, 15*, 351–357.

Roos, L. L., Jr., Roos, N. P., & Henteleff, P. D. (1978). Assessing the impact of tonsillectomies. *Medical Care, 16*, 502–518.

Rosenbaum, P. R. (1984). From association to causation in observational studies: The role of strongly ignorable treatment assignment. *Journal of the American Statistical Association, 79*, 41–48.

Rosenbaum, P. R. (1986). Dropping out of high school in the United States: An observational study. *Journal of Educational Statistics, 11*, 207–224.

Rosenbaum, P. R. (1987). The role of a second control group in an observational study (with discussion). *Statistical Science, 2*, 292–316.

Rosenbaum, P. R. (1991a). Discussing hidden bias in observational studies. *Annals of Internal Medicine, 115*, 901–905.

Rosenbaum, P. R. (1991b). Sensitivity analysis for matched case-control studies. *Biometrics, 47*, 87–100.

Rosenbaum, P. R. (1994). Coherence in observational studies. *Biometrics, 50*, 368–374.

Rosenbaum, P. R. (1995). *Observational studies*. New York: Springer-Verlag.

Rosenbaum, P. R., & Rubin, D. (1983). The central role of the propensity score in observational studies for causal effects. *Biometrika, 70*, 41–55.

Rosenbaum, P. R., & Rubin, D. (1984). Reducing bias in observational studies using subclassification on the propensity score. *Journal of the American Statistical Association, 79*, 516–524.

Rosenthal, R., & Rubin, D. (1980). Comparing within- and between-subjects studies. *Sociological Methods and Research, 9*, 127–136.

Ross, H. L., Campbell, D. T., & Glass, G. V. (1970). Determining the social effects of a legal reform: The British "breathalyser" crackdown of 1967. *American Behavioral Scientist, 13*, 493–509.

Rossi, J. S. (1990). Statistical power of psychological research: What have we gained in 20 years? *Journal of Consulting and Clinical Psychology, 58*, 646–656.

Rubin, D. B. (1974). Estimating causal effects of treatments in randomized and nonrandomized studies. *Journal of Educational Psychology, 66*, 688–701.

Rubin, D. B. (1977). Assignment to treatment group on the basis of a covariate. *Journal of Educational Statistics, 2*, 1–26.

Rubin, D. B. (1978). Bayesian inference for causal effects. *The Annals of Statistics, 6*, 34–58.

Rubin, D. B. (1986). Which ifs have causal answers. *Journal of the American Statistical Association, 81*, 961–962.

Rubin, D. B., & Thomas, N. (1996). Matching using estimated propensity scores: Relating theory to practice, *Biometrics, 52*, 249–264.

Sackett, D. L., & Gent, M. (1979). Controversy in counting and attributing events in clinical trials. *New England Journal of Medicine, 301*, 1410–1412.

Schachter, S. (1959). *The psychology of affiliation*. Stanford, CA: Stanford University Press.

Schwarz, N. B., & Hippler, H. J. (1995). Subsequent questions may influence answers to preceding questions in mail surveys. *Public Opinion Quarterly, 59*, 93–97.

Sears, D. O. (1986). College sophomores in the laboratory: Influences of a narrow data base on social psychology's view of human nature. *Journal of Personality and Social Psychology, 51*, 515–530.

Seaver, W. B., & Quarton, R. J. (1976). Regression discontinuity analysis of the dean's list effects. *Journal of Educational Psychology, 68*, 459–465.

Sechrest, L., West, S. G., Phillips, M. A., Redner, R., & Yeaton, W. (1979). Some neglected problems in evaluation research: Strength and integrity of treatments. In L. Sechrest, S. G. West, M. A. Phillips, R. Rodner, & W. Yeaton (Eds), *Evaluation studies review annual* (Vol. 4, pp. 15–35). Beverly Hills, CA: Sage.

Shadish, W. R. (in press). The empirical program of quasi-experimentation. In L. Bickman (Ed.), *Contributions to research design: Donald Campbell's legacy* (Vol. 2). Thousand Oaks, CA: Sage.

Shadish, W. R., Cook, T. D., & Campbell, D. T. (in press). *Experimental and quasi-experimental design for generalized causal inference*. Boston: Houghton-Mifflin.

Shadish, W. R., Hu, X., Glaser, R. R., Knonacki, R., & Wong, S. (1998). A method for exploring the effects of attrition in randomized experiments with dichotomous outcomes. *Psychological Methods, 3*, 3–22.

Shadish, W. R., & Ragsdale, K. (1996). Random versus nonrandom assignment to psychotherapy experiments: Do you get the same answer? *Journal of Consulting and Clinical Psychology, 64*, 1290–1305.

Sidman, M. (1960). *Tactics of scientific research*. New York: Basic Books.

Sörbom, D. (1979). An alternative to the methodology for analysis of covariance. In K. G. Jöreskog & D. Sörbom (Eds.), *Advances in factor analysis and structural equation models* (pp. 219–234). Cambridge, MA: Abt Books.

Sporer, S. L., Penrod, S., Read, D., & Cutler, B. (1995). Choosing, confidence, and accuracy: A meta-analysis of the confidence–accuracy relation in eyewitness identification studies. *Psychological Bulletin, 118*, 315–327.

"Student" (W. S. Gosset). (1931). The Lanarkshire milk experiment. *Biometrika, 23*, 398–406.

Stolzenberg, R. M., & Relles, D. A. (1990). Theory testing in a world of constrained research design. *Sociological Methods and Research, 18*, 395–415.

Swingle, P. G. (Ed.). (1973). *Social psychology in natural settings*. Chicago: Aldine.

Tebes, J. K., Snow, D. L., & Arthur, M. W. (1992). Panel attrition and external validity in the short-term follow-up study of adolescent substance use. *Evaluation Review, 16*, 151–170.

Trochim, W. M. K. (1984). *Research design for program evaluation: The regression-discontinuity approach*. Beverly Hills, CA: Sage.

Trochim, W. M. K., & Cappelleri, J. C. (1992). Cutoff assignment strategies for enhancing randomized clinical trials. *Controlled Clinical Trials, 13*, 571–604.

Trochim, W. M. K., Cappelleri, J. C., & Reichardt, C. S. (1991). Random measurement error does not bias the treatment effect estimate in the regression-discontinuity design: II. When an interaction effect is present. *Evaluation Review, 15,* 571–604.

Velicer, W. F., & Colby, S. M. (1997). Time series analysis of prevention and treatment research. In K. Bryant, M. Windle, & S. G. West (Eds.), *The science of prevention: Methodological advances from alcohol and substance abuse research* (pp. 211–250), Washington, DC: American Psychological Association.

Velicer, W. F., & Harrop, J. W. (1983). The reliability and accuracy of time series model identification. *Evaluation Review, 7,* 551–560.

Velicer, W. F., & MacDonald, R. P. (1984). Time series analysis without model identification. *Multivariate Behavioral Research, 19,* 33–47.

Vinokur, A. D., Price, R. H., & Caplan, R. D. (1991). From field experiments to program implementation: Assessing the potential outcomes of an experimental intervention program for unemployed persons. *American Journal of Community Psychology, 19,* 543–562.

Virdin, L. M. (1993). *A test of the robustness of estimators that model selection in the nonequivalent control group design.* Unpublished doctoral dissertation, Arizona State University.

Weiner, B. (Ed.). (1974). *Achievement motivation and attribution theory.* Morristown, NJ: General Learning Press.

West, S. G., & Aiken, L. S. (1997). Towards understanding individual effects in multiple component prevention programs: Design and analysis strategies. In K. Bryant, M. Windle, & S. G. West (Eds.), *The science of prevention: Methodological advances from alcohol and substance abuse research* (pp. 167–210). Washington, DC: American Psychological Association.

West, S. G., Aiken, L. S., & Todd, M. (1993). Probing the effects of individual components in multiple component prevention programs. *American Journal of Community Psychology, 21,* 571–605.

West, S. G., & Hepworth, J. T. (1991). Statistical issues in the study of temporal data: Daily experiences. *Journal of Personality, 59,* 611–662.

West, S. G., Hepworth, J. T., McCall, M. A., & Reich, J. W. (1989). An evaluation of Arizona's July 1992 drunk driving law: Effects on the city of Phoenix. *Journal of Applied Social Psychology, 19,* 1212–1237.

West, S. G., Newsom, J. T., & Fenaughty, A. M. (1992). Publication trends in *JPSP*: Stability and change in the topics, methods, and theories across two decades. *Personality and Social Psychology Bulletin, 18,* 473–484.

West, S. G., & Sagarin, B. (in press). Subject selection and loss in randomized experiments. In L. Bickman (Ed.), *Contributions to research design: Donald Campbell's legacy* (Vol. 2, pp. 117–154). Thousand Oaks, CA: Sage.

Wilkinson, L. and the Task Force on Statistical Inference (1999). Statistical methods in psychology journals: Guidelines and explanations. *American Psychologist, 54,* 594–604.

Willett, J. B., & Sayer, A. G. (1994). Using covariance structure analysis to detect correlates and predictors of change. *Psychological Bulletin, 116,* 363–381.

Winer, B. J. (1971). *Statistical principles in experimental design* (2nd ed.). New York: McGraw-Hill.

Wolchik, S. A., West, S. G., Sandler, I. N., Tein, J.-Y., Coatsworth, D., Lengua, L., Weiss, L., Anderson, E. R., Greene, S. M., & Griffin, W. A. (in press). An experimental evaluation of theory mother and mother-child programs for children of divorce. *Journal of Consulting and Clinical Psychology.*

CHAPTER FOUR

Computer Simulation Methods for Social Psychology

REID HASTIE AND GAROLD STASSER

A great teacher once described the activity of science as "the orderly arrangement of what, at the moment, appear to be facts" (Patrick Suppes in a philosophy of science course attended by one of the authors of this chapter). One implication of this quotation is that the activity of constructing "orderly arrangements" (theories) is as important as the other primary scientific activity of collecting "what at the moment, appear to be facts." It is important to remember that the ultimate goal of scientific research is not to analyze data or to calculate significance tests, but to produce theories that provide understanding and control of their subject phenomena. However, the methods of creating, using, and modifying scientific theories are neglected in our educational curricula in all of the sciences (cf. McGuire, 1983, 1989, 1997). Whereas the other chapters in this volume are about methods used to collect and extract descriptions of empirical phenomena from data, this chapter is about methods for "doing theorizing."

The defining characteristic of a scientific theory is that its function is to represent some aspects of the world in an abstract conceptual system. Usually scientific representations emphasize causal relationships among the events they describe, in contrast to other types of representations in theological, philosophical, or artistic theories. In applying a theory, the investigator maps objects and relations in the world onto elements and relations in an orderly, usually formal system. Consequently, the theory is an abstract representation of the world. Once a theory has been constructed, its implications about conditions in the empirical phenomena that lie within its scope may be derived. In psychology, this derivation process is usually relatively informal; the theorist thinks as hard and as clearly as he or she can about what the theory implies.

Given a specific interpretation of the theory, its consequences can be treated as predictions to be compared with data collected from the world to determine the degree of correspondence between the theory and the world. This stage of the process involves "operational," top-down interpretations, predictions, or models, as well as statistical, bottom-up interpretations of the data. The data usually lead to revisions or extensions of the original theory, and the theory is then modified in order to incorporate new data. This cycle of interpretation, empirical testing, and revision continues thoughout the life of a scientific theory. This is the essence of the scientific enterprise.

A summary of this process is presented in Figure 4.1 (based on Coombs, Raiffa, & Thrall, 1954, and Deutsch & Krauss, 1965). The figure describes the relations among several phases of the scientific process. The stages of research are interdependent and the directions of the arrows are often reversed. The goal of this process is to construct a valid theory of the world that is tested by comparing its implications to the observed data. The problem of evaluating theories by testing their empirical consequences has both statistical and logical aspects. The statistical problems involved in the verification process are those of determining how well the model fits the data and how likely it is to be correct given the empirical evidence. Most of the other

Partial support for the preparation of this chapter was provided by National Science Foundation (NSF) Grant SBR9410288 to Reid Hastie and NSF Grant SBR9410584 to Garold Stasser. We thank J. R. Gleason, Chick Judd, and Harry Reis for their valuable comments on simulation methods and on this chapter.

Correspondence should be directed to Reid Hastie, Psychology Department, Box 345, University of Colorado, Boulder, CO 80309 (e-mail: reid.hastie @ colorado.edu).

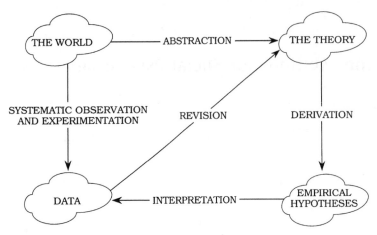

Figure 4.1. A summary of the major activities and "objects" that are involved in scientific investigation (based on Coombs, Raiffa, & Thrall, 1954).

chapters in this volume are about these methods; they are most relevant to the lower lefthand corner of Figure 4.1, whereas the present chapter focuses on the upper righthand corner.

From a logical viewpoint it is important to understand that a theory can only be rejected on the basis of data, not proved. If a theory implies certain characteristics of the data, then the absence of these characteristics is sufficient to reject the model. But the presence of these characteristics does not imply the model – although this presence does give the model inductive support. As the physicist Albert Einstein put it:

The scientific theorist is not to be envied. For Nature, or more precisely the experiment, is an inexorable and not very friendly judge of his (sic) work. It never says "Yes" to a theory. In the most favorable cases it says "Maybe," and in a great majority of cases simply "No." If an experiment agrees with a theory it means for the latter "Maybe," and if it does not agree it means "No." Probably every theory will some day experience its "No" – most theories, soon after conception.

For example, if a particular theory of social judgment predicts that an on-line impression will exhibit a primacy effect (early information about the person described has a larger impact on the impression than later information), then the failure to observe a primacy effect would lead us to reject the model. However, the observation of a primacy effect (as predicted) is not sufficient to establish the validity of the model, because this empirical phenomenon may be predicted by other models too. The theory is a sufficient condition for the existence of the predicted characteristics of the data, but these data characteristics are only necessary conditions for the validity of the theory.

One more preliminary: We find it useful to divide psychological theories into three levels of abstraction. At the top is the most abstract framework of background assumptions, usually stated verbally (N. H. Anderson, 1981, pp. 2–10; J. R. Anderson, 1990, pp. 23–38; for good examples of top-level frameworks). For example, these frameworks might include general assumptions, such as that behavior is multiply caused by conscious and unconscious thoughts, that a primary goal of cognition is to create a mental model of the situation in which the thinker is located, that many judgments and behaviors can only be understood when that situation model has been measured, that behavior is fundamentally rationally adaptive, etc. This abstract framework is what philosophers call a "scientific paradigm" (Kuhn, 1970) or a "research tradition" (Laudan, 1977; see Von Eckardt, 1993, for a comprehensive discussion of these concepts with an explication of the structure of modern theories of cognitive science).

At the next level "down," at a medium level of abstraction, is what most psychologists refer to as "The Theory": a collection of principles that is specific enough to serve as the basis to derive predictions of behavioral phenomena. In cognitive psychology, this level is often referred to as the "cognitive architecture." N. H. Anderson's "averaging model" (1981, pp. 58–73) and Leon Festinger's "social communication theory" (1950) are good examples of this level of a theory in social psychology (the more abstract framework for N. H. Anderson's theory was his information integration theory, N. H. Anderson, 1981; and the framework for Festinger's theories was Kurt Lewin's "gestalt field theory," Lewin, 1951).

Finally, and most concrete, when theories are used to make predictions that can be compared with behavioral data, they are specified to apply to a concrete, usually experimental task. For example, N. H. Anderson's (1981) averaging model is applied to the Asch (1946) impression formation task to yield predictions of order effects in the task or Festinger's "social communication theory" is applied to a committee policymaking task to predict the contents of discussion (Schachter, 1951). We call this most concrete level the "task-specific model." Obviously, our usage of these terms (framework, theory, and model) is not followed by everyone in social psychology, but we find the distinctions and their ordering by abstractness to be helpful.

There are three popular media for social psychological theories. We briefly introduce verbal statements and mathematical modeling approaches and then spend the rest of the chapter describing the computer simulation approach. Our pedagogical approach is to teach by example, and we explicate the motivations, details, and achievements of two computer simulation models, one of individual social cognition and the other of the group decision-making process.

A survey of social psychological theories would reveal that most of them are expressed in the form of verbal statements. Sometimes these verbal summaries are frustratingly obscure and difficult to pin down (Greenwald, 1975; Harris, 1976). But, historically, the most influential, productive, and brilliant social psychological theories have been written in the verbal medium (e.g., Festinger's theories of social influence [1950], social comparison [1951], and cognitive dissonance [1957]; McGuire's information processing theory of attitude change [1968]; Kelley's attribution theory [1973]). In our view, the best style for the expression of a verbal theory is in the form of a succinct set of well-formed axioms or principles. But, even here there is enormous variation in the style with which such theoretical axioms are written (cf. Wyer & Srull, 1986; vs. Festinger, 1950).

The second most popular medium for theorizing in social psychology is the mathematical modeling approach. Historically, the most enduring examples have appeared in research on attitude change (McGuire, 1969) and cognitive consistency (Abelson et al., 1968; although their popularity in these areas may have waned; cf. Eagley & Chaiken, 1993). The most ambitious approach to the mathematical modeling of social phenomena is the work of Norman Anderson and his colleagues (N. H. Anderson, 1981, 1991, 1996). N. H. Anderson applied his "cognitive algebra" models to phenomena ranging from husband and wife decision making to the psychophysics of color perception. His best-known models of social phenomena describe the impression-formation process. His famous averaging principle for impression formation is one of the most general and established psychological "laws" in the history of the field (although as Anderson recognized, there are many exceptions; cf. Hogarth & Einhorn, 1992).

The present chapter is an introduction to the third approach to "doing theory" in social psychology, computer simulation or computational modeling.

The computer simulation approach has a long history in social psychology (Abelson, 1968; Hovland, 1960; Ostrom, 1988), although it has caught on more slowly in social than in the cognitive and neuroscience areas of psychology. But, computational modeling is becoming increasingly popular, as we become more and more high-tech. Most graduate students entering the field of social psychology today are "computer literate," and many already have programming skills. Nonetheless, computer simulation is still less popular than the other two approaches to theory, particularly in the social sciences. This chapter is written to convince you that it should be more widely used.

The theoretical strategy in computer modeling is to create a software "program" that mimicks the essential behaviors of the system that is the subject of the theory. For example, if the program were intended to simulate a social judgment process, it would take as input a representation of the information available to the social perceiver and produce as output a social judgment. A program intended to mimic small group decision making would begin with a collection of simulated group members, each endowed with a background of decision-relevant information, simulate their interaction, and output a group decision.

We want to emphasize that the computer program is a medium for theorizing, but it does not prescribe a necessary form for the theory. Just because a theory that describes a "social cognition process" is implemented in the medium of a computer programming language does not mean that the theorist has assumed that the mind operates like a particular electronic computer. For example, theories of neural functioning in biological-chemical systems or physical events in meterological systems occur in substances that are very different from electronic circuits, but these theories are still implemented in the computer simulation medium. Another common confusion is the belief that computer simulation is not a good medium in which to represent a theory about human emotions or unconscious, implicit mental processes; after all, a computer doesn't "have" emotions or consciousness. This misconception also stems from a misunderstanding of the use of the computer as a theoretical medium. The computer is used to represent and "run" the theory (represented as a computer program). But the machine itself is not assumed to provide a physical analogy to the mind; the theory is "in" the concepts embodied in the program. (This point about the difference between a theoretical medium and the theory's subject matter is confusing because there are many theorists [see Gardner, 1985; and Von Eckardt, 1993, for examples] who do believe that the electronic computer, the machine, is a good inspiration for a theory of the human mind as well as a good medium for such a theory.)

As with other behavioral theories, the goals of simulation are to predict and explain the behaviors of the system that is under study. Simulation models are just trying to do what the other kinds of social theories do – predict and explain social behaviors. However, computer models are often more complex and more "dynamic" than the other kinds of theories. Nonetheless, computer simulation is subject to the same rules of good style, successful performance, and good practice that apply to the other forms of theorizing. The creation of an original, insightful theory is as difficult in the computer simulation medium as it is in any other format. Just like the other approaches to social psychological theory, computer simulation models can fail because they are incomplete, internally inconsistent, incomprehensible, or simply poor descriptions of the empirical phenomena they are intended to explain.

Computer models are subject to the critical scrutiny of the scientific community as are all theoretical expressions, but the process of developing and implementing computer models promotes several desirable characteristics in the end product. First, the construction of a computer model helps its author create an internally consistent theory. Second, the flexibility of the computer simulation medium (the representational power of modern programming languages) encourages theorists to state their theories more "completely" and to leave fewer assumptions implicit than when working with the alternative theoretical media. Finally, the computer model provides an efficient deductive tool whose power to derive theoretical implications cannot be matched by other forms of theory.

CURRENT COMPUTER SIMULATION MODELS OF SOCIAL PSYCHOLOGICAL PHENOMENA

As we wrote this chapter (in 1998), a search through the major social psychological journals unearthed about two dozen examples of computer simulation models. This number is approximate because it is impossible to draw a bright line to indicate where social psychology stops and cognate fields like experimental economics, sociology, and political science begin, and the number is constantly changing as more examples are published. The models can be grouped by the level of social phenomena to which they were applied: individual social cognition, social interactions in dyads and small groups (fewer than 20 members), and social phenomena in large organizations and social systems.

The social psychological simulation models place a heavy emphasis on "fitting" empirical findings from specific experiments (this emphasis seems to be heavier than in cognitive science; cf. Simon & Kaplan, 1989). Another distinctive, but not unique, characteristic of these models is that they almost all mimic behavioral phenomena "across time." That is, the principles underlying each simulation program, the implementation, and the type of data to which the model's behavior is compared all involve temporally ordered sequences of behavior. This is in contrast to the characteristics and applications of most verbal and mathematical models in social psychology; usually these models predict input and output relationships, but do not prescribe the details of events across time.

Among the more empirically driven simulations there are several clusters of related models. First, there is a collection of models that fall within the "connectionist" approach to theorizing about individual cognition. These would include the models proposed by Smith (1996); Read, Vanman, and Miller (1997); Kashima and Kerekes (1994); Kunda and Thagard (1996); Shultz and Lepper (1996), and McClelland, Rumelhart, and Hinton (1986). Second, there is a collection of simulation models that are based on the principle of reasoning from concrete exemplars or instances; these are the models described by Linville, Fischer, and Salovey (1989) and by Smith and Zarate (1992; see also Smith, 1991). Third, there are models of social cognition based on associative network representations of social information (Bond & Brockett, 1987; Bond, Jones, & Weintraub, 1985; Lui & Brewer, 1983). Fourth, there are many models that rely on information-pooling and opinion updating to characterize the consensus-seeking process in small groups, including models by Stasser (1988); Hastie, Penrod, and Pennington (1983; Penrod & Hastie, 1980); and Gigone and Hastie (1996). Fifth, there is a collection of models based on social exchange processes represented in hypothetical payoff matrices underlying social interactions (e.g., models by Messick & Liebrand, 1993; Kelley, 1985; Huesmann & Loevinger, 1976; and Axelrod, 1984; Axelrod & Hamilton, 1981). We would also direct the reader's attention to reviews by Carley (1996) and MacKinnon (1994; see also Heise, 1985) for models of more global sociological and organizational phenomena.

Some simulation models are not focused on specific empirical findings, but are intended to provide sufficiency or existence demonstrations that certain qualitative effects can be produced by (usually unexpectedly) simple sets of idealized assumptions. Axelrod and

Hamilton's (1981) seminal work on the evolution of cooperation in tournaments among adaptive social exchange algorithms is an example of such a demonstration. Axelrod and Hamilton (1981; and Axelrod, 1984) showed that completely self-interested "robots" could exhibit cooperative behavior when following certain highly adaptive strategies in a simulated prisoner's dilemma game environment. Nowak, Szamrej, and Latané (1990) provided another seminal example: A surprisingly simple model of social influence and attitude change processes yielded unexpected stable, coherent, clusters of polarized individuals in a hypothetical geographic space. And, Kalick and Hamilton (1986, 1988; Aron, 1988) showed that a population of mate-seeking individuals would exhibit "matching" (individuals with similar levels of social attractiveness were paired at a much higher than chance rate), even though the individuals' goals were to "maximize" the attractiveness of their mates.

AN INTRODUCTION TO THE ACTIVITY OF CONSTRUCTING COMPUTER SIMULATION MODELS

We describe two computer simulation models from our own research to illustrate the essential features of the approach. The first example is from the domain of individual social cognition. It is a model of the social judgment and memory processes that occur naturally when one person meets another (Hastie, 1988). The second example is a model of group consensus-seeking processes, including the kinds of interpersonal phenomena that occur in committees, panels, and juries that make social decisions (Stasser, 1988, 1990).

The Impression and Memory Processor (IMP) Model of Cognitive Processes in Impression Formation

The impression formation process that occurs when one person meets another for the first time is a frequent and important social event. It is a rare person who can overcome a "bad first impression" to achieve success in the political, business, or informal social world. Social psychologists have developed several experimental versions of the naturally occurring impression-formation situation that make it easier for the researcher to control, repeat, and measure the phenomena under study (N. H. Anderson, 1965; Asch, 1946). The experimental task that we model is most like the impression-formation process that occurs outside the laboratory when one person ("source") tells

another ("perceiver") about a third person ("target"); the perceiver forms an impression of the target based on the secondhand information communicated by the source. The experimenter plays the role of the "source" and the participant plays the role of the "perceiver."

The simulation model, IMP, was designed to perform the impression formation and memory tasks according to one modal strategy. The human participant is shown a list of trait adjectives and then a collection of film clips that depict the target character engaging in behaviors that have implications for his personality attributes. The participant is instructed to form an impression of the character and, after the traits and behaviors are presented, the participant rates the likeability, intelligence, and sociability of the target person. Subsequently, the participant recalls as many of the descriptive behaviors as possible: a "free recall" memory test.

The empirical phenomena that are the focus of the computer simulation modeling effort have been obtained in many experiments (N. H. Anderson, 1965; Hastie & Kumar, 1979; Srull, 1981). The best-known findings in these studies are that the impression resembles an "average" of the implications of the individual items of information and that information that is unexpected tends to be well-remembered and has an especially large impact on the impression. The so-called "incongruity-enhanced recall" effect has been observed in dozens of experiments (Rohan & Pettigrew, 1992; Stangor & McMillan, 1992).

A Model of the Task Environment

About one third of the IMP model is composed of hypotheses about what the task environment is like for the perceiver. It is an important, but neglected, point that computer simulation models cannot leave the theorist's assumptions about the nature of the environment implicit. In some cases, where the psychological theory is a theory about human behavior in an artificial environment, the environment can be literally incorporated in the theory (e.g., when the task itself is implemented in an electronic tutorial program or display-based technological environment; J. R. Anderson, 1996; Meyer & Kieras, 1997). In most psychological theories, the environment must be described theoretically, and the theorist's assumptions about the environment may be as critical in determining the success of the model as his or her assumptions about the mind that adapts to the environment (cf. J. R. Anderson, 1990; Brunswik, 1956; Fiedler, 1996; Pinker & Prince, 1988). One important advantage of computer modeling is that it forces researchers to answer theoretical questions explicitly; a simulation model won't run on implicit assumptions.

The experimental impression-formation task can be divided into four parts: (a) the "learning phase," in which the participant studies information about the hypothetical person (the adjectives and the behavior descriptions), forms an impression of the kind of person described, and stores this information in long-term memory; (b) the judgment task, in which the participant reports the impression; (c) the "retention interval," in which information is retained in long-term memory and some forgetting occurs; and (d) the recall task, in which the participant searches long-term memory and reports as many of the to-be-remembered behavior descriptions as possible.

Essentially, the environment is defined by the lists of stimulus information that describe the "characters" (target persons) about whom impressions are to be formed. IMP was not designed to address the daunting problem of reading and comprehending information from text. The solution we chose was to use human participants as translators to encode the stimulus trait words and sentences (describing trait-relevant behaviors) into numerical scale values representing the implications of the information for the sociability, intelligence, and likeability of a person who exhibited the trait or performed the behavior (see Fuhrman, Bodenhausen, & Lichtenstein, 1989, for published norms for similar materials). Thus, the sentence, "He beat another player to win the chess tournament," received an average sociability rating of 3.8 (on a 0–9 scale), an intelligence rating of 8.2, and a likeability rating of 4.2 from pretest participants. These numbers (3.8, 8.2, and 4.2) were provided to the computer program as input whenever a human participant had received the "chess tournament" sentence. The program operated on these numbers to form its impression and to perform other cognitive functions.

Because the trait and sentence materials were presented as lists in which all the contents referred to a single "target" stimulus person, the simulation program was designed with several flexible parameters that could change to accommodate varying list lengths and orderings of stimulus information. The specific values for these parameters were set to match the design of each experiment for which the simulation model attempted to mimic human participants' performance. For example, if the experimental lists presented to humans had contained 10 descriptive items, the list length parameter in the simulation model was set to 10 items. If the first item in this list of 10 items was the "chess tournament" item, the first set of impression values input to the program was 3.8, 8.2, and 4.2 (see example above). Essentially the program was given parameters that told it what form of input to expect (list lengths, impression scale value vectors, etc.). Because the program's responses were impression rating numbers and lists of items recalled from memory, the response was simply a list of the impression numbers and item labels. These numbers and symbols could be compared directly with individual human participants' ratings and recall protocols (although most comparisons were between average, grouped data from the simulation and from the human participants).

A Model of the Individual's Mind

A second collection of theoretical assumptions composes a model of the human mind. This collection of relatively immutable concepts, operators, and processing system structures is referred to as the architecture of the cognitive system (J. R. Anderson, 1983; Newell, Rosenbloom, & Laird, 1989). The overarching organization of IMP follows the multiple memory store "geography" that was popularized by Atkinson and Shiffrin (1968).

In IMP, the central feature of the cognitive architecture is a limited capacity working memory. (Initially the capacity was variable, but initial tests of IMP fixed the capacity at three to-be-remembered items of information.) The second component of the architecture is an unlimited capacity long-term memory. Information about the target person is initially deposited in working memory and eventually transferred into long-term memory. No information is completely lost from memory, and forgetting is conceptualized as a retrieval-based phenomenon. Information in long-term memory is effectively forgotten if it cannot be "found" during retrieval.

Information is stored in a person memory structure composed of slots or addressable locations in the computer's memory (Figure 4.2). Each slot contains the description of a behavior, the impression numbers (including summary impression values as well as the individual item values), and links or "pointers" to other slots within the structure. These pointers allow the computer program to move from information in one slot to information in another slot if the two are linked by a directional pointer. These pointers simulate the associative activation of one item of information following another that could occur in deliberate memory retrieval or in free associative rumination.

We assume that the human information processor can create and apply many different mental strategies

NO.	LABEL	SOC	INT	EVAL	ASSOCIATIVE LINKS
I9	Won the chess tournament	2.8	8.2	4.2	
F3	Sold door-to-door	8.6	4.1	3.1	
I2	Published the *New Yorker* article	4.2	7.2	6.1	
F6	Helped a neighbor	6.2	5.2	7.1	

	SOC	INT	EVAL
IMPRESSION	5.2	5.8	5.0

Figure 4.2. The format for memories of one "target" individual in the IMP computer simulation.

to solve the various problems posed for such systems by human experimenters, but the IMP model is a one-strategy model. Other, more complex simulation models attempt to create strategies for novel tasks when presented feedback about the successfulness of their initial strategies (e.g., Soar is a model that creatively learns cognitive strategies from feedback; Newell, 1990). At present there are few multistrategy models that attempt to represent the diversity of strategies that are exhibited by human participants in laboratory tasks (Payne, Bettman, & Johnson , 1993, provide a good example of a multistrategy model).

The initial version of IMP was designed only for the impression-formation and person memory task, and it performed this task according to one strategy. The set of operations, elementary information processes, that are needed to write the dynamic portions of the simulation model are also part of the cognitive architecture. In the initial version of IMP, the list of these more elementary operations includes operators that write and read information in working memory, operators that read and write information in long-term memory, operations to form links between items of information (these operations are applied in working memory, and the links are transferred into the long-term memory representation), operators that search memory by moving from node to node along the associative links, and, finally, operators that compute an impression value from the numerical inputs that are associated with each of the behavior descriptions.

Another approach to simulating the cognitive architecture is now available. Researchers can obtain computer programs (really programming environments) from theoretical psychologists that embody assumptions about a cognitive architecture. For example, one can purchase a Parallel Distributed Processing (PDP) connectionist architecture (McClelland & Rumelhart, 1989), the A Cognitive Theory–Rational (ACT–R) architecture (Anderson, 1993), the Executive-Process Interactive Control (EPIC) architecture (Meyer & Kieras, 1997), or the Concurrent Capacity Constrained Activation-based Production System (3CAPS) architecture (Just & Carpenter, 1992) from their inventors. If, for example, a researcher accepted the assumptions of the ACT–R theory of cognitive architecture, he or she could implement the basic ACT–R modeling environment on his or her own computer (this programming environment is sold with copies of the introduction to the theoretical system; J. R. Anderson, 1993). Then the researcher could proceed to account for behavior in the tasks of interest (e.g., impression formation and person memory) within the constraints imposed by the ACT–R assumptions about the operations of working

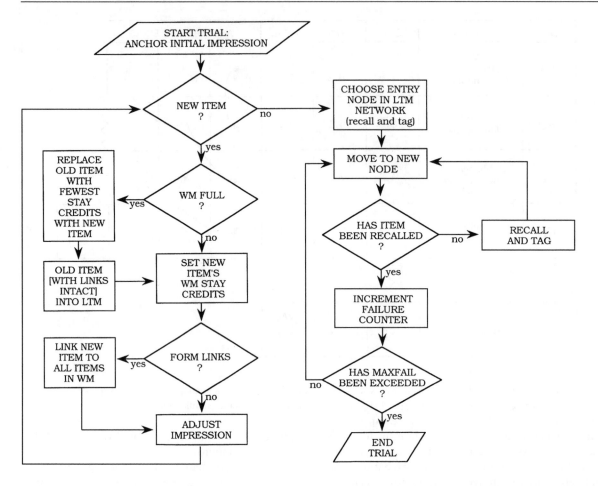

Figure 4.3. Summary of the flow of information and control in the IMP computer simulation program.

memory, associative structuring of long-term memory, memory retrieval, and inference to an induced impression.

There are many advantages from adopting another theorist's well-designed simulation environment: generality, systematic development, and the benefits of being able to share solutions to common methodological problems of task analysis, cognitive strategy design, and even approaches to data analysis and model evaluation with other like-minded modelers. (We might have chosen this route in the development of IMP, but IMP was developed before these cognitive architectures were available.)

The Operation of the IMP Computer Simulation

Once a cognitive architecture has been designed, the task of developing the simulation model becomes one of writing a program within the constraints of the architecture that can accomplish the impression-formation and memory recall tasks. The IMP model is divided into two basic parts. The first part acquires new information, forming an impression of the stimulus person "on-line" and creating an associatively linked long-term memory structure (Hastie & Park, 1986). The second part goes into operation when the experimenter signals the program that it is time to recall the information on which the original impression was based. Then the model enters its long-term memory store and searches to locate and report information about the descriptive items that it learned in the first part of the task.

The IMP model was implemented in the Turbo Pascal programming language on IBM/PC microcomputers. The model was composed of many subroutines or components. A flow chart summarizing the organization of the basic processing model (Figure 4.3) is a common way of outlining the substages in a processing task strategy and of displaying the flow of control and information in the simulation. The impression-formation process in the model is an anchor and adjusts algebraic computation that implements the weighted averaging principle for impression formation (N. H. Anderson, 1965, 1981). The initial anchor for this impression is provided by the ensemble of trait adjectives that is presented to the participant before the behavior descriptions are presented. These adjectives induce an initial impression of the target character as relatively intelligent (or unintelligent), sociable (or unsociable), etc.

The anchor and adjust process updates the initial impression by calculating an average of the old impression value and the new information. In the present application we simply weighted the old impression and new information equally. Such equal weighting emulates a recency process, as the last item of information will contribute one half of the value of the final impression. The computation was performed separately for each of the trait dimensions representing the scaled meaning of each new behavior description. (Remember, these scale values were obtained prior to the experiments, by asking pretest participants to rate the experimental materials on 0–9 scales).

Working memory is conceptualized as a limited capacity store, in which items are held while key processes such as impression updating and the formation of associative links between items occur. In the applications of the model reported in this chapter, a three-item capacity was selected. The value of three was selected by systematically trying several plausible values for working memory capacity and then using the value that yielded the best fits to the human participants' behavioral data. This method of parameter selection is a common technique in computer applications. By considering various working memory sizes, we are implicitly accepting the claim that working memory does not have a fixed capacity, at least as measured in units like numbers of words or phrases. That is, working memory capacity varies depending on factors such as the nature of the to-be-retained items of information, the participant's expertise at the task, motivation to perform, and other demands on the participant's cognitive resources (Ericsson & Kintsch, 1995). Of course, the acceptable values for such a theory-laden parameter must be consistent with findings from research by other psychologists who are concerned with the basic capacity of working memory in comprehension tasks (e.g., a value of 20 sentences would not "make sense" in the context of other theoretical proposals for the capacity of working memory).

Three slots within working memory are allocated to maintaining the current impression (the updated value computed according to the weighting and averaging anchor and adjust rule), and three item slots are allocated to contain the currently active and available behavior descriptions. At the beginning of one run of the model, average impressions are computed from the trait ensemble and stored in the impression slots associated with likability, sociability, and intelligence impressions. The three behavior description item slots are, of course, empty at the beginning. When the first behavior description is presented to the model its contents are written into one of the working memory slots, and numerical information attached to the behavior description is entered into algebraic computations to adjust the three impressions.

The fundamental "background process" of working memory is the determination of which behavior description items will remain in the three-item store. This decision is governed by the system's goal of forming an accurate impression of another person. In IMP, when working memory is full (after the third item has been presented), new items replace old items with an item's priority to remain in working memory determined by its relevance to the impression judgment and by the duration of its stay in working memory. As they enter working memory, items receive "credits" that they "spend" on each cycle of the model (a cycle is counted every time a new stimulus item is presented and enters working memory). Items that are informative about the impression (i.e., items that have strong implications represented as extreme scale values on the trait dimensions) and recent items have an advantage (i.e., they have the most "stay-time credits") to remain in working memory.

Without going into exact details, relevance is determined for each item by consulting the extremity of its value (extremity from the midpoint on the trait rating dimension, which was equal to 4.5 on the 0–9 scale) so that items close to 0 or 9 on the scale (according to pretest participants' ratings) are deemed more informative, more relevant, and have an advantage to stay longer in working memory. Relevance is determined when the item is first entered into working memory by consulting the extremity of the item on each of the three trait dimensions. The result of this inspection of the item's extremity is to assign a stay-time credit value to the item that ranges from 0 to 10. This number is the number of cycles that item would remain in working memory, if the three-item working memory store were not overloaded by the input of a fourth item.

On each cycle all items' stay-time credit values are decremented by 1; when an item's value reaches 0, it is "kicked out" into long-term memory. When working memory is full (it contains three items) and a new item is presented, the old item with the lowest number of stay credits is displaced into long-term memory. When an item is moved into long-term memory it is not forgotten and is still linked to other items in memory. Thus, the second critical process that occurs in working memory is the formation of these interitem long-term memory associative links.

The formation of links is modeled as a stochastic process that is influenced by the unexpectedness of a new item in the context of the current impression of the stimulus person. If a new item's trait implications (the scale values on the three 0–9 social trait dimensions) are highly discrepant from the current impression, the probability of all items in working memory being linked to the new item is high (e.g., .90). But, if the item is close to the current impression, we might think of it as providing redundant information about the stimulus character, then the probability of link formation is much lower (e.g., .20). The probability of an item being linked to other items in working memory is a direct, linear function of its discrepancy from the current impression, ranging from a low of .20 to a high of 1.00.

The link formation rule is a specification of the principle that surprising items will have an advantage in being linked to other items in memory compared with less surprising items. The critical mediating variable that ultimately determines recall of information about the character is the number of links or the elaboration of the memory trace in the context of other memory traces (Bradshaw & Anderson, 1982). Hastie (1984; see also Hastie & Kumar, 1979, and Srull, 1981) found that the surprising, informative items were especially likely to trigger explanatory thinking when a person was trying to form an impression of another person. He hypothesized that a byproduct of this explanatory reasoning process was a more elaborated memory trace for the information that the perceiver was attempting to explain.

Items that are displaced from working memory are transferred into a long-term memory where they remain in an associative network of nodes representing each behavior description within a pattern of connections determined by the stochastic linking process in working memory. As we noted, these connections are the pathways for retrieval during subsequent attempts to recall information. When recall starts, an entry point is selected from all the nodes in the network, and a serial node-by-node search process starts at that point. The selection is driven probabilistically by the number of links emanating from each node; nodes with more links are more likely to be selected as entry points. Only items that are connected to the entry point nodes

(directly or indirectly via intermediate nodes) can be recalled. The search process proceeds by recalling information about the current node (i.e., writing out a description of the behavior represented by that node), if it has not been recalled before. Then a departing link is selected at random, and the retrieval process searches down that link to focus on the next node.

The search process monitors the number of times it moves to a new node that represents an "old" (already recalled) item, and the model terminates its search when it has failed to find a "new" item on five trials cumulatively. Like the value for the capacity of working memory, the value of five was selected after systematically trying several values for this parameter, to maximize the goodness of fit between the model's performance and human participants' behavior. The device of modeling memory search as a random path selection process with a failure counter stopping rule was based on earlier suggestions by J. R. Anderson and Bower (1973) and more recently by Gillund and Shiffrin (1984).

Note that the model incorporates a "cue-dependent forgetting" principle; items are never lost from long-term memory, they are just "inaccessible" to the associative search process (Tulving, 1974). In the development of the model, we experimented with various forms of forgetting processes (e.g., items are "erased" from long-term memory and forgotten forever), but found that the permanent "availability," selective "accessibility" process provided the best acccount of our participants' behavior (e.g., they usually performed at almost perfect levels of accuracy on straightforward recognition memory tests).

COMMENT: RANDOM PROCESSES IN THE MODEL. One aspect of computer simulation modeling that stands out as virtually unique is the use of pseudorandom number generators to introduce variation into a model's performance. Verbal theoretical statements could include references to random or haphazard processes, although we cannot think of any examples. Mathematical models sometimes include stochastic, probabilistic components, so that derivations of predictions include predictions of the variability of distributions of outcomes. But, we know of no approaches except for some forms of computer simulation modeling in which the model "deliberately" consults a separate "machine" that provides it with random inputs to inject into its behavior. (Although, not all computer simulation models include random components; many simulation models are "deterministic" [e.g., Newell & Simon's, 1972, models of thinking].)

Both of the models we are using as examples in this chapter include random components. For example, the operation of forming links between a new item in working memory and other items currently in working memory is governed partly by a random process. After the probability of link formation has been calculated deterministically (based on the difference between the new item's scale values and the current impression scale values), a random number algorithm is run by the computer, and the number that is returned is used to decide "randomly" whether or not that particular item on that particular run of the simulation forms links (Marsaglia, Zaman, & Tsang, 1990). For example, suppose an item enters working memory and the summary difference between its scale values and the current impression values is calculated to be 2; then the probability of forming links is deterministically calculated to be .40. But, then a random number generator produces a value in the program (a value that can range from 0.00 to 1.00) and every time that value is less than or equal to .40, a link will be formed; otherwise (when the value is greater than .40) no links are formed. Thus, on one run of the model a link might be formed, but on the next run with identical list and impression values a link might not be formed. If everything is running correctly, on 40% of the runs links would be formed.

It is instructive to consider the question: Why would a theoretician deliberately add random processes to a theory? Many theorists argue that it is a mistake to include random components in a model. Cotton (1982) provided a useful discussion of this issue with examples from cognitive psychology. Poincaré (1908/1952) provided a seminal and remarkably prescient discussion of the circumstances under which deterministic prediction is likely to fail (although, he assumes this world is fundamentally deterministic). Poincaré's discussion identifies the conditions under which we believe that it is reasonable to consider including a random process in a simulation model:

1. When a process follows deterministic laws, but miniscule changes in initial conditions produce large differences in the outcomes produced by the process (i.e., what we might call a chaotic system today), random process models may be useful. For example, Vallacher and Nowak (1994) have concluded that the time course of ruminative evaluations follows complex nonlinear dynamical patterns, such that a person's evaluation at any point in time is predictable, but heavily dependent on precisely where the person's thoughts started. It may be theoretically effective to simply use a random process to simulate

these patterns, at least until the chaotic dynamics are better understood.

2. When a process follows deterministic laws, but the outcome is multiply determined by many interacting causal effects, random process models may be useful. For example, whether links will be formed between a new item in working memory and other items currently "active" in memory depends on many subtle aspects of the individual participant's interpretation of those items, the availability of cognitive resources, the participant's interpretation of the experimental instructions, individual differences in the participant's appetite for thinking (Blair, Jarvis, & Petty, 1996), etc. Although, in principle, most of the variability in performance could be "explained" by measuring dozens of relevant variables, the theorist may want to ignore those subtleties to focus on the molar judgment process. Summarizing (and simplifying) the causal dynamics by incorporating a random process may be a useful theoretical strategy to allow the theoretical enterprise to move ahead on important questions.

3. When a process follows deterministic laws, but the values of some of the events that are causal in the process are unknown, random process models may be useful. This situation is likely to arise when we attribute the underlying causes to a lower, substrate level of causal activity. For example, we may believe that some of the determinants of link formation derive from the physical state of a person's brain at the time that an item of information is perceived and comprehended. For example, the blood flow to one part of the brain might be momentarily low and prevent the formation of associative links. Although, hypothetically these lower level events could be measured and used to explain variation in cognitive activity, no current researchers would attempt to introduce this level of causation into their theoretical model of social judgment. In a simulation model, the influence of the lower level events could be relegated to a random process in the model.

Our point is that a modeler should carefully think through the reasons for using a random mechanism before including one in a model, and then be explicit about those reasons in reports of the model. As a general rule, scientists avoid explanations that include references to randomness. But, the image of the scientific enterprise as the continual rennovation of a ship while it is sailing is apt. There are many circumstances where the careful postulation of stochastic processes allows us to concentrate on solving one theoretical problem while explicitly acknowledging (by treating a process as a random mechanism) that we are ignorant about related phenomena.

COMMENT: SETTING PARAMETERS IN A MODEL. Scientists use the term *parameter* to refer to a value of a variable in a model that is set at a constant level during one application of the model, but which can assume different values in new applications. The size of working memory is a good example of such a parameter in a psychological model. We settled on the parameter value of three items for all of the applications of the IMP model reported in this chapter. But, we would have changed the value of that parameter if we had applied the model to different materials (e.g., if our participants had based their impressions on lists of trait adjectives) or if we were trying to predict individual behavior (because we know that the effective size of working memory can vary across individuals; Ericsson & Kintsch, 1995; Just & Carpenter, 1992).

It is useful to distinguish between parameters that refer to aspects of the experimental tasks (e.g., the list lengths in the IMP experiments, the group sizes in the DISCUSS experiments) and to characteristics of the human participants (e.g., working memory capacity and the retrieval stopping rule value in IMP, or the parameters that determine probability of speaking and probability of forgetting in the DISCUSS model; see below). Usually task parameters are determined simply by consulting the conditions of the experimental situation that is being modeled, but the behavioral parameters are chosen to maximize the performance of the model.

Kerr, Stasser, and Davis (1979) identified two approaches to choosing parameter values: model fitting and model testing. In model fitting, the parameters are allowed to assume values that result in the best fit of the model's predictions to the actual data. That is, the range of permissible or interpretable values for a parameter is systematically explored to identify optimal values for reproducing a particular set of data. In model testing, the parameter values are based on theoretical considerations or empirical data. Often there are competing theoretical notions or conflicting empirical results that suggest different choices for the parameter values in question. In these cases, the success of the model can be competitively evaluated under the different conditions suggested by a priori evidence.

Efficient model fitting requires a way of computing the "best-fitting" parameter values from characteristics of the data. An approach that is familiar to all psychol-

ogy students is to choose parameters (e.g., the coefficients in a linear regression equation) to minimize the squared differences between a model's estimates and the to-be-fitted data, but there are many other techniques for maximizing the goodness-of-fit of a theoretical model (e.g., Dutton & Starbuck, 1971). In the case of IMP we settled for searches of the multidimensional parameter space (one dimension for each parameter being fitted) to find good values of parameters such as working memory capacity and the maximum failures retrieval stopping. We minimized a least-squares criterion value ([model prediction − human data]^2) to identify the best parameter values. These searches produced fits that were successful in reproducing the qualitative properties of human participants behavior.

Evaluating the IMP Model

The IMP model was used to model human behavior in several of the experimental tasks that Hastie, Srull, and their colleagues used to study impression formation. We will use one model–human comparison to illustrate the method (see Hastie, 1988, for more details). An experimental study of social impression formation was conducted by Hastie and Mazur (1981). Women college students were shown "letters from a dormitory counselor" (e.g., a letter describing the target character as, "One of the most intelligent people I've ever met") followed by a series of filmed behavior vignettes (e.g., a film clip of the protagonist winning a chess tournament) as the basis to form impressions of a male student. The film clips included two kinds of behaviors, labeled congruent (with the impression conveyed by the dormitory counselor's letter) and incongruent. Under some of the experimental conditions the incongruent behaviors were sharply inconsistent; the stimulus character performed a series of actions that were both denotatively and conotatively incongruent with the initial personality trait impression (e.g., the "high incongruent" acts implied he was stupid). Under other conditions, the "medium incongruity" actions were only conotatively inconsistent (e.g., the intelligent impression and actions [positive evaluation] were paired with socially hostile actions [negative evaluation]); and under still other conditions the "low incongruent" actions depicted a consistent, collateral aspect of the character's personality (e.g., intelligent impression and actions were mixed with friendly actions). The second experimental manipulation was of the relative numbers of the two types of actions in the film clips; the total set of 10 actions was composed of 9 congruent and 1 incongruent, 7 congruent and 3 incongruent, or 5 congruent and 5 incongruent actions. The guiding hypothesis was that the three types of "incongruent" actions would be treated differently during the impression-formation task and would be remembered at different rates.

Each of the stimulus traits and episodes was rated by an independent sample of participants, and the average "intelligence," "friendliness," and "likeability" ratings were used as scale values to create versions of the experimental stimuli to use as inputs to IMP. The experimental design was then recreated as a set of data files for IMP. Because IMP included two stochastic processes (link formation during the impression formation process and path selection during memory search) a Monte Carlo simulation procedure was applied to obtain estimates of the model's behavior on the experimental task. Essentially this amounted to running 1,000 simulation trials for each experimental condition (with different random number generator seeds for the stochastic processes) and using averages of the 1,000 trial samples as descriptive statistics to compare with the averages from the human participants.

Average human and IMP performances on the memory measures are displayed in Figure 4.4. In the top panel we can see that the human data exhibit the predicted patterns, with degree of incongruity and number of incongruent behaviors affecting the impression and memory measures. The second panel displays IMP's performance, and it is clear that, qualitatively, it is similar to the human behavior. The lower panels compare IMP's performance with the summaries of human behavior. The correlation between the average human and model performances was .84. However, correlation coefficients can be misleading (cf. N. H. Anderson, 1982, pp. 158–178), and so we display 95% confidence bounds around the empirical mean values to highlight any cases where the model and human performance were discrepant at the $p < .05$ level (Estes, 1997; interestingly, as Estes points out, confidence intervals are often mistakenly interpreted to show the range of values within which the mean of a replication is likely to fall, "95% of the time." However, the correct interpretation, as the interval within which the population mean is expected to fall 95% of the time is exactly appropriate for comparisons between a model like IMP and behavioral data). Obviously, IMP fits the human data quite well; only 1 human performance mean (out of 18) is outside of the confidence intervals.

It is important to notice that simulation models usually yield "point predictions" of behavior. Thus, a major contribution of the simulation modeling approach is that it puts the emphasis on evaluating theories by

their ability to make a priori and a posteriori (the IMP model-fitting example) predictions of where performance will be, rather than merely predicting directional differences (Meehl, 1967; see the large literature on the pathologies of overreliance on significance testing in psychological research; recently, Cohen, 1994; Loftus, 1996; Schmidt, 1996).

These tests of the model's performance follow the conventional logic of hypothesis testing learned in elementary statistics, but the differences being tested are between the theory's predictions and the data, not as in most textbook comparisons between two estimates from the data. The enterprise of using goodness-of-fit tests to evaluate a theoretical model's fit requires some subtle changes in the researcher's conceptualization about the hypothesis-testing logic. First, the aim is often to find an adequately fitting or best-fitting theoretical model, rather than to find out if empirical differences are reliable enough to warrant further investigation or interpretation. This shift of perspective requires rethinking issues such as alpha significance levels and statistical power. In our discussion of the DISCUSS simulation model (below) we introduce some more sophisticated competitive model testing approaches.

Another point about the tests of IMP is that they involved comparisons between average model performance and average human behavior. The model performed the experimental task many times (1,000 "simulation runs"), and then the average of the model's behavior (averaged across "runs" and lists) was compared with the average of the human behavior (averaged across participants and lists). This is a common practice in evaluating simulations; the focus is on average behavior, not on individual behavior on one experimental trial. However, the simulation approach is flexible enough to model individual behavior. For example, Newell and Simon's (1972) landmark simulation models were aimed at accounting for one participant's performance on one trial of their experimental tasks. Simulation models also offer special advantages in the endeavor of accounting for individual differences through adjustments of individual difference parameters (e.g., differences in working memory capacity or motivation to recall) or task strategies.

Another advantage of computer simulation models over the verbal and mathematical approaches is that because they can exhibit relatively complex "behaviors," they make predictions for multiple mediating and outcome variables. For example, the IMP simulation not only produced outputs that could be summarized as proportions of behaviors recalled but also serial position curves, output order sequences, plus other

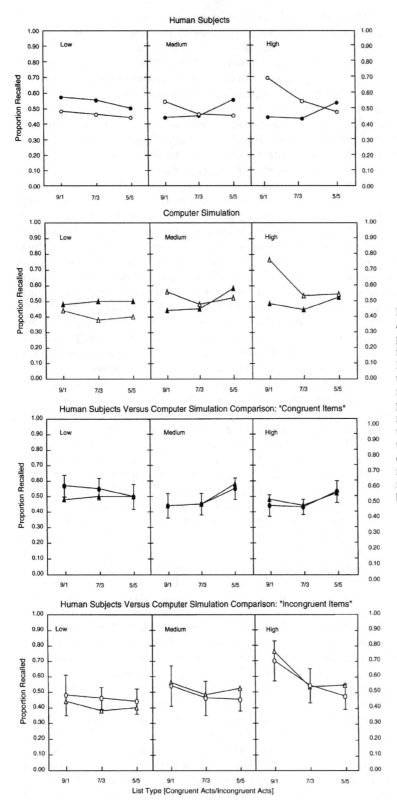

Figure 4.4. Comparison of human behavior and the IMP computer simulation model's performance in the Hastie and Mazur (1981) impression formation and memory task. From top to bottom, the first panel presents the human subjects' performance on the free recall memory task (circles), the second panel presents the computer simulation model's performance (triangles), and the bottom two panels compare the human and the model's performance with 95% confidence intervals around the human performance mean values (filled symbols represent recall of "congruent items" and unfilled symbols represent recall of "incongruent items").

"behaviors" such as impression ratings. All of these aspects of the model can be compared with the human behavioral data. Indeed, running a simulation model often prompts the researcher to invent new dependent variables to be measured in studies of human participants (see Hastie, Penrod, & Pennington, 1983, for examples of this kind of inventive process).

Empirical tests of a theory that examine the goodness-of-fit of several dependent (outcome) variables are much more informative than single measure comparisons, especially when the measures reflect processing at several points in time and not just ultimate outcomes. Computer simulations promote the development of process measures as well as outcome measures (cf. Taylor & Fiske, 1981) and encourage researchers to design studies that provide data on mediating processes as well as behavioral outcomes.

Further Evaluations of the Success of the IMP Model

The tests of IMP were all post hoc. The previously measured behavior of human participants was the focus of the model-fitting procedure. Of course, a priori predictive hypotheses will follow from any successful modeling application. Here, simulation models may be even more likely than the alternatives to provide the "deductive power" to derive new predictions of previously unobserved behavior. Shifrin and Nobel (1997) provided an instructive case study of their experiences developing and evaluating a model for recognition and cued-recall processes. Their account included many wise precepts about how to develop a model in the first place, how to proceed with goodness-of-fit tests, and, most important, how to evaluate the results of those tests.

In the case of post hoc model-fitting most of the deductions occur in the cycles of implementing, testing, revising, and reimplementing a model. In the case of IMP most of the unexpected implications of the theoretical assumptions concerned the detailed structure of the free-recall data. For example, we discovered that the shapes of the output serial position curves showed a small, but consistent negative recency effect. The very last items in the list tended to have relatively few associative links to other items, because the study process ended before they had much "stay time" in working memory when links might be formed with incoming items (i.e., there weren't any more incoming items). We also verified some deductions that had already been made informally by Thom Srull (1981) concerning the probabilities that an item of one type (congruent, incongruent) would be followed by items of either type when it had been recalled. The basic result is that congruent items tend to be followed by incongruent items in the recall sequence at a distinctively high rate.

The empirical signature of the incongruity enhanced recall effect is that when incongruent items are added to a list, recall of other items in the same list is increased (in the Hastie & Mazur [1981] experiment this would mean only congruent items). This is an unusual result in the context of the resource trade-offs and constant levels of overall recall commonly observed in free-recall learning tasks (Crowder, 1976). It is also a prediction (and finding) that discriminates between IMP and another popular account for the incongruity enhanced recall phenomenon in terms of a "pointer + tag" model of memory structure (cf. Graesser, Woll, Kowalski, & Smith, 1980). We found that there was a subtle interaction between the presence of items in working memory and the impression process. One way in which a surprising item could have a larger than average impact on the impression was for it to remain in working memory for a long time, where it was repeatedly averaged into the updated impression as part of the anchor-and-adjust impression formation process. There were also many other modest insights into the implications of the model that are part of the routine experience of implementing and testing a simulation model.

A final appeal of IMP derives from its "psychological plausibility." When we perform the experimental tasks to which the model has been fitted our subjective experiences seem to match processes embedded in the model. For example, when we hear or see a person behaving in an unexpected manner, we have a subjective impression of heightened attention and even notice that we are attempting to "explain" why the unexpected event occurred. Or, when we attempt to recall a set of facts about a person, we have an impression of increasing resistance caused by a "clogging" of our retrieval system. Subjectively, we keep recalling the same information and seem unable to "get around it" to find new, unrecalled information. These experiences have direct analogs in the encoding and retrieval processes of the IMP model.

Most of the component mechanisms within IMP are further supported by empirical analyses of related phenomena. For example, there is considerable empirical evidence for averaging models of impression-formation processes (N. H. Anderson, 1981) that unexpected events instigate attribution processes (Hastie, 1984; Weiner, 1985), that causal inferences enhance recall (Black & Bern, 1981; Myers, Shinjo, & Duffy,

1987), and that retrieval is terminated by retrieval failures (Gillund & Shiffrin, 1984; Roediger, 1978). As with any theory, the convergence among findings from diverse sources adds to the overall argument for the model's plausibility.

The DISCUSS Model of Social Processes in Small Group Decision Making

Whereas IMP is a model of how individuals process social information, DISCUSS is a model of how individuals process information in a social context. The social context of interest is a small group or team that endeavors to reach a collective choice based on information that is available to its members. DISCUSS is based on an information-processing view of group interaction (Hinsz, Tindale, & Vollrath, 1997; Larson & Christensen, 1993). The guiding metaphor in the development of DISCUSS was one of "minds" working together, interacting and reacting to one another.

Modeling a social system ordinarily involves identifying component processes that unfold over time. In the case of group decision making, relevant components include prediscussion information distribution (Who knows what prior to discussion?), discussion (Who speaks and what is said?), individual choice (How do members integrate information to form a preference?), and collective choice (How do members combine their preferences to yield a collective choice?). Each of these components can be further divided. For example, discussion entails memory (How is information retrieved during discussion?) and social processes (How are speaking turns allocated?).

In DISCUSS, group members are viewed as information integrators and are presumed to develop ledger-like representations of the supporting and opposing information about each decision alternative. Members' preferences are based on the weight of the evidence in their ledger. From this perspective, group discussion fills in the ledger by reminding members of items that they have momentarily forgotten or by giving them items that they never had. As old items are reinstated or new items enter the ledger, members reevaluate their preferences. A group decision is reached when a sufficient number of members agree to satisfy the operative decision rule (e.g., majority, unanimity, etc.).

A Model of the Environment

In models of collective behavior, representations of the environment tend to be complex because they involve multiple actors who are connected through some form of social communication or interaction. In articulating a theoretical model, the challenge is to capture the important aspects of the environment but to keep the representation manageable. In the DISCUSS model, the task environment is defined by the informational features of the decision task, and the social environment is limited to small groups (viz., 20 or fewer members). Additionally, the model presumes that a group is choosing from among a small set of well-defined, discrete decision alternatives.

DECISION ALTERNATIVES. A major component of the task environment is a set of informational items. Items in this set are linked to decision alternatives and have a valence. The sign of the valence determines whether the item supports or opposes the associated decision alternatives. The absolute size of the valence determines the relative weight of an item in evaluating alternatives. Thus, the number of items linked to each alternative and their valences define the informational characteristics of the alternatives. For example, consider an information-impoverished, binary decision task. In this task, Alternative X is associated with four items whose valences are 2, 1, 0, and -0.5. Alternative Y is linked to six items with the valences, 0.5, 0.5, 0, 0, 0, and -1. In this case, both Alternatives X and Y have two items of supporting information but X's supporting items are weighted more than Y's (indicating that X's are subjectively more important, relevant, or diagnostic). Moreover, three of Y's items are neutral (i.e., zero weight), implying that they are viewed as unimportant, irrelevant, or ambivalent with respect to the decision at hand.

THE SOCIAL ENVIRONMENT. The social environment is a population of "people" from which DISCUSS will compose groups of a target size. These potential group members are partly defined by relationships to the information set comprising the task environment – namely, their individual evaluations of, and access to, informational items. In the simplest case, DISCUSS assigns the same item valences to everyone in the population. For many kinds of social judgments, assuming equal weights is probably too simplistic. As an option, DISCUSS will treat item valences as the typical value for the population of group members, but permit individual members' values to deviate from these typical values. The degree of deviation permitted is determined by a *valence disparity* parameter whose value is

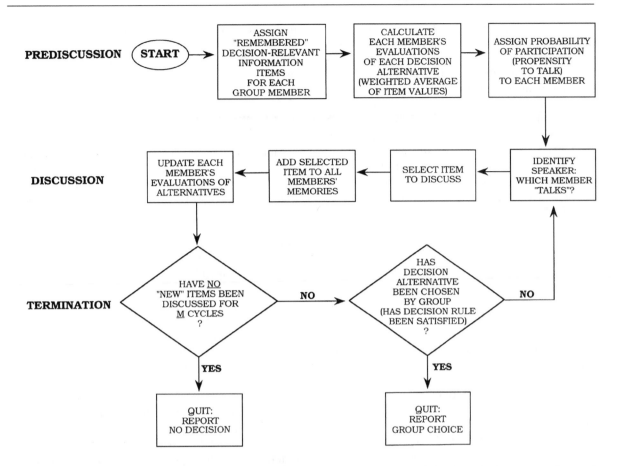

PREDISCUSSION → START → ASSIGN "REMEMBERED" DECISION-RELEVANT INFORMATION ITEMS FOR EACH GROUP MEMBER → CALCULATE EACH MEMBER'S EVALUATIONS OF EACH DECISION ALTERNATIVE (WEIGHTED AVERAGE OF ITEM VALUES) → ASSIGN PROBABILITY OF PARTICIPATION (PROPENSITY TO TALK) TO EACH MEMBER

DISCUSSION UPDATE EACH MEMBER'S EVALUATIONS OF ALTERNATIVES ← ADD SELECTED ITEM TO ALL MEMBERS' MEMORIES ← SELECT ITEM TO DISCUSS ← IDENTIFY SPEAKER: WHICH MEMBER "TALKS"?

TERMINATION HAVE NO "NEW" ITEMS BEEN DISCUSSED FOR M CYCLES ? — NO → HAS DECISION ALTERNATIVE BEEN CHOSEN BY GROUP (HAS DECISION RULE BEEN SATISFIED) ? — NO

YES ↓ QUIT: REPORT NO DECISION   YES ↓ QUIT: REPORT GROUP CHOICE

Figure 4.5. Summary of the flow of information and control in the DISCUSS computer simulation program.

supplied by the user. Here DISCUSS resorts to a pseudo-random mechanism to produce individual differences. DISCUSS samples the values that each member assigns to items from a population of values that are distributed normally around the item valences specified in defining the task environment. The standard deviation of this population of potential valences is equal to the disparity parameter.

The model of the social environment also prescribes how access to information is distributed among members. The simplest possibility is that members have access to all information. However, many of the more interesting applications of the model are to situations in which information access across individuals is not uniform, but may be biased in various ways. In practice, groups are frequently composed of members who differ in their backgrounds, social networks, or expertise. Experimental reconstructions of such cases induce systematic differences in the information that members of a group can access (e.g., Gigone & Hastie, 1993, Stasser & Titus, 1985, 1987).

A Model of the Individual Group Member's Mind

One advantage of computer simulation is that it allows the theorist to connect models of very different kinds of phenomena relatively easily. In the case of group decision making what is needed is the capacity to implement models of the mental processes and the initial stages of communication that occur within individuals and then to embed these models in the social environment of other group members. That is, individual and group level phenomena must be modeled simultaneously. Figure 4.5 is a flowchart that summarizes the computational steps that put the model in motion. The process is divided into three major stages: prediscussion, discussion, and termination. Prediscussion involves mostly individual cognitive processes: memory and judgment leading to initial preferences among the decision alternatives.

MEMORY. In constructing the social environment, each member is linked to a set of information about each decision alternative. However, access to information does not imply that the information is remembered later during discussion. Members are assumed to have imperfect recall that conforms to two guidelines. First, as the number of items to be remembered increases, the probability of recalling any one item decreases. Second, members remember more, on average, as the number of available items increase. The current versions of DISCUSS use a reciprocal function of information load to calculate the probability of recalling an item, $p(R)$ (see Murdock, 1960, for a similar formulation):

$$p(R) = 3.33/L + 0.37, \qquad (1)$$

where L is the number of items a member can access. The constants, 3.33 and 0.37, are least-squares estimates obtained from free recall protocols of participants who participated in two studies using a political caucus task (Stasser & Titus, 1985, 1987). These values are subject to revision depending on the nature of the materials participants have to recall, the amount of rehearsal time, and so forth. Here, again, DISCUSS uses a pseudo-random process to simulate a process that is undoubtedly multiply determined. For each member, DISCUSS counts the number of items received, calculates the probability of item recall given the information load, and uses a lottery to determine whether each item is permanently stored in memory.

JUDGMENT. The current version of DISCUSS includes two alternative strategies for the individual's formation and revision of evaluations of the choice alternatives: a summative submodel and an averaging submodel. Both submodels presume that individuals form an evaluation of the alternatives under consideration based on the information that they can recall at a given point in time. The summative submodel uses the simple sum of (recalled) item valences to obtain a summary evaluation for an alternative. The averaging submodel computes the evaluation by dividing the sum by the number of items recalled. Linear models, such as the summative and averaging submodels, are noted for their ability to approximate many nonlinear integration processes (Dawes, 1979; Dawes & Corrigan, 1974). Nonetheless, any model that specifies how information is integrated computationally to yield a preference could be substituted as a submodel in DISCUSS (e.g., Payne, et al., 1993; Pennington & Hastie, 1981).

DISCUSS has a simple individual choice rule: A member prefers the alternative with the highest evaluation. If two or more alternatives tie, then the individual is undecided for the moment unless a prior preference existed. If two or more tie and a prior preference existed, the prior preference is maintained. (A random "tie-breaker" procedure is also available if the user does not want to permit "indifference.")

A Model of Social Interaction

As depicted in Figure 4.5, DISCUSS represents social interaction in decision-making groups as a series of "speaking turns." Each turn consists of speaker selection, item selection (speech content), memory update, preference reassessment, and "voting." Because social interaction is simulated as a series of speaking turns, producing realistic patterns of participation in discussion is important. How frequently a member speaks directly affects the likelihood that his or her information will be considered by the group.

SPEAKER SELECTION. Fortunately, there is an extensive literature on participation patterns in small group discussions (see Stasser & Vaughan, 1996, for a recent review of this work). Having such an extensive theoretical and empirical record to inform and constrain the construction of a central component of a model is an advantage. A common theme in the participation literature is that discussion produces a *participation hierarchy*. Members of a group do not participate equally, and they characteristically produce a rank ordering from the highest to the lowest participator. DISCUSS uses a formulation originally suggested by Stephan and Mishler (1952). They concluded that participation rates drop by a constant fraction at each step in the ranking. The DISCUSS model incorporates the notion of ranked participation by computing the probability of participation, P_i, for the member in the ith rank as

$$P_i = r^i \left| \sum_{j=1}^{N} r^j \right., \qquad (2)$$

where N is group size, and r is the proportional change in speaking rates between adjacent ranks ($0 < r < 1$). If $r = 1$ in this expression, members are equally likely to speak. As the value of r decreases, high participators dominate more and more of the interaction. DISCUSS accepts as input the value of r. Empirical estimates of this value obtained from groups of varying sizes typically range from .5 to .8 (see Stasser, 1988; Stasser & Taylor, 1991, for more detail). At the onset of discussion, DISCUSS computes the hierarchy of participation rates and assigns members to locations in the ranking. At the onset of each speaking turn, DISCUSS conducts a lottery to identify the speaker; the chances of each member's winning the lottery is determined by location in the speaking hierarchy.

ITEM SELECTION. Once a speaker is identified, DISCUSS samples an item from the speaker's memory. This selection can be biased to varying degrees by the speaker's current preference. At one extreme (advocacy), the speaker will not contribute an item that does not support the current preference. Thus, for example, an advocacy simulation would not select a negatively valenced item about the speaker's preferred option. At the other extreme (nonadvocacy), an item is selected at random from memory, and the selection is not affected by the current preference. Between these extremes, item selection can be biased in varying degrees by the current preference; the degree of bias is controlled by an input parameter. Thus, the model can simulate discussion styles ranging from an adversarial debate to an open-minded search for relevant information.

MEMORY AND PREFERENCE UPDATE. If new information is introduced during a speaker cycle, DISCUSS surveys each member's memory and adds the item if a member does not already have it in memory. Whereas DISCUSS represents people as having fallible memories, they are never inattentive during group discussion. When the contents of a member's memory is changed, the member's preference is recomputed.

VALENCE ADJUSTMENTS. Recall that members of DISCUSS groups can acquire different valences for informational items during the composition of groups. When disparate valences exist, discussion may serve both to disseminate information and to resolve differences in the evaluative implication attached to information (see Wittenbaum & Stasser, 1999, for an empirical investigation of this process). A *norm adjustment* parameter determines the degree to which discussion of an item reduces differences in members' associated valences. In a nonnormative version of the model, discussion serves only to convey information but not to resolve differences in attached valences. In a normative version, discussion not only conveys the information but also reduces the disparity in valences among group members. This reduction can be complete (i.e., members attach the same valence to an item after it is discussed) or partial (discussion reduces the disparities by some proportion). If valence adjustments occur, members' preferences are recomputed using the new valences.

VOTING. At the end of each speaker cycle, members "vote." Voting is meant to include not only formal polls but other, often subtle, expressions of preferences. The assumption is that changes of opinion are registered in some fashion when they occur and that the group detects when it has reached the necessary agreement to identify a group choice.

TERMINATION. If there are changes of preferences as a result of an item being discussed, the simulation checks the updated distribution of opinions and terminates discussion if the requisite consensus (e.g., majority, unanimity, etc.) exists. Additionally, if nothing new has been contributed over a series of speaking turns, the simulation produces stalemate and terminates discussion with no decision. In default mode, the model terminates discussion if nothing new is added in N turns, where N is group size. The number of "no news" turns permitted can be changed by the user. The model assumes that a speaker will contribute something new unless everything she or he remembers has already been discussed (or, under extreme advocacy, counters her or his current preference.)

Comment: Complexity and Parsimony

An advantage of computer simulation is that it permits the theorist to incorporate complex and dynamic relationships into a "runable" model of human behavior. The medium not only permits but also encourages the theorist to build more and more complex representations of the phenomena under consideration. However, good style requires that one balance the quest for more elaborate, and perhaps empirically accurate, models with an appreciation for parsimony (Broadbent, 1987).

DISCUSS contains shortcuts in representing both cognitive and social processes (e.g., "voting" is sincere, never strategic; speakers contribute something new if they can; discussion is terminated after a fixed number of "no news" turns). Chief among these shortcuts is the way that DISCUSS simulates individual memory processes. DISCUSS incorporates the ideas that human memory is faulty, has a limited but elastic capacity, and retrieval may be motivationally biased. But, DISCUSS also ignores a lot of what we know about human memory. There are no primacy, recency, or novelty effects in DISCUSS simulations. Moreover, associative links are not formed among informational items. An attractive possibility is to wed DISCUSS to a more elaborate memory model such as IMP. Such a marriage would permit one to pursue phenomena that cannot be addressed by the current program. For example, one might explore how associative networks (arising perhaps from members' background information about the decision domain or order effects in access to information) might interact with different ways of distributing information among members.

Stasser and Vaughan (1996) considered the merits of such a wedding between computational models. They added a model of participation (SPEAK, Stasser & Taylor, 1991) to the speaker selection routine in DISCUSS. SPEAK not only incorporates the notion of a participation hierarchy but also reproduces cyclical patterns of participation that characteristically occur in face-to-face, unstructured discussions. In adding SPEAK to DISCUSS, Stasser and Vaughan (1996) also added the option of forming participation hierarchies that were connected to task-relevant attributes of persons (e.g., members who remember more, talk more). Consideration of parsimony raises the question of whether the added theoretical value justifies the added complexity in the speaker selection routine of DISCUSS. A related, and perhaps more manageable, question is whether the added complexity changes the simulation results in theoretically interesting cases. For example, Stasser and Vaughan (1996) found that the more empirically accurate speaking patterns produced by SPEAK did not affect other pertinent features of the simulated process (e.g., discussion content and group choices) when group size was small (4 members) or when all information was accessible to all members before discussion. However, SPEAK did change decision outcomes when participation was linked to amount of recall, groups were larger (6 or 12 members), and information was not completely shared before discussion. Stasser and Vaughan concluded that SPEAK offers two advantages over the original speaker selection routine in DISCUSS. First, the SPEAK algorithm produces characteristic temporal patterns in speaking turn allocation in unstructured, face-to-face discussion (Parker, 1988; Stasser & Taylor, 1991). Second, the original routine and SPEAK-based routines produce different outcomes under some theoretically and practically interesting conditions.

Evaluating the DISCUSS Model

As was illustrated with the IMP model, one approach to evaluating a computer model is to assess the fit of its predictions to data. Moreover, given the inherent complexity of social interaction, it is often possible and desirable to assess fit at different points in time and to multiple process measures. Stasser (1988) illustrated this strategy by comparing the output of DISCUSS to the seminal findings of Stasser and Titus (1985).

THE DATA. Stasser and Titus (1985) devised a method of distributing information across group members to create a hidden profile. To illustrate a hidden profile, suppose that a personnel committee is considering two job applicants. When full information about both applicants is available, it is clear that one applicant is better. However, suppose that access to the information is distributed across partly informed committee members so that everyone knows the "bad news" about the better applicant but the "good news" is distributed piecemeal so that each member only knows a couple of "good news" items. In this manner, we can create a hidden profile situation where, perversely, the better applicant looks relatively bad to each individual member. When the group convenes, they can uncover the favorable, but hidden profile of the better applicant if the unshared "good news" is exchanged during discussion.

Stasser and Titus (1985, 1987) examined whether groups would reveal hidden profiles and identify the most preferred option by pooling information effectively in discussion. Their groups failed, with few exceptions, to uncover the hidden profile. Others have obtained similar findings (e.g., Gigone & Hastie, 1993; Hollingshead, 1996; Stasser & Stewart, 1992). Stasser (1988) asked whether the information-processing view of collective choice as represented in DISCUSS could account for these findings. Also of interest was whether the failure of groups to discover hidden profiles is due to their tendency to discuss information that supports initial opinions in the group. Or, alternatively, would the groups have failed even if they engaged in an evenhanded exploration of the information during discussion?

Some of the results from the Stasser and Titus (1985) experiment are summarized in Table 4.1. In this experiment, information about the three candidates for student body president was presented to four-member student groups following one of three distribution plans. A fully *shared* plan gave every member access to all of the information. In an *unshared–consensus* plan, a hidden profile was created in order to hide Candidate A's winning qualities and to make Candidate B appear (falsely) most attractive. In an *unshared–conflict* plan, Candidate A's winning qualities were again obscured, but Candidate B appeared most attractive to two members and Candidate C appeared most attractive to the other two members of a group. The prediscussion preferences in Table 4.1 show that these manipulations of information accessibility affected the initial popularity of candidates in the expected ways. Moreover, the group decision data document the failure of groups to uncover the hidden profiles in the unshared–

consensus and the unshared–conflict conditions. In these conditions, the opportunity to exchange information during group discussion apparently did not help groups identify the normatively best option.

THE SIMULATION OF HIDDEN PROFILE EFFECTS. Stasser (1988) competitively evaluated several versions of the DISCUSS model using the results of Stasser and Titus (1985; see Table 4.1). Here we summarize the findings for four versions of DISCUSS obtained by crossing discussion style (advocacy vs. nonadvocacy) with the degree of reduction in valence disparity for discussed information (none vs. complete). We also include a baseline, "random choice" model in order to illustrate comparative fit approaches to model testing. The information distribution plans that defined the shared, unshared–consensus, and unshared–conflict conditions in Stasser and Titus's (1985) original study were reproduced in the information access array of DISCUSS. For each version of DISCUSS, the discussions of 100 four-person groups were simulated within each of these three conditions. The outputs of interest here are the predicted distributions of prediscussion preferences and group decisions.

COMPARATIVE MODEL TESTING. In addition to the quantitative assessment provided by a goodness-of-fit statistic, it is informative to competitively evaluate several versions of a model. Moreover, it is useful to include a baseline model that is conceptually empty for comparative purposes. Stasser (1988) used the likelihood ratio statistic to evaluate fit:

$$G = -2 \sum f_o \ \ln(f_e/f_o) \qquad (3)$$

where f_o is the observed frequency in a response category, f_e is the predicted frequency, and the summation is across response categories (Feinberg, 1977). The values of this likelihood statistic are distributed approximately as a chi-square variate with appropriate degrees of freedom. Table 4.2 gives the values of G for prediscussion preferences and group

TABLE 4.1. Data Summarizing the Relative Frequencies of Member Predecision Preferences and Group Decisions from Human Participants in the Stasser & Titus (1985) Experiment

Condition	Candidate			No decision	N
	A	B	C		
	Prediscussion preferences				
Shared	0.67	0.17	0.17	—	72
Unshared–consensus	0.25	0.61	0.14	—	84
Unshared–conflict	0.21	0.46	0.33	—	72
	Group decisions				
Shared	0.83	0.11	0.06	0.00	18
Unshared–consensus	0.24	0.71	0.05	0.00	21
Unshared–conflict	0.11	0.50	0.33	0.06	18

decisions, aggregated across the three experimental conditions in Stasser and Titus (1985). These values of G provide the traditional comparison of theoretical point predictions with data point estimates (see discussion above of goodness-of-fit evaluations for the IMP model).

The results of a goodness-of-fit test by itself can be ambiguous. On the one hand, obtaining a "significant" value signals poor fit. However, even minor discrepancies between predicted and observed outcomes can produce a significant result when statistical power is sufficiently large. For example, the values of G for the

TABLE 4.2. Goodness-of-Fit (G) and Incremental Fit (D) of Observed Preferences and Decision Distributions to the Predictions of DISCUSS and Baseline Models

Model	Prediscussion preferences		Group decisions	
	G	D	G	D
DISCUSS				
Advocacy-norm	9.35**	.86	5.44*	.92
Nonadvocacy-norm	8.52**	.88	5.87*	.91
Advocacy-nonnorm	9.26**	.86	55.98***	.17
Nonadvocacy-nonnorm	9.63**	.86	72.82***	−.08
Baseline				
Equiprobability	68.50***	—	67.23***	—

Note: There are 6 degrees of freedom for tests of fit for preference data and 9 degrees of freedom for tests of fit for decision data.
* $p > .25$. ** $p > .10$. *** $p < .05$.

TABLE 4.3. DISCUSS Model Predicted Proportion of Prediscussion Preferences and Group Decisions for Advocacy and Nonadvocacy

Condition	Candidate			No decision	N
	A	B	C		
Nonadvocacy model					
Prediscussion preferences					
Shared	0.68	0.15	0.17	—	400
Unshared–consensus	0.18	0.60	0.22	—	400
Unshared–conflict	0.14	0.43	0.43	—	400
Group decisions					
Shared	0.84	0.06	0.09	0.01	100
Unshared–consensus	0.21	0.61	0.15	0.03	100
Unshared–conflict	0.17	0.44	0.36	0.03	100
Advocacy					
Prediscussion preferences					
Shared	0.65	0.20	0.15	—	400
Unshared–consensus	0.20	0.59	0.21	—	400
Unshared–conflict	0.12	0.43	0.44	—	400
Group decisions					
Shared	0.81	0.12	0.07	0.00	100
Unshared–consensus	0.16	0.68	0.15	0.01	100
Unshared–conflict	0.08	0.51	0.40	0.01	100

DISCUSS predictions of prediscussion preferences reported in Table 4.2 are all "marginally significant." How damning are these results? The answer is not clear when one considers that the prediscussion preferences are individual-level data and thus based on a relatively large sample (viz., a total 228 observed cases). On the other hand, two of the models provided very good accounts of the group decision data yielding nonsignificant discrepancies between predicted and observed. Here we have the flip side of the aforementioned concern: Was there enough statistical power to detect material discrepancies given that the sample size for group decisions is much smaller than for members' prediscussion preferences (by a factor of four)? Judd and McClelland (1989) provide a thorough discussion of the logic of the model-comparison approach to hypothesis testing.

One way of putting goodness-of-fit tests in perspective is to compare the fit of theoretically inspired models to a baseline. In this case, Stasser (1988) included an equiprobability model that simply assumes that all responses are equally likely and used the performance of this "null" model as a baseline for computing Bentler and Bonett's (1980) normed fit index, D. This index describes how well a model is doing relative to a baseline model. When D is zero, a model is performing no better than the baseline model. When D is one, the model's predictions fit the observed data perfectly.

Comparative indices, such as D, are less affected by statistical power than are goodness-of-fit tests such as G. In the present case, the values of D in Table 4.2 suggest that both the advocacy-norm and nonadvocacy-norm versions of DISCUSS provide good accounts of the prediscussion preferences and the group decisions. However, the nonnorm versions do little better than the baseline model in accounting for group decisions.

OLD DATA: NEW INSIGHTS. We have emphasized the role of data in evaluating models. Nonetheless, the street between data and models is two-way (Figure 4.1). Simulations often suggest revised or new interpretations of existing findings. Consider the predictions of the advocacy- and nonadvocacy-norm models given in Table 4.3. The predictions of the two models are surprisingly similar across the three experimental conditions and reflect the actual results quite closely (see Table 4.1). The similarity of predictions was unexpected because the two models simulate the retrieval of information during discussion quite differently. The advocacy model assumes that members do not contribute information that opposes their preferences, whereas the nonadvocacy model assumes that members sample without bias from their memories.

By tracking multiple process measures, it is possible to gain insight into the dynamics underlying outcomes. For example, the DISCUSS model provides a record of the items mentioned in simulated discussions. These discussion records yielded one clue for why both the advocacy-norm and the nonadvocacy-norm models accounted equally well for the inability of Stasser and Titus's (1985) groups to discover hidden profiles. The discovery of hidden profiles depends on the discussion of unshared information. Discussion of shared information merely perpetuates the biased preferences that members bring to discussion when a hidden profile exists. In the nonadvocacy simulations of the hidden profile conditions, simulated discussions contained, on average, 42% of the shared information but only 15% of the unshared information. Similarly, in the advocacy simulations, 26% of the shared and 75% of the unshared items were contained in the discussion records. Thus, both the advocacy and nonadvocacy simulated discussions were dominated by shared information. Adding to the credibility of these simulated discussion content data, Stasser, Taylor, and Hanna (1989) recorded the discussions of three- and six-person groups and observed comparable patterns of information sampling.

Stasser and Titus (1985) attributed failures to discover the superiority of Candidate A in the hidden profile conditions partly to members' arguing for their preferences. The simulation results demonstrate that this tendency to advocate may not have occurred. The success of the nonadvocacy DISCUSS model implies that, even if members had been completely unbiased in their recall and contribution of information, most groups in the hidden profile conditions would still not have discovered the superiority of Candidate A.

Comment: Sensitivity Analyses

There are potentially two sources of residual uncertainty about conclusions based on retrospective simulations. First, there may be uncertainty about the appropriate values of some input parameters (e.g., item valences or participation inequality parameters in DISCUSS), and it is possible that the pattern of values used inadvertently and spuriously compensate for inadequacies in the model. Or, in comparative tests, chosen input values may compensate for limitations in one version while adversely affecting another version of the model. The other source of uncertainty is the design of the original study itself. Extraneous features of the experiment may have unexpectedly impacted the findings.

Sensitivity analyses provide a way of assessing the generalizability of findings from either a simulation or an empirical study. In sensitivity analyses, the values of input parameters are systematically varied over a range of plausible possibilities and the impact (if any) on model predictions noted. Stasser (1988) conducted sensitivity analyses by varying the values of item valences, the valence disparity parameter, and the participation inequality in DISCUSS. The nonadvocacy-norm and advocacy-norm versions of the DISCUSS model performed comparably across different combinations of these parameter values (see Stasser, 1988, for details).

Similarly, one can assess whether the findings of an empirical study may be sensitive to particular features of the method or design. For example, Stasser and Titus (1985) used four-person groups and 16 items of information about each of three alternatives. Stasser (1988) ran DISCUSS simulations varying group size (4, 8, and 12) and reducing information load from 16 to 8 items per alternative. These combinations of group size and information load yielded patterns of preferences and decisions that were similar to the empirical findings (Table 4.1). Thus, the results for the original study do not appear to have been unduly influenced by the specific choices of group size and information load.

THE VALUE OF COMPUTER SIMULATION MODELING

We will conclude with some remarks about the functions of psychological theories and about how we think the success of a theory should be evaluated (see Abelson, 1968; Hintzman, 1991; Lewandowsky, 1993, for other reviews of the pros and cons of simulation theories). We want to emphasize that we are referring to good, well-formed theories in each of the media. A bad theory (vaguely stated, internally inconsistent, incomplete, or empirically invalid) is going to be lousy in whatever form it appears. We hope the detailed examples we have presented convey a sense of good practice in simulation modeling.

A good theory provides an insightful, useful view of known facts about behavior. The best social psychological theories allow their users to exceed intuitive, "folk psychology" predictions of human behavior in important situations. A good theory is like a good method in that it allows its user to see deeper into the phenomena under study than he or she could see without the theory. A good method yields new, useful views of phenomena because it has several properties that are missing from everyday experience: control over conditions associated with the context in which the subject phenomena occur, "bird's eye" and multiple simultaneous views of the phenomena, and the possibility of creating comparison conditions and using random assignment to rule out alternative causal interpretations. By analogy, a good theory organizes the relevant phenomena, allows the theoretician to consider alternative views of the phenomena, examines detailed substages and events, and discerns the causal structure among its events and variables.

Good theories are stated clearly (the writings of great theoreticians like Robert Abelson, Roger Brown,

Leon Festinger, Harold Kelley, William McGuire, and Norman Anderson are distinguished by their clarity and elegance of statement) to promote communication among theorists and other researchers. A theory should be communicable, and the relations between fundamental assumptions and task-specific models should be "transparent." The process of constructing a computer simulation model promotes the development of clear, complete, and consistent theoretical statements. But, there are still examples of computer simulation theories that are difficult to comprehend (see the discussion of "Bonini's Paradox" in Dutton & Starbuck, 1971). Usually, when computer simulation theories are hard to comprehend, it is because they are too ambitious. The author keeps extending the theory, but his or her exposition lags behind the program and he or she does not carefully summarize (in English, not just in computer "code") the fundamental assumptions and organization of the theory (see J. R. Anderson, 1993, and Newell, 1990, for positive examples of how to make ambitious computer simulation theories clear and comprehensible). The problem of clarity of expression or transparency is not unique to simulation models. In fact, we believe the problem arises less often in computer models than in verbal and mathematical expressions (see Harris, 1976, for a criticism of the clarity of several social psychological theories).

Computer simulations have an advantage in promoting completeness and internal consistency. Both the IMP and the DISCUSS models started as verbal or verbal plus mathematical statements, and we cannot overemphasize the increased precision and completeness that we achieved by shifting to the computer simulation medium (see Broadbent, 1987; Hintzman, 1991; Lewandowsky, 1993, for several more examples where simulation modeling improved these aspects of theory construction). The other theoretical media (words, equations) are not as flexible and do not support nearly the variety of representations that can be implemented in typical programming languages like BASIC, FORTRAN, C, PASCAL, LISP, and PROLOG. Futhermore, there are substantial requirements on completeness and consistency that are imposed on the theory stated as a computer program if it is to succeed in running at all without "crashing."

A second set of issues concern the ease with which valid implications can be derived from a theory's assumptions, especially predictions of new relationships to look for in empirical data. Here, the deductive power of simulations is an order of magnitude greater than the derivational power of the alternative approaches. We would cite deductive power as the major advantage of computer modeling over other approaches to theory representation. New users are immediately struck by the ease with which a rich collection of predictions can be derived from a theory once it has been implemented as a simulation (Broadbent, 1987, presents several illustrations of the power of simulations to "derive" implications from apparently simple sets of theoretical assumptions). We cannot count the number of times that running a simulation model surprised us by revealing implications of our theoretical assumptions that contradicted our intuitions and "folk theories" about social behavior. Hintzman (1991) made this argument by summarizing the limits on human reasoning that have been identified by cognitive psychologists (e.g., Nisbett & Ross, 1980; Tversky & Kahneman, 1974) and then citing examples where computer simulation modeling overcomes our inherent cognitive limits to produce "valid surprises."

The third set of evaluative considerations is related to the primary functions of all psychological models, to represent behavioral phenomena analogically in an abstract system of ideas. The theory should provide an account of the major, reliable empirical findings; usually through a collection of theoretical statements that generate predictions that match empirical findings. The theory should be linked closely enough to data to be testable; usually this means the theory is a basis for precise predictions that can be falsified empirically. The reverse relationship should also hold: When empirical findings contradict a prediction derived from the model, it should be as easy as possible to decide which parts of the theory need revision (space prevents us from discussing the difficulties inherent in the theory revision process; see Quine & Ullian, 1970, for a good introduction to these important issues). Mathematical and simulation theories have an advantage over verbal formulations because they naturally operate on quantities and ordered relationships. It is also easier to trace the deductive path that leads to new predictions in formal modeling approaches. A special advantage of computer models is that they produce complex simulations of behavior and support predictions of multiple aspects of human behavior, as illustrated throughout this chapter.

Some critics have denounced simulation models as an obstacle to scientific progress because they are so difficult to falsify. G. R. Loftus (1985) and Luce (1989), for example, have argued that simulation modeling encourages theories to become unnecessarily complex. Thus, progress will be slowed by hard-to-falsify simulation models, and theorists will miss fundamental, simple laws of nature. Here we think our distinction between the three levels of abstraction in most psychological theories is relevant. At the lowest level, task-specific models, we would argue that computer simulations are the most precise, produce predictions of the greatest number of aspects of human behavior (predict many dependent variables), and, thus, are the most falsifiable of the three kinds of models.

The confusion arises because although the task-specific models are eminently falsifiable in the simulation approach, the more general theoretical principles may actually be less falsifiable, because the creation of alternative specific models is so easy within a computer simulation medium (see Greenwald, Pratkanis, Leippe, & Baumgardner, 1986, for a discussion of the tendency for theories in any medium to induce a "confirmation bias" in their adherents). Thus, the general theory may be insulated from empirical attacks, because it is so easy to posit task-specific models. However, verbally stated theories are also difficult to disconfirm (cf. Harris, 1976). With reference to theory falsifiability, the mathematical modeling approach probably has the edge over the other approaches. The history of mathematical modeling is littered with more cases of the "death of a beautiful theory at the hands of ugly facts" than any other theoretical tradition in psychology (e.g., Bjork, 1973; Estes, 1961, 1975; Luce, 1985; Restle, 1965; Townsend & Kadlec, 1990).

Fourth, a theory should be stated in a form that makes it as easy as possible to relate it to other theories. For example our discussion of the IMP model showed how easy it was to combine the essential assumptions of well-supported preexisting theories of social judgment and theories of human memory and then to investigate the interrelations and interactions between the two source theories. Similarly, the presentation of the DISCUSS model illustrated how originally separate theories of individual memory, opinion change, and group communication could be combined into one overarching theory. Lewandowsky (1993) cited several examples of the successful generalization of a simulation model by providing unified accounts of first one, then several tasks (e.g., category classification learning and recognition memory; recognition, recall, confidence judgments, and amnesic deficits).

A good theory should also be as easy as possible to relate to other theories at higher and lower levels of abstraction (Estes, 1977). For example, it should be possible to connect a theory of social judgment to "lower level" neural theories of brain functions in decision making (e.g., Cacioppo, Gardner, & Berntson, 1997; Damasio, 1994; Grossberg & Gutowski, 1987) to historically extended theories of evolutionary selection and behavioral genetics (e.g., Barkow, Cosmides, & Tooby, 1992; Gigerenzer, 1996; Plomin, DeFries, & McClearn,

1990) and also to "higher level" theories of rational adaptation and behavior in social and economic "markets" (e.g., Axelrod, 1984; Camerer, 1990; Kalick & Hamilton, 1986). The theory should also facilitate the analysis of individual differences within the behavioral scope of the theory (e.g., it should be obvious where to "locate" individual differences in accuracy, optimism, or valuation in a theory of social judgment [cf. Blair, Jarvis, & Petty, 1996; Cacioppo, Petty, Feinstein, & Jarvis, 1996] or individual differences in talkativeness, persuasiveness, or expertise in a theory of social interaction [e.g., Bavelas, Hastorf, Gross, & Kite, 1965; Stephan & Mischler, 1952]).

The relative advantages of the different media in supporting the integration of different theories obviously depend on what kind of theory is being related to what kind of theory. If the two theories are both implemented in the same medium, integration will be easiest. The simulation approach clearly has the advantage when the two theories are in different media (e.g., trying to embed a cognitive computational theory in a model of its neural substrate, trying to infer the optimal adaptive behavior of an organism in a realistic model of its environment, etc.). Simulation, because it is representationally the most flexible and richest of the media, has the advantage.

The simulation approach has also encouraged new theoretical strategies that depart from the traditional function of accounting for specific empirical phenomena. For example, simulation models are often used to project the implications of new ideas in the absence of empirical data. Usually this is a first step on the way to hypothesis formation and data collection. Examples would include Nowak, Szamrej, and Latané's (1990) theoretical research on attitudes: Assuming a simple model of attitude change and a simple spatial environment inhabited by individuals, what spatial distributions of attitudes will emerge from a dynamic simulation of attitude contagion? Kelley (1985; see also Thorngate & Carroll, 1987): What information about an "opponent" in a simple social interaction will enable an actor to maximize his or her outcomes across a sequence of "games?" Axelrod and Hamilton (1981; Axelrod, 1984): What are the conditions for the emergence of adaptive cooperative social strategies? And, Kalick & Hamilton (1986, 1988; see also Aron, 1988): If individuals choose the most attractive mates they can, does "matching" on attractiveness still occur in the population of pairs that are formed?

This chapter has attempted to communicate the nature and the advantages of the computer simulation modeling approach to theory construction and evaluation in social psychology. We believe the approach is often better than the alternatives (verbal and mathematical modeling). But, simulation modeling has not yet "caught on" in social psychology. We hope this chapter will help remedy that situation. Try it, you'll like it, and it will improve practice and raise the standards for theorizing in social psychology.

REFERENCES

Abelson, R. P. (1968). Simulation of social behavior. In G. Lindzey & E. Aronson (Eds.), *The handbook of social psychology* (2nd ed., Vol. 2, pp. 274–356). Reading, MA: Addison-Wesley.

Abelson, R. P., Aronson, E., McGuire, W. J., Newcomb, T. M., Rosenberg, M. J., & Tannenbaum, P. H. (1968). *Theories of cognitive consistency: A sourcebook.* Chicago: Rand McNally.

Anderson, J. R. (1983). *The architecture of cognition.* Cambridge, MA: Harvard University Press.

Anderson, J. R. (1990). *The adaptive character of thought.* Hillsdale, NJ: Erlbaum.

Anderson, J. R. (1993). *Rules of the mind.* Hillsdale, NJ: Erlbaum.

Anderson, J. R. (1996, November). *A working theory of human cognition.* Paper presented at the 37th Annual Meeting of the Psychonomic Society, Chicago, IL.

Anderson, J. R., & Bower, G. H. (1973). *Human associative memory.* Washington, DC: Winston.

Anderson, N. H. (1965). Averaging versus adding as a stimulus-combination rule in impression formation. *Journal of Experimental Psychology, 70,* 394–400.

Anderson, N. H. (1981). *Foundations of information integration theory.* New York: Academic Press.

Anderson, N. H. (1982). *Methods of information integration theory.* New York: Academic Press.

Anderson, N. H. (Ed.). (1991). *Contributions to information integration theory* (3 Vols.). Hillsdale, NJ: Erlbaum.

Anderson, N. H. (1996). *A functional theory of cognition.* Mahwah, NJ: Erlbaum.

Aron, A. (1988). The matching hypothesis reconsidered again: Comment on Kalick and Hamilton. *Journal of Personality and Social Psychology, 54,* 441–446.

Asch, S. E. (1946). Forming impressions of personality. *Journal of Abnormal and Social Psychology, 41,* 258–290.

Atkinson, R. C., & Shiffrin, R. M. (1968). Human memory: A proposed system and its control processes. In K. W. Spence & J. T. Spence (Eds.), *The psychology of learning and motivation: Advances in research and theory* (Vol. 2, pp. 89–195). New York: Academic Press.

Axelrod, R. (1984). *The evolution of cooperation.* New York: Basic Books.

Axelrod, R., & Hamilton, W. D. (1981, 27 March). The evolution of cooperation. *Science, 211,* 306–318.

Barkow, J. H., Cosmides, L., & Tooby, J. (Eds.). (1992). *The adapted mind: Evolutionary psychology and the generation of culture.* New York: Oxford University Press.

Bavelas, A., Hastorf, A. H., Gross, A. E., & Kite, W. R. (1965). Experiments on the alteration of group structure. *Journal of Experimental Social Psychology, 1,* 55–70.

Bentler, P. M., & Bonett, D. G. (1980). Significance testing and goodness of fit in the analysis of covariance structures. *Psychological Bulletin, 88,* 588–606.

Bjork, R. A. (1973). Why mathematical models? *American Psychologist, 28,* 426–433.

Black, J. B., & Bern, H. (1981). Causal inference and memory for events in narratives. *Journal of Verbal Learning and Verbal Behavior, 20,* 267–275.

Blair, W., Jarvis, G., & Petty, R. E. (1996). The need to evaluate. *Journal of Personality and Social Psychology, 79,* 172–189.

Bond, C. F., Jr., & Brockett, D. R. (1987). A social context–personality index theory of memory for acquaintances. *Journal of Personality and Social Psychology, 52,* 1110–1121.

Bond, C. F., Jr., Jones, R. L., & Weintraub, D. L. (1985). On the unconstrained recall of acquaintances: A sampling-traversal model. *Journal of Personality and Social Psychology, 49,* 327–337.

Bradshaw, G. L., & Anderson, J. R. (1982). Elaborative processing as an explanation of levels of processing. *Journal of Verbal Learning and Verbal Behavior, 21,* 165–174.

Broadbent, D. (1987). Simple models for experimentable situations. In P. Morris (Ed.), *Modelling cognition* (pp. 169–185). Chichester, England: Wiley.

Brunswik, E. (1956). *Perception and the representative design of psychological experiments.* Berkeley: University of California Press.

Cacioppo, J. T., Gardner, W. L., & Berntson, G. G. (1997). Beyond bipolar conceptualizations and measures: The case of attitudes and evaluative space. *Personality and Social Psychology Review, 1,* 3–25.

Cacioppo, J. T., Petty, R. E., Feinstein, J. A., & Jarvis, W. B. G. (1996). Dispositional differences in cognitive motivation: The life and times of individuals varying in need for cognition. *Psychological Bulletin, 119,* 197–253.

Camerer, C. F. (1990). Behavioral game theory. In R. M. Hogarth (Ed.), *Insights in decision making* (pp. 311–336). Chicago: University of Chicago Press.

Carley, K. M. (1996). Computational and mathematical organization theory: Perspective and directions. *Computational and Mathematical Organization Theory, 1,* 39–56. (This paper is a review; see also, for example: Carley, K. M. [1991]. A theory of group stability. *American Sociological Review, 56,* 331–354.)

Cohen, J. (1994). The earth is round (p < .05). *American Psychologist, 49,* 997–1003.

Coombs, C. H., Raiffa, H., & Thrall, R. M. (1954). Some views on mathematical models and measurement theory. *Psychological Review, 61,* 132–144.

Cotton, J. W. (1982). Where is the randomness for the human computer? *Behavior Research Methods & Instrumentation, 14,* 59–70.

Crowder, R. G. (1976). *Principles of learning and memory.* Hillsdale, NJ: Erlbaum.

Damasio, A. R. (1994). *Descartes' error: Emotion, reason, and the human brain.* New York: G. P. Putnam's Sons.

Dawes, R. M. (1979). The robust beauty of improper linear models in decision making. *American Psychologist, 34,* 571–582.

Dawes, R. M., & Corrigan, B. (1974). Linear models in decision making. *Psychological Bulletin, 81,* 95–106.

Deutsch, M., & Krauss, R. M. (1965). *Theories in social psychology.* New York: Basic Books.

Dutton, J. M., & Starbuck, W. H. (1971). *Computer simulation of human behavior.* New York: Wiley.

Eagley, A. H., & Chaiken, S. (1993). *The psychology of attitudes.* Orlando, FL: Harcourt Brace Jovanovich.

Ericsson, K. A., & Kintsch, W. (1995). Long-term working memory. *Psychological Review, 102,* 211–245.

Estes, W. K. (1961). Growth and function of mathematical models for learning. In W. Dennis (Ed.), *Current trends in psychological theory* (pp. 134–151). Pittsburgh, PA: University of Pittsburgh Press.

Estes, W. K. (1975). Some targets for mathematical psychology. *Journal of Mathematical Psychology, 12,* 263–282.

Estes, W. K. (1977). On the descriptive and explanatory functions of theories of memory. In L.-G. Nilsson (Ed.), *Perspectives on memory research* (pp. 35–60). Hillsdale, NJ: Erlbaum.

Estes, W. K. (1997). On the communication of information by displays of standard errors and confidence intervals. *Psychonomic Bulletin & Review, 4,* 330–341.

Feinberg, S. E. (1977). *The analysis of cross-classified categorical data.* Cambridge, MA: MIT Press.

Festinger, L. (1950). Informal social communication. *Psychological Review, 57,* 271–282.

Festinger, L. (1951). A theory of social comparison processes. *Human Relations, 7,* 117–140.

Festinger, L. (1957). *A theory of cognitive dissonance.* Stanford, CA: Stanford University Press.

Fiedler, K. (1996). Explaining and simulating judgment biases as an aggregation phenomenon in probabilistic multiple-cue environments. *Psychological Review, 103,* 193–214.

Fuhrman, R. W., Bodenhausen, G. V., & Lichtenstein, M. (1989). On the trait implications of social behaviors: Kindness, intelligence, goodness, and normality ratings for 400 behavior statements. *Behavior Research Methods, Instruments, & Computers, 21,* 587–597.

Gardner, H. (1985). *The mind's new science.* New York: Basic Books.

Gigerenzer, G. (1996). The modularity of social intelligence. In A. Whiten & R.W. Byrne (Eds.), *Machiavellian intelligence II* (pp. 71–95). Cambridge, England: Cambridge University Press.

Gigone, D. M., & Hastie, R. (1993). The common knowledge effect: Information sharing and group judgment. *Journal of Personality and Social Psychology, 65,* 959–974.

Gigone, D., & Hastie, R. (1996). The impact of information on group judgment: A model and computer simulation. In E. H. Witte & J. H. Davis (Eds.), *Understanding group behavior: Consensual action by small groups* (Vol. 1, pp. 221–251). Mahwah, NJ: Erlbaum.

Gillund, G., & Shiffrin, R. M. (1984). A retrieval model for both recognition and recall. *Psychological Review, 91,* 1–59.

Graesser, A. C., Woll, S. B., Kowalski, D. J., & Smith, D. A. (1980). Memory for typical and atypical actions in scripted activities. *Journal of Experimental Psychology: Human Learning & Memory, 6,* 503–515.

Greenwald, A. G. (1975). On the inconclusiveness of "crucial" cognitive tests of dissonance versus self-perception theories. *Journal of Experimental Social Psychology, 11,* 490–499.

Greenwald, A. G., Pratkanis, A. R., Leippe, M. R., & Baumgardner, M. H. (1986). Under what conditions does theory obstruct research progress? *Psychological Review, 93,* 216–229.

Grossberg, S., & Gutowski, W. E. (1987). Neural dynamics of decision making under risk: Affective balance and cognitive-emotional interactions. *Psychological Review, 94,* 300–318.

Harris, R. J. (1976). The uncertain connection between verbal theories and research hypotheses in social psychology. *Journal of Experimental Social Psychology, 12,* 210–219.

Hastie, R. (1984). Causes and effects of causal attribution. *Journal of Personality and Social Psychology, 46,* 44–56.

Hastie, R. (1988). A computer simulation model of person memory. *Journal of Experimental Social Psychology, 24,* 423–447.

Hastie, R., & Kumar, A. P. (1979). Person memory: Personality traits as organizing principles in memory for behaviors. *Journal of Personality and Social Psychology, 37,* 25–38.

Hastie, R., & Mazur, J. E. (1981). *Memory for information about people presented on film.* Unpublished manuscript, Harvard University, Cambridge, MA.

Hastie, R., & Park, B. (1986). The relationship between memory and judgment depends on whether the judgment task is memory-based or on-line. *Psychological Review, 93,* 258–268.

Hastie, R., Penrod, S. D., & Pennington, N. (1983). *Inside the jury.* Cambridge, MA: Harvard University Press.

Heise, D. (1985). Affect control theory: Respecification, estimation, and tests of the formal model. *Journal of Mathematical Sociology, 11,* 191–222.

Hinsz, V. B., Tindale, R. S., & Vollrath, D. A. (1997). The emerging conceptualization of groups as information processors. *Psychological Bulletin, 121,* 43–64.

Hintzman, D. L. (1991). Why are formal models useful in psychology? In W. E. Hockley & S. Lewandowsky (Eds.), *Relating theory and data: Essays on human memory in honor of Bennet B. Murdock* (pp. 39–56). Hillsdale, NJ: Erlbaum.

Hogarth, R. M., & Einhorn, H. J. (1992). Order effects in belief updating: The belief-adjustment model. *Cognitive Psychology, 24,* 1–55.

Hollingshead, A. B. (1996). The rank order effect on group decision making. *Organizational Behavior and Human Decision Processes, 68,* 181–193.

Hovland, C. I. (1960). Computer simulation of thinking. *American Psychologist, 15*, 687–693.

Huesmann, L. R., & Loevinger, G. (1976). Incremental exchange theory: A formal model for progression in dyadic social interaction: In L. Berkowitz & E. Walster (Eds.), *Advances in Experimental Social Psychology, 19*, pp. 191–229. New York: Academic Press.

Judd, C. M., & McClelland, G. H. (1989). *Data analysis: A model-comparison approach*. Orlando, FI: Harcourt Brace Jovanovich.

Just, M. A., & Carpenter, P. A. (1992). A capacity theory of comprehension: Individual differences in working memory. *Psychological Review, 99*, 122–149.

Kalick, S. M., & Hamilton, T. E., III. (1986). The matching hypothesis reexamined. *Journal of Personality and Social Psychology, 51*, 673–682.

Kalick, S. M., & Hamilton, T. E., III. (1988). Closer look at a matching simulation: Reply to Aron. *Journal of Personality and Social Psychology, 54*, 447–451.

Kashima, Y., & Kerekes, A. R. Z. (1994). A distributed memory model for averaging phenomena in person impression formation. *Journal of Experimental Social Psychology, 30*, 407–455.

Kelley, H. H. (1973). The processes of causal attribution. *American Psychologist, 28*, 107–128.

Kelley, H. H. (1985). A theoretical analysis, by means of computer robots, of single interactions in 2 × 2 games. *Electronic Social Psychology, 1*, 1–78 (Article No. 8501011).

Kerr, N. L., Stasser, G., & Davis, J. H. (1979). Model testing, model fitting, and social decision schemes. *Organizational Behavior and Human Performance, 23*, 399–410.

Kuhn, T. (1970). *The structure of scientific revolutions*. Chicago: University of Chicago Press.

Kunda, Z., & Thagard, P. (1996). Forming impressions from stereotypes, traits, and behaviors: A parallel-constraint-satisfaction theory. *Psychological Review, 103*, 284–308.

Larson, J. R., Jr., & Christensen, C. (1993). Groups as problem-solving units: Toward a new meaning of social cognition. *British Journal of Social Psychology, 32*, 5–30.

Laudan, L. (1977). *Progress and its problems*. Berkeley, CA: University of California Press.

Lewandowsky, S. (1993). The rewards and hazards of computer simulations. *Psychological Science, 4*, 236–243.

Lewin, K. (1951). *Field theory in social science*. New York: Harper.

Linville, P. W., Fischer, G. W., & Salovey, P. (1989). Perceived distributions of the characteristics of in-group and out-group members: Empirical evidence and a computer simulation. *Journal of Personality and Social Psychology, 57*, 165–188.

Loftus, G. R. (1985). Johannes Kepler's computer simulation of the universe: Some remarks about theory in psychology. *Behavior Research Methods, Instruments, & Computers, 17*, 149–156.

Loftus, G. R. (1996). Psychology will be a much better science when we change the way we analyze data. *Current Directions in Psychological Science, 5*, 161–171.

Luce, R. D. (1985). Mathematical modeling of perceptual, learning, and cognitive processes. In S. Koch & D. E. Leary (Eds.), *A century of psychology as a science* (pp. 654–677). New York: McGraw-Hill.

Luce, R. D. (1989). Mathematical psychology and the computer revolution. In J. A. Keats, R. Taft, R. A. Heath, & S. H. Lovibond (Eds.), *Mathematical and theoretical systems* (pp. 123–137). Amsterdam: North-Holland.

Lui, L., & Brewer, M. B. (1983). Recognition accuracy as evidence of category-consistency effects in person memory. *Social Cognition, 2*, 89–107.

MacKinnon, N. J. (1994). *Symbolic interactionism as affect control*. Albany, State University of New York Press.

Marsaglia, G., Zaman, A., & Tsang, W. W. (1990). Toward a universal random number generator. *Statistics & Probability Letters, 8*, 35–39.

McClelland, J. L., & Rumelhart, R. E. (1989). *Explorations in parallel distributed processing: A handbook of models, programs, and exercises*. Cambridge, MA: MIT Press.

McClelland, J. L., Rumelhart, D. E., & Hinton, G. E. (1986). The appeal of parallel distributed processing. In D. E. Rumelhart, J. L. McClelland, and the PDP Research Group (Eds.), *Parallel distributed processing: Explorations in the microstructure of cognition* (Vol. 1, pp. 3–44). Cambridge, MA: MIT Press.

McGuire, W. J. (1968). Personality and attitude change: An information-processing model. In A. G. Greenwald, T. C. Brock, & T. M. Ostrom (Eds.), *Psychological foundations of attitudes* (pp. 171–196). New York: Academic Press.

McGuire, W. J. (1969). The nature of attitudes and attitude change. In G. Lindzey & E. Aronson (Eds.), *Handbook of social psychology* (2nd ed., Vol. 3, pp. 136–314). Reading, MA: Addison-Wesley.

McGuire, W. J. (1983). A contextualist theory of knowledge: Its implications for innovation and reform in psychological research. In L. Berkowitz (Ed.), *Advances in experimental social psychology* (Vol. 16, pp. 1–47). San Diego, CA: Academic Press.

McGuire, W. J. (1989). A perspectivist approach to the strategic planning of programmatic scientific research. In B. Gholson, W. R. Shadish, Jr., R. A. Neimeyer, & A. C. Houts (Eds.), *The psychology of science: Contributions to metascience* (pp. 214–245). New York: Cambridge University Press.

McGuire, W. J. (1997). Creative hypothesis generating in psychology: Some useful heuristics. *Annual Review of Psychology, 48*, 1–30.

Meehl, P. E. (1967). Theory testing in psychology and physics: A methodological paradox. *Philosophy of Science, 34*, 103–115.

Messick, D. M., & Liebrand, W. B. (1993). Computer simulations of the relation between individual heuristics and global cooperation in prisoner's dilemmas. *Social Science Computer Review, 11*, 301–312.

Meyer, D. E., & Kieras, D. E. (1997). A computational theory of executive cognitive processes and multiple-task performance: Part 1. Basic mechanisms. *Psychological Review, 104,* 3–65.

Murdock, B. B., Jr. (1960). The immediate retention of unrelated words. *Journal of Experimental Psychology, 60,* 222–234.

Myers, J. L., Shinjo, M., & Duffy, S. A. (1987). Degree of causal relatedness and memory. *Journal of Memory and Language, 26,* 453–465.

Newell, A. (1990). *Unified theories of cognition.* Cambridge, MA: Harvard University Press.

Newell, A., Rosenbloom, P. S., & Laird, J. E. (1989). Symbolic architectures for cognition. In M. I. Posner (Ed.), *Foundations of cognitive science* (pp. 93–131). Cambridge, MA: MIT Press.

Newell, A., & Simon, H. A. (1972). *Human problem solving.* Englewood Cliffs, NJ: Prentice-Hall.

Nisbett, R. E., & Ross, L. (1980). *Human inference: Strategies and shortcomings of social judgment.* Englewood Cliffs, NJ: Prentice-Hall.

Nowak, A., Szamrej, J., & Latané, B. (1990). From private attitude to public opinion: A dynamic theory of social impact. *Psychological Review, 97,* 362–376.

Ostrom, T. M. (1988). Computer simulation: The third symbol system. *Journal of Experimental Social Psychology, 24,* 381–392.

Parker, K. (1988). Speaking turns in small group interaction: A context-sensitive event sequence model. *Journal of Personality and Social Psychology, 54,* 965–971.

Payne, J. W., Bettman, J. R., & Johnson, E. J. (1993). *The adaptive decision maker.* New York: Cambridge University Press.

Pennington, N., & Hastie, R. (1981). Juror decision making models: The generalization gap. *Psychological Bulletin, 89,* 246–287.

Penrod, S. D., & Hastie, R. (1980). A computer model of jury decision making. *Psychological Review, 87,* 133–159.

Pinker, S., & Prince, A. (1988). On language and connectionism: Analysis of a parallel distributed processing model of language acquisition. *Cognition, 28,* 73–193.

Plomin, R., DeFries, J. C., & McClearn, G. E. (1990). *Behavioral genetics: A primer* (2nd ed.). New York: Freeman.

Poincaré, H. (1952). *Science and method.* London: Dover. (Original work published 1908.)

Quine, W. V., & Ullian, J. S. (1970). *The web of belief.* New York: Random House.

Read, S. J., Vanman, E. J., & Miller, L. C. (1997). Connectionism, parallel constraint satisfaction processes, and Gestalt principles: (Re)introducing cognitive dynamics to social psychology. *Personality and Social Psychology Review, 1,* 26–53.

Restle, F. (1965). Significance of all-or-none learning. *Psychological Bulletin, 64,* 313–325.

Roediger, H. L., III. (1978). Recall as a self-limiting process. *Memory & Cognition, 6,* 54–63.

Rohan, K., & Pettigrew, T. F. (1992). Memory for schema-relevant information: A meta-analytic resolution. *British Journal of Social Psychology, 31,* 81–109.

Schachter, S. (1951). Deviation, rejection, and communication. *Journal of Abnormal and Social Psychology, 46,* 190–207.

Schmidt, F. L. (1996). Statistical significance testing and cumulative knowledge in psychology: Implications for training of researchers. *Psychological Methods, 1,* 115–129.

Shiffrin, R. M., & Nobel, P. A.(1997). The art of model development and testing. *Behavior Research Methods, Instruments, & Computers, 29,* 6–14

Shultz, T. R., & Lepper, M. R. (1996). Cognitive dissonance reduction as constraint satisfaction. *Psychological Review, 103,* 219–240.

Simon, H. A., & Kaplan, C. A. (1989). Foundations of cognitive science. In M. I. Posner (Ed.), *Foundations of cognitive science* (pp. 1–47). Cambridge, MA: MIT Press.

Smith, E. R. (1991). Illusory correlation in a simulated exemplar-based memory. *Journal of Experimental Social Psychology, 27,* 107–123.

Smith, E. R. (1996). What do connectionism and social psychology offer each other? *Journal of Personality and Social Psychology, 70,* 893–912.

Smith, E. R., & Zarate, M. A. (1992). Exemplar-based model of social judgment. *Psychological Review, 99,* 3–21.

Srull, T. K. (1981). Person memory: Some tests of associative storage and retrieval models. *Journal of Experimental Psychology: Learning, Memory, and Cognition, 7,* 440–563.

Stangor, C., & McMillan, D. (1992). Memory for expectancy-congruent and expectancy-incongruent information: A review of the social and social developmental literatures. *Psychological Bulletin, 111,* 42–61.

Stasser, G. (1988). Computer simulation as a research tool: The DISCUSS model of group decision making. *Journal of Experimental Social Psychology, 24,* 393–422.

Stasser, G. (1990). Computer simulation of social interaction. In C. Hendrick & M. S. Clark (Eds.), *Research methods in personality and social psychology* (Vol. 11, pp. 120–141). Newbury Park, CA: Sage.

Stasser, G., & Stewart, D. (1992). The discovery of hidden profiles in decision-making groups: Solving a problem versus making a judgment. *Journal of Personality and Social Psychology, 63,* 426–434.

Stasser, G., Taylor, L. A. (1991). Speaking turns in face-to-face discussions. *Journal of Personality and Social Psychology, 60,* 675–684.

Stasser, G., Taylor, L. A., & Hanna, C. (1989). Information sampling in structured and unstructured discussions of three- and six-person groups. *Journal of Personality and Social Psychology, 57,* 67–78.

Stasser, G., & Titus, W. (1985). Pooling of unshared information in group decision making: Biased information sampling during discussion. *Journal of Personality and Social Psychology, 48,* 1467–1478.

Stasser, G., & Titus, W. (1987). Effects of information load and percentage shared information on the dissemination of unshared information during group discussion. *Journal of Personality and Social Psychology, 53,* 81–93.

Stasser, G., & Vaughan, S. I. (1996). Models of participation in face-to-face unstructured discussions. In J. H. Davis &

E. Witte (Eds.), *Understanding group behavior: Consensual action by small groups* (Vol. 1, pp. 165–192). Hillsdale, NJ: Erlbaum.

Stephan, F. F., & Mishler, E. G. (1952). The distribution of participation in small groups: An exponential approximation. *American Sociological Review, 17,* 598–608.

Taylor, S. E., & Fiske, S. T. (1981). Getting inside the head: Methodologies for process analysis in attribution and social cognition. In J. H. Harvey, W. Ickes, & R. F. Kidd (Eds.), *New directions in attribution research* (Vol. 3, pp. 459–524). Hillsdale, NJ: Erlbaum.

Thorngate, W., & Carroll, B. (1987). Why the best person rarely wins: Some embarrassing facts. *Simulation & Games, 18,* 299–320.

Townsend, J. T., & Kadlec, H. (1990). Psychology and mathematics. In R. E. Mickens (Ed.), *Mathematics and science* (pp. 224–248). Singapore: World Scientific.

Tulving, E. (1974). Cue-dependent forgetting. *American Scientist, 62,* 74–82.

Tversky, A., & Kahneman, D. (1974, 27 September). Judgement under uncertainty: Heuristics and biases. *Science, 185,* 1124–11131.

Vallacher, R. R., & Nowak, A. (1994). The stream of social judgment. In R. R. Vallacher & A. Nowak (Eds.), *Dynamical systems in social psychology* (pp. 251–293). San Diego, CA: Academic Press.

Von Eckardt, B. (1993). *What is cognitive science?* Cambridge, MA: MIT Press.

Weiner, B. (1985). "Spontaneous" causal thinking. *Psychological Bulletin, 97,* 74–84.

Wittenbaum, G. M., & Stasser, G. (1999). The reevaluation of information during group discussion. *Group Processes and Interpersonal Relations, 1,* 21–34.

Wyer, R. S., Jr., & Srull, T. K. (1986). Human cognition in its social context. *Psychological Review, 93,* 322–359.

PART TWO

PROCEDURAL POSSIBILITIES

Using Physiological Indexes of Psychological Processes in Social Psychological Research

JIM BLASCOVICH

Many researchers tout the value of objective measures of psychological constructs. In particular, covert physiological measures enjoy a certain positive mystique among social psychologists. This mystique derives in part from the assumption shared by scientists and research participants alike that bodily processes, particularly less consciously controllable, covert ones, enjoy an unbiased veridical relationship to psychological constructs and processes. Not surprisingly, the mystique surrounding physiological measures, like most others, partially derives from a sense of the unknown.

Jones and Sigall (1971) exploited this mystique very creatively. They convinced research participants that physiological measures recorded through electrode sensors connecting their bodies to the researchers' sophisticated looking physiological recording devices would reveal their true thoughts and feelings even though the researchers did not really record physiological responses. Their "bogus pipeline" presumably motivated human participants to self-report what the machines would supposedly reveal objectively. The rationale underlying the bogus pipeline underlies the success of much lie-detection work. Whether or not physiological measures index psychological constructs veridically, when individuals believe that they do they are more likely to reveal their hidden thoughts and feelings. Most lie-detection experts, or "polygraphers" as they prefer, realize this fact. Their success stems more from confessions of likely suspects than from physiological patterns unequivocally associated with truth and lying actually recorded from suspects (Saxe,

This work was partially funded by National Science Foundation Grant SBR93-10202. Correspondence should be addressed to Jim Blascovich, Department of Psychology, University of California, Santa Barbara, CA 93106.

Dougherty, & Cross, 1987). Jones and Sigall also realized this fact.

Social psychologists no longer need rely on this mystique or illusion. We can now often successfully test our theories using validated physiological response patterns associated with important psychological constructs and processes in addition to the more traditional self-report and behavioral indexes. Valid physiological indexes of psychological processes represent "real," rather than bogus, pipelines. The methodological tools to distinguish physiologically between even a few sets of major psychological states enables social psychological researchers to critically evaluate models that assume the existence of one or more of such states as a function of theoretically specified circumstances and provide even more power to multimethod triangulation. This chapter concerns some of the apparent successes, that is, the real pipelines.

Imagine the existence of an assortment of assessment tools, or indexes, that would allow researchers to distinguish objectively and accurately appetitive from aversive motivational states, positive from negative affect, attention from inattention, and linguistic from nonlinguistic processing. Imagine further that these indexes used participant responses outside of their conscious control. Further, imagine that the indexes were available continuously, fluctuating as the underlying psychological states fluctuate over time. Such indexes would allow social psychologists to test the motivational, affective, and cognitive underpinnings of a wide range of theories within typical empirical contexts guided by powerful experimental designs. Physiological responses can provide such indexes.

Today, social psychologists can avail themselves of important physiological indexes of psychological processes, including motivational, affective, and cognitive ones. We hope to help the reader understand the nature of psychophysiological processes and the utility of psychophysiological measures as state-of-the-art empirical indexes of constructs fundamental to social psychological theories. Casual readers should benefit as consumers of social psychological research that includes psychophysiological measures. More thorough and resourceful readers should be able to begin to implement psychophysiological measures in their own research.

In this chapter, we cover relevant background information, including the evolution of social psychophysiology, a brief discussion of relevant epistemological issues, and the nature of physiological indexing. We also briefly review and integrate general information regarding physiological control processes and general technological approaches to their measurement. We move on to a brief discussion of threats to validity in physiological measurement. Next, we present illustrations of state-of-the-art physiological indexes of important motivational and affective constructs. Finally, we conclude with a general assessment and summary.

BACKGROUND INFORMATION

The Evolution of Social Psychophysiology

HISTORY. Though the use of heart rate to index interpersonal attraction places ancient Greek and Roman physicians at its historical beginnings, social psychophysiology began taking shape early in the 20th century. Researchers such as Riddle (1925), Lasswell (1936), Mittleman and Wolff (1939), and Boyd and DeMascio (1954) explored the relationships of specific psychological constructs, such as motivation, speech rate, emotions, and the nature of relationships to specific unitary physiological responses including respiration, pulse rate, finger temperature, and skin conductance. These early explorations, though mostly eventual failures substantively, exemplified the forward thinking of at least some investigators who believed that combining biological and psychological approaches could provide useful information to proponents of each.

We can learn from the early history of social psychophysiology by asking the question, "Why did these initial explorations fail to fulfill their promise?" They failed for many reasons: the naive integration of relatively unsophisticated physiological and psychological theoretical frameworks, weak logical and epistemological bases for drawing inferences, and primitive methodologies and technological apparati. Yet, in some sense,

these weaknesses, the errors in a sort of transcendent methodological trial-and-error scheme, provided some necessary steps in the evolution of social psychophysiology. Consequently, these weaknesses represent problems that we can learn about and avoid.

The promise of physiological indexes drove remedies for problems inherent in the integration of social psychology and psychophysiology. These began appearing in the literature with Shapiro and Crider's (1969) classic *Handbook of Social Psychology* chapter on physiological approaches to social psychology. Cacioppo and Petty's (1983) and Waid's (1984) edited volumes, respectively entitled *Social Psychophysiology* and *Sociophysiology*, showcased the works of newer, more fruitful investigations integrating social psychological and psychophysiological methodologies. The intensive summer "Program for Advanced Study and Research in Social Psychophysiology" (sometimes fondly referred to as "bootcamp"), sponsored by the National Science Foundation and led by John Cacioppo and his colleagues during the summers of 1986 through 1990, provided over 60 mostly social psychological researchers a firm grounding in psychophysiological theory and measurement techniques as well as in important logic, epistemology, and psychophysiological data analytic techniques.

FUNCTION. Social psychophysiology functions in the broadest sense as a methodology. Its value for social psychologists lies primarily in its provision of a growing set of objective measures or indexes of theoretical and empirical constructs. To be sure, valid use of these indexes or "pipelines" requires important background information about theory and technology. Fortunately, more and more sophisticated information of this type has become available. The advantages of social psychophysiological methodology accrue from its stipulation of relatively unbiased, real-time based measures of psychological constructs and indexes related to motivational, affective, and cognitive constructs – ones that often prove difficult to quantify without bias or artifact in the absence of such objective assessments and impossible to quantify otherwise in vivo. The disadvantages accrue from the difficulty in attaining appropriate background information and sometimes cumbersome (i.e., obtrusive) equipment, as well as cost. Though appropriate and less obtrusive equipment constantly becomes more reasonably priced, utilizing social psychophysiological indexes usually involves an investment in equipment above that involved in utilization of more traditional social psychological methodologies.

Epistemological Issues

The gradual rejection of Cartesian dualism by many life scientists has opened up several new avenues of exploration linking mind and body (cf. DeMascio, 1994). The emergence and growth of new and intellectually exciting fields, such as social psychophysiology, psychoneuroimmunology, and psychoneuroendocrinology, give testimony to the value of multilevel or multisystemic approaches to understanding the interconnections of body and mind. Social psychophysiology, like these other approaches, assumes the *identity thesis*. Specifically, social psychophysiologists assume that biological structures and physiological processes embody all human behaviors, including thoughts and feelings as well as overt actions. Consequently, researchers can turn to these structures and processes in order to learn more about social behavior (Cacioppo & Tassinary, 1990b).

Unfortunately, a one-to-one correspondence between specific behaviors and unitary physiological responses rarely exists. (Parenthetically, one-to-one relationships rarely exist for self-report or behavioral indexes either.) This lack of singular correspondence derives both from the multifunctionality of physiological processes and the complexity of behavior. Heart rate, as one example, generally increases during overt physical activities such as aerobic exercise, but it also increases during covert mental activities such as anticipation of the arrival of a romantic partner at an airport, completion of a written examination, or speech preparation. Thus, an increase in heart rate, or any other "single" physiological response for that matter, typically fails to unambiguously index specific behaviors.

In order for biological responses to be useful methodologically to social psychologists, we must understand both the biological and psychological contexts within which these responses occur. Unfortunately, sufficient understanding and familiarity with the biological context has eluded many of us. In the not-so-distant past, social psychologists, like many others, simply assumed the interchangeability of, particularly but not necessarily, autonomic and somatic physiological responses such as heart rate, blood pressure, skin conductance, and muscle tension as indexes of emotional and motivational constructs. Although not as frequently, we still see this rather naive type of approach reported in the social psychological literature.

On the other hand, psychophysiologists (as opposed to social psychophysiologists) have traditionally ignored much of the social psychological context. Traditionally, psychophysiologists assume that error variance in the relationships between specific behaviors and specific physiological responses derives not only from random measurement error but also from the contributions of systematic individual and situational influences. Thus, "individual response stereotypy" and "situational response stereotypy" provide catch-all categories accounting for individual differences in responses to similar situations and for differences in responses between situations as sources of error among traditional psychophysiologists.

Psychophysiologists do not assume the interchangeability of psychologically related physiological responses, and social psychologists do not treat individual and situational influences on any kind of responses as uninteresting or as error. Social psychophysiologists should do neither. The researcher employing a social psychophysiological approach must base his or her assumption of the critical identity thesis on thorough knowledge of its biopsychosocial underpinnings.

The Nature of Physiological Indexes of Psychological Constructs

Invariance defines the ideal relationship between a construct and its index. At the nominal level of measurement, invariance means that the construct and the index always co-occur. If the construct is there, so is the index and vice versa. For example, immunologists often index the occurrence of specific viral infections by the presence of specific viral antibodies. If the individual shows any evidence of the antibody, immunologists assume that the individual is or was once infected. If the individual shows no evidence of the antibody, they assume the individual has never been infected. At the ordinal level of measurement, invariance means that the construct and the index always co-occur and covary in a ranked or ordinal manner. For example, angiographers index coronary artery disease using ordinally increasing categories of occlusion for each coronary artery that they assess from cineangiographic (or "moving") x-rays of the coronary arteries in vivo. Consequently, level 3 occlusion indexes more disease than level 2 occlusion and less than level 4 occlusion.[1] At the interval-ratio level, invariance means that the construct and the index always co-occur and covary

---

[1] Though angiographers usually express the degree of arterial occlusion as percentages, their discrimination is traditionally based on six ordinal categories labeled inaccurately and inappropriately as "0," "25," "50," "75," "99," and "100" percent. The terminology "level 1, level 2," etc. in this text is chosen so as not to confuse the reader.

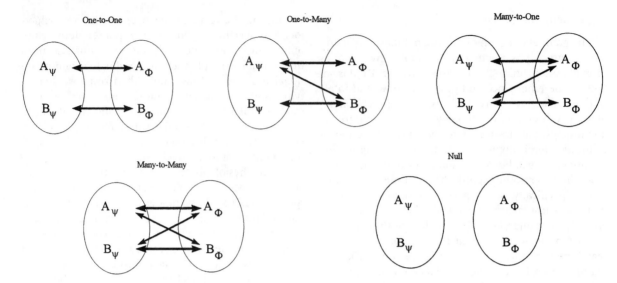

Figure 5.1. General relationships between psychological constructs (ψ) and physiological responses (ϕ).

monotonically. For example, exercise physiologists index muscle movement from integrated muscle action potentials. The greater the integrated muscle action potential, the greater the muscle flexion.

Unfortunately, despite many attempts, physiological invariants of psychological constructs have proven difficult to establish for at least two reasons. First, invariant indexes, whether subjective or objective, of social psychological constructs often prove elusive because of target constructs; for example, risk-taking, love, prejudice, self-concept, themselves prove difficult to define (Blascovich & Ginsburg, 1978). Second, as suggested above, a one-to-one correspondence between specific psychological constructs and unitary physiological responses rarely exists. Both domains are quite complex. Nevertheless, one can still devise valid physiological indexes or indicators of psychological constructs, perhaps even invariant ones.

We contend that, in general, as one narrows or limits the behavioral construct and expands the constellation of physiological responses forming the index, one can approach the one-to-one correspondence necessary to the development of valid physiological indexes of the behavioral constructs. Limiting the psychosocial context often limits the behavioral construct. Expanding the constellation of physiological responses can be accomplished by examining multiple physiological responses over time (Blascovich & Kelsey, 1990; Cacioppo & Tassinary, 1990a). Consequently, a constellation of physiological responses can constitute an

index that serves as a marker, if not an invariant, of context-specific psychological constructs.

Cacioppo and Tassinary (1990a, 1990b), building on the work of Troland (1929), described the general nature of relationships between specific behavioral constructs and specific physiological responses in five categories: one-to-one, one-to-many, many-to-one, many-to-many, and null (see Figure 5.1). As implied above, one-to-one relationships form the basis for meaningful and specific physiological (as well as other types) indexes of psychological constructs. In a sense, a one-to-one relationship forms the goal for development of social psychophysiological indexes.

Figure 5.1 (upper left panel) depicts one-to-one relationships between different psychological constructs (represented by A_ψ and B_ψ) and different sets of physiological responses (represented by A_ϕ and B_ϕ) symbolically. The development of valid and useful physiological indexes of the constructs is more likely if the following four propositions hold:

1. *The psychological constructs, A_ψ and B_ψ are conceptually distinct.* This proposition assumes the necessity of appropriate conceptual analysis and operational definition of the constructs of interest. One cannot index a psychological construct until one defines it explicitly and operationalizes it validly (Blascovich & Ginsburg, 1978). To the extent that psychological constructs are conceptually clear and nonoverlapping (e.g. threat and challenge; joy and sadness) rather than overlapping (e.g., threat and fear; compassionate and companiate love), distinctive physiological indexes are more likely. This proposition applies to physiological and nonphysiological indexes alike.

For this reason, physiological indexes are as unlikely as any to allow us to differentiate easily related but fuzzy concepts such as liking and loving, sadness and depression, peripheral and heuristic cognitive processing, achievement and intrinsic motivation, etc. Furthermore, the strategy of equating a psychological construct with a specific set of physiological responses creates the problem of definitional operationism (e.g., intelligence is what intelligence tests measure) unless an invariant relationship has been demonstrated.

2. *The sets of physiological responses, A_ϕ and B_ϕ, are each more inclusive (e.g., cardiac, hemodynamic, and vascular) rather than less inclusive (e.g., heart rate).* According to this proposition, although a single physiological response comprises the logically minimal response set defining a physiological index, given the many interrelationships among psychological and physiological processes, sets including two or more responses are considerably more desirable if not essential. Two major arguments support this proposition. First, statistically, n responses occurring in predictable ways are less likely to occur by chance then $n - 1$ responses. Hence, the problem of Type I error becomes reduced, and the basis for inference becomes stronger. Second, because the body's physiological systems predictably work in concert, sometimes in a complementary and sometimes in an oppositional fashion, the greater the number of physiological responses comprising an index, the more convergent and divergent validation of the psychological construct they provide.

3. *The sets of physiological responses, A_ϕ and B_ϕ, overlap in substance but not in form.* Stronger inference results when differing internal patterns of a common set of physiological responses, rather than different sets of physiological responses, distinguish the psychological constructs. Hence, differential patterns involving the same sets of physiological responses provide distinguishing information. From a purely logical point of view it matters little whether every physiological response in a set differs from its counterpart in the other set, only that at least one does.

4. *The sets of physiological responses, A_ϕ and B_ϕ, are assessed continuously over time.* Continuous time-series assessment of physiological responses increases the likelihood of distinguishing differential patterns of responses between sets of overlapping responses above and beyond that of single time-point samples of each response or even averaged n-point samples. For example, multiple time-point assessments allow us to discern patterns involving

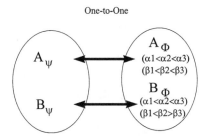

One-to-One

Figure 5.2. Expanded notion of one-to-one relationships between constructs (ψ) and physiological responses (ϕ).

linear increases versus decreases, accelerations versus decelerations, and polynomial trends versus linear ones; whereas, single time-point samples or averaged n-point samples do not. Figure 5.2 illustrates the incorporation of these four propositions into the graphic illustrating one-to-one relationships.

One must note two points of logic. First, it is not a necessary condition of valid indexing that any of these propositions hold. Single response indexes are logically possible and arguably valid as we see below. Second, conditions satisfying all four propositions are not sufficient for valid indexing. Thus, even if all these propositions hold, a reasonable basis for one-to-one relationships and, hence, indexes, is not achieved unless a reasonable theoretical basis for relating the specific construct with a specific pattern of physiological responses exists. However, satisfaction of these propositions increases the confidence with which we can theoretically propose or empirically apply an index.

As we will illustrate later in the chapter, the development of an appropriate theoretical basis for a physiological index may occur deductively, inductively, or a combination of the two. That is, one may derive or deduce differential patterns among physiological responses as a function of the mediation of distinctive psychological processes on the basis of existing physiological and social psychological theory, or one may establish the association of specific patterns with specific psychological processes and develop and test a theoretical explanation or basis for the relationship.

BASIC PHYSIOLOGICAL PROCESSES

Understanding of bodily processes and their relevance to psychological processes continues for scholars at a rapidly advancing pace. Likewise, new technological approaches to observation and recording of bodily processes appear constantly. The more we know about each, the better we can justify, develop, and implement psychophysiological indexes of psychological constructs and processes. Clearly, those interested in social psychophysiology can avail themselves of more sophisticated physiological indexes of psychological constructs today than a decade ago. Just as clearly, those interested will be able to avail themselves of even more sophisticated indexes in the future. In this section, we can only sketch some of the important aspects of physiological processes. We encourage readers wishing to use physiological indexes to avail themselves of physiological background material from excellent sources such as Cacioppo and Tassinary (1990a), Coles, Donchin, and Porges (1986), and specialty sources as necessary.

The ways that the body meets the requirements of life maintenance and environmental demands continues to amaze. Biochemical, electrochemical, hydraulic, and mechanical processes operate in fantastically complicated but well-organized and integrated ways to operate and maintain anatomical structures as well as life-sustaining (i.e., metabolic) processes efficiently and to produce behaviors involving simultaneous psychological processes, including motivation, cognition, affect, and movement.

We can describe the body from a systems or subsystems perspective dichotomizing bodily systems, albeit somewhat fuzzily, into control and operational ones. The former include neural, endocrine, and immunological systems. The latter include cardiovascular, digestive, electrodermal, respiratory, somatic systems, etc. Both system types involve basic cellular and intercellular tissues and processes. Hierarchically, the neural systems generally control or at least influence the other control systems directly and the operational systems both directly and indirectly through the endocrine and immunological systems, although endocrine and immunological control systems also may influence neural systems directly.

CONTROL SYSTEMS

Neural Processes

STRUCTURE AND FUNCTION. The structure of the neural system has traditionally been organized anatomically because gross neural functions generally follow structure and location. However, one should note that the gross components of the neural system are quite well integrated and that various neural control mechanisms are not necessarily specific to different anatomical neural structures. Thus, the classic structures and

substructures of the nervous system, such as the central nervous system (brain and spinal cord), autonomic nervous system (sympathetic and parasympathetic), and somatic nervous system, do not operate autonomously.

The nervous system functions in large measure as a communication and control system. Nearly every part of the body communicates with the brain by sending signals to the central nervous system via afferent peripheral nerves. Peripheral nerves enter (or "project" to) the brain through the spinal cord and brain stem. The brain internally transfers these signals to reception areas called somatosensory cortices. Projections from the somatosensory cortices directly and indirectly signal (i.e., communicate with) other areas and structures of the brain, which "interpret" these signals and, in turn, generate outgoing neural (i.e., efferent) and endocrine signals that control distal or peripheral physiological processes. These control areas of the brain are somewhat specialized and include areas such as the amygdala and hypothalamus, involved in control of visceral and other autonomically controlled organs and areas, and the motor cortices and subcortical motor nuclei, involved in control of the musculoskeletal system.

CELLULAR PROCESSES. Single-cell neurons provide the basic building blocks of the nervous system. Billions of neurons exist in the overall system with most located in the brain. Configurations of neurons allow signal transmissions within and between the peripheral and central nervous systems, transmissions fundamental to macrolevel neural processes. Although neurons can be distinguished on the basis of several dimensions, including size, length, and location (e.g. central or peripheral), all neurons operate in the same general way, receiving and transmitting biochemical and bioelectric signals organized and generated by bodily or brain structures or by other neurons. Neuronal cell structure and physiology facilitates this function.

Endocrine Processes

The relatively simple organization and structure of the endocrine system belies its power. Upon neural stimulation, the pituitary gland generally initiates endocrine processes vis-á-vis the release of specific target chemical substances known as hormones into the blood stream which, in turn, stimulate various bodily tissues including neural tissues and other endocrine tissues. The various specific endocrine glands secrete still other hormones and neurotransmitters that affect various physiological processes. Direct neural stimulation of specific endocrine glands also occurs. The endocrine system functions directly to regulate growth and maturation and indirectly to modulate neural control of various operational systems. Psychophysiologists recognize the latter function as quite important.

TECHNOLOGICAL BACKGROUND

That the connection of sensors between participants' bodies and sophisticated appearing electronic recording equipment within "bogus pipeline" experiments required little or no technological expertise on the part of researchers undoubtedly played a role in the popularity of such experiments. In contrast, that such connections within the context of real pipelines or valid physiological indexes require technological expertise has undoubtedly inhibited the adoption of social psychophysiological methods. However, in our humble opinion, such sophistication does not lie outside the grasp of social psychologists, and its value far outweighs its cost. Here we focus on an overview of "dry" technology, namely, the technology of electrophysiological recording. This focus does not devalue the worth of "wet" technology, namely, the technology of biochemical analysis within the social psychophysiological approach. Rather, it merely reflects the major technology employed to date by the majority of social psychologists using psychophysiological indexes and the technology most appropriate to the indexes of motivation and affect described below (but see Grunberg & Singer, 1990, for interesting exceptions to the use of "dry" technology).

The technology of electrophysiological recording includes all steps between acquisition of physiological response signals and their recording. As depicted in Figure 5.3, in the most complete case, physiological responses or signals are sensed, transduced, conditioned, and recorded. Successful implementation of physiological indexing of psychological constructs requires at least a conceptual understanding on the part of the investigator of what occurs technologically at each of the steps in the signal path. Fortunately, less detailed technical knowledge is required as the availability, sophistication, and user-friendliness of physiological recording equipment continues to improve.

Figure 5.3. Signal path.

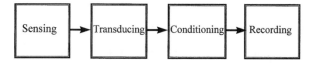

Physiological Response Signals

Historically, psychophysiologists have focused their technological expertise primarily on noninvasive[2] measurement techniques developing and implementing ways of recording internal physiological responses of interest from the surface of the body. The success of this approach stems in no small part from the fact that various physiological events or responses produce surface detectable signals including both electrical and nonelectrical ones. The former include actual changes in electrical potentials as a function of specific physiological processes (e.g., changes in electrical potential across the heart as it complete its cycle, changes in muscle action potentials as muscle bundles contract). The latter include changes in pressure (e.g., intraarterial blood pressure, intraocular pressure), movement (e.g., heart, lungs, digestive organs, blood flow), temperature, and tissue (e.g., production of sweat).

Signal Path

The path of physiological response signals for measurement purposes leads from the surface of the body to recording (see Figure 5.3). The signal path for electrical signals requires three steps, whereas the signal path for nonelectrical signals requires four steps. The additional step, signal transducing, changes nonelectrical physiological signals into analog electrical signals.

SENSORS. Electrodes provide the sensors for electrical physiological signals. Although varied in size, shape, and electrical conducting characteristics according to their intended purpose (i.e., specific signal of interest), all electrodes function identically in terms of picking up changes in electrical potentials. If some part of the body (e.g., the heart, a muscle) emits changes in electrical potential of interest to the investigator, careful placement of electrodes[3] will allow the investigator to optimize recording of that electrical potential.

Sensors for nonelectrical physiological signals include electrodes and other devices. Electrodes in this

---

[2] Noninvasive here refers to measurement techniques requiring no "invasion" of the tissues of the body below the epidermis (layer of dead skin cells on the surface of the body).

[3] Electrode configurations include both unipolar (requiring 2 electrodes) and bipolar (requiring 3 electrodes) types, with the latter regarded as more reliable. An adequate discussion of electrode configurations and placements lies beyond the scope of this chapter. However, one can find the necessary details in a variety of excellent sources, including Marshall-Goodell, Tassinary, and Cacioppo (1990).

case help researchers discern tissue changes not from changes in electrical potentials emitted by bodily organs, but rather by enabling the investigator to deliver safe levels of electrical current to tissues, which by nature of specified physiological changes (e.g., increased levels of sweat in a sweat duct, blood flow through the heart) reliably influence current flow and measure changes in such flow. Using similar principles, other sensing devices help researchers discern physiological changes by delivering nonelectrical stimulation to the body and sensing changes in physiological response to such stimulation. For example, a photoplethysmograph uses a small lamp to deliver light to the surface of the skin (e.g., on the distal phallange of a finger or on the ear lobe) combined with a photosensitive cell a short distance away sensing changes in light diffusion through the skin as a function of blood flow. Various other devices sense important nonelectrical physiological signals, including movement-sensitive devices such as strain gauges and temperature-sensitive devices such as thermistors.

TRANSDUCERS. As mentioned above, nonelectrical physiological response signals (e.g., blood flow, sweat levels) must be converted or *transduced* to analog electrical (i.e., voltage) signals. This occurs early in the signal path. Most transducers operate through principles of electrical bridging.[4] Bridge circuits produce a continuous voltage signal representing bioelectrical physiological responses measured with electrode sensors such as skin conductance and thoracic impedance. If one uses a fluctuating physical resistance device driven by an apparatus sensitive to nonelectrical physiological responses (e.g., strain gauge, thermistor, photoelectric cell), a bridge circuit will similarly produce a voltage analog signal corresponding to the underlying physiological cause of the nonelectrical physiological responses (e.g. movement, temperature, blood flow).

CONDITIONING. The next step in the signal path alleviates signal acquisition problems stemming from two factors: signal specificity and signal strength. The former relates to other physiological potentials and to ambient electronic noise, Here, the researcher must be able to focus on the signal of interest despite the fact that the myriad organs and tissues of the body constantly produce electrical signals that become

diffused throughout the body as they near its surface and despite the pervasiveness of ambient electronic noise generated by electrical equipment. Generally, the researcher must also magnify the signals of interest in order to record them because recording devices generally require more powerful input signals than the body produces. Physiological potentials range from microvolt (0.000001 V) to millivolt (0.001 V) levels depending on the target physiological response. Many nonelectrical signals also require amplification because voltage and current levels applied to bodily tissue to assess changes in physiological responses such as sweat or blood volume activity must necessarily be quite weak for safety purposes.

Signal filtering and amplification represent the two primary modes of dealing with the problems of signal specificity and signal strength. Because physiological response potentials of interest to psychologists generally cycle at different frequencies, ranging from as much as 500 Hz (cycles per second) for muscle action potentials to less than 1 Hz for cardiac potentials and less than 0.1 Hz for gastric contractions, psychophysiologists use electronic filters to prevent signals outside the frequency range of the target signal from obfuscating the signal of interest. Electronic amplification provides psychophysiologists with the tools necessary to boost the strength of signals without altering signal topography.

RECORDING. The last step in the signal path requires storage. Historically various devices have performed this function. Indeed, the polygraph takes its name from the first of these, the multichannel paper recording device. This device transformed analog voltage signals into pen excursions, which recorded voltage changes as waveforms on graph paper moving right to left under the pens. Actual manual measurements of various aspects of these waveforms provided necessary data values. With the advancement of electronic technology, analog voltage waveforms could be stored on magnetic tape. Today, widely available laboratory computers incorporating analog-to-digital converters allow on-line and high fidelity digitization of analog waveforms, allowing recording on mass media storage devices such as disk drives. Software algorithms have replaced manual measurement thereby automating scoring of these analog signals and decreasing data errors (e.g., Kelsey & Guethlein, 1990).

SPECIFIC METHODOLOGICAL CONCERNS

In addition to knowledge of specialized signal path technology, proper use of psychophysiological indexes

---

[4] Detailed discussion of the role of bridge circuits in physiological transducers lies beyond the scope of this chapter. Again, one can find the necessary details in a variety of excellent sources, including Marshall-Goodell, Tassinary, and Cacioppo (1990).

within the experimental domain requires attention to specific threats to validity. Although social psychologists know well the labels and the logical and substantive bases for many such threats (thanks in large part to Campbell & Stanley, 1963; see Smith this volume, Ch. 2), we generally lack familiarity with their manifestations within the psychophysiological domain. In addition to general concern regarding all the threats to validity, researchers must take special care to ameliorate the effects of maturation, testing, and instrumentation when using psychophysiological indexes.

Threats to Validity

MATURATION. Maturation poses special considerations for psychophysiological researchers not only in terms of gross cross-sectional maturational differences among research participants but also in terms of relatively short-lived within- and between-participant differences. Regarding the former, one should usually avoid including participants from grossly different age groups (e.g., adolescents, senior citizens) in the same study because the nature of many psychophysiological meaningful responses often changes dramatically over the lifespan. For example, muscles atrophy with age. Using certain somatic electromyographic (EMG) measures of teenagers and octogenarians could increase the ratio of unwanted to meaningful variance to levels rendering the statistical power of a design quite low.

Perhaps less obviously, biological processes related to fatigue, digestion, drug intake, environment, etc. moderate physiological and therefore psychophysiological responses. Investigators employing psychophysiological indexes should take into account normal individual and diurnal maturational variations in various behaviors such as eating, drinking, exercise, and sleep, as well as environmental factors including temperature and humidity. Experimentally controlling individual and diurnal variations in metabolic processes clearly requires not only random assignment of participants to experimental sessions during normal, nonprandial waking hours but also often requires specific instructions regarding sleeping, eating, and drug taking (e.g., alcohol, caffeine, medications, nicotine) behaviors prior to experimental sessions.

TESTING. Our physiological systems usually adapt to environmental stimuli and demands. Novel stimuli and demands generally elicit stronger physiological responses than familiar ones. Physiological responses can habituate to repeated stimulus presentation or situational demands relatively quickly, often within a couple of minutes.[5] Consequently, if repeated stimulus presentations or if repetitive behaviors (including cognitions) prove experimentally necessary, one must often control for habituation effects. In social psychological investigations, this can usually be accomplished by changing the content or form of the stimuli or task demands. For example, cardiovascular responses to a serial subtraction task will quickly return to baseline unless the subtractand is periodically changed.

Another unique effect of testing in psychophysiological experiments involves iatrogenic changes in the nature of the target variable or measure itself. For example, repeated blood pressure readings involving occlusive blood pressure cuffs can temporarily compress vascular tissue underneath the cuff causing less than normal vascular elasticity, which in turn leads to erroneous blood pressure readings as well as the discomfort of experimental participants. The solution involves either decreasing the frequency of such intrusive measurement procedures allowing underlying tissues to recover fully between measurements or the use of minimally intrusive monitoring equipment (which in most cases, including blood pressure equipment, is available).

INSTRUMENTATION. Although physiological measurement apparati have become substantially more reliable than even a few years ago, operating characteristics of such equipment as well as those of the measurement environment can and do change. A controlled, noise-free (electronically and otherwise) environment optimizes physiological recording reliability. A well-trained, noise-free operator, one who understands the nature of the measurement devices, proper participant hookup, calibration, and recording also usually prove beneficial.

Design Implications

Valid studies involving psychophysiological measures invariably employ pretest–posttest control group designs (Campbell & Stanley, 1963). Multiple or continuous measurements are included both prior to and during or following experimental manipulations. The pretest measurements constitute "baseline" or resting levels allowing a check on desired physiological adaptation to the recording environment itself and a check on physiological comparability of randomly assigned groups. This multiple or continuous within-participant

---

[5] Sensitization effects can also occur but are relatively rare. Nonetheless, the same logic for control as for habituation effects applies here.

measurement strategy proves advantageous for the indexing strategy already delineated (see propositions above) and allows the investigator to statistically minimize individual differences in basal physiological responses. For more complicated versions of the pretest–posttest designs, counterbalancing strategies minimize adaptation effects for multiple within-subjects manipulations (West, Biesanz, & Pitts, this volume, Ch. 3).

USEFUL PHYSIOLOGICAL INDEXES OF PSYCHOLOGICAL CONSTRUCTS

To this point, we have reviewed information important to psychophysiological indexing albeit briefly (though we encourage interested readers to avail themselves of more of the same on their own). Although this information might prove interesting in its own right, its value would certainly shrink (and this chapter would be premature) if valid and reliable psychophysiological indexes of critical constructs for theory testing in social psychological did not exist. Fortunately, several important psychophysiological indexes have appeared, and we expect that more will follow. Indeed, we hope this chapter further promotes their use and the development of additional ones.

Although we have chosen not to exhaust all plausible physiological indexes of psychological constructs of interest to social psychologists here, our illustrations stem not just from the limits of a chapter of prescribed length but also from our judgment that the specific indexes described below assess critical motivational and affective states or processes and are well-validated.

Psychophysiological Indexes of Motivational States: Challenge and Threat

Do academic performance stereotypes really threaten minority group members as Steele and his colleagues (Steele & Aronson, 1995) have hypothesized? Are low self-esteem individuals challenged by task failure as Swann (1983) has suggested? Do self-protective strategies such as self-handicapping reduce threat as Berglas and Jones (1978) have hypothesized? What coping strategies increase challenge or reduce threat? Does actual intergroup contact promote challenge or threat? Testing of these and myriad other hypotheses can benefit from the utilization of a psychophysiological index of challenge and threat developed over the past 5 years or so in our laboratory. Here, we review the rationale underlying the index and its validation and provide an example or two of its use.

RATIONALE

CONSTRUCTS. Recall from the discussion above that fuzzy or implicit definitions of many psychological constructs impede the successful development of indexes of them, including psychophysiological ones. We can, however, explicitly define motivational constructs such as challenge and threat. We define challenge and threat in terms of individuals' relative assessments of situational demands and available resources to meet those demands (Blascovich & Tomaka, 1996). Accordingly, *challenge* results from the evaluation of resources as meeting or exceeding demands, and *threat* results from the evaluation of demands exceeding resources.

CONTEXT. Recall also our contention that one can develop strong psychophysiological indexes of a construct by narrowing or limiting the psychosocial context. For example, one cannot necessarily interpret the increases in cardiac performance such as ventricular contractility and cardiac output that occur in metabolically demanding situations such as jogging in the same way that one interprets increases that occur in situations without such metabolic demands. Likewise, even within nonmetabolically demanding situations, one must evaluate increases in cardiac performance in situations requiring active cognitive responses differently than in those situations requiring passive endurance (Obrist, 1981).

Of course, limiting the psychosocial context of psychophysiological indexes precludes the possibility of invariant indexes. However, we do not view the downside as particularly problematic as invariance can be claimed for relatively few indexes in psychology and because limiting the generality does not mean rendering the index meaningless. Provided the context represents a large or meaningful cross section of the behavioral domain, one can aim for a marker, thereby providing the basis for strong inference within the specified type of context.

In the development of our cardiovascular indexes of challenge and threat, we limited the context to what we label *motivated performance situations*. Motivated performance situations are goal-relevant to the individual thereby engendering some degree of self- or other evaluation. Furthermore, motivated performance situations require instrumental cognitive responses and often overt actions on the part of the performer. We further limited motivated performance situations to nonmetabolically demanding ones, that is, ones excluding gross, repetitive muscle movements. Although these limits rule out many social psychologically relevant situations, they rule in a very important and large behavioral domain. Taking academic and other examinations, preparing and giving speeches, conducting interpersonal negotiations, making decisions and judgments, initiating close relationships, and interviewing for a job all qualify as nonmetabolically demanding motivated performance situations. Individuals encounter these situations every day, and many are quite goal-relevant for them. Furthermore, social psychologists have traditionally utilized motivated performance tasks in a wide variety of experimental contexts, testing an even wider variety of theories.

ONE-TO-ONE RELATIONSHIPS. Even though challenge and threat clearly represent different motivational states, each of which likely involves different physiological responses, psychologists have only recently focused on differences between physiological markers of these motivational states in what we have come to label as motivated performance situations. The failure to distinguish between different patterns of cardiovascular responses associated with positive and negative motivational states in the past propelled both a large literature connecting cardiovascular performance increases, as indexed conveniently but perhaps naïvely by unitary measures such as heart rate changes, to the negative consequences of stress or threat on the cardiovascular system (e.g., Blascovich & Katkin, 1993; Matthews et al., 1986; Turner, 1994) and a separate literature using virtually the same indexes connecting cardiovascular increases to the positive consequences of motivation and positive performance (e.g., Brehm & Self, 1989; Wright & Dill, 1993).

Thus, cardiovascular changes such as increases in heart rate and blood pressure were used by different researchers to index oppositional motivational states creating a dilemma for those interested in using cardiovascular indexes to identify distinctively one or the other superordinate motivational states (e.g., challenge or threat). This dilemma stems, of course, from the one-to-many relationships that hold for measures such as heart rate. Recently, however, the dilemma has been increasingly recognized and dealt with at theoretical and methodological levels.

Working within the tradition of cardiovascular reactivity and psychological stress, Dienstbier (1989) challenged the view that increased cardiovascular performance during potentially stressful situations is necessarily associated with malignant psychological states and, on the basis of both human and animal research, theorized that increases in cardiovascular performance could be and are often associated with positive or nonmalignant states. Dienstbier posited that increased sympathetic-adrenomedullary (SAM) activity is associated with benign states and improved performance and that increased pituitary-adrenocortical (PAC) activity is associated with malignant states when such activation occurs alone or concomitant with SAM activation.

Interestingly, about the same time as Dienstbier's (1989) article appeared, Kasprowicz and his colleagues (Kasprowicz, Manuck, Malkoff, & Krantz, 1990) published a piece categorizing individuals, based on the preponderance of specific types of cardiovascular responses as either "cardiac" or "vascular" responders. The former respond primarily with changes in activity in the heart, the latter in activity in the arteries. Later, Manuck, Kamarck, Kasprowicz, and Waldstein, (1993) suggested that so-called vascular reactivity appeared to be the more pernicious of the two heart-healthwise.

Encouraged by the theoretical work of Dienstbier (1989) and the empirical work of Kasprowicz et al. (1990), and keeping in mind that we wished to ensure the viability of one-to-one relationships between selected physiological measures and challenge and threat motivational states, we applied Dienstbier's theoretical rationale to the selection and collection of a set cardiovascular responses of participants in motivated performance situations. Based on the work of Dienstbier (1989) as well as on the work of Gray (1982) and McNaughton (1993), we posited that the benign pattern of physiological activation marked by SAM activation caused (a) sympathetic neural stimulation of the myocardium increasing cardiac performance and (b) adrenal medullary release of epinephrine causing vasodilation in the large muscle beds and lungs and an overall decrease in systemic vascular resistance, as well as some additional enhancement of cardiac performance. We posited that the malignant pattern marked by dual activation of the PAC and SAM axes caused (a) elevations of cardiac performance over resting levels (SAM activity), and (b) decreased release of epinephrine and norepinephrine from the adrenal medulla (PAC activity) causing moderate increases in cardiac output without accompanying decreases in systemic vascular resistance.

Logically, then, we needed a set of measures including separate unambiguous measures of both cardiac and vascular performance. And, of course, we needed to be able to assess these measures practically in a technological sense. Because of their ambiguity in terms of cardiac and vascular underpinnings, simple heart rate and blood pressure measures could not be used as unambiguous measures. Indeed, their ambiguity led to the indexing dilemma described above in the first place. Fortunately, the use of impedance cardiography had emerged in psychophysiology (see Sherwood et al., 1990), enabling researchers to assess less ambiguous measures of cardiac performance, such as pre-ejection period (PEP), stroke volume (SV), and cardiac output (CO). In addition, continuous blood pressure monitoring became available, which together with the impedance-derived measures allowed the noninvasive assessment and derivation of total peripheral resistance (TPR), an unambiguous measure of vascular performance.

According to Dienstbier's (1989) physiological toughness theory, challenge and threat could be indexed by different patterns of cardiac and vascular responses over time. Specifically, we expected that challenged individuals, those for whom resources outweighed the demand, (i.e., danger, uncertainty, and required effort) in a motivated performance situation should show relatively large increases in cardiac performance (as indexed by PEP, SV, and CO) and relatively large decreases in vascular performance (as indexed by TPR). We expected that threatened individuals, those for whom demands in a motivated performance situation outweighed resources, should also show increases in cardiac performance (as indexed by PEP, SV, and CO) and no change or increases in vascular performance (as indexed by TPR). Figure 5.4 depicts the predicted changes as change or difference scores from rest to task performance.

Validational Research

In order to validate these indexes, we conducted three types of studies: correlational, experimental, and manipulated physiology. We wanted to know if our

Figure 5.4. Predicted cardiovascular markers of challenge and threat (change scores).

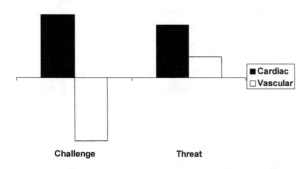

predicted patterns of cardiovascular responses (see Figure 5.4) were associated with free evaluations of challenge and threat, if we could evoke the patterns by manipulating the motivated performance situation in ways likely to cause challenge and threat motivational states, and whether the psychological states drive the cardiovascular responses or vice versa.

CORRELATIONAL STUDIES. These studies involved an initial one as well as a cross-sectional replication (Experiments 2 and 3 in Tomaka, Blascovich, Kelsey, & Leitten, 1993). In these studies, participants in an experimentally created motivated performance situation received instructions regarding an upcoming mental arithmetic task requiring quick and accurate vocal serial subtractions (e.g. "7s," "13s," etc. from a four-digit number).[6] After receiving instructions, but prior to actual task performance, self-reported demand and ability evaluations were solicited from participants, allowing us to assess overall evaluations by calculating demand–resource ratios. On the basis of these ratios, we were able to divide participants into challenge and threat groups. Subsequent analyses in both studies revealed the same patterns of cardiovascular responses associated with free challenge and threat evaluations as those predicted above. Specifically, as illustrated in Figure 5.5, in both studies challenged participants exhibited the benign pattern of cardiovascular responses described above, including relatively large increases in cardiac activity accompanied by decreases in total systemic vascular resistance. Threatened participants exhibited the less benign pattern, including increases in cardiac activity and increases in total systemic vascular resistance.

In addition, challenged participants in both studies recalled less stress during their task performance, perceived greater effort, and perceived better performance than threatened participants.

EXPERIMENTAL STUDIES. Because these studies were essentially correlational in nature, we needed to determine if the challenge and threat patterns of cardiovascular response could be evoked by experimental manipulation (Experiment 1 in Tomaka, Blascovich, Kibler, & Ernst, 1997). Again, participants performed a mental arithmetic task, in this experiment after receiving an instructional set emphasizing either

---

[6] Serial subtraction tasks like this are commonly used in cardiovascular reactivity research in laboratories around the world.

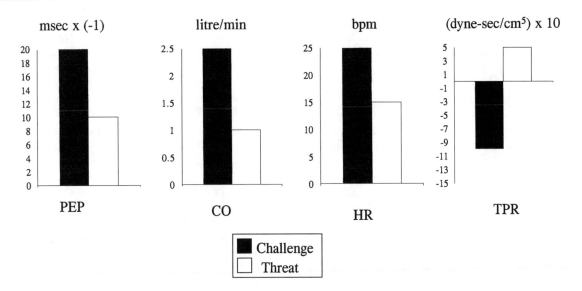

Figure 5.5. Free-appraisal study 1 results.

threat (highlighting accuracy of task performance and potential evaluation) or challenge (highlighting effort and doing one's best). Cognitive evaluations were assessed after instructions but prior to performing the task. Physiological responses were recorded continuously during the task and during a quiet rest period preceding the task.

Analyses indicated that instructional set had the expected effects on demand/resource ratios such that participants receiving instructions emphasizing threat showed greater demand–resource ratios than participants receiving instructions emphasizing challenge. Furthermore, those receiving challenge instructions exhibited the benign pattern of cardiovascular responses and those receiving threat instructions exhibited the less benign and predicted pattern.

MANIPULATED PHYSIOLOGY STUDIES. Although clearly supporting the logic of our cognitive appraisal approach to the validation of cardiovascular indexes of challenge and threat motivation in motivated performance situations, the results of the studies described above do not exclude the possibility that physiological responses drive the psychological responses. To test the latter notion, distinct patterns of autonomic physiological activity consistent with threat and challenge were evoked nonpsychologically, and the resulting effects of such manipulations on evaluations were examined (Experiments 2 and 3 in Tomaka et. al., 1997).

Two different patterns of physiological activation, each having a distinct physical mode of elicitation, were employed. The first was a manipulation of cardiovascular reactivity consistent with challenge. For this manipulation, participants pedaled a stationary bike for a relatively short period of time, but long enough to achieve relatively high cardiac reactivity coupled with a decline in systemic vascular resistance. The second was a manipulation of vascular reactivity consistent with threat accomplished by exposing participants to the cold pressor task. Cold pressor tasks have been shown to produce vasoconstrictive responses and increases in systemic vascular resistance (Allen, Shelley, & Boquet, 1992). Checks revealed that the nonpsychological manipulations produced appropriate challenge- and threat-like patterns of cardiovascular responses. However, no effects were found on overall challenge and threat evaluations.

SUMMARY OF VALIDATIONAL RESEARCH. These studies affirmed our notion that critically different patterns of cardiovascular responses accompany challenge and threat motivation in nonmetabolically demanding motivated performance situations. The distinctive challenge (i.e., large increases in cardiac performance and decreases in vascular resistance) and threat (i.e., increases in cardiac performance and increases in vascular resistance) held in both correlational and experimental studies involving both freely generated and manipulated evaluations related to challenge and threat motivation. Nonpsychological manipulations of the different patterns of cardiovascular responses themselves did not produce differences in psychological motivational states affirming the theoretical rationale underlying the indexes.[7]

RESEARCH EXAMPLES

BELIEF IN A JUST WORLD. The availability of the cardiovascular indexes of threat and challenge enabled us to examine dispositional influences on evaluation processes in motivated performance situations. One disposition we (Tomaka & Blascovich, 1994) explored is "belief in a just world" (BJW), which is the extent to which individuals believe that people generally "get what they deserve" from life or conversely the extent to which individuals believe that "life is inherently unfair" (Lerner, 1980). According to several theorists (e.g., Lazarus & Folkman, 1984; Lerner, 1980; Lerner & Miller, 1978), dispositional belief in a just world protects individuals, allowing them to adapt better to the demands of everyday life. In a motivated performance situation, high-BJW individuals should exhibit challenge motivation compared with low-BJW individuals.

In our study, which involved a motivated performance situation incorporating mental arithmetic, we blocked participants on dispositional BJW. As expected, task evaluations, cardiovascular response patterns, and performance differed as a function of BJW. High-BJW participants made more challenging overall evaluations, exhibited the challenge pattern (i.e., strong increases in cardiac performance coupled with decreased peripheral resistance), and performed better than low-BJW participants, who exhibited the threat pattern (i.e., increases in cardiac performance coupled with slight vasoconstriction).

ATTITUDE FUNCTIONALITY. Functionally, attitudes should facilitate decision making, (Allport, 1935; Fazio, 1989; Katz, 1960) by providing individuals with relatively accessible knowledge enabling them to make decisions in demanding situations more easily. Task object-relevant attitudes should increase the probability of a challenge rather than threat in a motivated performance situation. We (Blascovich et al., 1993; Experiment 2) explored these issues.

In this study, individuals participated in a two-phase experiment. In the first phase, participants developed attitudes toward sets of novel objects (abstract paintings) using Fazio's procedure (e.g., Fazio, Chen, McDonel, & Sherman, 1982). Half of the participants rehearsed attitudes toward one subset (15) of the abstract paintings, and the other half toward a second mutually exclusive subset (15). In the second phase, a motivated performance situation, participants expressed rapid pairwise preferences for 34 slides of randomly paired abstract paintings (i.e., attitude objects). Half of each participant group vocalized preferences within paired abstract paintings selected from the subset toward which they had rehearsed attitudes, whereas the other half vocalized preferences within pairs selected from the unfamiliar subset. Participants in the rehearsed painting condition exhibited increased cardiac response and vasodilation, the challenge pattern, whereas those in the novel painting condition exhibited increased cardiac response and vasoconstriction, the threat pattern.

A WORD ON TECHNOLOGY. The assessment of the cardiovascular indexes of challenge and threat discussed above requires the incorporation of impedance cardiographic and blood pressure recording devices into the social psychology laboratory. Fortunately, these devices are not only reliable and relatively self-contained but also physically small, about the size of a small bread box and a VCR, respectively. These devices perform the transducing and conditioning processes in the signal path described above. Turnkey software is also available, allowing direct recording of continuous cardiac (e.g., PEP, SV, CO) and blood pressure responses and the calculation of vascular response (i.e., total peripheral resistance). Technical details regarding the placement of sensors, operation of the equipment, and software are beyond the scope of this chapter and are available in several sources, including Sherwood et al. (1990), Sherwood (1993), and Kelsey and Guethlein (1990).

Psychophysiological Indexes of Affective States: Positive and Negative Affect

Testing of theoretical hypotheses related to affect can also benefit from the use of psychophysiological indexes. Here, we review two such indexes: facial

---

[7] It should be noted that the validational work reported here was not confined to a single laboratory or a single university. The challenge–threat manipulation study (Experiment 1 in Tomaka, Blascovich, Kibler, & Ernst, 1997, was conducted at the University of Otago and the University of Dunedin). Furthermore, by press time replications of the basic cardiovascular patterns in correlational and experimental studies have been conducted or reported to the author via personal communication by L. Feldman-Barrett (personal communcation, 1996) but were not yet submitted for publication.

electromyography and startle eyeblink reflex responses. First, however, we attend to some general issues regarding the psychophysiological indexing of affect.

CONSTRUCTS. Explicit definitions of positive and negative affect have proven no less daunting than definitions of motivational constructs such as challenge and threat although arguably more theoreticians agree on definitions of positive and negative affect than on the definitions of moods or specific emotions. Basically, positive and negative affect represent superordinate emotion or feeling categories (cf. Shaver, Schwartz, Kirson, & O'Connor, 1987) encompassing several specific basic and many subordinate emotions. Phenomenologically, positive affect occurs during the experience of any specific positive mood or emotion, and negative affect occurs during the experience of any specific negative mood or emotion. Most indexes, nonphysiological as well as physiological, of affect rest on the idea of something phenomenologically shared among the positive emotions as a group and something else among the negative emotions as a group.

CONTEXT. In the development of physiological indexes of positive and negative affect, researchers have generally limited the empirical context to situations requiring relatively little movement and involving passive receipt of stimuli or information by individuals. These empirical limits, however, do not preclude the extension of physiological indexes of affect to more psychologically and physically active situations, such as motivated performance situations, at least theoretically. However, for physiological indexes of affect, which involve small muscle assessments (see below), practical aspects of physiological recording (i.e., secure attachment of sensor and high signal/noise ratios) generally limit research to contexts involving relatively little physical movement.

ONE-TO-ONE RELATIONSHIPS. Positive and negative affect represent different feeling states, each of which according to the identity thesis (see above) presumably involves some physiological response. Cacioppo, Petty, Losch, and Kim (1986) and Lang, Bradley, and Cuthbert (1990) have challenged the validity of physiological indexes of affect valence such as skin conductance or heart rate changes because of a lack of one-to-one relationship with affect constructs (albeit leaving open the possibility that these unitary physiological indexes might relate to the in-

tensity but not the valence of affect). As researchers have sought more sophisticated psychophysiological indexes, those with one-to-one relationships to affective states, they have focused on patterns of facial electromyographic recordings specific to the facial muscles associated with the expression of affect, and on the inhibition–facilitation of reflexes (i.e., startle eyeblink responses) during the experience of positive and negative affective states.

FACIAL EMG INDEXES OF POSITIVE AND NEGATIVE AFFECT.

RATIONALE. Cacioppo and his colleagues (e.g., Cacioppo & Petty, 1981; Cacioppo, Petty, & Marshall-Goodell, 1984; Cacioppo et al., 1986) proposed the value of using electromyograms specific to targeted facial muscles as physiological indexes of positive and negative affect. They based their rationale on long-lived scholarly interest in the muscles of facial expression beginning in the modern era with the work of Darwin (1872/1965) on the evolutionary significance of facial expressions to the more recent facial expression work of Ekman and his colleagues (e.g., Ekman, 1993). Cacioppo's group reasoned that because the "somatic nervous system is the final pathway through which people interact with and modify their physical and social environments" (Cacioppo et al., 1986, p. 261) and particularly because the face is the locus of most emotional expression, targeted facial muscle responses represented fertile ground for psychophysiological indexing of affect.

Cacioppo's group focused in particular on the corrugator supercilii (i.e., "frown muscles") and the zygomaticus majori (i.e., "smile muscles"). Figure 5.6 depicts these and other facial muscle sites. This focus derived from earlier work (e.g., Fridlund, Schwartz, and Fowler, 1984) demonstrating that zygomaticus and corrugator EMG activity varied with participants' emotional reactions to videotapes and during emotional imagery states. Cacioppo and his colleagues were also convinced that the highly sensitive EMG recordings could detect covert movement in the targeted facial muscle groups and reveal affectively meaningful psychological states not detectable by visual observation. This latter point becomes important as individuals can exert control over overt facial expressions leading to a disparity between overt expressions and covert affective states.

Figure 5.7 depicts Cacioppo et al.'s (1986) description of the basic patterns of facial EMG responses marking positive and negative affect. Accordingly

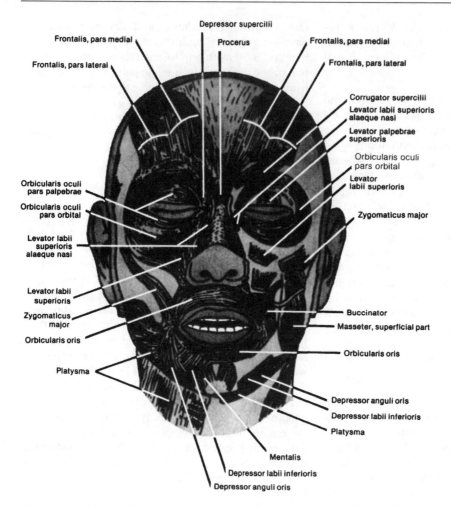

Figure 5.6. Facial Muscles.

corrugator supercilii EMG increases and zygomaticus majori EMG decreases during negative affect, and corrugator supercilii EMG decreases and zygomaticus majori EMG increases during positive affect.

Figure 5.7. Predicted facial electromyographic markers of positive and negative affect.

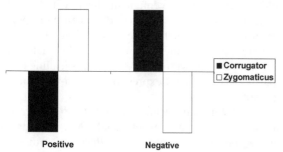

VALIDATIONAL RESEARCH. Cacioppo et al. (1986) reported two very similar studies validating their proposed EMG indexes of affect. In the major study reported, the investigators presented 28 participants with affectively valenced (positive and negative) visual stimuli both mild and moderate in intensity, as well as neutral and buffer stimuli. The investigators recorded facial and nonfacial EMG during each stimulus presentation (5 s) including muscles hypothetically related (e.g., corrugator supercilii and zygomaticus majori) and unrelated (e.g., superficial forearm flexor, medial frontalis) to affect. The researchers gathered self-reports of liking, arousal, and familiarity following each stimulus presentation. Basically, Cacioppo et al. (1986) confirmed the utility of the proposed EMG indexes of affect. Zygomaticus majori and corrugator supercilii EMG varied as a function of valence with the former being greater during positively valenced stimuli and the latter greater during negatively valenced stimuli. The investigators found no differences among the set of hypothetically nonrelated muscles (i.e., orbicularis oris, medial frontalis, and superficial forearm flexor), thus ruling out any contribution of general muscle tension to the indexes. Orbicularis oculi (muscles around the eyes) activity varied as a function of valence and intensity inversely but essentially redundant to the corrugator supercilii activity. Because of the proximity of the orbicularis oculi muscles to the corrugator, the orbicularis oculi finding is not surprising.

Cacioppo et al. (1986) not only tested for predictable relationships between facial EMG markers and affective states but also between visual markers (i.e., facial expressions) and affective states. Human judges simply were unable to distinguish between positive and negative affective states based on videotapes made during physiological recording undoubtedly because the carefully chosen stimuli elicited minimal levels of affect. Both the validation of the EMG markers and the lack of same for the visual markers caused Cacioppo et al. (1986) to conclude that, "facial EMG can mark the valence and intensity of transient and specific affective reactions even in the absence of emotional expressions that are noticeable, at least under normal viewing conditions" (p. 267).

RESEARCH EXAMPLE: ATTITUDE INDUCTION AND EXTREMITY. One theoretical question related to the attitude functionality research involving the cardiovascular indexes of challenge and threat described above concerns the dimension or feature of attitudes underlying the functionality effects. On one hand, as Fazio (1989) has maintained, accessibility or the strength of association between object and attitude underlies the functionality effect. On the other hand, extremity or polarization effects might account for the observed functionality. The attitude induction procedure used in the functionality studies required repeated vocal rehearsal of liking judgments of objects (e.g., abstract paintings) involving simple ordinal self-reports of attitude strength (i.e., like strongly, like, dislike, dislike strongly). Although analyses of these self-reported ratings indicated no extremity or polarization effects brought on by attitude rehearsal, the sensitivity of the 4- point scale to such effects may simply have been too low.

Such should not be the case, however, for psychophysiological indexes of affect, that is, continuous facial EMG recordings of the zygomaticus and corrugator muscle groups targeted by Cacioppo et al. (1986). These measures should be especially sensitive to polarization or extremity effects because they are continuous and unconstrained by scale limits or anchors. Consequently, we conducted an additional attitude functionality study in our laboratory (Salomon, Blascovich, Ernst, & Tomaka, 1996), in which we included appropriate facial EMG assessment during attitude induction. These EMG data revealed the predictable effects for valence (like vs. dislike) and intensity (low vs. high). However, within the relevant conditions, the EMG data failed to show that repeated associations of specific ordinal liking ratings with specific attitude objects increased attitude extremity. The EMG data were as stable over repeated stimulus presentations as were the rehearsed self-report ratings.

TECHNOLOGY. The assessment of the facial somatic indexes of positive and negative affect requires EMG technology. Such technology covers the entire signal path described above. Technical details regarding the placement of sensors, operation of the equipment, and software are beyond the scope of this chapter but are available in several sources, including Cacioppo, Tassinary, and Fridlund (1990).

STARTLE EYE-BLINK REFLEX INDEXING OF POSITIVE AND NEGATIVE AFFECT

RATIONALE. Lang and his colleagues (Lang, Bradley, & Cuthbert, 1990, 1992) proposed the value of using electromyograms specific to reflexive eye blinks to index affective valence. Guided by the work of Schneirla (1959), Konorski (1967), Dickinson and Dearing (1979), and Masterson and Crawford (1982), Lang et al. (1990, 1992) based their rationale on the assumption that brain states organize behavior along an appetitive-aversive dimension. They postulated that positive affect is associated with a brain state favoring approach, attachment, and consummatory behavior and that negative affect is associated with a brain state favoring avoidance, escape, and defense. They argued further that, "The efferent system as a whole (including exteroceptive reflexes) is presumably tuned according to the current states of this central affect-motivational organization" (p. 377).

Accordingly, Lang et al. (1990) hypothesized that reflexes associated with positive affect would be enhanced during the ongoing experience of a positive emotional state and that reflexes associated with negative affect would be enhanced during the ongoing experience of a negative emotional state. Furthermore, they hypothesized that affectively valenced reflexes would be inhibited during the ongoing experience of the affectively opposite emotional state. Thus, changes (i.e., facilitation or inhibition) in affectively toned reflexes could be used to index the basic ongoing affective state of an individual.

Lang and his colleagues focused on the startle eye-blink reflex, the reflexive blinks that occur when individuals perceive an unexpected and relatively intense stimulus, particularly, but not limited to, an acoustic stimulus. The startle eye-blink reflex is negatively toned and, hence, should be enhanced during ongoing negative affect and inhibited during ongoing positive affect. The eye blink is also relatively easy to measure physiologically using orbicularis oculi EMG.

VALIDATIONAL RESEARCH. In an elegant series of studies (see Lang et al., 1990, for a review), Lang and his colleagues provided convincing evidence for the startle eye-blink index of ongoing affect. Vrana, Spence, and Lang (1988) tested the hypothesis that the valence of ongoing affect enhances or inhibits acoustically driven startle eye-blink reflexes according to the match or mismatch between the valence of the underlying affective state and this negatively toned reflex. These investigators presented 36 negative, neutral, and positive photographs via slides to participants for 6-s periods during which they presented unpredictable loud white-noise bursts binaurally to participants while using orbicularis oculi EMG to measure the strength of reflexive eye-blink responses. As predicted, the data supported their hypothesis. A conceptual replication and extension by Bradley, Cuthbert, and Lang (1988) produced the same pattern of data, this time allowing participants to control the length and duration of stimulus slide presentation. Bradley, Cuthbert, and Lang (1990) produced the same effects substituting visually evoked startle eye-blink reflexes proving the eye-blink reflex effects were independent of startle stimulus modality.

Vrana and Lang (1990) demonstrated that the startle reflex methodology indexed affective state during affectively relevant imagery and memories. This study provided the crucial evidence that the startle reflex methodology is sensitive to internally generated affective states, a necessary assumption if social psychological investigators are to benefit from the techniques of physiological indexing of covert affect suggested by Lang and his colleagues.

STARTLE REFLEX RESPONSES AND SOCIAL PSYCHOLOGICAL RESEARCH. Although the startle eye-blink reflex measure of Lang and his colleagues has enjoyed increasing popularity among psychophysiolo-

gists, this relatively new index has attracted the attention of social psychologists more slowly. Nevertheless, we expect that empirical investigations in which startle reflex measurement testing social psychological theories incorporating affective state as a key variable will soon begin to appear in the literature. The startle eye-blink reflex index is relatively simple to employ and its validity is based on a wealth of research.

TECHNOLOGY. The assessment of the startle eye-blink reflex index of positive and negative affect generally requires EMG technology. As with facial EMG measures of affect described above, such technology covers the entire signal path described above. Technical details regarding the placement of sensors, operation of the equipment, and software are beyond the scope of this chapter but are available in several sources, including Cacioppo, Tassinary, and Fridlund (1990) and Lang et al. (1990).

Other Physiological Indexes of Psychological Constructs Important to Social Psychologists

Although the limits of this chapter preclude detailed illustrations of additional physiological indexes of psychological constructs, the reader should feel no such constraints. Indeed, other valid psychophysiological indexes exist and more continue to appear as psychophysiological theory and technology advances. In particular, several promising physiological indexes of cognitive processes have surfaced (see Heinze, Munte, & Mangun, 1994, for a review). For example, orbicularis oris EMG activity has been proposed to index verbal processing (Cacioppo & Petty, 1981). Startle reflex techniques have been used to index attention (Anthony & Graham, 1985). Event-related potentials have been investigated as indexes of memory processes (Nielsen-Bohlman & Knight, 1994).

ASSESSMENT AND SUMMARY

We foresee steady growth in the use of physiological indexes in social psychology as more and more researchers recognize their unique benefits and avail themselves of necessary biological and methodological background opportunities. Physiological indexes will not replace more traditional self-report and behavioral indexes in social psychology. However, we dare say that physiological indexes when properly employed and understood will increase the impact of social psychological research substantially. Here, we summarize the general points we have made in this chapter in terms of brief answers to a number of general questions.

How Should Interested Social Psychologists Begin the Process of Implementing Psychophysiological Indexes?

Researchers must think about using physiological indexes in the same ways they think of using subjective and behavioral indexes, convincing themselves and others of the validity and reliability of such indexes as markers and invariants of (i.e., bearing one-to-one relationships) the psychological constructs under scrutiny. We have noted that specific psychophysiological indexes derive their validity from psychophysiological theory confirmed via systematic empirical work. Furthermore, we have noted that derivation of successful physiological indexes, like nonphysiological indexes, largely depends on conceptual explication of target psychological constructs, on identification of key physiological response patterns across multiple physiological measures, and on specification of appropriate situational contexts.

What Sorts of Ideas Are Better or Worse Served by Psychophysiological Indexes?

Physiological indexes lend themselves to assessment of continuously fluctuating psychological states and processes especially affective, motivational, and cognitive ones. Thus, physiological responses are unlikely to index usefully specific attitudes, beliefs, and dispositions. However, to the extent that specific attitudes, beliefs, and dispositions influence affective, motivational, and cognitive processes, physiological indexes of the latter processes can be used effectively to test theoretical arguments and hypotheses regarding specific constructs.

What Advantages Accrue to Physiological Indexes?

Because physiological indexes are objective and covert, avoidance of self-report bias presents one of the major advantages of physiological indexes. However, because physiological indexes are also continuous, other advantages accrue. Thus, one can assess psychological states and processes continuously over time providing data for powerful time-series analytic statistical techniques. More importantly one can assess psychological states and processes in the background concurrently with other types of measures including self-report and behavioral ones or while research participants engage in other activities. Thus, physiological measures do not interfere with experimental treatments, and such indexes can eliminate the need for post hoc or retrospective accounts of target states and processes.

Do Physiological Indexes Provide the "Gold Standard" for Psychological Measurement?

That physiological measures enjoy intrinsic superiority over other types is naïve and perhaps results from the mystique of physiological measurement discussed at the outset of this chapter. Rather, physiological indexes provide a third set of measurement methods in addition to subjective and behavioral ones. Together with the other types of measures physiological ones add to the power of multimethod triangulation as discussed elsewhere in this text.

Where Can One Find a Catalog of Valid Physiological Indexes of Psychological Constructs?

In theory, a cataloging of psychophysiological indexes would be pragmatic. However, in reality, such a listing would prove difficult to create, easily become outdated, and be potentially misleading to researchers. We did not attempt to provide exhaustive coverage of physiological indexes here. Rather, we have tried to impart principles and provide illustrations of what we believe are valid indexes of superordinate psychological constructs. We hope that readers understand the epistemological principles we have presented regarding the development of psychophysiological indexes and that they are able to judge the validity of proposed physiological indexes in the literature and their application to the assessment of social psychological constructs.

REFERENCES

Allen, M. T., Shelley, K. S., Boquet, A. J (1992). A comparison of cardiovascular and autonomic adjustments to three types of cold stimulation tasks. *International Journal of Psychophysiology, 13,* 59–69.

Allport, G. W. (1935). Attitudes. In C. Murchison (Ed.), *Handbook of social psychology* (pp. 798–884). Worchester, MA: Clark University Press.

Anthony, B. J., & Graham, F. K. (1985). Blink reflex modification by selective attention: Evidence for the modulation of 'autonomic' processing. *Biological Psychology, 21,* 43–59.

Berglas, S., & Jones, E. E. (1978). Drug choice as a self-handicapping strategy in response to noncontingent success. *Journal of Personality and Social Psychology, 36,* 405–417.

Blascovich, J., Ernst, J. M., Tomaka, J., Kelsey, R. M., Salomon, K. A., & Fazio, R. H. (1993). Attitude as a moderator of autonomic reactivity. *Journal of Personality and Social Psychology, 64,* 165–176.

Blascovich, J., & Ginsburg, G. P. (1978). Conceptual analysis of risk taking in "risky shift" research. *Journal for the Theory of Social Behavior, 8,* 217–230.

Blascovich J., & Katkin, E. S. (Eds.). (1993). *Cardiovascular reactivity to psychological stress and disease.* Washington, DC: American Psychological Association.

Blascovich, J., & Kelsey, R. M. (1990). Using cardiovascular and electrodermal measures of arousal in social psychological research. *Review of Personality and Social Psychology, 11,* 45–73.

Blascovich, J., & Tomaka, J. (1996). The biopsychosocial model of arousal regulation. In M. Zanna (Ed.), *Advances in experimental social psychology* (Vol. 28, pp. 1–51). New York: Academic Press.

Boyd, R. W., & DeMascio, A. (1954). Social behavior and autonomic physiology: A sociophysiological study. *Journal of Nervous and Mental Disease, 120,* 207–212.

Bradley, M. M., Cuthbert, B. N., & Lang, P. J. (1988). Lateral presentation of acoustic startle stimuli in a varying affective foreground [abstract]. *Psychophysiology, 25,* 436.

Bradley, M. M., Cuthbert, B. N., & Lang, P. J. (1990). Startle reflex modification: Attention or emotion? *Psychophysiology, 27,* 513–522.

Brehm, J. W., & Self, E. (1989). The intensity of motivation. In M. R. Rozenweig & L. W. Porter (Eds.), *Annual Review of Psychology* (pp. 109–131). Palo Alto, CA: Annual

Cacioppo, J. T., & Petty, R. E. (1981). Electromyograms as measures of extent and affectivity of information processing. *American Psychologist, 36,* 441–456.

Cacioppo, J. T., & Petty, R. E. (Eds.). (1983). *Social psychophysiology: A sourcebook.* New York: Guilford Press.

Cacioppo, J. T., Petty, R. E., Losch, M. E., & Kim, H. S. (1986). Electromyographic activity over facial muscle regions can differentiate the valence and intensity of affective reactions. *Journal of Personality and Social Psychology, 50,* 260–268.

Cacioppo, J. T., Petty, R. E., & Marshall-Goodell, B (1984). Electromyographic specificity during simple physical and attitudinal tasks: Location and topographical features of integrated EMG responses. *Biological Psychology, 18,* 85–121.

Cacioppo, J. T., & Tassinary, L. G. (1990a). Inferring psychological significance from physiological signals. *American Psychologist, 45,* 16–28.

Cacioppo, J. T., & Tassinary, L. G. (1990b). Psychophysiology and psychophysiological inference. In J. T. Cacioppo & L. G. Tassinary (Eds.), *Principles of psychophysiology: Physical, social, and inferential elements* (pp. 3–33). New York: Cambridge University Press.

Cacioppo, J. T., Tassinary, L. G., & Fridlund, A. J. (1990). The skeletomotor system. In J. T. Cacioppo & L. G. Tassinary (Eds.), *Principles of psychophysiology: Physical, social, and inferential elements* (pp. 325–384). New York: Cambridge University Press.

Campbell, D. T., & Stanley, J. (1963). *Experimental and quasi-experimental designs for research.* Chicago: Rand-McNally.

Coles, M. G. H., Donchin, E., & Porges, S. W. (Eds.). (1986). *Psychophysiology: Systems, processes, and applications.* New York: Guilford Press.

Darwin, C. (1965). *The expression of the emotions in man and animals.* Chicago: University of Chicago Press. (Original work published 1872.)

DeMascio, A. R. (1994). *Descartes' error: Emotion, reason, and the human brain.* New York: Avon Books.

Dickinson, A., & Dearing, M. F. (1979). Appetitive-aversive interactions and inhibitory processes. In A. Dickinson & R. A. Boakes (Eds.), *Mechanisms of learning and motivation* (pp. 287–324). New York: Academic Press.

Dienstbier, R. A. (1989). Arousal and physiological toughness: Implications for mental and physical health. *Psychological Review, 96,* 84–100.

Ekman, P. (1993). Facial expression of emotion. *American Psychologist, 48,* 384–392.

Fazio, R. H. (1989). On the power and functionality of attitudes: The role of attitude accessibility. In A. R. Pratkanis, S. J. Breckler, & A. G. Greenwald (Eds.), *Attitude structure and function* (pp. 153–179). Hillsdale, NJ: Erlbaum.

Fazio, R. H., Chen, J., McDonel, E. C., & Sherman, S. J. (1982). Attitude accessibility, attitude-behavior consistency, and the strength of the object-evaluation association. *Journal of Experimental Social Psychology, 18,* 339–357.

Fridlund, A. J., Schwartz, G. E., & Fowler, S. C. (1984). Pattern recognition of self-reported emotional states from multiple-site facial EMG activity during affective imagery. *Psychophysiology, 21,* 622–637.

Gray, J. A. (1982). *The neuropsychology of anxiety: An enquiry into the functions of the septo-hippocampal system.* Oxford, England: Oxford University Press.

Grunberg, N. E., & Singer, J. E. (1990). Biochemical measurement. In J. T. Cacioppo & L. G. Tassinary (Eds.), *Principles of psychophysiology: Physical, social, and inferential elements* (pp. 149–176). New York: Cambridge University Press.

Heinze, H.-J., Munte, T. F., & Mangun, G. R. (Eds.). (1994). *Cognitive electrophysiology.* Boston: Birkhauser.

Jones, E. E., & Sigall, H. (1971). The bogus pipeline: A new paradigm for measuring affect and attitude. *Psychological Bulletin, 76,* 359–364.

Kasprowicz, A. L., Manuck, S. B., Malkoff, S. B., & Krantz, D. S. (1990). Individual differences in behaviorally evoked cardiovascular response: Temporal stability and hemodynamic patterning. *Psychophysiology, 27,* 605–619.

Katz, D. (1960). The functional approach to the study of attitudes. *Public Opinion Quarterly, 24,* 163–204.

Kelsey, R. M., & Guethlein, W. (1990). An evaluation of the ensemble averaged impedance cardiogram. *Psychophysiology, 28,* 24–33.

Konorski, J. (1967). *Integrative activity of the brain: An interdisciplinary approach.* Chicago: University of Chicago Press.

Lang, P. J., Bradley, M. M., & Cuthbert, B. N. (1990). Emotion, attention, and the startle reflex. *Psychological Review, 97,* 377–395.

Lang, P. J., Bradley, M. M., & Cuthbert, B. N. (1992). A motivational analysis of emotion: Reflex-cortex connections. *Psychological Science, 3,* 44–49.

Lasswell, H. D. (1936). Certain changes during trial (psychoanalytic) interviews. *Psychoanalytic Review, 23,* 241–247.

Lazarus, R. S., & Folkman, S. (1984). *Stress, appraisal, and coping.* New York: Springer.

Lerner, M. J. (1980). *The belief in a just world: A fundamental delusion.* New York: Plenum Press.

Lerner, M. J., & Miller, N. H. (1978). Just world research and the attribution process: Looking back and ahead. *Psychological Bulletin, 85,* 1030–1051.

Manuck, S. B., Kamarck, T. W., Kasprowicz, A. S., & Waldstein, S. R. (1993). Stability and patterning of behaviorally evoked cardiovascular reactivity. In J. Blascovich & E. S. Katkin (Eds.), *Cardiovascular reactivity to psychological stress and disease: An examination of the evidence* (pp. 83–108). Washington, DC: American Psychological Association.

Marshall-Goodell, B. S., Tassinary, L. G., & Cacioppo, J. T. (1990). Principles of bioelectric measurement. In J. T. Cacioppo & L. G. Tassinary (Eds.), *Principles of psychophysiology: Physical, social, and inferential elements* (pp. 113–148). New York: Cambridge University Press.

Masterson, F. A., & Crawford, M. (1982). The defense motivation system: A theory of avoidance behavior. *The Behavioral and Brain Sciences, 5,* 661–696.

Matthews, K. A., Weiss, S. M., Detre, T., Dembroski, T. N., Falkner, B., Manuck, S. B., & Williams, R. B. (1986). *Handbook of stress, reactivity, and cardiovascular disease.* New York: Wiley.

McNaughton, N. (1993). Stress and behavioral inhibition. In S. C. Stanford & P. Salmon (Eds.), *Stress: An integrated approach* (pp. 91–109). New York: Academic Press.

Mittleman, B., & Wolff, H. G. (1939). Affective states and skin temperature: Experimental study of subjects with "cold hands" and Raynaud's syndrome. *Psychosomatic Medicine, 1,* 271–292.

Nielsen-Bohlman, L., & Knight, R. T. (1994). Event-related potentials dissociate immediate and delayed memory. In H. J. Heinze, T. F. Munte, & G. R. Mangun (Eds.), *Cognitive electrophysiology* (pp. 169–182). Boston: Birkhauser.

Obrist, P. A. (1981). *Cardiovascular psychophysiology: A perspective.* New York: Plenum.

Riddle, E. M. (1925). Aggressive behavior in a small social group. *Archives of Psychology,* No. 78.

Salomon, K., Blascovich, J., Ernst, J. M., & Tomaka, J. (1996). Accessibility as a predictor of attitude functionality [abstract]. *Psychophysiology, 33,* S72.

Saxe, L., Dougherty, D., & Cross, T. (1987). Lie detection and polygraph testing. In L. S. Wrightsman, C. E. Willis, & S. Kassin (Eds.), *On the witness stand* (pp. 14–36). Newbury Park, CA: Sage.

Schneirla, T. C. (1959). An evolutionary and developmental theory of biphasic processes underlying approach and withdrawal. In *Nebraska Symposium on Motivation: 1959* (pp. 1–42). Lincoln: University of Nebraska Press.

Shapiro, D., & Crider A. (1969). Psychophysiological approaches in social psychology. In G. Lindzey & E. Aronson (Eds.), *Handbook of social psychology* (Vol. 3, pp. 1–49). Reading, MA: Addison-Wesley.

Shaver, P. R., Schwartz, J., Kirson, D., & O'Connor, C. (1987). Emotion knowledge: Further explorations of a prototype approach. *Journal of Personality and Social Psychology, 52,* 1061–1086.

Sherwood, A. (1993). Use of impedance cardiography in cardiovascular reactivity research. In J. Blascovich & E. S. Katkin (Eds.), *Cardiovascular reactivity to psychological stress and disease: An examination of the evidence* (pp. 157–200). Washington, DC: American Psychological Association.

Sherwood, A., Allen, M. T., Fahrenberg, J., Kelsey, R. M., Lovallo, W. R., & van Doornen, L. J. P. (1990). Methodological guidelines for impedance cardiography. *Psychophysiology, 27,* 1–23.

Steele, C. M., & Aronson, J. (1995). Stereotype threat and the intellectual test performance of African Americans. *Journal of Personality and Social Psychology, 69,* 797–811.

Swann, W. B. (1983). Self-verification: Bringing social reality into harmony with the self. In J. Suls & A. G. Greenwald (Eds.), *Social psychological perspectives on the self* (Vol. 2, pp. 33–66). Hillsdale, NJ: Erlbaum.

Tomaka, J., & Blascovich, J. (1994). Effects of justice beliefs on cognitive appraisal of and subjective, physiological, and behavioral responses to potential stress. *Journal of Personality and Social Psychology, 67,* 732–740.

Tomaka, J., Blascovich, J., Kelsey, R. M., & Leitten, C. L. (1993). Subjective, physiological, and behavioral effects of threat and challenge appraisal. *Journal of Personality and Social Psychology, 65,* 248–260.

Tomaka, J., Blascovich, J., Kibler, J., & Ernst, J. M. (1997). Cognitive and physiological antecedents of threat and challenge appraisal. *Journal of Personality and Social Psychology, 73,* 63–72.

Troland, L. T. (1929). *The principles of psychophysiology: A survey of modern scientific psychology* (Vols. 1–3). New York: Van Nostrand.

Turner, J. R. (1994). Cardiovascular rectivity and stress: Patterns of physiological response. New York: Plenum Press.

Vrana, S. R., & Lang, P. J. (1990). Fear imagery and the startle-probe reflex. *Journal of Abnormal Psychology, 99,* 181–189.

Vrana, S. R., Spence, E. L., & Lang, P. J. (1988). The startle-probe response: A new measure of emotion? *Journal of Abnormal Psychology, 97,* 487–491.

Waid, W. M. (1984). *Sociophysiology.* New York: Springer-Verlag.

Wright, R. A., & Dill, J. C. (1993). Blood pressure responses and incentive appraisals as a function of perceived ability and objective task demand. *Psychophysiology, 30,* 152–160.

CHAPTER SIX

Behavioral Observation and Coding

ROGER BAKEMAN

Some time ago students of behavior discovered a land called observational methods (Weick, 1968, 1985), but even today exactly where this land lies and the extent of its domain continue to be debated. Some observational nationalists claim almost unlimited territory. After all, almost every method – from unconstrained narratives (Brandt, 1972) to observing the pointer reading of an instrument measuring the amount of testosterone in saliva – depends on observation in some sense. Others define observational studies as nonexperimental (e.g., Good, 1994, p. 112) because participants are only observed to belong to one group or another and not randomly assigned. Still others (e.g., Pedhazur & Schmelkin, 1991) severely limit the land, describing only ratings and checklists as exemplars of systematic observation.

Nonetheless, I agree with Pedhazur and Schmelkin (1991) that observational methods are located not among the grand lands of independent theory (e.g., behavioral or cognitive) or overarching method (e.g., experimental or correlational) but in the important (one might say foundational) province of measurement. One of the founders was S. S. Stevens (1951), who defined measurement as the assignment of numerals to objects or events according to rules. In the context of observational methods, measurement occurs when codes are assigned to events of interest in the passing stream of behavior, which may be either live or recorded, according to definitions and rules clearly described in explicit coding schemes. Thus observational methods may be used whenever the behavior of interest is clearly defined and available to external observers.

Often observational methods are used when studying human infants and animals other than humans, presumably because such nonverbal organisms can not respond to questions or answer questionnaires. Topics studied include such diverse matters as birds courting, monkeys fighting, children playing, and mothers and infants exchanging gleeful vocalizations (Bakeman & Gottman, 1986). But observational methods are also useful for studying verbal behavior, such as couples discussing and therapists and clients conversing, and can even probe internal processes, for example, by having participants view videotapes of their own behavior and provide comments and explanations (Ickes, Bissonnette, Garcia, & Stinson, 1990). Thus the methods can be used in a variety of research contexts (e.g., experimental and correlational) and in the service of diverse theoretical orientations. Still, the methods seem especially useful when the behavior of interest is social, involving interaction between two or more participants, and when hypotheses emphasize not outcomes but process, that is, the ways and means by which interaction unfolds in time.

The remainder of this chapter describes issues, concepts, and techniques that are relevant when systematic behavioral observation and coding are used as a means of measuring behavior. The intent is to

I am greatly indebted to Vicenç Quera, with whom I co-authored *Analyzing Interaction: Sequential Analysis with SDIS and GSEQ*, and to John M. Gottman, with whom I co-authored *Observing Interaction: An Introduction to Sequential Analysis*. These two colleagues have been a pleasure to work with and have profoundly influenced my thinking regarding many of the matters presented in this chapter. I also thank Connie Russell, Craig Davis, and other students in my graduate observational methods course who provided helpful comments on an earlier draft.

Correspondence should be directed to Roger Bakeman, Department of Psychology, Georgia State University, University Plaza, Atlanta, GA 30303-3083 (e-mail: bakeman@gsu.edu).

provide readers with enough sense of the lay of the land (the work required, tools currently available, etc.) that they can decide whether their theories and concepts are compatible with, and whether their research would profit from, the application of observational methods.

Still, some general guidance is possible. Think of observational methods as another measurement tool in your toolbox, lying alongside the self-report instruments and other questionnaires that are probably already there. Ask yourself: Do you ever have questions about the validity of the scores derived from pencil and paper measures? How is the behavior of interest to you manifest? Is it private, in the sense that only the target of your investigations can tell you about it? Or is it public, accessible to view by others in some way? Remember, accessible behavior includes, for example, viewing children negotiate how they will play a game (either live or on videotape later), viewing two people discussing topics of dissension between them or reading transcripts of their discussion made from audio or video recordings, or even reading diaries that individuals made about their social interactions. Do your questions concern how often particular behaviors occur, such as conflicts during negotiation, agreements during discussion, or lies during social interaction? Or are you interested in process, and so pose questions concerning how particular behaviors are sequenced? Do you think that using more than one measurement modality would enhance the validity of your study? If you answered yes to any of these questions, you may well find observational methods a useful addition to your measurement toolbox.

BEHAVIORAL OBSERVATION IS SYSTEMATIC

The statement, behavioral observation is systematic, is part definitional, part desire – a goal that is sometimes only imperfectly achieved. In this chapter, I focus on methods of behavioral observation that are systematic; thus *systematic*, even when not stated explicitly, is understood as part of the definition. To qualify as systematic, procedures, should be public (all details of method are clearly described and so accessible to others) and replicable (given similar circumstances, other observers would provide similar results); thus personal characteristics of observers are ordinarily not an issue for systematic observation.

Unsystematic observation is perhaps the least satisfactory term for the alternatives because it does not convey their richness, historical depth, and continued importance. Long before academic social science

attracted adherents (primarily in Europe and North America, primarily in the 20th century), insightful studies of human behavior appeared in the form of plays, novels, essays, and other treatises, from Lady Murasaki's *The Tale of Genji* to Machiavelli's *The Prince*, among others. In this century, the tradition of humanistic studies has continued to exert influence in the social sciences, although some modern names for it include participant observation, ethnomethodology, phenomenology, qualitative research, or plain old-fashioned journalism. Examples are legion, but include books such as Erving Goffman's *Asylums* (1962), Robert Coles's *Children of Crisis* (1967), and Oscar Lewis's *Children of Sanchez* (1961) and films such as Frederick Wiseman's *Titticut Follies*, Jenny Chamberlin's *Paris is Burning*, and James, Marx, and Gilbert's *Hoop Dreams*.

At their best, qualitative studies such as those just listed represent lively intelligence and informed sensibility. But when not done well, such studies can seem ill-informed, self-contained, and self-indulgent. Yet how do we judge? How do we know when work is good, or at least acceptable? How do we respond to the criticism that authors may have viewed phenomena from a certain preconceived point of view that unduly biased their reports and interpretations? Systematic methods of quantification – including observational methods – have been developed, in part, to solve the sorts of problems qualitative studies present. The intent is to insulate findings from the biases and desires of observers. Systematic observations may have their limits (e.g., predefined codes limit what is seen, or at least recorded) but normally allow us to judge results independently of the observers' personal qualities (other than training). When judging qualitative studies, qualities of the interpreter strongly influence the judgment, but data that result from systematic measurement are rarely acclaimed or discounted because of the particular observers used. As a result, whereas qualitative studies are often viewed as idiosyncratic, we expect quantitative studies to be replicable.

Nonetheless, qualitative studies play an important, precursory role in systematic behavioral observation. Such studies are essential when developing behavioral codes, as discussed in a subsequent section, and often cause investigators to rethink their hypotheses. Thus, for some investigators qualitative studies are an end in themselves, but for users of behavioral observation they help inform development of both research questions and the measuring instruments used (Bakeman, 1991).

SYSTEMATIC OBSERVATION IS CATEGORICAL MEASUREMENT

As I define matters, observation becomes systematic when measurement occurs, that is, when a code (i.e., a category) is assigned an event. In ways I discuss later, this sentence is deceptively simple, but as an example consider how we might measure the act of measurement itself. S. S. Stevens (1951) provided what has become a widely accepted coding scheme for measurement scales. He named four types. To determine which applies (i.e., to measure the act of measurement), all we need do is consider the responses to a series of three yes–no questions:

1. Are codes ordered in some natural way?
   a. No, then the scale is *categorical*.
   b. Yes, then:
2. Are intervals between codes equivalent?
   a. No, then the scale is *ordinal*.
   b. Yes, then:
3. Does zero indicate truly none of the quantity measured?
   a. No, then the scale is *interval*.
   b. Yes, then the scale is *ratio*.

This example presents a coding scheme consisting of four codes. Arguably, these codes are themselves ordinal, in the sense that the quantitative meaning of the scale points increases from categorical, to ordinal, to interval, to ratio scale (although one could argue that the distinction between categorical and other scale types is itself categorical). Usually, however, the codes applied to behavioral observations are clearly categorical (e.g., agrees, approves, complains, excuses, interrupts); that is, the order of the codes is arbitrary and not dictated by some underlying common dimension. Furthermore, determining the appropriate code is an act of measurement, one that defines systematic observation.

The statement, systematic observation involves categorical measurement, is somewhat arbitrary and (deliberately) limiting. Measurement is essential, by definition, but events might be measured on scales other than categorical. For example, we might apply valances to codes like agrees, approves, and so forth, representing some underlying scale of positiveness. Then a sequence of coded statements would become a sequence of numbers representing points on an ordinal scale; or every 5 seconds we might rate a person's sensitivity when interacting with a partner on a 1–7 scale; or, a physiological measure like heart rate could be sampled every second, resulting in a sequence of numbers measured on a ratio scale (Gottman & Bakeman, 1996).

The last example does not quite fit the definition used here for behavioral observation because numbers are recorded automatically by an instrument, unaided by human judgment, and ordinal scaling as in the first two examples is relatively rare. All three examples, however, are amenable to other sorts of analyses; possibilities include time series analysis (Gottman, 1981), hierarchical linear models (Bryk & Raudenbush, 1992), and event history analyses (Allison, 1984; Singer & Willet, 1993).

In this chapter, I limit discussion to behavioral observations made by human observers (not automatic instruments) using categorical codes. Human observers and categorical data entail particular approaches to reliability and data analysis, and both are discussed later. Instruments entail a different set of problems (see Gottman & Bakeman, 1996) and usually result in at least ordinal data, which require different analytic approaches (see Gottman, 1981) than the ones discussed here for categorical data. Still, readers should be familiar with other possibilities and recognize that the approaches detailed here can often be combined with other approaches in extremely fruitful ways.

BEHAVIORAL SEQUENCES CAPTURE PROCESS

The measurement approach described here – human observers assigning codes to selected events – can be labor intensive and time consuming so it is reasonable for investigators to ask what might justify such effort. For example, if one wanted only an assessment of the effectiveness of a discussion group leader or the sensitivity of a mother when interacting with her infant, a rating scale approach (observers rating effectiveness or sensitivity from 1 to 5 after watching for a period of time) might seem preferable to a more microanalytic system (observers recording onset and offset times for a list of selected behaviors). Yet if one wants to capture process – What leadership strategies push groups into conflict as opposed to agreement? What maternal behavioral gambits seem to capture infants' attention? – some characterization of behavior unfolding in time and utilizing more detailed codes seems required.

Still, observational methods need not be sequential in a moment-by-moment continuous sense. For example, in a classic study Parten (1932) coded the play behavior of toddlers and preschoolers. One-minute time samples for selected days occurring over several months were coded unoccupied, onlooking, and solitary, parallel, associative, and cooperative play. From these data Parten was able to derive time-budget profiles (estimated proportions of time that different children devoted to the various activities) for each child, but she was not able to describe how play unfolded for these children during play sessions. In contrast, Bakeman and Brownlee (1980) coded successive play states for individual children continuously during play sessions, and so were able to discover that parallel play often served as a bridge into more complex play (i.e., more complex play was coded after parallel play more often than chance would suggest; for additional details, see Bakeman & Gottman, 1986).

All of these possibilities – summary assessments (based, e.g., on rating scales), time-budget profiles, and more fine-grained characterizations of process – have their uses. The largest investment of resources is demanded when detailed sequential records are made (typically, using current technology, by recording onset and offset times for selected behaviors, usually from videotape). Summary assessments and time-budget profiles can be derived from the more detailed sequential records (and usually are), but almost always an investigation of process provides the justification for collecting such records in the first place. Thus, although observational methods do not always result in behavioral sequences being recorded, the uses emphasized in the remainder of this chapter assume that behavioral sequences and not isolated codes were recorded.

DEVELOPING BEHAVIORAL CODES

As noted previously, behavioral codes, structured into coding schemes or sets of coding schemes, form the measuring instruments of observational research. Each code can be regarded as a category of behavior (asks question, waves arm, etc.), and each scheme as a dimension of interest (speech function, body movement, etc.). Almost always, codes grouped in a scheme are mutually exclusive (only one code applies) and exhaustive (some code applies), although codes from different schemes may cooccur; indeed, such cooccurrences are often of considerable substantive interest. Thus the essential activity of code development begins with attempts to define the relevant dimensions and the codes each comprises.

Where Do Codes Come From?

It is easy enough to ask colleagues to define the relevant dimensions of the phenomena they are studying currently. Far more difficult is providing clear and coherent answers when similar questions are put to us. Considerable conceptual clarity is required. Further, once dimensions are named, the categories that

appropriately characterize each dimension do not always follow automatically. Ultimately, of course, answers to where-do-codes-come-from questions depend on our ontological commitments. For example, some students of animal behavior, when constructing an ethogram, might claim they are only listing the discrete behaviors of which a particular species is capable (e.g., Tuculescu & Griswold, 1983); in that sense, the codes simply reflect physical reality, and discovering the codes is an important part of the research endeavor. In contrast, some students of human development, when developing codes, might emphasize that the codes – like human language itself – are arbitrary constructions, useful within a specified theoretical or cultural context (e.g., Rogoff, Mishy, Göncü, & Musier, 1993).

On a more practical level, and no matter one's philosophical underpinnings, coding schemes – to be useful – should derive in a fairly direct manner from the research questions asked. As a first step, we should identify other investigators who have asked similar questions using observational methodology and attempt to adopt their coding schemes outright or else adapt them appropriately. Common coding schemes used by several investigators introduce comparability, which permits the accumulation of results and so strengthens the research literature. Marital interaction, for example, is an area of research that has benefited from common coding schemes developed and used by a coherent cadre of investigators (e.g., see Weiss & Summers, 1983; cf. Bakeman & Casey, 1995).

Yet, arising perhaps from some misplaced territorial imperative, too often investigators create measuring instruments anew (coding schemes as well as personality and other scales) without first determining that no others exist. This makes as much sense as each student of heat developing his or her own thermometer. Thus, coding schemes should be adopted, or at least adapted, from ones existing in the literature whenever possible, but not if doing so violates a superior principle: Codes must fit both the behavior observed and the questions asked.

Several steps can help ensure that this is so. First, of course, questions need to be refined and clarified. Then the behavior of interest needs to be observed, carefully and openly, as though one planned qualitative narrative reports. Tentative coding schemes need to be piloted, discussed, and refined in the presence of the behavior (or, more conveniently, a videotaped record). All of this takes time and emotional and intellectual energy and requires continual clarification of both underlying questions and individual codes. Often the list of codes grows to include behaviors that can be discriminated and seem momentarily important, or at least salient, but that ultimately should be pruned in the interests of economy. A simple test helps: If investigators can explain how each proposed code will help answer a research question, it should be retained, but if not, perhaps it should be discarded. In any event, the importance of well-designed and appropriate coding schemes should not be underestimated. They serve as the lens of observational research; if initially faulty, subsequent data manipulation rarely improves the view.

Codes and Coding Units

The definitions of codes cannot easily be separated from the entities (events, time intervals, etc.) to which they are assigned. It makes sense to call the thing coded a *coding unit* because this reminds us of the presence in any study of different kinds of units, each of which may serve a different purpose. For example, participants assigned to treatment conditions are often called *experimental units*, whereas participants (individuals, dyads, families, etc.) in nonexperimental studies are called *study units*. Assumptions are often made concerning such units (e.g., their independence), and such units often figure prominently in statistical analyses. Thus, experimental or study units form components of the design of a study, whereas coding units reflect data recording procedures. Further, as we discuss shortly, representing the recorded data for analysis may depend on yet different units (e.g., units of time).

Often observational studies use only one kind of coding unit. For example, only turns of talk during marital interaction or only play states during preschooler free play might be coded. Other studies might use two or more coding units; for example, an investigator might code both infants' attention states and mothers' interactive strategies. However, there is a third possibility, which often turns out to be quite interesting: Coding units may be related hierarchically, much as real-life behavior seems to be. A good example is the child negotiation study conceived by David Bearison with the help of Bruce Dorval and other colleagues at the Graduate School and University Center of the City University of New York and presented here in a simplified version (Bearison, Dorval, LeBlanc, Sadow, & Plesa, in press). Like many of their colleagues, they used video recorders initially to preserve behavior of interest. Subsequently, coders viewed the videotapes, detecting and recording occurrences of various behaviors. Often onset times for some behaviors, and onset and offset times for others, are noted, using the time

display that is easily made a part of the picture with the sort of video equipment readily available today.

Bearison is not interested in every moment on the tape but only in certain times when the children (who have been instructed to coinvent a board game) enter into what he terms a *negotiation episode*. Asking coders first to identify episodes of a certain sort before moving on to another level of coding is a relatively common and useful strategy. For example, other investigators might be interested in episodes of children's conflict or cooperation, spouses' argument or tenderness, and client–therapist stalemate or breakthrough. The primary coding unit for Bearison consists of a negotiation episode but, reflecting his interest in the process of negotiation itself, he asks coders to consider a second coding unit: the conversational turns individuals take, which are related hierarchically to (i.e., are nested or embedded within) negotiation episodes. Thus coding proceeds on two levels. First negotiation episodes are detected and coded, then the conversational turns within them are coded.

Examples of Coding Schemes That Have Proved Useful

As argued earlier, coding schemes must reflect whatever ideas and questions drive a particular research endeavor; thus principled adaptation but not indiscriminate borrowing is encouraged. Nonetheless, examples are helpful. Literally hundreds are to be found in the literature, several are presented in Bakeman and Gottman (1986, chapter 2) and Bakeman and Quera (1995a, chapter 2), and a few have already been presented here (e.g., Parten's, 1932, scheme for coding children's play). Three additional examples, both of which reflect a moderate amount of complexity and a particular theoretical base, are the child negotiation study introduced earlier, a second study concerned with mother–infant–grandmother triadic interaction, and a third study concerning lying in everyday life.

As described earlier, negotiation episodes and the conversational turns nested within them were coded for the child negotiation study. Several dimensions of negotiation episodes were of concern, including their *topic* and their *outcome*. Topic codes included

1. rules or methods of play and
2. goals or purpose of playing;

and negotiation outcome codes included

1. unresolved,
2. passive acquiescence,

3. active acceptance,
4. joint compromise, and
5. joint elaboration.

Additionally, two dimensions of conversational turns were coded: their *function* and the *justification* provided. Function codes included

1. initial proposal,
2. counter proposal,
3. disagreement, and
4. agreement;

and justification codes included

1. none,
2. factual, and
3. perspective-taking (justifications that consider the other child's point of view in some way).

The actual study included more dimensions, more codes, and a coding manual that contained extended definitions for the codes, but the examples given here should give some sense of what a realistic and relatively complex set of coding schemes might look like. Some of these codes may not seem immediately obvious or familiar to all readers, but this only illustrates how codes necessarily reflect the theoretical context of the study they serve, in this case a study of relations between social context and cognitive development based on the works of Piaget and Vygotsky. If these codes seem strange to you, you should ask yourself the following: To which of your colleagues would codes you might use seem strange (and why)? And what theories would underpin the codes you might use?

A second example of a moderately complex approach to coding is provided by Sonya Rowland's dissertation research (Rowland, 1995). Adolescent mothers who lived at home were videorecorded interacting with their infants and mothers (the infants' grandmothers) during laboratory-based free play. Simplifying somewhat, the first of the three coding schemes characterized the infant's attention. Codes included

1. active attending to one or both adults (evidenced primarily by facial expressions, vocalizations, or motor responses),
2. passive attending to one or both adults (evidenced primarily by looking), and
3. not attending to either adult.

The second and third schemes characterized mothers' and grandmothers' actions with respect to their infant's activity and were coded separately for each. These codes included

1. actively maintaining infant's attention (by verbal comments, facial expressions, etc.),
2. forcibly redirecting infant's attention (e.g., introducing a new toy or activity),
3. passively supporting infant's attention (i.e., looking at the infant but little else), and
4. not attending to the infant's current activity.

These schemes, their constituent codes, extended definitions, and a number of coding rules (e.g., a behavior must last at least three seconds to be coded) were detailed in an extensive coding manual prepared by the investigator. Indeed, evidence of successful code development is usually reflected in a comprehensive coding manual. This document details the coding scheme or schemes in use, notes how they are structured (i.e., related to each other) if more than one is defined, and provides detailed definitions, often with extensive examples, for all individual codes.

A third example is provided by DePaulo's study of lying in everyday life (DePaulo, Kashy, Kirkendol, Wyer, & Epstein, 1996). DePaulo and her colleagues asked a sample of college students and a second sample of community members to keep a diary, in which they recorded all of their social interactions (that lasted over 10 min or that included a lie) and all of the lies they told during those interactions, every day for a week. Participants were told that a lie occurred any time they intentionally tried to mislead someone and that to count as a lie both the intent to deceive and the actual deception must occur. Subsequently, coding schemes that characterized four dimensions of lies were developed. The first dimension was the lie's *content*. Thus lies were coded as being about

1. feelings,
2. achievements or knowledge,
3. actions, plans, or whereabouts, or
4. facts or possessions.

The second dimension was the *reason* given for the lie. Reasons were coded as

1. self-oriented (told to protect or enhance the liars or their interests) or
2. other-oriented (told to protect or enhance other persons or their interests).

The third dimension was the *type* of lie, coded as

1. outright (a total falsehood),
2. exaggeration (overstating facts), or
3. subtle (evading or omitting relevant details).

Finally, the fourth dimension was the *referent* of the lie, coded as lies that refer to something about

1. the liar,
2. the target,
3. another person, or
4. an object or event.

The codes DePaulo and her colleagues (1996) used were based on a theoretical orientation that emphasizes impression management and the presentation of self in everyday life. The specific codes were developed through a multistep process that included reflection, piloting, and successive refining. Applying these codes to the participants' diaries allowed DePaulo et al. to report, for example, that participants told more self-centered lies than other-oriented lies, except in dyads involving only women. For present purposes, their work presents an excellent and clear example of a moderately complex coding scheme, firmly based in a theoretical orientation and a set of research questions that has proved productive and useful.

RECORDING BEHAVIORAL OBSERVATIONS

Once coding schemes have been developed and refined and the coding manual prepared, measurement – the assignment of codes to events – can take place. Only then does it make sense to talk of data. Occasionally investigators speak of videotapes as data, but this seems a misnomer. Videotapes, such as those used by Rowland (1995) in the triadic interaction study just described, are raw material, not data. Data (at least in the restrictive sense of quantified information organized for analysis) are the product of measurement; videotapes are no more data than a hunk of marble is sculpture. And just as sculpture can be realized in many media, so too the products of measurement may be committed to history in a variety of forms, each of which combines merits with disadvantages.

Pencil and Paper Have Their Pleasures

Pencil and paper should not be overlooked or dismissed due to their seeming lack of sophistication. As noted earlier (Bakeman & Gottman, 1986), no other recording instrument costs less or is easier to replace. Pencil and paper are easy to transport and relatively unobtrusive in use. They do not include batteries, whose charge may be found dissipated at extremely inconvenient moments. And although paper can be lost, it almost never malfunctions.

Moreover, there is a satisfying physicality about pencil marks on paper, a level of immediacy and control that observers often find attractive. For example, in several studies Lauren Adamson and I (Adamson & Bakeman, 1984; Bakeman & Adamson, 1984) have asked observers to locate onset and offset times for codes similar to those used by Rowland. Observers use time-stamped videotapes (the current time, accurate to the nearest second at least, is displayed as part of the picture) and a video player with a shuttle control (which allows the tape to be played forward and backward, maintaining a picture). As described shortly, the recording of codes can be quite automated, but even when more technical alternatives are available, we find that observers may prefer pencil and paper. Pencil and paper can easily be held in a variety of ways, passed among observers, flipped to relevant pages, and modified with nothing more complex than an eraser. Thus, even when videotapes are coded in a well-equipped laboratory, pencil and paper may still have their partisans. They are most likely to be preferred when coding decisions are relatively complex and made only every several seconds or so, not more frequently, as with both the child negotiation and triadic interaction studies described earlier.

Computers Offer Cheap and Easy Alternatives

Pencil and paper were touted in the previous paragraph, not to make Luddittes but observers happy. Once codes are assigned events, however, no matter how they are recorded initially, almost inevitably those codes will be rendered machine readable and subjected to analysis by computer at some point. Why bother with pencil and paper then? Why not let observers key codes directly into some sort of computer device and bypass the need to key in data later? Devices that record codes and store the information electronically for later processing once were specialized and expensive. Now electronic recording can be performed by any number of small, general purpose computers (e.g., notebook computers). All that is needed is a keyboard, an internal clock for real-time applications, an internal storage medium, and some way to transfer (i.e., upload) the recorded information later.

Electronic recording devices are especially useful for live coding (or any real-time coding for that matter). Different keys are associated with particular codes, and whenever one is depressed that code along with its associated time can be stored in memory. Even when videotapes are coded, some observers may prefer to enter codes and times (i.e., the time stamp on the tape) directly into a computer rather than writing the information on paper and keying it in later. For such purposes, a simple word processing program or text editor suffices, although tailored programs are available and may be somewhat easier for observers to use.

Sometimes Full Automation Pays

In some cases, more automatic, computer-assisted systems for recording observational data may be worth the cost and time spent learning their effective use. There are a number of ways that time information can be recorded in machine-readable form directly onto videotape. Using an appropriately programmed computer, observers viewing such videotapes need only depress keys corresponding to particular behaviors when those behaviors are observed, almost like playing a piano. The computer both reads the current time from the videotape and stores it along with the appropriate code in the computer's memory (e.g., see Long, 1996).

Another level of complexity and function is possible. In addition to reading time codes from videotapes into a computer, the video player can be controlled directly from the computer keyboard. Then, with appropriate hardware and software, coders can instruct the system, for example, to review all segments of tape previously coded for a particular code or set of codes or perform other desirable functions. Such systems are very useful (e.g., see Tapp & Walden, 1993; Gottman & Bakeman, 1996) but, as might be expected, have a relatively high entry cost both in terms of money and time. They are most likely to be viewed as cost-effective by relatively large and ongoing projects that require many coders working over several months or years to complete their tasks.

BEHAVIORAL SEQUENCES REPRESENTING

When recording the codes observers assign to events, observers' needs and desires should be paramount. As discussed in the previous section, the best system is one that the observers involved find workable and comfortable, and so a variety of arrangements are permissible. Representing (literally, re-presenting) the behavioral sequences recorded initially for subsequent analysis is another matter. Here standardization has immense benefits. Historically, investigators who coded sequences of behavior represented their data

in a variety of ways closely tied to their individual circumstances. As a result, few general purpose analysis programs were developed; instead, each group of researchers usually spent resources reinventing wheels. A common language was lacking.

The Sequential Data Interchange Standard (SDIS)

The Sequential Data Interchange Standard (SDIS; Bakeman & Quera, 1992, 1995a), a powerful and inclusive standardized format for sequential data, is intended to remedy this situation. As just noted, in the absence of a recognized standard most investigators have developed their own conventions and analysis programs, usually so tailored to a particular laboratory's work that they could not easily be used by others. A commonly recognized data standard not only allows investigators to share the tools they develop, but encourages the development of general purpose analytic programs that all can use. Indeed, Vicenç Quera and I have developed a powerful and flexible program – the Generalized Sequential Querier (GSEQ; Bakeman & Quera, 1995a) – for describing and analyzing sequential data expressed in SDIS format.

For ease of use and to reflect procedures that have been used and found useful historically, four data forms are recognized by SDIS. The four are event, state, timed event, and interval sequences, each of which is defined and described further in subsequent sections. Usually, the form in which investigators record data will dictate the SDIS form they use; almost always behavioral sequences recorded by investigators can be expressed in one or another of these four forms. We presented these as four separate forms because we thought that made them easier to learn and easier to use with different data recording approaches. Actually, there are logical similarities among them, as detail-oriented readers will note, and SDIS converts them all to a common format, which facilitates analysis by GSEQ.

UNTIMED EVENT SEQUENCES. Event sequences consist simply of coded events; duration of individual events is not of interest. By definition, event sequential data consist of a single stream of coded events without any sort of time information for the individual events. Thus, the coded events are necessarily mutually exclusive; only one can occur at a time. Sometimes, depending on the nature of the codes, two identical codes can follow themselves in the stream (e.g., A B A A B C C C etc.), and sometimes not (e.g., A B A B C etc.). Events may be observed live or on videotape, but because the form is so simple, often recording requires nothing more elaborate than pencil and paper.

Codes are common to all four forms and may be represented by any combination of letters and digits (the SDIS program limits their length to 16 although often only 7 are displayed so 7 is recommended; see Bakeman & Quera, 1995a). Thus, unlike some earlier programs (e.g., Bakeman, 1983; Quera & Estany, 1984) that allowed only numeric codes, SDIS permits users to define codes that have mnemonic value. For example, codes for Parten's (1932) parallel play scheme might be *Unoc, Onlk, Sol, Prll, Asso,* and *Coop* for unoccupied, onlooking, and solitary, parallel, associative and cooperative play, respectively. Then,

Event; <Cindy> Unoc Prll Unoc Sol Prll Asso Sol . . . /

might represent a fragment of an SDIS event sequential data file, where the angled brackets contain identifying information and the right slash indicates the end of one child's data.

STATE SEQUENCES. After event sequences, this is probably the simplest of the four data types. State sequences consist of one or more streams of coded events or states recorded in a way that preserves time information for each state. In its simplest form, only one stream is recorded. The duration of individual states, and perhaps the cooccurrence of states in different streams, is usually of interest. The states within each stream or set are defined to be mutually exclusive and exhaustive; hence the beginning of a new state necessarily implies the end of the previous one. By SDIS definitions, a single stream of states is like an event sequence to which time information has been added; thus the coding unit is a state but states are presented using time units. Sometimes consecutive codes may repeat, sometimes not; it depends on the behavior coded and is not part of the definition of a state sequence (cf. Sackett, 1979). Recording requires some sort of timing device, which could be a stop watch, a clock internal to an electronic recording device, or a clock internal to a video recorder that records time directly on the videotape.

For example, if duration were important, the SDIS state-sequential representation for the segment given in the previous paragraph would be

State; <Cindy> Unoc=12 Prll=8 Unoc=21 Sol=34 Prll=6 Asso=13 Sol=25. . . /

Assuming a time unit of 1 s, this fragment indicates that unoccupied lasted 12 s, followed by 8 s of parallel play, followed by 21 s unoccupied, and so forth. The fragment just given can also be represented as

State; <Cindy> ,2:30 Unoc,2:30 Prll,2:42 Unoc,2:50 Sol,3:11 Prll,3:45 Asso,3:51 Sol,4:04 . . . /

Here, the initial 2:30 (for minutes:seconds) indicates the clock setting when recording began and the 2:30 applied to Unoc indicates that the child was unoccupied then. At 2:42, 12 s later, parallel play began, and so forth. For state sequences, the onset of one state implies the offset of the preceding state, so only onset and not offset times need to be entered.

Multiple streams of states are also permitted, separated by an ampersand. For example,

State; <MI pair #27> 0, Mon,1 Moff,4 Mon,8 & Ion,3 Ioff,5 Ion,7 Ioff,9 ,10/

represents a 10-s session (assuming a unit of 1 s), during which the mother was on (Mon) 5 s, the infant was on (Ion) 4 s, and both were on together 2 s (seconds 3 and 8). This example is presented to illustrate multiple streams of states. With different codes (e.g., a separate code for both on together) the session could be presented as a single stream. It could also be presented as a timed event sequence as described in the next section. Any of these forms produce identical results, so the choice depends on individual preference.

TIMED EVENT SEQUENCES. In general, timed event sequences allow for more complexity than the previous two data forms and may be the most general of the four. Codes may represent momentary or frequency behaviors (only frequency and not duration is of interest), in which case only onset times need be recorded. Or codes may represent duration behaviors, in which case both onset and offset times would be preserved. Events need not be mutually exclusive; indeed, often the cooccurrence of various events is of interest to the investigator. Usually procedures for recording timed event sequences require electronic assistance, for example, video recorders that can record the time on the videotape or microcomputers or similar recording devices with internal clocks.

As an example, consider the schematic representation in Figure 6.1, which depicts a 22-s fragment from the triadic interaction study, during which the mother was inactive (Mnot). Infant attention codes include active attention (AcAt), passive attention (PaAt), and no attention (NoAt). During 17 of those seconds the grandmother was active: Codes include

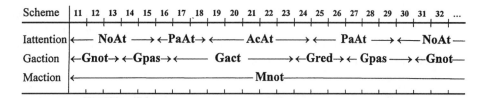

Figure 6.1. Schematic representation of a 22-s segment from the triadic interaction study. *Iattention, Gaction,* and *Maction* refer to the infant attention and grandmother and mother action coding schemes, respectively. See text for definitions of individual codes.

grandmother actively maintaining (Gact), forcibly redirecting (Gred), and passively supporting (Gpas) her infant's attention; the code for grandmother inactive was Gnot. Following SDIS conventions for timed event sequential data, this segment would be represented as

Timed; <family 25> ,11 NoAt,11-16 Gnot,11-14 Mnot,11-*t* Gpas,14-17 PaAt,16-19 Gact,17-24 AcAt,19-25 Gred,24-27 PaAt,25-30 Gpas,27-31 NoAt,30-*t* Gnot,31-*t* ... /

where *t* indicates an offset time beyond the range depicted. The schematic (Figure 6.1) assumes that coded behaviors began and ended precisely on the boundaries between seconds. Thus the onset is the first time unit (here, a second) coded for the behavior, and the offset is the first time unit not coded for the behavior. For example, the onset and offset for the grandmother actively attending episode was 17 and 24, for a total duration of 7 s.

Momentary behaviors could easily be added to this example. For example, if Burp were a momentary code, then Burp,27 might appear in the data stream. Otherwise, state and timed event sequences, both of which are represented using time units, are quite similar. Indeed, the present example could easily be recast as three streams of state sequences (regarding infant attention, grandmother action, and mother action as three states as shown in Figure 6.1; for additional examples, see Bakeman & Quera, 1995a) and would be somewhat simpler than the timed event representation given here. SDIS defines both forms so that when coding schemes include a variety of duration and momentary codes their full complexity can be represented as timed event sequences, but that when several sets of mutually exclusive and exhaustive codes are used (as for the triadic interaction study), the slightly simpler representation afforded by state sequences is available. For example, the SDIS state-sequential representation for the fragment presented in the previous paragraph is

State; <#25> ,11 NoAt,11 PaAt,16 AcAt,19 PaAt,25 NoAt,30 ... & GNot,11 Gpas,14 Gact,17 Gred,24 Gpas,27 Gnot,31 ... & Mnot,11 ... /

where streams are separated by ampersands.

INTERVAL SEQUENCES. Interval sequences are more flexible than their name implies and might better be called multidimensional event sequences. In the usual case, interval sequences consist of a series of successive time intervals to which codes may be assigned, but intervals could also be identified not with a stretch of a time but with a particular event or episode, as is demonstrated shortly. One or more codes (or no codes) may occur per interval, and the interval (when defined by elapsed time) may be quite short, only 5 or 10 s for example. Procedures that yield interval sequences are typically inexpensive and reliable (pencil, paper, and stop watch) but do not always provide the most accurate information; hence often interval sequences have been recorded when only approximate time information was desired and more accurate recording procedures were not feasible.

Interval recording is especially common in older literature and in situations where simple equipment is desirable (e.g., see Bakeman, Adamson, Konner, & Barr, 1990, for an analysis of interval sequential data collected by Konner on !Kung infant interaction in the 1970s) but is becoming less common with the advent of modern electronic equipment. It seems likely that many investigators who used interval sequences in the past would have preferred the greater accuracy provided by timed event sequences, but only recently has recording the onsets and offsets of frequency and duration behaviors become relatively inexpensive and easy to do.

As examples, consider the schematics shown in Figures 6.2–6.4. Figure 6.2 is loosely based on the study of !Kung infants referenced earlier. The fragment shows seven intervals (int$_i$). Codes include adult entertains (AEnt) and offers (AOfr); infant vocalizes (IVoc), offers (IOfr), and smiles (ISmi); and the environmental code (Rain). The SDIS representation for the intervals

...	IVoc AEnt	IVoc AEnt	AOfr Rain	IOfr IVoc ISmi Rain	Rain	Rain	IVoc Rain	...
	int_1	int_2	int_3	int_4	int_5	int_6	int_7	

Figure 6.2. Schematic representation of a fragment of infant interaction. Each interval represents 5 s. See text for definitions of codes.

shown in Figure 6.2 is

> Interval=5; <Infant 8> ... AEnt IVoc *2, Rain+
> AOfr, ISmi IVoc IOfr, *2, IVoc, ... /

Intervals are separated by commas. Successive intervals that contain the same codes (as int_1 and int_2 here) need not be repeated; instead the number of identical intervals may be entered after an asterisk. And a code that occurs in many successive intervals need be entered only once followed by a plus sign. For other useful conventions, see Bakeman and Quera (1995a).

Figure 6.3 shows a fragment consisting of seven child negotiation episodes (ne_i), so here intervals are equated with episodes. Codes include rule and goal topics as well as unresolved (unre), passive (pas) and active (act) acquiescence and joint compromise (comp) and elaboration (elab) outcomes. In contrast, Figure 6.4 shows a fragment consisting of four conversational turns nested within the first negotiation episode and three conversational turns nested within a second episode, so here intervals are equated with conversational turns (ct_i), and episode attributes are repeated in each interval as appropriate to provide context. Conversational turn codes include the functions of initial proposal (ipro), counterproposal (cpro), disagreement (dis), and agreement (agr) and the justifications of none, factual (fact), and perspective-taking (pers). The SDIS representation for the negotiation episodes shown in Figure 6.3 is

> Interval; <dyad 11n> ... rule unre, goal act, goal
> elab, rule comp, rule pas, rule pas, goal act, ... /

and for the conversational turns shown in Figure 6.4 is

> Interval; <dyad 11t> ... rule+ unre+ ipro none, dis
> none, cpro fact, agr none, goal+ act+ ipro none,
> agr pers, agr fact, ... /

The plus after a code indicates that the code continues for successive intervals until turned off explicitly or until another context code belonging to the same

...	unre rule	act goal	elab goal	comp rule	pas rule	pas rule	act goal	...
	ne_1	ne_2	ne_3	ne_4	ne_5	ne_6	ne_7	

Figure 6.3. Schematic representation of seven child negotiation episodes coded as interval sequences. See text for definitions of individual codes.

mutually exclusive and exhaustive set occurs (for details, see Bakeman & Quera, 1995a).

COMMONALTIES. The four forms are treated separately here because this connects most easily with what investigators actually do and have done historically; thus the four forms facilitate human use and learning. A general purpose computer program like GSEQ (Bakeman & Quera, 1995a), however, is better served by a common underlying format because this allows for greater generality (and less computer code); thus the SDIS program converts SDS files (files containing data that follow SDIS conventions) into a common format (called MDS or modified SDS files) that is easily read by GSEQ. The technical details need not concern users of these computer programs, but understanding the conceptual unity of the four forms can be useful. Common to all four is an underlying metric. For event sequences, the underlying metric is the discrete event itself. For state and timed event sequences, the underlying metric is a unit of time, often a second. And for interval sequences, the underlying metric is a discrete interval, usually (but not necessarily) defined in terms of time.

The metric can be imagined as cross marks on a time line, where the space between cross marks is thought of as bins to which codes may be assigned, each representing the appropriate unit. For event sequences, one code and one code only is placed in each bin. Sometimes adjacent bins may be assigned the same code (consecutive codes may repeat), sometimes not (for logical reasons, consecutive codes cannot repeat). For state sequences, one (single stream) or more codes (multiple streams)

...	none ipro unre rule	none dis unre rule	fact cpro unre rule	none ign unre rule	none ipro act goal	pers agr act goal	fact agr act goal	...
	ct_1	ct_2	ct_3	ct_4	ct_5	ct_6	ct_7	

Figure 6.4. Schematic representation of conversational turns nested within two child negotiation episodes and coded as interval sequences. See text for definitions of individual codes.

may be placed in each bin. Depending on the time unit used and the typical duration of a state, often a stretch of successive bins will contain the same code. For timed event sequences, one or more codes or no codes at all may be placed in each bin; likewise for interval sequences. Thus for all forms, successive bins represent successive units (whether events, time units, or intervals equated with a unit of time or episodes of some sort) and, depending on the form, contain zero, one, or more codes.

Any standardization of sequential data that became widely used would represent an important advance in observational methodology, although to my knowledge the SDIS is the only one proposed in the literature and implemented in computer programs. It is simple, flexible, and permits its users to avail themselves of analysis and other programs written by anyone who adheres to the standard. Observers can easily record data in this format directly or, when investigators possess recording equipment that uses a different format or wish to analyze data from an existing archive, it is a simple matter to write programs (e.g., in Basic or Pascal) that reformat existing data into the SDIS format. Once sequential data are expressed using SDIS conventions, the considerable power of programs like GSEQ can be brought to bear (for details see Bakeman & Quera, 1995a), including its ability to modify existing codes (e.g., recoding or lumping existing codes), create new ones (e.g., combining existing codes using standard *and*, *or*, and *not* logical operations or defining new codes keyed to onsets and offsets of existing ones, such as the 5 s after the onset of crying, or the two intervals after the onset of smiling), and produce any number of cross-classified counts (e.g., the number of intervals after one containing an adult offer that contain an infant offer, or the number of seconds within 5 s of the onset of crying that contain an onset of other comforting). Moreover, any additional analytic programs investigators write that assume SDIS data can be shared with others. Thus standardization confers considerable benefits and for that reason should be considered.

ASSESSING OBSERVER AGREEMENT AND RELIABILITY

Terms such as observer agreement and reliability seem central to behavioral observation, and so common definitions might be assumed, yet in practice they admit to a variety of meanings (Suen, 1988). Most writers share a common concern with accuracy and so seek to gauge how close measures come to reflecting the true state of affairs. Yet different writers use terms like agreement, reliability, and validity and mean quite different things by them, and readers need to be alert to the way key terms, assumptions, and concepts vary.

According to a common contemporary view (e.g., Judd & McClelland, 1998; see also John and Benet-Martinez, this volume, Ch. 13), variables consist of variance due to the construct we want to measure, variance due to systematic error, and random error variance. Thus, the measure would be deemed reliable when two judges agree, but if systematic error were high for both, construct validity would not be established. The classic psychometric view is less nuanced. Usually reliability is defined as the ratio of true to observed score variance (Nunnally, 1978), which would be regarded as construct validity by the more nuanced view. In this section, I attempt to finesse these important but complex matters and discuss simple observer agreement, unfreighted with additional conceptual baggage to the extent possible. Still, I recognize that the interpretation of observer agreement varies, depending on one's psychometric commitments and models, and that interobserver agreement only addresses potential errors among observers and ignores many other sources of potential errors, which in the context of observational research may be many (Pedhazur & Schmelkin, 1991, pp. 114–115, 145–146).

Agreement Is the Sine Qua Non of Observational Research

When two independent observers agree the usual presumption is that they are therefore accurate, even though it is possible that they simply share a similar but nonetheless deviant worldview. Yet, as Pedhazur and Schmelkin (1991) noted, the presumption of accuracy is questionable because other sources of error may be present. Usually in observational research interobserver agreement is emphasized, but it is important to remember that indices of interobserver agreement, although important, are not necessarily indices of reliability or validity, however defined.

Nonetheless, observer agreement can be viewed as the sine qua non of observational research because without it we know the data to be unreliable by most definitions (see also C. Smith's, this volume, Ch.12; Bartholomew, Henderson, & Marcia, this volume, Ch. 11). In the absence of agreement, we would view the stream of codes as simply one individual's narrative and, due to the restrictive nature of coding schemes, an impoverished one at that. A weakness of much observational research may well be the tendency to regard codes assigned to events as accurate (Gardner, 1995), thereby ignoring the usual psychometric distinction between true and observed scores. But surely a strength of most observational research – a necessary strength due to the relatively subjective nature of many codes – has been the emphasis on demonstrating interobserver agreement.

Some Point-by-Point Methods Ignore Time

Agreement statistics are useful, first, as a means of providing feedback to observers during training and, second, as a way of indicating the trustworthiness of observational data to colleagues (and journal editors). Some agreement statistics focus on the occurrence but not the timing of events. For example, older literature often contained reports of percent agreements, usually computed as a ratio of agreements to the sum of agreements and disagreements (multiplied by 100). However, there are two problems (at least) with such percents: The units coded for agreement and disagreement are by no means always clear, and agreement percentages do not control for chance. Two observers guessing randomly will agree some of the time, and the extent of their agreement will depend on the number of codes and their marginal distributions. Thus percentage agreements cannot be compared across studies, and there is no rational basis for assigning meaning to a particular value (e.g., 90%). This renders percentage agreements essentially useless, as most investigators now recognize.

COHEN'S KAPPA. The most commonly used index of agreement is Cohen's (1960) kappa, which does correct for chance. Kappa is an index that characterizes agreement in applying a coding scheme; it varies from zero (indicating no agreement) to one (indicating perfect agreement). It does not yield values for individual codes, although useful information concerning sources of disagreement can be gleaned from the agreement matrix on which kappa is based. For example, imagine that two coders both coded the function of successive negotiation episodes. Let k represent the number of codes in the scheme. Then agreement can be tallied in a $k \times k$ matrix. Rows represent the first coder, columns the second, and both are labeled identically with the k codes. When observers primarily agree, most tallies fall on the upper-left to lower-right diagonal. Off-diagonal cells indicate disagreements (e.g., what the first observer coded as A the second observer coded as B), and noting off-diagonal cells with many tallies provides useful feedback when training observers.

Kappa is a summary index derived from the agreement matrix. Let x_{ij} indicate a cell of the matrix. Plus signs indicate summation, so x_{i+} indicates the total for the ith row, and x_{++} indicates the total number of tallies in the matrix. Then

$$P_{obs} = \frac{\sum_{i=1}^{k} x_{ii}}{x_{++}}$$

represents the proportion of agreement actually observed, and

$$P_{exp} = \frac{\sum_{i=1}^{k} x_{+i} x_{i+}}{x_{++}^2}$$

represents the proportion of agreement expected due to chance. Then

$$\kappa = \frac{P_{obs} - P_{exp}}{1 - P_{exp}} \tag{1}$$

indicates how kappa is computed.

WEIGHTED KAPPA. When codes are roughly ordinal or for other reasons investigators may wish to regard some disagreements as more serious than others, Cohen (1968) has specified a way of weighting disagreements. Three $k \times k$ matrices are involved: one for observed frequencies, one for expected frequencies, and one for weights. Let x_{ij}, m_{ij}, and w_{ij} represent elements from these three matrices respectively; then $m_{ij} = (x_{+j} \times x_{i+}) \div x_{++}$, and the w_{ij} indicate how seriously we choose to regard various disagreements. Usually the diagonal elements of the weight matrix are 0, indicating agreement (i.e., $w_{ii} = 0$ for $i = 1$ through k); cells just off the diagonal are 1, indicating some disagreement; cells further off the diagonal are 2, indicating more serious disagreement, and so forth. Then

$$\kappa_{wt} = 1 - \frac{\sum_{i=1}^{k} \sum_{j=1}^{k} w_{ij} x_{ij}}{\sum_{i=1}^{k} \sum_{j=1}^{k} w_{ij} m_{ij}} \tag{2}$$

indicates how weighted kappa is computed. If all off-diagonal elements are 1 and all diagonal elements are 0, then κ as defined earlier and κ_{wt} yield identical results. A worked example for both kappa and weighted kappa is given in Figure 6.5. A Windows 95 program that computes kappa and weighted kappa is described by Robinson and Bakeman (1998) and can be downloaded from www.gsu.edu/psychology/bakeman.

Fleiss, Cohen, and Everitt (1969) described how to compute variance for kappa and weighted kappa, so it is possible to determine whether kappas differ significantly from zero, but mere significance is almost always too low a standard for observer agreement. Just as correlations that account for little variance may be

Counts:

	A	B	C	D	Total
A	32	5	3	1	48
B	3	21	2	0	26
C	0	3	18	0	21
D	0	5	4	47	56
Total	35	34	27	55	141

Weights:

	A	B	C	D
A	0	1	2	3
B	1	0	1	2
C	2	1	0	1
D	3	2	1	0

$$\kappa = 0.75, \quad \kappa_{wt} = 0.81$$

Figure 6.5. Agreement data (counts) for two observers, their corresponding weights, and the resulting values of kappa and weighted kappa.

statistically significant given enough cases, values of kappa that are quite low also may be significant. Absolute magnitude and not significance should be our guide. For example, Fleiss (1981) characterized kappas of .40 to .60 as fair, .60 to .75 as good, and over .75 as excellent, which seems a reasonable guideline. However, when codes are very few (e.g., $k = 2$ or 3), and their simple probabilities quite skewed, reasonable observer accuracy may nonetheless yield quite low values of kappa; see Bakeman, Quera, McArthur, and Robinson (1996) for details.

Describing and assessing interobserver agreement using kappa or weighted kappa can be characterized as a point-by-point method because, used as just described, kappa and weighted kappa take into account agreement at each sequential point. Typically the units considered are successive events, turns of talk, or the like. Such methods are appropriate when agreement as to the sequence of events matters but agreement with respect to the precise duration of events is not of concern, which is why they are described here as methods that ignore time.

Other Point-by-Point Methods Take Time into Account

Reflecting current technology, increasingly coders record onset and offset times of events so that, in addition to sequences, the durations of individual events are preserved. When such times are available,

and agreement with respect to duration matters, then time units can be tallied using an agreement matrix, and kappa can be computed exactly as just described. In such cases, the number of tallies in the agreement matrix reflects the time coded (e.g., if 500 s were coded, and 1-s units were tallied, then the matrix would contain 500 tallies). Some readers, recognizing that time units are arbitrary, may wonder if their arbitrary nature is problematic. One could as well tally half-second as 1-s units, after all, thereby doubling the number of units tallied. However, this does not affect the value of kappa (as it would, e.g., a chi-square statistic). Given the same amount of agreement, kappa is unaffected by the number of tallies; thus one need not be so concerned with the arbitrary choice of time unit.

Moreover – and this may not be immediately obvious – checking point-by-point agreement taking time into account (i.e., tallying time units) solves a common problem. As an example, consider the child negotiation study described earlier. Although coders may think of the process of coding negotiation episodes as a seamless task, it can be divided into two parts. First coders need to detect episodes, then code the episodes detected, and agreement with respect to detecting when episodes occurred is almost impossible to establish unless time is taken into account.

Assume, for example, a 1-s time unit. Two coders observe Bearison's videotapes (Bearison, in press), recording onset and offset times for all negotiation episodes (other coding is left for later). Then each second can be tallied into a 2×2 agreement matrix; rows represent the first coder, columns the second coder, and both are labeled *yes* and *no*, indicating whether a second is coded as occurring during a negotiation episode or not. Kappa is computed as described earlier. In this way, observers get credit for agreeing both when an episode did and did not occur, as only seems fair, and their agreement is quantified with kappa, correcting for chance. One further refinement is possible. Investigators might decide to tally 1-s disagreements (Observer A coded yes for a given second when Observer B coded no but coded the following second yes) as agreements if they believe such disagreements are not consequential.

In general, kappa is an index that corrects for chance and assesses observers' point-by-point agreement with reference to a given coding scheme. Time can be taken into account by tallying not events or some other unit of varying duration but time units themselves. Taking time into account is especially recommended when investigators want to establish that two observers agreed as to when a particular type of event occurred (e.g., a negotiation episode). It may or may not be taken into account when investigators want to establish that two observers agreed as to the characteristics of the event (e.g., the specific topic or outcome code for the negotiation episode).

Summary Methods Can Be Useful

Point-by-point agreement seems desirable when training observers, and its stringency probably provides the most certainty that observers are performing similarly, but methods that assess the reliability of the summary measures actually analyzed may provide the best basis for communicating with colleagues concerning the accuracy of our measures.

The sequential data themselves are far too numerous to present in any direct way. Almost always, they are reduced to a series of summary statistics – simple probabilities, conditional or transitional probabilities, other indices such as Yule's Q (defined in the next section), and so forth – that are then subjected to further analysis. For example, in the context of the triadic interaction study described earlier, among other associations Rowland (1995) was interested in how often infants passively attended when their mothers or grandmothers redirected their infants' activity. Thus summary measures of interest included pairs of appropriate conditional probabilities (one for the mother and one for the grandmother) and their associated Yule's Qs (defined in the next section) because analysis of these pairs of scores permitted Rowland to compare mothers' with grandmothers' effectiveness when interacting with their infants. Having found reasonable kappas, and thereby having demonstrated point-by-point observer agreement for the sequential data, investigators might reason that any summary measures based on the sequential data (such as those used by Rowland) surely would be at least as accurate and so might feel little need to consider reliability further.

As noted earlier, agreement is not the same as reliability; thus, in addition to kappa calculations, many investigators may want to analyze the reliability of their summary measures more formally. One fairly standard approach is based on concepts of generalizability (Cronbach, Gleser, Nanda, & Rajaratnam, 1972; also see Brennan, 1983; Wiggins, 1973). For example, imagine that five persons were observed by two observers, that the observers' scores were as shown in Table 6.1 (assume these are summary indices derived from sequential data), and that we want to generalize over the facet of observers (Bakeman & Gottman, 1997). That is, we want to estimate the reliability when,

TABLE 6.1. Hypothetical Data for Determining Observer Reliability

Person	Observer 1	Observer 2	Person average
1	2	1	$\bar{P}_1 = 1.5$
2	20	14	$\bar{P}_2 = 17.0$
3	30	22	$\bar{P}_3 = 26.0$
4	3	7	$\bar{P}_4 = 5.0$
5	120	84	$\bar{P}_5 = 102.0$
	$\bar{O}_1 = 35.0$	$\bar{O}_2 = 25.6$	$\bar{M} = 30.3$ (grand mean)

at some future time, we use observers similar to those in our generalizability study.

The setup of the data in Table 6.1 is the same as for a simple repeated-measures ANOVA. The within-subject factor is observer (in this case, with two levels, i.e., data from two observers) and there is no between-subject factor as such; persons represent total between-subject variability. The ANOVA source table for these data is given in Table 6.2 (showing R^2 and ΔR^2 as recommended by Bakeman, 1992). Given these data and the current question, an appropriate coefficient of generalizability, or reliability, is:

$$\alpha = \frac{MS_P - MS_r}{MS_P + (n_o - 1)MS_r}, \tag{3}$$

where n_o is the number of observers (2 in this case), and MS_p and MS_r are the mean squares for persons and residual (or error; in this case, the $P \times O$ interaction), respectively (Wiggins, 1973). This is an intraclass correlation coefficient based on the classical assumption that observed scores can be divided into a true and an error component ($X = T + e$), so that the appropriate intraclass correlation is defined as

$$\alpha = \frac{\sigma_T^2}{\sigma_T^2 + \sigma_e^2}. \tag{4}$$

Equation 3 is based on recommendations made by

TABLE 6.2. ANOVA Source Table for the Generalizability Study of Observer Reliability

Source	R^2	ΔR^2	SS	df	MS
Person	0.95	0.95	13,611.6	4	3,402.9
Observer	0.97	0.02	220.9	1	220.9
$P \times O$	1.00	0.03	485.6	4	121.4
Total			14,318.1	9	

Hartmann (1982) and Wiggins (1973, p. 290) and is derived from Equation 4 by substitution and algebraic manipulation.

The alpha of Equation 3 estimates the reliability of observations made by a randomly selected observer, selected from the pool that contained the two observers used for the reliability study (Table 6.2). It further assumes that data will be interpreted within what Suen (1988) termed a "norm-referenced" (i.e., values are meaningful only relatively; rank-order statistics like correlation coefficients are emphasized) as opposed to a criterion-referenced framework (i.e., interpretation of values references an absolute external standard; statistics like unstandardized regression coefficients are emphasized). For example, for the data shown in Table 6.2,

$$\alpha = \frac{MS_P - MS_r}{MS_P + (n_0 - 1)MS_r} = \frac{3402.9 - 121.4}{3402.9 + (2 - 1)121.4}$$
$$= .931.$$

For other possible intraclass correlation coefficients (sometimes termed generalizability coefficients) based on other assumptions, see Fleiss (1986, chapter 1), Shrout and Fleiss (1979), and Suen (1988).

In summary, point-by-point methods are useful for observer training and are usually regarded as sufficiently stringent that most arbiters (such as journal reviewers and editors) seldom require a more formal reliability study. Such studies, however, based as they are on the psychometric literature and the scores actually analyzed, have considerable merit. Moreover, sometimes point-by-point agreement will suggest limited agreement when a reliability study will reveal that the reliability is quite acceptable. For all these reasons, it makes sense to include reliability assessments of summary scores whenever feasible.

DESCRIBING AND ANALYZING BEHAVIORAL OBSERVATIONS

All the foregoing done – coding schemes defined, events coded and the codes recorded, sequences of coded events represented for subsequent analysis, and acceptable observer agreement and reliability established – finally we are able to begin describing the data and unraveling the stories contained therein.

Simple Statistics: Frequencies, Rates, and Bouts

As mentioned earlier, when discussing observer agreement, sequential data are almost always reduced to summary statistics for subsequent analysis. Some summary statistics are useful descriptively even when they do not exploit the sequential aspect of the data. For example, simple frequencies with which selected codes occurred can be informative, but better yet are their rates (occurrences per unit time), because rates are comparable even when different persons, dyads, or whatever were observed differing lengths of times. Additionally, when onset and offset times are recorded, proportions of total time devoted to different activities can be reported along with the activity.

For example, Rowland (1995) reported that bouts of joint mother–grandmother infant-directed actions were observed 32.8 times per hour (i.e., 1 every 1.83 min), that such bouts lasted 30.7 s on average, and that 28% of the total time was devoted to these bouts. Normally only two of these three partially redundant statistics (rates, mean bout durations, and percents of time) would be reported because values for one can be deduced from the other two (e.g., if proportion of time is relatively high but bouts are relatively infrequent, then necessarily mean bout length must be long).

Often more than a single individual, dyad, family, or whatever, is observed. Typically such study units are embedded in a design because investigators want to ask questions about the importance of their research factors. For example, a two-group design might include clinic and nonclinic couples or mothers and grandmothers, and investigators might want to know whether a particular sequential pattern was more characteristic of one group than the other. Usually such questions are analyzed using standard parametric techniques such as t-tests, ANOVAs, and multiple regression (for an alternative approach using permutation tests see Bakeman, Robinson, & Quera, 1996; see also Edgington, 1995; Good, 1994). However, care must be exercised when selecting individual statistics for analysis. For simple summary statistics such as the rates, mean durations, and proportions mentioned in the previous section, the usual parametric precautions apply (e.g., a reasonably normal distribution of scores). Additional considerations should be taken into account when analyzing conditional summary statistics.

Conditional Statistics: Measures of Association

Conditional associations can reflect cooccurrences (e.g., what is the probability that an infant was actively attending given that the grandmother was acknowledging the infant's activity) or lagged relations (e.g., what is the probability that counter proposals were followed by agreements during negotiation episodes). As the examples suggest, the association can be expressed as a conditional probability (the probability of B given A), which is called a transitional probability when lagged relations are under consideration (e.g., the probability of B at Time 1 given A at Time 0).

Conditional probabilities are useful descriptively but are not good candidates as scores for parametric analyses because their absolute values can be affected by the corresponding simple probabilities. For example, if the probability of B is much higher for Participant 1 than Participant 2, then a higher probability of B given A for Participant 1 may reflect only the higher simple probability and not anything inherently conditional or sequential. The z-score is another useful and often mentioned statistic; although it may be computed in a variety of ways (see Bakeman & Quera, 1995b), it has the merit of expressing the extent to which an observed value for a conditional probability differs from its expected value (and, granted assumptions, may be tested for significance). However, despite an earlier suggestion (Bakeman & Gottman, 1986), z-scores are not good candidates for parametric analyses either. If the number of tallies in the appropriate cells doubled but the association remained the same, the z-score would increase. Thus, except when the total number of tallies happens to be the same for all participants (i.e., study units), z-scores are not comparable across study units (individual participants, dyads, families, etc.). Far better candidates for subsequent parametric analyses are strength of association or effect size measures. As Wampold (1992) noted, they are unaffected by the number of tallies and should be analyzed instead of z-scores.

Strength of association or effect size measures are especially well-developed for 2×2 tables (to give just two examples from an extensive literature, see Conger & Ward, 1984; Reynolds, 1984; much of the material in this and subsequent paragraphs is summarized from Bakeman, McArthur, & Quera, 1996). This is fortunate because, when interest centers on one cell in a larger two-dimensional table, the larger table can be collapsed into a 2×2, and statistics developed for 2×2 tables can be used (as Morley, 1987, noted with respect to phi). Assume, for example, that we want to know whether Event B is particularly likely after Event A. In this case, we would label rows A and $\sim A$ and columns B and $\sim B$ (where rows represent Lag 0, columns Lag 1, and $\sim$ represents not). Then the collapsed 2×2 table can be represented as

| | Lag 1 | |
Lag 0	B	~B
A	a	b
~A	c	d

where individual cells are labeled a, b, c, and d as shown and represent cell frequencies. Thus a is the number of times Event A was followed by Event B.

ODDS RATIO. One of the most common statistics for 2×2 tables (perhaps more so in epidemiology and sociology than in psychology) is the odds ratio. As its name implies, it is estimated by the ratio of a to b divided by the ratio of c to d,

$$\text{est. odds ratio} = \frac{a/b}{c/d} \tag{5}$$

(where a, b, c, and d refer to observed frequencies for the cells of a 2×2 table as noted earlier; notation varies, but for definitions in terms of population parameters, see Bishop, Fienberg, & Holland, 1975; Wickens, 1993). Multiplying numerator and divisor by d/c, this can also be expressed as

$$\text{est. odds ratio} = \frac{ad}{bc}. \tag{6}$$

Equation 6 is more common, although Equation 5 reflects the name and renders the concept more faithfully. Consider the following example:

| | Lag 1 | | |
Lag 0	B	~B	
A	10	10	20
~A	20	60	80
	30	70	100

The odds for B after A are 1:1, whereas the odds for B after any other (non-A) event are 1:3, thus the odds ratio is 3. In other words, the odds for B occurring after A are three times the odds for B occurring after anything else. When the odds ratio is greater than 1 (and it can always be made ≥ 1 by swapping rows), it has the merit, lacking in many indices, of a simple and concrete interpretation.

YULE'S Q. The odds ratio varies from 0 to infinity and equals 1 when the odds are the same for both rows (indicating no effect of the row classification). Yule's Q is a related index. It is a transformation of the odds ratio designed to vary, not from 0 to infinity with 1 indicating no effect, but from -1 to $+1$ with 0 indicating no effect, just like the familiar Pearson product-moment correlation. For that reason many investigators find it more descriptively useful than the odds ratio. First, c/d is subtracted from the numerator so that Yule's Q is zero when a/b equals c/d. Then, a/b is added to the denominator so that Yule's Q is $+1$ when b or c or both are zero and -1 when a or d or both are zero, as follows:

$$\text{Yule's Q} = \frac{\dfrac{a}{b} - \dfrac{c}{d}}{\dfrac{c}{d} + \dfrac{a}{b}} = \frac{\dfrac{ad - bc}{bd}}{\dfrac{bc + ad}{bd}} = \frac{ad - bc}{ad + bc}. \quad (7)$$

Yule's Q can be expressed as a monotonically increasing function of the odds ratio; thus these two indices are equivalent in the sense of rank ordering participants the same way (Bakeman, McArthur, & Quera, 1996).

PHI. Another extremely common index for 2×2 tables is the phi coefficient. This is simply the familiar Pearson product-moment correlation coefficient computed using binary coded data (Cohen & Cohen, 1983; Hays, 1963). A common definition for phi is

$$\phi = \frac{z}{\sqrt{N}}, \quad (8)$$

where z is computed for the 2×2 table and hence equals $\sqrt{\chi^2}$. Thus phi can be viewed as a z-score corrected for sample size. In terms of the four cells, phi is

$$\phi = \frac{ad - bc}{\sqrt{(a + b)(c + d)(a + c)(b + d)}}. \quad (9)$$

Like Yule's Q it varies from -1 to $+1$ with zero indicating no association. The differences between Yule's Q and phi are relatively subtle (see Bakeman, McArthur, & Quera, 1996, for details), so as a practical matter it rarely matters which is used (or whether another index such as the odds ratio or log odds ratio is used instead; see Wickens, 1993). Less satisfactory as an index of conditional association is transformed kappa (Wampold, 1989, 1992); for reasons see Bakeman, McArthur, and Quera (1996).

Analyzing Conditional Association

In an ideal confirmatory world, investigators would pluck the one transition from a larger table needed to answer their most important research question, compute a single Yule's Q or phi based on a collapsed $A|\sim A \times B|\sim B$ table such as the one shown earlier, and

proceed to test for group differences (or other questions as their design permits). But much of the world is rankly exploratory. Indeed, it is tempting to compute some index for each cell of a table, one set for each participant, and then subject all indices to standard parametric tests (t-test, ANOVAs, etc.). This courts Type I error in a fairly major way. At the very least, no more indices should be derived than the degrees of freedom associated with the table, which at most is $(R-1)(C-1)$, where R is the number of rows and C the number of columns. This is somewhat analogous to decomposing an omnibus ANOVA into single-degree-of-freedom planned comparisons or contrasts.

One systematic way to derive indices from a larger table requires that one code be regarded as something of a baseline, or base for comparison, such as unengaged or no activity or other. For example, recall that Rowland (1995) coded infants as actively attending, passively attending, or not attending and categorized mothers' and grandmothers' actions as forcibly redirecting, actively maintaining, passively acknowledging, or not attending to the infants' current activity. This allowed her to tally seconds as follows:

	Infant attention		
Adult action	Active	Passive	Not
Redirecting	a	b	c
Maintaining	d	e	f
Acknowledging	g	h	i
Not attending	j	k	l

Then, following Reynold's (1984) suggestion for decomposing the odds ratio in tables larger than 2×2, six tables examining associations between redirecting–active, redirecting–passive, maintaining–active, and so forth, were formed. For example, the 2×2 table for redirecting–passive was

	Passive	Not
Redirecting	b	c
Not attending	k	l

where b, c, k, and l represent cells from the larger table. The first row and column indicate the association selected, whereas the second row and column indicate the base for comparison (here adult not attending and infant not attending).

For each of the six associations, Rowland (1995) formed two such tables, one for each mother and grandmother in her study, and computed a Yule's Q for each. Values for Yule's Q can be interpreted quite directly. If positive, they indicate the extent to which an observed association was greater than (or if negative, less than) the value predicted from the base rates, assuming no association. For example, for the redirecting–passive association, values above zero indicate that at times when the partner (mother or grandmother) was attempting to redirect her infant's attention, the infant passively attended more often than expected. Similarly, values below zero indicate that the infant passively attended less often than expected at those times. Finally, values of zero indicate that the infant passively attended exactly as often as expected at those times. However, there is a fourth possibility. Data may be insufficient to give credence to the value computed for Yule's Q, in which case the value should be regarded as missing.

SUFFICIENT DATA. Criteria for determining insufficiency are somewhat arbitrary. If one or both of the behaviors under consideration (here, passive attending and redirecting) never occurred, Yule's Q cannot be computed (the divisor is zero and so the quotient is undefined). However, if one or both of the behaviors occur very seldom, there is no reason to regard the value of Yule's Q (or any other summary statistic) as accurate; in such cases a shift of a single tally from one cell to another can result in quite dramatic changes in the value of Yule's Q. In my view, it does not make sense to compute a Yule's Q unless all marginal sums (row and column totals) are at least five, but this is only an arbitrary rule of thumb. Investigators should always be alert to the scanty-data problem and interpret results cautiously when summary statistics are based on few instances of critical codes.

GROUP DIFFERENCES. Rowland's (1995) study provides an excellent demonstration of the use of conditional indices coupled with standard analyses. She applied the at-least-five rule, which gave her complete data for 21 of 36 infants (infants were observed at 6 and 12 months of age so complete data implies four scores, one for mothers and one for grandmothers at 6 and 12 months, respectively). Almost always, data were incomplete because grandmothers had not been observed redirecting, whereas mothers almost always were. This was Rowland's first finding when attempting to explore the redirecting–passive attending association. Next, she performed a repeated

measures ANOVA for the 21 infants for whom complete data were available (the two within-subject variables were age and partner). Only the partner effect was significant: The mean Yule's Q was higher for mothers than grandmothers ($M = .378$ vs. $-.056$), $F(1, 20) = 5.81$, $p < .05$, suggesting that the mothers might actually be more competent than the grandmothers.

INDIVIDUAL PATTERNS. This ANOVA is somewhat unsatisfactory for at least two reasons. First, as is always true with repeated-measures analyses, any missing datum removes the entire case from consideration, which can leave considerable data unused, and, second, as is true of ANOVAs generally, means (and mean differences) are emphasized but individual cases are slighted. From the typical ANOVA we learn about average cases but not how many cases exemplify the average. Thus, for her third set of analyses Rowland (1995) counted the number of Yule's Q scores that were above zero.

These results, which were analyzed with a simple sign test, were in general agreement with the ANOVA just described but provided greater detail, particularly with respect to individual cases. Considering those cases for which a Yule's Q was computed, Rowland (1995) found that for 27 of 33 and 22 of 28 mothers at 6 and 12 months, respectively, mothers redirecting and infants passively attending cooccurred in more seconds than expected by chance ($p < .01$ for both). However, no such association was noted for grandmothers: For only 15 of 27 at both 6 and 12 months of age were cooccurrences of redirecting and passively attending greater than chance. Substantively, Rowland's results suggested that, at least in some instances, infants responded differently to their mothers than grandmothers, and in some cases the adolescent mothers appeared quite competent. Methodologically, this example alerts us to the usefulness of indices like Yule's Q (for either cooccurrence as here, or for sequential pattern as might be used in the negotiation study), the importance of screening all scores for reasonable distribution and a basis in sufficient data, and the usefulness of considering individually based alternatives (such as the sign test) to the more typical group-based t-test or ANOVA.

Guarding against Type I Error

In the previous several paragraphs I have suggested that associations between two particular events can be assessed with an index like Yule's Q or phi, whether cooccurrences as in the redirecting–passive attending example based on Rowland's (1995) data or lagged sequential transitions as Bearison computed for his conversational-turn functional codes. These statistics gauge the magnitude of the effect and, unlike chi-squares or z-scores, are unaffected by the number of tallies. Thus they are reasonable candidates for subsequent analyses such as the familiar t-tests, ANOVAs, and multiple regressions routinely used by social scientists to assess individual differences and effects of various research factors. But the events under consideration may be many in number, leading to many tests and thereby courting Type I error.

It goes without saying (which may be why it is so necessary to restate) that guiding ideas provide the best protection against Type I error. Given k codes and an interest in Lag 1 effects, for example, a totally unguided and completely exploratory investigator might examine occurrences of all possible k^2 two-event chains. In this section I have suggested that a more justifiable approach would limit the number of transitions examined to the $(R - 1)(C - 1)$ degrees of freedom associated with the table and have demonstrated one way that this number of 2×2 subtables could be extracted from a larger table. Presumably a Yule's Q or some other statistic would be computed for each subtable and, assuming sufficient occurrences, would then be analyzed further.

Investigators are quite free – in fact, encouraged – to investigate a smaller number of associations (i.e., form a smaller number of 2×2 tables). For example, a larger table might be collapsed into a smaller one, combining some codes together that seem functionally similar, or only those associations required to address the investigator's hypotheses might be subjected to analysis in the first place. Other transitions might be examined later, and those analyses labeled exploratory instead of confirmatory. For further discussion of this "less is more" and "least is last" strategy for controlling Type I error, see Cohen and Cohen (1983, pp. 169–172).

Multiway Frequency Tables

As mentioned previously, observational data are often and conveniently summarized by multiway frequency tables (i.e., multidimensional contingency tables). Techniques for analyzing such tables have long been understood (e.g., Bishop et al., 1975; Fienberg, 1980; Haberman, 1978, 1979), but only now is information about these techniques (i.e., log-linear analysis) beginning to filter into graduate programs in psychology. Log-linear analysis is extremely useful, not only for sequential observational data, but whenever data are categorical and organized in multiway frequency tables. Other sources describe these techniques well for a general audience (e.g., Bakeman & Robin-

son, 1994; Kennedy, 1983, 1992; Wickens, 1989), even emphasizing sequential aspects (e.g., Bakeman, Adamson, & Strisik, 1995; Bakeman & Quera, 1995b; Gottman & Roy, 1990) so no further detail is provided here. Instead, interested readers should consult the sources cited.

SUMMARY

Systematic observation of behavior – assigning predefined codes to behavioral events – is one of many measurement avenues open to investigators, but this avenue often seems to lead to a lively district. Observational methods may be applied to verbal and nonverbal behavior, and participants may be observed in a laboratory or field setting and in the context of experimental or nonexperimental designs; thus the methods are remarkably flexible. Observational methods are especially useful when investigators are interested in understanding process, making the unfolding of behavior in time particularly salient. Often, observational methods permit investigators to render behavior of interest with considerable fidelity, which permits more compelling tests of key hypotheses.

Coding schemes – usually sets of mutually exclusive and exhaustive codes – serve as measuring instruments, and their development requires considerable attention and careful piloting. When observing behavior, a variety of devices can be used to record codes, including simple pencil and paper or more elaborate computer-assisted systems. However, representing such data for subsequent analysis using SDIS confers considerable benefits, including access to GSEQ, a computer program designed for sequential analysis of observational data.

Observational data are collected by human observers making judgments; thus issues of training observers, agreement among them, and the reliability of summary scores based on the data they record require careful attention. In particular, observer agreement can be regarded as the sine qua non of observational research. Assuming sufficient occurrences for individual codes, their rates, proportions, and other simple statistics, as well as various indices that capture conditional aspects of the data (whether cooccurrences or lagged transitions), may be analyzed with standard parametric techniques such as t-tests, ANOVAs, and multiple regression; or log-linear analysis may be used to analyze the multiway frequency tables that are often used to summarize data from behavioral observations. Together and used wisely, this ensemble of techniques permits investigators to unlock the stories that may otherwise remain trapped in their data.

REFERENCES

Adamson, L. B., & Bakeman, R. (1984). Mothers' communicative actions: Changes during infancy. *Infant Behavior and Development, 7,* 467–478.

Allison, P. D. (1984). *Event history analysis: Regression for longitudinal event data.* Newbury Park, CA: Sage.

Bakeman, R. (1983). Computing lag sequential statistics: The ELAG program. *Behavior Research Methods and Instrumentation, 15,* 530–535.

Bakeman, R. (1991). Counts and codes: Analyzing categorical data. In B. M. Montgomery & S. Duck (Eds.), *Studying interpersonal interaction* (pp. 255–274). New York: Guilford Publications.

Bakeman, R. (1992). *Understanding social science statistics: A spreadsheet approach.* Hillsdale, NJ: Erlbaum.

Bakeman, R., & Adamson, L. B. (1984). Coordinating attention to people and objects in mother-infant interaction. *Child Development, 55,* 1278–1289.

Bakeman, R., Adamson, L. B., Konner, M., & Barr, R. (1990). !Kung infancy: The social context of object exploration. *Child Development, 61,* 794–809.

Bakeman, R., Adamson, L. B., & Strisik, P. (1995). Lags and logs: Statistical approaches to interaction (SPSS Version). In J. M. Gottman (Ed.), *The analysis of change* (pp. 279–308). Hillsdale, NJ: Erlbaum.

Bakeman, R., & Brownlee, J. R. (1980). The strategic use of parallel play: A sequential analysis. *Child Development, 51,* 873–878.

Bakeman, R., & Casey, R. L. (1995). Analyzing family interaction: Taking time into account. *Journal of Family Psychology, 9,* 131–143.

Bakeman, R., & Gottman, J. M. (1986). *Observing interaction: An introduction to sequential analysis.* New York: Cambridge University Press.

Bakeman, R., & Gottman, J. M. (1997). *Observing interaction: An introduction to sequential analysis* (2nd ed.). New York: Cambridge University Press.

Bakeman, R., McArthur, D., & Quera, V. (1996). Detecting group differences in sequential association using sampled permutations: Log odds, kappa, and phi compared. *Behavior Research Methods, Instruments, and Computers, 28,* 446–457.

Bakeman, R., & Quera, V. (1992). SDIS: A sequential data interchange standard. *Behavior Research Methods, Instruments, and Computers, 24,* 554–559.

Bakeman, R., & Quera, V. (1995a). *Analyzing interaction: Sequential analysis with SDIS and GSEQ.* New York: Cambridge University Press.

Bakeman, R., & Quera, V. (1995b). Log-linear approaches to lag-sequential analysis when consecutive codes may and cannot repeat. *Psychological Bulletin, 118,* 272–284.

Bakeman, R., Quera, V., McArthur, D., & Robinson, B. F. (1996). Detecting sequential patterns and determining their reliability with fallible observers. *Psychological Methods, 2,* 357–370.

Bakeman, R., & Robinson, B. R. (1994). *Understanding log-linear analysis with ILOG: An interactive approach.* Hillsdale, NJ: Erlbaum.

Bakeman, R., Robinson, B. F., & Quera, V. (1996). Testing sequential association: Estimating exact *p* values using sampled permutations. *Psychological Methods, 1,* 4–15.

Bearison, D. J. Dorval, B., LeBlanc, G., Sadow, A., and Plesa, D. (in press). Collaborative cognition: Children negotiating their ways of knowing. *Monographs of the Society for Research in Child Development.*

Bishop, Y. M. M., Fienberg, S. R., & Holland, P. W. (1975). *Discrete multivariate analysis: Theory and practice.* Cambridge, MA: MIT Press.

Brandt, R. M. (1972). *Studying behavior in natural settings.* New York: Holt, Rinehart & Winston.

Brennan, R. L. (1983). *Elements of generalizability theory.* Iowa City, IA: ACT Publications.

Byrk, A. S., & Raudenbush, S. W. (1992). *Hierarchical linear models: Application and data analysis methods.* Newbury Park, CA: Sage.

Cohen, J. A. (1960). A coefficient of agreement for nominal scales. *Educational and Psychological Measurement, 20,* 37–46.

Cohen, J. (1968). Weighted kappa: Nominal scale agreement with provision for scaled disagreement or partial credit. *Psychological Bulletin, 70,* 213–220.

Cohen, J., & Cohen, P. (1983). *Applied multiple regression/correlation analysis for the behavioral sciences.* Hillsdale, NJ: Erlbaum.

Conger, A. J., & Ward, D. G. (1984). Agreement among 2×2 agreement indices. *Educational and Psychological Measurement, 44,* 301–314.

Cronbach, L. J., Gleser, G. C., Nanda, H., & Rajaratnam, N. (1972). *The dependability of behavioral measurements: Theory of generalizability for scores and profiles.* New York: Wiley.

DePaulo, B. M., Kashy, D. A., Kirkendol, S. E., Wyer, M. M., & Epstein, J. A. (1996). Lying in everyday life. *Journal of Personality and Social Psychology, 70,* 979–995.

Edgington, E. S. (1995). *Randomization tests* (3rd ed.). New York: Marcel Dekker.

Fienberg, S. E. (1980). *The analysis of cross-classified categorical data* (2nd ed.). Cambridge, MA: MIT Press.

Fleiss, J. L. (1981). *Statistical methods for rates and proportions.* New York: Wiley.

Fleiss, J. L. (1986). *The design and analysis of clinical experiments.* New York: Wiley.

Fleiss, J. L., Cohen, J., & Everitt, B. S. (1969). *Statistical methods for rates and proportions.* New York: Wiley.

Gardner, W. (1995). On the reliability of sequential data: Measurement, meaning, and correction. In J. M. Gottman (Ed.), *The analysis of change* (pp. 339–359). Hillsdale, NJ: Erlbaum.

Good, P. (1994). *Permutation tests: A practical guide to resampling methods for testing hypotheses.* New York: Springer-Verlag.

Gottman, J. M. (1981). *Time-series analysis: A comprehensive introduction for social scientists.* New York: Cambridge University Press.

Gottman, J. M., & Bakeman, R. (1996). *Systematic observational techniques or building life as an observational researcher.* Unpublished document, University of Washington.

Gottman, J. M., & Roy, A. (1990). *Sequential analysis: A guide for behavioral research.* New York: Cambridge University Press.

Haberman, S. J. (1978). *Analysis of qualitative data* (Vol. 1). New York: Academic Press.

Haberman, S. J. (1979). *Analysis of qualitative data* (Vol. 2). New York: Academic Press.

Hartmann, D. P. (1982). Assessing the dependability of observational data. In D. P. Hartmann (Ed.), *Using observers to study behavior* (pp. 51–65). San Francisco: Jossey-Bass.

Hays, W. L. (1963). *Statistics.* New York: Holt, Rinehart, and Winston.

Ickes, W., Bissonnette, V., Garcia, S., & Stinson, L. L. (1990). Implementing and using the dyadic interaction paradigm. In C. Hendrick & M. S. Clark (Eds.), *Research methods in personality and soical psychology* (pp. 16–44). Newbury Park, CA: Sage.

Judd, C. M., & McClelland, G. H. (1998). Measurement. In D. Gilbert, S. Fiske, & G. Lindzey (Eds.), *Handbook of social psychology* (4th ed., pp. 180–232). New York: McGraw Hill.

Kennedy, J. J. (1983). *Analyzing qualitative data: Introductory log-linear analysis for behavioral research.* New York: Praeger.

Kennedy, J. J. (1992). *Analyzing qualitative data: Log-linear analysis for behavioral research* (2nd ed.). New York: Praeger.

Long J. (1996). *Video coding system reference guide.* Caroga Lake, NY: James Long Company.

Morley, D. D. (1987). Revised lag sequential analysis. In M. L. McLaughlin (Ed.), *Communication yearbook* (Vol. 10, pp. 172–182). Beverly Hills, CA: Sage.

Nunnally, J. C. (1978). *Psychometric theory* (2nd ed.). New York: McGraw-Hill.

Parten, M. B. (1932). Social participation among preschool children. *Journal of Abnormal and Social Psychology, 27,* 243–269.

Pedhazur, E. J., & Schmelkin, L. P. (1991). *Measurement, design, and analysis: An integrated approach.* Hillsdale, NJ: Erlbaum.

Quera, V., & Estany, E. (1984). ANSEC: A BASIC package for lag sequential analysis of observational data. *Behavior Research Methods, Instruments, and Computers, 16,* 303–306.

Reynolds, H. T. (1984). *Analysis of nominal data.* Beverly Hills, CA: Sage.

Rabinson, B. F., & Bakeman, R. (1998). ComKappa: A Windows 95 program for calculating kappa and related statistics. *Behavior Research Methods, Instruments, and Computers, 30,* 731–732.

Robinson, B. F., & Bakeman, R. (1998). ComKappa: A Windows 95 program for calculating kappa and related statistics. *Behavior Research Methods, Instruments, and Computers, 30,* 731–732.

Rogoff, B., Mishy, J. Göncü, A., Musier, C. (1993). Guided participation in cultural activity by toddlers and caregivers. *Monographs of the Society for Research in Child Development, 58,* (8, series no. 236).

Rowland, S. B. (1995). *Effects of adolescent mother-infant and grandmother-infant interaction on infant attention: A normative study of an African American sample.* Unpublished doctoral dissertation, Georgia State University, Atlanta.

Sackett, G. P. (1979). The lag sequential analysis of contingency and cyclicity in behavioral interaction research. In J. Osofsky (Ed.), *Handbook of infant development* (pp. 623–649). New York: Wiley.

Shrout, P. E., & Fleiss, J. L. (1979). Intraclass correlations: Uses in assessing rater reliability. *Psychological Bulletin, 86,* 420–428.

Singer, J. D., & Willet, J. B. (1993). It's about time: Using discrete-time survival analysis to study duration and timing of events. *Journal of Educational Statistics, 18,* 155–195.

Stevens, S. S. (1951). Mathematics, measurement, and psychophysics. In S. S. Stevens (Ed.), *Handbook of experimental psychology* (pp. 28–42). New York: Wiley.

Suen, H. K. (1988). Agreement, reliability, accuracy, and validity: Toward a clarification. *Behavioral Assessment, 10,* 343–366.

Tapp, J., & Walden, T. (1993). PROCODER: A professional tape control coding and analysis system for behavioral research using videotape. *Behavior Research Methods, Instruments, & Computers, 25,* 53–56.

Tuculescu, R. A., & Griswold, J. G. (1983). Prehatching interactions in domestic chickens. *Animal Behavior, 31,* 1–10.

Wampold, B. E. (1989). Kappa as a measure of pattern in sequential data. *Quality and Quantity, 23,* 171–187.

Wampold, B. E. (1992). The intensive examination of social interaction. In T. R. Kratochwill & J. R. Levin (Eds.), *Single-case research design and analysis: New directions for psychology and education* (pp. 93–131). Hillsdale, NJ: Erlbaum.

Weick, K. E. (1968). Systematic observational methods. In G. Lindzey & E. Aronson (Eds.), *Handbook of social psychology* (2nd ed., Vol. 2, pp. 357–451). Reading, MA: Addison-Wesley.

Weick, K. E. (1985). Systematic observational methods. In G. Lindzey & E. Aronson (Eds.), *Handbook of social psychology* (3rd ed., Vol. 1, pp. 567–634). New York: Random House.

Weiss, R. L., & Summers, K. J. (1983). Marital interaction coding system: III. In E. E. Filsinger (Ed.), *Marriage and family assessment: A source book for family therapy* (pp. 85–115). Beverly Hills, CA: Sage.

Wickens, T. D. (1989). *Multiway contingency tables analysis for the social sciences.* Hillsdale, NJ: Erlbaum.

Wickens, T. D. (1993). Analysis of contingency tables with between-subjects variability. *Psychological Bulletin, 113,* 191–204.

Wiggins, J. S. (1973). *Personality and prediction: Principles of personality assessment.* Reading, MA: Addison-Wesley.

CHAPTER SEVEN

Methods of Small Group Research

NORBERT L. KERR, JOEL ARONOFF, AND LAWRENCE A. MESSÉ

This chapter seeks to inform the reader about how research on group process and outcomes is conducted. But before turning to these topics, we thought that it would be useful to describe just what such research actually studies. The word "group" has a time-honored place in social psychology (cf. Allport, 1924). However, as with many terms with a long history in social psychology, this word has been used in a number of different ways over the years. For instance, the term has often been used – particularly by scholars of stereotyping and intergroup relations – to refer to any aggregate of people who share some socially salient characteristic(s), for example, a racial, ethnic, gender, or national "group." In this chapter, however, "group" refers to something different and quite distinct, a type of social entity that in the literature often has been called the *small group* (e.g., Bales, Strodtbeck, Mills, & Roseborough, 1951; Hare, 1976; Haythorn, 1953).

More specifically, the *small group* refers to a collective of persons whose history of shared fate, common purpose, and interaction has led to the perception, by participants and outsiders alike, that this collective is a social unit (Campbell, 1958; Heider, 1958).[1] As we discuss at greater length below, we view the idea of common purpose – particularly as it involves coordinated task activity – as the essential feature that distinguishes

the small group from other types of social units (e.g., close relationships; cf. Weber & Harvey, 1994).

Moreover, many phenomena that occur in small groups also occur in situations that do not involve a real social entity; rather, they occur in settings in which participants (temporarily) work together to accomplish some goal(s) with few, if any, feelings of "groupness." We will refer to the inclusive set of contexts – including both small groups (as defined above) and temporary, task-oriented collectives – as *group contexts*. A broad concern with group contexts rather than more narrowly on small groups, per se, can be justified for many reasons, not the least of which is that most investigations of group process and outcomes (cf. Forsyth, 1990) have studied these issues by examining people in temporary group contexts rather than actual small groups.

The enduring and often indeterminate time frame of "real" groups, to say nothing of their inherent complexities, makes their systematic study a daunting enterprise. And even the study of collective activities in more easily structured group contexts can be challenging enough, given the complicated phenomena of interest (see Table 7.1). Students who are drawn to the complex problems of individuals interacting in groups often ask, as they consider committing themselves to such a labor-intensive enterprise, "What questions are so special to this field that it is worth expending the great effort needed to answer them? What can be learned, what rewards obtained, that can justify investments of such magnitude." In this chapter we also make an attempt to address these questions, to explain why the exploration of people's behavior in group contexts is a critical task for social psychology. In doing so, we argue that the phenomena are unique, the methods robust, the personal satisfactions high, and the outcomes of

---

[1] Historically, the defining features of the small group have also been the focus of some debate (cf. Forsyth, 1990). As a way of demarking a set of research question and substantive phenomenon, we like McGrath's (1984) flexible, fuzzy-set definition of the group: "an aggregation of two or more people who are to some degree in dynamic interrelation with one another" (p. 8). However, in the present context, we believe that the definition that we present here is both serviceable and consistent with most perspectives on group phenomena (cf. Forsyth, 1990).

TABLE 7.1. Major Topics, Paradigms, and Variables of Group Research

Substantive Topic/Area & Core Questions	Representative Paradigms (& Articles)	Representative Independent Variables	Representative Dependent Variables
Intragroup processes			
Group formation & development What functions does group membership serve? How are group members recruited and socialized? Do groups go through standard phases of development or work?	Festinger's cohesiveness paradigm ⟨p. 238⟩ (Back, 1951) Bales (IPA) paradigm ⟨p. 142⟩ (Bales et al., 1951) Newcomb's acquaintance-process paradigm ⟨p. 188⟩ (Newcomb, 1961) The affiliation paradigm ⟨p. 193⟩ (Schachter, 1959) Levine & Moreland's newcomer paradigm (Moreland, 1985)	Relevance of task to the group Other members' resources & knowledge Task type Group size	Level of group cohesiveness Distribution of speech acts Desire to affiliate
Group structure What is the pattern of relationships (liking, power, status, communication, etc.) among group members? What is the effect of such patterns on group functioning? What expectations of member behavior (e.g., roles & norms) develop and guide behavior in the group?	The communication network paradigm ⟨p. 168⟩ (Leavitt, 1951) Schachter's productivity-norm paradigm ⟨p. 123⟩ (Schachter et al., 1951) Adam's inequity paradigm ⟨p. 204⟩ (Walster, Walster, & Bersheid, 1978)	Task features Allowed patterns of communication Group cohesion	Task performance Evaluation of group members Allocations to self vs. others Perceived social norms/role
Social influence processes What are the basic processes through which group members exert influence on one another? What personal and situational factors lead to leadership emergence and effectiveness?	Asch's conformity paradigm ⟨p. 235⟩ (Asch, 1951) Sherif's group norm paradigm ⟨p. 234⟩ (Sherif, 1936) Milgram's obedience paradigm ⟨p. 181⟩ (Milgram, 1974) Bystander-intervention paradigm ⟨p. 231⟩ (Lataré, & Darley 1970) Social-learning paradigm ⟨p. 230⟩ (Bandura, 1962) Reaction to deviate paradigm ⟨p. 239⟩ (Schachter, 1951) The leader style paradigm ⟨p. 255⟩ (Lewin, Lippett, & White, 1939)	Task type Level of group cohesiveness Levels of power/status of influencer Relationships between members Leadership styles	Level of compliance Imitative behavior Inclusion/exclusion from the group Group performance
Group productivity How do member, group, and task features affect group productivity? What factors affect whether groups achieve, fall short of, or even exceed their nominal potential productivity?	Social-facilitation paradigm ⟨p. 228⟩ (Zajonc, 1965) Laughlin's concept-attainment paradigm ⟨p. 70⟩ (e.g., Laughlin & Johnson, 1966) Participatory decision making paradigm ⟨p. 123⟩ (Coch & French, 1948) Social loafing paradigm (Lataré, Williams, & Harkins, 1979)	Presence of others Distribution of member abilities, personalities, etc. Group size	Task performance Member arousal Member contributions

(continued)

TABLE 7.1 (*continued*)

Substantive Topic/Area & Core Questions	Representative Paradigms (& Articles)	Representative Independent Variables	Representative Dependent Variables
Group decision making Are there systematic rules linking individual and group choices? Under what conditions are group decisions of higher or lower quality than individual decisions? What unique processes distinguish group from individual decision making processes?	Lewin's group discussion paradigm (p. 232) (Lewin, 1953) The Risky-shift paradigm ⟨p. 81⟩ (Wallack, Kogan, & Bem, 1962) Davis' mock-jury, SDS paradigm ⟨p. 85⟩ (Davis, Kerr, Atkin, Holt, & Meek, 1975) Groupthink paradigm (Janis, 1982) Collective induction paradigm (Laughlin, 1996)	Public vs. private discussion Type of decision task Procedural factors Group composition	Fulfilling intentions expressed in groups Contrast of individual and group judgment Distribution of group decisions Functional relation between individual and group decisions (social decision scheme)
Intragroup conflict How do patterns of group member interdependence guide member behavior? What are the ways members exchange resources to resolve such conflicts (e.g., through bargaining, negotiation, coalition formation) How do group members reconcile conflicts between personal and collective interest?	The prisoner's/social dilemma paradigm (p. 103) (Rapoport, 1976; Brewer & Kramer, 1986; Dawes, McTavish, & Shaklee, 1977) The bargaining paradigm (p. 99) ⟨Siegal & Fouraker, 1960⟩ Deutsch's Trucking game (p. 106) ⟨Deutsch & Krauss, 1962⟩ The Coalition paradigm (p. 110) ⟨Komorita & Chertkoff, 1973⟩	Game/task features Prior training & experience Social motives	Absolute & relative gain of group members Levels of cooperation and competition
Environmental processes How do features of the physical environment affect group and group-member behavior? How do groups regulate their use of physical environments	The Westgate-Westgate West paradigm (Festinger, Schacter, & Back, 1950) Sommer's personal space paradigm ⟨p. 217⟩ (Sommers, 1959) Groups-in-isolation paradigm ⟨p. 218⟩ (Altman & Haythorn, 1967) Crowding-performance paradigm (Freedman, Klevansky, & Ehrlich, 1971)	Functional distance between group members Seating positions Temporal demand	Territorial behavior Task performance Interpersonal attraction/hostility
Extra-group processes			
Groups as contexts for action How does being in a group, particularly in a very large groups or crowd, alter thinking and action?	The deindividuation paradigm (Diener, Lusk, DeFour, & Flax, 1980) Kelley's emergency-escape paradigm (Kelley, Condry, Dahlke, & Hill, 1965)	Group/crowd size Level of anonymity	Antisocial behavior Counternormative behavior
Intergroup relations What are the causes and cures of intergroup conflict? How does group membership alter social perception?	Sherif's Robber's Cave paradigm ⟨p. 118⟩ (Sherif et al., 1961) The minimal-group paradigm (Tajfel, Billig, Bundy, & Flament, 1971) The in-/outgroup homogeneity paradigm (Judd & Park, 1988)	Group membership Permeability of group boundaries Level of intergroup conflict of interest	Intergroup conflict Allocation of resources to in/outgroup members Perception/evaluation of in/outgroup members

Note: All page references enclosed in ⟨ ⟩ brackets refer to McGrath (1984).

great importance to social psychology. The pages that follow, then, attempt to explore contemporary methods for conducting research on group phenomena and to convince the reader that investigating something as complex as individual behavior in groups can be stimulating and rewarding – whether as a one-time venture or the focus of a career.

HOW CAREERS BEGIN

Some careers begin in paradise. As a graduate student, Joel Aronoff was invited to spend a summer as a supportive spouse on a field trip to the island of St. Kitts, in the West Indies. Driving around the island searching for a place to live, my wife and I stopped our car in a village at the head of a street leading down to the sea. Looking down toward the sandy beach we saw a blue lagoon framed by a barrier reef crowned with white spray thrown up from breaking waves. Two young boys came up to us to ask if we wanted to buy some lobsters that they had just caught. "How much?" we asked. "Twenty-five cents each," they answered. "Well," we thought, "This must be the place!"

We found a place to live and set about to begin work. But what was our work? How do you study human beings as they live their lives? We walked about and found some people willing to talk. They told us that St. Kitts was a small island, that most of the people in the village worked on the sugar cane estates, that the island was emerging toward independence through the efforts of an active local government, that schools and health clinics were expanding, and that a small group of fishermen were able to harvest a moderate amount of delicious food. Although we could watch some people fish and others cut sugar cane, what was the work of a social psychologist in this community?

Experience the previous term as a teaching assistant (TA) in a human motivation course made personality constructs highly salient. Although the task of a TA in that course was to explain the distinctions between arcane terms, somehow the presence in mind of the constructs led to a very simple question that captures one of the major dimensions of social psychology: "If there was such a thing as personality, what should we see in the behavior of people on the street?" More specifically, watching people throughout the day showed that they spent most of their time working and visiting with each other. Following this line of thinking, an obvious task for a social psychologist visiting in this community would be to explore the sources of the behavior these people displayed in their interactions with each other on village streets, in work groups, and in their families.

This particular anecdote illustrates a fairly common way that research begins (e.g., Brannigan & Merrens, 1995; W. McGuire, 1983) and the importance of observation as a useful initial stage of scientific work in social psychology. Observation – at least the kind of observation done at St. Kitts – is usually not a way to test hypotheses, to function in the *context of justification* (Herschel, 1987). Rather, such observation is a way to find new questions and an activity that helps us imagine ways that potential variables may be related, that is, to function in the *context of discovery* (Herschel, 1987). As Yogi Berra said, "You can see a lot by watching." In this case, watching the very ordinary matters of the villagers' everyday lives led to a simple research question. What we observed was that, throughout the day, the people of the village spent their time interacting with others in regular and predictable ways – at home, on walks to the fields, in coordinated work in the fields or on the sea, in negotiation over the sale of fish, and in playing dominos, drinking, and dancing when the day's work was done. These observations became a question: What was the connection between the motives of the individuals observed and the way they conducted their interpersonal behavior? And this question was clear enough so that it could become a researchable question.

We begin our discussion of method by emphasizing that research frequently begins with a serendipitous observation that creates new problems that need to be solved. The history of social psychology offers many notable illustrations (e.g., for dissonance theory, Festinger, 1957; obedience, Milgram, 1974; bystander intervention, Latané, & Darley, 1970; groupthink, Janis, 1982; group performance, Triplett, 1898). Of course, this initial stage needs to be followed by one in which one's ideas and questions become more focused, developing propositions about relationships among variables that can be sharply defined and accurately measured, and in contexts that are narrow enough to permit some relationship to be sufficiently isolated so that systematic observation can make some limited proposition more (or less) plausible than it was before. Ideally, scientific work strives for a balance between posing the big questions (what really drives behavior in real-world settings of interest?) and posing smaller but more tractable questions (what's the nature of the relationship between certain variables in certain, concrete contexts?). We will use the research that followed from the St. Kitts observation to illustrate some of the trade-offs (e.g., between realism and control; cf. Runkle & McGrath, 1972) that need to be made when choosing different research methods.

In the research begun on St. Kitts, the decision was made to focus on the normative structure of the economic work groups as the primary dependent variable. In summary, in the first study (Aronoff, 1967), it was learned that, in their work groups, the cane workers were organized in a hierarchical structure, with a great deal of power over work flow decisions vested in the "head cutter," with little solidarity among the men when faced with a destructive decision by the head cutter, with status based on external rather than personal attributes, and with pay based on each piece of cane that each man cut individually. In contrast, the fishing crews were organized in an egalitarian structure, with decision-making authority vested in each fisherman, with intense solidarity among the fishermen when confronted by irresponsible behavior of a captain, with status based on personal rather than external attributes, and with income based on investment and risk of time and capital. Note that these features of the two work groups are standard variables of small group research – leadership, status, reward, power, role networks, cooperation, and conflict (e.g., Cartwright & Zander, 1968; Forsyth, 1990).

Why was there this difference? To an economist or sociologist it seems self-evident that sugar plantation and fishing economies "need" to organize their work groups this way and that individual workers were "socialized" to maintain existing organizations. But observation suggested that the men in each type of work group not only "behaved" differently – in ways that were congruent with the principles of group organization, as articulated by the men (i.e., the normative culture of the groups) – but also that the men in one group seemed very different from those in the other. Briefly put, cane workers seemed very anxious, mistrustful, and dependent, whereas fishermen seemed not only secure and able but also very concerned with demonstrating their competence. Watching the men at work, it seemed easiest to say that the different kinds of men needed to work with each other in these different kinds of ways because such arrangements both drew on the capacities available to them and satisfied their predominant concerns.

This hypothesis helps explain the basic reason we study group phenomena in social psychology. Why study groups? The answer seemed rather simple when watching people in groups. When you watch people in their natural habitat, as an ethologist watches ducks or deer, it is clear that the small human group is a (perhaps, the) primary unit of social psychology. Ordinary human behavior, which can be observed on any street corner, occurs between people who live within groups and who go between groups. In their ongoing behavior, people affect each other in ways that cannot be sufficiently explained by knowledge of the attributes of one of the actors individually. Groups are one of the primary devices human beings have to accomplish their purposes. What else should a social psychologist study? If individuals form groups to accomplish their purposes, or if different kinds of people structure different kinds of groups to meet different purposes, then useful knowledge can result from well-executed research programs in this area. Many questions quickly come to mind that together could constitute a research program. Are there certain working arrangements that are best for everyone? Are there certain kinds of people who are most productive? Are there special fits between certain group arrangements and the capacities and the purposes of certain types of individuals?

DEFINITIONAL CONSIDERATIONS

As is obvious from our everyday experiences, people engage in social activities in a wide variety of settings and for a wide variety of reasons. Social psychologists, of course, are interested in studying the antecedents and consequences of social activities wherever, and in whatever form, they occur. For this purpose, it can be useful to differentiate among the many forms that social encounters can take. Thus, in order to study the distinct phenomena that are integral to groups and group processes, we must delineate the essential qualities that set these two constructs apart from other constructs, as well as from each other.

Group Contexts

What would distinguish groups from other social entities (e.g., all Presbyterians, people who happen to be passengers on the same bus one Monday morning, and so on)? What makes a group such as the cane-cutting gang and its activities different from such social entities? To be consistent with the perspective of many social psychologists (e.g., Zander, 1985), as noted earlier, in this chapter we use the term *group context* to refer to settings in which task accomplishment is a predominant (but not necessarily exclusive) concern; participants in these situations attempt to coordinate their activities to reach some shared goal(s). In other words, group contexts are settings in which people engage in collective task activities, and group process and group outcomes are the mediators, moderators, or consequences of such activities.

Although group contexts have much in common with the myriad of other social settings in which humans can and do interact, the group's unique focus on getting something done merits special attention in social psychology. We should note, however, that in this framework the term *task* is not meant to be taken as a synonym for renumerated work. Although many, if not all, formal work situations are group contexts (in that they have a collective task focus), there also exist other group settings in which the participants would not be seen as performing "work" (i.e., as engaging in "job" activities for which they are being compensated) but do need to collaborate to accomplish some task. For instance, in this framework we would consider a group of undergraduates who come together to build a float for a homecoming parade to be participating in a group context to the same degree that employees participating in a sales meeting would be.

We also should note that the distinction between group contexts and other social situations is not always sharp and is often easier to make in the abstract than for many actual, everyday social experiences. Consider, for instance, what is a very important social entity for many people – their family. Family members typically engage in all kinds of activities together. Many are meant to accomplish some task or achieve some goal. For example, meal preparation or household chores often are collective enterprises that at least a subset of the family typically performs as a team. But even then, the activities that occur during these times are not just aimed at getting the job done; working together, family members can argue, play, express affection or jealousy, and so forth.

Moreover, other events and activities that families share – for example, enjoying a picnic outing together, comforting a family member in distress, behaving affectionately – are not the least bit task-oriented and are expressed for a variety of noninstrumental reasons. As you can see, then, many social situations have elements of, but are not exclusively, group contexts, and group activities – particularly behaviors that reflect people's attempts to collectively accomplish something – are often mixed in with behaviors that are meant to serve other purposes (Bales, 1965; Cattell, 1948; Moreno, 1953).

It should be obvious why the cane-cutting gang, the example with which we began this chapter, constitutes a group context, as we have defined this term. It is a work setting in which participants (the head cutter and his subordinates) have joined together to achieve a common purpose: to cut sugar cane in order to make money. Similarly, the fishing crew discussed previously also qualifies as a group context because many of the activities in which the boat captain and his men engaged were aimed at performing the specific tasks necessary to accomplish the collective goal of catching fish, although crew members probably engaged in other activities as well.

Group Processes and Outcomes

Social psychologists routinely study non-task-related phenomena in group contexts. For instance, Segal (1979) investigated some mediators of interpersonal attraction (i.e., the positive feelings that some participants come to have for each other) among members of sports teams and police squads. And more recently, Moreland and his colleagues (e.g., Liang et al., 1995) have examined *transactive memory* – the allocation of "things to remember" among persons who find themselves in a situation of interdependence – in group contexts, thereby extending past work that had studied this phenomenon in intimate interpersonal relationships (Wegner, Erber, & Raymond, 1991).

In this chapter we focus on methods appropriate to the study of activities and outcomes that are distinctly related to the task emphasis that we view as the essential feature that differentiates the group context from other contexts. What are these task-relevant activities and outcomes? Although no listing is likely to be exhaustive, we believe that the topics that we present in Table 7.1 reflect the primary questions addressed in classic and contemporary research on group functioning (cf. Forsyth, 1990; Levine & Moreland, 1997; Wheelan, 1994; readers interested in obtaining detailed information about these phenomena may consult one or more of these excellent reviews of the empirical literature on group processes).

Methods for investigating these phenomena are presented below. Before turning to this review of research methods, one additional conceptual issue needs to be addressed: the distinction between groups and group processes or outcomes.

Studying Groups versus Group Processes or Outcomes

As we discussed above, the word "group" is one of those terms in social psychology that has taken on a number of distinct meanings over the years. The definition of group that is most relevant to the topics of this chapter – usually referred to as the "small group" – incorporates the ideas of endurance, interdependence, entitivity, and task focus. Both the cane-cutting gangs and fishing crews of St. Kitts, described previously, satisfy our definition of a small group. First, their respective members shared a common goal – making money by working to harvest a resource (sugar cane or fish). Second, members were behaviorally interdependent because they had to coordinate their activities to succeed at their tasks; and, they were outcome interdependent because for both cane gangs and fishing crews, each member's pay was determined by how well the group performed as a whole. Finally, both the members, themselves, and those who knew them saw them as part of a social entity (e.g., "Big Ed's Crew").

Real groups are hard to study in the controlled manner favored by most social psychologists, in part, because it takes time for groups to evolve (cf. Moreland & Levine, 1982; Worchel, Coutant-Sassic, & Grossman, 1992), and this process tends to require that participants have rather unconstrained opportunities to interact. Furthermore, when researchers study existing real groups, they have no control over the groups' histories, and it often is difficult to impose experimental manipulations on the groups' experiences.

We are not suggesting that short-term laboratory studies of so-called ad hoc groups have not made substantial contributions to understanding small group phenomena nor are we recommending that such efforts be abandoned in the future. Quite the contrary, we would maintain that group processes and outcomes of the sort that we listed earlier can profitably be studied in controlled settings; and, in doing so, much insight can be gained about what happens in group contexts, generally, and in real, functioning groups, specifically. We are merely noting that such research usually does not really study genuine (i.e., goal-directed, interdependent, high entativity) groups, per se, and these differences are important to keep in mind when generalizing from knowledge gained in the laboratory to the "real world."

WHY STUDY GROUP PHENOMENA?

Earlier we briefly posed the question, "why study groups?" and offered a rather glib answer, "what else should a social psychologist study?" However, before turning to the real substance of this chapter – methods for the study of groups and group processes – we want to take a moment to offer a more thoughtful answer to this important question. One common and reasonable answer is that group phenomena (defined restrictively or not) are ubiquitous. We will never have a comprehensive understanding of human social behavior without an understanding of human social groups.

This proposition probably would not be very controversial among social psychologists, yet even though practically every social psychologist would say that what he or she studies is highly relevant to a full understanding of behavior in groups, only a minority of our discipline would say they study group phenomena. What distinguishes this remnant of what was once a thriving enterprise in social psychology (cf. McGrath & Altman, 1966; Steiner, 1974) from the currently-more-dominant individualistic–cognitive paradigm (Steiner, 1986)? One thing is a conviction on the part of group researchers that we shall come to that universally desired understanding of group behavior faster and more deeply by focusing our attention on behavioral settings that have certain properties, properties that we might term the "four Is": interaction (between humans), interdependence (between humans), identification (with something bigger, more inclusive than the self), and imbeddedness (in interpersonal social structures, such as role structures, power relationships, normative systems, etc.).

Implicit, we think, in the working assumptions of most small group researchers is the conviction that it is not always productive to analyze phenomena at the most molecular level possible and that some issues are better, more insightfully addressed by investigating them at a more molar level of analysis (see Steiner, 1974, 1986). For example, it is possible, in principle, to describe the "behavior" of the helium in a balloon as the net effect of the movements of billions of individual helium molecules. Such an approach might depend on describing the "actions" and interactions of individual molecules and would, of necessity, result in enormously complex descriptive or explanatory models. However, the basic laws of thermodynamics turn out to offer simple relationships between certain summaries of the behavior of those billions of individual molecules – such as the temperature, volume, and pressure of the gas – which are much more useful for most purposes than (literally) more molecular models. Likewise, group researchers assume that there will be times when concepts defined at the group level may be more powerful or efficient for advancing our understanding of behavior than concepts defined at more molecular (e.g., individual) levels. (A similar presumption pervades all of social psychology – we take for granted that analyses of social behavior undertaken at the level of the individual can often be more useful or tractable than analyses at more molecular levels [e.g., physiological, neuronal, cellular, genetic].) This is not just an article of faith; there are many good illustrations in the social–behavioral sciences of the greater utility of molar analytic approaches. For instance, it has been hypothesized (Steiner, 1972) and shown (e.g., Hill, 1982, for a review) that task groups usually fall short of their productive potential. Bray, Kerr, and Atkin (1978), for example, showed that for a certain kind of intellectual task, this suboptimality increased as groups became larger. Now, this phenomenon could be analyzed at the individual level, in terms of the effects of increasing group size on the different perceptions and actions of individual group members. But a simple and efficient understanding of the full pattern of data results from the use of a group-level concept (viz., the group's functional size, which is that group size $\hat{n}$ whose productivity matches the observed productivity of the n-person group). In particular, for simple intellective problems, Bray et al. found that $\hat{n}$ was 1 (or, sometimes as much as 2), no matter how large the group actually is. That is, when participants take turns talking about such problems in a face-to-face group, the group ends up functioning about as well as would be expected if there were only one person in the group (cf. Diehl & Stroebe, 1987). Although one could probably also describe this phenomenon by reference to individual perception (e.g., perceived competition for speaking time, felt individual responsibility), in terms of predicting and understanding group performance, little is gained in doing so.

There is a final reason for studying group contexts: They are fascinating behavioral settings. This is fortunate for the group researcher because there are also many special methodological difficulties that can arise in the study of groups.

GENERIC STRATEGIES FOR SMALL GROUP RESEARCH

It is well-recognized that any single study can, at best, test only some aspects of a proposition (cf. Brewer, this volume, Ch. 1). It is certainly true that a single study cannot test all aspects of all related propositions. In group research, students need to assume that not only are multiple studies that target different aspects of a proposition needed to confirm a hypothesis but also that entirely different methods may be needed as well. Different methods are required to compensate for the inherent weaknesses in any particular choice of method (e.g., Runkle & McGrath, 1972). Furthermore, interesting new research questions often emerge from one's current results. In this section we identify some of the advantages and limitations inherent in common generic methodological strategies by using the series of studies that followed the original St. Kitts investigation

to illustrate Campbell's (1969) important concept of triangulation of methods. The proposition tested in those studies was that psychologically insecure people favor (are most rewarded by, are most comfortable with, etc.), and thus function best with, a hierarchical group structure, whereas secure people favor and function best with an egalitarian group structure.

Field and Archival Research on Groups

Group processes and outcomes can be, and often have been, studied outside the laboratory using nonexperimental methods (e.g., Aronoff, 1967; Moreno, 1953; Roethlisberger & Dickson, 1939; Whyte, 1943), and a good portion of this work has investigated actual small groups. Such field and archival research has a rich tradition in social science, generally, but is not frequently conducted in contemporary social psychology (Reis & Stiller, 1992). Moreover, a detailed exploration of these approaches would require much more space than we can devote in a single chapter on group process research. Thus, in this section, we provide only a basic overview of these methods as they have been applied to the study of group phenomena, primarily by citing some representative examples from the literature. Readers should note, however, that other sources are available that discuss these techniques much more comprehensively (e.g., Hyman, 1978; Judd, Smith, & Kidder, 1991; Weick, 1968, 1985).

Observational Field Methods

As we noted at the start of this chapter, much can be learned about group processes and outcomes – as well as a host of social phenomena in general – by carefully observing people's everyday (and not-so-everyday) experiences as they occur. For example, Muzafer Sherif (one of the founding fathers of social psychology) studied the evolution of group structure, entitivity, cohesiveness, and actual intergroup conflict by observing the activities of participants at a boys' summer camp (Sherif, 1951; Sherif & Sherif, 1953; Sherif, Harvey, White, Hood, & Sherif, 1961). In this context, subsets of campers (who had never previously met) were formed into aggregates as a function of cabin assignment, given group names (e.g., "Red Devils," "Bull Dogs"), and assigned to perform a number of activities (e.g., preparing a cookout meal, practicing baseball as a team, etc.). Although participants were informally interviewed periodically, the bulk of the data that Sherif collected was derived from careful observations that he and his staff made of the campers' activities. For instance, Sherif gained understanding into emergent social structure by observing how the boys acted with regard to one another as they went about performing tasks. Here is how Sherif (1966) described the cookout:

The staff supplied the boys with unprepared food. When they got hungry, one boy started to build a fire, asking for help in getting wood. Another attacked the raw hamburger to make patties.... A low-ranking member took a knife and started toward the melon. Some of the others protested. The most highly regarded boy in the group took the knife, saying, "You guys who yell the loudest get yours last." (p. 77)

These and other observations yielded many useful insights into group development and functioning.

The distinctive strength (cf. Runkel & McGrath, 1972) of a field study is its naturalness; one can examine behaviors of interest as they naturally occur. Field studies – such as Sherif's (1966) classic work on intra/intergroup relations in groups of boy campers or a study of psychological motivation and group structure in sugar-cane gangs – ideally exploit this strength. One common purpose is to discover natural phenomena that need to be understood. As noted earlier, many of the classic topics in social psychology (rumor transmission, opinion change, organizational effectiveness, obedience, conformity, helping, attraction, prejudice, etc.) began with a special experience or arresting example from some aspect of ordinary life. Another common purpose of a field study is to confirm that our knowledge of those phenomena – based largely on more controlled research methods used in settings that are necessarily more artificial – generalizes to natural behavioral settings. Field studies can be difficult, expensive, and tedious, but no other method can better establish whether a social process is important, in terms of its actual effects in real social settings, what range of attributes need to be examined, and its full network of associations with other social factors (Reis, 1983). Although the curriculum of social psychology, as an experimental science, is typically focused on past and future controlled experiments (usually conducted in a laboratory), to be maximally useful as a body of knowledge, ideally it should be able to relate the importance, meaningfulness, and strength of its findings to observations of behavior in natural settings.

The experience on St. Kitts offered all the benefits, as well as the limitations, of a field study. In the same small, remote locale, two strongly contrasting types of group process and group-member personality were dramatically visible to an observer. Simple observation of ongoing activity in each group suggested links between the personality of group members and the structure and functioning of groups. The methods available to study group phenomena in field settings include the usual variations of observation and interview (also see Bakeman, Ch. 6; Bartholomew, Henderson, & Marcia, Ch. 11, in this volume) as well as usual experimental and quasi-experimental designs (see Brewer, Ch. 1; West et al., Ch. 3, in this volume). The design of the St. Kitts study was simple. All the cane-cutting gangs and fishing crews in the village constituted the sample of groups and members. To verify the descriptive information collected through participant observation (a method discussed later), objective information on the structure and functioning of the groups was obtained through structured questionnaires given to all group members. Personality tests were given at a separate time to the same sample of men. The comparison between cane cutters and fishermen on the personality variables described earlier, as measured through these tests, strongly supported the hypotheses, as did the comparisons between work practices.

The weaknesses of studying group phenomena in this way are as clear as its strengths. Beyond certain potential biases discussed later (e.g., bias that can result when an outsider intrudes on a natural groups' functioning or when the author of a hypothesis is directly involved in data collection), the hypothesis is causal but the data in a field study are, at best, correlational. Other uncontrolled, unmeasured, and confounding variables may always be involved, and the ones studied may well be markers for quite different, but even more important, variables. There is often no way to know. In principle, one might be able to resolve such ambiguities by additional measurement or manipulation, but this possibility requires one to have control of the phenomena in question, and the essence of the natural field setting is that events are controlled by natural processes, not by the investigator. At best, a series of correlational tests can be conducted to disconfirm competing hypotheses, but all that such tests can ultimately accomplish is to make the primary hypotheses seem more plausible and to direct more controlled approaches to the question.

Traditionally, observational field methods have been divided into two principal types: those in which the researcher strictly maintains his bystander status as events unfold (*nonparticipant observation*) and those in which the researcher, at least to some extent, participates in the activities of interest (*participant observation*). Both types are used to study group processes and outcomes, so each is briefly discussed below.

NONPARTICIPANT OBSERVATION. The initial St. Kitts work illustrates nonparticipant observational research. The researcher watched (listened, etc.) as others behaved, taking care not to become involved in any of the events that were transpiring. The "Bank Wiring Room" Study, which was part of one of the first attempts by behavioral scientists to systematically study the industrial workplace, is another and a classic example of nonparticipant observation field research on group phenomena (Mayo, 1933; Roethlisberger & Dickson, 1939; Whitehead, 1938). For this study, researchers received permission from a large telephone equipment manufacturing company to relocate a work group, whose job it was to produce banks of electrical switches, to a smaller room that was off to the side of the main plant area. A member of the research team sat at a desk off to the side for the many weeks that the group used this room. This person was basically "a fly on the wall," who observed and recorded what the group members did. Some of the data that the observer recorded were specific regular activities (e.g., who initiated interactions with whom), whereas others were summaries of more singular events (e.g., an incident in which one of the members ventured into the main plant, to return a short while later with some much-needed supplies).

These records were handwritten – an arduous and labor-intensive task – and the researcher was often required to both observe and record at the same time. However, there have been substantial advances in recording technology since the time of this study. Contemporary research of this type would be likely to utilize videotaping equipment to collect data because such techniques have many advantages over the use of human observers in vivo. Among such advantages are the following: (a) Videotaping yields essentially permanent, verbatim records of what transpired. As such, researchers do not have to make decisions about what is important to observe before the events in question take place. They can review the tapes over and over again, before deciding what data should be distilled. (b) Data distillation itself is less stressful and potentially much more accurate from videotape than from coding "on-line." Judges and coders who work with recorded tapes essentially are nonparticipant observers with two major advantages: They can "collect" data at their own pace, rather than be forced to record at the speed with which events are unfolding; and they can use the rewind button to reexamine ambiguous behavior. (c) Videotapes tend to be a much richer data archive than written records because, by their nature, the latter can

only be predetermined summaries or condensations of the actual events. In contrast, videotape records are a "rawer" form of raw data and, as such, have the potential to yield a wide array of interesting information to any researcher who mines them. (d) The miniaturization of video equipment now permits a camera to be truly unobtrusive.

The truly raw-data nature of videotape observational records can also be a major disadvantage. Videos capture everything that the camera "witnesses," for as long as the camera is operating. Recording all the time that the work group spent in the bank wiring room, for instance, would have used a massive amount of tape. It would have been a daunting task just to have coders view the tapes to edit out unnecessary footage. And, coding tapes for particular events of interest, rather than recording this information as the events occur, imposes another step in the research process that sometimes is a source of inefficiency and time delays.

Of course, researchers can opt to time-sample the events of interest (see Bakeman, this volume, Ch. 6), but this solution also has some potential problems. Because the equipment lacks the capacity to judge when to record, the researchers must make that decision. Employing some sort of a priori, intermittent, fixed or variable sampling scheme leaves open the possibility that an important incident will be missed. Another approach is to have a researcher present at all times during observation periods to make moment-by-moment decisions about what should be recorded. This is pertinent when a discrete event is of interest (e.g., a particularly important decision in a group discussion). However sampling is optimal when an extensive record has been obtained and the relative frequency of different "kinds" of behavior (e.g., leadership behavior) needs to be obtained across all members of a group.

From the foregoing discussion, it should be clear that there are no simple criteria for deciding whether to observe and record on-line or use recording equipment to produce verbatim accounts for later use. As with much of the research process generally, such decisions have to be made by informed researchers who understand both their particular circumstances and various advantages and disadvantages of each approach.[2]

---

[2] Note that consideration of observation-recording techniques is also relevant to some laboratory-based research, particularly the type, discussed more fully later, that has participants interact face-to-face with few constraints on behavior.

PARTICIPANT OBSERVATION. As noted, field researchers sometimes "observe from within," by becoming actual participants in a group's experiences. Historically, participant observation has been used much less frequently in social psychology than in other social sciences, particularly anthropology and sociology, but there do exist a few instances of its use in our discipline. One example (Festinger, Riecken, & Schachter, 1956) involved participant observation of a very unusual group, whose task was to make sure that some humans survived a prophisized destruction of the world.

The group that Festinger et al. (1956) studied, which called itself "the Seekers," formed during the early 1950s as a result of some unusual events. A woman residing in a small Michigan town claimed to be receiving telepathic messages from extraterrestrial aliens warning her that at a specific date and time in the very near future, a catastrophe (massive flooding caused by the reemergence of two lost continents) was going to destroy the Earth. These messages went on to say that the aliens were on their way to her planet to rescue any humans who happened to be at the farm when they arrived just before the catastrophe.

Of course, the woman and her husband immediately started spreading the word about this impending tragedy and inviting people to join in their crusade to save humankind. Some people did, in fact, band together with the couple to work on this problem. They held meetings, issued press releases, and so forth. And, when the appointed time of destruction drew close, most moved to the farm where they prepared themselves for departure.

Included among these activists was the social psychologist, Leon Festinger, and a few of his associates, who had joined the group to study its members' behaviors, particularly their behaviors when the critical moment came and (they presumed) went without incident – no alien spaceship, no cataclysm of any sort. Meanwhile, Festinger and his colleagues watched the unfolding events from "the inside." Even though they attempted to maintain a low profile and not do anything that would affect what was transpiring, the researcher still had to "behave normally" as group members; as such they took part in the group's activities and behaved in much the same way as everyone else. (Needless to say, the moment of reckoning did come and go as Festinger et al. [1956] had hoped, and the investigators were able to pass along their interesting observations of what happens psychologically when prophecy fails.)

This brief description should provide a sense of what participant observation typically entails. The researcher joins the group as a full-fledged participant; she or he attempts to act like every other group member. The obvious advantage of this approach is that it provides the researcher with a unique opportunity to observe particular group processes and outcomes first-hand and in situ. In this way, she or he has the potential to learn about phenomena of interest that are unavailable to external observers.

Of course, participant observation has some obvious pitfalls as well. Some major concerns about participant observation center on data quality. To some researchers, this method can never really be scientific because observations are usually impressionistic and nonsystematic. Although such criticisms may be somewhat overstated, it is the case that participant observations tend not to lend themselves to independent verification.

A related problem involves the role that the researcher can play in influencing the phenomena being observed. For example, Festinger and his collaborators (1956) participated fully in the group's activities. Thus, the extent to which their behaviors affected what happened is an open question. Ideally, participant observers act in ways that have no impact on the phenomena of interest. But, behaving with complete neutrality is no easy feat, and because there typically is no way to verify that the researcher's presence, appearance, and actions did not influence events, the naturalness which is the distinctive advantage of all field methods may be compromised.

Participant observation also tends to be very time consuming and costly. The researcher may have to forego many of her or his usual professional and personal activities to become the full participant in the group that the method requires. On the positive side, however, this time could be considered well spent to the extent that participant-observer experiences yield creative insights, ideas for future research, and hypotheses to be systematically tested.

ARCHIVAL STUDIES. Most hypotheses in social psychology are stated as basic processes that hold true for all human beings. Few propositions are examined in more than one society and even fewer have been subjected to a true cross-cultural test in which the societies, themselves, constitute a sample of independent entities (e.g., one could argue that Great Britain and her North American offspring should be treated as a single society). Yet, for example, a universalist proposition suggesting a gender basis for role differentiation in natural groups, such as the family (i.e., Parsons & Bales, 1955), can only be examined in a cross-cultural test examining the allocation of family functions by sex in a sample of independent societies.

As it is usually infeasible for any individual to conduct parallel studies in 50–200 societies (cf. Buss, 1989), more indirect methods need to be used. There are a wealth of underutilized archives of many different kinds available to test our hypotheses cross-culturally as well as within any particular culture. Here, we wish to illustrate this approach to hypothesis testing by describing briefly how hypotheses such as that of Parsons and Bales (1955) or the one developed in St. Kitts can be tested using one particular, rich archive of cross-cultural data on all the world's described primitive cultures, The Human Relations Area Files. Murdock and his associates (Murdock et al., 1987) developed an outline of cultural material and organized existing information on each society drawn from standard ethnographic sources into separate files. Samples of primitive societies can be drawn from this source, variables of interest derived from the ethnographic record can be identified, and the relationship among such variables examined through customary procedures. Interested researchers should consult C. R. Ember and Ember (1988), M. Ember (1977), and Levinson and Malone (1980) for descriptions of these files and the research they make possible.

We can illustrate this approach from an in-progress study by Aronoff and Crano (in preparation), which examined a variation of the hypothesis developed on St. Kitts – that societies in which individuals are more insecure will exhibit a sharper division of tasks and labor between the sexes than will societies in which the individuals are more secure. The societies described in the standard cross-cultural sample (a 186-society sample of primitive cultures that has been used in a wide variety of studies) constituted the sample. The quality of childhood experience (rated as a continuum from warm to harsh experience) in the societies in this sample have been examined by Rohner (1975). These scores constitute an indirect measure of the degree of psychological insecurity in the primitive societies in this sample. Scores on the allocation of economic and social functions to each sex were drawn from studies by Aronoff and Crano (1975) and Crano and Aronoff (1978). Available results, at present, show that societies that treat their children in harsher ways also possess significantly more division of function between the sexes than societies that treat their children more warmly. Archival studies such as this could, in principle, be conducted to test the cross-cultural generality of many of the most interesting propositions in social psychology.

Field Experiments

A field experiment introduces direct manipulation of some variable of interest within a field setting. This method can combine the strengths of a field study with the distinctive strengths of an experiment – the ability to draw causal inferences. Such methods are rarely used because having all the necessary elements in place at the right time can require special access to and control of field settings, as well as a great deal of good luck.

But occasionally one has such good luck. Four years after the St. Kitts field study was completed, Joel Aronoff returned to the island for a Christmas holiday. Visiting with sugar cane workers, he learned of a period of intense industrial conflict that resulted in the cane gangs being reorganized so that they had the structure of fishing crews. This was very disturbing because a book describing the original study – and the former working conditions – was to appear within the year; follow-up research seemed in order. Thus, the original study was replicated that summer; comparisons between the original and the new study constituted a kind of natural quasi-experiment, in which the effects of a naturally occurring "manipulation" (here, a reorganization of cane-cutting crews) could be examined. It was found that there had been a very large turnover of personnel in the years since the original study was done, that the new cane workers had the same personality profile and life history (e.g., degree of parental loss) as the fishermen (i.e., their level of psychological security was found to be equal to that of the fisherman and substantially greater than that of their predecessors in the cane gangs), and that significant aspects of the structure of their work group had changed to be more compatible with their psychological characteristics. In this real-world situation, a change in the psychological functioning of workers was associated with a change in the organizational structure of their group. As illustrated, taking advantages of such "natural experiments," when they occur – assuming a social psychologist is fortunate enough to be present when they happen – can provide further evidence of a particular causal process. Even better evidence can be obtained when the investigator initiates and controls the manipulations in field experiments (e.g., Freedman & Fraser, 1966; Milgram, 1969).

Experiments

A "true experiment" (Anderson, 1966) is designed to advance the causal argument a good deal further. Although a single laboratory experiment cannot provide confidence that a phenomenon is important (in any real-world setting of interest), robust, or widely relevant to aspects of the larger society, it nevertheless provides the best evidence that we have a reasonable grasp on the causal antecedents of a social process (see Brewer, this volume, Ch. 1). Consider the causal hypothesis outlined earlier: One constellation of personality characteristics will lead people to structure their working groups hierarchically, whereas another constellation of personality characteristics will lead people to structure their working groups in more egalitarian ways. In the field situation, the observed relationships between personality and group structure were subject to many alternative explanations, ranging from observer bias to an open-ended list of potentially confounding historical, cultural, geographical, political, organizational, social, economic, racial, and demographic variables. In a field situation, the social process of interest is loosely tied to significant variables of every kind, and there is usually no practical way to test all the alternative hypotheses that imaginative and vigilant critics can propose.

Yet, consider what a laboratory experiment can contribute to exploring the hypothesis at this point in the process of theoretical development. What if the same assessment instrument that had been used to determine personality characteristics among very poor, nonliterate, adult, Afro-Caribbean male cane cutters and fishermen, which had been administered verbally by a highly self-interested, Caucasian graduate student, was given to a large group of comparatively affluent, late adolescent, Caucasian men attending a huge midwestern-U.S. university? Moreover, what if these data were collected in large testing situations that were very unlikely to be contaminated by experimenter expectations? What if the same scoring rules were used to identify in this student sample the same two types of personality constellations that were identified in the St. Kitts sample? What if 5-person laboratory groups were created, homogeneous for each personality constellation, and these college students were asked by research assistants, who were unaware of their personality scores, to work at a set of interactive tasks for an hour while their group behavior was videotaped? What if these videotapes were then scored by research assistants (unaware of the personality information) who had been trained in the use of the Interaction Process Scores (IPS) coding system (Borgatta & Crowther, 1965) to identify the acts of directing and structuring exhibited by each member of a group? And, what if the variance of such individual leadership scores was taken as the measure of the degree of social hierarchy for each group (the lower the variance, the more equal the distribution of directing acts, and thus the more egalitarian the group's structure; the higher the variance, the more concentrated this activity, and thus the more hierarchical the groups's structure)?

This scenario depicts a way to examine propositions about the effect of group membership characteristics on social functioning in group contexts. What if the midwestern college students, chosen because they were anxious, dependent, and mistrustful (as were the original cane cutters), interacted with each other in more hierarchical ways (i.e., the leadership/directing function was concentrated in few members), whereas those students chosen because they were secure, able, and concerned with demonstrating their competence (as were the fishermen) interacted with each other in more egalitarian ways (i.e., the leadership function was dispersed across many members)? Such a replication of the primary findings from St. Kitts (Aronoff & Messé, 1971), obtained under conditions that eliminated many of the alternative hypotheses to which the field research data were vulnerable (because only the personality scores [and their correlates] remained as the antecedent variable) constituted a powerful test of the hypothesis that only experimental methods could provide.

Finally, the experimental method easily permits a host of contributing factors to be examined systematically. For example, the St. Kitts hypothesis argued that specific personality factors lead individuals to behave in ways that conform to their capacities and purposes. The experiment described above is the most direct way to test such a hypothesis. However, a more powerful technique capitalizes on the ease with which the experimenter is able to directly manipulate group structures by varying the experimental task or instructions. Thus, it is possible to ask midwestern undergraduates, whose personality scores indicate that they are, psychologically speaking, fishermen or cane cutters, to work under relatively egalitarian versus hierarchical conditions. The combination of manipulated situational factor (viz., group structure) and manipulated personal factor (viz., personality composition of the group) permits one to test the hypothesis by examining one of its extensions – studying the joint effects of personality and group-structure on the productivity of the group. An experiment that performed this particular test (Wilson, Aronoff, & Messé, 1975) showed that each type of person was more productive under the preferred conditions of group structure (the structure that they generate when given free rein to interact as they chose).

Systematic Observation of Groups

Observers have tended to identify two very different sets of activities as characterizing the social behavior of human beings pursuing common goals, a classification whose dimensions are so significant that this typology pervades most scientific depictions of social interaction across a variety of contexts (e.g., the family, the workplace, the therapy session, etc.). In the first type of behavior, the observer notes that members of a group direct collective and individual efforts to address the tasks with which they are confronted. In the second type of behavior, the observer notes that members of the group engage in a variety of actions in attempts to maintain warm and expressive emotional bonds. In Bales's (1950) pioneering terminology, these two distinct types respectively comprise the instrumental and the socioemotional dimensions of social interaction. This contrast between stereotypic instrumental and expressive forms of social activity also appears today in works as disparate as Gilligan's (1982) description of the characteristic behavior of men and women to that of Triandis's (1995) categorization of the behaviors representative of members of individualistic and collective cultures.

It is not difficult to convert this typology into clear definitions that permit the various forms of individual activity to be measured reliably. Borgatta and Crowther (1965) provided a valuable overview of the pioneering work in this area, as well as a manual with which to train observers to score group activities according to a number of specific coding systems – including, for example, their refinement of Bales's classic (1950) system (Interaction Process Analysis [IPA]) that defines instrumental and socioemotional behavior. This manual was so successful as a training instrument that it remains as the single most useful source for learning how to score interpersonal behavior.

According to Bales (1950), all groups face the same six common problems, involving (a) orientation, (b) evaluation, (c) control, (d) decision, (e) tension management, and (f) group integration. The conceptualization of group functioning and associated measurement techniques that Bales developed were designed to capture behaviors that reflect such instrumental and socioemotional problems. Thus, in the instrumental sphere, statements by individuals asking for orientation ("What should we do next?") or evaluation ("What do you think of this?) are examples of behaviors that individuals might use in a group setting to deal with completing the group's task. Similarly, in the socioemotional sphere, the group might become better

integrated because one member makes a complimentary remark about another, or a member relieves a moment of tension by making a joke.

These six problem areas, of course, can be subdivided further to make increasingly finer behavioral distinctions (see, e.g., Carter, Haythorn, Meirowitz, & Lanzetta, 1951, for an example of a much more elaborated typology that was developed in conjunction with the Bales group's initial work). How fine a set of distinctions needs be drawn is a problem with which all behavioral coding systems must grapple. Thus, Carter et al. (1951) developed codes that distinguish between individuals who "propose a course of action for self" and those who "propose a course of action for others"; and similarly, this scheme also distinguishes "giving bald commands – in a disagreeable fashion" from other actions, such as "disagreeing with others" and "deflating others." Still other categories reflect such prominent social behavior (from the point of view of group productivity) as "standing around doing nothing."

In this case conceptual refinements of definitions that seem both appropriate and necessary to the researcher can tax the researcher's ability to produce reliable codes of activities. The popularity of Bales's IPA system (as well as Borgatta & Crowther's [1965] modification) is likely due to its demonstrated capacity to capture – in a simple, straightforward way – the two overriding problems that all groups confront: the problem of control and the problem of bonding between group members.

These instrumental and socioemotional codes can be readily employed to identify major orientations of group members' behaviors. For example, Slater (1955) used the Bales system to show that groups evolve roles that differentiate task and socioemotional specialists and that two different group members tend to assume each one of these "jobs." Similarly, this coding scheme can be used to conduct validity studies of the materials used in many social psychology experiments. For example, in preparing materials to be used in a person perception experiment, Woike and Aronoff (1992) needed to create a videotape of a male and a female student who were similar in the amount of instrumental and socioemotional behaviors that they displayed. To confirm the presumption that the actors and the script indeed presented the desired social event, the behavior of the male and the female actors on the videotape was scored using IPA for the presence of each type of behavior.

Further, these behavioral definitions can be used to define complex interpersonal roles. Thus, Bennis and Sheats (1948) combined different elements of Bales's codes to define a number of important task roles (e.g., initiator, opinion seeker, evaluator) and maintenance roles (e.g., encourager, compromiser, standard setter) in the group. Broad social roles, defined objectively through such means, can be much more descriptive of the complex and differentiated behaviors that seem to be important in actual work, social, and therapy groups (Forsyth, 1990).

The half-century of research in social science that has attempted to systematically codify behaviors in group contexts has provided valuable lessons and guidelines for future work. One lesson to be learned from this literature is that any attempt to capture the full spectrum of such activities must include categories of both task-oriented and socioemotional behaviors. Second, it now seems apparent that researchers should use observational schemes that are congruent with their studies' objectives. Systematic coding of behavior – despite numerous technological advances (e.g., the use of computers to aid in this task) – remains a labor-intensive endeavor. As such, it is essential for a researcher to use the most efficient and applicable procedure possible. For instance, as discussed earlier, the laboratory studies that attempted to link personality and group structure (Aronoff & Messé, 1971; Wilson et al., 1975) focused on a specific type of task behavior (acts of direction and control); as such, it was reasonable to code other, non-issue-relevant activities as "other," or not to code them at all. In contrast, it was necessary for Woike and Aronoff (1992) to code for both task-oriented and socioemotional activities in order to make sure the actors in the social event that participants were to observe were broadly equivalent in their group behaviors.

Methods for Analyzing the Structural Properties of Groups

As the preceding discussion of group observational methods suggests, a central question in the study of groups is how groups are structured – that is, what is the pattern of relationships (power, influence, status, liking, etc.) among the members of the group? A number of special techniques for analyzing group structure have been developed to address this central question.

SOCIOMETRY. A traditional method of exploring the structure property of relations among group members is Moreno's (e.g., 1953) sociometric technique. It begins with each group member choosing some number of other group members preferred on one or more dimensions. The simplest (and probably most common) choice is for each group member to choose the single other group member he or she likes best, but the dimension(s) of judgment could reflect any interest of the investigator (e.g., who are preferred coworkers?; who are most respected?). These preferences are recorded in a *sociomatrix*, where rows represent judges, columns represent targets, and the entries are the (presence or absence of) expressed preferences. Column totals summarize each target's social acceptance or *sociometric status*. Other summary indices can be derived from this matrix, such as the number of group members choosing one (social receptiveness or choice status) or the number of mutual choices in the group (as an index of group cohesiveness; Northway, 1967).

A *sociogram*, a graphical summary of the information contained in the sociomatrix, can also be created. Every group member is designated by a geometric shape (typically a circle, although one can represent subtypes of interest [e.g., men and women] with different shapes). Then group members' preferences (typically their first or strongest preferences on a single dimension) are indicated by arrows connecting judge to preferred target. A more easily comprehended picture of the group's structure can usually be created by rearranging the group members on the page to highlight patterns of choice (e.g., by putting a person chosen by many group members in the middle of a cluster; by putting those rarely chosen at the edges of the figure). Group members who are distinctive can be easily identified in the final sociogram. These designated individuals include those who are preferred by many group members (so-called *stars*), those preferred by few or no group members (so-called *isolates*), those who comprise subsets or cliques within the group that are mutually connected (so-called *chains*), and pairs of group members that choose one another (*reciprocated pairs* or *friends*). There are also more complex statistical techniques (Kafer, 1976; Lindzey & Borgatta, 1954; Sherwin, 1975) and software (e.g., Levin, 1976; Noma & Smith, 1978) that can be used when one's data set is large or varied (e.g., containing preferences on several dimensions).

SOCIAL NETWORK ANALYSIS. Social network analysis is similar to Moreno's (1953) sociometric approach, but is a far more flexible, powerful, and widely used (primarily in sociology, political science, and anthropology) method for analyzing a group's structural properties. Like sociometry, network analysis utilizes dyadic relationships as the basic unit of analysis, matrix summaries of the raw data, indices summarizing aspects of group members' position in the group, and occasionally (particularly for smaller groups) graphical summaries of the structure relationships. However, social network analysis has a much more fully developed set of analytic techniques (exploiting advances in graph theory; cf. Scott, 1991) and can and has been applied to a much larger variety of relationships, to relationships varying in strength as well as existence, to summarizing aspects of the full network, and to structural patterns in much larger and more complex social aggregates (e.g., at the organizational, national, or international levels).

It is well beyond the scope of this chapter (and the authors' abilities) to provide a full overview of the techniques of social network analysis. Rather, we shall simply note a few basics of these techniques. There are a number of good introductory texts available (e.g., Knoke & Kuklinski, 1982; Scott, 1991; Wellman & Berkowitz, 1988; Wasserman & Faust, 1994) where interested readers can pursue the study of this sophisticated technique.

Network analysis begins with a set of *nodes* or *actors*. In small group research, this is likely to be the set of group members, but it could also be other objects, either social (e.g., organizations, clubs) or nonsocial (e.g., events, locations). The set of actors examined may represent a tractable and well-delimited collective (e.g., an intact group), but could also be a random or snowballed sample from some very large or amorphous collective. When the objective is to construct an *egocentric network*, based on a single actor's perception of relationships with other actors, the sample could even be a single person. The basic relational data reflect the existence, nonexistence, and/or strength and frequency of relationships (or *links* or *ties*) between these actors. What kind of relationship is assessed will depend on the investigators' objectives and hypotheses, but could, in principle, be of any sort. Commonly studied relationships include sentiment (e.g., liking) relationships, exchanges of information or commodities, social influence relations, workflows, or kinship relations.

Network data can be obtained in any of several ways (e.g., from archives, by direct observation of group interaction, by self report via questionnaire or interview). The raw data can be tabulated in any of several equivalent matrix forms. Probably the most straightforward means of compilation is the $N \times N$ (where N is the number of actors) sociomatrix described earlier. When the relational data are uni- or nondirectional, the matrix is symmetric, and the $N(N-1)/2$ elements below the diagonal suffice; when the relational data are directed (i.e., Actor A's relationship to Actor B cannot be assumed to be equivalent to Actor B's relationship to A) then the matrix need not be symmetric, and entries both above and below the diagonal must be specified.

Network analysis presumes that "the structure of relations among actors and the location of individual actors in the network have important behavioral, perceptual, and attitudinal consequences, both for the individual units and for the system as a whole" (Knoke & Kuklinski, 1982, p. 13). Thus, this technique seeks to relate behavior of interest to features of the network. The latter can be statistics associated with specific actors, such as an actor's number of direct links with other actors (*degree*), the ease of an actor reaching all others (*closeness*), an actor's *centrality* in the network, or relative level of being the object rather than the source of relations (*prestige*). Actors who occupy distinctive positions in the network may be assigned distinctive roles. Some of these (e.g., star, isolate) are similar to sociometric roles mentioned previously; other roles of note include an actor who connects clusters of which he or she is not a member (*liaison*), an actor who belongs to two or more clusters (*bridge*), or an actor who connects one part of the network with another (*gatekeeper*). Other features describe a particular or the average link, such as its temporal stability, symmetry, or directness. Such analyses can be extended to focus on aspects of a particular or the average triad (e.g., what's the degree of transitivity of links?). Finally, the analysis may focus on features of the entire network, such as its size, the average path distance between actors (*connectivity*), the ratio of mutually reachable pairs of actors to all possible pairs (*connectedness*), the relative centrality of the most central actor to all other actors (*centralization*), the ratio of connected to possible links (*density*), etc. Such analyses are aided by social network analyses software packages (see Appendix, Scott, 1991; http://indy1.gamma.rug.nl/sibweb/cgi-bin/index.pl?links=/sibweb/menucat.html&rechts=/sibweb/bvcat.html).

Study of the range of applications of social network analysis (e.g., see Brass, 1995; Wasserman & Faust, 1994) can provide a much fuller appreciation of this technique's power and versatility than this brief overview.

INNOVATIVE METHODS AND TOOLS FOR GROUP RESEARCH

Traditionally, research on small group processes has been a fairly low-tech affair. For example, early observation of group process (e.g., Stephan & Mishler, 1952) relied on on-line coding by live observers. Clearly, the quantity and quality of data that could be obtained were severely limited. Similarly, manipulation of interesting features of groups' environment, structure, or process were generally crude and intrusive in many early studies. For example, the structure of group communication might be varied by physically arranging group members so that written notes could be passed physically only through certain slots (e.g., Guetzkow, 1968). The apparent content of intermember communications might be manipulated by the investigator originating or intercepting and replacing such written notes (e.g., Schachter, Ellertson, McBride, & Gregory, 1951).

The rapid growth of technology during the last few decades has certainly increased the potential (if not the reality) for more detailed, reliable, varied, and sophisticated small group research. Below, we will describe a number of the particular ways in which modern technology has been and could be applied to such research. We make no claims (nor harbor any illusions) that this overview is comprehensive. Comprehensiveness is precluded, in part, by the fact that new types of hardware and software are appearing all the time; "cutting edge" technologies can become obsolete in even the relatively short lag time between writing a chapter and its publication. We also wish to stress that whenever we mention a particular piece of technology, we do so only to provide an illustration of how technology has been or might be applied, and not as an endorsement. Interested readers should take any of our illustrations only as starting points, and undertake their own investigation into the advisability of applying any particular technology to their own particular substantive questions. To aid in such investigations, we occasionally provide addresses on the World Wide Web that contain and maintain product descriptions, reviews, and other sources of relevant information. (Also note that although these websites appear useful at present, they may or may not continue to be in the future.)

Audio-Video Hardware and Software

As we mentioned earlier, arguably the most important technological innovations for observational research on small groups is the development of reliable, affordable, compact, and easy-to-use equipment to make audio or video recordings of group interaction. Of course, audiotaping or filming group interaction has technically been possible since the advent of modern social psychology, but these technologies either lost much information that was of interest (e.g. identity of speaker, target of communications,

all other overt nonverbal behaviors in the case of audio recordings) or were expensive and cumbersome to use (in the case of film and early, reel-to-reel video). However, with the advent of compact video cameras, video cassettes, and video-cassette recorders (VCRs), it has become fairly simple and inexpensive to make high resolution video recordings of group behavior.

Earlier we noted some of the advantages of video recording over live observation – for example, multiple observers and investigators can examine and code the same interactions at their convenience and with less risk of fatigue, slow-motion replay can reveal subtle or easily missed behaviors, and distracting or biasing information can be masked. Easily available video technologies such as remote camera controls, video-mixing boards, and video-editing hardware also make it feasible to focus on particular and quite subtle aspects or combinations of observable behavior (e.g., a particular group member, simultaneous actions of a speaker and listener). Technology on the horizon promises to make possible even more detailed recordings.

With or without permanent video recordings, observational research of group behavior can be extremely labor-intensive. However, there are also a number of technologies currently available that make the task less onerous and more flexible. For example, there are a number of computer programs (e.g., Eventlog, The Observer 3.0; http://www.york.ac.uk/inst/ctipsych/dir/researchtools.html or http://indy1.gamma.rug.nl/sibweb/cgi-bin/index.pl?links=/sibweb/menucat.html&rechts=/sibweb/bvcat.html) that enable one to use the desktop or portable computer keyboard to encode multiple events of interest in real time. These are particularly useful where videorecording is not feasible for reasons of practicality (lack of hardware) or methodology (e.g., the use of a camera would be intrusive or unethical). There are also a number of hardware/software packages (e.g., MacSHAPA, Camera, PROCODER, VTLOGANL; see, e.g., Sanderson, 1994; Tapp & Walden, 1993; or http://www.york.ac.uk/inst/ctipsych/dir/researchtools.html or http://indy1.gamma.rug.nl/sibweb/cgi-bin/index.pl?links=/sibweb/menucat.html&rechts=/sibweb/bvcat.html or http://www.aviation.uiuc.edu/institute/acadprog/epjp/MacShapa.html on the Web) that are designed for coding data from videotape. Such programs can include a number of useful features, such as large numbers of possible coding categories, keyboard control of the VCR, precise timing of event occurrence and duration, visual or auditory feedback of entered codes, and the ability to annotate event coding. Thus, rather than coding a single variable of interest through laborious procedures (e.g., manually rewinding, using the tape counter or visual content to find the start of the event), using such technology one can simultaneously code several features of interaction, mark and automatically return to points of interest, and use feedback features to detect unanticipated patterns in the data. One can also either do a number of standard (e.g., interjudge reliability) or not-so-standard (e.g., lag sequential analyses, transition analyses, analyses of cyclic activity; see Bakeman, this volume, Ch. 6) analyses within such programs or export the data for analysis with other statistical packages.

Such video software still requires the decisions of human judges. For certain simple aspects of group interaction, one may design equipment to obviate the human judge. For example, Dabbs and Swiedler (1983) developed a system for automatically monitoring the onset and ending of speech in group discussions. As technological advances occur in shape, movement, and voice recognition by computer, it is likely that it will be possible to automate many other coding tasks, which should bring attendant gains in accuracy and efficiency of coding.

Computer Technology: Data Collection at Arbitrary Group Tasks

An even more revolutionary technological innovation of the late 20th century for social psychology (as for nearly every other discipline, as well as for the general public) is certainly the development of powerful, small, and affordable microcomputers. Software and hardware is now commonplace for such standard tasks as word processing, electronic mail, and statistical analysis. Here, though, we focus our attention on how the computer can and might be used as a tool for conducting group research.

Three generic approaches to computer-mediated experimentation on groups might be distinguished for our immediate purposes.

1. The first approach has a group working together at a single computer. In this setting, the computer serves as an instruction and/or stimulus-presentation device, and/or as a data recording device (typically for group responses through the keyboard, but possibly for individual member responses [e.g., via turn-taking] and via other input devices, such as joysticks, analog/digital boards, etc.). For example, rather than have a single pad for recording ideas generated by a brainstorming group (cf. Diehl & Stroebe,

1987), one could provide the group with a computer to record ideas, making possible richer data collection (e.g., the rate as well as the number of ideas generated).

2. The second approach has each member of a real or purported group working at separate, stand-alone computer stations. This approach is particularly appropriate for research questions about those group processes that do not involve any actual interpersonal activity (e.g., social facilitation) or that, at most, involve restricted patterns of interaction (e.g., a context in which group members are allowed to talk to one another as they work at their computers; cf. Olson, Olson, Storreston, & Carter, 1994), but it can also be used for certain group simulations where the experimenter programs in and controls the apparent responses or communications of other group members. For example, Messick et al. (1983) led participants to believe that they could monitor each other's harvests from a shared resource pool through computer feedback. In fact, there was no feedback of actual choices, but rather false feedback preprogrammed by the experimenters to examine participants' reactions to various patterns of resource use (e.g., a steadily declining resource pool; high vs. low variance in members' harvests).

3. The third approach provides each group member with his or her own station and permits intermember communication via a computer network. A striking recent example of this approach is Latané, and L'Herrou's (1996) study of different allowable communication links – modeling different spatial arrangements of group members – and their effect on patterns of social influence. The use of asynchronous computer communication (e.g., e-mail) allowed these investigators to both control channels of communication and overcome the difficult logistic problem of composing 24-person groups for several rounds of communication.

There are, in turn, several generic means of acquiring the software needed to undertake these approaches:

1. One can identify and obtain existing software (most typically from other investigators who have authored or used it). There are many such application-specific programs that have been developed for small group research (e.g., in social dilemma research, see Messick et al., 1983, for an illustration). Such software is usually identified through careful study of the existing empirical literature, by word of mouth,

or by examining databases of psychological software (cf. http://www.york.ac.uk/inst/ctipsych; Hornby & Anderson, 1994; Huff & Sobiloff, 1993). Of course, the chief drawback of using such preexisting software is that it is generally inflexible, not permitting alterations in procedure or experimental parameters. In a very few cases, investigators have tried to build flexibility into their programs so that other investigators could adapt them to new purposes. Good illustrations are CDS (Li, Seu, Evens, Michael, & Rovick, 1992), which captures typed dyadic communication, and GROUPCOM (Levine, 1978), which permits interpersonal communication among up to six group members.

2. If one is (or can afford to hire) a talented computer programmer, one can use machine or macrolanguages (e.g., Pascal, C) to program one's computer or computer network and apply any one of these approaches to one's substantive research question. This approach, of course, carries maximal flexibility, but is beyond the training or resources of many investigators.

3. There also exist a number of general-purpose programs developed specifically for psychological experimentation (cf. http://www.york.ac.uk/inst/ctipsych/dir/experiment.html or http://indy1.gamma.rug.nl/sibweb/cgi-bin/index.pl?links=/sibweb/menucat.html&rechts=/sibweb/bvcat.html). Most of these packages have been developed by experimental and cognitive psychologists for the Mac platform (e.g., Cohen, MacWhinney, Flatt, & Provost, 1993; Chute, 1993; Haxby, Parasuraman, LaLonde, & Abboud, 1993; Hunt, 1994; Vaughan & Yee, 1994), although there are some for the PC platform as well (e.g., MEL, Schneider, 1988, http://www.pstnet.com/melpro/melpro.htm; E-prime, http://www.pstnet.com/eprime/eprime.htm; SuperLab, http://www.superlab.com). These packages typically include many useful tools for conducting experiments, such as options that permit counterbalancing orders of stimulus presentation, precise timing of stimulus and response, etc. Unfortunately, at present, none of them is designed to take advantage of computer networking, so that they can only be used for what we have called Type I and II applications (i.e., without actual interaction among group members). Although, to our knowledge, there currently is no general-purpose experiment generator that is networked, there have been attempts to extend general-purpose authoring software from use for stand-alone experimental applications (e.g., Wolfe, 1992; http://www.york.ac.uk/inst/ctipsych/dir/experiment.html) to networked applications (e.g., Hoffman & MacDonald, 1993).

4. The market for sales of hardware and software for all of experimental psychology is a relatively small one (Schneider, 1991). Consequently, little research and development in the computer industry has focused on the requirements of psychological researchers in general, let alone those interested in the study of small group behavior in particular. However, there is both a considerable market for and commercial interest in technology that aids in interpersonal communication – what McGrath and Hollingshead (1994) generically termed group communication support systems (GCSSs) – and that assists organizational groups or teams to improve their productivity – group performance (or decision) support systems (GPSSs; McGrath & Hollingshead, 1994). So, a final means of applying technology to the study of group process is to directly utilize or adapt technology developed for these more applied purposes as group research tools.

GCSSs are simply tools for extending human communication beyond its most basic form (viz., face-to-face verbal/nonverbal interaction). GCSS technologies currently exist that permit synchronous or distributed (in both time and space) communication via various modalities (audio, video, video & audio, typed text, handwritten text, graphics; McGrath & Hollingshead, 1994). These technologies range from the mundane (telephones, surface mail) to the increasingly commonplace (e.g., cellular phones, voice mail, electronic mail) to the relatively novel (e.g., interactive chat rooms, video conferencing via the Internet; see http://thinkofit.com/webconf/ or http://www11.informatik.tumuenchen.de/cscw/ for introductions to a few of the possibilities currently available). Although such GCSSs are not commonly used as tools in small group research at present, we believe that they have considerable potential to be used in this way (see T. McGuire, Kiesler, & Siegel, 1987, or Hollingshead, McGrath, & O'Connor, 1993, for illustrations of this potential).

GPSSs attempt to do more than simply facilitate communication among group members. They attempt to restructure common group tasks, often incorporating innovative communication technology, so as to enhance group productivity. GPSS technologies have given birth not only to an industry aiming to exploit the commercial possibilities of developing and marketing such systems (e.g., http://www.ventana.com) but also to a burgeoning group of scholars with sophisticated research centers (http://www.uasabilityfirst.com/

groupware), major conferences (e.g., the biennial Computer Supported Cooperative Work [CSCW] meetings; the annual Human Computer Interaction [HCI] meetings; cf. http://www.acm.org/events/), and specialized scientific journals (e.g., *Communications of the ACM, Information Systems Research*).

One product of this marriage of commercial and scholarly pursuits is a rich empirical literature (see McGrath & Hollingshead, 1994). Another is an impressive and varied collection of "groupware," hardware and software products designed to facilitate collaborative work (see http://www.telekooperation.de/cscw/) – ranging from collaborative editing tools to message systems to group meeting support systems to conferencing systems. Ventana Corporation's GroupSystems package is a nice illustration of a GPSS. It contains modules for generating and categorizing ideas, outlining topics, commenting on ideas, and evaluating and voting on proposals.

Of course, the scientific study of group performance has been a major topic of social psychology since its inception (Baron, Kerr, & Miller, 1992; Kravitz & Martin, 1986; McGrath, 1984). It is thus a bit surprising to find so few social psychologists actively involved in the study and application of technology to group work (see McGrath & Hollingshead, 1994; Sproull & Kiesler, 1991; Kielser, 1997, for noteworthy exceptions). We suspect that these emerging disciplines hold tremendous potential not only to provide us with useful tools for controlling and observing group behavior but also to raise fascinating new questions about group behavior that would never occur to us without the many new possibilities for structuring group work that modern technologies create. The study of brainstorming in electronically linked groups, described below, is an excellent illustration.

GROUPS AS A CONTEXT/MEANS FOR RESEARCH AND APPLICATION

Thus far we have been emphasizing methodological tools that are useful when the primary goal is the study of group behavior, per se. In this section, however, we shift focus somewhat. Here we examine a number of methodologies in which some guided form of group interaction has been held to provide a useful context and means for achieving some other goal, such as solving a problem, assessing opinion, generating ideas, and so on. In effect, these are also "group productivity/decision support systems," but ones which require no exotic technologies. For the most part, these methodologies have not been developed by

nor are they commonly used by social psychologists; in these senses, they represent innovative group techniques. And, for the most part, there is little conclusive research evidence on the efficacy of these techniques. However, because they are employed (at times quite widely) outside social psychology and because the use and goals of these techniques pose a number of interesting and patently social psychological questions, we have chosen to describe them here. We have been somewhat selective, however; in particular, we have excluded methods of using groups for various therapeutic ends (see Forsyth, 1990, chapter 15, for an introduction to the latter methods).

Below we briefly present the genesis, rationale, basic procedures, a sourcebook or two, and (when available) evidence for efficacy for each of the following: group brainstorming, focus groups, quality circles, nominal group technique, and the Delphi method. These are roughly ordered in terms of increasing structure and constraint on interpersonal interaction.

Group Brainstorming

Brainstorming was developed by advertising executive A. F. Osborn (1957) as a means of facilitating the generation of creative ideas through face-to-face group interaction. Osborn prescribed four rules for such brainstorming groups. First, members are instructed to express any ideas that come to mind without concern for their quality, practicality, etc. Spontaneous and uninhibited "free-wheeling" is encouraged. Second, during brainstorming there should be no evaluation of any ideas expressed. Emphasis should be entirely on the generation of ideas, not their evaluation. Third, the brainstorming group should strive for as many ideas as possible; the more ideas, the better. Fourth, group members should try to build on others' ideas, combining, improving, and extending wherever possible.

Osborn (1957) made rather extravagant claims for the efficacy of group brainstorming – for example, "the average person can think up twice as many ideas when working with a group than when working alone" (Osborn, 1957, p. 229). Unfortunately, systematic research has failed to substantiate these claims. To the contrary, a sizeable literature (see Diehl & Stroebe, 1987; Mullen, Johnson, & Salas, 1991, for reviews) has consistently shown that brainstorming groups produce both fewer and poorer quality ideas than equal-sized, identically instructed nominal groups (i.e., groups whose members work in isolation and whose total output is determined by pooling members' output, eliminating any redundant ideas).

Substantial progress has been made in identifying the sources of this process loss in brainstorming groups, with production blocking (i.e., the fact that only one person at a time can talk [and, perhaps, think] at a time in the face-to-face group), production matching (i.e., social comparison and modeling of low levels of productivity), and evaluation apprehension (i.e., fear of negative evaluation for voicing ideas in the group context) all emerging as contributing processes (Diehl & Stroebe, 1987; Paulus & Dzindolet, 1993; Stroebe & Diehl, 1994). Hence, procedural variations that neutralize these mechanisms (e.g., individual recording of ideas, including periods of silence, turn taking) may close the gap between nominal and brainstorming" groups (Philipsen, Mulac, & Dietrich, 1979; Ruback, Dabbs, & Hopper, 1984).

The most exciting recent procedural innovation in brainstorming is so-called "electronic brainstorming" (EBS). Each group member has a terminal that is networked with all other terminals. Group members type in ideas at will. At any time, a group member can see a sample of the ideas generated by the group simply by hitting a key; by repeatedly doing so, he or she can examine all the ideas generated so far. Because ideas are not attributed to particular group members, member anonymity is maintained. Recent research suggests that for small- to moderate-sized groups (less than 10 persons), EBS groups perform as well as comparably sized nominal groups, and for larger groups (around a 12 or more), the EBS groups actually outperform the nominal group baseline (Dennis & Valacich, 1993; Valacich, Dennis, & Connolly, 1994). Such apparent "process gain" – group performance exceeding the group's apparent potential productivity – has been very rare in the social psychological literature (e.g., Williams & Karau, 1991) and is of special interest for theory development and application. The source of this apparent process gain in EBS groups remains to be identified. (See Osborn, 1957, for a more detailed description of group brainstorming; Gallupe & Cooper, 1993, for an introduction to the electronic variant.)

Focus Groups

The *focus group* has been used most in marketing and advertising research. It is a qualitative, semistructured interview technique, in which a small group, typically of 8–10 people, discusses a topic of interest under the supervision of a moderator. The information sought is usually fairly narrowly delimited (e.g., how do consumers react to a new product or product idea?; how is a product actually used?; how do competing products compare?). The information gleaned from focus groups may directly guide decision making or may prompt more systematic and quantitative techniques.

Considerable preparation should precede focus group sessions. The objectives of the sessions first need to be specified – what information is desired? The moderator(s) must be selected and briefed on the objectives. A moderator guide must be prepared. This guide is a detailed outline of topics that should be covered in the focus group, when each might be addressed, and how available time will be used. The appropriate respondent population must be identified and a method of participant recruiting settled on. Because the sample sizes of focus group studies, even those including several groups, are rarely large, and quantitative data (e.g., population estimates with confidence intervals) are not sought, a probability sample of the target population is usually not attempted. Consequently, generalization to larger populations is very problematic. Instead, certain participant characteristics are specified (e.g., women between 30 and 45 years of age who regularly use a particular product) and the groups are then composed of samples of paid volunteers obtained in any of several ways (e.g., from community groups, via telephone or mail screenings, from firms providing names). For a number of reasons (to avoid distractions, to target specific respondent populations), focus groups are typically fairly homogeneous demographically. If information is sought from diverse subpopulations (e.g., men and women; old and young), this is typically achieved by running separate homogeneous focus groups.

Focus group sessions follow no specific set of procedures. However, in practice, there are a number of common features. Although they sometimes are conducted via teleconference, the discussion is nearly always conducted face-to-face and is recorded; these days, video recordings are the norm. Also, interested observers (e.g., clients of a marketing research firm) may observe the focus group live through a one-way mirror. The moderator leads the focus group through usual stages of group discussion – general orientation (introductions, ground rules), orientation to the topic (via more general discussion), focus on specific topics of interest (defined in the moderator guide), and wrap up. The moderator attempts to act as a facilitator, encouraging and guiding but not dominating discussion. Any of a number of mechanical (e.g., presenting product samples or commercials; having respondents write down ideas before discussion) and social (e.g., soliciting views of quiet participants; seeking reactions to most active participants) methods can be used in this pursuit. A number of special steps may be taken with unusual respondent groups (e.g., children, experts). There may be postgroup discussions among investigators (e.g., the moderator and the client). There may also be a formal report prepared by the moderator to summarize and interpret the content of the focus group discussion.

The purported benefits of the focus group technique include the following: (a) it can often be easier and less expensive to use focus groups than more traditional survey or interview techniques (although the cost-per-respondent can be considerably higher for some focus groups); (b) the group setting can provide insights into social forces of interest (e.g., peer pressure on product use); (c) the group setting encourages greater honesty, spontaneity, involvement, and thoroughness of responding; and, consequently, (d) one has access to more useful information, including respondents' emotional reactions, vivid anecdotes, novel ideas, etc. Unfortunately, such claims, as well as prescriptions for focus group practice, are based primarily on "experienced validity" – the informal observations and experiences of focus group users and proponents. There is very little published research documenting these claims (Bristol & Fern, 1996; Calder, 1977). If these purported benefits could be established, focus groups might provide an effective technique for assessing attitudes, probing for suspicion postexperimentally, doing introspective process analyses of social processes, or for exploratory hypothesis-generating research. (See Goldman, 1987; Greenbaum, 1993; Vaughn, Schumm, & Sinagub, 1996, for more detailed descriptions of focus group methods.)

Quality Circles

Quality circles (or quality control circles; QCs) are used primarily in business and industrial settings. They are seen as an alternative to more traditional and hierarchical systems of management, an alternative which involves workers themselves more actively and directly in their work and organization. QCs were developed in the 1960s in Japan and have rapidly grown in popularity in many Western industries over the last few years.

Hutchins (1985) defined a QC as

a small group of between three and twelve people who do the same or similar work, voluntarily meeting together regularly for about one hour per week in paid time, usually under the leadership of their own supervisor, and trained to identify, analyze, and solve some of the problems in their work, presenting solutions to management and, where possible, implementing solutions themselves. (p.1).

To this end, a number of group techniques and principles are incorporated into QC procedures. For example, heavy reliance is placed on group brainstorming techniques for identifying workplace problems and solutions, the groups are limited in size to permit general participation in face-to-face meetings, and decision making is democratic – one person, one vote. There are also a number of aspects of the QCs' functioning that are not distinctively social in nature, such as collecting relevant data, analyzing the causes of workplace problems, and preparing clear and persuasive presentations of recommendations to management. Implementation of QCs and achieving their purported benefits (described below) is not simply a matter of forming groups of coworkers, but requires fairly extensive organizational commitment and support (e.g., a willingness to invest organizational resources, a willingness to seriously consider QC proposals).

The participation and involvement of workers achieved through QCs is alleged to have extensive benefits: reduced turnover, fewer grievances, improvements in productivity, improvements of quality, higher worker morale, and stronger corporate loyalty and identification. Attempts to verify these claims empirically have produced rather mixed results (see Barrick & Alexander, 1987; Steel & Shane, 1986); about half of the studies have reported mixed, negative, or null results. There are indications that the duration of the QCs is positively related to the magnitude of benefits. Although there are very difficult methodological problems in the evaluation of QCs (e.g., participant self-selection; reliance on quasi-experimental designs), the growing popularity of QCs and the early indications of positive results certainly justify more careful empirical attention. Besides posing interesting substantive questions for research on group and organizational processes, QCs might be usefully applied within research teams, themselves. (See Hutchins, 1985; Ingle, 1982, for more detailed descriptions of QCs.)

Nominal Group Method

The nominal group technique (NGT), developed by Delbecq and Van de Ven (e.g., Delbecq, Van de Ven, & Gustafson, 1975), was designed to overcome certain aspects of unconstrained face-to-face discussion that can interfere with effective group problem solving and decision making. Of particular concern were those small group processes that tend to prevent full and thorough participation by all group members. These included (a) the reluctance of some members to participate, especially in larger groups; (b) domination of group discussion by an opinionated, loquacious, repetitive, or high-status individual or faction; (c) the diversion of time and effort that might be devoted to generating and evaluating ideas to organize and maintain the group; (d) getting stuck on a single line of argument for long periods; and (e) hurrying to reach a speedy decision before all relevant information has been considered. NGT attempts to counter such problems by using nominal groups (as described above for brainstorming research) for idea generation.

Another set of problems can arise from explicit requirements or implicit pressures to achieve consensus in groups. Group members might (f) become overcommitted to their initial publicly expressed opinion (cf. Kerr & MacCoun, 1985), (g) decline to participate or defend a position to avoid social sanctions from a leader or the majority faction, or (h) compromise or shift position simply to avoid such sanctions. NGT attempts to minimize such problems by having no explicit consensus requirement or decision rule and by pooling preferences statistically to define a group product.

Formally, there are four stages in the NGT. First, a moderator poses the problem to a group. The members of the group are given time (typically 10–20 minutes) to silently write down as many ideas or solutions as they can, much as the nominal groups used in brainstorming research. It is recommended that the group be large enough to generate a substantial pool of ideas but not too large to make the following stages unwieldy; 7–10 group members are thought to be optimal. During the second stage, group members state the ideas that they have written using a round-robin procedure. After each idea is stated, the moderator writes it down on a blackboard or flip-chart. Stage 3 consists of open group discussion of the recorded ideas. The emphasis here is on clarifying and evaluating each idea; there is no goal of group consensus. A group decision or a preference ordering for ideas is determined by a nominal voting procedure at the fourth and final stage. Nominal voting requires each group member to privately evaluate the alternatives (e.g., rank ordering one's favorite five alternatives). The moderator pools these evaluations (e.g., computes mean rank orders) to identify the group's overall preference(s). Optional additional stages are another group discussion (this time focusing on the group decision) and another vote.

Proponents of the NGT take the sizeable literature demonstrating the superiority of nominal to brainstorming groups as indirect evidence for a superiority of the NGT to normal, face-to-face groups for idea generation. Van de Ven (1974) confirmed this claim empirically and also found that group members were more satisfied under a NGT than free interaction, a finding which he attributed to fuller, more uniform input under the NGT. There is also some evidence that allowing group members first to share likelihood-ratio estimates before group discussion (consistent with Stages 1 and 2 of the NGT) produces more accurate aggregated postdiscussion estimates (Gustafson et al., 1973), relative to groups without such prediscussion sharing. It seems fair to conclude that the evidence for the NGT, although fragmentary, is encouraging. The availability of GCSSs also raises new opportunities to examine innovative modifications of the traditional NGT, much as it has for group brainstorming. (See Delbecq & Van de Ven, 1971; Delbecq et al., 1975; Van de Ven, 1974, for more detailed descriptions of the nominal group technique.)

Delphi Technique

The Delphi technique seeks to pool the opinions of a group of people who are well-informed or expert on some topic of interest, but without direct, face-to-face interaction. Rather, an iterated sequence of questionnaires are sent to the group by a monitor. The monitor (who could be an individual or project team) is the conduit through which all communications are channeled. The monitor begins by identifying a panel of experts to whom an initial questionnaire is sent. In addition to dealing with several preliminary issues (e.g., explaining the projects' purposes and procedures, seeking respondent commitment to the project), the initial questionnaire poses some root questions on which subsequent rounds of the procedure are built. These questions would typically be few, very general, and open-ended; the goal is to let the group members (and not the moderator) define the domain of relevant opinions or issues. After the questionnaires are returned to the moderator, his or her next task is to develop a new questionnaire which (a) accurately and objectively summarizes group members' opinion from the initial questionnaire and (b) poses a revised, more focused set of questions for the next round. The new questionnaire is then sent back to group members. The feedback from the previous round keeps group members' identities anonymous and should ideally provide more than indices of central tendency. For example, in a Delphi application seeking technology forecasts, respondents might be given the median and interquartile range for estimates of when each of several events is expected to occur (e.g., "when will 90% of all university faculty have and use electronic mail?"), along with summaries of the supporting arguments provided by advocates of high, middling, and low estimates. Ideally, the procedure of questioning, summarizing responses, and requestioning is repeated as long as there seems to be progress (e.g., opinion continues to converge; positions are not static). At least two rounds are required for Delphi; the original developers recommended four rounds as optimal.

Delphi technique was developed at the Rand Corporation (cf. Brown, 1968; Dalkey & Rourke, 1971; Helmer, 1966) as a means of pooling expert opinion. It has often been used to make technological forecasts, but is not restricted to such tasks; "it can be used for any purpose for which a committee can be used" (Martino, 1983, p. 16). It is seen as particularly useful when informed yet subjective judgments are the only or best data available for decision making, when face-to-face discussions are impractical (e.g., because the best-informed respondents are numerous, dispersed, or hard to schedule), or where one wants to avoid certain social psychological consequences of face-to-face discussion, which are presumed to undermine effective decision making (e.g., see the factors listed above in our discussion of the NGT).

The Delphi technique also has its drawbacks. It requires respondents to complete and return several questionnaires. This requirement is likely to be a special problem when group members are busy (as genuinely expert respondents are likely to be) and the questionnaires seem complex or the iterated versions seem redundant. The process can also be expensive and time consuming (typically taking at least a few weeks when mail questionnaires are used); the advent of computer-mediated communication has helped reduce the latter problems.

A final problem with Delphi, as with several of the other techniques described here, is that there is not very much empirical research documenting its efficacy. There are some suggestive findings by Dalkey (e.g., Dalkey, 1968, 1969–1970), which reported that Delphi was superior to face-to-face interaction group estimates for almanac-type questions, but the validity and generality of the claims made for Delphi await systematic research attention. (See Alder & Ziglio, 1996; Linstone & Turoff, 1975; Martino, 1983, for more detailed descriptions of the Delphi technique. See Sackman, 1975, for a pointed critique of the method.)

Afterword: On the Illusion of Group Effectiveness

A curious anomaly has been reported by brainstorming researchers (Paulus & Dzindolet, 1993;

Stroebe et al., 1992). Although interacting brainstorming groups consistently perform less well than comparable nominal groups, participants in both conditions believe that they are and were more productive in a group than working alone.

In this section we have considered a number of methods, all of which extol the particular effectiveness of group settings for accomplishing varied tasks. And indeed, as Steiner (1972) has shown theoretically, for most tasks the potential productivity of a group is greater than mean individual productivity. The illusion of group effectiveness documented in brainstorming groups may stem (in part or in whole) from some confusion between what the average individual can do and what a nominal group of such individuals can do. It may also stem from the greater stimulation and excitement of group interaction; in this regard, it is noteworthy that those working in brainstorming groups also report greater task enjoyment and satisfaction than members of nominal groups. The reasons for the illusion of group effectiveness are not yet well established. Nevertheless, it is important to keep this illusion in mind when considering group methods that are highly touted but inadequately evaluated.

CONCLUSIONS

We hope that we have been able to show that the distinction between individual and group phenomena is an important one. Group processes are fundamentally different from individual psychological phenomena in important ways. In this area of social psychology (as well as related areas, such as the study of interpersonal relationships) we must examine the behavior of individuals as they are simultaneously being affected by the overt or implicit behaviors of others. The experimenter must ensure that his or her methods create such a truly "social" experience. Hence, to study group and other interpersonal phenomena routinely requires not only a different, more complex set of concepts and units of analyses but also a different, more complex set of methods than is needed to study individual behavior.

Allport (1924) suggested that the contrast of individual and group behavior represents the master question of social psychology. In this chapter, we have focused on the methods available to address this master question. After discussing some key conceptual distinctions (e.g., what distinguishes a small group from other social entities?), we have briefly surveyed and illustrated the range of methods currently available for the empirical study of group behavior, noted how technological innovations have created many new opportunities for the study of group phenomena, and described a few techniques that may be used for a number of purposes (e.g., assessment, problem-solving, and decision making) and that rely on group interaction.

Steiner (1986) has suggested that the dominant meta-paradigm of social psychology at the end of the 20th century features individual-level analyses and focuses on single-factor, intrapsychic, cognitive mediators of behavior. He argues persuasively that this meta-paradigm is inimical to the study of group phenomena. The many forces – theoretical, professional, and cultural – that have produced this meta-paradigm (cf. McGrath & Altman, 1966; Steiner, 1986) are powerful and show no signs of abating. Yet as scientific social psychology prepares to enter its second century, we continue to be optimistic that it will not lose sight of the master question that dominated the initial decades of its first century. Recent analyses of publication trends (Moreland, Hogg, & Hains, 1994) have suggested that interest in group phenomena has been increasing after several decades of decline. A hopeful sign is that much of this new interest reflects the integration of traditional topics of intragroup process (see Table 7.1) with some topics that have received much attention during social psychology's past few decades, such as social cognition and intergroup relations. Although the study of group phenomena does present a number of special difficulties, both conceptual and methodological, whether these trends continue will have less to do with overcoming such difficulties than with how clearly we recognize the centrality of group phenomena for human social behavior and accept the challenge of tackling the master question of our field.

REFERENCES

Alder, M., & Ziglio, E. (1996). *Gazing into the oracle: The Delphi method and its application to social policy and public health.* London: Jessica Kingsley.

Allport, F. (1924). *Social psychology.* New York: Houghton-Mifflin.

Altman, I., & Haythorn, W. W. (1967). The effects of social isolation and group composition on performance. *Human Relations, 20,* 313–340.

Anderson, B. F. (1966). *The psychology experiment: An introduction to the scientific method.* Belmont, CA: Wadsworth.

Aronoff, J. (1967). *Psychological needs and cultural systems: A case study.* New York: Van Nostrand.

Aronoff, J., & Crano, W. D. (1975). A re-examination of the cross-cultural principles of task segregation and sex role differentiation in the family. *American Sociological Review, 40,* 12–20.

Aronoff, J., & Crano, W. D. (1999). *Personality and the complexity of role structure in the family.* Manuscript in preparation.

Aronoff, J., & Messé, L. A. (1971). Motivational determinants of small group-structure. *Journal of Personality and Social Psychology, 17,* 319–324.

Asch, S. (1951). Effects of group pressure upon the modification and distortion of judgment. In H. Guetzkow (Ed.), *Groups, leadership and men* (pp. 177–190). Pittsburgh, PA: Carnegie Press.

Back, K. (1951). Influence through social communication. *Journal of Abnormal and Social Psychology, 46,* 9–23.

Bales, R. F. (1950). *Interaction process analysis.* Reading, MA: Addison-Wesley.

Bales, R. F. (1965). The equilibrium problem in small groups. In T. Parsons, R. F. Bales, & E. A. Shils (Eds.), *Working papers in the theory of action* (pp. 111–161). New York: Free Press.

Bales, R. F., Strodtbeck, F. L., Mills, T. M., & Roseborough, M. E. (1951). Channels of communication in small groups. *American Sociological Review, 16,* 461–468.

Bandura, A. (1962). Social learning through imitation. In M. R. Jones (Ed.), *Nebraska symposium on motivation.* Lincoln: University of Nebraska Press.

Baron, R. S., Kerr, N. L., & Miller, N. (1992). *Group process, group decision, group action.* Pacific Grove, CA: Brooks/Cole.

Barrick, M. R., & Alexander, R. A. (1987). A review of quality circle efficacy and the existence of positive-findings bias. *Personnel Psychology, 40,* 579–592.

Benne, K. D., & Sheets, P. (1948). Functional roles of group members. *Journal of Social Issues, 4,* 41–49.

Borgatta, E. F., & Crowther, B. (1965). *A workbook for the study of social interaction processes.* Chicago: Rand-McNally.

Brannigan, G. G., & Merrens, M. R. (Eds.). (1993). *The undaunted psychologist.* New York: McGraw-Hill.

Brannigan, G. G., & Merrens, M. R. (1995). *The social psychologist: Research adventures.* New York: McGraw-Hill.

Brass, D. J. (1995). A social network perspective on human resource management. In J. B. Shaw et al. (Eds.), *Research in personnel and human resources management* (Vol. 13) Greenwich, CT: JAI Press.

Bray, R., Kerr, N. L., & Atkin, R. (1978). Effects of group size, problem difficulty, and sex on group performance and member reactions. *Journal of Personality and Social Psychology, 36,* 1224–1240.

Brewer, M. B., & Kramer, R. M. (1986). Choice behavior in social dilemmas: Effects of social identity, group size, and decision framing. *Journal of Personality and Social Psychology, 50,* 543–549.

Bristol, T., & Fern, E. F. (1996). Exploring the atmosphere created by focus group interviews: Comparing consumers' feelings across qualitative techniques. *Journal of the Market Research Society, 38,* 185–195.

Brown, B. B. (1968). *Delphi Process: A methodology used for the elicitation of opinions of experts.* Santa Monica, CA: Rand Corporation.

Buss, D. M. (1989). Sex differences in human mate preferences: Evolutionary hypotheses tested in 37 cultures. *Behavioral and Brain Sciences, 12,* 1–49.

Calder, B. J. (1977). Focus groups and the nature of qualitative marketing research. *Journal of Marketing Research, 14,* 353–364.

Campbell, D. T. (1958). Common fate, similarity, and other indices of the status of aggregates of persons as social entities. *Behavioral Science, 3,* 14–25.

Campbell, D. T. (1969). Definitional versus multiple operationism. et al., *2,* 14–17.

Carter, L. F., Haythorn, W., Meirowitz, B., & Lanzetta, J. (1951). A note on a new technique of interaction recording. *Journal of Abnormal and Social Psychology, 46,* 258–260.

Cartwright, D., & Zander, A. (1968). *Group dynamics: Research and theory.* New York: Harper & Row.

Cattell, R. B. (1948). Concepts and methods in the measurement of group syntality. *Psychological Review, 55,* 48–63.

Coch, L., & French, J. R. (1948). Overcoming resistance to change. *Human Relations, 1,* 512–532.

Cohen, J., MacWhinney, B., Flatt, M., & Provost, J. (1993). PsyScope: An interactive graphic system for designing and controlling experiments in the psychology laboratory using Macintosh computers. *Behavior Research Methods, Instruments, & Computers, 25,* 257–271.

Chute, D. L. (1993). MacLaboratory for psychology: Successes, failures, economics, and outcomes over its decade of development. *Behavior Research Methods, Instruments, & Computers, 25,* 180–188.

Crano, W. D., & Aronoff, J. (1978). A cross-cultural study of expressive and instrumental role complementarity, in the family. *American Sociological Review, 43,* 463–471.

Dabbs, J. M., & Swiedler, T. C. (1983). Group AVTA: A microcomputer system for group voice chronography. *Behavior Research Methods and Instrumentation, 15,* 79–84.

Dalkey, N. C. (1968). *Experiments in group prediction.* Santa Monica, CA: Rand Corporation.

Dalkey, N. C. (1969–1970). *The Delphi method* (#s RM-5888-PR, RM-5957-PR, RM-6115-PR, RM-6118-PR). Santa Monica, CA: Rand Corporation.

Dalkey, N. C., & Rourke, D. L. (1971). *Experimental assessment of Delphi procedures with group value judgments.* Santa Monica, CA: Rand Corporation.

Davis, J. H., Kerr, N. L., Atkin, R., Holt, R., & Meek, D. (1975). The decision processes of 6- and 12-person mock juries assigned unanimous and 2/3 majority rules. *Journal of Personality and Social Psychology, 32,* 1–14.

Dawes, R. M., McTavish, J., & Shaklee, H. (1977). Behavior, communication, and assumptions about other people's behavior in a commons dilemma situation. *Journal of Personality and Social Psychology, 35,* 1–11.

Delbecq, A. L., & Van de Ven, A. H. (1971). A group process model for problem identification and program planning. *Journal of Applied Behavioral Science, 7,* 466–492.

Delbecq, A. L., Van de Ven, A. H., & Gustafson, D. H. (1975). *Group techniques for program planning.* Glenview, IL: Scott, Foresman.

Dennis, A. R., & Valacich, J. S. (1993). Computer brainstorms: More heads are better than one. *Journal of Applied Psychology, 78,* 531–537.

Deutsch, M., & Krauss, R. M. (1962). Studies of interpersonal bargaining. *Journal of Conflict Resolution, 6,* 52–76.

Diehl, M., & Stroebe, W. (1987). Productivity loss in brainstorming groups: Toward the solution of a riddle. *Journal of Personality and Social Psychology, 53,* 497–509.

Diener, E., Lusk, R., DeFour, D., & Flax, R. (1980). Deindividuation: Effects of group size, density, number of observers, and group member similarity on self-consciousness and disinhibited behavior. *Journal of Personality and Social Psychology, 39,* 449–459.

Ember, C. R., & Ember, M. (1988). *Guide to cross-cultural research using the HRAF archive.* New Haven, CT: Human Relations Area Files.

Ember, M. (1997). Evolution of the Human Relations Area Files. *Cross-Cultural Research, 31,* 3–15.

Festinger, L. (1957). *A theory of cognitive dissonance.* Evanston, IL: Row, Peterson.

Festinger, L., Reicken, H. W., & Back, K. (1956). *When prophesy fails.* Minneapolis: University of Minnesota Press.

Festinger, L., Schachter, S., & Back, K. (1950). *Social pressures in informal groups.* New York: Harper.

Forsyth, D. R. (1990). *Group dynamics* (2nd ed.). Pacific Grove, CA: Brooks/Cole.

Freedman, J. L., & Fraser, S. C. (1966). Compliance without pressure: The foot-in-the-door technique. *Journal of Personality and Social Psychology, 4,* 195–202.

Freedman, J. L., Klevansky, S., & Ehrlich, P. R. (1971). The effect of crowding on human task performance. *Journal of Applied Social Psychology, 1,* 7–25.

Gallupe, R. B., & Cooper, W. H. (1993, Fall). Brainstorming electronically. *Sloan Management Review,* 27–36.

Gilligan, C. (1982). *In a different voice.* Cambridge, MA: Harvard University Press.

Goldman, A. E. (1987). *The group depth interview: Principles and practice.* Englewood Cliffs, NJ: Prentice-Hall.

Greenbaum, T. (1993). *The handbook for focus group research* (2nd ed.). New York: Lexington Books.

Guetzkow, H. (1968). Differentiation of roles in task-oriented groups. In D. Cartwright & A. Zander (Eds.), *Group dynamics: Research and theory* (pp. 512–526). New York: Harper & Row.

Gustafson, D. H., Shukla, R. K., Delbecq, A., & Walster, G. W. (1973). A comparative study of differences in subjective likelihood estimates made by individuals, interacting groups, Delphi groups, and nominal groups. *Organizational Behavior and Human Decision Processes, 9,* 280–291.

Hare, A. P. (1976). *Handbook of small group research* (2nd ed.). New York: Free Press.

Haxby, J., Parasuraman, R., LaLonde, F., & Abboud, H. (1993). SuperLab: General-purpose Macintosh software for human experimental psychology and psychological testing. *Behavior Research Methods, Instruments, & Computers, 25,* 400–405.

Haythorn, W. (1953). The influence of individual members on the characteristics of small groups. *Journal of Abnormal and Social Psychology, 48,* 276–284.

Heider, F. (1958). *The psychology of interpersonal relations.* New York: Wiley.

Helmer, O. (1966). *The use of the Delphi technique in problems of educational innovations.* Santa Monica, CA: Rand Corporation.

Herschel, J. F. W. (1987). *A preliminary discourse on the study of natural philosophy.* Chicago: University of Chicago Press.

Hill, G. W. (1982). Group versus individual performance: Are n+1 heads better than one? *Psychological Bulletin, 91,* 517–539.

Hoffman, R., & MacDonald, J. (1993). Using HyperCard and Apple events in a network environment: Collecting data from simultaneous experimental sessions. *Behavior Research Methods, Instruments, & Computers, 25,* 114–126.

Hollingshead, A. B., McGrath, J. E., & O'Connor, K. M. (1993). Group task performance and communication technology: A longitudinal study of computer-mediated versus face-to-face work groups. *Small Group Research, 24,* 307–333.

Hornby, P. A., & Anderson, M. D. (1994). COMPsych: The electronic software information service and PC software archive for psychology. *Behavior Research Methods, Instruments, & Computers, 26,* 57–59.

Huff, C., & Sobiloff, B. (1993). MacPsych: An electronic discussion list and archive for psychology concerning the Macintosh computer. *Behavior Research Methods, Instruments, & Computers, 25,* 60–64.

Hunt, S. M. J. (1994). MacProbe: A Macintosh-based experimenter's workstation for the cognitive sciences. *Behavior Research Methods, Instruments, & Computers, 26,* 345–351.

Hutchins, D. (1985). *Quality circles handbook.* London: Pitman.

Hyman, H. H. (1978). *Interviewing in social research.* Chicago: University of Chicago Press.

Ingle, S. (1982). *Quality circles master guide.* Englewood Cliffs, NJ: Prentice-Hall.

Janis, I. (1982). *Groupthink: Psychological studies of policy decisions and fiascos* (2nd ed.). New York: Houghton-Mifflin.

Judd, C. M., & Park, B. (1988). Out-group homogeneity: Judgments of variability at the individual and group levels. *Journal of Personality and Social Psychology, 54,* 778–788.

Judd, C. M., Smith, E. R., & Kidder, L. H. (1991). *Research methods in social relations* (6th ed.). Fort Worth, TX: Harcourt, Brace, Jovanavich.

Kafer, N. F. (1976). A sociometric method for identifying group boundaries. *Journal of Experimental Education, 45,* 71–74.

Kelley, H. H., Condry, J. C., Dahlke, A., & Hill, A. (1965). Collective behavior in a simulated panic situation. *Journal of Experimental Social Psychology, 1,* 20–54.

Kerr, N. L., & MacCoun, R. (1985). Effects of jury size and polling method on the process and product of jury decision making. *Journal of Personality and Social Psychology, 48,* 349–363.

Kiesler, S. (1997). *Culture of the Internet.* Mahwah, NJ: Erlbaum.

Knoke, D., & Kuklinski, J. H. (1982). *Network analysis.* Beverly Hills, CA: Sage.

Komorita, S. S., & Chertkoff, J. M. (1973). A bargaining theory of coalition formation. *Psychological Review, 80,* 149–162.

Kravitz, D. A., & Martin, B. (1986). Ringelmann rediscovered: The original article. *Journal of Personality and Social Psychology, 50,* 936–941.

Latané, B., & Darley, J. M. (1970). *The unresponsive bystander: Why doesn't he help?* New York: Appleton-Century-Crofts.

Latané, B., & L'Herrou, T. (1996). Spatial clustering in the conformity game: Dynamic social impact in electronic groups. *Journal of Personality and Social Psychology, 70,* 1218–1230.

Latané, B., Williams, K. D., & Harkins, S. (1979). Many hands make light the work: The causes and consequences of social loafing. *Journal of Personality and Social Psychology, 37,* 822–832.

Laughlin, P. R. (1996). Group decision making and collective induction. In E. Witte & J. H. Davis (Eds.), *Understanding group behavior* (Vol 1., pp. 61–80). Mahwah, NJ: Erlbaum.

Laughlin, P. R., & Johnson, H. H. (1966). Groups and individual performance on a complementary task as a function of initial ability level. *Journal of Experimental Social Psychology, 2,* 407–414.

Leavitt, H. J. (1951). Some effects of certain communication patterns on group performance. *Journal of Abnormal and Social Psychology, 46,* 38–50.

Levin, M. L. (1976). Displaying sociometric structures: An application of interactive computer graphics for instruction and analysis. *Simulation and Games, 7,* 295–310.

Levine, J. M. (1978). GROUPCOM: A computer program for investigating social processes in small groups. *Behavior Research Methods, Instruments, & Computers, 10,* 191–195.

Levine, J. M., & Moreland, R. L. (1997). Small groups. In D. Gilbert, S. Fiske, & G. Lindzey (Eds.), *The handbook of social psychology* (4th ed.). Boston: McGraw-Hill.

Levinson, D., & Malone, M. J. (1980). *Toward explaining human culture.* New Haven, CT: HRAF Press.

Lewin, K. (1953). Studies in group decision. In D. Cartwright & A. Zander (Eds.), *Group dynamics: Research and theory.* Evanston, IL: Row, Peterson.

Lewin, K., Lippett, R., & White, R. (1939). Patterns of aggressive behavior in experimentally created "social climates." *Journal of Social Psychology, 10,* 271–299.

Li, J., Seu, J., Evens, M., Michael, J., & Rovick, A. (1992). Computer dialogue system (CDS): A system for capturing computer-mediated dialogue. *Behavior Research Methods, Instruments, & Computers, 24,* 535–540.

Liang, D. W., Moreland, R. L., & Argote, L. (1995). Group vs. individual training and group performance: The mediating factor of transactive memory. *Personality and Social Psychology Bulletin, 21,* 384–393.

Lindzey, G., & Borgatta, E. F. (1954). Sociometric measurement. In G. Lindzey (Ed.), *Handbook of social psychology* (pp. 405–448). Cambridge, MA: Addison-Wesley.

Linstone, H. A., & Turoff, M. (1975). *The Delphi method: Techniques and applications.* Reading, MA: Addison-Wesley.

Martino, J. P. (1983). *Technological forecasting for decision making* (2nd ed.). New York: North-Holland.

Mayo, E. (1933). *The human problems of an industrial civilization.* Cambridge, MA: Harvard University Press.

McGrath, J. E. (1984). *Groups: Interaction and performance.* Englewood Cliffs, NJ: Prentice-Hall.

McGrath, J. E., & Altman, I. (1966). *Small group research: A synthesis and critique of the field.* New York: Holt.

McGrath, J. E., & Hollingshead, A. B. (1994). *Groups interacting with technology.* Thousand Oaks, CA: Sage.

McGuire, T., Kiesler, S., & Siegel, S. (1987). Group and computer-mediated discussion effects in risk decision making. *Journal of Personality and Social Psychology, 52*, 917–930.

McGuire, W. (1983). Toward social psychology's second century. In S. Koch & D. E. Leary (Eds.), *A century of psychology as science* (pp. 558–590). New York: McGraw-Hill.

Messick, D. M., Wilke, H. A. M., Brewer, M. B., Kramer, R. M., Zemke, P. E., & Lui, J. (1983). Individual adaptations and structural change as solutions to social dilemmas. *Journal of Personality and Social Psychology, 44*, 294–309.

Milgram, S. (1969). The lost-letter technique. *Psychology Today, 3*, 30–33, 66–68.

Milgram, S. (1974). *Obedience to authority: An experimental view.* New York: Harper & Row.

Moreland, R. L. (1985). Social categorization and the assimilation of "new" group members. *Journal of Personality and Social Psychology, 48*, 1173–1190.

Moreland, R. L., Hogg, M. A., & Hains, S. C. (1994). Back to the future: Social psychological research on groups. *Journal of Experimental Social Psychology, 30*, 527–555.

Moreland, R. L., & Levine, J. M. (1982). Socialization in small groups: Temporal changes in individual-group relations. In L. Berkowitz (Ed.), *Advances in experimental social psychology* (Vol. 15, pp. 137–192). New York: Academic Press.

Moreno, J. L. (1953). *Who shall survive?* (Rev. ed.). Beacon, NY: Beacon House.

Mullen, B., Johnson, C., & Salas, E. (1991). Productivity loss in brainstorming groups: A meta-analytic integration. *Basic and Applied Social Psychology, 12*, 3–24.

Murdock, G. P., Ford, C. S., Hudson, A. E., Kennedy, R., Simmons, L. W., & Whiting, J. W. M. (1987). *Outline of cultural materials* (5th ed., rev.). New Haven, CT: Human Relations Area Files.

Newcomb, T. M. (1961). *The acquaintance process.* New York: Holt.

Noma, E., & Smith, D. R. (1978). SHED: A FORTRAN IV program for the analysis of small group sociometric structure. *Behavior Research Methods & Instrumentation, 10*, 60–62.

Northway, M. L. (1967). *A primer of sociometry* (2nd ed.). Toronto, Ontario, Canada: University of Toronto Press.

Olson, J. S., Olson, G., Storreston, M., & Carter, M. (1994). Groupwork close up: A comparison of the group design process with and without a simple group editor. *ACM Transactions on Information Systems, 11*, 321–348.

Osborn, A. F. (1957). *Applied imagination* (Rev. ed.). New York: Scribner.

Parson, T., & Bales, R. F. (1955). *Family, socialization and interaction process.* Glencoe, IL: Free Press.

Paulus, P. B., & Dzindolet, M. T. (1993). Social influence processes in group brainstorming. *Journal of Personality and Social Psychology, 64*, 575–586.

Philipsen, G., Mulac, A., & Dietrich, D. (1979). The effects of social interaction on group idea generation. *Communication Monographs, 46*, 119–125.

Rapoport, A. (1967). Optimal policies for the prisoner's dilemma game. *Psychological Review, 74*, 136–148.

Reis, H. T. (1983). The promise of naturalistic methods. *New Directions for Methodology of Social & Behavioral Science, 15*, 1–4.

Reis, H. T., & Stiller, J. (1992). Publication trends in *JPSP*: A three-decade review. *Personality and Social Psychology Bulletin, 18*, 465–472.

Roethlisberger, F. J., & Dickson, W. J. (1939). *Management and the worker.* Cambridge, MA: Harvard University Press.

Rohner, R. P. (1975). *They love me, they love me not.* New Haven, CT: The HRAF Press.

Ruback, R. B., Dabbs, J. M., & Hopper, C. H. (1984). The process of brainstorming: An analysis with individual and group vocal parameters. *Journal of Personality and Social Psychology, 47*, 558–567.

Runkle, P. & McGrath, J. E. (1972). *Research on human behavior: A systematic guide to method.* New York: Holt.

Sackman, H. (1975). *Delphi critique: Expert opinion, forecasting, and group process.* Lexington, MA: Lexington Books.

Sanderson, P. M. (1994). Handling complex real-world data with two cognitive engineering tools: COGENT and MacSHAPA. *Behavior Research Methods, Instruments, & Computers, 26*, 117–124.

Schachter, S. (1951). Deviation, rejection, and communication. *Journal of Abnormal and Social Psychology, 46*, 190–207.

Schachter, S. (1959). *The psychology of affiliation.* Stanford, CA: Stanford University Press.

Schachter, S., Ellertson, N., McBride, D., & Gregory, D. (1951). An experimental study of cohesiveness and productivity. *Human Relations, 4*, 229–238.

Schneider, W. (1988). Micro Experimental Laboratory: An integrated system for IBM PC compatibles. *Behavior Research Methods, Instruments, & Computers, 20*, 206–217.

Schneider, W. (1991). Equipment is cheap, but the field must develop and support common software for psychological research. *Behavior Research Methods, Instruments, & Computers, 23*, 114–116.

Scott, J. (1991). *Social network analysis: A handbook.* London: Sage.

Segal, M. W. (1979). Varieties of interpersonal attraction and their interrelationships in natural groups. *Social Psychology Quarterly, 42,* 253–261.

Sherif, M. (1936). *The psychology of social norms.* New York: Harper.

Sherif, M. (1951). A preliminary experimental study of inter-group relations. In J. H. Rohrer & M. Sherif (Eds.), *Social psychology at the crossroads* (pp. 388–424). New York: Harper.

Sherif, M. (1966). *In common predicament: Social psychology of intergroup conflict and cooperation.* New York: Houghton Mifflin.

Sherif, M., Harvey, O. J., White, B., Hood, W., & Sherif, C. (1961). *Intergroup conflict and cooperation.* Norman, OK: Institute of Group Relations.

Sherif, M., & Sherif, C. W. (1953). *Groups in harmony and tension.* New York: Harper.

Sherwin, R. G. (1975). Structural balance and the sociomatrix: Finding triadic valence structures in signed adjacency matrices. *Human Relations, 28,* 175–189.

Siegal, S., & Fouraker, L. E. (1960). *Bargaining and group decision making: Experiments in bilateral monopoly.* New York: McGraw-Hill.

Slater, P. E. (1955). Role differentiation in small groups. *American Sociological Review, 20,* 300–310.

Sommers, R. (1959). Studies in personal space. *Sociometry, 22,* 247–260.

Sproull, L., & Kiesler, S. B. (1991). *Connections: New ways of working in the networked organization.* Cambridge, MA: MIT Press.

Steel, R. P., & Shane, G. S. (1986). Evaluation research on quality circles: Technical and analytical implications. *Human Relations, 39,* 449–468.

Steiner, I. (1972). *Group process and productivity.* New York: Academic Press.

Steiner, I. (1974). Whatever happened to the group in social psychology? *Journal of Experimental Social Psychology, 10,* 94–108.

Steiner, I. (1986). Paradigms and groups. In L. Berkowitz (Ed.), *Advances in experimental social psychology* (Vol. 19, pp. 251–292). Orlando, FL: Academic Press.

Stephan, F. F., & Mishler, E. G. (1952). The distribution of participation in small groups: An exponential approximation. *American Sociological Review, 17,* 598–608.

Stroebe, W., & Diehl, M. (1994). Why groups are less effective than their members: On productivity losses in idea-generating groups. *European Review of Social Psychology, 5,* 271-303.

Stroebe, W., Diehl, M., & Abakoumkin, G. (1992). The illusion of group effectivity. *Personality and Social Psychology Bulletin, 18,* 643–650.

Tajfel, H., Billig, M., Bundy, R., & Flament, C. (1971). Social categorization and intergroup behavior. *European Journal of Social Psychology, 1,* 149–178.

Tapp, J., & Walden, T. (1993). PROCODER: A professional tape control, coding, and analysis system for behavioral research using videotape. *Behavior Research Methods, Instruments, & Computers, 25,* 53–56.

Triandis, H. C. (1995). *Individualism and collectivism.* Boulder, CO: Westview Press.

Triplett, N. (1898). The dynamogenic factors in pacemaking and competition. *American Journal of Psychology, 9,* 507–533.

Valacich, J. S., Dennis, A. R., & Connolly, T. (1994). Idea generation in computer-based groups: A new ending to an old story. *Organizational Behavior & Human Decision Processes, 57,* 448–467.

Van de Ven, A. H. (1974). *Group decision making and effectiveness: An experimental study.* Kent, OH: Kent State University Press.

Vaughan, J., & Yee, P. L. (1994). Using PsyScope for demonstrations and student-designed experiments in cognitive psychology courses. *Behavior Research Methods, Instruments, & Computers, 26,* 142–147.

Vaughn, S., Schumm, J. S., & Sinagub, J. (1996). *Focus group interviews in education and psychology.* Thousand Oaks, CA: Sage.

Wallack, M. A., Kogan, W., & Bem, D. J. (1962). Group influence in individual risk taking. *Journal of Abnormal and Social Psychology, 65,* 75–86.

Walster, E., Walster, G., & Bersheid, E. (1978). *Equity: Theory and research.* Boston: Allyn & Bacon.

Wasserman, S., & Faust, K. (1994). *Social network analysis: Methods and applications.* New York: Cambridge University Press.

Weber, A. L., & Harvey, J. H. (Eds.). (1994). *Perspectives on close relationships.* Boston: Allyn & Bacon.

Wegner, D. M., Erber, R., & Raymond, P. (1991). Transactive memory in close relationships. *Journal of Personality and Social Psychology, 61,* 923–929.

Weick, K. E. (1968). Systematic observational methods. In G. Lindzey & E. Aronson (Eds.), *The handbook of social psychology* (2nd ed., pp. 357–451). Reading, MA: Addison-Wesley.

Weick, K. E. (1985). Systematic observational methods. In G. Lindzey & E. Aronson (Eds.), *The handbook of social psychology* (3rd ed., pp. 567–634). New York: Random House.

Wellman, B., & Berkowitz, S. D. (1988). *Social structures: A network approach.* New York: Cambridge University Press.

Wheelan, S. A. (1994). *Group processes: A developmental perspective.* Boston: Allyn & Bacon.

Whitehead, T. N. (1938). *The industrial worker.* Cambridge, MA: Harvard University Press.

Whyte, W. F. (1943). *Street corner society.* Chicago: University of Chicago Press.

Williams, K. D., & Karau, S. J. (1991). Social loafing and social compensation: The effects of expectations of coworkers' performance. *Journal of Personality and Social Psychology, 61,* 570–581.

Wilson, J. P., Aronoff, J., & Messé, L. A. (1975). Social structure, member motivation, and productivity. *Journal of Personality and Social Psychology, 32,* 1094–1098.

Woike, B. A., & Aronoff, J. (1992). Antecedents of complex social cognitions. *Journal of Personality and Social Psychology, 63,* 97–104.

Wolfe, C. (1992). Using Authorware Professional for developing courseware. *Behavior Research Methods, Instruments, & Computers, 24*, 273–276.

Worchel, S., Coutant-Sassic, D., & Grossman, M. (1992). A developmental approach to group dynamics: A model and illustrative research. In S. Worchel, W. Wood, & J. A. Simpson (Eds.), *Group process and productivity* (pp. 181–202). Newbury Park, CA: Sage.

Zajonc, R. B. (1965). Social facilitation. *Science, 149*, 269–274.

Zander, A. (1985). *The purposes of groups and organizations.* San Francisco: Jossey-Bass.

CHAPTER EIGHT

Event-Sampling and Other Methods for Studying Everyday Experience

HARRY T. REIS AND SHELLY L. GABLE

With increasing frequency social and personality psychologists are relying on a research strategy known by the generic name, *everyday experience methods*. This designation refers not to a specific instrument or procedure but rather to a paradigm for studying social processes by examining ongoing experience as it occurs in the ebb and flow of everyday life. "Everyday experience" offers more than yet another methodological alternative; the focus on everyday activity allows researchers to evaluate theoretical models and other hypotheses from a perspective that differs fundamentally from traditional social psychological methods. The payoff is a detailed, accurate, and multifaceted portrait of social behavior embedded in its natural context.

Under the heading of "everyday experience methods" we compile diverse procedures and measures. Some protocols involve daily reports of mood or behavior for periods as short as 1 week, or as long as several months. Others ask participants to relate their thoughts, feelings, or activities when signaled at random moments throughout the day, or to describe selected events (e.g., social interaction, lies, cigarette smoking) whenever they occur. There are many different techniques by which researchers can study daily experience. What they share is an appreciation for the complexity, richness, and informativeness of ordinary activity.

For exceptionally helpful comments on earlier drafts of this chapter, we are grateful to William Graziano and Charles Judd. We are also indebted to Ladd Wheeler, John Nezlek, Philippe Delespaul, and Marten deVries for their contributions over many years to our thinking about everyday experience research. Correspondence should be directed to Harry T. Reis, Department of Clinical and Social Sciences in Psychology, University of Rochester, Rochester, NY 14627 (e-mail: reis@scp.rochester.edu).

Everyday experience methods are designed to provide detailed descriptions of specific moments or events in a person's life, from which researchers can extract information about "the persistence, cyclicity, change, and temporal structure of thought, emotion, and behavior" (Tennen, Suls, & Affleck, 1991, p. 333), as well as identifying situational and dispositional correlates of these patterns. In general terms, we conceive of these methods as a tool for "structured contemporaneous self-observation," by which we mean that participants are asked to monitor and describe ongoing activity according to schedules and formats defined and regulated by the investigator. As such, the method is akin to unobtrusively following participants through their day, observing and questionning them at relevant points. Through fixed-format and open-ended items, everyday experience data sets may include both relatively objective information (e.g., number of social contacts) as well as subjective descriptions of constructs that are intrinsically impressionistic or that reflect mental processes (e.g., mood, sense of self-worth).

To some extent, the rationale for everyday experience methods is methodological: Descriptions of current feelings and activities minimize, and often eliminate, retrospection bias. Moreover, because data are provided moment-by-moment, day-by-day, or event-by-event, distortions inherent in asking individuals to recall and summarize many events varying in recency and memorability (a documented shortcoming of global self-reports; Schwarz & Sudman, 1996) are precluded. The added benefits of relying on observations that aggregate across multiple occasions and settings are well-known (Epstein, 1979).

Everyday experience studies have the further advantage of examining behavior within its natural, spontaneous context. As Asch (1952) taught social psychologists many years ago, perception and action in the social world are determined by the situational context of behavior: "Most social acts have to be understood in their setting, and lose meaning if isolated. No error in thinking about social facts is more serious than the failure to see their place and function" (p. 61). Although social psychology rightly celebrates itself as the science of situations, often we fail to consider fully the extent to which our phenomena depend on the contexts in which we study them. McAdams (1995) made a similar point about personality psychology: "There is no particular reason that the language of nonconditional and decontextualized dispositions should work well to describe constructs that are situated in time, place, and role" (p. 379). Everyday experience studies permit researchers not only to understand the relevance of social processes within everyday, self-selected situations but also to characterize those contexts in some detail.

The advantages of the everyday experience approach to social psychology go beyond methodology. As elaborated later, these methods allow one to acquire knowledge not easily obtained with other techniques. For example, everyday experience studies may help establish the real-world prevalence and impact of particular processes and phenomena; may identify situational contexts in which effects are more or less likely to occur; may determine boundary conditions necessary or sufficient for the operation of basic processes; may isolate patterns of cyclicity and covariation among social, cognitive, emotional, and psychophysiological variables; and may clarify interactions with other, naturally occurring processes. In other words, the procedures we present in this chapter complement standard research strategies conceptually and methodologically. We believe that the next generation of established social psychological principles will have greater validity, comprehensiveness, and applicability if researchers add everyday experience methods to their toolbox.

In this chapter we describe everyday experience methods from both conceptual and practical vantage points. We begin with a conceptual rationale, covering the paradigm's special perspective on social behavior and its contribution to social psychological methodology. Beyond methodology, we show how everyday experience methods offer a unique conceptual window on a phenomenon or theory. We then review several specific protocols relevant to research in social and personality psychology. The two subsequent sections address practical matters arising in everyday experience research and special statistical techniques for capitalizing on the extensive data sets typically obtained.

Finally, we consider the role of everyday experience studies to complement other methods in programmatic research. Our goal is to make readers aware of the potential benefits of everyday experience methods and to provide a practical guide for incorporating them into a research program.

THEORETICAL CONSIDERATIONS IN EVERYDAY EXPERIENCE METHODOLOGY

Research Aims

Everyday experience studies have three general purposes: establishing the prevalence and/or qualities of phenomena, testing theoretically generated hypotheses and propositions, and serving as a "discovery" technique.

Diary data are commonly used for tallying and describing particular phenomena or constructs. The frequency of given events in everyday life, such as social interaction or exercise, may be estimated from reports of each occurrence, whereas their qualities can be characterized from detailed descriptions contained in each report. Protocols based on sampling units of time, with either random or fixed schedules, yield estimates of the frequency and pattern of given activities. When recording immediately follows the events being described, retrospection biases are greatly diminished, resulting in highly accurate accounts, at least from the respondent's point of view.

Here are a few examples. Wheeler and Nezlek (1977) used social interaction diaries, one for each interaction lasting 10 min or longer, to characterize college students' socializing along several dimensions, including frequency, distribution across partners, intimacy, and satisfaction. Diener, Larsen, Levine, and Emmons (1985) examined the relative frequency of high- and low-intensity emotional states with daily mood reports. Robinson and Godbey (1997) used daily time logs to describe allocation of time among various obligatory and leisure activities. Adolescent emotional states, and how they vary across settings such as school and home, were studied by Csikszentmihalyi and Larson (1984) with a random time-sampling protocol. Leigh (1993) kept track of alcohol consumption and sexual activity with records completed at the end of every day.

Beyond their inherent interest value, accurate and detailed descriptive data are essential for theory development. "Before we inquire into origins and functional relations, it is necessary to know the thing we are trying to explain" (Asch, 1952, p. 65). Kelley (1997) noted that to develop comprehensive and useful theories, "we need to know more than what are all the possible variations in situations, persons, and interaction. We must also know what the frequent and important variations are" (p. 166). Similarly, McClelland argued that behavioral frequencies may be the best place for personality theorists to begin (McClelland, 1957). Finally, coming from a background in ethology, Hinde (1995) discussed the importance of descriptive observation in identifying regularities and generating an ordered set of explanatory principles. The biological and physical sciences, after all, began with detailed, systematic descriptions of phenomena. For many topics in social–personality psychology, including some for which elegant conceptual models have become standard lore, theoretical refinements may have outpaced basic description. To carve nature at its joints, one must first locate those joints.

Everyday experience data may also be used to test theoretically derived hypotheses. In some cases, time- or event-sampled data are indispensable – for example, hypotheses about cyclicity and variability of emotional states over time (Larsen, 1987; Larsen & Kasimatis, 1990) or about reactions to stressful events (Stone & Neale, 1984). In other instances, by evaluating in natural contexts hypotheses also tested with other methods, daily experience studies contribute to the generalizability of a research program (Brewer, this volume, Ch. 1).

Hypothesis tests conducted with daily experience data may serve any of the functions routine in social psychological theory-building. For example:

1. *Comparing competing predictions.* Wheeler and Miyake (1992) used a social comparison diary to contrast self-enhancement, which predicts downward comparison following negative mood, with cognitive priming, which expects upward comparison. Upward comparison was supported.
2. *Identifying conditions under which processes operate.* Pietromonaco and Feldman-Barrett (1997) showed that the affective consequences of attachment dispositions are most evident during conflict and other anxiety-provoking interactions, as predicted by attachment theory.
3. *Evaluating alternative explanations for a phenomenon.* Bolger and Schilling (1991) compared three explanations for the observed correlation between trait neuroticism and distress. Best supported was the predisposition of persons high in neuroticism to react more strongly to stress.
4. *Unconfounding within-person processes from individual differences.* Reis, Sheldon, Gable, Roscoe, and Ryan (in press) showed that satisfaction of autonomy, competence, and relatedness needs in everyday activity was associated with greater well-being, over and above the impact of individual differences.
5. *Establishing phenomena outside the laboratory context.* As previously shown with laboratory groups of unacquainted individuals, Pemberton, Insko, and Schopler (1996) found that intergroup relations in everyday life are more competitive than are interpersonal relations.

In short, there is no reason why theoretical propositions cannot be evaluated with everyday experience data, much as they are traditionally tested in laboratory experiments. Of course, causal inference requires experimental manipulation and random assignment, conditions rarely achieved in naturalistic contexts. However, everyday experience methods are meant to complement, not substitute for, experimentation. Establishing a theory's validity, scope, and importance demands more than simply demonstrating that predictable effects can be evoked under controlled laboratory conditions (Brewer, this volume, Ch. 1; E. Smith, this volume, Ch. 2). Although laboratory research is best suited for establishing cause and effect, everyday experience studies indicate whether the same effect occurs under voluntary, self-determined conditions, when additional, perhaps unexpected, factors may come into play. Moreover, the advent of sophisticated procedures for evaluating causal models and propositions (e.g., sequential analysis, structural equation modeling), discussed below and elsewhere in this volume (Bakeman, Ch. 6; Wegener & Fabrigar, Ch. 16), makes everyday experience research increasingly useful for theory-building.

Finally, everyday experience methods sometimes play a serendipitous role. McGuire (1997) noted that the task of generating creative hypotheses is perhaps the most difficult and poorly understood step in the research process. Among many strategies he recommends are several techniques for sensitively observing natural occurrences. By assembling large data sets with multiple predictor, outcome, and moderator variables, diary studies lend themselves to exploration and the possibility of theory-advancing insights. Hypotheses so generated can be tested in subsequent studies. For example, Reis, Nezlek, and Wheeler (1980) found that facial attractiveness was more strongly correlated with the quantity and quality of men's than women's social participation. L. A. Clark and Watson (1988) found that high negative and low positive mood were associated with physical illness, whereas only negative affect had previously been linked with illness in between-subjects analyses. In both examples, later studies confirmed the effect.

To sum up, everyday experience methods are equally adept at description and hypothesis testing. Their main advantage is enhanced ecological validity, an important criterion that often receives short shrift in social and personality psychology (but see Brewer, this volume, Ch. 1). Because phenomena are assessed within natural social contexts, artifacts attributable to setting or other incidental aspects of the research process are greatly reduced (Stone & Shiffman, 1994). Although maximum internal validity is sacrificed, the emphasis on contemporaneous reports repeated over time and context minimizes retrospection and other forms of self-report bias, making the loss of construct validity significantly less than with other nonexperimental methods.

Conceptualizing Everyday Experience

DOMAINS OF EXPERIENCE. Although researchers often choose their tools for methodological and practical reasons, paradigms also reflect conceptual distinctions. Reis (1994) described three complementary domains of inquiry, each scrutinizing the same phenomena and processes from a distinct perspective. Research programs that incorporate all three perspectives are likely to be most informative.

The first perspective, termed *exemplary experience*, consists of studies in which behavior is observed in specific, restricted, or otherwise special settings. Included are laboratory experiments, in which behavior is observed under controlled conditions, and observational studies, which are carried out in uniform, often intrinsically relevant settings, such as playgrounds, worksites, and living rooms. Behavior displayed in these settings may be exemplary in two ways, corresponding to definitions as either "commendable; worthy of being imitated" or as "serving as an illustration; typical" (American Heritage Dictionary, 1976). Regarding the first definition, participants aware of being monitored may exhibit optimal rather than typical performance (Ickes & Tooke, 1988). Well-known processes such as impression management, social desirability, demand characteristics, politeness, evaluation apprehension, and the desire to be helpful or agreeable, may impel behavior that would differ away from the scrutiny of experimenters. Thus, in the lab, a bully might react calmly to a confederate's provocation, knowing that his responses were being recorded.

Particular settings may induce optimal behavior even when participants are unaware or unconcerned about being observed. Many contexts, notably including research laboratories, elicit polite, formal, cooperative, or thoughtful behavior that departs from behavior displayed in everyday settings. Marital interaction observed in the laboratory may differ from marital interaction at home (Larson, Richards, & Perry-Jenkins, 1994); for example, in the laboratory, participants rarely turn on the television when asked to self-disclose or carry out an unpleasant task. Situational cues provided by research laboratories have not been studied extensively, although it seems clear that expectations, moods, goals, and action scripts may be primed, affecting thought and behavior in both intentional and unintentional ways.

Exemplary in the sense of typicality refers to the assumption, inherent in laboratory work, that participants' reactions typify their natural responses to the conditions recreated in the lab. However, the cardinal rule of experimentation – carefully controlled context – necessarily constrains the range of possible behavior. Social judgment studies, for example, usually do not allow participants to change the topic, qualify their answers, or simply say nothing, as people so often do in real life. Seasoned experimenters know that slight changes in context sometimes beget large changes in behavior. To be sure, careful control of the context gives experimentation its extraordinary power for validating causal propositions. However, the contextual background customarily receives far less attention than does the manipulation and outcome, even though that background may involve influential boundary conditions (i.e., moderators).

In short, although there are valid and important reasons for studying behavior in exemplary contexts, knowledge garnered from such investigations may be limited. A controlled context, although adding precision to observations, "inevitably fails to incorporate the broader pattern of behaviors and contexts that make up daily life" (Funder, 1991, p. 36). Such findings are therefore likely to be enhanced by complementary insights from other approaches.

The second perspective, also familiar in social psychology, is *reconstructed experience*. Herein, researchers seek to characterize phenomena from the participant's own perspective, as he or she perceives them, past, present, or hypothetical. Participants are typically asked to evaluate, summarize, or otherwise describe in questionnaire or interview format their experiences with specific entities or in particular situations. Self-generated global assessments, a valuable source of information about perceptions, often differ from on-line experience (Kahneman, Fredrickson, Schreiber, & Redelmeier, 1993), due to the many processes that influence encoding, storage, retrieval, and evaluation of episodic memories (discussed below and by Visser, Krosnick, & Lavrikas this volume, Ch. 9). Beyond limits in our ability to recall and summarize past experiences, even spanning relatively brief intervals, motivated processes such as cognitive efficiency and self-esteem maintenance commonly transform event-by-event or moment-by-moment memories. Responses to global questions are therefore better considered as reconstructions and interpretations of personal experience than as direct accounts of that experience.

Comparison of contemporaneous and reconstructed evaluations of the same experience may illuminate these processes. In some cases, as in Stone et al.'s (1998) comparison of momentary and every-2-days retrospections about coping, there is little or no correspondence.[1] In other cases, divergences highlight processes of interest. Redelmeier and Kahneman (1996) showed that recall of pain from unpleasant medical procedures was based primarily on the most intense level of pain experienced and the most recent, or end, level (termed the "peak-end" rule). Reconstructed impressions also may reflect implicit theories about events rather than recall of actual content (Ross, 1989) or may bolster current beliefs. For example, in a 4-year longitudinal study, Sprecher (1999) found that although yearly ratings of love in successful relationships were stable, spouses supported the belief that love had grown over time by lowering recollections of prior love.

How episodic or momentary information contributes to general impressions represents an important substantive question applicable to many social psychological topics (Carlston & Smith, 1996). How, for example, do repeated interactions with a partner, some very intimate and others more mundane, evolve into impressions of a relationship (Duck & Sants, 1983; Hinde, 1995)? How do momentary moods contribute to global feelings of life satisfaction or dissatisfaction (Diener, 1996)? To understand reconstructions as the product of cognitive and self-serving transformations enacted on actual experience, it is useful to investigate the transformational process directly, by comparing global

impressions with data from the third domain, that of ongoing experience.

The domain of *ongoing experience* focuses on direct, usually immediate reports of everyday experience. Verifying causal antecedents with maximum internal validity is generally not the overriding concern; rather, these studies are designed to examine specific processes or phenomena within the stream of routine, voluntary activity. With suitable analysis, they permit specification of contexts in which target behaviors do and do not occur, they identify natural patterns of variation in target behaviors and covariation with predictors and spontaneous consequences, and they document the prevalence and nature of phenomena.

What type of research fits this category? Generally, these studies share an interest in the ongoing, often mundane moments and occurrences of everyday life. They are concerned with the diverse feelings, thoughts, and activities that occur spontaneously, filling people's waking time and occupying most of their conscious thoughts and attention. Daily life events have a structure and rhythm of their own. Sometimes they are variable and fleeting; at other times they are stable and continuous. Some are vivid and arousing, others are dull and inconsequential. The central assumption behind this approach is that these experiences are important, and that when examined carefully, may provide useful insights about human behavior.

For example, many studies have examined patterns and correlates of day-to-day and within-day variations in mood (e.g., L. A. Clark & Watson, 1988; David, Green, Martin, & Suls, 1997). Other studies have looked at cognitive activity and motivation among high school students (e.g., Moneta & Csikszentmihalyi, 1996) and psychiatric patients (Delespaul, 1995) by randomly sampled momentary reports. DePaulo, Kashy, Kirkendol, Wyer, and Epstein (1996) had participants keep daily logs of their lies, whereas Wheeler and Miyake's (1992) participants completed a record whenever social comparisons occurred. The Rochester Interaction Record (RIR; Reis & Wheeler, 1991) obtains detailed descriptions of all social interactions lasting 10 min or longer, and has been applied to studies of social involvement, relationships, and intergroup relations. Momentary or daily reports are commonly used to identify determinants and health consequences of coping and stress (e.g., Bolger, DeLongis, Kessler, & Schilling, 1989; Repetti, 1989; Stone et al., 1998). Fluctuations in self-concept and self-focused attention have also been studied (Campbell, Chew, & Scratchley, 1991; Hormuth, 1990;

---

[1] Note that here and elsewhere we refer to retrospections about events in one's relatively recent, adult experience. The limitations of retrospection for recalling early life experience are even greater (Brewin, Andrews, & Gotlib, 1993). Henry, Moffitt, Caspi, Langley, and Silva (1994) correlated retrospections of adolescents at age 18 with data collected prospectively since their birth. Correlations varied markedly as a function of timespan and content; for variables such as family conflict and maternal mental health, they were generally very small ($rs < .20$).

Kernis, Cornell, Sun, Berry, & Harlow, 1993). Additional examples are provided below.

Our discussion of domains assumes that each perspective offers a different but no less valuable perspective on the same process or phenomena. Studies of exemplary experience are informative about behavior in particular, well-specified contexts and help establish the causal impact of those contexts. Studies of reconstructed experienced tell us how people understand their lives and activities. Studies of everyday experience provide information about thoughts, feelings, and activities that occur in natural settings. Irrespective of methodological considerations, important conceptual benefits arise from including all three domains in a research program.

MAJOR VERSUS MINOR EVENTS. Longstanding interest in major life events, such as marriage, bereavement, and employment changes, has revealed important associations with mood, health, and social activity, for example (Kessler, 1997). Other, more recent studies have explored the impact of minor, or mundane, daily events on the same general outcomes, based on the assumption that ordinary evenings spent in quiet conversation with a partner or irritating days at work may also have important consequences, especially when recurrent. Enduring patterns of emotion or interaction may matter in the long run, even if any single episode is negligible – habitual types of communication between spouses, ongoing differential treatment by teachers or employers, or chronic styles of social cognition, for example.

That daily hassles influence health and well-being has been shown in several studies (e.g., DeLongis, Folkman, & Lazarus, 1988; Stone, Neale, & Shiffman, 1993). Mundane daily events, such as helping a friend move or riding on a crowded bus, relate to daily mood and symptoms, even after controlling for major life events (L. A. Clark & Watson, 1988). Although the effects of major events are undeniable, their significance may be limited by infrequency and because their impact tends to subside over time. Suh, Diener, and Fujita (1996) found that only life events during the past 3 months mattered for emotional well-being, a finding consistent with studies of adaptation to major traumas (Wortman & Silver, 1989). In contrast, mundane events occur far more often: The vast majority of affects experienced in everyday life are low intensity (Diener et al., 1985), and the vast majority of interactions are routine and superficial, even in very intimate relationships (Hays, 1989). Their impact is therefore more likely to be evident in more or less continuous patterns.

The study of minor life events and states lends itself well to the daily experience approach. By definition mundane, these events tend to be unmemorable, rendering retrospective methods problematic. Moreover, people have difficulty perceiving regularities or cyclical variations within a series of relatively inaccessible events, so that global descriptions may be misleading. In contrast, repeated, contemporaneous reports of even the most forgettable feelings or events allow researchers to identify whatever meaningful patterns may exist and whatever consequences there may be.

Everyday experience studies may also reveal repercussions of major events. For example, Caspi, Bolger, and Eckenrode (1987) suggested that some life events, such as divorce or spousal loss, have greatest impact by disrupting everyday routines and altering ongoing mood and thought. Retrospective impressions of these changes may elicit naive theories about the presumptive impact of transitional events rather than objective accounts (Ross, 1989). On the other hand, their actual impact can be established with diary records, in either longitudinal or cross-sectional designs.

DISTINGUISHING BETWEEN-PERSON AND WITHIN-PERSON EFFECTS. Whereas most researchers are aware of the need to differentiate between-person and within-person effects for statistical reasons, the conceptual distinction is often overlooked. Consider the following hypothetical studies of trust and self-disclosure. In Study 1, 100 participants are asked how much they trust their best friend. Self-disclosure is also rated, yielding a correlation of .50. Participants in Study 2 are asked to rate trust and self-disclosure for each of 10 different friends and acquaintances. Correlations between trust and self-disclosure are computed for each participant across their 10 ratings, and then averaged across all participants. The resulting correlation is also .50. Do these two correlations document the same phenomenon?

No. The first correlation indicates that people high in trust (particularly with best friends) also tend to be high in self-disclosure. Several explanations are possible, prominent among them the dispositional alternative, which is that trait predispositions to be trusting also incline people to high self-disclosure. The second correlation shows that the more one trusts a particular other, the more self-disclosing one is with that person. Because the correlations are computed within-person, dispositional explanations are irrelevant, supporting an interpretation that trust and self-disclosure covary as a function of relationship qualities.

Conceptually, it is easy to see why these levels of explanation are independent. Correlations computed between-persons address dispositional effects, that is, whether persons scoring high on one variable tend to score similarly high on another variable. When the research question involves dispositional processes, this design is appropriate, but when covariation across conditions, circumstances, or occasions is of interest, within-person correlations that rule out dispositional explanations are more suitable. Methods for studying within-person processes are not as well-known as between-person methods are, so within-person processes are sometimes investigated (erroneously) in between-person designs (Gable & Reis, in press).

Two examples highlight implications of this distinction. Epstein (1982) found a positive correlation between daily reports of sadness and anger, suggesting that people predisposed to experience one emotion were also more likely to experience the other emotion. On the other hand, the average within-person correlation for the same variables was negative, indicating that individuals were less likely to feel anger on days they felt sad. (Of course, both findings are readily integrated theoretically.) Second, in between-person analyses Emmons (1991) found no significant difference in the extent to which personal strivings moderated reactivity to different daily events, but within-person analyses indicated that achievement-oriented participants were more reactive to good achievement events, whereas affiliation-oriented participants were more affected by interpersonal events.

Methodological Considerations and Self-Reports

Most survey researchers agree that cognitive and motivational processes tend to bias responses to global questions. Consider questions like, "All things considered, how satisfying are your interactions with friends?" or "How stressed have you felt during the past week?" Respondents must retrieve from memory the full set of qualifying events, selecting among them the most relevant subset. Features germane to satisfaction or stress must then be remembered, rated, and combined with some sort of decision rule into an overall impression. Of course, no one carries out this exercise. Instead, cognitive shortcuts allow people to respond quickly and efficiently, albeit with varying accuracy (Ajzen, 1996; Carlston & Smith, 1996; Fiske & Taylor, 1991). It is not surprising, therefore, that recollection is often flawed.

Wentland (1993) meta-analyzed studies that used objective criteria to evaluate the accuracy of self-reports. (Attitudes, feelings, and impressions were excluded because they cannot be verified independently.) Across a diverse list of both sensitive and nonthreatening behaviors, accuracy ranged from 23% to 100%. The main factor influencing accuracy was information accessibility, operationally defined with specific variables, such as length of recall period, event salience, and question and response clarity. Wentland's analysis, which is consistent with other analyses of self-report bias (e.g., Schwarz & Sudman, 1996), suggested that concrete, specific questions close in time to the event tend to be least inaccurate. It seems likely that the accuracy of subjective variables, of equal or greater prominence in social psychology, would follow the same principles.

Although much inaccuracy is probably random, systematic errors have dominated the field's attention (Schwarz, Groves, & Schuman, 1998), with reconstruction often described as a heuristic-driven process. Among the more important heuristics for social psychological research are the following:

- *Recency*. The more recent the event, the better it is recalled and the more likely it is to influence retrospection. For example, Bernard, Killworth, Kronenfeld, and Sailer (1984) reported a series of experiments examining informant accuracy in recalling social network or communication contacts. Overall, fewer than half were remembered correctly, but more recent events were recalled better than less recent events. Even memory for relatively distinctive events degrades daily, for up to 2 months, between the event and its recall (Skowronski, Betz, Thompson, & Shannon, 1991). Also, end-of-day summaries of mood are sensitive to recent occurrences (e.g., Stone et al., 1993), consistent with Kahneman et al.'s (1993) peak-end rule.
- *Salience*. More distinctive events, in terms of intensity, emotionality, unusualness, or personal significance, tend to be more influential. For example, summary ratings of daily or weekly emotion reflect moments of peak intensity more than they reflect average levels (Parkinson, Briner, Reynolds, & Totterdell, 1995; Thomas & Diener, 1990). Similarly, general impressions of relationships follow from salient emotional interactions better than from representative events (Pietromonaco & Feldman-Barrrett, 1997).
- *Sense-making*. Events tend to be reinterpreted in light of later developments or to confirm implicit theories

and beliefs (Ross, 1989). For example, women's recollections about menstrual symptoms during a 4–6 week span better resembled their general beliefs about such symptoms than their daily symptom reports (McFarland, Ross, & DeCourville, 1989).

• *State of mind.* Retrospections, especially of affect and attitude, may reflect mood at the time of report (Blaney, 1986). For example, global summaries of mood over various intervals tend to resemble current mood (Parkinson et al., 1995; Stone et al., 1993), perhaps through availability biases. Similarly, certain motives and perceptions are assessed more accurately when relevant states of mind are activated (McClelland, Koestner, & Weinberger, 1989), for example, ratings of perceived social support following emotional arousal (M. S. Clark & Brissette, in press).

These and related biases are the prime rationale for event-sampling methods that require instantaneous reports (Stone, Shiffman, & DeVries, 1999). Note that all of the sampling schemes discussed below may involve instantaneous reports. Momentary reports are by definition more accurate, although not necessarily more important, than recollections, which may relate better to certain outcomes. Comparisons of event-sampled and retrospective data may be helpful in keeping this critical distinction clear.

DIARY DATA AS SELF-REPORTS. Some researchers propose event-sampling as a method of correcting the oft-noted shortcomings of self-report. Others, however, criticize diary data because they are still, after all, self-reports. Although this is of course correct, event-sampling differs from global recollections and evaluations in the key respect of focusing on momentary, and usually contemporaneous, accounts. The presumption, then, is that this strategy obviates or at least minimizes many of the specific biases that plague global self-reports.

Support for this premise is found in several sources. Survey research has found that decompositional approaches, which ask circumscribed questions about the smallest possible units, are superior to open-ended, global questions, which invite heuristic processing (Menon, 1997). Similarly, observer ratings tend to be more accurate the less global and the more concrete they are, and the more they focus on discrete behaviors rather than general impressions (Bakeman, this volume, Ch. 6; Ritter & Langlois, 1988), a principle that probably generalizes to self-report. In this regard, Penner, Shiffman, Paty, and Fritzsche (1994) showed

that within-person estimates of mood variability across diary reports were free of response-bias artifacts. The advantages of a componential approach to assessment dovetail with the benefits of aggregation across time or situations, either by computation of composites or from covariation analysis. Aggregated data generally identify stable patterns of behavior better than do data from single situations or assessments, which may be influenced by atypical or random factors (Epstein, 1982).

Verifying the advantages of event-sampling approaches is complicated by the difficulty of defining appropriate criteria. Criteria that are themselves global representations (e.g., subjective well-being or school achievement) may relate better to other global variables due to shared method variance. One way to assess the relative accuracy of different methods relies on comparison of independent observations. For example, Conrath, Higgins, and McClean (1983) asked participants to keep track of 100 interactions with coworkers. Concurrence between two individuals that an interaction had taken place was nearly twice as great with diaries than with a global "communications" questionnaire. Reis and Wheeler (1991) reported several studies showing high correspondence between roommates in reporting that an interaction had taken place. As for more subjective variables, earlier we discussed evidence that event-sampled data are substantially less influenced by self-report biases than are global self-reports. Independent verification of subjective variables is more problematic, because disagreement may denote differences of opinion or perspective rather than inaccuracy. Reis, Senchak, and Solomon (1985) found that participants' RIR ratings of intimacy for a single interaction were highly correlated with judgments by independent observers, however.

To be sure, event-sampled data are self-reports, and as such are not distortion-free. Nevertheless, it seems clear that event-sampling protocols characterize ongoing experience with substantially greater accuracy than do global self-reports. Self-reports are unlikely to disappear anytime soon from social psychological research, if only because many important phenomena depend on the individual's interpretation of his or her circumstances (and also because they are occasionally more accurate than archival data; Elander, West, & French, 1993). As Kagan (1984) said, "The child's personal interpretation of experience, not the event recorded by camera or observer, is the essential basis for the formation of and change in . . . beliefs, wishes, and actions" (p. 241). Moreover, many phenomena would be impractical, if not impossible, to study otherwise.

Event-sampling offers a substantial improvement in our methods for obtaining self-reports.

TYPES OF EVERYDAY EXPERIENCE PROTOCOLS

In this section we describe three general protocols for everyday experience studies, a typology proposed by Wheeler and Reis (1991). The three models differ primarily in the sampling frame used to obtain data. These distinctions are not merely procedural details; each protocol is tailored to fit particular operational circumstances and theoretical goals, and findings depend to some extent on the choice of method. After presenting the typology, we provide guidelines for choosing among them.

Interval-contingent Recording

With this method, sometimes called *time-contingent recording*, participants report their experiences at regular, predetermined intervals. Typically, these intervals represent theoretically or logically meaningful units of time, such as the end of each day or every 4 (waking) hours. Interval-contingent reports are commonly used in two ways: to describe events that have transpired since the previous report or to depict behavior at the moment of recording. Either way, it is important to space intervals reasonably. If the range is too great, natural cycles (e.g., diurnal rhythms) may be obscured, or important intervening events may be excluded. If the span is too short, the signal-to-noise ratio may be too small, and the burden on participants may be excessive. Reactivity may also become a problem.

By far the most common interval sampling unit is the day. A good example is the National Study of Daily Experiences (Almeida, 1997), in which a national sample of 1,484 adults completed telephone interviews about their daily experiences on eight consecutive evenings. Other examples include daily reports for periods of up to 3 months for mood and events (L. A. Clark & Watson, 1988); conflicts, coping, and distress (Bolger & Zuckerman, 1995); lies (DePaulo et al., 1996); time allocation across activities (Robinson & Godbey, 1997); health maintenance practices and symptoms (Lawrence & Schank, 1995); need satisfaction (Reis et al., in press); motives (Woike, 1995); and self-focussed attention and coping (Wood, Saltzberg, Neale, Stone, & Rachmiel, 1990). The value of once-daily recording is consistent both with intuition and empirical evidence that sleep-and-awakening provides a discrete break in biological and psychological cycles (Williams, Suls, Alliger, Learner, & Wan, 1991).

Other fixed intervals used in social psychological research include self-esteem ratings twice a day, at 10 a.m. and 10 p.m. (Kernis et al., 1993); physical symptoms described at noon, dinnertime, and bedtime (Larsen & Kasimatis, 1991); mood ratings at 9 a.m., 1 p.m., 4 p.m., and 7 p.m. (Hedges, Jansdorf, & Stone, 1985); and mood and activity ratings every 15 min for 1 day (Stone, Smyth, Pickering, & Schwartz, 1996). Although intervals are often chosen by intuition or for convenience, spectral analysis can recognize repetitive cycles in states or behaviors, which in turn may help researchers select optimally spaced intervals (Larsen, 1990). For example, a weekly mood cycle is well-documented, peaking on weekends (Larsen & Kasimatis, 1991).

Signal-contingent Recording

With signal-contingent reports, participants describe current activity when signals are delivered, most often by pagers, programmable wristwatches, or handheld computers. Signals may follow fixed or random schedules, or a combination of the two (random within predetermined blocks, such as every 2 hours). If schedules are random (or at least unrelated to participants' activities) and if participants comply with instructions to respond immediately, signal-contingent data may be used to estimate the prevalence and distribution of activities and states over time. Signals that are regular, predictable, or open to the respondent's discretion may produce unrepresentative data because of self-selection or regularities in activities or states of mind. Randomness is also desirable so that participants cannot modify their activities in anticipation of a signal.

The original and best-known example of signal-contingent recording is the experience sampling method (ESM), developed by Csikszentmihlayi and colleagues and first used to describe the "ecology of adolescent experience" (Csikszentmihlayi, Larson, & Prescott, 1977). ESM reports of self-described activity, thoughts, and feelings are cued by an electronic signal programmed to occur at random (and hence unpredictable) moments throughout the day. In a typical study, Delespaul (1995) divided the time between 7:30 a.m. and 10:30 p.m. into ten 90-min intervals, randomly beeping participants once during each period (with the constraint that beeps be at least 15 min apart). Questions may be rating scales or open-ended. Although most ESM studies rely on predistributed booklets, some studies use computerized presentation and recording (e.g., Affleck et al., 1998; Parkinson et al., 1995; Penner et al., 1994), which has the added benefit of verifying that data entry coincided with the signal.

A slightly more general version of ESM is ecological momentary assessment (EMA), developed by Stone and Shiffman (1994). EMA has been used to link self-reports with ambulatory physiological states in natural environments. For example, Schwartz, Warren, and Pickering (1994) related mood ratings to ambulatory blood pressure readings taken every 15 min. Rapid technological advances in portable physiological monitors and in the flexibility, accessibility, and convenience of handheld computers for administering complex self-report protocols strongly suggest that research of this sort will become increasingly common (Suls & Martin, 1993).

The flexibility of signal-contingent recording for tracking diverse, naturally fluctuating phenomena has made it especially popular for studies of mood and health symptoms, both because they tend to vary in theoretically interesting ways in everyday circumstances, and because recollections tend to deteriorate rapidly (Stone & Shiffman, 1994). Other topics studied by signal-contingent recording include adolescents' thoughts and feelings (Csikszentmihalyi & Larson, 1987), coping with everyday stressors (Stone et al., 1999), self-relevant cognition (Hormuth, 1986), motives (Emmons & King, 1988; 1989), mental life and activity among people with schizophrenia (Delespaul, 1995), interaction between adolescents and their parents (Larson & Richards, 1994), and personality–affect covariation (Brown & Moskowitz, 1997; David et al., 1997).

Event-contingent Recording

Event-contingent recording requires a report whenever events meeting a predetermined definition have occurred. For example, the RIR, developed by Wheeler and Nezlek (1977), entails completion of rating scales and descriptive items after every social interaction lasting 10 min or longer. Similar protocols have been used to study conversations (Duck, Rutt, Hurst, & Strejc, 1991), lies (DePaulo et al., 1996), conflict (Jensen-Campbell, 1996), social comparisons (Wheeler & Miyake, 1992), self-presentation (Leary et al., 1994), smoking (Shiffman et al., 1994), food and drink consumption (Decastro & Pearcey, 1995), and sex (D. F. Hurlbert & Apt, 1995).

Key to event-contingent recording is unambiguous definition of the events to be described, as well as timeliness. If participants are permitted to select from events, or if it is unclear whether a given event

should be reported, systematic distortions are likely. Event-contingent recording is useful when events are relatively low-frequency (in which case signal-contingent methods would capture few instances), especially when subtypes are of interest (e.g., same-sex vs. opposite-sex interaction; comparisons of drinking alone, with romantic partners, or with others). Event criteria often take participant burden into account, such as by requiring that only certain subtypes be recorded (such as interactions involving specific others or lasting 20 min or longer).

Comparison of Protocols

Selection among these three protocols reflects several considerations: research goals, the relative frequency with which the central variables occur or vary, the time frame in which report accuracy is likely to degrade, and participant burden. Interval-contingent methods are usually chosen to examine how a variable fluctuates over time (e.g., day-by-day variations in mood, perceived competence, or alcohol consumption). Because the time span from one record to the next is constant, interval-contingent methods are ideally suited to time-series analysis, for which the irregular gaps of signal-contingent and event-contingent recording adds complexity. Interval sampling is also appropriate when the time unit itself has inherent meaning. For example, experience is often summarized in single-day units (e.g., "How was your day?"), or one might examine hourly variations in cognition and affect among psychotherapists.

Interval-contingent recording has the further advantage of minimizing participant burden, inasmuch as intervals are relatively lengthy and predictable, facilitating data collection over longer periods. Because respondents have some control over the exact moment of data entry, intrusiveness is substantially less than with protocols requiring immediate reports whenever a signal or relevant event occurs – be it during a party, meeting, or while preparing chateaubriand. Participants need simply remember to complete a record at the appropriate time, or be available for regular, pre-arranged telephone interviews (Almeida, 1997; Stone, Kessler, & Haythornthwaite, 1991).

A major disadvantage of interval-contingent recording is that events may be removed in time from reports, allowing possible retrospection bias, as discussed earlier. Furthermore, target variables may have fluctuated or occurred more than once during the interval, circumstances that participants may find difficult to describe. Thus, the same cognitive biases that daily experience studies are designed to minimize may distort to some extent interval-contingent responses, depending on the length of time between event and description and on memorability. Weekly reports of social interaction probably would contain substantial inaccuracies, for example, whereas hourly time budgets and weekly exercise reports would probably be reasonably precise. Of course, recollection bias is much less of a concern for variables that inherently involve impressions aggregated over time and experience (e.g., how stressful was work today?). Finally, systematic biases may be introduced by repeatedly assessing behavior or feelings at fixed times or in the same setting. For example, people may be lethargic at bedtime or may exclude certain information if their spouse is present.

Signal-contingent recording tends to be somewhat more intrusive than event-contingent recording. Signals, even when inaudible to others (e.g., vibratory settings), require immediate interruption of ongoing activity, whereas event-contingent reports are provided after its natural completion. For practical reasons, most signal-contingent protocols allow participants to postpone responding at inopportune moments or to switch off the signaling device when they do not wish to be disturbed. This concession works against the necessary randomization and representativeness, however. On the other hand, because some events vary

within themselves – interactions that begin superficially and become progressively more intimate, for example – event-contingent recording may involve some degree of aggregation within a single report.

Either signal- or event-contingent formats are preferable for determining the prevalence of events and states in everyday life, mostly because they obtain data close in time to the phenomenon being studied, minimizing distortion. However, event-sampling is effective only when the event can be defined unambiguously, so that relevant exemplars are not overlooked, and only when a single class of events is to be identified. Signal-contingent methods are preferable for assessing the relative frequency of activities (e.g., time budgets; Robinson & Godbey, 1997) or states (e.g., intense vs. mild emotions; Diener et al., 1985). Otherwise, participants would need to complete a record for almost everything they did, an onerous task. Signal- and interval-contingent data collected electronically have the added advantage of recording the time of signal and response, which can verify compliance with the sampling protocol. Whether participants have faithfully followed an event-contingent scheme can be ascertained only from informants or independent observers.

Finally, event-contingent sampling is most effective when the events are rare, or when variations within a class of events, some of which are rare, are important. For example, even with 7–9 signals per day for 1 week, high school students reported only 4.16 instances of studying (Wong & Csikszentmihalyi, 1991), a small number for representatively estimating mental states while studying. Similarly, event-sampling with college students yielded an average of only 3.90 interactions with opposite-sex romantic partners per week (Tidwell, Reis, & Shaver, 1996). Random sampling would be unlikely to obtain more than one or two instances, unless data collection continued for a prohibitively long time. Cross-matched categories – studying with friends as opposed to alone – are even rarer. In that comparisons of mental states during different activities (e.g., studying vs. socializing, or same-sex vs. opposite-sex interaction) are likely to interest social psychologists, methods that sample rare events efficiently are often needed. Table 8.1 summarizes

---

TABLE 8.1. Comparison of Everyday Experience Protocols

Protocol	Situations Favoring Protocols
Interval-contingent	When susceptibility to retrospection bias is low
	To minimize participant burden
	When aggregated time intervals are inherently meaningful
	To conduct time-series analyses and evaluate cyclical patterns of variation and covariation
Signal-contingent	When susceptibility to retrospection bias is high
	To establish the relative distribution of different activities or mental states
	To compare different domains of activity or mental states during different activities
	To verify time of recording
Event-contingent	When susceptibility to retrospection bias is high
	When interested in a specific class of events or states, especially rare, clearly defined events
	To compare relatively infrequent variations within a class of events
	When it is important to obtain many episodes of the event or state in question

this discussion, listing advantages and disadvantages of each protocol.

REPRESENTATIVE AREAS OF EVERYDAY EXPERIENCE RESEARCH

To paraphrase an adage, if one compelling illustration is worth a thousand exhortations, the many illustrations included below should provide a good introduction to the everyday experience literature. Our aim is twofold: to show how everyday experience findings have contributed to the theoretical literature and to portray the kinds of phenomena and theories that can be investigated with these methods. In each case, findings from the special perspective of everyday experience add to the development of social psychological knowledge in a manner unattainable with traditional methods. Our review is highly selective, in part due to the sheer number of existing studies, but also to emphasize topics of greater relevance to social–personality psychology. Other topical reviews are offered by Tennen et al. (1991), Delespaul (1995), and Stone, Shiffman, and DeVries (1999).

Social Interaction Processes

The RIR and related measures have been used to investigate the impact of structural features of the social environment. In the original RIR study, Wheeler and Nezlek (1977) examined social participation during adaptation to a new environment – the first year of college. Students reported all social contacts lasting 10 min or longer for 2 weeks early in the fall semester and late in the spring semester. Changes in the distribution and intensity of interaction indicated that women relied on interpersonal resources more than men did to adapt to their new environment. A similar study conducted at four points during the freshman year showed that social activity became more stable over time, especially among close and same-sex acquaintances, both in terms of consistency across interactions and correlations among various features of social interaction (Nezlek, 1993).

A longitudinal study by Reis, Lin, Bennett, and Nezlek (1993) examined change and consistency in social interaction from the college environment to adult life approximately 10 years later. Again using the RIR, they found that over time, socializing became more focused on opposite-sex partners and generally more intimate but no more satisfying. Individuals also showed marked relative consistency over the decade in key social indicators. For example, among students studied

first as college seniors, the average level of intimacy across all interactions was strongly correlated between college and adulthood ($r = .59$, $p < .01$). Number of interactions and time spent socializing correlated significantly over time for all students. Milardo, Johnson, and Huston (1983) investigated a somewhat different structural change, courtship, with a variant of the RIR. As predicted by the dyadic withdrawal hypothesis, when romantic relationships deepened, partners tended to interact less with others in their social network. Lydon, Jamieson, and Holmes (1997) studied the transition from superficial to close friendship. Consistent with their theorizing that individual interactions have greater significance in transitional relationships, they found larger correlations between perceptions of closeness and actual interaction features, as assesssed by the RIR, in developing friendships than in acquaintanceships or existing close relationships.

Diary studies have also shown that culture and sex matter. For example, people in individualistic cultures tend to interact more often but more superficially than people in collective cultures (Wheeler, Reis, & Bond, 1989). Reviewing a series of diary studies of intimacy, Reis (1998) concluded that sex differences were minimal in opposite-sex interaction, but in same-sex interaction, men's interaction was consistently and substantially less intimate than that of women. This latter difference was not found in non-Western cultures, however, implicating a cultural values explanation.

Other research has focussed on particular types of interaction. For example, attachment theory posits that dispositional attachment styles should be most evident when attachment concerns are activated. Consistent with this hypothesis, Pietromonaco and Feldman-Barrett (1997) found that intimacy, emotion, and liking for partners were most strongly related to attachment styles during high-conflict interactions. Similarly, Tidwell et al. (1996) found that attachment style predicted differences in intimacy, emotions, and the distribution of social contacts across close and superficial partners in opposite-sex, but not same-sex, interaction.

To study conflict, a relatively rare social occurrence, Drigotas, Whitney, and Rusbult (1995) asked respondents to record their thoughts and feelings whenever they or their partners felt dissatisfied about the relationship. In long-term dating couples, they found that although both active ("voice") and passive ("loyalty") constructive responses produced more favorable outcomes than destructive responses did, passive responses were more likely to be overlooked or misconstrued by partners. Participants in a study by Downey, Freitas, Michaelis, and Khouri (1998) completed an end-of-day report for 28 days describing conflict, satisfaction, and feelings of acceptance and rejection. On the day after feeling rejected, high rejection-sensitive women were more likely than low rejection-sensitive women to engage in conflict with their partners; also, their male partners were more likely to report feeling dissatisfied with the relationship. Jensen-Campbell (1996) had 6th–8th graders keep diary records of conflict during a 2-week span. Trait agreeableness predicted lesser intensity conflict and better conflict resolution strategies (e.g., less force and insults, more negotiation) among girls.

Social support is particularly amenable to diary research, depending as it does on the occurrence of stressful circumstances. Cutrona (1986a) demonstrated that perceived supportive actions by others may buffer the impact of daily stress on mood. Internal conflict about emotions, however, makes people less likely to perceive social support enacted by others (Emmons & Colby, 1995). Moreover, the type of support sought may depend on one's social goals. Using a combination of signal-contingent and end-of-day reports, Harlow and Cantor (1995) showed that persons focused on social outcomes tended to rely on emotional support when their social lives were going poorly, whereas persons focused on self-improvement were more likely to rely on informational support, especially from partners who represented their ideals.

Other interaction processes familiar to social psychologists have been explored with event-sampling methods. For example, Leary et al. (1994) showed that the salience of several self-presentational goals varied as a function of acquaintance and same-sex/opposite sex pairing. A series of studies by DePaulo and colleagues examined everyday lies with a "lie diary" based on the RIR (DePaulo & Kashy, 1998; DePaulo et al., 1996; Kashy & DePaulo, 1996). They found, for example, that lies told to close friends tend to be altruistic rather than self-serving (although altruistic lies also make interaction less intimate and enjoyable). Various features of daily social interaction (e.g., intimacy, conflict, control) have been related to the Extraversion, Neuroticism, and Agreeableness factors of the "Big Five" model of personality (Feldman-Barrett & Pietromonaco, 1997). Finally, appearance plays a role in social participation. Attractive men, but not women, interact more with the opposite sex; attractive persons of both sexes report higher quality interaction (Reis et al. 1980; Reis et al., 1982). Persons with more favorable self-perceptions of body attractiveness rate intimacy higher across all interactions, and facially ma-

ture men report lower intimacy, but more control, over opposite-sex interaction (Berry & Landry, 1997).

Motivation

Everyday experience studies of motivation take either of two general forms: between-persons, relating aggregated event-by-event reports to individual differences, or within-persons, linking activity variations to momentary or daily outcomes. Exemplifying the former, several ESM studies have shown that high affiliation motivation predicts less time spent alone (e.g., Wong & Csikszentmihalyi, 1991), in part due to a homeostatic mechanism that maintains social contact at desired levels (O'Connor & Rosenblood, 1996). McAdams and Constantian (1983) found that intimacy motivation was a better predictor of affectively positive interactions and thoughts about others than was affiliation motivation. Individuals who pursue goals concordant with personal values tend to have higher quality interactions (Hodgins, Koestner, & Duncan, 1996). Differences between implicit (operating outside of awareness) and explicit (operating with awareness) motives have also been explored. For example, Woike (1995) showed that implicit motives relate better to people's most memorable daily affective experience, whereas explicit motives relate better to routine daily activities. Motivational significance, defined in terms of goal relevance, also predicts the frequency of conscious attention to various activities (Klinger, Barta, & Maxeiner, 1980).

As for within-person processes, fulfillment through daily activity of three basic psychological needs posited by Deci and Ryan (1985) – autonomy, competence and relatedness – accounted for daily fluctuations in well-being around personal baselines (Reis et al., in press; Sheldon, Ryan, & Reis, 1996). Several studies by Csikszentmihalyi and colleagues, in which the ESM was first devised and refined, document the emotional and cognitive consequences of "flow," or feeling unselfconscious, absorbed, and optimally challenged in ongoing activity (Csikszentmihalyi, 1990). For example, among adolescents, this state is least common while studying or watching television.

Some of the most ambitious event-sampling studies mix these levels of analysis in demonstrating differential impact of events as a function of their personal significance. For example, participants in a diary study by Lavallee and Campbell (1995) described their most bothersome event twice each day for 2 weeks. To the extent that events were relevant to personal goals, more negative affect and stronger self-regulatory responses (e.g., rumination, self-focused attention) were elicited. Similarly, in a 20-day event-contingent diary study, Moskowitz and Côté (1995; Côté & Moskowitz, 1998) found support for a "behavioral concordance" model, which states that interpersonal events generate affect to the extent that they draw on salient traits (e.g., agreeableness, quarrelsomeness, dominance, and neuroticism). The importance of "fit" between person characteristics and events is also shown in end-of-day diary studies by Gable and Reis (1999) and Suls, Martin, and David (1998).

Affect

Event-sampling is especially popular for studying affect and emotional well-being, probably because important questions about moment-to-moment and day-to-day variability lend themselves readily to these methods. Moreover, distortions inherent in recollecting affect, even over short durations, and difficulties in creating significant emotional ups-and-downs by experimental manipulation, make diary methods prominent in the emotion literature. For example, daily diaries are ideal for studying natural mood cycles and their correlates. Well-known is the so-called "day-of-the-week" effect – that positive affect tends to be higher, and negative affect lower, on weekends than weekdays (Stone, Hedges, Neale, & Satin, 1985). The increase in positive mood appears mostly on measures that stress pleasantness; mood measures emphasizing activation tend not to rise on weekends (Egloff, Tausch, Kohlmann, & Krohne, 1995; Kennedy-Moore, Greenberg, Newman, & Stone, 1992). Differences in the desirability and personal meaningfulness of weekend and weekday activities appear to underlie these effects (Kennedy-Moore et al., 1992; Reis et al., in press). More generally, weekly rhythms have been estimated to account for approximately 40% of daily mood variation (Larsen & Kasimatis, 1990). Deviations from normative mood cycles offer an innovative method for studying emotionality and other behavioral expressions of personality (Larsen & Cutler, 1996; Moskowitz, Brown, & Côté, 1997; Penner et al., 1994). For example, extraverts are less entrained to this cycle than introverts are, presumably because of their greater responsiveness to influences outside the self (Larsen & Kasimatis, 1990). Mood also reveals a predictable diurnal (within-day) structure – positive activation tends to be higher mid-day, whereas pleasantness is higher in the evening – even after activity patterns have been controlled (Egloff et al., 1995; Stone et al., 1996).

Individual differences are important moderators of affective responses to daily events. For example, as mentioned above, Moskowitz and Côté's (1995) test of the concordance model found that affect was influenced by behavioral events only when those events were directly relevant to salient traits (see also Suls et al., 1998). However, other studies have supported both main effects – that certain traits predispose persons to experience particular events – and reactivity models – that certain traits may exacerbate reactions to events once they occur. Suls and colleagues (David et al., 1997; Marco & Suls, 1993), for example, found that trait negative affectivity is associated with reports of more frequent negative events and greater distress following such events (see also Bolger & Zuckerman, 1995). Gable and Reis (1999) found a similar result for persons high in behavioral inhibition. Evidence for a corresponding link between positive traits (extraversion, behavioral activation) and events was more a matter of differential exposure than of differential reactivity in these studies. Traits may similarly influence accuracy of mood recollection. In global retrospections after 90 days of thrice-daily emotion reports, people high in neuroticism tend to recall more negative emotion than their diaries indicate, whereas people high in extraversion tend to overreport positive emotion (Feldman-Barrett & Pietromonaco, 1997).

The consistent finding that positive and negative affect have distinguishable event predictors contributes to the ongoing debate concerning the independence of these affects. Momentary mood reports often find independence of positive and negative mood in time periods as brief as hourly ESM data (Larson, 1987). Moreover, positive and negative moods have distinguishing predictors. For example, in both aggregated and within-person studies, positive mood tends to derive from friendly or intimate social engagement and choiceful activity, whereas negative mood is predicted by stressful events (e.g., L. A. Clark & Watson, 1988; Langston, 1994; Reis et al., in press; Vittengl & Holt, 1998). It is important to note that in each of these studies, positive and negative events were statistically controlled for each other, indicating that the absence of stress and conflict may minimize bad moods, but it takes a different kind of event to generate good moods.

A few other studies demonstrate the theory-building role of event-sampling in emotion research. Feldman-Barrett, Robin, Pietromonaco, and Eyssell (1998) compared momentary and retrospective reports of emotional experiences. Men and women differed in the latter but not the former, suggesting that sex differences in emotion may be more a matter of stereotype-guided recollection than of actual experience. On the other hand, Seidlitz and Diener (1998) suggested that women may encode the affective details of experience, especially emotionally positive experience, better than men do. Event-sampling can also address emotional interdependence within relationships. In an extensive ESM study that simultaneously included several family members, Larson and Richards (1994) found, for example, that emotional contagion tended to flow from husbands to wives rather than the reverse. Also noteworthy is their finding that whereas mothers' affect tended to be best when away from home, fathers' affect was highest while at home. They attribute this asymmetry to activity divergences between men and women in these two settings, highlighting the role of everyday experience in global life satisfaction (Larson, Richards, & Perry-Jenkins, 1994). Finally, Martin and Watson (1997) studied expressed and unexpressed anger, finding that the former predicted poorer mood and greater problems, whereas the latter was unrelated to these outcomes.

Stress and Health

A consistent finding is that stressful events relate to daily reports of distress (e.g., Bolger et al., 1989; Buunk & Peeters, 1994; Stone, Neale, & Shiffman, 1993) and physical symptoms (e.g., DeLongis et al., 1988; Larsen & Kasimatis, 1991). In these studies, typical stressors refer to annoyances, hassles, and workload, rather than major life events, which tend to be rare in everyday life. Given the reliability of the daily stress–distress correlation, research has turned to questions about causal mechanisms and potential moderators. Trait neuroticism, for example, is considered important, because of its association with elevated reports of both variables, especially when the data aggregation period is long (Watson & Pennebaker, 1989). In a series of path analyses, Bolger and colleagues found that persons high in neuroticism, in addition to reacting more extremely to given stressful events, also experience more negative events and use poorer methods of coping (Bolger & Schilling, 1991; Bolger & Zuckerman, 1995). Brown and Moskowitz (1997), collecting event-contingent and signal-contingent records several times each day, found a strong link between unpleasant affect and symptoms, independent of trait neuroticism. Similarly, women's higher levels of daily distress than men's has been attributed to their relatively greater exposure to certain daily stressors, over and above reactivity differences (Almeida & Kessler, 1998). These studies

illustrate the flexibility of daily experience methods for comparing alternative causal explanations.

Diary studies have also examined consequences of stress. For example, stress at work or in school, especially among men, may affect subsequent interactions with spouses and other family members (Crouter, Perry-Jenkins, Huston, & Crawford, 1989; Repetti, 1989, 1993, 1996; Thompson & Bolger, 1999). Interpersonal stress also may be transmitted within families, such as when marital conflict spills over to parent–child interaction (Almeida, Wethington, & Chandler, 1999). This spillover, even from one day to the next, is particularly characteristic of distressed families (Margolin, Christensen, & John, 1996).

Diary studies are particularly valuable for behavioral health research, given the bias that retrospective symptom reports may introduce (Stone & Shiffman, 1998). For example, Affleck et al. (1998) and Stone, Broderick, Porter, & Kaell (1997) used diaries to track contextual factors predicting the intensity of chronic pain, whereas Shiffman and colleagues have identified precursors and consequences of smoking and smoking cessation (e.g., Shiffman, Paty, Gnys, Kassel, & Hickcox, 1996). Reis, Wheeler, Nezlek, Kernis, and Spiegel (1985) showed that social participation, assessed by the RIR, correlated with visits to a college health care facility for physical health problems. A particularly promising approach links the typical diary reports of emotion or activity to physiological markers. For example, using ambulatory cardiovascular monitors and handheld computers, Kamarck et al. (1998) obtained reports of cardiovascular activity and descriptions of ongoing activity every 45 min for 6 days (during waking hours). Among various findings, blood pressure and heart rate increased with emotional activation and decreased with greater task control. Momentary moods and stressful events have been related to increased cortisol levels (van Eck, Berkhof, Nicolson, & Sulon, 1996). Longer time frames are also feasible. In one example, weekly reports of interpersonal stress covaried with elevated immune activity in rheumatoid arthritis patients (Zautra et al., 1998). It seems likely that technological advances in ambulatory recording will make this type of research increasingly common.

In the mental health realm, ESM has been used to describe everyday behavior, emotions, and cognition characteristic of psychiatric disorders, such as schizophrenia, anxiety disorder, depression, and bulimia (Delespaul, 1995; DeVries, 1987; R. T. Hurlburt, 1990, 1997; Johnson & Larson, 1982). The advantage of this approach over traditional methods of clinical assessment is in detecting nonobvious symptoms. Also, treatment effectiveness and possible side effects can be verified through comparison of pre–post diaries. In addition, diary studies have established experiential correlates of less debilitating conditions, such as loneliness (Wheeler, Reis, & Nezlek, 1983) and dysphoria (Gable & Nezlek, 1998; Nezlek, Imbrie, & Shean, 1994).

The Self

The advantage of daily experience methods for studying the self resides primarily in tracking variability for determining temporal and contextual correlates. For example, using an event-contingent protocol, Wheeler and Miyake (1992) examined naturally occurring social comparisons. Among their findings was strong support for a dysphoria-priming model: Negative mood makes upward comparison more likely, which in turn lowers subjective well-being. Downward comparison, in contrast, which is more common with strangers than with friends, tends to raise well-being. Skowronski et al. (1991) studied self-relevance effects in memory by asking participants how well they remembered each event from a list of events that had occurred to self and one other person, as reported daily for 10 weeks. Self-events were recalled better than other-events, especially when those events were pleasant (rather than unpleasant), and both highly typical and highly unusual events were recalled better than moderately typical events.

Other studies have shown that low self-esteem individuals experience wider emotional swings in response to negative daily events (Campbell et al., 1991); that self-esteem instability, over and above mean levels, predicts greater reactivity to interpersonal evaluations (Kernis et al., 1993); that positive events such as success and acceptance have less impact on self-concept clarity than do negative events such as failure and rejection (Nezlek & Plesko, 1999); that narcissism is associated with more variable self-esteem and mood, especially in response to interpersonal experiences (Rhodewalt, Madrian, & Cheney, 1998); and that negative daily events may exacerbate depression when attention is self-focused as opposed to externally focused (Larsen & Cowan, 1988).

Intergroup Relations

In one of the first applications of these methods to group process, Pemberton et al. (1996) adapted the RIR to intergroup competition. As predicted by their discontinuity model, intergroup interactions were seen as more competitive and less cooperative than inter-individual and within-group interactions. McLaughlin-Volpe, Aron, Wright, and Reis (1999) studied the relationship between outgroup prejudice and social interaction with the RIR. Contrary to the simplest version of the "contact hypothesis," prejudice was unrelated to the frequency of social activity with ethnic outgroups. There was, however, a strong correlation between prejudice and the quality of interactions, defined as closeness and intimacy. Everyday experiences with racism and sexism also have been studied with an event-sampling protocol developed by Swim, Cohen, Hyers, Fitzgerald, and Bylsma (1997).

PRAGMATIC CONSIDERATIONS

As with all methods, event-sampling involves many mundane decisions and practices that, if mishandled, can adversely influence research outcomes. Often, these decisions reflect tradition ("that's how we've always done it"), expedience, or human participant realities, although it is to be hoped that they do not counter conceptual priorities. Developing procedures and materials for event-sampling research can be daunting to new investigators, due to their novelty and because they are labor-intensive for participants and researchers alike. In that every study entails different theoretical aims and pragmatic issues, universal procedures are unlikely to be helpful. Nevertheless, below we offer general guidelines for designing and conducting everyday experience research.

Designing the Protocol

The choice among interval-, signal-, and event-contingent schemes should be based on two main considerations: the type of question(s) being studied and the incidence of target behaviors. Earlier we discussed appropriate and inappropriate applications of each model. It is imperative that the sampling frame and duration of recording provide a sufficient number of representative reports.

With interval-contingent recording, researchers must first determine the necessary number and timing of reports. Intervals should represent meaningful time units and not just convenience. Meaningfulness depends on the target behavior's natural cycle, as well as the manner in which participants segment their activity. In general, intervals should be long enough to allow variability from one interval to the next, but not so long that successive fluctuations are masked or that forgetting or retrospection bias is likely. Intervals should be regular, with records scheduled at the same approximate point within each interval. For many behaviors, day's end meets these criteria.

The logic of signal-contingency mandates a random schedule, although to enhance representativeness, normal waking hours are often divided into fixed blocks, each with one random signal. The frequency and distribution of target activities and states in everyday life dictate the number and scheduling of blocks. Too few signals may bypass important occurrences, because only the moment of signal is described; too many signals may create excessive burden without incremental information yield. Typical ESM studies use 8–12 signals per day for 1–2 weeks. Delespaul (1992, 1995) provided a thorough discussion of various signaling plans.

Event-contingent sampling is predicated on unambiguous definition of the events to be recorded. Criteria should not be so inclusive as to overburden participants (and thereby invite sloppiness or noncompliance), but should be broad enough to include all instances of the target event. Because event-contingent sampling is commonly used to probe subtypes of general categories, some of which may be rare, data collection should continue as long as needed to obtain a reasonable number of each subtype for as many participants as possible. This period is likely to vary from topic to topic. Social participation studies, for example, typically require no more than 1–2 weeks, whereas studies of experience with prejudice might considerably longer. In some cases, a sampling scheme (e.g., every third meal) or more restrictive definition (e.g., interactions lasting 20 min or longer) may minimize participant burden while still yielding representative data.

All three formats require foreknowledge of the natural incidence and distribution of target events and states. Because researchers must depend on spontaneous variations rather than manipulation, data collection should be planned not only with base rates in mind, but also the frequency of cross-categorized activities. For example, one might be interested in the cooccurrence of alcohol consumption and sexual activity or social rejection after outgroup contact, relatively rare conjunctions. Pilot data is therefore a must. Too many studies have been completed without piloting, only to discover that the target phenomena had been sampled insufficiently.

Several methods of administration are feasible. Most common is paper-and-pencil, usually with printed booklets that are convenient to keep handy. Interval-contingent designs lend themselves to prearranged telephone interviews (Almeida, 1997) or computerized data collection (Gable & Nezlek, 1998). Particularly promising are portable or palmtop computers (e.g.,

Parkinson et al., 1995; Penner et al., 1994; Stone et al., 1998), which offer several major advantages: time can be recorded to verify compliance with the sampling scheme and to justify matching with other measures (e.g., another person's responses or ambulatory physiological data); complex "branched" protocols, asking different questions randomly or as a function of prior responses, can be administered; response duration can be registered; question order can be randomized; and data can be uploaded automatically, eliminating the cost and tedium of data entry. As this technology and software becomes more accessible in the near future, palmtop computers will likely become the method of choice.

Because event-sampling is designed to obtain data about representative events, it is best to avoid unusual circumstances. We would not study social interaction during final examinations, major holidays, or honeymoons, for example (unless they were the research focus). Nonetheless, uniform times of the week or year may inadvertently confound research. Enjoyable social interaction occurs more often on weekends than weekdays, for example, and depressed affect is more common in winter than in summer. These factors should be controlled by using multiple assessment periods. Of course, even the best plans may be affected by unpredictable events. When such events are sample-wide (e.g., natural disasters), researchers may consider themselves fortunate to have stumbled onto an entirely new research focus!

Designing the Instrument

Specific content depends, of course, on substantive interests. In hypothesis-driven studies, items should focus on the effect in question and its putative mechanisms, as well as alternative explanations and potential moderators. In exploratory research, items should be diverse, reflecting the full range and variability of a phenomenon, relevant contextual factors, and expected or possible covariates. Information about likely predictors and consequences is often desirable. Instruments are usually designed expressly for every study, although specific items are best selected on the basis of prior research.

Three kinds of items are popular: open-ended questions, fixed-format rating scales, and checklists. Open-ended questions ask respondents to describe activity in their own words (e.g., "What were you thinking when the signal occurred?"). These responses are descriptively rich, but must be content-analyzed (Bartholomew, Henderson, & Marcia, this volume,

Ch. 11). It may be risky to use open-ended items for hypothesis testing, in that lay persons' spontaneous wordings may not correspond to critical dimensions or features.

Traditional rating scales are used to quantify the degree to which particular qualities are present (e.g., mood, stress, perceived control, intimacy). Likert-type and other rating scales facilitate quantitative analysis, the main method for extracting information from diary data. As we discuss later, the repeated sequential nature of daily experience data offers special opportunities and challenges for quantitative analysis. Because the same protocol is completed repetitively within a narrow timespan, care must be taken to avoid reactivity and response style artifacts (Stone et al., 1999, discuss distinguishing internal consistency from response style artifacts).

Checklists are used primarily for indicating which events within a series did and did not occur during a given interval, and then (possibly) rating some aspect of them. For example, checklists of stressful life events or of different social activities are common. Checklists require extensive development and pilot testing (Stone et al., 1991). Because they must be reasonably exhaustive without overwhelming respondents, they are usually limited to normatively common events, a practice that may omit rare or idiosyncratic but significant occurrences. (An open-ended "other event" category can be used, but may add error.) Event definitions should be unambiguous and mutually exclusive, so that the same event is not tallied in separate categories at different times or by different respondents. A clear, standard format tends to help.

We have sometimes noticed confusion regarding the distinction between objective and subjective material. Whereas appraisals and similar ratings are clearly subjective, other information, such as whether an interaction took place, in principle may be recorded objectively. Nevertheless, the practice of treating these latter variables as totally objective markers may be misleading. Aside from the failure to follow instructions, respondents sometimes differ in perceiving that a given event meets reporting criteria. For example, spouses may disagree whether a conversation has been supportive, and some events are considered stressful by some persons but challenging by others. Because diary studies are intended to maximize accuracy, protocols can and should be made as objective as possible by minimizing subjectivity whenever conceptually appropriate. (For example, we would prefer the item "disagreed with my spouse" to "fought with my spouse.") In our opinion, objectivity is a matter of degree, and although diary data generally come closer to that standard than other self-report methods do, the possibility of subjectivity should not be ignored.

The format of a protocol depends on several factors. Length and complexity depend on the abilities and motivation of participants. Because excessive length inevitably degrades response quality, it is better to err on the side of brevity. We recommend that once-daily reports not exceed 15 min, and that more-than-daily reports not exceed 5–7 min. Presentation format can make a big difference. A well-organized form that locates related items in boxed sections with judicious use of bolding, highlighting, and varied fonts simplifies responding and improves data quality. Pocket-sized booklets are helpful for encouraging timeliness. Questions presented by computer should be organized for clarity and simplicity, particularly if respondents will not be able to scroll backwards.

Two final suggestions. First, it is often useful to include general items about the topic being studied, both for general description and to enhance the cover story (see below). For example, in studying daily workload stress, we might ask how many hours the participant had worked that day and include an open-ended question about their activities, even if this material is not central. Second, signal-contingent diaries should ask if anything important has happened since the prior signal, which may clarify unusual circumstances.

Participant Issues

By nature, event-sampling research depends on participants' ability and willingness to comply with instructions. Diaries are usually burdensome and intrusive, necessitating care in participant relations. We always make the participant's task clear early on, in that dropouts compromise sampling and are costly. Incentives should be commensurate with workload: not so large as to attract freeloaders but not so small as to only attract research-eager volunteers. We find it helpful to highlight participants' role as collaborators in the "descriptive geography" of our work – that is, the need to develop a comprehensive factual base about everyday social activity. (For example, we sometimes recruit participants by asking them to think about questions like, "How many hours per day do people spend socializing?") Aside from diverting attention from theoretical aims, intuitively engaging questions may enhance compliance. Protecting confidentiality, and being sure that participants are aware of safeguards, is essential, especially when diaries tap potentially embarrassing, compromising, or illegal behaviors and mental states. In couple studies, partners should not have access to each others' records.

Detailed training to explain the protocol and item content is important. Some studies include 1 or 2 training days, whose data are excluded, so that questions and ambiguities can be clarified. To facilitate and verify compliance, it is usually desirable to collect completed records and distribute new ones as often as possible, but certainly every few days. Debriefing interviews at the conclusion of record-keeping is generally useful for detecting problems such as noncompliance or misunderstanding of terms.

Documenting compliance is a growing concern. The only iron-clad assurance is interview or in-person administration (useful only for interval-contingent recording) and computer-generated time stamps (although computer clocks can be altered). Recent evidence suggests that partial compliance may be a significant problem. Litt, Cooney, and Morse (1998) studied drinking urges and behavior for 21 days with a combined signal- and event-contingent protocol. After extensive probing, 70% of the participants admitted delaying or omitting records at some time. Gable and Reis (1999) used computerized data collection to unobtrusively monitor the time at which daily activity records were completed. More than two thirds of their sample recorded at least 2 days simultaneously, and 40% recorded 4 or more days at once.

For some topics, partial compliance probably creates minimal distortion. People seem unlikely to forget that they were paid yesterday or that they spent the day alone. In other cases, particularly when the delay is long and the possibility of retrospection bias is substantial, meaningful inaccuracy may be introduced. When timeliness matters (as by definition it does with signal-contingent methods like ESM and EMA), procedures to monitor and promote compliance should be adopted, such as telephone calls, computer signals, daily collection of materials, and added incentives for timeliness. Excluding nontimely responses or full cases that exceed a predetermined noncompliance threshold is suboptimal, in our view. One reason is that delayed recording is unlikely to be random; it occurs most often when participants wish not to be interrupted. Furthermore, false negatives are more likely than false positives – omitting an event, signal, or interval rather than adding a nonexistent one.[2] The impact

of these and other systematic distortions remains to be established.

DOES RECORD-KEEPING ALTER EXPERIENCE? Because ecological validity is a prime justification for daily event studies, researchers sometimes worry that the process of record-keeping itself may alter the experiences being monitored (Tennen et al., 1991). Anticipation of the need to describe an event, unavoidable with repetitive recording, may affect people's experience of that event (Hormuth, 1986). Even more pointedly, attention to natural occurrences may foster unaccustomed levels of self-monitoring and introspection, modifying self-perceptions and perhaps changing behavior. For example, realizing that one has described a full day's social contacts as superficial may motivate intimacy strivings.

Although this variant of the better-known reactivity problem in repeated measurement has received little empirical scrutiny, indirect evidence has suggested that its impact may be minimal. Bernard et al. (1984) reported that recollections by participants who habitually kept records of contacts were no more accurate than those of participants new to record-keeping. Although 70% of the participants in another study (Litt et al., 1998) reported that signal-contingent reports made them more aware of their drinking problems, behavioral comparisons suggested few differences from a control group. Momentary mood reports collected several times during the day do not enhance accuracy over end-of-day summaries in predicting retrospective reports several weeks later (Thomas & Diener, 1990). The impact of repeated self-recording on behavior and subjective experience warrants study not only as a methodological question but also as an intrinsically interesting phenomenon.

This type of reactivity is often indistinguishable from the more general problem of response decay, implicated when response rates decline over time or when event descriptions and subjective ratings become less thoughtful. Response decay may be caused by participant burnout, for example, when protocols are overly burdensome or a study runs too long. Diagnostic signs include diminished event frequency without apparent justification and ratings stereotypy (e.g., logically inconsistent answers; decreased variance across time, items, or events; and increased use of scale anchors or midpoints). It is best to identify such problems in

---

[2] This is one instance in which event-sampling methods may be preferable to signal-contingent methods, which usually allow participants to turn off the signaling device when intrusion would be unacceptable. Although this provision is needed to obtain cooperation, event records, which can be provided after the fact, would not omit the event.

pilot-testing and revise procedures accordingly; alternatively, Stone et al. (1991) discussed procedures for weighting and model-based corrections.

DATA ANALYTIC STRATEGIES

The unique nature of event-sampling data requires special consideration in data analysis. The simplest issue, managing the sheer mass of data that repeated self-recording provides, is easily addressed; other issues, such as nesting, serial dependence, and imbalance in the number and variance of data points, are more complex. The commitment of time and effort that event-sampling research requires makes maximization of information yield a career-management necessity. It is therefore desirable to have a firm grasp of data analytic strategies and practices in the earliest stages of design and planning. In this section, we review design and conceptualization issues rather than technical or computational details. More thorough treatments are provided by Kenny, Kashy, and Bolger (1998); Schwartz and Stone (1998); and West and Hepworth (1991).

The standard event-sampling study has two levels of analysis, implying three general questions. One level usually involves differences between individuals, incorporating between-persons effects and hypotheses (e.g., does extraversion relate to everyday social activity?). Nested within persons is the second level, the repeated assessments defined by the sampling framework (e.g., does subjective well-being vary on different days of the week?). Interactions between these levels can also be examined, indicating whether the within-person trend varies systematically as a function of between-person factors (e.g., do daily stress and perceived social support relate differently for men and women?). Designs with more than two levels are also feasible, as discussed below.

Two preliminary notes are in order. First, researchers should be careful to frame questions at the appropriate level of analysis. As discussed earlier, within-person hypotheses are sometimes framed in between-person terms for simplicity, leading to conceptual, and occasionally statistical, misspecification (Gable & Reis, in press). Although event-sampling is often used to address purely between-person hypotheses, within-person and mixed questions represent more compelling models for daily experience research.

Second, event-sampling data frequently compel a choice between relatively simple, heuristically clear techniques and more elegant but complex statistical methods. Often, the consequences and quirks of sophisticated procedures developed to exploit specific designs or to manage certain data circumstances are unknown. In part, this is why the American Psychological Association (1999) task force on statistical inference recommended that complex statistics be eschewed when simpler methods will suffice. Although we subscribe to the maxim of simplicity, we firmly believe that statistical advances inevitably enhance the quality of insights that our data produce. We therefore encourage aspiring analysts to seek an optimal synthesis of heuristic simplicity, time-worn practice, and the enhanced precision of newer methods.

A method of analysis that we do not endorse treats each record (i.e., day, event, signal) as an independent entry, in essence ignoring nesting in the data structure. Aside from the prospect of introducing substantial bias by ignoring dependency (Kashy & Kenny, this volume, Ch. 17), this approach bypasses the most interesting feature of daily experience research – how a person's behavior varies from one context to another.

Aggregation and Composites

The simplest and most common way to analyze event data is to calculate numerical composites across all of an individual's records. For example, from 2 weeks of data, one might compute the total number of social interactions, lies, or counterfactual thoughts; mean levels of stress, perceived rejection, or attempted suppression of emotion; variability of mood or self-esteem within a fixed interval; or proportion of all social contacts that involve one's spouse or in-group. Using standard statistical tests, these composites can be related to predictors, such as personality or demographic or situational variables; or to outcomes, such as health, well-being, or productivity. A slight variation on this theme entails computing indices separately within subcategories; for example, to compare mean affect ratings during social, work, and alone time; to contrast the consequences of upward and downward social comparison or of emotional suppression and expression; or to examine the frequency of self-handicapping strategies during stressful and stress-free periods. Ordinary repeated measures ANOVA is commonly used for such questions (but see below).

This strategy builds on the well-known advantages of composites for maximizing reliability (Epstein, 1982) and has the added benefit of simplicity in data management and interpretation. There are several liabilities, however, beginning with the loss of potentially valuable information, which to us seems unfortunate, given the great effort that event-sampling research entails. Another drawback concerns reliability: To the extent that the number of records per person varies or the within-person variance differs from one person to another, the resulting statistics may improperly estimate standard errors and significance levels. (This is because heteroskedasticity engenders systematic discrepancies in the degree to which each person's observed mean deviates from his or her true mean.) Per-person record counts are likely to vary sharply in event-contingent sampling, but this issue also applies to time-contingent and signal-contingent sampling, in which the relative frequency of subcategories may differ (e.g., one adolescent signaled 100 times may be alone 10 times and with others 90 times, whereas a second adolescent may display the inverse ratio). Setting a minimum number of instances for valid representation of a category does not resolve disproportionality across participants and may yield empty cells, which further complicates analyses.

There are good reasons to rely on the computational and heuristic simplicity of composites. Nevertheless, possibilities for misleading conclusions should always be explored. We advocate a two-tiered approach for researchers wishing to use simple composites. Aggregation should be accompanied by examination of the relative frequency of records and between-person variability. If nontrivial differences emerge, basic findings should be confirmed with more sophisticated analyses, such as weighted least squares (WLS; Kenny et al., 1998) and maximum likelihood estimation (ML; Bryk & Raudenbush, 1992).

The Logic of Within-Person Regression

Suppose a research team wanted to know whether momentary mood was related to perceptions of control, as assessed by a signal-contingent diary. To partition chronic dispositional factors from other explanations for whatever association is obtained, separate regression equations might be computed for each participant, predicting mood from ratings of perceived control (Michela, 1990). In this analysis, each signal-contingent record corresponds to a "case," yielding a slope (i.e., unstandardized regression coefficient) for each participant.[3] These slopes can be examined in much the same manner as any score – for example, averaged across participants to estimate the population mean slope (i.e., the average relationship between mood and perceived control in the population) and

tested for significance. Similarly, to determine whether variations in magnitude are meaningful, the person-by-person slopes might be correlated with dispositional variables (e.g., attributional style or depression). This two-step method is used mostly with continuous predictors, although coded categorical variables are also feasible.

This approach has the same strengths and weaknesses as composites do, described under the previous heading. It is heuristically and computationally clear and is unlikely to yield anomalous results (especially if individual scatterplots have been inspected for outliers and skew; McClelland, this volume, Ch. 15). On the other hand, as discussed earlier, frequency and variability differences may bias significance tests, so this approach is not usually recommended by itself. It is useful, however, for descriptive purposes and as a robust alternative to more complex analyses.

A related method involves partialing a set of $n - 1$ dummy-coded variables to remove variance associated with person factors. This procedure, promoted by Cohen and Cohen (1983) as a regression analogue to repeated measures ANOVA for experimental designs, does not transfer well to event-sampling designs. This is because it treats participants as a fixed rather than a random effect, resulting in misspecified error terms (as shown by Equation 5) and incorrect degrees of freedom. Only when individual differences in slopes and intercepts are negligible will this method yield approximately correct results. An additional disadvantage of the dummy-code approach is that serial autocorrelation – the tendency of scores obtained close in time to be correlated – is not controlled.

As with other aggregates, results obtained from pooled within-person regressions should be examined carefully for variability and reliability differences. Nevertheless, the conceptual clarity of slopes embodies an important use of the event-sampling methodology. Covariation among features of the natural social environment, whether it be among several ratings by the individual or between contextual factors and the individual's reaction, may provide a unique and useful window into social processes. This is because the range of situations being described represents naturally occurring variation and because indexes of covariation are estimated within-person, over and above the impact of individual differences.

Multilevel Modeling

Multilevel modeling (also called hierarchically nested models and hierarchical linear models) is a

---

[3] Unstandardized coefficients yield better – that is, more generalizable – estimates than standardized values, which is why we focus on slopes rather than correlations. The logic is the same, however.

relatively new development that, although not very different in the terms it estimates from the more modest techniques described above, offers several important advantages. Multilevel models allow simultaneous estimation of between- and within-persons effects and their interaction; they readily handle multiple continuous predictors with an unbalanced number of cases per person (including missing data); and they simplify treating variables as random rather than fixed effects. This is important because fixed effects apply only to the specific exemplars of a predictor variable included in a particular study, whereas random effects can be generalized to the full population from which those exemplars are sampled.[4] Finally, multilevel modeling takes ready advantage of maximum likelihood estimation, which, although computationally complex, is more precise and efficient than least squares estimation.

Because the conceptual logic of multilevel modeling follows straightforwardly from within-person regression, readers should keep in mind the familiar concepts of slopes and intercepts (a more comprehensive introduction is given by Bryk & Raudenbush, 1992). Imagine a study in which, for 14 consecutive days, participants report levels of a predictor variable, social support received, and an outcome variable, mood. A dispositional measure, attachment style, is also available, which may moderate the support–mood relationship. The upper-level unit of analysis here is the person, whereas the lower-level unit, nested within persons, is the day. For each person, daily mood is estimated as follows:[5]

$$Y_{ij} = b_{0j} + b_{1j}X_{ij} + e_{ij}, \tag{1}$$

where Y_{ij} refers to each individual's mood on a given

day (i.e., the ith day for the jth participant), b_{0j} refers to that individual's average mood across all 14 days, X_{ij} is the individual's support rating for that day, b_{1j} is the regression coefficient indicating the degree of mood change produced by a one-unit change in support on a given day, and e_{ij} is error.

The innovative part of multilevel modeling is in estimating b_{0j} and b_{1j}. The constant term (or intercept) for each individual, b_{0j}, is represented as

$$b_{0j} = a_0 + a_1 Z_i + u_{0i}, \tag{2}$$

where a_0 refers to the sample-wide mean mood score, Z_i is the individual's attachment style rating, a_1 is the regression coefficient indicating the degree of change in individual's mean mood produced by a one-unit change in attachment style, and u_{0i} is error.

The slope term for each individual, b_{1j}, is

$$b_{1j} = c_0 + c_1 Z_i + u_{1i}, \tag{3}$$

where c_0 represents the average effect of support on mood in the sample, Z_i is the attachment style score, c_1 is the regression coefficient now indicating the degree of change in the mood–support slope produced by a one-unit change in attachment style, and u_{1i} is error. In other words, c_1 tells us whether the mood–support relationship is moderated by attachment style. If c_1 is trivial, the slope for most individuals in the data set computed separately will be about the same. If c_1 is large, individual slopes will be larger or smaller than the sample average, depending on whether their attachment style score is higher or lower than the sample mean.

From Equations 1 and 2, it is easy to see that on an average support day (i.e., $X_{ij} = 0$, after centering), an individual's predicted mood score is solely a function of dispositions. Similarly, Equations 1 and 3 reveal that for someone whose attachment rating is average (i.e., $Z_i = 0$), the magnitude of daily mood fluctuations mirrors the sample-wide average effect.

Kenny et al. (1998) highlighted the divergence between multilevel approaches and standard ANOVA regression by substituting Equations 2 and 3 into Equation 1:

$$Y_{ij} = a_0 + a_1 Z_i + u_{0i} + (c_0 + c_1 Z_i + u_{1i})X_{ij} + e_{ij} \tag{4}$$

or, more simply,

$$Y_{ij} = a_0 + a_1 Z_i + c_0 X_{ij} + c_1 Z_i X_{ij} + u_{0i} + u_{1i}X_{ij} + e_{ij}. \tag{5}$$

The second, third, and fourth terms on the right side of the equation are main effects for Z, X, and their

---

[4] As Kenny et al. (1998) insightfully noted, stimuli in social psychological research (e.g., vignettes, photographs, or who one interacts with) should be treated as random effects, because rarely do researchers limit inferences to those particular stimuli. This is particularly true for event-sampling research, in which predictor variables are instantiated not by manipulation and counterbalancing but by participants' spontaneous activities. Unfortunately, most ANOVA programs treat predictor variables as fixed rather than as random.

[5] Centering data before analysis has important implications for interpretability of the obtained coefficients. In most applications, it is desirable to center data at the corresponding unit of analysis (Bryk & Raudenbush, 1992). Thus, in the example that follows, day-level predictors (support) would be centered around the person's mean; person-level predictors (attachment style) would be centered around the sample mean. The resulting values are therefore interpretable as deviations from the corresponding mean.

interaction, and e_{ij} is the customary ANOVA-regression error term. But standard ANOVA regression omits u_{0i} and $u_{1i}X_{ij}$, both of which are necessary to draw unbiased inferences in a random effects model. These terms represent the random effect for the intercept and slope, respectively; without them, inferences about the predictor variables should not be generalized to the population.

We can now illustrate how these equations address the sorts of questions likely in event-sampling research. The classic between-persons question is "Do attachment styles relate to average mood?" and is quantified by the intercept term a_1 from Equation 2. The strictly within-persons question, "On days in which others are perceived to be supportive, is mood higher?," is assessed by the sample-average slope, c_0, from Equation 3. This effect is independent of dispositional differences in mood or perceived support. The third and final question asks about the interaction: "Does the support–mood relationship vary in magnitude as a function of attachment style?" The term c_1 in Equation 3 provides the appropriate test. Because interpretation of interactions can be tricky, to determine their specific nature we recommend recomputing Equation 3 for attachment scores one standard deviation above and below the mean. Significant interactions should be evident in nonparallel slopes.

There are three general methods for estimating multilevel effects (Kenny et al., 1998). Although differing in certain assumptions and procedures, the basic constructs (and hence information provided) are similar. The simplest estimation method is ordinary least squares (OLS) or unweighted regression, with which most social psychologists are familiar. This method computes slopes and intercepts following the above equations, weighting all participants equally. A second method, WLS, is designed to improve precision in Equation 4 by differentially weighting cases according to their expected accuracy. This is desirable because, all other things being equal, coefficients obtained from cases with a larger number of observations or that have more variance can be expected to better estimate population values and therefore should have more influence on the sample-wide result.

The third method, embodied in popular programs such as HLM (Bryk, Raudenbush, & Congdon, 1996) and PROC MIXED within SAS, is based on the greater efficiency and accuracy of ML estimation. Aside from a different method of estimation, ML focuses on the same basic constructs as least squares methods do (i.e., slopes and intercepts); therefore the main difference is in statistical precision rather than information provided.

Although both the statistical logic and computational details of ML estimation are complex, existing programs are rapidly becoming more convenient and flexible; given its mathematical superiority, it seems likely that ML-analyses of event-sampled data will become standard practice in the near future.

MULTILEVEL MODELS IN PERSPECTIVE. Multilevel models can be expanded to incorporate multiple predictors at each level of analysis, for example to compare the relative contribution to mood of daily perceived support and stress, and their interaction. Several dispositional factors can also be included.

Of growing appeal to daily experience researchers is the ability of multilevel models to accommodate additional levels of nesting (although in current practice models with more than three levels are difficult to analyze). Two-level analyses are most popular. The lower-level unit is time in interval-contingent sampling, the signal in signal-contingent sampling, and the event in event-contingent sampling. The higher-level unit is usually the person. If our support–mood example had been conducted at several points during the year, days might be nested within seasons, which are then nested within individuals. Or, one might investigate the nature of relationship types by comparing RIR diaries for romantic partners, close friends, acquaintances, and strangers. In this instance, interactions are nested within partners, which in turn are nested within persons. Of course, the highest-level unit of nesting need not be the person – any grouping in which scores are correlated is appropriate. For example, in studies conducted within organizational units such as schools, businesses, or families, days might be nested within persons, who are in turn nested within groups.

In some instances it may be desirable to aggregate across one level of nesting prior to analysis. For example, one might calculate composites for all interactions of a given sort, with particular partners, or on certain days of the week. Although this procedure likely violates the equal reliability assumption discussed above, implications of this violation for overall findings are not known. In this regard, we concur with Stone et al. (1991), who noted that the familiar psychometric criterion of high internal consistency (John & Benet-Martinez, this volume, Ch. 13) may not be reasonable for event-sampling, because there is little reason to assume "that the experience of one event is related to other events" (p. 588). The great advantage of preaggregation is to simplify data management and to reduce some of the inherent (and perhaps conceptually irrelevant) variability in everyday events. Collapsing across minor variations within a category may also provide more meaningful indicators of a construct.

Existing multilevel modeling programs were developed to capitalize on ML estimation, especially with unbalanced data sets, but they have come to offer daily experience researchers a different sort of benefit – the ability to maximize information retrieval from large, hierarchically nested data sets. We think it probable (and desirable) that multilevel modeling will become the gold standard for analyzing daily experience data. As with all such technically complex methods, however, it is critical to not lose sight of the conceptual foreground. This means thinking about slopes and intercepts, two elementary mathematical constructs. It also means not abandoning simple statistics, both when appropriate and for heuristic confirmation of results obtained by more sophisticated procedures.

Analysis of Temporal Patterns

Although temporal issues are present in all daily experience data sets, they are rarely addressed explicitly. This is unfortunate. Variations in how the passage of time is experienced and how circumstances at a given moment may influence subsequent behavior embody potentially fruitful questions for understanding social life. Moreover, sequential data provide substantive opportunities for studying cyclical patterns, as well as for causal analysis. Disregarding sequence in diary data, such as by collapsing across all observations, therefore represents underutilization of a valuable resource.

There is another, more statistical basis for attending to sequence: the possibility of serial dependency, which may produce spurious correlations between observations adjacent in time. There are several reasons for this, the most common being that error terms in two consecutive observations are unlikely to be independent (as standard analyses assume). For example, mood ratings taken at 2 p.m. and 4 p.m. on the same day may be influenced by the same outside factors (e.g., weather, office environment); thus error in Time 1 mood ratings is correlated with error in Time 2 mood. All other things being equal, the closer in time or more similar in context two observations are, the larger these effects may be. With many closely spaced observations, such as in signal-contingent recording, serial dependency may be substantial, spanning several observations. Correlated residuals, as this problem is also called, may bias standard errors (and hence the results of significance tests) and may distort correlations between two sets of sequential within-person variables. Spurious effects may also occur.

West and Hepworth (1991) offered an excellent introduction to strategies for identifying and contending with serial dependency. Using standard time-series analysis procedures (e.g., the Durbin-Watson test or Box-Jenkins autocorrelation function), the first step is to determine the extent of serial dependency: a *lag 1 effect* indicates correlated errors between one observation and the next one, a *lag 2 effect* means that correlated errors extend to the next two measurements, and so on. Although few daily event researchers report these statistics, those that do reveal conflicting results, some showing substantial carryover from one observation to the next, and others finding no effect. The extent of carryover probably depends on the variables under study and the time between assessments. We therefore recommend that researchers routinely scan their data sets for serial dependency.

Serial dependency may be controlled in several ways. The most formal methods, developed for time-series analysis and available in most statistical packages, are rare in psychology but common in other social sciences. A more familiar technique involves partialing the outcome variable for the prior observation, which removes all variance associated with the prior outcome, including error.[6] The unit of analysis then becomes a residual, $Y_t - b_{t(t-1)}Y_{t-1}$. The main drawback to this approach is that longer or more complex lags may be difficult to control, although in principle any function that can be modeled in regression terms can be incorporated (Judd, this volume, Ch. 14). Complex lags also tend to be hard to explain theoretically.

Social psychologists may find sequential patterns and cycles interesting for conceptual reasons. Some phenomena are most likely to be revealed in sequential processes. For example, Margolin, Christensen, and John (1996) obtained daily telephone reports of family conflict for 2 weeks, subdivided into mornings, afternoons, and evenings. Distressed and nondistressed families were differentiated by continuance of tension at lag 3 (i.e., from one day to the same time the next day), but not at lags 1 and 2. In other words, the duration of a conflictual atmosphere may be the hallmark of familial distress.

Spectral analysis, a general class of methods for detecting cycles and rhythms in sequential data (Larsen, 1990), is rarely applied in social–personality psychology, despite the prevalence of cycles in our phenomena. One well-known cycle is the day, characterized by

---

[6] This is the procedure recommended by Cohen and Cohen (1983) to analyze change. Both techniques use partialing to create outcome variables uncorrelated with earlier scores.

regularities in activity schedules and diurnal rhythms in internal states such as mood, fatigue, and attentiveness. People also experience weekly cycles – in one study, 40% of the variance in daily mood was attributed to this cycle (Larsen & Kasimatis, 1990). Mood tends to be more positive and less negative on weekends than weekdays, although there is disagreement about whether mood varies reliably from Monday to Friday (Stone et al., 1985). Larsen (1987) also identified a monthly mood cycle. Other relevant temporal cycles include seasons and academic semesters, in which predictable markers (e.g., weather, stress, study patterns) may affect less obvious variables.

Once identified, cycles and rhythms may contribute to social psychological theory in several ways. Mediators can be sought, helping to explain basic processes. For example, Reis et al. (in press) suggested that weekend activity is more likely than weekday activity to satisfy autonomy and relatedness needs, perhaps accounting for the weekly mood cycle. Individual and group differences might also be explored, as in Larsen and Kasimatis's (1990) finding that extraverts were less entrained to the weekly mood cycle than introverts were. It may also be desirable to control for cycle-related artifacts and error variance. For example, loneliness effects tend to be greater on weekends than weekdays, suggesting that findings may depend on when data are collected (Gable & Reis, in press).

It should be noted that sequential analysis is facilitated by equally, or at least systematically, spaced intervals. The irregular gaps of signal-contingent and especially event-contingent sampling may complicate computation (by requiring specification of the length of each interval) and interpretation of lags and sequences, unless data are aggregated over fixed intervals prior to analysis.

Finally, although spurious causation cannot be discounted in the absence of experimental manipulation, temporal precedence in sequentially structured data allows supporting certain hypotheses while ruling out others (West, Biesanz, & Pitts, this volume, Ch. 3). Most such tests involve lagged effects – variable Y at time t predicted from variable X at time $t - 1$, controlling for variable Y at time $t - 1$. Synchronous correlations are significantly less persuasive evidence of causal influence, even when the prior observation is partialed. Lagged tests of causation, although rare in social psychology, are especially impressive due to the repetitive nature of event-sampling data – in a 14-day daily diary study, the lagged effect is tested for 13 paired days. Downey et al. (1998), as noted earlier, is a good illustration. They collected daily ratings of perceived rejection, conflict, and relationship satisfaction from romantic partners for 4 weeks. Following days in which they felt rejected, rejection-sensitive women were more likely to interact conflictually, and their partners reported diminished satisfaction. By establishing the lagged effect, Downey et al. demonstrated temporal precedence, supporting a causal interpretation, while simultaneously ruling out the reverse causal path (i.e., that conflict engenders feelings of rejection).

A Note of Perspective

The quantitative methods described above are not like your graduate advisor's t-test (or even his or her regression equation). Devised to handle and capitalize on features common to large, multilevel, often sequential, data sets, their robustness to unusual data, sampling anomalies, and assumption failure is as yet mostly unknown. Consequently, researchers must be prepared to inspect data thoroughly and to rely on multiple strategies before "going to the bank" with findings. Distributions, univariate and multivariate, should be scrutinized carefully, particularly for outliers, heteroscedasticity, and correlated errors. Models should be developed on the basis of substantive theory, taking full advantage of the ability of daily experience data to address propositions from between-person, within-person, and temporal perspectives, but also to be consistent with statistical requirements. Above all, we urge that results be confirmed with multiple procedures. Appeasing the competing muses of statistical precision and heuristic clarity is a fine art that all daily experience analysts must master.

INTEGRATING EVENT-SAMPLING IN PROGRAMMATIC RESEARCH

In the opening chapter of this *Handbook*, Brewer argued that construct validity is better considered a property of research programs than of individual studies. Brewer's position suggests that the value of event-sampling for social psychology should be appraised not in isolation but rather in how it complements other methods. Every method has benefits and drawbacks, insights that it can and cannot impart. Methodological triangulation, embracing diverse strategies and procedures, is the best way to keep social psychological knowledge from becoming method-bound. Of course, methods ought not to be chosen willy-nilly; they should complement one another in addressing key conceptual issues and methodological shortcomings.

Webb, Campbell, Schwartz, and Sechrest (1966) introduced the idea of multiple operationalism to suggest that because all methods have strengths and weaknesses, multiple perspectives are needed from methods that complement each other's limitations. All empirical tests include not only substantive but also methodological components, both of which contribute, albeit to varying degrees, to research outcomes. Determining the degree to which results (whether supporting or failing to support a theory) should be attributed to each component (as well as to the many specific facets of each) is fundamentally impossible, as Houts, Cook, and Shadish (1986) noted, without corroboration from "aggressively sought alternative explanations" (p. 56), including, of course, both conceptual and methodological explanations. They therefore argued for "critical multiplism," which replaces the notion of a single critical test or paradigm with reliance on diverse theoretical and methodological alternatives.

Daily experience studies represent a valuable addition to the social–personality psychology toolbox in this regard. For example, one might explore behavioral confirmation processes, as identified and interpreted in laboratory experiments, with an event-contingent sampling scheme. Corroborated principles can be held in greater confidence; propositions not confirmed suggest the need for further theorizing. Certain effects may occur only in the presence of particular moderating conditions, for example. Or, a process may be confounded with another process or procedural detail, implying incorrect specification of the underlying theory. Still other findings may suggest clarifications or extensions of a theory, leading to further experiments. In any or all of these eventualities, the synthesis of laboratory and daily experience approaches can be expected to yield fascinating insights and more compelling theories.

Event-sampling might also be the starting point in a research program. As noted earlier, daily experience studies describe the relative prevalence of phenomena and their predictors, covariates, and consequences. Establishing the scope and nature of a phenomenon, as well as its natural context, is central to basic science, as the history of the biological and physical sciences has shown, and we are confident that social psychology would benefit from such data. John Bowlby (1988) said as much:

[The wise researcher] will concentrate attention on a limited aspect of a limited problem. If in making his selection he proves sagacious, or simply lucky, he may not only elucidate the problem selected but also develop ideas applicable to a broader range. If his selection proves unwise or

unlucky he may merely end up knowing more and more about less and less. (pp. 40–41)

We do not mean to imply that the benefits of everyday experience research reside only, or even primarily, in replicating existing findings or in identifying phenomena to be taken apart and put back together in the laboratory. At the outset of this chapter, we discussed direct theoretical uses of everyday experience studies, including tests of hypotheses in natural contexts, comparison of competing predictions and models, delineation of moderating conditions, evaluation of alternative explanations, and separation of within-person (including temporal) processes from dispositional factors. Many of the specific examples cited earlier demonstrate the benefits of theory-testing with event-sampling data. If event-sampling is valued for its detailed descriptions of naturally occurring behavior with minimal retrospection bias, is it also not important to evaluate theories with such data?

To be sure, the sine qua non of theoretical specification in social psychology is cause-and-effect. Internally valid causal inference requires three conditions (Kenny, 1979): correlation, temporal precedence, and nonspuriousness. This last factor is most definitively established with experimenter-manipulated conditions, carefully controlled contexts, and random assignment. Causal relations are, and should remain, a central focus of social psychological research, but, as described earlier and elsewhere in this *Handbook*, laboratory experiments have limitations. Everyday experience studies provide an alternative perspective, complementing the laboratory not only in method but also in the kind of behavior examined and in the contexts in which they are evidenced. This is of course the logic behind multiple operationalism.

Likewise, momentary reports offer a useful counterpart to global self-reports. Although many phenomena are inherently global and subjective (e.g., certain attitudes and self-perceptions), for other constructs such measures inevitably beg the question of whether actual experience or after-the-fact reconstruction is being assessed. Comparison of findings from diary and retrospective accounts can shed light on these important processes.

Lest we mislead readers, we do not recommend daily experience research universally. At least six situations seem ill-suited to this form of research: when an effect is unlikely to be evident without careful control of other, simultaneous processes; when, in fine-tuning a theory, it is necessary to create unusual, rare, or even implausible conditions; when ruling out spurious causation is paramount; when global, general impressions are the theoretical focus; when participants are unlikely to comply with sampling protocols; and when phenomena are inaccessible to self-report.

On the other hand, event-sampling is ideal in at least five circumstances: when it is desirable to observe phenomena in natural, voluntary, and spontaneously arising contexts; when retrospection and certain other biases are likely to produce misleading accounts; when social processes are such that they cannot be created ethically or impactfully in the laboratory; when within-person and temporal patterns are likely to be revealing; and when ecological validity is foremost.

In short, to us it seems tantamount to obvious that validity, defined in the broadest possible sense, requires methodological triangulation. Our general impression is that social and personality psychologists often pursue methodological variety with relatively minor variations on the same theme. Everyday experience methods, in conjunction with laboratory and global self-report strategies, offer a substantial alternative with which to enhance the validity of a research program.

CONCLUDING COMMENTS

Social psychology's special niche in the behavioral and social sciences concerns the impact of the social environment on behavior. Most social psychologists take as an article of faith the importance of understanding the situational context in which behavior is displayed. Reflected throughout the literature, this orientation is most evident in the popular construct of Personality × Situation interactionism – that dispositions are reflected in the situations that people select, in differential reactions to existing situations, and in the way that one person's behavior may alter the situation for others.

Yet too often research seems oblivious to this core principle. For example, many studies treat behavior as essentially static or acontextual or as a fixed quality of individuals (even if theorizing from a more dynamic contextual view). Our measurement practices often seem to assume that behavior doesn't depend on the context of observation or the manner of assessment. Methodology is construed as a search for operations that yield significant effects, and self-reports are cast either as prima facie accurate or irreparably biased. Of course we know better than this. The Fourth *Handbook of Social Psychology* has been published, but this is only the first methods handbook. An entire handbook devoted to methods suggests that the research process in social psychology is changing and that methodology

has become a fundamentally more complex and diverse business than before.

If nothing else, social psychological theorizing is increasingly sophisticated, detailed, and differentiated. Whereas studies were once focused on uncovering the field's core phenomena, the cumulative knowledge produced by decades of research directs our attention to second-order questions: identifying moderator variables and boundary conditions for basic processes, verifying underlying mechanisms and mediating processes for established phenomena, and determining the relevance and applicability of competing theories and predictions (Reis & Stiller, 1992). The growing complexity of theories, and hence the most cutting-edge questions, inevitably requires adoption of more diverse methods, both to pose a broader, more comprehensive range of questions and to compensate for the unavoidable limitations of any single method. In short, the need for – but also the opportunities provided by – multiple operationalism is greater than ever.

Everyday experience studies offer one avenue for bridging some of the field's more imposing gaps: between laboratory experiments and survey questionnaires, between one-shot observations and global retrospections, between theorizing about contextual variations and examining them empirically, between internal and ecological validity, between highly controlled situations and those encountered in natural activity; and between theory and the details of ordinary life. Integrated with the many other methods represented in this *Handbook*, everyday experience methods can help the next generation of research fulfill our legacy of understanding how social behavior is embedded in situational contexts.

REFERENCES

Affleck, G., Tennen, H., Urrows, S., Higgins, P., Abeles, M., Hall, C., Karoly P., & Newton, C. (1998). Fibromyalgia and women's pursuit of personal goals: A daily process analysis. *Health Psychology, 17,* 40–47.

Ajzen, I. (1996). The social psychology of decision making. In E. T. Higgins & A. W. Kruglanski (Eds.), *Social psychology: Handbook of basic principles* (pp. 297–325) New York: Guilford Press.

Almeida, D. M. (1997). *National study of daily experiences: The MIDUS in-depth diary study.* Chicago: MacArthur Foundation Research Network on Successful Midlife Development.

Almeida, D. M., & Kessler, R. C. (1998). Everyday stressors and gender differences in daily distress. *Journal of Personality and Social Psychology, 75,* 670–680.

Almeida, D. M., Wethington, E., & Chandler, A. L. (1999). Daily transmission of tensions between marital and parent-child tensions. *Journal of Marriage and the Family, 61*, 49–61.

American Heritage Dictionary (1976). Boston: Houghton Mifflin.

American Psychological Association Task Force on Statistical Inference (1999). Statistical methods in psychology journals. *American Psychologist, 54*, 594–604.

Asch, S. E. (1952). *Social psychology.* New York: Prentice Hall.

Bernard, H. R., Killworth, P., Kronenfeld, D., & Sailer, L. (1984). The problem of informant accuracy: The validity of retrospective data. *Annual Review of Anthropology, 13*, 495–517.

Berry, D. S., & Landry, J. C. (1997). Facial maturity and daily social interaction. *Journal of Personality and Social Psychology, 72*, 570–580.

Blaney, P. H. (1986). Affect and memory: A review. *Psychological Bulletin, 99*, 229–246.

Bolger, N., DeLongis, A., Kessler, R. C., & Schilling, E. A. (1989). Effects of daily stress on negative mood. *Journal of Personality and Social Psychology, 57*, 808–818.

Bolger, N., & Schilling, E. A. (1991). Personality and the problems of everyday life: The role of neuroticism in exposure and reactivity to daily stressors. *Journal of Personality, 59*, 355–386.

Bolger, N., & Zuckerman, A. (1995). A framework for studying personality in the stress process. *Journal of Personality and Social Psychology, 69*, 890–902.

Bowlby, J. (1988). *A secure base: Parent-child attachment and healthy human development.* New York: Basic Books.

Brewin, C. R., Andrews, B., & Gotlib, I. H. (1993). Psychopathology and early experience: A reappraisal of retrospective reports. *Psychological Bulletin, 113*, 82–98.

Brown, K. W., & Moskowitz, D. S. (1997). Does unhappiness make you sick? The role of affect and neuroticism in the experience of common physical symptoms. *Journal of Personality and Social Psychology, 72*, 907–917.

Bryk, A. S., & Raudenbush, S. W. (1992). *Hierarchical linear models.* Newbury Park, CA: Sage.

Bryk, A. S., Raudenbush, S. W., & Congdon, R. T. (1996). *HLM: Hierarchical linear and nonlinear modeling with the HLM/2L and HLM3/L Programs.* Chicago: Scientific Software International, Inc.

Buunk, B. P., & Peeters, M. C. W. (1994). Stress at work, social support and companionship: Towards an event-contingent recording approach. *Work and Stress, 8*, 177–190.

Campbell, J. D., Chew, B., & Scratchley, L. S. (1991). Cognitive and emotional reactions to daily events: The effects of self-esteem and self-complexity. *Journal of Personality, 59*, 473–505.

Carlston, D. E., & Smith, E. R. (1996). Principles of mental representation. In E. T. Higgins & A. W. Kruglanski (Eds.), *Social psychology: Handbook of basic principles* (pp. 184–210). New York: Guilford Press.

Caspi, A., Bolger, N., & Eckenrode, J. (1987). Linking person and context in the daily stress process. *Journal of Personality and Social Psychology, 52*, 184–195.

Clark, L. A., & Watson, D. (1988). Mood and the mundane: Relations between daily life events and self-reported mood. *Journal of Personality and Social Psychology, 54*, 296–308.

Clark, M. S., & Brissette, I. (in press). Experiencing, expressing and interpreting emotions: Relationship context matters. In N. Frijda, A. Manstead, & S. Bem. (Eds.), *Emotion and beliefs.* Cambridge, England: Cambridge University Press.

Cohen, J., & Cohen, P. (1983). *Applied multiple regression/correlation analysis for the behavioral sciences.* Hillsdale, NJ: Erlbaum.

Conrath, D. W., Higgins, C. A., & McClean, R. J. (1983). A comparison of the reliability of questionnaire versus diary data. *Social Networks, 5*, 315–322.

Côté, S., & Moskowitz, D. S. (1998). On the dynamic covariation between interpersonal behavior and affect: Prediction from neuroticism, extroversion, and agreeableness. *Journal of Personality and Social Psychology, 75*, 1032–1046.

Crouter, A. C., Perry-Jenkins, M., Huston, T. L., & Crawford, D. W. (1989). Temporal rhythms in family life: Seasonal variation in the relation between parental work and family processes. *Developmental Psychology, 29*, 273–292.

Csikszentmihalyi, M. (1990). *Flow: The psychology of optimal experience.* New York: Harper & Row.

Csikszentmihalyi, M., & Larson, R. (1984). *Being adolescent: Conflict and growth in the teenage years.* New York: Basic Books.

Csikszentmihalyi, M., & Larson, R. (1987). Validity and reliability of the experience-sampling method. *Journal of Nervous and Mental Disease, 175*, 526–536.

Csikszentmihalyi, M., Larson, R., & Prescott, S. (1977). The ecology of adolescent activity and experience. *Journal of Youth and Adolescence, 6*, 281–294.

Cutrona, C. E. (1986a). Behavioral manifestations of social support: A microanalytic investigation. *Journal of Personality and Social Psychology, 51*, 201–208.

Cutrona, C. E. (1986b). Objective determinants of perceived social support. *Journal of Personality and Social Psychology, 50*, 349–355.

David, J. P., Green, P. J., Martin, R., & Suls, J. (1997). Differential roles of neuroticism, extraversion, and event desirability for mood in daily life: An integrative model of top-down and bottom-up influences. *Journal of Personality and Social Psychology, 73*, 149–159.

Decastro, J. M., & Pearcey, S. M. (1995). Lunar rhythms of the meal and alcohol intake of humans. *Physiology & Behavior, 57*, 439–444.

Deci, E. L., & Ryan, R. M. (1985). *Intrinsic motivation and self-determination in human behavior.* New York: Plenum.

Delespaul, P. A. E. G. (1992). Technical note: Devices and time-sampling procedures. In M. W. de Vries (Ed.), *The experience of psychopathology: Investigating mental disorders in their natural settings* (pp. 363–373). Cambridge, England: Cambridge University Press.

Delespaul, P. A. E. G. (1995). *Assessing schizophrenia in daily life: The experience sampling method.* Maastricht, The Netherlands: International Institute for Psycho-Social and Socio-Ecological Research.

DeLongis, A., Folkman, S., & Lazarus, R. S. (1988). The impact of daily stress on health and mood: Psychological and social resources as mediators. *Journal of Personality and Social Psychology, 54,* 486–495.

DePaulo, B. M., & Kashy, D. A. (1998). Everyday lies in close and casual relationships. *Journal of Personality and Social Psychology, 74,* 63–79.

DePaulo, B. M., Kashy, D. A., Kirkendol, S. E., Wyer M. M., & Epstein, J. A. (1996). Lying in everyday life. *Journal of Personality and Social Psychology, 70,* 979–995.

DeVries, M. W. (1987). Investigating mental-disorders in their natural settings: Introduction. *Journal of Nervous and Mental Disease, 175,* 509–513.

Diener, E. (1996). Traits can be powerful, but are not enough: Lessons from subjective well-being. *Journal of Research in Personality, 30,* 389–399.

Diener, E., Larsen, R. J., Levine, S., & Emmons, R. A. (1985). Intensity and frequency: Dimensions underlying positive and negative affect. *Journal of Personality and Social Psychology, 48,* 1253–1265.

Downey, G., Freitas, B. L., Michaelis, B., & Khouri, H. (1998). The self-fulfilling prophecy in close relationships: Rejection sensitivity and rejection by romantic partners. *Journal of Personality and Social Psychology, 75,* 545–560.

Drigotas, S. M., Whitney, G. A., & Rusbult, C. E. (1995). On the peculiarities of loyalty: A diary study of responses to dissatisfaction in everyday life. *Personality and Social Psychology Bulletin, 21,* 596–609.

Duck, S., Rutt, D. J., Hurst, M. H., & Strejc, H. (1991). Some evident truths about conversations in everyday relationships: All communications are not created equal. *Human Communication Research, 18,* 228–267.

Duck, S., & Sants, H. (1983). On the origin of the specious: Are personal relationships really interpersonal states? *Journal of Social and Clinical Psychology, 1,* 27–41.

Egloff, B., Tausch, A., Kohlmann. C. W., & Krohne, H. W. (1995). Relationships between time of day, day of the week, and positive mood: Exploring the role of the mood measure. *Motivation and Emotion, 19,* 99–110.

Elander, J., West, R., & French, D. (1993). Behavioral correlates of individual differences in road-traffic crash risk: An examination of methods and findings. *Psychological Bulletin, 113,* 279–294.

Emmons, R. A. (1991). Personal strivings, daily life events, and psychological and physical well-being. *Journal of Personality, 59,* 453–472.

Emmons, R. A., & Colby, P. M. (1995). Emotional conflict and well-being: Relation to perceived availability, daily utilization, and observer reports of social support. *Journal of Personality and Social Psychology, 68,* 947–959.

Emmons, R. A., & King, L. A. (1988). Conflict among personal strivings: Immediate and long-term implications for psychological and physical well-being. *Journal of Personality and Social Psychology, 54,* 1040–1048.

Emmons, R. A., & King, L. A. (1989). Personal striving differentiation and affective reactivity. *Journal of Personality and Social Psychology, 56,* 478–484.

Epstein, S. (1979). The stability of behavior: I. On predicting most of the people much of the time. *Journal of Personality and Social Psychology, 37,* 1097–1126.

Epstein, S. (1982). A research paradigm for the study of personality and emotions. *Nebraska Symposium on Motivation,* 91–154.

Feldman-Barrett, L. F. (1997). The relationships among momentary emotion experiences, personality descriptions, and retrospective ratings of emotions. *Personality and Social Psychology Bulletin, 23,* 1100–1110.

Feldman-Barrett, L. F., & Moganstein, M. (1997). *Sex differences in the experience of emotion: Retrospective versus momentary ratings.* Unpublished manuscript, Boston College.

Feldman-Barrett, L. F., & Pietromonaco, P. R. (1997). Accuracy of the five-factor model in predicting perceptions of daily social interactions. *Personality and Social Psychology Bulletin, 23,* 1173–1187.

Feldman-Barrett, L. F., Robin, L., Pietromonaco, P. R., & Eyssell, K. M. (1998). Are women the "more emotional" sex? Evidence from emotional experiences in social context. *Cognition and Emotion, 12,* 555–578.

Fiske, S. T., & Taylor, S. E. (1991). *Social cognition.* New York: McGraw-Hill.

Funder, D. C. (1991). Global traits: A neo-Allportian approach to personality. *Psychological Science, 2,* 31–39.

Gable, S. L., & Nezlek, J. B. (1998). Level and instability of day-to-day psychological well-being and risk for depression. *Journal of Personality and Social Psychology, 74,* 129–138.

Gable, S. L., & Reis, H. T. (1999). *Approach and avoidance dispositions, daily events, and affect.* Unpublished manuscript, University of Rochester.

Gable, S. L., & Reis, H. T. (in press). Now and then, them and us, this and that: Studying relationships across time, partner, context, and person. *Personal Relationships.*

Harlow, R. E., & Cantor, N. (1995). To whom do people turn when things go poorly? Task orientation and functional social contacts. *Journal of Personality and Social Psychology, 69,* 329–340.

Hays, R. B. (1989). The day-to-day functioning of close versus casual friendships. *Journal of Social and Personal Relationships, 6,* 21–37.

Hedges, S. M., Jansdorf, L., & Stone, A. A. (1985). Meaning of daily mood assessments. *Journal of Personality and Social Psychology, 48,* 428–434.

Henry, B., Moffitt, T. E., Caspi, A., Langley, J., & Silva, P. A. (1994). On the "remembrance of things past": A longitudinal evaluation of the retrospective method. *Psychological Assessment, 6,* 92–101.

Hinde, R. A. (1995). A suggested structure for a science of relationships. *Personal Relationships, 2*, 1–15.

Hodgins, H. S., Koestner, R., & Duncan, N. (1996). On the compatibility of autonomy and relatedness. *Personality and Social Psychology Bulletin, 22*, 227–237.

Hormuth, S. E. (1986). The sampling of experiences in situ. *Journal of Personality, 54*, 262–293.

Hormuth, S. E. (1990). *The ecology of the self: Relocation and self-concept change.* Cambridge England: Cambridge University Press.

Houts, A. C., Cook, T. D., & Shadish, W. R. (1986). The person-situation debate: A critical multiplist perspective. *Journal of Personality, 54*, 52–105.

Hurlburt, D. F., & Apt, C. (1995). The coital alignment technique and directed masturbation: A comparative study on female orgasm. *Journal of Sex and Marital Therapy, 21*, 21–29.

Hurlburt, R. T. (1990). *Sampling normal and schizophrenic inner experience.* New York: Plenum Press.

Hurlburt, R. T. (1997). Randomly sampling thinking in the natural environment. *Journal of Consulting and Clinical Psychology, 65*, 941–949.

Ickes, W., & Tooke, W. (1988). The observational method: Studying the interaction of minds and bodies. In S. Duck & D. F. Hay (Eds.), *Handbook of personal relationships: Theory, research, and interventions* (pp. 79–97). Chichester, England: Wiley.

Ickes, W., Tooke, W., Stinson, L., Baker, V. L., & Bissonnette V. (1988). Naturalistic social cognition: Intersubjectivity in same-sex dyads. *Journal of Nonverbal Behavior, 12*, 58–84.

Jensen-Campbell, L. A. (1996). *Perceptions of interpersonal conflict during early adolescence.* Unpublished doctoral dissertation, Texas A&M University.

Johnson, C., & Larson, R. (1982). Bulimia: An analysis of moods and behavior. *Psychosomatic Medicine, 44*, 341–351.

Kagan, J. (1984). *The nature of the child.* New York: Basic Books.

Kahneman, D., Fredrickson, B. L., Schreiber, C. A., & Redelmeier, D. A. (1993). When more pain is preferred to less: Adding a better end. *Psychological Science, 4*, 401–405.

Kamarck, T. W., Shiffman, S. M., Smithline, L., Goodie, J. L., Paty, J. A., Gnys, M., & Jong, J. Y. K. (1998). Effects of task strain, social conflict, and emotional activation on ambulatory cardiovascular activity: Daily life consequences of recurring stress in a multiethnic adult sample. *Health Psychology, 17*, 17–29.

Kashy, D. A., & DePaulo, B. M. (1996). Who lies? *Journal of Personality and Social Psychology, 70*, 1037–1051.

Kelley, H. H. (1997). The "stimulus field" for interpersonal phenomena: The source of language and thought about interpersonal events. *Personality and Social Psychology Review, 1*, 140–169.

Kennedy-Moore, E., Greenberg, M. A., Newman, M. G., & Stone, A. A. (1992). The relationship between daily events and mood: The mood measure may matter. *Motivation and Emotion, 16*, 143–155.

Kenny, D. A. (1979). *Correlation and causality.* New York: Wiley.

Kenny, D. A., Kashy, D. A., & Bolger, N. (1998). Data analysis in social psychology. In D. T. Gilbert, S. T. Fiske, & G. Lindzey (Eds.), *The handbook of social psychology* (Vol. 1, 4th ed., pp. 233–265). New York: McGraw-Hill.

Kernis, M. H., Cornell, D. P., Sun, C. R., Berry, A., & Harlow, T. (1993). There's more to self-esteem than whether it is high or low: The importance of stability of self-esteem. *Journal of Personality and Social Psychology, 65*, 1190–1204.

Kessler, R. C. (1997). The effects of stressful life events on depression. *Annual Review of Psychology, 48*, 191–214.

Klinger, E., Barta, S. G., & Maxeiner, M. E. (1980). Motivational correlates of thought content frequency and commitment. *Journal of Personality and Social Psychology, 39*, 1222–1237.

Langston, C. A. (1994). Capitalizing on and coping with daily-life events: Expressive responses to positive events. *Journal of Personality and Social Psychology, 67*, 1112–1125.

Larsen, R. J. (1987). The stability of mood variability: A spectral analytic approach to daily mood assessments. *Journal of Personality and Social Psychology, 52*, 1195–1204.

Larsen, R. J. (1990). Spectral analysis of psychological data. In V. Von Eye (Ed.), *Statistical methods in longitudinal research, Volume II: Time series and categorical longitudinal data* (pp. 319–349). Boston: Academic Press.

Larsen, R. J., & Cowan, G. S. (1988). Internal focus of attention and depression: A study of daily experience. *Motivation and Emotion, 12*, 237–249.

Larsen, R. J., & Cutler, S. E. (1996). The complexity of individual emotional lives: A within-subject analysis of affect structure. *Journal of Social and Clinical Psychology, 15*, 206–230.

Larsen, R. J., & Kasimatis, M. (1990). Individual differences in entrainment of mood to the weekly calendar. *Journal of Personality and Social Psychology, 58*, 164–171.

Larsen, R. J., & Kasimatis, M. (1991). Day-to-day physical symptoms: Individual-differences in the occurrence, duration, and emotional concomitants of minor daily illnesses. *Journal of Personality, 59*, 387–423.

Larson, R. W. (1987). On the independence of positive and negative affect within hour-to-hour experience. *Motivation and Emotion, 11*, 145–156.

Larson, R. W., & Richards, M. H. (1994). *Divergent realities: The emotional lives of mothers, fathers, and adolescents.* New York: Basic Books.

Larson, R. W., Richards, M. H., & Perry-Jenkins, M. (1994). Divergent worlds: The daily emotional experience of mothers and fathers in the domestic and public spheres. *Journal of Personality and Social Psychology, 67*, 1034–1046.

Lavallee, L. R., & Campbell, J. D. (1995). Impact of personal goals on self-regulation processes elicited by daily negative events. *Journal of Personality and Social Psychology, 69*, 341–352.

Lawrence, D. M., & Schank, M. J. (1995). Health care diaries of young women. *Journal of Community Health Nursing, 12*, 171–182.

Leary, M. R., Nezlek, J. B., Downs, D., Radford-Davenport, J., Martin, J., & Mcmullen, A. (1994). Self-presentation in everyday interactions: Effects of target familiarity and gender composition. *Journal of Personality and Social Psychology, 67*, 664–673.

Leigh, B. C. (1993). Alcohol consumption and sexual activity as reported with a diary technique. *Journal of Abnormal Psychology, 102*, 490–493.

Litt, M. D., Cooney, N. L., & Morse, P. (1998). Ecological momentary assessment (EMA) with treated alcoholics: Methodological problems and potential solutions. *Health Psychology, 17*, 48–52.

Lydon, J. E., Jamieson, D. W., & Holmes, J. G. (1997). The meaning of social interactions in the transition from acquaintanceship to friendship. *Journal of Personality and Social Psychology, 73*, 536–548.

Marco, C. A., & Suls, J. (1993). Daily stress and the trajectory of mood: Spillover, response assimilation, contrast, and chronic negative affectivity. *Journal of Personality and Social Psychology, 64*, 1053–1063.

Margolin, G., Christensen, A., & John, R. S. (1996). The continuance and spillover of everyday tension in distressed and nondistressed families. *Journal of Family Psychology, 10*, 304–321.

Martin, R., & Watson, D. (1997). Style of anger expression and its relation to daily experience. *Personality and Social Psychology Bulletin, 23*, 285–294.

McAdams, D. P. (1995). What do we know when we know a person? *Journal of Personality, 63*, 365–398.

McAdams, D. P., & Constantian, C. A. (1983). Intimacy and affiliation motives in daily living: An experience sampling analysis. *Journal of Personality and Social Psychology, 45*, 851–861.

McClelland, D. C. (1957). Toward a science of personality psychology. In H. P. David & H. von Bracken (Eds.), *Perspective in personality theory* (355–382). New York: Basic Books.

McClelland, D. C., Koestner, R., & Weinberger, J. (1989). How do self-attributed and implicit motives differ? *Psychological Review, 96*, 690–702.

McFarland, C., Ross, M., & DeCourville, N. (1989). Women's theories of menstruation and biases in recall of menstrual symptoms. *Journal of Personality and Social Psychology, 57*, 522–531.

McGuire, W. J. (1997). Creative hypothesis generating in psychology: Some useful heuristics. *Annual Review of Psychology, 48*, 1–30.

McLaughlin-Volpe, T., Aron, A., Wright, S. C., & Reis, H. T. (1999). *Intergroup social interactions and intergroup prejudice: Quantity versus quality.* Unpublished manuscript, SUNY-Stony Brook.

Menon, G. (1997). Are the parts better than the whole? The effects of decompositional questions on judgments of frequent behaviors. *Journal Of Marketing Research, 34*, 335–346.

Michela, J. L. (1990). Within-person correlational design and analysis. In C. Hendrick & M. S. Clark (Eds.), *Research methods in personality and social psychology* (pp. 279–311). Newbury Park, CA: Sage.

Milardo, R. M., Johnson, M. P., & Huston, T. L. (1983). Developing close relationships: Changing patterns of interaction between pair members and social networks. *Journal of Personality and Social Psychology, 44*, 964–976.

Moneta, G. B., & Csikszentmihalyi, M. (1996). The effect of perceived challenges and skills on the quality of subjective experience. *Journal of Personality, 64*, 275–310.

Moskowitz, D. S., Brown, K. W., & Côté, S. (1997). Reconceptualizing stability: Using time as a psychological dimension. *Current Directions in Psychological Science, 6*, 127–132.

Moskowitz, D. S., & Côté, S. (1995). Do interpersonal traits predict affect: A comparison of 3 models. *Journal of Personality and Social Psychology, 69*, 915–924.

Nezlek, J. B. (1993). The stability of social interaction. *Journal of Personality and Social Psychology, 65*, 930–941.

Nezlek, J. B., Imbrie, M., & Shean, G. D. (1994). Depression and everyday social interaction. *Journal of Personality and Social Psychology, 67*, 1101–1111.

Nezlek, J. B., & Plesko, R. M. (1999). *Day-to-day relationships among self-concept clarity, self-esteem, daily events, and mood.* Unpublished manuscript, College of William & Mary.

O'Connor, S. C., & Rosenblood, L. K. (1996). Affiliation motivation in everyday experience. *Journal of Personality and Social Psychology, 70*, 513–522.

Parkinson, B., Briner, R. B., Reynolds, S., & Totterdell, P. (1995). Time frames for mood: Relations between monetary and generalized ratings of affect. *Personality and Social Psychology Bulletin, 21*, 331–339.

Pemberton, M. B., Insko, C. A., & Schopler, J. (1996). Memory for and experience of differential competitive behavior of individuals. *Journal of Personality and Social Psychology, 71*, 953–966.

Penner, L. A., Shiffman, S., Paty, J. A., & Fritzsche, B. A. (1994). Individual differences in intraperson variability in mood. *Journal of Personality and Social Psychology, 66*, 712–721.

Pietromonaco, P. R., & Feldman-Barrett, L. (1997). Working models of attachment and daily social interactions. *Journal of Personality and Social Psychology, 73*, 1409–1423.

Redelmeier, D. A., & Kahneman, D. (1996). Patients' memories of painful medical treatments: Real-time and retrospective evaluations of two minimally invasive procedures. *Pain, 66*, 3–8.

Reis, H. T. (1994). Domains of experience: Investigating relationship processes from three perspectives. In R. Erber & R. Gilmour (Eds.), *Theoretical frameworks for personal relationships* (pp. 87–110). Hillsdale, NJ: Erlbaum.

Reis, H. T. (1998). Gender differences in intimacy and related behaviors: Context and process. In D. J. Canary & K. Dindia (Eds.), *Sex differences and similarities in communication: Critical essays and empirical investigations of sex and gender in interaction* (pp. 203–231). Mahwah, NJ: Erlbaum.

Reis, H. T., Lin, Y., Bennett, M. E., & Nezlek, J. B. (1993). Change and consistency in social participation during early adulthood. *Developmental Psychology, 29,* 633–645.

Reis, H. T., Nezlek, J. B., & Wheeler, L. (1980). Physical attractiveness in social interaction. *Journal of Personality and Social Psychology, 38,* 604–617.

Reis, H. T., Senchak, M., & Solomon, B. (1985). Sex differences in the intimacy of social interaction: Further examination of potential explanations. *Journal of Personality and Social Psychology, 48,* 1204–1217.

Reis, H. T., Sheldon, K. M., Gable, S. L., Roscoe, J., & Ryan, R. (in press). Daily well-being: The role of autonomy, competence and relatedness. *Personality and Social Psychology Bulletin.*

Reis, H. T., & Stiller, J. (1992). Publication trends in *JPSP*: A three-decade review. *Personality and Social Psychology Bulletin, 18,* 465–472.

Reis, H. T., & Wheeler, L. (1991). Studying social interaction with the Rochester Interaction Record. *Advances in Experimental Social Psychology, 24,* 269–318.

Reis, H. T., Wheeler, L., Nezlek, J., Kernis, M. H., & Spiegel, N. (1985). On specificity in the impact of social participation on physical and psychological health. *Journal of Personality and Social Psychology, 48,* 456–471.

Reis, H. T., Wheeler, L., Spiegel, N., Kernis, M. H., Nezlek, J., & Perri, M. (1982). Physical attractiveness in social interaction: II. Why does appearance affect social experience? *Journal of Personality and Social Psychology, 43,* 979–996.

Repetti, R. L. (1989). Effects of daily workload on subsequent behavior during marital interaction: The roles of social withdrawal and spouse support. *Journal of Personality and Social Psychology, 57,* 651–659.

Repetti, R. L. (1993). Short-term effects of occupational stressors on daily mood and health complaints. *Health Psychology, 12,* 125–131.

Repetti, R. L. (1996). The effects of perceived daily social and academic failure experiences on school-age children's subsequent interactions with parents. *Child Development, 67,* 1467–1482.

Rhodewalt, F., Madrian, J. C., & Cheney, S. (1998). Narcissism, self-knowledge organization, and emotional reactivity: The effect of daily experiences on self-esteem and affect. *Personality and Social Psychology Bulletin, 24,* 75–87.

Ritter, J. M., & Langlois, J. H. (1988). The role of physical attractiveness in the observation of adult–child interactions: Eye of the beholder of behavioral reality? *Developmental Psychology, 24,* 254–263.

Robinson, J. P., & Godbey, G. (1997). *Time for life: The surprising ways Americans use their time.* University Park, PA: Pennsylvania State University Press.

Ross, M. (1989). Relation of implicit theories to the construction of personal histories. *Psychological Review, 96,* 341–357.

Schwartz, J. E., & Stone, A. A. (1998). Strategies for analyzing ecological momentary assessment data. *Health Psychology, 17,* 6–16,

Schwartz, J. E., Warren, K., & Pickering, T. G. (1994). Mood, location and physical position as predictors of ambulatory blood pressure and heart rate: Application of multi-level random effects model. *Annals of Behavioral Medicine, 16,* 210–220.

Schwarz, N., Groves, R. M., & Schuman, H. (1998). Survey methods. In D. T. Gilbert, S. T. Fiske, & G. Lindzey (Eds.), *The handbook of social psychology* (Vol. 1, 4th ed., pp. 143–179). New York: McGraw-Hill.

Schwarz, N., & Sudman, S. (Eds.). (1996). *Answering questions: Methodology for determining cognitive and communicative processes in survey research.* San Francisco: Jossey-Bass.

Seidlitz, L., & Diener, E. (1998). Sex differences in the recall of affective experiences. *Journal of Personality and Social Psychology, 74,* 262–271.

Sheldon, K. M., Ryan, R. M., & Reis, H. T. (1996). What makes for a good day? Competence and autonomy in the day and in the person. *Personality and Social Psychology Bulletin, 22,* 1270–1279.

Shiffman, S., Fischer, L. A., Paty, J. A., Gnys, M., Kassel, J. D., Hickcox, M., & Perz, W. (1994). Drinking and smoking: A field study of their association. *Annals of Behavioral Medicine, 64,* 366–379.

Shiffman, S., Paty, J. A., Gnys, M., Kassel, J. D., & Hickcox, M. (1996). First lapses to smoking: Within-subjects analysis of real-time reports. *Journal of Consulting and Clinical Psychology, 64,* 366–379.

Skowronski, J. J., Betz, A. L., Thompson, C. P., & Shannon, L. (1991). Social memory in everyday life: Recall of self-events and other-events. *Journal of Personality and Social Psychology, 60,* 831–843.

Sprecher, S. (1999). "I love you more today than yesterday": Romantic partners' perceptions of changes in love a related affect over time. *Journal of Personality and Social Psychology, 76,* 46–53.

Stone, A. A., Broderick, J. E., Porter, L. S., & Kaell, A. T. (1997). The experience of rheumatoid arthritis pain and fatigue: Examining momentary reports and correlates over one week. *Arthritis Care and Research, 10,* 185–193.

Stone, A. A., Hedges, S. M., Neale, J. M., & Satin, M. S. (1985). Prospective and cross-sectional mood reports offer no evidence of a blue Monday phenomenon. *Journal of Personality and Social Psychology, 49,* 129–134.

Stone, A. A., Kessler, R. C., & Haythornthwaite, J. A. (1991). Measuring daily events and experiences: Decisions for the researcher. *Journal of Personality, 59,* 575–607.

Stone, A. A., & Neale, J. M. (1984). Effects of severe daily events on mood. *Journal of Personality and Social Psychology, 46,* 137–144.

Stone, A. A., Neale, J. M., & Shiffman, S. (1993). Daily assessments of stress and coping and their association with mood. *Annals of Behavioral Medicine, 15*, 8–16.

Stone, A. A., Schwartz, J. E., Neale, J. M., Shiffman, S., Marco, C. A., Hickcox, M., Paty, J., Porter, L. S., & Cruise, L. J. (1998). A comparison of coping assessed by ecological momentary assessment and retrospective recall. *Journal of Personality and Social Psychology, 74*, 1670–1680.

Stone, A. A., & Shiffman, S. (1994). Ecological momentary assessment (EMA) in behavioral medicine. *Annals of Behavioral Medicine, 16*, 199–202.

Stone, A. A., Shiffman, S., & DeVries, M. (1999). Ecological momentary assessment. In D. Kahneman, E. Diener, & N. Schwarz (Eds.), *Well-being: The foundations of hedonic psychology.* (pp. 26–39). New York: Sage.

Stone, A. A., Smyth, J. M., Pickering, T., & Schwartz, J. (1996). Daily mood variability: Form of diurnal patterns and determinants of diurnal patterns. *Journal of Applied Social Psychology, 26*, 1286–1305.

Suh, E., Diener, E., & Fujita, F. (1996). Only recent events matter. *Journal of Personality and Social Psychology, 70*, 1091–1102.

Suls, J., & Martin, R. E. (1993). Daily recording and ambulatory monitoring methodologies in behavioral medicine. *Annals of Behavioral Medicine, 15*, 3–7.

Suls, J., Martin, R., & David, J. P. (1998). Person-environment fit and its limits: Agreeableness, neuroticism, and emotional reactivity to interpersonal conflict. *Personality and Social Psychology Bulletin, 24*, 88–98.

Swim, J. K., Cohen, L. L., Hyers, L. L., Fitzgerald, D. C., & Bylsma, W. H. (1997). *The experience of everyday prejudice: A daily diary study.* Unpublished manuscript, Pennsylvania State University.

Tennen, H., Suls, J., & Affleck, G. (1991). Personality and daily experience: The promise and the challenge. *Journal of Personality, 59*, 313–337.

Thomas, D. L., & Diener, E. (1990). Memory accuracy in the recall of emotions. *Journal of Personality and Social Psychology, 59*, 291–297.

Thompson, A., & Bolger, N. (1999). Emotional transmission in couples under stress. *Journal of Marriage and the Family, 61*, 38–48.

Tidwell, M. C. O., Reis, H. T., & Shaver, P. R. (1996). Attachment, attractiveness, and social interaction: A diary study. *Journal of Personality and Social Psychology, 71*, 729–745.

van Eck, M. M., Berkhof, H., Nicolson, N., & Sulon, J. (1996). The effects of perceived stress, traits, mood states and stressful daily events on salivary control. *Psychosomatic Medicine, 58*, 447–458.

Vittengl, J. R., & Holt, C. S. (1998). A time-series diary study of mood and social interaction. *Motivation and Emotion, 22*, 255–275.

Watson, D., & Pennebaker, J. W. (1989). Health complaints, stress, and distress: Exploring the central role of negative affectivity. *Psychological Review, 96*, 234–254.

Webb, E. J., Campbell, D. T., Schwartz, R. D., & Sechrest, L. (1966). *Unobtrusive measures.* Skokie, IL: Rand McNally.

Wentland, E. J. (1993). *Survey responses: An evaluation of their validity.* New York: Academic Press.

West, S. G., & Hepworth, J. T. (1991). Statistical issues in the study of temporal data: Daily experiences. *Journal of Personality, 59*, 609–662.

Wheeler, L., & Miyake, K. (1992). Social comparison in everyday life. *Journal of Personality and Social Psychology, 62*, 760–773.

Wheeler, L., & Nezlek, J. B. (1977). Sex differences in social participation. *Journal of Personality and Social Psychology, 35*, 742–754.

Wheeler, L., & Reis, H. T. (1991). Self-recording of everyday life events: Origins, types, and uses. *Journal of Personality, 59*, 339–354.

Wheeler, L., Reis, H. T., & Bond, M. H. (1989). Collectivism–individualism in everyday social life: The middle kingdom and the melting pot. *Journal of Personality and Social Psychology, 57*, 79–86.

Wheeler, L., Reis, H. T., & Nezlek, J. B. (1983). Physical attractiveness in social interaction. *Journal of Personality and Social Psychology, 38*, 604–617.

Williams, K. J., Suls, J., Alliger, G. M., Learner, S. M., & Wan C. K. (1991). Multiple role juggling and daily mood states in working mothers: An experience sampling study. *Journal of Applied Psychology, 76*, 664–674.

Woike, B. A. (1995). Most-memorable experiences: Evidence for a link between implicit and explicit motives and social cognitive processes in everyday life. *Journal of Personality and Social Psychology, 68*, 1081–1091.

Wong, M. M., & Csikszentmihalyi, M. (1991). Motivation and academic achievement: The effects of personality traits and the quality of experience. *Journal of Personality, 59*, 539–574.

Wood, J. V., Saltzberg, J. A., Neale, J. M., Stone, A. A., & Rachmiel, T. B. (1990). Self-focused attention, coping responses, and distressed mood in everyday life. *Journal of Personality and Social Psychology, 58*, 1027–1036.

Wortman, C. B., & Silver, R. D. (1989). The myths of coping with loss. *Journal of Consulting and Clinical Psychology, 57*, 349–357.

Zautra, A. J., Hoffman, J. M., Matt, K. S., Yocum, D., Potter, P. T., Castro, W. L., & Roth, S. (1998). An examination of individual differences in the relationship between interpersonal stress and disease activity among women with rheumatoid arthritis. *Arthritis Care and Research, 11*, 271–279.

CHAPTER NINE

Survey Research

PENNY S. VISSER, JON A. KROSNICK, AND PAUL J. LAVRAKAS

Social psychologists have long recognized that every method of scientific inquiry is subject to limitations and that choosing among research methods inherently involves trade-offs. With the control of a laboratory experiment, for example, comes an artificiality that raises questions about the generalizability of results. And yet the "naturalness" of a field study or an observational study can jeopardize the validity of causal inferences. The inevitability of such limitations has led many methodologists to advocate the use of multiple methods and to insist that substantive conclusions can be most confidently derived by triangulating across measures and methods that have nonoverlapping strengths and weaknesses (see, e.g., Brewer, this volume, Ch. 1; Campbell & Fiske, 1959; Campbell & Stanley, 1963; Cook & Campbell, 1969; Crano & Brewer, 1986; E. Smith, this volume, Ch. 2).

This chapter describes a research methodology that we believe has much to offer social psychologists interested in a multimethod approach: survey research. *Survey research* is a specific type of field study that involves the collection of data from a sample of elements (e.g., adult women) drawn from a well-defined population (e.g., all adult women living in the United States) through the use of a questionnaire (for more lengthy discussions, see Babbie, 1990; Fowler, 1988;

This chapter was completed while the second author was a Fellow at the Center for Advanced Study in the Behavioral Sciences, supported by National Science Foundation Grant SBR-9022192. Correspondence should be directed to Penny S. Visser, Department of Psychology, Princeton University, Princeton, New Jersey 08544 (e-mail: pvisser@Princeton.edu), or Jon A. Krosnick, Department of Psychology, Ohio State University, 1885 Neil Avenue, Columbus, Ohio 43210 (e-mail: Krosnick @osu.edu).

Frey, 1989; Lavrakas, 1993; Weisberg, Krosnick, & Bowen, 1996). We begin the chapter by suggesting why survey research may be valuable to social psychologists and then outline the utility of various study designs. Next, we review the basics of survey sampling and questionnaire design. Finally, we describe procedures for pretesting questionnaires and for data collection.

REASONS FOR SOCIAL PSYCHOLOGISTS TO CONDUCT SURVEY RESEARCH

Social psychologists are interested in understanding how people influence, and are influenced by, their social environment. And to the extent that social psychological phenomena are universal across different types of people, it makes little difference precisely with whom social psychological research is conducted – even data collected from samples that are decidedly unrepresentative of the general population can be used to draw inferences about that population.

In recent years, however, psychologists have become increasingly sensitive to the impact of dispositional and contextual factors on human thought and social behavior. Instead of broad statements about universal processes, social psychologists today are far more likely to offer qualified accounts of which people, under which conditions, are likely to exhibit a particular psychological phenomenon or process. And accordingly, social psychologists have increasingly turned their attention to interactions between various social psychological processes and characteristics of the individual, such as personality traits, identification with a social group or category, or membership in a distinct culture. In many cases, the nature of basic social psychological processes has been shown to depend to a large degree on characteristics of the individual.

The process by which attitude change occurs, for example, has been shown to differ for people who are low and high in what Petty and Cacioppo (1986) have termed "need for cognition," a general enjoyment of and preference for effortful thinking. Attitude change among people high in need for cognition tends to be mediated by careful scrutiny of the arguments in a persuasive appeal, whereas attitude change among people low in need for cognition tends to be based on cues in the persuasive message or context, such as the attractiveness of the source.

Similarly, attributions have been shown to differ depending on social group membership (see, e.g., Hewstone, Bond, & Wan, 1983). People tend to attribute positive behaviors by members of their own social group or category to stable, internal causes. Those same positive behaviors performed by a member of a different social group, however, are more likely to be attributed to transitory or external factors.

According to much recent research, culture may also moderate many social psychological phenomena. Markus and Kitayama (1991), for example, have argued that members of different cultures have different construals of the self and that these differences can have a profound impact on the nature of cognitive, emotional, and motivational processes. Similarly, Nisbett and his colleagues (Cohen, Nisbett, Bowdle, & Schwarz, 1996; Nisbett, 1993; Nisbett & Cohen, 1996) have explored what they termed the "culture of honor" of the American South and have demonstrated marked differences in the cognitive, emotional, behavioral, and even physiological reactions of southern men (relative to their northern counterparts) when confronted with insult.

These kinds of process-by-individual-difference interactions suggest that precisely who participates in social psychological research can have a profound impact on what results are obtained. And of course, for the vast majority of social psychological research, that "who" has been the infamous college sophomore. Sears (1986) has argued that the field's overwhelming reliance on this narrow base of research participants may represent a serious problem for social psychology. Pointing to various attributes that are characteristic of young adults, Sears (1986) suggested that the "college sophomore" participant pool is unrepresentative of the general population in a number of important ways. Among other things, young adults are more susceptible to attitude change (Alwin, Cohen, & Newcomb, 1991; Glenn, 1980; Krosnick & Alwin, 1989; Sears, 1983), exhibit less stable personality traits (Caspi, Bem, & Elder, 1989; Costa, McCrae,

& Arenberg, 1983; Nesselroade & Baltes, 1974), have more weakly established self-images (Mortimer, Finch, & Kumka, 1982), and have less well-developed social identities (Alwin et al., 1991) than older adults.

Because of these kinds of differences, Sears (1986) argued, the field's reliance on participant pools of college-aged adults raises questions about the generalizability of some findings from social psychological laboratory research and may have contributed to a distorted portrait of "human nature." However, the evidence Sears (1986) cited largely reveals the prevalence of certain characteristics (e.g., the frequency of attitude change or the firmness of social identities), rather than differences in the processes by which these characteristics or others emerge in different age groups. We currently know so little about the operation of social psychological processes in other subsets of the population that it is impossible to assess the extent of bias in this regard.

Doing so will require studies of samples that are representative of the general population, and inducing most members of such samples to visit a laboratory seems practically impossible. Studying a representative sample through field research, however, is relatively easy and surprisingly practical. Using the basic tenets of probability theory, survey researchers have developed a number of efficient strategies for drawing representative samples that are easy to contact. And when samples have been selected in such a manner, social psychologists can confidently generalize findings to the entire population. Furthermore, survey research provides ideal conditions for the exploration of Process × Individual Difference interactions because carefully selected samples reflect the full heterogeneity of the general population.

There are two primary limitations of survey research for social psychologists. First, surveys are more expensive and time-consuming than most laboratory experiments using captive participant pools. However, many cost-saving approaches can be implemented. Second is the impracticality of executing elaborate scripted scenarios for social interaction, especially ones involving deception. Whereas these sorts of events can be created in labs with undergraduate participants, they are tougher to do in the field. But as we discuss shortly, many experimental procedures and manipulations can be incorporated in surveys.

Put simply, social psychology can happily proceed doing most of our research with college sophomores, assuming that our findings generalize. And we can live with the skepticism of scholars from other disciplines who question that generalizability, having documented the profound impact that context and history have on social processes. Or we can accept the challenge and explore the replicability of our findings in the general population. Either we will confirm our assumptions of generalizability or we will refine our theories by adding to them new mediators and moderators. The explication of the survey method offered below is intended to help those who accept the challenge.

TOTAL SURVEY ERROR

Even researchers who recognize the value of survey methodology for social psychological inquiry are sometimes reluctant to initiate survey research because of misconceptions regarding the feasibility of conducting a survey on a limited budget. And indeed, the cost of prominent large-scale national surveys conducted by major survey organizations are well outside of the research budgets of most social psychologists. But survey methodologists have recently begun to rekindle and expand the early work of Hansen and his colleagues (e.g., Hansen & Madow, 1953) in thinking about survey design issues within an explicit cost–benefit framework geared toward helping researchers make design decisions that maximize data quality within the constraints of a limited budget. This approach to survey methodology, known as the "total survey error" perspective (cf. Dillman, 1978, Fowler, 1988; Groves, 1989; Lavrakas, 1993), can provide social psychologists with a broad framework and specific guidelines for making decisions to conduct good surveys on limited budgets while maximizing data quality.

The total survey error perspective recognizes that the ultimate goal of survey research is to accurately measure particular constructs within a sample of people who represent the population of interest. In any given survey, the overall deviation from this ideal is the cumulative result of several sources of survey error. Specifically, the total survey error perspective disaggregates overall error into four components: coverage error, sampling error, nonresponse error, and measurement error. *Coverage error* refers to the bias that can result when the pool of potential survey participants from which a sample is selected does not include some portions of the population of interest. *Sampling error* refers to the random differences that invariably exist between any sample and the population from which it was selected. *Nonresponse error* is the bias that can result when data are not collected from all of the members of a sample. And *measurement error* refers to all distortions in the assessment of the construct of interest, including systematic biases and random variance

that can be brought about by respondents' own behavior (e.g., misreporting true attitudes, failing to pay close attention to a question), interviewer behavior (e.g., misrecording responses, providing cues that lead participants to respond in one way or another), and the questionnaire (e.g., ambiguous or confusing question wording, biased question wording or response options).

The total survey error perspective advocates explicitly taking into consideration each of these sources of error and making decisions about the allocation of finite resources with the goal of reducing the sum of the four. In the sections that follow, we consider each of these potential sources of survey error and their implications for psychologists seeking to balance pragmatic budget considerations against concerns about data quality.

STUDY DESIGNS

Surveys offer the opportunity to execute studies with various designs, each of which is suitable for addressing particular research questions of long-standing interest to social psychologists. In this section, we will review several standard designs, including cross-sectional, repeated cross-sectional, panel, and mixed designs, and discuss when each is appropriate for social psychological investigation. We will also review the incorporation of experiments within surveys.

Cross-Sectional Surveys

Cross-sectional surveys involve the collection of data at a single point in time from a sample drawn from a specified population. This design is most often used to document the prevalence of particular characteristics in a population. For example, cross-sectional surveys are routinely conducted to assess the frequency with which people perform certain behaviors or the number of people who hold particular attitudes or beliefs. However, documenting prevalence is typically of little interest to social psychologists, who are usually more interested in documenting associations between variables and the causal processes that give rise to those associations.

Cross-sectional surveys do offer the opportunity to assess relations between variables and differences between subgroups in a population. But although many scholars believe their value ends there, this is not the case. Cross-sectional data can be used to test causal hypotheses in a number of ways. For example, using statistical techniques such as two-stage least squares regression, it is possible to estimate the causal impact of variable A on variable B, as well as the effect of variable B on variable A (Blalock, 1972). Such an analysis rests on important assumptions about causal relations among variables, but these assumptions can be tested and revised as necessary (see, e.g., James & Singh, 1978). Furthermore, path analytic techniques can be applied to test hypotheses about the mediators of causal relations (Baron & Kenny, 1986; Kenny, 1979), thereby validating or challenging notions of the psychological mechanisms involved. And cross-sectional data can be used to identify the moderators of relations between variables, thereby also shedding some light on the causal processes at work (e.g., Krosnick, 1988b).

A single, cross-sectional survey can even be used to assess the impact of a social event. For example, Krosnick and Kinder (1990) studied priming in a real-world setting by focusing on the Iran/Contra scandal. On November 25, 1986, the American public learned that members of the National Security Council had been funneling funds (earned through arms sales to Iran) to the Contras fighting to overthrow the Sandinista government in Nicaragua. Although there had been almost no national news media attention to Nicaragua and the Contras previously, this revelation led to a dramatic increase in the salience of that country in the American press during the following weeks. Krosnick and Kinder suspected that this coverage might have primed Americans' attitudes toward U.S. involvement in Nicaragua and thereby increased the impact of these attitudes on evaluations of President Ronald Reagan's job performance.

To test this hypothesis, Krosnick and Kinder (1990) took advantage of the fact that data collection for the 1986 National Election Study, a national survey, was underway well before November 25 and continued well after that date. So these investigators simply split the survey sample into one group of respondents who had been interviewed before November 25 and the others, who had been interviewed afterward. As expected, overall assessments of presidential job performance were based much more strongly on attitudes toward U.S. involvement in Nicaragua in the second group than in the first group.

Furthermore, Krosnick and Kinder (1990) found that this priming effect was concentrated primarily among people who were not especially knowledgeable about politics (so-called "political novices"), a finding permitted by the heterogeneity in political expertise in a national sample of adults. From a psychological viewpoint, this suggests that news media priming occurs most when opinions and opinion-formation processes are not firmly grounded in past experience and in supporting knowledge bases. From a political viewpoint, this finding suggests that news media priming may not be especially politically consequential in nations where political expertise is high throughout the population.

Repeated Cross-Sectional Surveys

Additional evidence consistent with a hypothesized causal relation would be that changes over time in a dependent variable parallel changes in a proposed independent variable. One way to generate such evidence is to conduct repeated cross-sectional surveys, in which data are collected from independent samples drawn from the same population at two or more points in time. If a hypothesized causal relation exists between two variables, between-wave changes in the independent variable should be mirrored by between-wave changes in the dependent variable. For example, if one believes that interracial contact may reduce interracial prejudice, an increase in interracial contact over a period of years in a society should be paralleled by a reduction in interracial prejudice.

One study along these lines was reported by Schuman, Steeh, and Bobo (1985). Using cross-sectional surveys conducted between the 1940s and the 1980s in the United States, these investigators documented dramatic increases in the prevalence of positive attitudes toward principles of equal treatment of Whites and Blacks. And there was every reason to believe that these general principles might be important determinants of people's attitudes toward specific government efforts to ensure equality. However, there was almost no shift during these years in public attitudes toward specific implementation strategies. This challenges the notion that the latter attitudes were shaped powerfully by the general principles.

Repeated cross-sectional surveys can also be used to study the impact of social events that occurred between the surveys (e.g., Weisberg, Haynes, & Krosnick, 1995). And repeated cross-sectional surveys can be combined into a single data set for statistical analysis, using information from one survey to estimate parameters in another survey (e.g., Brehm & Rahn, 1997).

Panel Surveys

In a panel survey, data are collected from the same people at two or more points in time. Perhaps the most obvious use of panel data is to assess the stability of psychological constructs and to identify the determinants of stability (e.g., Krosnick, 1988a; Krosnick & Alwin, 1989). But with such data, one can test causal hypotheses in at least two ways. First, one can examine whether individual-level changes over time in an independent variable correspond to individual-level changes in a dependent variable over the same period of time. So, for example, one can ask whether people who experienced increasing interracial contact manifested decreasing racial prejudice, while at the same time, people who experienced decreasing interracial contact manifested increasing racial prejudice.

Second, one can assess whether changes over time in a dependent variable can be predicted by prior levels of an independent variable. So, for example, do people who had the highest amounts of interracial contact at Time 1 manifest the largest decreases in racial prejudice between Time 1 and Time 2. Such a demonstration provides relatively strong evidence consistent with a causal hypothesis, because the changes in the dependent variable could not have caused the prior levels of the independent variable (see, e.g., Blalock, 1985; Kessler & Greenberg, 1981, on the methods; see Rahn, Krosnick, & Breuning, 1994, for an illustration of its application).

One application of this approach occurred in a study of a long-standing social psychological idea called the *projection hypothesis*. Rooted in cognitive consistency theories, it proposes that people may overestimate the extent to which they agree with others whom they like, and they may overestimate the extent to which they disagree with others whom they dislike. By the late 1980s, a number of cross-sectional studies by political psychologists yielded correlations consistent with the notion that people's perceptions of the policy stands of presidential candidates were distorted to be consistent with attitudes toward the candidates (e.g., Granberg, 1985; Kinder, 1978). However, there were alternative theoretical interpretations of these correlations, so an analysis using panel survey data seemed in order. Krosnick (1991a) did just such an analysis exploring whether attitudes toward candidates measured at one time point could predict subsequent shifts in perceptions of presidential candidates' issue stands. And he found no projection at all to have occurred, thereby suggesting that the previously documented correlations were more likely due to other processes (e.g., deciding how much to like a candidate based on agreement with him or her on policy issues; see Byrne, 1971; Krosnick, 1988b).

The impact of social events can be gauged especially powerfully with panel data. For example, Krosnick and Brannon (1993) studied news media priming using such data. Their interest was in the impact of the Gulf War on the ingredients of public evaluations of presidential job performance. For the 1990–1991 National Election Panel Study of the Political Consequences of War, a panel of respondents had been interviewed first in late 1990 (before the Gulf War) and then again in mid-1991 (after the war). The war brought with it tremendous news coverage of events in the Gulf, and Krosnick and Brannon suspected that this coverage might have primed attitudes toward the Gulf War, thereby increasing their impact on public evaluations of President George Bush's job performance. This hypothesis was confirmed by comparing the determinants of presidential evaluations in 1990 and 1991. Because the same people had been interviewed on both occasions, this demonstration is not vulnerable to a possible alternative explanation of the Krosnick and Kinder (1990) results described above: that different sorts of people were interviewed before and after the Iran/Contra revelation and their preestablished presidential evaluation strategies may have produced the patterns of regression coefficients that would then have been misdiagnosed as evidence of news media priming.

Panel surveys do have some disadvantages. First, although people are often quite willing to participate in a single cross-sectional survey, fewer may be willing to complete multiple interviews. Furthermore, with each additional wave of panel data collection, it becomes increasingly difficult to locate respondents to reinterview them, because some people move to different locations, some die, and so on. This may threaten the representativeness of panel survey samples if the members of the first-wave sample who agree to participate in several waves of data collection differ in meaningful ways from the people who are interviewed initially but do not agree to participate in subsequent waves of interviewing.

Also, participation in the initial survey may sensitize respondents to the issues under investigation, thus changing the phenomena being studied. As a result, respondents may give special attention or thought to these issues, which may have an impact on subsequent survey responses. For example, Bridge et al. (1977) demonstrated that individuals who participated in a survey interview about health subsequently considered the topic to be more important. And this increased importance of the topic can be translated into changed behavior. For example, people interviewed about politics are subsequently more likely to vote in elections (Granberg & Holmberg, 1992; Kraut & McConahay, 1973; Yalch, 1976). Even answering a single survey question about one's intention to vote increases the likelihood that an individual will turn out to vote on election day (Greenwald, Carnot, Beach, & Young, 1987).

Finally, panel survey respondents may want to appear consistent in their responses across waves. Therefore, people may be reluctant to report opinions or behaviors that appear inconsistent with what they had reported during earlier interviews. The desire to appear consistent could mask genuine changes over time.

Researchers can capitalize on the strengths of each of the designs discussed above by incorporating both cross-sectional and panel surveys into a single study. If, for example, a researcher is interested in conducting a two-wave panel survey but is concerned about carry-over effects, he or she could conduct an additional cross-sectional survey at the second wave. That is, the identical questionnaire could be administered to both the panel respondents and to an independent sample drawn from the same population. Significant differences between the data collected from these two samples would suggest that carry-over effects were, in fact, a problem in the panel survey. In effect, the cross-sectional survey respondents can serve as a "control group" against which panel survey respondents can be compared.

Experiments within Surveys

Additional evidence of causal processes can be documented in surveys by building in experiments. If respondents are randomly assigned to "treatment" and "control" groups, differences between the two groups can then be attributed to the treatment. Every one of the survey designs described above can be modified to incorporate experimental manipulations. Some survey respondents (selected at random) can be exposed to one version of a questionnaire, whereas other respondents are exposed to another version. Differences in responses can then be attributed to the specific elements that were varied.

Many social psychologists are aware of examples of survey research that have incorporated experiments to explore effects of question order and question wording (see, e.g., Schuman & Presser, 1981). Less salient are the abundant examples of experiments within surveys that have been conducted to explore other social psychological phenomena.

RACISM. One experimental study within a survey was reported by Kinder and Sanders (1990), who were interested in the impact of public debates on public opinion on affirmative action. Sometimes, opponents

of affirmative action have characterized it as entailing reverse discrimination against qualified White candidates; other times, opponents have characterized affirmative action as giving unfair advantages to minority candidates. Did this difference in framing change the way the general public formed opinions on the issue?

To answer this question, Kinder and Sanders (1990) asked White respondents in a national survey about whether they favored or opposed affirmative action programs in hiring and promotions and in college admissions. Some respondents were randomly assigned to receive a description of opposition to affirmative action as emanating from the belief that it involves reverse discrimination. Other respondents, again selected randomly, were told that opposition to affirmative action emanates from the belief that it provides unfair advantages to minorities.

This experimental manipulation of the framing of opposition did not alter the percentages of people who said they favored or opposed affirmative action, but it did alter the processes by which those opinions were formed. When affirmative action was framed as giving unfair advantage to minorities (thereby making minority group members salient), it evoked more anger, disgust, and fury from respondents, and opinions were based more on general racial prejudice, on intolerance of diversity in society, and on belief in general moral decay in society. But when affirmative action was framed as reverse discrimination against qualified Whites (thereby making Whites more salient), opinions were based more on the perceived material interests of the respondent and of Whites as a group.

Because Kinder and Sanders (1990) analyzed data from a national survey, respondents varied a great deal in terms of their political expertise. Capitalizing on this diversity, Kinder and Sanders found that the impact of framing was concentrated nearly exclusively among political novices. This reinforced the implication of Krosnick and Kinder's (1990) finding regarding political expertise in their research on news media priming described earlier.

Sniderman and Tetlock (1986) and Sniderman, Tetlock, & Peterson (1993) have also conducted experiments within surveys to assess whether conservative values encourage racial prejudice in judgments about who is entitled to public assistance and who is not. In their studies, respondents were told about a hypothetical person in need of public assistance. Different respondents were randomly assigned to receive different descriptions of the person, varying in terms of previous work history, marital and parental status, age, and race. Interestingly, conservatives did not exhibit prejudice against Blacks when deciding whether he or she should receive public assistance, even when the person was said to have violated traditional values (e.g., by being a single parent or having a history of being an unreliable worker). And in fact, when presented with an individual who had a history of being a reliable worker, conservatives were substantially more supportive of public assistance for Blacks than for Whites. However, conservatives were significantly less supportive of public policies designed to assist Blacks as a group and were more likely to believe that Blacks are irresponsible and lazy. Sniderman and Tetlock (1986) concluded that a key condition for the expression of racial discrimination is therefore a focus on groups rather than individual members of the groups and that a generally conservative orientation does not encourage individual-level discrimination.

Peffley and Hurwitz (1997; Peffley, Hurwitz, & Sniderman, 1997) also conducted experiments within surveys to explore the impact of racial stereotypes on judgments regarding crime. These investigators hypothesized that although some Americans may hold negative stereotypes of Blacks, those stereotypes may only be used to make judgments about criminal acts or public policies regarding crime when the perpetrators have characteristics consistent with those negative stereotypes. Therefore, when debates about government policy focus on counterstereotypic African American perpetrators, public attitudes may not be especially driven by stereotypes.

In one experiment, respondents in a representative sample survey were told about a man accused of committing a crime and were asked how likely he was to have actually committed it and how likely he was to commit a similar crime in the future. Respondents were randomly assigned to be told that the accused was either Black or White, and they were randomly assigned to be told that the crime was either violent or not violent. When the perpetrator was Black and the crime was violent (and thereby consistent with some negative stereotypes of Black criminals), respondents who held especially negative stereotypes of Blacks were more likely than others to say the person had committed the crime and would do so again. But when the crime was not violent or when the perpetrator was White, stereotypes of Blacks had no impact on judgments of guilt or likelihood of recidivism. In another experiment, respondents with especially negative stereotypes of Blacks were more opposed than others to furlough programs for Blacks convicted of committing violent crimes, but were not especially opposed to furlough programs for Whites or for Blacks who were described as having been model prisoners. This suggests that stereotypes can have relatively little impact on public policy debates if discussions focus on counterstereotypic perpetrators.

MOOD AND LIFE SATISFACTION. Schwarz and Clore (1983) conducted an experiment in a survey to explore mood and misattribution. They hypothesized that general affective states can sometimes influence judgments via misattribution. Specifically, these investigators presumed that weather conditions (sunny vs. cloudy) influence people's moods, which in turn may influence how happy they say they are with their lives. This presumably occurs because people misattribute their current mood to the general conditions of their lives, rather than to the weather conditions that happen to be occurring when they are asked to make the judgment. As a result, when people are in good moods, they may overstate their happiness with their lives.

To test this hypothesis, Schwarz and Clore (1983) conducted telephone interviews with people on either sunny or cloudy days. Among respondents who were randomly selected to be asked simply how happy they were with their lives, those interviewed on sunny days reported higher satisfaction than people interviewed on cloudy days. But among people randomly selected to be asked first, "By the way, how's the weather down there?", those interviewed on sunny days reported identical levels of life satisfaction to those interviewed on cloudy days. The question about the weather presumably led people to properly attribute some of their current mood to current weather conditions, thereby insulating subsequent life satisfaction judgments from influence.

THE BENEFITS OF EXPERIMENTS WITHIN SURVEYS. What is the benefit of doing these experiments in representative sample surveys? Couldn't they instead have been done just as well in laboratory settings with college undergraduates? Certainly, the answer to this latter question is yes; they could have been done as traditional social psychological experiments. But the value of doing the studies within representative sample surveys is at least three-fold. First, survey evidence documents that the phenomena are widespread enough to be observable in the general population. This bolsters the apparent value of the findings in the eyes of the many nonpsychologists who instinctively question the generalizability of laboratory findings regarding undergraduates.

Second, estimates of effect size from surveys provide a more accurate basis for assessing the significance that any social psychological process is likely to have in the course of daily life. Effects that seem large in the lab (perhaps because undergraduates are easily influenced) may actually be quite small and thereby much less socially consequential in the general population. And third, general population samples allow researchers to explore whether attributes of people that are homogeneous in the lab but vary dramatically in the general population (e.g., age, educational attainment) moderate the magnitudes of effects or the processes producing them (e.g., Kinder & Sanders, 1990).

SAMPLING

Once a survey design has been specified, the next step in a survey investigation is selecting a sampling method (see, e.g., Henry, 1990; Kalton, 1983; Kish, 1965; Sudman, 1976). One need not look far in the social science literature to find examples where the conclusions of studies were dramatically altered when proper sampling methods were used (see, e.g., Laumann, Michael, Gagnon, & Michaels, 1994). In this section, we explain a number of sampling methods and discuss their strengths and weaknesses. In this discussion, the term *element* is used to refer to the individual unit about which information is sought. In most studies, elements are the people who make up the population of interest, but elements can also be groups of people, such as families, corporations, or departments. A *population* is the complete group of elements to which one wishes to generalize findings obtained from a sample.

Probability Sampling

There are two general classes of sampling methods: nonprobability and probability sampling. *Nonprobability sampling* refers to selection procedures in which elements are not randomly selected from the population or some elements have unknown probabilities of being selected. *Probability sampling* refers to selection procedures in which elements are randomly selected from the sampling frame and each element has a known, nonzero chance of being selected. This does not require that all elements have an equal probability, nor does it preclude some elements from having a certain (1.00) probability of selection. However, it does require that the selection of each element must be independent of the selection of every other element.

Probability sampling affords two important advantages. First, researchers can be confident that a selected sample is representative of the larger population from which it was drawn only when a probability sampling method has been used. When elements have been selected through other procedures or when portions of the population had no chance of being included in the sample, there is no way to know whether the sample is representative of the population. Generalizations beyond the specific elements in the sample are therefore only warranted when probability sampling methods have been used.

The second advantage of probability sampling is that it permits researchers to precisely estimate the amount of variance present in a given data set that is due to sampling error. That is, researchers can calculate the degree to which random differences between the sample and the sampling frame are likely to have diminished the precision of the obtained estimates. Probability sampling also permits researchers to construct confidence intervals around their parameter estimates, which indicate the precision of the point estimates.

SIMPLE RANDOM SAMPLING. Simple random sampling is the most basic form of probability sampling. With this method, elements are drawn from the population at random, and all elements have the same chance of being selected. Simple random sampling can be done with or without replacement, where replacement refers to returning selected elements to the population, making them eligible to be selected again. In practice, sampling without replacement (i.e., so that each element has the potential to be selected only once) is most common.

Although conceptually a very straightforward procedure, in practice, simple random sampling is relatively difficult and costly to execute. Its main disadvantage is that it requires that all members of the population be identified so that elements can be independently and directly selected from the full population listing (the sampling frame). Once this has been accomplished, the simple random sample is drawn from the frame by applying a series of random numbers that lead to certain elements being chosen and others not. In many cases, it is impossible or impractical to enumerate every element of the population of interest, which rules out simple random sampling.

SYSTEMATIC SAMPLING. Systematic sampling is a slight variation of simple random sampling that is more convenient to execute (e.g., see Ahlgren, 1983). Like simple random sampling, systematic sampling requires that all elements be identified and listed. Based on the number of elements in the population and the desired sample size, a sampling interval is determined. For example, if a population contains 20,000 elements and a sample of 2,000 is desired, the appropriate sampling interval would be 10. That is, every 10th element would be selected to arrive at a sample of the desired size.

To start the sampling process, a random number between one and 10 is chosen, and the element on the list that corresponds to this number is included in the sample. This randomly selected number is then used as the starting point for choosing all other elements. Say, for example, the randomly selected starting point was 7 in a systematic sample with a sampling interval of 10. The 7th element on the list would be the first to be included in the sample, followed by the 17th element, the 27th element, and so forth.[1]

It is important to note that systematic sampling will yield a sample that is representative of the sampling frame from which it was drawn only if the elements composing the list have been arranged in a random order. When the elements are arranged in some nonrandom pattern, systematic sampling will not necessarily yield samples that are representative of the populations from which they are drawn. This potential problem is exacerbated when the elements are listed in a cyclical pattern. If the cyclical pattern of elements coincided with the sampling interval, one would draw a distinctly unrepresentative sample.

To illustrate this point, consider a researcher interested in drawing a systematic sample of men and women who had sought marital counseling within the last 5 years. Suppose he or she obtained a sampling frame consisting of a list of individuals meeting this criterion, arranged by couple: each husband's name listed first, followed by the wife's name. If the researcher's randomly chosen sampling interval was an even number, he or she would end up with a sample composed exclusively of women or exclusively of men, depending on the random start value. This problem is referred to as *periodicity*, and it can be easily avoided by randomizing the order of elements within the sampling frame before applying the selection scheme.

---

[1] Some have argued that the requirement of independence among sample elements eliminates systematic sampling as a probability sampling method, because once the sampling interval has been established and a random start value has been chosen, the selection of elements is no longer independent. Nevertheless, sampling statisticians and survey researchers have traditionally regarded systematic sampling as a probability sampling method, as long as the sampling frame has been arranged in a random order and the start value has been chosen through a random selection mechanism (e.g., Henry, 1990; Kalton, 1983; Kish, 1965). We have therefore included systematic sampling as a probability sampling method, notwithstanding the potential problem of nonindependence of element selection.

STRATIFIED SAMPLING. Stratified sampling is a slight variation of random and systematic sampling, where the sampling frame is divided into subgroups (i.e., strata), and the sampling process is executed separately on each stratum (e.g., see Ross, 1988; Stapp & Fulcher, 1983). In the example above, the sampling frame could be divided into categories (e.g., husbands and wives), and elements could be selected from each category by either a random or systematic method. Stratified sampling provides greater control over the composition of the sample, assuring the researcher of representativeness of the sample in terms of the stratification variable(s). When the stratification variable is related to the dependent variable of interest, stratified sampling reduces sampling error below what would result from simple random sampling.

Stratification that involves the use of the same sampling fraction in each stratum is referred to as proportional stratified sampling. Disproportional stratified sampling – using different sampling fractions in different strata – can also be done. This is typically done when a researcher is interested in reducing the standard error in a stratum where the standard deviation is expected to be high. By increasing the sampling fraction in that stratum, he or she can increase the number of elements allocated to the stratum. This is often done to ensure large enough subsamples for subpopulation analyses. For example, survey researchers sometimes increase the sampling fraction (often called oversampling) for minority groups in national surveys so that reliable parameter estimates can be generated for such subgroups.

Stratification requires that researchers know in advance which variables represent meaningful distinctions between elements in the population. In the example above, gender was assumed to be an important dimension, and substantive differences were expected to exist between men and woman who had sought marital counseling in the past 5 years. Otherwise, it wouldn't matter if the sample included only men or only women. As Kish (1965) pointed out, the magnitude of the advantage of stratification depends on the relation between the stratification variable and the variable(s) of substantive interest in a study; the stronger this relation, the greater the gain from using a stratified sampling strategy.

CLUSTER SAMPLING. When a population is dispersed over a broad geographic region, simple random sampling and systematic sampling will result in a sample that is also dispersed broadly. This presents a practical (and costly) challenge in conducting face-to-face interviews, because it is expensive and time-consuming to transport interviewers to widely disparate locations, collecting data from only a small number of respondents in any one place.

To avoid this problem, researchers sometimes implement cluster sampling, which involves drawing a sample with elements in groups (called "clusters") rather than one-by-one (e.g., see Roberto & Scott, 1986; Tziner, 1987). Then all elements within a cluster are sampled. From the full geographic region of interest, the researcher might randomly select neighborhoods, for example, and collect data from all of the households in each selected neighborhood. In fact, face-to-face interviewing of the American adult population is typically done in clusters of 80 to 100 households within randomly selected neighborhoods, keeping the cost of national interviewing staffs at a manageable level.

Cluster sampling can also be implemented in multiple stages, with two or more sequential steps of random sampling; this is called *multistage* sampling (e.g., see Himmelfarb & Norris, 1987). To assemble a national sample for an in-person survey, for example, one might begin by randomly selecting 100 or so counties from among the more than 3,000 in the nation. Within each selected county, one could then randomly select a census tract; and from each selected tract, one could select a specific block. Then a certain number of households on each selected block could be randomly selected for inclusion in the sample. To do this, a researcher would only need a list of all counties in the United States, all of the census tracts in the selected counties, and all the blocks within the selected tracts, and only then one would one need to enumerate all of the households on the selected blocks, from which to finally draw the sample elements.

Cluster sampling can substantially reduce the time and cost of face-to-face data collection, but it also reduces accuracy by increasing sampling error. Members of a cluster are likely to share not only proximity, but a number of other attributes as well – they are likely to be more similar to one another along many dimensions than a sample of randomly selected individuals would be. Therefore, interviews with a cluster of respondents will typically yield less precise information about the full population than would the same number of interviews with randomly selected individuals.

Furthermore, clustering creates problems because it violates an assumption underlying most statistical tests: independence of observations. That is, all the people in a particular cluster are likely to be more similar to each other than they are to people in other clusters. For statistical tests to be unbiased, this sort of nonindependence needs to be statistically modeled and incorporated in any analysis, thus making the enterprise more cumbersome.

Threats to Sample Representativeness

Ideally, these sampling processes will yield samples that are perfectly representative of the populations from which they were drawn. In practice, however, this virtually never occurs. Two of the four sources of error within the total survey error perspective can distort survey results by compromising representativeness: sampling error and nonresponse error.

SAMPLING ERROR. Sampling error refers to the discrepancy between the sample data and the true population values that are attributable to random differences between the sample and the sampling frame. When one uses a probability sample, estimates of sampling error can be calculated, representing the magnitude of uncertainty regarding obtained parameter estimates. Sampling error is typically expressed in terms of the standard error of an estimate, which refers to the variability of sample estimates around the true population value, assuming repeated sampling. That is, the standard error indicates the probability of observing sample estimates of varying distances from the true population value, assuming that an infinite number of samples of a particular size are drawn from the same population. Probability theory provides an equation for calculating the standard error for a single sample from a population of "infinite" size:

$$SE = \sqrt{\text{sample variance}/\text{sample size}}. \quad (1)$$

Once the standard error has been calculated, it can be used to construct a confidence interval around a sample estimate, which is informative regarding the precision of the parameter estimate. For example, a researcher can be 95% confident that an observed sample statistic (e.g., the sample mean for some variable) falls within 1.96 standard errors of the true population parameter. A small standard error, then, suggests that the sample statistic provides a relatively precise estimate of the population parameter.

As Equation 1 shows, one determinant of sampling error is sample size – as sample size increases, sampling error decreases. This decrease is not linear, however. Moving from a small to a moderate sample size produces a substantial decrease in sampling error, but further increases in sample size produce smaller and smaller decrements in sampling error. Thus, researchers are faced with a trade-off between the considerable costs associated with increases in sample size and the relative gains that such increases afford in accuracy.

The formula in Equation 1 is correct only if the population size is infinite. If the population is finite, then a correction factor needs to be added to the formula for the standard error. Thus, the ratio of sample size to population size is another determinant of sampling error. Data collected from 500 people will include more sampling error if the sample was drawn from a population of 100,000 people than if the sample was drawn from a population of only 1,000 people. When sampling from relatively small populations (i.e., when the sample to population ratio is high), the following alternative sampling error formula should be used:

$$SE = \sqrt{\left(\frac{\text{sample variance}}{\text{sample size}}\right)\left(\frac{\text{population size} - \text{sample size}}{\text{population size}}\right)} \tag{2}$$

As a general rule of thumb, this correction only needs to be done when the sample contains over 5% of the population (Henry, 1990). However, even major differences in the ratio of the sample size to population size have only a minor impact on sampling error. For example, if a dichotomous variable has a 50/50 distribution in the population and a sample of 1,000 elements is drawn, the standard sampling error formula would lead to a confidence interval of approximately 6 percentage points in width. If the population were only 1,500 in size (i.e., two thirds of the elements were sampled), the confidence interval width would be reduced to 5 percentage points.

As Equations 1 and 2 illustrate, sampling error is also dependent on the amount of variance in the variable of interest. If there is no variance in the variable of interest, a sample of 1 is sufficient to estimate the population value with no sampling error. And as the variance increases, sampling error also increases. With a sample of 1,000, the distribution of a dichotomous variable with a 50/50 distribution in the population can be estimated with a confidence interval 6 percentage points in width. However, the distribution of a dichotomous variable with a 10/90 distribution would have a confidence interval of approximately 3.7 percentage points in width.

The standard formula for calculating sampling error, and that used by most computer statistical programs, is based on the assumption that the sample was drawn using simple random sampling. When another probability sampling method has been used, the sampling error may actually be slightly higher or slightly lower than the standard formula indicates. This impact of sampling strategy on sampling error is called a design effect. Defined more formally, the design effect associated with a probability sample is "the ratio of the actual variance of a sample to the variance of a simple random sample of the same elements" (Kish, 1965, p. 258).

Any probability sampling design that uses clustering will have a design effect in excess of 1.0. That is, the sampling error for cluster sampling will be higher than the sampling error for simple random sampling. Any stratified sampling design, on the other hand, will have a design effect less than 1.0, indicating that the sampling error is lower for stratified samples than for simple random samples. Researchers should be attentive to design effects, because taking them into account can increase the likelihood of statistical tests detecting genuinely significant effects.

NONRESPONSE ERROR. Even when probability sampling is done for a survey, it is unlikely that 100% of the sampled elements will be successfully contacted and will agree to provide data. Therefore, most survey samples include some elements from whom no data are gathered.[2] A survey's findings may be subject to nonresponse error to the extent that the sampled elements from whom no data are gathered differ systematically from those from whom data are gathered.

To minimize the potential for nonresponse error, researchers implement various procedures to encourage as many selected respondents as possible to participate (see, e.g., Dillman, 1978; Fowler, 1988; Lavrakas, 1993). Stated generally, the goal here is to minimize the apparent costs of responding, maximize the apparent rewards for doing so, and establish trust that those rewards will be delivered (Dillman, 1978). One concrete approach to accomplishing these goals is sending

---

[2] Most researcher use the term "sample" to refer both to (a) the set of elements that are sampled from the sampling frame from which data ideally will be gathered and (b) the final set of elements on which data actually are gathered. Because almost no survey has a perfect response rate, a discrepancy almost always exists between the number of elements that are sampled and the number of elements from which data are gathered. Lavrakas (1993) suggested that the term "sampling pool" be used to refer to the elements that are drawn from the sampling frame for use in sampling and that the term "sample" be preserved for that subset of the sampling pool from which data are gathered.

letters to potential respondents informing them that they have been selected to participate in a study and will soon be contacted to do so, explaining that their participation is essential for the study's success because of their expertise on the topic, suggesting reasons why participation will be enjoyable and worthwhile, assuring respondents of confidentiality, and informing them of the study's purpose and its sponsor's credibility. Researchers also make numerous attempts to contact hard-to-reach people and to convince reluctant respondents to participate and sometimes pay people for participation or give them gifts as inducements (e.g., pens, golf balls). Nonetheless, most telephone surveys have difficulty achieving response rates much higher than 60%, and most face-to-face surveys have difficulty achieving response rates much higher than 70%.

In even the best academic surveys with such response rates, there are significant biases in the demographic composition of samples. For example, Brehm (1993) showed that in the two leading, recurring academic national surveys of public opinion (the National Election Studies and the General Social Surveys), certain demographic groups have been routinely represented in misleading numbers. For example, young adults and old adults are underrepresented; males are underrepresented; people with the lowest levels of education are overrepresented; and people with the highest incomes are underrepresented. Likewise, Smith (1983) reported evidence suggesting that people who don't participate in surveys are likely to have a number of distinguishing demographic characteristics (e.g., living in big cities and working long hours).

Although a response rate may seem far from 100%, such a high rate of nonresponse does not necessarily mean that a study's implications about nondemographic variables are contaminated with error. If the constructs of interest are not correlated with the likelihood of participation, then nonresponse would not distort results. So investing large amounts of money and staff effort to increase response rates might not translate into higher data quality.

A particularly dramatic demonstration of this fact was reported recently by Visser, Krosnick, Marquette, and Curtin (1996). These researchers compared the accuracy of self-administered mail surveys and telephone surveys forecasting the outcomes of statewide elections in Ohio over a 15-year period. Although the mail surveys had response rates of about 20% and the telephone surveys had response rates of about 60%, the mail surveys predicted election outcomes much more accurately (average error = 1.6%) than the telephone surveys (average error = 5.2%). In addition, the

mail surveys documented the demographic characteristics of voters more accurately than did the telephone surveys. Therefore, simply having a low response rate does not necessarily mean that a survey suffers from a large amount of nonresponse error.

Studies exploring the impact of response rates on correlational results have had mixed implications. For example, Brehm (1993) found that statistically correcting for demographic biases in sample composition had very little impact on the substantive implications of correlational analyses. However, Traugott, Groves, and Lepkowski (1987) reached a different conclusion. These investigators conducted identical telephone interviews with two equivalent samples of respondents. A higher response rate was achieved with one of the samples by mailing letters to them in advance, notifying them about the survey (this improved response rates from about 56% to about 70%). Correlations between some pairs of variables were the same in the two samples. Correlations between other pairs of variables were weakly positive in the sample with the lower response rate and much more strongly positive in the sample with the higher response rate. And correlations between still other pairs of variables were strongly positive in the sample with the lower response rate and zero in the sample with the higher response rate. Thus, substantive results can change substantially as response rates are improved.

Consequently, it is worthwhile to assess the degree to which nonresponse error is likely to have distorted data from any particular sample of interest. One approach to doing so involves making aggressive efforts to recontact a randomly selected sample of people who refused to participate in the survey and collect some data from these individuals. One would especially want to collect data on the key variables of interest in the study, but it can also be useful to collect data on those dimensions along which nonrespondents and respondents seem most likely to differ substantially (see Brehm, 1993). A researcher is then in a position to assess the magnitude of differences between people who agreed to participate in the survey and those who refused to do so.

A second strategy rests on the assumption that respondents from whom data were difficult to obtain (either because they were difficult to reach or because they initially declined to participate and were later persuaded to do so) are likely to be more similar to nonrespondents than are people from whom data were relatively easy to obtain. Researchers can compare responses of people who were immediately willing to participate with those of people who had to be recontacted and persuaded to participate. The smaller the discrepancies between these groups, the less of a threat nonresponse error would seem to be (though see Lin & Schaeffer, 1995).

COVERAGE ERROR. One other sort of possible error deserves mention at this point: coverage error. For reasons of economy, researchers sometimes draw probability samples not from the full set of elements in a population of interest but rather from more limited sampling frames. The greater the discrepancy between the population and the sampling frame, the greater potential there is for coverage error. Such error may invalidate inferences about the population that are made on the basis of data collected from the sample.

By way of illustration, many national surveys these days involve telephone interviewing. And although their goal is to represent the entire country's population, the sampling methods used restrict the sampling frame to households with working telephones. Although the vast majority of American adults do live in households with working telephones (about 95%; Congressional Information Service, 1990), there is a 5% gap between the population of interest and the sampling frame. To the extent that people in households without telephones are different from those in households with telephones, generalization of sample results may be inappropriate.

As compared with residents of households with working telephones, those in households without working telephones tend to earn much less money, have much less formal education, tend to be much younger, and are more often racial minorities (Thornberry & Massey, 1988). If attitudes toward government-sponsored social welfare programs to help the poor are especially positive in such households (as seems quite likely), then telephone surveys may underestimate popular support for such programs. Fortunately, however, households with and without telephones tend not to differ much on many behavioral and attitudinal measures that are unrelated to income (Groves & Kahn, 1979; Thornberry & Massey, 1988). Nonetheless, researchers should be aware of coverage error due to inadequate sampling frames and, when possible, should attempt to estimate and correct for such error.

Nonprobability Sampling

Having considered probability sampling, we turn now to nonprobability sampling methods. Such methods have been used frequently in studies inspired by the recent surge of interest among social psychologists in the impact of culture on social and psychological processes (e.g., Kitayama & Markus, 1994; Nisbett & Cohen, 1996). In a spate of articles published in top journals, a sample of people from one country has been compared with a sample of people from another country, and differences between the samples have been attributed to the impact of the countries' cultures (e.g., Benet & Waller, 1995; Han & Shavitt, 1994; Heine & Lehman, 1995; Rhee, Uleman, Lee, & Roman, 1995). In order to convincingly make such comparisons and properly attribute differences to culture, of course, the sample drawn from each culture must be representative of it. And for this to be so, one of the probability sampling procedures described above must be used.

Alternatively, one might assume that cultural impact is so universal within a country that any arbitrary sample of people will reflect it. However, hundreds of studies of Americans have documented numerous variations between subgroups within the culture in social psychological processes, and even recent work on the impact of culture has documented variation within nations (e.g., Nisbett & Cohen, 1996). Therefore, it is difficult to have much confidence in the presumption that any given social psychological process is universal within any given culture, so probability sampling seems essential to permit a conclusion about differences between cultures based on differences between samples of them.

Instead, however, nearly all recent social psychological studies of culture have employed nonprobability sampling procedures. These are procedures where some elements in the population have a zero probability of being selected or have an unknown probability of being selected. For example, Heine and Lehman (1995) compared college students enrolled in psychology courses in a public and private university in Japan with college students enrolled in a psychology course at a public university in Canada. Rhee et al. (1995) compared students enrolled in introductory psychology courses at New York University with psychology majors at Yonsei University in Seoul, Korea. Han and Shavitt (1994) compared undergraduates at the University of Illinois with students enrolled in introductory communication or advertising classes at a major university in Seoul. And Benet and Waller (1995) compared students enrolled at two universities in Spain with Americans listed in the California Twin Registry.

In all of these studies, the researchers generalized the findings from the samples of each culture to the entire cultures they were presumed to represent. For example, after assessing the extent to which their two samples manifested self-enhancing biases, Heine and Lehman (1995) concluded that "people from cultures representative of an interdependent construal of the self," instantiated by the Japanese students, "do not self-enhance to the same extent as people from cultures characteristic of an independent self," instantiated by the Canadian students (p. 605). Yet the method of recruiting potential respondents for these studies rendered zero selection probabilities for large segments of the relevant populations. Consequently, it is impossible to know whether the obtained samples were representative of those populations, and it is impossible to estimate sampling error or to construct confidence intervals for parameter estimates. As a result, the statistical calculations used in these articles to compare the different samples were invalid, because they presumed simple random sampling.

More important, their results are open to alternative interpretations, as is illustrated by Benet and Waller's (1995) study. One of the authors' conclusions is that in contrast to Americans, "Spaniards endorse a 'radical' form of individualism" (p. 715). Justifying this conclusion, ratings of the terms "unconventional," "peculiar," and "odd" loaded in a factor analysis on the same factor as ratings of "admirable" and "high-ranking" in the Spanish sample, but not in the American sample. However, Benet and Waller's American college student sample was significantly younger and more homogeneous in terms of age than their sample of California twins (the average ages were 24 years and 37 years, respectively; the standard deviations of ages were 4 years and 16 years, respectively). Among Americans, young adults most likely value unconventionality more than older adults, so what may appear in this study to be a difference between countries attributable to culture may instead simply be an effect of age that would be apparent within both cultures.

The sampling method used most often in the studies described above is called *haphazard sampling*, because participants were selected solely on the basis of convenience (e.g., because they were enrolled in a particular course at a particular university). In some cases, notices seeking volunteers were widely publicized, and people who contacted the researchers were paid for their participation (e.g., Han & Shavitt, 1994). This is problematic because people who volunteer tend to be more interested in (and sometimes more knowledgeable about) the survey topic than the general public (see, e.g., Bogaert, 1996; Coye, 1985; Dollinger & Leong, 1993), and social psychological processes seem likely to vary with interest and expertise.

Yet another nonprobability sampling method is *purposive sampling*, which involves haphazardly selecting members of a particular subgroup within a population.

This technique has been used in a number of social psychological studies to afford comparisons of what are called "known groups" (e.g., Hovland, Harvey, & Sherif, 1957; Webster & Kruglanski, 1994). For example, in order to study people strongly supporting prohibition, Hovland et al. (1957) recruited participants from the Women's Christian Temperance Union, students preparing for the ministry, and students enrolled in religious colleges. And to compare people who were high and low in need for closure, Webster and Kruglanski (1994) studied accounting majors and studio art majors, respectively.

In these studies, the groups of participants did indeed possess the expected characteristics, but they may have had other characteristics as well that may have been responsible for the studies' results. This is so because the selection procedures used typically yield unusual homogeneity within the "known groups" in at least some regards and perhaps many. For example, accounting majors may have much more training in mathematics and related thinking styles than studio art majors. Had more heterogeneous groups of people high and low in need for closure been studied by Webster and Kruglanski (1994), it is less likely that they would have sharply differed in other regards and less likely that such factors could provide alternative explanations for the results observed.

Snowball sampling is a variant of purposive sampling, where a few members of a subpopulation are located, and each is asked to suggest other members of the subpopulation for the researcher to contact. Judd and Johnson (1981) used this method in an investigation comparing people with extreme views on women's issues to people with moderate views. To assemble a sample of people with extreme views, these investigators initially contacted undergraduate women who were members of feminist organizations and then asked them to provide names of other women who were also likely to hold similar views on women's issues. Like cluster sampling, this sampling method also violates the assumption of independence of observations, complicating analyis.

Probably the best known form of nonprobability sampling is *quota sampling*, which involves selecting members of various subgroups of the population to assemble a sample that accurately reflects known characteristics of the population. Predetermined numbers of people in each of several categories are recruited to accomplish this. For example, one can set out to recruit a sample containing half men and half women, and one third people with less than high school education, one third high school graduates, and one third people with at least some college education. If quotas are imposed on a probability sampling procedure (e.g., telephone interviews done by random digit dialing) and if the quotas are based on accurate information about a population's composition (e.g., the U.S. Census), then the resulting sample may be more accurate than simple random sampling would be, though the gain would most likely be very small.

However, quotas are not usually imposed on probability sampling procedures but instead are imposed on haphazard samples. Therefore, this approach can give an arbitrary sample the patina of representativeness, when in fact only the distributions of the quota criteria match the population. A particularly dramatic illustration of this problem is the failure of preelection polls to predict that Truman would win his bid for the U.S. Presidency in 1948. Although interviewers conformed to quotas in selecting respondents, the resulting sample was quite unrepresentative in some regards not explicitly addressed by the quotas (Mosteller, Hyman, McCarthy, Marks, & Truman, 1949). A study by Katz (1942) illustrated how interviewers tend to over-sample residents of one-family houses, American-born people, and well-educated people when these dimensions are not explicit among the quota criteria.

Given all this, we urge researchers to recognize the inherent limitations of nonprobability sampling methods and to draw conclusions about populations or about differences between populations tentatively, if at all, when nonprobability sampling methods are used. Furthermore, we encourage researchers to attempt to assess the representativeness of samples they study by comparing their attributes with known population attributes in order to bolster confidence in generalization when appropriate and to temper such confidence when necessary. To scholars in disciplines that have come to recognize the necessity of probability sampling in order to describe populations (e.g., sociology and political science), social psychological research attempting to generalize from a college student sample to a nation looks silly and damages the apparent credibility of our enterprise.

Are we suggesting that all studies of college sophomores enrolled in introductory psychology courses are of minimal scientific value? Absolutely not. The value of the vast majority of social psychological laboratory experiments does not hinge on generalizing their results to a population. Instead, these studies test whether a particular process occurs at all, to explore its mechanisms, and to identify its moderators. Any demonstrations along these lines enhance our understanding of the human mind, even if the phenomena documented occur only among select groups of American college sophomores.

After an initial demonstration of an effect or process or tendency, subsequent research can assess its generality. Therefore, work such as Heine and Lehman's (1995) is valuable because it shows us that some findings are not limitlessly generalizable and sets the stage for research illuminating the relevant limiting conditions. We must be careful, though, about presuming that we know what these limiting conditions are without proper, direct, and compelling tests of our conjectures.

QUESTIONNAIRE DESIGN AND MEASUREMENT ERROR

Once a sample is selected, the next step for a survey researcher is questionnaire design. When designing a questionnaire, a series of decisions must be made about each question. First, will it be open-ended or closed-ended? And for some closed-ended question tasks, should one use rating scales or ranking tasks? If one uses rating scales, how many points should be on the scales and how should they be labeled with words? Should respondents be explicitly offered "no-opinion" response options or should these be omitted? In what order should response alternatives be offered? How should question stems be worded? And finally, once all the questions are written, decisions must be made about the order in which they will be asked.

Every researcher's goal is to maximize the reliability and validity of the data he or she collects. Therefore, each of the above design decisions should presumably be made so as to maximize these two indicators of data quality. Fortunately, thousands of empirical studies provide clear and surprisingly unanimous advice on the issues listed above. Although a detailed review of this literature is far beyond the scope of this chapter (see Bradburn, et al., 1981; J. M. Converse & Presser, 1986; Krosnick & Fabrigar, in press; Schuman & Presser, 1981; Sudman, Bradburn, & Schwarz, 1996), we will provide a brief tour of the implications of these studies.

Open versus Closed Questions

An open-ended question permits the respondent to answer in his or her own words (see, e.g., C. Smith, this volume, Ch. 12; Bartholomew, Henderson, & Marcia, this volume, Ch. 11). For example, one commonly asked open-ended question is "What is the most important problem facing the country today?" In contrast, a closed-ended question requires that the respondent select an answer from a set of choices offered explicitly by the researcher. A closed-ended version of the above question might ask "What is the most important facing the country today: inflation, unemployment, crime, the federal budget deficit, or some other problem?"

The biggest challenge in using open-ended questions is the task of coding responses. In a survey of 1,000 respondents, nearly 1,000 different answers will be given to the "most important problem" question if considered word-for-word. But in order to analyze these answers, they must be clumped into a relatively small number of categories. This requires that a coding scheme be developed for each open-ended question. Multiple people must read and code the answers into the categories, the level of agreement between the coders must be ascertained, and the procedure must be refined and repeated if agreement is too low. The time and financial costs of such a procedure, coupled with the added challenge of requiring interviewers to carefully transcribe answers, have led many researchers to favor closed-ended questions, which in essence ask respondents to directly code themselves into categories that the researcher specifies.

Unfortunately, when used in certain applications, closed-ended questions have distinct disadvantages. Most important, respondents tend to confine their answers to the choices offered, even if the researcher does not wish them to do so (Jenkins, 1935; Lindzey & Guest, 1951). Explicitly offering the option to specify a different response does little to combat this problem. If the list of choices offered by a question is incomplete, even the rank ordering of the choices that are explicitly offered can be different from what would be obtained from an open-ended question. Therefore, a closed-ended question can only be used effectively if its answer choices are comprehensive, and this can often be assured only if an open-ended version of the question is administered in a pretest using a reasonably large sample. Perhaps, then, researchers should simply include the open-ended question in the final questionnaire, because they will otherwise have to deal with the challenges of coding during pretesting. Also supportive of this conclusion is evidence that open-ended questions have higher reliabilities and validities than closed-ended questions (e.g., Hurd, 1932; Remmers, Marschat, Brown, & Chapman, 1923).

One might hesitate in implementing this advice because open-ended questions may themselves be susceptible to unique problems. For example, some researchers feared that open-ended questions would not work well for respondents who are not especially articulate, because they might have special difficulty explaining their feelings. However, this seems not to be a problem (England, 1948; Geer, 1988). Second, some researchers feared that respondents would be especially likely to answer open-ended questions by mentioning the most salient possible responses, not those that are truly most appropriate. But this, too, appears not to be the case (Schuman, Ludwig, & Krosnick, 1986). Thus, open-ended questions seem to be worth the trouble they take to ask and the complexities in analysis of their answers.

Rating versus Ranking

Practical considerations enter into the choice between ranking and rating questions as well. Imagine that one wishes to determine whether people prefer to eat carrots or peas. Respondents could be asked this question directly (a ranking question), or they could be asked to rate their attitudes toward carrots and peas separately, and the researcher could infer which is preferred. With this research goal, asking the single ranking question seems preferable and more direct than asking the two rating questions. But rank-ordering a large set of objects takes much longer and is less enjoyed by respondents than a rating task (Elig & Frieze, 1979; Taylor & Kinnear, 1971). Furthermore, ranking might force respondents to make choices between objects toward which they feel identically, and ratings can reveal not only which object a respondent prefers but also how different his or her evaluations of the objects are.

Surprisingly, however, rankings are more effective than ratings, because ratings suffer from a significant problem: *nondifferentiation*. When rating a large set of objects on a single scale, a significantly number of respondents rate multiple objects identically as a result of survey satisficing (Krosnick, 1991b). That is, although these respondents could devote thought to the response task, retrieve relevant information from memory, and report differentiated attitudes toward the objects, they choose to shortcut this process instead. To do so, they choose what appears to be a reasonable point to rate most objects on the scale and select that point over and over (i.e., nondifferentiation), rather than thinking carefully about each object and rating different objects differently (see Krosnick, 1991b; Krosnick & Alwin, 1988). As a result, the reliability and validity of ranking data are superior to those of rating data (e.g., Miethe, 1985; Munson & McIntyre, 1979; Nathan & Alexander, 1985; Rankin & Grube, 1980; Reynolds & Jolly, 1980). So although rankings do not yield interval-level measures of the perceived distances between objects in respondents' minds and are more statistically cumbersome to analyze (see Alwin & Jackson, 1982), these measures are apparently more useful when a researcher's goal is to ascertain rank orders of objects.

Rating Scale Formats

When designing a rating scale, one must begin by specifying the number of points on the scale. A great number of studies have compared the reliability and validity of scales of varying lengths (for a review, see Krosnick & Fabrigar, in press). For bipolar scales (e.g., running from positive to negative with neutral in the middle), reliability and validity are highest for about 7 points (e.g., Matell & Jacoby, 1971). In contrast, the reliability and validity of unipolar scales (e.g., running from no importance to very high importance) seem to be optimized for a bit shorter scales, approximately 5 points long (e.g, Wikman & Warneryd, 1990). Techniques such as magnitude scaling (e.g., Lodge, 1981), which offer scales with an infinite number of points, yield data of lower quality than more conventional rating scales and should therefore be avoided (e.g., Cooper & Clare, 1981; Miethe, 1985; Patrick, Bush, & Chen, 1973).

A good number of studies suggest that data quality is better when all scale points are labeled with words than when only some are (e.g., Krosnick & Berent, 1993). Furthermore, respondents are more satisfied when more rating scale points are verbally labeled (e.g., Dickinson & Zellinger, 1980). When selecting labels, researchers should strive to select ones that have meanings that divide up the continuum into approximately equal units (e.g., Klockars & Yamagishi, 1988). For example, "very good, good, and poor" is a combination that should be avoided, because the terms do not divide the continuum equally: the meaning of "good" is much closer to the meaning of "very good" than it is to the meaning of "poor" (Myers & Warner, 1968).

Researchers in many fields these days ask people questions offering response choices such as "agree–disagree," "true–false," or "yes–no" (see, e.g., Bearden, Netemeyer, & Mobley, 1993). Yet a great deal of research suggests that these response choices sets are problematic because of acquiescence response bias (see, e.g., Couch & Keniston, 1960; Jackson, 1979; Schuman & Presser, 1981). That is, some people are inclined to say "agree," "true," or "yes," regardless of the content of the question. Furthermore, these responses are more common among people with limited cognitive skills, for more difficult items, and for items

later in a questionnaire, when respondents are presumably more fatigued (see Krosnick, 1991b). A number of studies now demonstrate how acquiescence can distort the results of substantive investigations (e.g., Jackman, 1973; Winkler, Kanouse, & Ware, 1982), and in a particularly powerful example, acquiescence undermined the scientific value of *The Authoritarian Personality's* extensive investigation of facism and antisemitism (Adorno, Frankel-Brunswick, Levinson, & Sanford, 1950). This damage occurs equally when dichotanous items offer just two choices (e.g., "agree" and "disagree") as when a rating scale is used (e.g., ranging from "strongly agree" to "strongly disagree").

It might seem that acquiescence can be controlled by measuring a construct with a large set of items, half of them making assertions opposite to the other half (called "item reversals"). This approach is designed to place acquiescers in the middle of the final dimension but will do so only if the assertions made in the reversals are equally extreme as the statements in the original items. This involves extensive pretesting and is therefore cumbersome to implement. Furthermore, it is difficult to write large sets of item reversals without using the word "not" or other such negations, and evaluating assertions that include negations is cognitively burdensome and error-laden for respondents, thus adding measurement error and increasing respondent fatigue (e.g., Eifermann, 1961; Wason, 1961). And even after all this, acquiescers presumably end up at the midpoint of the resulting measurement dimension, which is probably not where most belong on subtantive grounds anyway. That is, if these individuals were induced not to acquiesce but to answer the items thoughtfully, their final index scores would presumably be more valid than placing them at the midpoint.

Most important, answering an agree–disagree, true–false, or yes–no question always involves answering a comparable rating question in one's mind first. For example, if a man is asked to agree or disagree with the assertion "I am not a friendly person," he must first decide how friendly he is (perhaps concluding "very friendly") and then translate that conclusion into the appropriate selection in order to answer the question he was asked ("disagree" to the original item). It would be simpler and more direct to ask the person how friendly he is. In fact, every agree–disagree, true–false, or yes–no question implicitly requires the respondent to make a mental rating of an object along a continuous dimension, so asking about that dimension is simpler, more direct, and less burdensome. It is not surprising, then, that the reliability and validity of other rating scale and forced choice questions are higher than those of agree–disagree, true–false, and yes–no questions (e.g., Ebel, 1982; Mirowsky & Ross, 1991; Ruch & DeGraff, 1926; Wesman, 1946). Consequently, it seems best to avoid long batteries of questions in these latter formats and instead ask just a couple of questions using other rating scales and forced choice formats.

The Order of Response Alternatives

The answers people give to closed-ended questions are sometimes influenced by the order in which the alternatives are offered. When categorical response choices are presented visually, as in self-administered questionnaires, people are inclined toward primacy effects, whereby they tend to select answer choices offered early in a list (e.g., Krosnick & Alwin, 1987; Sudman, Bradburn, & Schwarz, 1996). But when categorical answer choices are read aloud to people, recency effects tend to appear, whereby people are inclined to select the options offered last (e.g., McClendon, 1991). These effects are most pronounced among respondents low in cognitive skills and when questions are more cognitively demanding (Krosnick & Alwin, 1987; Payne, 1949/1950). All this is consistent with the theory of satisficing (Krosnick, 1991b), which posits that response order effects are generated by the confluence of a confirmatory bias in evaluation, cognitive fatigue, and a bias in memory favoring response choices read aloud most recently. Therefore, it seems best to minimize the difficulty of questions and to rotate the order of response choices across respondents.

No-Opinion Filters and Attitude Strength

Concerned about the possibility that respondents may feel pressure to offer opinions on issues when they truly have no attitudes (e.g., P. E. Converse, 1964), questionnaire designers have often explicitly offered respondents the option to say they have no opinion. And indeed, many more people say they "don't know" what their opinion is when this is done than when it is not (e.g., Schuman & Presser, 1981). People tend to offer this response under conditions that seem sensible (e.g., when they lack knowledge on the issue; Donovan & Leivers, 1993), and people prefer to be given this option in questionnaires (Ehrlich, 1964). However, most "don't know" responses are due to conflicting feelings or beliefs (rather than lack of feelings or beliefs all together) and uncertainty about exactly what a question's response alternatives mean or what the question is asking (e.g., Coombs & Coombs, 1976). It is

not surprising, then, that the quality of data collected is no higher when a "no opinion" option is offered than when it is not (e.g., McClendon & Alwin, 1993). That is, people who would have selected this option if offered nonetheless give meaningful opinions when it is not offered.

A better way to accomplish the goal of differentiating "real" opinions from "nonattitudes" is to measure the strength of an attitude using one or more follow-up questions. Krosnick and Petty (1995) proposed that strong attitudes can be defined as those that are resistant to change, are stable over time, and have powerful impact on cognition and action. Many empirical investigations have confirmed that attitudes vary in strength, and the respondent's presumed task when confronting a "don't know" response option is to decide whether his or her attitude is sufficiently weak as to be best described by selecting that option. But because the appropriate cutpoint along the strength dimension seems exceedingly hard to specify, it would seem preferable to ask people to describe where their attitude falls along the strength continuum.

However, there are many different aspects of attitudes related to their strength that are all somewhat independent of each other (see, e.g., Krosnick, Boninger, Chuang, Berent, & Carnot, 1993). For example, people can be asked how important the issue is to them personally or how much they have thought about it or how certain they are of their opinion or how knowledgeable they are about it (for details on measuring these and many other dimensions, see Wegener, Downing, Krosnick, & Petty, 1995). Each of these dimensions can help to differentiate attitudes that are crystallized and consequential from those that are not.

Question Wording

The logic of questionnaire-based research requires that all respondents be confronted with the same stimulus (i.e., question), so any differences between people in their responses are due to real differences between the people. But if the meaning of a question is ambiguous, different respondents may interpret it differently and respond to it differently. Therefore, experienced survey researchers advise that questions always avoid ambiguity. They also recommend that wordings be easy for respondents to understand (thereby minimizing fatigue), and this can presumably be done by using short, simple words that are familiar to people. When complex or jargony words must be used, it is best to define them explicitly.

Another standard piece of advice from seasoned surveyers is to avoid double-barreled questions, which actually ask two questions at once. Consider the question, "Do you think that parents and teachers should teach middle school students about birth control options?" If a respondent feels that parents should do such teaching and that teachers should not, there is no comfortable way to say so, because the expected answers are simply "yes" or "no." Questions of this sort should be decomposed into ones that address the two issues separately.

Sometimes, the particular words used in a question stem can have a big impact on responses. For example, Smith (1987) found that respondents in a national survey were much less positive toward "people on welfare" than toward "the poor." But Schuman and Presser (1981) found that people reacted equivalently to the concepts of "abortion" and "ending pregnancy," despite the investigators' intuition that these concepts would elicit different responses. These investigators also found that more people say that a controversial behavior should be "not allowed" than say it should be "forbidden," despite the apparent conceptual equivalence of the two phrases. Thus, subtle aspects of question wording can sometimes make a big difference, so researchers should be careful to say exactly what they want to say when wording questions. Unfortunately, though, this literature does not yet offer general guidelines or principles about wording selection.

Question Order

An important goal when ordering questions is to help establish a respondent's comfort and motivation to provide high-quality data. If a questionnaire begins with questions about matters that are highly sensitive or controversial or that require substantial cognitive effort to answer carefully or that seem poorly written, respondents may become uncomfortable, uninterested, or unmotivated and may therefore terminate their participation. Seasoned questionnaire designers advise beginning with items that are easy to understand and answer on noncontroversial topics.

Once a bit into a questionnaire, grouping questions by topic may be useful. That is, once a respondent starts thinking about a particular topic, it is presumably easier for him or her to continue to do so, rather than having to switch back and forth between topics, question by question. However, initial questions in a sequence can influence responses to later, related questions, for a variety of reasons (see Tourangeau & Rasinski, 1988). Therefore, within blocks of related questions,

it is often useful to rotate question order across respondents so that any question order effects can be empirically gauged and statistically controlled for if necessary.

Questions to Avoid

It is often of interest to researchers to study trends over time in attitudes or beliefs. To do so usually requires measuring a construct at repeated time points in the same group of respondents. An appealing shortcut is to ask people to attempt to recall the attitudes or beliefs they held at specific points in the past. However, a great deal of evidence suggests that people are quite poor at such recall, usually presuming that they have always believed what they believe at the moment (e.g., Bem & McConnell, 1970; Ross, 1989). Therefore, such questions vastly underestimate change and should be avoided.

Because researchers are often interested in identifying the causes of people's thoughts and actions, it is tempting to ask people directly why they thought a certain thing or behaved in a certain way. This involves asking people to introspect and describe their own cognitive processes, which was one of modern psychology's first core research methods (Hothersall, 1984). However, it became clear to researchers early in this century that it did not work all that well, and Nisbett and Wilson (1977) articulated an argument about why this is so. Evidence produced since their landmark paper has largely reinforced the conclusion that many cognitive processes occur very quickly and automatically "behind a black curtain" in people's minds, so they are unaware of them and cannot describe them. Consequently, questions asking for such descriptions seem best avoided as well.

PRETESTING

Even the most carefully designed questionnaires sometimes include items that respondents find ambiguous or difficult to comprehend. Questionnaires may also include items that respondents understand perfectly well, but interpret differently than the researcher intended. Because of this, questionnaire pretesting is conducted to detect and repair such problems. Pretesting can also provide information about probable response rates of a survey, the cost and timeframe of the data collection, the effectiveness of the field organization, and the skill level of the data collection staff. A number of pretesting methods have been developed, each of which has advantages and disadvantages, as we review next.

Pretesting Methods for Interviewer-Administered Questionnaires

CONVENTIONAL PRETESTING. In conventional face-to-face and telephone survey pretesting, interviewers conduct a small number of interviews (usually between 15 and 25) and then discuss their experiences with the researcher in a debriefing session (see, e.g., Bischoping, 1989; Nelson, 1985). They describe any problems they encountered (e.g., identifying questions that required further explanation, wording that was difficult to read or that respondents seemed to find confusing) and their impressions of the respondents' experiences in answering the questions. Researchers might also look for excessive item-nonresponse in the pretest interviews, which might suggest a question is problematic. On the basis of this information, researchers can make modifications to the survey instrument to increase the likelihood that the meaning of each item is clear to respondents and that the interviews proceed smoothly.

Conventional pretesting can provide valuable information about the survey instrument, especially when the interviewers are experienced survey data collectors. But this approach has limitations. For example, what constitutes a "problem" in the survey interview is often defined rather loosely, so there is potential for considerable variance across interviewers in terms of what is reported during debriefing sessions. Also, debriefing interviews are sometimes relatively unstructured, which might further contribute to variance in interviewers' reports. Of course, researchers can standardize their debriefing interviews, thereby reducing the idiosyncrasies in the reports from pretest interviewers. Nonetheless, interviewers' impressions of respondent reactions are unavoidably subjective and are likely to be imprecise indicators of the degree to which respondents actually had difficulty with the survey instrument.

BEHAVIOR CODING. A second method, called behavior coding, offers a more objective, standardized approach to pretesting. Behavior coding involves monitoring pretest interviews (either as they take place or via tape recordings of them) and noting events that occur during interactions between the interviewer and the respondent (e.g., Cannell, Miller, & Oksenberg, 1981). The coding reflects each deviation from the script (caused by the interviewer misreading the questionnaire, for example, or by the respondent asking for additional information or providing an initial response that was not sufficiently clear or complete). Questions that elicit frequent deviations from the script are presumed to require modification.

Although behavior coding provides a more systematic, objective approach than conventional pretest methods, it is also subject to limitations. Most important, behavior coding is likely to miss problems centering around misconstrued survey items, which may not elicit any deviations from the script.

COGNITIVE INTERVIEWING. To overcome this important weakness, researchers employ a third pretest method, borrowed from cognitive psychology. It involves administering a questionnaire to a small number of people who are asked to "think aloud," verbalizing whatever considerations come to mind as they formulate their responses (e.g., Forsyth & Lessler, 1991). This "think aloud" procedure is designed to assess the cognitive processes by which respondents answer questions, which presumably provides insight into the way each item is comprehended and the strategies used to devise answers. Interviewers might also ask respondents about particular elements of a survey question, such as interpretations of a specific word or phrase or overall impressions of what a question was designed to assess.

COMPARING THESE PRETESTING METHODS. These three methods of pretesting focus on different aspects of the survey data collection process, and one might expect that they would detect different types of interview problems. And indeed, empirical evidence suggests that the methods do differ in terms of the kinds of problems they detect, as well as in the reliability with which they detect these problems (i.e., the degree to which repeated pretesting of a particular questionnaire consistently detects the same problems).

Presser and Blair (1994) demonstrated that behavior coding is quite consistent in detecting apparent respondent difficulties and interviewer problems. Conventional pretesting also detects both sorts of potential problems, but less reliably. In fact, the correlation between the apparent problems diagnosed in independent conventional pretesting trials of the same questionnaire can be remarkably low. Cognitive interviews also tend to exhibit low reliability across trials, and they tend to detect respondent difficulties almost exclusively.

However, the relative reliability of the various pretesting methods is not necessarily informative about the validity of the insights gained from them. And one might even imagine that low reliability actually reflects the capacity of a particular method to continue to reveal additional, equally valid problems across pretesting iterations. But unfortunately, we know of no empirical studies evaluating or comparing the validity of the various pretesting methods. Much research along these lines is clearly needed.

Self-Administered Questionnaire Pretesting

Pretesting is especially important when data are to be collected via self-administered questionnaires, because interviewers will not be available to clarify question meaning or probe incomplete answers. Furthermore, with self-administered questionnaires, the researcher must be as concerned about the layout of the questionnaire as with the content; that is, the format must be "user-friendly" for the respondent. A questionnaire that is easy to use can presumably reduce measurement error and may also reduce the potential for nonresponse error by providing a relatively pleasant task for the respondent.

Unfortunately, however, pretesting is also most difficult when self-administered questionnaires are used, because problems with item comprehension or response selection are less evident in self-administered questionnaires than face-to-face or telephone interviews. Some researchers rely on observations of how pretest respondents fill out a questionnaire to infer problems in the instrument – an approach analogous to behavior coding in face-to-face or telephone interviewing. But this is a less than optimal means of detecting weaknesses in the questionnaire.

A more effective way to pretest self-administered questionnaires is to conduct personal interviews with a group of survey respondents drawn from the target population. Researchers can use the "think aloud" procedure described above, asking respondents to verbalize their thoughts as they complete the questionnaire. Alternatively, respondents can be asked to complete the questionnaire just as they would during actual data collection, after which they can be interviewed about the experience. They can be asked about the clarity of the instructions, the question wording, and the response options. They can also be asked about their interpretations of the questions or their understanding of the response alternatives and about the ease or difficulty of responding to the various items.

DATA COLLECTION

The survey research process culminates in the collection of data, and the careful execution of this final step is critical to success. Next, we discuss considerations relevant to data-collection mode (face-to-face, telephone, and self-administered) and interviewer selection, training, and supervision (for comprehensive discussions, see, e.g., Bradburn & Sudman, 1979; Dillman, 1978; Fowler & Mangione, 1990; Frey, 1989; Lavrakas, 1993).

Mode

FACE-TO-FACE INTERVIEWS. Face-to-face data collection often requires a large staff of well-trained interviewers who visit respondents in their homes. But this mode of data collection is not limited to in-home interviews; face-to-face interviews can be conducted in a laboratory or other locations as well. Whatever the setting, face-to-face interviews involve the oral presentation of survey questions, sometimes with visual aids. Until recently, interviewers always recorded responses on paper copies of the questionnaire, which were later returned to the researcher.

Increasingly, however, face-to-face interviewers are being equipped with laptop computers, and the entire data-collection process is being regulated by computer programs. In computer-assisted personal interviewing (CAPI), interviewers work from a computer screen, on which the questions to be asked appear one by one in the appropriate order. Responses are typed into the computer, and subsequent questions appear instantly on the screen. This system can reduce some types of interviewer error, and it permits researchers to vary the specific questions each participant is asked based on responses to previous questions. It also makes the incorporation of experimental manipulations into a survey easy, because the manipulations can be written directly into the CAPI program. In addition, this system eliminates the need to enter responses into a computer after the interview has been completed.

TELEPHONE INTERVIEWS. Instead of interviewing respondents in person, researchers rely on telephone interviews as their primary mode of data collection. And whereas computerized data collection is a relatively recent development in face-to-face interviewing, most large-scale telephone survey organizations have been using such systems for the past decade. In fact, computer-assisted telephone interviewing (CATI) has become the industry standard, and several software packages are available to simplify computer programming. Like CAPI, CATI involves interviewers reading from a computer screen, on which each question appears in turn. Responses are entered immediately into the computer.

SELF-ADMINISTERED QUESTIONNAIRES. Often, questionnaires are mailed or dropped off to individuals at their homes, along with instructions on how to return the completed surveys. Alternatively, people can be intercepted on the street or in other public places and asked to compete a self-administered questionnaire, or such questionnaires can be distributed to large groups of individuals gathered specifically for the purpose of participating in the survey or for entirely unrelated purposes (e.g., during a class period or at an employee staff meeting). Whatever the method of distribution, this mode of data collection typically requires respondents to complete a written questionnaire and return it to the researcher.

Recently, however, even this very simple mode of data collection has benefited from advances in computer technology and availability. Paper-and-pencil self-administered questionnaires have sometimes been replaced by laptop computers, on which respondents proceed through a self-guided program that presents the questionnaire. When a response to each question is made, the next question appears on the screen, permitting respondents to work their way through the instrument at their own pace and with complete privacy. Computer assisted self-administered interviewing (CASAI), as it is known, thus affords all of the advantages of computerized face-to-face and telephone interviewing, along with many of the advantages of self-administered questionnaires. A very new development is audio CASAI, where the computer "reads aloud" questions to respondents, who listen on headphones and type their answers on computers.

Choosing a Mode

Face-to-face interviews, telephone interviews, and self-administered questionnaires each afford certain advantages, and choosing among them requires trade-offs. This choice should be made with several factors in mind, including cost, characteristics of the population, sampling strategy, desired response rate, question format, question content, questionnaire length, length of the data-collection period, and availability of facilities.

COST. The first factor to be considered when selecting a mode of data collection is cost. Face-to-face interviews are generally more expensive than telephone interviews, which are usually more expensive than self-administered questionnaire surveys of comparable size.

THE POPULATION. A number of characteristics of the population are relevant to selecting a mode of data collection. For example, completion of a self-administered questionnaire requires a basic proficiency in reading and, depending on the response format, perhaps writing. Clearly this mode of data collection is inappropriate if a nonnegligible portion of the population being studied does not meet this minimum proficiency requirement. Some level of computer literacy is necessary if CASAI is to be used, and again, this may be an inappropriate mode of data collection if a nonnegligible portion of the population is not computer literate. Motivation is another relevant characteristic – researchers who suspect that respondents may be unmotivated to participate in the survey should select a mode of data collection that involves interaction with trained interviewers. Skilled interviewers can often increase response rates by convincing individuals of the value of the survey and persuading them to participate and provide high-quality data (Cannell, Oksenberg, & Converse, 1977; Marquis, Cannell, & Laurent, 1972).

SAMPLING STRATEGY. The sampling strategy to be used may sometimes suggest a particular mode of data collection. For example, some preelection polling organizations draw their samples from lists of currently registered voters. Such lists often provide only names and mailing addresses, which limits the mode of data collection to face-to-face interviews or self-administered surveys.

DESIRED RESPONSE RATE. Self-administered mail surveys typically achieve very low response rates, often less than 50% of the original sample when a single mailing is used. Techniques have been developed to yield strikingly high response rates for these surveys, but they are complex and more costly (see Dillman, 1978). Face-to-face and telephone interviews often achieve much higher response rates, which reduces the potential for nonresponse error.

QUESTION FORM. If a survey includes open-ended questions, face-to-face or telephone interviewing is often preferable, because interviewers can, in a standardized way, probe incomplete or ambiguous answers to ensure the usefulness and comparability of data across respondents.

QUESTION CONTENT. If the issues under investigation are sensitive, self-administered questionnaires may provide respondents with a greater sense of privacy and may therefore elicit more candid responses than telephone interviews and face-to-face interviews (e.g., Bishop & Fisher, 1995; Cheng, 1988; Wiseman, 1972).

QUESTIONNAIRE LENGTH. Face-to-face data collection permits the longest interviews, an hour or more. Telephone interviews are typically quite a bit shorter, usually lasting no more than 30 min, because respondents are often uncomfortable staying on the phone for longer. With self-administered questionnaires, response rates typically decline as questionnaire length increases, so they are generally kept even shorter.

LENGTH OF DATA COLLECTION PERIOD. Distributing questionnaires by mail requires significant amounts of time, and follow-up mailings to increase response rates further increase the overall turnaround time. Similarly, face-to-face interview surveys typically require a substantial length of time in the field. In contrast, telephone interviews can be completed in very little time, within a matter of days.

AVAILABILITY OF STAFF AND FACILITIES. Self-administered mail surveys require the fewest facilities and can be completed by a small staff. Face-to-face or telephone interview surveys are most easily conducted with a large staff of interviewers and supervisors. And ideally, telephone surveys are conducted from a central location with sufficient office space and telephone lines to accommodate a staff of interviewers, which need not be large.

Interviewing

When data are collected face-to-face or via telephone, interviewers play key roles. We therefore review the role of interviewers, as well as interviewer selection, training, and supervision (see J. M. Converse & Schuman, 1974; Fowler & Mangione, 1986, 1990; Saris, 1991).

THE ROLE OF THE INTERVIEWER. Survey interviewers usually have three responsibilities. First, they are often responsible for locating and gaining cooperation from respondents. Second, interviewers are responsible to "train and motivate" respondents to provide thoughtful, accurate answers. And third, interviewers are responsible for executing the survey in a standardized way. The second and third responsibilities do conflict with one another. But providing explicit cues to the respondent about the requirements of the interviewing task can be done in a standardized way while still establishing rapport.

SELECTING INTERVIEWERS. It is best to use experienced, paid interviewers, rather than volunteers or students, because the former approach permits the researcher to be selective and choose only the most skilled and qualified individuals. Furthermore, volunteers or students often have an interest or stake in the substantive outcome of the research, and they may have expectancies that can inadvertently bias data collection.

Whether they are to be paid for their work or not, all interviewers must have good reading and writing skills, and they must speak clearly. Aside from these basic requirements, few interviewer characteristics have been reliably associated with higher data quality (Bass & Tortora, 1988; Sudman & Bradburn, 1982). However, interviewer characteristics can sometimes affect answers to questions relevant to those characteristics.

One instance where interviewer race may have had impact along these lines involved the 1989 Virginia gubernatorial race. Preelection polls showed Black candidate Douglas Wilder with a very comfortable lead over his White opponent. On election day, Wilder did win the election, but by a slim margin of 0.2%. According to Finkel, Guterbock, and Borg (1991), the overestimation of support for Wilder was due at least in part to social desirability. Some survey participants apparently believed it was socially desirable to express support for the Black candidate, especially when their interviewer was Black. Therefore, these respondents overstated their likelihood of voting for Wilder.

Likewise, Robinson and Rohde (1946) found that the more clearly identifiable an interviewer was as being Jewish, the less likely respondents were to express anti-Jewish sentiments. Schuman and Converse (1971) found more favorable views of Blacks were expressed to Black interviewers, though no race-of-interviewer effects appeared on numerous items that did not explicitly ask about liking of Blacks (see also Hyman, Feldman, & Stember, 1954). It seems impossible to eliminate the impact of interviewer race on responses, so it is preferable to randomly assign interviewers to respondents and then statistically control for interview race and the match between interviewer race and respondent race in analyses of data on race-related topics. More broadly, incorporating interviewer characteristics in statistical analyses of survey data seems well worthwhile and minimally costly.

TRAINING INTERVIEWERS. Interviewer training is an important predictor of data quality (Fowler &

Mangione, 1986, 1990). Careful interviewer training can presumably reduce random and systematic survey error due to interviewer mistakes and nonstandardized survey implementation across interviewers. It seems worth the effort, then, to conduct thorough, well-designed training sessions, especially when one is using inexperienced and unpaid interviewers (e.g., students as part of a class project). Training programs last 2 days or longer at some survey research organizations, because shorter training programs do not adequately prepare interviewers, resulting in substantial reductions in data quality (Fowler & Mangione, 1986, 1990).

In almost all cases, training should cover topics such as

- how to use all interviewing equipment,
- procedures for randomly selecting respondents within households,
- techniques for eliciting survey participation and avoiding refusals,
- opportunities to gain familiarity with the survey instrument and to practice administering the questionnaire,
- instructions regarding how and when to probe incomplete responses,
- instructions on how to record answers to open- and closed-ended questions, and
- guidelines for establishing rapport while maintaining a standardized interviewing atmosphere.

Training procedures can take many forms (e.g., lectures, written training materials, observation of real or simulated interviews), but it is important that at least part of the training session involve supervised practice interviewing. Pairs of trainees can take turns playing the roles of interviewer and respondent, for example. And role playing might also involve the use of various "respondent scripts" that present potential problems for the interviewer to practice handling.

SUPERVISION. Carefully monitoring ongoing data collection permits early detection of problems and seems likely to improve data quality. In self-administered surveys, researchers should monitor incoming data for signs that respondents are having trouble with the questionnaire. In face-to-face or telephone surveys, researchers should maintain running estimates of each interviewer's average response rate, level of productivity, and cost per completed interview.

The quality of each interviewer's completed questionnaires should be monitored, and if possible, some of the interviews themselves should be supervised. When surveys are conducted by telephone, monitoring the interviews is relatively easy and inexpensive and should be done routinely. When interviews are conducted face-to-face, interviewers can tape record some of their interviews to permit evaluation of each aspect of the interview.

VALIDATION. When data collection occurs from a single location (e.g., telephone interviews that are conducted from a central phone bank), researchers can be relatively certain that the data are authentic. When data collection does not occur from a central location (e.g., face-to-face interviews or telephone interviews conducted from interviewers' homes), researchers might be less certain. It may be tempting for interviewers to falsify some of the questionnaires that they turn in, and some occasionally do. To guard against this, researchers often establish a procedure for confirming that a randomly selected subset of all interviews did indeed occur (e.g., recontacting some respondents and asking them about whether the interview took place and how long it lasted).

CONCLUSIONS

Over the last several decades, social psychological researchers have come to more fully appreciate the complexity of social thought and behavior. In domain after domain, simple "main effect" theories have been replaced by more sophisticated theories involving moderated effects. Statements such as "People behave like this" are being replaced by "Certain types of people behave like this under these circumstances." More and more, social psychologists are recognizing that psychological processes apparent in one social group may operate differently among other social groups and that personality factors, social identity, and cultural norms can have a profound impact on the nature of many social psychological phenomena.

And yet, the bulk of research in the field continues to be conducted with a very narrow, homogeneous base of participants – the infamous college sophomores. As a result, some scholars have come to question the generalizability of social psychological findings, and some disciplines look with skepticism at the bulk of our empirical evidence. Although we know a lot about the way college students behave in contrived laboratory settings, such critics argue, we know considerably less about the way all other types of people think and behave in their real-world environments.

In this chapter, we have provided an overview of a research methodology that permits social psychologists to address this concern about the meaning and value of our work. Surveys enable scholars to explore social psychological phenomena with samples that accurately represent the population about whom generalizations are to be made. And the incorporation of experimental manipulations into survey designs offers special scientific power. We believe that these advantages of survey research make it a valuable addition to the methodological arsenal available to social psychologists. The incorporation of this methodology into a full program of research enables researchers to triangulate across measures and methods, providing more compelling evidence of social psychological phenomena than any single methodological approach can.

Perhaps a first step for many scholars in this direction might be to make use of the many archived survey data sets that are suitable for secondary analysis. The University of Michigan is the home of the Inter-University Consortium for Political and Social Research (ICPSR), which stores and makes available hundreds of survey data sets on a wide range of topics, dating back at least five decades. Regardless of what topic is of interest to a social psychologist, relevant surveys are likely to have been done that could be usefully reanalyzed. And the cost of accessing these data is quite minimal to scholars working at academic institutions that are members of ICPSR and only slightly more to others. Also, the Roper Center at the University of Connecticut archives individual survey questions from thousands of surveys, some in ICPSR and some not. They do computer-based searches for questions containing particular key words or addressing particular topics, allowing social psychologists to make use of data sets collected as long ago as the 1940s.

So even when the cost of conducting an original survey is prohibitive, survey data sets have a lot to offer social psychologists. We hope that more social psychologists will take advantage of the opportunity to collect and analyze survey data in order to strengthen our collective enterprise. Doing so may require somewhat higher levels of funding than we have had in the past, but our theoretical richness, scientific credibility, and impact across disciplines are likely to grow as a result, in ways that are well worth the price.

REFERENCES

Adorno, T. W., Frenkel-Brunswik, E., Levinson, D. J., & Sanford, R. N. (1950). *The authoritarian personality.* New York: Harper & Row.

Ahlgren, A. (1983). Sex differences in the correlates of cooperative and competitive school attitudes. *Developmental Psychology, 19,* 881–888.

Alwin, D. F., Cohen, R. L., & Newcomb, T. M. (1991). *The women of Bennington: A study of political orientations over the life span.* Madison: University of Wisconsin Press.

Alwin, D. F., & Jackson, D. J. (1982). Adult values for children: An application of factor analysis to ranked preference data. In K. F. Schuessler (Ed.), *Sociological methodology 1980.* San Fransisco: Jossey-Bass.

Babbie, E. R. (1990). *Survey research methods.* Belmont, CA: Wadsworth.

Baron, R. M., & Kenny, D. A. (1986). The moderator-mediator variable distinction in social psychological research: Conceptual, strategic, and statistical considerations. *Journal of Personality and Social Psychology, 51,* 1173–1182.

Bass, R. T., & Tortora, R. D. (1988). A comparison of centralized CATI facilities for an agricultural labor survey. In R. M. Groves, P. P. Beimer, L. E. Lyberg, J. T. Massey, W. L. Nicholls, & J. Waksberg (Eds.), *Telephone survey methodology* (pp. 497–508). New York: Wiley.

Bearden, W. Q., Netemeyer, R. G., & Mobley, M. F. (1993). *Handbook of marketing scales.* Newbury Park, CA: Sage.

Bem, D. J., & McConnell, H. K. (1970.). Testing the self-perception explanation of dissonance phenomena: On the salience of premanipulation attitudes. *Journal of Personality and Social Psychology, 14,* 23–31.

Benet, V., & Waller, N. G. (1995). The big seven factor model of personality description: Evidence for its cross-cultural generality in a Spanish sample. *Journal of Personality and Social Psychology, 69,* 701–718.

Bischoping, K. (1989). An evaluation of interviewer debriefing in survey pretests. In C. F. Cannell, L. Oskenberg, F. J. Fowler, G. Kalton, & K. Bischoping (Eds.), *New techniques for pretesting survey questions* (pp. 15–29). Ann Arbor, MI: Survey Research Center.

Bishop, G. F., & Fisher, B. S. (1995). "Secret ballots" and self-reports in an exit-poll experiment. *Public Opinion Quarterly, 59,* 568–588.

Blalock, H. M. (1972). *Causal inferences in nonexperimental research.* New York: Norton.

Blalock, H. M. (1985). *Causal models in panel and experimental designs.* New York: Aldine.

Bogaert, A. F. (1996). Volunteer bias in human sexuality research: Evidence for both sexuality and personality differences in males. *Archives of Sexual Behavior, 25,* 125–140.

Bradburn, N. M., & Sudman, S. (1979). *Improving interview method and questionnaire design.* San Francisco: Jossey-Bass.

Bradburn, N. M., Sudman, S., & Associates. (1981). *Improving interview method and questionnaire design.* San Francisco: Jossey-Bass.

Brehm, J. (1993). *The phantom respondents.* Ann Arbor: University of Michigan Press.

Brehm, J., & Rahn, W. (1997). Individual-level evidence for the causes and consequences of social capital. *American Journal of Political Science, 41*, 999–1023.

Bridge, R. G., Reeder, L. G., Kanouse, D., Kinder, D. R., Nagy, V. T., & Judd, C. M. (1977). Interviewing changes attitudes – sometimes. *Public Opinion Quarterly, 41*, 56–64.

Byrne, D. (1971). *The attraction paradigm.* New York: Academic Press.

Campbell, D. T., & Fiske, D. W. (1959). Convergent and divergent validation by the multitrait-multimethod matrix. *Psychological Bulletin, 56*, 81–105.

Campbell, D. T., & Stanley, J. C. (1963). Experimental and quasi-experimental designs for research. In N. L. Gage (Ed.), *Handbook of research on teaching* (pp. 171–246). Chicago: Rand McNally.

Cannell, C. F., Miller, P., & Oskenberg, L. (1981). Research on interviewing techniques. In S. Leinhardt (Ed.), *Sociological methodology* (pp. 389–437). San Francisco: Jossey-Bass.

Cannell, C. F., Oskenberg, L., & Converse, J. M. (1977). *Experiments in interviewing techniques: Field experiments in health reporting. 1971–1977.* Hyattsville, MD: National Center for Health Services Research.

Caspi, A., Bem, D. J., & Elder, G. H., Jr. (1989). Continuities and consequences of interactional styles across the life course. *Journal of Personality, 57*, 375–406.

Cheng, S. (1988). Subjective quality of life in the planning and evaluation of programs. *Evaluation and Program Planning, 11*, 123–134.

Cohen, D., Nisbett, R. E., Bowdle, B. F., & Schwarz, N. (1996). Insult, aggression, and the southern culture of honor: An "experimental ethnography." *Journal of Personality and Social Psychology, 70*, 945–960.

Congressional Information Service. (1990). *American statistical index.* Bethesda, MD: Author.

Converse, J. M., & Presser, S. (1986). *Survey questions: Handcrafting the standardized questionnaire.* Beverly Hills, CA: Sage.

Converse, J. M., & Schuman, H. (1974). *Conversations at random.* New York: Wiley.

Converse, P. E. (1964). The nature of belief systems in the mass public. In D. E. Apter (Ed.), *Ideology and discontent* (pp. 206–261). New York: Free Press.

Cook, A. R., & Campbell, D. T. (1969). *Quasi-experiments: Design and analysis issues for field settings.* Skokie, IL: Rand McNally.

Coombs, C. H., & Coombs, L. C. (1976). 'Don't know': Item ambiguity or respondent uncertainty? *Public Opinion Quarterly, 40*, 497–514.

Cooper, D. R., & Clare, D. A. (1981). A magnitude estimation scale for human values. *Psychological Reports, 49*, 431–438.

Costa, P. T., McCrae, R. R., & Arenberg, D. (1983). Recent longitudinal research on personality and aging. In K. W. Schaie (Ed.), *Longitudinal studies of adult psychological development* (pp. 222–263). New York: Guilford Press.

Couch, A., & Keniston, K. (1960). Yeasayers and naysayers: Agreeing response set as a personality variable. *Journal of Abnormal and Social Psychology, 60*, 151–174.

Coye, R. W. (1985). Characteristics of participants and non-participants in experimental research. *Psychological Reports, 56*, 19–25.

Crano, W. D., & Brewer, M. B. (1986). *Principals and methods of social research.* Newton, MA: Allyn and Bacon.

Dickinson, T. L., & Zellinger, P. M. (1980). A comparison of the behaviorally anchored rating and mixed standard scale formats. *Journal of Applied Psychology, 65*, 147–154.

Dillman, D. A. (1978). *Mail and telephone surveys: The total design method.* New York: Wiley.

Dollinger, S. J., & Leong, F. T. (1993). Volunteer bias and the five-factor model. *Journal of Psychology, 127*, 29–36.

Donovan, R. J., & Leivers, S. (1993). Using paid advertising to modify racial stereotype beliefs. *Public Opinion Quarterly, 57*, 205–218.

Ebel, R. L. (1982). Proposed solutions to two problems of test construction. *Journal of Educational Measurement, 19*, 267–278.

Ehrlich, H. J. (1964). Instrument error and the study of prejudice. *Social Forces, 43*, 197–206.

Eifermann, R. R. (1961). Negation: A linguistic variable. *Acta Psychologica, 18*, 258–273.

Elig, T. W., & Frieze, I. H. (1979). Measuring causal attributions for success and failure. *Journal of Personalty and Social Psychology, 37*, 621–634.

England, L. R. (1948). Capital punishment and open-end questions. *Public Opinion Quarterly, 12*, 412–416.

Finkel, S. E., Guterbock, T. M., & Borg, M. J. (1991). Race-of-interviewer effects in a preelection poll: Virginia 1989. *Public Opinion Quarterly, 55*, 313–330.

Forsyth, B. H., & Lessler, J. T. (1991). Cognitive laboratory methods: A taxonomy. In P. Biemer, R. Groves, L. Lyberg, N. Mathiowetz, & S. Sudman (Eds.), *Measurement error in surveys* (pp. 393–418). New York: Wiley.

Fowler, F. J. (1988). *Survey research methods* (2nd ed.). Beverly Hills, CA: Sage.

Fowler, F. J., Jr., & Mangione, T. W. (1986). *Reducing interviewer effects on health survey data.* Washington, DC: National Center for Health Statistics.

Fowler, F. J., Jr., & Mangione, T. W. (1990). *Standardized survey interviewing.* Newbury Park, CA: Sage.

Frey, J. H. (1989). *Survey research by telephone* (2nd ed.). Newbury Park, CA: Sage.

Geer, J. G. (1988). What do open-ended questions measure? *Public Opinion Quarterly, 52*, 365–371.

Glenn, N. O. (1980). Values, attitudes, and beliefs. In O. G. Brim & J. Kagan (Eds.), *Constancy and change in human development* (pp. 596–640). Cambridge, MA: Harvard University Press.

Granberg, D. (1985). An anomaly in political perception. *Public Opinion Quarterly, 49*, 504–516.

Granberg, D., & Holmberg, S. (1992). The Hawthorne effect in election studies: The impact of survey participation on voting. *British Journal of Political Science, 22*, 240–247.

Greenwald, A. G., Carnot, C. G., Beach, R., & Young, B. (1987). Increasing voting behavior by asking people if they expect to vote. *Journal of Applied Psychology, 72*, 315–318.

Groves, R. M. (1989). *Survey errors and survey costs*. New York: Wiley.

Groves, R. M., & Kahn, R. L. (1979). *Surveys by telephone: A national comparison with personal interviews*. New York: Wiley.

Han, S., & Shavitt, S. (1994). Persuasion and culture: Advertising appeals in individualistic and collectivist societies. *Journal of Experimental and Social Psychology, 30*, 326–350.

Hansen, M. H., & Madow, W. G. (1953). *Survey methods and theory*. New York: Wiley.

Heine, S. J., & Lehman, D. R. (1995). Cultural variation in unrealistic optimism: Does the west feel more invulnerable than the east? *Journal of Personality and Social Psychology, 68*, 595–607.

Henry, G. T. (1990). *Practical sampling*. Newbury Park, CA: Sage.

Hewstone, M., Bond, M. H., & Wan, K. C. (1983). Social factors and social attribution: The explanation of intergroup differences in Hong Kong. *Social Cognition, 2*, 142–157.

Himmelfarb, S., & Norris, F. H. (1987). An examination of testing effects in a panel study of older persons. *Personality and Social Psychology Bulletin, 13*, 188–209.

Hothersall, D. (1984). *History of psychology*. New York: Random House.

Hovland, C. I., Harvey, O. J., & Sherif, M. (1957). Assimilation and contrast effects in reactions to communication and attitude change. *Journal of Personality and Social Psychology, 55*, 244–252.

Hurd, A. W. (1932). Comparisons of short answer and multiple choice tests covering identical subject content. *Journal of Educational Psychology, 26*, 28–30.

Hyman, H. A., Feldman, J., & Stember, C. (1954). *Interviewing in social research*. Chicago: University of Chicago Press.

Jackman, M. R. (1973, June). Education and prejudice or education and response-set? *American Sociological Review, 38*, 327–339.

Jackson, J. E. (1979). Bias in closed-ended issue questions. *Political Methodology, 6*, 393–424.

James, L. R., & Singh, B. H. (1978). An introduction to the logic, assumptions, and the basic analytic procedures of two-stage least squares. *Psychological Bulletin, 85*, 1104–1122.

Jenkins, J. G. (1935). *Psychology in business and industry*. New York: Wiley.

Judd, C. M., & Johnson, J. T. (1981). Attitudes, polarization, and diagnosticity: Exploring the effect of affect. *Journal of Personality and Social Psychology, 41*, 26–36.

Kalton, G. (1983). *Introduction to survey sampling*. Beverly Hills, CA: Sage.

Katz, D. (1942). Do interviewers bias poll results? *Public Opinion Quarterly, 6*, 248–268.

Kenny, D. A. (1979). *Correlation and causality*. New York: Wiley.

Kessler, R. C., & Greenberg, D. F. (1981). *Linear panel analysis: Models of quantitative change*. New York: Academic Press.

Kinder, D. R. (1978). Political person perception: The asymmetrical influence of sentiment and choice on perceptions of presidential candidates. *Journal of Personality and Social Psychology, 36*, 859–871.

Kinder, D. R., & Sanders, L. M. (1990). Mimicking political debate within survey questions: The case of White opinion on affirmative action for Blacks. *Social Cognition, 8*, 73–103.

Kish, L. (1965). *Survey sampling*. New York: Wiley.

Kitayama, S., & Markus, H. R. (1994). *Emotion and culture: Empirical studies of mutual influence*. Washington, DC: American Psychological Association.

Klockars, A. J., & Yamagishi, M. (1988). The influence of labels and positions in rating scales. *Journal of Educational Measurement, 25*, 85–96.

Kraut, R. E., & McConahay, J. B. (1973). How being interviewed affects voting: An experiment. *Public Opinion Quarterly, 37*, 398–406.

Krosnick, J. A. (1988a). Attitude importance and attitude change. *Journal of Experimental Social Psychology, 24*, 240–255.

Krosnick, J. A. (1988b). The role of attitude importance in social evaluation: A study of policy preferences, presidential candidate evaluations, and voting behavior. *Journal of Personality and Social Psychology, 55*, 196–210.

Krosnick, J. A. (1991a). Americans' perceptions of presidential candidates: A test of the projection hypothesis. *Journal of Social Issues, 46*, 159–182.

Krosnick, J. A. (1991b). Response strategies for coping with the cognitive demands of attitude measures in surveys. *Applied Cognitive Psychology, 5*, 213–236.

Krosnick, J. A., & Alwin, D. F. (1987). An evaluation of a cognitive theory of response order effects in survey measurement. *Public Opinion Quarterly, 51*, 201–219.

Krosnick, J. A., & Alwin, D. F. (1988). A test of the form-resistant correlation hypothesis: Ratings, rankings, and the measurement of values. *Public Opinion Quarterly, 52*, 526–538.

Krosnick, J. A., & Alwin, D. F. (1989). Aging and susceptibility to attitude change. *Journal of Personality and Social Psychology, 57*, 416–425.

Krosnick, J. A., & Berent, M. K. (1993). Comparisons of party identification and policy preferences: The impact of survey question format. *American Journal of Political Science, 37*, 941–964.

Krosnick, J. A., Boninger, D. S., Chuang, Y. C., Berent, M. K., & Carnot, C. G. (1993). Attitude strength: One construct or many related constructs? *Journal of Personality and Social Psychology, 65*, 1132–1151.

Krosnick, J. A., & Brannon, L. A. (1993). The impact of the Gulf War on the ingredients of presidential evaluations:

Multidimensional effects of political involvement. *American Political Science Review, 87,* 963–975.

Krosnick, J. A., & Fabrigar, L. R. (in press). *Designing great questionnaires: Insights from psychology.* New York: Oxford University Press.

Krosnick, J. A., & Kinder, D. R. (1990). Altering popular support for the president through priming: The Iran-Contra affair. *American Political Science Review, 84,* 497–512.

Krosnick, J. A., & Petty, R. E. (1995). Attitude strength: An overview. In R. E. Petty & J. A. Krosnick (Eds.), *Attitude strength: Antecedents and consequences* (pp. 1–24). Hillsdale, NJ: Erlbaum.

Laumann, E. O., Michael, R. T., Gagnon, J. H., & Michaels, S. (1994). *The social organization of sexuality: Sexual practices in the United States.* Chicago: University of Chicago Press.

Lavrakas, P. J. (1993). *Telephone survey methods: Sampling, selection, and supervision* (2nd ed.). Newbury Park, CA: Sage.

Lin, I. F., & Shaeffer, N. C. (1995). Using survey participants to estimate the impact of nonparticipation. *Public Opinion Quarterly, 59,* 236–258.

Lindzey, G. E., & Guest, L. (1951). To repeat – checklists can be dangerous. *Public Opinion Quarterly, 15,* 355–358.

Lodge, M. (1981). *Magnitude scaling: Quantitative measurement of opinions.* Beverly Hills, CA: Sage.

Markus, H. R., & Kitayama, S. (1991). Culture and the self: Implications for cognition, emotion, and motivation. *Journal of Personality and Social Psychology, 98,* 224–253.

Marquis, K. H., Cannell, C. F., & Laurent, A. (1972). Reporting for health events in household interviews: Effects of reinforcement, question length, and reinterviews. In *Vital and health statistics* (Series 2, No. 45) (pp. 1–70). Washington, DC: U.S. Government Printing Office.

Matell, M. S., & Jacoby, J. (1971). Is there an optimal number of alternatives for Likert Scale items? Study I: Reliability and validity. *Educational and Psychological Measurement, 31,* 657–674.

McClendon, M. J. (1991). Acquiescence and recency response-order effects in interview surveys. *Sociological Methods and Research, 20,* 60–103.

McClendon, M. J., & Alwin, D. F. (1993). No-opinion filters and attitude measurement reliability. *Sociological Methods and Research, 21,* 438–464.

Miethe, T. D. (1985). The validity and reliability of value measurements. *Journal of Personality, 119,* 441–453.

Mirowsky, J., & Ross, C. E. (1991). Eliminating defense and agreement bias from measures of the sense of control: A 2×2 index. *Social Psychology Quarterly, 54,* 127–145.

Mortimer, J. T., Finch, M. D., & Kumka, D. (1982). Persistence and change in development: The multidimensional self-concept. In P. B. Baltes & O. G. Brim, Jr. (Eds.), *Life-span development and behavior* (Vol. 4, pp. 263–312). New York: Academic Press.

Mosteller, F., Hyman, H., McCarthy, P. J., Marks, E. S., & Truman, D. B. (1949). *The pre-election polls of 1948: Report to the Committee on Analysis of Pre-Election Polls and Forecasts.* New York: Social Science Research Council.

Munson, J. M., & McIntyre, S. H. (1979). Developing practical procedures for the measurement of personal values in cross-cultural marketing. *Journal of Marketing Research, 16,* 48–52.

Myers, J. H., & Warner, W. G. (1968). Semantic properties of selected evaluation adjectives. *Journal of Marketing Research, 5,* 409–412.

Nathan, B. R., & Alexander, R. A. (1985). The role of inferential accuracy in performance rating. *Academy of Management Review, 10,* 109–115.

Nelson, D. (1985). Informal testing as a means of questionnaire development. *Journal of Official Statistics, 1,* 179–188.

Nesselroade, J. R., & Baltes, P. B. (1974). Adolescent personality development and historical change: 1970–1972. *Monographs of the Society for Research in Child Development, 39* (No. 1, Serial No. 154).

Nisbett, R. E. (1993). Violence and U.S. regional culture. *American Psychologist, 48,* 441–449.

Nisbett, R. E., & Cohen, D. (1996). *Culture of honor: The psychology of violence in the south.* Boulder, CO: Westview Press.

Nisbett, R. E., & Wilson, T. D. (1977). Telling more than we can know: Verbal reports on mental processes. *Psychology Review, 84,* 231–259.

Patrick, D. L., Bush, J. W., & Chen, M. M. (1973). Methods for measuring levels of well-being for a health status index. *Health Services Research, 8,* 228–245.

Payne, S. L. (1949/1950). Case study in question complexity. *Public Opinion Quarterly, 13,* 653–658.

Peffley, M., & Hurwitz, J. (1997). Public perceptions of race and crime: The role of racial stereotypes. *American Journal of Political Science, 41,* 375–401.

Peffley, M., Hurwitz, J., & Sniderman, P. M. (1997). Racial stereotypes and Whites' political views of Blacks in the context of welfare and crime. *American Journal of Political Science, 41,* 30–60.

Petty, R. E., & Cacioppo, J. T. (1986). *Communication and persuasion: Central and peripheral routes to attitude change.* New York: Springer-Verlag.

Presser, S., & Blair, J. (1994). Survey pretesting: Do different methods produce different results? In P. V. Marsden (Ed.), *Sociological methodology, 1994* (pp. 73–104). Cambridge, MA: Blackwell.

Rahn, W. M., Krosnick, J. A., & Breuning, M. (1994). Rationalization and derivation processes in survey studies of political candidate evaluation. *American Journal of Political Science, 38,* 582–600.

Rankin, W. L., & Grube, J. W. (1980). A comparison of ranking and rating procedures for value system measurement. *European Journal of Social Psychology, 10,* 233–246.

Remmers, H. H., Marschat, L. E., Brown, A., & Chapman, I. (1923). An experimental study of the relative difficulty of true-false, multiple-choice, and incomplete-sentence types of examination questions. *Journal of Educational Psychology, 14*, 367–372.

Reynolds, T. J., & Jolly, J. P. (1980). Measuring personal values: An evaluation of alternative methods. *Journal of Marketing Research, 17*, 531–536.

Rhee, E., Uleman, J. S., Lee, H. K., & Roman, R. J. (1995). Spontaneous self-descriptions and ethnic identities in individualistic and collectivist cultures. *Journal of Personality and Social Psychology, 69*, 142–152.

Roberto, K. A., & Scott, J. P. (1986). Confronting widowhood: The influence of informal supports. *American Behavioral Scientist, 29*, 497–511.

Robinson, D., & Rohde, S. (1946). Two experiments with an anti-semitism poll. *Journal of Abnormal and Social Psychology, 41*, 136–144.

Ross, M. (1989). Relation of implicit theories to the construction of personal histories. *Psychological Review, 96*, 341–357.

Ross, M. W. (1988). Prevalence of classes of risk behaviors for HIV infection in a randomly selected Australian population. *Journal of Sex Research, 25*, 441–450.

Ruch, G. M., & DeGraff, M. H. (1926). Corrections for chance and "guess" vs. "do not guess" instructions in multiple-response tests. *Journal of Educational Psychology, 17*, 368–375.

Saris, W. E. (1991). *Computer-assisted interviewing.* Newbury Park, CA: Sage.

Schuman, H., & Converse, J. M. (1971). The effects of Black and White interviewers on Black responses in 1968. *Public Opinion Quarterly, 35*, 44–68.

Schuman, H., Ludwig, J., & Krosnick, J. A. (1986). The perceived threat of nuclear war, salience, and open questions. *Public Opinion Quarterly, 50*, 519–536.

Schuman, H., & Presser, S. (1981). *Questions and answers in attitude surveys.* San Diego, CA: Academic Press.

Schuman, H., Steeh, C., & Bobo, L. (1985). *Racial attitudes in America: Trends and interpretations.* Cambridge, MA: Harvard University Press.

Schwarz, N., & Clore, G. L. (1983). Mood, misattribution, and judgments of well-being: Informative and directive functions of affective states. *Journal of Personality and Social Psychology, 45*, 513–523.

Sears, D. O. (1983). The persistence of early political predispositions: The role of attitude object and life stage. In L. Wheeler (Ed.), *Review of personality and social psychology* (Vol. 4, pp. 79–116). Beverly Hills, CA: Sage.

Sears, D. O. (1986). College sophomores in the laboratory: Influences of a narrow data base on social psychology's view of human nature. *Journal of Personality and Social Psychology, 51*, 515–530.

Smith, T. W. (1983). The hidden 25 percent: An analysis of nonresponse in the 1980 General Social Survey. *Public Opinion Quarterly, 47*, 386–404.

Smith, T. W. (1987). That which we call welfare by any other name would smell sweeter: An analysis of the impact of question wording on response patterns. *Public Opinion Quarterly, 51*, 75–83.

Sniderman, P. M., & Tetlock, P. E. (1986). Symbolic racism: Problems of motive attribution in political analysis. *Journal of Social Issues, 42*, 129–150.

Sniderman, P. M., Tetlock, P. E., & Peterson, R. S. (1993). Racism and liberal democracy. *Politics and the Individual, 3*, 1–28.

Stapp, J., & Fulcher, R. (1983). The employment of APA members: 1982. *American Psychologist, 38*, 1298–1320.

Sudman, S. (1976). *Applied sampling.* New York: Academic Press.

Sudman, S., & Bradburn, N. M. (1982). *Asking questions.* San Francisco: Jossey-Bass.

Sudman, S., Bradburn, N. M., & Schwarz, N. (1996). *Thinking about answers: The application of cognitive processes to survey methodology.* San Francisco: Jossey-Bass.

Taylor, J. R., & Kinnear, T. C. (1971). Numerical comparison of alternative methods for collecting proximity judgements. *American Marketing Association Proceeding of the Fall Conference,* 547–550.

Thornberry, O. T., Jr., & Massey, J. T. (1988). Trends in United States telephone coverage across time and subgroups. In R. M. Groves, P. P. Biemer, L. E. Lyberg, J. T. Massey, W. L. Nicholls, & J. Waksberg (Eds.), *Telephone survey methodology* (pp. 25–50). New York: Wiley.

Tourangeau, R., & Rasinski, K. A. (1988). Cognitive processes underlying context effects in attitude measurement. *Psychological Bulletin, 103*, 299–314.

Traugott, M. W., Groves, R. M., & Lepkowski, J. M. (1987). Using dual frame designs to reduce nonresponse in telephone surveys. *Public Opinion Quarterly, 51*, 522–539.

Tziner, A. (1987). Congruency issues retested using Rineman's achievement climate notion. *Journal of Social Behavior and Personality, 2*, 63–78.

Visser, P. S., Krosnick, J. A., Marquette, J., & Curtin, M. (1996). Mail surveys for election forecasting? An evaluation of the Columbus Dispatch poll. *Public Opinion Quarterly, 60*, 181–227.

Wason, P. C. (1961). Response to affirmative and negative binary statements. *British Journal of Psychology, 52*, 133–142.

Webster, D. M., & Kruglanski, A. W. (1994). Individual differences in need for cognitive closure. *Journal of Personality and Social Psychology, 67*, 1049–1062.

Wegener, D. T., Downing, J., Krosnick, J. A., & Petty, R. E. (1995). Measures and manipulations of strength-related properties of attitudes: Current practice and future directions. In R. E. Petty & J. A. Krosnick (Eds.), *Attitude strength: Antecedents and consequences* (pp. 455–487). Hillsdale, NJ: Erlbaum.

Weisberg, H. F., Haynes, A. A., & Krosnick, J. A. (1995). Social group polarization in 1992. In H. F. Weisberg (Ed.), *Democracy's feast: Elections in America* (pp. 241–249). Chatham, NJ: Chatham House.

Weisberg, H. F., Krosnick, J. A., & Bowen, B. D. (1996). *An introduction to survey research, polling, and data analysis* (3rd ed.). Newbury Park, CA: Sage.

Wesman, A. G. (1946). The usefulness of correctly spelled words in a spelling test. *Journal of Educational Psychology, 37,* 242–246.

Wikman, A., & Warneryd, B. (1990). Measurement errors in survey questions: Explaining response variability. *Social Indicators Research, 22,* 199–212.

Winkler, J. D., Kanouse, D. E., & Ware, J. E., Jr. (1982). Controlling for acquiescence response set in scale development. *Journal of Applied Psychology, 67,* 555–561.

Wiseman, F. (1972). Methodological bias in public opinion surveys. *Public Opinion Quarterly, 36,* 105–108.

Yalch, R. F. (1976). Pre-election interview effects on voter turnouts. *Public Opinion Quarterly, 40,* 331–336.

CHAPTER TEN

The Mind in the Middle

A Practical Guide to Priming and Automaticity Research

JOHN A. BARGH AND TANYA L. CHARTRAND

Though it might be hard for fledgling researchers of today to believe, for most of the 20th century, invoking cognitive mechanisms and processes to explain and model psychological phenomena was not allowed. The reason for this was because the only known research technique to examine these internal mental states was introspection and self-report. This method was seen to be fatally flawed in that an objective outside observer could not make the measurements, and so the data could not be independently verified. Other sciences did not confuse the observer with the observed, and so, it was said, neither should psychology if it wanted to be considered a science. In his book, *The Ghost in the Machine*, Arthur Koestler (1967) observed that this dedicated neglect of its natural subject matter caused psychology to go nowhere, at a time in history when the other sciences, in contrast, were making giant strides forward.

But things are very different today. The research methods and techniques described in this chapter are a major reason why we now have a scientific social cognitive psychology. The methods described are not of self-report; they are made by outside observers and are replicable by other outside observers. Instead of introspection, as a field we have learned how to make inferences about cognitive process and structure from response latencies, and from the order in which our participants recall stimuli about people and events and about what happens when the mental system is put under stress, as when the individual has to do several different things at once. For the most part, we do not have to rely solely on the person's own description of their internal state – like the nuclear physicist inferring atomic structure from lines on a photographic plate, we can infer mental structure from 25 ms differences in the time taken to pronounce a specific word. One cannot "see" inside another's mind, but neither can the physicist "see" quarks and muons inside the atom. Just as do other sciences, we infer, deduce, and build theories about the mind based on observables, generating falsifiable predictions and putting them to the test. (And we can even use introspection and self-report, because we are able to verify and check these data against the other, independent means.)

The present chapter is a summary of the methods commonly used to explore the cognitive representations and processes that mediate between environmental events and psychological reactions to them – whether those responses be impressions, evaluations, goals, or behavior. We focus primarily on passive, or unintentional, forms of cognitive mediation in an attempt to keep it distinct from motivational mediation as much as possible. Goal effects on information processing and behavior are purposive and strategic (by definition) and not strictly due to cognitive structure or process per se (for a comprehensive recent review, see Gollwitzer & Moskowitz, 1996). But motivation and cognition are highly if not inextricably related (Gollwitzer & Bargh, 1996; Sorrentino & Higgins,

This chapter was written while the senior author was a visiting professor at the University of Konstanz. Its preparation was supported in part by Grant SBR-9409448 from the National Science Foundation, and by a fellowship from the Alexander von Humboldt Foundation. We thank the editors and Miguel Brendl, Peter Gollwitzer, Asher Koriat, Katelyn McKenna, James Uleman, Wolfgang Wasel, and Gifford Weary for their advice and suggestions. Correspondence should be directed to John A. Bargh at Department of Psychology, New York University, Seventh Floor, 6 Washington Place, New York, NY 10003, or Tanya L. Chartrand, Department of Psychology, Ohio State University, Columbus, Ohio 43210.

1986), and the reader of the present chapter will find many references to the intersection of the two – for instance, in the unintended carry-over effects of a goal chosen intentionally in one context to a subsequent context. We hope by maintaining a focus on passive or unintentional effects, we keep to the theme of how to study the mental representations and processes that mediate and moderate social psychological phenomena.

Priming and automaticity research techniques share a concern with the ways that internal mental states mediate, in a passive and hidden manner, the effects of the social environment on psychological processes and responses. Automaticity techniques enable an experimenter to measure the particular mental procedures or representations that are assumed, in his or her theory, to correspond to the individual differences in a phenomenon. For example, Dodge (e.g., 1993) has argued that violent boys differ from other boys in the ways that they automatically perceive the aggressive intentions of others. Many depression researchers, starting with Aaron Beck (1967), have proposed that depressed individuals tend to automatically think of themselves in negative terms and so suffer low self-worth, without having much awareness of how those feelings come about. Priming studies, on the other hand, are more concerned with effects of the current situational context and how these environmental features cause the average individual to think, feel, and behave differently than otherwise.

Today, a quarter century after Mischel (1973) proposed the mergence of social and personality psychology – that is, the study of individual differences in reactions to situational forces – the existence of individual differences in perception is well established in the field. Yet only 50 years ago it was a radical thing (in experimental psychology) to suggest that one's experience of the outside world was determined by anything other than the stimulation "out there." We start our treatment of cognitive research methods by presenting a brief history of cognitive mediation in psychology: first, the breakthrough idea that people could differ in what they perceived in the environment, and how they perceived it, followed by the various reasons found for these individual variations. The mind was not always in the middle of psychological explanation; here is how it got there.

THE INFLUENCE OF INTERNAL STATES ON PERCEPTUAL EXPERIENCE

The early elementalist approach of Wundt and Titchener held that perception was explicable entirely in terms of discrete sensory events; indeed, any reference to perception of objects per se by the introspecting perceiver (instead of to the sensory features present in that object) was held to be going beyond the information present – an inference, not something actually perceived (see Boring, 1950). The Gestalt movement, in fact, arose in direct opposition to the elementalist approach. The Gestaltists argued that people did indeed go beyond the information given, perceiving objects as wholes according to precise principles of form and relations that were not reducible to the sensory stimulation alone (Koffka, 1922).

The study of visual illusions provided the Gestalt movement with many powerful demonstrations that these emergent properties of the stimulus – and not merely the actual stimulus present – produced perceptions of size, distance, and brightness (see Boring, 1950). For example, a black and white photograph of a woman in a white dress, standing next to a man wearing a dark suit, appears phenomenally the same under varying lighting conditions. This is despite the fact that the dark suit under the brighter lighting is actually the same (physically speaking) shade of grey as the white dress had been under the darker lighting.

INDIVIDUAL DIFFERENCES IN PERCEPTUAL EXPERIENCE

When Christian Dior launched his "New Look" in fashion design in 1947, little did he know that he was also supplying the name for a radical movement in human perception research. What we know now as the "New Look" in perception was a break from the then dominant assumption that perceptual experience was determined solely by properties of the stimulus field (including the Gestaltists' emergent properties). For the first time, it was proposed that there could be individual differences in perceptual processing.

Although the Gestaltists showed that people go beyond the information present in the environment, the mechanisms by which they did so were still regarded as universal. Individual variation around the grand mean of judgments of intensity or other stimulus features was treated as error variance. But it had been noticed that there were consistent individual differences in these errors. Some experimental participants were consistently on the low side of the mean, with others usually on the high side, and this became known, somewhat oxymoronically, as the "constant error."

If these deviations had been merely random noise, a given individual would have been expected to vary randomly – not systematically – around the mean in his or her judgments. Recognizing this, Bruner and

Postman (1947) proposed that these constant errors were not errors at all, but true individual differences in perceptual experience. Moreover, they surmised that the observed individual differences were perhaps correlated with other individual differences, such as in motivations, needs, and values. The New Look in perception was born.

Suddenly, entire areas of psychological inquiry – attitudes and values, emotion, motivation and goal research, personality, clinical and psychodynamic theory – had a bridge to experimental psychology. New Look research boomed as these researchers explored the effects of their particular brand of individual difference on perceptual experience (see reviews by Allport, 1955; Bruner, 1957; Dixon, 1971; Erdelyi, 1974). In a very real way, it was the birth not just of a fruitful avenue of perception research, but of a truly general experimental psychology, as the laboratory techniques that had long been associated with "scientific" psychology could now be exploited by these other areas.

THE ROOTS OF PRIMING RESEARCH

Although the New Look did champion the role played by individual differences in motives and needs in perceptual experience, nowhere in it was there a mention of what we now refer to as *priming* – how recent or current experience passively (without an intervening act of will) creates internal readinesses. Bruner's (1957) classic statement of category accessibility theory described how current goals and purposes caused representations relevant to achieving those goals to become more accessible and ready to be activated by their corresponding objects and events in the environment. But this was a quite active and intentional internal state.

Recent Experience as an Individual Difference

A closer historical precedent to present-day research on passive contextual effects is Duncker's (1945) pioneering work on mindsets and creativity. Duncker showed that a person's usual way of thinking about objects and their functions sometimes gets in the way of coming up with novel, creative solutions to problems. For example, let's say Joe is given the task of tying together two pieces of string dangling far enough apart that he can't grasp the one piece without letting go of the other. Joe also has a hammer at his disposal, but on his own he can't figure out how it could help him to complete the task. However, as soon as the experimenter sets one of the dangling threads into motion, it occurs to Joe to tie the hammer to the end of the string in order to set it in motion like a pendulum. Importantly, Joe is not aware of the effect that the experimenter's knocking the string into motion had on his (Joe's) arrival at the correct solution. Today, we understand this phenomenon as a case of passive conceptual priming – the concept, in this case, being that of motion. This activated concept becomes more likely than before to influence conscious judgments and problem solving.

In fact, Higgins and Chaires (1980) demonstrated how solutions to the Duncker candle problem could be produced using the more modern priming techniques discussed in this chapter. By exposing the participant repeatedly to the word "or" as part of an apparently unrelated experiment, he or she was more likely to see a box of tacks as two separate objects, a box and some tacks, compared with participants previously exposed to the word "and." This was shown by the or-primed participants' greater success rate in solving a puzzle in which the box had to be tacked to a wall in order to form a platform for the candle.

The first use of the term "priming" to refer to the temporary internal activation of response tendencies was by Karl Lashley in a 1951 article. Lashley was dealing with the problem of how serial response sequences, as in speech production, flow so quickly and apparently effortlessly. He argued that there had to be a mediating state intervening between the act of will or intention and the production of the intended behavior, which assembled the action into the proper serial sequence. This he called the priming of the response.

The idea of priming thus entered the literature to refer to a preparedness of mental representations to serve a response function. Yet the activation Lashley described came from internal, and even intentional, sources. It took a bit of serendipity for the phenomenon of passive priming influences to be discovered.

This was provided by Storms (1958), who first gave his participants a list of words to memorize, and then had them free associate to a series of stimulus words. Unexpectedly, Storms found that the words presented in the memory task became more likely than usual to be given as associates (compared with standard free associate norms). Storms reported this effect but could not explain it, concluding that "the mechanisms of this recency effect remain unexplored" (p. 394).

It was Segal and Cofer (1960) who first used the term "priming" to refer to this effect of recent use of a concept in one task on its probability of usage in a subsequent, unrelated task.[1] Segal and Cofer replicated Storms's finding, but, critically, without the use

---

[1] For some reason, we feel compelled to point out that priming research thus originated at New York University.

of explicit recall instructions; merely exposing participants to the list of words had the effect of increasing the probability that those words would be used in the subsequent free-association task.

Following this initial demonstration, priming began to be used as an experimental technique, especially to show how information had been stored in memory despite the individual's inability to recall it (Grand & Segal, 1966; Koriat & Feuerstein, 1976; Segal, 1967). That is, words presented in a first task still were more likely than usual to show up as free associates in a subsequent task, even though participants had failed to recall them at the end of the first task. These early priming studies were thus the forerunners of the important contemporary distinction between implicit and explicit forms and uses of memory (e.g., Greenwald & Banaji, 1995; Schacter, 1987).

Priming in Social Psychology

For social psychology, the ground-breaking priming study came when Higgins, Rholes, and Jones (1977) showed that personality trait concepts (such as "adventurous" or "independent") – not just single words – could be primed by recent use. Using the same unrelated studies paradigm as had Segal and his colleagues, Higgins et al. (1977) exposed participants to synonyms of certain personality traits as part of a first, memory experiment. Next, in what participants believed to be an unrelated experiment, they read about a target person named Donald who behaved in ways ambiguously related to the primed traits, such as sailing across the ocean alone and preferring to study by himself. Those participants who had been exposed to words such as "adventurous" and "independent" formed more positive impressions of Donald than did participants who had been previously exposed to relevant terms such as "reckless" and "aloof." Importantly, participants evidenced no awareness of having been influenced by their prior exposure to trait terms in the earlier memory experiment.

The advance beyond previous priming studies was that the participants' responses did not involve using the prime words themselves, as in the free-association task studies; instead their overall impression or evaluation of Donald was requested. What had been primed was not just the single, concrete lexical memory locations corresponding to the stimulus words, therefore, but also the abstract trait concepts. These in turn became more likely to capture the relevant but ambiguous behavioral information, thus slanting final impressions in the positive or negative direction.

The Higgins et al. (1977) study revealed for the first time how an individual's recent experience could affect – in a passive and unintended way – his or her perceptual interpretation of another person's behavior. In their study, all participants read about the same target person doing the same things, yet they came away from their reading with markedly different impressions of that person, differences that were only accountable by reference to the manipulated differences in their recent use of the trait concepts.

THE ROOTS OF AUTOMATICITY RESEARCH

Priming and automaticity research have a common purpose: to explore the effects of individual differences in accessibility of mental representations on perception, evaluation, motivation, and behavior. However, whereas priming research centers on the temporary activation of an individual's mental representations by the environment and the effect of this activation on various psychological phenomena, automaticity research focuses on more permanent, "hardwired" sources of activation – that is, chronic accessibility of social knowledge structures. We now turn to the development of the present-day conception of automaticity.

It is now widely held that automatic processing is not a singular entity, but rather a grab bag of the various types of processing that are considered *not conscious* (Bargh, 1989, 1994, 1996; Logan & Cowan, 1984; Neumann, 1984; Wegner & Bargh, 1998). That is, although there has been consensus over the years as to the qualities of deliberate or controlled processing, different kinds of "not-conscious" processes had been noted and studied. Conscious processing, by all accounts, is serial (sequential), rather than parallel, in nature; is limited in the amount of information it can handle at any one time; corresponds roughly to the contents of phenomenal awareness; and is directed by the individual's intentions and goals. The latter quality enables control processing to be flexible and strategic and able to override (nearly always) the usual or habitual response in a situation.

And so, if a process or effect was discovered that did not have one or more of these features, it was considered to be "automatic" under the assumption that there were two and only two basic types of information processing: conscious and automatic (see, e.g., Johnson & Hasher, 1987; Posner & Snyder, 1975; Shiffrin & Schneider, 1977). Over the past century of research, however, two distinct strains of not-conscious processing had been discovered and studied. These two separate programs of research have led today to two major types of automaticity: goal-dependent and preconscious.

Goal-Dependent Automaticity and Skill-Acquisition Research

One type of not-conscious processing concerns acquired skills that through a great deal of practice or experience come to be executed very efficiently, needing minimal if any attention or guidance (see Newell & Rosenbloom, 1981; Shiffrin & Schneider, 1977). Examples of such skills are driving and typing, abilities that can operate without conscious guidance once started, but which are nonetheless intentional in that they require an act of conscious will to begin operation.

Although William James was not fond of the nonconscious as a scientific construct, his concept of habit did provide the heritage for modern-day conceptions of automaticity. James (e.g., 1890) placed great importance on habit in daily life and believed that habits are ingrained by consistent and diligent practice. James's notion that activities frequently and consistently engaged in require less and less conscious effort over time became the foundation of skill-acquisition research (see Anderson, 1982; Newell & Rosenbloom, 1981).

For example, Shiffrin and Schneider (1977) proposed that perceptual skills can become automatized over time. They conducted a series of studies in which the participants' task was to detect a single letter or digit target within a rapidly presented array of letters and digits. After thousands of such trials, attention was automatically directed to the target. This pointed to the importance of frequency for the development of automaticity. Shiffrin and Schneider (1977) also showed the importance of consistency, in that automatic detection capabilities were only achieved when a stimulus was always a target or always a distractor; when the participants' response to the target varied, automatic responses did not develop.

It is important to note that in all of the skill-acquisition research, past and present, there is an underlying assumption that an initial conscious act of will is required to set the effects into motion. One does not drive, type, or find targets in a perceptual display without having the intention of doing so, regardless of how efficient and automatic the processing is once one is engaged in the activity. This form of automaticity is called *goal-dependent* (Bargh, 1989) because unlike the other major form (see next section), it requires an initial intention or act of will to put the process into motion.

Preconscious Processing

The New Look was concerned with immediate reactions to a stimulus prior to it reaching conscious awareness. Today, the idea that a substantial amount of information processing occurs immediately on an environmental event – for instance, the activation of an individual's stereotype of a social group on the mere presence of a member of that group – has found wide acceptance. But at the time, the New Look's focus on motivational and personality determinants of conscious perceptual thresholds was very controversial. This was due to its notion of perceptual defense, which, with its basis in Freudian notions of defense mechanisms, argued that perceptual thresholds were higher for emotionally threatening stimuli. However, if this were true, it would have violated the ingrained and implicit assumption of the time that perception was a conscious act (see Erdelyi, 1974). The New Look's ideas about preconscious analysis were about 25 years ahead of their time, but eventually the assumption that all of perceptual activity is fully conscious was overthrown.

Mainly this occurred through research on selective attention, beginning with Broadbent's (1958) seminal work. Broadbent held that an individual is equipped with an internal, and intentionally operated, selection mechanism that "tunes" attention to focus on certain information in the environment and to disregard other information. But whereas Broadbent argued for an "early selection" theory of attention – that is, information to be selected is determined very early, prior to a complete analysis of the input for meaning – Treisman (1960) demonstrated that in fact some to-be-ignored contents do in fact receive analysis for meaning, prior to attentional selection. Although her participants were very good at ignoring the to-be-unattended ear in a dichotic listening task, in which they were to repeat out loud a story played to one ear but not the other, there nonetheless were times when they would repeat the contents of the unattended channel. This occurred when the attended story switched to that ear. Thus the idea of pure early selection was dispelled. Such a theory could not account for the switching of attention to an unattended channel based on the meaning of the information presented there.

After this demonstration that some selection outside of conscious awareness does indeed occur, a lively debate began as to exactly how much. Although many argued for a relatively early-selection model, in which only a limited amount of informational input is analyzed for meaning (e.g., Neisser, 1967), others (e.g., Deutsch & Deutsch, 1963) argued for a late-selection, complete analysis model. According to this model, there is a full and complete preconscious analysis of all sensed information for meaning and importance, and information enters consciousness depending on its importance for the individual.

In a historic synthesis of the two positions, Norman (1968) proposed that the extent of preconscious analysis varied, depending on the match between the external information and the readiness or accessibility of internal memory representations relevant to that information. And so cognitive psychology had come full circle back to the discredited ideas of the New Look, which had originally proposed that individual differences in internal states (i.e., due to emotions, needs, and goals) affected perception prior to the attainment of the conscious percept.

Finally, in a very influential paper, Posner and Snyder (1975) put forth a model suggesting that automatic processes at encoding are triggered directly by the presence of the relevant stimulus. However, strategic conscious processes can override automatic ones to determine the response to the stimulus when the responses suggested by the two are incompatible – but only if the conscious process has enough time to develop and attentional capacity to operate. The basic proposals of this model were supported in a series of experimental tests by Neely (1977).

PRIMING AND AUTOMATICITY TOGETHER

This is the heritage of contemporary priming and automaticity research in social and personality psychology. Priming studies are concerned with the temporary activation states of an individual's mental representations and how these internal readinesses interact with environmental information to produce perceptions, evaluations, and even motivations and social behavior (see Bargh, 1997). Automaticity research is conceptually quite similar to priming studies, but generally concerns chronic individual differences in mental representations that transcend the current context. Both types of research focus on the accessibility or ease of activation of social knowledge structures and how these influence psychological phenomena without the individual being aware of or intending such influences.

Moreover, because priming produces for a short time a level of activation and accessibility in a representation that is comparable to that of a long-term, automatic process (Bargh, Bond, Lombardi, & Tota, 1986), priming techniques also have been exploited as a way to experimentally manipulate what are theoretically posited as chronic, automatic effects. (For

examples of this use of priming, see Bargh, Raymond, Pryor, & Strack, 1995, Experiment 2; Chen, Shechter, & Chaiken, 1996; Fazio, Sanbonmatsu, Powell, & Kardes, 1986, Experiment 3; Roskos-Ewoldsen & Fazio, 1992.) Thus priming techniques can be used either to research the passive, unintended influences of the current and recent environmental context or to experimentally simulate automaticity effects.

PRIMING RESEARCH TECHNIQUES

There are a variety of experimental techniques that fall under the general umbrella of priming research. *Conceptual priming* involves the activation of mental representations in one context, so that they exert a passive, unintended, and nonaware influence in subsequent unrelated contexts until their activation dissipates. Examples of such research are the many trait concept priming studies in which using the word "honest," for instance, as part of a language test causes one to perceive a subsequent target person as more honest. In this research, the participants' task in processing the concept-relevant information (i.e., the priming task) is not the same – in fact is kept as different as possible – as their task in the subsequent part of the experiment that assesses the priming effect. In this way, the priming effect is shown to be due to the concepts primed (independent of processing goal) and not the priming of a particular mental procedure, which distinguishes this type of priming from the next.

Mindset priming manipulations have the participant actively engage (or read about someone else so engaged) in a goal-directed type of thought in one context, to show that this mindset (Gollwitzer, 1990) – what goal to pursue in the situation – is more likely to operate later in an unrelated context. Thus, what is primed is a procedure or purposive way of thinking about information or a situation. For example, Wilson and Capitman (1982) had some of their male participants read a "boy meets girl" story in an allegedly unrelated first experimental task, and they smiled more and generally behaved in a more friendly way to a female confederate in the next part of the experiment.

Unlike the other two types of priming studies, *sequential priming* techniques do not examine the residual effects of recent experience. Rather, they test for chronic connections between two representations, across which activation automatically spreads, for example between an attitude object and its evaluation or between two different concepts. Sequential priming is therefore the technique of choice for studying the associative structure of the mind. The discussion of sequential priming techniques therefore is postponed until the section on automaticity research, which is also concerned with long-term structural effects.

What all three types of priming have in common is a concern with the unintended consequences of an environmental event on subsequent thoughts, feelings, and behavior. They address the residual effects of one's use of a representation in comprehending or acting on the world, which leaves the primed representation, or any other representation automatically associated with it, active for some time thereafter. During the time it remains active, it exerts a passive effect on the individual, one that he or she is not aware of and does not intend – and is therefore unlikely to control (see Bargh, 1994; Bruner, 1957; Higgins, 1989, 1996).

CONCEPTUAL PRIMING

In conceptual priming, manipulations are used that activate the internal mental representation of interest in a first task, in such a way that the participant does not realize the relation between that activation event and the later influence or use of that representation in an unrelated context. The priming task must use the concept or representation in some way, but not in a way that tips the participant off to the relation between the two tasks. To show it is just the mere activation of the representation that is important, and not its particular use in, say, person perception, tasks have commonly exposed the participant to representation-relevant stimuli (i.e., words or pictures) in an unobtrusive way.

Supraliminal Priming

There are different degrees to which an individual may be aware (or unaware) of the actual stimuli priming a given construct. In supraliminal or "conscious" priming, the participant is exposed to the priming stimuli as part of a conscious task. That is, the individual is fully aware of the priming stimuli itself, but is not aware of some underlying pattern that serves to prime the construct. A very frequently used supraliminal priming technique is the "scrambled sentence test," first devised by Costin (1969) as a clinical projective test but adapted by Srull and Wyer (1979) in their trait construct priming research. An example is given in Appendix A. Participants are told that the task is designed to measure their language ability, and they are instructed to make coherent, grammatical sentences out of each string of words. In the course of doing so, they are exposed to some words that are related to the concept the experimenter wishes to prime.

Generally, priming stimuli are selected by consulting a standard thesaurus for close synonyms of the to-be-primed concept. Pretesting can also be used to supplement this set of synonyms if more or varied priming stimuli are needed, by having a separate group of participants rate the degree to which each potential prime is related to the target concept. It is a good idea to use as many different words that are synonyms of the target concept in the scrambled sentence test as possible, because repeating a given word increases the chances that the participant may clue in to the purpose of the task, or at least become consciously aware that the experiment seems to be focusing on that particular concept.[2] At the same time, one must be careful not to sacrifice direct activation of just the single concept of import by using only peripherally related primes.

One wants, of course, to have the most powerful manipulation possible, while at the same time not overstepping the line that leads to the participant's awareness. There is no easy rule to achieve the "right" level of subtlety, but we can offer a few guidelines based on experience. One is to engage in extensive debriefing of the participant to ensure he or she is not cognizant of the relation between the priming manipulation and the subsequent experimental task. The best way of doing this is through a "funneled debriefing" (see Chartrand & Bargh, 1996; Eagly & Chaiken, 1993). Appendix B gives an example of this technique. Briefly, the idea is to probe in a systematic way for any suspicions or actual knowledge the participant has about the intended effect of the prime on their subsequent performance in the experiment.

In general, if a participant evidences any genuine awareness of a relation between the prime and experimental task, his or her data should not be included in the analyses. By "genuine awareness" we mean any answer in the debriefing that is "in the ballpark" as to what could have affected responses. In our research, we take a conservative stance and err on the side of overexclusion if there is any doubt.

If an alarmingly high proportion of participants are being excluded for this reason – and those alarms should go off if upwards of 5% or so are showing awareness of the priming influence on their responses – it is likely that even participants who remain in the data set might have had some degree of awareness.

---

[2] Note that this is not normally a problem in subliminal priming, in which the same set of words directly related to the primed concept can be repeatedly presented over the course of the priming task (see Bargh & Pietromonaco, 1982).

The second tactic that we recommend is to replicate priming effects that are obtained with "conscious" or supraliminal priming techniques (e.g., the scrambled sentence test) using subliminal prime presentation instead (see next section). Although subliminal priming is a weaker manipulation, obtaining the same significant effect using it goes a long way toward dispelling doubts about the "demand" or conscious, strategic nature of the obtained priming effects.

Subliminal Priming

Subliminal priming studies in social psychology may be carried out, therefore, not only to demonstrate effects of nonconsciously perceived stimuli but also to conclusively rule out alternative explanations for priming effects. (Discussion of subliminal priming is also relevant to the topic of automaticity, in its sense of processing without awareness; see Bargh, 1994.) That was the reason why Bargh and Pietromonaco (1982)

Figure 10.1. Subliminal priming: the foveal and parafoveal visual fields.

performed the first subliminal trait construct priming study – to ensure that the original findings of Higgins et al. (1977) and Srull and Wyer (1979, 1980) had not been due to demand or other active strategies on the part of the experimental participants. All of those previous studies had presented the critical primes to participants as part of a first, explicit task. Similarly, Devine's (1989) use of the same procedure to prime the African American stereotype was motivated by a wish to eliminate self-presentational strategies on the part of the experimental participants that could mask the true effects of the stereotype.

The mechanics of conducting subliminal priming studies are straightforward, and hinge on three principles: (a) very brief presentation of the prime, (b) its immediate masking by another stimulus, and (c) appropriate awareness checks.

Brevity of presentation translates into the amount of internal activation of the corresponding representation. Roughly speaking, the amount of internal activation is given by the formula $D \times I = A$, where D is the duration of the stimulus, I is its intensity, and A is the amount of activation. Using a tachistoscope,

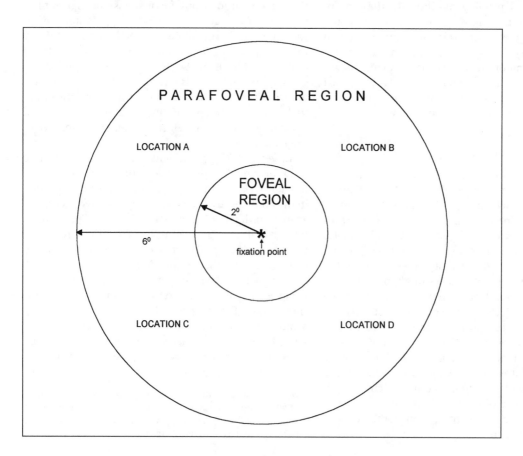

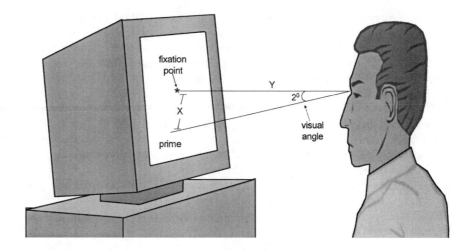

$$Y = X / \tan(2^0)$$

Figure 10.2. Determining the parafoveal region of the computer display and calculating the required distance of the participant from the computer screen.

as was used in many of the New Look and perceptual microgenesis studies, one could vary the illumination level of the stimulus or use gelatin filters (similar to the effect of sunglasses) to make the stimulus harder to see. But the great majority of subliminal presentations in modern research accomplish their purpose by varying the duration, not the intensity, of the stimulus.

How long can a stimulus be presented and still be subliminal? Given that recognition thresholds are often if not usually measured in terms of millisecond duration and that there are individual differences in these thresholds (see Greenwald, Klinger, & Liu, 1989), no single answer can be given. Establishing individual thresholds is a laborious and time-consuming process (e.g., a half hour of dark adaptation; see Greenwald et al., 1989), so the practical solution is to use a duration brief enough for most, if not all, participants and to conduct a conservative awareness check on these same participants (more on this below).

The appropriate duration depends on whether the stimulus will be masked and whether it is presented to the participant's foveal or parafoveal visual field. Roughly speaking, *foveal processing* is given to information in the center or focus of conscious visual attention, and *parafoveal processing* is of information in the fringe or periphery of the attended region. The foveal processing area extends from 0 to 2 degrees of visual angle from the focal point of attention (see Figure 10.1). In experiments involving a tachistoscope or computer screen, foveal presentation is accomplished through presenting a "fixation point" (such as an asterisk) and the critical stimulus at the same position.

The parafoveal visual field extends beyond the foveal, from about 2 to 6 degrees of visual angle.

Determining the parafoveal area of computer display screens involves taking into account the distance between the participant's eyes and the screen; the farther away the participant is seated from the screen the greater the area on the screen that falls in the foveal region (see Figure 10.2 and Bargh et al., 1986, for details on calculating the visual angle).

Information presented in the parafoveal region does not reach conscious awareness, at least as concerns its meaning or identity. One does become aware of movement and changes in this region, which automatically attract attention. However, such information is processed subconsciously to some extent. One can therefore "get away with" longer presentation durations with parafoveal compared with foveal presentation. The study of parafoveal processing has been a major topic in research on reading, specifically on one's ability to anticipate or "look ahead" in order to facilitate the conscious processing of the material (see Raynor, 1978).

MASKING. It is usually not sufficient to present a prime briefly and then remove it from the display. This is because the effective duration of the stimulus is longer, for two reasons. First, the decay rate of the medium in which the stimulus is electronically presented (this is not a problem for tachistoscopic display) is greater than zero. Older monitors (ca. 1980s) used a phosphor medium that sometimes took so long to decay that you could watch it happen. More modern computer monitors have much faster decay rates, but it is important to look into this specification before purchasing equipment. The best of today's monitors have such fast decay rates that it is no longer a problem, at least for the kind of subliminal studies usually done in social psychology.

But even if one is using a tachistoscope or the best computer monitor on the market, one still needs to mask the stimulus. This brings us to the second reason why a stimulus duration could be longer than intended (and attain conscious awareness): because it tends to persist in the participant's visual iconic memory store for a time after it has physically disappeared from the display (see Sperling, 1960, for the first demonstration of the existence of visual iconic storage). To erase or overwrite the visual buffer, so that the effective presentation duration of the prime is the same as its actual duration on the screen, a pattern mask should be presented at the same location, overwriting the prime on the display, and for as long as – and preferably longer than – the prime had been presented (Marcel, 1983; Turvey, 1973).

A pattern mask contains the same features as does the prime so that the same mental feature detectors are used in perceiving it. However, so as not to interfere with the effect of the prime, the pattern mask should not correspond to any higher level meaning. Thus, for example, the primes in the Bargh et al. (1986) study were all words, and so the masking string ("XQFBZR-MQWGBX") was made up of the same features – that is, letters – but was not itself a word. In this way the same feature detectors are employed for prime and mask, disrupting the visual iconic storage.

With immediate pattern masking, the prime can be presented outside of awareness at durations of 15 ms or below for foveally presented faces (Bargh, Chen, et al., 1996, Experiment 3; Edwards, 1990) and schematic line-art renderings (i.e., cartoon-like drawings) of faces (Niedenthal, 1990).[3] When parafoveal presentation is used instead of foveal, longer durations can be used: 60 ms in Bargh et al. (1986), 125 ms in Erdley and D'Agostino (1988), 90 ms in Bargh et al.

(1995, Experiment 1), and 60 ms in Chartrand and Bargh (1996, Experiment 2).[4]

With parafoveal presentation it is important to ensure that the prime is really presented parafoveally; that is, that the participant's visual focus is on the desired fixation point. Only then can one be entirely sure that the prime was parafoveally and not foveally presented. For instance, if the parafoveal prime is always presented at the same point in time in a trial (say, 1 s after a warning signal), it can easily be anticipated, and the participant's attention can move away from the instructed fixation point to the location of the flash (making it phenomenally foveal regardless of the experimenter's intention).

To avoid that possibility, we have often inserted a random delay of from 2 to 7 s between the trial warning signal and the presentation of the prime (see Bargh & Pietromonaco, 1982; Bargh et al., 1986; Chartrand & Bargh, 1996). In addition, the prime was presented in one of four possible locations ("quadrants") on the screen (all in the parafoveal region). Which one of these was used for a given trial was determined randomly by the computer, thus minimizing the possibility of anticipations by the participant.

Could the participant move his or her eyes quickly enough after the presentation of the prime to "catch" it before it is masked and thereby consciously see its content? The answer is no, as long as the parafoveal presentation is short enough. The normal speed of saccadic jumps of the eye from one location to another is about 220 ms, by which time the presented prime and mask are long gone from the display. (There is some controversy over the existence of even faster saccadic jumps of 100 ms, called "express saccades" [Fischer & Weber, 1993], but if the parafoveal presentation is 60 ms or so even these could not get there in time.)

One way to ensure that the participant's attention is focused on the fixation point at the time of the parafoveal "flash" is to give him or her some task to perform involving stimuli presented at the fixation point. For instance, the participant could be asked to repeat out loud each of a series of digits presented at the

---

[3] Perdue, Dovidio, Gurtman, and Tyler (1990) presented words (related to the group concepts of "us" and "them") foveally for 55 ms, with immediate pattern masking, but as they did not run awareness checks (basing claims of subliminality instead on the reports of pretest participants), one should be extremely cautious in the use of such a lengthy foveal presentation time. Seamon, Brody, and Kauff (1983), for example, found greater than chance recognition of polygons presented foveally (and pattern masked) at 5 ms.

[4] When using computer-generated displays and monitors, the minimum presentation time is constrained by the monitor hardware – specifically, the screen refresh rate. For example, a 60 Hz monitor updates its display 60 times a second, or once every 16.7 ms; a 70 Hz monitor every 1/70th of a second or 14.3 ms. Even if the program controlling the display instructs that a stimulus be displayed for a shorter time than this, the stimulus will nonetheless be displayed for the full duration of the screen refresh cycle.

fixation point, with the experimenter keeping track of correct performance. The prime could be presented immediately following the presentation of the final digit so that if the participant reported it correctly, visual attention could be safely assumed to not have been at the presentation location. (One could go further and vary the number of digits presented on each trial and in this way prevent the participant from anticipating the moment of prime presentation.)

AWARENESS CHECKS FOR SUBLIMINAL PRIMING TASKS. With subliminal priming, one should probe for actual awareness of the relation between the priming and experimental tasks, just as with supraliminal priming. It is always possible for the participant to "get lucky" and happen to be looking right at the prime location at the moment it was presented, all of the experimenter's precautions notwithstanding. And it only takes conscious awareness of one prime to possibly make the participant aware of the nature of the priming stimuli and consequently raise the specter of demand effects.

As an awareness check, the experimenter could follow up the experimental trials with a short representation of some of the original priming trials. The participant should be informed this time that words (or pictures) are being presented and to try to guess what they are. If the participant is not able to guess any of the words or identify the gist of the pictorial content, it is safe to say that subliminal presentation has been achieved. An even more conservative test would be to give participants the correct answer along with one or more distractor items prior to each trial of the awareness check and compare performance with that of a control group to which no actual primes are presented (Bargh et al., 1986).

Note in this regard that comparing performance to chance levels (e.g., 50% on two-item tests) is not an appropriate awareness check, because the particular distractors that are used can vary in how likely they are to be chosen given no primes. Factors such as word frequency or relevance to psychological issues (e.g., personality trait terms vs. vegetable names as distractors) play a role in the frequency with which both distractors and target primes are chosen (see Fowler, Wolford, Slade, & Tassinary, 1981). Thus comparisons need to be made between the frequency with which the distractors are chosen in the prime and a no-prime control condition.

Our recommendation is to forego giving the participant options from which to choose and to base judgments of awareness on his or her ability to con-

sciously report the prime stimulus after each trial of the awareness check task. Better than chance performance in selecting the correct item from a set of options could come from actual awareness, but it also could be the result of priming itself! (Indeed, such a result might well be expected on theoretical grounds.) If one instead uses any effect of the prime on task performance as the definition of awareness, subliminal effects are defined out of existence (see, e.g., Holender, 1986) – and this does not seem a very interesting or productive route to take.

Supraliminal and Subliminal Priming Compared

This brings us to an important point about the role of awareness in priming effects. The same effects have been repeatedly obtained with subliminal and supraliminal priming manipulations alike: assimilation of ambiguous but relevant input into the primed category or activation of the primed goal. For example, in the subliminal priming studies described above, the same assimilative priming effect was obtained as in the original Higgins et al. (1977) and Srull and Wyer (1979) studies that used supraliminal primes. Thus, awareness of the priming stimuli's presentation does not matter for the obtained effect.

However, awareness of the potential effect or influence of the priming events does matter. This may specifically become an issue when using supraliminal priming procedures. If the primes are very extreme exemplars of the category (e.g., Hitler and Dracula as primes for "hostile"; see Herr, Sherman, & Fazio, 1984), they are especially memorable and likely to be used as a conscious standard of comparison subsequently. Target person Donald's refusal to pay his rent pales in comparison as an example of hostile behavior next to the exploits of Torquemada; if one has just read about the horrors of the Spanish Inquisition, one would probably see Donald as less, not more, hostile than otherwise. Strack and Hannover (1996) provided a thorough analysis of when such "contrast" effects are to be expected. The most important factor seems to be whether the priming event is still in conscious awareness (or working memory) at the later, critical moment (see Lombardi, Higgins, & Bargh, 1987; Newman & Uleman, 1990).

So, if a person is aware of the relevance of the priming event to the later perception or judgment, there is an adjustment away from the presumed effect of that event (i.e., the person's "theory" of how they would have been influenced; see Wegener & Petty, 1995;

Wilson & Brekke, 1994). But in the usual case, in which one is not aware of the potential influence, bias in the direction of the primed representation occurs.

Clearly, then, what matters for the occurrence of unintended effects of the environment on one's thought, feeling, and behavior is not the lack of awareness of the occurrence of the event – which is how cognitive psychologists typically define unconscious influences (see Greenwald 1992; Greenwald, Draine, & Abrams, 1996; Shevrin, 1992) – but instead a lack of awareness of the potential influence of that event. One can be consciously aware of the event and still have it affect or even control one's thought or behavior. (For the vigorous historical debate as to one's degree of awareness of mental processes more generally, see Ericsson & Simon, 1980; Nisbett & Wilson, 1977.)

Strength of Priming Manipulations

In general, the more priming stimuli presented to the participant, the stronger the obtained priming effects. Srull and Wyer (1979) varied both the number of items in the scrambled sentence test (30 or 60) and the proportion of the items containing trait-relevant primes (20% or 80%). Both factors produced significant main effects, meaning that the more total primes and the greater the concentration of relevant primes within the task, the stronger were the priming effects on impressions.

As a general rule, the scrambled sentence test or other "conscious" priming tasks – that is, tasks in which the individual is aware of the priming material – produce stronger priming effects than does subliminal priming. Activation from a conscious, intentional processing of the primes is stronger than subconscious activation, in the same way that increasing the brightness or duration of a stimulus on a tachistoscope eventually raises it from being invisible to visible. The stronger the activation of a concept, the greater its accessibility and likelihood of subsequent use (Higgins & King, 1981).

Moreover, the stronger the priming manipulation, the longer the priming effect lasts. Higgins, Bargh, and Lombardi (1985) explicitly tested a "synapse" model of concept accessibility in which the frequency of priming was pitted against recency of priming. Stimuli related to two different trait constructs (e.g., "adventurous" and "reckless") were presented in a scrambled sentence test, but with one trait primed more frequently during the course of the task and the other primed more recently (i.e., on the final trial). Then, in the ostensibly unrelated task that followed, participants read about a target person who behaved in a way applicable to both primed concepts (e.g., sailing alone across the Atlantic). Participants' impressions of the target person were more consistent with the evaluative implications of the recently primed trait if they were asked their opinion right after the priming task, but more consistent with the evaluative implications of the frequently primed trait if asked a few minutes later.

However, in the quest for a powerful priming effect, one must be careful not to overdo it. Great care should be taken when designing and conducting priming research in order to rule out active effects of the priming manipulations – the most notorious of these being demand effects. A manipulation that is too heavy-handed, such as having every one of the 20 items in a scrambled sentence test contain a synonym of the trait construct being primed, is likely to tip off the participant as to the nature of the study, especially when they see the "Donald" story served up next in which the protagonist behaves somewhat in line with that trait.

Beyond Perception: Goal and Behavior Priming

A fairly recent development in priming research is the opening up of the range of psychological phenomena that can be primed. For many years priming research focused exclusively on effects in perception and impression formation (see reviews in Bargh, 1994; Higgins, 1989; Wyer & Srull, 1989). Although some studies did employ a dependent variable that was not a judgment – for example, the participants' behavior toward another person or toward an attitude object (see Carver, Ganellen, Froming, & Chambers, 1983; Fazio, Chen, McDonel, & Sherman, 1982; Herr, 1986; Neuberg, 1988) – it was a priming effect on an evaluation or judgment that mediated the behavioral effect.

Recently it has been shown that the same priming manipulations used in the past to produce perceptual effects, such as the scrambled sentence test, produce behavioral or motivational effects as well, if that kind of dependent measure is employed instead. That is, it is possible to prime a behavioral tendency or prime a particular goal via the same manipulation (supraliminal or subliminal) originally employed to produce perceptual effects. For example, Bargh, Chen, et al. (1996, Experiment 1) used a scrambled sentence test to activate the concept of rudeness or politeness and then waited to see if the participant would interrupt a conversation in order to get his or her next task from the experimenter. Those primed with rude stimuli were far more likely to interrupt (63%) than nonprimed participants (38%), and those primed with politeness interrupted the least often of all (17%). Importantly, this effect was not mediated by the participants' impressions of the experimenter, so it appeared to be a direct effect of priming on behavioral tendencies (as predicted from the theoretical position that there is a direct passive effect of perception on action; see especially Prinz, 1990, in press).

Motivations and goals can also be primed. Bargh and Gollwitzer (1994) reported several experiments in which achievement or affiliation motives were activated by having participants first perform a "word search" task. Embedded in a matrix of letters were words synonymous with one or the other motivation. Those primed with achievement worked harder and found more words in subsequent word search tasks compared with participants primed with affiliation, who were more concerned with interacting with the confederate than with working on the task.

The purpose of the Chartrand and Bargh (1996) studies was to show that primed information-processing goals operated the same way as did consciously and intentionally activated goals. Our first experiment used a scrambled sentence test to prime either the goal of forming an impression or of memorization (shown in Appendix A). Next, in an ostensibly unrelated second experiment, participants were presented with the set of social behaviors used in Hamilton, Katz, and Leirer (1980b). We obtained the same results as in the Hamilton et al. (1980b) study – higher free recall of the behaviors and a greater degree of thematic organization of them in memory in the impression than in the memory condition – even though we primed those goals instead of giving them to participants directly through experimental instructions. And in our second experiment, we replicated previous findings of on-line impression formation (Bargh & Thein, 1985; Hastie & Park, 1986) using subliminal priming of the impression goal instead of explicit conscious instructions to the participant to form an impression.

What Have We Been Priming All These Years?

It is noteworthy that the same priming methods – such as the scrambled sentence test and subliminal prime presentation – produce motivational and behavioral as well as perceptual effects. The inescapable conclusion from this fact is that in a given experiment, a priming manipulation simultaneously produces all of these various effects. Just because the dependent variable of interest in a given study is, say, impressions of a target person, this does not mean that the only effect of the priming manipulation was on the participants' social perception. If the experimenter had instead placed the participant in a situation in which he or she could behave in line with the primed construct, behavioral effects would have been obtained instead.

Priming effects, along with automaticity effects, occur and operate in parallel. Priming manipulations have more effects on the participants (and on people in real life) than happen to be measured by the experimenter. It is in our view one very important direction for priming and automaticity research in the future to sort out how these various simultaneous processes interact with one another (for an example, see Moskowitz, Gollwitzer, Wasel, & Schaal, 1999).

MINDSET PRIMING

Mindset priming studies, reviewed in this section, also prime motivations or processing goals but do so by having the participant first engage in that goal or intentionally use the mental procedure in question. Because the priming involves active and intentional use of the procedure, and not just the passive activation of the goal concept, we consider mindset priming to be of a different variety than conceptual priming. Mindset priming is characterized better as a carry-over of an intentionally pursued goal or mental procedure to a new context. An act of conscious will on the part of the participant is required, unlike in conceptual priming.

As a result, there is a greater role played by intention and awareness in mindset priming, which makes studies using this technique more susceptible to demand effects. Nevertheless, it is sometimes more appropriate to use a "carry-over" priming paradigm than a conceptual one. For instance, if the concept to be primed is too abstract or too procedural to prime with a single word in a scrambled sentence task or subliminal priming procedure, it might be more reasonable to use a carry-over priming task. Moreover, it is a legitimate matter of interest whether intentional goal pursuits in one context influence the individual's decisions and behavior in subsequent contexts, without their awareness (or choosing) of this goal at the later point in time.

The original study of this kind was performed by Gollwitzer, Heckhausen, and Steller (1990). The participant was instructed to think about a personal problem in one of two ways: either to dwell on the pros and cons of a specific way to solve the problem (inducing a *deliberative* mindset) or to generate a specific detailed plan to accomplish an important personal life-project (inducing an *implemental* mindset). (Control condition participants merely looked at a book of photographs during the same time period.) In the ostensibly unrelated second experiment, participants were given the first few lines of several novel "fairy tales" and were instructed to complete each tale. They could complete the story any way they liked, but as predicted, those who had previously been given an implemental (action-oriented) mindset were more likely than the other participants to continue the story with what the protagonist actually did in order to accomplish a chosen goal, whereas those participants previously in a deliberative mindset more often wrote endings in which the protagonist considered and chose between various action alternatives. These findings suggested that the goal or mindset used in the first experiment continued to be active and operate in the second task, without participants being aware of or intentionally choosing this mode of thought while writing the story endings.

A second example of mindset priming comes from research by Bator and Cialdini (1995; see Cialdini, 1994). In a first experiment, motivations to hold consistent beliefs (i.e., cognitive consistency) were primed in some participants. This was done in the following manner. Participants were told that they would be interacting with another person and then read an essay purportedly written by that person. The content of this essay either indicated that the other person very much valued consistency in beliefs and behavior, or it did not indicate this. Next, in what was presented as an unrelated experiment, all participants were asked to write an essay in favor of having comprehensive examinations instituted as a graduation requirement – something nearly all of these college students personally opposed. Participants wrote this counterattitudinal essay either under free choice (i.e., they were asked to by the experimenter but could ostensibly say no) or no choice (i.e., they were instructed to by the experimenter) conditions, following which they were asked for their own positions on the issue.

According to cognitive dissonance theory (e.g., Wicklund & Brehm, 1976), writing counterattitudinal essays under free choice conditions should cause the participant to become more favorable toward the issue, compared with participants who felt they had no choice in writing the essay. However, Bator and Cialdini (1995) obtained this effect only for those participants whose consistency motivation had been primed. Participants in the control (not primed) condition held the same final position on the comprehensive exam issue regardless of whether they had written the essay under free-choice or no-choice conditions.

Other research programs have recently used the unrelated task paradigm to preactivate specific motivations. In an interesting variant of the mindset priming technique, Chaiken and her colleagues (Chaiken, Giner-Sorolla, & Chen, 1996; Chen et al., 1996) first gave their experimental participants a scenario to read in which the target person was portrayed either as being concerned with accurately understanding what was going on or with making a good first impression on another person. This was to manipulate whether an accuracy or an impression-management goal was activated. In the apparently unrelated second experiment, participants were given an attitude issue (e.g., gun control) that they would be discussing with another participant, who was described either as holding a pro or con position on that issue.

Participants then read an essay containing arguments on both sides, and while reading it they wrote down any reactions they had to the essay. Finally, participants gave their own attitude about the issue. As predicted, the attitudes of participants for whom the impression motive had been primed were closer to that of the other person they had expected to meet, compared with the expressed positions of the accuracy-motive primed participants.

To us, this technique – in which participants read about and so vicariously experience the story protagonist's goals and purposes – represents a mixture of the more passive or conceptual goal priming technique and the more active, mindset priming in which the participant him- or herself has pursued in the particular goal being studied. On the one hand, it seems that something more is occurring in this priming technique than the passive activation of the goal, because the participant is reading about and perceiving a target person actively pursuing that goal – and yet because the participant is not explicitly engaging in the relevant intention or act of will, it seems less active than the Gollwitzer et al. (1990) mindset priming study. Although we cannot offer a definitive solution at this very early stage of motivational priming research, the Chaiken et al. (1996) priming study does show that our present distinction between conceptual and mindset priming is fuzzier than we would wish and should be seen as more tentative than definitive.[5]

Unwanted Effects of Priming

Priming is an experimental sword that cuts both ways. That is to say, a participant's recent experience

---

[5] More interesting to us about the Chaiken et al. (1996) study than where it fits into our particular classification scheme is its implications for how an individual's own motives might be automatically triggered by those of other people he or she is currently perceiving in another person.

in an experimental setting will potentially affect his or her subsequent responses whether or not such an effect was intended by the experimenter. Having participants complete questionnaires prior to another dependent measure can be a major source of unwanted priming effects (i.e., unless of course the experimenter has planned for and wants this influence). This is because in the course of the questionnaire the participant will consider and use concepts that then become more accessible and likely to be used, if relevant, in subsequent experimental tasks. This is especially a problem if the experimenter wishes to draw conclusions about the chronic or long-term nature of the effects found in the latter tasks, because the temporarily primed state of the influential concepts might have produced the effects instead.

This has now been demonstrated in several studies. When Skelton and Strohmetz (1990) had some participants first rate a series of words on their health connotations, those participants subsequently reported having a greater number of health problems as measured by symptom checklists. Marks, Sinclair, and Wellens (1991) gave their depressed and nondepressed participants the Beck Depression Inventory (BDI) at the beginning of the experimental session and thereby produced different self-judgments compared with those of participants who had not earlier completed the BDI.

Any good experimental design is informed by a task analysis, in which the experimenter carefully considers how the various manipulations and tasks will affect the psychological state of the participant. Our advice is to include in such task analyses a consideration of how tasks positioned earlier in the experimental session could possibly, through conceptual or mindset priming, influence dependent measures positioned later in the session. A failure to do this yourself at the design stage runs the risk of having a careful journal reviewer do it for you later on, when it is too late.

Demand Characteristics and Mindset Priming

Priming manipulations seek to activate concepts in one context to study the passive effects of this activation in a subsequent task. Conceptual priming produces this activation with a first task that is as different from the experimental task as possible, to show that it is the mere activation of the concept – not the source of or reason for the activation[6] – that matters. Mindset prim-

[6] In fact, if participants are aware of the source or reason for activation when performing the second task, and believe it has an unwanted influence, they may correct or overcorrect for that influence.

ing, however, involves the active use of a certain way of thinking (at least, vicariously) by the participant in the first experiment, that is then more likely than otherwise to be employed in the second task.

Because of this, one has to be much more worried about experimental demand as an explanation for mindset than for conceptual priming results. The skeptic could argue that by being told to deal with information in one way in the first task by the experimenter, the participant assumes that this is what he or she is supposed to do with the information presented in the second task. Extra care should be taken, therefore, to camouflage the relation between the two tasks as much as possible (e.g., by using different rooms and experimenters for them) and to probe carefully for awareness of the relation between the two tasks (see Appendix B).

AUTOMATICITY RESEARCH TECHNIQUES

As discussed in the section on the history of automaticity, there never was such a thing as a single type of processing, called "automatic," that could be studied with just a single paradigm or methodology. Instead, different paradigms and tests have evolved to study the separate qualities of the not-conscious processes that are grouped under the umbrella category of "automaticity." These separate qualities are (a) whether the individual is aware of the operation of the process, (b) whether the process is efficient, (c) whether it is unintentional, and (d) whether the individual can control the process. Although tests of awareness of a process have already been discussed in the Subliminal Priming section (see also S. T. Murphy, Monahan, & Zajonc, 1995; S. T. Murphy & Zajonc, 1993), there are distinct methods of testing for the presence of each of the other three qualities of automaticity, to which we now turn.

Efficiency

Efficiency in processing is important to study because there are usually many demands on our limited attention, or working memory, at any given moment. Processes that do not require much if any conscious attention to operate will therefore have an advantage under these busy circumstances. They will occur more consistently over time in a given situation and constitute the default set of reactions to most occasions (Bargh, 1997; Brewer, 1988; Fiske & Neuberg, 1990; Gilbert & Osborne, 1989; Gilbert, Pelham, & Krull, 1988; Rothbart, 1981). Therefore, it is important for us as social psychologists, who are in the business of studying the general and typical reactions to situations, to study the efficiency of any process on which we are focused. As Langer (1978) noted two decades ago, we as researchers are not on sure footing when we generalize to the noisy real world the results of laboratory studies in which our participants are given plenty of time and nothing else to do while the critical phenomenon is being scrutinized.

Contemporary models of stereotyping (e.g., Devine, 1989), causal attribution (e.g., Gilbert, 1989; Trope, 1986), and impression formation (e.g., Bargh & Thein, 1985; Brewer, 1988; Fiske & Neuberg, 1990) posit two stages of processing. One is the default and is described as very efficient; the second stage is more effortful and can only occur if the person has the time, attention, and motivation to use them. We leave a consideration of the motivational variable to the next section on unintentional processing. Efficiency per se allows a process to operate in both of two "real-world" conditions of information overload: when there is no time to consider and integrate the various available sources of information (such as a rapid stream of behavior, emotional reactions, and so forth during impression formation) and when one's current goals and purposes take attention away from what is going on in the environment.

The attentional demands made by a mental process can be measured directly, typically through reaction time techniques, or the attentional demands of a task can be manipulated to assess if performance is affected. Either method can yield information about the efficiency of the underlying process – its ability to operate under conditions of scarce attentional resources.

MEASUREMENT OF EFFICIENCY. It is possible to measure the efficiency of a mental process in terms of how much time a person requires to engage in it. Smith (e.g., 1994) and his colleagues have performed a series of studies demonstrating the development of procedural automaticity in the domain of social judgments. In their paradigm, participants judge whether each of a series of behaviors is or is not an instance of a particular personality trait. The speed with which this yes–no decision is made is measured (in milliseconds). It is shown that the time to make these trait categorizations of behaviors decreases with practice, demonstrating an increase in procedural efficiency or automaticity. This proceduralization has two components: a general component in that judging behaviors with regard to a particular trait (e.g., kindness) becomes faster even with novel behaviors (not judged previously) and a specific component in that the same behavior judged in terms of the same trait is done still more efficiently (Smith, Branscombe, & Bormann, 1988; Smith

& Lerner, 1986; Smith, Stewart, & Buttram, 1992). The speed-up with practice was also found to follow the same inverse power function that characterized nonsocial mental process proceduralization (e.g., Anderson, 1982).

Although it is true that the more efficient a mental process, the less time it requires to run to completion (because conscious attention can only be deployed over time; Logan, 1980), the converse does not follow. That is, one cannot directly infer from the amount of time participants take to make a judgment or decision, for example, how efficient or automatic it is. This is because other factors influence and contribute to response times besides the procedural efficiency of an underlying process – most notably, strategic self-presentation. We treat this issue in more detail later (see "Some issues regarding the use of reaction times as a dependent variable"). The research of Smith and colleagues is a good example of a paradigm in which one is able to draw conclusions about underlying procedural efficiency from raw response times, because the same behaviors are being judged by the same participants repeatedly, in a within-subjects design. Thus, other influences on response times, such as how long it takes the participant to read the behavior, are held constant across trials. Moreover, because the participant is not making self-referential decisions about the behaviors, no self-presentational strategy is likely to be operative.

An interesting variant of measuring efficiency through response times can be found in the work by Macrae and his colleagues (e.g., Macrae, Milne, & Bodenhausen, 1994) on the automaticity of stereotype activation. Instead of measuring latencies in the primary task given to participants, as in the research by Smith and colleagues, these researchers made use of a dual task procedure to measure response times to a secondary task. Participants were instructed to monitor a tape-recorded informational passage about Indonesia at the same time as viewing information on a computer screen about a target individual and forming an impression of him. Some participants were given a stereotypic label (e.g., "skinhead") about the target. The interesting twist on the usual dual task paradigm was that it was performance on the secondary task that was the dependent variable of interest. It was found that performance on the prose-monitoring task, as tapped by later memory for it, was better if stereotype-relevant information had been presented in the course of the impression-formation task. This confirmed the authors' hypothesis about the efficiency with which stereotypes process relevant information.

MANIPULATION OF ATTENTIONAL DEMANDS. One can also assess efficiency of a process by manipulating the attentional demands of a task, to see if this changes task performance. To the extent that it does, attention is needed for the task; to the extent that it does not, the process is unaffected by attentional shortage and is thus quite efficient. Accordingly, laboratory manipulations of these conditions either present information very rapidly (information overload) or give the participant a secondary task to "load" attentional capacity (what Gilbert et al., 1988, called "cognitive busyness").

As an example, Bargh and Thein (1985) conducted a person memory study in which a series of 24 behaviors related to the trait of honesty (either honest, dishonest, or neutral behaviors as developed by Hastie & Kumar, 1979) was presented one at a time on a computer screen, and participants were instructed to form an impression of the target person who had performed these behaviors. In one condition, participants could read each behavior at their leisure, pressing the space bar to move on to the next behavior. (This technique had the additional advantage of allowing us to measure how much attention and consideration were given to the various types of information, as operationalized by looking time; see also Fiske, 1980.) But in the rapid-paced condition, each behavior was presented for only 1 s, with a 1-s pause before the next behavior came on the screen. This was just enough time for the participant to read each behavior one time through, preventing any further conscious deliberation about a given piece of behavioral information or its integration with others to form a coherent impression on-line. Results confirmed that this manipulation prevented participants from forming an impression on-line (at the time of reading the behaviors), forcing them to do so only later, based on those behaviors they could recall.

Another type of efficiency manipulation is the *dual-task paradigm*. This involves giving the participant a second task to do at the same time as the experimental task, such as holding a number or word in memory during a trial. One such study compared the automaticity of the self-concept in depressed and nondepressed people and employed a memory load task to do so (Bargh & Tota, 1988). The main experimental task required participants to answer yes or no as quickly as possible, indicating whether each of a series of positive and negative adjectives described themselves (or, on other trials, described the average other person). Half of the participants were required to hold a six-digit number in memory during each trial, with a different number presented each time. The number to remember appeared on the computer screen first, then the referent of the

judgment task for that trial (i.e., self or other), and then the adjective. After the participant had answered by pressing the "yes" or "no" key (recording the response latency in milliseconds on each trial), a message appeared on the screen asking them to repeat the six-digit string out loud. The indication of automaticity, in the efficiency sense of the term, was the degree to which this second, attention-demanding task caused judgment latencies to increase. Results confirmed the predicted differences in the positivity–negativity of the self concept that becomes active automatically in depressed people versus nondepressed people.

Gilbert and Osborne (1989) used a variation of the memory-load technique that has become a popular methodology because of its simplicity and effectiveness (e.g., Macrae, Hewstone, & Griffiths, 1993; Wegner & Erber, 1992). They gave participants a single eight-digit number to remember throughout the entire time that the critical person information was presented (via a videotape) and only after all of the information had been presented did they ask participants to repeat the number back. They found predicted differences in attributions and judgments as a function of this "cognitive busyness" manipulation; the memory load prevented participants from being able to take situational influences into account in their behavioral attributions. Thus participants were more likely to make dispositional attributions under memory load even when clear situational forces were operating to constrain or shape behavior.

It is extremely important when conducting dual-task studies of this sort to make sure of some things. First, the "load" task must be sufficiently attention-demanding that little attention remains with which to perform the primary task. Imagine, for example, if in the above studies participants had been given a one- or two-digit number to remember instead of a six- or eight-digit number. Judgment latencies, or the type of attribution made across all experimental conditions, would likely not be any different from the nonload conditions, but it would be erroneous to conclude from this that making judgments never requires any attention or that situational attributions are made automatically. We would have the usual interpretational problem of null results. Thus it is best to include in a design conditions under which one does expect the memory load to have an effect, so that one is confident that the load was sufficiently strong to affect the dependent variables in conditions where it is theoretically expected to do so, whereas not affecting them in the conditions where one's theory predicts relatively attention-free task performance.

One difficulty with having participants remember the same digit string throughout the experiment is that they learn it; that is, they store it in long-term memory, so that they may not need to keep rehearsing it in short-term memory. If a participant successfully learns the string – and in the Gilbert and other studies using this procedure the participant is given a minute or so before the experimental task starts to rehearse the number – then clearly the demands on his or her attention capacity would not have increased to any significant degree.

To show that the load manipulation is strong enough, it should be shown independently in a manipulation check to be of sufficient difficulty that participants do not perform it perfectly. In other words, it is good to show that they make errors in reporting the material they were to hold in memory (if that is their secondary task). But if they make too many errors, one can't be sure if they were trying hard enough to perform that secondary task. One strategy the participant might take for coping with the attention load situation might be to disregard one of the two tasks and focus on one or the other exclusively, to the detriment of performance on the other. If the participant adopts this strategy, nothing can be concluded about the attention demands of the primary task.

And so we want the participant to make some errors, but not too many. The solution to this problem adopted by Gilbert et al. (1988) and Gilbert and Hixon (1991) was to omit data from participants if they did not report at least half of the digit string correctly. An alternative is to include, as either a between-subjects (separate set of participants) or within-subjects (additional repeated measure on the same participants) control condition, an even stronger load manipulation. If this additional condition produces the same results as the original load condition, then the latter was most likely completely loading the participants' working memory; if the results differ, then the original load manipulation was not completely using available attentional resources.

It is also possible to test out one's load manipulation through a pretest in which participants are given a task or manipulation known to require conscious effort; the no-load condition should replicate previous findings on this task but the load manipulation should knock out this effect. This load manipulation check technique was employed by Moskowitz et al. (1999) using outcome dependency as the test manipulation; the load effect successfully knocked out the effect of outcome dependency to increase effortful scrutiny of the target person.

In dual-task paradigms, it is important that the participant consider the experimental task to be the primary one – that is, the more important of the two (see Kantowitz, 1974). In order to assess the attentional demands of a primary task, everything should be kept as similar as possible about that task in the load and nonload conditions other than the load itself. If in the load condition the participant believes the primary task to not be as important, and so is not as motivated to perform it compared with participants in the load condition, more than just the attention demands have changed to potentially affect the dependent measures. Thus participants should not be told that the tasks are equally important but instead that – although it is important for them to perform both tasks, not just one or the other – the focal (judgment, attribution, etc.) task is the crucial one for the experiment.

An interesting variant of the memory load procedure was introduced by Tice, Butler, Muraven, and Stillwell (1995). They were interested in the relative automaticity of self-presentational strategies to friends versus to strangers. The content of self-presentations to friends was found to be more modest than those to strangers. But the automaticity of these self-presentational strategies was assessed by the participants' subsequent recall of the interaction. The authors reasoned that the more that attention is focused inward, on one's own interaction performance, the less should be available for external events. Consequently, one's later memory for those events will be poorer. (This phenomenon used to be known as the "next-in-line effect"; see Brenner, 1973). Tice et al. (1995) used this fact to measure the ease or relative automaticity of the different self-presentational strategies. As predicted, when participants were instructed to engage in their natural tendencies – to be modest with friends and self-enhancing with strangers – their later recall of the interaction was better than if they had been instructed to engage in the contrary strategy (i.e., self-enhancement with friends and modesty with strangers).

Unintended Processing Effects

A major source of unintended effects on thinking, feeling, and doing is automatic associative connections in memory. If the (intended or unintended) activation of representation "A" then proceeds to activate representation "B" automatically, without any conscious intent or awareness involved, this latter representation can have an unintended effect on judgments, evaluations, and behavior. For example, Devine (1989) designed her study to show that (White) participants "went beyond the information given" in their stereotypic assumptions by priming them with some aspects of the African American stereotype, but not directly with "hostility," which is also an element of that stereotype. The priming manipulation nevertheless did influence subsequent judgments about a target person's hostility, an effect that could only have occurred if hostility had been activated unintentionally because of the automatic spread of activation within the stereotype. Bargh et al. (1995) showed how the activation of the concept of power spread automatically to the concept of sex for those likely to sexually harass or aggress, as indicated by their greater attraction toward a female confederate after only power, not sex, was primed.

There are two major ways of establishing the existence of such automatic connections: through analyses of output order in free-recall memory measures ("clustering") and through sequential priming techniques.

CLUSTERING MEASURES OF MEMORY ORGANIZATION. Free-recall measures of memory can be utilized to get at the underlying structure and organization of memory. The guiding logic here is that the order with which participants remember and hence write down what they remember about a person or event reflects the way it has been encoded in memory. The connections formed between the elements of the person or event memory help determine what is most easily recalled later on. Given that judgments and decisions are often made based on what is later most easily recalled from memory about the person or event (see Hastie & Park, 1986), the organization of material in memory can later determine, in a passive way, the outcome of those judgments.

Before one can examine clustering, free-recall protocols must first be coded for whether each item written by the participant should be considered "correct." Whereas the appropriate unit of analysis (i.e., what is coded as correct or incorrect) is clear with single-word recall paradigms, it is not so clear when the stimulus materials involve behavioral phrases or prose paragraphs. Although either a strict "verbatim" criterion or a more lenient "general meaning" or "gist" criterion may be used in these cases, researchers have normally not found significant differences in their results based on the use of these different criteria. Many end up basing their final analyses solely on the leniently scored "gist" protocols, in which an item is scored as correct if it captures the primary concept or meaning expressed in the original item (see Chartrand & Bargh, 1996;

Hamilton et al., 1980a, 1980b). However, researchers should choose the criterion most appropriate for their particular study based on whether verbatim recall is theoretically necessary to show or not.

A related issue concerns "intrusions" in free recall, which are items "recalled" by participants that were not present in the original stimulus material (see Srull, 1984, for a more in-depth discussion of intrusions). Because intrusion rates may vary across experimental conditions in a systematic way, they should be analyzed and reported by researchers. It is possible to use intrusions in free recall as an indication of information "added in" to a memory by the schema or stereotype used to encode the original information, but as intrusions in free recall are typically rare, such studies have mainly used recognition memory tests in which "hit rates" (yeses to actually presented items) and "false alarm rates" (yeses to test foils that had never been presented) can be compared to separate out accurate retrieval from guessing biases (see Grier, 1971; Srull, 1984; Wyer & Gordon, 1982).

The most common method of determining the amount of clustering in free-recall protocols is to use one of various objective clustering techniques, in which the conceptual categories organizing the information are specified a priori by the experimenter. Many different clustering methods exist, each with their own equation that yields an overall clustering "score" for each recall protocol. One of the most widely used measures of category clustering in free recall, the Bousfield and Bousfield (1966) deviation (BBD) measure, was one of the first to be developed. Essentially, this measure is a ratio of observed category repetitions to the number of such repetitions expected on the basis of chance.

One limitation of the BBD is that there is no fixed upper bound; a positive score indicates clustering above chance, but it is impossible to determine whether the score reflects perfect or less than perfect clustering. Specifically, the score for perfect or maximum possible clustering changes with the number of categories that the participant recalls and with the distribution of the total items recalled across categories. Furthermore, the BBD is affected by the total number of items recalled. Finally, because it does not reflect a proportion of actual to total category repetitions above chance, it is difficult to make comparisons between experiments or between participants.

Alternative clustering measures do exist, however, such as the modified ratio of repetition (MRR; Bower, Lesgold, & Tieman, 1969), the clustering (C) index, and the deviation (D) index (Dalrymple-Alford, 1970).

Robertson's (1985) model-based measure of clustering, $\kappa\alpha$, is highly related to the clustering index, but requires an iterative procedure to calculate its value. It has the advantage of placing more weight on those repetitions occurring at the beginning of the recall list, less to those in the middle of the recall list, and no weight to any repetitions occurring at the end of the recall list. (Also see Robertson, 1995, for a model of recall order that incorporates the clustering information with the serial order in which they are recalled and any interaction between presentation order effects and clustering.)

Many researchers have argued that the adjusted-ratio-of-clustering (ARC) index developed by Roenker, Thompson, and Brown (1971) is the best overall measure currently available (M. D. Murphy, 1979; Ostrom, Pryor, & Simpson, 1981; Srull, 1984; Wyer & Gordon, 1982). Unlike many of the alternative measures, ARC yields a clustering score ranging from 0, indicating no clustering beyond what would be expected by chance, to 1, indicating perfect clustering. Moreover, it corrects for different numbers of categories that are presented as well as the number of categories recalled. Finally, ARC appears to be the least confounded with extraneous factors (M. D. Murphy, 1979). The computational formula for ARC is

$$ARC = \frac{R - E(R)}{N - K - E(R)}, \qquad (1)$$

where R = number of observed category repetitions, N = total number of all items recalled, K = number of conceptual categories represented in the presentation list, and $E(R)$ = expected number of category repetitions, $(\Sigma m(I)^2/N) - 1$, where m is the number of items from category I that are recalled.

Although researchers should choose clustering measures carefully, it should be noted that the various formulas are often highly intercorrelated. For instance, Hamilton et al. (1980b) and Chartrand and Bargh (1996) used both the BBD and ARC measures in their analyses of clustering and found the same pattern of means with both indices.

Although these objective clustering measures are very popular, there exist alternative techniques for recall output analysis. One such alternative involves calculating conditional probabilities and is best exemplified by Srull's research on person memory (Srull, 1981; Srull, Lichtenstein, & Rothbart, 1985; Srull & Wyer, 1989). Participants were presented with a series of behaviors by a target person and instructed to form an impression of him or her. Most of the behaviors were consistent with a certain personality trait (e.g., honest) but a minority were inconsistent (e.g., dishonest) or unrelated to the trait in question. By examining the order in which the behaviors could later be recalled and calculating conditional probabilities of recalling one type (e.g., inconsistent), given that the same or another type (e.g., consistent) had just previously been recalled, Srull and his colleagues could construct a sophisticated process model of the process of impression formation.

This model could make accurate, detailed predictions about how people give consideration to unexpected, impression-inconsistent information and attempt to reconcile and integrate these behaviors into an overall, coherent impression of the target. These predictions were generated from a model of associative structure, deduced backwards from a fine-grained analysis of recall output order, tracing the mental route participants took to retrieve each target behavior. Importantly, calculating conditional probabilities was the more appropriate method of analysis in these studies, as levels of category clustering by the objective measures were at near-chance levels. Yet there did exist a highly systematic nature to the order of items recalled, which was uncovered using this different technique.

SEQUENTIAL PRIMING TECHNIQUES. The sequential priming task permits conclusions about the automaticity of associative connections between memory representations. By varying the time delay between the presentation of a prime stimulus and of a target stimulus, and assessing the effect of the prime on responses to the target under these different time gaps, inferences can be drawn as to whether the effect was immediate and automatic or conscious and strategic. Essentially, if presentation of the prime affects responses to the target at time gaps too short for temporary, strategic responses to have been responsible, then the prime and target concepts can be said to be structurally associated in long-term memory. Accordingly, sequential priming tasks have become one of the most widely used experimental techniques in social psychological research on memory structure and automaticity.

Associative network theory (e.g., Anderson & Bower, 1973; Srull, 1981; Wyer & Carlston, 1979) holds that memory consists of interconnected nodes, with activation spreading automatically from one node to another. Activation will only spread if there is an associative link that has been formed, and the stronger the association the more and faster the activation will spread to the related node. Early experiments testing associative network theory showed that responses to a target item (e.g., NURSE) were faster if an associated node (e.g., DOCTOR) had just been activated (Meyer & Schvaneveldt, 1971). Presumably, activation had spread from the node representing the prime to that representing the target so that when the target was presented, that location was already activated and so required less time to be activated in the response process.

Posner and Snyder (1975) added a strategic mode or component to spreading activation theory. They held that automatic activation effects were the default, but could be overruled by a current goal or strategy in the task if sufficient time were allowed for this attention-demanding strategy to operate. Automatic sequential priming effects for prime–target pairs such as doctor–nurse or sun–moon were relatively fast, occurring in 300 ms or less. Temporary strategic effects, on the other hand, take longer to develop, because they require attentional (effortful) resources that take time to accrue (Logan, 1980). However, if there is attentional capacity and sufficient time, strategic expectancies are capable of inhibiting and overruling the automatic activation (see also Shallice, 1972).

Neely (1977) tested this model by varying the amount of time between the prime presentation onset and the target presentation onset, known as the "stimulus onset asynchrony" or SOA. On each trial, a prime appeared in the center of the display for a certain amount of time, then was erased, and the target word was presented at the same location. Target words were members of the category BODY (i.e., parts of the body such as heart or leg) or the category FURNITURE (e.g., chair, table), or were nonwords (e.g., trone). The prime stimulus was either the word BODY or the word FURNITURE. The participants' task was one of lexical decision, in which they were to respond whether a target was a word or a nonword as quickly as they could.

A key element of Neely's (1977) design was to vary the delay between prime and target presentation. With brief delays (e.g., 250 ms), only automatic effects should be able to occur; thus, the prime BODY should facilitate (speed up) responses to names of parts of the body (and likewise for FURNITURE and

names of pieces of furniture) because strong, automatic connections are assumed to exist between these target concepts and their higher-order category concept. Only with longer delays (e.g., 750 ms) should strategic conscious expectations be able to influence responses. In the critical experimental condition, participants had a conscious expectancy for the opposite of the semantically consistent prime–target combination. In other words, they expected the BODY prime to be followed by names of pieces of furniture and for FURNITURE to be followed by names of body parts. However, the automatic effect would remain the same as always, as it reflects long-term associations and can not flexibly adapt to temporarily altered circumstances. In line with the Posner–Snyder model, Neely (1977) found that under these conditions the category-name primes continued to facilitate responses to members of that category under the short prime–target delay conditions, but that under the longer prime–target delay, category-name primes facilitated responses to members of the alternative category.

The sequential priming paradigm used by Meyer and Schvaneveldt (1971) and Neely (1977) has been employed increasingly to study social psychological phenomena. Fazio et al. (1986) based their original study of automatic attitude activation on the Neely (1977) paradigm. The names of various attitude objects (e.g., basketball, Reagan, ice cream) were presented as primes, and positive and negative adjectives (e.g., beautiful, terrible) appeared as targets. The SOA between prime and target was also varied, either 300 or 1,000 ms. Instead of the lexical decision task used by previous researchers, Fazio et al. (1986) instructed their participants to evaluate the target adjective as quickly as they could on each trial, by pressing one of two buttons, labeled "good" and "bad" (see Figure 10.3).

Results showed a reliable effect of at least some sets of attitude object primes on latencies to evaluate the target adjectives, with participants faster to respond when prime and target were of the same, rather than the opposite, valence. Importantly, this effect was

Figure 10.3. The sequential priming paradigm.

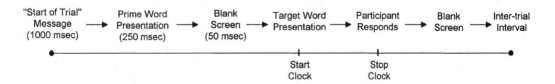

found only for the short and not the long SOA conditions. For the attitude objects to affect the target evaluations at such short SOAs, the attitude object prime had to have activated its own evaluation before the target was presented – that is, within 300 ms – and this is too quickly to have been the product of some conscious and intentional process. Moreover, the effect did not occur when participants did have enough time (i.e., the 1,000 SOA condition) to prepare, strategically, a response based on the prime valence. This was presumably because prime valence was not diagnostic as to the valence of the target that followed; positive primes were followed half of the time by positive and half by negative primes, and the same was true for negative primes.

The outcome of these and subsequent studies on automatic attitude activation (Bargh, Chaiken, Govender, & Pratto, 1992; Bargh, Chaiken, Raymond, & Hymes, 1996; Roskos-Ewoldsen & Fazio, 1992) have been uniformly consistent with the hypothesis that attitude objects immediately and automatically activate their associated evaluations in memory.[7] Because the evaluations are made so quickly and without conscious intention, many researchers have now made use of the paradigm to investigate social attitudes that people are reticent to admit, such as stereotypic or negative views of social groups (e.g., Perdue et al., 1990). Because the dependent measure is the latency to respond in an innocuous task, there is no way for participants to strategically respond in a way that hides these automatic evaluations.

Fazio, Jackson, Dunton, and Williams (1995) used the automatic attitude effect itself as a predictor of prejudicial behavior. By assessing the degree to which African American faces primed responses to negative adjectives, and slowed down responses to positive adjectives, a measure of the participants' implicit stereotypic beliefs could be constructed unobtrusively. This measure was found to predict the negativity of the participants' behavioral reactions to an African American experimenter, whereas a self-report measure of racial attitudes did not.

Although the evaluation task has become a popular one to use in sequential priming paradigms, a pronunciation task may often be preferable. Because the purpose in using the sequential priming paradigm is to

establish the unintentional and immediate activation of social concepts and evaluations, conscious and intentional strategies on the part of participants should be eliminated from the paradigm as much as possible. Having participants intentionally evaluate adjectives in the test of attitude automaticity, for example, was problematic for drawing conclusions about the goal-independence or unintentionality of the effect. Participants were consciously thinking in terms of evaluation and were trying to evaluate the target adjectives – would the effect occur when this goal of evaluation was not currently operating? By having participants pronounce as quickly as possible rather than evaluate the targets, it was shown that the effect did not depend on the conscious goal of evaluation (Bargh, Chaiken, et al., 1996).

Balota and Lorch (1986) showed that the pronunciation task has advantages even over some apparently strategy-free tasks, such as lexical decision. For one thing, a researcher usually has to discard half of the data gathered in a lexical decision task because the responses to the nonword trials are not of theoretical meaning or importance. For another, lexical decision still involves a decision (i.e., word or nonword) about the stimulus, and this increases the time needed to respond and also the variance due to individual differences in the judgment process. In line with these reasons, Balota and Lorch found that pronunciation was a more sensitive measure of spreading activation than was lexical decision.

The sequential priming paradigm has the potential for illuminating many of the important situational effects that are at the heart of traditional social psychology (e.g., Ross & Nisbett, 1991). Instead of restricting ourselves to tracing the strong associative connections between internal abstract concepts, such as between elements in a stereotype, or between an object and its attitude, one can examine the immediate and unintentional reactions to social situations. This is quite simply accomplished by having the priming stimuli related to the situational features. A first attempt at extending the paradigm to situation–concept relations was successful in demonstrating automatic sexually related cognitions as a result of priming the situational feature of having power (Bargh, Raymond, Pryor, & Strack, 1995). Participants identified as likely to be sexual harassers or aggressors showed the sequential priming effect of power on sexually related stimuli in a pronunciation task, and in a second experiment were more attracted to a female confederate (compared with other participants) if the concept of power had been primed. Thus the sequential priming paradigm would seem to have

---

[7] There is a difference of opinion about the generality of the effect and whether it is moderated by the "strength" of the attitude in memory (see, e.g., Chaiken & Bargh, 1993; Fazio, 1993), but a great deal of consensus as to the existence of the automaticity effect itself.

great promise for investigating other automatic effects of situations, as well as individual differences in these reactions.

Some Issues Concerning the Use of Response Latencies as a Dependent Variable

The key dependent variable in the automatic evaluation studies, as in many other lines of social cognition research (e.g., the content of the self-schema; see Markus, 1977), is the speed with which a response can be made to the target stimulus. Response latencies can be very informative as to the accessibility and automaticity of concept activation and as to the automaticity of connections between two concepts (i.e., prime and target stimuli), but there are two important caveats to keep in mind.

First of all, there are usually more components to a response latency than just the one that is of experimental interest. This is true for evaluation, lexical decision, and even pronunciation tasks. Take, for example, the operational definition of attitude strength in terms of latency of responding "good" or "bad" to the name of the attitude object (Fazio et al., 1986). The shorter this latency, the stronger the corresponding attitude was considered to be. However, many other factors influence the latency to respond to a given attitude stimulus, such as word length (it takes more time to read longer words) and word frequency, to name a few. These theoretically uninteresting features of the stimuli proved to be significantly correlated with evaluation latencies in further studies (Bargh et al., 1992). If one uses simple latencies alone, as if the only influence on them were attitude strength, one ends up making some erroneous inferences (e.g., concluding attitudes toward gum are stronger in general than attitudes toward abortion).

Perhaps more important, conscious response strategies can influence response latencies, especially those resulting from evaluation tasks. It should be noted, however, that researchers can avoid this particular problem by employing a pronunciation task for the sequential priming procedure, for pronunciation tasks are not as susceptible to response biases as are other tasks.

Rogers (1974) was the first to analyze response latencies to trait terms in self-judgment tasks in terms of both the degree to which the concept was part of the self-concept and in terms of the participant's strategy in answering the questions. This distinction between the actual latency component of interest and mere response strategy was an important one to make. One common strategy is positive self-presentation, causing fast latencies when saying "no" to negative items and "yes" to positive items rather than vice versa. This result could occur either because self-concepts are generally positive or because the participant has adopted a strategy of basing his or her response not on the true self-concept but on merely matching the response to the positivity or negativity of the item.

Because such response strategies are effortful and require attentional resources, we recommend separating the activation and strategic components by loading attention with a secondary task to see if latencies are affected by the load. To the extent that the latencies are not affected by the load manipulation, this signals the true automaticity or chronic accessibility of the judgment process or underlying mental representation; to the extent memory load increases the latency of response to that item, it can be concluded that the concept could only be responded to effortfully. Without assessing latencies under attentional load, the role played by response strategies remains unclear.

The second important caveat, which holds for all types of sequential priming tasks, is that the distribution of response latencies is typically positively skewed, in that they are constrained at the fast end and not at the slow end. This means a transformation must be carried out to normalize the distribution. There are a variety of possible transformations, such as taking the square root, the natural logarithm, or the reciprocal of the raw latency. The natural logarithm is a milder transformation, whereas taking the reciprocal or square root is somewhat stronger in that they alter the original distribution to a greater extent. The question of which of these transformations should be used has been a matter of some debate. Fazio (1990) recommended the reciprocal transformation, but Winer (1971, p. 400) argued against this as too strongly altering the underlying distribution, recommending instead the natural logarithm. (See also Box, Hunter, & Hunter, 1978, for a comparison of the effects of different transformations.) Perhaps the most reasonable method is to try several transformations (moving from mildest to strongest), examine their relative success in removing the positive skew, and then choose accordingly. Different sorts of tasks may have varying degrees of positive skew associated with them, and one wants to pick the transformation that does the best job in each specific context.

Along with distribution transformation comes the issue of what to do with outliers. These are very long latencies that can greatly affect the means and thus the outcome and conclusions from the experiment.[8] It is usual and accepted practice to trim outliers to remove this distorting influence on the results. Some rules of thumb can be suggested:[9]

First of all, the same policy of trimming (and for that matter, of transformation) should be used in all of one's experiments as a matter of course.

Second, common sense as to what is a reasonable response latency for the task at hand should play a role in determining whether a long response is a true response or an error. For instance, if the task is merely to pronounce each stimulus word as quickly as possible after presentation, latencies of 1.5 or 2 s or longer would seem to indicate either an equipment error (e.g., the participant spoke too softly for the microphone to pick up the response) or a failure to follow instructions. But the same latency if the task is to say whether an adjective describes oneself is quite reasonable; it may easily take this long for the person to decide.

Latencies that are too fast to have been reasonable responses should also be trimmed; these are almost always anticipations and not true responses. Typically, latencies shorter than 300 ms are trimmed (and these are usually quite rare) for this reason. (Even the National Basketball Association endorses this 300-ms "minimal response time" rule – if less than 0.3 of a second remains on the game clock, no shot is allowed to count after play is resumed, as it is deemed impossible to get one off in this short a time.)

Third, only truly extreme latencies should be trimmed; for example, those that are over 3 standard deviations above the mean (as in Blair & Banaji, 1996), or only the most extreme 2% of all responses. In the dozen or so published automatic attitude experiments, for instance, only between 1% and 2% of responses were trimmed in each study.

Fourth and finally, it should be established that the deleted reaction times are equally distributed across conditions. If a disproportionate number of them fall in a given condition or subset of conditions, this implies that they are not random events or errors, but systematic effects of the experimental manipulations.

Because of the usual and recognized need in response latency research to trim and transform the data, it is more important than usual to earn and keep the trust of the consumers of your research by not taking advantage of the situation. Readers of research are rightly suspicious when data are omitted or transformed, as it is easy to imagine the temptation to trim and transform until the "right" results are obtained. The above guidelines should go a long way toward quelling such skepticism.

Uncontrollability

Thus far we have been concerned with the case in which a person is not aware of and does not intend to be perceiving or feeling or behaving in a certain way; it happens in the absence of a conscious intention. But what if the person was made aware of the effect? Could they control responses based on it if they wanted to? Uncontrollability of a process is another quality of automaticity, but one that need not follow from the others. That is, it is very possible and probably even likely for one to be affected unintentionally by, say, the current environmental context (as in priming effects) but be able to counteract such effects on judgments or behavior if one becomes aware of the potential influence (Strack & Hannover, 1996). Devine (1989) showed that stereotype activation may be unintended, but with the appropriate values, motivation, and task, one can control the effect of the stereotype on responses (see also Fiske, 1989).

This leads to the general observation that although the initial activation events, such as in stereotyping, may not be easily if at all controlled, the overt responses based on those activated representations are controllable in most cases. Take the classic paradigm for studying uncontrollable activation, the Stroop color–word task (Stroop, 1935; see reviews in Logan, 1980; MacLeod, 1991). In this task, the participant is to name the color in which a word is presented. It is easily shown that people take longer when the word itself

---

[8] It might be questioned why it is acceptable to routinely perform such trimming with reaction time data when one is not routinely permitted to trim outliers in other forms of dependent measures (e.g., responses at the opposite end of questionnaire scales as are most other responses). Although we do not claim to offer a definitive answer to this provocative objection, in a first pass at an answer we would point to the usually small, though meaningful differences between conditions typically obtained with reaction time methods, which can be easily swamped and distorted by just a single outlier; secondly, unlike outliers in questionnaires that are the product of conscious choice, those in reaction time studies are most usually errors of some form and not psychologically meaningful (e.g., a response time of 4 s to pronounce "elephant" for a native English speaker).

[9] For a recent example of careful outlier analysis and elimination, see Uleman, Hon, Roman, and Moskowitz (1996, pp. 381–382). These researchers also provide useful guidelines for dropping participants with high error rates and for eliminating the effects of practice, fatigue, and boredom that can occur during experiments with many response trials.

– which is irrelevant to the task of naming the color – is the name of a different color (e.g., the word RED presented in green ink).[10] Researchers have shown that this effect holds for any stimuli to which the participant is perceptually sensitive, such as those related to his or her chronically accessible social constructs (Bargh & Pratto, 1986) or to discrepancies between his or her actual and ideal self-concepts (Higgins, VanHook, & Dorfman, 1988).

What is often overlooked in this paradigm is that the participants' actual responses in this task are overwhelmingly the correct ones. It is not that people say "red" to the word RED in green ink; they say "green" but take longer to do so, because of the need to inhibit the automatically activated competing response "red" (see Logan, 1980). So it has always been the case that findings of "uncontrollable" automatic effects refer not to uncontrollable responses but to uncontrollable internal activation events.

Again, the key is whether the individual is aware of the possibility of influence. If he or she is not, as in priming or stereotype-activation events, biased judgments and even behavior (Bargh et al., 1996) can be the result. But if the participant is made aware, he or she may be able to adjust for and control the effect (though overadjustment may occur; see Strack & Hannover, 1996). Take, for example, the study by Schwarz and Clore (1983) in which participants were contacted by telephone and asked questions about their life satisfaction. They were called either on a rainy or a sunny day, and if the interviewer did not mention the weather at all, it did affect their responses. Those contacted on a rainy day reported less satisfaction with their entire life than did those contacted on a sunny day, apparently misattributing their feelings due to the weather in the process. But if the experimenter casually referred to the current weather conditions, the effect disappeared. Calling the

participants' attention to the weather made it a piece of information in current working memory and more salient as a potential cause for their mood later on when they were asked about their life satisfaction.

An interesting variant on this theme is the *opposition* paradigm developed by Jacoby and his colleagues (e.g., Jacoby, 1991; Jacoby, Lindsay, & Toth, 1992). The essence of this procedure is to place conscious and unconscious influences in opposition to each other, so that the unconscious effects happen despite being contrary to intended, conscious purposes. In one study (Jacoby, Kelley, Brown, & Jasechko, 1989), for example, participants were exposed to a series of proper names as part of one experimental session. Half of the participants studied the list under full attention conditions, and the remaining participants studied it under divided attention conditions, having to perform a secondary task at the same time. The point of this attention manipulation was to decrease some participants' ability to later remember the names they had been shown.

Coming back to the lab the next day, the participants were asked to judge the fame of a list of names, which included new famous and new nonfamous names as well as some from the list of the previous day. Participants were told that all of the names they had studied the day before were nonfamous. Thus, if they consciously remembered seeing a name from that prior list, their response would be to say it was nonfamous. But participants from the divided attention condition of the day before would be less able to remember those names, and so less able to sort out whether the felt familiarity of those names came from their actual fame, or from having seen them during the study phase of the experiment. And, as predicted, the divided attention condition participants were more likely than the full attention participants to mistakenly say that the previous day's nonfamous names were actually famous – a demonstration, the authors concluded, of "becoming famous overnight."

Note that neither the current weather conditions, in the Schwarz and Clore study, nor the original list of nonfamous names, in the Jacoby et al. (1989) experiment, were presented "subliminally" to participants, below their threshold of conscious awareness. All of the influential information was originally available to consciousness. The subliminality or supraliminality of the influential stimulus was not the critical factor in being influenced unintentionally and being unable to attempt to control that influence, but the participants' awareness of the potential effect of that (consciously perceived) stimulus.

---

[10] There is no reason to limit this technique to the task of color-naming; the logic applies equally well to any task in which an irrelevant dimension of the stimuli suggests the same or a competing response to that dictated by the relevant dimension. In the original Stroop task, the meaning of the stimulus word is an irrelevant dimension, and its color the relevant dimension, but participants cannot help but process the irrelevant feature. But if the task is instead to indicate whether a stimulus word was presented above or below a fixation point, then the word "above" facilitates response times (compared with other words) when presented above the fixation point and slows down response times when presented below the fixation point (contrariwise for the word "below"; see Logan, 1980).

How Control Attempts Can Produce Uncontrollability

Wegner and his colleagues (e.g., Ansfield & Wegner, 1996; Wegner, 1994; Wegner & Erber, 1992) have generated a substantial body of evidence on uncontrollable processing effects. The basic experimental technique involves having participants engage in an attention-demanding secondary task while they are trying to prevent something from happening. Wegner's (1994) ironic process model makes the specific prediction that distraction and other strains on attentional capacity actually increase the likelihood that the counterintentional process will occur. That is, trying not to do something involves keeping in mind what it is that one does not want to happen, in order to maintain vigilance against it. But this has the ironic side effect of increasing the activation or accessibility of precisely those thoughts and behavior representations that one desires to control or prevent. Because the act of inhibiting or controlling them is effortful and attention-demanding (see Logan, 1980; Posner & Snyder, 1975; Shallice, 1972), trying not to do something under divided attention conditions will often have the ironic effect of making it more, not less, likely that one will do it. This is because one is left with the increased activation without the inhibition.

Ansfield and Wegner (1996) reported a series of experiments based on the Chevreul pendulum illusion, in which one is told to keep a pendulum still and not to let it move in a certain direction. As predicted by ironic process theory, having participants count backwards from 1,000 by 7s while holding the pendulum caused the pendulum to move – as if by magic – exactly in the unintended direction. Ironic process theory identified a very large domain of uncontrollable mental processes – all of those one intends to control, but cannot because of a current deficit in the attentional capacity needed to do so.

CONCLUSIONS

Priming is a very useful technique for studying the role played by situational context in cognition, motivation, and behavior. Such contextual effects are, if anything, more pervasive in everyday life than many social psychological theories allow. One's ongoing stream of consciousness continually creates ripples of influence that persist well after the conscious focus has flowed on to other things. And our conscious goals and purposes also continue to influence us after their originally intended task has been completed or abandoned.

Priming is also used to experimentally manipulate states of mind that are analogous to individual differences in automatic processing. One can select people based on these chronic differences, such as those high on achievement motivation or those with a chronically accessible trait construct for honesty, and compare their performance on a task or their perceptions of a target person with those of participants without these chronic states. However, these groups of individuals could well differ in other ways as well, and they are self-selecting into the experimental conditions. A researcher's confidence in the focal independent variable as the real cause of an effect in individual difference research is bolstered if he or she can also produce the effect experimentally. Thus priming research is a natural complement to automaticity research.

The importance of studying automaticity resides in the ecological importance of the particular quality of automaticity that is under scrutiny. That is, it is important to study the efficiency or attention-free nature of a process when one wants to see if it would occur even in cognitively busy circumstances, and it is our feeling that these conditions are more the rule than the exception in life. And it is important to study whether a process occurs unintentionally because of the implications it has, in conjunction with lack of awareness, for the individual's ability to control it. If the process only happens when the person intends it, those with good intentions have nothing to fear. But in many cases good intentions go for naught because the person does not choose and is not aware of the perceptual or motivational process affecting him or her. And this lack of both intention and awareness may preclude controllability of the process.

Research into such automatic effects helped to raise the general public's consciousness in the 1970s and 1980s about the possibility of nonconscious bias, especially in racial and gender stereotyping. Further study of these unseen hands of automatic influence can only continue to do more such good. After all, it is only with such knowledge and awareness that one can hope to counteract those influences. An exciting contemporary trend in research, in fact, is aimed at discovering the conditions under which unwanted automatic influences, as in stereotyping, can be controlled or even changed.

But not all automatic influences are unwanted and counterproductive – quite the opposite. There is a natural tendency to assume, based on the findings of an automatic or nonconscious role in such social and personal problems as prejudice, sexual harassment, and depression, that automatic mental processes are always associated with negative outcomes, and conscious mental control with positive outcomes. Indeed, several influential authors have made just this argument (e.g., Bandura, 1986; Langer, 1989; Mischel, Cantor, & Feldman, 1996). Yet it is the natural purview of social psychologists to study social problems, and so the problematic ones are likely to be overrepresented in the roll call of researched automatic phenomena.

Habits of thought and behavior can be helpful as well as harmful: William James (1890) famously advised the young to make habitual as soon as possible all the useful behaviors one could. Just as negative stereotypes can be activated automatically, so too can chronic fairness motives (Moskowitz et al., 1997). Just as depressed people think about themselves automatically in negative terms, so too do nondepressed people think about themselves in automatically positive terms (Bargh & Tota, 1988), which turns out to be an important component of psychological health (e.g., Taylor & Brown, 1988). Therefore, another good tack for future research – besides the continued probe of how to control undesired automatic and contextual (priming) effects – might be to investigate the roles played by priming and automaticity in psychological health and socially constructive behavior. After all, nonconscious phenomena can be created and developed, as well as controlled and changed.

REFERENCES

Allport, F. H. (1955). *Theories of perception and the concept of structure*. New York: Wiley.

Anderson, J. R. (1982). Acquisition of cognitive skill. *Psychological Review, 89*, 369–406.

Anderson, J. R., & Bower, G. H. (1973). *Human associative memory*. New York: Winston.

Ansfield, M. E., & Wegner, D. M. (1996). The feeling of doing. In P. M. Gollwitzer & J. A. Bargh (Eds.), *The psychology of action: Linking cognition and motivation to behavior* (pp. 482–506). New York: Guilford Press.

Balota, D. A., & Lorch, R. F., Jr. (1986). Depth of automatic spreading activation: Mediated priming effects in pronunciation but not in lexical decision. *Journal of Experimental Psychology: Learning, Memory, and Cognition, 12*, 336–345.

Bandura, A. (1986). *Social foundations of thought and action: A social cognitive theory*. Englewood Cliffs, NJ: Prentice-Hall.

Bargh, J. A. (1989). Conditional automaticity: Varieties of automatic influence in social perception and cognition. In J. S. Uleman & J. A. Bargh (Eds.), *Unintended thought* (pp. 3–51). New York: Guilford Press.

Bargh, J. A. (1994). The four horsemen of automaticity: Awareness, intention, efficiency, and control in social cognition. In R. S. Wyer & T. K. Srull (Eds.), *Handbook of social cognition* (2nd ed., Vol. 1, pp. 1–40). Hillsdale, NJ: Erlbaum.

Bargh, J. A. (1996). Principles of automaticity. In E. T. Higgins & A. Kruglanski (Eds.), *Social psychology: Handbook of basic principles* (pp. 169–183). New York: Guilford Press.

Bargh, J. A. (1997). The automaticity of everyday life. Target chapter in R. S. Wyer, Jr. (Ed.), *Advances in social cognition* (Vol. 10, pp. 1–61). Mahwah, NJ: Erlbaum.

Bargh, J. A., Bond, R. N., Lombardi, W. J., & Tota, M. E. (1986). The additive nature of chronic and temporary sources of construct accessibility. *Journal of Personality and Social Psychology, 50*, 869–878.

Bargh, J. A., Chaiken, S., Govender, R., & Pratto, F. (1992). The generality of the automatic attitude activation effect. *Journal of Personality and Social Psychology, 62*, 893–912.

Bargh, J. A., Chaiken, S., Raymond, P., & Hymes, C. (1996). The automatic evaluation effect: Unconditionally automatic attitude activation with a pronunciation task. *Journal of Experimental Social Psychology, 32*, 185–210.

Bargh, J. A., Chen, M., & Burrows, L. (1996). Automaticity of social behavior: Direct effects of trait construct and stereotype activation on action. *Journal of Personality and Social Psychology, 71*, 230–244.

Bargh, J. A., & Gollwitzer, P. M. (1994). Environmental control of goal-directed action: Automatic and strategic contingencies between situations and behavior. In W. Spaulding (Ed.), *Integrations of motivation and cognition: The Nebraska Symposium on Motivation* (Vol. 41, pp. 71–124). Lincoln: University of Nebraska Press.

Bargh, J. A., & Pietromonaco, P. (1982). Automatic information processing and social perception: The influence of trait information presented outside of conscious awareness on impression formation. *Journal of Personality and Social Psychology, 43*, 437–449.

Bargh, J. A., & Pratto, F. (1986). Individual construct accessibility and perceptual selection. *Journal of Experimental Social Psychology, 22*, 293–311.

Bargh, J. A., Raymond, P., Pryor, J., & Strack, F. (1995). The attractiveness of the underling: An automatic power–sex association and its consequences for sexual harassment and aggression. *Journal of Personality and Social Psychology, 68*, 768–781.

Bargh, J. A., & Thein, R. D. (1985). Individual construct accessibility, person memory, and the recall–judgment link: The case of information overload. *Journal of Personality and Social Psychology, 49*, 1129–1146.

Bargh, J. A., & Tota, M. E. (1988). Context-dependent automatic processing in depression: Accessibility of negative constructs with regard to self but not others. *Journal of Personality and Social Psychology, 54*, 925–939.

Bator, R. J., & Cialdini, R. B. (1995). *Priming a consistency motivation enhances cognitive dissonance effects*. Manuscript submitted for publication, Arizona State University.

Beck, A. T. (1967). *Depression: Clinical, experimental, and theoretical aspects*. New York: Harper & Row.

Blair, I., & Banaji, M. (1996). Automatic and controlled processes in stereotype priming. *Journal of Personality and Social Psychology, 70*, 1142–1163.

Boring, E. G. (1950). *A history of experimental psychology* (2nd ed.) New York: Appleton-Century-Crofts.

Bousfield, A. K., & Bousfield, W. A. (1966). Measurement of clustering and sequential constancies in repeated free recall. *Psychological Reports, 19*, 935–942.

Bower, G. H., Lesgold, A. M., & Tieman, D. (1969). Grouping operations in free recall. *Journal of Verbal Learning and Verbal Behavior, 8*, 481–493.

Box, G. E. P., Hunter, W. G., & Hunter, J. S. (1978). *Statistics for experimenters*. New York: Wiley.

Brenner, M. (1973). The next-in-line effect. *Journal of Verbal Learning and Verbal Behavior, 12*, 320–323.

Brewer, M. B. (1988). A dual process model of impression formation. In T. K. Srull & R. S. Wyer, Jr. (Eds.), *Advances in social cognition* (Vol. 1, pp. 1–36). Hillsdale, NJ: Erlbaum.

Broadbent, D. E. (1958). *Perception and communication*. London: Pergamon.

Bruner, J. S. (1957). On perceptual readiness. *Psychological Review, 64*, 123–152.

Bruner, J. S., & Postman, L. (1947). Value and need as organizing factors in perception. *Journal of Abnormal and Social Psychology, 42*, 33–44.

Carver, C. S., Ganellen, R. J., Froming, W. J., & Chambers, W. (1983). Modeling: An analysis in terms of category accessibility. *Journal of Experimental Social Psychology, 19*, 403–421.

Chaiken, S., & Bargh, J. A. (1993). Occurrence versus moderation of the automatic attitude activation effect: Reply to Fazio. *Journal of Personality and Social Psychology, 64*, 759–765.

Chaiken, S., Giner-Sorolla, R., & Chen, S. (1996). Beyond accuracy: Defense and impression motives in heuristic and systematic information processing. In P. M. Gollwitzer & J. A. Bargh (Eds.), *The psychology of action* (pp. 553–578). New York: Guilford Press.

Chartrand, T. L., & Bargh, J. A. (1996). Automatic activation of impression formation and memorization goals: Nonconscious goal priming reproduces effects of explicit task instructions. *Journal of Personality and Social Psychology, 71*, 464–478.

Chen, S., Shechter, D., & Chaiken, S. (1996). Getting at the truth or getting along: Accuracy and impression-motivated heuristic and systematic processing. *Journal of Personality and Social Psychology, 71*, 262–275.

Cialdini, R. B. (1994, October). *The strain for consistency: A history, a measure, and a surprise*. Plenary address to the annual meetings of the Society for Experimental Social Psychology, Lake Tahoe, NV.

Costin, F. (1969). The scrambled sentence test: A group measure of hostility. *Educational and Psychological Measurement, 29*, 461–468.

Dalrymple-Alford, E. C. (1970). The measurement of clustering in free recall. *Psychological Bulletin, 1*, 32–34.

Deutsch, J. A., & Deutsch, D. (1963). Attention: Some theoretical considerations. *Psychological Review, 70*, 80–90.

Devine, P. G. (1989). Stereotypes and prejudice: Their automatic and controlled components. *Journal of Personality and Social Psychology, 56*, 680–690.

Dixon, N. F. (1971). *Subliminal perception: The nature of a controversy*. New York: McGraw-Hill.

Dodge, K. A. (1993). Social-cognitive mechanisms in the development of conduct disorder and depression. *Annual Review of Psychology, 44*, 559–584.

Duncker, K. (1945). On problem solving. *Psychological Monographs, 58* (5, Whole No. 270).

Eagly, A. H., & Chaiken, S. (1993). *The psychology of attitudes*. New York: Harcourt Brace Jovanovich.

Edwards, K. (1990). The interplay of affect and cognition in attitude formation and change. *Journal of Personality and Social Psychology, 59*, 202–216.

Erdelyi, M. H. (1974). A new look at the New Look: Perceptual defense and vigilance. *Psychological Review, 81*, 1–25.

Erdley, C. A., & D'Agostino, P. R. (1988). Cognitive and affective components of automatic priming effects. *Journal of Personality and Social Psychology, 54*, 741–747.

Ericsson, K. A., & Simon, H. A. (1980). Verbal reports as data. *Psychological Review, 87*, 215–251.

Fazio, R. H. (1990). A practical guide to the use of response latencies in social psychological research. In C. Hendrick & M. S. Clark (Eds.), *Review of Personality and Social Psychology* (Vol. 11, pp. 74–97). Newbury Park, CA: Sage.

Fazio, R. H. (1993). Variability in the likelihood of automatic attitude activation: Data reanalysis and commentary on Bargh, Chaiken, Govender, and Pratto (1992). *Journal of Personality and Social Psychology, 64*, 753–758.

Fazio, R. H., Chen, J., McDonel, E. C., & Sherman, S. J. (1982). Attitude accessibility, attitude-behavior consistency, and the strength of the object-evaluation association. *Journal of Experimental Social Psychology, 18*, 339–357.

Fazio, R. H., Jackson, J. R., Dunton, B. C., & Williams, C. J. (1995). Variability in automatic activation as an unobtrusive measure of racial attitudes: A bona fide pipeline? *Journal of Personality and Social Psychology, 69*, 1013–1027.

Fazio, R. H., Sanbonmatsu, D. M., Powell, M. C., & Kardes, F. R. (1986). On the automatic activation of attitudes. *Journal of Personality and Social Psychology, 50*, 229–238.

Fischer, B., & Weber, H. (1993). Express saccades and visual attention. *Behavioral and Brain Sciences, 16*, 553–610.

Fiske, S. T. (1980). Attention and weight in person perception: The impact of negative and extreme behavior. *Journal of Personality and Social Psychology, 38*, 889–906.

Fiske, S. T. (1989). Examining the role of intent: Toward understanding its role in stereotyping and prejudice. In J. S. Uleman & J. A. Bargh (Eds.), *Unintended thought* (pp. 253–283). New York: Guilford Press.

Fiske, S. T., & Neuberg, S. E. (1990). A continuum of impression formation, from category-based to individuating processes: Influences of information and motivation on attention and interpretation. In M. P. Zanna (Ed.),

Advances in experimental social psychology (Vol. 23, pp. 1–74). San Diego, CA: Academic Press.

Fowler, C. A., Wolford, G., Slade, R., & Tassinary, L. (1981). Lexical access with and without awareness. *Journal of Experimental Psychology: General, 110,* 341–362.

Gilbert, D. T. (1989). Thinking lightly about others: Automatic components of the social inference process. In J. S. Uleman & J. A. Bargh (Eds.), *Unintended thought* (pp. 189–211). New York: Guilford Press.

Gilbert, D. T., & Hixon, J. G. (1991). The trouble of thinking: Activation and application of stereotypic beliefs. *Journal of Personality and Social Psychology, 60,* 509–517.

Gilbert, D. T., & Osborne, R. E. (1989). Thinking backward: Some curable and incurable consequences of cognitive busyness. *Journal of Personality and Social Psychology, 57,* 940–949.

Gilbert, D. T., Pelham, B. W., & Krull, D. S. (1988). On cognitive busyness: When persons perceivers meet persons perceived. *Journal of Personality and Social Psychology, 54,* 733–740.

Gollwitzer, P. M. (1990). Action phases and mind-sets. In E. T. Higgins & R. M. Sorrentino (Eds.), *Handbook of motivation and cognition* (Vol. 2, pp. 53–92). New York: Guilford Press.

Gollwitzer, P. M., & Bargh, J. A. (Eds.). (1996). *The psychology of action.* New York: Guilford Press.

Gollwitzer, P. M., Heckhausen, H., & Steller, B. (1990). Deliberative and implemental mind-sets: Cognitive tuning toward congruous thoughts and information. *Journal of Personality and Social Psychology, 59,* 1119–1127.

Gollwitzer, P. M., & Moskowitz, G. B. (1996). Goal effects on action and cognition. In E. T. Higgins & A. W. Kruglanski (Eds.), Social psychology: *Handbook of basic principles* (pp. 361–399). New York: Guilford Press.

Grand, S., & Segal, S. J. (1966). Recovery in the absence of recall. *Journal of Experimental Psychology, 72,* 138–144.

Greenwald, A. G. (1992). New Look 3: Unconscious cognition reclaimed. *American Psychologist, 47,* 766–779.

Greenwald, A. G., & Banaji, M. R. (1995). Implicit social cognition: Attitudes, self-esteem, and stereotypes. *Psychological Review, 102,* 4–27.

Greenwald, A. G., Draine, S. C., & Abrams, R. L. (1996). Three cognitive markers of unconscious semantic activation. *Science, 273,* 1699–1702.

Greenwald, A. G., Klinger, M. R., & Liu, T. J. (1989). Unconscious processing of dichoptically masked words. *Memory and Cognition, 17,* 35–47.

Grier, J. B. (1971). Nonparametric indexes for sensitivity and bias: Computing formulas. *Psychological Bulletin, 75,* 424–429.

Hamilton, D. L., Katz, L. B., & Leirer, V. O. (1980a). Cognitive representation of personality impression: Organizational processes in first impression formation. *Journal of Personality and Social Psychology, 39,* 1050–1063.

Hamilton, D. L., Katz, L. B., & Leirer, V. O. (1980b). Organizational processes in impression formation. In R. Hastie, T.

M. Ostrom, E. B. Ebbesen, R. S. Wyer, Jr., D. L. Hamilton, & D. E. Carlston (Eds.), *Person memory: The cognitive basis of social perception* (pp. 121–153). Hillsdale, NJ: Erlbaum.

Hastie, R., & Kumar, P. A. (1979). Person memory: Personality traits as organizing principles in memory for behaviors. *Journal of Personality and Social Psychology, 37,* 25–38.

Hastie, R., & Park, B. (1986). The relationship between memory and judgment depends on whether the judgment task is memory-based or on-line. *Psychological Review, 93,* 258–268.

Herr, P. M. (1986). Consequences of priming: Judgment and behavior. *Journal of Personality and Social Psychology, 51,* 1106–1115.

Herr, P. M., Sherman, S. J., & Fazio, R. H. (1984). On the consequences of priming: Assimilation and contrast effects. *Journal of Experimental Social Psychology, 19,* 323–340.

Higgins, E. T. (1989). Knowledge accessibility and activation: Subjectivity and suffering from unconscious sources. In J. S. Uleman & J. A. Bargh (Eds.), *Unintended thought* (pp. 75–123). New York: Guilford Press.

Higgins, E. T. (1996). Knowledge activation: Accessibility, applicability, and salience. In E. T. Higgins & A. Kruglanski (Eds.), *Social psychology: Handbook of basic principles* (pp. 133–168). New York: Guilford Press.

Higgins, E. T., Bargh, J. A., & Lombardi, W. (1985). Nature of priming effects on categorization. *Journal of Experimental Social Psychology, 11,* 59–69.

Higgins, E. T., & Chaires, W. M. (1980). Accessibility of interrelational constructs: Implications for stimulus encoding and creativity. *Journal of Experimental Social Psychology, 16,* 348–361.

Higgins, E. T., & King, G. A. (1981). Accessibility of social constructs: Information-processing consequences of individual and contextual variability. In N. Cantor & J. F. Kihlstrom (Eds.), *Personality, cognition, and social interaction* (pp. 69–122). Hillsdale, NJ: Erlbaum.

Higgins, E. T., Rholes, W. S., & Jones, C. R. (1977). Category accessibility and impression formation. *Journal of Experimental Social Psychology, 13,* 141–154.

Higgins, E. T., VanHook, E., & Dorfman, D. (1988). Do self-attributes form a cognitive structure? *Social Cognition, 6,* 177–217.

Holender, D. (1986). Semantic activation without conscious identification in dichotic listening, parafoveal vision, and visual masking: A survey. *Behavioral and Brain Sciences, 9,* 1–66.

Jacoby, L. L. (1991). A process dissociation framework: Separating automatic from intentional uses of memory. *Journal of Memory and Language, 30,* 513–541.

Jacoby, L. L., Kelley, C., Brown, J., & Jasechko, J. (1989). Becoming famous overnight: Limits on the ability to avoid unconscious influences of the past. *Journal of Personality and Social Psychology, 56,* 326–338.

Jacoby, L. L., Lindsay, D. S., & Toth, J. P. (1992). Unconscious influences revealed: Attention, awareness, and control. *American Psychologist, 47,* 802–809.

James, W. (1890). *Principles of psychology*. New York: Holt.

Johnson, M. K., & Hasher, L. (1987). Human learning and memory. *Annual Review of Psychology, 38*, 631–668.

Kantowitz, B. H. (1974). Double stimulation. In B. H. Kantowitz (Ed.), *Human information processing* (pp. 320–342). Hillsdale, NJ: Erlbaum.

Koestler, A. (1967). *The ghost in the machine*. London: Hutchinson & Co.

Koffka, K. (1922). Perception: An introduction to the Gestalt-theorie. *Psychological Bulletin, 19*, 531–585.

Koriat, A., & Feuerstein, N. (1976). The recovery of incidentally acquired information. *Acta Psychologica, 40*, 463–464.

Langer, E. J. (1978). Rethinking the role of thought in social interaction. In J. H. Harvey, W. I. Ickes, & R. F. Kidd (Eds.), *New directions in attribution research* (Vol. 2, pp. 35–58). Hillsdale, NJ: Erlbaum.

Langer, E. J. (1989). *Mindfulness*. New York: Allyn & Bacon.

Lashley, K. S. (1951). The problem of serial order in behavior. In L. A. Jeffress (Ed.), *Cerebral mechanisms in behavior: The Hixon symposium* (pp. 112–136). New York: Wiley.

Linville, P. (1996). Attention inhibition: Does it underlie ruminative thought? In R. S. Wyer, Jr. (Ed.), *Advances in social cognition* (Vol. 9, pp. 121–133). Mahwah, NJ: Erlbaum.

Logan, G. D. (1980). Attention and automaticity in Stroop and priming tasks: Theory and data. *Cognitive Psychology, 12*, 523–553.

Logan, G. D., & Cowan, W. (1984). On the ability to inhibit thought and action: A theory of an act of control. *Psychological Review, 91*, 295–327.

Lombardi, W. J., Higgins, E. T., & Bargh, J. A. (1987). The role of consciousness in priming effects on categorization. *Personality and Social Psychology Bulletin, 13*, 411–429.

MacLeod, C. (1991). Half a century of research on the Stroop effect: An integrative review. *Psychological Bulletin, 109*, 163–203.

Macrae, C. N., Hewstone, M., & Griffiths, R. J. (1993). Processing load and memory for stereotype-based information. *European Journal of Social Psychology, 23*, 77–87.

Macrae, C. N., Milne, A. B., & Bodenhausen, G. V. (1994). Stereotypes as energy-saving devices: A peek inside the cognitive toolbox. *Journal of Personality and Social Psychology, 66*, 37–47.

Marcel, A. J. (1983). Conscious and unconscious perception: Experiments on visual masking and word recognition. *Cognitive Psychology, 15*, 197–237.

Marks, M. M., Sinclair, R. C., & Wellens, T. R. (1991). The effect of completing the Beck Depression Inventory on self-reported mood state: Contrast and assimilation. *Personality and Social Psychology Bulletin, 17*, 457–465.

Markus, H. (1977). Self-schemata and processing information about the self. *Journal of Personality and Social Psychology, 35*, 63–78.

Meyer, D. E., & Schvaneveldt, R. W. (1971). Facilitation in recognizing pairs of words: Evidence of a dependence between retrieval operations. *Journal of Experimental Psychology, 90*, 227–234.

Mischel, W. (1973). Toward a cognitive social learning reconceptualization of personality. *Psychological Review, 80*, 252–283.

Mischel, W., Cantor, N., & Feldman, S. (1996). Principles of self-regulation: The nature of willpower and self-control. In E. T. Higgins & A. W. Kruglanski (Eds.), *Social psychology: Handbook of basic principles* (pp. 329–360). New York: Guilford Press.

Moskowitz, G. B., Gollwitzer, P. M., Wasel, W., & Schaal, B. (1999). Preconscious Control of Stereotype activation through chronic egalitarian goals. *Journal of Personality and Social Psychology, 77*, 167–184.

Murphy, M. D. (1979). Measurement of category clustering in free recall. In C. R. Puff (Ed.), *Memory organization and structure* (pp. 51–83). San Diego, CA: Academic press.

Murphy, S. T., Monahan, J. L., & Zajonc, R. B. (1995). Additivity of nonconscious affect: Combined effects of priming and exposure. *Journal of Personality and Social Psychology, 69*, 589–602.

Murphy, S. T., & Zajonc, R. B. (1993). Affect, cognition, and awareness: Affective priming with optimal and suboptimal stimulus exposures. *Journal of Personality and Social Psychology, 64*, 723–739.

Neely, J. H. (1977). Semantic priming and retrieval from lexical memory: Roles of inhibitionless spreading activation and limited-capacity attention. *Journal of Experimental Psychology: General, 106*, 226–254.

Neisser, U. (1967). *Cognitive Psychology*. New York: Appleton-Century-Crofts.

Neuberg, S. L. (1988). Behavioral implications of information presented outside of conscious awareness: The effect of subliminal presentation of trait information on behavior in the Prisoner's Dilemma Game. *Social Cognition, 6*, 207–230.

Neumann, O. (1984). Automatic processing: A review of recent findings and a plea for an old theory. In W. Prinz & A. F. Sanders (Eds.), *Cognition and motor processes* (pp. 255–293). Berlin: Springer-Verlag.

Newell, A., & Rosenbloom, P. S. (1981). Mechanisms of skill acquisition and the law of practice. In J. R. Anderson (Ed.), *Cognitive skills and their acquisition* (pp. 1–55). Hillsdale, NJ: Erlbaum.

Newman, L. S., & Uleman, J. S. (1990). Assimilation and contrast effects in spontaneous trait inference. *Personality and Social Psychology Bulletin, 16*, 224–240.

Niedenthal, P. M. (1990). Implicit perception of affective information. *Journal of Experimental Social Psychology, 26*, 505–527.

Nisbett, R. E., & Wilson, T. D. (1977). Telling more than we can know: Verbal reports on mental processes. *Psychological Review, 84*, 231–259.

Norman, D. A. (1968). Toward a theory of memory and attention. *Psychological Review, 75*, 522–536.

Ostrom, T. M., Pryor, J. B., & Simpson, D. D. (1981). The organization of social information. In E. T. Higgins, C. P. Herman, & M. P. Zanna (Eds.), *Social cognition: The Ontario Symposium* (Vol. 1, pp. 3–38). Hillsdale, NJ: Erlbaum.

Perdue, C. W., Dovidio, J. F., Gurtman, M. B., & Tyler, R. B. (1990). Us and them: Social categorization and the process of intergroup bias. *Journal of Personality and Social Psychology, 59,* 475–486.

Posner, M. I., & Snyder, C. R. R. (1975). Attention and cognitive control. In R. L. Solso (Ed.), *Information processing and cognition: The Loyola symposium* (pp. 55–85). Hillsdale, NJ: Erlbaum.

Postman, L., Bruner, J. S., & McGinnies, E. (1948). Personal values as selective factors in perception. *Journal of Abnormal and social Psychology, 43,* 142–154.

Pratto, F., & Bargh, J. A. (1991). Stereotyping based on apparently individuating information: Trait and global components of sex stereotypes under attention overload. *Journal of Experimental Social Psychology, 27,* 26–47.

Prinz, W. (1990). A common coding approach to perception and action. In O. Neumann & W. Prinz (Eds.), *Relationships between perception and action* (pp. 167–201). Heidelberg, Germany: Springer-Verlag.

Prinz, W. (in press). Perception and action planning. *European Journal of Cognitive Psychology.*

Rayner, K. (1978). Foveal and parafoveal cues in reading. In J. Requin (Ed.), *Attention and performance VIII* (pp. 149–161). Hillsdale, NJ: Erlbaum.

Robertson, C. (1985). A measure of categorical clustering based upon a model of recall order. *British Journal of Mathematical and Statistical Psychology, 38,* 141–151.

Robertson, C. (1995). Modeling recall: Clustering and order effects. *British Journal of Mathematical and Statistical Psychology, 48,* 29–50.

Roenker, D. L., Thompson, C. P., & Brown, S. C. (1971). Comparison of measures for the estimation of clustering in free recall. *Psychological Bulletin, 1,* 45–48.

Rogers, T. B. (1974). An analysis of two central stages underlying responding to personality items: The self-referent decision and response selection. *Journal of Research in Personality, 8,* 128–138.

Roskos-Ewoldsen, D. R., & Fazio, R. H. (1992). On the orienting value of attitudes: Attitude accessibility as a determinant of an object's attraction of visual attention. *Journal of Personality and Social Psychology, 63,* 198–211.

Ross, L., & Nisbett, R. E. (1991). *The person and the situation: Perspectives of social psychology.* New York: McGraw-Hill.

Rothbart, M. (1981). Memory processes and social beliefs. In D. L. Hamilton (Ed.), *Cognitive processes in stereotyping and intergroup behavior* (pp. 272–298). Hillsdale, NJ: Erlbaum.

Schacter, D. L. (1987). Implicit memory: History and current status. *Journal of Experimental Psychology: Learning, Memory, and Cognition, 13,* 501–518.

Schwarz, N., & Clore, G. L. (1983). Mood, misattribution, and judgments of well-being: Informative and directive functions of affective states. *Journal of Personality and Social Psychology, 45,* 513–523.

Seamon, J. G., Brody, N., & Kauff, D. M. (1983). Affective discrimination of stimuli that are not recognized: Effects of shadowing, masking, and cerebral laterality. *Journal of Experimental Psychology: Learning, Memory, and Cognition, 9,* 544–555.

Segal, S. J. (1967). The priming of association test responses. *Journal of Verbal Learning and Verbal Behavior, 6,* 216–221.

Segal, S. J., & Cofer, C. N. (1960). The effect of recency and recall on word association. *American Psychologist, 15,* 451.

Shallice, T. (1972). Dual functions of consciousness. *Psychological Review, 79,* 383–393.

Shevrin, H. (1992). Subliminal perception, memory, and consciousness: Cognitive and dynamic perspectives. In R. Bornstein & T. Pittman (Eds.), *Perception without awareness* (pp. 123–142). New York: Guilford Press.

Shiffrin, R. M., & Schneider, W. (1977). Controlled and automatic human information processing: II. Perceptual learning, automatic attending, and a general theory. *Psychological Review, 84,* 127–190.

Skelton, J. A., & Strohmetz, D. B. (1990). Priming symptom reports with health-related cognitive activity. *Personality and Social Psychology Bulletin, 16,* 449–464.

Smith, E. R. (1994). Procedural knowledge and processing strategies in social cognition. In R. S. Wyer & T. K. Srull (Eds.), *Handbook of social cognition* (2nd ed., Vol. 1, pp. 99–152). Hillsdale, NJ: Erlbaum.

Smith, E. R., Branscombe, N., & Bormann, C. (1988). Generality of the effects of practice on social judgment tasks. *Journal of Personality and Social Psychology, 54,* 385–395.

Smith, E. R., & Lerner, M. (1986). Development of automatism of social judgments. *Journal of Personality and Social Psychology, 50,* 246–259.

Smith, E. R., Stewart, T. L., & Buttram, R. T. (1992). Inferring a trait from a behavior has long-term, highly specific effects. *Journal of Personality and Social Psychology, 62,* 753–759.

Sorrentino, R. M., & Higgins, E. T. (1986). Motivation and cognition: Warming up to synergism. In R. M. Sorrentino & E. T. Higgins (Eds.), *Handbook of motivation and cognition* (Vol. 1, pp. 3–19). New York: Guilford Press.

Sperling, G. (1960). The information available in brief visual presentations. *Psychological Monographs, 74,* Whole No. 498.

Srull, T. K. (1981). Person memory: Some tests of associative storage and retrieval models. *Journal of Experimental Psychology: Human Learning and Memory, 7,* 440–462.

Srull, T. K. (1984). Methodological techniques of the study of person memory and social cognition. In R.S. Wyer, Jr., & T. K. Srull (Eds.), *Handbook of social cognition* (pp. 73–150). Hillsdale, NJ: Erlbaum.

Srull, T. K., Lichtenstein, M., & Rothbart, M. (1985). Associated storage and retrieval processes in person memory. *Journal of Experimental Psychology: Learning, Memory, and Cognition, 11,* 316–345.

Srull, T. K., & Wyer, R. S., Jr. (1979). The role of category accessibility in the interpretation of information about persons: Some determinants and implications. *Journal of Personality and Social Psychology, 37,* 1660–1672.

Srull, T. K., & Wyer, R. S., Jr. (1980). Category accessibility and social perception: Some implications for the study of person memory and interpersonal judgments. *Journal of Personality and Social Psychology, 38,* 841–856.

Srull, T. K., & Wyer, R. S., Jr. (1989). Person memory and judgment. *Psychological Review, 96,* 58–83.

Storms, L. H. (1958). Apparent backward association: A situational effect. *Journal of Experimental Psychology, 55,* 390–395.

Strack, F., & Hannover, B. (1996). Awareness of influence as a precondition for implementing correctional goals. In P. M. Gollwitzer & J. A. Bargh (Eds.), *The psychology of action* (pp. 579–596). New York: Guilford press.

Stroop, J. R. (1935). Studies of interference in serial verbal reactions. *Journal of Experimental Psychology, 18,* 643–662.

Taylor, S. E., & Brown, J. D. (1988). Illusion and well-being: A social psychological perspective on mental health. *Psychological Bulletin, 103,* 193–210.

Tice, D. M., Butler, J. L., Muraven, M. B., & Stillwell, A. M. (1995). When modesty prevails: Differential favorability of self-presentation to friends and strangers. *Journal of Personality and Social Psychology, 69,* 1120–1138.

Treisman, A. M. (1960). Contextual cues in selective listening. *Quarterly Journal of Experimental Psychology, 12,* 242–248.

Trope, T. (1986). Identification and inferential processes in dispositional attribution. *Psychological Review, 93,* 239–257.

Turvey, M. T. (1973). On peripheral and central processes in vision: Inferences from an information-processing analysis of masking with patterned stimuli. *Psychological Review, 80,* 1–52.

Uleman, J. S., Hon, A., Roman, R. J., & Moskowitz, G. B. (1996). On-line evidence for spontaneous trait inferences at encoding. *Personality and Social Psychology Bulletin, 22,* 377–394.

Wegener, D. T., & Petty, R. E. (1995). Flexible correction processes in social judgment: The role of naive theories in corrections for perceived bias. *Journal of Personality and Social Psychology, 68,* 36–51.

Wegener, D. M. (1994). Ironic processes of mental control. *Psychological Review, 101,* 34–52.

Wegener, D. M., & Bargh, J. A. (1998). Control and automaticity in social life. In D. T. Gilbert, S. T. Fiske, & G. Lindzey (Eds.), *Handbook of social psychology* (4th ed., pp. 446–496). Boston: McGraw-Hill.

Wegener, D. M., & Erber, R. (1992). The hyperaccessibility of suppressed thoughts. *Journal of Personality and Social Psychology, 63,* 903–912.

Wicklund, R. A., & Brehm, J. W. (1976). *Perspectives on cognitive dissonance.* Hillsdale, NJ: Erlbaum.

Wilson, T. D., & Capitman, J. A. (1982). Effects of script availability on social behavior. *Personality and Social Psychology Bulletin, 8,* 11–19.

Wilson, T. D., & Brekke, N. (1994). Mental contamination and mental correction: Unwanted influences on judgments and evaluations. *Psychological Bulletin, 116,* 117–142.

Winer, B. J. (1971). *Statistical principles in experimental design* (2nd ed.). New York: McGraw-Hill.

Wyer, R. S., Jr., & Carlston, D. E. (1979). *Social cognition, inference, and attribution.* Hillsdale, NJ: Erlbaum.

Wyer, R. S., Jr., & Gordon, S. E. (1982). The recall of information about persons and groups. *Journal of Experimental Social Psychology, 18,* 128–164.

Wyer, R. S., Jr., & Srull, T. K. (1989). *Memory and cognition in its social context.* Hillsdale, NJ: Erlbaum.

APPENDIX A: EXAMPLES OF SCRAMBLED SENTENCE TESTS

Instructions: For each set of words below, make a grammatical four word sentence and write it down in the space provided.

For example:

flew   eagle   the   plane   around

The eagle flew around.

* *

(from Bargh, Chen, & Burrows, 1996, Experiment 2)

1. him was *worried* she always
2. from are *Florida* oranges temperature
3. ball the throw toss silently
4. shoes give replace *old* the
5. he observes occasionally people watches
6. be will swear *lonely* they
7. sky the seamless *grey* is
8. ate she it selfishly all
9. be to back *careful* better
10. prepare the gift wrap neatly
11. sew *sentimental* buy item the
12. he *wise* drops only seems
13. are we *stubborn* courteous sometimes
14. the push wash frequently clothes
15. us *bingo* sing play let
16. should now withdraw *forgetful* we
17. somewhat prepared I was retired
18. sunlight makes temperature *wrinkle* raisins

19. is *rigid* he usually studying
20. a have *traditional* wedding holiday
21. picked throw apples hardly the
22. drink this looks seems *bitter*
23. they obedient him often meet
24. there are they *conservative* going
25. knits *dependent* he occasionally them
26. studies she texts *ancient* him
27. helpless it hides there over
28. is he *gullible* plant so
29. *cautious* alone very are they
30. send I mail it over

(from Chartrand & Bargh, 1996, Experiment 1)

1. from are Florida *preserve* they
2. a smile parrot what great

3. watches *recalls* he occasionally people
4. ball the hoop toss normally
5. saw hammer he train the
6. good dislikes *recognizes* she deals
7. maintain she to composure try
8. should withdraw *keep* now we
9. the machine wash frequently clothes
10. somewhat *memory* prepared I was
11. save does *study* usually he
12. be to *remember* back careful
13. sky the seamless red is
14. a have June holiday wedding
15. they *retain* him often meet

Note: Words in italics are the critical priming stimuli (for the "elderly" stereotype and the goal of memorization, respectively); they are not italicized in the actual task.

APPENDIX B: EXAMPLE OF FUNNELED DEBRIEFING PROCEDURE FOR SUPRALIMINAL PRIMING TASK

The experimenter proceeds to ask the participant the following questions and records the answers given:

1. What do you think the purpose of this experiment was?
2. What do you think this experiment was trying to study?
3. Did you think that any of the tasks you did were related in any way?
   (if "yes") In what way were they related?
4. Did anything you did on one task affect what you did on any other task?
   (if "yes") How exactly did it affect you?
5. When you were completing the scrambled sentence test, did you notice anything unusual about the words?
6. Did you notice any particular pattern or theme to the words that were included in the scrambled sentence test?
7. What were you trying to do while reading the behavioral phrases on the computer monitor? Did you have any particular goal or strategy?

(Source: Chartrand & Bargh, 1996, Experiment 1)

CHAPTER ELEVEN

Coded Semistructured Interviews in Social Psychological Research

KIM BARTHOLOMEW, ANTONIA J. Z. HENDERSON, AND JAMES E. MARCIA

In 1991, Bartholomew and colleagues began a research project in which they followed 77 young established couples over 2 years to investigate how individuals represent and process information about close relationships (Bartholomew, 1997; Scharfe & Bartholomew, 1994, 1995). In addition to various self-report measures and couple tasks, each participant completed four semistructured interviews: the Peer Attachment Interview (PAI) at Time 1, a second PAI and the Family Attachment Interview (FAI) at Time 2, and then the PAI again at Time 3. Each interview ranged from 45 min to 1.5 hours, and two independent coders rated each interview according to a particular model of individual differences in adult attachment representations (Bartholomew & Horowitz, 1991). Research personnel required approximately 250 hours of training to become effective interviewers and reliable coders. In order to ensure sufficient numbers of independent coders and interviewers, 40 graduate and undergraduate students were trained over four separate, 8-month long, training sessions. Of these original 40 trainees, some never became reliable, some moved, and about half stayed with the project long enough to conduct and code interviews. By the time all interviews were coded, 16 independent coders and approximately 32 hours of researcher time, not including training and supervision time, were required for each couple.

We thank Karen Tee, Ingrid Sochting, and Sandra Vermeulen for talking with us at length about their experiences in using and developing coded semistructured interviews. We are also grateful to Cheryl Bradley and Colleen MacQuarrie for their helpful comments on earlier drafts of this chapter. Correspondence should be directed to Kim Bartholomew Department of Psychology, Simon Fraser University, Burnaby, B.C., Canada, V5A IS6 (e-mail: bartholo@sfu.ca).

What would justify the time, the effort, and the expense of employing such a demanding research methodology? And why do we persist in relying on coded semistructured interviews in our research projects? We persist because in some research domains coded research interviews are the ideal research method, in some cases perhaps the only appropriate method. The coded semistructured interview allows us to go beyond the content of our participants' words and thoughts and capture the psychological processes that might be at work. We are convinced that some fascinating and important research questions simply are not amenable to study through other means.

This chapter focuses on the development and use of the coded semistructured interview, or CSSI, thus named for its two essential components: Expert coders make judgments about particular psychological constructs, and a flexible semistructured interview method is used to generate information from which to make these judgments. Our focus on the CSSI reflects both our areas of expertise and what we feel to be of the most value to prospective readers. Although there are many reviews of survey interviewing (including Visser, Krosnick, & Lavrakas, this volume, Ch. 9) and of qualitative research interviewing, there are few sources that discuss coded research interviews in quantitative research. Before discussing how to develop and use CSSIs, we review the key components of the CSSI, clarify how the CSSI differs from related research methods, and discuss its advantages and disadvantages.

What makes the coded semistructured interview *structured* is its repeated form from respondent to respondent. What makes it *semi*structured is the variability, within the limits of a repeated form, in questions from interview to interview. The interviewer has the flexibility to track any respondent so that the questions asked are always germane both to the information required and to the flow of the conversation. No other testing method can provide this degree of relevancy to the construct under investigation and responsivity to the participant.

What makes the coded semistructured interview *coded* is that expert raters or coders make judgments on one or more constructs of interest based on the content, organization, and tone of the interview record. Most coded SSIs focus on internal psychological processes, how individuals interpret and represent their life experiences, and how their psychological functioning is organized. Constructs that call for a CSSI method are not generally expected to be accessible to participants' conscious awareness and thus not easily captured in a self-report measure. Although participants are not expected to provide the desired ratings directly, they do provide information from which a trained coder can make a judgment. Perhaps the most common reason for reliance on expert judgments is to assess process variables. As demonstrated by Nisbett and Wilson (1977), in many (if not most) domains, individuals are not consciously aware of their own psychological processes. For instance, if research participants are asked to respond to a hypothetical moral dilemma, they can readily report the content of their moral decisions (i.e., what is the correct course of action in the dilemma), but they are probably unable to directly report the thinking process that brought them to this conclusion. In some domains, participants may not be able to create sufficient distance from a construct to assess themselves, as might be the case in trying to assess one's own degree of defensiveness. Or participants may be unfamiliar with the constructs of interest and therefore not be qualified to judge their standing on them. For example, an individual may be aware that he or she is struggling to decide on ideological values and has not yet made a commitment to occupational, ideological, or interpersonal positions. Yet, he or she would not interpret these characteristics as typical of a moratorium identity structure, as would be done based on the Ego Identity Interview (Marcia, 1966). Finally, participants simply may never have thought about the constructs of interest from a self-analyzing perspective.

CSSIs allow for the assessment of complex higher-order constructs, such as identity status, attachment strategy, or cognitive complexity, that integrate a good deal of information. To illustrate, in our attachment coding system (Poole & Bartholomew, 1996), the relatively abstract construct of "attachment security" is assessed by examining a number of factors in combination: feelings about the self in relation to others, strategies to cope with emotional upsets, trust in others' willingness to offer support in particular situations, ability to coherently discuss close attachment relationships, how attachment relevant information is processed, and so on. The coder must look at how these factors are organized to define a general strategy of regulating negative affect in close relationships within the context of the individual's social world. As previously mentioned, it takes approximately 250 hours to train coders to accurately assess degree of attachment security from an interview record. It would be extremely difficult to design a self-report measure to assess attachment security in a comparable manner, even if we were to assume that individuals are capable of accurately reflecting on the behaviors, thoughts, feelings, and processes that the construct of security encompasses.

Although we have implied that psychological variables can be dichotomized into those that participants can directly report on and those that they cannot, in practice variables vary along a continuum in their degree of conscious accessibility. It is ultimately up to the judgment of the researcher as to which psychological constructs call for expert coders. And the semistructured interview is one way, though by no means the only way, for expert coders to make judgments about complex process variables. Coded research methods can also be applied to written materials (see Smith, this volume, Ch. 12). For example, Tetlock and Suedfeld (1988) developed a system to assess integrative complexity that can be applied to political texts or transcripts of public speeches. The assessment of integrative complexity focuses on the structure or style of thought, rather than content, and encompasses two cognitive stylistic attributes: evaluative differentiation, the capacity to acknowledge the legitimacy of opposing perspectives on an issue or event, and conceptual integration of competing perspectives. Projective techniques, such as the Thematic Apperception Test, Rorschach, and sentence completion tests, also employ expert coding systems without the use of a semistructured interview.

In our research, we prefer the semistructured interview method over other coded research methods primarily because of its greater flexibility. Examples of such interviews are the Ego Identity Interview (Marcia, 1966), assessing ego identity status; the Intimacy Status Interview (Orlofsky, Marcia, & Lesser, 1973), assessing intimacy status; the PAI (Bartholomew & Horowitz, 1991), assessing representations of close attachment relations; the Ethic of Care Interview (Skoe, 1993), assessing levels of care-oriented moral reasoning; and the Camberwell Family Interview (Vaughn & Leff, 1976), assessing expressed emotion. Semistructured interviews differ from observational, questionnaire, and projective techniques in that they are more interactional, provide more latitude for participant response, permit flexibility of "stimulus" presentation to match the flow of the situation, and yield a rich source of information.

FORMS OF RESEARCH INTERVIEWS

Interviews have a specific purpose and are usually conducted within a specific context. Although there are forms of interviews other than the research interview (e.g., intake, therapeutic, counseling, personnel selection, medical, etc.), the research interview is designed to obtain information relevant to investigating a scientific question. The most common forms are survey interviews, various forms of qualitative interviews, uncoded SSIs, and the CSSI.

Survey Interviews

Telephone or face-to-face interviews are a common means of conducting survey research (see Visser et al., this volume, Ch. 9) and are probably the most common form of research interview. Survey interviews are used to assess a range of information, including behaviors, attitudes, preferences, and intentions, usually with the goal of generalizing the findings to a particular population. For instance, public opinion polls assess political opinions and voting intentions, marketing surveys canvas consumer preferences and interests, and government censuses yield demographic information. In contrast to the CSSI, the survey interview is designed to collect information on variables that are relatively circumscribed and to which the informant is assumed to have conscious access. In these cases, there is no need for expert coders; rather, participants can assess their own standing on the variables of interest.

Survey interviews are generally highly structured and standardized in order to avoid bias that may be introduced by the interviewer. However, the interview format does give the interviewer some flexibility to clarify questions or answers if needed and to deal with unique interview situations. Because the goal of such interviews is to collect information that can be generalized to a particular population, key issues are sampling methods, ways to maximize participant response rates, and the optimal design of questions in order to obtain valid information. Excellent treatments of survey interviewing are found in Visser et al. (this volume,

Ch. 9), Fowler (l988), Cannell and Kahn (1968), and Schuman and Kalton (1985).

Qualitative Interviews

Within the qualitative research tradition, unstructured interviews are typically the primary source of data. Although the focus of the qualitative interview may be informed by theory, this approach is nontheory driven in that the researcher has not predetermined what is to be derived or coded from the interview. Rather, the findings emerge more inductively from an intensive study of interview records and are organized into themes using a range of analytic methods. Major issues arising in qualitative research interviews are the nature of the relationship between the interviewer and the interviewee, how to conceptualize reliability and validity, and how to organize and present findings. For discussions of qualitative research interviewing see Alcoff (1991), Gluck and Patai (1991), Merriam (1988), and Mishler (1986).

Exploratory, pilot, and poststudy interviews can also be considered forms of qualitative interviewing. Open-ended pilot interviews can be invaluable for theory development and hypothesis generation. Somewhat more structured pilot interviews are useful for more focused tasks such as the generation of items for a new questionnaire. The poststudy interview can be useful to clarify participants' understanding of the experimental situation, to generate new insights and hypotheses, and to provide an opportunity for debriefing. For example, a number of years ago, Podd (1972) was interested in the relationship between ego identity development and performance in Milgram's obedience task. Although there were no differences among identity statuses in level of (bogus) shock participants thought that they had administered to "victims," poststudy interviews revealed that only one group of participants, those with a foreclosed identity status, would be willing to repeat administration of maximum shock were they to participate in the study again.

A primary difference between "pure" qualitative interviews and exploratory or pilot interviews is that the former are considered the major component of a qualitative research project, whereas the latter are typically the starting point for larger quantitative research projects. And unlike the qualitative interview, the CSSI is designed to assess specific constructs in a replicable manner; hence, they fall squarely within the quantitative domain. Qualitative researchers sometimes differentiate qualitative and quantitative methods on features such as holistic versus reductionistic, contextual versus decontextual, and concern with meaning and process versus facts and outcomes (e.g., Merriam, 1988). As we hope will become clear, such dichotomies are not accurate. Although there are important distinctions between these two research approaches, the characterization of quantitative methods as capable of assessing only content stripped of context seems to stem from unfamiliarity with many quantitative methods (including the CSSI) that assess complex psychological processes. In fact, both qualitative and coded interviews are primarily concerned with process and meaning; and, in both cases, the context of interview responses can be considered.

Participant Coded Semistructured Interviews

There are many semistructured research interviews that do not involve expert coding. For example, the Social Support Interview (Fiore, Becker, & Coppel, 1983) probes how helpful and how upsetting participants have found 10 members of their social networks across five content domains. Participants themselves, rather than expert coders, provide quantitative ratings of the helpfulness and upset variables. In such cases, an SSI is used to facilitate the participant making accurate self-judgments and to ensure that participants understand the variables of interest. SSIs are especially helpful for assessing complicated sets of variables, such as social networks, or variables that participants may not be used to thinking about.

ADVANTAGES AND DISADVANTAGES OF CSSIs

For understanding certain kinds of complex psychological constructs, the coded semistructured interview is invaluable. It permits researchers to investigate complex psychological constructs that would be extremely difficult to get at through other methods. Another advantage is that it allows researchers to understand the theory, the constructs, and the findings in a way that literature reviews and analysis of self-report data cannot. We often obtain information from participants that leads us to question our initial theoretical conceptions, providing a kind of ongoing test of the phenomenological validity of our constructs. In our research labs, carefully listening to how participants' think about themselves and their social lives has been the strongest factor in hypothesis generation and development of theory.

The primary disadvantage of the CSSI, as our opening example illustrates, is the time and expense required. Interviews are more time-consuming than questionnaires or projective measures, which can be modified for group administration. Also some unreliability is introduced as result of the method's most telling advantage: its flexibility in varying questions. Interviewers and coders must be well-trained and intimately familiar with scoring criteria. Whereas an intelligent fourth grader can score, and sometimes even interpret, many questionnaires, a fairly highly skilled interviewer and coder (or coders) are required for the CSSI. Thus, finding and keeping competent research personnel is an ongoing struggle.

We therefore urge researchers to carefully estimate the time, expense, and complexity involved in using coded interviews before making a commitment to this research method. Because of the tremendous investment required, we advocate exploring other options before undertaking an interview study. Are there other methods available that could address the same question, such as open-ended written questions or projective tests? To explore new constructs that may be amenable to assessment through self-reports, it may be possible to use interviews in the piloting phase of a new project and then use the pilot findings to guide the construction of a self-report measure. Finally, it is sometimes possible to apply a coding system to interviews that have been collected as part of a previous project, thus saving the time and expense of recruiting and interviewing a new sample. If the interviews are sufficiently rich, the coding system sufficiently flexible, and the coders sufficiently experienced, this approach can work. In our lab, we have successfully applied our attachment coding system to therapy-intake sessions, clinical interviews with individuals experiencing bereavement (Bartholomew & Shaver, 1998), and unstructured interviews with battered women (Henderson, Bartholomew, & Dutton, 1997).

OVERVIEW

The remainder of the chapter will focus on the use of coded semistructured interviews in social psychological research. In the beginning of this chapter our goal was to define the CSSI and outline when it might be the research method of choice. The next section focuses on development – first of the research interview and then of the coding system, including discussions of discrete versus continuous constructs, use of secondary variables, development of the coding manual, and reliability and validity issues. The third section focuses on training of both interviewers and coders and deals with such issues as choosing interviewers and coders, ongoing supervision, and how to deal with interviewer and coder biases. The fourth section deals with conducting CSSIs and touches on questions of the interview setting, types of questions, note-taking, and difficult interviews. The final section discusses three ethical issues relevant to research using the CSSI method: informed consent, effects on the participant, and dissemination of findings. This progression from development of the interview and coding system to training of interviewers and coders to conducting the CSSI only loosely corresponds to the actual process of employing a CSSI. In practice, the various phases often cooccur (e.g., development of the interview and coding system), and difficulties arising in one phase will have implications for other phases (e.g., training difficulties may lead to modifications to the coding system). We have maintained a somewhat arbitrary division of material into development, training, and conducting sections for ease of presentation.

DEVELOPMENT OF THE CSSI

To illustrate some of the steps involved in the development of the CSSI, we describe Marcia's experience in developing and refining the Ego Identity Status Interview. In initially considering how to investigate ego identity, a construct drawn from Erikson's (1959) ego psychoanalytic theory, Marcia considered three techniques: Kelly's Role Construct Repertory Grid, an ad hoc sentence completion test, and a CSSI. Although the first measure had the advantages of being a relatively easy to score, established technique, Marcia thought it was too indirect a method to serve as a primary indicator of the presence or absence of an identity structure. The sentence completion technique could be tailored to capture a complex variable such as identity, but, because this was one of the first attempts at measuring the construct, Marcia felt that its scope would be too limited.

Deciding on an interview method, Marcia first conducted exploratory interviews to see if Erikson's description of identity formation matched the experiences of his college students. He constructed questions to assess identity in two key content domains identified by Erikson, occupation and ideology. Although male respondents indicated that Erikson's description of identity was applicable to them, it became evident that the process by which they had arrived at committed or uncommitted positions was important. Hence, although Marcia had begun interviews expecting only two identity positions, achievement and diffusion, he concluded these initial interviews by postulating four styles of identity resolution (achievement, diffusion,

EXPLORATION

	Present	Absent
Present	Identity Achieved	Foreclosure
Absent	Moratorium	Identity Diffusion

COMMITMENT

Figure 11.1. Marcia's identity status model.

moratorium, and foreclosure). In addition, he refined the criteria for identity formation, so that it encompassed two process variables: exploration and commitment (see Figure 11.1). He then constructed further interview questions that kept responses within the topic areas, furnished information on the criteria of exploration and commitment, and still permitted freedom of response. The semistructured format allowed the interviewer to continue probing until sufficient information was generated to make such difficult determinations as the genuineness of exploration and the extent of commitment.

The construction of the interview was accompanied by development of a scoring manual describing the criteria underlying the identity statuses and giving sample responses from pilot interviews. The interplay between reworking the interview format and manual criteria with research group discussion was ongoing as intercoder agreement was sought. After an acceptable level of intercoder agreement was attained, both interview and manual were deemed to be in the first of their many "final" forms, and construct validity studies proceeded. Over the past 30 years, interview questions and manual content have changed, interview areas have been expanded or modified to include different populations, and additional identity statuses have been proposed (Marcia, Waterman, Matteson, Archer, & Orlofsky, 1993).

Preliminary Steps in the Development of the CSSI

The design of a coded SSI should be guided by its objective, normally the assessment of one or more clearly defined constructs. Thus, development of the coded SSI begins with theory. The literature review is a practical starting point, as it provides the theoretical foundation for the constructs under study. Tee (1996) discussed the importance of the literature review in refining her research question concerning cultural assumptions of first- and second-generation South Asian women. Previous work revealed that women in transition from an Eastern to Western culture were considered either traditional in their cultural values or modern (i.e., having adopted and embraced Western culture). Building on this review, Tee conjectured that there may be transitional positions between traditional and modern positions, and she used pilot interviews to investigate this possibility. In addition to providing a solid basis for beginning the research, previous literature can furnish a useful ongoing resource as a guide to problems in development, training, and practice.

Design of the Interview

Although the primary researcher may draw up an initial outline of interview questions, we suggest that this soon be submitted to a research team for brainstorming, so that as many relevant questions as possible may be generated. Other potential question sources are related interviews and suggestions of colleagues with expertise in the focal area. Ideally, every question in an interview aids in assessing the constructs of interest. Questions may also serve to establish rapport at the outset of an interview, provide a context for interpretation of other answers, or facilitate the transition between topics. An SSI is designed to let interviewers follow up on key questions in order to ensure that sufficient information is gained for coding purposes. It is helpful to have multiple follow-up questions available, especially for beginning interviewers.

The next step is to organize questions into a logical sequence, by theory or content domain, or to facilitate a narrative history of respondents' lives. Cannell and Kahn (1968) suggested an hourglass-shaped organization, in which an interview opens with general questions, then progressively funnels toward more specific and personal questions, and broadens again toward the close of the interview. The FAI (Bartholomew & Horowitz, 1991), which deals with participants' accounts of their childhood family relationships, begins with demographic information (family composition, changes of residence, etc.), then moves to a general description of participants' relationships with their caregivers, and only toward the middle of the interview focuses on more personal issues such as feelings of acceptance by parents and experiences of abuse and loss. The last section of the interview broadens to a series of evaluative questions, such as effects of participants' childhood experiences on their current functioning and changes they would have liked to see in their relationships with parents.

Interview length is influenced by a number of factors including the constructs of interest, the particular sample, the pragmatics of data collection, and financial constraints. Identity and attachment interviews have varied in length from 30 min to 2 hours depending on available resources, the age of participants, and the complexity of participants' responses. And longer is not necessarily better. With increasing length, one often reaches a plateau of diminishing returns. A relatively constrained time frame ensures that participants are not exhausted; and it forces interviewers to stay focused on questions and responses relevant to constructs of interest.

Recording of the Interview

Coded research interviews can be audiotaped or videotaped, and then may be transcribed, depending on the constructs being assessed. Although interviews may also be recorded by note-taking, this method is usually insufficient to permit reliable coding of the interview record. If constructs involve a strong affective component, researchers may prefer videotaping which can capture nonverbal behavior. However, participants may be less comfortable with this method, and coders may be biased by participants' physical appearance. Audiotaping is less expensive, less intrusive for participants, and avoids bias due to attractiveness. Some coding systems require written transcripts (usually taken from audio recordings) because excerpts from written output must be marked and counted for coding purposes (see Colby and Kohlberg's [1987] 17-step procedure for coding Moral Judgment Interviews). Researchers whose coding systems necessitate transcribing often comment that this task is valuable, particularly in piloting stages, for getting close to the data, genuinely understanding participants' stories, and refining both interview and coding system. However, the time and effort involved in transcribing is considerable. Proficient transcribers working with a transcribing machine suggest a 3:1 to 4:1 ratio of transcribing time to interview length. In addition, when working from transcriptions, information that is carried in the participant's tone and delivery is lost. An alternative is to have coders work simultaneously with a transcription and audiotape (e.g., Tee, 1996). However, for most applications, it is almost as effective, and certainly much cheaper, to develop a system that does not necessitate transcribing.

Piloting

One should do as much piloting as time and resources afford. We suggest, at minimum, a two-phase approach: refinement of the interview and interviewers' skills, followed by testing the interview along with the coding system. Although we are focusing on development of research interviews in this section, in practice, development of the interview and its associated coding system are likely to occur in tandem during the pilot phase. The first pilot serves to test the interview and, in the process, may provide insights for the development of the coding system. Pilot participants can provide valuable feedback on the content, flow, and clarity of questions. The purpose of the second phase of piloting is to use the revised interview in conjunction with the coding system to ensure that interview and coding system are integrated (cf. Bakeman, this volume, Ch. 6). One may find that interview information is clear, but that some constructs are ill-defined and, thus, difficult to code. Hence, this is also the time to begin work on the coding manual or interpretive guide, to be discussed in a subsequent section.

There are no rules as to when piloting can cease and the actual study begins. Unfortunately, this decision is often based on time and resource requirements, rather than the level of refinement of interview and coding system. And even with the most exhaustive piloting, the format of a research interview can always be improved. CSSIs permit flexibility to make modifications that improve the interviewer's ability to assess the constructs of interest. With both our identity status and attachment interviews, we find ourselves continuing to make changes years after the initial development. In particular, whenever an interview designed for use with a particular population is to be applied to a new population, it is essential to conduct further pilot tests and make needed revisions. We caution against skipping this piloting phase, even if the researcher is familiar with a given interview and population under investigation. For example, the Ethic of Care Interview (Skoe, 1993) was developed initially for use with college women to assess their standing on Gilligan's (1982) conceptions of care-based moral reasoning. One of four moral dilemmas concerns a young woman involved in an affair with a married man and facing an unplanned pregnancy. In revising the interview for use with men, male participants were asked to discuss what the married man, not the pregnant woman, should do in the situation. It is not surprising that men and women responded quite differently to this dilemma, introducing difficulties in comparing their levels of reasoning. Ideally, a new dilemma appropriate for both women and men should have been designed in the piloting phase (Sochting, Skoe, & Marcia, 1994).

DEVELOPMENT OF A CODING SYSTEM

In our experience, developing and implementing a reliable coding system is the most challenging aspect of using CSSIs. The constructs of interest are, to varying degrees, abstract and complex and, therefore, difficult to clearly define and operationalize. Interview protocols are also complex. Because each participant's interview responses will be unique, the system must be sufficiently flexible and abstract to allow the same set of constructs to be assessed from an unlimited number of interview responses. And yet the system must also be sufficiently detailed and concrete to ensure that independent coders will reach the same conclusions when presented with the same interview record.

In some cases, coding systems are primarily theory-based. For example, Skoe and Marcia (1991) developed an interview and coding system to operationalize Gilligan's (1982) proposed levels of moral reasoning evident in a care-based conception of morality. The resulting coding system was based directly on Gilligan's theorizing, derived, itself, from qualitative interviews. In contrast, coding systems may be developed inductively from insights gained in extensive piloting or qualitative interviews. Tee (1996) began her piloting phase with open-ended questions designed to explore the experiences of first- and second-generation South Asian women living in Canada. In her pilot interviews, she identified five different "voices" or responses and reactions to cultural values and belief systems. These voices ranged from unquestioning acceptance of cultural values to increasing psychological resistance and questioning of belief systems to an integration of traditional cultural assumptions with modern Western values.

Most often, coding systems are informed by a combination of theory, previous research findings, and analysis of pilot interviews. Although researchers may initially develop a research question based on existing literature and a conceptual analysis of the field of study, extensive piloting is usually essential to develop a workable coding system. For example, Bartholomew (1990) published a theoretical paper reviewing two independent lines of research in adult attachment, those of Hazan and Shaver (1987) and of Main, Kaplan, and Cassidy (1985), and proposed an expanded four-category model of adult attachment to integrate these lines of work. This model was based largely on pilot interviews suggesting that previous conceptualizations of adult attachment were inadequate to capture the full range of individual differences observed, both in terms of specific attachment patterns and in terms of the use of categorical systems. The final conceptualization of adult attachment and corresponding coding system emerged from an analysis of pilot interviews in light of basic theory and previous empirical work in the area (Bartholomew, 1993).

Categorical and Continuous Coding Schemes

Probably the most common measurement strategy in coding research interviews is to assess one or more categorical or grouping variables. Each participant's interview is judged to reflect one or more of a limited number of discrete categories that are assumed to differ qualitatively from one another (e.g., forms of reasoning, personality types, defense mechanisms, etc.). Classification systems differ in terms of whether categories are seen as reflecting an underlying structure or a set of common dimensions. For example, four identity statuses (Marcia, 1966), based on the dimensional criteria of exploration and commitment, can be derived from a 2×2 classification system: exploration – present or absent; commitment – present or absent (see Figure 11.1). Other systems have a one-dimensional ordering, notably developmental conceptions such as levels of moral reasoning (see Figure 11.2). In contrast, some categorical systems assess groups that have no defined relation to one another. For example, four qualitatively different representational patterns or states of mind with respect to attachment (autonomous, dismissing, preoccupied, and unresolved) are assessed by the Adult Attachment Interview (Main et al., 1985; see Figure 11.3).

There are good reasons for the popularity of categorical coding systems. People, including research psychologists, seem to think and process information in terms of categories (Mayer & Bower, 1986). Categories are intuitively appealing and permit easy communication of findings. They can describe and summarize complex patterns of individual differences or interview components that may be characteristic of

Level I: PRECONVENTIONAL
Stage 1: Heteronomous morality
　　Motivation: Avoidance of punishment, and the superior power of authorities.
Stage 2: Individualism, instrumental purpose, and exchange
　　Motivation: To serve one's own needs or interests in a world where you have to recognize that other people have their interests too.

Level II: CONVENTIONAL
Stage 3: Mutual interpersonal expectations, relationships, and interpersonal conformity.
　　Motivation: The need to be a good person in your own eyes and those of others. Caring for others, belief in the Golden Rule. Desire to maintain rules and authority which support stereotypical good behavior.
Stage 4: Social system and conscience
　　Motivation: To keep the institution going as a whole, to avoid the breakdown in the system "If everyone did it" or the imperative of conscience to meet one's obligations. (Easily confused with stage 3 belief in rules and authority).

Level III: POSTCONVENTIONAL OR AUTONOMOUS
Stage 5: Social contract or utility and individual rights
　　Motivation: A sense of obligation to law because of one's social contract to make and abide by laws for the welfare of all and for the protection of all people's rights. A feeling of contractual commitment, freely entered upon, to family, friendship, trust, and work obligations. Concern that laws and duties can be based on rational calculation of overall utility, "the greatest good for the greatest number."
Stage 6: Universal ethical principles
　　Motivation: The belief as a rational person in the validity of universal moral principles, and a sense of personal commitment to them.

Figure 11.2. Kohlberg's developmental stages of moral thought. Adapted from Kohlberg, 1976.

different "types" of people, representational systems, or styles of cognitive processing. However, categorical coding systems are often adopted because of habit or convention, rather than appropriateness. The unwarranted imposition of categories on constructs that are actually dimensional in nature introduces measurement error, reduces statistical power, and even constrains the kinds of research questions that are asked (Fraley & Waller, 1998). Researchers therefore need to consider carefully whether or not their constructs are best represented by discrete categories. Is it difficult to define categories in terms of necessary and sufficient conditions? Is there meaningful variation among responses or individuals within a given category? In mutually exclusive systems, do some interview records

Autonomous-secure: parents may or may not have been supportive; topic of relationships is easily discussed; speech is not rehearsed; strong sense of personal identity involving understanding of self and others.

Preoccupied: parents were lacking in love but not necessarily rejecting; extensive but confused discussion of relationships; often angry and/or passive speech.

Dismissing: parents were somewhat rejecting; false claim to normality, independence, invulnerability; deleterious consequences of negative experiences go unacknowledged.

Unresolved: Anomalous resolution of death of attachment figure or of past trauma; irrational thought processes with regard to loss or trauma; often fearful.
Note: Unresolved interviews are also assigned to one of the three major adult patterns above (autonomous/secure, preoccupied or dismissing).

Figure 11.3. Adult patterns of attachment coded from the Adult Attachment Interview. Adapted from Steele and Steele, 1994.

indicate more than one classification? Are there some underlying dimensions or defining characteristics of categories that could be assessed directly? If the answer to any of these questions is "yes," then an alternative measurement approach is probably called for. For example, with the four-category model of adult attachment (Bartholomew & Horowitz, 1991), there are no absolute defining criteria for category membership. Further, Griffin and Bartholomew (1994a) have demonstrated that there is considerable meaningful (and predictive) variance in attachment ratings within attachment categories and that the large majority of individuals show evidence of two, three, or even four attachment patterns. Finally, as illustrated in Figure 11.4, a dimensional structure is hypothesized to underlie the four attachment patterns (Griffin & Bartholomew, 1994b). See Gangestad and Snyder (1985), Griffin and Bartholomew (1994a), and Meehl (1992) for discussions of categorical versus dimensional approaches to conceptualizing individual differences.

The prototype approach to categorization recognizes explicitly that most natural categories (including psy-

chological categories) cannot be defined by necessary and sufficient criteria as classical categorization models imply (Rosch, 1978). A prototype is an ideal category member, or an exemplar of a particular category. From this perspective, categories are fuzzy sets that may overlap with one another, and they contain members that differ in their correspondence with the prototypic group member. The prototype approach to categorization maintains the advantages of a person-centered classification scheme, but takes into consideration within-group variation. It permits individuals to be assessed on their degree of fit with multiple prototypes (using continuous ratings), rather than forcing coders to choose a single category. This allows for a more fine-grained assessment than is possible with simple grouping approaches. A related advantage is that, with prototype ratings, it is possible to examine categories that are uncommon in the sample under study. For example, in samples of individuals in violent spousal relationships, too few individuals are rated as securely attached to permit reliable comparisons with individuals in other attachment categories. However, there is still adequate variance within these samples in degree of fit with the prototype of secure attachment, in spite of the truncated range, to permit testing of associations between degree of security and other variables of interest (e.g., Dutton, Saunders, Starzomski, & Bartholomew, 1994; Henderson et al., 1997).

Finally, dimensional rating systems are appropriate if there is an underlying continuum on the construct of interest, such as degree of interview coherence (high to low) or strength of emotional expression. Looking again at Tee's (1996) coding system for responses to cultural values, after intensive line-by-line analysis of interview transcripts, participants are given a 0–9 rating indicating the degree to which each voice or perspective is expressed. Alternatively, dimensional ratings can be derived from a series of categorical judgments. If interview units (such as clauses, sentences, or interview sections) are separately coded on some dichotomous category, then unit judgments can be pooled to provide dimensional ratings of the number of times that a particular classification was made, or of the proportion of units in which a particular categorical judgment was made.

It is not uncommon for categorical measures to evolve into dimensional measures based on coding difficulties that arise in applying simpler categorical systems. For example, Lyons (1982) devised a scoring system to classify moral judgments according to Gilligan's (1982) distinction between care-oriented and justice-

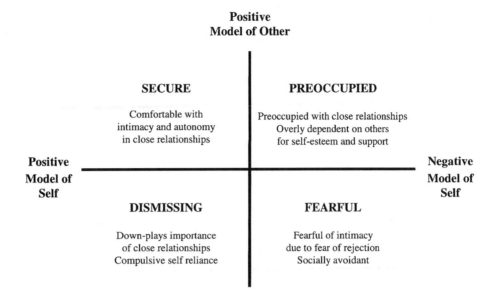

Figure 11.4. Two dimensional, four-category model of adult attachment.

oriented moral judgments (C and J), a two-category distinction. Subsequently, Gilligan and Attanucci (1988) introduced a combined care/justice category (C/J) to allow for judgments that showed evidence of both orientations. Then Krebs, Vermeulen, Denton, and Carpendale (1994) added two intermediate possibilities, primarily care and secondarily justice, C(J) and the converse J(C), yielding a 5-point dimensional rating of the proportional presence of care and justice in a judgment. This "evolution" suggests that the initial categories were inappropriately imposed on underlying dimensions.

Secondary Variables

We recommend incorporating secondary variables in coding systems, rather than relying exclusively on ratings of key constructs. A *secondary variable* is one that is subsumed by, and a constituent of, the primary constructs under investigation. In the Ego Identity Interview, identity status is determined in a number of distinct areas (vocational choice, religious convictions, sexuality, etc.), and these domain-specific status ratings inform an overall status rating, the key construct. This approach forces coders to take into account participant responses across the entire interview and is likely to increase the reliability of final ratings. In effect, different sections of the interview function as multiple items on a measure. In addition, ratings in each domain or section can be examined separately to clarify the gen-

eral phenomenon. For instance, in the Ego Identity Interview, consideration of identity status ratings in specific domains may clarify the process of identity formation (e.g., Waterman, 1982).

Judgments of higher-order constructs can also be supplemented by secondary ratings of more specific variables that need to be considered by coders in making their final judgments. Such secondary codes are particularly useful to supplement very complex or difficult coder judgments. In the original PAI, 15 secondary variables were assessed in addition to the four prototype-based attachment patterns (Bartholomew & Horowitz, 1991). These variables range from relatively straightforward judgments, such as quality of same and opposite sex friendships, to judgments of key attachment-related variables, such as proneness to separation anxiety and, finally, to judgments of the overall interview record such as internal coherence of participants' relationship accounts. When coders encounter problems in making overall attachment assessments, it is often possible to pinpoint the source of their coding errors by reviewing their ratings on secondary variables. As with the previously described strategy of assessing different components of the interview, multiple secondary variables can also be helpful in explicating the key constructs. For illustrations, see Bartholomew and Horowitz (1991) and Kobak and Sceery (1988).

Updating of Coding System

Coding systems, like interview schedules, need to be refined and updated, especially in the early stages. Changes to a coding system can be driven by a number of factors, including new theoretical ideas, new relevant empirical findings, and insights gained from studying interview records. For example, a section on attitudes toward gender roles was added to the Identity Status Interview in the mid-1970s as gender roles that were previously culturally prescribed began to be reexamined. Changes may also be prompted by difficulties in attaining intercoder agreement that indicate lack of clarity in the coding system. For example, in an early version of the PAI coding system, a Reciprocity scale assessed degree of mutuality in close relationships. Problems in coding this scale arose in training groups, and reliabilities for the scale were consistently low. Upon revisiting the coding criteria, it became evident that the scale combined two distinct forms of reciprocity, relative dominance and relative emotional involvement, that do not always cooccur.

Another common impetus to revise coding systems is the researcher's desire to apply the system to a new population. A system developed on middle-class Caucasian college women may or may not be workable with men, working young adults, younger or older individuals, or other social or ethnic groups. Cross-cultural applications are likely to be especially problematic (see Marcia et al., 1993 for illustrations for the Ego Identity Interview). Ideally, pilot work with the new population of interest will reveal where modifications are required. In practice, unfortunately, changes often follow from unsuccessful attempts to apply an established coding system to a new population.

Even in cases where, theoretically, we would not expect a system to be appropriate for a different population, it is sometimes possible to build on or adapt the original coding system. Consider Tee's (1996) system assessing Canadian South Asian women's cultural values. Though the particular cultural "voices" that Tee identified may not characterize individuals moving between a different set of cultures (or even men in the same position), her research strategy of developing a coding system based on voices identified in pilot interviews could be used with other populations. Similarly, Marcia's notion of identity statuses, and the underlying processes associated with the varying statuses, has been successfully applied to other domains such as ethnic identity (Phinney, 1989). Sometimes, however, piloting may lead to the conclusion that the system is not applicable to the new popu-

lation of interest. Such problems in applying a research interview and associated coding system to a new population can be informative findings in their own right.

The Coding Manual

The most important function of a coding manual is to facilitate training new coders and interviewers, even when an expert is guiding the training process. A manual continues to be an invaluable reference for coders even after they have become reliable. And by documenting coding procedures, a coding manual serves as a vehicle for disseminating the work to other researchers. The actual construction of a coding manual serves another, less obvious, function: It compels the researcher to clarify his or her thinking about the concepts under study in order to describe them in terms understandable to others. This can be surprisingly hard work.

The primary objective of coding manuals is to lay out coding criteria for all the key and secondary variables and, where applicable, a definition of marker points on continuous rating scales. Coding manuals must be sufficiently detailed for coders to make all necessary distinctions, but sufficiently abstract to be applicable to an unlimited number of novel responses. To make general descriptions more vivid, interview excerpts demonstrating possible rating outcomes are valuable. Manuals should also contain a copy of interview questions and any interview instructions specific to the measure. For researchers new to working with coded interviews, we recommend starting by studying other coding manuals (for instance, see Marcia et al., 1993), perhaps steering clear of such lengthy examples as Colby and Kohlberg's (1987) 1,200-page manual for the Moral Judgment Interview.

Bradley's (1996) manual for the Generativity Status Measure is a good example of detail and comprehensiveness. It begins with an overview of basic theory and the conceptual model that is being assessed (Bradley & Marcia, 1997). Bradley defines five prototypical resolutions of Erikson's psychosocial stage of Generativity–Despair in terms of underlying dimensional criteria of vital involvement and inclusivity as they relate to self and others. She then describes secondary variables (aspects of involvement and inclusivity) to be coded along 9-point rating scales. The bulk of the manual focuses on the five generativity statuses, including a description of each prototypic status and interview excerpts demonstrating how each status manifests itself in each of four content domains covered in the interview (work, community, family, and personal concerns). See Appendix A for an excerpt from Bradley's manual.

RELIABILITY OF MEASUREMENT

Reliability refers to the repeatability of scores. In the case of CSSIs, reliability is typically assessed by intercoder or interjudge agreement; that is, how well two or more independent coders agree on the interpretation of interview protocols according to the guiding coding scheme. Thus, a reliability estimate can be obtained for each judgment made by coders. In practice, however, it is not uncommon to compute only the reliability of key coding variables (e.g., attachment patterns, generativity statuses). Another method of assessing reliability that could be applied to interview ratings is test–retest reliability, the consistency of ratings over a brief period of time (usually somewhere between 2 weeks and a few months). However, this method is rarely used with interview measures because of the demands on participant and researcher and because participants may be able to remember their interview responses, thereby inflating reliability estimates. Also, if the construct under investigation is developmental in nature, participants might be expected to change, thereby deflating reliability estimates. We therefore focus on coder agreement in our discussion of reliability.

Most commonly, interjudge agreement on continuous ratings is assessed by Pearson product moment correlations between two coders' ratings. If two or more coders rate an entire sample of interviews, then their averaged (or summed) ratings are used as final ratings. In this case, reliabilities of averaged ratings can be estimated with an intraclass correlation coefficient (see Bakeman, this volume, Ch. 6; Shrout & Fleiss, 1979). We recommend that correlational reliability indices be supplemented by other methods of describing coder agreement, especially when conducting reliability checks during training. First, mean differences between coders can indicate coder biases in use of rating scales. Second, if coders fail to appropriately use the full range of scale scores (a common problem with overly cautious beginning coders), obtained reliabilities will be attenuated. Third, in cases where different rating scales should show a particular pattern of intercorrelations, each coder's ratings can be intercorrelated separately as another check of his or her appropriate application of the coding system. Where there is reason to suspect that some participant characteristic, such as sex, could affect scale reliabilities, we recommend conducting reliability analyses separately for subsamples defined by the given characteristic. For example, we conduct reliability checks of attachment ratings separately by gender of interviewee because beginning coders sometimes have difficulties coding a particular gender. Finally, confidence intervals can be calculated for population values of reliability indices.

Percent agreement, the percentage of cases in which two coders agree on the participants' standing on a particular variable, is probably the most common approach to assessing reliability of categorical variables. However, simple percentage of agreement is not a sufficient measure of intercoder agreement because it does not control for chance agreement. Therefore, an index of agreement that takes chance agreement into account, such as coefficient Kappa (Cohen, 1968), needs to be included in addition to percent agreement. See Fleiss (1981), Liebetrau (1983), and Bakeman (this volume, Ch. 6) for discussions of various approaches to assessing categorical agreement.

Number of Coders Required

At a minimum, it is necessary to have all interviews in a sample coded once and a subset of interviews rated by a second independent coder to establish reliability. The first set of codings would then be used in all analyses, and the obtained reliability would refer to agreement expected between any two randomly selected coders. This procedure is acceptable if the coders employed have previously demonstrated high levels of interscorer agreement. Although less than ideal, this approach may also be adopted if a researcher lacks the resources to obtain multiple codings of all interviews. The number of reliability codings required depends on the estimated population value of the reliability index: the higher the value, the fewer codings required (because the standard error of the reliability index will be lower). Thus, if coders have previously demonstrated high levels of reliability, as few as 20 cases may be sufficient. However, if reliability has not been established prior to beginning or if the complexity of the coding system tends to preclude high reliability, we recommend an absolute minimum of 30 reliability codings.

A second approach is to have two or more independent coders assess all interviews. With continuous rating scales, ratings of multiple coders are then averaged for use in data analysis, and reliability estimates refer to the expected agreement if the combined ratings of two (or more) randomly chosen coders were compared with the combined ratings of a second set of two (or more) randomly chosen coders. Rosenthal and Rosnow (1984) referred to reliability of the mean of two or more judges' ratings as *effective reliability*. The reliability of the mean of two ratings will always be greater than that of an individual rating, and reliability can always be increased (at least in theory) by adding additional coders. The expected increase in reliability afforded by the addition of one or more coders can be estimated with the Spearman Brown prophecy formula. Alternatively, Rosenthal and Rosnow provided a table indicating the effective reliability for various numbers of judges and mean reliabilities among any two judges. Just as the determination of sample size should be guided by a power analysis, the number of coders required for a desired level of reliability should be determined prior to undertaking a project involving coding of SSIs.

The same logic applies to categorical coding systems: Multiple coders will lead to increased reliability. For instance, judged presence or absence of a particular category can be given a dichotomous 0 or 1 rating, and then these ratings can be averaged across multiple coders. This procedure converts dichotomous judgments into a dimensional variable – the proportion of coders that agree on a particular categorical judgment. In this case, similar gains in reliability can be obtained as with continuous ratings (see Horowitz, Inouye, & Siegelman, 1979, for an example). It is interesting to consider that the obtained proportional values are equivalent to continuous ratings of the prototypicality of group membership. It would be much simpler to recognize at the outset of the study that category members differ in their prototypicality and use a coding scheme that takes this variability into consideration. Thereby, higher reliability can be obtained with fewer coders.

Coder Discrepancies

With continuous rating scales, it is not necessary to resolve coder discrepancies. Whether two (or more) coders agree or disagree, their pooled or averaged ratings make up the final data. It is not even clear what would constitute disagreement on a given rating scale: a 1-point difference on a 7-point scale would presumably be fine; would a 2-point difference be a disagreement?; perhaps a 3-point or greater difference? By averaging across coders, final ratings will, at least in theory, be closer to the "true" score than each individual rating. Thus, if overall reliabilities of continuous ratings are acceptable, there is no need to resolve dis-

crepancies. If reliabilities are not acceptable, we recommend adding additional coders or, if necessary, replacing an unreliable coder.

In contrast, categorical coding systems necessitate resolving coder disagreements because it is not possible to average discrepant categorical judgments. There are three common approaches to dealing with categorical discrepancies. If two coders disagree on a categorical assignment, a third rater can be added, and the classification agreed on by two of three raters becomes the final rating. If three coders all disagree, then a fourth coder is added, and the category judgment agreed on by two of the four is used. We have never seen a case where more than four coders are required to reach agreement, though in principle additional coders could be required. With this procedure, coefficients of agreement are reported for the original two coders, and agreement for the best two of three coders (hopefully 100%) is also reported. Alternatively, differences can be resolved by discussion, in which case the consensus classification is used for data analysis. In this case, no new coders are required, and there is no need to compute new reliabilities. However, there is no way using the consensus approach to assess reliabilities of the final ratings or to ensure that "consensus" does not merely reflect the ratings of the more persuasive of the two coders. A final method for resolving disagreements is to bring in an expert coder (such as the developer of the coding system) to resolve discrepancies. However, again, reliabilities can no longer be assessed for final ratings; there is also the possibility that the expert will not agree with either of the original coders. Therefore, we recommend the first approach of adding additional raters until agreement is reached.

Sources of Unreliability

What is an acceptable level of reliability? The answer depends on the coding system, the norms in the field of research, and even the individual researcher's standards. Also, different methods of assessing reliability will yield different estimates. For instance, kappas will always lead to lower reliability estimates than proportion agreement. However, as a general rule, reliabilities above .80 are acceptable by most standards, and somewhat lower reliabilities (.60 to .80) are often considered acceptable for more difficult coding schemes. Even lower reliabilities are not necessarily disastrous. However, if the researcher's hypotheses are not confirmed, then it is not possible to interpret the lack of findings: Unreliable ratings may have led to attenuation of existing associations or the predicted associations may not, in fact, exist.

There are three key sources of unreliability in interview ratings: poorly conducted interviews, a poorly constructed coding system, and poorly trained and supervised coders. All of these situations can be avoided. Adequate training and supervision of interviewers should ensure that interview protocols contain enough relevant information on which to assess constructs of interest. With adequate training and reliability checks, coding ambiguities will be brought to light long before coders begin their task, and adequate piloting will reveal if revisions are required to the coding system. Reliability problems stemming from inadequate understanding of coding criteria by coders can also be avoided by proper training prior to commencement. There are instances, however, in which the inherent complexity and level of abstraction of the coding system constrains the reliability of ratings, despite the best efforts of the researcher to clarify rating criteria and train coders. Alternatively, in some projects interview protocols are inherently limited, for example, in cases where interviews originally conducted for another purpose are being coded. In such cases, introduction of additional coders will increase reliability. However, in most applications, additional coders are an expensive substitute for good interviewing technique, precise coding guidelines, and thorough training.

Should Interviewers Be Coders?

Interviewers who are also trained coders generally make better interviewers than those less familiar with the coding system. However, should interviewers also code interviews they are conducting? Interviewer/coders will be aware of characteristics of participants (notably physical attractiveness) and of participants' behavior in the interview sessions (such as eye contact, smiling, and nervous gestures) that will not be captured on interview recordings or transcripts. Though this information would probably have little or no effect on more cognitive judgments, such as level of moral reasoning, it may well affect judgments such as attachment organization in which participant affect in the interview is considered in the coding system. If interviewers are coding from face to face interaction with participants and reliability coders are coding from an audiotape, transcript, or videotape, systematic errors of measurement may be introduced. Even if interviewers subsequently code from a tape or transcript of interview sessions, they will have had access to additional information. We encountered a vivid example of this problem with a participant who has since been nicknamed "Mr. 9 on Warmth" (so named because he obtained the highest possible rating on an Interpersonal Warmth scale). This participant's disarming manner and striking physical beauty appeared to lead his interviewers to rate him more positively on all scales in the coding system (including security of attachment) than did coders who were working from an audiotape. Mr. 9 on Warmth was part of a 3-year longitudinal study, and this effect was consistent across all three time points.

Potential biases such as that described above may arise whenever coders are working from different forms of information (audio vs. transcript, in person vs. videotaping, etc.). Ideally, all coders should work from the same source of information and interviewers would not serve as coders. In practice, however, use of dual interviewers/coders is sometimes the only feasible option. With some forms of research interviews, an experienced interviewer/coder can code immediately on completion of the interview, dramatically reducing coding time and cost. If this approach must be taken, it is especially important to establish that coders are reliable before beginning and to closely monitor coders throughout the study. Also, the dual role should be clearly described in research reports.

Uncodable Interviews

There are circumstances when an interview protocol is uncodable, for instance, due to poor tape quality, an incomplete interview, or an incoherent participant. In these cases, there is little option but to remove such an interview from the study. Other situations are more questionable: a poorly conducted interview, an extremely complex and difficult to code interview, a hard to comprehend participant, or a barely audible tape. How to deal with these situations depends on the research interview, the coding system, the particular study, and, ultimately, the principal researcher's judgment. In our work, we use all interviews that are comprehensible to coders. We feel that deleting interviews because they are difficult to code is akin to deleting participants whose responses do not fit our research hypotheses. Not all researchers will agree with our very conservative guidelines for identification of uncodable interviews. It is important, therefore, that researchers with more liberal definitions of "uncodable" clearly indicate in their research reports how many (if any) interviews were judged to be uncodable and on what basis.

VALIDITY ASSESSMENT

Validity refers to the extent to which an instrument is measuring what it is intended to measure, the relationship between empirical indicators and the constructs of interest. Whereas reliability is basically an empirical issue, validity is more of a theoretical issue and, therefore, its assessment is less straightforward. There are various approaches to assessing validity that are more or less applicable to any given coded research interview. In each form of validity assessment, a comparison is made to some standard: an informed judgment, a comparison with something that ratings ought to agree with or be different from, or some outcome that ratings ought to predict.

Often in interview studies, inferences about validity are made primarily on the basis of face or content validity, whether the measure reflects an appropriate domain of content. There is no clear procedure to establish content validity, although one approach would be to submit interview questions and scoring criteria to a panel of theoretically knowledgeable judges. Ultimately, it is based on the informed judgment of the researcher. Content validity, while an important consideration in the early phases of developing an interview measure, is only a first step in furnishing adequate validity for a measure. *Concurrent validity*, assessing correspondence of the new measure with other measures of the same construct (or constructs), is not always applicable to CSSIs. In many cases, if other valid measures of a construct were already available, there would have been no need to develop the research interview in the first place. Rather, one often starts with an interview measure and subsequently attempts to develop simpler self-report measures using interview ratings as the standard of comparison (as has been done in the field of ego identity, e.g., Grotevant & Adams, 1984). In contrast, *discriminant validity*, distinguishing the measure from other measures with which there should not be an association, can be very useful in the interview domain. For instance, it may be important to demonstrate that interview ratings of a construct such as attachment pattern or ego identity are distinguishable from, and therefore not reducible to, verbal ability or IQ (e.g., Bakermans-Kranenburg & van IJzendoorn, 1993). Finally, criterion or predictive validity is relevant when the purpose of a measure is to predict some outcome or behavior that is external to the measure itself (Nunnally, 1978). However, with the sorts of complex constructs that are typically assessed by coded research interviews, there is rarely any specific external criterion. For a notable exception, see van Ijzendoorn's (1995) meta-analysis on the predictive validity of the Adult Attachment Interview (AAI). In this case, the AAI was designed to assess parental attachment representations associated with corresponding infant attachment patterns (as assessed in an observational procedure, the "Strange Situation").

Construct validity, the extent to which associations between a given measure and various other measures are consistent with theoretically derived hypotheses (Cronbach & Meehl, 1955), subsumes and integrates the various types of validity previously described, and it involves simultaneous assessment of the theory and the measures. As described by Cronbach (1988), a weak form of construct validity emphasizes examining associations between measure scores and a "nomological network" of external variables. For illustrations, see Marcia's (1966) work validating ego identity statuses and Bartholomew and Horowitz's (1991) work validating their model of adult attachment. In contrast, a strong form of construct validity is the multitrait, multimethod matrix (MTMMM) procedure described by Campbell and Fiske (1959). See Griffin and Bartholomew (1994b) for an example of an MTMMM analysis including coded interview data. Latent variable analysis was used to simultaneously assess convergent validity of two attachment dimensions across three methods (interview ratings, self-reports, and reports of significant others) and discriminant validity across attachment dimensions assessed by the same methods.

TRAINING OF INTERVIEWERS AND CODERS

When discussing training of interviewers and coders, we face a dilemma of artificially separating interviewing and coding. This separation is particularly inappropriate when discussing training because, more often than not, individuals learn to interview and code simultaneously. We recommend that interviewers also be trained coders, though the reverse need not be the case. Interviewers who understand the coding system will be in a better position to know what questions to follow up, to spontaneously create more meaningful probes, and to redirect participants toward issues that are relevant to the coding scheme.

Choosing Interviewers and Coders

In choosing potential interviewers and coders, we try to choose psychologically minded individuals who demonstrate good social skills, have an ability to recognize and to control their own biases, and have performed any similar tasks well in the past. It is also important that interviewer and coder candidates be keenly interested in the research domain and believe in the potential value of the work. Interviewers who lack such interest are likely to communicate their lack of enthusiasm in the research interview and are less likely to follow through on the sometimes arduous work of becoming a reliable coder.

Some researchers have proposed that the most effective interviewers and coders will be those who score high or optimally on the construct of interest (e.g., Loevenger & Wessler, 1970). (Of course, not all constructs have such a clear evaluative component.) Matteson (1993) suggested that individuals who are identity achieved, the optimal outcome in the Ego Identity Interview coding scheme, make the best coders. He further recommended that potential interviewers and coders be interviewed and coded for their identity status to aid in the selection process. In more cognitive domains, it could be argued that individuals operating at a relatively low level will be incapable of recognizing and comprehending cognitive processes more developed than their own. For example, according to Kohlberg's theory of moral reasoning, a Stage 2 coder (whose moral reasoning is motivated by rewards and self-interest) may not be capable of recognizing, understanding, or coding a Stage 4 participant (whose moral judgments are based on the value of upholding social law and order). We do not endorse choosing research personnel based on their standing on constructs under study. This approach is based on impressions rather than empirical study, and it is clearly not justified in all domains. Though we have never systematically rated coders in our research in adult attachment, we are quite confident that not all of our reliable coders would be rated high on attachment security, the most optimal outcome in the attachment model. In addition, we question the ethics of screening potential members of a research team based on their standing on psychological constructs.

Training Interviewers

Interviewers need to understand the goals of the study and to be familiar with the theoretical constructs of the project, the basics of the scoring system, and the purpose of each interview question. This is especially important if it is not feasible for interviewers to also be trained coders. Therefore, the first step of training is a review of relevant theory and the coding system. The next step involves some combination of observation, role playing, and practice, with discussion and feedback throughout the process. In this stage, it is essential for at least some interviews to be taped in order to obtain feedback on interviewing technique. We recommend a combination of feedback sources: the expert trainer, other members of the training group, and the trainee themselves, listening to their own tapes.

Regardless of initial skill level, it takes time for interviewers to become accustomed to and comfortable with an interview format. In less structured interviews, it can take considerable practice with an interview format for an interviewer to cover key questions while remaining sensitive to how participants prefer to move through the material. It is critical that interviewers come to understand the purpose of every question in order to follow up with meaningful and useful probes. For example, in the FAI participants are asked about being lost as a child. As the purpose of this question is to judge separation anxiety, probes focusing on how the participant felt about being lost, and eventually, found provide much more useful information than probes into the circumstantial details of the separation.

An often overlooked area of training concerns the mechanics of taping an interview, whether via audiotape or videotape. Over the course of thousands of interviews we have committed many technological gaffs: placing the microphone too far away from the participant, putting the microphone on top of the tape recorder, leaving a loud air purifier on during the interview, forgetting to check the batteries in the microphone, and so on. Most of these problems can be averted by drilling interviewers in interviewing procedure. We now include "procedure" as a critical component to our training and are not hesitant about stating and restating the obvious, the most important being to test the tape or video recorder every time before starting an interview. For more detailed treatments of training procedures for interviewers see Gorden (1987) and Matteson (1993).

ONGOING SUPERVISION OF INTERVIEWERS. When time and money are scarce, there may be a tendency to give interviewers minimal training and set them free. However, we have discovered (the hard way) the importance of continuing to monitor interviewers throughout the research project and subsequent projects. A relatively painless way to provide ongoing feedback to interviewers is to have coders provide brief written or oral feedback as they are coding interviews. If the interviewer is inappropriately leading the participant or failing to follow up certain responses or in any other way not ideally facilitating the interview process, a good coder will be immediately aware of the problem. Coders should be asked to note the interviewer's strengths as well as weaknesses. It is also a good strategy to encourage (or perhaps insist) that interviewers periodically listen to their own interview tapes. There is nothing like the power of listening to one's own recorded words to draw attention to an inappropriate or untimely question, or an affected mannerism.

INTERVIEWER BIASES. There has been much discussion in the survey research literature concerning potential interviewer effects attributable to overt characteristics of the interviewer, such as sex, age, race, ethnicity, and social class (e.g., Cannell & Kahn, 1968; Gorden, 1987). In survey research, there are concerns that differences on such characteristics could influence participants' comfort with the interview and their willingness to disclose particular information. In more in-depth interviewing, a complementary concern is that an interviewer who cannot identify with the participant may not be capable of understanding the participant's feelings and experiences. At an extreme, it could be argued that interviewers should match the sample under study on all core demographic characteristics – a requirement that would quickly bring to a halt many research projects.

The research looking at such interviewer effects is thin, but, overall, it appears that interviewer effects are only evident in cases where interviewer characteristics are directly relevant to the content of the study (Gorden, 1987). Thus, Schuman and Converse (1971) found that race of interviewer only influenced responses of Black participants to questions that related directly to race relations (such as hostility toward Whites). With coded interviews, common sense can dictate where such interviewer effects are likely. For instance, when working with battered women we would only employ female interviewers, to facilitate disclosure and ensure comfort of the participants. But in most cases it is the skill of the individual interviewer that will ensure the success of the interview. One of the outstanding sets of interviews we have encountered was conducted by a male interviewer with women (generally considerably older than himself) suffering from breast cancer (Bellg, 1995). Conversely, we have encountered interviewers who were strongly identified with study participants but who were painfully incompetent interviewers. We advocate choosing interviewers based on their competence, not their standing on overt characteristics.

A more serious concern is that an interviewer's expectations regarding the subject material or an interviewer's personal agenda could lead to confirmation biases. That is, by unintentionally directing the interview (by emphasizing certain topics, avoiding other topics, asking leading questions, etc.), the interviewer could influence participant responses and, thereby, effect the eventual coding of the interview. For example, we encountered an interviewer who systematically steered participants away from emotionally upsetting material, apparently because of her own discomfort with strong emotions. In another case, an interviewer of women who had recently left abusive relationships very actively attempted to lead participants to adopt a feminist analysis of their experiences of abuse. If we were simply coding the *content* of these interviews or even the participants' standing on specific attitudinal or affective scales (e.g., attitudes toward one's spouse or emotional expressiveness), ratings could be strongly influenced by such interviewer biases. However, such interviewer biases are less problematic when high-order process variables are being assessed from an SSI. A biased interviewer would be less likely to lead a participant to shift their moral reasoning to a higher (or lower) level than to influence the content of their moral judgments. With a CSSI, well-trained coders also provide a safeguard against potential interview biases by identifying interview bias and taking it into consideration in their ratings. For example, when the interviewer of abused women failed to follow up participant responses that were incompatible with her perspective, coders attributed these gaps to the interviewer rather than to the participant. Moreover, the coders gained relevant information from observing how participants responded to the interviewer's attempts to lead them in particular directions. Thus, although interviewer biases will compromise the quality of interview data (thereby introducing random measurement error in ratings), they are less likely to introduce systematic error in codings.

Nevertheless, the possibility of interviewer bias should be taken seriously in all research with CSSIs. Although it may not be possible to eliminate all forms of interviewer bias, there are a number of measures that can be taken to avoid and control for potential biases. The same interviews should not provide the basis of independent and dependent variables, even if independent raters assess the two sets of variables. For instance, it would be inappropriate to test for associations between childhood abuse and current attachment security by assessing both variables in the same research interview. More generally, as far as possible, interviewers should be unaware of participants' standing on all other measures in the study and of the study hypotheses. If two or more CSSIs are used in a study, interviewers must be independent. Where the same CSSI is used on multiple occasions (such as in a longitudinal study), or when CSSIs are administered to dependent participants (such as both members of a couple), then independence of interviewers must be maintained. We also recommend use of multiple interviewers in a single study to attenuate the impact of any one interviewer's biases. Finally, close monitoring of interview quality throughout the course of a study can serve to identify and correct most interviewer problems.

Training of Coders

There are a number of approaches to training coders, including workshops of various lengths, tutorial type seminars, and more formal classes. In many instances, a group of trainees is supervised by an expert coder. Alternatively, they may work from a detailed manual, preferably with access to a trained coder for consultation when necessary. Whatever the format, coding is most readily learned in small groups in which group discussion is encouraged; coders learn as much from each other as they do from a trainer.

To give a concrete example of one model of training, we briefly describe how we train coders to assess attachment interviews in a weekly tutorial format. As a prerequisite, trainees are required to demonstrate a solid background in attachment theory and research. In the first classes, students review and discuss the conceptual model guiding the research and become familiar with the coding manual. The major focus of training is working through a set of 30–40 sample interviews. Trainees code taped interviews with the guidance of the coding manual in between sessions and bring finished codings, along with notes justifying their rating decisions, to class for discussion. During the class, trainees are given the correct codings (based on a consensus reached by at least three reliable coders) and discuss all scales on which they experienced difficulties.

At the end of the semester, trainees code an additional 30 tapes, this time without discussion, for a reliability check. Researchers skip this step at their peril. It is extremely risky to have coders begin working with study interviews as soon as they appear to have successfully grasped the coding scheme in a training class. A formal reliability check will indicate which coders have attained reliability, which coders need additional training to become reliable (and where, specifically, their problems lie), and which coders are unlikely

to become reliable. Naturally, the complexity of the coding system will determine the length of time it takes coders to become reliable.

When we asked researchers who work with CSSIs about problems that arise in the research process, a recurrent theme was the challenge of dealing with unreliable coders. In the worst scenarios, researchers did not pay sufficient attention to establishing reliability before coders began their tasks nor to monitoring coders in the course of their work. As a result, coders were sometimes discovered to be unreliable only after having devoted hundreds of hours to the project. At this point, the only recourse is to have another coder begin from scratch; sometimes it is even necessary to begin training new coders. If a researcher follows the training procedures we have advocated, however, such scenarios can be avoided.

ONGOING SUPERVISION OF CODERS. Ongoing supervision of coders is as important as ongoing supervision of interviewers. There may be a tendency for some coders to become less reliable over time, whether through sloppiness in applying coding criteria or gradual adoption of idiosyncratic coding biases, referred to as *coder drift*. The obvious way to avert such problems is to periodically check the reliability of coders in the midst of projects rather than after all ratings have been completed. Of course, it is not acceptable for coders to change ratings after discussions. Another useful strategy is to have all coders on a project meet regularly to discuss difficult cases (again, not changing prior ratings). Sochting (personal communication, February 16, 1996) recommended having coders periodically rate the same randomly chosen research protocol and meet to discuss their ratings. Such meetings not only ensure that coding difficulties are quickly identified and corrected, but may be valuable in keeping coders motivated. As with interviewing, additional training and more reliability checks are often required if a coder is asked to work with a new population.

CODER BIASES. We find that coding biases, apparently resulting from coders' particular backgrounds (personal, cultural, ethnic, etc.), values, and psychological make-up, often surface in training classes. Coders have a tendency to use their own experiences and expectations as a baseline from which to judge others. For example, a new coder of the FAI was asked why she gave a rather uninvolved and undemonstrative, but not actively rejecting, father a relatively high rating on parental acceptance. She explained, "But he was pretty good for a *father!*" It is not reasonable to expect that sufficient training can always produce perfectly objective coders. What is crucial, however, is that coders are willing to non-defensively examine their blind spots and take them into account in the coding process. Coders can learn to correct for their particular coding biases and to be much more careful in making coding judgments in areas in which they are aware that they experience difficulties. As with interviewer bias, a number of measures can be taken to avoid coder bias. Thorough training of coders, including performing reliability checks prior to beginning coding for a research project, and close supervision of coders are absolutely essential. As with interviewers, coders should be unaware of participants' standing on all other variables in the study and, where possible, to the study hypotheses. Independent coders are required if the study involves multiple CSSIs (whether more than one SSI is used or the same SSI is given on more than one occasion). In the longitudinal study of attachment processes in young couples described earlier (Scharfe & Bartholomew, 1994, 1995), two independent coders rated each research interview. It was necessary to maintain independence of coders across partners in a couple, across the two CSSIs administered (the PAI & FAI), and across time, because the PAI was administered at three points in time. Therefore, 16 independent coders were required for each couple.

CONDUCTING SEMISTRUCTURED INTERVIEWS

The primary goal of coded research interviews is to glean enough relevant information from participants to reliably code the interview. It is also important for the researcher to create a safe, comfortable, even enjoyable, interview experience for participants. The goal of gaining information must not take place at the expense of participants. In our experience, the attainment of each goal augments the other. The value of a well-constructed interview schedule, a valid coding system, and highly reliable coders may be compromised if the actual research interview is poorly conducted. Because much has been written about the practical aspects of conducting interviews (see Gorden [1987] for an extensive overview), in this section we concentrate on those issues that are relevant to CSSIs and that have received less attention in previous literature. We discuss the physical and psychological setting of the research interview, types of questions, note-taking, and strategies for dealing with difficult interviewees.

The Physical Setting of the Interview

In setting up the interview space, the objective is to achieve a balance between comfort and professionalism. Although it is ideal to provide consistent interview conditions for all participants, sometimes practical constraints require researchers to accept some variability in setting. For example, if working with a sample of persons with AIDS, some participants may not be well enough to travel to the researcher's office. In such a case, we would conduct interviews in the participant's home or even in a hospital room, if necessary. Rather than losing participants because they don't fit into a researcher's preordained structure, we suggest accommodating the participant's needs and reducing variability where possible.

The Psychological Setting of the Interview

A critical factor in creating a comfortable psychological climate is the initial establishment of interviewer–participant rapport. Participants are more likely to be comfortable when they are prepared for what is to follow. Therefore, participants should be told at the outset what to expect in terms of procedure, kinds of questions, and approximate length of the interview. The voluntary nature of their participation and responses should be described (both verbally and on the consent form), and the nature of the confidentiality of their responses should be explained.

A key ingredient in maintaining rapport is for interviewers to leave their value systems and their judgments outside the interviewing room. Consider, for example, the experience of the second author interviewing a young man about his long-term romantic relationship. Having learned to hold her judgments at bay, the interviewer was able to create a climate where the young man felt comfortable openly expressing blatantly misogynist views (such as comparing fidelity with being forced to restrict one's choice of candy bars to one). This openness facilitated coders accurately assessing this participant's representations of close relationships.

Active or effective listening is critical in research interviewing. By this, we are referring to an interviewer's skill in actively listening to and attempting to understand the participant's responses (cf. Gorden, 1987). This can take many forms, such as asking for clarification of apparent inconsistencies in the participant's narrative, connecting questions to previous responses of the participant, acknowledging where the participant has already touched on a particular issue, or noticing a participant's misunderstanding of a question and rewording the question accordingly. By attentively listening and asking subsequent questions that take into consideration previous content, interviewers can simultaneously make participants feel understood and facilitate relevant interview responses. In contrast, it is not the role of research interviewers to emotionally support participants, nor to aid participants in understanding or coming to terms with their experiences. Reflecting meaning or affect, expressions of empathy, interpretations of participant experiences, and so on are not appropriate in a research interview. Interviewers with counseling or clinical backgrounds quickly learn to put on different hats when moving from the therapeutic to the research interview.

A question that commonly arises with SSIs is whether interviewers should encourage or discourage emotional content. Matteson (1993) stated unequivocally that "it is not appropriate in a research interview to encourage opening up deeper feelings" (p. 144). In contrast, we maintain that the answer to this question depends on the nature of the interview. In Skoe's Ethic of Care interview (1993), where the focus concerns states of cognitive reasoning, interviewers are instructed to tactfully steer participants away from deeper feelings. However, in the Identity Status Interview, a defining characteristic distinguishing the moratorium status from the identity diffusion status is the presence of some sense of struggle and conflict. Similarly, affect is directly relevant in the PAI, and good interviewers know how to allow the expression of deeper feelings without turning the interview into a therapy session.

Types of Questions

Much has been written on the advantages and disadvantages of various kinds of questions that can be used in interviews – open versus closed, probes, clarifying questions, leading or loaded questions, etc. (see Gorden, 1987). We would like to emphasize that almost every question has its place, and there are no absolute rules about what questions are or are not acceptable. For instance, some interviewing guides suggest that leading questions should always be avoided. However, we have found that leading questions can sometimes make it easier for a participant to admit a socially unacceptable feeling, belief, or behavior. Consider this original question from the FAI: "Would you have liked your parents to be different in any way?" Dissatisfied with the uninformative "no" response this question often elicited, it was reworded to "How would you have liked your parents to be different?". This leading question allows participants to freely express any negative feelings they might have about their parents and results in much more informative responses. As we discuss later in this section, there are also specific instances where both open and closed questions are appropriate.

Note-Taking

We strongly encourage interviewers to take notes during interview sessions. Note-taking, if not excessive, can be rapport-enhancing by indicating to the participant that the interviewer is interested, and it can offer the participant a break from the intensity of constant face-to-face contact. For the interviewer, it ensures that he or she stay focused, it can be used as a breathing space to think or regroup, and it allows the interviewer to make "probe notes" (Gorden, 1987) concerning issues they may want to address later. Finally, interview notes can serve as a last resort backup if technology has failed you.

The Difficult Interview

Though not a comprehensive list, we briefly discuss some of the more common difficulties that have surfaced in our interviewing experience and provide illustrations of how we have dealt with them.

PARTICIPANT DOES NOT WANT TO BE TAPED. Participants will generally feel more comfortable about being audiotaped or videotaped if they are made aware of the taping ahead of time. If a participant still feels ambivalent about being taped, a useful strategy is to ask if taping can proceed with the understanding that the participant will be free to choose to keep the tape at the end of the interview session. In our experience, if the interviewer has even minimal rapport-building skills, the reluctant participant is predictably happy to allow their tape to be included in the research project by the end of the interview.

PARTICIPANT IS TOO TALKATIVE. If one has unlimited time to interview, the overly talkative participant is not necessarily problematic. However, more typically, one must consider time constraints and the extra work produced for coders who have to wade through irrelevant material. With an overly talkative participant, the experienced interviewer imposes structure early on, uses more closed-ended questions, focuses only on the most important questions in the interview, and tactfully interrupts when necessary. As a final strategy, we suggest turning off the recorder and telling the participant that, although you appreciate how forthcoming they are being, you are concerned about getting the interview finished in the allotted time. For all but the most socially insensitive participant, this strategy can work wonders.

PARTICIPANT IS NOT TALKATIVE ENOUGH. Participants can be less than forthcoming for a variety of reasons, and the interviewer's response should vary accordingly. If a participant is shy, anxious, or self-conscious, open-ended questions and probes are useful. It is also important for interviewers to accept some silence in an interview. Often participants are silent because they need time to think about a question. However, sometimes the problem arises from the interviewer's own interviewing limitations. Perhaps the interviewer seems insensitive by having an overly brusque and efficient manner, or, conversely, perhaps the interviewer is overly intense for the shy participant. Whenever there are difficulties establishing rapport with a participant, we recommend that interviewers obtain feedback on the taped interview to isolate any potential interviewing problems.

PARTICIPANT IS DIFFICULT OR HOSTILE. In general, we have found that it is best to be direct in dealing with difficult participants. For example, a former participant's one-word answers and clipped tone made it immediately evident that she did not want to be interviewed. An experienced interviewer turned off the tape and said, "I get the sense that you really don't want to do this interview today. Would you prefer to put it off to another time? Or perhaps you would prefer not to do it at all? What do you think?" The participant admitted that she was tired, had had a hard day, and felt coerced into participating in the study by her spouse. But she agreed to continue with the interview. In fact, the remainder of the interview proceeded smoothly, and during debriefing she said she had enjoyed the experience. For a description of a number of possible strategies to deal with difficult participants, see Gorden's (1987) chapter on "Dealing with Resistance."

PARTICIPANT BECOMES UPSET. Depending on the nature of the interview, crying or other emotional outbursts may or may not be something to be discouraged. Assuming that emotion need not be avoided, in many instances no particular response is required. If the participant is relatively comfortable continuing, then we encourage our interviewers to do so. If the participant is too emotional to continue, it may be necessary to stop for a few moments to let him or her gain composure. If the interviewer is not sure whether to continue, he or she can check this out with the participant. Sometimes simply normalizing the experience for the participant is helpful:

Participant: "I don't know what's the matter with me, crying like this. I've never talked about this stuff before. I'm so sorry."

Interviewer: "It's O.K. Lots of people become emotional when talking about this material."

Interviewers should always have on hand referral sources that will see individuals on a walk-in or phone-in basis. These agencies should be selected with reference to the population being interviewed (e.g., college counseling services, battered spouse services). If a participant becomes extremely distraught or if it becomes clear that the participant is in a situation that calls for immediate intervention, then the needs of the participant should take precedence over the research agenda, and the interview should be terminated.

INTERVIEWER IS UNCOMFORTABLE WITH QUESTIONS. If interviewers are uncomfortable asking a question, it usually follows that participants will be uncomfortable answering it. Generally the best cure for this dilemma is practice. Many of our interviewers were initially uncomfortable asking questions about the sexual aspects of participants' relationships and conveyed this discomfort to participants. With practice, however, topics that are initially difficult because of socialized taboos become relatively straightforward.

ETHICAL CONSIDERATIONS

It is beyond the scope of this chapter to consider all of the ethical issues that may arise with CSSIs. Therefore, we will briefly discuss three ethical issues of particular relevance to CSSIs: informed consent, effects of participating in the research, and dissemination of findings.

Informed Consent

A standard participant consent form for a questionnaire study usually includes a brief description of the procedure, an assurance of participant confidentiality, an indication of the voluntary nature of participation, and so on. When one moves to an interview measure, we recommend that consent be requested for any foreseeable future applications of interview material: use of interview excerpts in publications, talks, or conferences; presentation of case studies in papers or presentations; use of interview tapes for training sessions, etc. This will avoid subsequent problems. For example, at one point we wanted to use some interview tapes for a training seminar, but this use of tapes was not included in the original consent forms. We considered a range of options to deal with this dilemma, from transcribing interviews and removing identifying information to obtaining written consent from the original study participants. We ended up tracking down the participants (up to 2 years after their participation) and asking for their verbal consent for this new use of their interviews. Clearly, it would have been preferable to obtain this consent at the outset.

Effects on the Participant

The process of being interviewed appears to be a rewarding experience for most participants. Not often in life do we have the chance to tell our stories to an attentive, encouraging audience. It has been our experience that participants generally find interview sessions to be interesting, informative, thought-provoking, and sometimes even beneficial. Cannell and Kahn (1968) explained why interviewing is typically very rewarding for participants:

The opportunity to talk to a good listener, to find one's opinions of serious interest to another person, to see that person making a real and successful effort to understand rather than to evaluate or criticize, to encounter the stimulation of moving sequentially and logically through a series of related issues – these are experiences which are rare for many people and which are intrinsically satisfying. (p. 580)

However, this rare satisfying experience may encourage some participants to disclose material or get in touch with feelings they wish they hadn't.

Those who have cautioned about the potential exploitative power of the semistructured interview have emphasized the power of the interviewer in the interviewer–participant hierarchy (e.g., Gluck & Patai, 1991). It has been our experience that in spite of stressing that participants are free to not answer questions, most participants respond to every question, even when they are clearly uncomfortable with or distressed by interview content. In addition to the potential experience of momentary discomfort in the interview situation, there is the possibility that longer-term negative effects could stem from the interview process. Participants may feel distressed knowing they have overdisclosed, or they may find themselves unable to stop thinking about difficult personal materials raised in the interview (such as negative childhood experiences), or the interview may facilitate a questioning or reevaluation of their lives that could be confusing and distressing.

We are aware of little empirical work examining potential longer-term consequences of research participation. However, it is likely that even very intimate research interviews rarely have long-term negative consequences for participants. In a 6-month telephone follow-up of a sample of 77 couples who had completed an attachment interview, the large majority of participants reported that their interview experience had no impact whatsoever, and a few said it had a slight positive impact. Similarly, Rubin and Mitchell (1976) asked young couples who had participated in a longitudinal study involving extensive self-report measures (and, in some cases, semistructured interviews as well) about the effects of their participation. The large majority felt that participation had no effect on their relationships, and just 4% said their participation had led them to become less close (though this was often seen as a positive development by participants). However, as Rubin and Mitchell pointed out, participants may not be able to accurately assess the impact of research participation on themselves or their relationships. It would be necessary to follow-up participants and a control group of potential participants who were not administered a research interview or other measure to determine the potential effects of research participation.

Until we have better empirical data to assess any potential short-term or long-term effects of participation, we recommend taking a very cautious stance and treating research participants with utmost consideration. In conducting interviews that deal with personal and sometimes emotional material, we take a number of steps to make respondents as comfortable as possible. Respondents are clearly informed that their participation is voluntary and that they are free to not answer any questions or to withdraw from the project at any time. Though consent forms tell participants that their responses will be kept confidential and anonymous, we find that participants also appreciate being explicitly told how their interview tapes will be used. We explain that at no point will names or phone numbers be associated with their interview responses, that only research personnel working on the project have access to interview tapes, and that research materials do not leave the lab. As some of our research involves individuals in abusive intimate relationships, we have also become acutely aware of issues concerning participant safety. In these cases, we often conduct interviews in locations that are less than ideal research conditions if this will create a safer and more comfortable environment for participants. In addition, we refer all participants experiencing distress in their lives to available community services and provide them with our contact number in case they wish to speak further with the interviewer or to receive help in finding appropriate support services in the community.

Dissemination of Findings

It is important to ensure that participants' input has been worth their effort. It is therefore crucial to make every reasonable effort to publish the results of your study. However, because most scientific publications are sufficiently specialized so as to be beyond the scope of most research participants, participants should be sent a simpler lay person's version of findings as soon as possible after completion of data analyses. Social responsibility can also extend beyond the immediate participants to the community at large. If the research has implications for a particular clinical or cultural group, one might consider giving a talk, training session, or seminar to disseminate the knowledge to people working with those groups. As an illustration, as part of her project looking at South Asian women, Tee (1996) organized a cultural sensitivity training workshop for therapists, transition house workers, and other professionals working with women in cultural transition.

CONCLUSIONS

Conducting and coding semistructured research interviews is hard and exacting work. As we have discussed in this chapter, extensive thought, time, and resources are required to develop semistructured interviews and associated coding systems; to choose, train, and monitor interviewers and coders; and to conduct and continually update the research interview. We have highlighted some of the key challenges that face researchers using CSSIs, such as conceptualizing the constructs of interest, avoiding potential interviewer and coder biases, establishing reliability and validity, handling difficult interview situations, and conducting the research in an ethical and responsible manner. Throughout, we have emphasized that most research problems can be avoided by exhaustive piloting of the CSSI and by thorough training and careful monitoring of all members of the research team.

In spite of the challenges, conducting research with coded SSIs can be extremely rewarding, thought provoking, and even exciting. The CSSI both requires and elicits high levels of intellectual and sometimes affective engagement on the part of participants and researchers. Especially for researchers in the habit of doing experimental work, or relying on self-reports and observations, it can be enlightening to carefully listen to individuals talking about themselves and their social worlds. No other method yields the richness of information furnished by participants who are treated as informed and valued respondents. Even after listening to hundreds of interviews, we are impressed by each individual's uniqueness. And we often find ourselves being pushed to think about our research area in new ways and to question the adequacy of our pet constructs.

REFERENCES

Alcoff, L. (1991). The problems of speaking for others. *Cultural critique, Winter 1991–1992*, New York: Oxford University Press.

Bakermans-Kranenburg, M. J., & van Ijzendoorn, M. H. (1993). A psychometric study of the Adult Attachment Interview: Reliability and discriminant validity. *Developmental Psychology, 29*, 870–880.

Bartholomew, K. (1990). Avoidance of intimacy: An attachment perspective. *Journal of Social and Personal Relationships, 7*, 147–178.

Bartholomew, K. (1993). From childhood to adult relationships: Attachment theory and research. In S. Duck (Ed.), *Understanding relationship processes: 2. Learning about relationships* (pp. 30–62), Beverly Hills, CA: Sage.

Bartholomew, K. (1997). Attachment processes: Individual and couple perspectives. *British Journal of Medical Psychology, 70*, 249–263.

Bartholomew, K., & Horowitz, L. M. (1991). Attachment styles among young adults: A test of a four-category model. *Journal of Personality and Social Psychology, 61*, 226–244.

Bartholomew, K., & Shaver, P. (1998). Methods of assessing adult attachment: Do they converge? In J. A. Simpson & W. S. Rholes (Eds.), *Attachment theory and close relationships* (pp. 25–45). New York: Guilford Press.

Bellg, A. J. (1995). *Adult attachment and adjustment to breast cancer.* Unpublished doctoral dissertation, University of Rochester, Rochester, New York.

Bradley, C. L. (1996). *Generativity status measure: Interview and scoring manual.* Unpublished manuscript, Simon Fraser University, Burnaby, British Columbia, Canada.

Bradley, C. L., & Marcia, J. E. (1997). Generativity-stagnation: Development of a status model. *Developmental Review, 17*, 262–290.

Campbell, D. T., & Fiske, D. W. (1959). Convergent and discriminant validation by the multitrait-multimethod matrix. *Psychological Bulletin, 56*, 81–105.

Cannell, C. F., & Kahn, R. L. (1968). Interviewing. In G. Lindzey & E. Aronson (Eds.), *The handbook of social psychology* (2nd ed., Vol. 2, pp. 526–595). Reading, MA: Addison-Wesley.

Cohen, J. (1968). A coefficient of agreement for nominal scales. *Educational and Psychological Measurement, 20*, 37–46.

Colby, A., & Kohlberg, L. (Eds.). (1987). *The measurement of moral judgement, Vols. 1–2.* Cambridge, MA: Cambridge University Press.

Cronbach, L. J. (1988). Five perspectives on the validity argument. In H. Wainer & H. I. Braun (Eds.), *Test validity* (pp. 3–17). Hillsdale, NJ: Erlbaum.

Cronbach, L. J., & Meehl, P. E. (1955). Construct validity in psychological tests. *Psychological Bulletin, 52,* 177–193.

Dutton, D. G., Saunders, K., Starzomski, A. J., & Bartholomew, K. (1994). Intimacy-anger and insecure attachment as precursors of abuse in intimate relationships. *Journal of Applied Social Psychology, 24,* 1367–1386.

Erikson, E. H. (1959). Identity and the life cycle. *Psychological Issues.* Monograph No. 1.

Fiore, J., Becker, J., & Coppel, D. B. (1983). Social network interactions: A buffer or a stress. *American Journal of Community Psychology, 11,* 423–439.

Fleiss, J. L. (1981). *Statistical methods for rates and proportions.* New York: Wiley.

Fowler, F. J. (1988). *Survey research methods: Vol. 1*(rev. ed.). Newbury Park, CA: Sage.

Fraley, R. C., & Waller, N. G. (1998). Adult attachment patterns: A test of the typological model. In J. A. Simpson & S. Rholes (Eds.), *Attachment theory and close relationships.* (pp. 77–114), New York: Guilford Press.

Gangestad, S., & Snyder, M. (1985). To carve nature at its joints: On the existence of discrete classes in personality. *Psychological Review, 92,* 317–349.

Gilligan, C. (1982). *In a different voice: Psychological theory and women's development.* Cambridge, MA: Harvard University Press.

Gilligan, C., & Attanucci, J. (1988). Two moral orientations: Gender differences and similarities. *Merrill-Palmer Quarterly, 34,* 223–237.

Gluck, S. B., & Patai, D. (Eds.). (1991). *Women's words: The feminist practice of oral history.* New York: Routledge.

Gorden, R. L. (1987). *Interviewing: Strategy, techniques and tactics* (4th ed.). Chicago: Dorsey Press.

Griffin, D. W., & Bartholomew, K. (1994a). The metaphysics of measurement: The case of adult attachment. In K. Bartholomew & D. Perlman (Eds.), *Advances in personal relationships: Volume. 5. Attachment processes in adulthood* (pp. 17–52), London: Jessica Kingsley.

Griffin, D. W., & Bartholomew, K. (1994b). Models of the self and other: Fundamental dimensions underlying measures of adult attachment. *Journal of Personality and Social Psychology, 67,* 430–445.

Grotevant, H. D., & Adams, G. R. (1984). Development of an objective measure to assess ego identity in adolescence: Validation and replication. *Journal of Youth and Adolescence, 13,* 419–438.

Hazan, C., & Shaver, P. (1987). Romantic love conceptualized as an attachment process. *Journal of Personality and Social Psychology, 52,* 511–524.

Henderson, A. Z., Bartholomew, K., & Dutton, D. G. (1997). He loves me; He loves me not: Attachment and separation resolution of abused women. *Journal of Family Violence, 12,* 169–191.

Horowitz, L. M., Inouye, D., & Siegelman, E. Y. (1979). On averaging judges' ratings to increase their correlation with an external criterion. *Journal of Consulting and Clinical Psychology, 47,* 453–458.

Kobak, R., & Sceery, A. (1988). Attachment in late adolescence: Working models, affect regulation, and representations of self and others. *Child Development, 59,* 135–146.

Kohlberg, L. (1976). Moral stages and moralization: The cognitive-developmental approach. In T. Lickona (Ed.), *Moral development and behavior: Theory, research, and social issues* (pp. 31–35). New York: Holt, Rinhart & Winston.

Krebs, D. L., Vermeulen, S. C., Denton, K. L., & Carpendale, J. I. (1994). Gender and perspective differences in moral judgment and moral orientation. *Journal of Moral Education, 23,* 17–26.

Liebetrau, A. M. (1983). *Measures of association.* Newbury Park, CA: Sage.

Loevinger, J., & Wessler, R. (1970). *Measuring ego development: Vol. 1.* San Francisco: Jossey-Bass.

Lyons, N. (1982). *The manual for analyzing responses to the question: How would you describe yourself to yourself?* Unpublished manuscript, Harvard Graduate School of Education.

Main, M., Kaplan, N., & Cassidy, J. (1985). Security in infancy, childhood, and adulthood: A move to the level of representation. *Monographs of the Society for Research in Child Development, 50* (1–2), 66–104.

Marcia, J. E. (1966). Development and validation of ego identity status. *Journal of Personality and Social Psychology, 3,* 551–558.

Marcia, J. E., Waterman, A. S., Matteson, D. R., Archer, S., & Orlofsky, J. (1993). *Ego identity: A handbook for psychosocial research.* New York: Springer-Verlag.

Matteson, D. R. (1993). Interviewers and interviewing. In J. E. Marcia, A. S. Waterman, D. R. Matteson, S. Archer, & J. Orlofsky (Eds.), *Ego identity: A handbook for psychosocial research* (pp. 137–155). New York: Springer-Verlag.

Mayer, J. D., & Bower, G. H. (1986). Learning and memory for personality prototypes. *Journal of Personality and Social Psychology, 51,* 473–492.

Meehl, P. E. (1992). Factors and taxa, traits and types, differences of degree and differences in kind. *Journal of Personality, 60,* 117–174.

Merriam, S. B. (1988). *Case study research in education: A qualitative approach.* San Francisco: Jossey-Bass.

Mishler, E. G. (1986). *Research interviewing: Context and narrative.* Cambridge, MA: Harvard University Press.

Nisbett, R. E., & Wilson, T. D. (1977). Telling more than we can know: Verbal reports on mental processes. *Psychological Review, 84,* 231–259.

Nunnally, J. C. (1978). *Psychometric theory* (2nd ed.) New York: McGraw Hill.

Orlofsky, J. L., Marcia, J. E., & Lesser, I. (1973). Ego identity status and the intimacy versus isolation crisis of young adulthood. *Journal of Personality and Social Psychology, 27,* 211–219.

Phinney, J. S. (1989). Stages of ethnic identity development in minority group adolescents. *Journal of Early Adolescence, 9,* 34–49.

Podd, M. H. (1972). Ego identity status and morality: The relationship between two developmental constructs. *Developmental Psychology, 6,* 497–507.

Poole, J. A., & Bartholomew, K. (1996). *Coding manual for the Peer Attachment Interview.* Unpublished manuscript, Simon Fraser University, British Columbia, Canada.

Rosch, E. (1978). Principles of categorization. In E. Rosch & B. B. Lloyd (Eds.), *Cognition and categorization* (pp. 27–48). Hillsdale, NJ: Erlbaum.

Rosenthal, R., & Rosnow, R. L. (1984). *Essentials of behavioral research: Methods and data analysis.* New York: McGraw-Hill.

Rubin, Z., & Mitchell, C. (1976). Couples research as couples counseling: Some unintended effects of studying close relationships. *American Psychologist, 34,* 17–25.

Scharfe, E., & Bartholomew, K. (1994). Reliability and stability of adult attachment patterns. *Personal Relationships, 1,* 23–43.

Scharfe, E., & Bartholomew, K. (1995). Accommodation and attachment representations in young couples. *Journal of Social and Personal Relationships, 12,* 389–401.

Schuman, H., & Converse, J. (1971). Effects on black and white interviewers on black responses in 1968. *Public Opinion Quarterly, 35,* 44–68.

Schuman, H., & Kalton, G. (1985). Survey methods. In G. Lindzey & E. Aronson (Eds.), *The handbook of social psychology* (3rd ed., Vol. 1, pp. 635–697). Reading, MA: Addison-Wesley.

Shrout, P. E., & Fleiss, J. L. (1979). Interclass correlations: Uses in assessing rater reliability. *Psychological Bulletin, 86,* 420–428.

Skoe, E. E. (1993). *The ethic of care interview manual.* Unpublished manuscript, University of Tromsö, Tromsö, Norway.

Skoe, E. E., & Marcia, J. E. (1991). A care-based measure of morality and its relation to ego identity. *Merrill-Palmer Quarterly, 37,* 289–304.

Sochting, I., Skoe, E. E., & Marcia, J. E. (1994). Care-oriented moral reasoning and prosocial behavior: A question of gender or sex role orientation. *Sex Roles: A Journal of Research, 31,* 131–147.

Steele, H., & Steele, M. (1994). Intergenerational patterns of attachment. In K. Bartholomew & D. Perlman (Eds.), *Advances in personal relationships: Volume 5. Attachment processes in adulthood* (pp. 93–120), London: Jessica Kingsley.

Tee, K. (1996). *Between two cultures: Exploring the voices of first and second generation South Asian women.* Unpublished doctoral dissertation, Simon Fraser University, Burnaby, British Columbia, Canada.

Tetlock, P. E., & Suedfeld, P. (1988). Integrative complexity coding of verbal behavior. In C. Antaki (Ed.), *Analyzing lay explanation: A casebook of methods* (pp. 72–87). Beverly Hills, CA: Sage.

van Ijzendoorn, M. H. (1995). Adult attachment representations, parental responsiveness, and infant attachment: A meta-analysis of the predictive validity of the Adult Attachment Interview. *Psychological Bulletin, 117,* 387–403.

Vaughn, C. E., & Leff, J. P. (1976). The measurement of expressed emotion in the families of psychiatric patients. *British Journal of Social and Clinical Psychology, 15,* 157–165.

Waterman, A. (1982). Identity development from adolescence to adulthood: An extension of theory and a review of research. *Developmental Psychology, 18,* 341–358.

APPENDIX A. EXCERPTS FROM THE GENERATIVITY STATUS MEASURE CODING MANUAL

In her coding manual Bradley discusses each of the 5 Generativity prototypes in depth. The following excerpts are taken from her description of the Agentic status.

The paragraph below introduces the Agentic prototype in a general way.

Agentic

Agentic is characterized by high involvement in self as self relates to the world: an identification of oneself with one's personal goals and achievements. *Agentic* individuals can be very productive, but may be spread too thin, or have too concentrated a focus to reliably guide others. Highly *Agentic* individuals may see others as peripheral to their own concerns and therefore uninteresting. Tolerance of limitations or impediments to personal goals may be lacking: they tend to perceive others as either contributing to or obstructing their path.

It is important not to be caught in a "workaholic" simplification of this prototype. *Agentic* is much more than simply busy. In fact, business can be characteristic of any of the prototypes. What distinguishes the *Agentic* style from others is that respondents tend to have difficulty guiding others when the others' pursuits differ from their own, or will cause some degree of personal inconvenience. Others are seen as needed extensions of the self more than as separate beings, and efforts on their part to disengage may be perceived as potential threats to the *Agentic*'s own objectives. Consequently, the *Agentic* prototype is less tolerant of others' independent aspirations and requirements. When conflict arises, *Agentic* respondents may reject or dismiss the individual and seek a replacement so that they may continue uninterrupted. *Agentic* individuals desire recognition from others because this confirms their power-base, provides credibility to continue carrying out their goals unimpeded, and brings more individuals to their cause. At their best, then, these individuals can be inspiring, committed to their ideals, and can be great artists, scientists, or impressive achievers; but their primary motivation will be personal rather than global, even though this may be a very real offshoot of their activities.

Next, Bradley describes the prototype in each of the specific content domains discussed in the interview. Below she illustrates how the Agentic prototype might look in the content domain of work.

Work

They may be very busy, and have a position of some responsibility. They seem to be constantly striving to meet deadlines, or maximize their output. They may have minimal contact with the people they deal with beyond work-related concerns.

She then gives several examples of actual interview excerpts from the work domain typical of individuals who would receive a low, moderate, or high scoring on the Agentic prototype. Her examples are numbered for clarity: A refers to Agentic, W refers to the work domain, and 4 refers to example # 4.

Example AW4

I: Do you feel that you've accomplished, or are on your way to accomplishing, your career goals?

R: Oh yeah, I far exceeded them, just blew them away.

I: What are your most valued accomplishments?

R: Currently, I have the best-selling book in the world in my field. As far as my occupation goes, I guess I'm a person who has always loved writing and wanted to do it. I tried to make some really original points, and in some chapters tried to tell the field where it should be going, not so much where it is now. I tried to point out this is telling the students what is happening now and more of it should happen, and I can do this by putting it in a textbook, and making sure every student and teacher has to read this year after year and think about it... And I get tons of fan mail, tons of it, from other writers, and so yeah, that's always been one of my goals, and I think it's a very important thing I did. Certainly I worked towards it for 6 years of my life, 6:00 a.m. every morning... I'm most happy when I'm striving, and it's starting to come clear that maybe I'm going to get it, that's the thrill... I've done very well as far as my career goes, I've published way beyond what most people do...

I: How would you react when someone questions your authority?

R: It depends on what... I would never be in a position of giving someone a direct order. Usually, my authority is such that I don't have to order people to do anything, I just suggest that it might be a good idea to do that, but would never say "you do this." Now if someone working for me said "Stuff it," they

wouldn't work for me anymore, but I guess on the other hand - do you know the concept "noblesse oblige?" I'm a strong advocate of that, and I can be a pretty aggressive person . . . .

She then comments on how this woman might be scored and why.

This excerpt rates in the high range on *Agentic* (a 9 would be appropriate). The respondent is extremely self absorbed, and has a remarkable opinion of her influence and skill. Others do not figure, except most peripherally, in her response. Inclusivity for other people's viewpoints and priorities appears to be minimal.

In the next section Bradley goes through the same process in a new content domain, this time in the area of family. In this section it is also interesting to note that Bradley spends some time clarifying an area that could potentially be confusing for coders, how the Agentic differs from the Conventional prototype in regards to attitudes about family.

Family

In the area of family concerns, the Agentic may look similar to the *Conventional*, in the desire to imbue the children with his or her own values and directions. The main difference will be either an isolation from the children, or difficulty perceiving family members' choices and desires as separate from his or her own.

Example AF4:

I: How would you describe your relationship with your children?

R: My family is a big priority of course. And as a family, we have goals, goals that everyone can share in. So take this business here – I built it up from nothing, and I've been very successful, my name means something in the community. And we're thinking of expanding into the European market, opening a branch in England. My son, he's 21 now, finished his university degree, and it's time he got involved. So we're sending him overseas to start up this new branch.

I: How did you and the family come to this decision?

R: Well, I wouldn't say it wasn't without some – ah, discussion, shall we say. My wife is really opposed, she doesn't want him to have to leave everything he knows. And frankly, the rest of the family doesn't see the benefits of him going either. But he's going, and I truly think it's our big chance to make a real splash with this business. So – he's over there now, getting things together for us to start. It's an exciting time, a real opportunity for him – and for the rest of us. So, people will come around. And he doesn't have to be there forever, after all.

Example AF4 describes a parent-child relationship in which the needs and desires of the child are quite secondary to the goals and ambitions of the parent. The key, in differentiating *Agentic* from *Conventional* responses with respect to children, is the level of involvement in the children, and the perception of these as separate individuals. While Conventional may have difficulty accepting a child's independent wishes, the child – and their interests, activities, or desires – will take shape in the response, whereas there may be little description of the child, in terms of a recognizable individual, in a strongly *Agentic* response. Thus in the excerpt above we learn very little about the children themselves; rather, we learn more about the parent, the parent's goals, and the means by which he intends to accomplish those goals... A very high rating on the *Agentic* dimension (8 or 9) is appropriate for this excerpt.

Excerpt from C. Bradley (1996). *Generativity status measure: Interview and scoring manual.* Unpublished manuscript, Simon Fraser University, Burnaby, British Columbia, Canada.

CHAPTER TWELVE

Content Analysis and Narrative Analysis

CHARLES P. SMITH

This chapter introduces two important approaches to the analysis of qualitative material. Content analysis deals primarily with verbal material, but may be used with nonverbal material as well; narrative analysis deals only with verbal material, usually stories or accounts of personal experiences. These techniques may be used to study individuals, groups, cultures, or historical periods by means of either qualitative or quantitative research.

Of what special value are these methods that deal primarily with the analysis of samples of language? For one thing, language is a major, and often distinctive, source of information for social and behavioral scientists. Language both facilitates and reveals the development of persons and cultures. Language permits inferences regarding subjective experiences, intentions, and internal structures that influence overt behavior. Moreover, many phenomena of interest occur largely in the form of overt verbal behavior, including communication, socialization, interpersonal relations, attribution, moral reasoning, role-playing, and stereotyping.

Content and narrative analysis can provide information that may or may not be accessible by other methods. Sometimes qualitative material can best reveal innermost thoughts, frames of reference, reactions to situations, and cultural conventions. In fact, language often tells more about people than they want to disclose, or than they know about themselves, and it can bring to light things a researcher might not think to ask about. Archival material such as letters, diaries, and speeches may provide the only source of information about persons who are dead, unavailable, or uncooperative, and written or oral materials may provide the only feasible way of studying individuals in depth, earlier historical periods, or large-scale social phenomena, such as differences among cultures.

Research methods employing written or spoken language have gone in and out of vogue. In the late 19th and early 20th centuries, when psychology was regarded as the science of the mind, eminent scholars, including Galton, William James, Wundt, Freud, G. Stanley Hall, and Piaget, made extensive use of accounts of personal experiences, and the use of personal documents in the work of Thomas and Znaniecki (1918, 1919, 1920) demonstrated the importance of the subjective aspects of social life. However, in the 1920s behaviorism redefined psychology as the science of behavior; rejected the subjective, introspective, and mentalistic; and sought basic laws, often in the behavior of inarticulate organisms. Fortunately, during this period attention to the inner life continued in the writings of those who were clinically, humanistically, phenomenologically, or existentially oriented.

When interest in cognition and affect returned to mainstream psychology during the 1950s and 1960s, a basis had been laid for a more rigorous scientific approach to these topics. For some researchers this entailed reliable measurement by means of "fixed response" methods such as inventories, questionnaires, and hypothetical situations about which judgments or attributions are requested in terms of provided alternatives. For other investigators these methods did not capture the complexity of human thought and behavior. Some turned to methods such as content

For their many insightful contributions, I am greatly indebted to my wife, Judith Smith, and to colleagues including Colette Daiute, Dan P. McAdams, Harry T. Reis, David Rindskopf, Jody Veroff, and Joseph Veroff.

Correspondence should be directed to Charles P. Smith, 1724 Allard Rd., Chapel Hill, NC 27514 (e-mail: cpjbsmith@earthlink.net).

analysis and narrative analysis that may be applied to phenomena that are less artificial and more reflective of an individual's constructs and contextual organization of experience.

The earlier-established method of content analysis is considered first and then compared with the more recent method of narrative analysis.

PART I: CONTENT ANALYSIS

Part I first considers the nature, scope, and applicability of content analysis and then explains how to conduct content-analytic research.

Characteristics and Uses of Content Analysis

DEFINITIONS AND TERMINOLOGY. *Content analysis* is a technique used to extract desired information from a body of material (usually verbal) by systematically and objectively identifying specified characteristics of the material (cf. Berelson, 1954; Holsti, 1969; Stone, Dunphy, Smith, & Ogilvie, 1966). The impartial and consistent application to all selected material of explicitly defined procedures of analysis is intended to be objective in the sense of yielding unbiased results that can be reproduced by other qualified investigators. Content analysis differs from clinical *interpretation*, which is more holistic and provisional, and for which specific criteria are not made explicit in advance.

Actually, the term "content" in content analysis is something of a misnomer, because verbal materials may be examined for content, form (e.g., style, structure), function (e.g., person gives suggestion), or sequence of communications (see Bakeman, this volume, Ch. 6).

By means of content analysis a large body of qualitative information may be reduced to a smaller and more manageable form of representation. In addition, qualitative information may be transformed into quantitative information, such as category frequencies or ratings. The term *coding* is commonly used to refer to the process of classifying or rating, and those who do the classifying are usually referred to as coders, although they are sometimes called judges, raters, or scorers.

Content analysis is applied to qualitative material, whether obtained from archival records, recording of naturally occurring behavior, or evoked responses (as from interviews or projective methods). Although the material to be analyzed may consist of recorded interactions, nonverbal behavior, photographs, filmed actions, graphic and artistic productions, or music (e.g., Simonton, 1994), content analysis usually employs written or transcribed verbal material that I sometimes refer to as "text." The categorization of observable speech and behavior, although conceptually similar to content analysis, is usually dealt with under the heading of observational methods (see Bakeman, this volume, Ch. 6).

A sample of written or spoken language is used verbatim, preserving misstatements, omissions, errors of spelling and grammar, and so forth. Words, phrases, or errors in material to be analyzed may be classified in terms of their "manifest" or ordinary meaning or in terms of their "latent" or inferred underlying meaning.

HISTORICAL BACKGROUND. Examples of content analysis date back to the classification of theological terms in hymns in 18th-century Sweden (Dovring, 1954–1955) and to the analysis in 1838 of visual imagery in the dreams of people who had become blind at different ages (Van de Castle, 1994). Journalistic studies of trends in topics covered in newspapers date from the 1890s (Berelson, 1954). In social science, the value of content analysis was recognized early in the 20th century by such scholars as Max Weber and Harold Lasswell. During the 1940s and 1950s, major figures, including Berelson, Lazarsfeld, Osgood, Pool, and R. K. White, introduced many of the conventions of content analysis used in contemporary communications research (Holsti, 1969). The practical utility of content analysis was demonstrated during World War II in studies of propaganda techniques and enemy morale.

Although the term *content analysis* was probably first used in the field of journalism, psychologists used similar procedures to study individuals and groups. Notable examples include the Thematic Apperception Test (TAT; Murray, 1938), the use of personal documents (Allport, 1942), the analysis of verbal exchanges in small groups (Bales, 1950), and the analysis of dream reports (Hall & Van de Castle, 1966). Early work on computer-assisted content analysis culminated in a landmark volume by Stone et al. (1966).

USES OF CONTENT ANALYSIS. Content analysis may be used for exploratory research, theory development, hypothesis testing, or applied research. It may be used for description or for inference. Most people are familiar with the concept of content analysis even if they do not know the term. For instance, on January 14, 1996, *The New York Times* reported that a computer-assisted analysis of the vocabulary of an unsigned Elizabethan elegy indicated that it was probably authored by Shakespeare.

Analyses of verbal and other symbolic materials may differentiate between individuals, groups, or cultures. For example, content analysis has been used to distinguish between stories told by women who were or were not victims of childhood sexual abuse (Arkhurst, 1994) and between suicide notes that were genuine or simulated (Ogilvie, Stone, & Schneidman, 1966).

Conversely, content analysis may be used to show that groups that are thought to differ in certain respects do not differ. For example, stereotypes regarding differences between men and women or ethnic groups may not be supported by the blind analysis of appropriate materials from each group. An historically influential study of this type was conducted by Hooker (1957), who asked expert clinicians to make a blind analysis of the projective test responses of heterosexual and homosexual men who were closely matched for age, education, and IQ. At the time of her research, homosexuality was regarded as a severe emotional disorder and was often treated with electroshock therapy. To their surprise, when the two groups of unlabeled responses were mixed together, the clinicians could not identify heterosexuals and homosexuals more accurately than would be expected by chance. Hooker's research was credited with contributing to the eventual removal of homosexuality from the list of psychiatric disorders (*The New York Times*, November 22, 1996). When categories of analysis are explicit, this type of study provides a powerful method for challenging ideas concerning invidious differences between groups.

Content analysis may reveal properties of texts that might go unnoticed by a reader, as evidenced by R. K. White's (1947) values analysis of Richard Wright's autobiography *Black Boy*. White comments:

Without making a systematic inventory of *all* the facts of a given kind, it is difficult to realize just how important and how insidious the errors of omission are in any ordinary subjective impression of a book or a personality. The errors of omission are, moreover, highly systematic errors; there is an inevitable selection of just those facts which fit most neatly into the interpreter's unacknowledged wishes and preconceptions. (1947, p. 441–442)

Also, unexpected information may be brought to light by content analysis. For example, contrary to their expectation, Osgood and Walker (1959) found "no evidence for greater *disorganization* of encoding behavior in suicide notes as compared with ordinary letters to friends and relatives" (p. 66).

Fixed response measures are clearly preferable to content analytic measures for obtaining some kinds of information. Alternatively, content analytic measures may reveal more adequately the complexity of phenomena such as childhood experiences, moral reasoning, or cognitive styles. Open-ended interview questions, for example, permit a respondent to express his or her own constructs and frame of reference. Even interview responses may be of limited value if the respondent is not candid or is unable to provide information about matters of which he or she is unaware, such as ambivalence toward parents or children. To obtain that kind of information it may be necessary to analyze material obtained by means of unobtrusive or projective methods. *Unobtrusive measures* are obtained from behavior that has occurred for some other reason than the investigator's research. Such measures are nonreactive in the sense that the person is not aware of, or affected by, the measurement process. Letters to a friend, for example, might reveal feelings about parents that the writer might not reveal to an interviewer. Projective techniques, such as the thematic apperceptive method, might reveal still deeper conflicts of which the person is not consciously aware.

McClelland, Koestner, and Weinberger (1989) pointed out that projective measures of motives yield different information than self-report measures of motives. The former (implicit motives) best predict spontaneous behavior and long-term behavioral trends, whereas the latter (self-attributed motives) best predict near-term performance in situations where explicit incentives elicit striving for normative goals. For some purposes prediction may be improved by combining both kinds of measures. Possible reasons why the two types of measures often are not correlated are discussed by McClelland et al. (1989).

Although some kinds of variables, such as explanatory style, appear to be measured equally well by content analysis and by self-report (Peterson, 1992), other kinds of variables, such as conceptual–integrative complexity and implicit motivation, are best reflected in "thought samples," which permit a subject to express her or his characteristic construction of experience.

SCOPE AND APPLICABILITY OF CONTENT ANALYSIS. Illustrative uses of content analysis in different fields of psychology are presented in Table 12.1. In social sciences other than psychology, the technique has been used to describe and compare cultures and to study such topics as cultural change, propaganda, media coverage of political campaigns, factors affecting voting behavior, political leadership, the decision-making of corporate executives, family dynamics, and suicide. Content analysis has also been used in research in education, geography, psychiatry, and psycholinguistics.

TABLE 12.1. Illustrative Topics Studied by Means of Content Analysis

Field of Psychology	Illustrative Topics
Clinical	Childhood physical and sexual abuse, depression, effects of psychotherapy, object relations, personality assessment, suicide
Developmental	Conceptions of motherhood, development of conceptual complexity, ego development, language acquisition, moral reasoning, preschool crisis situations
Educational	Classroom climate, learning logs, problem-solving, readability of text, writing skills
Health	Emotional expression, factors affecting the immune system, causal explanations, quality of life, stress and coping, self-help groups
Industrial-organizational	Buyer–seller interaction, ethnicity and gender in advertisements, leadership, managerial success
Personality	Anxiety, creativity, cognitive and attributional styles, dependency, dreams, emotions, moods, motivation, personal causation, values
Social	Aggression, attributions, authoritarianism, belief systems, generativity, groupthink, gender roles, interpersonal relations, leadership, propaganda, self-definition, stereotypes, stigma

ARCHIVAL RESEARCH. Archival studies have employed personal and public documents to obtain information about such topic areas as attitudes and beliefs, aggression and violence, and leadership (Simonton, 1981). Winter (1992) has reviewed archival research including studies of eminent persons, societal motive patterns related to war and peace, the relationship of conceptual–integrative complexity to professional eminence, and the relationship of explanatory style to the electability of presidential candidates (see also Suedfeld, Tetlock, & Streufert, 1992).

The following studies illustrate the archival approach. Snowdon et al. (1996) found that a measure of idea density taken from autobiographies written by nuns in their 20s was strongly predictive of which nuns would develop Alzheimer's disease six decades later. When the autobiographies were written, Alzheimer's disease was unknown, and the use to which the archived materials would be put could not have been anticipated.

McClelland (1961) used both verbal and nonverbal archival material in a study of determinants of the rise and wane of economic growth in ancient Greece. Measures of economic growth at different historical periods were related to two different content-analytic measures of achievement motivation, one from Greek literature and one from designs on Greek vases (Aronson, 1958). Analyses revealed that signs of high achievement motivation were most frequent in a period of economic growth and significantly less frequent prior to economic decline.

COMMUNICATIONS RESEARCH. Content analysis has been applied most extensively in the cross-disciplinary field of communication (a) to study the substantive or formal characteristics of communications, (b) to make inferences about the characteristics and intentions of communicators, and (c) to make inferences from content about its effects on, or the characteristics of, its recipients. Berelson (1954), Holsti (1969), and Krippendorff (1980) summarized research on: (a) trends in communication content, (b) the comparison of different media, (c) style, (d) propaganda techniques, (e) military intelligence, (f) the intentions and psychological states of persons or groups, and (g) the attitudes, interests, and values of media audiences.

Two examples of contemporary research on communication and the mass media follow. Davis (1990) analyzed personal advertisements from a newspaper for evidence of sex-role stereotypes. He found that for desired attributes of a companion, women were more likely than men to specify "employment, financial, and intellectual status, as well as commitment, while men emphasized physical characteristics" (p. 43). Davis concluded that these differences were consistent with traditional sex-role stereotypes.

Taylor, Lee, and Stern (1995) analyzed photographic advertisements from business, women's general interest, and technical magazines and concluded that "Hispanic Americans are significantly underrepresented in magazine advertising, portrayals of Asian Americans reflect societal stereotypes, and [relative to prior research findings] portrayals of African Americans have become less stereotyped over the years" (p. 608).

INTERVIEWS, SURVEYS, AND OPEN-ENDED QUESTION-NAIRES. Content analysis is the primary method of obtaining information from responses to "unstructured" or "open-ended" questions. Interviews are used in many kinds of research, including communications research, cross-cultural research, life history research, and narrative analysis (see Visser, Krosnick, & Lavrikas, this volume, Ch. 9).

Note that it may be possible to locate interview responses obtained by another researcher (or survey organization) who has already asked some or all of the questions contemplated for new research – possibly with a larger and more representative sample than many researchers can afford. For example, archived open-ended questionnaires, completed for the Harvard Study of Adult Development, made possible longitudinal research by Peterson, Seligman, and Vaillant (1988), who showed that pessimistic causal explanations given in 1946 predicted physical illness three decades later.

The analysis of material from group interviews by Schneider, Wheeler, and Cox (1992) illustrates research in industrial–organizational psychology. These authors analyzed notes from 97 panel (group) interviews with 350 employees from three financial service companies. The groups were asked to discuss the service climate of their organizations. "Quantitative analyses of the 33 coded themes revealed the routines and rewards most strongly related to service passion: responsiveness to consumers, hiring procedures... [etc.]" (p. 705). The analysis also suggested which procedures could be modified in order to improve organizational functioning.

Finally, the interview setting may be used for additional purposes. Veroff (1992) and his associates have made extensive use of thematic apperceptive measures of motivation in survey research. Veroff explained how to select stimuli and code stories obtained from survey interviews.

PERSONALITY THEORY AND ASSESSMENT. Content-analytic research in personality ranges from intensive studies of individuals to cross-cultural research, using archival materials, interview responses, psychotherapy transcripts, reported dreams and daydreams, and responses to projective methods, including the TAT, the Rorschach, and sentence completion.

Qualitative research, with cross-cultural implications, is illustrated by the following study of personality taxonomy. Many Western psychologists have obtained evidence for a five-factor model of personality attributes, such as extraversion, emotional stability, and conscientiousness. To find out whether this model extends to non-Western cultures, Narayanan, Menon, and Levine (1995) asked students in two universities in India "to describe two 'critical incidents' observed in others or themselves that were particularly revealing about their personality" (p. 57). Coders not familiar with the five-factor model sorted incidents into a set of mutually exclusive meaningful categories. Ratings revealed that all but one of these categories were representative of the five factors, indicating that "the personality dimensions obtained with this qualitative culture-specific method were very similar to the Big Five structure" (p. 60), with only a few characteristics being specific to a non-Western culture.

Employing a projective technique, Ames & Riggio (1995) undertook to develop adolescent maladjustment norms for the Rotter Incomplete Sentences Blank. Such norms serve as guidelines for deciding whether to refer a student for counseling or therapy. High school and college students were asked to complete sentences "to express *your real feelings.*" Responses were scored for degree of conflict (0–6). The results led to a recommended maladjustment cut-off score for adolescents and to recommendations to bring coding criteria in line with contemporary social mores.

A procedure for validating a coding system is illustrated in a study by McAdams and Constantian (1983) who obtained a measure of intimacy motivation by means of content analysis of stories written about six TAT-type pictures by 50 male and female college students. To validate their measure, they used the motive scores to predict intimacy-relevant thought and behavior at a later date. An experience sampling method (ESM) was used to obtain reports from the students regarding the situations they were in and their thoughts and behaviors over the course of a week. Participants wore pagers and, when signaled, took out a form and wrote answers to open-ended questions regarding what they were doing and thinking about when they were paged. As expected, the higher the intimacy motive scores, the more often participants were thinking of interpersonal situations and were engaged in interpersonal behavior. (For more information about ESM, see Reis & Gable, this volume, Ch. 8.)

Much of the literature on dream research has been reviewed by Hall and Van de Castle (1966; Van de Castle, 1994), whose sophisticated content analyses of dream reports have provided information bearing on the validity of psychoanalytic theory, gender differences, and contextual factors affecting dream content.

Steps in Content-Analytic Research

Content-analytic research typically involves the steps described below. Although listed sequentially, some of the steps may overlap or be carried out concurrently.

1. State the research problem and the goal of the research. What is to be identified, described, or measured? State hypotheses, if any.
2. Decide whether content analysis will provide the needed information, either by itself or in conjunction with another method.
3. Decide what type of qualitative material will best provide the information needed.
4. Decide how to select the chosen material and the amount needed.
5. Decide on a content analysis (coding) system – either a preexisting one or one that you develop. What categories or rating dimensions will best yield the information you want?
6. Obtain pilot material on which to try out the coding system. Does the material yield the desired information? If you have devised a new coding system, does it need to be revised?
7. Train coders. Make sure that satisfactory intercoder agreement can be obtained using the pilot material.
8. Obtain the final material to be analyzed.
9. Code the material, with identifying characteristics removed, and determine intercoder agreement; or perform computer-assisted content analysis.
10. Analyze the data; carry out cross validation if appropriate.
11. Interpret the results. Compare your findings with norms, if available.

Some of the key steps will now be discussed in greater detail.

DECIDING ON THE TYPE OF MATERIAL TO BE ANALYZED. Obviously, the material selected should reflect the phenomenon being studied. For example, to learn about the values transmitted by a culture, one might choose material from mass media or from products assumed to be representative of the culture, such as films, folktales, or selections from children's readers.

Some types of material are more informative than others. A study by Combs (1947), for example, demonstrated that autobiographical material was less likely to reveal socially or personally unacceptable motives than TAT stories. Dreams, daydreams, TAT stories, narratives of personal experiences, and ESM responses are not equivalent (see Emmons & King, 1992; Gottschalk & Gleser, 1969; McAdams & Zeldow, 1993; Winter, 1992, among others). Other factors affecting the choice of material include its availability, the time and expense required to obtain it, and whether unobtrusive measures are needed.

ARCHIVAL MATERIALS. Archival materials include symbolic cultural products, personal documents, publications, records and official documents, broadcast media transcriptions, and so on. The selection and use of archival materials is discussed by Simonton (1981) and Winter (1992). Two major archives, with informative websites, include the Murray Research Center at Radcliffe College and the Inter-University Consortium for Political and Social Research (ICPSR). There are many other archives that are more specialized.

NATURALLY OCCURRING MATERIALS. To capture naturally occurring behavior one might record broadcasts of live events or, with appropriate permission, conversations, psychotherapy sessions, e-mail exchanges, or group deliberations. Depending on the circumstances, the persons involved may or may not be aware that they are being studied. Somewhere between naturally occurring materials and elicited materials are those obtained by the experience sampling method.

ELICITED MATERIALS. Elicited material, such as responses to interview questions or projective methods, is obtained specifically for research purposes. Such material "is usually taken to be indicative of something beyond itself. A particular statement, for example, . . . has significance to the researcher because it may be taken to indicate the presence of a certain attitude, value, cognitive structure, or the like" (Cartwright, 1953, p. 423).

The selection of pictorial or verbal cues for thematic apperceptive measures is discussed by Smith, Feld, and Franz (1992). To a large extent cues determine the type and amount of imagery obtained, and special cues may have to be developed for special populations, as was done by Henry (1951) for research with Native Americans.

ADVANTAGES AND DISADVANTAGES OF DIFFERENT TYPES OF MATERIAL. Each type of material has its own advantages. One is availability. If one wants to study survivors of the Holocaust, it would be expensive and time-consuming to identify and interview them. However, there are several archives where videotaped interviews of survivors are available for research (Suedfeld, 1996). Some archival materials also have the advantage of being nonreactive. On the other hand, archival materials may not be available in sufficient quantity or for the population of interest, or they may not constitute a representative sample of the population of interest.

Naturally occurring behavior may be of value for its spontaneity and ecological validity, but it may be difficult to record and time-consuming to transcribe, and it may not be possible to study naturally occurring behavior in a representative sample of some population.

With material elicited specifically for research purposes, the researcher has greater control over the sources of the information, the amount and kind of information obtained, and the conditions under which it is obtained. In an interview study, for example, the researcher can determine who the interviewers and respondents will be, how many interviews will be obtained, and what questions will be asked. However, the responses will be reactive and may be obtained only from persons who are willing and available to respond.

Different types of elicited material are preferable for different purposes. For example, in a study of leadership among Naval officers, Winter (1992) found that "motive scores based on 'ordinary' verbal material (in this case, critical-incident interviews) predicted leadership performance far better than did scores based on thematic apperceptive methods" (p. 111). Similarly, Emmons and King (1992) show that for some purposes ESM responses are preferable to thematic apperceptive stories for the assessment of motives.

OBTAINING THE MATERIAL TO BE ANALYZED (SAMPLING). For a few research problems the entire body of available material can be used (e.g., all of the existing letters of an important historical figure). More often, however, the total body of relevant material is too large to be analyzed (e.g., all major newspapers in the United States published during a 10-year period). On what basis is a selection to be made? This is a very important question, because sample selection and sample size affect the informativeness, reliability, and generalizability of the findings. Of many possible factors that can undermine the value and credibility

of content-analytic research, the most common, in my judgment, is inappropriate sampling and insufficient sample size.

Content analytic research usually requires selection of both (a) the material to be analyzed (e.g., interview responses, articles, folktales) and (b) the sources of that material (e.g., persons, publications, societies). To select sources and materials, one may use a probability or a nonprobability sampling plan. Probability sampling permits the selection of an unbiased sample that is representative of the population and makes it possible to generalize the findings from the sample to the entire population. (Sampling theory and procedures are reviewed by Visser, Krosnick, & Lavrikas, this volume, Ch. 9).

However, with the exception of survey and communications research, probability sampling is not common in content-analytic studies. For one thing, it may not be possible to identify all the members of the total relevant population (e.g., all people with AIDS). More often, the researcher may feel that it is not necessary to select a probability sample, particularly if the research is exploratory or involves theory development and the emphasis is on internal rather than external validity (see Judd, Smith, & Kidder, 1991). In such cases a nonprobability sample may be used.

Unfortunately, there is no way of knowing the extent to which any type of nonprobability sample is representative. The least desirable type of nonprobability sample is that chosen on the basis of convenience, that is, participants or materials are used because they are easily available. Patton (1990) reviewed preferable kinds of nonprobability samples and their rationales. In-depth qualitative study of one or a small number of cases can provide valuable insights into phenomena that can subsequently be studied by quantitative methods.

SAMPLING CONVENTIONS. Somewhat different sampling issues arise for different types of material. Perhaps the most elaborate set of sampling considerations arise in media research. For example, to sample personal ads, Davis (1990) made decisions about sampling newspapers, seasons, and days of the week. Taylor et al. (1995) sampled 1,616 pictorial advertisements from a cross section of magazines over a 1-year period. Berelson (1954) noted that it may be necessary in communications research to sample each of three layers: (a) publications or other sources (e.g., radio stations), (b) issues or dates, and (c) content within issues. In sampling publications or other sources of communications, one may need to take account of such factors as geographical location, frequency of publication, time of publication (morning or evening), target audience (women, sports fans), and size of circulation. For greater detail, see Holsti (1969) and Krippendorff (1980).

Sampling decisions encountered in cross-cultural research are illustrated in the work of Kalin, Davis, and McClelland (1966), who used folktales to study psychological correlates of heavy drinking in preliterate societies. In their research, the selection of societies and folktales was contingent on such factors as geographical area, separation of cultures, adequacy of folktale collections, and type of folktale.

In research using projective methods the sampling of content sometimes poses complex issues (see Smith et al., 1992). The sentence completion study described earlier (Ames & Riggio, 1995) illustrated some sampling decisions involving a projective method. The authors tested male and female students from public and private high schools in two geographical areas that differed in socioeconomic status. The material to be analyzed was sampled by the sentence stems, which had been selected on the basis of their ability to elicit responses that would reveal various kinds of inner conflicts. Although no actual population of items (sentence-completion stems) exists, one may construct a set of items intended to be representative of all possible items in the relevant domain (see Nunnally, 1978). The high internal consistency reliability (alpha = .91) of the scores suggests that a sufficient sample of items ($N = 40$) was used. Although the authors took some steps to ensure "varied representation," one could not safely generalize their findings to all U.S. adolescents, much less to those in other countries. Also, they did not obtain sufficient information to permit the recommendation of norms for different social and ethnic subgroups.

SAMPLE SIZE. After a rationale is adopted for selecting some elements from a larger population of elements, the researcher must decide how many elements to select. Sample size affects the range, reliability, and accuracy of the values measured. Simply put, too little material will not provide enough information on which to make a sound estimate of whatever is being assessed. The optimal size for a sample will depend on the aim and characteristics of the proposed research and such extrinsic factors as the amount of time, money, and personnel available. The chapter by Visser, Krosnick, & Lavrikas, in this volume, discusses how to determine sample size if one wishes to use sample values to estimate values in the total population. If

population values are not important, then sample size will be determined by the kinds of statistical analyses to be carried out and the level of power desired for those analyses. For qualitative research it is not possible to calculate the effects of different sample sizes, but the same general considerations of reliability and precision should be kept in mind in deciding on the size of a sample (see Patton, 1990).

CONTENT ANALYSIS (CODING) SYSTEMS. This section describes the properties of content analysis systems, explains how such systems are devised, how qualitative material can be quantified, and how computers may be used for content analysis.

The coding system is the heart of the content analytic method. It specifies the information to be obtained from the material to be analyzed. If appropriate categories of analysis are not used, vital information may not be detected, and the analysis may reveal nothing of interest (McAdams & Zeldow, 1993). The coding system is also the primary basis for the objectivity of the method. It makes distinctions explicit and public, so that other researchers can use the same procedure.

Coding systems comprise (a) definitions of units of material to be analyzed, (b) categories or dimensions of classification, and (c) rules for applying the system. This information is recorded in a *coding manual* that also provides examples of what to code and what not to code for each category or dimension. The manual may also contain practice materials.

UNITS. Units provide a standard basis of comparison of one text with another. The absolute amount of some behavior is often less informative than its rate of occurrence or frequency per unit (Hall & Van de Castle, 1966). The advantages and disadvantages of different kinds of units (e.g., narrow vs. broad) are discussed by Holsti (1969, pp. 104ff.) and by Krippendorff (1980). There is no single best unit; what is best depends on the objectives of the research.

The term *text unit* is used here to refer to the largest body of material subjected to analysis in a particular investigation (e.g., an essay, an editorial, or an interview). Although a text unit usually has natural boundaries, as in the examples given above, it may have arbitrary boundaries (e.g., Snowden et al., 1996, coded only the last 10 sentences of each autobiography).

The term *coding unit* (or recording unit) is used to refer to that part of the text unit to which coding categories or dimensions are applicable. A coding unit may be a designated portion or segment of the text, or it may be a designated aspect of the text, such as themes or characters.

Segments that have been used as coding units include (a) the entire text unit (e.g., an essay), (b) linguistically defined segments (e.g., words, clauses, sentences), (c) response segments (e.g., a response to an interview question), (d) physically defined segments (e.g., newspaper column inches), and (e) temporal segments (e.g., minutes of broadcast time).

Perhaps the most important aspect of the text that has been used as a coding unit is the *theme*, by which is meant the expression of a single idea, a statement about a topic, or a motif (e.g., themes of loneliness or accomplishment). A theme may be expressed in a few words, a phrase, or one or more sentences. When the theme is the coding unit, each theme in a text unit is identified by some specified criterion and then classified according to its properties. The character has also been used as a coding unit, in which case each character is classified according to some scheme, such as sex, role, or type of behavior (see Hall & Van de Castle, 1966).

Finally, the term *context unit* refers to the largest body of material that may be considered in order to make a coding decision (cf. Berelson, 1954). For example, to classify a word as a part of speech, it may be necessary to consider the entire sentence in which it appears; to interpret and classify a response to a particular interview question, it may be necessary to consider responses to the preceding and succeeding questions.

CATEGORIES AND DIMENSIONS. Categories and dimensions specify the information sought by the researcher – the variables to be assessed. Their application yields either a qualitative description or a quantitative measure of the variables of interest. Categories provide for classification into two or more alternatives, such as present–absent, or Christian–Jewish–Muslim, etc. Categories may represent underlying continuous variables, such as favorable, no opinion, unfavorable; or they may represent discrete nominal classes that belong in no quantitative order.

Some discussions of coding systems have not made clear that the terms character and theme can be used to refer to coding units in one system and to coding categories in another. When each character in a story is identified and then classified, the character is the coding unit. However, when the information desired is the number of characters in a story, the story is the coding unit, and the number of characters is the category.

Themes are coding units when each theme is identified and then classified. The coding systems developed by David McClelland, John W. Atkinson, and their colleagues to measure motivation (e.g., McClelland, Atkinson, Clark, & Lowell, 1953) used stories as coding units, and themes, or types of "imagery," as coding categories. For example, in a story, feeling good about winning an essay contest would be indicative of the category "positive goal affect." An achievement motive score for each story is obtained by counting the number of thematic coding categories present.

Different kinds of coding categories or dimensions may be needed for the analysis of the formal properties of a text, such as psychological styles. For example, a category used for scoring stories for *self-definition* (Stewart, 1992) does not employ substantive themes but rather the presence or absence of causal thinking, regardless of content. As this example indicates, units for coding formal properties tend to be defined at a more abstract level than content units. For other examples, refer to the coding systems for explanatory style (Peterson, 1992) and conceptual–integrative complexity (Suedfeld et al., 1992).

Discussions of classification (e.g., Holsti, 1969, pp. 95ff.) usually specify that categories should be unidimensional, exhaustive, mutually exclusive, and independent (i.e., an entry in one category does not affect an entry in another category). These properties of categories have important implications for the statistical analysis of the data, including calculations of intercoder agreement. However, some researchers intentionally have employed coding categories that are not unidimensional, or not independent, or not mutually exclusive (e.g., Funkhouser, 1973; McAdams, 1992; Suedfeld et al., 1992; Weber, 1990, pp. 23ff., 32ff.).

Categories can also differ in breadth or inclusiveness, abstractness, and degree of inference required. Idiographic categories can be developed to apply only to a single individual and may be used for the intensive study of one person (e.g., throughout psychotherapy). However, most coding systems employ general categories that enable comparisons among individuals or groups.

Coding dimensions represent continuous variables. Intensity or degree can be measured by means of a numerical scale such as 0 (*no conflict*) to 6 (*extreme conflict*). Coding for intensity is problematic, however. When intensity is implied by words in the text (e.g., apprehensive vs. terrified; miffed vs. enraged), a researcher may wish to preserve that information. However, it is often difficult for a coder to make reliable judgments of degree or for a classification system to specify appropriate intervals on a quantitative scale. For example, for degree of aggression, does killing an animal represent more or less aggression than injuring a human being?

Another way of assessing the degree of importance of a variable is to record the frequency of occurrence of some type of imagery, such as that indicative of aggression. Usually, each instance is given equal weight. The number of tallies in a coding unit is taken to be a measure of degree of aggression on the assumption that the greater the importance of the variable to the source, the more often it will be mentioned. When a frequency count is made, however, it is usually important to control for the length of the coding unit, because longer material tends to yield higher frequency counts. To help offset the effect of differences in length, many coding systems do not employ frequency counts; instead a category like aggression is scored only once per coding unit, no matter how many times it appears.

Although measures of intensity and frequency of the same variable from the same text tend to be positively correlated, they measure different aspects of the variable. Partly for this reason, frequency measures have also been considered problematic as measures of the importance or strength of a variable. Hall and Van de Castle (1966), Holsti (1969, pp. 122ff.), and Stone et al. (1966) discussed issues involved in measures of frequency and intensity. In their scales for anxiety, hostility, and other variables, Gottschalk and Gleser (1969) dealt with intensity, frequency, and length of material by obtaining a scale score based on summing the number of weighted categories coded per 100 words (see also Gottschalk, 1995).

RULES. Rules explain how to apply the coding system and how to deal with instances not explicitly addressed by the system. Rules may tell how to distinguish units, apply categories, and record coding decisions. An example of a rule is "Do not infer the presence of emotion on the basis of the setting or activity in which the character is engaged" (Hall & Van de Castle, 1966).

CHARACTERISTICS OF CODING SYSTEMS. Coding systems vary in their explicitness and detail. At the least explicit end of the continuum are systems that provide general guidelines for the classification of verbal material, together with a few examples. Generally such systems assume prior mastery of some theoretical orientation such as psychoanalytic ego psychology. Such systems are often intended to be used primarily for clinical or other applied purposes rather than for research. Although explicitness is a matter of degree,

guidelines alone usually do not constitute a content analysis system as commonly understood, due to their insufficient specificity and the resulting insufficient interjudge agreement among coders who are not immersed in the theoretical orientation underlying the guidelines.

Coding systems also differ in their simplicity or complexity. Complex systems may require chapter or book-length exposition, in part because they may contain more categories, but also because the categories may be more abstract. In their intimacy motive validation study, McAdams and Constantian (1983) employed both simple and moderately complex coding systems. For example, ESM responses to the question "What were you thinking about?" were given a "1" for mention of specific people in the participant's life or of relationships between people, or a "0" if no specific people or relationships were mentioned. In contrast, each participant's score for intimacy motivation was derived from an elaborate set of coding categories that require chapter-length exposition (McAdams, 1992).

Some coding systems are complex because they assess more than one dimension and then combine components from different dimensions in order to assign an individual to a stage or level (e.g., moral reasoning, Colby & Kohlberg, 1987; conceptual-integrative complexity, Suedfeld et al., 1992).

Some coding systems specify two or more stages of coding. For example, in the study of pessimistic causal explanations by Peterson et al. (1988), the text unit was first coded to identify instances of bad events for which causal explanations were given. Each explanation then became a coding unit that was rated on 7-point scales for stability, globality, and internality.

Another level of complexity, "contingency analysis," identifies the cooccurrences of symbols in a text (Osgood, 1959; Stone et al., 1966). This procedure can be used to study the associated thoughts of a single individual, the associations common to members of a group (e.g., Van de Castle, 1994), or sequential contingencies (see Bakeman, this volume, Ch. 6).

A different type of contingency is built into some scoring systems. Only if certain primary categories are coded as present is the text then coded for secondary categories. For example, for each story, the intimacy score consists of the number of primary and secondary categories present (McAdams, 1992).

QUANTIFICATION. Quantification is most often achieved by recording the presence or absence of specified information, or its frequency of occurrence. Less often a scale number or rating may be given, or a physical or temporal measurement may be made, such as the number of column inches or the amount of broadcast time devoted to a news story. In some systems scores are obtained by summing the categories in a text unit that are indicative of a variable, such as the need for achievement. Typically each category is given equal weight, and sums are usually treated as if they were equal interval scores, although ordinal statistics are sometimes used.

DECIDING ON A CODING SYSTEM. Sometimes a researcher can use an existing coding system to obtain the information needed. If not, a new one must be devised, or it may be possible to supplement a preexisting coding system with additional categories of the investigator's own making.

PREEXISTING SYSTEMS. Coding systems of many kinds have been developed, as illustrated in Table 12.2. Additional coding systems are described in chapters in this volume by Bakeman and by Bartholomew, Henderson, and Marcia. One advantage of using coding systems that were developed from surveys or archival materials is that norms derived from large samples may be available.

DEVISING NEW CODING SYSTEMS. The approach to developing a new coding system will vary depending on several factors, including (a) whether a researcher wishes to test an existing theory, develop a new theory, or address an applied problem, as in market research; (b) the nature of the material to be analyzed; and (c) the population for which the system is intended (e.g., children or adults). Complementary discussions of the development of new coding systems are given by Bakeman (this volume, Ch. 6) and by Viney (1983).

Coding categories and dimensions should be defined explicitly, clearly, and in detail, so that different coders can agree on what material is included or not included in a category. A category may be defined either by an exhaustive list of what is to be included or by a statement of the meaning of the category (the class of responses to be treated as equivalent), together with illustrative examples of what kind of material is or is not included.

TABLE 12.2. Some Coding Systems Developed for Social Science Research

Adjustment and adaptation
  Personal problem-solving skills (Ronan et al., 1995)

Cognitive and personality orientations
  Agency (Wessman & Ricks, 1966)
  Causal thinking (Pennebaker, Mayne, & Francis, 1997)
  Origin–Pawn[c,d]
  Psychological time perspective (Wessman & Ricks, 1966)
  Responsibility[c]
  Uncertainty orientation[c]

Cognitive and attributional styles
  Conceptual–integrative complexity (Suedfeld et al., 1992)
  Explanatory style (Peterson, 1992)

Interpersonal relations
  Affiliation, aggression, dependency, intimacy[b]
  Agency and communion (Mansfield & McAdams, 1996)
  Interpersonal scripts (Demorest et al., 1999)
  Social alienation[a]
  Sociality[d]

Life-span development
  Ego development (Hy & Loevinger, 1996)
  Moral reasoning (Colby & Kohlberg, 1987)
  Psychological stances toward the environment[c]

Moods and emotions
  Anger, happiness, sadness, tension[b]
  Anxiety, hope, hostility[a,d]
  Depression[a]
  Emotional expression (Pennebaker et al., 1997)
  Positive affect, experienced quality of life[d]

Motives
  Achievement (McClelland & Koestner, 1992)
  Affiliation, motive to avoid success, power[c]
  Fear of failure (Birney, Burdick, & Teevan, 1969)
  Intimacy (McAdams, 1992)

Psychoanalytically oriented constructs
  Anality, castration anxiety, defensive projection, ego strength, Genitality, masochism, orality, regression[b]
  Object relations (McKay, 1992; Westen, 1991)

Self and identity
  Generativity (McAdams & St. Aubin, 1992)
  Self-definition and social definition (Stewart, 1992)

Values
  Value analysis (White, 1951)

---

[a] See Gottschalk, 1995
[b] See Hall & Van de Castle, 1966
[c] See Smith, 1992a
[d] See Viney, 1983

New coding systems may originate from two contrasting orientations: the *a priori* (the categories are specified before the material is examined) and the *empirical* (the categories emerge from the material to be analyzed). A priori categories of analysis most often derive from psychoanalytic theory. For example, categories indicative of authoritarianism might be derived from a theory of cognitive structure. A priori categories might also derive from an applied purpose, such as to assess factors that affect morale and productivity. One possible problem with a priori categories is that they may not reflect the frame of reference of the source. For example, Cartwright (1953) found that terms used by professional economists could not successfully be applied in coding popular conceptions of how to control wartime inflation.

Empirical approaches may be either *inductive* or *experimental*. A purely inductive approach allows categories to emerge from the material without the influence of preconceptions. The inductive approach is most likely to be used in preliminary, exploratory, or qualitative research. For example, in preliminary research a researcher might review interview responses to a certain question, listing each different response. Next, similar responses would be classified into a smaller number of higher-order categories. These categories might then be used for content analysis, or they could be used as fixed alternative responses for questions to be used in a survey.

An inductive approach might also be used when one wants a summary description of some phenomenon in terms of the frame of reference of the respondent. For example, research in environmental psychology investigated "the assumption that favourite places can be used to regulate pleasurable and painful feelings" (Korpela, 1992, p. 249). From essays, categories were derived inductively for reasons for going to a favorite place. The article on service climate by Schneider et al. (1992) also provided a helpful description of the inductive derivation and subsequent refinement of coding categories.

Categories derived by the experimental approach reflect the effect of variations in an independent variable on the type of material to be analyzed. This approach was a major contribution made by McClelland, Atkinson, and their associates (e.g., McClelland et al., 1953) in research on the measurement of human motives. Previous studies of the effects of fear and hunger on perception had suggested an experimental procedure for the development of a motive scoring system, namely, to arouse a motivational state and then identify its effects on imaginative stories. Atkinson and

McClelland (1948) began by demonstrating that story content changed with increasing hours of food deprivation. However, not all of the changes that occurred had been anticipated. This led to a distinctive feature of their procedure: All changes in imaginative content (thematic imagery) that occurred as a result of motive arousal were considered indicative of the presence of the motive and constituted the motive scoring system.

Subsequent studies employed experimental arousal, or naturally occurring changes in motive-arousing conditions, to develop scoring systems for a number of additional motives. In addition, scoring systems were developed by comparing stories from naturally occurring groups that might be expected to differ with respect to motives such as power (see Smith, 1992a).

In practice the a priori and empirical approaches are usually combined. A theory suggests what to look for, and analysis suggests modifications and additions to the a priori scheme. For example, a priori categories that occur infrequently would be dropped, as might empirically derived categories that have no theoretical or practical significance.

The application of an a priori system also may suggest modifications in the underlying theory. The scoring systems and theories developed by Murray (1938) and his associates for the TAT and by Kohlberg and his associates (Colby & Kohlberg, 1987) evolved by means of the empirical refinement of criteria derived from guiding theoretical orientations.

In field research, a coding system may evolve over a period of time as field notes are taken and analyzed (see Miles & Huberman, 1994). Usually, however, before using a coding system for research, it is desirable to conduct preliminary research until the system requires no further modification.

It is a good idea to cross-validate a scoring system in order to ensure that the same scoring categories will emerge from a different population or will apply to a different population. The nature of the population for which a coding system was intended may limit its generality. For example, coding systems developed from material obtained from only one gender must be demonstrated to be applicable with the other. Finally, the nature of the text can affect the coding categories derived. For example, people may express a different kind of reasoning about hypothetical moral dilemmas than about moral dilemmas they have encountered in their lives.

INTERCODER AGREEMENT. Two kinds of reliability are of interest in content-analytic research: one is the reliability of the coder as a measuring instrument, called intercoder, interjudge, or interscorer agreement; the other, as is discussed later, is the reliability of the frequencies or scores derived for quantitative research.

A high degree of agreement between two or more independent coders, blind to all identifying characteristics of the material, is a prerequisite for using a coding system for research. To enable a high level of agreement, the coding system must be clear and explicit. Agreement demonstrates the objectivity of the system and is a necessary, but not sufficient, condition for the validity of classifications or scores. An index of intercoder agreement should be reported either between a researcher and an independent coder or between two researchers coding independently. Less satisfactory are indexes of agreement between two separate codings of the same material by the same researcher or between a researcher and practice materials scored by an expert.

Indexes of intercoder agreement considered here deal with (a) categories and (b) scores. Illustrations are taken from the achievement motive scoring system (McClelland et al., 1953). The simplest, and most frequently reported, category index is the *percentage of agreement* between two or more coders in classifying material into two or more categories. For example, two coders might agree 80% of the time. Although it is better than no measure of agreement, there are two problems with this index. First, it will be affected by the frequency with which a category is present. Second, it does not take account of the amount of agreement that would be expected purely by chance.

The first problem is most evident with low or high frequency occurrences. Suppose that the category *achievement imagery* is present in only 2 of 100 stories. If the first person correctly codes 2 present and 98 absent, and the second person codes 100 absent, their percentage agreement will be 98, even though the second coder has missed all the instances of achievement imagery. To correct percentage of agreement for the frequency with which a category occurs, the following index was developed by McClelland et al. (1953); see also Smith, Feld, and Franz (1992, p. 529).

$$\frac{2 \ (\# \text{ of agreements between scorers on presence of category})}{(\# \text{ scored present by scorer 1}) + (\# \text{ scored present by scorer 2})}$$

It is helpful to compute this index for each category, both to assess agreement and to discover categories that may need to be dropped or revised. Although low or high frequency occurrences may lead to overestimation of agreement, some authors recommend that agreement include both occurrences and nonoccurrences (see McDowell & Acklin, 1996).

To correct for agreement due to chance, when coding categories are independent, mutually exclusive, and exhaustive, the Kappa index is recommended. To evaluate agreement when ordinal categories are employed, a weighted Kappa may be used. Kappa and weighted Kappa are explained by Bakeman (this volume, Ch. 6).

Some coding systems yield scores instead of category frequencies. For example, the achievement motive score for each story is the sum of the various imagery categories scored (e.g., achievement imagery, need, goal anticipation, etc.). The scores for each story are then summed to obtain the total score for each storyteller. The index of agreement between the scores assigned by two coders is usually a correlation coefficient (rank-difference or product moment).

How high should agreement be to be satisfactory? Published research has tended to regard as satisfactory percentage of agreement, or category present agreement, of approximately 85% or more or interscorer correlations of .85 or more (see Smith, Feld, & Franz, 1992). A Kappa of .80 or more is generally regarded as satisfactory (see, e.g., McDowell & Acklin, 1996). Although these are arbitrary standards, they derive from the consideration that accurate measurement would be represented by 100% agreement. In exploratory research, or in the application of a coding system to a new kind of verbal material (e.g., when a system developed for adults is applied to adolescents), a somewhat lower degree of intercoder reliability may be acceptable. A test of statistical significance is rarely, if ever, relevant for a measure of intercoder reliability. The question is not whether agreement is significantly better than chance, but how close it is to perfect.

Finally, after calculating agreement, coders usually discuss their differences and resolve them. In this process, one coder often realizes that he or she missed something, or misinterpreted something, and that the other coder's decision was correct. Thus, the resolved coding is likely to be somewhat more accurate than the index of agreement indicates.

CODER TRAINING. The following are required for training: a clear coding manual, ample practice materials, and an opportunity to discuss coding decisions with an expert scorer. A coder should learn to point to the portion of the text that led to a coding decision. The amount of practice required depends primarily on the size and complexity of the coding system. Smith, Feld, and Franz (1992) and Veroff (1992), among others, discuss the training of coders for the scoring of thematic materials, and the training of interview coders is described in the preceding chapter on coded semistructured interviews (this volume). A researcher may train more coders than are needed and then use only those coders who demonstrate the greatest aptitude.

COMPUTER-ASSISTED CONTENT ANALYSIS. Early approaches to computer-assisted content analysis are reviewed by Krippendorff (1980). Of these, the most influential led to the development of the General Inquirer (Stone et al., 1966), a set of computer programs that recognized and classified English words using software "dictionaries" prepared by researchers. Some "general-purpose" dictionaries, such as the Harvard Psycho-Sociological Dictionary, were prepared to deal with a wide variety of social science research problems. Other broadly applicable dictionaries include an anthropological dictionary and dictionaries for categorizing values, group processes, and attitudes (based on the semantic differential). In the research on alcoholism by Kalin et al. (1966) described earlier, a "special-purpose" dictionary was prepared for the General Inquirer consisting of approximately 4,000 words and 95 theoretically relevant categories. By means of preliminary analyses on half of the folktales, the dictionary was refined and was then cross-validated on the other half of the material.

The General Inquirer, now extended to languages other than English, is also useful for information retrieval. It can list all instances of some specified type (e.g. all verbs), search for contingencies (the cooccurrence of two or more categories within a coding unit), or call up for inspection all sentences in which specified words are used. Systematic categorization of all text words and their contexts may disclose aspects of the material that had been overlooked. The General Inquirer has been used to resolve issues of disputed authorship and to discriminate between two sources of verbal material (e.g., genuine and simulated suicide notes).

Aspects of computer-assisted analysis, such as text entry, preediting, and dictionary preparation can be time-consuming; however, software preparation forces the researcher to be explicit about the coding distinctions to be made. The problems of having to preedit text and deal with idioms and syntax have been addressed in software developed by Gottschalk (1995) and his associates for the content-analytic assessment of a number of psychological states and traits. In some instances text entry may be facilitated by optical scanning devices. Alternatively, some kinds of elicited materials may be collected on the computer. For example,

Blankenship and Zoota (1998) found no differences in power motivation scores obtained from handwritten as compared with computer written TAT stories by college men and women.

Pennebaker, Mayne, and Francis (1997) used Linguistic Inquiry and Word Count (LIWC) software to identify empirically four predictors of health-related outcomes from writing samples. Computerized text assessment of these four variables in the bereavement narratives of partners of gay men who had died of AIDS predicted partner adjustment 1 year later.

Miles and Huberman (1994) discussed types of codes for computer-assisted qualitative research and the use of software to identify emergent themes or configurations and to facilitate cross-case analysis. They provided a helpful appendix on choosing computer programs for qualitative data analysis. For example, code and retrieve programs, such as ATLAS, NUDIST, and The Ethnograph, among others, help to divide the text into chunks and attach codes to the chunks. Weitzman and Miles (1995) authored a subsequent volume on computer programs for qualitative data analysis. Also, Hesse-Biber, Dupuis, and Kinder (1997) described a computer-assisted procedure for the qualitative analysis of multimedia data.

At present, the drawbacks of computer use for content analysis include the time required to construct special purpose dictionaries and the limitations of preexisting general purpose dictionaries (see, e.g., McAdams & Zeldow, 1993). Computer-assisted software that requires thematic or abstract conceptual analysis of text, such as that developed for coding achievement motivation, is not yet satisfactory, so far as I am aware. At present the computer may be of greatest value in dealing with large amounts of material, large numbers of variables, contingencies, patterns, and analyses that permit coding categories to emerge, and/or take account of context. Also, text already in the computer can be reanalyzed in terms of revised or alternative coding schemes.

STATISTICAL ANALYSIS. Statistics used for the analysis of content-analytic data are illustrated in the references cited (see also Krippendorff, 1980, Ch. 10). Prior to statistical analysis, it may be advisable to correct for the effect on scores of differences in the length of the coded material. Winter (1992) discussed the correction of archival materials for length. For other ways of dealing with differences in length, see Gottschalk and Gleser (1969), Hall and Van de Castle (1966), Pennebaker et al. (1997), and Smith, Feld, and Franz, (1992).

RELIABILITY AND VALIDITY. In quantitative research, the *reliability* of scores can refer to one or more aspects of consistency of measurement, namely, internal consistency, consistency between alternative forms, or test–retest consistency. Reliability assessments provide information about the repeatability, unidimensionality, and stability over time of the frequencies or ratings derived from content analysis. "For example, using scores assigned to thematic apperceptive stories, one may obtain measures of repeatability (from alternate forms), homogeneity (internal consistency among scores from different stories) and stability (test-interval-retest)" (Smith, 1995, p. 128). Steps to take to maximize the reliability of thematic measures are recommended by Smith (1992b). Further information about reliability is provided by Holsti (1969) and Krippendorff (1980), as well as in chapters in this volume by Bakeman; Bartholomew, Henderson, and Marcia; and John and Benet-Martinez. In particular, a different approach to reliability, that of generalizability theory, is presented in the chapters by Bakeman and by John and Benet-Martinez (see also a TAT study by Ronan, Date, & Weisbrod, 1995).

The *validity* of content analysis refers to whether coding assesses what it was intended to assess. An unbiased sample and a reliable assessment are necessary, but not sufficient, conditions for validity. High internal consistency is not necessary for validity (see Smith, 1992b). Several different kinds of validity have been distinguished. For content analytic measures the following are most relevant: *concurrent validity* (a measure can discriminate between existing groups, such as adults high or low in generativity; see Mansfield & McAdams, 1996); *predictive validity* (a measure can predict subsequent events or behaviors); *construct validity* (a measure is related as theoretically expected to other relevant variables; see McClelland & Koestner, 1992); and *external validity* (findings obtained with a measure can be generalized to other populations or contexts).

CONCLUSIONS REGARDING CONTENT ANALYSIS. Although labor intensive, content analysis can extract valuable information from qualitative material – information that may not be obtainable by fixed-response methods. Content analysis may be used when sources are aware of being studied and when they are not. And when sources are not available, or cannot remember, surviving documents may provide at least some of the information that is sought. Few other general procedures can be used to study individuals in depth, communications between persons, personal and social changes over time, and societies, past and present.

PART II: NARRATIVE ANALYSIS[1]

Overview

Narrative analysis both complements, and differs from, content analysis. Whereas there is general agreement about the characteristics of the content-analytic method, there is no such agreement about narrative analysis. Content analysis is derived from mainstream social science and is used primarily in quantitive research, whereas narrative-analytic systems are derived as much from literary and philosophical analysis as from social science and are used predominantly in qualitative research. Proponents of narrative analysis vary widely in their attitudes toward mainstream social science. Many emphasize subjectivity and reject the "objective," "realist," "positivist–empiricist," and "mechanistic" assumptions of traditional science with its goal of "context-free" and value-neutral laws (e.g., Gergen, 1985; Mishler, 1995; Polkinghorne, 1988; Riessman, 1993; Sarbin, 1986).

Although literary discussions of narrative go back at least to Aristotle's *Poetics*, contemporary narrative analysis dates back only to approximately the 1960s. Early-20th century influences on the study of narrative include Russian literary criticism and linguistics, Russian psychological theories regarding the social determinants of language and thought, and, in England, Bartlett's (1932) research on memory. More recent continental and Anglo-American influences on narrative analysis include structuralism, poststructuralism, hermeneutics, social constructionism, postmodernism, interpretive approaches in anthropology and sociology, and contributions from linguistics and cognitive psychology. For more detail, see Manning and Cullum-Swan (1994) and Riessman (1993).

WHY STUDY NARRATIVES? Narrative is regarded as a basic and universal mode of verbal expression (Bruner, 1986; McAdams, 1993; Miller, Hoogstra, Mintz, Fund, & Williams, 1994). Telling about past events is one of the earliest forms of children's discourse (McCabe & Peterson, 1991b; Nelson, 1989). In everyday conversation we recount experiences or tell stories to inform, instruct, entertain, impress, empower, exonerate, or cathart, among other things.

Narrative analysis permits a holistic approach to discourse that preserves context and particularity

[1] I am especially indebted to my colleague, Colette Daiute, and to her course on Narrative Analysis. Her organization of the subject matter and her assigned readings have made a major contribution to my presentation of the topic.

(Riessman, 1993). Advocates believe that narratives yield information that may not be available by other methods (Bruner, 1986; Polkinghorne, 1988; Veroff, Sutherland, Chadiha, & Ortega, 1993). Language transduces thoughts, feelings, and sensory experiences into a shared symbolic form. Thus, language is the medium through which meaning and socially constructed reality can best be studied. Narrative language provides access to subjective experience, providing insights into conceptions of self and identity and opening up new ways of studying memory, language and thought, and socialization and culture. Narratives can also be used for academic and clinical assessment as well as for academic and therapeutic interventions.

DEFINITIONS. Most narrative researchers would probably agree that a *narrative* is an oral, written, or filmed account of events told to others or to oneself (monologue), but is *not* verbal material that is purely descriptive, expository (e.g., an explanation of how to assemble furniture), disconnected, or abstract. For our purposes narrative is used to refer to accounts of personal experiences, or the experiences of others, or to fictional accounts, such as stories, myths, folktales, and fairy tales. According to Spence (1982), for most purposes the literal truth of an account of one's experience is not relevant. Spence contrasted historical truth ("what really happened") with narrative truth – "the criterion we use to decide when a certain experience has been captured to our satisfaction" (1982, p. 31).

A related literature on accounts has developed in sociology and in social psychology (see Orbuch, 1997). *Accounts* have been defined as "storylike constructions containing description, interpretation, emotion, expectations, and related material" (Harvey, 1995, p. 3). Harvey sees the sociological heritage of this literature in treatments of saving face, justifications of behavior, and ascriptions of responsibility for problematic events. The social psychological heritage is the attribution literature on the way people interpret events.

PERSPECTIVE, CONTEXT, AND FRAME. Narratives are characterized by perspective and context. *Perspective* refers to the fact that a narrative contains a point of view toward what happened, telling us what is significant (Gee, 1991). Perspective may also refer to a narrator's taking into account what the listener needs to know (McCabe, Capron, & Peterson, 1991). *Context*, and the related term *frame*, are used variously to refer to (a) external influences on the narrator, (b) ways in which the narrator constructs the narrative, and

(c) characteristics of the resulting text. External influences include the historical period, physical surroundings, and culture (Gee, 1991), as well as the immediate social setting, that is, to whom the person is speaking and for what purpose (Miller et al., 1994; Tannen, 1993). Within the narrative, context has been "variously defined, in terms of an ongoing narrative ("plot"), the immediate semantic environment, [and] the literary tropes operating" (Manning & Cullum-Swan, 1994, p. 464). In narrative the particulars of an episode are embedded in a setting. One part cannot be understood in isolation ("taken out of context") from the rest.

One definition of frame is "an expectation about the world, based on prior experience, against which new experiences are measured and interpreted" (Tannen, 1993, p. 17). The narrator is influenced by frames representing different settings, roles, and cultural backgrounds.

VARIETIES OF NARRATIVE. Some authors believe that narrative structure is common to all cultures, whereas others have identified both cultural and individual differences in narrative structure (McCabe, 1997). A common structure was suggested by Propp's (1928/1968) analysis of Russian fairy tales. And indeed, the traditional European American tale tends to include certain common characteristics: a setting, a time-ordered sequence of events, a problem-solving or goal orientation, and a conflict or difficulty to be resolved (Mandler & Johnson, 1977). However, this Eurocentric view has given way to an appreciation that narratives from different cultures differ considerably in their customary form and properties (Gee, 1991; Invernizzi & Abouzeid, 1995; McCabe, 1997), although most narratives, except those of young children, include context, perspective, pattern, coherence, and human or human-like (animate) characters.

FUNCTIONS OF NARRATIVE. Reflecting back on events and telling about them can (a) provide meaning and coherence to, and perspective on, experience and one's social traditions (Bruner, 1990); (b) construct a person's knowledge (Bruner, 1986; Daiute, 1995), including a person's sense of self or identity (McAdams, 1993; Miller et al., 1994); (c) produce an organizing principle for human action (McAdams, 1993; Sarbin, 1986); (d) alter the teller's way of thinking about events, and/or sense of identity (McAdams, 1993; Polkinghorne, 1988; Schafer, 1992; Spence, 1982); and (e) bring about emotional adjustment and healing (e.g., McAdams, 1993; Pennebaker et al., 1997). For listeners, narrative can "raise consciousness," create a shared history and a shared group identity, and preserve and transmit culture.

Approaches to Narrative Analysis

Approaches are presented here by academic discipline. Mishler (1995) provided a more detailed review, particularly of the anthropological approach. Other treatments of the topic are given by Cortazzi (1993) and Riessman (1993). Helpful resources include *The Journal of Narrative and Life History*, and a Sage Publications series on narratives edited by Josselson and Lieblich.

LINGUISTICS. Linguists have studied such properties of narrative as units of meaning, macrostructure, cohesion between sentences, and perspective. Psycholinguists have dealt with language acquisition, development, processing, and pathology, whereas sociolinguists have focused on language in its social context.

HIGH POINTS ANALYSIS. Labov's sociolinguistic approach to the semantic function and structure of narrative has been broadly influential. Labov regarded narrative as "one method of recapitulating past experience by matching a verbal sequence of clauses to the sequence of events which actually occurred" (Labov & Waletzky, 1967, p. 20). Labov later modified his view of the temporal sequence in narrative (Mishler, 1995).

For Labov, *referential* clauses present the sequence of events (e.g., "this person had. . .too much to drink and he attacked me"). *Evaluative* clauses indicate the relative importance of the events (e.g. "He was beat up real, real bad"). The structure of a narrative reflects the way the narrator has organized and made sense of experience. According to Labov, a complete narrative consists of an abstract (summary), orientation (person, place, time, situation), complication (series of events terminated by a result), evaluation (point or significance of events, attitude of the narrator), resolution (outcome), and coda (returns perspective to the present; Labov, 1972). Like Aristotle, Labov and Waletzky (1967) stated that the narrator typically emphasizes "the point where the complication has reached a maximum [high point]: the break between the complication and the result" (p. 35). Using a modified high points analysis, Peterson and McCabe (1983) found structural changes in children's narratives between the ages of 3 and 9.

EPISODIC ANALYSIS. Episodic or story grammar analysis emphasizes the purposive and goal-seeking aspects of stories (see Peterson & McCabe, 1983). It derives from the work of Rumelhart (1975) and Mandler and Johnson (1977), among others. The basic structure includes one or more characters with motives that cause goal-directed actions ("attempts") that, in turn, cause consequences. This method lends itself to the study of developmental changes in narrative structure and children's understanding of motives, causality, perspective-taking, and planning. Peterson and McCabe (1983) compared the high points and episodic systems and discussed their strengths and weaknesses.

POETIC STRUCTURE. Gee (1991) regarded narrative as "a perspective that human beings take on the way in which certain themes fall into a satisfying pattern, a perspective stemming from their social identity and the resources their social group(s) make available to them" (p. 13). Temporal and causal elements are not emphasized. For Gee (1991) "all speech is produced in terms of *lines* (often a clause long) and *stanzas* (a small group of lines with one perspective and a narrow topic)" (p. 9). Gee gives an example of the poetic structure of an oral story told by a 7-year-old that exemplifies an African American cultural tradition of using rhythmic and poetic patterning to construct meaning, rather than linear progress to "the point."

DEVELOPMENTAL PSYCHOLOGY AND EDUCATION. Kathryn Nelson (1989, 1993) presented information on young children's narratives beginning with memories of experiences as early as 12 months of age and progressing to relatively complete stories by about the age of 8. Nelson (1989) obtained tape recordings of a female child's spontaneous presleep monologues from 21 months to 36 months of age. Possible functions served by "Emily's" speech are considered, including comprehending experience, self-regulation, problem-solving, and development of self.

Daiute (1995) has studied the construction of knowledge by third- and fourth-graders by means of written accounts of school-related events. She showed that Western-European norms applied to accounts of school-related experiences may not reveal the way children attempt to make sense of academic assignments. For example, the account of a class trip, written on a computer by Brant, a third-grade African American boy, makes no mention of the Renaissance, the intended focus of the outing.

LH SKOOI GO;S TO GARDNER MUSEUM
miss Gardner was loveubewul women she lived on the top
of the museum she payed the tackes her husbend did the woerk
when he died she was left olune all by her self but she
made the best of it . . . THE END (Daiute, 1995, p. 3)

This and other assignments suggest that "Brant tended
to take a person-centered approach, focusing . . . on
a character, the character's relationships, trials, and
tribulations. . . . [This] suggests a more general theme –
his meta-narrative perhaps – that life is difficult, and
people spend considerable action and thought adjusting to the difficulties they face" (p. 24). Daiute (1995)
derived an interpretive profile for each child that reflects his or her unique interpretive stance. Such information can help a teacher to understand why a child
like Brant is not doing well in school.

The period from middle childhood through adolescence is studied from a feminist perspective by Debold
(1995). Her interview procedure stems from prior research on female moral conflicts. Her analysis attempted to identify shifts in self-representation, as well
as thoughts or feelings girls cannot or do not wish to
talk about.

Other developmental research deals with the effect on children's narratives of parental interaction and
of schools (McCabe & Peterson, 1991a), and with accounts of female experiences of moral conflict (Brown,
Debold, Tappan, & Gilligan, 1991). Vitz (1990) recommended the use of narrative in moral education as contrasted with exercises in abstract moral reasoning.

PERSONALITY. The study of lives by means of narrative materials dates back to Henry Murray, Robert
White, and their associates (Murray, 1938). The contemporary narrative analysis of lives began around
the 1980s (see Cohler, 1982; McAdams, 1988; Sarbin,
1986). Life stories in social context have been reported
by social psychologists, sociologists, and anthropolo-
gists (e.g., Angrosino, 1995; Josselson & Lieblich, 1993;
Rosenwald & Ochberg, 1992).

McAdams, (1993) life span theory of identity illustrates a narrative approach to the study of lives. It
traces the determinants and development of the life
story from an enduring narrative tone of optimism or
pessimism acquired during infancy to the beginning of
myth-making in adolescence through the generativity and integrity phases of middle and late adulthood.
McAdams (1993) believed that each person constructs
the core themes of a life story – a personal myth –
that is revised throughout life. The story we compose
defines who we are; it gives coherence to experience,
and unity and purpose to life. A life story may contain one or more imagoes (personified idealizations of
the self such as "the rebel," "the loyal friend," or "the
survivor"). Imagoes representing high or low agency
and/or communion are found to be consistent with
scores for power and intimacy motivation. McAdams
(1993) reported many case studies that illustrate the
complex dynamics of life-story construction and show
a trend toward the integration of conflicting imagoes
in later life.

Many forms of psychotherapy facilitate accounts of
personal experiences. Some therapists participate in
the coconstruction of a life story that is beneficial for
the patient (Schafer, 1992; Spence, 1982). Of current
interest is a movement called "narrative therapy," in
which both therapists and clients engage in narrative
procedures (see White & Epston, 1990).

COGNITION. Because most cognitive approaches
are not of direct relevance to research in social psychology, they will not be dealt with in detail. Suffice it
to say that important work has been carried out on the
relation of narrative to encoding (Mandler & Johnson,
1977), schemata (Rumelhart, 1975), and memory
(McCabe et al., 1991; Nelson, 1993). *Advances in Social
Cognition* (1995, Vol. 8) contains discussions of many of
these topics.

**SOCIAL PSYCHOLOGY, SOCIOLOGY, AND ANTHRO-
POLOGY.** Narrative research from these disciplines
shares a social and cultural perspective. Some of it reflects a social constructionist viewpoint (e.g., Gergen,
1985), and/or the interpretive approach to culture
(e.g., Geertz, 1973). The social construction of emotion,
and of self and identity, are dealt with in the *Journal of
Narrative and Life History* (1995, Vol. 5). Work, identity,
and narrative are dealt with by Mishler (1992), and
The Narrative Study of Lives (Lieblich & Josselson, 1994)
is devoted to the topics of identity and gender.

Narrative research on the marital experiences
of African American and White couples has been
conducted by Joseph Veroff and his associates. These
researchers developed a joint-narrative interview procedure in which a couple is asked to tell the story of
their relationship beginning with how they met (see
Veroff et al., 1993). Among other findings, narrative affect measures predicted marital happiness in the third
year to a significant extent beyond the predictions of
self-report affect measures.

Other topics addressed from a social perspective
include abortion activists (Ginsberg, 1989), divorce

(Riessman, 1993), effects on family relationships of disclosure by gay and lesbian children (Ben-Ari, 1995), interpersonal scripts (Demorest et al., 1999) mass media (Berger, 1996), women's health (Riessman, 1993), and comparison of narratives of different social class, ethnic, and cultural groups (Gee, 1991; Invernizzi & Abouzeid, 1995; McCabe, 1997; Tannen, 1993).

Methodological Considerations

Narrative research methods vary widely, and few sources are devoted primarily to narrative methodology (see Cortazzi, 1993; Mishler, 1986; Peterson & McCabe, 1983; Riessman, 1993). The analysis of life history narratives is discussed by Angrosino (1995) and Geiger (1986).

In general, the steps in narrative research are similar to those of content-analytic research. A clear formulation of the objectives of the research will guide the selection of a system of analysis, the kind of material to be analyzed, and the participants, groups, or societies from which the narratives originate.

A researcher may decide to use one or more existing analysis systems, adapt an existing system, or develop a new one. To teach narrative research methods, Riessman (1993) described her analysis of interview material using three different systems to study such topics as divorce, the effect of welfare policies on single mothers, and women's health.

The research topic, and the system(s) of analysis selected, usually delimit the kind of material (usually accounts of personal experiences or fictional stories) that will yield the desired information. For example, many studies of narrative *structure* have employed story recall. Narrative material may be elicited from participants; recorded from naturally occurring behavior, such as a "talk show"; or obtained from preexisting sources, such as personal documents or collections of folktales. Elicited material may be obtained by means of interviews, recall of a story or a film, or writing samples (e.g., an essay, thematic apperceptive stories). However, interview responses and recalled stories may have different properties (e.g., structural features).

There should be a rationale for the type and number of participants selected and whether one or a few persons are to be studied in depth or many persons are to be studied in less detail (see the earlier discussion of sampling). Developmental studies, such as those reviewed earlier, indicate the ages at which children can provide more or less complete narrative accounts in response to interview or recall procedures.

Transcription of oral narratives is a complex process that can affect interpretations (Mishler, 1986; Riessman, 1993, pp. 11–13, 20, 56ff.). Normally interviews are tape recorded. A videotaped interview provides more information, but may also induce greater self-consciousness. Responses must be transcribed in such a way as to preserve all information that might affect interpretation (e.g., pauses, emphasis, nonverbal communication).

A written or transcribed account is sometimes cast in the form of clauses, or even reorganized in temporal order (Mishler, 1995). Decisions about such matters can affect interpretations. Riessman (1993) discussed transformations and how to decide where interview narratives begin and end. For any transformation or interpretation of accounts, evidence of agreement between independent decisions increases confidence in conclusions.

Validity issues in narrative research are similar to those in any quantitative or qualitative research. However, some advocates of narrative analysis, and of qualitative research, do not regard the concept of validity as directly applicable to narrative research. Riessman (1993, p. 64–69) discussed this issue as well as criteria for judging the quality of narrative research.

Content Analysis and Narrative Analysis in Perspective

Content analysis has developed within mainstream social science. There is little discussion of its epistemological presuppositions, although some researchers assume, implicitly or explicitly, that language reflects subjective experience. The replicability, internal validity, and external validity of content-analytic research are a function of recognized sampling, measurement, and research design conventions. More consideration has been given in content-analytic than in narrative research to the possibility that third-person accounts (e.g., TAT stories) can reveal information that may be omitted or altered in first-person accounts, such as interview responses.

Content-analytic coding systems might benefit from greater emphasis on information often obtained in narrative analyses regarding context, structure, and linguistic devices indicative of evaluation. Narrative research also suggests caution in assuming the cross-cultural applicability of content-analytic coding systems.

Narrative research may obtain information not usually available by other methods, such as in-depth understanding of the subjective experience of particular individuals or the modes of thought and emotion characteristic of different cultures. Individual differences in the importance of narrative for personal functioning have received little attention. It seems likely that research employing a variety of methods in addition to narrative analysis to study phenomena such as emotion, self-image, or memory would reveal distinctive contributions made by each method.

Narrative analysis strongly reflects the influence of disciplines outside the behavioral and social sciences. Instead of seeking the explanation of natural phenomena, some narrative analysts seek the interpretation of meaning. Whereas explanations require empirical verification or falsification, interpretations do not. However, some narrative researchers appear to want to have it both ways, that is, to reject traditional science; interpret a relatively small number of narratives, often without evidence of independent agreement; and then attempt empirical generalizations about differences due to age, gender, ethnic groups, or cultures.

Advocates of both content and narrative analysis believe their methods produce information that is not attainable by other means. Although narrative analysis is still seeking its identity, it has already suggested new questions and insights for further study by means of mainstream social science. The future will reveal the distinctive possibilities of both types of analysis.

Finally, social psychological research might benefit from more often availing itself of information provided by different research methods. In some instances information from one method may agree with, or supplement, that obtained by another method. In other instances information from different methods may not be compatible. For example, checklist or scenario-based measures may or may not be consistent with content-analytic measures. In the past some researchers have assumed that objective self-report measures were superior to content-analytic measures because the former were more reliable, even though there was scant evidence for their construct validity. This chapter indicates that an acceptable level of reliability is often attainable for content-analytic or narrative measures and that such measures not only can possess construct validity and predictive validity, but may be the best available measures according to these criteria.

REFERENCES

Allport, G. W. (1942). *The use of personal documents in psychological science* (Bulletin No. 49). New York: Social Science Research Council.

Ames, P. C., & Riggio, R. E. (1995). Use of the Rotter Incomplete Sentences Blank with adolescent populations: Implications for determining maladjustment. *Journal of Personality Assessment, 64,* 159–167.

Angrosino, M. V. (1995). Metaphors of ethnic identity: Projective life history narratives of Trinidadians of Indian descent. *Journal of Narrative and Life History, 5,* 125–146.

Arkhurst, C. (1994). *The thematic apperception test stories of women with and without histories of childhood sexual abuse.* Unpublished master's thesis, City College of New York.

Aronson, E. (1958). The need for achievement as measured by graphic expression. In J. W. Atkinson (Ed.), *Motives in fantasy, action, and society* (pp. 249–265). Princeton, NJ: Van Nostrand.

Atkinson, J. W., & McClelland, D. C. (1948). The projective expression of needs: II. *Journal of Experimental Psychology, 38,* 643–658.

Bales, R. F. (1950). *Interaction process analysis: A method for the study of small groups.* Cambridge, MA: Addison-Wesley.

Bartlett, F. C. (1932). *Remembering.* Cambridge, England: Cambridge University Press.

Ben-Ari, A. T. (1995). It's the telling that makes the difference. In R. Josselson & A. Lieblich (Eds.), *The narrative study of lives* (Vol. 3, pp. 153–172). Thousand Oaks, CA: Sage.

Berelson, B. (1954). Content analysis. In G. Lindzey (Ed.), *Handbook of social psychology* (Vol. 1, pp. 488–522). Cambridge, MA: Addison-Wesley.

Berger A. A. (1996). *Narratives in popular culture, media, and everyday life.* Newbury Park, CA: Sage.

Birney, R. C., Burdick, H., & Teevan, R. C. (1969). *Fear of failure.* New York: Van Nostrand-Reinhold.

Blankenship, V., & Zoota, A. L. (1998). Comparing power imagery in TATs written by hand or on the computer. *Behavior Research Methods, Instruments, and Computers, 30,* 441–448.

Brown, L. M., Debold, E., Tappan, M., & Gilligan, C. (1991). Reading narratives of conflict and choice for self and moral voices: A relational method. In W. M. Kurtines & J. L. Gewirtz (Eds.), *Handbook of moral behavior and development: Volume 2. Research* (pp. 25–61). Hillsdale, NJ: Erlbaum.

Bruner, J. S. (1986). *Actual minds, possible worlds.* Cambridge, MA: Harvard University Press.

Bruner, J. S. (1990). *Acts of meaning.* Cambridge, MA: Harvard University Press.

Cartwright, D. P. (1953). Analysis of qualitative material. In L. Festinger & D. Katz (Eds.), *Research methods in the behavioral sciences* (pp. 421–470). New York: Dryden.

Cohler, B. J. (1982). Personal narrative and life course. In P. Baltes & O. G. Brim, Jr. (Eds.), *Life span development and behavior* (Vol. 4, pp. 205–241). New York: Academic Press.

Colby, A., & Kohlberg, L. (1987). *The measurement of moral judgment* (2 vols.). Cambridge, England: Cambridge University Press.

Combs, A. W. (1947). A comparative study of motivations as revealed in thematic apperception stories and autobiography. *Journal of Clinical Psychology, 3,* 65–75.

Cortazzi, M. (1993). *Narrative analysis.* London: Falmer.

Daiute, C. (1995, June). *Imposing the self on school.* Paper presented at the Twenty-fifth Annual Symposium of the Jean Piaget Society, Berkeley, CA.

Davis, S. (1990). Men as success objects and women as sex objects: A study of personal advertisements. *Sex Roles, 23,* 43–50.

Debold, E. (1995, June). *Knowing distress and controlling passion: Development of abstract reasoning and mind–body dissociations in adolescent girls.* Paper presented at the Twenty-fifth Annual Symposium of the Jean Piaget Society, Berkeley, CA.

Demorest, A., Crits-Christoph, P., Hatch, M., & Luborsky, L. (1999). A comparison of interpersonal scripts in clinically depressed versus nondepressed individuals. *Journal of Research in Personality, 33,* 265–280.

Dovring, K. (1954–1955). Quantitative semantics in 18th century Sweden. *Public Opinion Quarterly, 18,* 389–394.

Emmons, R. A., & King, L. (1992). Thematic analysis, experience sampling, and personal goals. In C. P. Smith (Ed.), *Motivation and personality: Handbook of thematic content analysis* (pp. 73–86). New York: Cambridge University Press.

Funkhouser, G. R. (1973). The issues of the Sixties: An exploratory study. *Public Opinion Quarterly, 37,* 62–75.

Gee, J. P. (1991). Memory and myth: A perspective on narrative. In A. McCabe & C. Peterson (Eds.), *Developing narrative structure* (pp. 1–25). Hillsdale, NJ: Erlbaum.

Geertz, C. (1973). *The interpretation of cultures.* New York: Basic Books.

Geiger, S. N. G. (1986). Women's life histories: Method and content. *Signs: Journal of Women in Culture and Society, 11,* 334–351.

Gergen, K. J. (1985). The social constructionist movement in modern psychology. *American Psychologist, 40,* 266–275.

Ginsburg, F. (1989). Dissonance and harmony: The symbolic function of abortion in activists' life stories. In Personal Narratives Group (Ed.), *Interpreting women's lives: Feminist theory and personal narratives* (pp. 59–84). Indianapolis: University of Indiana Press.

Gottschalk, L. A. (1995). *Content analysis of verbal behavior.* Hillsdale, NJ: Erlbaum.

Gottschalk, L. A., & Gleser, G. C. (1969). *The measurement of psychological states through the content analysis of verbal behavior.* Berkeley: University of California Press.

Hall, C. S., & Van de Castle, R. L. (1966). *The content analysis of dreams.* New York: Appleton-Century-Croft.

Harvey, J. H. (1995). Accounts. In A. S. R. Manstead & M. Hewstone (Eds.), *The Blackwell encyclopedia of social psychology* (pp. 3–5). Oxford, England: Basil Blackwell.

Henry, W. E. (1951). The thematic apperception technique in the study of group and cultural problems. In H. H. Anderson & G. L. Anderson (Eds.), *An introduction to projective techniques* (pp. 230–278). Englewood Cliffs, NJ: Prentice-Hall.

Hesse-Biber, S., Dupuis, P. R., & Kinder, T. S. (1997). New developments in video ethnography and visual sociology – analyzing multimedia data qualitatively. *Social Science Computer Review, 15,* 5–12.

Holsti, O. R. (1969). *Content analysis for the social sciences and humanities.* Reading, MA: Addison-Wesley.

Hooker, E. (1957). The adjustment of the male overt homosexual. *Journal of Projective Techniques, 21,* 18–31.

Hy, L-X., & Loevinger, J. (1996). *Measuring ego development* (2nd ed.). Hillsdale, NJ: Erlbaum.

Invernizzi, M. A., & Abouzeid, M. P. (1995). One story map does not fit all: A cross-cultural analysis of children's written story retellings. *Journal of Narrative and Life History, 5,* 1–19.

Josselson, R., & Lieblich, A. (Eds.). (1993). *The narrative study of lives* (Vol. 1). Newbury Park, CA: Sage.

Judd, C. M., Smith, E. R., & Kidder, L. H. (1991) *Research methods in social relations* (6th ed.). Fort Worth, TX: Holt, Rinehart & Winston.

Kalin, R., Davis, W. N., & McClelland, D. C. (1966). The relationship between use of alcohol and thematic content of folktales in primitive societies. In P. J. Stone, D. C. Dunphy, M. S. Smith, & D. M. Ogilvie (Eds.), *The general inquirer: A computer approach to content analysis* (pp. 569–588). Cambridge, MA: MIT Press.

Korpela, K. M. (1992). Adolescents' favourite places and environmental self-regulation. *Journal of Environmental Psychology, 12,* 249–258.

Krippendorff, K. (1980). *Content analysis: An introduction to its methodology.* Beverly Hills, CA: Sage.

Labov, W. (Ed.). (1972). *Language in the inner city: Studies in the Black English vernacular.* Philadelphia: University of Pennsylvania Press.

Labov, W., & Waletzky, J. (1967). Narrative analysis: Oral versions of personal experience. In J. Helm (Ed.), *Essays on the verbal and visual arts* (pp. 12–44). Seattle: University of Washington Press.

Lieblich, A., & Josselson, R. (Eds.). (1994). *The narrative study of lives: Vol. 2. Exploring identity and gender.* Newbury Park, CA: Sage.

Mandler, J., & Johnson, N. (1977). Remembrance of things parsed: Story structure and recall. *Cognitive Psychology, 9,* 111–151.

Manning, P. K., & Cullum-Swan, B. (1994). Narrative, content, and semiotic analysis. In N. K. Denzin & Y. S. Lincoln (Eds.), *Handbook of qualitative research* (pp. 463–477). Thousand Oaks, CA: Sage.

Mansfield, E. D., & McAdams, D. P. (1996). Generativity and themes of agency and communion in adult autobiography. *Personality and Social Psychology Bulletin, 22,* 721–731.

McAdams, D. P. (1988). Biography, narrative, and lives: An introduction. In D. P. McAdams & R. L. Ochberg (Eds.), *Psychobiography and life narratives* [Special issue]. *Journal of Personality, 56,* 1–18.

McAdams, D. P. (1992). The intimacy motivation scoring system. In C. P. Smith (Ed.), *Motivation and personality:*

Handbook of thematic content analysis (pp. 229–253). New York: Cambridge University Press.

McAdams, D. P. (1993). *Personal myths and the making of the self*. New York: William Morrow.

McAdams, D. P., & Constantian, C. A. (1983). Intimacy and affiliation motives in daily living: An experience sampling analysis. *Journal of Personality and Social Psychology, 45*, 851–861.

McAdams, D. P., & St. Aubin, E. de. (1992). A theory of generativity and its assessment through self-report, behavioral acts, and narrative themes in autobiography. *Journal of Personality and Social Psychology, 62*, 1003–1015.

McAdams, D. P., & Zeldow, P. B. (1993). Construct validity and content analysis. *Journal of Personality Assessment, 61*, 243–245.

McCabe, A. (1997). Cultural background and storytelling. *The Elementary School Journal, 97*, 453–473.

McCabe, A., Capron, E., & Peterson, C. (1991). The voice of experience: The recall of early childhood and adolescent memories by young adults. In A. McCabe & C. Peterson (Eds.), *Developing narrative structure* (pp. 137–173). Hillsdale, NJ: Erlbaum.

McCabe, A., & Peterson, C. (Eds.). (1991a). *Developing narrative structure*. Hillsdale, NJ: Erlbaum.

McCabe, A., & Peterson, C. (1991b). Getting the story: A longitudinal study of parental styles in eliciting narratives and developing narrative skill. In A. McCabe & C. Peterson (Eds.), *Developing narrative structure* (pp. 217–254). Hillsdale, NJ: Erlbaum.

McClelland, D. C. (1961). *The achieving society*. Princeton, NJ: Van Nostrand.

McClelland, D. C., Atkinson, J. W., Clark, R., & Lowell, E. L. (1953). *The achievement motive*. New York: Appleton-Century-Crofts.

McClelland, D. C., & Koestner, R. (1992). The achievement motive. In C. P. Smith (Ed.), *Motivation and personality: Handbook of thematic content analysis* (pp. 143–152). New York: Cambridge University Press.

McClelland, D. C., Koestner, R., & Weinberger, J. (1989). How do self-attributed and implicit motives differ? *Psychological Review, 96*, 690–702.

McDowell, C., & Acklin, M. W. (1996). Standardizing procedures for calculating Rorschach interrater reliability: Conceptual and empirical foundations. *Journal of Personality Assessment, 66*, 308–320.

McKay, J. R. (1992). Affiliative trust-mistrust. In C. P. Smith (Ed.), *Motivation and personality: Handbook of thematic content analysis* (pp. 254–266). New York: Cambridge University Press.

Miles, M. B., & Huberman, A. M. (1994). *Qualitative data analysis* (2nd ed.). Thousand Oaks, CA: Sage.

Miller, P. J., Hoogstra, L., Mintz, J., Fung, H., & Williams, K. (1994). Troubles in the garden and how they get resolved: A young child's transformation of his favorite story. In C. A. Nelson (Ed.), *Memory and affect in development. The Minnesota Symposium on Child Psychology: Vol. 26* (pp. 87–114). Hillsdale, NJ: Erlbaum.

Mishler, E. G. (1986). *Research interviewing: Context and narrative*. Cambridge, MA: Harvard University Press.

Mishler, E. G. (1992). Work, identity and narrative: An artist-craftman's story. In G. C. Rosenwald & R. L. Ochberg (Eds.), *Storied lives: The cultural politics of self-understanding* (pp. 21–40). New Haven, CT: Yale University Press.

Mishler, E. G. (1995). Models of narrative analysis: A typology. *Journal of Narrative and Life History, 5*, 87–123.

Murray, H. A. (1938). *Explorations in personality*. New York: Oxford University Press.

Narayanan, L., Menon, S., & Levine, E. L. (1995). Personality structure: A culture-specific examination of the five-factor model. *Journal of Personality Assessment, 64*, 51–62.

Nelson, K. (Ed.). (1989). *Narratives from the crib*. Cambridge, MA: Harvard University Press.

Nelson, K. (1993). Events, narratives, memory: What develops? In C. A. Nelson (Ed.), *Memory and affect in development. The Minnesota symposia on child psychology: Vol. 26* (pp. 1–24). Hillsdale, NJ: Erlbaum.

Nunnally, J. (1978). *Psychometric theory* (2nd ed.). New York: McGraw Hill.

Ogilvie, D. M., Stone, P. J., & Schneidman, E. S. (1966). Some characteristics of genuine versus simulated suicide notes. In P. J. Stone, D. C. Dunphy, M. S. Smith, & D. M. Ogilvie (Eds.), *The general inquirer: A computer approach to content analysis* (pp. 527–535). Cambridge, MA: MIT Press.

Orbuch, T. L. (1997). People's accounts count: The sociology of accounts. *Annual Review of Sociology, 23*, 455–478.

Osgood, C. E. (1959). The representational model and relevant research methods. In I. D. S. Pool (Ed.), *Trends in content analysis* (pp. 33–88). Urbana: University of Illinois Press.

Osgood, C. E., & Walker, E. G. (1959). Motivation and language behavior: A content analysis of suicide notes. *Journal of Abnormal and Social Psychology, 59*, 58–67.

Patton, M. Q. (1990). *Qualitative evaluation and research methods* (2nd ed.). Newbury Park, CA: Sage.

Pennebaker, J. W., Mayne, T. J., & Francis, M. E. (1997). Linguistic predictors of adaptive bereavement. *Journal of Personality and Social Psychology, 72*, 863–871.

Peterson, C. (1992). Explanatory style. In C. P. Smith (Ed.), *Motivation and personality: Handbook of thematic content analysis* (pp. 376–382). New York: Cambridge University Press.

Peterson, C., & McCabe, A. (1983). *Developmental psycholinguistics: Three ways of looking at a child's narrative*. New York: Plenum.

Peterson, C., Seligman, M. E. P., & Vaillant, G. E. (1988). Pessimistic explanatory style is a risk factor for physical illness: A 35-year longitudinal study. *Journal of Personality and Social Psychology, 55*, 23–27.

Polkinghorne, D. E. (1988). *Narrative knowing and the human sciences*. Albany: State University of New York Press.

Propp, V. (1968). *The morphology of the folktale* (2nd ed., rev.). Austin: University of Texas Press. (Original work published 1928.)

Riessman, C. K. (1993). *Narrative analysis.* Newbury Park, CA: Sage.

Ronan, G. C., Date, A. L., & Weisbrod, M. (1995). Personal problem-solving scoring of the TAT: Sensitivity to training. *Journal of Personality Assessment, 64,* 119–131.

Rosenwald, G. C., & Ochberg, R. L. (Eds.). (1992). *Storied lives: The cultural politics of self-understanding.* New Haven CT: Yale University Press.

Rumelhart, D. E. (1975). Notes on a schema for stories. In D. G. Bobros & A. Collins (Eds.), *Representation and understanding: Studies in cognitive science* (pp. 211–236). New York: Academic Press.

Sarbin, T. R. (Ed.). (1986). *Narrative psychology: The storied nature of human conduct.* New York: Praeger.

Schafer, R. (1992). *Retelling a life: Narration and dialogue in psychoanalysis.* New York: Basic Books.

Schneider, B., Wheeler, J. K., & Cox, J. F. (1992). A passion for service: Using content analysis to explicate service climate themes. *Journal of Applied Psychology, 77,* 705–716.

Simonton, D. K. (1981). The library laboratory: Archival data in personality and social psychology. In L. Wheeler (Ed.), *Review of personality and social psychology* (Vol. 2, pp. 217–244). Beverly Hills, CA: Sage.

Simonton, D. K. (1994). Computer content analysis of melodic structure. *Psychology of Music, 22,* 31–43.

Smith, C. P. (Ed.). (1992a). *Motivation and personality: Handbook of thematic content analysis.* New York: Cambridge University Press.

Smith, C. P. (1992b). Reliability issues. In C. P. Smith (Ed.), *Motivation and personality: Handbook of thematic content analysis* (pp. 126–139). New York: Cambridge University Press.

Smith, C. P. (1995). Content analysis. In A. S. R. Manstead & M. Hewstone (Eds.), *The Blackwell encyclopedia of social psychology* (pp. 125–130). Oxford, England: Blackwell.

Smith, C. P., Feld, S. C., & Franz, C. E. (1992). Methodological considerations: Steps in research employing content analysis systems. In C. P. Smith (Ed.), *Motivation and personality: Handbook of thematic content analysis* (pp. 515–536). New York: Cambridge University Press.

Snowdon, D. A., Kemper, S. J., Mortimer, J. A., Greiner, L. H., Wekstein, D. R., & Markesbery, W. R. (1996). Linguistic ability in early life and cognitive function and Alzheimer's disease in late life. *Journal of the American Medical Association, 275,* 528–532.

Spence, D. P. (1982). *Narrative truth and historical truth: Meaning and interpretation in psychoanalysis.* New York: Norton.

Stewart, A. J. (1992). Self-definition and social definition. In C. P. Smith (Ed.), *Motivation and personality: Handbook of thematic content analysis* (pp. 481–488). New York: Cambridge University Press.

Stone, P. J., Dunphy, D. C., Smith, M. S., & Ogilvie, D. M. (1966). *The general inquirer: A computer approach to content analysis.* Cambridge, MA: MIT Press.

Suedfeld, P. (1996). Thematic content analyses: Nomothetic methods for using Holocaust survivor narratives in psychological research. *Holocaust and Genocide Studies, 10,* 168–180.

Suedfeld, P., Tetlock, P. E., & Streufert, S. (1992). Conceptual/integrative complexity. In C. P. Smith (Ed.), *Motivation and personality: Handbook of thematic content analysis* (pp. 393–400). New York: Cambridge University Press.

Tannen, D. (1993). What's in a frame? Surface evidence for underlying expectations. In D. Tannen (Ed.), *Framing in discourse* (pp. 14–55). New York: Oxford University Press.

Taylor, C. R., Lee, J. Y., & Stern, B. B. (1995). Portrayals of African, Hispanic, and Asian Americans in magazine advertising. *American Behavioral Scientist, 38,* 608–621.

Thomas, W. I., & Znaniecki, F. (1918, 1919, 1920). *The Polish peasant in Europe and America* (Vols. I & II [1918]; Vol. III [1919]; Vols. IV & V [1920]. Boston: Gorham Press.

Van de Castle, R. L. (1994). *Our dreaming mind.* New York: Ballantine.

Veroff, J. (1992). Thematic apperceptive methods in survey research. In C. P. Smith (Ed.), *Motivation and personality: Handbook of thematic content analysis* (pp. 100–109). New York: Cambridge University Press.

Veroff, J., Sutherland, L., Chadiha, L., & Ortega, R. M. (1993). Predicting marital quality with narrative assessment of marital experience. *Journal of Marriage and the Family, 55,* 326–327.

Viney, L. L. (1983). The assessment of psychological states through content analysis of verbal communications. *Psychological Bulletin, 94,* 542–563.

Vitz, P. C. (1990). The use of stories in moral development: New psychological reasons for an old education method. *American Psychologist, 45,* 709–720.

Weber, R. P. (1990). *Basic content analysis* (2nd ed.). Newbury Park, CA: Sage.

Weitzman, E. A., & Miles, M. B. (1995). *Computer programs for qualitative data analysis.* Thousand Oaks, CA: Sage.

Wessman, A. E., & Ricks, D. F. (1966) *Mood and personality.* New York: Holt, Rinehart and Winston.

Westen, D. (1991). Clinical assessment of object relations using the TAT. *Journal of Personality Assessment, 56,* 56–74.

White, M., & Epston, D. (1990). *Narrative means to therapeutic ends.* New York: Norton.

White, R. K. (1947). Black boy: A value analysis. *Journal of Abnormal and Social Psychology, 42,* 440–461.

White, R. K. (1951). *Value analysis: The nature and use of the method.* Glen Gardiner, NJ: Libertarian Press.

Winter, D. G. (1992). Content analysis of archival materials, personal documents, and everyday verbal productions. In C. P. Smith (Ed.), *Motivation and personality: Handbook of thematic content analysis* (pp. 110–125). New York: Cambridge University Press.

PART THREE

DATA ANALYTIC STRATEGIES

CHAPTER THIRTEEN

Measurement: Reliability, Construct Validation, and Scale Construction

OLIVER P. JOHN AND VERONICA BENET-MARTÍNEZ

Is an alpha reliability of .70 high enough? How do I know my questionnaire scale is unidimensional? What do I need to do to show that my measure is valid? These are the kinds of questions that methodologists are often asked. The answers to these questions are important for everybody who does empirical research in social–personality psychology, and they all involve basic issues in measurement. Yet, when we teach courses on measurement and test construction, we seldom encounter much enthusiasm. In fact, most students think that measurement is outright boring. However, without measurement there would be no empirical science.

Consider an unusual and extreme but illustrative example: recent research on the vast societal problem of child molestation (see Harris & Rice, 1996). Theory suggested a crucial variable: Child molesters may sexually prefer and be responsive to children, whereas nonmolestors are more responsive to adults. The researchers were faced with what seemed to be insurmountable measurement problems – how could they measure a construct such as "sexual responsiveness to children" in individuals who had reason to deny to others and themselves that they are attracted to children? Self-report did not seem a viable option

when studying sex offenders and sexual aggression. Eventually, the researchers developed an ingenious phallometric procedure that allowed them to measure genital blood flow in response to slides depicting pictures of nude adults and children. Even though they had a seemingly fool-proof physiological measure, the investigators took painstaking care to attend to measurement issues: Do the blood-flow measurements generalize across equivalent kinds of pictures? Do they replicate over time and testing situations? Do they validly differentiate groups of known offenders from (presumed) nonoffenders? Do they converge with measures obtained with other methods, such as reports from clinicians, and would they predict future abuse?

SOME GENERAL CONSIDERATIONS IN MEASUREMENT

These questions – traditionally discussed under the headings of reliability and validity – all illustrate the fundamental concern of empirical science with *generalizability*, that is, the degree to which we can make inferences from our measurements or observations to other samples, items, measures, methods, outcomes, and so on (Cronbach, Gleser, Nanda, & Rajaratnam, 1972). If we cannot make such generalizations, our measurements are obviously much less useful than if we can provide explicit evidence for generalizability.

The notion of generalizability also reminds us that good measurement implies not only that we can reproduce or replicate the same measurement but also that we can trust that the measurement has a particular meaning – we want to be able to make inferences about other variables that interest us. In the phallometric example, the blood-flow measurements

The preparation of this chapter was supported, in part, by Grant MH49255 and 43948 from the National Institute of Mental Health and a sabbatical award from the University of California, Berkeley, to the first author. We are indebted to Harry Reis and Chick Judd for their enormous editorial efforts on behalf of this chapter and to Lewis R. Goldberg and Richard W. Robins for their helpful comments on an earlier draft. Correspondence may be addressed to Oliver P. John, Department of Psychology, University of California, Berkeley, CA 94720-1650 (e-mail: ojohn@socrates.berkeley.edu).

would be useless if they failed to help us understand differences between offenders and nonoffenders. Another basic idea implicit in the idea of generalizability is that all psychological measurement – self-reports, observer ratings, even physiological measures – is prone to errors and that we cannot simply assume that a single measurement will generalize. Any one measurement may be distorted by numerous sources of error (e.g., there may have been something about the particular slide used, the blood-flow meter may have shifted slightly, etc.), and the resulting observation (or score) is only imperfectly related to what we want to measure, namely sexual responsiveness. To counteract this limitation of single measurements, psychologists obtain multiple measurements (e.g., across different stimuli, experimenters, or observers) and then aggregate them into a more generalizable composite score.

Defining Measurement as Building and Evaluating Models

Admonished that psychologists often talk "at great length" about phenomena and concepts they have not defined (Dawes & Smith, 1985, p. 509), we shall briefly consider what measurement is and how it may be defined. An early definition comes from Stevens (1951), one of the founders of measurement theory, who suggested that measurement is the assignment of numbers to objects or events according to rules. However, it is now generally agreed that measurement requires more than that, and Dawes and Smith, Himmelfarb (1993), and Judd and McClelland (1998) present excellent discussions of the relevant historical and conceptual issues. We agree that it is most useful to think of measurement as the process of building models that represent the phenomena of interest, typically in quantitative form. Judd and McClelland (1998) articulated this point of view:

The raw data...of the social and behavioral sciences ...consist of infinitely minute observations of ongoing behavior and attributes of individuals, social groups, social environments, and other entities or objects that populate the social world. Measurement is the process by which these infinitely varied observations are reduced to compact descriptions or *models* that are presumed to represent meaningful regularities in the entities that are observed ...Accordingly, measurement consists of rules that assign scale or variable values to entities to represent the constructs that are thought to be theoretically meaningful (pp. 181, emphasis added).

Like most models, measurement models (e.g., tests, scales, or variables) have to be reductions or simplifications to be useful. Although they should represent the best possible approximation of the phenomena of interest, we must expect them, like all "working models," to be eventually proven wrong and to be superseded by successively better models. For this reason, measurement models must be specified explicitly so that they can be evaluated, disconfirmed, and improved. Moreover, we should not ask whether a particular model is true or correct; instead, we should build several plausible alternative models and ask: Given everything we know, which models can we rule out and which model is best at representing our data? Or, even more clearly: which model is the least wrong? This kind of comparative model-testing (e.g., Judd, McClelland, & Culhane, 1995) is the best strategy for evaluating and improving our measurement procedures.

Psychometric and Representational Approaches to Measurement

The present chapter focuses on what has become known as the psychometric or nonrepresentational approach to measurement. Representational measurement has been discussed in several extensive reviews, especially in the context of attitude measurement (Dawes & Smith, 1985; Himmelfarb, 1993). In brief, the basic assumption of representational measurement is that numbers are assigned to entities such that the properties of the numbers (e.g., "greater than," "multiplication") represent empirical relations. A good example of representational measurement is the Mohs Scale of Hardness, which measures the hardness of rocks in terms of an ordinal scale (Dawes & Smith, 1985, p. 532): Rock X is harder than Rock Y if and only if X can scratch Y. The key feature of representational measurement in this example is the empirical relation that can be shown to exist between any pair of rocks and that can be represented by the "greater-than" relation among real numbers. One advantage of these kinds of measurement models is that they make predictions about the behavior of the individual entities being measured and thus provide internal consistency checks that can be used to disconfirm the model. For example, the ordinal hardness scale for rocks has to follow the transitivity rule, such that if Rock X is harder than Rock Y and Y is harder than Z, then X has to be harder than Z, and this prediction can be verified empirically by checking whether X does indeed scratch Z.

In contrast, the psychometric approach does not afford such internal consistency checks. For example, although the responses participants make on rating scales are often assigned numbers (e.g., 1 = *disagree strongly* and 5 = *agree strongly*), these numbers are not imbued with strong representational meaning that would permit consistency checks (see Dawes & Smith, 1985, for samples and a discussion of rating scales). Instead, the psychometric approach relies on aggregate patterns of data to evaluate a proposed measurement model. It does so because it assumes that each individual response or observation is so prone to error that consistency checks at this level of measurement are simply not meaningful and informative. For example, consider the two self-report items "I am a generous person" and "I am a stingy person" (Hampson, 1998). Although responses to these two items tend to be negatively correlated (i.e., most respondents claim one of the two traits but not both), the correlations are not even close to −1.0, the number we would expect if people were semantically consistent. Instead, only some people are very consistent; there are vast individual differences, even among college students, and more verbally intelligent students show greater consistency (Goldberg & Kilkowski, 1984). In other words, people are not like rocks – they are much less consistent in their behavior, scratching or otherwise. Thus, the psychometric approach tends to ignore consistency checks at the level of the individual and instead relies on patterns of variances and covariances that reflect relations at the aggregate level in probabilistic form (e.g., in this sample, individuals who gave relatively high ratings to "generous" were unlikely to give high ratings to "stingy").

Although representational measurement promised to provide a strong and defensible foundation for psychological measurement, it has so far failed to deliver on that promise. During the 1970s and 1980s a slew of studies, inspired by Tversky and Kahneman's (1974) pioneering work, showed that people's preferences, risk perceptions, political attitudes, and so on often violate the transitivity rule required for ordinal scaling and that judgments may shift substantially depending on the framing of the questions or items. Dawes and Smith (1985) noted that "representational measurement is rare in the field of attitude; instead, this field is permeated by questionnaires and rating scales" (pp. 511–512). More recently, Cliff (1992) called representational measurement "the revolution that never happened" (p. 186), and Dawes (1994) concurred. For these reasons, and because Judd and McClelland (1998) provided an excellent up-to-date review and discussion of the representational approach, the present chapter is devoted to the psychometric approach.

Overview

The remainder of this chapter is organized into three parts. We begin with the historically early conceptions of reliability and then move to more recent and increasingly complex views that emphasize construct validation and model-testing as a broader, more integrative approach. In the first part of this chapter, we consider issues traditionally discussed under the heading of reliability; review several still persistent definitions or "types" of reliability coefficients; discuss in some detail the problems and misuses of coefficient alpha, the most commonly used psychometric index in social–personality psychology; and then suggest generalizability theory as a broader and more heuristic perspective. In the second part, we examine issues related to construct validation, beginning with early definitions and designs to establish validity, followed by a broader view that considers construct validation as the crucial issue in psychological measurement and includes a broad range of validity evidence, focusing on convergent and discriminant aspects. In the third part, we consider model-testing in construct validation and scale construction. After a brief introduction to measurement models in structural equation modeling (SEM), we discuss an empirical example that reexamines the issue of dimensionality as an aspect of structural validity, and then we consider issues in questionnaire construction, reviewing three classical strategies (external–criterion, rational–intuitive, and internal–factor analytic) and suggesting an integrated model adopting the construct-oriented approach.

It sometimes seems that methodologists write papers that are of great interest to other methodologists. Instead, the present chapter is focused on what in our experience has proven useful and of interest to graduate and postdoctoral students, with the goal of devising sound measurement models and evaluating them, rather than covering mathematical formulae or statistical derivations. Respecting the glacial pace of methodological advances (Cohen, 1990), we do discuss current practice, even when it is outmoded, and then point to more recent conceptualizations. Finally, whenever possible, we have avoided technical language, omitted Greek symbols, and used examples to make this chapter as concrete and accessible as possible.

RELIABILITY AND GENERALIZABILITY

It should by now be obvious that most measurement procedures in psychology are subject to "error." Many different sources may contribute to such error. In the social–personality literature, the observations, ratings, or judgments that constitute the measurement procedure are typically made by humans who are subject to a wide range of frailties. Research participants may become careless or inattentive, bored or fatigued, and may not always be motivated to do their best. The particular conditions and point in time when ratings are made or recorded may also contribute error. Further errors may be introduced by the rating or recording forms given to the raters to obtain their judgments; the instructions, definitions, and questions on these forms may be difficult to understand or require complex discriminations, again entering error into the measurement. In short, characteristics of the participant, the testing situation, the test or instrument, and the experimenter can all affect reliability.

Reliability refers to the consistency of a measurement procedure, and indices of reliability describe the extent to which the scores produced by the measurement procedure are reproducible. Consider the example of a bathroom scale; if it gives different readings in three successive weighings of the same person, we would hardly call the scale reliable.

Classical Test Theory

Issues of reliability have traditionally been treated within the framework of classical test theory (Gulliksen, 1950; Lord & Novick, 1968). If a given measurement X is subject to error e, then the measurement without the error, $X - e$, would represent the accurate or "true" measurement T (e.g., the person's actual weight). This seemingly simple formulation, that each measurement can be partitioned into a true score, T, and measurement error, e, is the fundamental assumption of classic test theory. Conceptually, each true score represents the mean of a very large number of measurements on a specific individual, whereas measurement error represents all of the momentary variations in the circumstances of measurement that are unrelated to the measurement procedure itself. Such errors are assumed to be random (a rather strong assumption to which we will return), and it is this assumption that permits the definition of error in statistical terms.

All conceptions of reliability involve the notion of repeated measurements. Classical test theory has relied heavily on the notion of *parallel tests* – that is, two tests that have the same mean, variance, and distributional characteristics, and that correlate equally with external variables (Lord & Novick, 1968). Under these assumptions, true score and measurement error can be treated as independent. It follows that the variance of the observed scores equals the sum of the variance of the true scores and the variance of the measurement error:

$$\text{Variance } (X) = \text{Variance } (T + e)$$
$$= \text{Variance } (T) + \text{Variance } (e).$$

Reliability can then be defined as the ratio of the true-score variance to the observed-score variance, which is equivalent to 1 minus the ratio of error variance to observed-score variance:

$$\text{Reliability} = \text{Variance } (T)/\text{Variance } (X)$$
$$= 1 - [\text{Variance}(e)/\text{Variance } (X)].$$

In other words, if there is no error, reliability would be 1; if there is only error and no true-score variance, reliability would be 0. The correlation between the observed variable and the true score is the square root of the reliability.

Specific Types of Reliability Evidence

Because classical test theory defined parallel tests in purely mathematical terms, it provided little substantive specification or restriction of the types of measurement procedures that might be considered parallel. Beginning in the 1950s, several experimental designs were distinguished, and they are summarized in Table 13.1: Retest (or stability), equivalence, and internal consistency (or split-half). These distinctions were meant to convey the idea that "reliability is a generic term referring to many types of evidence" (American Psychological Association [APA], 1954, p. 28). Clearly, the different designs spelled out in Table 13.1 take into account quite different sources of error. *Retest* (or stability) designs estimate how much responses vary within individuals across time and situation, thus reflecting error due to differences in the situation and conditions of test administration or observation.[1] *Equivalence*

---

[1] As noted in Table 13.1, both Pearson and intraclass correlations can be used to index stability. Pearson correlations only reflect changes in the relative standing of participants from one time to the other, which is typically the prime concern in research on individual differences. When changes in mean levels or variances are of interest, too, then the intraclass correlation is the appropriate index.

TABLE 13.1. Reliability: Facets of Generalizability, Traditional Definitions of Reliability Coefficients, and Estimation Procedures

Facet of generalizability	Major sources of error	Traditional reliability coefficient	Procedure	Statistical analysis
Times	Change of participant's responses over time; change in testing situation	Retest (or stability)	Test participants at different times with same form	Pearson or intraclass correlation
Forms	Differences in content sampling across "parallel" forms	Equivalence	Test participants at one time with two forms covering same content	Pearson or intraclass correlation
Items	Content heterogeneity and low content saturation in the items	(a) Split-half (b) Internal consistency	Test participants with multiple items at one time	(a) Correlation between test halves (Spearman-Brown corrected) (b) Coefficient alpha
Judges or observers	Disagreement among judges	Internal consistency	Obtain ratings from multiple judges on one form and occasion	(a) Pairwise interjudge correlation (b) Coefficient alpha (c) Intraclass correlation

procedures estimate error due to different content-sampling and item-selection in two alternate forms of the test. *Internal-consistency* procedures offer an estimate of error associated with the particular selection of items; error is high (and internal consistency is low) when items are heterogeneous in content and lack content saturation.

Coefficient Alpha: Ubiquitous but Not a Panacea

We now consider coefficient alpha (Cronbach, 1951) because this internal consistency index plays such an important role in the social–personality literature. A perusal of the articles published in the *Journal of Personality and Social Psychology* and *Personality and Social Psychology Bulletin* shows that de facto alpha is the index of choice when authors want to claim that their measure is reliable. Moreover, contrary even to the recommendations in the *Standards* (APA, 1985), alpha is usually the only reliability evidence considered.

Why has alpha become the Bill Gates of measurement reliability? We suspect it is the relative ease with which alpha is both obtained and computed. Alpha does not require collecting data at two different times

from the same participants, as retest reliability would, or the construction of two alternate forms of a scale, as parallel-form reliability would require. Alpha is the "least effort" reliability index; it can be used as long as the same participants responded to multiple items thought to indicate the same construct. And computationally, today's SPSS and statistical software packages allow the user to view the alpha of many alternative scales formed from any motley collection of items with just a few mouse clicks. However, although alpha has many important uses, it also has some important limitations. Although long known to methodologists, these limitations are often underappreciated by researchers and are therefore reviewed here in some detail.

TWO DETERMINANTS OF ALPHA. Cronbach's (1951) alpha is a generalization of split-half reliability, representing the mean of the reliabilities computed from all possible split halves of the test. As such, alpha is a function of two parameters: (a) the interrelatedness of the items in a test or scale and (b) the length of the test. Consider Table 13.2, which shows the interitem correlation matrices for two hypothetical tests,

TABLE 13.2. Interitem Correlation Matrices for Two Hypothetical Tests with the Same Coefficient Alpha Reliability of .81

				Test A with 10 items										Test B with 6 items				
Variable	1	2	3	4	5	6	7	8	9	10	Variable	1	2	3	4	5	6
1.	—										1.	—					
2.	.3	—									2.	.6	—				
3.	.3	.3	—								3.	.6	.6	—			
4.	.3	.3	.3	—							4.	.3	.3	.3	—		
5.	.3	.3	.3	.3	—						5.	.3	.3	.3	.6	—	
6.	.3	.3	.3	.3	.3	—					6.	.3	.3	.3	.6	.6	—
7.	.3	.3	.3	.3	.3	.3	—										
8.	.3	.3	.3	.3	.3	.3	.3	—									
9.	.3	.3	.3	.3	.3	.3	.3	.3	—								
10.	.3	.3	.3	.3	.3	.3	.3	.3	.3	—							

one with 10 items and one with 6 items, constructed by Schmitt (1996).[2] Both tests have the same alpha of .81 but they achieve that alpha in two rather different ways. Test B has only 6 items but, on average, these items are more highly intercorrelated (mean $r = .42$) than the 10 items of Test A (mean $r = .33$).

The idea that test length can compensate for lower levels of interitem correlation is formalized in the Spearman–Brown prophecy formula, which specifies the relation between test length and reliability (see, e.g., Lord & Novick, 1968). Given a particular level of mean interitem correlation, the Spearman–Brown formula allows the researcher to derive the number of items needed to achieve a certain level of alpha. Figure 13.1 shows this relation for mean interitem correlations of .20, .40, .60, and .80 in graphic form. Three points are worth noting. First, the alpha reliability of the total scale always increases as the number of items increases (as long as adding items does not lower the mean interitem correlation). Second, the utility of adding ever more items diminishes quickly, so that adding the 15th item leads to a much lesser increase in alpha than adding the 5th item, just like consuming the 15th chocolate bar or beer adds less enjoyment than did the earlier ones. Third, less is to be gained from adding more items if those items are highly intercorrelated (e.g., .60) than when they show little content saturation (e.g., .20). The lesson here is that we need to be careful in interpreting alpha: We cannot interpret

empirical findings without considering scale length. In contexts where the researcher is interested in the homogeneity of the items, a direct index of item content saturation (e.g., the mean interitem correlation) may be more informative than alpha.

ALPHA DOES NOT INDEX UNIDIMENSIONALITY. The examples in Table 13.2 also illustrate a second issue with alpha: Contrary to popular belief, alpha does not measure the homogeneity of the interitem intercorrelations, nor does it indicate that a scale is unidimensional. In fact, although Tests A and B in Table 13.2 have the same alpha, they differ radically in the homogeneity (vs. dispersion) of the correlations among their items. For Test A, they are completely homogeneous (all are .3, with a standard deviation (SD) of 0 in this hypothetical example), whereas for Test B they vary considerably (from .3 to .6, with an SD of .15). Because alpha does not represent this variability, Cortina (1993) derived an index that reflects the spread of interitem correlations and argued that this index should be reported along with alpha. A large spread in interitem correlations is a bad sign because it suggests that either the test is multidimensional or the interitem correlations are distorted by substantial sampling error.[3] In the example, the pattern of item intercorrelations for Test B suggests that the problem here is multidimensionality. Clearly, the responses to these six items are a function not of one, but two, factors: Items 1, 2, and 3 correlate much more substantially (mean $r = .6$) with each other than they correlate (mean $r = .3$) with items

[2] Consistent with Schmitt (1996), the examples are presented in correlational terms (rather than in covariance terms) simply for ease of interpretation and convenience. Alphas are in fact standardized alphas (i.e., after standard scoring all variables).

[3] Cortina's (1993) index should not be confused with the standard error of alpha, which can be computed under certain distributional assumptions (cf. Feldt, Woodruff, & Salih, 1987).

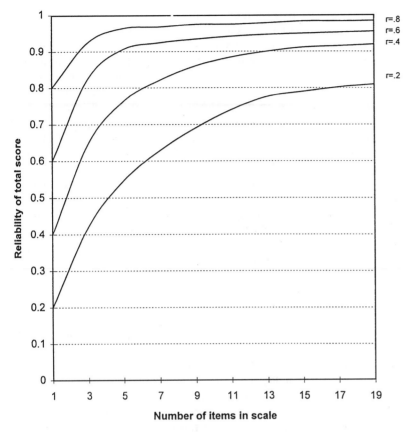

Figure 13.1. Alpha reliability as a function of the number of items included in the scale at four levels of mean interitem correlation.

4, 5, and 6, which in turn correlate more highly with each other (mean $r = .6$). Alpha disguises this rather important difference between Tests A and B.

Because alpha cannot address it, unidimensionality needs to be established in other ways. The most rigorous approach is to use the confirmatory factor analysis part of SEM (Jöreskog & Sörbom, 1981; see also Bentler, 1980; Wegener & Fabrigar, this volume, Ch. 16). SEM allows us to test how well the interitem correlation matrix fits a single-factor, rather than multifactor, model. In other words, how well can the loadings on a single factor reproduce the correlation matrix actually observed? Not surprisingly in these artificial data, the SEM results show that the one-factor model describes the data pattern for Test A perfectly; all items have a factor loading of .548 (i.e., the square root of .3, which is the size of all interitem correlations in this example) and an error term of .837. In contrast, for Test B the fit of the one-factor model was unacceptable even though the item loadings of .648 (i.e., the square root

of .42, which is the mean interitem correlation) were higher than for the truly unidimensional Test A. As expected, a two-factor model significantly increased fit for Test B, and perfect fit was obtained when we specified a model with two correlated factors. Reflecting their .60 correlation with each other, items 1, 2, and 3 loaded .775 on factor 1 and 0 on factor 2, whereas items 4, 5, and 6 loaded 0 on factor 1 and .775 on factor 2; the mean intercorrelation of .3 between the items in these two sets gave rise to a .50 correlation estimated between the two latent factors.

It is important to emphasize that the issue of error (or unreliability) present in an item is separate from the issue of multidimensionality (which is discussed in later sections on structural validity). In the SEM analyses summarized above, the item loadings represent how much of the item variance is shared across items (thus generalizable), whereas error is captured by the residual item variance (i.e., 1 minus the squared loading) indicating how much variance is unique to that item; the proportion of shared to total item variance is often referred to as *content saturation*. Dimensionality, on the other hand, is captured by the relative fit of the one-factor model over multiple-factor models. Thus, comparing again Tests A and B in Table 13.2, the longer Test A is clearly more unidimensional than Test B, yet its items do not show greater content saturation (i.e., higher factor loadings and lower error terms). In other words, unidimensionality does not imply lower levels of measurement error (i.e., unreliability) and vice versa. We return to these issues later in this chapter when we discuss the measurement model in SEM.

Once we know that a test is multidimensional, can we go ahead and still use alpha as a reliability index? Unfortunately, the answer is no. As Cronbach (1947, 1951) recognized early on, we can estimate the reliability of a multidimensional test or scale only through parallel forms, and the two parallel forms must show the same factor structure. In fact, if the test is not unidimensional, then alpha underestimates reliability (see Schmitt, 1996, for an example). Thus, if a test is found to be multidimensional, one should score two unidimensional subscales and then use alpha to index their reliabilities separately.[4]

HOW LARGE SHOULD ALPHA BE? IT DEPENDS ON THE CONSTRUCT. Students often ask questions like "my scale has an alpha of .70 – isn't that good enough?" and they are frustrated when the answer is "that depends." Although it would be nice to have a simple cookbook for measurement decisions, there is no particular level of alpha that is necessary, adequate, or even desirable in all contexts. Although Nunnally (1978) suggested that "reliabilities of .7 or higher will suffice" (p. 245), an alpha of .70 is not a benchmark every scale must pass. It is easy to find examples in the literature that use this arbitrary standard. For example, Gray-Little, Williams, and Hancock (1997) noted that alphas between .72 and .88 are usually taken to indicate "acceptable to high reliability" (p. 444). However, as we have seen above, alpha needs to be interpreted in terms of its two main parameters – interitem correlation as well as scale length – and in the context of how these two parameters fit the nature and definition of the construct to be measured. In any one context, a particular alpha may be just right, or too low, or too high. As Pedhazur and Schmelkin (1991) put it,

Does a .5 reliability coefficient stink? To answer this question, no authoritative source will do. Rather, *it is for the user to determine what amount of error variance he or she is willing to tolerate, given the specific circumstances of the study.* (p. 110)

The definition of the construct to be measured is a crucial parameter in interpreting alpha. Consider a researcher who wants to measure the broad construct of extraversion, which includes sociability, assertiveness, and talkativeness, and has constructed a scale with the following items: "I like to go to parties," "Parties are a lot of fun for me," "I do not enjoy parties," (reverse scored) and "I'd rather go to a party than spend the evening alone." Note that these items are essentially paraphrases of each other and represent the same

item content (liking parties) stated in slightly different ways. Cattell (1972) called these kinds of scales "bloated specifics" – they have high alphas simply because the item content is so redundant and interitem correlations are very high. Thus, alphas in the high .80s or even .90s, especially for short scales, may not indicate an impressively reliable scale but instead signal redundancy or narrowness in item content.

For example, the 10-item Rosenberg (1979) Self-Esteem Scale has alphas approaching .90 in student samples, and the pairwise correlations between some items approach .70 (Gray-Little et al., 1997). Some of these self-esteem items turn out to be almost synonymous, such as "I certainly feel useless at times" and "At times I think I am no good at all." Although such redundant items increase alpha, they do not add unique (and thus incremental) information and can often be omitted in the interest of efficiency, suggesting that the scale can be abbreviated without much loss of information (see Robins & Hendin, 1999).

This phenomenon is also known as the *attenuation paradox* because increasing the internal consistency of a test beyond a certain point will not enhance construct validity and may even come at the expense of validity when the added items emphasize one part of the construct (e.g., party-going) over other important parts (e.g., assertiveness). This paradox emphasizes an important point in this chapter: Our goal in measurement is to maximize validity rather than internal consistency, and issues of meaning and conceptualization play a key role in all decisions about measurement.

The party-going items on our imaginary extraversion scale illustrate how easy it is to boost alpha by adding redundant items to a scale. However, unless one is specifically interested in party-going behavior, this strategy is not very useful: The narrow content representation (i.e., high content homogeneity) would make this scale less useful as a measure of sociability and even less useful as a measure of the broader construct of extraversion. Although the scale may predict the frequency of party attendance with great precision (or fidelity), it is less likely to relate to anything else of interest because of its narrow bandwidth. Conversely, broad-bandwidth measures (e.g., an extraversion scale or a general attitude measure of conservatism) can predict a wider range of outcomes or behaviors but do so with lower fidelity. This phenomenon is known as the bandwidth-fidelity trade-off (Cronbach & Gleser, 1957) and has proven to be of considerable importance in the literature on attitudes (Eagly & Chaiken, 1993; Fishbein & Ajzen, 1974) and personality traits (Epstein, 1980; John, Hampson, & Goldberg, 1991). In general, then, the attitude or trait serving as the

---

[4] There is an important exception where this internal-consistency conception does not apply. In most social–personality measurement, the indicators of a construct are seen as effects caused by the construct; individuals endorse particular attitude statements because of underlying individual differences in attitudes. However, as Bollen (1984) noted, constructs such as socioeconomic status (SES) are different. SES indicators, such as education and income, cause changes in SES, rather than SES causing changes in education or income. In these cases of "cause indicators," the indicators are not necessarily correlated and the internal-consistency conception does not apply.

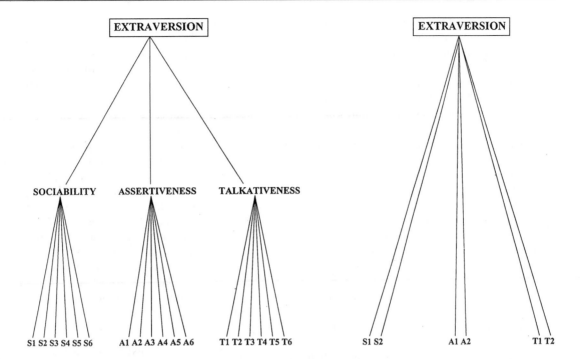

Figure 13.2. Relation between hierarchical level and content homogeneity in interpreting the size of alpha reliability.

predictor should be measured at a similar level of abstraction as the criterion to be predicted, so that predictive relations are not going to be attenuated.

The close connection between the hierarchical level of the construct to be measured and the content homogeneity of the items is illustrated in Figure 13.2. Sociability, assertiveness, and talkativeness are three scales that are positively intercorrelated and together define the broader construct of extraversion. (Our earlier example of the party-going scale might be represented as an even lower-level scale, representing one of the components of the sociability scale.) Consider the assertiveness scale. Because its six items are selected to represent a narrow range of content (e.g., all the assertiveness items have to do with dominance and self-assertion in various situations), item content should be relatively homogeneous, leading to a substantial mean interitem correlation. Now consider an equally long extraversion scale (shown on the right side of Figure 13.2), made up of two sociability items, two assertiveness items, and two talkativeness items. Compared with the lower-level scales, the item content on this scale is much more heterogeneous, leading to a lower mean interitem correlation and thus a lower alpha.

One implication of Figure 13.2 is that if one wants to measure broader constructs, one should probably include a larger number of items to compensate for the greater content heterogeneity; for example, one might use all 18 items to measure the superordinate extraversion construct defined on the left side of Figure 13.2.

This principle underlies the construction of many hierarchically organized assessment instruments, such as in the literature on the self-concept (e.g., Marsh, Byrne, & Shavelson, 1992) and on personality traits. For example, in Costa and McCrae's (1992) NEO PI–R, each of the Big Five personality dimensions is defined by six more specific "facet" scales, which, in turn, are each measured with eight items; the resulting 48-item superordinate Big Five scales all have reliabilities exceeding .90.

Correcting for Attenuation

According to classical test theory (e.g., Lord & Novick, 1968), researchers should be concerned about reliability because the reliability of a measure constrains how strongly that measure may correlate with another variable (e.g., an external criterion). If error is truly random, as classical test theory assumes, the upper limit of the correlation for a measure is not 1.0 but the square root of its reliability (i.e., the correlation of the measure with itself). Thus, the true correlation between the measure and another variable may be underestimated (i.e., attenuated) when reliability is inadequate. For example, for a reliability of .70, the expected upper limit for a correlation would be the square root of .70, namely .84, and for a reliability as low as

.60, the limit would be .77. These numerical examples show that lower reliabilities can reduce estimates of external correlations and, everything else equal, higher reliabilities are to be preferred.

However, other properties of the instrument need to be considered as well in planning one's research. As Burisch (1984, 1986) has shown, "short scales not only save testing time but also avoid subject boredom and fatigue ... there are subjects ... from whom you won't get any response if the test looks too long." Consider, for example, the 48-item long Big Five trait scales from the NEO PI–R (Costa & McCrae, 1992). Despite their reliabilities above .90, they are used less frequently by other researchers than are shorter scales that have reliabilities in the .70s and .80s. When participant time and attention is at a premium, the trade-off between length and reliability may well be worth it – note that the drop in reliabilities from .90 to .80 and to .70 lowers the upper limits for external correlations only from .95 to .89 and to .84 for the shorter scales.

Researchers sometimes use reliability indices (typically alpha) to correct observed correlations between two measures for attenuation due to unreliability. Such corrections are sometimes used to estimate the correlation between the latent constructs underlying their measures (see also the section on SEM below) – that is, what would the correlation be if both measures were assessed with perfect reliability? This can be useful to compare effect sizes across variables or studies. Another application is in contexts where researchers want to distinguish the long-term stability of attitudes or personality from the reliability of measurement or compare stability estimates for different groups, such as

men and women (J. Block & Robins, 1993). The correction formula (Cohen & Cohen, 1975; Lord & Novick, 1968) is simple: Divide the observed correlation by the square root of the product of the two reliabilities. This correction expresses the size of the association relative to the maximum correlation attainable given the imperfect reliabilities of the two measures.

However, the ease of this correction should not lead to sloppy measurement. Appealing to the relative brevity of one's measures to excuse low reliability is, as we have seen above, not the only explanation for low alphas, and certainly not an excuse. In many situations, low reliability will create problems for estimating effect sizes and testing hypotheses. This is especially true in multivariate applications, such as multitrait multimethod matrices (discussed below), where unequal reliabilities might bias conclusions about convergent and discriminant validity (West & Finch, 1997). In general, then, researchers are well-advised to invest the time and effort needed to construct reliable measures.

Reporting Basic Psychometric Data

Whereas most social–personality researchers do report alpha reliabilities for their scales, few report their intercorrelations. This information is often crucial, for example, when multiple scales are scored from the same data source (e.g., a self-report attitude measure) and when the research question implies relative independence among the constructs measured. For example, intercorrelations among predictors are important for understanding the results of multiple regression analyses (e.g., see the numerical examples provided by Goldberg, 1991), and concerns have been raised about the correlations among constructs postulated to be conceptually unrelated, such as the Big Five personality dimensions (e.g., J. Block, 1995; John & Srivastava, 1999). Thus, we agree with Schmitt (1996), who argued that, at the very least, research reports should regularly present a matrix that includes reliability information for the key measures (on the diagonal), the intercorrelations among these measures (below the diagonal), and probably also the intercorrelations corrected for attenuation due to unreliability (above the diagonal). Table 13.3 gives an example from our own research on the

---

TABLE 13.3. How to Report Simple Psychometric Information for Multiple Scales: Alpha Coefficients, Observed Correlations, and Corrected Correlations among the Big Five Inventory (BFI) Scales

Scales	E	A	C	N	O
Extraversion (E)	(.88)	.17	.28	− .34	.30
Agreeableness (A)	.14	(.79)	.34	− .38	.06
Conscientiousness (C)	.24	.27	(.82)	− .22	.10
Neuroticism (N)	− .29	− .31	− .18	(.84)	− .17
Openness (O)	.25	.05	.08	− .14	(.81)

Note: N = 711 U.S. college students. Data from Benet-Martínez and John (1998). Alpha coefficients are presented on the diagonal, observed correlations below the diagonal, and correlations corrected for attenuation above the diagonal.

Big Five Inventory scales (John, Donahue, & Kentle, 1991; John & Srivastava, 1999). The inclusion of the uncorrected intercorrelations allows the reader to evaluate the size of the reliability coefficients relative to the overlap among the scales; reliabilities should be substantially larger than these intercorrelations. The inclusion of corrected intercorrelations is helpful because it removes differences among the intercorrelations that are simply due to differential reliability, thus making comparisons among intercorrelations much easier. The corrected coefficients are also useful for identifying pairs of scales that lack discriminance – that is, they are so highly intercorrelated that postulating two separate underlying constructs is not sensible either theoretically or practically.

Beyond Classical Test Theory: Generalizability Theory

The distinctions among "types of reliability" emphasized in the literature and summarized in Table 13.1 had a number of unfortunate consequences. First, they masked a major shortcoming of classical test theory: If all these measures were indeed parallel and all errors truly random, then all these approaches to reliability should yield the same answer. Unfortunately, they do not; reliability depends on the particular facet of generalization being examined (Cronbach, Rajaratnam, & Gleser, 1963). Second, what had been intended as heuristic distinctions became reified as "the Stability Coefficient" or "the Alpha Coefficient," even though the notion of reliability was intended as a general concept. Third, the classification itself was too simple, equating particular kinds of reliability evidence with only one source of error and resulting in a restrictive terminology that cannot fully capture the broad range and combination of multiple error sources that are of interest in most research and measurement applications (Shavelson, Webb, & Rowley, 1989).

Therefore, the APA (e.g., 1985) recommended in subsequent editions of the *Standards for Educational and Psychological Testing* that these distinctions and terminology be abolished and replaced by the broader view advocated by generalizability theory (Cronbach et al., 1963). Regrettably, however, practice has not changed sufficiently over the years, and generalizability theory has not fully replaced these more simplistic notions. To emphasize that the classical conception of random error is outdated, the very first column in our Table 13.1 spells out the facet of generalizability that is being varied and studied in each of these generalizability designs.

Generalizability theory holds that we are interested in the "reliability" of an observation or measurement because we wish to generalize from this observation to some other class of observations. For example, as shown by the last row in Table 13.1, concern with interjudge agreement may actually be a concern with the question of how accurately we can generalize from a given set of ratings to ratings by another set of judges. Or we might want to know how well scores on an attitude scale constructed according to one set of procedures generalize to another scale constructed according to different procedures. Or we might want to test the generalizability of a scale originally developed in English to a Chinese language and cultural context.

All these facets of generalizability represent legitimate research concerns that we will reconsider later in this chapter under the heading of construct validation; they can be studied systematically in generalizability designs, both individually and together. These designs allow the researcher to deliberately vary the facets that potentially influence observed scores and estimate the variance attributable to each facet (Cronbach et al., 1972). In other words, whereas classical test theory tries to estimate the portion of variance that is attributable to "error," generalizability theory aims to estimate the extent to which specific sources of variance contribute to test scores under carefully defined conditions. Thus, instead of the traditional reliability coefficients listed in Table 13.1, we should use more general estimates, such as intraclass correlation coefficients (see Shrout & Fleiss, 1979), to probe particular aspects of the dependability of measures. For example, the intraclass correlation coefficient (see Judd & McClelland, 1998, for numerical examples) can be used to index the generalizability of one set of judges to a universe of similar judges.

It is perplexing: Generalizability theory should hold considerable appeal for personality–social psychologists because the extent to which we can generalize across items, instruments, contexts, groups, languages, and cultures is crucial to the claims we can make about our findings. Despite excellent and readable introductions (e.g., Shavelson et al., 1989), generalizability theory is not used as widely as it should be. A recent exception is the flourishing research on determinants of consensus among personality raters (Kenny, 1994; see also Kashy & Kenny, this volume, Ch. 17) and the determinants of self–other agreement (John & Robins, 1993).

Generalizability theory is especially useful when data are collected in nested designs and multiple facets may influence reliability. A nice illustration is King and

Figueredo's (1997) study of chimpanzee personality differences. They collected ratings of chimpanzees differing in age and sex (subject variables) on 40 traits (stimulus variables) at several different zoos (setting variables) from animal keepers familiar with the animals to varying degrees (observer variables). They then used a generalizability design to show how these facets affected agreement among the judges; fortunately for their purposes, setting and subject variables turned out to be unimportant. It is a shame that generalizability theory, as well as Kenny's (1994) social relations model, have been perceived as "technical." With clear and accessible introductions available, it is high time that these important approaches to variance decomposition achieve greater popularity with a broader group of researchers.

Item Response Theory

The measurement model and procedures of classical test theory have also been criticized by psychometricians advocating item response theory (IRT) as an alternative and more advanced approach (Embretson, 1996; Mellenbergh, 1996). In the classical conception of reliability, the characteristics of the individual test-taker and the characteristics of the test cannot be separated (Hambleton, Swaminathan, & Rogers, 1991). That is, the person's standing (or level) on the underlying construct is defined only in terms of responses on the particular test; thus, the same person may appear quite liberal on a test that includes many items measuring extremely conservative beliefs but quite conservative on a test that includes many items measuring radical liberal beliefs. Furthermore, the psychometric characteristics of the test depend on the particular sample of respondents being measured; for example, whether a belief item from a conservatism scale reliably discriminates high and low scorers depends on the level of conservatism of the sample, so that the same test may work well in an undergraduate student sample but fail to make reliable distinctions among bible-belt evangelists. In short, classical test theory is not helpful if we want to compare individuals who have taken different tests measuring the same construct or if we want to compare items answered by different groups of individuals.

Another limitation of classical test theory is the assumption that the error of measurement is the same for all individuals in the sample, an implausible assumption given that tests and items differ in their ability to discriminate among respondents at different levels of the underlying construct (Lord, 1984). Moreover, classical theory is test-oriented rather than item-oriented and thus does not make predictions about how an individual or group will perform on a particular item.

These limitations can be addressed in IRT, which describes the relation between individuals' responses to a particular item and the construct underlying those responses with a function called the *item characteristic curve*. This curve depicts the probability that individuals at different levels of the construct would endorse the item; it thus provides information about how well the item discriminates those with high versus low levels of the underlying trait and also about how difficult the item is. This information is particularly useful to researchers interested in detecting biases in their items; according to IRT, an item is an unbiased measure of a construct, say conservatism, if individuals who are equally conservative have the same expected score on the item, regardless of conceptually unrelated memberships in gender, ethnic, or cultural groups.

In the context of constructing and evaluating scales and other multi-item measures, IRT procedures have two attractive features. First, they permit researchers to select items on the basis of both difficulty and discrimination, rather than relying on the item–total correlations offered by classical test theory. Second, IRT procedures can be used to assess a person's standing on the construct without having to administer the entire scale, a procedure known as computerized adaptive testing (Waller & Reise, 1989).

Until recently, IRT was limited computationally to dichotomous (true–false) response formats and unidimensional constructs. It was therefore much more useful for educational and achievement research (where item difficulty has an inherent psychological meaning) than for social–personality research, which relies heavily on multistep rating scales. However, with the recent extensions of IRT and IRT software to rating scales and multidimensional models (Kelderman & Rijkes, 1994), IRT's "new rules of measurement" (Embretson, 1996, p. 341) may soon appear more frequently in our journals. For example, Gray-Little et al. (1997) used IRT to explore the properties of the 10 items on the Rosenberg Self-Esteem Scale. Results indicated that the 10 items indeed define a unidimensional trait. However, given the uniformity of the item discrimination parameters, the scale could easily be shortened without compromising the measurement of global self-esteem, a conclusion consistent with our earlier discussion of construct definitions and item redundancy (Robins & Hendin, 1999). The IRT analyses also indicated that the items discriminate better at low and moderate levels of self-esteem than at higher levels.

With its current selection of items, the scale may fail to differentiate reliably between truly high levels of self-esteem and narcissistically exaggerated, grandiose self-views (John & Robins, 1994).

More generally, then, IRT provides quantitative procedures to describe the relation of a particular item to the latent construct being measured in terms of difficulty and discrimination parameters. This information can be useful for item analysis and scale construction, permitting researchers to select items that best measure a particular level of the construct of interest and detecting items that are biased for particular groups of individuals.

To summarize, in this section we focused on classical test theory approaches to reliability, specific types of reliability indices, issues with coefficient alpha (test length, unidimensionality, and construct definitions), and the practice of correcting for attenuation. In discussing these issues, we mentioned such concepts as latent (or underlying) constructs, construct definitions, dimensionality, criterion variables, and discriminant relations, but did not discuss them systematically. These concepts raise complex conceptional issues and highlight that the meaning and interpretation of measurements is crucial to evaluating the quality of our measurements. Traditionally, issues of score meaning and interpretation are discussed under the heading of validity. We focus on the validity of measured variables here; the validity of manipulated variables is discussed in Chapters 1 and 2 of this volume.

CONSTRUCT VALIDATION

Traditional Definitions of Validity

As described by Cronbach and Meehl (1955), the APA committee on psychological tests initially distinguished among several types of validity, which are given in the top part of Table 13.4. Content validity is established by demonstrating that the items are a representative sample of the universe of item content relevant to the construct. This aspect of validity is typically established deductively; first the investigator defines a universe of items (i.e., a hypothetical set of all possible kinds of relevant item content) and then samples systematically from that universe to assemble the test items. Face validity concerns theoretical considerations about the appropriateness of the items, particularly whether they appear to assess attributes and behaviors relevant to the intended construct; that is, do the items look reasonable and sensible as indicators of the construct they are supposed to measure?

Criterion-oriented (or external) validity had traditionally been considered most central because a test or measure that fails to predict or relate to anything else of interest would be of little use. At the time, it seemed useful to distinguish concurrent validity (the extent to which the test relates to relevant criteria obtained at the same time) and predictive validity (the extent to which the test can predict relevant variables, events, and outcomes in the future).

The "chief innovation" (Cronbach & Meehl, 1955, p. 281), however, was the notion of construct validity. Many researchers had come to appreciate the so-called "criterion problem" – that any one external criterion is also only a "measure" that is itself an imperfect indicator of the construct to be measured and thus cannot, by itself, truly and fully represent the construct. If there is no gold standard, no single criterion against which the test can be validated, how should we establish inferences about the proper interpretation or meaning of the scores on the test? The question thus became "What constructs account for variance in test performance?" (Cronbach & Meehl, 1955, p. 282).

An Integrated Conception of Construct Validity

It was soon recognized that the early view of several distinct types of validity was fragmented and misguided. Loevinger (1957) extended the theoretical implications of construct validity by proposing that all scientific issues in test construction, validation, and test use be evaluated from the construct point of view. A *construct* is a hypothetical attribute, process, or other regularity in the behavior of individuals, groups, or other entities (e.g., liberal values, extraversion, self-monitoring tendencies), and procedures for determining the validity of a measure are similar to the general scientific procedures for developing and confirming theories. That is, what seemed like different types of validity are really just different sources of evidence that address particular questions of construct validity.

It is now generally agreed that the construct validity of our observed variables is the central concern in measurement. This is quite a departure from classical test theory, which holds that measures are imperfect indicators of constructs because they contain some degree of random measurement error or unreliability. The construct view, in contrast, argues that the variables we observe or measure are imperfect indicators not only because of random errors; more important, they are imperfect because they also measure constructs we did not intend to measure and thus include *systematic* error (e.g., error introduced by the particular method used to

TABLE 13.4. Types of Validity and Validity Evidence: Major Approaches

Early Approaches (e.g., Cronbach & Meehl, 1955)

Content validity: Extent to which the items are a representative sample of the behavior domain to be measured

Face validity: Extent to which the items appear to measure the intended construct

Criterion-oriented (or external) validity:

   (a) Predictive: Extent to which an individual's future score on a criterion is predicted from prior test scores
   (b) Concurrent: Extent to which the test scores estimate an individual's present criterion score

Construct validity: Whether the measure accurately reflects the construct intended to measure

Elaboration of Construct Validity (e.g., Loevinger, 1957; Messick, 1989)

Content validity: Evidence of content relevance, representativeness, and technical quality of items

Substantive validity: Evidence for response consistencies or performance regularities that are reflective of domain processes

Structural validity: Evidence for internal structure of the scores that is consistent with the internal structure of the construct domain

Generalizability: Evidence for score properties and interpretations that generalize to and across population groups, settings, and tasks

Consequential validity: Rationale and evidence for evaluating the intended and unintended consequences of score interpretation and use, including test bias and fairness

External validity: Convergent and discriminant evidence from multitrait multimethod comparisons, as well as criterion relevance

Examples of Validation Procedures

Expert judgments and review: Test whether experts agree that items are relevant and represent construct domain; use ratings to assess item characteristics, such as comprehensibility and unambiguity

Differentiation between criterion (or contrast) groups: Test size and direction of expected differences between groups on the construct of interest

Factor analysis: Test hypothesized structure of the construct domain (e.g., whether items thought to define the construct load on the same factor and not on other factors)

Correlation: Test relation between measure of construct and measure of other distinct constructs

Multitrait multimethod: Test whether different measures of the same construct correlate more highly than measures of different constructs using same and different methods (e.g., instruments, data sources, languages)

collect the data). In this view (e.g., Judd & McClelland, 1998), scores on observed variables potentially reflect three sources of variance: (a) the construct we intend to measure (convergent aspects of validation), (b) a variety of other constructs (or sources of influence) we would like to avoid measuring (discriminant aspects of validation), and (c) random error (or unreliability). This broad construct view thus highlights convergent and discriminant validity and considers reliability as just another piece of evidence for the construct validity of the proposed measurement.

Messick (1989, 1995) has articulated a comprehensive program of construct validation that addresses the meaning of test scores in test interpretation and use. His view highlights that validity is an "integrative evaluative judgment of the degree to which evidence and theoretical rationales support the *adequacy* and *appropriateness*" of the theoretical specification of the construct (Messick, 1989, p. 13). Thus, validity is considered a property of the interpretation of a measure, rather than a property of the measure itself; for example, there may be substantial evidence to support the interpretation of a particular attitude scale as a measure of individual differences in liberal values but no validity evidence for its interpretation as a measure of intelligence or extraversion. Of course, if the theoretical account of the construct is specified clearly and in detail, specific predictions about relations to other constructs and criteria can be readily made, thus simplifying the process of collecting evidence that supports or disconfirms a particular interpretation of the test score.

Like any other theory or model, the validity of the particular score interpretation can never be established but is always evolving to form an ever-growing "nomological network" of validity-supporting relations (Wiggins, 1973). Given that multiple pieces of evidence will accumulate to support the hypothesized construct, it is often difficult to summarize the available validity evidence with a simple quantitative index, and investigators have had to resort to qualitative and tabular summaries. For example, Snyder (1987) wrote a whole book to summarize what has been learned about the self-monitoring construct in more than 20 years of empirical research and construct development. More recently, meta-analytic techniques (see Johnson & Eagly, this volume, Ch. 19) have proven useful to make such data summaries more manageable and objective (Schmidt, Hunter, Pearlman, & Hirsch, 1985).

Types of Evidence for Construct Validity

In his integrative account, Messick (1989) specified six forms of evidence that should be sought to examine construct validity. The six forms of evidence are listed and defined briefly in the middle section of Table 13.4.

The first is evidence for *content* validity; such evidence is provided most easily if the construct has been explicated theoretically in terms of specific aspects that exhaust the content domain to be covered by the construct. Common problems involve underrepresenting an important aspect of the construct definition in the item pool and overrepresenting another one. An obvious example are the multiple-choice exams we often construct to measure student performance in our classes; if the exam questions do not sample fairly from the relevant textbook and lecture material, we cannot claim that the exam validly represented what students were supposed to learn (i.e., the course content).

Arguments about content validity arise not only between professors and students, but also in research. For example, when revising his self-monitoring scale, Snyder (1987) excluded a number of items measuring other-directed self-presentation, thus representing behavioral variability and attitude–behavior inconsistency to a lesser extent in the revised scale; because all items measuring public performing skills were retained, the construct definition in the new scale shifted toward a conceptually unrelated construct, extraversion (John, Cheek, & Klohnen, 1996). This example shows that discriminant aspects are also important in content validation; to the extent that the items measure aspects not included in the construct definition, the measure would be contaminated by construct-irrelevant variance. For example, when validating scales to measure positive and negative emotion expression, these scales should not assess variance that must be attributed to theoretically unrelated constructs, such as social desirability or self-esteem (e.g., Gross & John, 1997).

As shown in the third section of Table 13.4, there are a number of validation procedures researchers might use (see also Smith & McCarthy, 1995). Researchers might ask expert judges to review the match between item representation and construct domain specification, and to add or delete items. Another procedure would be to use factor analysis to verify the hypothesized structure of the content domain.

Substantive validity evidence makes use of substantive theories and process models to further support the interpretation of the test scores. Relevant procedures might involve differentiation between criterion (or contrast) groups assumed to differ in the relevant processes. For example, Cacioppo and Petty (1982) developed the Need for Cognition Scale to measure individual differences in the preference and enjoyment of effortful thinking; as part of their construct validation program, they conducted a study contrasting college professors (assumed to need cognition) and assembly line workers (assumed to not need cognition). Even stronger evidence for substantive validity comes from studies that use experimental manipulations that directly vary the processes in question. For example, Petty and Cacioppo (1986) showed that the process of attitude change was mediated by the need for cognition: Individuals scoring high on the scale were influenced by careful examination of the arguments presented in a message, whereas those scoring low were more influenced by extraneous aspects of the context or message (e.g., the attractiveness of the source of the message).

Structural validity evidence requires that the correlational (or factor) structure of the measure is consistent with the hypothesized internal structure of the construct domain. We noted the issue of multidimensionality in the section on reliability, pointing out that coefficient alpha does not allow inferences about the dimensionality of a measure. The structure underlying a measure or scale is not an aspect of reliability; rather, it is central to the interpretation of the resulting scores and thus needs to be addressed as part of the construct validation program. Researchers have used both exploratory and confirmatory factor analysis for this purpose, and we will return to this important issue below in the context of evaluating measurement with structural equations models.

Generalizability evidence, as used here by Messick (1989, 1995), is needed to demonstrate that score interpretations apply across tasks or contexts, times or occasions, and observers or raters. The inclusion of generalizability evidence here makes explicit that construct validation includes consideration of "error associated with the sampling of tasks, occasions, and scorers (that) underlie traditional reliability concerns" (Messick, 1995, p. 746). In this context, we should note that the notion of generalizability encompasses traditional conceptions of both reliability and criterion validity; they may be considered on a continuum, differing only in how far generalizability claims can be extended (Thorndike, 1997). Traditional reliability studies provide relatively "weak" tests of generalizability, whereas studies of criterion validity provide "stronger" tests of generalizability.

As suggested by Figure 13.3, generalizing from a test score to another test constructed according to parallel procedures does increase our confidence in the test but does so only modestly. If we find we can also generalize to other times or occasions, our confidence is further strengthened, but not by quite as much as when we can show generalizability to other methods or even to nontest criteria related to the construct the test was intended to measure. Figure 13.3 thus resembles the layers of an onion, showing how far the test allows us to generalize, with the inner layers representing relatively modest levels of generalization and the outer layers representing farther-reaching generalizations to contexts that are more and more removed from the central core (i.e., dissimilar from the initial measurement operation).

The kind of validity evidence Messick (1989) considered under the generalizability rubric is crucial for establishing the limits or boundaries beyond which the interpretation of the measure cannot be extended. An issue of particular importance for social–personality researchers is the degree to which findings generalize from "convenience" samples, such as American college students, to groups that are less educated, older, or come from different ethnic or cultural backgrounds.

Consequential validity evidence focuses on the personal and societal consequences (both intended and unintended) of score interpretation and use. It requires the test-user to confront issues of test bias and fairness and is of paramount importance in contexts where tests are used to make important decisions about individuals. Thus, it is more about valid use of the test than about the validation of the test per se. Consequential validity is a greater concern in educational and employment settings than in social–personality research contexts, where scale scores and performances in experimental tasks have little, if any, consequence for the research participant. Finally, *external* validity covers such a broad range of both convergent and discriminant evidence that we consider it in more detail.

External Validation: Convergent and Discriminant Aspects

External validity evidence refers to the ability of a test to predict conceptually related behaviors, outcomes, or criteria, and has been emphasized by a wide range of writers. For example, in their review of attitude measurement, Dawes and Smith (1985, p. 512) argued that "the basis of all measurement is empirical prediction," and in his review of personality measurement, Wiggins (1973, p. 406) argued that prediction "is the sine qua non of personality assessment." Obviously, it makes sense that a test or scale should predict construct-relevant criteria. It is less apparent that we also need to show that the test does not predict conceptually unrelated criteria. In other words, a full demonstration of external aspects of construct

Figure 13.3. How far can we generalize from a test score? The onion model of generalizability.

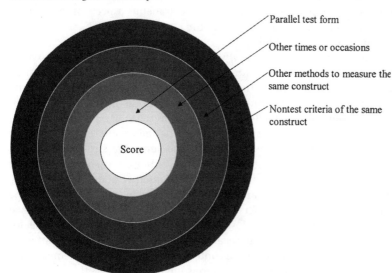

Parallel test form

Other times or occasions

Other methods to measure the same construct

Nontest criteria of the same construct

Score

validation requires requires a demonstration of both what the test measures and what it does not measure.

MULTITRAIT MULTIMETHOD MATRIX. Campbell and Fiske (1959) introduced the terms *convergent* and *discriminant* to distinguish demonstrations of what a test measures from demonstrations of what it does not measure. The convergent validity of a self-report scale of need for cognition could be assessed by correlating the scale with independently obtained peer ratings of the participant's need for cognition and with frequency of effortful thinking measured by beeping the participant several times during the day. Discriminant validity could be assessed by correlating the self-report scale with peer ratings of extraversion and a beeper-based measure of social and sports activities. Campbell and Fiske (1959) were the first to formalize these ideas of convergent and discriminant validity into a single systematic design that crosses multiple traits or constructs (e.g., need for cognition and extraversion) with multiple methods (e.g., self-report, peer ratings, and beeper methodology). They called this design a multitrait multimethod (MTMM) matrix, and the logic of the MTMM is both intuitive and compelling.

What would we expect for our example? Certainly, we would expect sizable convergent validity correlations among the need for cognition measures across the three methods (self-report, peer report, beeper); because these correlations involve the same trait but different methods, Campbell and Fiske (1959) called them monotrait–heteromethod coefficients. Moreover, given that need for cognition is theoretically unrelated to extraversion, we would expect small discriminant correlations between the need-for-cognition measures and the extraversion measures; this condition should hold even if both traits are measured with the same method, leading to so-called heterotrait–monomethod correlations. Certainly, we want each of the convergent correlations to be substantially higher than the discriminant correlations involving the same trait. And finally, the same patterns of intercorrelations among the constructs should emerge, regardless of the method used; in other words, the relations among the constructs should generalize across methods.

METHOD VARIANCE. One important recognition inherent in the MTMM is that we can never measure the trait or construct by itself; rather, we measure the trait intertwined with the method used: "each measure is a trait-method unit in which the observed variance is a combined function of variance due to the construct being measured and the method used to measure

that construct" (Rezmovic & Rezmovic, 1981, p. 61). The design of the MTMM is so useful because it allows us to estimate variance in our scores that is due to method effects – that is, errors systematically related to our measurement methods and thus conceptually quite different from the notion of random error in classical test theory. These errors are systematic because they reflect the influence of unintended constructs on scores, that is, unwanted variance – something we did not wish to measure but that is confounding our measurement (Ozer, 1989).

Method variance is indicated when two constructs measured with the same method (e.g., self-reported attitudes and self-reported behavior) correlate more highly than when the same constructs are measured with different methods (e.g., self-reported attitudes and behavior coded from videotape). For example, it has been argued that positivity bias in self-perceptions is psychologically healthy (Taylor & Brown, 1988); however, if positivity bias is measured with self-reports and the measure of psychological health is a self-report measure of self-esteem, then the positive intercorrelation between these measures may not represent a valid hypothesis about the two constructs (positivity bias and psychological health) but shared self-report method variance associated with narcissism (John & Robins, 1994); that is, individuals who see themselves too positively may be narcissistic and also rate their self-esteem too highly. Discriminant validity evidence is needed to rule out this alternative hypothesis, and the construct validity of the positivity bias measure would be strengthened considerably if psychological health were measured with a method other than self-report, such as ratings by clinically trained observers (Robins & John, 1997).

MULTIPLE SOURCES OF DATA: LOTS. Beginning with Cattell (1957, 1972), psychologists have tried to classify the many sources researchers can use to collect data into a few broad categories. Because each data source has unique strengths and limitations, the construct validation approach emphasizes that we should collect data from *lots* of different sources, and so the acronym LOTS has particular appeal (J. H. Block & Block, 1980).

L data refer to life-event data that can be obtained fairly objectively from the individual's life history or life record, such as graduating from college, getting married or divorced, moving, socioeconomic status, memberships in clubs and organizations, and so on. Examples of particularly ingenious measures derived from *L* data are counts of bottles and cans in garbage containers to measure alcohol consumption (Webb, Campbell, Schwartz, Sechrest, & Grove, 1981) and police records of arrests and convictions to measure juvenile delinquency (Moffitt, 1993).

O data refer to observational data, ranging from observations of very specific aspects of behavior to more global ratings (see Bakeman, this volume, Ch. 6; Kerr, Aronoff, & Messe, this volume, Ch. 7). Examples are careful and systematic observations recorded by human judges, such as in laboratory settings or carefully defined situations; behavior coded or rated from videotape; and reports from knowledgable informants, such as peers, roommates, spouses, teachers, and interviewers that may aggregate information across a broad range of relevant situations in the individual's daily life. *O* data obtained through unobtrusive observations or coded later from videotape can be particularly useful to make inferences about the individual's attitudes, prejudices, preferences, emotions, and other attributes of interest to social scientists. A nice illustration is a study that recorded seating position relative to an outgroup member to measure ethnocentrism (Macrae, Bodenhausen, Milne, & Jetten, 1994).

T data refer to information from test situations that provide standardized measures of performance, motivation, or achievement, and from experimental procedures that have clear and objective rules for scoring performance. Reaction times are frequently used in studies of social cognition, providing an objective measure of an aspect of performance. An intelligence test is another kind of example. A third is the length of time an individual persists on a puzzle or delays gratification in a standardized situation (Mischel, 1990).

Last, but not least, *S* data refer to self-reports. *S* data may take various forms. Global self-ratings of general characteristics and true–false responses to questionnaire items have been used most frequently. However, self-reports are also studied in detailed interviews (see Bartholomew, Henderson, & Marcia, this volume, Ch. 11), in narratives and life stories (see C. Smith, this volume), and in survey research (Visser, Krosnick, & Lavrikas, this volume, Ch. 9). Daily experience sampling procedures (see Reis & Gable, this volume, Ch. 8) can provide very specific and detailed self-reports of moment-to-moment functioning in particular situations.

The logic underlying *S* data is that individuals are in a good position to report about their psychological processes and characteristics – unlike an outside observer, they have access to their private thoughts and experiences and they can observe themselves over time and across situations. However, the validity of self-reports depends on the ability and willingness of the individual to provide valid reports, and self-reports may be influenced by various constructs other than the intended one. Systematic errors include, most obviously, individual differences in response or rating scale use, such as acquiescence (see Visser, Krosnick, & Lavrikas, this volume, Ch. 9) and response extremeness (Hamilton, 1968).

Moreover, some theorists have argued that self-reports are of limited usefulness because they may be biased by social desirability response tendencies. Two kinds of desirability biases have been studied extensively (for a review, see Paulhus & John, 1998). Impression management refers to deliberate attempts to misrepresent one's characteristics (e.g., "faking good"), whereas self-deceptive enhancement reflects honestly held but unrealistic self-views. Impression management appears to have little effect in research contexts where individuals participate anonymously and are not motivated to present themselves in a positive light; self-deception is not simply a response style but related to substantive personality characteristics, such as narcissism.

Fortunately, although social–personality psychologists use self-reports most frequently, other methods are available and used. Thus, measures based on *L*, *O*, and *T* data can help evaluate and provide evidence for the validity of more easily and commonly obtained self-report measures tapping the same construct. Unfortunately, research using multiple methods to measure the same construct has not been very frequent. Overall, it seems that multimethod designs have been underused in construct validation efforts. In a way, researchers seem more likely to talk about the MTMM approach than to go to the trouble of actually using it.

There is an extensive and useful methodological literature on the MTMM, which took off in the 1970s when SEM became available and provided powerful analytical tools to estimate separate trait and method factors (Kenny, 1976; Kenny & Kashy, 1992; Schwarzer, 1986; see also Wegener & Fabrigar, this volume, Ch. 16). A number of excellent reviews and overviews have appeared recently. For example, West and Finch (1997, pp. 155–159) provided hypothetical data to illustrate three scenarios: (a) convergent and discriminant validity with minimal method effects, (b) strong method effects, and (c) effects of unreliability and lack of discriminant validity. Judd and McClelland (1998, Tables 13.11–13.15) provide a series of examples that illustrate Campbell and Fiske's (1959) original principles of convergent and discriminant validation as well as the application of SEM techniques to estimate separate trait and method effects (see Kenny & Kashy, 1992, for specific issues in fitting SEM models).

To summarize, in this section we reviewed Messick's (1989) six forms of evidence relevant to construct validation (see Table 13.4), and then considered one of them, external validation, in some detail, focusing on convergent and discriminant aspects, such as the multitrait–multimethod approach, the nature of method variance, and multiple sources of data. Although one might quibble with some of Messick's (1989) particular categories (e.g., some of them seem to overlap), we view his formulation as comprehensive and heuristically useful. Most important, we agree with Messick's view that evidence concerning traditional issues of reliability are part of the construct validation program, namely under the heading of generalizability, and that evidence about dimensionality must be considered in the context of structural validity. In the following section, we reconsider these issues, now from the perspective of the measurement model in SEM.

MODEL TESTING IN CONSTRUCT VALIDATION AND SCALE CONSTRUCTION

The measurement model in SEM is based on confirmatory factor analysis (CFA); Loehlin (1998), McArdle (1996), and Bollen and Long (1993) provided recent introductions (see also Wegener & Fabrigar, this volume, Ch. 16). CFA is particularly promising because it provides a general analytic approach to assessing construct validity. As will become clear, convergent validity, discriminant validity, and random error can all be addressed within the same general framework. To illustrate these points, we briefly discuss a simple numerical example.

Measurement Models in SEM: Convergent Validity, Discriminant Validity, and Random Error

Like all factor analytic procedures (Floyd & Widaman, 1995; Tinsley & Tinsley, 1987), CFA assumes that a large number of observations or items are a direct result (or expression) of a smaller number of *latent* sources (i.e., unobserved, hypothetical, or inferred constructs). However, CFA eliminates some of the arbitrary features often criticized in exploratory factor analysis (Gould, 1981; Sternberg, 1985). First, CFA techniques require the researcher to specify an explicit model (or several competing models) of how the observed (or measured) variables are related to the hypothesized latent factors. Second, CFA offers advanced statistical techniques that allow the researcher

to test how well the a priori model fits the particular data; even more important, CFA permits comparative model testing to establish whether the a priori model fits the data better (or worse) than plausible alternative or competing models.

CFA models can be displayed graphically, allowing us to effectively communicate the various assumptions incorporated in each model. Some examples are shown in Figure 13.4. Figure 13.4a shows a common-factor model, in which a single underlying construct S (shown as a circle on the top) is assumed to give rise to the correlations among the six items or responses R_1 to R_6 (the observed variables, shown in squares). Following established convention (Bentler, 1980), circles are used to represent latent variables, whereas squares represent measured (or manifest) variables; arrows with one head represent directed or regression parameters, whereas two-headed arrows (which are often omitted) represent covariance of undirected parameters. Note that each measured variable R_m has two arrows leading to it. The arrow from the latent construct S is a factor loading L_m that represents the strength of the effect that the latent construct has on each observed variable. The other arrow involves another latent variable for each observed variable – these are unique factor scores (e_m) that represent the unique or residual variance (U^2) remaining in each observed variable.

Conceptually, this model captures a rather strong structural hypothesis, namely that the six observed variables covary only because they all measure the same underlying construct S. In other words, we hypothesize that the only thing the items have in common is this latent construct, and all remaining or residual item variance is idiosyncratic to each item and thus unshared. This structural model provides a new perspective on how to define two important terms we have used in this chapter: the convergent validity of the item and random error. In particular, the loading of an item on the construct of interest represents the convergent validity of the item, whereas its unique variance represents random error. However, in this simple measurement model, we cannot address discriminant validity.

Compare the measurement model in Panel a of Figure 13.4 with the one in Panel b that postulates two factors S_1 and S_2 influencing responses to six items. Here we are hypothesizing two distinct constructs, rather than one. Note that this model incorporates another condition, known as *simple structure*: The convergent validity loadings (represented by arrows from the latent constructs to the observed items) indicate that the first two items are influenced by the first construct but not the second construct, whereas the

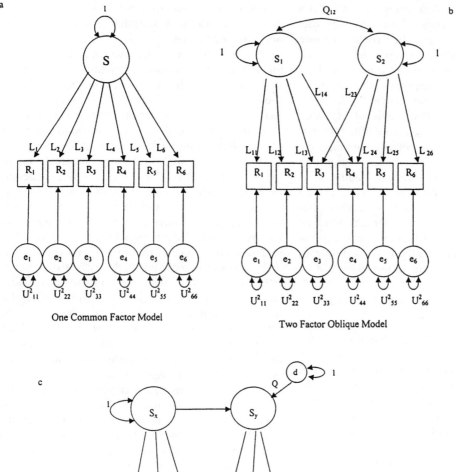

Figure 13.4. Measurement models in structural equation modeling: (a) a one-common-factor model, (b) a two-factor oblique model, and (c) a model showing one common factor related to a criterion.

last two items are influenced only by the second construct and not the first. In other words, these items can be uniquely assigned to only one construct, which much simplifies the measurement model. With two constructs in the measurement model, we can also address issues of discriminant validity. Whereas the item's loading on the construct of interest represents convergent validity and its unique variance random error, its loading on constructs other than the intended one is relevant to discriminant validity.

Note that this model includes an arrow between the two constructs, indicating a correlation or covariance; the two constructs are not independent (orthogonal) but related (oblique). At the level of the constructs, this correlation tells us about discriminant validity. If the correlation is very high (e.g., .90), we would worry that the two constructs are not distinguishable and that we really have only one construct; if the correlation is quite low (e.g., .10), we would be reassured that the two concepts show good discriminant validity with respect to each other. There is another possibility here, namely that the two constructs could be components of a broader, superordinate construct that includes them both. These issues involve questions about the dimensionality and internal structure of the constructs being measured. We discussed these issues earlier in the section on reliability but, as we argued in the section on validity, dimensionality issues are part of the construct validation program (see Table 13.4) because they concern the structural validity of the interpretation of our measure.

STRUCTURAL VALIDITY EXAMINED WITH SEM: AN EMPIRICAL EXAMPLE. Structural validity issues resurface with great regularity in the social–personality literature. Some of the most popular constructs have endured protracted debates about their validity: self-monitoring, attributional style, hardiness, Type A coronary-prone behavior pattern, and most recently need for closure (Hull, Lehn, & Tedlie, 1991; Neuberg, Judice, & West, 1997). Part of the problem is that many of these constructs, and the scales designed to measure them, were initially assumed to be unidimensional, but later evidence challenged those initial assumptions. It is therefore instructive instructive to consider how SEM approaches can help address the underlying issues and to provide a

provide a numerical though manageable example as an illustration.

For the purpose of this illustration we constructed two hypothetical scales and then used actual data from participants who had rated themselves on a number of personality-descriptive adjectives and phrases (Benet-Martínez & John, 1998); we used a large sample ($N =$ 450) because small sample sizes can create problems for SEM estimation procedures (McArdle, 1996).

The first scale was intended as a measure of impulsivity (vs. inhibition), a construct of long-standing interest and debate (e.g., J. Block, 1995; Kagan & Snidman, 1991). To address content validation early on, we defined our universe of item content from the perspective of generalizability theory, using a design that varied two facets of generalizability: context (task vs. social) and construct pole (impulsive vs. inhibited). For the high (impulsive) pole, we selected from our existing item pool three items to represent task contexts (careless, disorganized, lazy) and two items to represent social contexts (enthusiastic and assertive); for the low (inhibited) pole of the construct, two items each for task contexts (persevering and thorough) and social contexts (reserved and shy).

The second scale, briefly, was intended as a measure of extraversion and sampled from previously studied content facets of the construct, namely talkativeness and self-assertion; again, it included both extraverted items (assertive, has an assertive personality, bold, verbal, is talkative, talkative) and introverted items (untalkative, tends to be quiet, and timid). To begin with, we assumed that each scale is unidimensional (of course, we had doubts about one of the scales, as will soon become clear).

What do we find when we apply the traditional analyses of internal consistency and exploratory factor analysis to these two scales? Table 13.5 summarizes the

---

TABLE 13.5. Structural Validity Example: Traditional Psychometric Characteristics of the "Impulsivity" and Extraversion Item Sets

	"Impulsivity" (two-dimensional)	Extraversion (one-dimensional)
Alpha of total scale	.79	.90
First principal component	38%	58%
Second principal component	20%	13%
Correlation between subscales	−.30	.67

Note. $N = 452$ college students. Data from Benet-Martínez and John (1998).

major results. As we cautioned earlier, one should not calculate alphas before the unidimensionality of a scale has been verified. Indeed, the alphas seem reasonably high for these relatively short scales, and most journal editors would consider even the lower alpha of .79 quite acceptable (in fact, the 25-item self-monitoring scale had a lower alpha than this 9-item scale; Snyder, 1987). Moreover, the item–total correlations were all substantial for all items on both scales.

What about the structural validity of these scales? Exploratory factor analyses resulted in eigenvalues (Table 13.5 shows the corresponding percentages of variance accounted for by the first and second unrotated principal component) that make it hard to tell conclusively if we need one or two factors, although for the impulsivity scale the evidence points to two factors. The loadings for two rotated factors, shown in Figures 13.5a and 13.5b, are more informative. For impulsivity, the items defining our four a priori facets nicely hang together, and the items show excellent simple structure. However, the exploratory factor solution seems inconsistent with a one-dimensional impulsivity theory because the social impulsivity items and the task impulsivity items formed two distinct factors.

To find out whether the social and task impulsivity factors have a substantial positive relation, as the

general impulsivity account would suggest, we formed two scales and intercorrelated them. Social impulsivity (enthusiastic and assertive vs. reserved and shy) correlated −.30 with task impulsivity (careless, lazy, and disorganized vs. thorough and persevering), thus failing to produce the predicted positive correlation – the facets do not hang together the way they should.

In contrast, if we rotate two factors for the extraversion scale (see Figure 13.5b), we find much less evidence for simple structure; instead, the variables all fall into a positive manifold (all items are either in the high-high or low-low quadrant), with the two a priori facets forming somewhat separable assertiveness and talkativeness clusters, especially within the upper-right quadrant. As expected from this loading pattern, the two clusters (when scored as scales) were correlated .67 – a positive and substantial correlation (see Table 13.4). These exploratory analyses leave us with some alternative hypotheses that we can test against the a priori models, using SEM.

The SEM analyses are summarized very briefly in Table 13.6. We begin with the one-factor model because it is the simplest or "compact model" (Judd et al., 1995). Because the models are all nested, we can statistically compare them with each other, testing the relative merits of more complex (i.e., full or augmented) models later. Without going into detail, the comparative fit indices show that we can clearly reject the one-factor model for the impulsivity scale; a test comparing it with the uncorrelated two-factor

Figure 13.5. Plot of exploratory factor loadings (after Varimax rotation) for (a) the items assumed to relate to Impulsivity, and (b) items assumed to relate to Extraversion.

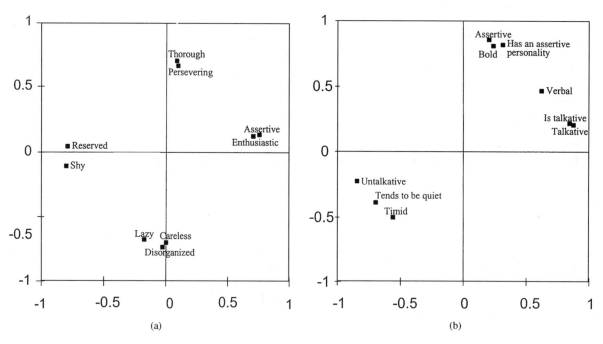

(a)   (b)

model shows that the latter provides a significantly better fit for the data. Not surprisingly, fit is improved further (and significantly) when correlations between the two factors are freely estimated. Note, however, that this model requires the estimation of another parameter, namely the −.30 correlation between the two factors.

These findings are inconsistent with the general impulsivity hypothesis: Because the two factors do not correlate positively, we cannot conclude that the scale consists of two impulsivity facets that together form the superordinate construct. Rather, we might conjecture that we are measuring abbreviated versions of the familiar Big Five factors of extraversion (defined by our social impulsivity items) and conscientiousness (defined by the task impulsivity items reversed-scored). Indeed, the present findings are quite consistent with numerous studies of much broader sets of personality descriptors (e.g., John, 1990; John & Srivastava, 1999).

CRITERIA FOR UNIDIMENSIONALITY. We can push the model comparison approach even farther. Rather than letting SEM estimate the correlation (or covariation) between the latent factors as a free parameter, we can fix it at a value that would allow us to make strong inferences about the independence of the two constructs. This is what we did in the last two models in Table 13.6: We set a specific decision rule, fixing the correlation to one of two decisive values and asking which one fit the data more closely.

Hattie (1985) emphasized that researchers need to formulate decision criteria that help them decide "how close a set of items is to being a unidimensional set" (p. 159). In most real data, just as in the present one, unidimensionality is not simply present or absent. Thus, we need to make a conceptual argument at what levels of intercorrelation we will call a measure relatively unidimensional or relatively multidimensional. Although reasonable people can disagree about any one cut-off point because it is inherently arbitrary, we are prepared to argue that factor intercorrelations as low as .20 would indicate relative independence, whereas correlations as high as .80 suggest such substantial overlap that a one-factor model should be preferred on the basis of parsimony.

As shown in Table 13.6, this decision rule allowed us to differentiate between the two models. The

TABLE 13.6. Structural Validity Example in the SEM Approach: Summary of Models Tested and Their Fit Indices

Model tested	df	Comparative fit index "Impulsivity"	Extraversion
One factor only	27	.57	.82
Two uncorrelated factors	27	.90	.83
Two correlated factors, r freely estimated	26	.93 (r = −.30)	.93 (r = .71)
Two correlated factors, r set to .20	27	.92	.87
Two correlated factors, r set to .80	27	.78	*.91*

Note. N = 452 college students. Data from Benet-Martínez and John (1998). Best-fitting models in the critical comparisons are set in italics.

low-intercorrelation model provided a significantly better fit for the "impulsivity" items than did the high-intercorrelation model, thus correctly identifying this item set as measuring two essentially independent constructs; we say "correctly" here because we had in fact constructed this set by drawing items from uncorrelated Big Five self-report scales for conscientiousness and extraversion, respectively. In contrast, note that the high-intercorrelation model provided a significantly better fit for the extraversion scale. This result suggests that this item set is best interpreted as measuring an essentially unidimensional construct with two highly correlated item clusters, which might be interpreted as talkative and assertive manifestations of extraversion.

MORE COMPLEX MODELS INCLUDING EXTERNAL VALIDITY. In a fully developed construct validation program, of course, we would not stop here. For the "impulsivity" item set, we would move on to testing the relations of these two SEM-based constructs with other measures of extraversion and conscientiousness, preferably drawn from other data sources, such as peer ratings or behavioral observations. Using an MTMM design to address external validity, we would gather evidence both about convergent validity (e.g., self-reported conscientiousness with measures of conscientiousness drawn from other data sources) and discriminant validity (e.g., measures of conscientiousness with measures of extraversion from the same data source).

Again, we would use SEM procedures for these additional validation steps, as suggested by the simplified model in Figure 13.4c. This model shows how we can represent a unidimensional measurement model for construct S_x and a unidimensional criterion construct S_y, along with a predictive (or convergent) validity relation represented by the arrow from S_x to S_y. Note that this model addresses the criterion problem that seemed so intractable in the early treatments of validity: The criterion itself is not treated as a "gold standard" but modeled as a construct that must also be measured with fallible observed indicator variables. We should note that the models used to represent trait and method effects in MTMM matrices are considerably more complex than the simple models considered here; for example, McArdle (1996, Figure 13.2) provided an elegant model for a more complete representation of the construct validation program.

Many readers might benefit from an example with more extensive numerical illustrations of SEM than we could provide here. We recommend an early paper by Judd, Jessor, and Donovan (1986), who examined the construct validity of a 9-item scale designed to measure attitudinal tolerance of deviance, including attitudes toward shoplifting, lying, and getting into fights. This construct postulates the existence of an underlying general attitude toward deviance manifested in self-reported attitudes about specific deviant behaviors. To elaborate four aspects of the construct validity of this measure, Judd et al. (1986) used various SEM procedures. First, to examine the convergent validity (or internal consistency) of the 9 items, they analyzed their intercorrelations (or covariances), testing hypotheses about structural validity (e.g., do all 9 items reflect a single common factor?). Second, to examine external (or criterion) validity, they tested whether the construct relates to other constructs in theoretically consistent ways (e.g., do these attitudinal items predict deviant behavior?). Third, to address discriminant validity, they measured discriminant relations regarding religious attitudes in terms of both structural validity (e.g., are the attitude-toward-deviance items reliably different from religious attitude items?) and criterion validity (e.g., are these items better at predicting deviant behaviors than are the religious attitude items?). Fourth, they investigated particular aspects of substantive validity, namely temporal stability and prediction of behavior over time; these substantive predictions are important because attitudes, like other personality constructs, refer to individual differences that are assumed to be relatively stable and enduring over time, rather than transitory states of short duration (Chaplin, John, & Goldberg, 1988).

Issues in Questionnaire Construction

So far, we have discussed construct validation as if the measure to be validated already existed. However, construct validation issues are central not only during the evaluation of existing psychological measures but also during each stage of their development. We now consider the somewhat specialized case of questionnaire (or scale) construction. The first questionnaires were developed in the early 1900s, and since the 1950s the construction of questionnaires began to proliferate (Goldberg, 1971). We will argue that questionnaire construction, like the development of any psychological measure, must be considered in the context of a program of construct validation. Historically, however, the construct validation approach was not articulated until the 1950s, and the consensus in its favor has been building slowly and quietly, mostly since the 1970s, and it is far from complete. Three distinct schools of thought preceded it and retain adherents even today.

EARLY APPROACHES: EXTERNAL, RATIONAL-INTUITIVE, AND INTERNAL. Three approaches to questionnaire construction emerged in the 1950s; each was inspired by one particular type of validity (see Table 13.4) and aimed to maximize that particular type of validity while ignoring all others (for reviews, see Burisch, 1984, 1986). Given today's perspective favoring an integrated construct approach, the ideological fervor of these three camps strikes us almost like self-parodies.

The so-called *external* approach emphasized maximizing criterion validity, seemingly lost in "a single-minded bivariate search for items that correlate with a chosen criterion" (Tellegen, 1985, p. 685). Typically, externally oriented researchers would administer large and atheoretically assembled sets of questionnaire items to preselected criterion and control groups (e.g., patients hospitalized for depression vs. patients admitted for surgical procedures) and then determine empirically which items significantly differentiated the two groups. The items that successfully differentiated between the groups would be retained to form the resulting scale (e.g., for depression), regardless of the actual item content or broader theoretical considerations. The most famous products of the external approach are the Minnesota Multiphasic Personality Inventory (MMPI; Hathaway & McKinley, 1943) for clinical populations and the California Psychological Inventory (CPI; Gough, 1987) for normally functioning adults. The continued popularity of these instruments, conceived in the 1950s, is testimony to the endurance of the approach. Although the obsession with criterion validity still persists in some literatures (e.g., on marital interaction and satisfaction), the external approach largely fell out of favor, primarily because the subtle and theoretically opaque items did not form psychologically coherent and heuristic constructs, were hard to replicate, and required a rather inefficient scale-construction process.

At the other extreme of the dust bowl empiricists were those psychologists who had detailed theories they did not doubt. Thus they felt free to focus solely on the content and face validity of their measures. Variously labeled the *rational*, *intuitive*, or *deductive* approach, they easily generated items on the basis of their theories. The resulting scales, face-valid with obvious item content, proved remarkably popular, if not always with other researchers then certainly with the test-taking public. In fact, this approach gave birth to the Myers-Briggs Type Indicator (MBTI; Myers & McCaulley, 1985), based partly on Carl Jung's type theories. Without much evidence for its external, structural, or substantive validity, the MBTI nonetheless became the most popular personality questionnaire in this country. To the eternal embarrassment of research psychologists, the MBTI continues to be used at major research universities in applied contexts, such as counseling and career advising. On the brighter side, the deductive approach eventually developed into the construct approach, which is, as we have described above, more interested in empirical evidence that might turn out to disconfirm one's favorite theory.

Finally, an emphasis on structural validity and the growing availability of exploratory factor analysis in the 1950s and 1960s gave rise to the *internal* or *inductive* approach to questionnaire construction. As the label suggests, the focus was on discovering the factor structure of large item sets, often assembled with little concern for particular content representation or selection. The early factor-analytic personality models of Cattell, Eysenck, and Guilford were based on this approach and dominated until the mid-1980s when they gave way to the emerging consensus on the Big Five dimensions (Goldberg, 1993; John, 1990; John & Srivastava, 1999). The preoccupation with the internal factor structure in self-reports came at the expense of other sources of validity evidence. Partly because the dimensions emerging from factor analyses were assumed to be "real," theoretical construct definitions, substantive validity evidence, and criterion validation against measures of behaviors were deemed of secondary interest.

It is easily apparent that each of these three approaches, in its pure form, had a great strength that was also its greatest failure, namely its single-minded pursuit of just one type of validity evidence. Obviously, some kind of integration was needed. Although the conceptual foundations had been laid already in the 1950s, the construct validation approach emerged only gradually, as the three earlier approaches grew softer around the edges and eventually became indistinguishable.

RECAPITULATION: MODERN CONSTRUCT-ORIENTED SCALE CONSTRUCTION. Few, if any, scales or measures today are constructed according to just one of the early approaches. Most researchers have adopted, implicitly or explicitly, many of the features of the construct validation program discussed in this chapter. In fact, much of our presentation here has spelled out, in considerable detail, the kinds of issues that researchers constructing a new measure must consider. There is no simple formula but the integrated conception of construct validity and the various validation procedures summarized in Table 13.4 provide a blueprint for the kinds of evidence to be gathered and procedures to be followed.

Questionnaire construction, like measurement more generally, involves theory-building and thus requires an iterative process. It begins with (a) generating hypotheses; (b) building a model and plausible alternatives; (c) generating items using construct definitions, generalizability facets, and content validation procedures as guides (for information about item and response formats, see Visser, Krosnick, & Lavrikas, this volume, Ch. 9); (d) gathering and analyzing data; (e) confirming and disconfirming the initial models; and (f) generating alternative hypotheses leading to improved models, additional and more content-valid items, more data gathering, and so on. The cycle continues, until a working model has been established that is "good enough" – one that the investigator can live with, at least for a while, given the constraints and limits of real-life research.

There are a few admirable individuals who have completed what amounts to a lifelong and thus exhaustive (and exhausting) program of construct validation. Developing and validating a sentence completion test to measure ego development would seem a hopeless undertaking to most. Yet, Jane Loevinger, one of the field's premier psychometricians and pioneer of construct validation in the 1950s (e.g., Loevinger, 1957), took on this project and devoted a good 30 years of work to it, with impressive results (Loevinger, 1998a).

However, eventually she came to view her work on that sentence completion test as "completing a life sentence" (Loevinger, 1998b, p. 347).

Other examples include Robert Altemeyer's (1988) tireless efforts to sift the real construct of authoritarianism from the ashes of the F scale; after some 20-plus years of validation studies, and probably an equal number of scale reconstructions, his right-wing authoritarianism scale is now firmly embedded in a nomological network of generalizable construct relations. Douglas Jackson's (1971, 1984) construction and validation of the Personality Research Form (PRF) offers a more circumscribed and manageable example of a construct validation program that may also serve as a blueprint for other efforts. Jackson emphasized four broad steps: (a) substantive definitions of scale content, (b) sequential strategy in scale construction, (c) appraisal of the structural component of validity (including the suppression of unwanted response style variance), and (d) evaluation of the external component of validity. At each of these steps, Jackson also tried to foster the goals of scale generalizability and convergent and discriminant validity.

It is easily apparent that these four steps and two key concerns closely map onto our discussion of construct validation. In other words, scale construction and construct validation go hand in hand, and one cannot be separated from the other. Our final topic is a unique special set of measurement issues that scale construction efforts need to address, namely the language and culture contexts within which the measure is developed and used.

CULTURAL AND TRANSLATION ISSUES IN QUESTIONNAIRE CONSTRUCTION. After years of relative neglect, interest in cross-cultural research has been growing in the 1990s (Van de Vijver & Leung, 1997). There are both theoretical and practical reasons for examining psychological measures in cultures other than the United States. First, cross-cultural studies are needed to test the generalizability of our psychological theories and models. Second, given the increasing multiculturalism in the United States, cultural research is necessary to understand the psychological reality of cultural and ethnic minorities.

Methodological considerations are very important in cross-cultural research. Consider a researcher who wants to test a theory that two culture groups differ on a measure or that they show different correlates with a measure. First, the researcher must demonstrate that the same characteristic has been measured in the same way across the two groups. The most common research strategy has been to translate an original U.S.-developed measure to assess the construct of interest in a new culture. This *imposed-etic* strategy (Berry, 1980) is economical and efficient when we want to examine how a particular measure generalizes to other cultures. However, when we want to identify culture-specific aspects of a construct, the imposed-etic approach has serious limitations; using translated measures simply assumes that the construct is universal, thus ignoring meanings and indicators of the construct that are potentially culture-specific (Church & Katigbak, 1988).

The question whether imposed-etic measures overlook important domains of the local culture is at the core of the longstanding *emic–etic* debate (Berry, Poortinga, Segall, & Dasen, 1992), which contrasts the supposedly interculturally comparable, universal (etic) aspects of a construct with its culture-specific, indigenous (emic) aspects (Berry, 1980). On the one hand, an imposed-etic strategy is useful in that it makes cross-cultural comparisons feasible (i.e., statements about the similarity of two cultures require dimensional equivalence), yet its use may distort the meaning of the construct. On the other hand, a fully emic strategy is well-suited to identify culture-specific aspects of a construct (i.e., it is ecologically valid), but it renders comparisons across cultures virtually impossible (Berry, 1980). Note that the emic–etic distinction is not "either–or" but a matter of degree. Overlap between measures taken in different cultures is not simply present or absent, but rather varies in strength and breadth (Berry et al., 1992).

The current view is that emic and etic approaches render two distinct (though related) types of information. Thus, the two approaches need to be combined to provide a complete picture of cultural specificity and overlap (Benet-Martínez & Waller, 1997; Church & Katigbak, 1988; Yang & Bond, 1990). The use of a combined emic–etic approach requires the researcher (a) to identify the emic (indigenous) elements of the construct (through focus groups, interviews, or content analyses of popular media), and develop and administer measures that adequately tap these constructs; (b) to administer translated measures tapping imposed-etic constructs; and (c) to assess the specificity and overlap between imported and indigenous measures. By comparing the information yielded by imposed-etic and emic measures, the researcher can assess how well imported and indigenous constructs correspond and identify indigenous elements not represented by the imported (translated) instrument (for an illustration of this procedure, see Benet-Martínez & Waller, 1997).

An indispensable requirement for valid cross-cultural comparisons is conceptual equivalence, that is, symmetry in the meaning of different-language versions of a measure (see Van de Vijver & Leung, 1997, for a discussion of construct, measurement, and scalar equivalence in cross-cultural comparisons). One way to foster conceptual equivalence is to use the back-translation procedure (Brislin, 1980). One fluent bilingual (ideally an expert on the construct of interest) translates the instrument from the original language into the language of interest. A second bilingual expert independently translates these materials back into the original language. The combination of (a) comparing the back-translated version to the original, (b) discussions between translators, and (c) back-and-forth translations should lead to a final set of translated items that are symmetrically translatable to the original language counterparts.

Following careful back-translation procedures, construct validation procedures must be used to check the success of the translation. In comparisons of two monolingual samples (e.g., one Spanish speaking, the other English speaking), discrepancies in item and scale statistics indicate lack of equivalence but fail to reveal its source – it might be due to poor translations but sample and culture differences could also play a role. Thus, ideally, the two language versions are compared across samples of both monolinguals and bilinguals (see Benet-Martínez & John, 1998, for an illustration of how a bilingual design can be used to disentangle these confounds). Most recently, IRT (see our earlier discussion) has become an effective and popular tool for examining cross-cultural and cross-linguistic measurement invariance (e.g., Ellis, Becker, & Kimmel, 1993). If sample sizes are large enough, measurement invariance across languages can also be tested with CFA (Benet-Martínez & John, 1998). Together, CFA and IRT hold much promise to help resolve these special measurement problems in cross-cultural research (see Reise, Widaman, & Pugh, 1993).

CONCLUSIONS AND RECOMMENDATIONS

In this chapter, we have tried to strike a balance between description and prescription, between "what is" and "what should be" the practice of measurement in social–personality research. We reviewed the traditional reliability coefficients but urged the reader to think about facets of generalizability, such as time, items, and observers, and to explicitly adopt a generalizability framework. We railed against some of our pet peeves, such as the indiscriminate use of alpha, pointing out its limitations and arguing for more complex interpretations of this ubiquitous index. We discussed a unified conception of construct validity, suggesting that systematic construct validation efforts are needed to develop a theoretical understanding of our methods; this goal is worth a sustained program of research, rather than a few isolated criterion correlations sprinkled throughout the literature. We noted the voracious appetite our field has for "fast data" (the so easily obtained self-reports) and argued for a more diversified diet, calling for multimethod investigations as a rule, rather than the rare exception. We illustrated, briefly, the power of the no-longer new SEM techniques to address measurement problems, calling for their routine use, at least in samples of large size (of which we would like to see more, too).

This chapter has noted shortcomings in the current practice of measurement that one could deplore, and practices that ought to be changed. Nonetheless, we are upbeat about the future of measurement in social–personality psychology. In writing this chapter, we became particularly persuaded by the simple logic of comparative model-testing: We now see it as the best strategy for evaluating and improving our measurement procedures. We are confident that even though our journals still practice the archaic preoccupation with significance tests, comparative model-testing will catch on, eventually, and so will the powerful tools provided by SEM. Of course, it won't happen tomorrow. As Jacob Cohen (1990) concluded from his 40 years of research on methodology, the "inertia" of methodological advance is enormous "but I do not despair . . . these things take time" (p. 1311).

REFERENCES

Altemeyer, R. (1988). *Enemies of freedom: Understanding right-wing authoritarianism*. San Francisco, CA: Jossey-Bass.

American Psychological Association. (1954). Technical recommendations for psychological tests and diagnosis techniques. *Psychological Bulletin, 51,* 201–238.

American Psychological Association. (1985). *Standards for educational and psychological testing*. Washington, DC: Author.

Benet-Martínez, V., & John, O. P. (1998). Los Cinco Grandes across cultures and ethnic groups: Multitrait multimethod analyses of the Big Five in Spanish and English. *Journal of Personality and Social Psychology, 75,* 729–750.

Benet-Martínez, V., & Waller, N. G. (1997). Further evidence for the cross-cultural generality of the "Big Seven" model: Imported and indigenous Spanish personality constructs. *Journal of Personality, 65,* 569–598.

Bentler, P. M. (1980). Multivariate analysis with latent variables: Causal modeling. *Annual Review of Psychology, 31*, 419–456.

Berry, J. W. (1980). Introduction to methodology. In H. Triandis & J. W. Berry (Eds.), *Handbook of cross-cultural psychology* (Vol. 2, pp. 1–28). Boston: Allyn & Bacon.

Berry, J. W., Poortinga, Y. H., Segall, M. H., & Dasen, P. R. (1992). *Cross-cultural psychology: Research and applications.* New York: Cambridge University Press.

Block, J. (1995). A contrarian view of the five-factor approach to personality description. *Psychological Bulletin, 117*, 187–215.

Block, J., & Robins, R. W. (1993). A longitudinal study of consistency and change in self-esteem from early adolescence to early adulthood. *Child Development, 64*, 909–923.

Block, J. H., & Block, J. (1980). The role of ego-control and ego-resiliency in the organization of behavior. In W.A. Collins (Ed.), *Development of cognition, affect, and social relations: The Minnesota symposia on child psychology* (Vol. 13, pp. 40–101). Hillsdale, NJ: Erlbaum.

Bollen, K. A. (1984). Multiple indicators: Internal consistency or no necessary relationship? *Quality and Quantity, 18*, 377–385.

Bollen, K. A., & Long, J. S. (Eds.). (1993). *Testing structural equation models.* Newbury Park, CA: Sage.

Brislin, R. W. (1980). Translation and content analysis of oral and written materials. In H. Triandis & J. W. Berry (Eds.), *Handbook of cross-cultural psychology* (Vol. 2, pp. 389–444). Boston: Allyn & Bacon.

Burisch, M. (1984). Approaches to personality inventory construction: A comparison of merits. *American Psychologist, 39*, 214–227.

Burisch, M. (1986). Methods of personality inventory development – A comparative analysis. In A. Angleitner & J. S. Wiggins (Eds.), *Personality assessment via questionnaire* (pp. 109–120). Berlin, Germany: Springer-Verlag.

Cacioppo, J. T., & Petty, R. E. (1982). The need for cognition. *Journal of Personality and Social Psychology, 42*, 116–131.

Campbell, D. T., & Fiske, D. W. (1959). Convergent and discriminant validation by the multitrait–multimethod matrix. *Psychological Bulletin, 56*, 81–105.

Cattell, R. B. (1957). *Personality and motivation structure and measurement.* New York: World Book.

Cattell, R. B. (1972). *Personality and mood by questionnaire.* San Francisco, CA: Jossey-Bass.

Chaplin, W. F., John, O. P., & Goldberg, L. R. (1988). Conceptions of states and traits: Dimensional attributes with ideals as prototypes. *Journal of Personality and Social Psychology, 54*, 541–557.

Church, A. T., & Katigbak, M. S. (1988). The emic strategy in identification and assessment of personality dimensions in a non-western culture. *Journal of Cross-Cultural Psychology, 19*, 140–163.

Cliff, N. F. (1992). Abstract measurement theory and the revolution that never happened. *Psychological Science, 3*, 186–190.

Cohen, J. (1990). Things I have learned (so far). *American Psychologist, 45*, 1304–1312.

Cohen, J., & Cohen, P. (1975). *Applied multiple regression/correlation analysis for the behavioral sciences.* Hillsdale, NJ: Erlbaum.

Cortina, J. M. (1993). What is coefficient alpha? An examination of theory and applications. *Journal of Applied Psychology, 78*, 98–104.

Costa, P. T., & McCrae, R. R. (1992). *NEO PI–R. The Revised NEO Personality Inventory.* Odessa, FL: Psychological Assessment Resources.

Cronbach, L. J. (1947). Test "reliability": Its meaning and determination. *Psychometrika, 12*, 1–16.

Cronbach, L. J. (1951). Coefficient alpha and the internal structure of tests. *Psychometrika, 16*, 297–334.

Cronbach, L. J., & Gleser, G. C. (1957). *Psychological tests and personnel decisions.* Urbana: University of Illinois Press.

Cronbach, L. J., Gleser, G. C., Nanda, H., & Rajaratnam, N. (1972). *The dependability of behavioral measurements: Theory of generalizability for scores and profiles.* New York: Wiley.

Cronbach, L. J., & Meehl, P. E. (1955). Construct validity in psychological tests. *Psychological Bulletin, 52*, 281–302.

Cronbach, L. N., Rajaratnan, N., & Gleser, G. C. (1963). Alpha coefficients for stratified-parallel tests. *Educational and Psychological Measurement, 25*, 291–312.

Dawes, R. M. (1994). Psychological measurement. *Psychological Review, 101*, 278–281.

Dawes, R. M., & Smith, T. L. (1985). Attitude and opinion measurement. In G. Lindzey & E. Aronson (Eds.), *Handbook of social psychology* (Vol. 1, pp. 509–566). New York: Random House.

Eagly, A. H., & Chaiken, S. (1993). *The psychology of attitudes.* Ft. Worth, TX: Harcourt Brace Jovanovich.

Ellis, B. B., Becker, P., & Kimmel, H. D. (1993). An item response theory evaluation of an English version of the Trier Personality Inventory (TPI). *Journal of Cross-Cultural Psychology, 24*, 133–148.

Embretson, S. E. (1996). The new rules of measurement. *Psychological Assessment, 8*, 341–349.

Epstein, S. (1980). The stability of behavior: II. Implications for psychological research. *American Psychologist, 35*, 790–806.

Feldt, L., Woodruff, D., & Salih, F. A. (1987). Statistical inference for coefficient alpha. *Applied Psychological Measurement, 11*, 93–103.

Fishbein, M., & Ajzen, I. (1974). Attitudes towards objects as predictors of single and multiple behavioral criteria. *Psychological Review, 81*, 59–74.

Floyd, F. J., & Widaman, K. F. (1995). Factor analysis in the development and refinement of clinical assessment instruments. *Psychological Assessment, 7*, 286–299.

Goldberg, L. R. (1971). A historical survey of personality scales and inventories. In P. McReynolds (Ed.), *Advances in psychological assessment* (Vol. 2, pp. 293–336). Palo Alto, CA: Science and Behavior Books.

Goldberg, L. R. (1991). Clinical versus statistical prediction. In D. Cicchetti & W. M. Grove (Eds.), *Thinking clearly about psychology: Essays in honor of Paul E. Meehl* (pp. 173–184). Minneapolis: University of Minnesota Press.

Goldberg, L. R. (1993). The structure of phenotypic personality traits. *American Psychologist, 48,* 26–34.

Goldberg, L. R., & Kilkowski, J. M. (1984). The prediction of semantic consistency in self-descriptions: Characteristics of persons and of terms that affect the consistency of responses to synonym and antonym pairs. *Journal of Personality and Social Psychology, 48,* 82–98.

Gough, H. G. (1987). *The California Psychological Inventory administrator's guide.* Palo Alto, CA: Consulting Psychologists Press.

Gould, S. J. (1981). *The mismeasure of man.* New York: W.W. Norton.

Gray-Little, B., Williams, S. L., & Hancock, T. D. (1997). An item response theory analysis of the Rosenberg Self-Esteem Scale. *Personality and Social Psychology Bulletin, 23,* 443–451.

Gross, J. J., & John, O. P. (1997). Revealing feelings: Facets of emotional expressivity in self-reports, peer ratings, and behavior. *Journal of Personality and Social Psychology, 72,* 435–448.

Gulliksen, H. (1950). *Theory of mental tests.* New York: Wiley.

Hambleton, R. K., Swaminathan, H., & Rogers, H. J. (1991). *Fundamentals of item response theory.* Newbury Park, CA: Sage.

Hamilton, D. L. (1968). Personality attributes associated with extreme response style. *Psychological Bulletin, 69,* 192–203.

Hampson, S. E. (1998). When is an inconsistency not an inconsistency? Trait reconciliation in personality description and impression formation. *Journal of Personality and Social Psychology, 74,* 102–117.

Harris, G. T., & Rice, M. E. (1996). The science in phallometric measurement of male sexual interest. *Current Directions in Psychological Science, 5,* 156–160.

Hathaway, S. R., & McKinley, J. C. (1943). *The Minnesota Multiphasic Personality Inventory* (rev. ed.). Minneapolis University of Minnesota Press.

Hattie, J. (1985). Methodology review: Assessing unidimensionality of tests and items. *Applied Psychological Measurement, 9,* 139–164.

Himmelfarb, S. (1993). The measurement of attitudes. In A. H. Eagly & S. Chaiken (Eds.), *The psychology of attitudes* (pp. 23–87). Ft. Worth, TX: Harcourt Brace Jovanovich.

Hull, J. G., Lehn, D. A., & Tedlie, J. C. (1991). A general approach to testing multi-faceted personality constructs. *Journal of Personality and Social Psychology, 61,* 932–945.

Jackson, D. N. (1971). The dynamics of structured personality tests: 1971. *Psychological Review, 78,* 229–248.

Jackson, D. N. (1984). *Personality Research Form manual.* Port Huron, MI: Research Psychologists Press.

John, O. P. (1990). The Big Five factor taxonomy: Dimensions of personality in the natural language and in questionnaires. In L. A. Pervin (Ed.), *Handbook of personality: Theory and research* (pp. 66–100). New York: Guilford Press.

John, O. P., Cheek, J. M., & Klohnen, E. C. (1996). On the nature of self-monitoring: Construct explication via Q-sort ratings. *Journal of Personality and Social Psychology, 71,* 763–776.

John, O. P., Donahue, E. M., & Kentle, R. L. (1991). *The "Big Five" Inventory: Versions 4a and 54* [Technical Report]. Institute of Personality and Social Research, University of California, Berkeley.

John, O. P., Hampson, S. E., & Goldberg, L. R. (1991). The basic level in personality-trait hierarchies: Studies of trait use and accessibility in different contexts. *Journal of Personality and Social Psychology, 60,* 348–361.

John, O. P., & Robins, R. W. (1993). Determinants of interjudge agreement on personality traits: The Big Five domains, observability, evaluativeness, and the unique perspective of the self. *Journal of Personality, 61,* 521–551.

John, O. P., & Robins, R. W. (1994). Accuracy and bias in self-perception: Individual differences in self-enhancement and the role of narcissism. *Journal of Personality and Social Psychology, 66,* 206–219.

John, O. P., & Srivastava, S. (1999). The Big Five taxonomy: History, measurement, and theoretical perspective. In L. A. Pervin & O. P. John (Eds.), *Handbook of personality: Theory and research* (2nd. ed.) (pp. 102–138). New York: Guilford Press.

Jöreskog, K. G., & Sörbom, D. (1981). *LISREL V: User's guide.* Chicago: National Educational Resources.

Judd, C. M., Jessor, R., & Donovan, J. E. (1986). Structural equation models and personality research. *Journal of Personality, 54,* 149–198.

Judd, C. M., & McClelland, G. H. (1998). Measurement. In D. T. Gilbert, S. T. Fiske, & G. Lindzey (Eds.), *Handbook of social psychology* (Vol. 2, pp. 180–232). Boston: McGraw-Hill.

Judd, C. M., McClelland, G. H., & Culhane, S. E. (1995). Data analysis: Continuing issues in the everyday analysis of psychological data. *Annual Review of Psychology, 46,* 433–465.

Kagan, J., & Snidman, N. (1991). Infant predictors of inhibited and uninhibited profiles. *Psychological Science, 2,* 40–44.

Kelderman, H., & Rijkes, C. M. (1994). Loglinear multidimensional IRT models for polytomously scored items. *Psychometrika, 59,* 149–176.

Kenny, D. A. (1976). An empirical application of confirmatory factor analysis to the multitrait-multimethod matrix. *Journal of Experimental Social Psychology, 12,* 247–252.

Kenny, D. A. (1994). *Interpersonal perception: A social relations analysis.* New York: Guilford Press.

Kenny, D. A., & Kashy, D. A. (1992). Analysis of the multitrait-multimethod matrix by confirmatory factor analysis. *Psychological Bulletin, 112,* 165–172.

King, J. E., & Figueredo, A. J. (1997). The five-factor model plus dominance in chimpanzee personality. *Journal of Research in Personality, 31,* 257–271.

Loehlin, J. C. (1998). *Latent variable models: An introduction to factor, path, and structural analysis* (3rd ed.). Mahwah, NJ: Erlbaum.

Loevinger, J. (1957). Objective tests as instruments of psychological theory. *Psychological Reports, 3,* 635–694.

Loevinger, J. (Ed.). (1998a). *Technical foundations for measuring ego development.* Mahwah, NJ: Erlbaum.

Loevinger, J. (1998b). Completing a life sentence. In P. M. Westenberg, L. Cohn, & A. Blasi (Eds.), *Personality development: Theoretical, empirical, and clinical investigations of Loevinger's conception of ego development* (pp. 347–354). Mahwah, NJ: Erlbaum.

Lord, F. (1984). Standard errors of measurement at different ability levels. *Journal of Educational Measurement, 21,* 239–243.

Lord, F., & Novick, M. R. (1968). *Statistical theories of mental tests.* New York: Addison-Wesley.

Macrae, C. N., Bodenhausen, G. V., Milne, A. B., & Jetten, J. (1994). Out of mind but back in sight: Stereotypes on the rebound. *Journal of Personality and Social Psychology, 67,* 808–817.

Marsh, H. W., Byrne, B. M., & Shavelson, R. J. (1992). A multidimensional, hierarchical self-concept. In T. M. Brinthaupt & R. P. Lipka (Eds.), *The self: Definitional and methodological issues* (pp. 44–95). Albany, NY: SUNY Press.

McArdle, J. J. (1996). Current directions in structural factor analysis. *Current Directions in Psychological Science, 5,* 11–18.

Mellenbergh, G. J. (1996). Measurement precision in test score and item response models. *Psychological Methods, 1,* 293–299.

Messick, S. (1989). Validity. In R. L. Linn (Ed.), *Educational measurement* (3rd ed., pp. 13–103). New York: Macmillan.

Messick, S. (1995). Validity of psychological assessment. *American Psychologist, 50,* 741–749.

Mischel, W. (1990). Personality dispositions revisited and revised: A view after three decades. In L. A. Pervin (Ed.), *Handbook of personality: Theory and research* (pp. 111–134). New York: Guilford Press.

Moffitt, T. E. (1993). Adolescence-limited and life-course persistent antisocial behavior: A developmental taxonomy. *Psychological Review, 80,* 252–283.

Myers, I. B., & McCaulley, M. H. (1985). *Manual: A guide to the development and use of the Myers-Briggs Type Indicator.* Palo Alto, CA: Consulting Psychologists Press.

Neuberg, S. L., Judice, T. N., & West, S. G. (1997). What the need for closure scale measures and what it does not: Toward differentiating among related epistemic motives. *Journal of Personality and Social Psychology, 72,* 1396–1412.

Nunnally, J. C. (1978). *Psychometric theory* (2nd ed.). New York: McGraw-Hill.

Ozer, D. J. (1989). Construct validity in personality assessment. In D. M. Buss & N. Cantor (Eds.), *Personality psychology: Recent trends and emerging directions* (pp. 224–234). New York: Springer-Verlag.

Paulhus, D. L., & John, O. P. (1998). Egoistic and moralistic biases in self-perception: The interplay of self-deceptive styles with basic traits and motives. *Journal of Personality, 66,* 1025–1060.

Pedhazur, E. J., & Schmelkin, L. P. (1991). *Measurement, design, and analysis: An integrated approach.* Hillsdale, NJ: Erlbaum.

Petty, R. E., & Cacioppo, J. T. (1986). *Communication and persuasion: Central and peripheral routes to attitude change.* New York: Springer-Verlag.

Reise, S. P., Widaman, K. F., & Pugh, R. H. (1993). Confirmatory factor analysis and item response theory: Two approaches for exploring measurement invariance. *Psychological Bulletin, 114,* 552–566.

Rezmovic, E. L., & Rezmovic, V. (1981). A confirmatory factor analysis approach to construct validation. *Educational and Psychological Measurement, 41,* 61–72.

Robins, R. W., & Hendin, H. M. (1999). *A single item measure of self-esteem: Evidence for its reliability and validity.* Manuscript submitted for publication.

Robins, R. W., & John, O. P. (1997). The quest for self-insight: Theory and research on the accuracy of self-perception. In H. Hogan, J. Johnson, & S. Briggs (Eds.), *Handbook of personality psychology* (pp. 649–679). New York: Academic Press.

Rosenberg, M. (1979). *Conceiving the self.* New York: Basic Books.

Schmidt, F. L., Hunter, J. E., Pearlman, K. & Hirsch, H. R. (1985). Forty questions about validity generalization and meta-analysis. *Personnel Psychology, 38,* 697–798.

Schmitt, N. (1996). Uses and abuses of coefficient alpha. *Psychological Assessment, 8,* 350–353.

Schwarzer, R. (1986). Evaluation of convergent and discriminant validity by use of structural equations. In A. Angleitner & J. S. Wiggins (Eds.), *Personality assessment via questionnaire* (pp. 192–213). Berlin, Germany: Springer-Verlag.

Shavelson, R. J., Webb, N. M., & Rowley, G. L. (1989). Generalizability theory. *American Psychologist, 44,* 922–932.

Shrout, P. E., & Fleiss, J. L. (1979). Intraclass correlations: Uses in assessing rater reliability. *Psychological Bulletin, 86,* 420–428.

Smith, G. T., & McCarthy, D. M. (1995). Methodological considerations in the refinement of clinical assessment instruments. *Psychological Assessment, 7,* 300–308.

Snyder, M. (1987). *Public appearances, private realities: The psychology of self-monitoring.* New York: Freeman.

Sternberg, R. J. (1985). Human intelligence: The model is the message. *Science, 230,* 1111–1118.

Stevens, S. S. (1951). Mathematics, measurement, and psychophysics. In S. S. Stevens (Ed.), *Handbook of experimental psychology* (pp. 1–49). New York: Wiley.

Taylor, S. E., & Brown, J. (1988). Illusion and well-being: A social psychological perspective on mental health. *Psychological Bulletin, 103,* 193–210.

Tellegen, A. (1985). Structures of mood and personality and their relevance to assessing anxiety, with an emphasis on self-report. In A. H. Tuma & J. Maser (Eds.), *Anxiety and the anxiety disorders* (pp. 681–706). Hillsdale, NJ: Erlbaum.

Thorndike, R. M. (1997). *Measurement and evaluation in psychology and education* (6th ed.). Upper Saddle River, NJ: Prentice Hall.

Tinsley, H. E., & Tinsley, D. J. (1987). Uses of factor analysis in counseling psychology research. *Journal of Counseling Psychology, 34*, 414–424.

Tversky, A., & Kahneman, D. (1974). Judgment under uncertainty: Heuristics and biases. *Science, 185*, 1124–1131.

Van de Vijver, F., & Leung, K. (1997). *Methods and data analysis for cross-cultural research*. Thousand Oaks, CA: Sage.

Waller, N. G., & Reise, S. P. (1989). Computerized adaptive personality assessment: An illustration with the Absorp-

tion scale. *Journal of Personality and Social Psychology, 57*, 1051–1058.

Webb, E. J., Campbell, D. T., Schwartz, R. D., Sechrest, L., & Grove, J. B. (1981). *Nonreactive measures in the social sciences* (2nd ed.). Boston: Houghton-Mifflin.

West, S. G., & Finch, J. F. (1997). Measurement and analysis issues in the investigation of personality structure. In R. Hogan, J. Johnson, & S. Briggs (Eds.), *Handbook of personality psychology* (pp. 143–164). Dallas, TX: Academic Press.

Wiggins, J. S. (1973). *Personality and prediction: Principles of personality assessment*. Menlo Park, CA: Addison-Wesley.

Yang, K., & Bond, M. H. (1990). Exploring implicit personality theories with indigenous and imported constructs: The Chinese case. *Journal of Personality and Social Psychology, 58*, 1087–1095.

CHAPTER FOURTEEN

Everyday Data Analysis in Social Psychology
Comparisons of Linear Models

CHARLES M. JUDD

One of the most impressive claims of social psychology is that it attempts to understand and explain human behavior, particularly social behavior, by focusing on a very wide range of potential explanatory constructs. The legacy of the discipline, from Kurt Lewin (1935) on, is that behavior is considered to result from the total life space of the individual actor, and this life space includes the person, the environment, and, importantly, their interaction.

A consequence of this scope is that the independent variables that social psychologists examine come in all shapes and sizes. Thus, for instance, we deal with macrolevel environmental forces that shape behavior; with immediate contextual cues that others communicate; with personal aspirations, goals, and histories; with cognitive processes and heuristics; and with emotions and affects. Although particular researchers or lines of work within social psychology may attend more to some of these explanatory constructs and less to others, it is not at all atypical for research reported in our leading journals to include a wide range of independent variables, sampling from both the environmental and personality side of the life space.

Although this diversity of explanatory constructs gives rise to much of the theoretical richness of social psychology, it has posed difficulties over the years in the areas of measurement and data analysis. The diverse shapes and sizes of our independent variables mean that both our measurement and analytic strategies must be very flexible. We need to be able to handle classification systems and typologies (e.g., this environment or experimental condition vs. that one, this type of person vs. that one) as well as much more finely graded continuua (e.g., degree or magnitude of some property of the environment or person).

Unfortunately, until very recently, the data analytic options available for social psychologists have not encouraged or even permitted this sort of flexibility. For 50 years, social psychologists have largely learned that there exist two forms of data analysis: analysis of variance with categorical independent variables, typically used with data from experimental designs, and correlation–regression procedures for data in which the independent variables varied more or less continously and were measured rather than manipulated. This dichotomy is in fact largely an historical accident dictated by two factors that importantly shaped the development of statistical procedures in the 20th century.

The first factor was the need for computational ease. In essence, Ronald Fisher developed factorial analysis of variance, with categorical independent variables, because of the need to simplify the computations involved in the more general multiple regression approach to data analysis. As Tatsuoka (1993) noted, in his discussion of the general linear model,

"Fisher . . . initially used multiple regression analysis . . . to carry out multigroup significance testing. The multiple regression approach was feasible for the simplest cases (i.e., one-way design problems) of ANOVA, but for factorial and more complicated designs the computational difficulty proved to be insurmountable in the precomputer days. It was largely for this reason that Fisher invented what we now know as the traditional variance partitioning approach to ANOVA. (p. 3)

The second factor derives from the fact that the history of data analysis is largely an applied history, with procedures and methods developed in large part to meet particular analytic needs of particular disciplines. And, unlike social psychology, most of these disciplines had independent variables that assumed characteristic or typical shapes and sizes. So, on the one hand correlation and regression procedures were largely utilized by economists, sociologists, and others where the independent variables were typically measured characteristics of entities, varying more or less continuously or at least ordinally. On the other hand, in disciplines where experimentation was feasible and desirable (e.g., agricultural research, experimental psychology), ANOVA procedures were employed and refined for dealing with categorical or discretely measured independent variables.

Most social psychologists receive their training in departments of psychology where the dominant approach historically has been an experimental one. Accordingly, the analytic courses to which first-year students in social psychology were typically exposed consisted largely of ANOVA and related procedures, where the emphasis was on experimentally manipulated independent variables. In some training programs, students might then take a further course, devoted to regression–correlation procedures, but here the focus was on measured, rather than manipulated, independent variables, and these were typically assumed to be measured on at least ordinal scales. As a result, a common assumption was that the two analytic approaches, ANOVA and multiple regression–correlation procedures, differed not only in the scale of measurement of the independent variables but also in the degree to which one could make causal claims about the effects of independent variables. Erroneously, many confounded analytic procedures with the sort of theoretical conclusions one could draw.

In the 1960s and 1970s, two very important individuals, Donald Campbell and Jacob Cohen, began the process of breaking down the barriers that had been constructed between analytic techniques and returning us to the original insights of Ronald Fisher. Donald Campbell (e.g., Campbell & Stanley, 1963; Cook & Campbell, 1979) made clear that the causal status of one's conclusions depended not on the scale of measurement of the independent variable, nor on the type of data analysis one conducted, but on the sort of research design employed. The critical design feature necessary to maximize internal validity was random assignment. The analysis one subsequently did on the data really had no impact. Then in the late 1960s, Jacob Cohen published a hugely influential article (1968) that made clear that multiple regression–correlation procedures were fully capable of handling categorical independent variables, and that when it did so, the results were equivalent to those emerging from traditional ANOVA procedures. The article was later

expanded into a very widely cited and influential book (Cohen & Cohen, 1975; 1983).

But the shift in analytic paradigms that these two individuals began has still not been totally and successfully completed. Although most graduate statistics courses in psychology currently pay lip service to the notion that analysis of variance procedures and multiple regression both involve the same underlying least-squares model estimation, it continues to be the case that the vast majority of courses taught in our graduate programs are either devoted to the analysis of variance and experimental data or to regression models and correlational data. Graduate courses that really integrate the two, that treat the analysis of both categorical independent variables and continuous ones, within the same general linear model analytic framework, remain rare (Aiken, West, & Sechrest, 1990). With a few exceptions, the same can be said about the textbooks in wide use in these courses. Although nearly all books on experimental design and analysis of variance now show the regression approach to these data (e.g., Keppel & Zedeck, 1989; Maxwell & Delaney, 1990; Myers & Well, 1991; Winer, Brown, & Michels, 1991), typically these translations are confined to an appendix or one chapter. Truly integrative books (e.g., Cohen & Cohen, 1983; Judd & McClelland, 1989; Pedhazur, 1982) remain rare. In spite of the lip service that data analysts now pay to the unity of regression and analysis of variance procedures, the reality of graduate training is that for most students they remain separate data analytic approaches.

Besides simple inertia, there is an additional explanation for why truly integrative data analysis courses are not widely taught. Many designs in psychological research employ what are called within-subject or repeated-measures factors, where the same participant is exposed to the various levels of the independent variables of interest. Although both Cohen and Cohen (1975, 1983) and Pedhauzer (1982) illustrated how the analyses of data from such designs could be accomplished using multiple regression, the procedures they promoted were cumbersome at best. No one in their right mind would give up their repeated-measures ANOVA programs to adopt the laborious procedures recommended for the analysis of data from such designs via a general multiple regression approach.

More recently, however, a much more efficient algorithm for including within-subject factors in multiple regression has been developed (Judd & McClelland, 1989). Accordingly, it is now possible and desirable to encourage social psychologists to abandon their ANOVA programs and accomplish all of their analyses with general multiple regression programs. The advantage of this is that we can include independent variables of all shapes and sizes, be they measured or manipulated, discrete or continuous, within-subject or between-subjects, in a single analytic approach. All too often, social psychologists have resorted to using median splits in order to create categorical variables out of continuous ones, so that the analysis can be accomplished via ANOVA programs. And, as a consequence, both a loss of statistical power and biased estimates have resulted (Maxwell & Delaney, 1993). Now, however, with the development of efficient approaches for within-subject analyses using multiple regression, the last remaining excuse for such a strategy seems to have disappeared.

The purpose of this chapter is to set forth a very general approach to data analysis, using multiple regression, that has the flexibility of including all shapes and sizes of independent variables, just as they are studied by social psychologists. These independent variables may be manipulated or measured, they may be continuous or discrete, and they may be within-subjects or between-subjects. Additionally, both their additive and interactive effects can be examined efficiently. Perhaps finally our analyses can do justice to the richness and diversity of the independent variables of interest to social psychologists.

THE BASICS OF MULTIPLE REGRESSION

Multiple regression involves the estimation of linear additive combinations of predictor or independent variables in order to predict a criterion or dependent variable with as little error as possible. Thus, in the following generic regression model,

$$Y_i = b_0 + b_1 X_{1i} + b_2 X_{2i} + (\ldots) + b_p X_{pi} + e_i,$$

the dependent variable is Y_i, the independent or predictor variables are X_{1i} through X_{pi}, and the various regression coefficients (b_0 through b_p) are values that are derived to make the errors of prediction (e_i) as small as possible. The error function that is minimized is traditionally a least squares function, so that the coefficients are derived to minimize the sum of the squared errors.

The regression coefficients in this model are readily interpretable. The intercept, b_0, is the predicted value of Y_i when the value of all p X_is equal zero. The regression coefficient associated with any particular predictor, equivalently called a slope, tells us about the predicted difference in the dependent variable associated with a one-unit difference in the predictor, holding constant all other predictors in the model. This last phrase is especially critical, because the power of multiple regression comes from its ability to estimate the "partial" slopes, statistically controlling or holding constant the other predictors in the model even in the presence of partial redundancy or multicollinearity among the independent variables.[1]

Nested multiple regression models can be compared, and these comparisons provide the basis for statistical inference. What we mean by "nested" models is that the comparison of two models for purposes of inference must always involve an augmented and a compact model (Judd & McClelland, 1989) where the compact model fixes some of the regression coefficients of the augmented model at a priori values rather than estimating them from the data at hand. Typically, these a priori values are zero, although in general they need not be.

Common examples of nested augmented and compact models that may be of interest include cases where one regression coefficient is set equal to zero in the compact model (or equivalently a predictor is not included), where a set of predictors is omitted from the compact model, and where the compact model has no predictor variables at all. These are discussed in more detail below. Although these comparisons are frequently of interest and routinely evaluated by most multiple regression programs, the model comparison approach permits any two nested models to be compared. It thus allows researchers to ask questions of interest that may not be routinely asked by multiple regression software (e.g., nonzero a priori values of coefficients, equality of coefficients; for further examples, see Judd & McClelland, 1989).

Statistical inference proceeds by asking whether the additional complexity of the augmented model over the compact one is worthwhile. It evaluates that question by examining the reduction in error of prediction achieved by the augmented model over the compact one, specifically comparing their sums of squared errors of prediction. The compact model can never have a sum of squared errors smaller than that of the augmented model, because regression coefficients are estimated to minimize the sum of squared errors. Thus, from the sums of squared errors of the two models, one can compute a reduction in the sum of squared

---

[1] Although this ability to "control" redundant independent variables is a very powerful aspect of multiple regression, it is not without its biases. So, for instance, the presence of measurement error in predictor variables will result in a general tendency to underestimate their impact and to "undercontrol" for their effects. See Campbell and Kenny (1999).

errors as one moves from the compact to the augmented model:

$$SSR = SSE(C) - SSE(A),$$

where SSE(C) and SSE(A) refer to the sums of squared errors of the compact and augmented model. And this can be converted to a proportional reduction in error by dividing it by the sum of squared errors from the compact model:

$$PRE = \frac{SSR}{SSE(C)}.$$

This proportional reduction in error statistic estimates the relative improvement in predictions made by the model when one relaxes the constraints imposed in the compact model.

Compact and augmented models differ in the number of coefficients that are estimated. In order to evaluate whether the proportional reduction in error from the compact to augmented models is substantial, we want to weight that reduction by the difference in the number of coefficients that are estimated in the two models. This is accomplished by converting PRE to an F statistic, according to the following equation:

$$F_{pa-pc, N-pa} = \frac{PRE/(pa - pc)}{(1 - PRE)/(N - pa)},$$

where pa and pc are the number of coefficients estimated in the augmented and compact models, and N is the total number of observations.[2] This F statistic can be equivalently expressed in terms of the sums of squares of the augmented and compact models (and their difference, SSR):

$$F_{pa-pc, N-pa} = \frac{SSR/(pa - pc)}{SSE(A)/(N - pa)}.$$

Under the assumptions that the errors are independently sampled from a single, normally distributed population of errors, this F statistic is distributed according to the tabled F distributions (with degrees of freedom equal to pa − pc and N − pa) and can be used to decide whether the restrictions imposed by the compact model lead to a significant deterioration in the overall fit of the model.

The above description of statistical inference in multiple regression is as general as possible. As we said above, in practice, inferential tests (and augmented and compact models) ask certain typical questions.

First, a very common question is to ask whether the regression coefficient associated with a particular independent variable is significantly different from zero. Equivalently, this asks whether that independent variable contributes to the quality of predictions over and above the others in the model. The compact model is one in which the regression coefficient for that independent variable is fixed at zero, or equivalently where that independent variable is no longer included as a predictor. The PRE that results from this model comparison is also known as the squared partial correlation, and the F statistic that is generated is routinely output by all multiple regression programs as the F statistic (or the squared t statistic) associated with each individual regression coefficient. Notice in this case that the number of estimated coefficients in the augmented model is only one more than the number in the compact model; thus the F statistic has only a single degree of freedom in its numerator.

A second common inferential question is to ask whether a set of predictors contributes over and above the others included in an augmented model. Here, a set of coefficients are fixed at zero in the compact model, or equivalently those predictors are not included in the compact model. The PRE that results from this comparison converts to an F statistic with multiple degrees of freedom in the numerator.

Finally, a common model comparison asks whether the entire set of predictors included in the augmented model significantly improves predictions of the dependent variable. In this case, all regression coefficients except the intercept are fixed at zero in the compact model, and the estimated least-squares intercept in this model then equals the mean value of the dependent variable. The resulting PRE is also known as the squared multiple correlation or the coefficient of determination, and the associated F statistic is the overall F commonly output to test whether the multiple correlation (or simple correlation in the case where the augmented model includes only a single predictor variable) is significantly different from zero.[3]

---

[2] One can think of this F statistic as the magnitude of the proportional error reduction per additional parameter estimated as we move from the compact to the augmented model, compared with the reduction per parameter that we would expect if we added all possible additional parameters (N − pa of them) to the augmented model. See Judd and McClelland (1989, pp. 83–85).

[3] The PRE statistic can be computed for any comparison between augmented and compact models. For particular comparisons, it is equivalent to widely known statistics of association. Thus, the squared Pearson correlation, the multiple r-squared or coefficient of determination, and the squared partial correlation are all special cases of PRE, comparing particular compact and augmented models.

EXAMINING INTERACTIONS IN MULTIPLE REGRESSION

Although multiple regression models are referred to as linear models, they are linear and additive in form only and substantial flexibility can be incorporated by including as predictors nonlinear transformations of other predictors. For instance, the product of two predictors can be included as a predictor. Its partial effect, controlling for the two predictors themselves, estimates the interaction between the two (Cohen, 1978). Similarly, the partial effect of a squared predictor, controlling for the predictor itself, estimates the quadratic effect of the predictor. Considerable care, however, must be taken in interpreting the partial effects of predictors in these models when those predictors are involved as components of product variables that are also included in the models.

To illustrate, suppose we create a product variable, multiplying X_1 and X_2 together and then we regress Y on X_1, X_2, and their product:

$$Y_i = b_0 + b_1 X_{1i} + b_2 X_{2i} + b_3 (X_{1i} X_{2i}) + e_i.$$

To interpret the various coefficients in this model, it is easiest to reexpress it as one of two equivalent simple effects models. These two reexpressions are obtained by factoring either X_1 or X_2 from the right-hand side of the equation. Factoring out X_1 yields

$$Y_i = (b_0 + b_2 X_{2i}) + (b_1 + b_3 X_{2i}) X_{1i} + e_i.$$

And when we factor out X_2 we obtain

$$Y_i = (b_0 + b_1 X_{1i}) + (b_2 + b_3 X_{1i}) X_{2i} + e_i.$$

In the first of these two reexpressions, we can consider the term $(b_1 + b_3 X_{2i})$ as the simple effect of X_1 on Y at particular levels of X_2. So, b_3 is interpreted exactly according to the definition of an interaction: It tells us how much the simple slope for X_1 increases (or decreases) as X_2 goes up by one unit. Alternatively, from the second reexpression b_3 estimates how much the simple slope for X_2 changes as X_1 goes up by one unit. Looking at the slopes for the X_1 and X_2 predictors in these reexpressions, it is clear that these partial regression coefficients have a very different meaning in this model that includes the product term than in a model that does not. According to the first reexpression, b_1, the regression coefficient for the X_1 predictor in this model estimates the simple effect of X_1 when and only when X_2 equals zero. In a parallel manner from the second reexpression, the coefficient for X_2, b_2, represents the simple effect of X_2 when and only when X_1 equals zero. Obviously these

slopes are interpreted very differently in the presence of the product in the model than in its absence.

The general interpretational point, given the presence of product predictors in multiple regression, is as follows: A regression coefficient associated with a predictor that is a component of a higher-order product included in the model estimates the simple relationship between that predictor and the dependent variable when the other predictor(s) with which this one is multiplied to form the product terms equals zero. As a result, to increase interpretability, a number of texts (Aiken & West, 1991; Judd & McClelland, 1989) have recommended using a centering transformation (i.e., subtracting the mean value from individual scores) on the component predictor variables, computing the product from these centered variables, and then including the centered variables and their product in the interactive model. As a result of centering the predictors, the regression coefficient associated with either predictor, when their product is included as a predictor, will equal the simple effect of that predictor at the mean value of the other predictor.

To illustrate, Table 14.1 presents three regression equations computed from a data set of mean course ratings of 5,446 courses taught at the University of Colorado over the last 20 or so years. For each course, the following variables are contained in the data set:

RATE   Mean course rating
        (1–4 scale; higher = more liking),
GRADE   Mean course grade given by
        instructor (1–4),
LEVEL   Mean level of course (1–4).

The first equation in the table shows the regression of RATE on GRADE and LEVEL. Then RATE is regressed on GRADE, LEVEL, and the variable INT, which is the product of GRADE and LEVEL. Finally, this latter model is reestimated, having first centered GRADE and LEVEL.

For each model we present the estimated coefficients, the t and PRE statistics associated with each regression coefficient (comparing the specified model with a compact one where that coefficient is set to zero), the overall R-squared (PRE) of the model and its associated F statistic (comparing the specified model with a compact one where just the intercept is estimated), and the sum of squared errors of the model. Given the sample size, it is hardly surprising that the tests of all hypotheses reported yield significant statistics.

From the first model, we see that average grade given in a class is strongly associated with the mean

TABLE 14.1. Predicting Average Course Ratings from Average Course Grades, Level of Course, and Their Interaction

RATE	=	0.87	+	0.69 GRADE	+	0.03 LEVEL	+ e
t (5442)		16.86		39.19		5.31	
PRE		.05		.22		.01	

R-square $= .24$ $F(2,5443) = 881.49$ $SSE = 1526.85$

RATE	=	0.37	+	0.86 GRADE	+	0.24 LEVEL	−	0.07 INT	+ e
t (5443)		3.21		21.95		5.57		−4.86	
PRE		.00		.08		.01		.01	

R-square $= .25$ $F(3,5442) = 597.97$ $SSE = 1520.26$

RATE	=	3.01	+	0.68 GRADE'	+	0.03 LEVEL'	−	0.07 INT'	+ e
t (5443)		408.21		38.90		5.41		−4.86	
PRE		.89		.22		.01		.01	

R-square $= .25$ $F(3,5442) = 597.97$ $SSE = 1520.26$

rating of the class, holding constant the course level. As the average course grade goes up by one unit (e.g., from a B [3] to an A [4]), the expected increase in the mean course rating is .69 points on a 4-point rating scale. Although significant, the effect of course level, over and above grade, is considerably smaller.

The interaction in the second equation is significant, although again its associated PRE statistic is quite small. To interpret the coefficients in this model, we can reexpress the model in terms of the RATE–GRADE simple relationship:

$$RATE = (0.37 + 0.24 \, LEVEL) \\ + (0.86 - 0.07 \, LEVEL)GRADE + e,$$

The regression coefficient association with GRADE in this model, 0.86, is the estimated difference in RATE associated with a one-unit increase in GRADE when and only when LEVEL equals zero. And because LEVEL in this data set only varies between 1 and 4, this coefficient tells us very little of interest. Similarly, the coefficient associated with LEVEL, 0.24, is the estimated difference in RATE associated with a one-unit increase in LEVEL when and only when GRADE equals zero, which it never actually does in the data set. Hence, if we wanted to talk about the "effect" of each of these variables, we would be mistaken if we took these coefficients and their associated inferential statistics as informative in any straightforward way. The coefficient for the interaction term, −0.07, tells us about the change in the simple relationship between RATE and GRADE as LEVEL increases by one unit. In other words, from the simple slope

for GRADE in the above reexpression, we can compute the estimated simple slope for GRADE at different LEVELs, simply by substituting for the values of LEVEL:

Value of LEVEL	Simple slope of GRADE
1	0.79
2	0.72
3	0.65
4	0.58

The interaction coefficient tells us about the decrease in those slopes as LEVEL increases one unit.

When we get to the third equation, in which GRADE and LEVEL have been centered by subtracting off their respective means (and importantly the product is computed from these centered variables), even though three of the four regression coeficients have changed from the second model, in a deep sense this model is identical to the second, as revealed by the fact that the sum of squared errors is the same. The regression coefficient associated with the GRADE predictor now equals 0.68, a value much closer to that in the first equation. And it estimates the simple slope for GRADE when LEVEL is at zero, or equivalently when LEVEL is at its mean, allowing that simple slope to change as LEVEL changes value. In a parallel manner, the regression coefficient for LEVEL estimates its simple slope when GRADE is at is mean value. The coefficient for the interaction is the same as it was in the second equation, because it still estimates the change in the simple slope for GRADE as LEVEL changes values.

INCLUDING CATEGORICAL PREDICTORS: BETWEEN-SUBJECTS ANOVA MODELS

Categorical predictors can easily be incorporated into multiple regression models by adopting numerical coding conventions for representing their values. With a categorical variable having m levels, a total of $m - 1$ predictors must be coded to fully represent all the information in the categorical variable. A variety of different coding conventions have been proposed. The most widely used convention involves contrast codes, and it is that convention that we adopt in this chapter. In Table 14.2, contrast codes for a categorical variable having four levels, A, B, C, and D, are illustrated. There are two rules for constructing contrast codes: First, the sum of the values of a coded variable, across levels of the categorical variable, must equal zero; second, the sum of the cross products of values between all pairs of coded variables, again across levels of the categorical variable, must also equal zero.[4] So, in Table 14.2, the sum of the values of $X1$, across A, B, C, and D, equals zero. Additionally, if we multiply the values of $X1$ and $X2$ and sum them across the four levels, that sum also equals zero.

Assuming that a complete set of contrast codes is used to represent a categorical variable, and then the dependent variable is regressed on these codes, the predicted values from the regression model will equal the category means. Additionally, the regression coefficients associated with the coded variables inform us about mean differences between the levels of the categorical variable. The regression coefficient for each contrast coded predictor equals the following comparison among the category means:

$$\frac{\sum \lambda_k \bar{Y}_k}{\sum \lambda_k^2},$$

where λ_k are the values of the contrast codes and $\bar{Y}_k$ are the category means, again assuming that a complete set of codes has been included. Thus, in the case of the contrast codes of Table 14.2, the regression coefficient associated with $X1$ will equal half the difference between the mean of the C and D category means and the mean of the A and B category means. The coefficient associated with $X2$ will equal half the difference between the category means of B and A, and that associated with $X3$ will equal half the difference for

---

[4] Actually, the second rule is necessary only if one want to create *orthogonal* contrast codes. There are occasions where nonorthogonal codes may be prefered although these are generally more difficult to interpret. (See Abelson & Prentice, 1997, for procedures to residualize nonorthogonal contrasts.)

TABLE 14.2. Illustration of Coding Conventions with a Four-Level Categorical Variable

| Contrast Codes | Level | | | |
	A	B	C	D
$X1$	-1	-1	1	1
$X2$	-1	1	0	0
$X3$	0	0	-1	1

categories D and C. Given that a full set of codes has been developed and included as predictors, this interpretation does not depend on having equal n in the various category levels.

Because the regression coefficients associated with the coded variables estimate mean differences, tests of their significance are equivalent to tests of those mean differences as conducted by traditional ANOVA procedures. In each case, the augmented model with a full set of contrast codes is compared with a compact one in which one of the coefficients is fixed at zero. The resulting reduction in the sum of squared errors due to that particular coded variable can also be expressed as a function of the cell means and the cell ns:

$$\text{SSR due to a contrast coded predictor} = \frac{\left(\sum \lambda_k \bar{Y}_k\right)^2}{\sum \lambda_k^2 / n_k}.$$

Additionally, when one compares the regression model that includes a full set of coded variables to a compact model that only includes the intercept, the test of the difference is equivalently an omnibus test (i.e., multiple df in the numerator of the F statistic) of whether there are any differences among the category means. The PRE statistic for this comparison is equivalent to the multiple r-squared, or the coefficient of determination, and hence testing the significance of the multiple r is equivalent to asking the omnibus ANOVA question about the significance of any group differences.

In summary, traditional between-subjects ANOVA procedures, both the omnibus tests and tests of individual focused comparisons, can be readily accomplished using appropriately coded predictors in the context of multiple regression. In fact, there is one distinct advantage to conducting the analysis via multiple regression rather than relying on ANOVA computer programs. Most ANOVA programs provide only the omnibus test of whether there are any mean differences (in the one-way case we have been considering so far), and the user must press further and define individual contrasts if the appropriate single degree of freedom tests are to be requested. Many researchers, however, erroneously believe that particular focused contrasts should be tested only if the omnibus test proves to be significant. The omnibus test is generally a very low power test and when researchers have particular focused comparisons that they wish to ask of their data, they should be encouraged to do so regardless of the outcome of the omnibus test (Rosenthal & Rosnow, 1985). The regression approach, because it forces the researcher to define contrast-coded predictors, necessarily provides the single degree of freedom tests of interest to the researcher, assuming he or she has coded those questions into one or more of the included predictors.

Multiple regression models can be easily extended to conduct higher-order factorial analysis of variance. One simply defines appropriate codes for each factor separately. Then additional codes to capture the interaction comparisons between factors are developed by taking the product of codes from the different factors. To illustrate, in Table 14.3, a 3 × 3 factorial design is defined, factor A having levels A1, A2, and A3, and factor B having levels B1, B2, and B3. With nine different cells defined by this crossed design, a total of eight contrast coded predictors need to be developed to fully code the design. $X1$ and $X2$ are contrasts that code the factor A comparisons, $X1$ examining the mean difference between levels A1 and A3, and $X2$ examining the mean difference between level A2 and the mean of levels A1 and A3. $X3$ and $X4$ are defined analogously for factor B. The four interaction contrasts, $X5$ though $X8$, are constructed by taking products of coded predictors from the two factors. For instance, $X5$ is the product of $X1$ and $X3$, and it examines whether the A1 versus A3 difference is different at level B1 than it is at level B3. Again, the regression coefficients for each of these codes will be an exact function of the category mean differences according to the formula that we have already given:

$$\frac{\sum \lambda_k \bar{Y}_k}{\sum \lambda_k^2}.$$

The full analysis of variance model is one where the dependent variable is regressed on all eight contrast-coded predictors. Tests of individual predictors in this model examine the significance of the mean differences coded by those individual contrasts. The omnibus main effects tests due to either factor A or factor B can

TABLE 14.3. Contrast Codes for a 3 × 3 Factorial Analysis of Variance

Factor A	A1			A2			A3		
Factor B	B1	B2	B3	B1	B2	B3	B1	B2	B3
Contrast codes									
$X1$	1	1	1	0	0	0	−1	−1	−1
$X2$	1	1	1	−2	−2	−2	1	1	1
$X3$	1	0	−1	1	0	−1	1	0	−1
$X4$	1	−2	1	1	−2	1	1	−2	1
$X5$	1	0	−1	0	0	0	−1	0	1
$X6$	1	−2	1	0	0	0	−1	2	−1
$X7$	1	0	−1	−2	0	2	1	0	−1
$X8$	1	−2	1	−2	4	−2	1	−2	1

be conducted by comparing this full model with a compact model in which the two codes from one factor or the other are omitted as predictors. The omnibus interaction test derives from a comparison of this full model with a compact one in which the four interaction contrasts, $X5$ through $X8$, are omitted as predictors. Finally, the test of the overall r-squared, or the comparison between this full model and one that includes only the intercept, provides the omnibus test of whether any of the nine cell means differ from each other.

A particular advantage to this regression-based approach to factorial analysis of variance is that it permits the researcher to ask the questions of the data that he or she is interested in, rather than the questions that may only have been dictated by tradition. So, for instance, in the above 3 × 3 example, although the main effect and interaction codes that we have presented would be those most typically of interest in the analysis of data from this design, there is nothing sacred about this particular set of codes. With nine cells or categories in the design, it is fully coded by any set of eight contrast codes, and any such set will end up providing predicted values of the various cell means and asking questions about differences among those cell means. For instance, a perfectly valid alternative coding scheme for this design is that given in Table 14.4 where we have defined the predictors as $Z1$ through $Z8$. $Z1$ asks whether the mean in the A1–B1 cell differs from the average of the means in the other cells of the design. It is entirely possible that this question and some of the other questions coded by this set of codes would be the primary questions of interest with a design such as this one (see the discussion of this issue contained in Judd, McClelland, & Culhane, 1995). The

TABLE 14.4. An Alternative Set of Contrast Codes for the 3 × 3 Design

Factor A	A1			A2			A3		
Factor B	B1	B2	B3	B1	B2	B3	B1	B2	B3
Contrast codes									
Z1	8	−1	−1	−1	−1	−1	−1	−1	−1
Z2	0	7	−1	−1	−1	−1	−1	−1	−1
Z3	0	0	6	−1	−1	−1	−1	−1	−1
Z4	0	0	0	5	−1	−1	−1	−1	−1
Z5	0	0	0	0	4	−1	−1	−1	−1
Z6	0	0	0	0	0	3	−1	−1	−1
Z7	0	0	0	0	0	0	2	−1	−1
Z8	0	0	0	0	0	0	0	1	−1

problem with traditional ANOVA approaches to such data is that they enforce certain questions upon the researcher and encourage him or her to think that those are the only questions that should be asked.

Once one realizes that factorial analysis of variance is equivalent to a one-way analysis of variance, simply using a particularly clever set of codes, then the analysis of data from designs with missing cells, or fractional factorial designs, can be accomplished in a relatively straightforward manner. Again, within a multiple re-

gression framework, one simply formulates the set of $m-1$ condition difference questions that one would like to ask of the data. There is no particular need to force the analysis into the "main effects and interactions" framework and, as a result, many of the difficulties of fractional factorial designs are avoided.

To illustrate, suppose we did a study in which male and female judges were asked to evaluate a job applicant under one of three conditions: the applicant was male, the applicant was female, or the gender of the applicant was left unspecified. All other information about the applicant was held constant. Twenty-four participants judged the overall suitability of the applicant for the job.

Table 14.5 presents the hypothetical cell means. A first analysis of these data uses traditional ANOVA contrasts, defined as follows:

$X1$ +1 if male judge; −1 if female judge.
$X2$ +1 if male applicant; −1 if female applicant; 0 if unspecified.
$X3$ +2 if gender of applicant unspecified; −1 otherwise.
$X4$ $X1 * X2$.
$X5$ $X1 * X3$.

The resulting multiple regression model, where the dependent variable Y is regressed on these five contrast coded predictors, is given in Table 14.5, right under the cell means. The individual regression coefficients in this model equal the differences among the cell means coded by the respective contrasts. The full analysis of variance source table is presented at the bottom of Table 14.5. The single degree of freedom tests in this source table are simply tests of the individual regression coefficients (comparing that augmented model with a compact one where a particular coefficient is set to zero). The multiple degree of freedom tests in the source table result from comparisons of the augmented model to models leaving out two or more predictors. So, for instance, the compact model for the multiple degree of freedom interaction test sets the coefficients of $X4$ and $X5$ at zero. The test of the overall R-squared represents a 5 degree of freedom test where this augmented model is compared with a compact

TABLE 14.5. Hypothetical Data and Analysis of Gender of Judge by Gender of Applicant Design

Gender of Judge	Gender of Applicant		
	Male	Female	Unspecified
Male	3.5	4.0	3.6
Female	3.1	3.9	3.5

$Y = 3.600 + 0.100\ X1 - 0.325\ X2 - 0.025\ X3 + 0.075\ X4 + 0.025\ X5 + e$

R-square = .24 SSE = 6.62

Source	SS	df	MS	F	PRE
Between	2.08	5	0.42	1.14	.24
Subj Gender ($X1$)	0.24	1	0.24	0.65	.03
App. Gender	1.72	2	0.86	2.32	.21
$X2$	1.69	1	1.69	4.57	.20
$X3$	0.03	1	0.03	0.08	.00
Subj. Gender by App. Gender	0.12	2	0.06	0.16	.02
$X4$	0.09	1	0.09	0.24	.01
$X5$	0.03	1	0.03	0.08	.00
Within	6.62	18	0.37		
Total	8.70	23			

TABLE 14.6. Alternative Coding Scheme for Gender of Judge by Gender of Applicant Design

$Z1$	+1 if judge male; −1 if judge female
$Z2$	+1 if judge male and applicant male; −1 if judge male and applicant female; 0 otherwise
$Z3$	+2 if judge male and applicant unspecified; −1 if judge male and applicant male or female; 0 otherwise
$Z4$	+1 if judge female and applicant male; −1 if judge female and applicant female; 0 otherwise
$Z5$	+2 if judge female and applicant unspecified; −1 if judge female and applicant male or female; 0 otherwise

$$Y = 3.600 + 0.100\, Z1 - 0.250\, Z2 - 0.030\, Z3 + 0.400\, Z4 + 0.00\, Z5 + e$$

R-square = .24 $SSE = 6.62$

one estimating simply the intercept (i.e., the grand mean).

An alternative (and equally valid from a statistical point of view) set of codes for analyzing these data is presented in Table 14.6 along with the regression model. Note that the overall R-squared for this model is equivalent to that for the model in Table 14.5, because both models use a full set of codes and therefore the predicted values from both models are the cell means. Most of the individual regression coefficients in this model have changed as a result of the use of different codes, asking about different comparisons among the cell means. So whereas $Z1$ still asks about the gender of judge main effect, the other questions concern simple differences due to applicant gender within levels of judge gender. For instance, the coefficient for $Z2$ estimates the difference between judgments of the male and female applicants for male judges only. $Z2$ through $Z5$ represents simply an alternative way of carving up the between-condition differences than that coded by the traditional main effects of applicant gender ($X2$ and $X3$) and the interaction of applicant gender with judge gender ($X4$ and $X5$).

CATEGORICAL AND CONTINUOUS PREDICTORS: BETWEEN-SUBJECTS ANALYSES OF COVARIANCE (ANCOVA)

Once one appreciates that categorical variables can be efficiently and flexibly analyzed within the context of multiple regression, and that those analyses are

identical to analysis of variance procedures, depending on the choice of codes used, then a wide range of more flexible analyses becomes possible, because regression procedures can of course include continuous predictor variables as well. So, for instance, the limitations of traditional analysis of variance procedures that all too often have led researchers to dichotomize (at the median or mean) continuously varying independent variables in order to include them in an ANOVA are no longer limitations. Assuming that a continuous independent variable has a linear relationship with a dependent variable, it is well-known that a two group analysis of variance dichotomizing the independent variable has less power than a regression analysis that preserves the original scale of the independent variable. And certainly a three group or higher division, again assuming a linear underlying relationship, loses considerable power, particularly if one follows the traditional (and misguided) practice of only looking at omnibus main effect tests. Additionally, Maxwell and Delaney (1993) have shown that when two continuously measured independent variables are dichotomized and included in an ANOVA, not only is power an issue but their effects and their interaction may well be estimated with bias compared with an analysis that preserves their original metric.

The ease of including continuous predictors in a regression model along with categorical ones makes, for instance, the analysis of covariance, with and without interactions between the covariate(s) and the categorical variables, entirely straightforward.[5] When one or more covariates are included in a regression model along with the contrast-coded categorical predictors, the regression coefficients associated with those contrast-coded predictors no longer tell us about the differences in the simple category means; rather they tell us about differences in what are called "adjusted" means in the ANCOVA terminology. So the regression coefficient for a contrast-coded predictor, when a covariate is included, is modified from what we gave

[5] Here and later we use the term "covariate" to refer to any continuously varying predictor that is included in a model along with contrast coded predictors. This somewhat outdated terminology derives from the analysis of covariance, which, as we show, is simply a model containing both sorts of predictors.

earlier and now equals:

$$\frac{\sum \lambda_k \bar{Y}'}{\sum \lambda_k^2},$$

where $\bar{Y}'_k$ is the adjusted mean for the kth cell of the design, given by the following formula:

$$\bar{Y}'_k = \bar{Y}_k - b_c(\bar{C}_k - \bar{C}),$$

where b_c is the regression coefficient for the covariate, $\bar{C}_k$ is the mean of the covariate for the kth cell of the design, and $\bar{C}$ is the mean of all the covariate cell means. In essence, the coefficients associated with the contrast-coded predictors now tell us about differences in the cell means on the dependent variable, getting rid of (or controlling for) any parallel differences in the covariate cell means.

A problematic assumption in analysis of covariance, as developed in the analysis of variance tradition, is the "homogeneity of regression" assumption, that the covariate–dependent variable relationship is homogeneous in all cells of the experimental design. This assumption is highlighted by the formula given above for the adjusted means, where the regression coefficient associated with the covariate, b_c, does not have a k subscript. In other words the weight for the adjustment is assumed to be constant across the cells of the design. Within a regression context, however, this assumption is not at all problematic, for it is equivalent to assuming that the covariate by categorical interactions are all nonsignificant. These interactions can be readily tested by comparing the analysis of covariance model with an augmented one that also includes the covariate by categorical variable products as predictors. Additionally, if the assumption is found not to hold, that is, that the covariate–dependent variable relationship does vary across the cells of the design, then one can interpret the augmented model that includes the covariate interactions. In this interpretation, one needs to attend to the warning given earlier about the subtleties involved in interpreting the coefficients of predictors when those predictors are components of product terms that are also used as predictors in the same model. So, the regression coefficients associated with the contrast-coded categorical predictors in this model that includes their interactions with the covariate tell one about simple mean differences between conditions when and only when the covariate equals zero. Centering transformations, that set the mean of the covariate at zero, make interpretation a bit easier, because then the regression coefficients associated with the contrast-coded categorical predictors

estimate condition differences at the mean value of the covariate.

Models that include categorical by continuous product predictors are of considerable interest outside of the context of experimental design and the analysis of covariance. For instance, a question that frequently arises in social psychological research is whether the relationship between some continuously measured independent variable and the dependent variable differs across different intact groups, such as gender or ethnic group membership. The common approach to this question is to compute correlations between the two variables for the different groups and then ask whether those correlations significantly differ from each other. Such an approach implicitly assumes that the variances of the independent variables in the different groups are homogeneous. In other words, if correlations are found to differ, it may be due either to differences in the magnitude of the slopes linking the dependent and independent variables in the various groups or to differences in the variances of the independent variables. Assuming that the independent and dependent variables are measured in the same metrics in all the groups, the real question we would like to know is whether a unit difference in the independent variable is associated with larger or smaller differences in the dependent variable across the various groups. And this question is best answered by comparing the unstandardized slopes in the groups. In a regression model that includes the independent variable, groups, and the Groups × Independent Variable interactions as predictors, the interactions inform us about the differences in these slopes. Hence, a better procedure than comparing correlations across groups is to test the interactions between the independent variable of interest and contrast-coded variables that represent groups.

To illustrate, we use data borrowed from Kerlinger and Pedhauzer (1973, p. 278). A researcher gathers data on achievement (measured on a 50-point scale) and achievement motivation (5-point scale) from 12 men and 10 women. The raw data are given in Table 14.7. Three regression models are also presented in that table. First, the analysis of variance model is presented where achievement (Y_i) is regressed on a contrast-coded variable representing gender (X_i, coded as $+1$ if female; -1 if male). Next, the analysis of covariance model is presented, regressing achievement on both gender and achievement motivation (M_i). The final model includes the product-predictor variable (XM_i).

From the first equation, we know that there is a significant mean difference between the two groups in achievement, $F(1, 20) = 15.71; p < .01; PRE = .44$.

The regression coefficient associated with X_i in this equation equals half the difference between the female and male achievement means, and the SSR due to X_i is 688.26.

In the second model, the regression coefficient associated with achievment motivation (M_i) is significant over and above gender, $F(1, 19) = 89.28$, $p < .01$; PRE $= .82$. And the gender coefficient is also significant, $F(1, 19) = 75.52$; $p < .01$; PRE $= .80$. Thus, the gender difference continues to be highly significant when controlling for motivation levels. The regression coefficient associated with gender in this equation, 5.31, equals half the difference between the female and male adjusted achievement means, where those adjusted means are:

Female: $28.10 - 4.10(3.10 - 3.175) = 28.41$.
Male: $39.33 - 4.10(3.25 - 3.175) = 39.02$.

Note that although the regression coefficient for gender is reduced in magnitude when motivation is controlled, it's PRE and associated F statistic are substantially larger than in the ANOVA model due to substantial reduction in error variance associated with the inclusion of motivation in the model.

The third equation includes the interaction and thereby provides a test of the homogeneity of regression assumption of the second model. A comparison between the third model and the second yields an SSR due to the interaction of 56.90, with an associated PRE of .37 and an $F(1, 18) = 10.51$, $p < .01$. Following the logic developed earlier when discussing models with interactions, this equation can be reexpressed by focusing on either the simple gender–achievement relationship within levels of motivation:

$$Y_i = (21.07 + 3.96M_i) + (-1.65 - 1.16M_i)X_i + e_i$$

or on the simple motivation–achievement relationship within levels of gender:

$$Y_i = (21.07 - 1.65X_i) + (3.96 - 1.16X_i)M_i + e_i.$$

The first of these reexpressions makes clear that the coefficient associated with gender in this third equation, -1.65, tells us about the predicted gender difference in achievement when and only when motivation equals zero. This value is basically uninformative because no one in the sample has a motivation score of zero. A centering transformation applied to the motivation variable prior to the computation of the product would result in a more meaningful coefficient for the gender variable in this interaction model. The coefficient for the interaction, following the first reexpression, informs us about the change in the gender difference as motivation increases in value. So the predicted gender difference, with men having higher achievement scores than women in these data, becomes greater as motivation increases.

The second reexpression shows that the coefficient associated with motivation in this interactive model (3.96) is the simple achievement–motivation slope when X_i, the contrast code for gender, equals zero. Because gender is contrast-coded, this then is the slope for the average of the two gender groups. The coefficient associated with the interaction, -1.16, tells us about how the simple slope for motivation changes as we move from the female group to the male group. So the simple slope in the female group is

---

TABLE 14.7. ANCOVA with Interactions Illustration (Data from Kerlinger & Pedhazur, 1973, p. 278)

	Males		Females	
	Achievement	Achievement Motivation	Achievement	Achievement Motivation
	25	1	22	1
	29	1	24	1
	34	2	24	2
	35	2	22	3
	35	3	29	3
	39	3	30	3
	42	4	30	4
	43	4	33	4
	46	4	32	5
	46	5	35	5
	48	5		
	50	5		
Mean	39.33	3.25	28.10	3.1

$Y_i = 33.72 - 5.61X_i + e_i$
SSE $= 879.60$ R-square $= .44$

$Y_i = 20.70 - 5.31X_i + 4.10M_i + e_i$
SSE $= 154.34$ R-square $= .90$

$Y_i = 21.07 - 1.65X_i + 3.96M_i - 1.16XM_i + e_i$
SSE $= 97.44$ R-square $= .94$

equivalent to

$$(3.96 - 1.16[+1]) = 2.80.$$

And for the males, it is equivalent to

$$(3.96 - 1.16[-1]) = 5.12.$$

And the test of the interaction is equivalently a test of the difference between these two simple achievement–motivation slopes. In fact, if we estimated two separate regression models, one for women and one for men, regressing achievement on motivation only using data from participants in each group, these would be the values of the estimated slopes in the two groups.

CATEGORICAL PREDICTORS THAT VARY WITHIN SUBJECTS: REPEATED MEASURES AND MIXED MODELS ANOVA

Although the general approach that we have outlined to incorporating categorical variables into multiple regression is fairly well-known, there has been considerable confusion about how experimental factors that vary within subjects might be analyzed using multiple regression programs. As we stated in the introduction to this chapter, suggested approaches to this issue have been quite cumbersome and therefore they are not widely used. As an unfortunate result, when researchers are faced with a situation involving one or more within-subject factors and other independent variables that vary continuously, there is an almost universal lack of knowledge about how continuous predictors can be incorporated into the analysis. It is in this case that one most often encounters the use of median splits to dichotomize continuous variables so that they might be included in standardly used repeated measures analysis programs.

In this section of the chapter, we present a relatively straightforward approach to the analysis of within-subject factors via least-squares regression procedures. We consider first designs with all factors within-subjects and then what are called mixed designs, where some are within and others are between-subjects. In the next section of the chapter, we demonstrate how continuous predictors can be incorporated into these analyses. Finally, we extend the analysis to designs where the within-subject independent variable(s) themselves can be considered to vary continuously.

A general comment is in order about what we are calling within-subject factors. Tests of coefficients in regression models, based on comparisons of augmented and compact models, make the assumptions that errors or residuals are independently sampled from a normal distribution with a single variance. Violations of these assumptions can have serious consequences, because then the Fs that are computed for these comparisons are not distributed according to the tabled F distribution. In the chapter in this volume by Gary McClelland, considerable attention is devoted to the normality and the homogeneity of variance assumptions. The problem with data where each participant is measured repeatedly, under the various levels of an experimental factor, is that the resulting observations are most certainly not independent, because they come from the same participant. Accordingly, an approach like the one we outline in this section must be used so that in fact the errors in any one regression model are independent of each other.

Repeated observations from the same participant are not the only way in which dependence can arise. In general, dependence of observations occurs whenever observations are linked in some way (because they come from the same participant, the same group of individuals, the same classroom, or whatever), and those linked observations are either more or less similar to each other than observations that are not so linked (Kenny & Judd, 1986, 1996). The approach that we outline is then an appropriate solution to the general problem of dependence of observations, regardless of the source of that dependence.

Repeated Measures Models: Factors Varying Only within Subjects

The general approach to within-subject categorical variables that we have outlined in detail elsewhere (Judd & McClelland, 1989) involves the computation of within-subject contrast or difference scores that are then analyzed using traditional least-squares regression models. So consider a design in which there is only a single experimental factor having three levels and every participant is measured under all three levels. Thus, each participant has scores $Y1_i$, $Y2_i$, and $Y3_i$. As was true in the case of between-subject categorical variables, with three levels we can code two within-subject contrasts or differences, using weights that follow the rules set out earlier for contrast coded variables. So, for instance, we might compute one within-subject contrast score that compares level 3 of the factor with level 1 and one that compares level 2 with the average of levels 1 and 3:

$$W1_i = Y3_i - Y1_i,$$
$$W2_i = 2 {}^* Y2_i - (Y1_i + Y2_i).$$

Note that unlike the between-subject case where every

participant had a score on the contrast-coded predictor corresponding to the condition in which that participant was found, in this case, we actually compute an individual contrast or difference score for each participant, weighting his or her dependent responses by contrast-code weights.

To ask whether there are significant differences in the dependent variable across levels of the independent variable, we want to ask whether the means of these two W_i scores differ significantly from zero. This is accomplished in each case by comparing an augmented model in which the intercept is estimated with a compact model in which the intercept is fixed at zero:

Augmented model: $W_i = b_0 + e_i$,

Compact model: $W_i = 0 + e_i$.

Thus, this model comparison is done for both $W1_i$ and $W2_i$.

Most multiple regression computer programs will not estimate models with the intercept only, without any predictor variables. But the above comparison is easily accomplished by recognizing that the sum of squared errors for the augmented model is simply the sum of squares of each W_i around its mean:

$$SSE(A) = \sum (W_i - \bar{W}_i)^2,$$

and the sum of squared errors of the compact model equals the sum of the squared values (not deviated from the mean) of each W_i:

$$SSE(C) = \sum (W_i)^2.$$

Given these two sums of squares and their difference,

$$SSR = (SSE[C] - SSE[A]) = n\bar{W}^2,$$

it is easy to show that the PRE and F statistics for these two inferential tests equal

$$PRE = \frac{n\bar{W}^2}{\sum W_i^2},$$

$$F(1, n - 1) = \frac{n\bar{W}^2}{\sum (W_i - \bar{W})^2/(n - 1)}.$$

These two tests are equivalent to conducting a repeated measures ANOVA with one within-subject factor having three levels, with one exception. The typical repeated measures program provides only the omnibus two degree of freedom test of any differences among the three levels of the factor, without testing the individual single degree of freedom contrasts that we have specified. As in the between-subject case, there is a considerable power benefit in focusing on those single degree of freedom tests that are of interest rather than

relying simply on unfocused omnibus tests. Additionally, there is a further compelling reason for avoiding the omnibus, multiple degree of freedom tests in the within-subject case. Unlike the between-subject situation where every F statistic for each single degree of freedom contrast is based on the same augmented model (and hence the denominator of all of the Fs is the same sum of squared errors), in this case each W_i defines its own augmented and compact models. Thus the test of each individual within-subject contrast involves its own unique error term (commonly refered to in the ANOVA literature as the interaction of that contrast with participants). The omnibus within-subject tests that are commonly reported by repeated measures ANOVA procedures routinely pool or average these individual error terms, thus implicitly assuming they are all of equivalent size. This assumption, commonly known as the homogeneity of within-subject differences or the sphericity assumption, is unfortunately often violated. By avoiding the multiple degree of freedom tests, and concentrating instead on particular within-subject contrasts of interest, this assumption is avoided altogether.[6]

Multiple within-subject factors are analyzed as an extension of what we have just presented, generating within-subject contrasts, or W_is that code the main effects and interactions of those factors. Each of these are then tested by asking whether the mean W_i differs from zero, using in each case its own individual error term. So, for instance, if we had two factors, one with two levels and one with three, both varying within-subjects, we would need to compute five W_is, one to code the main effect of the two-level variable, two to code the main effects of the three-level variable, and two to code the interactions. Each of these would be tested by asking whether the mean W_i differs from zero, using the augmented and compact models defined in the preceding paragraphs.

Mixed Models: Within- and Between-Subject Factors

Mixed models, where some factors vary within-subjects and others between them, involve the computation of both within-subject contrast scores and between-subject contrast predictor variables. Consider

---

[6] A number of corrections have been developed for the omnibus test when the sphericity assumption is violated. Although these corrections seem to work reasonably well, the whole issue is fortunately avoided when individual within-subject contrasts are computed and tested as we have recommended.

TABLE 14.8. Mixed Design				
Level of Factor A	Subject	Level of Factor B		
		1	2	3
A1				
	S1			
	S2			
	S3			
A2				
	S4			
	S5			
	S6			
A3				
	S7			
	S8			
	S9			

the mixed design in Table 14.8. Here participants have been assigned to the three levels of one experimental factor, A, and have been crossed with the second factor B. Each participants thus is measured on the dependent variable three times ($Y1$, $Y2$, and $Y3$), once in each level of the within-subject factor B. The general linear model analysis of data from designs such as this is accomplished by, first, coding the between-subject factor (or factors in higher order designs) into a set of contrast-coded predictors. In this case, factor A is represented by two contrast-coded predictors, $X1$ and $X2$. For levels 1, 2, and 3 of factor A, the contrast weights might be 1, 0, -1, and -1, 2, and -1 for $X1$ and $X2$, respectively. To code the three levels of factor B, the within-subject factor, one computes two W_is to code two within-subject contrasts or differences. Let us define $W1$ and $W2$ as we did above coding the level 3 versus 1 difference as $W1$ and the level 2 versus other two levels as $W2$. Additionally, in this mixed design, we want to compute an additional W for each participant, $W0$, that is simply the average of each participant's $Y1$, $Y2$, and $Y3$ scores. As will become clear shortly, this $W0$ variable allows us to estimate the main effects of factor A, the between-subject factor, coded by $X1$ and $X2$.

To conduct the full analysis of variance on this design, one computes three regression equations, regressing $W0$, $W1$, and $W2$ on $X1$ and $X2$:

$$W0 = b_{00} + b_{01}X1 + b_{02}X2,$$
$$W1 = b_{10} + b_{11}X1 + b_{12}X2,$$
$$W2 = b_{20} + b_{21}X1 + b_{22}X2.$$

In the $W0$ equation, there are two coefficients of interest, b_{01} and b_{02}. The first asks if the average Y score

increases as $X1$ changes values, or equivalently as we go from level 3 of factor A to level 1. The second asks about the difference between level 2 of factor A and the average of levels 1 and 3 in the average Y scores. Note that because the dependent variable in this equation collapses across the levels of factor B, these two tests represent the two degrees of freedom of the main effects of factor A.

The main effects of factor B are estimated and tested by the intercepts in the $W1$ and $W2$ equation. The $W1$ intercept, b_{10}, is the predicted value of $W1$ when both $X1$ and $X2$ equal zero, which they do on average, collapsing across levels of factor A. Hence, this intercept estimates the mean difference between levels 3 and 1 of factor B and a test of the null hypothesis that this intercept equals zero tests the significance of that mean difference. The $W2$ intercept, b_{20}, asks whether level 2 of factor B differs from the mean of levels 1 and 3, on average collapsing across levels of factor A.

Finally, the four degrees of freedom for the A by B interaction are estimated and tested by the regression coefficients associated with the $X1$ and $X2$ predictors in the $W1$ and $W2$ regression equations. For instance, the b_{11} coefficient in the $W1$ equation estimates how different the level 3 versus level 1 difference of factor B is when A is level 3 compared with when A is level 1.

An Illustration

Eight participants are run in a social facilitation study where they complete four different tasks, either in the presence of someone else or by themselves. So there is one between-subject factor having two levels (audience versus no) and one within-subject factor having four levels (task). The raw data are given in Table 14.9.

The analysis of these data proceeds by first coding the between-subject independent variable using a single contrast-coded predictor variable (X) because there are only two levels to this between-subject factor:

$$X = +1 \text{ if audience present; } -1 \text{ if no audience.}$$

The within-subject factor, task, has four levels, and so in total three different within-subject contrast or differences scores can be coded from these four levels. These three contrasts should be chosen to address the particular theoretical questions of interest. In the present case, we have somewhat arbitrarily created contrasts to compare task 1 with the remaining three tasks ($W1$), task 2 with the remaining two tasks ($W2$), and task 3 with task 4 ($W3$):

$$W1_i = ([3 * Y1_i] - Y2_i - Y3_i - Y4_i).$$
$$W2_i = ([2 * Y2_i] - Y3_i - Y4_i).$$
$$W3_i = (Y3_i - Y4_i).$$

Additionally, we compute $W0$ as the average of the four Y scores for each participant:

$$W0_i = (Y1_i + Y2_i + Y3_i + Y4_i)/4.$$

The analysis of these data consists of four augmented models, one for each of these W scores regressed on the between-subject contrast-coded predictor variable, X. These models are given below the raw data in Table 14.9. In the case of the $W0$ equation, the coefficient associated with X estimates half the difference between the mean Y value in the presence of the audience versus not, collapsing across the four tasks. A comparison with a compact model in which it is set at zero tests the significance of the between-subject main effect.

In the $W1$, $W2$, and $W3$ models, the intercepts estimate the mean differences due to the within-subject factor of task. More specifically, the $W1$ intercept estimates the difference between task 1 and the other three, the $W2$ intercept estimates the difference between task 2 and tasks 3 and 4, and the $W3$ intercept estimates the task 3–task 4 difference. Each of these intercepts may be tested by comparing each augmented model with a compact one in which the intercept is set equal to zero. Note that each of the resulting F statistics will have a different denominator or error term, since each is based on a different augmented model. In these data, all three intercepts are negative (and the intercepts in the $W2$ and $W3$ equation are significantly so), indicating higher scores on later tasks.

The regression coefficients associated with the contrast-coded predictor variable, X, in each of the $W1$, $W2$, and $W3$ equations estimate the audience by task interactions. Specifically, the coefficient associated with X in the $W1$ equation estimates whether the audience effect is different on task 1 than on the other three tasks. And the coefficients associated with X in the other two equations inform us about differences in the audience effect on task 2 versus tasks 3 and 4 and on task 3 versus task 4. Of these coefficients, the only significant one is in the $W3$ equation, indicating that the audience effect was greater on task 4 than on task 3.

The analysis that we have outlined for these data results in the same F statistics and conclusions as those

TABLE 14.9. Mixed Design Data Example

		Y1	Y2	Y3	Y4
Audience Present	Participant 1	6	5	7	9
	Participant 2	7	7	8	9
	Participant 3	3	5	6	7
	Participant 4	3	4	4	6
No Audience	Participant 5	1	3	4	3
	Participant 6	6	6	5	4
	Participant 7	6	4	6	6
	Participant 8	2	1	3	3

$$W0 = 4.97 + 1.03\,X + e$$
$$SSE = 15.67$$

$$W1 = -2.87 - 2.12\,X + e$$
$$SSE = 84.75$$

$$W2 = -2.50 - 1.00\,X + e$$
$$SSE = 42.00$$

$$W3 = -0.50 - 1.00\,X + e$$
$$SSE = 2.00$$

which would result if these data were analyzed using traditional repeated measures analysis of variance programs. However, generally these programs only provide the omnibus multiple degree of freedom tests for factors having more than two levels, unless the researcher specifies that particular single degree of freedom contrasts are desired. So, in the example we have just given, a repeated measures analysis of variance program would typically only provide a three degree of freedom test for the main effect of task and a three degree of freedom test for the audience by task interaction. Again, the problem with these tests is that each single degree of freedom within-subject comparison involves a different model with a different error term. The omnibus tests implicitly assume that these error terms, across our $W1$, $W2$, and $W3$ equations, are all homogeneous, an assumption that is frequently inappropriate.

CONTINUOUS INDEPENDENT VARIABLES IN THE CONTEXT OF WITHIN-SUBJECT FACTORS

Between-Subjects Covariate

A major advantage of the within-subject contrast approach to repeated measures models that we outlined above is that continuously varying independent variables can readily be included in such models as well. For instance, let's return to the mixed model data structure that was used as an example in Table 14.8. In that design, participants are measured under each of the three levels of factor B and each participant is randomly assigned to one of the three levels of factor A. Equivalently, factor A is between-subjects and factor B within them. Let us first consider a modification of this design in which factor A, rather than being a categorical variable under which subjects are grouped (i.e., an experimentally manipulated factor), is a continuously measured independent variable of interest. To lend some substance to this example, suppose factor B consists of three task types with subjects completing all three. And suppose A is an individual difference measure of achievement motivation. Traditional approaches to repeated measures analysis of variance have considerable difficulties with this sort of design, unless the motivation variable, A, is dichotomized or otherwise broken up into categories (with resulting information loss). The within-subject contrast analysis that we outlined above imposes no such constraints.

Recall that we computed for each subject three different W scores:

$$W0 = (Y1 + Y2 + Y3)/3,$$
$$W1 = (Y3 - Y1),$$
$$W2 = (Y1 + Y3 - [2*Y2]).$$

And then we estimated three different regression equations in which these three Ws were regressed on two contrast-coded variables, X1 and X2, that were used to code the three levels of factor A. Now we simply regress the three W scores on the continuously scored motivation variable:

$$W0 = b_{00} + b_{01}A,$$
$$W1 = b_{10} + b_{11}A,$$
$$W2 = b_{20} + b_{21}A.$$

Interpretation of the various regression coefficients in these models is relatively straightforward. From the first equation, the intercept, b_{00}, is unlikely to be of much interest; it is the predicted value of subjects' average Y scores when A equals zero. The regression coefficient for motivation in this equation, however, b_{01}, is of considerable interest: It tells us how average Y scores vary as motivation (A) goes up or down. In the traditional analysis of variance parlance, it represents the linear "main effect" of the continuously varying motivation variable.

The intercepts in the second and third equations, b_{10} and b_{20}, tell us about the expected values of the within-subject differences attributable to task (factor B), and

coded by the respective within-subject contrasts, when and only when the motivation variable equals zero. In other words, these coefficients are estimating simple effects of factor B at level zero of variable A. The first one, from the W1 equation, estimates the simple difference between condition B3 and condition B1 when A equals zero. And the second, from the W2 equation, examines whether scores in level 2 of factor B differ from the average of scores in levels 1 and 3, again when A equals zero.

Turning to the two slopes for A in the W1 and W2 models, b_{11} and b_{21}, these regression coefficients inform us about whether the within-subject task differences coded by the W1 and W2 contrasts vary as motivation varies. Conceptually, they represent the two single-degree-of-freedom interactions between factor B and the continuously varying A. The first one, b_{11}, examines the extent to which the difference between levels 3 and 1 of factor B changes in magnitude as motivation increases. The second one, b_{21}, estimates the extent to which the difference between level 2 of factor B and the average of levels 1 and 3 changes in magnitude as motivation increases.

We previously noted that the interpretation of simple effects in models with interactions involving continuously varying independent variables is facilitated if those variables are centered or transformed so their means equal zero. The same is true in these models, so we might estimate the following three models:

$$W0 = b_{00} + b_{01}A',$$
$$W1 = b_{10} + b_{11}A',$$
$$W2 = b_{20} + b_{21}A'.$$

where A' equals A minus its mean. The slope coefficients in these models, b_{01}, b_{11}, and b_{21}, and their interpretations are unaltered by this transformation. So b_{01} continues to tell us about the overall or main linear effect of motivation, collapsing across levels of factor B. In the W1 and W2 equations, b_{11} and b_{21} continue to tell us about the A × B interaction and are interpreted exactly the same as previously. What is different as a result of the transformation of A are the three intercepts, b_{00}, b_{10}, and b_{20}. The first one continues to be of relatively little interest; it simply estimates the average Y score for subjects at the mean level of achievement motivation. In essence, it estimates the grand mean of the data. The intercepts in the W1 and W2 equations continue to estimate simple differences due to factor B coded by the two within-subject contrasts, but now those effects are simple differences due to factor B when A is at its mean, or for subjects with the mean level of motivation. In other words, they now estimate the mean differences due to factor B on average, again analogous to "main effects" in analysis of variance parlance.

In this exposition, we have assumed that the primary interest is in the experimentally manipulated factor, factor B, and have focused our explanation of these models on its effects and the moderation of its effects due to the continuously varying motivational variable. But, in fact, we might be interested in these models from the other point of view, asking questions about how the relationship between motivation, A, and the outcome, Y, varies under the three different tasks (i.e., levels of factor B). This is analogous to the situation, discussed in the analysis of covariance section earlier in this chapter, where we were interested in differences in a relationship between a continuously varying independent variable and the dependent variable for three different groups of subjects. Now however, the grouping variable is within-subjects, representing different tasks or conditions under which the dependent variable (presumably performance) is measured.

To examine the achievement motivation–performance relationship on each of three tasks, one could correlate A with $Y1$, A with $Y2$, and A with $Y3$ and then use the somewhat cumbersome and laborious procedures that are available for testing differences among dependent correlations (Olkin & Finn, 1990). The approach we have outlined, however, seems considerably more straightforward, testing the task type by achievement motivation interactions (Judd, McClelland, & Smith, 1996).

Covariate That Varies within Subjects

The models we have just explored involve a continuous predictor that is only measured a single time for each subject in the context of the repeated measures design where each subject is observed under multiple treatment conditions. An alternative design is one in which the continuously measured variable is measured at each level of the within-subject treatment conditions. Suppose participants are given two detailed job applications to read. For each participant one of these applications is attributed to a minority applicant and one to a nonminority applicant, and the specific application is conterbalanced with race of applicant across subjects. So applicant race is a within-subject factor having two levels. Additionally, subjects are randomly assigned to one of two conditions: either they are told that their job is to evaluate each applicant or they are told that they should attempt to remember as much as

they can about each applicant. Subsequently all participants are given a recall test and the amount recalled from the minority application (YM_i) and the amount recalled from the nonminority application (YN_i) are the primary dependent variables of interest. So the design is a two by two mixed design with applicant race within-subjects and task instructions (evaluate versus remember) between them. Additionally, because the researcher believes that amount recalled for each application should be a function in part of study time, she records the amount of time each participant spent studying each of the two applications. This then is the continuously measured covariate, measured at each level of the within-subject factor.

We first analyze the recall data ignoring the study time covariate. Two W scores are computed from the two recall dependent variables:

$$W0_i = (YM_i + YN_i)/2,$$
$$W1_i = (YM_i - YN_i).$$

And these are regressed on the contrast coded predictor, X_i, that equals $+1$ if the participant was in the evaluation instruction condition and -1 if the participant was in the memory instruction condition.

$$W0_i = b_{00} + b_{01}X_i,$$
$$W1_i = b_{10} + b_{11}X_i.$$

In the first equation, b_{01} estimates whether there is an overall recall difference between the two conditions, collapsing across applicant type. In the second equation, the intercept, b_{10}, estimates the difference in amount recalled between the minority and nonminority applicants, on average across levels of task instructions. Finally, the coefficient for X_i in the $W1_i$ equation, b_{11}, estimates the applicant type by task instruction interaction. More specifically, it will equal half the difference in the minority versus nonminority recall difference between the evaluation condition and the memory condition.

These analyses ignore study time. One would like to ask about these effects controlling for study time as well. Assume SM_i and SN_i are the two measures of study time, the first for the minority application and the second for the nonminority one. From these we compute two WS scores defined in a parallel manner to the W scores used for the recall dependent variable:

$$WS0_i = (SM_i + SN_i)/2,$$
$$WS1_i = (SM_i - SN_i).$$

And then we regress each of the W scores from the recall measures on the contrast-coded X_i variable and the parallel form of the *WS* score:

$$W0_i = b_{00} + b_{01}X_i + b_{02}WS0_i$$
$$W1_i = b_{10} + b_{11}X_i + b_{12}WS1_i$$

Now the coefficient for X_i in the first equation, b_{01}, estimates the task instruction main effect in recall, controlling for mean study time levels. In other words, it asks about this main effect over and above any average study time differences that may exist between the two task instruction conditions. The coefficient for $WS0_i$ in this equation, b_{02}, asks whether average study time, collapsing across the two applications, is predictive of average recall, again collapsing across the two applications, within task instruction conditions.

Turning to the coefficients in the $W1_i$ equation, the intercept, which previously estimated the mean recall difference between the minority and nonminority applicants, collapsing across task instruction conditions, now estimates that expected difference when and only when the difference between study times for the two applicants equals zero. In other words, it now tells us about the expected recall difference between applicants after adjusting for any differences in mean study time between the two, within levels of task instructions. The coefficient associated with X_i continues to inform us about whether the difference between the applicants in recall depends on instruction condition, but this time it does so controlling for the difference in study time between the two applicants. Note that the interpretation of this slope does not depend on the study time differences being equal to zero. It simply estimates the interaction between applicant ethnicity and task instructions in recall holding constant study time differences. Finally, the coefficient associated with the difference in study time, $WS1_i$, estimates the extent to which recall differences between the two applicants depend upon study time differences, within task instruction conditions.

These models can be made more complex if the theoretical questions merit the additional complexity. For instance, in the $W0_i$ equation, one might include an additional predictor that is the product of X_i with $WS0_i$. Its coefficient would inform us about the interaction between task instruction conditions and average study time levels (across the two applicants) in predicting average recall. So, for instance, it might tell us that study time on average was more highly related to average recall in the recall instruction condition than in the evaluation instruction condition. The inclusion of this product would of course affect the interpretation of other coefficients in this model, following the warning mentioned earlier about the interpretation of coefficients of predictor variables when those variables are components of products also included as predictor variables.

A parallel product might be included in the $W1_i$ equation, representing the interaction between X_i and $WS1_i$. Its coefficient would inform us about whether study time differences between the two applicants are more predictive of recall differences between the two in one task instruction condition than in the other.

Finally, a potentially interesting question concerns the relationship between the covariate, study time, and the dependent variable, recall, for each level of the within-subject experimental factor of applicant ethnicity. One might be interested in the interaction of study time and applicant ethnicity, predicting for instance that study time ought to relate to recall more strongly for the nonminority applicant than for the minority one. Judd, McClelland, and Smith (1996) have shown that this interaction can be tested by regressing the recall difference dependent variable, $W1_i$, on the average study time predictor, $WS0_i$. If one makes the assumption that study time for one applicant has no effect on recall for the other candidate (holding constant its own study time), then the coefficient for $WS0_i$ estimates the difference in the simple study time–recall relationships between the two levels of applicant ethnicity.

INDEPENDENT VARIABLES THAT VARY CONTINUOUSLY WITHIN-SUBJECTS

Although the above examples illustrate how continuously varying independent variables may be incorporated into the analysis of data where some factors are within subjects, the within-subject factors themselves have been categorical. That is, either subjects were recalling information about the minority applicant or they were recalling information about the nonminority candidate. Sometimes, however, within-subject independent variables vary more or less continuously and the general approach that we have outlined in the preceding sections of this chapter can be extended to this situation.

Suppose a researcher was interested in how exercise was related to subjective feelings of happiness. He has a set of alternative research designs at his disposal and one way to define the differences among these designs is to consider the nature of the independent variable, exercise. There are four possible cases, three of which we have already considered. These four are defined by whether the independent variable varies between or within-subjects and whether it is treated as a categorical or a more or less continous variable. The between-subject categorical case occurs when each subject is assigned to one excercise level, say high and low, and his or her happiness is then assessed. The between-subject continuous case occurs if each participant's level of excercise were measured as well as his or her happiness. The within-subject categorical case is when subject's happiness is measured both following high and low exercise, perhaps couterbalancing the order in which each subject is exposed to these two levels of the independent variable. The final case, and the only one not considered so far in this chapter, is when each subject's exercise levels and happiness are repeatedly assessed, with exercise levels varying more or less continuously from day to day. Actually, it is exceedingly likely that the independent variable in this last case varies between-subjects as well as within them. Within subjects, there are day to day fluctuations in exercise levels and one would like to know how these fluctuations relate to subjective happiness levels. Additionally, it is probably the case that subjects differ in their mean excercise levels and this variation may also be related to variation in their mean levels of subjective happiness.[7]

Consider the hypothetical (and unreasonably small) dataset given in the top half of Table 14.10. Each of 6 participants is monitored for 8 days, recording both their level of exercise (E_{ij}) and subjective happiness (H_{ij}) on each day (for both of these variables the i subscript refers to participant and the j subscript refers to day). Exercise levels are recorded as number of minutes during the day devoted to exercise. Subjective happiness is measured on a 1 to 7 rating scale and was always completed at the end of the day. In these data, there is variation in the independent variable, exercise, both between subjects and within-subjects. That is, some participants, exercise more on average than

other participants; additionally, within any given participant there are day to day fluctuations in exercise levels. What we would like to do is examine how both of these sources of variation in the independent variable relate to variation in the dependent variable.

The general strategy that we adopted for within-subject designs can be extended to this situation. Recall that in the earlier analyses we outlined, we formed within-subject composite scores on the dependent variable, either averaging over the various responses given by each participants the $W0_i$ score, or calculating one or more within-subject difference or contrast scores, $W1_i$, that estimated for each participant the difference in the dependent variable across the levels of the independent variable. We can take the same general approach here. First, we compute an average score on subjective happiness for each participant, $\bar{H}_i$, and we also compute a within-subject (linear) difference score for each participant, estimating for each participant how much subjective happiness goes up or down across days as exercise level fluctuates. The most straightforward way of computing such a within-subject difference score is to do a separate regression for each participant, treating day as the unit, and estimating the simple slope for each participant when subjective happiness is regressed on exercise level. These within-subject regression equations are presented in the lower half of Table 14.10. Each of the resulting slopes are conceptually identical to the within-subject differences or contrasts that we computed earlier, because each one estimates the difference in subjective happiness for a given participant as that participant increases his or her exercise by 1 minute.

Now we want to ask two questions about these composite variables. First, to examine how between-subject differences in typical exercise levels relate to between-subject differences in typical happiness, we can regress the mean happiness score for each participant on his or her mean exercise level. The participant means on these two variables are given in Table 14.10, and the resulting regression equation is

$$\bar{H}_i = 2.372 + 0.086\bar{E}_i + e_i.$$

Comparing this model with a compact one in which the slope for mean exercise level is fixed at zero yields a PRE of .56 and an $F(1, 4) = 5.02$, $p = .09$. Given the small number of observations and the resulting lack of statistical power, one probably should conclude that there is a fairly substantial, although not statistically significant, relationship between the independent variable and the dependent variable at the between-subject level. That is, as participants typically exercise more, disregarding the day to day fluctuations in their

---

[7] It is important to underline that the design distinctions that we have made in this paragraph focus on the presumed level of measurement of the independent variable (i.e., whether it is treated categorically or more or less continuously) and whether it varies within subjects or only between them. These design distinctions have implications for the analysis one conducts to estimate the relationship between the independent and dependent variables and it is these implications that are of central interest in this chapter. However, these design distinctions do not have necessary implications for the types of conclusions that can be drawn from this relationship, and more specifically whether one can infer causality from that relationship. Confidence that a causal relationship exists depends on the use of a random assignment variable for assignment of specific observations to the various levels of the independent variable, regardless of whether those levels are treated categorically or continuously in the analysis and regardless of whether there are multiple observations from each subject or only one. The reader may want to refer to the chapters by Brewer and by Smith (both this volume) for further discussion of these important issues.

TABLE 14.10. Data Example with Independent Variable Varying within and between Subjects

Participant		1	2	3	4	5	6	7	8	M
1										
	E	0	15	0	25	15	0	10	15	10
	H	3	4	4	5	5	3	4	4	4
2										
	E	35	45	0	25	35	0	45	60	30.62
	H	5	6	4	4	5	4	5	6	4.88
3										
	E	15	20	25	35	0	10	15	20	17.50
	H	2	3	4	4	3	4	2	4	3.25
4										
	E	45	30	60	45	30	15	30	45	37.50
	H	5	6	6	4	4	4	5	5	4.88
5										
	E	0	10	0	15	15	0	0	10	6.25
	H	2	3	3	2	3	1	2	1	2.13
6										
	E	25	25	30	30	25	15	25	35	26.25
	H	6	7	7	7	6	4	6	6	6.13

Header spanning columns 1–8: Day

Within-Subject Regressions

Participant 1: $H_{1j} = 3.33 + 0.067 E_{1j} + e_{1j}$
Participant 2: $H_{2j} = 3.82 + 0.034 E_{2j} + e_{2j}$
Participant 3: $H_{3j} = 2.67 + 0.033 E_{3j} + e_{31j}$
Participant 4: $H_{4j} = 3.83 + 0.028 E_{4j} + e_{41j}$
Participant 5: $H_{5j} = 1.96 + 0.026 E_{5j} + e_{51j}$
Participant 6: $H_{6j} = 2.95 + 0.121 E_{6j} + e_{61j}$

exercise levels, they show a tendency to report higher subjective happiness.

To examine whether within-subject variations in exercise level are predictive of within-subject differences in subjective happiness, we want to ask whether the mean within-subject contrast or slope is significantly different from zero. As we did earlier, this is accomplished by comparing an augmented model in which the intercept is estimated from the data to a compact one in which the intercept is fixed at zero. The dependent variable in these models are the within-subject slopes that we have previously estimated by regressing subjective happiness on exercise level across days within each subject. The mean of these slopes equals 0.051, which differs significantly from zero, PRE $= .70$, $F(1, 5) = 11.46$, $p < .05$. At this level, looking only within subjects across days, there is a large

and significant relationship between exercise level and subjective happiness, such that day to day variations in exercise are positively associated with day to day variation in subjective happiness, ignoring the mean differences between the various participants.

It is important to note that the two different estimates of the relationship between the independent and dependent variables, one within subjects and the other between subjects, need not reach similar conclusions. That is, it is entirely possible for the magnitude of the relationship to differ depending on whether we are looking within or between subjects, because the process that is responsible for that relationship may be rather different at the two different levels. That said, however, it is entirely appropriate to compare the magnitude of the effects at the two different levels and interpret the slope estimates consistently. So, in the between-subjects analysis, the slope for mean exercise level, .086, tells us that our best expectation from these data is that participants who exercise one more minute on average across days are .086 units happier on the subjective happiness scale. Within subjects, the mean slope was .051, telling us that if the typical participant exercises one more minute one day compared to another day, our best estimate is that his or her subjective happiness rating will be higher by .051 units. Interestingly, of course, the latter estimate is significantly different from zero whereas the former is not, a difference produced by the fact that error variation between subjects around the mean predicted value of subjective happiness for each participant is greater than the error variation between subjects in their within-subject slopes.

The approach we have just outlined for examining the effects of an independent variable that varies more or less continuously within-subjects can readily be extended to handle more complex data structures and more complex questions. Suppose, for instance, that we also measured for each participant how intensely they typically exercised. So for each participant we measured the percentage of maximum heart rate typically achieved by that participant when he or she exercised. We could then ask whether this intensity variable moderates the exercise–subjective happiness relationship both within and between subjects. The between-subject case follows the earlier analysis where mean subjective happiness for each participant is regressed on mean exercise level for each participant. Additionally, assuming we had sufficient degrees of freedom, we could also include exercise intensity as an additional predictor and the product of intensity and mean exercise level. If this product was predictive of subjective happiness levels, controlling for its two components, then we would have evidence that intensity of exercise level moderates the exercise–subjective happiness between-subject relationship.

The moderation of the within-subject relationship is examined by regressing each subject's slope, from the within-subject regression of exercise level on subjective happiness, on the intensity variable. If intensity is predictive of these slopes, then it indicates that the magnitude of the within-subject relationship between exercise and subjective happiness is affected by exercise intensity. If intensity is centered in this analysis, that is, if it is transformed by subtracting off the mean intensity score from each individual's intensity score, then the intercept in this regession will equal the mean value of the slope. Assuming intensity is predictive of the slope, then a test of whether the mean slope differs from zero is more powerfully conducted by testing whether this

intercept is significantly different from zero than by conducting the analysis recommended earlier in this section. In other words, the two estimated regression coefficients in this model tell us both about whether there is on average a within-subject relationship between exercise and subjective happiness (the intercept) and whether that within-subject relationship depends on the intensity with which subjects typically exercise.

In addition to permitting tests of within and between-subject moderation as just outlined, this analytic approach can very flexibly handle missing data and differences between subjects in the number of data points available. Even if data from certain days were missing from some subjects, or if some subjects were observered for many more days than others, both mean values on the independent and dependent variables and within-subject slopes still could be computed, assuming there was some day-to-day variation in exercise levels. And then the analyses outlined above still could be conducted, although we might want to do a weighted analyses, weighting cases by the number of valid data points they each contribute or some other index of the reliability of the measurement at the level of the individual subject.

The analytic approach that we have just outlined, where the independent variable varies within and between subjects and where it is treated in a more or less continuous manner, is conceptually equivalent to other approaches to what are called multilevel or hierarchically-nested data (see Kashy & Kenny, this volume, Ch. 17; Collins & Sayer, this volume, Ch. 18). These other approaches are a bit more sophisticated, in that they estimate the various effects simultaneously rather than as separate regression equations, and they use weighted least squares or maximum likelihood criteria to do the estimation, rather than ordinary least squares as we have outlined. There exist specialized computer programs to accomplish these analyses (e.g., HLM). Although these approaches and programs have obvious advantages over the ordinary least squares approach that we have outlined, the fundamental point of this chapter is that nearly all analyses of interest to social psychologists can be readily accomplished by making comparisons between models that are estimable using widely available general linear model or multiple regression programs.

CONCLUSION

The purpose of this chapter has been to outline a very general analytic approach to data that social psychologists typically collect. This approach permits one to analyze the effects of independent variables that are considered to vary either categorically or continuously. Additionally they may vary either between subjects, within subjects, or both within and between them. And all of these analyses can be readily accomplished by a model comparison approach, with such models being estimated by widely-available multiple regression statistical programs. As a result, social psychologists can now be remarkably flexible in the analyses they conduct. They are not restricted to particular computer programs that only conduct certain sorts of analyses and not others. And they can treat their variables in the metrics in which they were measured, rather than forcing the metrics to fit the confines of one particular analysis procedure or another. Given the richness of the data that social psychologists collect, with some independent variables measured and others manipulated, with some independent variables varying within subjects and some between them, and with focused questions concerning the simple effects and interactions of those variables, a single comprehensive approach to data analysis such as that put forward in this chapter is long overdue.

In retrospect, it may seem a little strange that a chapter such as the current one, focusing on data analysis issues, should be part of a handbook on research methods. But we hope that we have convinced the reader that design issues and analysis issues are tightly entwined. All too often in the past, design considerations have been dictated by the vagaries of the limited analytic approaches taught in our graduate courses and available in the specificalized computer programs used. A much more flexible analytic approach, such as that outlined in this chapter, frees the researcher from those restrictions and permits optimal design and measurement to be utilized.

REFERENCES

Abelson, R. P., & Prentice, D. A. (1997). Contrast tests of interaction hypotheses. *Psychological Methods, 2*, 315–329.

Aiken, L. S., & West, S. G. (1991). *Multiple regression: Testing and interpreting interactions.* Newbury Park, CA: Sage.

Aiken, L. S., West, S. G., & Sechrest, L. (1990). Graduate training in statistics, methodology, and measurement in psychology: A survey of PhD programs in North America. *American Psychologist, 45*, 721–735.

Campbell, D. T., & Kenny, D. A (1999). *A primer on regression artifacts.* New York: Guilford.

Campbell, D. T., & Stanley, J. C. (1963). *Experimental and quasi-experimental designs for research.* Chicago: Rand McNally.

Cohen, J. (1968). Multiple regression as a general data-analytic system. *Psychological Bulletin, 70*, 426–443.

Cohen, J. (1978). Partialed products are interactions; partialed powers are curve components. *Psychological Bulletin, 85*, 858–866.

Cohen, J., & Cohen, P. (1975). *Applied multiple regression/correlation analysis for the behavioral sciences.* Hillsdale, NJ: Erlbaum.

Cohen, J., & Cohen, P. (1983). *Applied multiple regression/correlation analysis for the behavioral sciences* (2nd ed.). Hillsdale, NJ: Erlbaum.

Cook, T. D., & Campbell, D. T. (1979). *Quasi-experimentation: Design and analysis issues for field settings.* Boston: Houghton Mifflin.

Judd, C. M., & McClelland, G. H. (1989). *Data analysis: A model comparison approach.* San Diego, CA: Harcourt, Brace, Jovanovich.

Judd, C. M., McClelland, G. H., & Culhane, S. E. (1995). Data analysis: Continuing issues in the everday analysis of psychological data. *Annual Review of Psychology, 46*, 433–465.

Judd, C. M., McClelland, G. H., & Smith, E. R. (1996). Testing treatment by covariate interactions when treatment varies within subjects. *Psychological Methods, 1*, 366–378.

Kenny, D. A., & Judd, C. M. (1986). Consequences of violating the independence assumption in analysis of variance. *Psychological Bulletin, 99*, 422–431.

Kenny, D. A., & Judd, C. M. (1996). A general procedure for the estimation of interdependence. *Psychological Bulletin, 119*, 138–148.

Keppel, G., & Zedeck, S. (1989). *Data analysis for research designs.* New York: W. H. Freeman.

Kerlinger, F. N., & Pedhazur, E. J. (1973). *Multiple regression in behavioral research.* New York: Holt, Rinehart, & Winston.

Lewin, K. (1935). *A dynamic theory of personality.* New York: McGraw-Hill.

Maxwell, S. E., & Delaney, H. D. (1990). *Designing experiments and analyzing data: A model comparison perspective.* Belmont, CA: Wadsworth.

Maxwell, S. E., & Delaney, H. D. (1993). Bivariate median splits and spurious statistical significance. *Psychological Bulletin, 113*, 181–190.

Myers, J. L., & Well, A. D. (1991). *Research design and statistical analysis.* New York: Harper Collins.

Olkin, I., & Finn, J. (1990). Testing correlated correlations. *Psychological Bulletin, 108*, 330–333.

Pedhazur, E. J. (1982). *Multiple regression in behavioral research.* New York: Holt, Rinehart, & Winston.

Rosenthal, R., & Rosnow, R. L. (1985). *Contrast analysis: Focused comparisons in the analysis of variance.* Cambridge, England: Cambridge University Press.

Tatsuoka, M. (1993). Elements of the general linear model. In G. Keren & C. Lewis (Eds.), *A handbook for data analysis in the behavioral sciences: Statistical issues* (pp. 3–41). Hillsdale, NJ: Erlbaum.

Winer, B. J., Brown, D. R., & Michels, K. M. (1991). *Statistical principles in experimental design.* New York: McGraw-Hill.

CHAPTER FIFTEEN

Nasty Data

Unruly, Ill-Mannered Observations Can Ruin Your Analysis

GARY H. McCLELLAND

Researchers confronting their own data often find those data to be more unruly, ill-mannered, and irascible than the well-behaved, cooperative data found in textbook examples. Irascible data that slap us in the face at least get our attention. More dangerous are those stealthy, sinister observations that can go undetected and yet have a disproportionate and untoward effect on our analyses. This chapter describes techniques for detecting and taming those nasty data that otherwise could ruin your analyses.

SOURCE OF PROBLEMS

The supposedly "tried-and-true" statistical methods can be remarkably fragile in some situations. In particular, those methods that minimize sums of squares – including the most common statistical procedures used by social psychologists such as t-tests, ANOVAs, and regression – are very sensitive to outliers. Estimates of group means or regression parameters can sometimes be dramatically affected by just a single outlier observation. Most textbooks from which social psychologists learn their statistics indicate that the standard procedures assume normality and homogeneity of variance (equal variances within each group or equal variances around each predicted criterion in regression). Tables of critical values or those "p-values" produced by statistical programs as well as statistical power analysis depend strongly on those assumptions being correct. But few textbooks provide information about how to detect violations of the normality and homogeneity of variance assumptions in one's data or what to do about

them when they are detected. The good news is that the standard statistical methods are remarkably robust against some violations of the assumptions. However, there are some violations of those assumptions that can wreak havoc on one's analysis. In this chapter we give advice about how to separate the benign from the killer violations.

There are many ways in which one's data can become nasty and ill-mannered. Data recording and data entry errors have the potential for introducing whopping outliers. We may believe we are sampling from what appears to us to be one population but which in fact is several distinct populations, one possibly much smaller than the others. Or nature may just throw us a curve ball now and then to keep the game interesting. In whatever ways our data become irascible, it is important for us to detect the potential problems.

Most statistical analyses are performed by computers, but unfortunately the standard output from many programs just provides the usual test statistics, intermediate steps in the calculation of those test statistics, and their associated probabilities under the null hypothesis. Such outputs seldom provide clues about nasty data that might be lurking in the analysis. However, almost all computer packages also now provide adequate graphical and statistical procedures for detecting outliers and data that violate the standard assumptions. And the relevant procedures are mostly graphical and fairly simple so there is no longer any excuse for not examining one's data for outliers and other ill-mannered data.

Why Worry?

Many psychologists, especially those far removed from their last statistics course in graduate school,

Direct correspondence to Gary McClelland, Department of Psychology, CB345, University of Colorado, Boulder, CO 80309-0345 (e-mail: gary.mcclelland@colorado.edu).

believe that the standard least-squares statistical procedures are relatively robust against all but the most serious kinds of nasty data. Indeed, early Monte Carlo studies (in which data were randomly sampled so as to violate specific assumptions) did indicate that basic tests such as Student's t-test were generally robust against certain violations. However, these studies have been greatly overgeneralized and more recent theoretical and Monte Carlo studies have identified some unruly types of data, data not that uncommon in real research, that can have killer effects on analyses.

The old claims for robustness found in many statistics textbooks written for psychologists should be discounted for three reasons. First, the early robustness studies often considered quite restricted violations. For example, the frequently cited study by Box (1964) of the effects of unequal variances on the Type I level of Student's t-test considered ratios of standard deviations no more extreme than $\sqrt{3}$ to 1. However, subsequent research has shown that Student's t-test is remarkably sensitive when standard deviation ratios are greater than that, especially if sample sizes are unequal. Wilcox (1996) gave this example: If the two group sizes are 21 and 41 and the standard deviation of the smaller group is four times that of the larger (Wilcox, 1987, demonstrates that such extreme ratios are not uncommon in the social sciences), then the putative $\alpha = 0.05$ Student's t-test actually has a Type I error rate of approximately 0.15.

A second reason for discounting the old claims for robustness is that robustness with respect to one issue, such as Type I error rate, does not imply robustness with respect to other important statistical issues. In particular, many test statistics whose Type I error rates are not appreciably altered by assumption violations often have greatly diminished statistical power. Wilcox (1996, p. 114) presents an example where a "contaminated" normal distribution (a small percentage of the cases are sampled from a normal distribution with a much larger standard deviation, but the same mean) reduces the power of Student's t-test from .99 to .33. Furthermore, there are few robustness studies of other statistical measures such as confidence intervals and effect sizes that are increasingly recommended for psychological research.

A third reason for ignoring robustness claims is that even if the inferential test statistics were robust against all assumption violations, the tools described here for assessing assumption violations would still be valuable for providing researchers with a better understanding of their data. Instead of just using statistical procedures canonically to "bless" one's data to the editor's satisfaction, the goal of statistical analysis should be to understand one's data better. We cannot identify nasty, inconsistent data unless we have successfully modeled most of our data, and in turn identifying inconsistencies often shows the way to a more complete model of the data. Velleman (1997) reminds us that this is not a new idea with this quotation from Bacon's *Novum Organum*:

errors of Nature, sports and monsters correct the understanding in regard to ordinary things, and reveal general forms. For whoever knows the ways of Nature will more easily notice her deviations; and, on the other hand, whoever knows her deviations will more accurately describe her ways. (II 29)

This chapter is devoted to methods for knowing the deviations so that we may more accurately describe Nature's ways. For didactic reasons, I first consider detection or diagnosis techniques, and then I suggest some useful remedies. However, the reader should be aware that in practice data analysis using these techniques is highly iterative with back and forth testing, using the same detection techniques, to assess whether the remedies have been successful.

METHODS FOR DETECTING NASTY AND ILL-MANNERED DATA

The methods for detecting nasty and ill-mannered data depend somewhat on the type of analysis. However, most of the ideas are common to all the methods. We will start by considering data from a single group, move on to comparisons among groups, and conclude with simple and multiple regression. In social psychology we seldom test statistical hypotheses with a single group because we seldom have adequate a priori null hypotheses to justify such tests. Nevertheless, examining the data for a single group is a good place to start because it provides a simple context in which to introduce several of the primary methods of detecting outliers and assumption violations.

Single Groups

NORMALITY ASSUMPTION. When applying standard least-squares statistical techniques to data from a single group, or to data from a single cell from a factorial design, we assume that the data are sampled from a normal distribution, such as the smooth curve depicted in Figure 15.1. However, the smooth density curve of Figure 15.1 only emerges if there are many, many observations. With small samples such as those

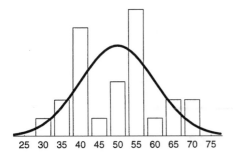

Figure 15.1. Density function for the normal distribution superimposed on histogram of 25 random observations from normal distribution.

commonly used in social psychology experiments and even with a couple of hundred observations in a field study, the empirical density function or histogram seldom closely approximates the normal density curve, even if the data are from a normal distribution. For example, the following 25 data values were sampled randomly from a normal distribution with mean 50 and standard deviation 10:

38 61 42 57 70 52 51 29 51 34 38 72 55
55 54 39 54 44 57 55 40 42 63 65 36.

The histogram for these data, also in Figure 15.1, shows considerable lumpiness. Using only the histogram, judging whether these data are from a normal distribution is difficult.

There are statistical tests for normality (Madansky, 1988, pp. 20–53, thoroughly describes the best methods). However, both these tests and viewing the histogram focus our attention on many types of nonnormality that are not problematic. Figure 15.2 displays a Cauchy distribution (which results from the ratio of two normally distributed variables) on the left and a uniform distribution on the right. Both visual inspection and the normality tests (if we performed them) easily reveal that the uniform distribution is not normal, but the case of the Cauchy distribution is not so clear. However, in terms of the effect on a least-squares analysis the Cauchy distribution is by far the more dangerous, while the uniform distribution poses virtually

no problems. Extreme observations in the tails of the distribution pose the greatest danger of overwhelming the other observations and distorting the analysis. The "squares" in least-squares analysis, inherent in ANOVA and regression, implicitly give extra weight to those extreme observations in the tails; thus, it is those observations that can most seriously distort a least-squares analysis. Although it is difficult to see in Figure 15.2, the tails of the Cauchy distribution are much thicker (that is, extreme observations are relatively more likely) than those of the normal distribution. In contrast, the tails of the uniform distribution are in a sense chopped off, so there is little threat to the analysis. Although eyeballing the empirical density or using the statistical tests of normality consider the whole distribution, it is really only the tails that require our close attention.

Fortunately, there are better and fairly simple ways to examine the tails of the empirical distribution. The normal quantile-quantile plot (Chambers, Cleveland, Kleiner, & Tukey, 1983; Wilk & Gnanadesikan, 1968) is one such graphical method for examining the tails. Normal q-q plots were popular when normal probability graph paper was available and have regained favor as they have become increasingly available in computer statistical packages. They are easy enough to construct directly and doing so makes clear what the computer packages do when they generate normal q-q plots. The idea is simple: We plot the empirical quantiles (the ordered data) against quantiles (i.e., z-scores) for the normal distribution. For example, one point in the normal q-q plot is the median of the data and the z-score $= 0$, which corresponds to the median of a normal distribution. In Table 15.1, the first column is the ordered data from the example of Figure 15.1, and i is just the index of the data. The next column is the fraction f_i of the observations that are equal to or less than the data value for the given row. We assume that each data value is in the middle of a histogram category by defining $f_i = (i - .5)/n$. Subtracting .5 avoids problems at the ends and ensures, for example, that for the median $f = .5$ (other definitions sometimes used for f_i to correct for problems at the ends are $f_i = i/[n + 1]$ and $f_i = [i - 3/8]/[n + 1/4]$). The

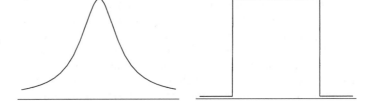

Figure 15.2. Examples of two nonnormal distributions: Cauchy (left) and uniform (right).

TABLE 15.1. Empirical and Normal Quantiles for Sample Data

Empirical Quantile Data	i	f_i	Normal Quantile $z(f_i)$
29	1	0.02	−2.05
34	2	0.06	−1.55
36	3	0.10	−1.28
38	4	0.14	−1.08
38	5	0.18	−0.92
39	6	0.22	−0.77
40	7	0.26	−0.64
42	8	0.30	−0.52
42	9	0.34	−0.41
44	10	0.38	−0.31
51	11	0.42	−0.20
51	12	0.46	−0.10
52	13	0.50	0.00
54	14	0.54	0.10
54	15	0.58	0.20
55	16	0.62	0.31
55	17	0.66	0.41
55	18	0.70	0.52
57	19	0.74	0.64
57	20	0.78	0.77
61	21	0.82	0.92
63	22	0.86	1.08
65	23	0.90	1.28
70	24	0.94	1.55
72	25	0.98	2.05

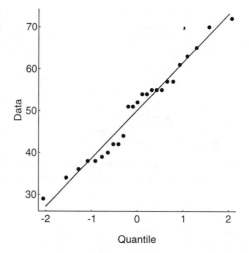

Figure 15.3. Normal quantile-quantile plot for sample data from a normal distribution.

last column in Table 15.1 is the z-score corresponding to each fraction f_i.

The normal q-q plot is simply a scatterplot of data against $z(f_i)$ as in Figure 15.3. If the data are from a normal distribution with mean μ and standard deviation σ, then data can be described by the following straight line.

$$\text{data} = \mu + \sigma z(f_i). \tag{1}$$

In other words, if the data are all telling more or less the same story, then the points should fall on a line with intercept equal to the mean and slope equal to the standard deviation. Points that deviate from the line, especially at either end, either because they are outliers or because the data distribution is skewed, are trying to tell a different story. In those cases, the one story told by the mean and the standard deviation does not apply to all the data points. In the example of Figure 15.3, however, the data do fall closely to the line representing a normal distribution with intercept equal

to the sample mean of 50.2 and a slope equal to the sample standard deviation of 11.5. Hence, these data are much more consistent with a normal distribution than implied by inspection of the lumpy histogram in Figure 15.1. (Note that Shapiro-Wilk's, 1968, W, one of the more popular statistical tests of normality, simply formalizes this regression concept in a manner accounting for the inherent nonindependence among the estimated residuals.)

Figure 15.4 shows four normal q-q plots. Those in the top row, data from normal and uniform distributions, respectively, are not threatening to a least-squares analysis because they indicate no more extreme observations in the tails than we would expect for a normal distribution. However, those in the bottom row, data from Cauchy and chi-square distributions, respectively, are very dangerous because they indicate the observations in the tails are more extreme than expected for a normal distribution. The plot for the normal distribution shows the linear pattern expected in a q-q plot. The plot for the uniform distribution is essentially linear in most of the middle range but, for at least one end, the slope flattens. Flat slopes at the ends imply that the tails of the distribution are thinner than those of a normal distribution. Thin tails generally are not problematic because they imply that unruly extreme observations, to which least-squares techniques are very sensitive, are less likely to occur than they would if normality were satisfied. In contrast, the plot for the Cauchy distribution illustrates a distribution with much thicker tails than the normal; the Cauchy plot is also essentially linear in most of the

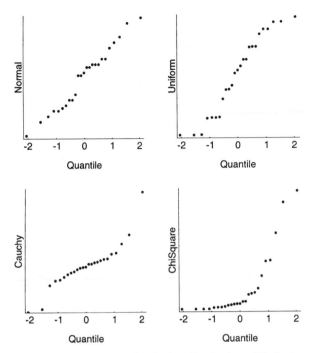

Figure 15.4. Normal q-q plots for four distributions: (Clockwise from upper left) normal, uniform, Cauchy, chi-square.

middle range but at either end the slope dramatically steepens. The data values on the steep part of the q-q plot are effectively outliers which have a disproportionate effect on a least-squares analysis. Finally, the q-q plot for the chi-square distribution illustrates the appearance of an asymmetric or skewed distribution; there are essentially two slopes – a flat slope below the median, indicating a thin tail, and a very steep slope above the median, indicating a thick tail. Skewed distributions can also have adverse effects on standard statistical procedures. Unless there is a steep slope at either end of the normal q-q plot, then you probably do not need to worry about violations of the normality assumption. In other words, thin-tail violations of normality are generally benign, whereas thick-tail violations can kill an analysis.

More and more software packages provide normal q-q plots. Although most plot the empirical data against the equivalent z-score quantiles as illustrated in Figures 15.3 and 15.4, some reverse the axes. For reversed axes, exchange "flat" for "steep" in the above descriptions. Also, some programs normalize the data on the vertical axis so that the slope of the line is necessarily one. Variants of normal q-q plots also exist. For example, Atkinson (1981, 1982) argues that half-normal plots, in which the absolute value of the stu-

dentized deleted residual (see below) is plotted against the normal quantiles increases diagnosticity for small and moderate samples (say, less than 60 observations).

OUTLIERS. If the data really are from a single group, then they all should more or less be telling the same story, especially the story about what the typical value is for the group. If one or a few observations are telling a very different story from the other observations, then the assumption that the data come from a single group ought to be questioned. Outliers often identify themselves by causing steep tails in the normal q-q plots considered above. There are also statistically principled methods for identifying outliers. One method is to compute the standardized residual for each observation; that is,

$$r_i' = \frac{Y_i - \bar{Y}}{s} \sqrt{\frac{n}{n-1}}. \tag{2}$$

Standardized residuals are often compared with z-scores from normal distributions. With the sample sizes used in social psychology experiments or even surveys, z-scores greater in absolute value than about 2.6 should be rare. For example, if the underlying distribution is normal, then only about 1 out of every 100 observations should have a z-score greater than 2.6. For 1,000 observations, only about four observations should have absolute z-scores greater than 3. One should clearly be very suspicious of any z-scores greater than 4 or 5.

One problem with using z-scores is that an outlier may distort the estimated mean and standard deviation so that the outlier no longer looks extreme. A solution is to leave out an observation, recalculate the mean and standard deviation of the remaining observations, and then calculate the z-score. Actually, it is more appropriate to compare the resulting number to Student's t-distribution, so we have

$$r_i^* = \frac{Y_i - \bar{Y}_{[i]}}{s_{[i]}} \tag{3}$$

is distributed as Student's t-distribution with $df = n - 2$, where the $[i]$ as a subscript indicates that the ith observation has been omitted from calculating the mean and standard deviation. This value is exactly the same as the t-statistic for testing the coefficient for a dummy code (= 1 for the ith observation and = 0 for all other observations) onto which Y was regressed. This value of t is also sometimes known as the *studentized deleted residual*. It would be tiresome to recompute n means and standard deviations, each time leaving out one observation. Fortunately, this is not necessary because, as shown by Atkinson (1985),

$$r_i^* = r_i' \sqrt{\frac{n - 1 - r_i'^2}{n - 2}}. \tag{4}$$

Additionally, many computer packages now compute studentized deleted residuals. SAS (1989) and many other programs refer to this outlier index as RSTUDENT.

Sometimes there are a priori suspicions that an observation might be an outlier. For example, one might suspect the data from a participant who completed a questionnaire in 10 minutes that all other participants required more than an hour to complete. Or one might be wary of data from a participant whose experimental session was interrupted by a fire alarm. If so, then it is appropriate to compare the studentized deleted residual for that observation against Student's t-distribution in a test of whether one can reject the null hypothesis that the observation is telling the same story as all the other observations.

Without a priori doubts about a few observations, it is still appropriate to use the studentized deleted residual to screen for outliers. However, computing the studentized deleted residual for all the observations increases the likelihood of Type I errors. Hence, it is prudent to use the Bonferroni adjustment – using α/n instead of α – when identifying statistically significant outliers. For 100 observations, any observation with a studentized deleted residual greater in absolute value than 3.6 is significantly different ($p < .05$) from the other observations; for 1,000 observations the critical value is 4.07. Thus, without worrying about tables of critical values and Bonferroni adjustments, any studentized deleted residual greater than 4 should be considered as an outlier.

Two Groups

A very common statistical test is the comparison of two groups such as control vs. treatment or the comparison of two demographically defined groups such as men vs. women. The assumptions underlying the standard statistical procedures such as Student's t-test are that the data from each group come from the same normal distribution except for a possible shift in location (i.e., the difference in the means). In particular, the variance of the normal distribution must be the same within each group. The procedures considered above for single groups can of course be applied to the data from each individual group. Rather than making two separate q-q plots, it is more common to plot the

errors – the deviations from the within-group means – in a single q-q plot. Such a plot assesses the normality assumption underlying Student's t-test for independent groups and can reveal outliers, but it does not assess the assumption that the variances are the same within each group (homogeneity of variance). The q-q plot of the errors should fall on a line having a mean of zero and a slope equal to the estimated common standard deviation (i.e., the root mean squared error).

HOMOGENEITY OF VARIANCE. Just like testing for normality, there are formal statistical procedures for testing homogeneity of variance (see Madansky, 1988, for a review of many such tests). However, these tests themselves are often not robust to violations of normality and the presence of outliers. Furthermore, even when they detect violations, they do not provide any diagnosis that might lead to a remedy. There are, fortunately, several graphical techniques that are both useful for detecting violations of homogeneity of variance and for assessing the cause of the violations. The mean and median coincide for a normal distribution so the difference in the 50th percentiles estimates the difference in the means. Not as well known is that equivalent quantiles, as illustrated in left column of Figure 15.5, from two identical normal distributions are also the same distance apart and so estimate the difference in the means. If the distributions for the two groups are not the same then the quantiles need not be equidistant. The right column of Figure 15.5 illustrates that the quantiles for two normal distributions with unequal variances will not be equidistant.

Figure 15.5. Quantiles are equidistant for equal variances (left) and not equidistant for unequal variances (right) [first quartile, median, and third quartile for top to bottom].

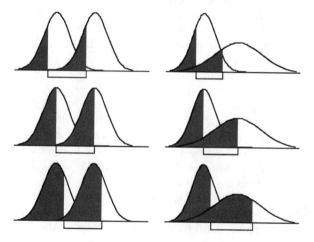

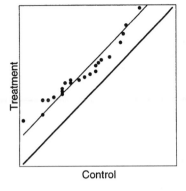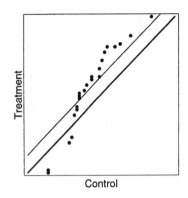

Figure 15.6. Quantile-quantile plot comparing control vs. treatment groups: equal variances (left) and unequal variances (right).

Plotting the quantiles of one group against the quantiles of the other group provides a simple method for visualizing whether the quantiles are consistent in their estimates of the mean difference between the groups. Such plots are called quantile-quantile plots (the normal is dropped because there is no need to assume normality). Figure 15.6 shows the q-q plots for control vs. treatment comparisons for (a) equal variance normal distributions such as those in the left column of Figure 15.5 and (b) unequal variance normal distributions such as those in the right column of Figure 15.5. If the observations were from the same normal distribution (i.e., if the means of the two groups were equal), then the points would fall on the diagonal line with slope 1 and intercept 0. In the left panel of Figure 15.6, the points fall along a line with slope 1 and intercept equal to the mean difference. Q-Q points falling on the line indicate that the corresponding quantile difference is consistent with the mean difference estimated from the other quantiles. In contrast, the q-q points in the right panel of Figure 15.6 clearly do not fall on a line with slope 1, indicating that different quantiles provide inconsistent estimates of the mean difference between the two groups. Lower quantiles estimate a negative difference (control exceeds treatment) while higher quantiles estimate a positive difference greater than the mean difference (the mean difference determines the intercept of the line). Note, if the number of observations is unequal in the two groups, then the empirical quantiles of the smaller group are plotted against the corresponding interpolated quantiles of the other group.

If many of the q-q points are far away from a common line defined by the mean and the standard deviation, then not all the quantiles are telling the same story about whether the treatment mean is higher than the control mean. In other words, q-q points not falling on this common line indicate that the two distributions are not the same. In this case, the two distributions are not the same because they have different variances. Substantially different distributions, whatever the reason, imply that the usual statistical comparison based on Student's t-test is inappropriate.

It is a popular myth among psychologists that unequal variances are only a serious problem in the comparison of two groups when the numbers of observations are very different in the two groups. Although it is true that the Type I error will largely be unaffected by the unequal variances (10,000 simulations of the unequal variance comparison of Figure 15.5 yielded a Type I error rate of .051 using a nominal $\alpha = .05$), the Type II error rate and other statistics such as confidence intervals and effect sizes can be adversely affected by the unequal variances. For example, the power for detecting the difference in Figure 15.5 is .97 (based on 10,000 simulations), but falls to .75 for the unequal variances depicted.

No matter what the aggregate statistical tests report, the scientist should strive to get the story right. Figure 15.5 demonstrates that the true story is considerably more complicated than the simple claim that the treatment group, on average, scores higher than the control group. In this illustration of unequal variances, there may be important consequences of not telling the whole story. Suppose that the treatment were a reading intervention program in the schools. If the data are as in the right graph of Figure 15.5, then the intervention is necessarily deleterious for some even though it is helpful on average. Although a within-subjects study would be required to know for sure, it is likely for a skill like reading that someone who scores low in the control group would also be amongst those scoring low in the treatment group. If the variances are unequal as illustrated in Figure 15.5, then the intervention program would be harmful to those most in need of help.

To avoid such errors, researchers must tell the whole story represented in their data.

A second method for detecting unequal variances is the *spread-location* or *s-l* plot suggested by Cleveland (1993). Such plots are particularly good for detecting *monotone spread* – a steady increase (or decrease) in the spread or variance of the observations as the location or typical value increases. An *s-l* plot is formed by graphing the absolute errors against the medians of each group. Cleveland (1993) recommends plotting absolute errors and medians because outliers can distort means and variances and therefore interfere with detection of unequal variances. Further, absolute errors are often severely skewed; plotting the square root of the absolute errors removes much of that skew. Figure 15.7 displays *s-l* plots for the same examples used in Figure 15.6. A line connects the two medians of the square roots of the absolute deviations and the positions along the horizontal axis have been "jittered" (a small amount of random error added) so that the points do not overlap. If the variances in the two (or more) groups are equal, then the line connecting the medians of the square roots of the absolute errors will be flat (as in the left panel), but if the variances are unequal the line will be sloped (as in the right panel). Displaying all the errors provides a visual context for judging the magnitude of the slope relative to the range of errors.

DETECTION OF OUTLIERS. The studentized deleted residual is easily generalized to two (or more groups). The studentized residual is given by:

$$r_{ij}^* = \frac{Y_{ij} - \bar{Y}_{[i]j}}{s_{[i]}} \qquad (5)$$

where j denotes group; this statistic can be compared to Student's t-distribution with $n - 3$ degrees of freedom. A short-cut formula exists that does not require recomputation after each deletion; however, it is easier

simply to use a standard regression program (regressing Y on a coded predictor – either contrast, effect, or dummy) that produces studentized deleted residuals.

Multiple Groups

The generalization of the detection techniques for two groups to experiments with multiple groups – using one-way ANOVA, two-way or higher factorial ANOVA – is straightforward. For testing normality, the normal q-q plot for all the errors is useful as well as normal q-q plots for the data (or errors) within each group. The spread-location plots are easily extended by using each groups median (or mean) to identify its location in the graph, regardless of the one-way or factorial structure of the groups. And the studentized deleted residual has the same definition and can be compared with the Student t-distribution with $n - g - 1$ degrees of freedom, where g is the number of groups. Again, it is much easier to obtain the studentized deleted residuals from a regression program; see Judd & McClelland (1989) for details on how to use regression programs to analyze ANOVA models. Only quantile-quantile plots comparing groups do not generalize almost exactly. One could make all $(g)(g - 1)/2$ possible q-q plots comparing one group against another. Also, in factorial designs, one can construct the q-q plot comparing one row against another or one column against another. In a 2×2 factorial design, the interaction compares the positive diagonal cells to the negative diagonal cells; the corresponding q-q plot can often be quite informative. Note that in these multigroup comparisons (e.g., a row against a row), the distributions need not be normal (indeed, if the row variable has an effect, these distributions are unlikely to even be unimodal); however, the assumptions underlying the q-q plot (which do not presume normality) should still hold.

Simple Regression

Anyone who answers a lot of statistical questions for psychologists is always amazed at the number of students and colleagues who arrive with their printouts asking for help in interpreting regression results but who have not looked at any graphs of their data and analyses. The most important diagnostic plot for simple regression is a scatterplot with the regression line superimposed. Anscombe (1973) demonstrated that very different datasets could produce the same regression analysis. The statistical results for all four

Figure 15.7. Spread-location plots for the examples of figure 15.6.

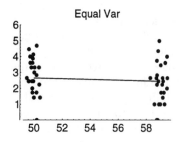
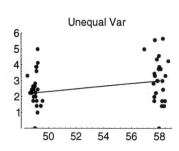

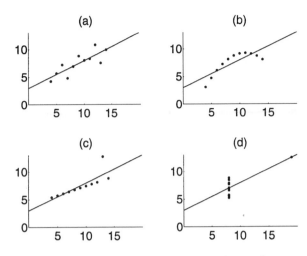

Figure 15.8. Anscombe's (1973) four datasets having the same statistical analysis ($Y = 3 + .5X, r = .82, t(9) = 4.24, p < .01$).

datasets in Figure 15.8 are identical: $Y = 3.0 + .5X, r = .82, t(9) = 4.24, p < .01$. Yet just a casual inspection of the respective scatterplots reveals that these are very different datasets with very different interpretations. Figure 15.8(a) is probably what is expected for a simple regression with those statistics. Figure 15.8(b) clearly has a curvilinear component. Figure 15.8(c) would be a perfect relationship except for a single outlier and in Figure 15.8(d) there would be no relationship except for a single outlier. Although the data in Figure 15.8(b–d) would be most unlikely to occur in a real study, the point is that a wide variety of datasets – only some of which are consistent with the simple regression model – can produce the same routine statistical analysis. To know what story the data are really telling, it is essential to examine the scatterplot for any simple regression analysis.

OUTLIERS. For simple regression there are three separate outlier questions. Given that there are two variables, a predictor and a criterion variable, two outlier questions are obvious. Is the predictor value for an observation unusual? Is the criterion value unusual? The third question pertains to the joint effect of the predictor and criterion values by asking about the influence of the observation on joint inferences about all the parameters in the model. That is, does the observation distort or have undue influence on the overall regression model? Each outlier issue is considered in turn.

Is the predictor value unusual? All observations contribute equally to estimating the mean; that is, each observation has a weight of $1/n$. In contrast, each ob-

servation does not contribute equally to the estimate of the slope in regression. To gain insight into this issue and its importance, it is useful to consider an equivalent, but conceptually different, way to estimate the slope of the best-fitting least-squares line. A common formula for calculating the slope of the regression line is given by:

$$b = \frac{\sum_{i=1}^{n}(X_i - \bar{X})(Y_i - \bar{Y})}{\sum_{j=1}^{n}(X_j - \bar{X})^2}. \tag{6}$$

A little algebra yields this equivalent formula for the slope

$$b = \sum_{i=1}^{n} w_i \left[\frac{Y_i - \bar{Y}}{X_i - \bar{X}} \right] \tag{7}$$

where $\quad w_i = \dfrac{(X_i - \bar{X})^2}{\sum_{j=1}^{n}(X_j - \bar{X})^2}.$

The term in brackets in Equation 7 is the slope "suggested" by each point – the change in Y between the point and the mean for the variable Y divided by the change in X between the point and the mean for the variable X, that is, the slope of a line between the data point and the mean point. The estimated slope for the regression is simply the weighted average of all the individual slopes suggested by each point. Figure 15.9, using the data from Figure 15.8(a), illustrates the individual slopes for each data point.

The weight given each data point when calculating the overall slope estimate is based on the unusualness

Figure 15.9. Slopes between each data point and the mean point.

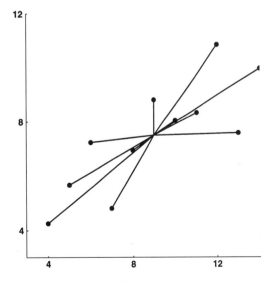

of the data point in terms of the predictor variable. The further the predictor variable is from the mean, the greater its weight. This makes sense because the slopes of long lines in Figure 15.9 are unlikely to be affected much by small changes, perhaps caused by error, in the criterion variable Y; hence, our confidence in the estimated slope is greater for long lines. In contrast, small changes in Y for short lines could dramatically alter the slope; hence, our confidence in the estimated slope is much less for short lines. The details of the calculations are presented in Table 15.2. One can think of each observation as having a vote on the slope that is to apply to all the observations, but with the votes of some observations counting more. If all the observations are telling more or less the same story, then all the observations ought to be voting for essentially the same slope. In the case of a perfect relationship, all the individual slopes would be identical and would equal the overall slope. In Figure 15.9, where the data had a correlation of .82, the individual slopes vary from .02 to infinity. However, those observations with extreme slopes generally receive little weight. In particular, the infinite slope receives a weight of 0. The weight is a measure of how much impact or leverage an observation has on the overall slope estimate. In this case, four observations (3, 6, 8, and 11) account for approximately 75% of the total weight. It would be undesirable for a single observation to have a very large percentage of the total weight, because in that case the slope votes of all the other data points are ignored in calculating the "overall" slope. In that case, the "overall" slope is really a description of only one data point. This occurs when one observation has a very unusual (relative to the other observations) predictor value; such is the case in Figure 15.8(d).

Most modern regression programs report the lever (sometimes unhelpfully referred to as the diagonal of the hat matrix) h, which represents the weight or leverage an observation has in determining the overall model. For simple regression, the lever is given by

$$h_i = \frac{1}{n} + \frac{(X_i - \bar{X})^2}{\sum_{j=1}^{n}(X_j - \bar{X})^2}. \tag{8}$$

The lever represents an observation's weight in determining the overall model. In simple regression, the model consists of two parts – the mean (or intercept) and the slope. Each observation has equal weight in the voting for the mean and weight proportional to the squared deviation of the predictor variable from its mean in the voting for the slope. The lever, as shown in Equation 8, is simply the sum of those two weights.

Unusually high values for the levers are undesirable because it means that what the regression program reports really only applies to the one or two observations with unusually high levers. It is inappropriate and misleading to report a regression equation as if it applies to all n observations if, because a few points have high levers, it actually only applies to a few observations. In judging the magnitude of levers it is useful to note that the sum of the levers necessarily equals the number of parameters, 2 for the case of simple regression. Hence, the average lever equals 2/n for simple regression. If a single lever is near 1, then it implies that one of the two parameters of the simple regression model is allocated to predict that single observation; this is clearly undesirable. An example is the unusual observation in the dataset of Figure 15.8(d); its leverage value is 1.0, whereas all the other observations have leverage values of 0.1. That one unusual observation effectively determines the slope.

It is well-known that restricting the range (more properly, restricting the variance) of the predictor variable attenuates the correlation. The converse applies when there is a single outlier with an extreme predictor value. That one observation artificially increases the range (variance) and thus inflates the correlation. Allowing one observation to inflate the correlation, or

TABLE 15.2. Slope Calculations for the Dataset of Figure 15.8(a)

	X1	Y1	Slope	Wt	Wt *slope
	10	8.04	0.54	0.01	0.00
	8	6.95	0.55	0.01	0.01
	13	7.58	0.02	0.15	0.00
	9	8.81	inf	0.00	0.00
	11	8.33	0.41	0.04	0.02
	14	9.96	0.49	0.23	0.11
	6	7.24	0.09	0.08	0.01
	4	4.26	0.65	0.23	0.15
	12	10.84	1.11	0.08	0.09
	7	4.82	1.34	0.04	0.05
	5	5.68	0.46	0.15	0.07
Sum	99	82.51		1.00	0.50
Mean	9	7.50			
Sum Sq Dev	110				

even to create one when otherwise there would be no relationship, obviously increases the chances of making Type I errors – rejecting the null hypothesis when the null hypothesis is in fact correct. Observations with unusual predictor values, assuming they do not also have unusual criterion values, often make regression models appear better than they actually are. In those cases, the story told by the regression model really only pertains to that one observation and it is very misleading to pretend that the regression story applies to all the data.

Is the criterion value unusual? This is the same outlier question we asked with respect to group comparisons and the answer is the same. The studentized deleted residual is defined as before as

$$r_i^* = \frac{Y_i - \hat{Y}_{[i]}}{s_{[i]}}. \tag{9}$$

Again, there are short-cut formulas, but these are seldom needed because most modern regression programs report, if requested, the studentized deleted residuals. For simple regression, these can be compared to Student's t-distribution with $n - 3$ degrees of freedom. Conceptually, it is important to note that the studentized deleted residual is equivalent to the value of the t-statistic one would obtain for testing the coefficient of a dummy variable added to the regression model with a value of 1 for the indicated observation and a value of 0 for all other observations. In other words, the studentized deleted residual asks whether the observation is so unusual, relative to the others, that it is worthwhile to add a separate parameter to the regression model just to account for that one observation. As an example, the studentized deleted residual for the unusual observation in the Anscombe (1973) dataset of Figure 15.8(c) equals 3.9, while the next highest (in absolute value) studentized deleted residual is only −.9.

A single unusual criterion value can dramatically inflate the variance of the criterion, variance that the predictor variable cannot possibly explain. This has the effect of greatly reducing the correlation and associated test statistics. A single unusual criterion value therefore greatly increases the chances of a Type II error – not rejecting the null hypothesis when the null hypothesis is in fact false. Observations with unusual criterion values, assuming they do not also have unusual predictor values, often make regression models appear much worse than they actually are and greatly reduce statistical power.

Does the observation have undue influence on the overall regression model? An observation might have

an unusual predictor value, but if its criterion value falls near the regression line determined by the other observations, then it will not unduly influence the estimates of the slope and intercept of the regression line. Similarly, although it will increase the mean squared error substantially, an observation with an unusual criterion value will have little effect on the estimates of the slope and intercept if it has a typical predictor value. The really nasty observations – the ones that have greatly disproportionate influence on the overall model – are those that have both predictor and criterion values that are at least a little bit weird. It is therefore useful to have an index that is the product of a function of leverage and a function of the residual, standardized or studentized. One popular such index is Cook's (1979) D, which is defined as

$$D_i = \frac{r_i'^2 h_i}{2s^2(1 - h_i)}. \tag{10}$$

Many computer programs will produce Cook's D, if asked, so this formula is more important for its conceptual than computational value. To be large, Cook's D requires that both the squared standardized residual and the lever h be reasonably large. Large values are those that stand out relative to the other values; a large gap between the largest Cook's D and the next largest value usually indicates a serious problem. As illustrated in an example later, an observation or two with large values of Cook's D can seriously distort the parameter estimates; if so, the effects on Type I and Type II errors are unpredictable. In short, observations with undue influence are very nasty and can really ruin an analysis. Watch out for them!

Many computer programs now provide an overwhelming choice of outlier indices. In general, the indices can be sorted into categories corresponding to one of the three outlier questions. The subtle differences among indices for the same question are generally not important; be sure to use one index from each category.

HOMOGENEITY OF VARIANCE. Many regression programs now provide a plot of the residuals against the fitted or predicted values from the regression equation. The most common violation of homogeneity of variance observable in these plots is a funnel shape – little spread for small predicted values and much greater spread for large predicted values. However, it is often easier to see the changing spread of the residuals as a function of the predicted values if the residuals are "folded" by either squaring them or taking the absolute values. Just as for the two-group comparison above,

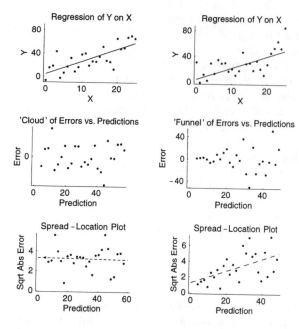

Figure 15.10. Plots for detecting violations of homogeneity of variance in regression analysis.

many find that spread is easiest to detect visually if the square root of the absolute value of the residuals is plotted against either the actual or predicted data values. One can even fit a regression line (or a robust curve) to verify any visually apparent change in the spread.

Figure 15.10 presents examples of the plots for detecting violations of homogeneity of variance. The plots in the left column of Figure 15.10 pertain to data generated using a fixed error distribution for all observations while those in the right column pertain to data generated using an error distribution proportional to the size of the respective predictor values. In the usual regression scatterplot (the top row of Figure 15.10), the data values should be scattered evenly about the regression line. It is possible, but somewhat difficult, to observe that the scatter about the regression line is increasing in the top right plot. Plots of the errors or raw residuals against the predicted values are in the second row of Figure 15.10; the errors in these plots should have a "cloud" appearance. However, the graph in the right column has an obvious "funnel" shape, indicating a clear violation of the homogeneity of regression assumption. Finally, spread-location plots are in the bottom row of Figure 15.10; these "folded" errors [sqrt(|error|)] should have no apparent trend as the predictions increase. That is the case in the left column where the dotted regression line essentially has a slope

of zero, but is definitely not the case in the right column where the folded errors steadily increase with the size of the predictions. Such graphs provide an easy visual method for detecting violations of the homogeneity of variance assumption in regression.

Multiple Regression

The techniques for detecting nasty observations for simple regression generalize easily to multiple regression. The generalizations of the formulas for levers, studentized deleted residuals, and Cook's D are not practical for hand computation, so we do not present them. Most modern regression programs will produce those outlier indices, or equivalent ones that answer the three outlier questions for regression. The interpretations of the studentized deleted residuals and Cook's D are exactly the same as for simple regression. There is one additional wrinkle for leverage in multiple regression. We could assess whether each predictor value is unusual with respect to that predictor. However, doing so we might miss an observation whose predictor values were not unusual within each predictor but whose pattern across all the predictors was unusual. For example, if we were using actual height and weight to predict satisfaction with body image among a sample of adolescent girls, a height of 5′ 9″ wouldn't be particularly unusual and a weight of 95 pounds wouldn't be particularly unusual, but the combination would be. Thus, we would like one index to assess the unusualness of the whole pattern of an observation's predictor values. The generalization of the leverage index h detects this kind of unusualness quite well.

The scatterplot of simple regression obviously does not generalize well for multiple regression. However, the partial regression leverage plot is a type of scatterplot for each variable that is useful in identifying unusual observations and relationships in multiple regression analyses. For a particular predictor X, instead of plotting Y against X, the partial regression leverage plot graphs the residual Y against the residual X after both Y and X have been predicted by all the other variables in the multiple regression model. The best fitting slope in this plot equals the regression coefficient for that variable in the full multiple regression model. Model deficiencies such as curvilinearity and unusual data points are often easy to spot in such plots (Velleman & Welsch, 1981, provided good examples). Many regression programs have options for generating the complete set of partial regression leverage plots.

REMEDIES

Once nasty and unruly data have been detected using the diagnostic graphs and statistical indices described above, it is important to take remedial action to prevent them from ruining the analysis. In this section we consider several remedial strategies that are likely to be effective. However, we first consider a commonly tried strategy – nonparametric statistics – that is not likely to be either effective or appropriate. It is ironic that an ineffective remedy like nonparametric statistics is accepted without question by social psychologists while effective remedies such as transformations and removing outliers remain controversial.

Nonparametric Statistics

When confronted with unruly, nasty data, many researchers turn to nonparametric statistics in the belief that all the strong assumptions required by statistical tests based on least-squares are relaxed. In fact, the only assumption that is relaxed is the normality assumption; assumptions about having the same distribution and homogeneity of variance still apply. For example, the Mann-Whitney U (also known as Wilcoxon Rank-Sum) and the Kruskal-Wallis tests, the nonparametric analogs to two-sample t-tests and one-way ANOVA, allow the data to have a weird distribution, but the same weird distribution must apply to the data within each group. When the data are nasty because of a few outliers, it is unlikely that each group will have the same nonnormal distribution. Most statistics textbooks written by psychologists fail either to describe the necessary assumptions underlying nonparametric tests or to warn of their reduced statistical power. As a consequence, nonparametric statistics are often used inappropriately in the psychological literature.

Note that the derivation of the quantile-quantile plots in Figure 15.5 still applies if the normal distribution is replaced by any other distribution. If two groups have distributions of the same shape, shifted only in location, then equivalent quantiles from each distribution should estimate the location shift. Thus, even with nonnormal distributions, plots of one group's quantiles against the other group's should yield a straight line parallel to the diagonal. The spacing of the points along the line won't be the same as if the data were from a normal distribution (e.g., the spacing between quantiles in the tail of a skewed distribution will be further apart), but the quantile-quantile line will be straight and parallel to the diagonal. Thus, any problems detected by examining quantile-quantile plots cannot possibly be remedied by using nonparametric

statistics, because the assumptions of such tests are necessarily violated.

Transformations

Nonlinear but monotonic transformations of the criterion or dependent variable can often correct violations of normality and homogeneity of variance. As an added bonus – Emerson (1991) and Tukey, Mosteller, and Hoaglin (1991) even argue it is the more important benefit – data transformed to solve such problems often yield a simpler model (i.e., fewer interactions and polynomial components). There are types of data that one can anticipate will benefit from transformation. Data that are constrained at one or both ends of their ranges are likely to violate the normality and homogeneity assumptions. Examples of such data include counts, completion times, proportions, and correlations (when used as data themselves). Generally the constrained end of the scale needs to be stretched and/or the unconstrained (or skewed) end needs to be pulled in. Appropriate transformations in these cases include square root for counts, logarithm for times, arcsin or logit for proportions, and Fisher's Z for correlations (see Judd & McClelland, 1989, for more details about these known transformation problems and Bargh & Chartrand, this volume, Ch. 10, for reaction time transformations). Data spanning several orders of magnitude are also likely to be problematic for the standard analysis assumptions. For example, when studying vocabulary size of pre-school children, the difference between knowing, say, 50 and 100 words is surely not the same as the difference between knowing 1,050 and 1,100 words. However, using untransformed word counts presumes such differences are equivalent.

Box and Cox (1964) and Tukey (1977) have popularized the family of power transformations, which are frequently useful for solving problems of nonnormality and heterogeneity of variance. Instead of analyzing the dependent variable Y, one analyzes

$$Y(\lambda) = \begin{cases} \dfrac{Y^\lambda - 1}{\lambda} & (\lambda \neq 0), \\ \log y & (\lambda = 0) \end{cases} \tag{11}$$

for an appropriate value of λ. The power transformation is undefined for the power zero, but conveniently the log function fills that role because it is the limit of the power function as the power approaches zero. Values of the power transformation are displayed in Figure 15.11 in what Tukey (1977) refers to as the "ladder of powers." The subtraction of 1 and division by λ

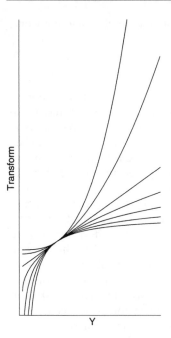

Figure 15.11. Family of power transformations. (Powers, descending on the right edge of the figure, are 3, 2, .5, 0, −.5, and −1).

serves the purpose of making the power transformation curves be aligned in Figure 15.11 at $Y = 1$; in practice, the extra arithmetic is not needed. Values of λ less than one pull in the tails of positively skewed distributions while powers greater than one pull in the tails of negatively skewed distributions. There are sophisticated statistical and graphical procedures for estimating the optimal power transformation for achieving normality and homogeneity of variance (see Madansky, 1988, for a review of many such procedures), but simply trying a few powers usually suffices to determine whether a transformation will help. That is, one usually generates a few alternative power-transformed criterion variables using, say, the whole number powers between −2 and +2. The diagnostic plots and indices described in this chapter are then generated for an analysis of each power-transformed criterion variables. The approximately best power – the one that produces an analysis with the fewest assumption violations and outliers – is generally clear. One could then repeat the process with a finer range of powers around the approximate best, but such precision is usually not necessary.

Transformations are sometimes controversial in social psychology, but they should not be. Statisticians readily accept the need for transformations (e.g., Atkinson, 1985). There is seldom reason to believe that the scale we happen to use ought to be linearly related to what we are trying to measure. In many areas of psychology where enough individual data have been obtained to assess linearity, nonlinear functions are the rule. Examples include psychophysical functions in perception and utility functions in decision making. There is no reason to presume that social psychology will escape such nonlinearity in our measurement scales. Psychologists sometimes mistakenly assume that because their response scale is measured in physical units that are interval or ratio scales that they need not worry about linearity. However, just because, for example, times to solve problems are measured on a ratio scale of time does not imply that those times represent even a linear scale of a psychological concept such as problem difficulty (see Judd & McClelland, 1998, for further discussion of this issue.)

Psychologists who think they are opposed to transformations are often surprised to learn that nonparametric statistics, of which they approve, are actually a transformation approach to data analysis. For example, Conover and Iman (1981) demonstrated that common nonparametric statistics are essentially equivalent to applying the usual least-squares methods to rank-transformed data, a transformation of the data that is usually less gentle than the family of power transformations. In this sense, power transformations offer an intermediate strategy between analyzing the raw data with problems of nonnormality and heterogeneity of variance and using nonparametric statistics. Anyone willing to use nonparametric statistics ought to be willing to consider the gentler power transformations. Transformations can often improve the health of sick data and social psychologists ought to consider them more often in data analysis.

Sometimes it is impossible to find a transformation that both achieves normality and stabilizes the variance. Judd, McClelland, and Culhane (1995) provide an overview of some more advanced transformation and analysis techniques to deal with such situations. However, if the data are so messy that a simple power transformation does not improve things, then most social psychologists ought to seek help from an expert because advice from a primer like this one will not be sufficient.

Outliers

Unfortunately, dealing with outliers is sometimes even more controversial than using transformations. If the identified outlier turns out to be the result of a typographical error or an impossible value (e.g., a meter reading in an energy conservation study that implies negative consumption since the previous reading), then almost no researchers would object to discarding or, if possible, correcting the data value. The controversies arise when the outliers have no obvious procedural explanation. In the early days of psychological research when identification of outliers was usually based on ad hoc rules proposed by the investigator, researchers were justified in being skeptical of such fiddling with the data. However, we now have principled, statistically based methods for identifying outliers. The outlier detection methods are no more nor no less sound than the methods, say, for determining if there is a difference between two means. While it certainly is unethical to delete observations just to get the result one wants, it is equally unethical to present a model (or story) for the data that really is determined by just a few of the observations (e.g., reporting a linear regression for the data in Figure 15.8[d]).

Dealing with outliers may be less controversial if we think in terms of a story metaphor. The model resulting from data analysis tells a story about our data. All observations ought to help us tell that story. It might be a very complicated story with subplots (interactions). If an observation is part of that story then it should not be necessary to add a dummy parameter to the model just for that observation. If it is necessary to add such a parameter (i.e., if the studentized deleted residual is large), then that observation is telling its own story (the dummy parameter is needed for that part of the story) and it is a different story than the other observations are telling. It is wrong to pretend that that observation is part of the same story as the other data. Even worse, if that observation has high leverage and a large Cook's D, then it will substantially distort the story told by all the other observations. The result may well be a story that doesn't apply to any of the data. At the very least, researchers should examine their data for outliers and then report analyses with and without the outliers included. Otherwise, there will be doubt as to what story the data are really telling.

Researchers in social psychology are often justifiably pleased when they are able to account for significant, but small proportions of the overall variance in their data. So too we should be pleased if we are able to provide models that provide good accounts of the data for a large proportion of our observations. If we are not embarrassed when we say that we understand, say, 15% of the variance in our data but that we don't have a clue about the other 85%, then we certainly should not be embarrassed to admit we have a model

of the data that applies to, say, 90% of our observations but we don't have a clue what the other 10% of the folks (outliers) were doing. A good model for most of our data is better than a poor model for all of our data.

Finally, it is important to identify those observations telling different stories, not so that we can discard them, but so that we can listen to the different stories they have to tell. For example, to design intervention programs it would be useful to find resilient children who had thrived and excelled despite being raised in adverse environments. Identifying outliers and figuring out why they are outliers often leads to new theoretical advances. That cannot occur if the outliers are left submerged within the story told by the other observations. For all these reasons, social psychologists should always examine their data for outliers.

EXAMPLE

An example will help elucidate the diagnostic and remedial tools described above. These data pertain to the relationship between the number of grants in the physical and social sciences awarded by the National Science Foundation (NSF) to various universities. These data were assembled by a colleague whose university's administration was concerned about the low number of NSF grants they received. They had decided to remedy the situation by providing extra resources to departments in the physical sciences. This colleague hoped to convince his administration that it was equally important to support social science departments because there was a strong relationship between the number of grants received in the physical and social sciences at peer institutions. The data analyzed here are the number of NSF grants of each type for the given state's two primary public universities and their self-identified peer institutions. Each university is categorized as either the state's flagship or land grant university. Figure 15.12 shows the data and best-fitting regression lines for the flagship and land grant universities. Despite the apparent divergence of the slopes, the difference in slopes (i.e., a test of the interaction between university category and number of social science grants) is not significant, $F(1, 15) = 1.9, \text{PRE} = .11, p = .19$ (note that PRE is the proportional reduction in error variance, equivalent to the squared partial correlation, when adding the tested predictor to a model containing all the other predictors; see Judd & McClelland, 1989). However, the plot reveals a potential outlier – a flagship university that has by far the greatest number of physical science grants – that

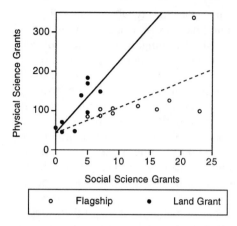

Figure 15.12. Relationship between NSF physical science and social science grants at flagship and land grant peer institutions.

may be distorting the regression line for the flagship universities. In any case, a visual check of the regression assumptions as well as an outlier analysis is needed.

Figure 15.13 displays the normal quantile plot (on the left) and the spread-location plot (on the right). One point, which corresponds to the apparent outlier in Figure 15.12, is far away from the normality line in the normal quantile plot; its steep slope relative to the other points identifies this as a normality violation that could have substantial impact on the analysis. The spread-location plot clearly shows that the square root of the absolute value of the residuals is increasing with the size of the predicted values from the regression; thus, the assumption of homogeneity of variance is violated. The studentized deleted residual for the unusual observation is 6.78, its leverage is .32, and its Cook's D is 1.33, about twice as large as

Figure 15.13. Normal quantile and spread-location plots for the untransformed analysis of the NSF grant data.

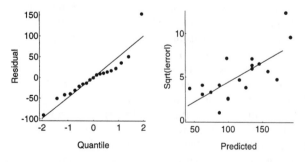

the next value of Cook's D. Its lever does not identify it as a particularly unusual observation in terms of its predictor values. However, the large studentized deleted residual ($p < .0001$) suggests that this university is telling a very different story about the relationship between the number of physical and social science NSF grants; the large value of Cook's D indicates that it is having a disproportionate effect on the overall model. If the outlier is omitted, the interaction is significant, $F(1, 14) = 15.38, \mathrm{PRE} = .53, p = .0015$. In other words, the story we tell about whether the relationship is different for flagship and land grant universities depends entirely on whether we include this one university. We should not allow one observation to dominate the story we tell about all the data! In this particular case, the unusual university has by far the highest total number of grants. And its number of physical science and social science grants fits neither the pattern of the land grant universities nor the pattern of the other flagship universities. In retrospect, this might not be a legitimate peer institution; it may have been included, wishfully, as a peer only because it was in the same intercollegiate athletic conference. For all these reasons, it is appropriate to conduct an analysis with that outlier removed. If the analysis changes appreciably without that university, that of course does not prove any of our post hoc suppositions above. Instead, those suppositions might provide hypotheses to be explored in a larger study including all the state universities.

Removing the one clear outlier does not repair the violation of homogeneity of variance apparent in the right panel of Figure 15.13 (the new graph is not presented here). Hence, a transformation may be appropriate. Also, there are a priori reasons for anticipating the need for a transformation of these data. The scale for the number of grants is not likely to be linear with an underlying scale of institution quality. For example, is the functional difference between, say, 5 and 10 grants equivalent to the difference between, say, 105 and 110 grants? We are likely to judge the second difference to be negligible while considering the first difference to be quite large. Analyzing the raw data implicitly treats these two differences as if they were equal. Also, counts are likely to follow a Poisson distribution rather than a normal distribution. In a Poisson distribution the variance is a function of the mean level. The square root transformation is well known for removing this dependency for count data. Although one need not transform on both sides, it seems appropriate in this case to transform both the criterion (number

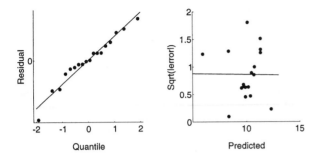

Figure 15.14. Normal quantile and spread-location plots for the square root transformed analysis of the NSF grant data with the outlier omitted.

of physical science grants) and the predictor (number of social science grants). Figure 15.14 shows the normal quantile plot of the residuals and the spread-location plot after the square root transformation has been applied with the outlier omitted (it remains an outlier, although not as extreme, after the transformation). Both plots suggest that the analysis of the transformed data without the outlier reasonably satisfy the normality and homogeneity of variance assumptions. Any weaker power transformation (i.e., a power between 0.5 and 1) leaves a positive slope in the spread-location plot, whereas any stronger transformation (such as the log or the inverse) induces a negative slope. Hence, the square root transformation (power = 0.5) is best for correcting the variance problems in these data.

Figure 15.15. Final analysis of square root transformed data with one outlier omitted.

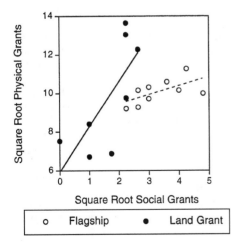

An analysis of the transformed data reveals a second problematical observation – a land grant university that has 56 NSF grants in the physical sciences but none in the social sciences. Some land grant universities have remained closer to their roots as agricultural and mechanical universities and so do not have the full complement of social science departments; this university may be such an instance. Fortunately, the story does not change appreciably if this observation is included or omitted. So, we will stop with the analysis of the square root transformed data with the first outlier omitted; this final analysis is depicted in Figure 15.15. There is no evidence for a relationship between the number of physical and social science grants at Flagship universities (slope = 0.46), $F(1, 14) = 0.6$, PRE = .04, $p = .45$, but there is a relationship for land grant universities (slope = 2.4), $F(1, 14) = 15.65$, PRE = .53, $p = .0014$. The difference between the two slopes is statistically significant (slope difference = 1.93), $F(1, 14) = 5.15$, PRE = .27, $p = .04$. (Omitting the second problematical observation would strengthen the land grant relationship and enhance the slope difference.) Transforming the original data and omitting the outlier yielded not only an analysis that satisfied the important statistical assumptions but also a clear and consistent story for these data. Including the outlier and not transforming the data yielded an analysis that violated the major assumptions underlying the analysis and produced a muddled and inconsistent story for the data.

CONCLUSION

Many social psychologists, including reviewers of an early draft of this chapter, when first considering remedies for outliers and assumption violations ask: "Isn't there a danger these methods can be abused?" Absolutely, any statistical method can be and probably has been abused by unscrupulous scientists. But that does not imply these methods for detecting outliers or assumption violations and remediating them should be denied to those careful social psychologists who want to understand everything their data have to say. Furthermore, the concern about abuse should not be one-sided. It is a serious abuse to report classical statistical tests when the data contain serious outliers or when the assumptions are substantially violated. In short, scientists seriously mislead their readers when they pretend that one consistent story applies to their data when the methods presented in this chapter would reveal multiple stories inconsistent with the main story. Unwittingly, many of us are guilty of that kind of abuse. The one-sided concern about possible abuses of outlier detection is akin to only worrying about Type I errors. Just as we are frequently reminded to also be concerned about Type II errors, so too we should be reminded that ignoring outliers and assumption violations is also a serious matter.

Probably the greatest psychological obstacle to using outlier detection methods is a belief that it is unethical to alter data for any reason. Although modern outlier detection statistics do provide a principled, rather than arbitrary, method for identifying observations that do not belong in an analysis, that is not the most important reason for their use. In programmatic research it is those unusual cases telling different stories that lead us to the next insights or that help us to sharpen our theories. If we don't use outlier methods to highlight those unusual cases, then we can't listen to the important stories they are trying to tell us. The ultimate worth of remedies such as removing outliers or transforming variables is not whether they solve a nasty data analysis problem in a single study, but rather whether they lead to a better understanding or a better theoretical account of an integrated series of studies. As Bacon told us long ago, mature theories facilitate the detection of deviations and in turn those deviations help us improve our theories. Rather than closing our eyes for fear of imagined abuses, we should instead gladly open our eyes wide to look for outliers, nonnormality, and heterogeneity of variance. Doing so will inevitably improve our understanding of our data.

In summary, nasty, unruly observations can ruin one's analysis. A few outliers can grab the analysis so that the resulting story applies to none or only a few observations. The typical statistical output from computer programs usually provides no clues that the analysis has been overwhelmed by a few observations or by systematic violations of the assumptions of normality and homogeneity of variance. However, if prodded, most modern programs will provide useful diagnostic plots and outlier indices. There is no excuse for not using these diagnostic tools. Failure to detect important assumption violations and outliers may mean that researchers report misleading stories about their data. Once nasty, unruly data are detected they can often be tamed through remedies such as transformations and the deletion of outliers. Principled methods exist for identifying appropriate transformations and marking outliers for possible deletion. Using those methods will mean that more data stories have happy endings.

REFERENCES

Atkinson, A. C. (1981). Two graphical displays for outlying and influential observations in regression. *Biometrika, 68,* 13–20.

Atkinson, A. C. (1982). Regression diagnostics, transformations and constructed variables (with discussion). *Journal of the Royal Statistical Society B, 44,* 1–36.

Aktinson, A. C. (1985). *Plots, transformations, and regression: An introduction to graphical methods of diagnostic regression analysis.* Oxford, England: Clarendon Press.

Anscombe, F. J. (1973). Graphs in statistical analysis. *American Statistician, 27,* 17–21.

Box, G. E. P. (1954). Some theorems on quadratic forms applied in the study of analysis of variance problems, I. Effect of inequality of variance in the one-way model. *Annals of Mathematical Statistics, 25,* 290–302.

Box, G. E. P., & Cox, D.R. (1964). An analysis of transformations (with discussion). *Journal of the Royal Statistical Society B, 26,* 211–246.

Chambers, J. M., Cleveland, W. S., Kleiner, B., & Tukey, P. A. (1983). *Graphical methods for data analysis.* New York: Chapman and Hall.

Cleveland, W. S. (1993). *Visualizing data.* Summit, NJ: Hobart Press.

Conover, W. J., & Iman, R. L. (1981). Rank transformations as a bridge between parametric and nonparametric statistics. *American Statistician, 35,* 124–129.

Cook, R. D. (1977). Influential observations in linear regression. *Journal of the American Statistical Association, 74,* 169–174.

Emerson, J. D. (1991). Introduction to transformation. In D. C. Hoaglin, F. Mosteller, & J. W. Tukey (Eds.), *Fundamentals of exploratory analysis of variance* (pp. 365–400). New York: Wiley.

Judd, C. M., & McClelland, G. H. (1989). *Data analysis: A model comparison approach.* San Diego, CA: Harcourt Brace Jovanovich.

Judd, C. M., & McClelland, G. H. (1998). Measurement. In D. Gilbert, S. Fiske, & G. Lindzey (Eds.), *Handbook of social psychology* (4th ed., pp. 180–232). New York: McGraw-Hill.

Judd, C. M., McClelland, G. H., & Culhane, S. E. (1995). Data analysis: Continuing issues in the everyday analysis of psychological data. *Annual Review of Psychology, 46,* 433–465.

Madansky, A. (1988). *Prescriptions for working statisticians.* New York: Springer-Verlag.

SAS Institute. (1989). *SAS/STAT user's guide* (Version 6, 4th ed.). Cary, NC: Author.

Shapiro, S. S., & Wilk, M. B. (1968). An analysis of variance test for normality (complete samples). *Biometrika, 52,* 591–611.

Tukey, J. W. (1977). *Exploratory data analysis*. Reading, MA: Addison-Wesley.

Tukey, J. W., Mosteller, F., & Hoaglin, D. C. (1991). Concepts and examples in analysis of variance. In D. C. Hoaglin, F. Mosteller, & J. W. Tukey (Eds.), *Fundamentals of exploratory analysis of variance* (pp. 1–23). New York: Wiley.

Velleman, P. F. (1997). The philosophical past and the digital future of data analysis: 375 years of philosophical guidance for software design on the occasion of John W. Tukey's 80th birthday. In D. R. Brillinger, L. T. Fernholz, and S. Morgenthaler (Eds.), *The practice of data analysis:*

Essays in honor of John W. Tukey (pp. 317–337). Princeton: Princeton University Press.

Velleman, P. F., & Welsch, R. E. (1981). Efficient computing of regression diagnostics. *American Statistician, 35,* 234–242.

Wilcox, R. R. (1987). New designs in analysis of variance. *Annual Review of Psychology, 38,* 29–60.

Wilcox, R. R. (1998). *Statistics for the social sciences*. San Diego, CA: Academic Press.

Wilk, M. B., & Gnanadesikan, R. (1968). Probability plotting methods for the analysis of data. *Biometrika, 55,* 1–17.

CHAPTER SIXTEEN

Analysis and Design for Nonexperimental Data
Addressing Causal and Noncausal Hypotheses

DUANE T. WEGENER AND LEANDRE R. FABRIGAR

A great deal of psychological inquiry is based on studies that do not use experimental manipulations. In this chapter, we review a variety of statistical methods that are useful in addressing both causal (directional) and noncausal research questions in such settings. Though a complete coverage of each of these techniques is not possible in a single chapter, we attempt to highlight some of the major issues in the use of these techniques and to provide references for more thorough and technical discussions. We begin by briefly reviewing some of the reasons why researchers use nonexperimental data and by noting the artificiality of the traditional distinction between "experimental" and "nonexperimental" statistical procedures. In discussing the statistical procedures themselves, we first review procedures that are commonly used to investigate noncausal hypotheses (i.e., hypotheses in which no directional relations are explicitly posited to exist among the constructs of interest) – exploratory factor analysis, confirmatory factor analysis, multidimensional scaling, and cluster analysis. Next, we turn our attention to statistical methods more typically used to address causal hypotheses (i.e., hypotheses in which directional relations are posited to exist among constructs). Our review begins by discussing the conditions necessary for

inferences of causality, notes different types of directional hypotheses that researchers might investigate, and then discusses the use of different statistical methods for addressing these questions. The procedures discussed are multiple regression, hierarchical linear modeling, and covariance structure modeling. It is important to note that all of the analyses applicable to causal hypotheses (and some of the analyses applicable to noncausal hypotheses) are often applicable to and useful for experiments in which the key constructs have been manipulated rather than measured.

WHEN DO PSYCHOLOGISTS CONDUCT NONEXPERIMENTAL STUDIES?

Though there are numerous contexts in which psychologists use nonexperimental data, many of these situations can be placed into three broad categories – situations in which (a) the question(s) of interest do not involve causal relations, (b) the variables of interest cannot or should not be manipulated, and (c) nonexperimental procedures increase the efficiency and expediency of research. Research questions that do not involve causal relations often include explorations of the number and nature of distinct psychological dimensions thought to underlie a domain of interest. For instance, Osgood, Suci, and Tannenbaum's (1957) classic studies on the meaning of language explored the number and nature of dimensions of connotative meaning underlying adjectives. Similarly, research in the areas of emotion and personality have sought to identify the distinct psychological dimensions underlying these domains (e.g., John, 1990; Larsen & Diener, 1992; Watson & Tellegen, 1985). Other "noncausal" research includes studies aimed at developing and validating a measure for a particular construct(s). In each of these examples,

Work on this chapter was supported by an NIH grant (P01-MH/DA56826) to DTW and by a grant to LRF by the Social Sciences and Humanities Research Council of Canada. We thank Bud MacCallum, Chick Judd, and Harry Reis for comments. Correspondence regarding the chapter can be addressed to Duane T. Wegener, Department of Psychological Sciences, Purdue University, West Lafayette, IN 47907-1364 (e-mail: wegener@psych.purdue.edu) or to Leandre R. Fabrigar, Department of Psychology, Queen's University, Kingston, Ontario, K7L 3N6 Canada (e-mail: fabrigar@psyc.queensu.ca).

the primary goal of the researcher is to determine how many dimensions underlie a set of variables and to understand the psychological nature of the dimensions. In some contexts, however, social psychologists might collect nonexperimental data because they are interested in variables that cannot be manipulated. For example, personality variables by their nature cannot be readily manipulated. Likewise, demographic variables such as sex, ethnicity, and age cannot be changed by experimenters. Socialization experiences and culture might also fit this category. In such cases, researchers must measure natural variation of variables and then assess their impact on other variables by nonexperimental means. In other cases it might be conceptually possible to manipulate variables but practical or ethical issues preclude such a strategy. For example, it might be theoretically possible to randomly assign children to be raised in complete isolation or with extensive human contact, but such a manipulation would be extremely difficult to implement and unethical to attempt.

Even in situations in which manipulation is feasible and desirable, nonexperimental aspects of the study are often useful. For example, hypotheses often involve complex consequences of a given predictor variable that can be usefully explored using both experimental and nonexperimental approaches. Consider a researcher interested in examining the role of three possible mediators of the impact of a manipulated independent variable (IV) on a dependent variable (DV). It might be possible to examine each stage of this chain through four separate manipulations (one examining the impact of the IV on the three mediators and three other manipulations, each examining the impact of one of the mediators on the DV). However, it might often be more efficient and feasible to use statistical procedures for assessing mediation in a study in which the IV is manipulated but the mediators are only measured (though at some stage, the manipulation of proposed mediators might afford the researcher greater leverage in concluding that the proposed mediators have a causal impact on the DV). In a later section of the chapter, we will explicitly discuss procedures for testing such hypotheses.

"EXPERIMENTAL" VERSUS "NONEXPERIMENTAL" STATISTICAL METHODS

Researchers have often regarded certain statistical procedures as "experimental" (e.g., ANOVA) and other statistical procedures as "nonexperimental" (e.g., correlation, covariance structure modeling [CSM]). This distinction is less than satisfactory because many statistical methods can be readily applied to both experimental and nonexperimental data.[1] Instead, it seems more useful to organize analysis procedures according to the types of research questions they are capable of addressing. Some statistical methods address only noncausal hypotheses involving relations among the constructs of interest (e.g., exploratory factor analysis, multidimensional scaling). Other procedures (e.g., multiple regression, hierarchical linear modeling) generally address directional (causal) hypotheses. Additionally, many of these procedures can be used to assess directional or nondirectional hypotheses (e.g., CSM). It is important to note that directional relations might be tested with data collected via experimental or nonexperimental means.[2] The choice of statistical procedure is more a function of the research question than the experimental versus nonexperimental nature of the design (see also Judd, this volume, Ch. 14).

ANALYSES ADDRESSING NONCAUSAL HYPOTHESES

Discussion of each of the "noncausal" procedures begins with an overview of the goals and nature of the statistical technique. Then, practical issues are discussed that influence the implementation of the analysis. Finally, design features of the study relevant to that particular statistical procedure are noted.

EXPLORATORY FACTOR ANALYSIS

Perhaps the most widely used form of noncausal analysis is exploratory factor analysis (EFA; sometimes

---

[1] One term that is often used instead of nonexperimental data is "correlational data." Although this term is generally understood, the former seems more desirable because it does not use a type of analysis to describe a characteristic of data. Correlational analysis is equally applicable to data collected using experimental or nonexperimental methods.

[2] Although directional models applied to nonexperimental data might sometimes provide a less than compelling case for attributing cause to the "causal" factor in the model, it is important to note that causes are modeled in those analyses. Such analyses therefore provide at least an initial basis for the plausibility of a causal role for a given factor. In circumstances in which threats to causal inference (e.g., existence of alternative explanations or existence of alternative but mathematically equivalent models, MacCallum, Wegener, Uchino, & Fabrigar, 1993) are minimal, some directional analyses can also provide a reasonably strong basis for making causal inferences. We return to these issues in a later section of the chapter.

referred to as unrestricted factor analysis). The primary objective of an EFA is to identify the number and nature of factors underlying a set of measured variables. EFA is typically used when a researcher is attempting to construct a scale or to develop a theory about the latent variables (constructs) underlying a conceptual domain. In the case of theory development, a researcher might be interested in a particular class of variables and wish to identify the basic constructs underlying these variables. For instance, in research on attitude structure, researchers could have investigated the tripartite theory (Rosenberg & Hovland, 1960) by using EFA to investigate the possibility of three latent classes of evaluative responding – affect, cognition, and behavior (see Fabrigar, Wegener, MacCallum, & Strahan, 1999). In the case of scale development, a researcher might be interested in identifying the dimensionality of a battery of items and the relation(s) of these items to the dimensions (e.g., see development of a scale measuring affective vs. cognitive bases of attitudes in Crites, Fabrigar, & Petty, 1994). Sometimes, a researcher might simply wish to deal with a small set of latent constructs underlying a set of measured variables rather than dealing with the larger set of measures. EFA is especially likely to be used if the researcher does not have a strong basis for predictions regarding the number of constructs or their relations to the measured variables (for additional discussion, see Fabrigar et al., 1999; Finch & West, 1997).

Common Factors or Principal Components?

Before undertaking an EFA, it is necessary to determine whether the nature of the research question is appropriate for this type of analysis. The purpose of EFA is to arrive at a more parsimonious conceptual understanding of a set of measured variables by determining the number and nature of the latent constructs needed to account for the correlations among the measures. This goal differs from data reduction, in which a researcher simply wishes to reduce a larger number of variables to a smaller set of composite variables that retain as much information from the original variables as possible. Data reduction does not involve an attempt to relate these composite variables to underlying constructs. Distinguishing between these goals is important because principal components analysis (PCA) is an appropriate data-reduction procedure, whereas EFA is more appropriate for identifying latent pshychological constructs (see Fabrigar et al., 1999).

EFA is based on the common factor model (Thurstone, 1947), which postulates that the variance in each measured variable is a linear function of one or more common factors and one unique factor. Common factors are unobservable latent variables that influence more than one measured variable in a battery and are presumed to account for the correlations (covariances) among the measured variables. Unique factors, in contrast, are unobservable latent variables that influence one and only one measured variable in a battery. Thus, the common factor model assumes that the variance in measured variables can be decomposed into common variance (i.e., the variance explained by the common factors; also referred to as the communality) and unique variance (including random measurement error). In contrast, the PCA model does not differentiate between common and unique variance. The principal components are defined as linear composites of the original measured variables (treated as if they contain no error) and thus contain both common and unique variance. Therefore, principal components are not latent variables and cannot be equated with common factors.

Despite this conceptual distinction, researchers have often (inappropriately) used PCA instead of EFA even when the goal is to understand the structure of correlations among measured variables. This is easily done because the two types of analysis produce information that appears similar. EFA procedures produce a matrix of factor loadings that reflects the extent to which each common factor influences each measured variable, and this matrix takes the same form as the PCA matrix of component loadings. However, as numerous methodologists have pointed out (and numerous studies have demonstrated), these two types of analysis can produce somewhat different results (e.g., see Fabrigar et al., 1999; Snook & Gorsuch, 1989; Widaman, 1990, 1993). Moreover, results of EFA are closer to population values in simulation data where random error is represented in the sample data (e.g., Snook & Gorsuch, 1989; Tucker et al., 1969). Given that almost all psychological measures are likely to have at least some random error (i.e., unique variance), the common factor model can be considered more realistic. Additionally, a variety of indices of model fit have been developed to assess the adequacy of the common factor model in a given set of data. In contrast, PCA offers little for assessing model adequacy. Therefore, as a general technique applicable across a variety of research settings, extraction of common factors seems to be the more reasonable choice (for more detailed discussion, see Fabrigar et al., 1999; Gorsuch, 1983).

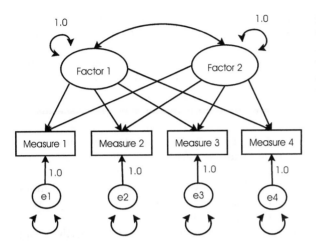

Figure 16.1. Path diagram of an EFA of four measures extracting two common factors.

Statistical Issues in Conducting EFA

An EFA begins with the matrix of correlations (or covariances) among measured variables. A particular model (i.e., a model with a particular number of factors) is specified and fit to the matrix of correlations. This process involves estimating model parameters that maximize the match between the predicted (model) and observed correlation matrices. These parameter estimates include loadings of the measured variables on the factors (i.e., the strength of the relations between factors and measures), communalities (i.e., the amount of variance in each measure accounted for by the factors), and correlations among factors (in the case of oblique rotations). Based on these parameter estimates, especially the factor loadings, the researcher interprets the nature of the factors according to the measured variables most strongly associated with each factor.

Figure 16.1 shows a factor analytic model in which two common factors are hypothesized to underlie the associations among four measured variables.[3] As depicted, in EFA (aka unrestricted factor analysis), each

factor can conceptually influence all of the measured variables.[4] EFA solutions are typically rotated in order to aid interpretation and simplify representation. Therefore, loadings (relations between the factors and the measured variables) for a given factor will typically be high for some subset of the measured variables. Perhaps more than any other commonly used statistical method in psychology, EFA requires a researcher to make a number of important decisions.

FACTOR EXTRACTION. A variety of methods have been developed to fit the common factor model to the data (e.g., maximum likelihood, noniterated and iterated principal factor – aka principal axis). The principal factor procedures can be useful because of their relaxed distributional assumptions. Unless multivariate normality is markedly violated, however, maximum likelihood (ML) factor analyses would be preferable. ML methods enable researchers to conduct significance tests of the factor loadings and correlations among factors (see Cudeck & O'Dell, 1994). In addition, most well-known indices of model fit have been developed based on ML procedures (see later discussion).[5] In most settings, however, ML and principal factors procedures will produce very similar parameter estimates and thus will be likely to lead to similar conclusions.

SELECTING THE NUMBER OF FACTORS. Deciding how many factors to include requires balancing parsimony (i.e., a model with relatively few common factors) against plausibility (i.e., a model with sufficient factors to adequately account for correlations among

---

[3] In the figures, common factors (i.e., latent variables) are represented by ellipses and measures are represented as rectangles. Error terms (unique variances) are also displayed as latent variables using circles or ellipses. Directional relations between variables are represented as single-headed arrows and nondirectional relations as double-headed arrows. Variances of latent variables are also represented by double-headed arrows from the variable to itself. Arrows without numerical values are free parameters, and numerical values of the arrows, or paths, are values of fixed parameters specified by the researcher.

[4] In order to actually fit the model, certain constraints are placed on the EFA at the factor extraction phase (i.e., when a second common factor is included, one of the measured variables is set with a loading of zero on the second factor; when a third common factor is included, the same measure and one other are set to load at zero on the third factor, etc.). When EFA solutions are rotated, however, factor loadings for all measured variables can take on nonzero values (see later discussion of rotation). Consistent with the notion that EFA and CFA follow from the same common factor model, CFA programs could actually be used to extract a specific number of factors, the loadings from which could be submitted to the same rotation procedures used in EFA programs.

[5] Significance tests for parameters in principal factors methods (aka principal axis or ordinary least squares, OLS methods) can also be computed (Browne, 1982). Indices of model fit have recently become available for such procedures in a free program, Comprehensive Exploratory Factor Analysis (CEFA; Browne, Cudeck, Tateneni, & Mels, 1998) that can be downloaded from http://quantrm2.psy.ohio-state.edu/browne/.

measured variables). In other words, the goal of the researcher is to determine the number of "major" factors underlying a set of measured variables. It is important to note that errors in selection of the number of factors can have a substantial impact on the results (e.g., Guertin, Guertin, & Ware, 1981; Wood, Tataryn, & Gorsuch, 1996). In most research settings, one can never know the "true" factor structure. However, in simulation studies where the factor structure is known, specifying too few factors in a model has often resulted in rotated solutions that combine multiple factors into one factor and increase error in estimates of factor loadings. Including too many factors, though often a less severe error than underfactoring (see Guertin et al., 1981; Wood et al., 1996), can also be problematic. Such models often result in solutions in which one or more of the factors has no substantially loading measured variables, in which one or more factors is defined by only a single measured variable, or in which a major factor is lost from the solution (see Gorsuch, 1983).

Given these consequences, it is not surprising that an extensive literature has developed regarding how to best determine the optimal number of factors. Perhaps the best known procedure is the Kaiser criterion of determining how many eigenvalues (i.e., sum of the squared loadings for each factor) for the correlation matrix of measured variables are greater than 1.0 (see Gorsuch, 1983). A model is then specified with the same number of common factors as there are eigenvalues meeting this criterion. Although the objectivity of this procedure is appealing, the approach has significant problems. For example, the procedure is rather arbitrary (i.e., it is not meaningful to claim that a factor with an eigenvalue of 1.01 is a "major" factor but a factor with an eigenvalue of .99 is not). Also, the procedure has been demonstrated in numerous simulation studies to lead to substantial overfactoring (e.g., Hakstian, Rogers, & Cattell, 1982; Tucker et al., 1969; see Fabrigar et al., 1999, for additional discussion).

Another common rule for determining the number of factors is the "scree test" (Cattell, 1966), in which the eigenvalues of the correlation matrix (or the reduced correlation matrix – with communality estimates in the diagonal) are computed and plotted in descending order. This graph is then examined to identify the last substantial drop in eigenvalue magnitude. A model with the same number of common factors as the number of eigenvalues prior to this substantial drop is then fit to the data. Because extraction of common factors utilizes the reduced matrix, it is conceptually most appropriate to base the scree test on the eigenvalues from the

reduced matrix. Determining what constitutes a "substantial" drop is somewhat subjective (Kaiser, 1970) and the procedure is potentially ambiguous if no substantial drop exists, but simulation studies indicate that this procedure tends to function reasonably well (e.g., Hakstian et al., 1982; Tucker et al., 1969).

A third procedure that has been investigated is parallel analysis (e.g., Horn, 1965; Humphreys & Montanelli, 1975). Using parallel analysis to identify common factors involves calculating the eigenvalues (from the reduced matrix) that would be expected from random data for a given sample size and number of measures. These values are then compared with the eigenvalues produced by the actual data (e.g., by comparing the scree plots). A model is specified with the same number of common factors as real eigenvalues that exceed the eigenvalues expected from random data (i.e., the number of factors is the number of eigenvalues prior to the point at which the two scree plots meet or cross). Like other objective mechanical rules, this procedure is arbitrary in that a factor just meeting the criterion is retained, whereas a factor falling just below the criterion is ignored. This procedure is not available in most major statistical programs. Nonetheless, parallel analysis has been found to function fairly well in simulation studies (e.g., Humphreys & Montanelli, 1975; Montanelli & Humphreys, 1976). Parallel analysis has also been developed for principal components analysis (see Longman, Cota, Holden, & Fekken, 1989).

The three methods described thus far have been traditionally used with principal-factor extraction. More recently, with ML extraction, indices of model fit have been used to determine the optimal number of common factors. The model fit approach involves computing goodness of fit for a series of models with differing numbers of factors – beginning with zero and increasing by one factor until some maximally interesting number. Fit measures for each model can then be examined to determine which model is most parsimonious while still providing an adequate fit to the data. For example, one might retain the number of factors necessary to reach some level of acceptable fit, or (more often) might retain the number of factors beyond which fit fails to improve (i.e., the factor that produces the last substantial improvement in fit). In some ways, this approach is similar to a scree plot (i.e., factors with large eigenvalues will tend to provide the largest increases in fit), but the goodness of fit approach also assesses overall model fit (and, as discussed later, for some fit indices confidence intervals are also available). Any of the model fit indices typically used for confirmatory factor analyses and covariance structure modeling can be used for EFA (see Browne and Cudeck, 1992; Fabrigar et al., 1999).

A number of procedures exist to determine the number of "major" factors, but none of the procedures is infallible. It is important to remember that this decision is a theoretical as well as statistical issue. A model that fails to produce an interpretable solution or is theoretically nonsensical has little value. Researchers should therefore rely on multiple criteria (including the model fit approach whenever possible) when deciding on the appropriate number of factors. The worst strategy would be to mechanically follow one of the more poorly performing procedures, such as the eigenvalues-greater-than-1 rule (for discussion and examples, see Fabrigar et al., 1999).

FACTOR ROTATION. For any given solution with two or more factors, there exists an infinite number of alternative orientations of the factors in multidimensional space that will account equally well for the correlations among measured variables. This means that a researcher must select a single orientation from among the infinite number of equally fitting solutions. The criterion most commonly used to accomplish this is the property of simple structure (Thurstone, 1947). Thurstone proposed that for any given set of mathematically equivalent solutions, those with the best "simple structure" would generally be most interpretable, psychologically meaningful, and replicable. Thurstone used the term simple structure to refer to solutions in which each factor was defined by a distinct subset of measured variables with large loadings relative to the other measured variables (i.e., high within-factor variability in loadings) and in which each measured variable loaded highly on only a subset of the common factors (i.e., low factorial complexity in defining variables). Thurstone suggested that factors be rotated in multidimensional space to arrive at the solution with the best simple structure.

Numerous studies have compared the utility of the various rotations that have been developed (e.g., Dielman, Cattell, & Wagner, 1972; Gorsuch, 1970; Hakstian, 1971). Although these methods differ in a number of respects, perhaps the most fundamental distinction is between orthogonal and oblique rotations. Orthogonal rotations constrain factors to be uncorrelated. Varimax (Kaiser, 1958) has generally been found to be the best and most widely used orthogonal rotation in psychological research. In contrast to orthogonal rotations, oblique rotations permit correlations among factors. A common misconception is that oblique rotations require correlated factors. This is not the case. If the best simple structure involves orthogonal factors, successful oblique rotations will estimate interfactor correlations that are close to zero and will produce factor loadings that are similar to successful orthogonal rotations. However, when the best simple structure includes correlated factors, oblique rotations will produce a solution with correlated factors. Unlike orthogonal rotation, there is no single method of oblique rotation that is clearly dominant in psychological research. The three most common oblique rotations are direct quartimin (Jenrich & Sampson, 1966), promax (Hendrickson & White, 1964), and Harris-Kaiser orthoblique (Harris & Kaiser, 1964).

There are a number of reasons to prefer oblique over orthogonal rotations. For many, if not most, constructs examined in psychology (e.g., personality traits, attitudes), there is substantial theoretical and empirical basis for expecting constructs to be correlated. Therefore, oblique rotations often provide a more accurate and realistic representation of how constructs are likely to be related, as well as an estimate of the extent to which constructs are related.[6] Because orthogonal rotations require factors to be uncorrelated, orthogonal rotations often produce solutions with poorer simple structure than oblique solutions (when the underlying factor structure is based on correlated factors), resulting in a less interpretable solution that provides less information about the underlying structure of the data (Ford, MacCallum, & Tait, 1986; see Fabrigar et al., 1999, for a comparison of orthogonal and oblique rotations using PCA and EFA on data addressing the tripartite model of attitude structure). Moreover, researchers using orthogonal rotations might assume that their labeled constructs are uncorrelated, when in reality, cleaner versions of the same latent variables (i.e., the same basic labels for latent variables with better simple structure) would be discovered as substantially correlated when oblique rotations are used. Given the advantages of oblique over orthogonal rotation and the likely ubiquity of correlated factors in psychology, there seems to be little justification for routine use of orthogonal rotation in seeking solutions with simple structure.

Each of the decisions discussed can influence the results of EFA. This makes it especially unfortunate that

[6] Each of the preceding discussions, with the exception of use of model fit in determining the number of factors, is also applicable to the use of PCA. However, PCA also often provides poorer simple structure than EFA, and can drastically underestimate the correlations among factors when oblique rotations are used (see Widaman, 1993; Fabrigar et al., 1999).

a large percentage of researchers do not make their decisions known to readers (see Fabrigar et al., 1999, for a review). Because of the marked differences that can occur when different combinations of procedures are used, we believe it is essential for authors (with the oversight of editors) to clearly state whether EFA or PCA was used. When using EFA, the factor extraction method, means of determining the number of factors, and factor rotation procedure should be clearly specified. Across many circumstances in social and personality psychology, EFA appears more appropriate than PCA, and use of ML factor extraction, multiple factor number criteria (especially use of model fit, scree tests, and parallel analysis), and oblique rotations will generally serve researchers well.

Design Issues in Conducting EFA

Researchers must also be sensitive to study design. There are two major issues that should be taken into account when designing studies to be analyzed using EFA: selection of measured variables and selection of sample.

SELECTION OF MEASURED VARIABLES. Common and unique factors that emerge in any EFA are a direct result of decisions concerning which measured variables to include, as illustrated in Figure 16.2. Four measures are shown to be influenced by two common factors and four unique factors. Measures 1 and 2 are primarily influenced by common factor 1 (the dark solid paths in the figure; the light dotted lines are paths included in the model that showed little or no

Figure 16.2. Path diagram of an EFA illustrating the impact of sampling of measures from the domain of interest.

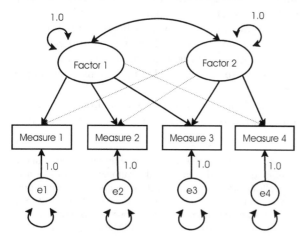

relation). Measure 3 is influenced by both common factors, and measure 4 is influenced by common factor 2. If a researcher had chosen not to include the fourth measured variable, a substantially different pattern of results would have emerged: Only common factor 1 would have been obtained. This is because common factors are defined as latent variables that influence more than one measured variable. If measured variable 4 were excluded, common factor 2 would only influence a single measured variable and would have become part of the unique factor (latent variable "e3") influencing measure 3.

If a researcher fails to select measured variables that adequately sample the domain of interest, he or she might not obtain important common factors. Alternatively, if measures irrelevant to the domain of interest are included, common factors unrelated to the domain of interest can emerge. It is often not sufficient to include only two measured variables representing each common factor. Although in theory including a minimum of two measures representing a common factor is sufficient to derive that common factor, results from such data sets are often less than optimal. Factor analytic procedures tend to provide much better estimates of population values when common factors are "overdetermined" (i.e., when numerous measured variables – at least 3 to 5 – represent each common factor; MacCallum, Widaman, Zhang, & Hong, 1999; Velicer & Fava, 1998).

Psychometric soundness of the measures should also be addressed. There are definite advantages to selecting measures that are relatively pure indicators of the major common factors of interest. Including measures that are influenced by many minor factors will result either in a model with poor fit (if only the major factors are in the model) or with good fit but low parsimony. Researchers should also attempt to select highly reliable measures (that contain relatively little random error). Accuracy of parameter estimates (e.g., factor loadings) tends to improve if factor analyses are conducted on measured variables with little unique variance (see Gorsuch, 1983; Tucker & MacCallum, 1997; MacCallum et al., 1999).

SELECTION OF RESEARCH PARTICIPANTS. Social and personality psychologists often select samples for convenience (e.g., student samples) rather than representativeness of the population as a whole. In many (perhaps most) cases, this is not likely to pose problems. However, if the sample is substantially more homogeneous than the population on one or more common factors, variance is reduced and can attenuate the correlations among measured variables, yielding falsely low estimates of the factor loadings and correlations among factors (see Gorsuch, 1983; Tucker & MacCallum, 1997). Sometimes results can be distorted because of selective sampling related to a unique (rather than common) factor. This is particularly likely when a test (or parallel test) used in participant selection is included in the analysis (e.g., including ACT scores when high SAT scores were used to select participants; Tucker & MacCallum, 1997).

A second question related to the issue of sampling is the number of participants needed to conduct an EFA. Unfortunately, a straightforward answer to this question is difficult because sample size is not independent of other design features. When each common factor is overdetermined (3 or more variables per factor) and communalities are high (an average of .7 or higher), accurate parameter estimates can be obtained with samples as small as 100 (MacCallum et al., 1999; see also Velicer & Fava, 1998). However, when such design features are poor, even samples as large as 400–800 might not be sufficient. When tests of model fit or of parameter estimates are an issue, determining an appropriate sample size might also be based on achieving a desired level of statistical power (MacCallum, Browne, & Sagawara, 1996).

CONFIRMATORY FACTOR ANALYSIS

Another widely used form of nondirectional analysis is confirmatory factor analysis (CFA; also referred to as restricted factor analysis). CFA is an extension of EFA and is similar in a number of ways. CFA is based on the same underlying conceptual model – the common factor model. In both cases, the primary objective is to identify the number and nature of factors underlying a set of measured variables. Like EFA, CFA is often used for theory development or scale construction. Despite these similarities, there are also substantial differences. Whereas EFA should be used when the researcher does not have a strong basis for predicting the number of constructs or their relations to the measures, CFA should be used when there is a strong basis for such predictions. That is, CFA requires an a priori specification of the number of common factors and the pattern of zero and nonzero loadings of measures on the factors (i.e., latent variables). Because of this, it is only plausible to consider a small number of theoretically meaningful alternative models.

For example, Breckler (1984) tested the tripartite model of attitude structure by specifically comparing a three-factor CFA (with correlated affect, behavior, and cognition factors) with a one-factor (evaluation) CFA. Because the three-factor model was found to fit the data better than the one-factor model, Breckler considered this as support for the tripartite conception (see later discussion of model comparisons).

Because CFA requires a priori specification of models, and therefore a relatively small number of meaningful models can be considered, it is less likely that the CFA analysis will capitalize on chance characteristics in the data. In contrast, because EFA places few restrictions on the pattern of loadings, the best-fitting of many potential patterns can be identified.[7] In many circumstances, it would make sense to use EFA and CFA within the same program of research. For example, an initial EFA might provide a basis for later specification of CFA models, or a large sample could be split and an EFA conducted on half of the sample, with a CFA conducted on the other half. Alternatively, if a specified CFA model fits poorly, subsequent EFA analyses might suggest alternative models or reasons why the model had poor fit (e.g., by identifying poor measures of certain constructs).

The CFA model in Figure 16.3 parallels the EFA in Figure 16.1. Rather than having all measures potentially loading on all factors (rotating to simple structure in EFA creates a pattern of high vs. low loadings, but the pattern is not restricted), this CFA model specifies that factor 1 loads on three measures and factor 2 loads on two measures. Note that the measures influenced by each factor may be nonoverlapping, but need not be.

CFA also differs from EFA regarding rotation. Rotations are common in EFA, but are extremely rare in CFA, because the expected simple structure of factor loadings has already been specified. Finally, CFA generally permits more flexible and focused hypothesis testing of model parameters. For example, in CFA a researcher can test whether certain factor loadings (or interfactor correlations or communalities) are equivalent to one another. It is also possible to

---

[7] One interesting bridge between EFA and CFA is target rotation (also known as Procrustes rotation). In this procedure, an initial EFA solution is rotated to be as close as possible to a specified pattern of zero and nonzero loadings (for additional discussion, see Browne, 1972; Gorsuch, 1983; Gower, 1975). Although a specified solution is targeted, use of the initial unrestricted EFA means that there are no guarantees that loadings specified to be zero will end up approximating zero in the final rotated solution. Also, in targeted rotation, fit of the model corresponds to the unrestricted solution, not to the specified target model per se (as is the case when CFA is used).

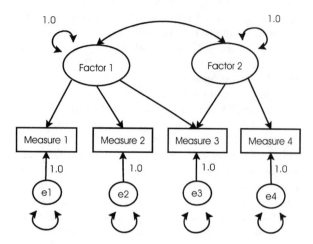

Figure 16.3. Path diagram of a CFA of four measures specifying two correlated factors.

conduct tests of the statistical significance of parameter estimates.[8]

Statistical Issues in CFA

MODEL SPECIFICATION. The first step in conducting a CFA is to specify the model(s) to be tested. That is, the researcher must mathematically define the model by specifying which parameters are free (i.e., parameters with unknown values to be estimated from the data, including loadings of measures on the latent factors, unique variances [errors of measurement], and interfactor correlations), fixed (i.e., parameters set to a specific numerical value), and constrained (i.e., parameters with unknown values that are estimated from the data but must hold a specified mathematical relation to one or more other parameters). There are a number of issues that must be considered.

The model must be identified (i.e., it must be possible to compute a unique solution for the specified model). Although a particular model might make conceptual sense, it might not be mathematically possible

to estimate the parameters with the available information (i.e., the complexity of the model might exceed the amount of information available from the measured variables). Unfortunately, there is no practical foolproof method for determining if a particular model is identified. Although it is in principle possible to algebraically determine if a given model is identified, this process is very complex with any but the simplest of models. There are some general procedures (such as the order condition or t-rule), mathematical algorithms, and empirical tests that can help reveal identification problems (e.g., see Bollen, 1989; Jöreskog & Sörbom, 1988; Kenny et al., 1998; Schumacker & Lomax, 1996). Although lack of model identification can pose serious problems, these difficulties can generally be avoided if the researcher pays attention to model parsimony. A model should include free parameters only when there is a reasonable theoretical or empirical basis for expecting nonzero values. If this is done, lack of model identification should be relatively rare.

During model specification, a researcher should also consider alternative models. Arguing in support of a particular preferred model on the basis of a CFA is most convincing when the preferred model is shown not only to adequately account for the data (see later section on model evaluation) but also to do so better than other conceptually plausible alternatives. Simply finding that a model provides an adequate account of the data is not particularly compelling evidence of the value of the model in that other conceptually plausible models might perform just as well (or better). Therefore, it is useful at the model-specification stage to propose and evaluate plausible alternative models.[9]

Alternative models might differ from one another and from the preferred model in several typical ways, such as the number of common factors necessary to account for relations among the measures. Consider the tripartite view of attitude structure, mentioned earlier (e.g., Breckler, 1984; Ostrom, 1969; Rosenberg & Hovland, 1960). Work on this topic could focus on a three-factor model, in which some measures load on an "affect" factor, others on a "cognition" factor, and still others on a "behavior" factor. Plausible alternative models might include a single-factor model in which

---

[8] Although it has long been possible to conduct tests of model fit in ML versions of EFA (see earlier discussion), methods for testing the statistical significance of factor loadings and correlations among factors are a rather recent development (Cudeck & O'Dell, 1994; Browne et al., 1998). To our knowledge, CEFA (Browne et al., 1998) is the only available EFA program that includes these capabilities. In contrast to CFA, EFA does not allow for tests of equivalence of parameter estimates within a model (e.g., testing whether two sets of factor loadings are equivalent – as in the equivalence of the CFA measurement model across two samples) and the like.

[9] We use the terms "preferred" and "alternative" models to highlight the differences between such a process and a situation in which a researcher considers only a single model. Of course, there are also settings in which a researcher might specify a number of plausible models with no a priori reason to prefer any one model. In a very real sense, any "preferred" model is simply one of the set of alternative models that might be used to account for the data.

all of the measures load on an "evaluative" factor (see Breckler, 1984). For the researcher to argue strongly for the tripartite conceptualization, he or she would need to show that the three-factor model accounts well for the data and that the three-factor model fits better than the one-factor model (i.e., that it is "worth" the additional complexity of two more factors).

Alternative models might also differ in other ways. Some alternative conceptions specify different patterns of zero and nonzero loadings without varying the number of factors. Imagine, for example, that a researcher collects responses to a number of positive and negative items designed to assess affective and cognitive reactions to an attitude object. The researcher might hypothesize two competing two-factor models – one with all of the "affective" items loading on one factor and all of the "cognitive" items loading on the other factor (Crites et al., 1994) and the second with all of the "positive" items loading on one factor and all of the "negative" items loading on the other factor (Cacioppo & Berntson, 1994). In this case, the number of factors is the same, but the conceptual meaning of the factors differs (i.e., affect–cognition vs. positive–negative). The extent to which each model accounts for the relations among the measured variables might then be compared (see later discussion concerning use of the Root Mean Square Error of Approximation, RMSEA, in such settings).

In other situations, alternative CFA models might utilize the same number of factors and might specify the same pattern of zero and nonzero loadings, but differ in the constraints on the parameter estimates. Such alternative models are most commonly specified when testing particular hypotheses regarding one or more parameters. For example, the researcher might wish to test whether a given factor correlates more highly with one factor than with another, or might wish to test whether a given item loads more highly on one factor than on another. To test such hypotheses, one could specify an alternative model in which the two between-factor correlations (or two loadings of the item on the two factors) are constrained to be equal, comparing this model with one in which the two parameters are not constrained. If the two parameter values differ substantially, then constraining them to be equal will substantially hurt the ability of the model to account for the data. Such comparisons can also take advantage of model-comparison procedures for "nested" models.

FITTING THE MODEL TO THE DATA. After specifying the model(s) of interest, the researcher must select a procedure by which to fit that model to the data. Model-fitting essentially involves arriving at a set of parameter estimates that minimizes the discrepancy between the model and the sample covariance (correlation) matrix (i.e., the observed associations among all measured variables). Typical fitting procedures are iterative. That is, starting values for parameters are substituted into the structural equations, a discrepancy value is found, and then new values of the parameters are substituted into the equations, the discrepancy value compared with the previous value, and so on, until the discrepancy value is minimized. A variety of procedures exist, differing in the mathematical function used to define the discrepancy between model and data.[10]

The most common model-fitting procedure in CFA is ML. ML is widely used because it has a strong underlying statistical rationale, allows for computation of confidence intervals around parameter estimates, and has a number of indices of model fit that have been developed for it. The ML procedure, along with significance tests and fit indices, is commonly available in existing statistical software. One limitation is that ML carries with it relatively stringent distributional assumptions (e.g., multivariate normality).

Tests of multivariate skewness and kurtosis (D'Agostino, 1986; Mardia, 1970) are available in some computer packages, but can identify even minor deviations from normality with large samples (Finch & West, 1997). The amount of nonnormality needed to create problems with ML estimation is difficult to specify (Curran, West, & Finch, 1996; West et al., 1995). Some investigations of various violations of normality have shown rather robust outcomes for ML procedures (Chou & Bentler, 1995; see also Browne, 1990; Browne & Shapiro, 1988), but other studies have noted consistent inflation of model fit with nonnormality (especially when more extreme violations of normality have been addressed; Curran et al., 1996; Hu, Bentler, & Kano, 1992). Therefore, when nonnormality is minimal, it is often safe for the researcher to treat ML procedures as likely to be robust and appropriate. However, when nonnormality is marked (e.g., skew > 2, kurtosis > 7; West et al., 1995), researchers might wish to (a) transform the measured variables in order to normalize the

---

[10] We confine our discussion to model-fitting procedures that assume at least interval level data. In recent years, substantial progress has also been made regarding procedures for fitting CFA (and covariance structure models more generally) to data with ordinal or nominal properties (e.g., Muthén, 1987; 1993).

distributions, (b) use item parcels (i.e., composites of multiple individual items – if the dimensionality of the parcels is well understood, if there is still a sufficient number of parcels per factor, and if the parcels have more normal distributions than the original items), (c) use corrections to the fit statistics and/or standard errors (e.g., Browne, 1984a; Satorra & Bentler, 1994), or (d) use alternative estimation procedures (such as asymptotically distribution free [ADF] estimation; Browne, 1984a) designed for conditions in which multivariate normality assumptions do not hold (see also Bollen, 1989; West et al., 1995).

Unfortunately, for psychologists, the ADF procedure might prove to be less than ideal, because the procedure works optimally for sample sizes considerably larger (e.g., $N = 1,000-5,000$) than are typically used (Raykov & Widaman, 1995; West et al., 1995). Using relatively small samples (e.g., Chou & Bentler, 1995) ML has performed better than ADF across various violations of multivariate normality, but with larger samples ADF has outperformed ML (e.g., Curran et al., 1996). At this point, little is known about how specific characteristics of data relate to the performance of the various estimation procedures. It is probably possible that any of the procedures perform better than other procedures under some distributional qualities.

EVALUATING MODELS. After obtaining parameter estimates, researchers must assess the adequacy of the model in accounting for the observed relations among measures. There are several issues to consider, including overall fit of the model, fit of the hypothesized model compared with alternative models, model parsimony, and interpretability of the solution.

Perhaps the most widely used basis for assessing model adequacy is overall fit. As noted previously, model fitting involves determining parameter values that minimize the discrepancy between the model and the sample covariance (correlation) matrix. Even these "best" parameter estimates are unlikely to reduce the discrepancy to zero. In a sense, such indices tell a researcher how successful the fitting process was at finding estimates that correspond to the observed data. Of course, in most settings (especially those with a complex factor structure), researchers will not be specifying the "true" model (any reasonably parsimonious models are likely to be "wrong" to some extent), but the fitting and evaluation process can help identify the most parsimonious model that corresponds well to the data. If no parameter values lead to small discrepancies between model and data (i.e., if the model fit is poor), then the model is regarded as an implausible representation of the structure underlying the data. If small discrepancies can be produced with a given model, then the model is regarded as plausible.

Over the years, many fit indices have been developed. The most common is the likelihood ratio or χ^2 goodness-of-fit test (for ML solutions, the form of which is $[N-1]F_{ML}$ [i.e., sample size minus one, times the discrepancy function for the ML procedure]). Under certain conditions, which differ slightly depending on the version of the likelihood ratio used, this value follows an approximate χ^2 distribution (Bollen, 1989). The null hypothesis for the likelihood ratio is that the model holds exactly in the population. Although there are a number of possible reasons to question the utility of the likelihood ratio test, perhaps the most important are that the hypothesis of exact fit is never realistic and that the likelihood ratio is inherently sensitive to sample size – such that large samples lead to rejection of virtually all models (MacCallum, 1990).

Because of these concerns, numerous alternative measures of model fit have been developed. These measures are often referred to as descriptive fit indices because they express fit in terms of the magnitude of discrepancy between the model and the data rather than as a formal hypothesis test of perfect fit. These descriptive fit indices are usually classified into two broad categories: incremental fit indices and absolute fit indices (see Hu & Bentler, 1998).[11]

Incremental fit indices compare a hypothesized model to the fit of a "null model," typically in which all measures are assumed to have variances but no relations with one another. It is important to note that the "variance only" null model has only been a convention. Other baseline models could be, but are rarely, chosen. Probably the best known and one of the better performing incremental fit indices (Hu & Bentler, 1998) is the Tucker–Lewis (1973) index (TLI; aka the Bentler-Bonett, 1980, Non-Normed Fit Index, NNFI). Simulations suggest that this index is only slightly influenced by sample size (e.g., Anderson & Gerbing, 1984), and this index is influenced by model parsimony. That is, adding inconsequential structural paths decreases the TLI–NNFI, so one is "punished" in terms of fit. Using the typical null model as a baseline, a TLI–NNFI of .9 and above has been traditionally regarded as reasonable fit,

---

[11] In this discussion, we focus on common classes of fit indices and on particular indices that are less common but possess some desirable properties that seem to merit more widespread usage. For more extensive discussions of a variety of fit indices, see Mulaik, James, Van Alstine, Bennett, Lind, and Stilwell (1989), and Tanaka (1993).

but recent work suggests that .95 might be a more appropriate benchmark (Hu & Bentler, 1998).

Other fit indices are referred to as absolute fit indices in that they express fit in terms of the absolute discrepancy between the model and the data rather than as a comparision between a target model and a baseline model. One such fit index that functions well (see Hu & Bentler, 1998) and explicitly accounts for model parsimony is Steiger's (1990; Steiger & Lind, 1980) Root Mean Square Error of Approximation (RMSEA). RMSEA is an estimate of discrepancy per degree of freedom for the model (Browne & Cudeck, 1992; Finch & West, 1997). Therefore, decreasing the parsimony of the model only improves fit if the discrepancy function is substantially reduced; if the discrepancy function changes little, adding parameters decreases model fit. To avoid the unrealistic hypothesis of exact fit, Browne and Cudeck (1992) recommended that a 0.05 value of RMSEA be regarded as indicative of close fit, 0.08 as reasonable fit, and 0.10 or greater as poor fit. One can also construct confidence intervals around the point estimate of RMSEA. If the lower limit of the confidence interval is zero, the hypothesis of exact fit is not rejected, but a nonzero lower limit to the confidence interval reminds the researcher that exact fit is not tenable. Confidence intervals around RMSEA point estimates are especially useful for comparisons of nonnested models (see later discussion of model comparison).

FIT COMPARED TO ALTERNATIVE MODELS. Model comparisons can be quite useful for evaluation of hypothesized models. One might classify model comparisons into two broad categories – comparisons of models whose fundamental conceptual nature differs, and comparisons of models that share a conceptual structure but differ in terms of a specific parameter estimate(s) within that structure.

Alternative models are often nested. Parameter "nesting" refers to a circumstance in which one model includes all of the free parameters of another model and adds one or more free parameters. For example, in the earlier example of the tripartite model of attitude structure, the single-factor "evaluative" model was nested within the more complex three-factor (affect–cognition–behavior) model. More general covariance nesting can also occur in which the covariances of one model are a subset of the covariances that make up another model.

The most typical way to compare nested models is to subtract the χ^2 (likelihood ratio) value for the less parsimonious model (i.e., the model with the fewest degrees of freedom) from the χ^2 value for the more parsimonious model (i.e., the model with the most degrees of freedom). This difference in χ^2s is itself approximately distributed as a χ^2 with degrees of freedom equal to the difference in degrees of freedom between the two nested models. In this case, the null hypothesis is that the χ^2 values for the two models are equal, so rejection of that hypothesis implies that the more complex model is "worth" the added complexity.

As with other χ^2 indices, the χ^2 difference test is influenced by sample size. For a given drop in the discrepancy function associated with addition of a set of free parameters, that change in discrepancy is more likely to show a significant increase in χ^2 to the extent that sample size is large. This characteristic of the χ^2 is often less than desirable when the alternative models postulate different sets of "major" factors underlying the data (Fabrigar et al., 1999). When seeking "major" factors, it seems less than optimal to use a test in which a given drop in discrepancy identifies a major factor in one setting (e.g., large sample size) but not in another (e.g., small but still substantial sample size).

A less formal comparison of models could involve comparison of RMSEA values, along with their associated confidence intervals. If their confidence intervals do not overlap, or do so very little, this would provide some basis for arguing that the model with the smaller RMSEA value is, in fact, superior. Because RMSEA is relatively unaffected by sample size, decision criteria comparing two models can be equitably applied across sample sizes. When identifying the number and nature of factors, it is generally preferable to use criteria beyond the χ^2 difference test in order to ensure that (significant) differences in fit are not largely a function of sample size.

It is interesting that almost all tests of individual parameter estimates can be cast as comparisons of nested models. That is, the same information as a significance test of a single free parameter could be obtained from a χ^2 difference test between two models – one in which the path is fixed at zero and one in which the path is left free to vary. Likewise, when one free parameter is hypothesized to differ from another, one could use a χ^2 difference test between models in which the two parameters are (vs. are not) constrained to be equal. If allowing the parameters to vary results in a significant increase in fit, the values of the two parameters are found to differ from one another. In tests of a specific parameter within or across models, overfactoring and underfactoring are not issues. Rather, if anything, one might argue that increases in sample size give one greater confidence that observed differences between parameter estimates are not due simply to chance (see later discussion of model comparison in multisample tests).

Sometimes, alternative models are not nested. As noted earlier, for example, a researcher might want to compare a model in which measures are associated with "affective" and "cognitive" vs. "positive" and "negative" factors. For such nonnested models, the difference in likelihood ratios cannot be used. However, when differences in RMSEA are substantial and confidence intervals show minimal overlap, reasonable grounds exist for preferring one model over the other.[12,13]

INTERPRETABILITY OF PARAMETER ESTIMATES. Of course, evaluation of models can also be influenced by the extent to which parameter estimates are interpretable or sensible. For example, multiple cross-boundary estimates (e.g., negative variance estimates) can undermine model interpretability, regardless of overall fit (alone or in comparison with alternative models). In many circumstances, one might justifiably prefer a model with adequate fit and no questionable parameter estimates even if another model with many cross-boundary estimates fits the data a bit better. One might also regard existing theory and data as factors that influence overall preferences for one model over another. For example, if a model includes one or more parameter estimates that fit well with existing theory and research, but an alternative solution provides one or more estimates that would be difficult to reconcile with existing data and theory, this might be enough to prefer the former to the latter, especially if the unexpected values have not been replicated.

[12] Confidence intervals of the RMSEA index will be influenced by sample size, but the RMSEA index provides a means for inspecting the amount of change in the discrepancy function that is relatively free of impact of sample size.

[13] Browne and Cudeck (1989; 1992) also discuss another type of information about models that might prove useful in model-comparison contexts – the expected cross-validation index (ECVI) which essentially indexes the extent to which a model (the parameters of which have been estimated from a given sample) would likely fit a new validation sample covariance matrix (with low values representing low discrepancy between model and new sample matrix). Confidence intervals can be computed to supplement the point estimate of ECVI, and the difference between two ECVI values can be tested for nested models (using FITMOD, Browne, 1992b). If two models have similar RMSEA values, but differ greatly in ECVI (e.g., such that the confidence intervals of the two ECVI indices do not substantially overlap), one would prefer the model with the low ECVI value. In recent years, ECVI has become available in a variety of software packages.

MODEL PARSIMONY. Finally, even if two models have roughly equivalent fit, a researcher might prefer the more parsimonious model. Even if model-sensitive fit indices (such as RMSEA) are used, a researcher might argue that additional parameters are only strongly justified if they substantially improve fit of the model to the data. Simple theories are often to be preferred unless the more complicated theory can substantially improve understanding of the phenomenon or can substantially broaden the types of phenomena understood under the same conceptual umbrella.

MODEL MODIFICATION. In many cases, a researcher's hypothesized model fits the data rather poorly. In such situations, the researcher is reasonably tempted to look for ways to improve the model. In fact, many computer packages include methods (e.g., the modification index, Lagrange multiplier test, or Wald test) that tell the researcher how fit will change if certain paths are added or deleted from the hypothesized model (MacCallum, Roznowski, & Necowitz, 1992). In practice, researchers frequently acknowledge that model parameters have been added to or deleted from a theoretical model based on these empirical indices of possible model modification (see Breckler, 1990; MacCallum et al., 1992). MacCallum (1986, 1995), however, cautions responsible researchers to be wary of empirically driven model modifications. Empirically based model modifications make an analysis exploratory rather than confirmatory. Because modification indices generated for a given sample can capitalize on chance, they often do not generalize across samples. In addition, modified models show poor cross-validation unless sample size is quite large (e.g., $N = 500-800$; MacCallum et al., 1992).

Moreover, simulation studies show that modification indices rarely identify a true model when it exists. For example, MacCallum (1986) simulated 160 data sets of sample sizes common in psychology ($N = 100$ and 300) in which the model was missing one or more parameters from the true model. For only 22 of the 160 samples (all with $N = 300$) was the correct model identified by modification indices. In addition, of the 22 successful modifications, only 4 occurred when the search was guided purely by the largest modification index, regardless of its theoretical meaning (or lack thereof); 18 occurred when knowledge of the true model (unusual in actual research) did not allow additional misspecifications to be introduced by blindly following the largest modification index.

Therefore, it seems clear that empirically driven indices of model modification should be utilized only with great caution. If used, the researcher should acknowledge that the procedure removes the confirmatory quality of the initial analysis, and substantially opens the model to capitalization on chance. Because of the instability of cross-sample validation of modified models, MacCallum et al. (1992) even question the utility of showing that a modified model has a better cross-validation index than the original model. Instead, MacCallum et al. recommend parallel modifications on two samples. If the two samples show inconsistent modification indices or cross validations, this would cast doubt on the new model(s). We concur with this conservative stance and urge researchers to be extremely cautious in considering empirically based model modifications.

Nonstandard CFA Models

Sometimes researchers have hypotheses that do not involve causal relations among latent variables but postulate relations between latent variables and measured variables or relations among latent variables that differ from the traditional unrestricted (EFA) or restricted (CFA) common factor model (e.g., nonlinear effects). In social and personality psychology, two common nontraditional cases include MTMM matrices and hypotheses of circumplex structure.

MULTITRAIT–MULTIMETHOD MODELS. MTMM–CFA models are often fit to data in which each of two or more measurement methods has been used to assess each of two or more psychological constructs (i.e., "traits," which could be attitudes, personality characteristics, performance, etc.). Data of this sort have typically been collected to assess the convergent and discriminant validity of measures by examining the pattern of correlations among measures (Campbell & Fiske, 1959; for an example, see Ostrom, 1969). However, this approach can be quite complicated when the data involve many traits and methods, leading methodologists to suggest CFA models that provide a simpler and more quantifiable summary of the structure of MTMM matrices (Judd & McClelland, 1998; Marsh & Grayson, 1995; Widaman, 1985). Most models have treated trait and method factors as additive (as independently influencing responses). Unfortunately, many versions of such models either have severe estimation problems because of their complexity or put constraints on the model that do not allow researchers to ask important questions about the data (e.g., whether various methods or traits are correlated with one another; see Marsh &

Grayson, 1995; Visser, Fabrigar, Wegener, & Browne, 1999).

One interesting alternative is the components of covariance approach suggested by Wothke (1984, 1996; see also Bock, 1960). This approach specifies a "g" factor that represents general performance (response) and conceptualizes trait and method factors as deviations from overall response. The components of covariance approach are also "additive" in that methods, traits, and unique variance independently influence responses (see Panel A of Figure 16.4 for one parameterization of a MTMM study with 2 traits and 2 methods using this model; see also Wothke, 1996). Because each trait and each method is conceptualized as contributing deviations from general response (and the sum of the deviations must therefore sum to zero), the model includes one less trait factor and one less method factor than was actually used in the study (see Visser et al., 1999). Following estimation of the model parameters, one can inspect the correlations among traits or among methods by constructing the correlations of "g + trait-deviation" or "g + method-deviation" terms (Browne, 1989). The components of covariance model avoids the estimation problems of previous MTMM–CFA models and does not require constraints of uncorrelated methods or traits (Browne, 1993).

Another interesting alternative is the direct product model originally proposed by Swain (1975) and extensively developed by Browne (1984b, 1989, 1993). Some researchers have suggested that it might be more plausible to represent trait factors and method factors as combining in a multiplicative fashion to influence measured variables (e.g., Campbell & O'Connell, 1967, 1982; Schmitt & Stults, 1986 – e.g., with strength of trait influences changing across methods). The direct product model postulates just such a relation (as depicted in Panel B of Figure 16.4). This model treats each measured variable as the product (rather than the sum) of the trait it is designed to assess and the method of measurement. The model also postulates that trait factors are inter-correlated and that method factors are inter-correlated. No correlations are permitted between trait and method factors. The model can be reparameterized for specification in programs such as LISREL (Wothke & Browne, 1990). However, a simpler approach is to use MUTMUM, a program specifically designed to fit the direct product model (Browne, 1992c, available at the same website as the CEFA program noted earlier). The direct product model produces parameter estimates that relate directly to the Campbell and Fiske (1959) criteria for MTMM data (Cudeck, 1988). It avoids estimation problems inherent in

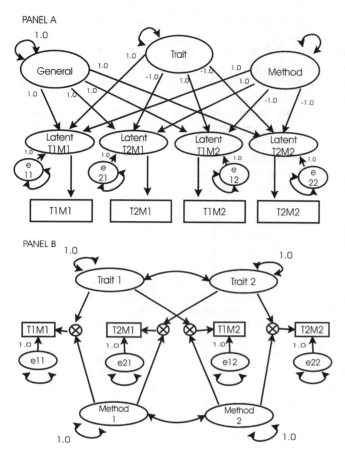

Figure 16.4. Path diagrams of the components of covariance and direct product models addressing MTMM data.

traditional MTMM–CFA additive models (Goffin & Jackson, 1992; Coovert, Craiger, & Teachout, 1997), and does not require constraints of uncorrelated methods or traits. Its assumption of multiplicative rather than additive trait/method effects might be more realistic in many cases.

CIRCUMPLEX MODELS. A circumplex refers to a set of variables ordered along the circumference of a circle. Circumplex representations have enjoyed considerable popularity in personality and social psychology, particularly within the domains of interpersonal behavior (e.g., Wiggins, 1980) and affect (e.g., Larsen & Diener, 1992). Typically, circumplex representations have been tested by constructing graphical representations from EFA or multidimensional scaling (MDS) analyses and then examining if the resulting picture corresponds to a circle. However, these methods have been criticized as being highly subjective and imprecise

(e.g., Romney & Bynner, 1997; Fabrigar, Visser, & Browne, 1997).

Browne (1992a) has proposed a nonstandard covariance structure model for testing circumplex structure. Like traditional CFA, this model postulates that measures are influenced by common and unique variance. It differs in postulating that the correlations among latent variables can be represented as an ordering on a circle with the magnitude and direction of the correlations among variables being a function of the distance along the circumference of the circle. This model can be fit to a sample correlation matrix to obtain indices of goodness of fit and parameter estimates of the locations of variables on the circle, of variable communalities, of the relation between distance on the circle and correlations between variables, and of the correlation between variables at opposite sides of the circle.

Browne's (1992a) model has a number of advantages over traditional EFA and MDS approaches in being more objective and precise. It also has advantages over other confirmatory models of circumplex data, most notably that the parameter estimates relate directly to a circumplex representation, are readily interpretable, and can be used to determine the adequacy of a researcher's hypothesized circumplex representations (see Fabrigar et al., 1997, for more detailed discussion).

Design Issues in Conducting CFA

As in EFA, design issues can have a substantial impact on the value of the results obtained from CFA. The primary design issues in CFA are similar to those of EFA. That is, CFA requires researchers to carefully attend to the selection of measured variables and research participants. However, the shift from an exploratory to a confirmatory approach requires some change in emphasis when addressing these issues.

SELECTION OF MEASURED VARIABLES. Because CFA is employed when a clear basis exists for postulating the number and nature of the common factors, a researcher should select the best available set of measured variables to represent each common factor, rather than being concerned about comprehensive representation of items throughout the conceptual domain (as in EFA). Therefore, when conducting CFA, existing data and theory should guide selection of optimal indicators of each common factor. As in EFA, CFA is most effective when each factor is overdetermined – when many measured variables are included as indicators of each common factor. Methodologists have generally recommended including at least three measured variables representing each factor (Bentler, 1980; Bollen, 1989).

Selecting measured variables with good psychometric properties is even more important in CFA than in EFA. As in EFA, CFA is likely to perform better if the measures have high reliability. However, it is particularly important in CFA that each measured variable be influenced substantially by the common factor(s) postulated to underlie that measure. Furthermore, each measured variable should not be substantially affected by common factors other than those specified to influence the measure. Including poor measured variables will generally diminish fit.

Therefore, when there is no sound basis for making strong assumptions about relations between common factors and measured variables, it is sensible to conduct an initial EFA study including a large set of measures likely to reflect each of the expected common factors. The EFA results can be used to predict common factors and to select subsets of measured variables that best relate to each common factor. Measured variables should have high communalities, large loadings on the relevant common factors, and small loadings on common factors posited to be irrelevant to those measures. A second study can then be conducted using these measures, and a CFA can be performed on these new data.

SELECTION OF RESEARCH PARTICIPANTS. As in EFA, a researcher should carefully consider sampling and the number of participants to be included. Issues of selective sampling in CFA are similar to those in EFA, and the quality of measured variables and number of measures for each factor are relevant when estimating needed sample size (Tanaka, 1987). When the measures have little unique variance and common factors are overdetermined, relatively accurate parameter estimates can be obtained with modest sample sizes.

However, because CFA usually involves more formal assessment of model fit and specific hypothesis tests, issues of statistical power are more prevalent. Satorra and Saris (1985; Saris & Satorra, 1993) have focused on power analysis using the likelihood ratio test to compare a model with an alternative assumed to be true in the population. More recently, MacCallum et al. (1996) proposed an alternative approach based on RMSEA. In this approach, one specifies a hypothesis regarding RMSEA, an assumed value of RMSEA

in the population, and a desired level of power (e.g., RMSEA $\leq$ 0.05, assumed population RMSEA of 0.08, power of .80). A researcher can then compute the sample size necessary to obtain the desired level of power given the assumed population value of RMSEA. The MacCallum et al. approach does not necessitate specification of an alternative model assumed to be true, and can be extended to other hypotheses regarding RMSEA (see MacCallum et al., 1996) and to fit indices other than RMSEA (e.g., MacCallum & Hong, 1997).

MULTIDIMENSIONAL SCALING

Multidimensional scaling (MDS) refers to a broad class of geometric models used to understand the underlying structure of (dis)similarities among objects (or concepts) by pictorially representing these objects as points in multidimensional space. MDS is sometimes used in social psychology when developing a typology for a particular domain of objects. For instance, Rusbult and Zembrodt (1983) identified constructiveness–destructiveness and activity–passivity as two dimensions underlying an exit-voice-loyalty-neglect typology of reactions to relationship dissatisfaction. MDS is also used to identify underlying dimensions by which people differentiate objects. For example, Feldman (1995) used MDS to address the dimensions (arousal and valence) that underlie perceptions of various emotions. As with EFA, MDS is often used in an exploratory fashion when there is no strong basis for predicting the number and nature of the dimensions. In some cases, however, use of dimensions can be used as a dependent measure, influenced by some independent conceptual variable. For instance, Halberstadt and Niedenthal (1997) examined the extent to which people in various moods used a valence (emotion) dimension in perceiving similarity between faces (see also DeSteno & Salovey, 1997).

MDS starts with a matrix of proximities among objects. In most applications, these proximities are similarity ratings, but other forms of data such as correlation coefficients can also be used (Borg & Groenen, 1997; Kruskal & Wish, 1978). The next step is to select and fit a model to the proximity matrix to derive a set of coordinates that specifies the location of each object in multidimensional space. This fitting process involves finding sets of values that minimize the discrepancy (as defined by some mathematical function) between the distance reconstructed from the MDS model and the observed matrix of proximities. The resulting pictorial representation of the objects is then examined to interpret the obtained dimensions and/or to develop typologies of objects.

Statistical Issues in Conducting MDS

When using MDS, a researcher must (a) choose which type of model to use, (b) determine the appropriate dimensionality in which to represent the objects, and (c) evaluate the adequacy of the resulting representation and interpret its substantive implications.

CHOICE OF MDS MODEL. One major distinguishing characteristic of MDS models is the manner in which distance in multidimensional space is defined (sometimes referred to as the "metric" of the model; Carrroll & Arabie, 1980; MacCallum, 1988). The most common metric is "Euclidean," and the most prevalent model is the "unweighted Euclidean distance model" (also called "classical MDS"). This model locates objects in multidimensional space using coordinates equal in number to the number of dimensions in the space, and the distances among objects are defined as simple distances (which can be measured with a ruler). Although the Euclidean metric is the most intuitively obvious way to define distances, some methodologists have proposed that other metrics might be more appropriate for certain types of data. Probably the best known non-Euclidean metrics are the "city-block metric" and the "dominance metric." All three are special cases of a family known as "Minkowski-p metrics," in which different members of the family are defined by different power functions. Several empirical and interpretational criteria have been proposed for choosing among metrics (see Borg & Groenen, 1997; Carroll & Arabie, 1980; MacCallum, 1988). It seems preferable to use the common and intuitively appealing Euclidean metric unless there is a compelling conceptual justification and strong empirical evidence that it is inappropriate. Unfortunately, it is unclear how robust Euclidean models are to violations of assumptions regarding the metric of the data (Borg & Groenen, 1997).

A second distinguishing characteristic among MDS models concerns level of measurement assumptions. Some models (called "metric MDS") assume interval-level proximities whereas other models (called "nonmetric MDS") assume only ordinal proximities. This distinction concerns the proximity measures themselves and has nothing to do with properties of the solutions. In almost all cases, both metric and nonmetric MDS produce coordinates with at least interval-level properties. In practice, metric and nonmetric MDS usually produce similar solutions (Schiffman, Reynolds, & Young; 1981; Borg & Groenen, 1997). Nonetheless,

the choice is not entirely inconsequential in that solutions are not always the same. Metric MDS offers greater resistance to local minima and degenerate solutions (two problems discussed later; Kruskal & Wish, 1978). Nonmetric MDS has the advantage of less stringent assumptions regarding measurement properties of data. Also, determining the appropriate dimensionality can be somewhat easier in nonmetric MDS (Kruskal & Wish, 1978).

A third important feature of MDS models is the "mode" of data. Mode refers to whether the model is appropriate for data from a single source (i.e., matrix) or multiple sources. One-mode MDS is used when a single matrix of proximities (e.g., a matrix of proximities from a single individual or a matrix consisting of proximities aggregated across individuals) is analyzed. In two-mode MDS, matrices could be two or more sets of aggregated proximities derived from participants in different experimental conditions or from the same participants at different points in time. Alternatively, matrices can be derived from individual participants. The term two-mode MDS is used because the data being analyzed are said to have two modes (i.e., objects and sources). The best known of the two-mode MDS models is probably the weighted Euclidean MDS model, also known as individual differences scaling (INDSCAL; see also Carroll & Arabie, 1980; MacCallum, 1988).

Weighted Euclidean MDS differs from one-mode MDS in several ways. One-mode MDS produces a single stimulus space that represents the multidimensional location of objects. Weighted MDS produces a similar "group stimulus space," but this group space is not necessarily appropriate for any individual matrix (e.g., because individuals likely use each dimension to differing degrees). A set of weights is computed and used to adjust the group stimulus space (i.e., dimensions are stretched or shrunk) to produce a "personal" stimulus space (see Schiffman et al., 1981). This feature is particularly useful to psychologists whose hypotheses involve differences among groups from different experimental conditions or personality types. For example, DeSteno and Salovey (1997) investigated the extent to which the dimensions underlying self-concept were influenced by temporarily induced mood states (see also Halberstadt & Niedenthal, 1997).

Unfortunately, researchers have often inappropriately compared groups on INDSCAL weights for a single dimension. Because INDSCAL normalizes data from each subject separately, the data are treated as "conditional" (i.e., the observations on one individual are not comparable to observations on another individual,

Takane et al., 1977). As demonstrated by MacCallum (1977), direct comparison of subject weights from IND-SCAL is inappropriate (e.g., if the data for each subject are fit well by a two-dimensional solution, subject INDSCAL weights will artifactually show a negative correlation between the two dimensions). Such problems are removed, however, if INDSCAL weights are only compared using weight ratios (i.e., ratios of use of one dimension compared to use of another dimension; MacCallum, 1977; Schiffman et al., 1981).

A second important difference between one-mode and weighted MDS regards orientation of the dimensions. In one-mode MDS, there is no unique solution – dimensions can be rotated without affecting the ability of the representation to account for proximities. Thus, a researcher must determine which orientation is most conceptually meaningful. In weighted MDS, there will be one particular orientation that best accounts for proximities. Although a unique solution does not ensure that this orientation will have conceptual meaning, empirically this is usually the case (Wish & Carroll, 1974).

DETERMINING DIMENSIONALITY. After selecting a model, a researcher must determine the appropriate dimensionality with which to represent the objects of interest. This task is similar to the task of selecting the appropriate number of factors in EFA. Like EFA, dimensionality in MDS is as much a theoretical question as a statistical question (Kruskal & Wish, 1978). Several statistical procedures exist to aid in this decision, but the issue of interpretability and theoretical plausibility must always be taken into account (Arabie, Carroll, & DeSarbo, 1987; MacCallum, 1988).

One common approach is to conduct a series of MDS analyses beginning with a one-dimensional solution and adding a dimension with each analysis until a solution includes three more dimensions than is expected to be needed (Harshman, 1984). A scree plot of the goodness of fit of each solution (as assessed by one of the fit indices discussed later) can then be constructed to locate the point at which adding dimensions no longer produces a substantial improvement in fit. This approach is analogous to use of plots of goodness of fit in determining the number of factors in EFA (see earlier discussion). Of course, as in EFA, identifying breaks in improvement of fit can be rather subjective.

Another approach is to compare the plot of goodness of fit for a series of analyses with plots of fit that would be expected to occur for data with varying numbers of underlying dimensions (Kruskal & Wish, 1978). Methodologists have compiled numerical values of

goodness of fit that would be obtained if the true underlying dimensionality were one-dimensional, two-dimensional, etc. (e.g., Wageneaar & Padmos, 1971; Isaac & Poor, 1974). These plots can be examined to see which plot most closely matches the plot generated from the actual data. Presumably, the underlying dimensionality is the same as the dimensionality of the best matching expected plot. Unfortunately, plots of expected fit have not been compiled for many types of models and indices of fit. Also, these plots reflect dimensions of relatively equal importance (Kruskal & Wish, 1978) whereas real data will often involve some dimensions that are substantially stronger than others. Thus, plots from actual data might not clearly match any plot of predicted values.

A third recommended basis for selecting dimensionality is the stability of solutions at different dimensionalities (Kruskal & Wish, 1978; MacCallum, 1988). Stability can be assessed by examining the solution for randomly split halves of the sample or by assessing changes in the solution when an object is deleted from the analysis. Thus, a researcher can examine the point at which introducing additional dimensions reduces the stability of the solution. Only a solution in which all dimensions are stable should be used as a basis for interpretation.

No method for determining dimensionality is foolproof. Therefore, it is most sensible for a researcher to use a combination of methods. One should also carefully consider the interpretability and plausibility of solutions at different dimensionalities.

EVALUATING AND INTERPRETING MDS SOLUTIONS. A number of fit indices have been developed to assess the adequacy of MDS models (for a review, see Borg & Groenen, 1997), most of which are of a form known as "stress." Stress is a numerical value reflecting how poorly the model fits the data. Thus, smaller values indicate better fit. Numerous formulae for defining stress have been proposed, of which two of the best known are Kruskal's (1964) "Stress 1" and Takane, Young, and de Leeuw's (1977) "S-stress." Although stress is the most common method of expressing model fit in MDS, nonstress indices of fit are also sometimes used (e.g., RSQ in weighted Euclidean MDS, Schiffman et al., 1981).

If a MDS analysis indicates poor fit, the results should be interpreted with caution. Fit guidelines have been proposed for various indices (e.g., Kruskal, 1964; Takane et al., 1977), but fit indices can be affected by a number of factors (Kruskal & Wish, 1978; MacCallum, 1988; Borg & Groenen, 1997). For example, as the ratio of the number of objects to the number of dimensions approaches 1:1, stress values become misleading. Kruskal and Wish (1978) recommend that the number of objects be more than four times the number of dimensions. Numerous ties and missing values can lead to overly low stress. In contrast, high levels of error in the data and the use of metric rather than non-metric MDS will tend to provide higher stress values. Sample size has been found to have little impact on fit, at least for weighted Euclidean models (MacCallum & Cornelius, 1977).

When evaluating solutions, researchers must also be attentive to the possibility of local minima and degenerate solutions. A local minimum occurs when an iterative MDS procedure fails to converge on a best-fitting solution. This problem can be detected by examining a plot of stress values at differing dimensionalities, which should show that stress either does not change or becomes smaller as the dimensionality increases. If increasing dimensionality is found to produce a larger stress value, this suggests the existence of a local minimum (Kruskal & Wish, 1978). One could also conduct several analyses for the same dimensionality and data using different initial start values for the parameter estimates (Harshman, 1984; Borg & Groenen, 1997). If differing start values produce the same stress value and parameter estimates, a local minimum is unlikely. A degenerate solution refers to a situation in which the index of fit can be made arbitrarily small regardless of the relation between the proximity data and the inter-object distances in the MDS solution (Borg & Groenen, 1997). Establishing when a degenerate solution has been obtained is difficult. However, these types of solutions typically have stress values that are zero or near zero and have a configuration of points that has little structure (Weinberg & Carroll, 1992). Degenerate solutions can generally be avoided by placing a sufficient number of constraints on the model (Borg & Groenen, 1997).

Several excellent discussions of substantive interpretation of MDS solutions are available (Kruskal & Wish, 1978; MacCallum, 1988; Schiffman et al., 1981; Weinberg & Carroll, 1992). Some procedures are relatively subjective whereas others have a clear statistical rationale. One widely used subjective technique is to examine the objects located at the extreme ends of each dimension (Schiffman et al., 1981). The dimension is interpreted by identifying characteristics common to all objects at the same end of the dimension. A more formal approach uses regression analysis (Kruskal & Wish, 1978; Schiffman, 1981). A researcher first identifies characteristics of the objects that he or she thinks

might constitute underlying dimensions, and then collects ratings of each object on these characteristics along with the similarity judgments among objects. Dimension coordinate values for each object are used as predictors in a regression analysis, and ratings of the characteristics for each object are used as DVs. Dimensions found to be particularly strong predictors of a characteristic are implied to reflect that characteristic.

For example, Rusbult, Onizuka, and Lipkus (1993) had participants make similarity judgments of different descriptions of romantic relationships. A two-dimensional MDS solution produced the most useful representation of the data. Next, Rusbult et al. (1993) had two trained judges rate the extent to which each relationship description reflected a variety of different attributes (e.g., intimacy, egalitarianism, commitment, intensity of feelings). The MDS coordinates for each description were used in regression analyses to predict the attribute ratings. These analyses revealed that the first dimension was strongly associated with attributes reflecting intimacy–superficiality, whereas the second dimension was strongly associated with attributes reflecting romance–practicality and traditional–nontraditional.

Design Issues in Multidimensional Scaling

A number of design features should be taken into account when collecting MDS data. Perhaps the most important issue is the selection and content of objects. As noted earlier, the stress of a model can be misleading when the number of objects relative to dimensions is low. Therefore, it is important to consider how many dimensions are expected to emerge and to ensure that a large number of objects relative to dimensions is included (i.e., at least 4:1 and if possible more; Kruskal & Wish, 1978; Schiffman et al., 1981). Also, in any MDS analysis, the dimensions that emerge depend on the objects that are included in the analysis. If a domain is inadequately sampled, important dimensions could fail to emerge. It is also important not to include irrelevant objects because results can be distorted by large differences between relevant and irrelevant objects.

Another design issue is the manner in which proximity data are collected. When direct similarity judgments are collected, a variety of possible judgment procedures can be used (Borg & Groenen, 1997; Schiffman et al., 1981). The researcher must also consider controlling for order effects in judgments and including ancillary measures of objects to aid in interpretation of dimensions. In some cases, the number of objects might be so great that it is not feasible to collect similarity ratings for all possible pairs. Procedures have been developed for collecting and analyzing data for incomplete proximity matrices (Borg & Groenen, 1997; MacCallum, 1988; Schiffman et al., 1981). In other cases, direct similarity judgments might not be available and thus some procedure must be used to convert data into a form of proximity data (see Borg & Groenen, 1997).

A final issue is the selection of research participants. As with other forms of analysis, samples should, when possible, represent the population of interest. It is also useful to consider measuring individual differences on constructs related to the manner in which participants judge the objects of interest. For instance, Carroll and Wish (1974) found that individuals' characteristics such as age, gender, political ideology, and religion influenced use of dimensions in similarity ratings of different types of interpersonal relationships. Similarly, one could measure individual differences such as affect intensity (Larsen & Diener, 1987) and investigate whether such differences relate to dimension use in affect-relevant judgment (as in Feldman, 1995; Halberstadt & Niedenthal, 1997).

CLUSTER ANALYSIS

Cluster analysis refers to a wide range of statistical procedures designed to assign a group of objects to relatively homogenous subgroups based on their similarity on a set of attributes. In social and personality psychology, the objects are most commonly individual people for whom the researcher has obtained measures on a set of attributes (e.g., measures on a set of personality characteristics, measures of attitudes on a set of social issues). However, virtually any group of objects is possible. Though cluster analyses might be more common in clinical settings (e.g., identifying personality profiles that form distinct groups related to some psychopathology or diagnosis), a researcher could certainly investigate the existence of clusters of attitudes toward particular political candidates or policies (and could even relate those clusters to characteristics like liberal versus conservative ideology of respondents).

Traditionally, cluster analysis has been used to accomplish one or more of five basic goals (Lorr, 1983): (a) to identify natural clusters (which can aid in determining how many subgroups exist as well as the characteristics of these subgroups), (b) to reduce data (from information about numerous individuals into information about a small set of subgroups), (c) to generate hypotheses when there are no clear expectations concerning the existence, number, or nature of clusters,

(d) to test the existence of specific a priori subgroups, and (e) to identify a classification scheme for later predictions.

Researchers can choose from diverse types of cluster analysis. Two features of particular importance are the type of cluster and hierarchical versus nonhierarchical organization of clusters (Lorr, 1983; Murtagh, 1985). One type of cluster is the "compact" cluster. Compact clusters are subgroups in which each member is more similar to every other member of that same subgroup than to members of any other subgroup. These clusters are often circular or spherical in shape. A second type is the "chained" or "connected" cluster. In chained clusters, each member is more similar to one other member of that cluster than to any member of another cluster. These clusters tend to be serpentine or amoeboid in shape.

A second major distinction is the mathematical procedure used to identify clusters, which can be classified as nonhierarchical methods and hierarchical methods. Hierarchical cluster analysis (with two or more levels of organization) identifies subordinate clusters within superordinate clusters, whereas nonhierarchical clustering represents all clusters within a single level of organization. Within the nonhierarchical category, a further subclassification involves methods that use iterative versus noniterative partitioning of objects into multiple clusters. Within the hierarchical category, most procedures can be classified as agglomerative (i.e., methods that begin at the most subordinate level and create increasingly superordinate clusters) or divisive (i.e., methods that begin at the most superordinate level and create increasingly subordinate clusters). Within each of these four broad subcategories, multiple procedures exist (Jain & Dubes, 1988; Lorr, 1983; Murtagh, 1985).

Although cluster analysis might be useful in some contexts, there are various limitations. For example, a clear set of conceptual guidelines for selecting among the many clustering procedures has yet to be fully articulated. Likewise, empirical comparisons have not yet provided a comprehensive picture of the extent to which different procedures produce optimal or even similar results. In addition, the validity of the resulting clusters is often in question. Even if the true underlying distribution of objects is relatively uniform throughout multidimensional space, sample data will almost always include some regions that are more densely populated than others. Therefore, it will almost always be possible to create clusters from data. However, when subgroups are not distinctly defined, the plausibility of representing objects as discrete subgroups becomes questionable. We urge readers to think carefully about the conceptual meaning of clusters in the specific research domain and about the reasonability of thinking in terms of distinct clusters (i.e., discrete homogeneous groups of objects) rather than continuous dispersion across a set of relevant dimensions. Unless homogeneous, distinct subgroups seem more likely – and there is some evidence of distinct groupings (e.g., from inspection of scatterplots) – EFA or MDS might provide a more conceptually valid and defensible approach.

SUMMARY AND COMPARISONS OF NONCAUSAL METHODS

We have described several procedures for addressing noncausal hypotheses regarding the number and nature of dimensions underlying a set of data. To some extent, methods are distinguished by the types of data they utilize and the types of questions they are designed to address. Whereas EFA and CFA investigate relations among measures of a given object, MDS addresses the dimensionality of a set of objects. Some research questions lend themselves to ratings of a given object, whereas others lend themselves to arrangement/judgment of multiple objects (especially on similarity). Some form of factor analysis is typically well-suited to the former type of question, whereas MDS is well-suited to the latter type of question. It is also important to note, however, that there might often be opportunities for addressing the same conceptual question from either approach (and there is nothing to say that one could not "factor analyze objects" by rating many objects on a single dimension or use MDS to spatially represent a set of traits relevant to a single object – though these are rarely done).

When a research question seems equally amenable to either strategy, we believe that there are reasons to favor factor-analytic methods. One reason is that the common factor model explicitly represents measurement error within the model. Thus, the existence of measurement error can to some degree be assessed and accounted for in the solution. MDS models do not incorporate measurement error, so it is difficult to determine the severity or impact of such error in a particular data set. A second advantage of factor analysis regards rotation. Although the orientation of dimensions in weighted Euclidan MDS is uniquely determined, this is not true in most other forms of MDS, so that rotation becomes an issue. In factor analysis, criteria and specific procedures for both orthogonal and oblique rotation have been well-developed and are available in software. This is much less true for MDS. Another major

advantage of factor analysis is the fact that ML estimation has been extensively studied and is available in virtually all major statistical programs. This allows for the computation of a wide range of indices of goodness of fit and provides the ability to compute confidence intervals and significance tests for parameter estimates. Although ML procedures have been developed for MDS (e.g., see Borg & Groenen, 1997; MacCallum, 1988; Young, 1984), they have not been as extensively studied nor are they widely available. Finally, confirmatory approaches to factor analysis have been extensively developed and computer software for implementing CFA is widely distributed. In contrast, although there is some work on confirmatory MDS (e.g., see Borg & Groenen 1997; MacCallum, 1988; Young, 1984), this literature is much less developed and software is not widely available.

There are certainly some situations in which MDS is desirable. These would include research questions that explicitly deal with dimensions along which people classify objects or with ways in which certain individuals or groups use particular dimensions to classify or perceive objects, and would also include situations where it is desirable to avoid explicit specification of the dimensions along which objects vary. However, when none of these research goals is central, the latent variable qualities of EFA and CFA, the extensive methodological research addressing those methods, and the ready availability of programs supporting rotation, overall fit, and parameter significance tests make factor analysis the better choice.

Finally, in certain respects, cluster analysis is similar to MDS in the types of questions it can address. Both methods can be used to represent the structure of similarities among objects. However, cluster analysis requires that one specify a set of attributes for judging the objects whereas MDS typically does not. Another difference is that cluster analysis represents similarities among objects in the form of assignment to distinct subgroups whereas MDS represents similarities in more continuous terms as points in multidimensional space. Objects could form distinct clusters in MDS but there is no such assumption. Factor analysis shares with MDS the more continuous nature of representing the data. In addition, the factor analytic advantages of representing measurement error and of extensive methodological development of fit indices and significance tests also apply to comparisons with cluster analysis. The greatest limitation of cluster analysis would seem to be the often questionable assumption that distinct homogeneous clusters are a meaningful way of conceptualizing the data.

ANALYSES INVOLVING CAUSAL HYPOTHESES

In many research settings, the key questions of interest go beyond determining the number and nature of constructs underlying a set(s) of measured variables or objects. In many social psychological settings, a researcher might wish to examine one or more potential causal relations among the constructs of interest. In the sections that follow, we review a series of statistical techniques used to test causal hypotheses. We begin our discussion with an overview of the major types of causal hypotheses. Then we discuss the conditions necessary for establishing causality relations and comment on study design features and statistical procedures that assist in establishing these conditions. Finally, we review statistical procedures used to test different types of causal hypotheses. Our review focuses on procedures that have traditionally been associated with the analysis of nonexperimental data. However, these procedures can fruitfully test causal hypotheses with either experimental or nonexperimental data (see also Judd, this volume, Ch. 14; E. Smith, this volume, Ch. 2).

TYPES OF CAUSAL HYPOTHESES

Several different types of causal hypotheses are commonly investigated in psychology. The simplest form of causal hypothesis is that a given IV (either measured or manipulated) is hypothesized to have a direct causal influence on a DV. For example, a researcher might hypothesize that increases in the value of an IV directly lead to increases in the value of a DV. We refer to such hypotheses as "direct causal" hypotheses. Obviously, within the context of a particular study, a researcher might be interested in testing more than one direct causal hypothesis. One might hypothesize that multiple IVs directly influence a DV, that one IV directly influences multiple DVs, or that multiple IVs directly influence multiple DVs.

In other cases, a researcher might hypothesize a more complex set of causal relations among one or more IVs and one or more DVs. One such type of hypothesis is a mediational hypothesis (see Baron & Kenny, 1986). *Mediation* refers to a case in which a researcher postulates that an IV exerts a causal influence on a DV at least in part indirectly – via its influence on another (mediating) variable. That is, a researcher postulates that an IV has a direct causal influence on a mediator variable, which in turn has a direct causal influence on the DV. Mediational hypotheses are often complex. For example, a researcher might postulate that more than one variable mediates the impact of

the IV on the DV. Alternatively, the researcher might be interested in multiple IVs or multiple DVs. Finally, a researcher might posit multiple steps in a mediational chain, such as when an IV causally influences a mediator which in turn causally influences a second mediator which then affects the DV.

A third type of causal hypothesis, *moderation* (Baron & Kenny, 1986), refers to a case in which the strength and/or valence of a relation between an IV and DV is thought to be regulated by a second IV (the moderator). For example, a researcher might hypothesize that the first IV will have a substantial influence on the DV at one level of the second IV but that this influence will become weaker at another level of the second IV. Alternatively, the researcher might predict that the first IV will have a positive causal relation with the DV at one level of the second IV but that it will have a negative causal relation at another level of the second IV.[14] Such moderator hypotheses are typically examined using interaction tests among IVs. However, as we will see, moderator hypotheses can also sometimes be addressed using methods that are conceptually similar, but do not include interaction tests per se. Complex moderator hypotheses are also often examined by researchers. For instance, a researcher might hypothesize that a moderator relation between two IVs is moderated by a third IV (i.e., that a three-way interaction exists).

Though rarely discussed, many psychological theories also involve "hybrid" hypotheses that combine different types of causal hypotheses. For instance, a researcher might hypothesize that a particular mediational relation varies across levels of some variable. That is, one variable moderates the mediational relations among a set of variables – *moderated mediation*. This might involve predicting that different variables mediate the relation between an IV and a DV at different levels of the moderator. For example,

---

[14] When examining moderator relations, there is often some ambiguity with respect to which IV might be designated as the moderator. In some cases, there might be conceptual reasons that make it more plausible or useful to conceptualize one IV as moderating the influence of the other IV on the DV. In other situations, it might be equally meaningful to designate either of the IVs as the moderator. When testing moderator hypotheses using interaction terms, this decision has little practical consequence as the interaction test does not require specifying which IV is the moderator. However, when other types of procedures are used (e.g., dividing participants into groups based on their scores on the moderator variable and then testing the impact of the IV on the DV within each group), this decision can have consequences for the manner in which the analysis is conducted.

the Elaboration Likelihood Model (Petty & Cacioppo, 1986) involves moderated mediation (Petty, Wegener, Fabrigar, Priester, & Cacioppo, 1993), with assessments of the central merits of attitude objects mediating the effects of persuasive appeals under conditions of high elaboration, but with simplified processes (e.g., heuristics or conditioning) mediating the effects of the same appeals under conditions of low elaboration (for similar models, see Chaiken & Trope, 1999). Alternatively, it might be hypothesized that an IV has a direct impact on a DV at one level of the moderator, but this relation is mediated at another level of the moderator (for additional discussion of moderated mediation see James & Brett, 1984).

Another form of hybrid hypothesis occurs when an IV moderates the impact of a second IV via its influence on some mediator variable – *mediated moderation*. A moderator might causally influence a mediator which in turn moderates the impact of another IV on the DV, for example. Such a hypothesis is actually implied by most moderation effects in social psychology. That is, a manipulation's effect on a psychological variable (often measured as a manipulation check) is hypothesized as responsible for the moderational impact of the manipulation. Of course, other examples exist as well. For instance, DeSteno, Petty, Wegener, and Rucker (in press) found that different negative emotions (i.e., anger vs. sadness) produced opposite patterns of likelihood judgments for angering versus saddening events (a moderation effect). DeSteno et al. went on to test the possibility that the moderating effect of emotions was mediated by global beliefs about whether the world was a maddening versus saddening place. There is also another type of *mediated moderation* in which there is a moderational effect of two IVs on the mediating variable and a direct effect of that mediator on the DV (see Baron & Kenny, 1986). This type of mediated moderation might be common in studies where the DV is some type of behavior. For example, one might find that choices of products are influenced by the content of product advertisements when the product appears to be personally relevant to consumers, but are not when the product appears low in personal relevance to consumers (e.g., Petty, Cacioppo, & Schumann, 1983). This moderational (content X relevance) effect on behavior, however, might take place because the moderational effect influenced attitudes (e.g., Petty, Cacioppo, & Goldman, 1981), and attitudes influenced behavior (either directly or through behavioral intentions; Fazio, 1990).

A final type of hybrid hypothesis occurs when noncausal relations among constructs or variables are mod-

erated by some variable. For instance, a researcher might postulate that a moderator variable (causally) influences the magnitude of correlations between two common factors underlying a set of measured variables. Alternatively, a researcher might hypothesize that the number of common factors underlying a set of measured variables differs across levels of a moderator variable or that the magnitude of factor loadings differs across levels of a moderator variable.

CONDITIONS FOR INFERRING CAUSALITY

These various hypotheses all share the common feature of implying at least some form of causality among the constructs of interest, which can be represented mathematically. Some statistical procedures permit representation of virtually any of these types of hypotheses whereas other procedures allow for representation of only some of the hypotheses. However, it is important to recognize that ability to use a statistical procedure to represent a hypothesized set of causal relations (and then estimate these relations for a given data set) does not necessarily imply that the hypothesized causal relations are correct. For example, a researcher can conduct a regression analysis assessing the impact of several IVs on a DV. Although this analysis models a directional impact of the IVs on the DV, finding significant effects of the IV's does not necessarily establish that the relations are causal.

A substantial literature addresses the conditions under which causality can be inferred (e.g., Cliff, 1983; Holland, 1986; Judd & Kenny, 1981; Platt, 1964; West, Biesanz, & Pitts, this volume, Ch. 3). Although such discussions vary, three commonly noted conditions are isolation, association, and direction (e.g., Bollen, 1989). A DV can only be said to be caused by an IV when impact of the IV on the DV has been isolated from all other influences. It must also be established that changes in the IV are associated with changes in the DV. Finally, the direction of the association must be that changes in the IV lead to changes in the DV rather than the reverse. Establishing the existence of these conditions can be challenging, and there are a number of features of both study design and statistical analysis that affect this determination (see E. Smith, this volume, Ch. 2; West et al., this volume, Ch. 3).

Satisfaction of the isolation, association, and direction conditions can be thought of as falling along a continuum. At one end of the continuum is simple measurement of the IV and DV, with no attempts to control for extraneous influences on the DV. Even if an association between the IV and DV is found, no claims about isolation or direction are possible. In fact, even the association between IV and DV could reflect some unmeasured third variable that correlates with both. Statistical techniques that control for the impact of alternative IVs, that control for measurement error, or both, can move one higher on the continuum toward building a credible case for the causal effect of an IV on a DV. Statistical techniques alone, however, are less effective than utilizing "pure" manipulations of the construct of interest, assuming design features such as random assignment (E. Smith, this volume, Ch. 2; Wegener, Downing, Krosnick, & Petty, 1995). Although causal inferences based on experimental manipulations pose additional issues, common design features of experiments can at least assure one that the manipulation itself causes change in the DV (Brewer, this volume, Ch. 1; E. Smith, this volume, Ch. 2).

In social psychology, the conduct of controlled experiments (in which manipulations of crucial constructs are developed and used) has become the standard approach for addressing causal hypotheses. However, as noted earlier, there are many reasons for conducting nonexperimental research (e.g., when manipulation of constructs is impractical, unethical, or undesirable). Given nonexperimental data, some statistical methods are more useful than others for establishing at least a modest level of confidence that the isolation, association, and direction conditions of causality have been satisfied. Because of this, these procedures have become widely used in these settings. In the sections that follow, we review a range of statistical procedures that are most commonly associated with testing causal relations in nonexperimental settings.

REGRESSION

Multiple linear regression has, in recent years, become a common, "everyday" method of analysis for both experimental and nonexperimental research in psychology. As detailed elsewhere in this volume (Judd, this volume, Ch. 14), regression is a general and flexible technique, capable of addressing many types of research questions involving both continuous and categorical predictor variables. In general, linear regression consists of a set of predictor variables (IVs) hypothesized to influence a single DV. These IVs can represent continuous or categorical measures of the constructs of interest and other relevant variables; DVs are continuous measures. Regression IVs are related to the DV through a set of linear equations (see Cohen & Cohen, 1983; Judd, this volume, Ch. 14).

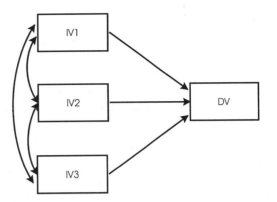

Figure 16.5. Path diagram of the multiple regression model for direct causal hypotheses.

As presented in Figure 16.5, multiple regression models are saturated, with all IV's correlated with one another, and all IV's influencing the DV. In addition, the IVs and DV are treated as perfect measures of the variables of interest. That is, there is no representation of measurement error. It is therefore impossible to separate errors in equations (predicting the DV from the IVs) from errors of measurement (see later discussion of CSM). The saturated nature of the model, with measures treated as perfect indicators, render the model nonfalsifiable (i.e., the model exhausts all degrees of freedom, such that model fit per se cannot be meaningfully assessed, though one can examine the amount of variance in the DV accounted for by the IVs). Thus, the focus is generally on parameter estimation as the researcher seeks to determine the extent to which the various IVs uniquely influence the DV (controlling for the impact of other predictor variables).

Types of Hypotheses

DIRECT CAUSE. The model represented in Figure 16.5 tests direct causal hypotheses. That is, the IV(s) of interest directly influence the DV, controlling for other potential influences. If a researcher wishes to distinguish the IV(s) of interest from related, but conceptually distinct, influences on the DV, he or she can measure these alternative predictors and include them in the model. For example, Abelson, Kinder, Peters, and Fiske (1982) investigated the influence of positive and negative affect on candidate evaluation using multiple regression. In addition, Abelson et al. included positive and negative traits of candidates and measures of party identification – Republican versus Democrat – in order to test whether the affect and trait measures were

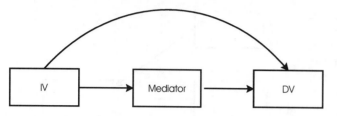

Figure 16.6. Path diagram of a simple mediational relation using measured variables.

"simple reflections of partisan orientation" (p. 625) rather than conceptually distinct predictors of candidate evaluation.

MEDIATION. Regression analyses can also address mediational relations among variables. For example, Figure 16.6 presents a simple mediational relation, with the effect of the IV on the DV mediated by the mediator variable. Often, such models also allow for direct influence of the IV on the DV. One instance of testing such a model would be in studies of the revised frustration-aggression hypothesis (Berkowitz, 1989), where the impact of frustration on aggression is posited to be mediated by negative affective experiences created by the frustrating event.

To conduct a test of such mediation, one regression analysis examines whether the IV (frustration) influences the DV (aggression). A second analysis tests whether the IV influences the mediator (negative affect), and a third tests whether the mediator influences the DV, controlling for the IV. This third regression, including both IV and mediator, also determines whether the IV has an influence on the DV independent of the mediator. Statistically testing the drop in influence of the IV when the proposed mediator is included in the model completes the test of mediation. If the tests show significant relations between IV and DV, IV and mediator, and mediator and DV, and the impact of the IV is significantly lower when the mediator is controlled, then evidence of mediation exists (Baron & Kenny, 1986; Kenny, Kashy, & Bolger, 1998). If the IV has a significant impact on the DV independent of the mediator, partial mediation is said to exist.

As the number of mediators increases, regression-based tests quickly become unwieldy. Although possible in many cases, the regression technique for testing such hypotheses is best abandoned in favor of analyses of covariance structures (see later discussion).

MODERATION. One strength of the regression approach is the ease with which it deals with modera-

tional relations. As depicted in Panel A of Figure 16.7, moderators are often tested by including a multiplicative term in the model (i.e., a product of the two interacting IVs). The interaction is tested as the unique influence of the multiplicative term when the lower-order (main effect) IVs are included in the model (Cohen & Cohen, 1983). For instance, Krosnick (1988) used moderated regression to show that issue stands influence evaluations of candidates more to the extent that the issues are important to potential voters. When using moderated regression, it is often desirable to center or "mean-deviate" the values of each IV (i.e., to set the mean of each IV to zero, Aiken & West, 1991; Judd, this volume, Ch. 14).

When a moderator variable is dichotomous or categorical, one might address moderational hypotheses by running separate regressions at each level of the moderator variable. As shown in Panel B of Figure 16.7, one might conduct separate analyses investigating the impact of an IV on the DV at each level of the moderator

Figure 16.7. Path diagrams of tests of simple moderational relations in multiple regression.

PANEL A

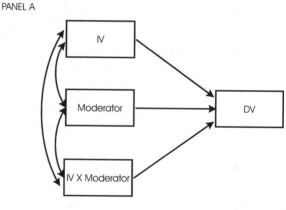

PANEL B

Moderator Group 1

Moderator Group 2

variable, then testing the difference in regression coefficients across pairs of groups (Cohen & Cohen, 1983). Although such a test is not identical to the interaction test, it does address the conceptual question of difference in impact of an IV across levels of the moderator. Such an approach is rare for straight moderational tests (and would often be less sensitive than the traditional test), but the split analysis becomes more useful when attempting to address some of the hybrid hypotheses using the regression technique. As discussed by E. Smith (this volume, Ch. 2) and Judd (this volume, Ch. 14), this split type of analysis should not be the default approach when dealing with continuous variables (i.e., one should not routinely dichotomize one of the variables in order to run separate regressions at each level of the split moderator). Aiken and West (1991) provided a general guide for dealing with continuous variables in moderated regression.

MODERATED MEDIATION. Moderated mediation, especially when the moderator is categorical, is most simply examined by separate mediational analyses at each level of the moderator. Then, one can conduct comparisons across levels of the moderator between the regression coefficients for each of the three critical paths (i.e., IV to mediator, mediator to DV partialing the IV, and IV to DV partialing the mediator). In some cases, moderated mediation might be caused primarily by changes in impact of the IV on the mediator, in others by changes in the impact of the mediator on the DV, or in others by both. Moderated mediation could occur when a moderator X IV interaction is observed (because of differences in IV to mediator and/or mediator to DV paths) or when no moderator X IV interaction is observed (because different mediators create the same magnitude of effect or a mediator operates at some levels of the moderator but direct effects occur at other levels). For example, Petty, Schumann, Richman, and Strathman (1993) found equal persuasion effects of mood under high- and low-elaboration conditions, despite differences in hypothesized mechanism (i.e., thought-mediated "biased processing" effects under high elaboration, but more direct "cue" effects under low elaboration).

One might also use interaction terms to identify moderated mediation effects. A moderator X IV interaction influencing the mediator would identify differences in the impact of the IV on the mediator. A moderator × mediator effect on the DV, partialing for the moderator X IV effect (and lower-order effects) and accompanied by a decrease in the moderator X IV effect, would identify differences in impact of the mediator

across levels of the moderator. A significant moderator X IV interaction in this last analysis suggests changes in the direct impact of the IV across levels of the moderator.

MEDIATED MODERATION. In other contexts, researchers might be interested in mediated moderation; e.g., when a moderator interacts with an IV to affect a DV, but the moderator has its effect via some mediating variable (which is the conceptual variable that actually interacts with the IV). Exactly this logic is at least implicit when researchers collect manipulation-check data. The manipulation is assumed to affect a conceptual variable (measured by the manipulation check), which is assumed to interact with another IV. Testing such an effect is relatively straightforward. First, one would test the moderator X IV interaction influencing the DV. As in tests of simple mediation, the influence of the moderator on the proposed mediator would be tested. Then, one would test the mediator X IV interaction influencing the DV, controlling for the moderator X IV interaction (and all lower-order effects). This would show the proximal moderational impact of the mediator when the mediator X IV effect is significant but the moderator X IV effect is substantially reduced. A significant moderator X IV interaction in the last analysis would provide evidence of partial rather than complete mediation.

For example, Wegener, Petty, and Smith (1995) used such a technique in a study of mood effects on processing of persuasive communications. In this research, the crucial effect was a Mood (happy, sad) × Content (uplifting, depressing) × Argument Quality (strong, weak) three-way interaction. Thus, the mood manipulation (the moderator) was found to interact with the other crucial variables; the manipulation was found to significantly influence mood manipulation checks (the mediator); and inclusion of regression terms using the mood manipulation check substantially reduced the obtained effects for the crucial three-way interactions involving the mood manipulation.

Testing the second type of *mediated moderation* is also relatively straightforward (Baron & Kenny, 1986). This begins with the same analysis that starts the previous test of mediated moderation, with the moderator X IV influencing the DV (partialing for lower-order effects – equivalent to an ANOVA if the moderator and IV are categorical). The second analysis uses the same model to predict the mediator (rather than the ultimate DV). For this type of mediated moderation, the moderator X IV effect should be substantial on both the DV (in the first analysis) and the mediator (in the second analysis).

Next, the mediator is added to the original set of predictors, and the ultimate DV is used as the outcome variable. This type of mediated moderation is supported if the mediator effect on the DV is significant but the moderator X IV effect on the DV is substantially reduced (comparing this last analysis with the first, in which the mediator was not included).

HIERARCHICAL LINEAR MODELS

In some contexts, researchers have data at more than one level of analysis, where each lower level is nested within a higher level. For example, imagine that a researcher is interested in the determinants of participation in group discussions. One might obtain lower-level measures of characteristics of individual group members (e.g., knowledge of the discussion topic, amount of participation in group discussion). These individuals are nested within groups (i.e., there is person-based variance within a given group), and the researcher might also obtain higher-level measures of characteristics of the groups (e.g., group size). The researcher might want to test whether topic knowledge and group size influence participation in the discussion.

One relatively recent development for examining nested data is hierarchical linear modeling (HLM; also called multilevel linear modeling; Bryk & Raudenbush, 1992; Collins & Sayer this volume, Ch. 18; Goldstein, 1995; Judd, this volume, Ch. 14; Reis & Gable, this volume, Ch. 8). HLM can be thought of as a multilevel form of multiple regression, in which ML estimation is typically used (see earlier discussion of ML estimation in CFA). At the lower level of analysis, the model is similar to traditional multiple regression, with a set of IVs predicting a DV (see Figure 16.8 for a simplified representation). In our example, each member's topic knowledge is an IV predicting that person's discussion participation. HLM models differ from traditional regression models in that a second level of analysis is also represented and in that observations at the lower level of analysis can be grouped together based on their membership in some higher-order level of organization. For instance, in our example, individuals can be grouped because they belonged to the same discussion group. Furthermore, each set of lower-level observations can be conceptualized as having its own parameter estimates. Thus, within each discussion group, it is possible to compute a regression coefficient and intercept for task knowledge predicting discussion participation. Importantly, the model also allows specification of IVs measured at the second level of analysis that are presumed to account for variations across sets of obser-

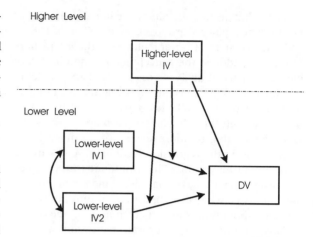

Figure 16.8. Simplified representation of two-level HLM.

vations (i.e., groups) in the value of the lower-level regression coefficients and intercepts. For instance, group size could be specified as a higher-level IV predicting variation across discussion groups in the regression coefficients and intercepts for topic knowledge influencing discussion participation. Although two-level models are the most common form of hierarchical model, it is possible to test models with more than two levels.

At the lower level of analysis, the same types of causal relations that can be examined in multiple regression (e.g., direct causal, mediational, moderational) can be explored in HLM. The use of higher-level IVs to account for variations in the lower-level regression coefficients can be conceptualized as moderator relations. That is, the effect of a higher-level IV on lower-level regression coefficients indicates that the influence of the lower-level IV (e.g., topic knowledge) on the DV (e.g., discussion participation) is not the same across different levels of a higher-level IV (e.g., group size). The test of whether a higher-level IV accounts for variations in the intercept of the lower-level model can have somewhat different conceptual implications depending on the scaling of the lower-level IVs. If the lower-level IVs are expressed as deviations from the mean value for that higher-level unit, an effect of a higher-level IV on the lower-level intercept would correspond to a direct causal relation between the higher-level IV and the DV (e.g., group size influences amount of member participation). In Figure 16.8, this effect is depicted using a direct arrow from the higher-level IV to the DV.

HLM also has potential for testing more complex relations. For instance, one might imagine using HLM to test moderated mediation. A higher-level variable could moderate a set of mediational lower-level relations. In fact, such moderated mediation questions fit naturally into the logic of the model. For example, individuals could be considered "grouped" by the fact that they all received the same manipulation in an experiment (i.e., experimental condition is the higher-level IV). Though rare in HLM, effects more complex than two-way interactions can also be addressed. One might also imagine testing whether the moderational impact of one higher-level IV on the lower-level regression coefficients or intercepts is mediated by another higher-level IV (i.e., mediated moderation).

HLM has several advantages over traditional regression models for analyzing multilevel data (Bryk & Raudenbush, 1992), including improved estimation of lower-level effects within higher-level units, the ability to test cross-level effects, and the ability to partition variances and covariances in lower-level measures into within-unit and between-unit higher-level components (Reis & Gable, this volume, Ch. 8). However, HLM is not the only way to deal with multilevel data. Traditional multiple regression models can be adapted (Judd, this volume, Ch. 14; Kenny et al., 1998), and certain CFA models are mathematically equivalent to some classes of HLM (MacCallum, Kim, Malarkey, & Kiecolt-Glaser, 1997). Much work remains to be done, but HLM appears to offer a useful approach to the analysis of multilevel data. For psychology, the HLM method seems especially useful in longitudinal studies of change (see Collins & Sayer, this volume, Ch. 18) and will likely receive greater attention in settings for which nonindependence of observations is an issue (Kenny & Kashy, this volume, Ch. 17).

For instance, one could study effectiveness of conflict resolution in couples by having different couples utilize different discussion techniques in conversations about controversial aspects of the relationship. In such a setting, HLM techniques could be used to examine couple characteristics (higher-level variables) such as length of relationship or availability of social support as well as characteristics of the individuals (lower-level variables) such as desire for control (Burger & Cooper, 1979), as well as interactions between these higher- and lower-level variables.

COVARIANCE STRUCTURE MODELING

CSM (sometimes called covariance structure analysis, structural equation modeling, or causal modeling) is a method of specifying and estimating relations between latent variables and measured variables and among la-

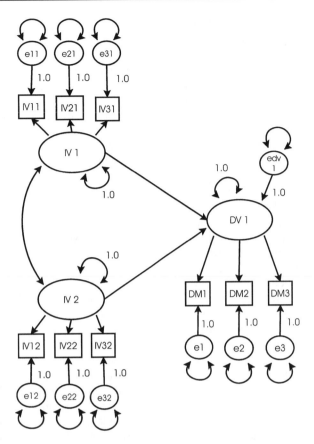

Figure 16.9. Path diagram of a CSM specifying two correlated latent variables that causally influence a third latent variable.

tent variables (Bollen, 1989; Hoyle, 1995; Schumacker & Lomax, 1996). CSM is a general mathematical framework that includes CFA (as well as regression, path analysis, and ANOVA) as a special case. One can think of CSM as a CFA model in which causal relations are permitted among the common factors. For example, the CSM depicted in Figure 16.9 includes three common factors in which IV1 and IV2 are correlated and each exerts a causal influence on the DV.

Statistical Issues in CSM

STEPS IN CONDUCTING CSM. A CSM analysis is very similar to CFA, and the overlapping material will not be repeated.

MODEL SPECIFICATION. CSM requires specification of a model (or models) to be tested. As in CFA, this is done by specifying which relations between variables are fixed at some value (often zero) or left free to vary (to be estimated during model fitting). CSM models have two components: the measurement model and the structural model. The measurement model refers to the pattern of relations between latent and measured variables. The structural model refers to the pattern of relations among latent variables. The inclusion of endogenous latent variables (i.e., latent DV's that receive causal influences) in CSM adds some features that were not present in CFA models. As shown in Figure 16.9, a new type of error term (latent variable "edv") is added. This term corresponds to errors in prediction of the latent variable by the variables hypothesized to influence it (aka "errors in equations"). Also, the scale of the endogenous latent variable must be set, either by fixing its variance at 1.0 (as in Figure 16.9) or by fixing at 1.0 a path to one of the latent variable's indicators. The ability to fix the variance of endogenous latent variables is not available in all CSM software packages.

Many of the same issues that arise in model specification in CFA also arise in CSM. The model must be identified (i.e., the model must have a unique mathematical solution). Couching the research question in terms of comparisons among a priori alternative models can also be beneficial. In CSM, researchers sometimes have substantive interest in testing hypotheses about the number and nature of common factors underlying the data (i.e., the measurement model), but in many cases, these questions have already been thoroughly explored or are not of particular interest. Often, the primary goal is to understand the relations among the latent variables (i.e., the structural model).

Some measurement models specify causal indicators rather than effects indicators (Bollen & Lennox, 1991). CSM models typically follow the common factor model convention of conceptualizing latent variables as influencing the measured variables. In such models, measured variables are referred to as effects indicators. However, for some constructs, this assumption is questionable. For example, Bollen and Lennox (1991) note that socioeconomic status (SES) might be plausibly conceptualized in the opposite causal direction, with indicators such as income and level of education (referred to as causal indicators) combining to produce SES (rather than representing SES as a latent variable influencing income and education level). Such models can present problems in practice because they sometimes imply unusual or improbable conceptual notions not immediately obvious from the path diagram (e.g., that large sets of measured variables are uncorrelated, despite the fact that their associated latent variables are hypothesized to be related, MacCallum & Browne, 1993). Such models also can suffer from identification

problems. Therefore, researchers should be cautious when specifying models that include causal indicators. It might often be more useful to compute a composite (e.g., a mean) score of the supposed causal indicators, which can be specified as a perfect (errorless) measure of the intended construct. Such a model retains the conceptual notion of the construct and is likely to avoid the unusual properties and identification problems of causal-indicator models.

Most commonly, alternative models in CSM focus on the structural model. In some cases, alternatives might include additional paths or might omit paths among latent variables. In other cases, alternatives might differ in the direction of one or more paths. Researchers also sometimes specify alternative models that involve setting constraints on specific parameter estimates of a model. As in CFA, these "constrained" models are nested within more general "unconstrained" models, so it is possible to conduct formal statistical tests of differences in fit (e.g., using the likelihood ratio statistic). This allows the researcher to test specific hypotheses regarding parameter estimates in a given model. For example, a researcher might be interested in testing whether the coefficients for two latent variables exerting causal influences on a third latent variable are equivalent (see Figure 16.9). This could be done by testing the difference in the likelihood ratio test statistic between a model with these parameter estimates constrained to be equal and a model without this constraint.

MODEL FITTING. The basic process for model fitting is identical to that of CFA (i.e., numerical estimates of free parameters are derived by minimizing the discrepancy between the model and the data). The same indices of fit can be used, and the same general issues arise.

MODEL EVALUATION. The next step in a CSM analysis is to evaluate the adequacy of the model(s). The basic criteria used in CFA model evaluation (overall model fit, interpretability of parameter estimates, and parsimony of the model) are also typically used in CSM. A researcher can separately assess fit of the measurement and structural portions of the model (Anderson & Gerbing, 1988; see Mulaik et al., 1989, for techniques to separate fit of the structural and measurement models). At a minimum, researchers should realize that overall model fit in CSM is a joint function of the plausibility of both aspects of the model (Schumacker & Lomax, 1996). One difficulty that sometimes arises in CSM (but not typically in CFA) is the problem of equivalent models (MacCallum et al., 1993). As noted earlier, for some models there exist one or more mathematically equivalent models. These models cannot be distinguished on the basis of their fit to the data.

No comprehensive set of rules has been developed for determining when an alternative model will be equivalent to a preferred model. However, rules for generating classes of equivalent models have been developed (Stelzl, 1986; Lee & Hershberger, 1990). These rules allow a researcher to determine changes in the direction of relations among latent variables (i.e., the structural model) that will result in a mathematically equivalent model. Because the resulting equivalent models will always have the same number of free parameters as the original model, they will have not only the same goodness of fit but also the same level of statistical parsimony. Thus, when such equivalent models exist, researchers will need to provide a rationale for preferring one model based on the greater interpretability of parameter estimates or the greater conceptual plausibility of the hypothesized pattern of relations (MacCallum et al., 1993).

MODEL MODIFICATION. The issues arising in modification of CFA models are equally applicable to CSM models. Indeed, if anything, the temptation to modify models is likely to be greater in CSM, because both the measurement and structural portions of the model provide opportunities for modification. Unfortunately, the problems inherent in empirically driven model modifications in CFA are also true of CSM. Thus, we recommend extreme caution in the use of empirically derived indices of model modification as a basis for modifying covariance structure models.

TYPES OF HYPOTHESES. CSM provides an extremely flexible mathematical framework in which a wide range of different forms of hypothesized causal relations can be represented and tested. Virtually all of the types of hypotheses discussed thus far can be examined in CSM. Furthermore, these hypotheses can be tested when the constructs are represented by measured variables (i.e., when there are only single indicators assessing each construct) or when constructs are represented by latent variables.

DIRECT CAUSE. CSM affords the ability to test virtually any form of direct causal relation (a single IV affecting a single DV, multiple IVs influencing a single DV, a single IV influencing multiple DVs, or multiple IVs affecting multiple DVs). Furthermore, the researcher can specify all IVs as intercorrelated, all IVs as uncorrelated,

or some subset of IVs as intercorrelated. CSM also allows one to specify models in which a given IV only influences a subset of DVs.

Another critical (and defining) feature of the CSM approach is the ability to specify IVs and/or DVs as latent variables. If the researcher has two or more measured variables that are designed to assess the same latent variable, the researcher can specify causal and/or noncausal relations between this latent variable and other variables in the model. A single measured variable that reflects a given construct can be represented in one of two ways. Some CSM programs represent such constructs as if they were latent variables, but with only the single measure as a perfect (errorless) indicator of the latent variable. Other programs (e.g., RAMONA) do not require specification of a latent variable, including measured variables themselves as part of the structural model (in Figures 16.9 and 16.10, we represent such "perfect measures" as rectangles – similar to the regression representations – rather than as latent variables with a single indicator). Models specified in either manner are mathematically equivalent, and a latent variable with a single indicator is not a latent variable in any real sense, because there is no representation of error.

Figure 16.10 provides an example of a model that incorporates many features previously described. This model includes three IVs with direct causal influences on two DVs. Two of these IVs are assumed to be correlated with one another whereas the third IV is assumed to be uncorrelated with the other IVs. Each DV is postulated to be influenced by only a subset of IVs. Two of the IVs and one of the DVs are latent variables with multiple indicators whereas the remaining IV and DV are measured variables treated as perfect representations of the constructs of interest.

MEDIATION. One of the most common and powerful uses of CSM is to address questions involving mediation. For example, consider a researcher who wants to assess mediation of frustration effects on aggression by examining not only frustration effects on negative emotions (see earlier discussion), but also effects of negative emotions on interpretation of actions by others (with different interpretations leading to different levels of ultimate aggression). Although this multi-step mediation would become rather unwieldy for regression-based tests, CSM techniques could easily handle such a model. In fact, virtually any mediational pattern among measured variables or latent variables can be specified (a single IV influencing a single mediator which in turn influences a single DV, multiple

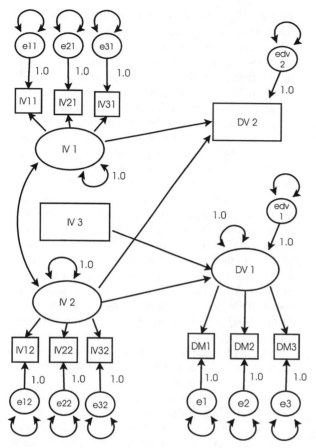

Figure 16.10. Path diagram of a CSM incorporating multiple IVs and DVs, both measured and latent structural variables, and a subset of IVs correlated with one another.

IVs, multiple mediators, multiple DVs, or any combination of these). As with direct causal CSM models, the researcher can allow for intercorrelations among IVs and can specify a model in which a specific IV influences only a subset of mediators and/or a given mediator influences only a subset of DVs. Under certain conditions, CSM also allows for non-recursive models that contain reciprocal causal relations or feedback loops among variables.

There are several important differences between CSM and other statistical procedures used to test mediation. CSM allows more flexibility in specifying different mediational models. Also, because CSM fits a single model to the data rather than requiring a series of analyses, it is possible to derive indices of model fit for the entire model. Finally, CSM allows researchers to specify latent variables and causal relations among them.

MODERATION. Moderational hypotheses can be tested in CSM in one of two ways. One method is through the use of interaction terms. When all variables in a model are single measured variables presumed to be perfect indicators of the constructs of interest, moderation can be tested using procedures analogous to those used in multiple regression (i.e., multiplicative products of the interacting variables). A model can then be specified that includes the IVs and the product of the IVs as causal influences on the DV(s) (along with correlations among the IV terms). Models of this sort are mathematically equivalent to regression models including interaction terms.

With multiple indicators of a latent variable, products of two or more latent variables would be a natural parallel to the single-indicator approach. There are potential advantages of specifying latent variable interaction models over measured variable interaction models. Busemeyer and Jones (1983) have demonstrated that product variables are less reliable than the component variables used to form them. Thus, it is often more difficult to detect moderator effects than direct causal effects (McClelland & Judd, 1993). Because latent variables do not include random error, interaction terms created from such variables have the potential to be more sensitive than measured-variable interaction terms.

Kenny and Judd (1984) proposed one approach to estimating interactions among latent variables (for alternative implementations of this general approach, see Hayduk, 1987; Jaccard & Wan, 1995). This approach involves computing all possible product terms between the indicators of the two latent variables presumed to interact with one another and then using these product terms as indicators of a latent variable multiplicative term. For example, imagine that a researcher has two latent variables (X and Z) each assessed by two measured variables (x_1, x_2, z_1, and z_2). Product terms would be computed between each x variable and each z variable (e.g., x_1z_1, x_1z_2, x_2z_1, x_2z_2). These four product terms would then be specified as indicators of a latent variable representing the XZ multiplicative term. Because variances of the product indicators depend on parameters in the measurement model associated with X and Z, this approach requires specifying a variety of additional latent variables influencing the indicators of the multiplicative term as well as some nonlinear constraints (Bollen, 1989; Kenny & Judd, 1984; Ping, 1996).

Although the Kenny and Judd (1984) method is conceptually sensible, there are practical limitations. First, the requirements of creating numerous product terms, additional latent variable error terms, and non-linear constraints in the model makes it complex and difficult to implement in all but the simplest models. Second, the complexity of the resulting model can lead to parameter estimation difficulties when fitting the model to the data (Ping, 1996).

An alternative two-step procedure proposed by Ping (1996) notes that, when sets of measured variables are influenced by only one latent variable, the estimates for parameters in the measurement model are unaffected by inclusion or exclusion of other latent variables. Therefore, Ping's procedure involves first specifying and fitting a measurement model for all latent variables other than the interaction latent variable. Because the loadings of product term indicators on the latent variable interaction term and the unique variances associated with product term indicators depend on values in the measurement model for the latent variables involved in the interaction, it is possible to compute these values from the parameter estimates provided by this measurement model. A second model is then specified that contains all latent variables including the "interaction" latent variable and the relations among these latent variables. This model specifies the structural model parameters (i.e., the impact of the two latent variables and the interaction latent variable on the dependent variable) as free parameters and the parameters in the measurement model as fixed parameters (with values estimated and/or calculated from the earlier measurement model). The estimates of the free structural parameters test the direct causal influences of the latent variables on the DV and whether one latent variable moderates the influence of the other latent variable.

The Ping (1996) approach is somewhat easier to program than the Kenny and Judd (1984) approach in that two simpler models are specified rather than a single extremely complex model. The approach might also be less prone to difficulties in parameter estimation. However, even this approach could prove difficult to implement with complex interaction models, because the number of parameters associated with the interaction latent variables is likely to become large, requiring numerous calculations and increasingly complex equations.

A considerably simpler approach, especially if a moderator is dichotomous, is to conduct a multisample CSM analysis (Jöreskog & Sorbom, 1988). This approach involves no computation of interaction variables and is analogous to the conduct of separate regression analyses at each level of a moderator. In this approach, a researcher categorizes participants according to the moderator. A covariance matrix among the measured variables other than the moderator variable is computed for each group. Then, a model specifying the IV(s) influencing the DV(s) is simultaneously fit to each of the matrices, and the parameter values for the model obtained from the different matrices are compared. Many programs (e.g., LISREL, EQS) permit CSM analysis in which a specified model is simultaneously fit to each group.

It is not meaningful to make comparisons of parameters in the structural model across groups unless equivalency of measurement model across groups is first established. The standard method of establishing equivalence is to constrain parameter estimates of the factor loadings to be equivalent across groups (Williams & Thomson, 1986). Therefore, researchers must begin by comparing a multisample model with no cross-group constraints to a model in which the measurement model is constrained to be equivalent across groups. If the constrained and unconstrained models do not differ significantly, measurement equivalence is assumed. The model with the equivalency of factor loading constraints is then used as the baseline model for subsequent tests of hypotheses regarding differences across groups in the structural model. The direct causal model of interest is specified and simultaneously fit to each group, allowing structural parameter estimates to vary across groups (the unconstrained model). Variation in the impact of the IV on the DV is tested by comparing the unconstrained model with a constrained model in which the path between the IV and the DV must be equivalent across groups. A significant difference in fit between the constrained and unconstrained models indicates that a moderation effect is present. It is regarded as more appropriate to conduct multisample analyses on covariance matrices rather than correlation matrices because variances of measured variables might differ across groups.

We have generally shown models in our figures that set the scale of measurement for latent variables by fixing their variance at 1.0 (a typical procedure in factor analysis). In multisample analysis, however, it is preferred that one set a latent variable's scale of measurement by allowing the variance of the latent variable to be free but fixing the path between the latent variable and one of its indicators at 1.0. This is preferred because it might not be reasonable to assume that the variance in factors will be the same across all groups (covariance rather than correlation matrices are used for similar reasons; Bielby, 1986; Williams & Thomson, 1986; Sobel & Arminger, 1986).

Multisample analyses provide a relatively simple and useful method for testing moderational hypotheses in CSM. However, there are certainly limitations. First, such analyses necessarily involve treating the moderator variable as categorical even if the moderator is measured on a continuous scale. This limitation exists because there will generally not be sufficient sample size to define a group for each score of the moderator variable. Additionally, even if the sample size is large enough, simultaneously fitting a model to many groups is extremely unwieldy and might pose difficulties to parameter estimation. A second limitation is that there is no way to represent the moderator variable as a latent variable in multisample analyses (because categorization of individuals on the moderator variable must be based on observed scores). Thus, some of the benefits of testing moderational hypotheses in CSM are lost (although it is still possible to treat other IVs and DVs as latent variables). Finally, multisample approaches become rather unwieldy for testing more complex moderational hypotheses (e.g., three-way interactions) because the number of groups becomes large and no direct overall test exists for more than a single moderator.

Hybrid hypotheses can also be tested in CSM. The most feasible way of addressing *moderated mediation* questions would be through multisample analysis strategies. That is, a researcher can specify the mediational model of interest and then simultaneously fit the model to covariance matrices for different groups (determined by scores on a moderator). Tests between groups on the paths in the structural model can then be conducted by including constraints in the model. Using latent variables, there is no feasible way of testing the first type of *mediated moderation* (where the mediator also serves as the moderator). Though never extensively discussed, the CSM approaches for simple moderation (e.g., Kenny & Judd, 1984; Ping, 1996) could potentially be extended by making the DV in those analyses into a mediator predicting a subsequent DV (in order to test the second type of mediated moderation). CSM could also implement regression-like tests of moderated mediation and mediated moderation when single rather than multiple indicators of constructs are used.

A final class of hypotheses that has not been previously discussed is moderation of noncausal relations among constructs of interest. In some cases, a researcher might be interested in examining differences in the factor loadings of a model across different groups, differences in the unique variances across groups, or differences in the correlations among factors across groups. Such hypotheses can be tested by multisample CFA. For example, Judd and Krosnick (1982) investigated a number of conceptual and methodological reasons why important rather than unimportant attitudes

might be more likely to correlate highly with one another. The procedures and computer software for multisample CFA would be the same as for multisample CSM.

Design Issues in the Use of CSM

Careful consideration of study design can greatly enhance the utility of results obtained from CSM. Many of the design issues in CFA, such as selection of measured variables and the nature and size of the sample, are equally relevant to CSM. However, because CSM generally involves formulating models that postulate certain causal relations among latent variables, additional considerations are necessary. Most notably, a researcher should consider how design features might strengthen the basis for making causal inferences. Experimental manipulation of key constructs provides a strong basis for causal inferences. Also, incorporating longitudinal features into the design can sometimes assist in establishing conditions of causality, though time ordering alone is often insufficient (MacCallum et al., 1993; West et al., this volume, Ch. 3).

CSM has proven to be one of the most important developments in quantitative methodology over the past 30 years. CSM can be used to specify a wide range of models involving direct causal or mediational relations among measured variables and latent variables. Many of these models would be difficult and sometimes impossible to specify in other common methods of analysis such as multiple regression and ANOVA.

SUMMARY OF METHODS ADDRESSING CAUSE

A variety of approaches can be brought to bear on hypotheses of cause in nonexperimental data. The techniques most commonly used (multiple regression, HLM, CSM) afford researchers some leverage in making a case for causal impact of the hypothesized IV(s).

Regression utilizes a rather simple mathematical model, but complex interaction effects fit easily within the framework, and it can be adapted to various mediational and moderational questions (Judd, this volume, Ch. 14; Kenny et al., 1998). Moreover, regression analyses can often be usefully applied with relatively small samples (at least substantially smaller than typically recommended for more complex analyses, such as CSM). Related to the conditions of isolation, association, and direction, the primary benefit of multiple regression is an increase in ability to isolate effects of the proposed IV on the DV. By measuring and statistically controlling alternative influences on the DV, confidence may increase that the influence of an IV is not due to other constructs included in the model. Overall confidence in the causal impact of the IV increases to the extent that all plausible alternative causes are included in the model. Because association assumes relation between the IV and the DV separate from alternative influences on the DV, increasing isolation also aids in meeting the condition of association. Especially compared to techniques limited to categorical IV's (e.g., ANOVA), the ability of regression to utilize continuous measures of IV's increases the ability to find associations between IV and DV.

However, regression also has limitations in this regard. Measures are treated as perfect (errorless) indicators of the constructs under study, though there is almost always some error in psychological measures. Such errors create underestimation of relations between constructs, and thus limit the extent to which complete partialing can take place. In addition to (lack of) representation of error in the model, regression techniques can be cumbersome for many kinds of advanced research questions. Even simple mediation questions require several regressions, and this gets more complex as the number of mediators increases.

The primary benefits of HLM for addressing issues of causation are largely shared with the traditional regression technique. Of course, to the extent that the hierarchical approach improves estimation and testing of certain effects (because of error terms for lower-level slopes and intercepts, see Reis & Gable, this volume, Ch. 8), they are better able to isolate effects and establish association. The utility of regression and HLM rests heavily on the ability of researchers to include in the model alternative influences on the DV that can be statistically controlled. Of course, such techniques are only successful to the extent that alternative causes of variation in the DV are exhaustively represented and measured well. Statistical techniques will be unable to isolate hypothesized influences on the DV when poor measures are utilized or alternative plausible causes are omitted (see Wegener et al., 1995).

The CSM latent-variable approach facilitates isolating causes and finding associations between IVs and DVs by accounting for random error in the model. When measures contain random error, relations among IVs are underestimated. Because latent variables are free of random error, CSM affords better statistical control of other IVs in the model, thereby allowing a researcher to more effectively establish the condition of isolation. The ability to establish association can also be improved through the use of latent variables. In addition to leading to underestimation of relations among IVs, random error also attenuates

relations between IVs and DVs. Thus, random error can mask true relations between IVs and DVs. The analysis of latent variables can help alleviate this problem. Inclusion of random error in the model is also more realistic than assuming an absence of error, especially in the analysis of psychological data.

Most common statistical procedures (e.g., regression) are used for parameter estimation (e.g., to assess the impact of an IV on a DV) and are based on mathematical models that are nonfalsifiable (i.e., for which fit of the overall model cannot be assessed). Although parameter estimation is extremely useful, in some contexts a researcher might also be interested in assessing the plausibility of a hypothesized pattern of relations among constructs. CSM allows a researcher to specify falsifiable models and provides a wide variety of model fit indices to address such questions. Model fit can also be useful when a researcher wishes to compare two models that postulate different directional relations among constructs. Thus, CSM affords some advantage in assessing the condition of directionality (though the existence of equivalent or near equivalent models will sometimes limit this potential advantage). As noted repeatedly in this volume, design features of the study (e.g., manipulation of crucial hypothesized causal factors) often have the most direct impact on the causal inferences that researchers can make.

REFERENCES

Abelson, R. P., Kinder, D. T., Peters, M. D., & Fiske, S. T. (1982). Affective and semantic components in political person perception. *Journal of Personality and Social Psychology, 42*, 619–630.

Aiken, L. S., & West, S. G. (1991). *Multiple regression: Testing and interpreting interactions.* Newbury Park, CA: Sage.

Anderson, J. C., & Gerbing, D. W. (1984). The effect of sampling error on convergence, improper solutions, and goodness of fit indices for maximum likelihood factor analysis. *Psychometrika, 49*, 155–173.

Anderson, J. C., & Gerbing, D. W. (1988). Structural equation modeling in practice: A review and recommended two-step approach. *Psychological Bulletin, 103*, 411–423.

Arabie, P., Carroll, J. D., & DeSarbo, W. S. (1987). *Three-way scaling and clustering.* Beverly Hills, CA: Sage.

Arabie, P., & Hubert, L. J. (1992). Combinatorial data analysis. *Annual Review of Psychology, 43*, 169–203.

Baron, R. M., & Kenny, D. A. (1986). The moderator-mediator distinction in social psychological research: Conceptual, strategic, and statistical considerations. *Journal of Personality and Social Psychology, 51*, 1173–1182.

Bentler, P. M. (1980). Multivariate analysis with latent variables: Causal modeling. *Annual Review of Psychology, 31*, 419–456.

Bentler, P. M., & Bonett, D. G. (1980). Significance tests and goodness of fit in the analysis of covariance structures. *Psychological Bulletin, 88*, 588–606.

Berkowitz, L. (1989). Frustration–aggression hypothesis: Examination and reformulation. *Psychological Bulletin, 106*, 59–73.

Bielby, W. T. (1986). Arbitrary metrics in multiple-indicator models of latent variables. *Sociological Methods and Research, 15*, 3–23.

Bock, R. D. (1960). Components of variance analysis as a structural and discriminal analysis of psychological tests. *The British Journal of Statistical Psychology, 13*, 151–163.

Bollen, K. A. (1989). *Structural equations with latent variables.* New York: Wiley.

Bollen, K. A., & Lennox, R. (1991). Conventional wisdom on measurement: A structural equation perspective. *Psychological Bulletin, 110*, 305–314.

Borg, I., & Groenen, P. (1997). *Modern multidimensional scaling.* New York: Springer-Verlag.

Breckler, S. J. (1984). Empirical validation of affect, behavior, and cognition as distinct components of attitude. *Journal of Personality and Social Psychology, 47*, 1191–1205.

Breckler, S. J. (1990). Applications of covariance structure modeling in psychology: Cause for concern? *Psychological Bulletin, 107*, 260–273.

Browne, M. W. (1972). Oblique rotation to a partially specified target. *British Journal of Mathematical and Statistical Psychology, 25*, 207–212.

Browne, M. W. (1974). Generalized least-squares estimators in the analysis of covariance structures. *South African Statistical Journal, 8*, 1–24.

Browne, M. W. (1982). Covariance structures. In D. M. Hawkins (Ed.), *Topics in multivariate analysis* (pp. 72–141). Cambridge, England: Cambridge University Press.

Browne, M. W. (1984a). Asymptotically distribution-free methods for the analysis of covariance structures. *British Journal of Mathematical and Statistical Psychology, 37*, 62–83.

Browne, M. W. (1984b). The decomposition of multitrait-multimethod matrices. *British Journal of Mathematical and Statistical Psychology, 37*, 1–21.

Browne, M. W. (1989). Relationships between an additive model and a multiplicative model for multitrait-multimethod matrices. In R. Coppi & S. Bolasco (Eds.), *Multiway data analysis* (pp. 507–520). North-Holland: Elsevier Science Publishers.

Browne, M. W. (1990). Asymptotic robustness of normal theory methods for analysis of latent curves. *Contemporary Mathematics, 112*, 211–225.

Browne, M. W. (1992a). Circumplex models for correlation matrices. *Psychometrika, 57*, 469–497.

Browne, M. W. (1992b). *FITMOD: A computer program for calculating point and interval estimates of fit measures.* Columbus: Ohio State University.

Browne, M. W. (1992c). *MUTMUM user's guide.* Columbus: Ohio State University.

Browne, M. W. (1993). Models for multitrait-multimethod matrices. In R. Steyer, K. F. Wender, & K. F. Widaman (Eds.), *Psychometric methodology: Proceedings of the 7th European meeting of the Psychometric Society in Trier* (pp. 61–73). Stuttgart, Germany: Gustav Fischer Verlag.

Browne, M. W., & Cudeck, R. (1989). Single sample cross-validation indices for covariance structures. *Multivariate Behavioral Research, 24*, 445–455.

Browne, M. W., & Cudeck, R. (1992). Alternative ways of assessing model fit. *Sociological Methods and Research, 21*, 230–258.

Browne, M. W., Cudeck, R., Tateneni, K., & Mels, G. (1998). *CEFA: Comprehensive exploratory factor analysis.* Columbus: Ohio State University.

Browne, M. W., & Du Toit, S. H. C. (1992). Automated fitting of nonstandard models. *Multivariate Behavioral Research, 27*, 269–300.

Browne, M. W., & Shapiro, A. (1988). Robustness of normal theory methods in the analysis of linear latent variate models. *British Journal of Mathematical and Statistical Psychology, 41*, 193–208.

Bryk, A. S., & Raudenbush, S. W. (1992). *Hierarchical linear models: Applications and data analysis methods.* Newbury Park, CA: Sage.

Burger, J. M., & Cooper, H. M. (1979). The desirability of control. *Motivation and Emotion, 3*, 381–393.

Busemeyer, J. R., & Jones, L. E. (1983). Analysis of multiplicative combination rules when causal variables are measured with error. *Psychological Bulletin, 93*, 549–563.

Cacioppo, J. T., & Berntson, G. G. (1994). Relationship between attitudes and evaluative space: A critical review, with emphasis on the separability of positive and negative substrates. *Psychological Bulletin, 115*, 401–423.

Campbell, D. T., & Fiske, D. W. (1959). Convergent and discriminant validation by the multitrait-multimethod matrix. *Psychological Bulletin, 56*, 81–105.

Campbell, D. T., & O'Connell, E. J. (1967). Method factors in multitrait-multimethod matrices: Multiplicative rather than additive? *Multivariate Behavioral Research, 2*, 409–426.

Campbell, D. T., & O'Connell, E. J. (1982). Methods as diluting trait relationships rather than adding irrelevant systematic variance. In D. Brinberg & L. Kidder (Eds.), *New directions for methodology of social and behavioral science: Forms of validity in research* (Vol. 12, pp. 93–111). San Francisco: Jossey-Bass.

Carroll, J. D., & Arabie, P. (1980). Multidimensional scaling. *Annual Review of Psychology, 31*, 607–649.

Carroll, J. D., & Wish, M. (1974). Models and methods for three-way multidimensional scaling. In D. H. Krantz, R. C. Atkinson, R. D. Luce, & P. Suppes (Eds.), *Contemporary developments in mathematical psychology: Measurement, psychophysics, and neural information processing* (Vol. 2, pp. 57–105). San Francisco: W. H. Freeman.

Cattell, R. B. (1966). The scree test for the number of factors. *Multivariate Behavioral Research, 1*, 245–276.

Chaiken, S., & Trope, Y. (Eds.). (1999). *Dual-process theories in social psychology.* New York: Guilford Press.

Chou, C., & Bentler, P. M. (1995). Estimates and tests in structural equation modeling. In R. H. Hoyle (Ed.),

Structural equation modeling: Concepts, issues, and applications (pp. 37–55). Newbury Park, CA: Sage.

Cliff, N. (1983). Some cautions concerning the application of causal modeling methods. *Multivariate Behavioral Research, 18,* 115–126.

Cohen, J., & Cohen, P. (1983). *Applied multiple regression/correlation analysis for the behavioral sciences (2nd ed.).* Hillsdale, NJ: Erlbaum.

Coovert, M. D., Craiger, J. P., & Teachout, M. S. (1997). Effectiveness of the direct product versus confirmatory factor model for reflecting the structure of multimethod-multirater job performance data. *Journal of Applied Psychology, 82,* 271–280.

Crites, S. L. Jr., Fabrigar, L. R., & Petty, R. E. (1994). Measuring the affective and cognitive properties of attitudes: Conceptual and methodological issues. *Personality and Social Psychology Bulletin, 20,* 619–634.

Cudeck, R. (1988). Multiplicative models and MTMM matrices. *Journal of Educational Statistics, 13,* 131–147.

Cudeck, R., & O'Dell, L. L. (1994). Applications of standard error estimates in unrestricted factor analysis: Significance tests for factor loadings and correlations. *Psychological Bulletin, 115,* 475–487.

Curran, P. J., West, S. G., & Finch, J. F. (1996). The robustness of test statistics to nonnormality and specification error in confirmatory factor analysis. *Psychological Methods, 1,* 16–29.

D'Agostino, R. B. (1986). Tests for the normal distribution. In R. B. D'Agostino & M. A. Stephens (Eds.), *Goodness-of-fit techniques* (pp. 367–390). New York: Dekker.

DeSteno, D., Petty, R. E., Wegener, D. T., & Rucker, D. D. (in press). Beyond valence in the perception of likelihood: The role of emotion specificity. *Journal of Personality and Social Psychology.*

DeSteno, D. A., & Salovey, P. (1997). The effects of mood on the structure of the self-concept. *Cognition and Emotion, 11,* 351–372.

Dielman, T. E., Cattell, R. B., & Wagner, A. (1972). Evidence on the simple structure and factor invariance achieved by five rotational methods on four types of data. *Multivariate Behavioral Research, 7,* 223–242.

Fabrigar, L. R., Visser, P. S., & Browne, M. W. (1997). Conceptual and methodological issues in testing the circumplex structure of data in personality and social psychology. *Personality and Social Psychology Review, 1,* 184–203.

Fabrigar, L. R., Wegener, D. T., MacCallum R. C., & Strahan, E. J. (1999). Evaluating the use of factor analysis in psychological research. *Psychological Methods, 4,* 272–299.

Fazio, R. H. (1990). Multiple processes by which attitudes guide behavior: The MODE model as an integrative framework. In M. P. Zanna (Ed.), *Advances in experimental social psychology* (vol. 23, pp. 75–109). San Diego, CA: Academic Press.

Feldman, L. A. (1995). Valence focus and arousal focus: Individual differences in the structure of affective experience. *Journal of Personality and Social Psychology, 69,* 153–166.

Finch, J. F., & West, S. G. (1997). The investigation of personality structure: Statistical models. *Journal of Research in Personality, 31,* 439–485.

Ford, J. K., MacCallum, R. C., & Tait, M. (1986). The application of exploratory factor analysis in applied psychology: A critical review and analysis. *Personnel Psychology, 39,* 291–314.

Goffin, R. D., & Jackson, D. N. (1992). Analysis of multitrait-multirater performance appraisal data: Composite direct product method versus confirmatory factor analysis. *Multivariate Behavioral Research, 27,* 363–385.

Goldstein, H. (1995). *Multilevel statistical models* (2nd ed.). New York: Halsted.

Gorsuch, R. L. (1970). A comparison of biquartimin, maxplane, promax, and varimax. *Educational and Psychological Measurement, 30,* 861–872.

Gorsuch, R. L. (1983). *Factor analysis* (2nd ed.). Hillsdale, NJ: Erlbaum.

Gower, J. C. (1975). Generalized Procrustes analysis. *Psychometrika, 40,* 33–51.

Guertin, A. S., Guertin, W. H., & Ware, W. B. (1981). Distortion as a function of the number of factors rotated under varying levels of common variance and error. *Educational and Psychological Measurement, 41,* 1–9.

Hakstian, A. R. (1971). A comparative evaluation of several prominent methods of oblique factor transformation. *Psychometrika, 36,* 175–193.

Hakstian, A. R., Rogers, W. T., & Cattell, R. B. (1982). The behavior of number-of-factors rules with simulated data. *Multivariate Behavioral Research, 17,* 193–219.

Halberstadt, J. B., & Niedenthal, P. M. (1997). Emotional state and the use of stimulus dimensions in judgment. *Journal of Personality and Social Psychology, 72,* 1017–1033.

Harris, C. W. (1967). On factors and factor scores. *Psychometrika, 32,* 363–379.

Harris, M. L., & Harris, C. W. (1971). A factor analytic interpretation strategy. *Educational and Psychological Measurement, 31,* 589–606.

Harris, C. W., & Kaiser, H. F. (1964). Oblique factor analytic solutions by orthogonal transformations. *Psychometrika, 29,* 347–362.

Harshman, R. A. (1984). "How can I know if it's real?" A catalog of diagnostics for use with three-mode factor analysis and multidimensional scaling. In H. G. Law, C. W. Snyder, Jr., J. A. Hattie, & R. P. McDonald (Eds.), *Research methods for multimode data analysis.* New York: Praeger.

Hayduk, L. A. (1987). *Structural equation modeling with LISREL: Essentials and advances.* Baltimore, MD: Johns Hopkins Press.

Hendrickson, A. E., & White, P. O. (1964). Promax: A quick method for rotation to oblique simple structure. *British Journal of Statistical Psychology, 17,* 65–70.

Holland, P. W. (1986). Statistics and causal inference. *Journal of the American Statistical Association, 81,* 945–960.

Horn, J. L. (1965). A rationale and technique for estimating the number of factors in factor analysis. *Psychometrika, 30,* 179–185.

Hoyle, R. H. (Ed.). (1995). *Structural equation modeling: Concepts, issues, and applications.* Thousand Oaks, CA: Sage.

Hu, L., & Bentler, P. M. (1998). Fit indices in covariance structure modeling: Sensitivity to underparameterized model misspecification. *Psychological Methods, 3,* 424–453.

Hu, L., Bentler, P. M., & Kano, Y. (1992). Can test statistics in covariance structure analysis be trusted? *Psychological Bulletin, 112,* 351–362.

Humphreys, L. G., & Montanelli, R. G., Jr. (1975). A investigation of the parallel analysis criterion for determining the number of common factors. *Multivariate Behavioral Research, 10,* 193–205.

Isaac, P. D., & Poor, D. D. S. (1974). On the determination of appropriate dimensionality in data with error. *Psychometrika, 39,* 91–109.

Jaccard, J., & Wan, C. K. (1995). Measurement error in the analysis of interaction effects between continuous predictors using multiple regression: Multiple indicator and structural equation approaches. *Psychological Bulletin, 117,* 348–357.

Jain, A. K., & Dubes, R. C. (1988). *Algorithms for clustering data.* Englewood Cliffs, NJ: Prentice-Hall.

James, L. R., & Brett, J. M. (1984). Mediators, moderators, and tests for mediation. *Journal of Applied Psychology, 69,* 307–321.

Jennrich, R. I., & Sampson, P. F. (1966). Rotation for simple loadings. *Psychometrika, 31,* 313–323.

John, O. P. (1990). The "Big Five" factor taxonomy: Dimensions of personality in the natural language and in questionnaires. In L. A. Pervin (Ed.), *Handbook of personality: Theory and research* (pp. 66–100). New York: Guilford Press.

Joreskog, K. G., & Sorbom, D. (1988). *LISREL 7: A guide to the program and applications.* Chicago: SPSS, Inc.

Judd, C. M., & Kenny, D. A. (1981). *Estimating the effects of social interventions.* New York: Cambridge University Press.

Judd, C. M., & Krosnick, J. A. (1982). Attitude centrality, organization, and measurement. *Journal of Personality and Social Psychology, 42,* 436–447.

Judd, C. M., & McClelland, G. H. (1998). Measurement. In D. Gilbert, S. Fiske, & G. Lindzey (Eds.), *The handbook of social psychology* (4th ed., pp. 180–232). New York: McGraw-Hill.

Kaiser, H. F. (1958). The varimax criterion for analytic rotation in factor analysis. *Psychometrika, 23,* 187–200.

Kaiser, H. F. (1970). A second generation of Little-Jiffy. *Psychometrika, 35,* 401–415.

Kaplan, D. (1995). Statistical power in structural equation modeling. In R. H. Hoyle (Ed.), *Structural equation modeling: Concepts, issues, and applications* (pp. 100–117). Thousand Oaks, CA: Sage.

Kenny, D. A., & Judd, C. M. (1984). Estimating the nonlinear and interactive effects of latent variables. *Psychological Bulletin, 96,* 201–210.

Kenny, D. A., Kashy, D. A., & Bolger, N. (1998). Data analysis in social psychology. In D. T. Gilbert, S. T. Fiske, & G. Lindzey (Eds.), *Handbook of social psychology* (4th ed.), Vol. 1, pp. 233–265. New York: McGraw-Hill.

Krosnick, J. A. (1988). The role of attitude importance in social evaluation: A study of policy preferences, presidential candidate evaluations, and voting behavior. *Journal of Personality and Social Psychology, 55,* 196–211.

Kruskal, J. B. (1964). Multidimensional scaling by optimizing goodness of fit to a nonmetric hypothesis. *Psychometrika, 29,* 1–27.

Kruskal, J. B., & Wish, M. (1978). *Multidimensional scaling.* Newbury Park, CA: Sage.

Larsen, R. J., & Diener, E. (1987). Affect intensity as an individual difference characteristic: A review. *Journal of Research in Personality, 21,* 1–39.

Larsen, R. J., & Diener, E. (1992). Promises and problems with the circumplex model of emotion. In M. S. Clark (Ed.), *Review of personality and social psychology: Emotion* (Vol. 13, pp. 25–59). Newbury Park, CA: Sage.

Lawley, D. N. (1940). The estimation of factor loadings by the method of maximum likelihood. *Proceedings of the Royal Society of Edinburgh, Section A, 60,* 64–82.

Lee, S., & Hershberger, S. (1990). A simple rule for generating equivalent models in covariance structure modeling. *Multivariate Behavioral Research, 25,* 313–334.

Loehlin, J. C. (1990). Component analysis versus common factor analysis: A case of disputed authorship. *Multivariate Behavioral Research, 25,* 29–31.

Longman, R. S., Cota, A. A., Holden, R. R., & Fekken, G. C. (1989). A regression equation for parallel analysis criterion in principal components analysis: Mean and 95th percentile eigen values. *Multivariate Behavioral Research, 24,* 59–69.

Lorr, M. (1983). *Cluster analysis for social scientists.* San Francisco: Jossey-Bass.

MacCallum, R. C. (1974). Relations between factor analysis and multidimensional scaling. *Psychological Bulletin, 81,* 505–516.

MacCallum, R. C. (1977). Effects of conditionality on INDSCAL and ALSCAL weights. *Psychometrica, 42,* 297–305.

MacCallum, R. C. (1986). Specification searches in covariance structure modeling. *Psychological Bulletin, 100,* 107–120.

MacCallum, R. C. (1988). Multidimensional scaling. In J. R. Nesselroade & R. B. Cattell (Eds.), *Handbook of multivariate experimental psychology* (2nd ed.), pp. 421–445. New York: Plenum Press.

MacCallum, R. C. (1990). The need for alternative measures of fit in covariance structure modeling. *Multivariate Behavioral Research, 25,* 157–162.

MacCallum, R. C. (1995). Model specification: Procedures, strategies, and related issues. In R. H. Hoyle (Ed.), *Structural equation modeling: Concepts, issues, and applications* (pp. 16–36). Newbury Park, CA: Sage.

MacCallum, R. C., & Browne, M. W. (1993). The use of causal indicators in covariance structure models: Some practical issues. *Psychological Bulletin, 114,* 533–541.

MacCallum, R. C., Browne, M. W., & Sugawara, H. M. (1996). Power analysis and determination of sample size for covariance structure modeling. *Psychological Methods, 1,* 130–149.

MacCallum, R. C., & Cornelius, E. T., III. (1977). A Monte Carlo investigation of recovery of structure by ALSCAL. *Psychometrika, 42*, 401–427.

MacCallum, R. C., & Hong, S. (1997). Power analysis in covariance structure modeling using GFI and AGFI. *Multivariate Behavioral Research, 32*, 193–210.

MacCallum, R. C., Kim, C., Malarkey, W. B., & Kiecolt-Glaser, J. K. (1997). Studying multivariate change using multilevel models and latent curve models. *Multivariate Behavioral Research, 32*, 215–253.

MacCallum, R. C., Roznowski, M., & Necowitz, L. B. (1992). Model modifications in covariance structure analysis: The problem of capitalization on chance. *Psychological Bulletin, 111*, 490–504.

MacCallum, R. C., Wegener, D. T., Uchino, B. N., & Fabrigar, L. R. (1993). The problem of equivalent models in applications of covariance structure analysis. *Psychological Bulletin, 114*, 185–199.

MacCallum, R. C., Widaman, K. F., Zhang, S., & Hong, S. (1999). Sample size in factor analysis. *Psychological Methods, 4*, 84–99.

Mardia, K. V. (1970). Measures of multivariate skewness and kurtosis with applications. *Biometrika, 57*, 519–530.

Marsh, H. W., & Grayson, D. (1995). Latent variable models for multitrait-multimethod data. In R. H. Hoyle (Ed.), *Structural equation modeling: Concepts, issues, and applications* (pp. 177–198). Thousand Oaks, CA: Sage.

McClelland, G. H., & Judd, C. M. (1993). Statistical difficulties of detecting interactions and moderator effects. *Psychological Bulletin, 114*, 376–390.

Montanelli, R. G., & Humphreys, L. G., (1976). Latent roots of random data correlations matrices with squared multiple correlations on the diagonal: A Monte Carlo study. *Psychometrika, 41*, 341–348.

Mulaik, S. A., James, L. R., Van Alstine, J., Bennett, N., Lind, S., & Stilwell, C. D. (1989). Evaluation of goodness-of-fit indices for structural equation models. *Psychological Bulletin, 105*, 430–445.

Murtagh, F. (1985). *Multidimensional clustering algorithms.* Vienna, Austria: Physica-Verlag.

Muthén, B. (1987). *LISCOMP: Analysis of linear structural equations with a comprehensive measurement model.* Mooresville, IN: Scientific Software, Inc.

Muthén, B. (1993). Goodness of fit with categorical and other nonnormal variables. In K. A. Bollen & J. S. Long (Eds.), *Testing structural equation models* (pp. 204–234). Newbury Park, CA: Sage.

Nunnally, J. C. (1978). Psychometric theory (2nd ed.). New York: McGraw-Hill.

Osgood, C. E., Suci, G. J., & Tannenbaum, P. H. (1957). *The measurement of meaning.* Urbana, IL: University of Illinois Press.

Ostrom, T. M. (1969). The relationship between the affective, behavioral, and cognitive components of attitude. *Journal of Experimental Social Psychology, 5*, 12–30.

Petty, R. E., & Cacioppo, J. T. (1986). *Communication and persuasion: Central and peripheral routes to attitude change.* New York, NY: Springer-Verlag.

Petty, R. E., Cacioppo, J. T., & Goldman, R. (1981). Personal involvement as a determinant of argument-based persuasion. *Journal of Personality and Social Psychology, 41*, 847–855.

Petty, R. E., Cacioppo, J. T., & Schumann, D. (1983). Central and peripheral routes to advertising effectiveness: The moderating role of involvement. *Journal of Consumer Research, 10*, 135–146.

Petty, R. E., Schumann, D., Richman, S., & Strathman, A. (1993). Positive mood and persuasion: Different roles for affect under high and low elaboration conditions. *Journal of Personality and Social Psychology, 64*, 5–20.

Petty, R. E., Wegener, D. T., Fabrigar, L. R., Priester, J. R., & Cacioppo, J. T. (1993). Conceptual and methodological issues in the Elaboration Likelihood Model of persuasion: A reply to the Michigan State critics. *Communication Theory, 3*, 336–363.

Ping, R. A. (1996). Latent variable interaction and quadratic effect estimation: A two-step technique using structural equation analysis. *Psychological Bulletin, 119*, 166–175.

Platt, J. (1964). Strong inference. *Science, 146*, 347–353.

Raykov, T., & Widaman, K. F. (1995). Issues in applied structural equation modeling research. *Structural Equation Modeling, 2*, 289–318.

Romney, D. M., & Bynner, J. M. (1997). Evaluating a circumplex model of personality disorders with structural equation modeling. In R. Plutchik & H. R. Conte (Eds.), *Circumplex models of personality and emotions* (pp. 327–346). Washington, DC: American Psychological Association.

Rosenberg, M. J., & Hovland, C. I. (1960). Cognitive, affective, and behavioral components of attitudes. In C. I. Hovland & M. J. Rosenberg (Eds.), *Attitude organization and change: An analysis of consistency among attitude components* (pp. 1–14). New Haven, CT: Yale University Press.

Rusbult, C. E., Onizuka, R. K., & Lipkus, I. (1993). What do we really want?: Mental models of ideal romantic involvement explored through multidimensional scaling. *Journal of Experimental Social Psychology, 29*, 493–527.

Rusbult, C. E., & Zembrodt, I. M. (1983). Responses to dissatisfaction in romantic involvements: A multidimensional scaling analysis. *Journal of Experimental Social Psychology, 19*, 274–293.

Saris, W. E., & Satorra, A. (1993). Power evaluations in structural equation models. In K. A. Bollen & J. S. Long (Eds.), *Testing structural equation models* (pp. 181–204). Newbury Park, CA: Sage.

Satorra, A., & Bentler, P. M. (1994). Corrections to test statistics and standard errors in covariance structure analysis. In A. Von Eye & C. C. Clogg (Eds.), *Analysis of latent variables in developmental research* (pp. 399–419). Newbury Park, CA: Sage.

Satorra, A., & Saris, W. E. (1985). The power of the likelihood ratio test in covariance structure analysis. *Psychometrika, 50*, 83–90.

Schiffman, S. S., Reynolds, M. L., & Young, F. W. (1981). *Introduction to multidimensional scaling: Theory, methods, and applications.* New York: Academic Press.

Schmitt, N., & Stults, D. M. (1986). Methodological review: Analysis of multitrait-multimethod matrices. *Applied Psychological Measurement, 10*, 1–22.

Schumacker, R. E., & Lomax, R. G. (1996). *A beginner's guide to structural equation modeling.* Hillsdale, NJ: Erlbaum.

Snook, S. C., & Gorsuch, R. L. (1989). Component analysis versus common factor analysis: A Monte Carlo study. *Psychological Bulletin, 106*, 148–154.

Sobel, M. E., & Arminger, G. (1986). Platonic and operational true scores in covariance structure analysis. *Sociological Methods and Research, 15*, 44–58.

Steiger, J. H. (1990). Some additional thoughts on components, factors, and factor indeterminacy. *Multivariate Behavioral Research, 25*, 41–45.

Steiger, J. H., & Lind, J. (1980). *Statistically based tests for the number of common factors.* Paper presented at the annual meeting of the Psychometric Society, Iowa City.

Stelzl, I. (1986). Changing a causal hypothesis without changing the fit: Some rules for generating equivalent path models. *Multivariate Behavioral Research, 21*, 309–331.

Swain, A. J. (1975). *Analysis of parametric structures for variance matrices.* Unpublished doctoral dissertation. University of Adelaide, Adelaide, Australia.

Takane, Y., Young, F. W., & De Leeuw, J. (1977). Nonmetric individual differences multidimensional scaling: An alternating least-squares method with optimal scaling features. *Psychometrika, 46*, 389–405.

Tanaka, J. S. (1987). "How big is big enough?": Sample size and goodness of fit in structural equation models with latent variables. *Child Development, 58*, 134–146.

Tanaka, J. S. (1993). Multifaceted conceptions of fit in structural equation models. In K. A. Bollen & J. S. Long (Eds.), *Testing structural equation models* (pp. 10–39). Newbury Park, CA: Sage.

Thurstone, L. L. (1947). *Multiple factor analysis.* Chicago: University of Chicago Press.

Tucker, L. R., Koopman, R. F., & Linn, R. L. (1969). Evaluation of factor analytic research procedures by means of simulated correlation matrices. *Psychometrika, 34*, 421–459.

Tucker, L. R., & Lewis, C. (1973). A reliability coefficient for maximum likelihood factor analysis. *Psychometrika, 38*, 1–10.

Tucker, L. R., & MacCallum, R. C. (1997). *Exploratory factor analysis.* Unpublished manuscript.

Velicer, W. F., & Fava, J. L. (1998). Effects of variable and subject sampling on factor pattern recovery. *Psychological Methods, 3*, 231–251.

Visser, P. S. Fabrigar, L. R. Wegener, D. T. & Browne M. W. (1998). *Analyzing multitrait-multimethod data in personality and social psychology.* In preparation. Princeton, NJ: Princeton University.

Wagenaar, W. A., & Padmos, P. (1971). Quantitative interpretation of stress in Kruskal's multidimensional scaling technique. *British Journal of Mathematical and Statistical Psychology, 24*, 101–110.

Watson, D., & Tellegen, A. (1985). Toward a consensual structure of mood. *Psychological Bulletin, 98*, 219–235.

Wegener, D. T., Downing, J., Krosnick, J. A., & Petty, R. E. (1995). Strength-related properties of attitudes: Measures, manipulations, and future directions. In R. E. Petty and J. A. Krosnick (Eds.), *Attitude strength: Antecedents and consequences* (pp. 455–487). Mahwah, NJ: Erlbaum.

Wegener, D. T., Petty, R. E., & Smith, S. M. (1995). Positive mood can increase or decrease message scrutiny: The hedonic contingency view of mood and message processing. *Journal of Personality and Social Psychology, 69*, 5–15.

Weinberg, S. L., & Carroll, J. D. (1992). Multidimensional scaling: An overview with applications in educational research. In B. Thompson (Ed.), *Advances in social science methodology* (Vol. 2, pp. 99–135). Stamford, CT: JAI Press.

West, S. G., Finch, J. F., & Curran, P. J. (1995). Structural equation models with nonnormal variables: Problems and remedies. In R. H. Hoyle (Ed.), *Structural equation modeling: Concepts, issues and applications* (pp. 56–75). Newbury Park, CA: Sage.

Widaman, K. F. (1985). Hierarchically tested covariance structure models for multitrait-multimethod data. *Applied Psychological Measurement, 9*, 1–26.

Widaman, K. F. (1990). Bias in pattern loadings represented by common factor analysis and component analysis. *Multivariate Behavioral Research, 25*, 89–95.

Widaman, K. F. (1993). Common factor analysis versus principal component analysis: Differential bias in representing model parameters? *Multivariate Behavioral Research, 28*, 263–311.

Wiggins, J. S. (1980). Circumplex models of interpersonal behavior. In L. Wheeler (Ed.), *Review of personality and social psychology* (Vol. 1, pp. 265–294). Beverly Hills, CA: Sage.

Williams, R., & Thomson, E. (1986). Normalization issues in latent variable modeling. *Sociological Methods and Research, 15*, 24–43.

Wish, M., & Carroll, J. D. (1974). Applications from individual differences scaling to studies of human perception and judgment. In E. C. Carterette & M. P. Friedman (Eds.), *Handbook of perception* (Vol. 2, pp. 449–491). New York: Academic Press.

Wood, J. M., Tataryn, D. J., & Gorsuch, R. L. (1996). Effects of under- and overextraction on principal axis factor analysis with varimax rotation. *Psychological Methods, 1*, 354–365.

Wothke, W. (1984). *The estimation of trait and method components in multitrait–multimethod measurement.* Unpublished doctoral dissertation, University of Chicago.

Wothke, W. (1996). Covariance components analysis of the multitrait-multimethod matrix. In P. E. Shrout & S. T. Fiske (Eds.), *Personality research, methods, and theory: A festschrift honoring Donald W. Fiske* (pp. 125–144). Hillsdale, NJ: Erlbaum.

Wothke, W., & Browne, M. W. (1990). The direct product model for the MTMM matrix parameterized as a second order factor analysis model. *Psychometrika, 55*, 255–262.

Young, F. W. (1984). Scaling. *Annual Review of Psychology, 35*, 55–81.

CHAPTER SEVENTEEN

The Analysis of Data from Dyads and Groups

DEBORAH A. KASHY AND DAVID A. KENNY

Much of social psychological theory and research studies individuals. This individualistic orientation is due in part to the fact that standard statistical methods such as ANOVA and multiple regression require independence between observations. Nonetheless many social psychological concepts intrinsically involve two persons (e.g., attraction, person perception, helping, aggression, communication, and influence), and several others require groups of persons (e.g., leadership, cohesiveness, productivity, conformity, norms, and group polarization). Before we can have a genuinely *social* psychology, our theories, research methods, and data analyses will have to take into account the truly interpersonal nature of the phenomena under study.

Because the phenomena that social psychologists study are social by definition, observations do not refer to a person, but rather to multiple persons embedded within a social context. Take for instance how much Harry likes Sally. Because the checkmark on a piece of paper is made by Harry, researchers all too often make the fundamental attribution error and treat the measurement as if it referred to only Harry. Almost certainly the liking Harry feels for Sally is driven in part by characteristics of Sally herself, such as how friendly or agreeable she is, as well as by the unique relationship that Harry and Sally have established. The measurement reflects both Harry and Sally and so is fundamentally dyadic.

The intrinsically social nature of the measurements in a social psychology study means that they are often

linked to other measurements in the study, and the strength of these links may be one of the most important research questions to be examined. Consider the following examples:

1. Both members in a romantic relationship evaluate whether they are satisfied with the relationship (Feeney, 1994).
2. The productivity of each of the members in a group is measured to determine social loafing (Williams & Karau, 1991).
3. The amount of self-disclosure of both interactants is measured to ascertain whether there is reciprocity (Reno & Kenny, 1990).
4. Two persons are asked to describe a common target to determine if there is consensus in person perception (Park & Judd, 1989).
5. To determine if leadership is a trait, a person's leadership is measured when the person is a member of multiple groups (Zaccaro, Foti, & Kenny, 1991).

In each of these cases, the issues of stability, consistency, and correlation between related measurements are interesting social psychological phenomena worth studying in their own right. Yet, none of them can be addressed easily by standard methods.

The dominant statistical method that social psychologists currently use (see Judd, this volume, Ch. 14, for a review), ANOVA, was developed for agricultural researchers. Those researchers knew that two ears of corn from the same stalk were similar to one another, and even two ears from the same row were similar due to cross-fertilization. So they created separate plots of land and computed the crop yields in the different plots. These plots served as "subjects." It could then be safely assumed that the yields from different plots

Supported in part by grants to the second author from the National Science Foundation (DBS-9307949) and the National Institute of Mental Health (R01-MH51964). We thank P. Niels Christensen, Jennifer Boldry, Radmila Prislin, and Renée Tobin for their helpful comments on earlier versions of this chapter.

were independent of one another. The key assumption of ANOVA (and multiple regression) is that once variation due to the independent variable(s) is controlled, the scores of different units are independent.

Why is the independence assumption so important for accurate statistical inference? The reason has to do with the amount of unique evidence contributing to a particular finding. Consider a study of the effects of leadership style (directive, facilitative, and laissez-faire) on group member attitudes toward outgroup members after a discussion of attitudes toward the outgroup occurs. If a sample of 48 individuals is broken into six 8-person groups, and the six groups are then randomly assigned to one of three leadership styles, there will be two groups (a total of 16 individuals) within each leadership style condition.

Say that each group discusses the target outgroup for 20 min and then individuals respond to a question on a 7-point scale concerning their attitudes toward the outgroup. One way to approach such a study would be to treat the individual as the unit of analysis and analyze the data treating the study as if there were simply 16 individuals within each level of leadership style. In this approach there would be a total of 48 data points contributing to estimates of differences in attitudes between the three leadership styles. However, because the group members discuss their attitudes, they may influence one another so that within a group all members may share the same consensual opinion of the outgroup. In this case, there are really only two unique or independent pieces of data within each leadership style, one from each group. Thus group, not individual, should be treated as the unit of analysis. If the nonindependence is ignored and individual is treated as the unit, the conclusion from the study will be based on 42 more pieces of evidence than it should be.

Social psychologists are keenly aware of the assumption of independence, and to ensure that it is not violated, they often have taken the approach of randomly assigning individuals to conditions and then testing them in isolation. If interaction is needed, they train confederates who behave in a predetermined or scripted fashion. In social cognition research, which dominates contemporary social psychology, stimulus persons are often presented in written materials, audiotapes, or videotapes. With computer-mediated interaction, the other "person" may even be a computer program. Too often what is "social" in a social psychology experiment is the interaction between a person and a piece of paper (Ickes & Gonzalez, 1994).

Investigation of dyadic or group processes requires that social psychologists use research designs and analysis strategies that recognize the interdependence of social behavior. Social psychologists should treat interdependence not as a statistical nuisance that should be controlled, but rather as an important social psychological phenomenon that should be studied. Reciprocity, agreement, accuracy, and consistency all imply some form of nonindependence of data. Thus, our discussion of nonindependence focuses on two issues: estimating nonindependence and the degree to which it results in biased hypothesis testing when standard data analytic techniques are used, and modeling interdependence in dyads and in groups to study it as a social psychological construct of importance in its own right.

In this chapter, we present methods that allow for the analysis of data taken from interacting persons in dyads and groups. We will see that standard methods (see Judd, this volume, Ch. 14) often cannot be used because the independence assumption is violated. Fortunately, over the last 20 years, new techniques have been developed that allow for the study of social interaction (e.g., Griffin & Gonzalez, 1995; Kashy & Snyder, 1995; Kenny, 1996c). We introduce the major techniques for the analysis of nonindependent data. The chapter by Bakeman (this volume, Ch. 6) covers methods for the analysis of sequential processes, and the chapter by Collins and Sayer (this volume, Ch. 18) covers methods for the analysis of change. We also refer the reader to Wasserman and Faust (1994) for the analysis of social network data.

Finally, our discussion includes both dyadic and group data, and because a dyad is a special case of a group, there are a number of parallels between analyses of these two types of data. However, because of the prevalence of dyadic research, we often explicitly discuss dyadic analysis instead of treating it simply as a special case of group research.

LEVEL OF MEASUREMENT FOR DYADIC AND GROUP DATA

There are two general types of measurement for outcome variables in dyadic research, and three such types for group research. Measurements in dyadic research can be obtained at the level of the dyad such that each dyad has only one score, or they can be obtained at the level of the individual such that each of the two members has his or her own score. For example, in a study of dating couples, the physical distance between the two persons would be a dyad-level measure, and the number of affectionate comments directed toward the partner would be an individual-level measure.

In a parallel fashion, data from group research can be measured at the level of the group, as would be the case if the measure were a single index of group productivity. Similarly, data from group research can be measured at the individual level so that each person within the group contributes a single score. An example of an individual-level measure for group data is when each group member rates his or her satisfaction with the group.

Group research also allows for more complex measurement. Specifically, measurements can be obtained at the dyad-level within a group so that each individual is paired with each of the other group members.[1] For example, in a four-person group (Persons A, B, C, and D) where each individual rates every other individual in the group on a measure of friendliness, there would be 12 dyadic ratings (AB, AC, AD, BA, and so on). This type of dyadic-level group data results in a fairly complex web of nonindependence but can address several important social psychological questions. A discussion of the analysis of group research with dyad-level measurement is presented in the second section of this chapter.

SINGLE OUTCOME MEASURES FOR THE DYAD OR GROUP

When outcomes are measured at the dyad or group level such that there is only a single score for each dyad or group, dyad or group should be the unit of analysis. In effect, treating dyad or group as the unit of analysis involves analyzing the data as if dyad or group were the "subject." It is obviously wrong to replicate the data so that each dyad or group member is assigned the same dependent variable score, and then treat individual as the unit of analysis. In general, when each group generates only one outcome score, such as a measure of overall group productivity or a single index of group cohesiveness, group must be treated as the unit of analysis. The statistical power of such a study depends on the number of groups rather than the number of persons. Thus, given that effect size does not vary as a function of group size, a study using group-level measures with 15 four-person groups would be more powerful than a study with 10 eight-person groups, even though the second study would have a higher overall number of participants.

The remainder of this chapter is divided into two major sections. In the first, we discuss the analysis of data in which each person participates in only one dyad or group, and as a result of that participation, each individual generates a single outcome score. In the second section we consider designs in which each person participates in multiple dyads and generates an outcome score from every pairing. We introduce the social relations model (SRM; Kenny & La Voie, 1984) for the analysis of these designs. In both sections, we emphasize that how a person responds depends not only on that person but also on the partners with whom the person interacts. We present the major formulas for the computation of statistics, but we avoid presenting extensive computational details. We do, however, cite the sources that present these computational details.

INDIVIDUAL-LEVEL OUTCOME MEASURES: DYADIC AND GROUP DESIGNS IN WHICH EACH INDIVIDUAL OCCURS IN ONLY ONE DYAD OR GROUP

Individual-level outcome measures are by far the most common type of measure in dyadic and group research, and therefore this chapter focuses on them. With individual outcome measures, each member of the dyad or group supplies an outcome score, and the members' scores may differ from one another.

There are three major issues addressed in our discussion of individual-level data. First, we consider how the degree of nonindependence can be measured. We then consider what effects nonindependence has on significance testing. Finally, we present data analytic techniques that control for nonindependence.

Assessing the Degree of Nonindependence in the Outcome Scores

Assessing the degree to which scores within a dyad or group are related (i.e., nonindependent) is an important first step in examining dyadic and group data. The amount of nonindependence has important consequences for both the extent to which standard hypothesis tests are biased, as well as whether alternative analyses are appropriate. In addition, the degree of nonindependence may be an important empirical and theoretical issue in and of itself. For example, one might wish to assess whether, and to what degree, a wife's marital satisfaction relates to her husband's marital satisfaction. Similarly, in a group study one could measure how much members agree in their assessments of the group's performance.

---

[1] It is possible to form all possible triads in a group (Bond, Horn, & Kenny, 1996) but we do not consider such an analysis in this chapter.

DYADIC DATA. One question that must be addressed before nonindependence can be measured in dyadic data is whether there is a natural distinction between the two dyad members. In heterosexual couples, the dyad members may be distinguished by their gender. Thus, if one wishes to assess whether there is significant nonindependence between the two persons' scores on an individual-level outcome measure such as relationship satisfaction, the woman's satisfaction score can be designated as the X variable, the man's satisfaction score as the Y variable, and the degree to which X and Y are nonindependent can be estimated using a standard Pearson product-moment correlation coefficient.

There are, however, many instances in which dyad members can be distinguished only by some arbitrary means, as would be the case for same-gender friendship dyads. In such cases, the assignment of persons to X and Y is arbitrary; the two individuals are interchangeable. Sometimes researchers adopt a strategy with such dyads of assigning members to X or Y randomly and then computing a Pearson correlation between the X and Y scores. The problem with this strategy is that other assignments would likely yield different estimates.

Consider as an example the data in Table 17.1 from a fictitious study of liking between same-gender roommates. In this data set there are 10 pairs of roommates, and persons are asked to rate on a 9-point scale how much they like their roommates. Say that because of how the data were entered, the 10 scores on the left column were treated as the X variable, and the 10 scores on the right column were treated as the Y variable. The Pearson correlation between X and Y is $r = .53$, $p = .12$. Now, because the assignment to X and Y was totally arbitrary, say that the scores for the last five roommate pairs were reversed (e.g., now the "X" score for the last dyad is 3 and the "Y" score is 2). The Pearson correlation now is $r = .79$, $p = .006$. Clearly, the fact that the size and so the statistical significance of the Pearson correlation can change substantially depending on such an arbitrary factor implies that this particular statistic is not well-suited for assessing the relatedness of scores from dyads with interchangeable members.

The intraclass correlation provides a unique estimate of the relationship between scores from indistinguishable members of dyads and groups. Intraclass correlations can be interpreted as the correlation between the scores from two individuals who are in the same group. Thus, if a group member has a high score on an outcome measure, and the intraclass correlation is positive, then other members of the same dyad or group also have relatively high scores; if the intraclass correlation is negative, then other members of the same dyad or group have relatively lower scores. A common alternative interpretation of a positive intraclass correlation is the proportion of variation in the outcome measure that is accounted for by dyad or group. That is, if the intraclass correlation equals .40, then 40% of the variation in the scores is accounted for by the particular dyad or group to which individuals belong.

To estimate the intraclass correlation for dyadic data, two composite scores must be computed for each of the k dyads. The first composite, m_i, is the average of the two members' scores in dyad i, and the second composite, d_i, is the difference between the two members' scores:

$$m_i = \frac{X_i + Y_i}{2}, \qquad d_i = X_i - Y_i.$$

Then the average of all the members' scores is computed as M. Thus, $M = \sum m_i / k$. Next, two statistics, a and b, are computed by summing over dyads:

$$a = \frac{2 \sum (m_i - M)^2}{k - 1}, \qquad b = \frac{\sum d_i^2}{2k}.$$

The intraclass correlation, or $\hat{\rho}$, is defined as $\hat{\rho} = (a - b)/(a + b)$. For the example data in Table 17.1, $a = 7.42$, $b = 2.40$, and $\hat{\rho} = .51$.

Like Pearson correlations, the intraclass correlation for dyadic data can range from -1 to $+1$ and is interpreted accordingly. The intraclass correlation can

TABLE 17.1. Intraclass Correlation Example Using Data from a Fictitious Study of Roommates

Dyad	Scores X_i	Y_i	m_i	d_i
1	8	6	7.0	2
2	5	3	4.0	2
3	7	2	4.5	5
4	8	5	6.5	3
5	8	7	7.5	1
6	5	6	5.5	-1
7	3	4	3.5	-1
8	8	9	8.5	-1
9	6	7	6.5	-1
10	2	3	2.5	-1

$M = 5.60$; $a = 7.42$; $b = 2.40$; $\hat{\rho} = .51$.
$F(9,10) = 3.09$, $p = .093$

be tested for statistical significance using an F statistic. Because the hypothesis of independence is rejected either if the intraclass correlation is positive or negative, a two-tailed F-test is used. If the intraclass correlation is positive then F is computed as $F = a/b$, with $df_{num} = k - 1$, and $df_{denom} = k$; if the intraclass correlation is negative then $F = b/a$, and $df_{num} = k$ and $df_{denom} = k - 1$. Because the test is two-sided, the p-value associated with the computed F should be doubled. For the example, $F(9, 10) = 3.09$, $p = .093$ (two-tailed). Griffin and Gonzalez (1995) discussed an alternative estimator of the intraclass correlation.

GROUP DATA. The intraclass correlation can also be used to estimate the degree of nonindependence present in data from groups. The estimation uses the mean squares derived from ANOVA and is a more general solution for the intraclass correlation than that presented for dyads (i.e., dyads could be treated as two-person groups).

As an example, consider a fictitious group study in which eight groups, each composed of six individuals, work on a set of problem-solving tasks. After each group has completed the tasks, all individuals within the group are asked to rate, on 9-point scales, how much they liked participating in their group. Table 17.2 contains the data from this study.

To estimate the intraclass correlation for group data, an ANOVA model is estimated in which there are two sources of variance: Groups (G) and participants within groups (S/G). That is, in the ANOVA the eight groups are treated as eight levels of an independent variable, and liking scores are the dependent variable. The formula for the intraclass correlation for group data is presented in Table 17.2, and for the example data, this correlation is estimated as .26. This correlation indicates that, to a moderate degree, if a person in the group said that he or she liked participating in the group, the other group members felt similarly. The test of whether the intraclass correlation differs significantly from zero is an F-ratio that tests whether the group effect is statistically significant, or $F = MS_G/MS_{S/G}$. In the example, $F(7, 40) = 3.10$, $p = .02$ (two-tailed).

This method for estimating the intraclass correlation does not take into account the effects of any independent variables that may be included in the design. When there are independent variables in the study, somewhat more complex procedures need to be used to estimate the intraclass correlation. These procedures are described at a later point in this chapter.

Note that whereas the upper bound for the intraclass correlation is always one, the lower bound is $-1/(n - 1)$ where n is the group size. Thus, although the intraclass correlation for dyadic data can vary from -1 to $+1$, the intraclass correlation for group data is bounded by a negative value that approaches zero as the size of the group increases. If the intraclass correlation is negative, the F-ratio to test its statistical significance should be inverted so that $F = MS_{S/G}/MS_G$ with the corresponding degrees of freedom.

TABLE 17.2. Intraclass Correlation Example Using Fictitious Group (G) Attraction Data

	G_1	G_2	G_3	G_4	G_5	G_6	G_7	G_8
	5	3	6	6	7	4	6	4
	4	6	7	3	6	5	5	5
	7	5	5	4	3	6	4	5
	5	3	7	3	8	4	7	4
	6	4	6	2	7	4	5	5
	4	6	6	5	6	5	6	3
Group M	5.17	4.50	6.17	3.83	6.17	4.67	5.50	4.33

Source	df	SS	MS	F
Groups (G)	7	30.92	4.42	3.10
Participants within groups (S/G)	40	57.00	1.42	

Intraclass correlation:

$$\hat{\rho} = \frac{MS_G - MS_{S/G}}{MS_G + (n - 1)MS_{S/G}} = .26$$

Note. n = number of participants per group; for the example $n = 6$

Although the presence of a statistically significant correlation between the dyad or group members' scores implies nonindependence, the absence of a significant sample correlation does not ensure independence in the population. In fact, Kenny, Kashy, and Bolger (1998) have shown that the test of the intraclass correlation has relatively low power, and so the likelihood of making a Type II error (failing to reject the null hypothesis when it is false) is high. We, and others (Myers, 1979), recommend that a liberal test ($\alpha = .20$) of nonindependence be used. In addition, even if the intraclass correlation is not significant using a liberal test, if there is a theoretical basis for assuming that the data are nonindependent, researchers should consider treating dyad or group as the unit of analysis. Kenny et al. (1998) have found that there is relatively little loss in power when data are treated as nonindependent when in fact they are independent.

Types of Independent Variables

The effect of nonindependence depends on the type of independent variable under investigation. There are three general classes of independent variables

in dyadic and group research: between, within, and mixed (Kenny, 1988; 1996c).

BETWEEN INDEPENDENT VARIABLES. For between independent variables (often referred to as nested independent variables in group research), within a dyad or group all persons have identical scores on the independent variable, but these scores vary from dyad to dyad or group to group. For example, in a study of the effects of stress on romantic relationship satisfaction, couples could be randomly assigned to a high-stress condition in which they are asked to discuss a difficult problem in their relationship, or they could be assigned to a low-stress condition in which they are asked to discuss a current event. The level of stress would be a between-dyads variable because some dyads would be in the high-stress condition, others would be in the low-stress condition, and for every dyad, both dyad members would be at the same level of stress.

Similarly, in group designs, groups (G) are nested within levels of the independent variable (A) so that all of the individuals (S) in a group have the same score on the independent variable. The top section of Table 17.3 illustrates the basic data structure for a

---

TABLE 17.3. Data Structure and Sources of Variance for Group Designs with Between Independent Variables

A_1				A_2				A_3			
G_1	G_2	G_3	G_4	G_5	G_6	G_7	G_8	G_9	G_{10}	G_{11}	G_{12}
S_1	S_7	S_{13}	S_{19}	S_{25}	S_{31}	S_{37}	S_{43}	S_{49}	S_{55}	S_{61}	S_{67}
$\vdots$	$\vdots$	$\vdots$	$\vdots$	$\vdots$	$\vdots$	$\vdots$	$\vdots$	$\vdots$	$\vdots$	$\vdots$	$\vdots$
S_6	S_{12}	S_{18}	S_{24}	S_{30}	S_{36}	S_{42}	S_{48}	S_{54}	S_{60}	S_{66}	S_{72}

Source	df	
	Formulas	Estimate
Between Groups		
A	$a - 1$	2
G/A	$a(g - 1)$	9
Within Groups		
$S/G/A$	$ag(n - 1)$	60
Total	$agn - 1$	71

Intraclass correlation controlling for the effects of A:

$$\hat{\rho}_{G/A} = \frac{MS_{G/A} - MS_{S/G/A}}{MS_{G/A} + (n - 1)MS_{S/G/A}}$$

$$F_{[a(g-1),ag(n-1)]} = \frac{MS_{G/A}}{MS_{S/G/A}}$$

Note. a = number of levels of A ($a = 3$ above), g = number of groups within a single level of A ($g = 4$ above), and n = number of participants per group ($n = 6$ above)

TABLE 17.4. Data Structure and Sources of Variance for Group Designs with Within Independent Variables

G_1		G_2		G_3		G_4		G_5		G_6		G_7		G_8	
A_1	A_2	A_1	A_2	A_1	A_2	A_1	A_2	A_1	A_2	A_1	A_2	A_1	A_2	A_1	A_2
S_1	S_4	S_7	S_{10}	S_{13}	S_{16}	S_{19}	S_{22}	S_{25}	S_{28}	S_{31}	S_{34}	S_{37}	S_{40}	S_{43}	S_{46}
$\vdots$	$\vdots$	$\vdots$	$\vdots$	$\vdots$	$\vdots$	$\vdots$	$\vdots$	$\vdots$	$\vdots$	$\vdots$	$\vdots$	$\vdots$	$\vdots$	$\vdots$	$\vdots$
S_3	S_6	S_9	S_{12}	S_{15}	S_{18}	S_{21}	S_{24}	S_{27}	S_{30}	S_{33}	S_{36}	S_{39}	S_{42}	S_{45}	S_{48}

Source	df	
	Formulas	Estimate
Between Groups		
G	$g-1$	7
Within Groups		
A	$a-1$	1
$G \times A$	$(a-1)(g-1)$	7
$S/G \times A$	$ag(n-1)$	32
Total	$agn-1$	47

Intraclass correlation for the Group main effect:

$$\hat{\rho}_G = \frac{MS_G - MS_{S/G \times A}}{MS_G + (an-1)MS_{S/G \times A}}, \qquad F_{[(g-1),ag(n-1)]} = \frac{MS_G}{MS_{S/G \times A}}$$

Intraclass correlation for the Group $\times$ Treatment interaction:

$$\hat{\rho}_{G \times A} = \frac{MS_{G \times A} - MS_{S/G \times A}}{MS_{G \times A} + (n-1)MS_{S/G \times A}}, \qquad F_{[(a-1)(g-1),ag(n-1)]} = \frac{MS_{G \times A}}{MS_{S/G \times A}}$$

Note. a = number of levels of A (here $a = 2$), g = number of levels of groups (here $g = 8$), and n = number of participants in a group that are in the same level of A (here $n = 3$)

between-groups design in which there are three levels of the independent variable, A, 12 groups total, four of which are at each of three levels of A, and 72 participants. Say that in this example a researcher investigated the effect of three types of conflict resolution strategies on group member motivation. The researcher forms 12 six-person groups, 4 of which use each strategy.

WITHIN INDEPENDENT VARIABLES. A within independent variable varies across members within the dyad or group, but when averaged across the dyad or group members, each dyad or group has an identical average score. A prototypical within-dyad independent variable in marital research is gender in that every couple is comprised of both a man and a woman. A less obvious example of a within-dyad independent variable is the actual proportion of housework done by two roommates. With this variable, the sum of the two proportions always equals one, yet within each dyad the amount of housework varies across the two roommates.

For group designs involving within independent variables, some members of each group are in one treatment condition, whereas other members of the same group are in other treatment conditions, with the restriction that the group average on the independent variable is the same for all of the groups. Thus, in this design, treatment condition and group are crossed. Table 17.4 shows the data structure for a group design involving a within independent variable with two levels, eight groups total, and within each group there are three persons in the first level of $A (A_1)$ and three other persons in the second level of $A (A_2)$. In this hypothetical study, the researcher examines the effect of a mood manipulation on the degree to which individuals within a group cooperate. The researcher forms eight groups so that in each group there are three individuals whose moods are manipulated to be anxious, and three individuals whose moods are manipulated to be angry.

MIXED INDEPENDENT VARIABLES. The third type of independent variable in dyadic and group research

TABLE 17.5. Errors in Hypothesis Testing When Individuals Are Treated as the Unit of Analysis in the Presence of Nonindependence (adapted from Kenny, 1988)

Type of independent variable	Direction of nonindependence[a]	
	Positive	Negative
Between	Type I increased	Type II increased
Within	Type II increased	Type I increased

[a]Direction of nonindependence refers to the direction of the correlation between dyad or group members' scores on the outcome variable.

is a mixed independent variable where variation exists both within the dyad or group and between dyads or groups. A mixed predictor variable is probably a new concept to social psychological researchers (Kenny & Cook, 1998; Kenny et al., 1998). Age is an example of a mixed independent variable in marital research because the two spouses' ages may differ from one another and in addition, some couples on average may be older than others. Many variables in dyadic research are mixed in nature such that the two partners' scores differ, and some dyads have higher average scores than others.

An example of a mixed independent variable in group research is an investigation of the degree to which attraction to the group predicts individual productivity within the group. In this case each individual has his or her own attraction score (the individual's independent variable score). These scores vary within a group, and in addition, in some groups the average level of attraction will be high and in other groups this average will be low. Although it is possible to manipulate a variable to create a mixed independent variable, mixed predictor variables are typically unmanipulated variables.

Bias in Significance Testing

If there is evidence of nonindependence, then the data analysis must take dyad or group into account, and individual should not be treated as the unit of analysis. If individual were mistakenly treated as the unit of analysis, the conclusions drawn would be biased in either the Type I error direction (concluding that there is an effect when there really is not) or in the Type II error direction (concluding that there is no effect when there really is) depending on the direction of

nonindependence as well as the type of independent or predictor variable being assessed (Kenny, 1995; Kenny & Judd, 1986; Kenny et al., 1998). Table 17.5 summarizes the effects of nonindependence on hypothesis testing.

As shown in Table 17.5, if the independent variable is between dyads or groups and the intraclass correlation for the dependent variable is positive, inferential statistics (e.g., F or t statistics) would be too large, resulting in obtained p values that are smaller than they should be. In this case the probability of making a Type I error is actually greater than the p-value obtained from the inferential test. For example, in dyadic research with a between-dyads predictor variable, if there were 50 dyads or 100 individuals, two treatment conditions, and the intraclass correlation for the dependent variable were .25, then test statistics that normally would be associated with an alpha of .05 would actually be associated with an alpha of .08. More dramatically, if the overall N were 100, group size were five, and the intraclass correlation were .25, the actual alpha level would be .17 (Kenny et al., 1998). Thus, in this case mistakenly treating individual as the unit of analysis when there is nonindependence can result in substantial increases in Type I errors.

When the intraclass correlation is negative and the independent variable is between dyads or groups, inferential tests are overly conservative. For example, with an intraclass correlation of $-.50$ in dyadic research in which there are 100 individuals and two treatment conditions, the actual alpha would be only .006, not .05. There would also be a corresponding increase in the probability of Type II errors and a drop in power.

If individual were treated as the unit of analysis with dyadic data when the independent variable is within-dyads, and the correlation between the dyad members' scores on the dependent variable is positive, the inferential statistic would be too small and the probability of making a Type II error would be increased. Thus, in this case the power of the test is lower than it would be if dyad were treated as the unit of analysis. Similarly, when groups are studied and the independent variable is within, treating person as the unit of analysis generally results in an overly conservative test and thus a reduction in power. The loss of power occurs because the group design with a within independent variable is, in essence, a repeated measures design in the sense that each group has participants in both treatment conditions. When group is treated as the unit of analysis, variance due to the group main effect is subtracted from the error term used to test the treatment effect. Thus, treating group as the unit increases power in exactly the same way as a within-subjects design has greater power than a between-subjects design.[2]

The effects of nonindependence with mixed independent variables are more complex because both the independent and dependent variables vary between and within dyads or groups. In fact, an intraclass correlation can be computed for the independent variable, X, and if the independent variable is mixed, the intraclass correlation, $\hat{\rho}_X$, will be between $-1/(n-1)$ and 1, where n is the number of persons within a group. (If the intraclass correlation for the independent variable, $\hat{\rho}_X$, is exactly equal to one then the independent variable is between, and if it is exactly equal to $-1/[n-1]$ then the independent variable is within.)

For mixed independent variables, if the intraclass correlations for both the predictor and outcome variables are positive, then inferential tests that treat individual as the unit of analysis will be too liberal. However, Kenny (1995) has shown that for dyads, when $\hat{\rho}_X$ and $\hat{\rho}_Y$ are both below .30, if individual were used as the unit of analysis rather than group with a nominal alpha level of .05, the actual alpha level never exceeds about .06. Thus there is relatively less bias in hypothesis testing when individual is treated as the unit of analysis and the independent variable is mixed rather than between or within, at least for dyads.

Analysis of Nonindependent Data Involving Between and Within Independent Variables

Analyses of nonindependent data for designs involving between or within independent variables are fairly straightforward and can be conducted using variations of standard techniques. In the following sections we first introduce methods for assessing the degree of nonindependence while controlling for the effects of the independent variable. This discussion is framed within the context of group data, but can be used for dyadic data by considering dyads as groups with an $n = 2$. We then describe data analytic methods appropriate for group designs when there is evidence of nonindependence. Finally, we briefly discuss analyses specifically tailored for dyadic data when the data are nonindependent.

[2] This discussion assumes that there is no Treatment × Group interaction. If such an interaction occurs, then the level of power in group designs with within independent variables is more complicated and the reader should consult Kenny et al. (1998) for details.

BETWEEN INDEPENDENT VARIABLES. As shown in the ANOVA source table in Table 17.3, there are three sources of variation in a design in which the independent variable is between. There is variation due to the independent variable, called strategy type in our earlier discussion of group data with between independent variables, which is denoted as Factor A in the table. One type of strategy may be more motivating than the other types of strategies. Second, within each level of A some groups may be more motivated than other groups (G/A). Finally, within the groups some persons may be more motivated than others $(S/G/A)$.

Recall that in our earlier discussion of how the intraclass correlation can be estimated for group data, we gave one solution for the intraclass correlation. That solution simply estimated the degree to which scores within groups are especially similar to one another relative to variation of scores between groups. The intraclass correlation can be estimated such that it controls for the effect of the between independent variable.[3] That is, if the independent variable has an effect, then scores will tend to be more variable between groups than within groups regardless of whether there actually is interdependence within the groups. The formula for estimating and testing the intraclass correlation that removes the effect of the between independent variable is included in Table 17.3.

There are several possible ways to test the effect of the between independent variable, A, and the appropriate choice depends on the level of nonindependence of scores within the groups. If the test of nonindependence is significant using alpha = .20, then group must be treated as the unit of analysis, and the $MS_{G/A}$ is used as the error term to test the A effect. For the example in Table 17.3, this would result in an F-test with two degrees of freedom for the numerator and nine degrees of freedom for the denominator. However, if there is no evidence of nonindependence, group can be ignored and person can be treated as the unit of analysis. To treat person as the unit, the G/A and $S/G/A$ sums of squares and degrees of freedom can be summed to obtain a pooled error term that will be the $MS_{S/A}$:

$$MS_{S/A} = \frac{SS_{G/A} + SS_{S/G/A}}{df_{G/A} + df_{S/G/A}}.$$

Pooling these two sources of error variation into a $MS_{S/A}$ is equivalent to reestimating the ANOVA dropping group from the model altogether so that there

[3] Whenever there are independent variables in the study, the effects of these variables should be removed from the intraclass correlation.

are only two sources of variation, A (with 2 degrees of freedom in the example) and S/A (with 69 degrees of freedom).

If the between independent variable is continuous and there is evidence of nonindependence, then a regression procedure can be used to analyze the data. In this case, the group average on the dependent variable serves as the outcome measure in a regression in which the between independent variable is the predictor. The effective n in such an analysis is the number of groups.

WITHIN INDEPENDENT VARIABLES. As shown in Table 17.4, there are potentially four sources of variation in a design involving a within independent variable. The first source of variation is the group main effect (G), which measures whether there are average differences between groups on the outcome variable, level of cooperation in the earlier group example with a within independent variable. The next source of variation is the effect of the within independent variable (A), which is typically the effect of most interest in the study. Recall that for the example of group research with a within independent variable, the independent variable was a mood manipulation in which each group included individuals whose moods were anxious as well as individuals whose moods were angry. The A effect thus measures the degree to which individuals' moods affect cooperation. In addition, there is an interaction between the treatment and group ($G \times A$). This interaction assesses the degree to which the mood effect varies from group to group. Finally, there is the persons within the treatment by group interaction ($S/G \times A$) source of variance. Note that for dyadic data, the $G \times A$ effect and the $S/G \times A$ effect cannot be separated because there is only one participant within each level of the $G \times A$ interaction. Thus, for dyadic data with a within-dyads independent variable, there are only three sources of variation: G, A, and $G \times A$.

Assessing nonindependence in group designs with within independent variables while controlling for the effect of the independent variable is relatively complex in that the nonindependence of scores within groups can derive from two sources: the group main effect and the Group $\times$ Treatment interaction. The measure of nonindependence for the group main effect, ρ_G, measures whether there are consistent differences from group to group after removing the effects of the independent variable.[4] The nonindependence due to

the Group $\times$ Treatment interaction, $\rho_{G \times A}$, measures whether individuals who are in the same group and the same level of treatment are especially similar to one another. The formulas to estimate and test these two intraclass correlations are presented in the bottom of Table 17.4.

Because dyadic designs lack the $S/G \times A$ effect, the nonindependence due to the Group $\times$ Treatment interaction cannot be estimated. Thus, for dyadic designs ρ_G provides the only measure of nonindependence controlling for the within-dyads independent variable.

For group data with categorical within independent variables, presence of nonindependence from either the group main effect or the Group $\times$ Treatment interaction implies that group should be included as a factor in the analysis. If there is evidence of nonindependence for the group main effect, but there is no evidence of a Group $\times$ Treatment interaction, then group is included as a factor in the analysis, but participant is treated as the unit of analysis, and the $MS_{S/G \times A}$ is the error term used to test the A effect. If there is nonindependence due to the Group $\times$ Treatment interaction, then group is treated as the unit of analysis. In this design, treating group as the unit requires using the mean square for the Group $\times$ Treatment interaction ($MS_{G \times A}$) as the error term when testing the treatment effect. If there is no indication of nonindependence from either source (using liberal tests), then person can be used as the unit of analysis by simply dropping the group factor from the model (thereby dropping the group main effect and the interaction with group) and treating the design as a single factor between-subjects ANOVA. Kenny et al. (1998) presented a more detailed discussion of the two sources of nonindependence in designs involving categorical within independent variables.[5]

For dyadic data, if there is evidence of nonindependence (from ρ_G) then the effects of the independent variable can be assessed by treating the difference between the two dyad members' scores as the outcome score. For categorical independent variables this could be accomplished using a paired t-test. If the independent variable were continuous (e.g., the proportion of

---

[4] In a group study with a within independent variable, the group main effect is analogous to the subject main effect in a within-subjects ANOVA design.

[5] In group research it is quite rare to have a continuous within independent variable, and so we have omitted a discussion of this case. In most instances, continuous independent variables that appear to be crossed or purely within in nature are actually mixed independent variables. However, a variable such as the proportion of work contributed by each member of a group (with equal n groups) would be fully crossed, and such a variable could be analyzed using the within-groups regression procedure described in the section discussing the analysis of mixed independent variables for group data.

housework done by each person), the difference between the two members' outcome scores would be regressed on the difference between the two members' scores on the independent variable. (The direction of differencing should be consistent for the predictor and outcome scores such that if Bob's housework score is subtracted from Jim's housework score, then Bob's outcome score should also be subtracted from Jim's outcome score.) This regression would estimate the degree to which larger discrepancies in housework related to larger discrepancies on the outcome measure. Because the direction of differencing may be arbitrary (as in the nondistinguishable case), the intercept should not be estimated in this regression. (Most computer packages have a no-intercept option for regression analyses. For example, in SAS, this is the NOINT option in PROC GLM or PROC REG.) Forcing the intercept to be zero ensures that the regression solution is the same even if the direction of differencing were switched for some dyads.

As was the case for between-dyads independent variables, if there is no evidence of nonindependence for dyadic data with within-dyads independent variables, then individual can be treated as the unit of analysis. Each individual would have a unique score on the independent variable, and each individual would have a score on the dependent variable, and t-tests, F-tests, or regressions could be computed across the individuals.

Analysis of Designs Including Mixed Independent Variables: The Actor–Partner Interdependence Model

Mixed independent variables vary across individuals within groups, and they vary on average across groups. We can then view such variables as really two different variables: the between-group variable, which is the group mean, $\bar{X}$, and the within-group variable, which is the deviation of each individual's score from the group mean, $X_{ij} - \bar{X}$. Before detailing the approach that we recommend to analyze the effects of mixed variables, we first present some alternative methods.

One possibility is simply to perform two analyses. The first analysis is at the "individual level," and in it X_{ij} is used to predict Y_{ij}. The second analysis is at the group level, and in it the group mean on X is used to predict the group mean on Y. The problem with such an approach is that the so-called "individual-level" analysis contains the group effect within it. Thus, the results from the individual-level analysis are partially confounded with the results from the group-level analysis.

This is perhaps most clearly understood by examining the most extreme case in which the variation in X is entirely between groups. In this case the results from the individual- and group-level analyses will be exactly the same. A further problem with this approach is that, because of nonindependence in the outcome scores, the significance tests of the individual-level analysis will be biased in ways that we have discussed earlier in this chapter.

Another approach to this data analytic issue, known as contextual analysis (Boyd & Iversen, 1979) has been applied in the sociological literature. In this approach, individual is treated as the unit of analysis but both the individual scores on the predictor variable (X_{ij}) as well as the group mean on the predictor ($\bar{X}$) are used in an analysis predicting the individual scores on the outcome measure (Y_{ij}). Although the contextual analysis approach is more sophisticated than the first approach we described, nonindependence of the outcome scores biases its significance tests.

To counteract these problems, one could conduct two analyses: one within-groups analysis and one between-groups analysis. The within-groups analysis would involve predicting the deviation of the outcome score from the group mean on the outcome score ($Y_{ij} - \bar{Y}$) using the deviation of the predictor score from the group mean on the predictor score ($X_{ij} - \bar{X}$) with suitable adjustments to the degrees of freedom. The between-groups analysis would simply involve predicting the group mean on the outcome score using the group mean on the predictor score. These two analyses are independent of one another, and so avoid the confounding problem discussed earlier. However, they seem to us to connect poorly with social psychological theory. It is for this reason we emphasize a new model for research involving mixed independent variables, the actor–partner interdependence model.

We should note that there is an alternative way of using the between groups and within groups relationships to make inferences at the group and individual levels, and these are described by Kenny and La Voie (1986), Griffin and Gonzalez (1995), and others. Because the approach described by these authors has not attracted much use to date by practicing social psychologists, we do not detail it.

The actor–partner interdependence model (APIM) focuses on an important ramification of nonindependence in dyadic and group research: One person's score on an independent variable may influence not only that person's score on an outcome variable, but also that person's partners' score on the outcome variable. This model can be applied to both dyadic and group research, and it can be used in dyadic research both when dyad members are distinguishable (e.g., married couples) and when dyad members are interchangeable (e.g., same-sex friends). In the following discussion of the model and analysis, we first discuss the dyadic context. The extension to group research follows.

As an example, consider the effects of depression on marital satisfaction. It may be that a wife's depression influences her own marital satisfaction as well as her husband's marital satisfaction. The effect of a wife's depression on her own marital satisfaction is called an *actor effect*, and the effect of her depression on her husband's satisfaction is called a *partner effect* (Kenny, 1996c). That is, an actor effect occurs when a person's score on a predictor variable affects that person's score on an outcome variable; a partner effect occurs when a person's score on a predictor variable affects his or her partner's score on an outcome variable.

The analysis implied by the APIM can be used to estimate actor and partner effects for both dyadic and group data when the independent variable is mixed, and it allows either categorical or continuous independent variables. It can also incorporate independent variables that are not mixed (i.e., those that are within or between); however, separation of actor and partner effects can occur only with mixed predictor variables.

As an example, consider a fairly complicated fictitious study of relationship satisfaction involving 10 cohabiting heterosexual dating couples. In this study five of the couples are randomly assigned to a high-stress condition and the other five are in a low-stress condition, and so stress is a between-dyads variable.

For each couple a series of measures is obtained. Couples are asked to jointly arrive at an estimate of the proportion of time each partner spends on housework. Housework then is a within-dyads independent variable (for each couple the sum across the man's score and the woman's score is always equal to one), as is gender (each couple has one man and one woman). Two mixed predictor variables also are assessed. The first variable is relationship anxiety: Each partner rates the degree to which he or she feels anxious about their relationship on a 9-point scale such that higher numbers indicate greater anxiety. The second variable is distrust: Each partner rates his or her level of distrust of his or her partner on a 9-point scale. Relationship satisfaction is the outcome measure. The fictitious data for this example are in Table 17.6.

There are several ways to estimate the APIM (Kenny & Cook, 1998). In this chapter we focus on the method that is simplest, yet very general.

SINGLE PREDICTOR VARIABLES. In describing the estimation of actor and partner effects we begin with the simple case in which a single mixed independent variable, anxiety, is used to predict relationship satisfaction. To estimate actor and partner effects two regression equations are computed. In the first regression, called the within-dyad regression, both the predictor and outcome variables are differenced across the two partners. For example, if the question of interest involves predicting satisfaction from relationship anxiety, for each dyad one person's score on satisfaction would be subtracted from the other person's score on

TABLE 17.6. Data for Fictitious Example of Dyadic Analysis with Mixed, Between-Dyad, and Within-Dyad Predictor Variables

Dyad	Satisfaction P_A	Satisfaction P_B	Distrust P_A	Distrust P_B	Anxiety P_A	Anxiety P_B	Stress	Housework P_A	Housework P_B	Gender P_A	Gender P_B
1	5	7	4	8	6	6	1	.4	.6	1	0
2	9	7	9	5	3	5	1	.6	.4	1	0
3	9	5	9	6	2	6	1	.8	.2	1	0
4	7	7	8	6	6	5	1	.5	.5	0	1
5	3	2	6	5	9	8	1	.6	.4	1	0
6	6	9	3	5	5	8	−1	.3	.7	0	1
7	6	8	8	8	4	3	−1	.3	.7	0	1
8	8	5	7	5	8	6	−1	.8	.2	1	0
9	6	6	9	9	5	6	−1	.4	.6	1	0
10	7	8	6	7	4	6	−1	.5	.5	1	0

Note. P_A represents scores for Person A and P_B represents scores for Person B

satisfaction. This difference between the two partners' scores on satisfaction (Person A's satisfaction score minus Person B's satisfaction score) serves as the outcome score in a regression in which the predictor score is the difference (subtracting in the same direction across the two dyad members: Person A minus Person B) between the two partners' anxiety scores. Using the data in Table 17.6, for the first three dyads, the outcome and predictor scores (respectively) would be: Dyad 1: $-2, 0$; Dyad 2: $2, -2$; and Dyad 3: $4, -4$. The intercept should not be estimated in the within-dyads regression (see the earlier discussion on page 461).

In the second regression, called the between-dyads regression, the average of the two satisfaction scores is computed for each dyad, as is the average of the two anxiety scores. The mean anxiety score for the dyad is then used to predict the mean satisfaction score for the dyad. Again using the data in Table 17.6, for the first three dyads the outcome and predictor scores (respectively) for the between-dyads regression would be: Dyad 1: 6, 6; Dyad 2: 8, 4; and Dyad 3: 7, 4.

The unstandardized regression coefficients derived from these two regressions, b_b from the between regression and b_w from the within regression, are then used to estimate actor and partner effects[6] as follows (Kenny, 1996a):

actor: $(b_b + b_w)/2$; partner: $(b_b - b_w)/2$.

For the anxiety and satisfaction data in Table 17.6, the between regression equation yields a b_b of $-.742$, and the within regression yields a b_w of $-.098$ and thus the actor effect is estimated to be $-.420$, and the partner effect is $-.322$. Both the actor and partner effect estimates can be interpreted as unstandardized regression coefficients. The actor effect in this example indicates that individuals who are one point higher in anxiety are less satisfied by .420 points with their relationship. The partner effect estimate indicates that individuals whose partners are one point higher in anxiety are less satisfied by .322 points.

To test whether the actor and partner effects differ significantly from zero, the standard errors associ-

---

[6] The results of the within and between regressions can be interpreted without transforming them into actor and partner effects. For the example, the between slope estimates whether dyads with higher mean anxiety levels have lower mean satisfaction, and the within slope estimates whether dyads who differ in anxiety also differ in satisfaction. Our focus is on the estimation of actor and partner effects because this is a new methodological approach that provides information that is more consistent with a social psychological, mutual influence perspective.

ated with the between and within regression coefficients ($s_b = .240$ and $s_w = .359$, respectively) must be pooled. (The standard error for each of these regression coefficients can be derived by taking the t-value associated with the regression coefficient and dividing it by the regression coefficient.) The formula to calculate the pooled standard error is

$$\text{Pooled Standard Error} = \sqrt{\frac{s_b^2 + s_w^2}{4}}.$$

For the anxiety example, the pooled standard error is .216. The estimate of the actor effect is divided by this pooled standard error to yield a t-test indicating whether the actor effect differs significantly from zero. In the example the t-value for the actor effect is $-.420/.216 = -1.94$. Similarly, the partner effect t-value is $-.322/.216 = -1.49$. The degrees of freedom for both of these tests are estimated as

$$df = \frac{\left(s_b^2 + s_w^2\right)^2}{\frac{s_b^4}{df_b} + \frac{s_w^4}{df_w}}.$$

If a fractional answer is obtained and a critical value is to be sought from a t-table, to be conservative one rounds down. For the example, the degrees of freedom are estimated to be 15.39 or 15. Thus the actor effect t-value is marginally significant ($p < .10$) and the partner effect is nonsignificant.

An additional relevant statistic in this analysis is the amount of variance explained by the actor and partner effects combined. To compute this statistic, the total variance that can potentially be explained by the actor and partner effects must be computed. To compute this total variance, two regressions are conducted: a between regression without the averaged mixed predictor variable, and a within regression (no intercept) without the differenced mixed predictor variable. The between regression without the mixed predictor yields a sum of squares error, SSE_b', and a mean square error, MSE_b'; the within regression without the mixed predictor also yields a sum of squares error, SSE_w', and a mean square error, MSE_w'. The total variance that can be explained is then $(MSE_b' + MSE_w')/2$. The total variance left unexplained by the mixed independent variable is computed from the regressions including the mixed variable as a predictor and equals $(MSE_b + MSE_w)/2$ where MSE_b is the mean square error from the between regression that included the averaged mixed independent variable as a predictor, and MSE_w is the mean square error from the within regression that included the differenced mixed independent variable as the predictor. To compute the proportion of variance explained by the actor and partner effects combined, the value of R^2 is

$$R^2 = 1 - \frac{SSE_b + SSE_w}{SSE_b' + SSE_w'},$$

where SSE_b is the sum of squares error from the between regression that included the averaged mixed independent variable, and SSE_w is the sum of squares error from the within regression that included the differenced mixed independent variable.

Finally, note that the degree of nonindependence in the outcome measure, after controlling for the effects of the mixed independent variable, can be assessed using the error mean squares from the between and within regressions. The intraclass correlation for dyads controlling for the mixed independent variable is

$$\hat{\rho} = \frac{MSE_b - MSE_w}{MSE_b + MSE_w}.$$

If the intraclass correlation is positive, it is tested using $F = MSE_b/MSE_w$ with numerator degrees of freedom equal to the error degrees of freedom from the between regression and denominator degrees of freedom equal to the error degrees of freedom from the within regression. If the intraclass correlation is negative, then the $F = MSE_w/MSE_b$ with a corresponding flip of the degrees of freedom.

MULTIPLE PREDICTOR VARIABLES. A major advantage of this method of analyzing the APIM is that multiple predictor variables can be examined simultaneously. In the multiple predictor variable extension, the two regressions (within- and between-dyads) are conducted as multiple regressions. For the within-dyads regression each of the mixed predictor variables, as well as the outcome variable, are differenced (always in the same direction across partners). For the between-dyads regression, each of the mixed predictor variables and the outcome variable are averaged across partners. Actor and partner effects for each mixed predictor can then be estimated using the formulas presented previously.

In some analyses there may be a purely between-dyads or a purely within-dyads predictor variable in the analysis. For both purely within- or purely between-dyads variables, separate actor and partner effects cannot be estimated. If a within-dyads variable is to be included as a predictor variable, the difference between the dyad members' scores is included as a predictor only in the within-dyads regression. Purely between-dyads variables are included only in the between-dyads regression. This analysis provides estimates of the general effects of the purely between- and purely within-dyads

variables as well as estimates of both actor and partner effects for all mixed variables.

Table 17.7 has the results of this analysis for the fictitious example data set. The between-dyads multiple regression includes the two averaged mixed variables, distrust and anxiety, as well as the between-dyads predictor variable, stress. The within-dyads regression includes the differenced mixed variables, distrust and anxiety, as well as the differenced within-dyads predictor variables, housework and gender. As before, the intercept is not estimated in the within regression.

For the distrust variable, the results in Table 17.7 indicate a nonsignificant actor effect and a significant partner effect. Thus, although there is little evidence that persons high in distrust were less satisfied, there is a significant partner effect in the fictitious data such that persons whose partners distrusted them were less satisfied in their relationships. For anxiety both the actor and partner effects differed significantly from zero. The actor effect indicates that individuals who were high in anxiety were less satisfied, and the partner effect indicates that individuals whose partners were high in anxiety were less satisfied.

The other three variables in the example, stress, housework, and gender, are interpreted directly from the regression estimates. The between-dyads regression indicates that stress condition did not have a significant effect on satisfaction; the negative coefficient for stress shows a nonsignificant tendency for dyads in the higher stress condition to have lower average satisfaction scores. The within-dyads regression indicates a nonsignificant effect for gender but a significant effect of housework. The housework coefficient indicates that persons who performed more housework than their partner were on average more satisfied. The gender coefficient indicates that men were slightly more satisfied than women.

EXTENSION TO GROUP RESEARCH. Mixed variables occur often in group research in the form of individual difference variables such as self-monitoring, self-esteem, or extroversion. For such variables individuals within the group will usually have different scores, and the group averages will likely differ from one another. Consider as an example the effects of self-esteem on how much a person contributes to the group output. As in the dyad case, according to the APIM the actor effect estimates the degree to which a person's own level on the predictor variable predicts the person's response on the outcome measure (i.e., to what degree does a person's self-esteem predict his or her level of contribution). The partner effect has a slightly

TABLE 17.7. Multiple Predictor Variable Estimates for the Fictitious Dating Satisfaction Study

Regressions
Between: $Y = 16.010 - .558$ (Distrust) $- 1.044$ (Anxiety) $- .376$ (Stress)
Within: $Y = .324$ (Distrust) $+ .009$ (Anxiety) $+ 4.128$ (Housework) $+ .217$ (Gender)

	Between				Within			
	b	s	t	p	b	s	t	p
Distrust	−0.558	.278	−2.01	.092	0.324	.118	2.76	.033
Anxiety	−1.044	.253	−4.13	.006	0.009	.097	0.09	.932
Stress	−0.376	.291	−1.29	.245	—	—	—	—
Housework	—	—	—	—	4.128	.958	4.31	.005
Gender	—	—	—	—	0.217	.253	0.86	.425

Actor and Partner Estimates and Tests
Distrust:
  Actor: $(-.558 + .324)/2 = -.117$
  Partner: $(-.558 - .324)/2 = -.441$
  Standard Error:

$$\sqrt{\frac{.278^2 + .118^2}{4}} = .151$$

  Degrees of Freedom:

$$\frac{[.278^2 + .118^2]^2}{\frac{.278^4}{6} + \frac{.118^4}{6}} = 8.094 \approx 8$$

Tests of Actor and Partner Effects
  Actor: $t(8) = -.117/.151 = -.774$, n.s.
  Partner: $t(8) = -.441/.151 = -2.921, p < .05$
Anxiety:
  Actor: $-.518$
  Partner: $-.526$
  Standard Error $= .136$
  Degrees of Freedom: $7.74 \approx 7$
  Tests of Actor and Partner Effects
    Actor: $t(7) = -3.821, p < .01$
    Partner: $t(7) = -3.885, p < .01$

different meaning in group research; it estimates the degree to which the average level of the predictor variable for other group members predicts the person's response on the outcome measure (i.e., to what degree does the self-esteem level of the other group members predict the person's contribution).

As in the dyadic analysis of mixed predictor variables, to estimate actor and partner effects two regressions must be computed. The first regression is the between-group regression. In this regression the group average on the predictor variable is used to predict the group average on the outcome measure.

The second regression is the within-group regression. The within regression first requires taking each individual's score on the predictor variable and subtracting from it the group mean of the predictor variable. Similarly, the group mean of the outcome variable is subtracted from each individual's score on the outcome measure. The within regression is then computed by using the predictor deviation scores to predict the outcome deviation scores. The error degrees of freedom for the within analysis are $k(n - 1) - p$, where k is the number of groups, n is the number of persons within each group, and p is the number of predictor variables in the within regression. The intercept should not be estimated in the within regression. To make sure that the degrees of freedom are correct for this within-groups regression, group should be dummy-coded with $k - 1$ codes. Including these codes in the regression removes variance due to groups.

The actor and partner effect estimates for a predictor variable are then computed by combining the between and within regression coefficients as follows:

$$\text{actor effect} = [b_b + (n - 1)b_w]/n;$$

$$\text{partner effect} = (n - 1)(b_b - b_w)/n,$$

where n is the group size and must be the same for all groups. The standard error and degrees of freedom to test the actor effect are

$$\text{Pooled Std. Err.} = \sqrt{\frac{s_b^2 + (n - 1)^2 s_w^2}{n^2}},$$

$$df = \frac{\left(s_b^2 + (n - 1)^2 s_w^2\right)^2}{\frac{s_b^4}{df_b} + \frac{(n-1)^4 s_w^4}{df_w}}$$

and the standard error and degrees of freedom to test the partner effect are

$$\text{Pooled Std. Err.} = \sqrt{\frac{(n - 1)^2 \left(s_b^2 + s_w^2\right)}{n^2}},$$

$$df = \frac{\left(s_b^2 + s_w^2\right)^2}{\frac{s_b^4}{df_b} + \frac{s_w^4}{df_w}}.$$

Computing the proportion of variance explained by the actor and partner effects combined is done following a similar procedure as that described for dyadic data. The total amount of variability that can potentially be explained by the actor and partner effects is computed using two regressions: a between regression without the averaged mixed predictor variables, and a within regression (no intercept) without the mixed predictor deviation scores. The between regression without the mixed predictor yields a sum of squares error, SSE_b'; the within regression without the mixed predictor also yields a sum of squares error, SSE_w'. The total variability left unexplained when the mixed independent variable is included in the analysis is computed from the original between and within regressions. The SSE_b is the sum of squares error from the between regression that included the averaged mixed independent variable as a predictor, and the SSE_w is the sum of squares error from the within regression that included the differenced mixed independent variable as the predictor. To compute the proportion of variance explained by the actor and partner effects combined, the value of R^2 is

$$R^2 = 1 - \frac{SSE_b + SSE_w}{SSE_b' + SSE_w'}.$$

The intraclass correlation for group data controlling for the mixed independent variable is

$$\hat{\rho} = \frac{MSE_b - MSE_w}{MSE_b + (n - 1)MSE_w},$$

again assuming equal group sizes.

Multilevel Models

Imagine a group research situation in which group size is not controlled by the experimenter: Some groups may have many members; other groups may have very few members. Imagine further that some of the important independent or predictor variables are group-level variables such as leadership style or group size, whereas other predictor variables are individual-level variables such as individuals' levels of motivation or perhaps their gender. In this context, the group level is what we will refer to as the upper level and the individual level will be referred to as the lower level. Note that at both levels some of these predictor variables may be categorical in nature and some may be continuous. In addition, the group-level variables are naturally between-groups predictors, whereas the individual-level variables may be either within-groups predictor variables or mixed predictor variables. The outcome variable is measured at the level of the individual, and in this case might be a measure of the degree to which the individual feels committed to working with the group.

As a second example, imagine a research situation in which individuals complete brief questionnaires every time some event, such as an interaction with a romantic partner, occurs. Some individuals may interact very frequently with their romantic partners, whereas others may report relatively few such interactions. In this study, one major question of interest might concern whether characteristics of the research participants affect the outcomes of their romantic interactions, and therefore measures of the participants attachment styles, their gender, their ethnicity, and their education level may be obtained. There also may be important situational variables involved in predicting the outcome of romantic interactions. For example, the researcher might want to know whether the couple was alone or in the company of others when an interaction occurred. The outcome variable is measured for each interaction, and might be a measure of the amount of conflict that occurs in the interaction. In this example, individuals are the upper level and interactions are the lower level.

These two examples, although seemingly quite different, share some important methodological issues that are very difficult, if not impossible, to address within the standard ANOVA framework:

1. There are unequal numbers of observations at a lower level that are nested within some upper level grouping.
2. There are independent variables at both the upper level and the lower level, and although the general effects of these variables may be important questions to address, the interaction between variables measured at the two levels might also be quite important.
3. The independent variables at both levels may be either categorical or continuous, and they may be between, within, or mixed.
4. The data within the upper level groupings are potentially nonindependent.

Although these are difficult problems for ANOVA, there is a very new data analytic method that can handle every one of them. In this section of the chapter we introduce multilevel modeling (also known as hierarchical linear models, mixed model ANOVA, and random coefficient estimation), which is one of the newest and most exciting data analytic developments in recent years. The multilevel approach can potentially replace every one of the analyses described in this chapter thus far, although the specific methods for doing so are beyond the scope of this chapter. We expect that the use of multilevel modeling in the social and behavioral sciences will increase rapidly in the near future. In this section our goal is simply to introduce multilevel modeling and we refer the reader to more detailed sources (e.g., Bryk & Raudenbush, 1992; Kenny et al., 1998) for more specific application information.

THE BASIC DATA STRUCTURE. The defining feature of multilevel data is that there is a hierarchy of observations. The lower level is the level at which the outcome variable is measured and is nested or grouped within an upper-level unit. In group research, the lower-level unit is person, and the upper-level unit is group whether that be small face-to-face groups, classrooms, or organizations. Applications of multilevel modeling are not, however, limited to group research. For example, in repeated measures research (e.g., diary studies, program evaluation studies), observation or time point can be treated as the lower-level unit, and person can be treated as the upper-level unit (see Reis & Gable, this volume, Ch. 8; West, Biesanz, & Pitts, this volume, Ch. 3). There is no requirement that each person has the same number of repeated measurements or that groups have the same number of persons.

As an example of the basic data structure, we consider a fictitious group study examining the effects of the number of hours spent in group training and member motivation on productivity. The participants in this study are 45 laboratory groups ranging in size from 3 to 8 members. In addition to the number of hours in training, each group member's motivation and productivity is assessed. This study is used to investigate several questions concerning motivation and productivity. First, are persons generally more productive in groups that received more or less training? This first question concerns the effects of a between-groups independent variable, and ANOVA could be used to analyze such data if the hours in training effect were the sole question of interest. Second, does motivation predict productivity? Motivation is almost certainly a mixed independent variable because some individuals likely are more motivated than others and some groups are likely more motivated on average than others. The third question that this study can address using a multilevel approach is the interaction between motivation and hours in training: Does motivation have different effects in groups that received more training relative to those that received less training?

In this example, person is the lower-level unit and group is the upper-level unit. Motivation is a lower-level predictor variable that we symbolize as X. Note that X can be either continuous or categorical (categorical Xs need to be contrast coded). When X is continuous, as is the case for motivation, to make the intercepts more interpretable, the X variable should be centered around a meaningful value, often the mean (Aiken & West, 1991). To center the variable, the grand mean of the variable (not the group mean) is subtracted from each score. Number of hours in training is an upper-level predictor variable and is denoted as Z. Like X, Z can be either continuous or categorical and should be centered or coded as needed. The outcome measure, an individual's level of productivity, is denoted as Y.

Note that partner effects are not estimated in this model (see the discussion of mixed variables in the previous section). For the example, the partner effect would refer to the effect of the motivation of the other group members on the person's productivity. Had we wished to allow for such effects, we would create an additional X variable: the mean motivation of those in the group besides the person (Kenny, 1996b). Although partner effects are not usually estimated in multilevel models, because of their social psychological importance, they should be given consideration.

ANALYSIS. As mentioned earlier, many different types of data fit into this general data structure. The basic requirement is that there should be some upper-level unit and a lower-level unit, and the outcome or dependent variable should be measured once for each lower-level unit. As indicated by the example, hierarchically nested designs are generally of this form. Repeated measures designs may also be of this form such that time point is the lower-level unit and person is the upper-level unit. Similarly, social interaction diary designs (see Reis & Gable, this volume, Ch. 8) typically have this structure. In diary studies, research participants report on their interactions with multiple partners for some period of time. Thus, the lower-level unit is partner and the upper-level unit is the research participant.

Multilevel modeling can be viewed as a two-step procedure in which a regression analysis is first performed within each upper-level unit (group), and then the results of all of these analyses are pooled across the upper-level units. That is, in the first step, the relationship between X and Y is estimated separately for each upper-level unit. In the example, the first step of the analysis estimates the relationship between motivation and productivity separately for each group. So for each group, a regression equation is computed treating productivity as the criterion and motivation as the predictor. These regressions yield an intercept and a slope for each group. Given that motivation was centered, the intercept estimates the level of productivity for someone of average motivation in the group and the slope estimates the effect of motivation on productivity for the group.

In the second step, the results from the step 1 analyses are pooled across the upper-level units and the effects of the upper-level predictor variable, Z, are assessed. In the example, the second step involves computing two regressions, both of which treat group as the unit of analysis. In the first regression, the intercepts from the first-step regressions are treated as the criterion measures and number of hours in training (the upper-level predictor variable) is treated as the predictor. The slope from this regression equation measures the general effect of hours in training on productivity: Are groups with more training more or less productive?

The second of the second-step regressions treats the slopes from the first-step regressions as the criterion variable and again hours in training is the predictor. When the upper-level predictor variable, hours in training in the example, is centered, the intercept from this regression is the average of the first-step regression slopes. This intercept estimates the typical relationship between motivation and productivity: Are groups with more highly motivated members more productive? The slope from this regression estimates the interaction between hours in training and member motivation: Does the effect of member motivation on productivity differ depending upon how much training a group received?

The first-step regression coefficients are likely to differ in their precision. Some are estimated more precisely than others because they are based on more observations and/or because X varies more. It seems reasonable to weight the second-step equation by the precision of the first-step estimates. That is, groups whose coefficients are well estimated should count more than groups whose coefficients are not well estimated. The standard way to weight the more precise first-step estimates is to use maximum likelihood estimation (Kenny et al., 1998).

In multilevel modeling there are two sources of nonindependence that are represented by two variances of effects. First, there is variance in the first-step regression intercepts. This variance measures the extent to which there are differences between upper-level units in their average scores on Y when X and Z are controlled. So it measures the degree to which groups differ in average levels of productivity controlling for both the levels of motivation in the groups and amount of training received. Thus, the variance of the intercepts is a measure of the degree of nonindependence between scores within the groups and when computed in terms of variance explained is analogous to the intraclass correlation. Note that the interpretation of the variance of the first-step regression intercepts is completely dependent on the meaning of zero in the X variable. Because motivation is centered around its mean, the intercept is the predicted level of productivity for a group that is average in motivation.

There is also variance in the first-step regression slopes. This variance measures the extent to which the relationship between X and Y varies across the upper-level units after removing variation due to Z. So for the example, this variance measures the degree to which the relationship between motivation and productivity varies across groups, controlling for amount of training received. Although not obvious, this variance taps the interaction of motivation with group.

There is now a wide array of specialized computer programs that calculate these maximum likelihood estimates and tests: HLM/2L and HLM/3L (Bryk, Raudenbush, & Congdon, 1994), MIXREG (Hedeker, 1993), MLn (Goldstein, Rasbash, & Yang, 1994), as well as 5V within BMDP and PROC MIXED within SAS. It should be noted that these programs actually accomplish the estimation in one step and do not take two steps as we have previously described. Also, most programs implement a variety of estimation approaches, the most common being restricted maximum likelihood. Introductions to maximum likelihood estimation of multilevel models can be found in Bryk and Raudenbush (1992) and Hedeker, Gibbons, and Flay (1994).

To accomplish the first-step regressions, the group size must be greater than the number of lower-level predictors plus two. This condition is satisfied for our example, but it is generally not satisfied when the group size is small. Thus, this condition generally is hardly ever satisfied for dyadic data. When the condition is not satisfied, one must drop from the model the variance in the first step regression slopes.

Also problematic is the way in which multilevel models conceptualize nonindependence. Because a variance is used and variances must be nonnegative, negative nonindependence (when the intraclass correlation for the outcome measure is negative) is not allowable. So if nonindependence is negative, the current formulation of most multilevel models would be inappropriate.

DYAD-LEVEL OUTCOME MEASURES IN GROUP RESEARCH: THE SOCIAL RELATIONS MODEL

Some research questions can only be addressed by designs in which persons participate in more than one dyad. For example, consider the question of whether affective evaluations are primarily determined by the unique relationship between two individuals. If individuals participate in only one dyad, then a measure of liking of the partner may not necessarily represent unique liking. That is, a high liking score from one member of the dyad may be due to the fact that the individual is a "liker" such that he or she likes everyone. Similarly, it may be that the partner is simply "likable" and is liked by everyone. Finally, it may be the case that liking is in fact relationally determined and that ratings of liking within dyads are unique. In order to separate these three factors, each individual would have to participate in more than one dyad. With multiple interactions, the degree to which a person is a "liker" can be assessed by looking at whether that person generally likes everyone with whom he or she interacts. Similarly, the degree to which a person is "likable" can be assessed by looking at whether everyone who interacts with that person likes him or her. Finally, if there is evidence that, over and above a person's tendency to be a "liker" and over and above the partner's tendency to be liked, one

person likes the other, then there is evidence that liking is uniquely determined by the specific relationship.

It is not uncommon for persons to participate in more than one dyad. One example of this is provided by Miller and Kenny (1986) who asked each member of a sorority how much they disclosed to every other sorority member. A second example would be a study in which each individual interacted with two different partners and each person's nonverbal behavior was measured (Duncan & Fiske, 1977). Another example might be a study involving groups of strangers who rated each other's personalities (Albright, Kenny, & Malloy, 1988).

Investigation of many important social psychological phenomena requires that individuals participate in more than one dyad. For example, investigations of the degree to which individuals agree in their evaluations of others (i.e., consensus) require such a data structure (e.g., Albright et al., 1997; Kenny, Albright, Malloy, & Kashy, 1994). Similarly, studies inquiring into the degree to which individuals know how they are seen by others require multiple dyads (e.g., Levesque, 1997; Kenny & DePaulo, 1993). Studies of reciprocity of verbal and nonverbal behavior also fit well into such a research paradigm (e.g., Miller & Kenny, 1986).

The Basic Data Structures

There are several data structures (see Kenny, 1990) for dyad-level outcome measures within group research, the most common of which is the round-robin design.

ROUND-ROBIN DESIGNS. As shown in Table 17.8, in round-robin data structures every member of the group interacts with or rates every other individual in the group; the key requirement is that each dyadic combination provides an outcome score. Consider as an example a group comprised of four members: Allison (A), Beth (B), Cathy (C), and Diane (D). Dyadic interactions can occur in the presence of the entire group (A, B, C, and D interact simultaneously), or they can occur one-on-one such that Allison and Beth interact in one room while Cathy and Diane interact in another, then A and C interact while B and D interact, and so on. An example of the former type of round robin is a study of perceptions of and by lonely people in which groups of four individuals scoring at differing levels of loneliness worked together on problem solving tasks and then rated one another on measures of social skills and intelligence (Christensen & Kashy, 1998). An example of the latter can be found in Levesque

TABLE 17.8. Common Data Structures that Can Be Analyzed Using the Social Relations Model

Round robin

	A	B	C	D
A	s	x	x	x
B	x	s	x	x
C	x	x	s	x
D	x	x	x	s

Full block

	A	B	C	D	E	F	G	H
A	s				x	x	x	x
B		s			x	x	x	x
C			s		x	x	x	x
D				s	x	x	x	x
E	x	x	x	x	s			
F	x	x	x	x		s		
G	x	x	x	x			s	
H	x	x	x	x				s

Half block

	E	F	G	H
A	x	x	x	x
B	x	x	x	x
C	x	x	x	x
D	x	x	x	x

and Kenny (1993). In their study of the accuracy of behavioral predictions, both behavioral measures and interpersonal perception measures were gathered from four-person groups in which the participants interacted in dyads.

Typically, though not required, round-robin data are directional so that Allison's rating of or behavior with Beth differs from Beth's rating of or behavior with Allison. The diagonal of a round-robin design represents self-data (see Table 17.8). Self-data occurs frequently in rating studies and generally involves having the research participants rate how they see themselves on the variables being measured. Self-data are uncommon in studies of behaviors such as self-disclosure or nonverbal behavior.

BLOCK DESIGNS. Dyad-level group data also occurs in the form of block designs. The block design is actually a family of designs including the full-block, half-block, and asymmetric-block designs. In the full-block design (see Table 17.8), a group is broken into two subgroups and individuals interact with only those in the other subgroup. So if the group includes 8 individuals, A through H, persons A, B, C, and D interact with persons E, F, G, and H. Thus, as indicated in Table 17.8, the full-block design results in two sets of observations:

the upper-right section and the lower-left section. Self-data can be collected in the block design, and are represented along the diagonal.

Sometimes data are collected from only one half of the block design, such that A, B, C, and D rate E, F, G, and H and not vice versa. This is called a half-block design. An example of a half-block design is presented in Kenny, Horner, Kashy, and Chu (1992, Study 1). In that study 113 participants rated 32 videotaped targets on ten personality traits. Finally, the asymmetric-block design is similar to the full-block design with the exception that in this design persons A through D can be distinguished from persons E through F on a meaningful variable. For example, in Kenny and DePaulo (1993), one subgroup were interviewers and the other were applicants for a hypothetical resident associate position.

The Social Relations Model

Using dyad-level measures and the specialized designs in Table 17.8 brings a substantial advantage over research using individual-level measures in that it allows individual-level effects to be separated from unique dyadic-combination effects. The SRM, developed by Kenny and his colleagues (Kenny, 1994; Kenny & La Voie, 1984; Warner, Kenny, & Stoto, 1979) provides a general framework from which both social behavior and interpersonal perception can be studied. In the SRM, dyadic outcome measures within groups can be broken into group-level effects, individual-level effects, and dyad-level effects. Because the social psychological meanings of the SRM effects differ depending upon whether the outcome scores are interpersonal ratings or measures of behavior such as self-disclosure, two example variables will be used to describe the SRM components, one of which will be rating data, and the other will be a behavioral measure.

To illustrate the SRM, consider as an example a study in which the group consisting of Allison, Beth, Cathy, and Diane is one of 10 groups of unacquainted individuals who interact dyadically in a round-robin pattern. Say that the interactions are videotaped and the tapes are coded for the amount of self-disclosure on the part of each dyad member. In addition, after each interaction the 2 dyad members rate one another on a measure of extroversion.

THE SRM COMPONENTS. According to the SRM, each dyadic score is composed of four components. Consider as examples Allison's rating of Beth's extroversion and the degree to which Allison self-discloses to

TABLE 17.9. Social Relations Model Components for Rating Measures and Behavioral Measures

Score	=	Group Mean	+	Allison's Actor Effect	+	Beth's Partner Effect	+	Allison's Relationship Effect with Beth
Rating Measure:								
Allison's rating of Beth's extroversion	=	Group mean for extroversion	+	Allison's tendency to see all partners as extroverted	+	Beth's tendency to be seen by all partners as extroverted	+	Allison's unique perception of Beth's extroversion
Behavioral Measure:								
Allison's level of self-disclosure with Beth	=	Group mean for self-disclosure	+	Allison's tendency to self-disclose to all partners	+	Beth's tendency to elicit self-disclosure from all partners	+	Allison's unique amount of self-disclosure to Beth

Beth. Table 17.9 presents the SRM break-down of these dyadic scores for both extroversion and self-disclosure.

First, at the group level, Allison and Beth's group might on average have scored high on extroversion relative to the other nine groups. That is, one component that contributes to Allison's rating of Beth's extroversion is the general level of extroversion in the group as a whole: Some groups are more extroverted than others. This first component is called the *group mean* and reflects the average level of the outcome score for the group. Similarly, the degree to which Allison self-discloses to Beth in part reflects the group mean for self-disclosure because some groups may self-disclose more than others.

Next, at the individual level Allison's ratings or behavior may be consistent across all of her interactions with the other group members (B, C, and D). For ratings of extroversion, Allison may tend to rate everyone as highly extroverted and so part of Allison's high rating of Beth's extroversion may be a function of Allison's general tendency to see others as extroverted. In terms of self-disclosure, one factor that contributes to Allison's level of self-disclosure with Beth is Allison's general tendency to disclose a great deal to others. The tendency for a person to exhibit a consistent level of response across all interaction partners is generally called an *actor effect*.[7] The meaning of the actor effect in the SRM differs dramatically from that for the APIM (see above). In the APIM, the actor effect is the impact of a person's score on a predictor variable on that person's score on his or her outcome variable. In the SRM, the actor effect is the degree to which an individual provides consistent scores on the outcome variable across multiple dyads, there being no predictor variable.

The *partner effect* is also an individual-level effect and it measures the tendency for others to be consistent with a particular partner. Thus, for Allison's rating of Beth's extroversion, the partner effect measures the tendency for Beth to be seen as extroverted by all of her interaction partners. When outcome measures are behavioral, the partner effect measures the degree to which certain individuals tend to elicit similar behavior from all of their interaction partners. In terms of self-disclosure, the partner effect measures the tendency for all group members to self-disclose a great deal to Beth. As was true for the actor effect, the partner effect has different meanings for the APIM and the SRM. For the APIM, the partner effect is the degree to which a person's partner's score on a predictor affected the person's score on the outcome. For the SRM, the partner effect is the degree to which others behave in consistent ways on the outcome measure when interacting with a particular partner.

The *relationship effect* is at the dyad level. For Allison's rating of Beth's extroversion, the relationship effect measures the degree to which Allison sees Beth as especially extroverted, over and above Allison's general tendency to see others as extroverted and over and above Beth's tendency to be seen by others as extroverted. Thus, the relationship effect reflects the unique combination of two individuals after removing their individual-level tendencies. For the self-disclosure example, the relationship effect measures the degree to which Allison discloses to Beth, after taking into account both Allison's actor effect for self-disclosure and Beth's partner effect for self-disclosure.

The relationship effect can be separated from error only if there are multiple measures of the same underlying construct. For example, Allison could rate Beth on two indicators of extroversion, such as sociability and talkativeness. These two measures could be treated as indicators of extroversion and the part of Allison's

---

[7] In rating studies using the SRM, the actor effect is usually referred to as the *perceiver effect* and the partner effect as the *target effect*.

unique rating of Beth that is consistent across the two indicators would be treated as the relationship effect and any inconsistency across the two indicators would be treated as error. Replications over time also may be used to partition relationship effects from error. That is, if Allison and Beth interact two times, and self-disclosure is measured at each, Allison's relationship effect for self-disclosure with Beth could be separated from noise due to chance fluctuations over time.

THE SRM AS A MODIFIED TWO-WAY RANDOM EFFECTS ANOVA DESIGN. The SRM can be thought of as a somewhat complex two-way random effects ANOVA model. Although it is possible to think of any SRM data structure in such a fashion, it is easiest to exemplify this connection with the half block design in which one set of individuals (say persons A, B, C, and D) rate a second set of individuals (say E, F, G, and H). Within the ANOVA framework, actor is the first factor with the "levels" being the individuals A, B, C, and D within the group. The second factor is partner, and its levels are persons E, F, G, and H. Using this framework, we can define the variance due to actor, the variance due to partner, and the variance due to relationship.

The actor variance, measuring the degree to which some individuals see all partners as high on a trait and other individuals see all partners as low on a trait, is essentially (but not exactly) the variance among the row marginal means after averaging across partners. Thus, the actor variance is the row main effect. The partner variance, measuring the degree to which some individuals are seen by all actors as high on a trait and other individuals are seen by all actors as low on the trait, is essentially (but not exactly) the variance among the column marginal means after averaging across actors; it is the column main effect. The relationship variance, measuring the degree to which trait ratings are unique to particular pairings of actors and partners, is the variance due to the interaction between actor and partner. That is, the relationship variance is the variance in the cells, after the row marginal means (the main effect of actor) and the column marginal means (the main effect of partner) have been removed.

The first panel of Table 17.10 contains an example data set in which there is only variance due to the actor effect. As you can see, the row marginal means vary,

---

TABLE 17.10. The Social Relations Model as a Two-Way Random Effects ANOVA

Actor variance only

| | | Partner | | | | |
		E	F	G	H	Row marginal means
	A	1	1	1	1	1.0
Actor	B	2	2	2	2	2.0
	C	3	3	3	3	3.0
	D	4	4	4	4	4.0
Column marginal means		2.5	2.5	2.5	2.5	

Partner variance only

| | | Partner | | | | |
		E	F	G	H	Row marginal means
	A	1	2	3	4	2.5
Actor	B	1	2	3	4	2.5
	C	1	2	3	4	2.5
	D	1	2	3	4	2.5
Column marginal means		1.0	2.0	3.0	4.0	

Relationship variance only

| | | Partner | | | | |
		E	F	G	H	Row marginal means
	A	1	2	3	4	2.5
Actor	B	2	3	4	1	2.5
	C	3	4	1	2	2.5
	D	4	1	2	3	2.5
Column marginal means		2.5	2.5	2.5	2.5	

but the column marginal means are constant. Further, once the variance in the row marginal means has been taken into account, there is no variation in scores from cell to cell. The second panel of Table 17.10 contains an example data set in which there is only partner variance. The third panel shows a situation in which scores vary as a function of the relationship effect (the interaction of actor and partner).

THE SRM VARIANCES. In a social relations analysis the variances for the three central components, actor, partner, and relationship, are estimated for each group, and then these variances are pooled across groups.[8] For example, in a rating study, the actor variance measures the degree of *assimilation* (the degree to which some individuals tend to rate all others as high on a trait whereas other individuals rate all others as low). The actor variance for a behavioral variable such as self-disclosure measures the degree to which some individuals are consistently high disclosers and others are consistently low disclosers. The partner variance in rating data measures *consensus* (the degree to which all individuals agree that some targets are high on a trait whereas other targets are low on the trait). For self-disclosure (behavioral data) the partner variance measures the degree to which, with some partners, everyone discloses a great deal but with other partners everyone discloses little. The relationship variance measures the degree to which ratings vary depending upon the specific individuals in the dyad, after partialling out variance due to those individuals' actor and partner effects. For rating data, the relationship variance measures the degree to which perceptions of individuals' standings on a trait are unique to the particular dyadic combinations. For behavioral data, the relationship variance measures the degree to which the exhibition of some behavior such as disclosure is uniquely determined by the dyadic combination.

THE SRM CORRELATIONS. The SRM also specifies two correlations between the SRM components of a variable. At the individual level, a person's actor effect can be correlated with that person's partner effect to assess generalized reciprocity. For the self-disclosure example, a positive generalized reciprocity correlation would indicate that individuals who disclose a great deal to all of their partners also receive a great deal of

disclosure from all of their partners. At the dyadic level, the two members' relationship effects can be correlated to assess dyadic reciprocity. That is, if Allison discloses to an unusually high degree when with Beth, does Beth also disclose to an unusually high degree when with Allison?

The individual-level SRM effects (actor and partner) can also be correlated with self-data and with individual difference measures. For example, the correlation between self-ratings of extroversion and actor effects for extroversion measures whether the way a person sees him or herself corresponds to how he or she sees others (this is sometimes referred to as *assumed similarity*). The correlation between self-ratings and partner effects of trait ratings measures self–other agreement: Do others see a person as that person sees him or herself? Correlations between the individual-level effects and personality data can address such questions as whether high self-monitors tend to disclose a great deal across all partners (this would be a correlation between personality scores and actor effects), or whether high self-monitors tend to be recipients of higher levels of self-disclosure from their partners (this would be a personality–partner correlation).

When multiple groups are studied, significance tests for the SRM treat group as the unit of analysis for tests of most of the variances and correlations. That is, separate estimates are derived for each group and then both the mean of the estimates as well as the standard error of the estimates are derived. The mean estimates are then tested to see if they differ significantly from zero. The correlations between self-data, personality data, and actor and partner effects treat individual within group as the unit of analysis.

Social Relations Analyses: An Example

The computational formulas for estimation of the SRM parameters (the variances and covariances) are fairly complex and are described in detail in Kenny (1994). Kenny has developed two computer programs that perform SRM analyses, SOREMO (Kenny, 1996d) for round-robin data structures, and BLOCKO (Kenny, 1996a) for block data structures. In this chapter, instead of describing the actual estimation procedure, we discuss the results from a simple fictitious example involving a single group of six individuals who interact in a round-robin fashion. The computer program SOREMO is used to estimate the SRM variances and correlations. Likely in the future, multilevel models (see above) will be modified to estimate the SRM variances and correlations.

---

[8] For groups in which persons have distinct roles (e.g., families), the variances can be estimated between groups through confirmatory factor analysis (Kashy & Kenny, 1990).

TABLE 17.11. Fictitious Round-Robin Data Set Of Participant Ratings of Liking and Coded Ratings of Smiling During Brief Dyadic Interactions

	Self-monitoring Score of Actor	Partner					
Actor		A	B	C	D	E	F
A	19	—	$6^a,7^b$	6,6	4,7	8,6	6,5
B	15	8,5	—	7,4	7,6	6,5	8,4
C	10	5,3	7,5	—	3,4	5,3	4,5
D	12	5,4	9,5	6,4	—	9,4	7,3
E	18	6,5	7,4	6,5	8,6	—	5,4
F	15	4,2	6,5	5,4	6,4	8,3	—

[a] Ratings of the degree to which the actor liked the partner on 9-point scales.
[b] Independent observer's codings of the degree to which the actor smiled at the partner on 9-point scales.

The example study examines the correspondence between ratings of liking, the degree to which individuals smile when interacting, and self-monitoring. Six individuals (A, B, C, D, E, and F) are recruited to serve as participants. After completing the self-monitoring scale (Snyder, 1974), the six individuals are broken into dyads (A with B, C with D, and E with F). The three dyads are videotaped while interacting for a period of 5 min, after which each person rates how much he or she likes his or her partner. Dyad composition then rotates, the new dyads interact, and ratings are again obtained. This procedure is followed until each individual has interacted with every other individual in the group and thus, each person participates in five interactions. The videotapes of the interactions are then coded by independent coders on a 9-point scale for the amount of each dyad member's smiling. The fictitious data set generated by this example study is given in Table 17.11. Note that because individuals did not provide data about how much they liked (or smiled at) themselves, the diagonal of the data in Table 17.11 is empty and so correlations between the individual-level effects and self-data cannot be estimated.

The group mean for liking was $M = 6.23$ and the mean for smiling was $M = 4.57$. The SRM variances and correlations are presented in Table 17.12. Examination of the variance partitioning for liking indicates that in this fictitious data set, such judgments largely depend on actor and relationship effects. About one quarter of the variation in ratings of liking is accounted for by who the rater or actor was. Only about 11% of the variation is dependent on the partner, indicating that there was a rather weak tendency for some group members to be liked by everyone and others to be liked by no one. Clearly, however, the majority of liking variance is at the level of the dyad or relationship (plus error).

The variance partitioning results for smiling indicate that 47% of the variation for this variable was accounted by actor. Some individuals were "smilers" (they smiled at all of their partners) and others were "non-smilers." The 14% partner variance shows a tendency for some individuals to elicit smiling from all of their partners. The remaining 39% of the variation in smiling was accounted for by the relationship effect plus error.

The generalized reciprocity correlation for liking is quite large and positive. This result indicates that individuals who liked all of their partners tended to be liked by their partners. The generalized reciprocity correlation for smiling is relatively small and negative, implying that individuals who smiled at all of their partners were not generally smiled at by all of their partners. In contrast, the positive dyadic reciprocity correlation for smiling indicates that individuals reciprocated unique

TABLE 17.12. Social Relations Model Estimates for the Fictitious Round-Robin Data Set in Table 17.11

Variance partitioning: absolute and (percentages)

	Actor	Partner	Relationship/Error
Liking	.644 (25.0)	.278 (10.8)	1.656 (64.2)
Smiling	.717 (46.7)	.217 (14.1)	.600 (39.1)

Reciprocity correlations

	Generalized	Dyadic
Liking	.78	.26
Smiling	−.19	.19

Correlations with a personality variable: self-monitoring (SelfM)

	SelfM-Actor	SelfM-Partner
Liking	.34	.48
Smiling	.75	−.58

levels of smiling. That is, if a person smiled a great deal at a particular partner, the partner reciprocated by smiling a great deal. Liking was also positively reciprocated at the dyad level such that if one person indicated an unusually high level of liking, his or her partner also indicated an unusually high level of liking. The divergence of smiling findings for generalized and dyadic reciprocity in the fictitious data set demonstrates how SRM analyses can simultaneously model different processes that occur at the individual and dyad levels.

The final set of correlations in Table 17.12 assess the degree to which self-monitoring relates to the two individual-level effects, actor and partner. The positive correlation between self-monitoring and actor effects in liking implies that high self-monitors tended to rate all of their partners as more likeable than did low self-monitors. Similarly, the positive correlation between self-monitoring and smiling indicates that high self-monitors tended to smile at all of their partners more than did low self-monitors. Self-monitoring was positively related to partner effects for liking and negatively related to partner effects for smiling. These correlations indicate that higher self-monitors were generally liked more but were smiled at less by all of their partners. Note that individual-level measures, such as personality data or self-data cannot be correlated with relationship effects.

SUMMARY AND CONCLUSION

In this chapter we have presented research designs and data analytic methods that recognize that individuals within a group or dyad may influence one another. We have described how the degree of interrelatedness of scores from dyads and groups can be assessed as well as the consequences of ignoring nonindependence in hypothesis testing. We have also described a number of data analytic approaches that, rather than assuming independence, instead explicitly model interdependence.

The APIM described in this chapter is one of the newest innovations in the analysis of nonindependent data, and it has tremendous potential for elaborating our understanding of dyad and group processes. The estimation procedure for this model allows for both univariate and multivariate analyses, it focuses on estimating actor and partner effects for mixed independent variables while allowing for inclusion of within or between independent variables, and it can be applied to either dyadic or group data. It is also an analysis that does not require especially complicated research designs or specialized data analysis methods in order to estimate the effects. The primary data requirement

is that each person provides a score on an outcome measure and a score on a mixed predictor variable; persons need not engage in multiple interactions and they need not provide multiple outcome scores over time.

Multilevel modeling is also a new data analytic method, and it too shows a great deal of promise for future research in many areas of psychology. Multilevel modeling can be applied across a wide range of research designs including repeated measures designs as well as group designs. This technique has a number of important advantages over more traditional ANOVA and regression approaches. One advantage is that, whereas repeated measures ANOVA requires equal numbers of observations from each unit sampled, multilevel analysis allows for unequal numbers of observations from each unit. More important, multilevel modeling provides a method for estimating interactions between variables that are measured at different levels of analysis. The primary data requirement for multilevel modeling is that there is a nesting of sampling units, and that the outcome measure is obtained once for each lower-level unit.

Over the past decade, the SRM has proven to be an important tool for social psychologists studying a range of interpersonal phenomena. This model provides a method for differentiating the unique effects that occur when two particular individuals interact with or rate one another from the two individuals' general tendencies. The data requirements for a Social Relations Analysis are somewhat stringent in that each individual must interact with or rate several partners.

This chapter is merely an introduction into the analysis of nonindependent data. There are a number of other important methods that we have not discussed. Social network analyses, for example, are a set of techniques that can be used to model the interrelatedness of individuals within a social group (see Wasserman & Faust, 1994). There are also specialized designs in which individuals are in more than one group (Kenny, Hallmark, Sullivan, & Kashy, 1993), and models for triadic processes (Bond, Horn, & Kenny, 1997).

The available research methodology plays a critical role in the development of scientific theory by constraining the types of questions the scientist can conceptualize. Thus, researchers who are familiar only with ANOVA methodology, for example, tend to conceive of questions that fit within an ANOVA framework. They may even begin to think that people think in terms of ANOVA (e.g., Kelley, 1973). Although ANOVA and multiple regression are important tools for discovering how variables affect an individual's behavior, they are not well-suited to the study of many research questions in social psychology. When questions concern issues of interdependence between individuals, the methods described in this chapter that directly measure and model interdependence will lead to theoretical and conceptual advances. As we noted in the introduction of this chapter, if social psychology is to grow and develop as the study of truly social behavior, researchers need to become proficient in the kinds of designs and analyses that allow them to study individuals within actual social contexts.

REFERENCES

Aiken, L. S., & West, S. G. (1991). *Multiple regression: Testing and interpreting interactions.* Newbury Park, CA: Sage.

Albright, L., Kenny, D.A., & Malloy, T. E. (1988). Consensus in personality judgments at zero acquaintance. *Journal of Personality and Social Psychology, 55,* 387–395.

Albright, L., Malloy, T. E., Dong, Q., Kenny, D. A., Fang, X., Winquist, L., & Yu, D. (1997). Cross-cultural consensus in personality judgments. *Journal of Personality and Social Psychology, 72,* 558–569.

Bond, C. F., Horn, E. M., & Kenny, D. A. (1997). A model for triadic relations. *Psychological Methods, 2,* 79–94.

Boyd, L., & Iversen, G. (1979). *Contextual analysis: Concepts and statistical techniques.* Belmont, CA: Wadsworth.

Bryk, A. S., & Raudenbush, S. W. (1992). *Hierarchical linear models: Applications and data analysis methods.* Newbury Park, CA: Sage.

Bryk, A. S., Raudenbush, S. W., & Congdon, R. (1994). *Hierarchical linear modeling with the HLM/2L and HLM/3L programs.* Chicago: Scientific Software International.

Christensen, P. N., & Kashy, D. A. (1998). Perceptions of and by lonely people in initial social interaction. *Personality and Social Psychology Bulletin, 24,* 322–329.

Duncan, S., & Fiske, D. W. (1977). *Face to face interaction: Research, methods, and theory.* Hillsdale, NJ: Academic Press.

Feeney, J. A. (1994). Attachment style, communication patterns, and satisfaction across the life cycle of marriage. *Personal Relationships, 1,* 333–348.

Goldstein, H., Rasbash, J., & Yang, M. (1994). *MLn: User's guide for version 2.3.* London: Institute of Education, University of London.

Griffin, D., & Gonzalez, R. (1995). Correlational analysis of dyad-level data in the exchangeable case. *Psychological Bulletin, 118,* 430–439.

Hedeker, D. (1993). *MIXREG: A FORTRAN program for mixed-effects linear regression models.* University of Chicago: Chicago, IL.

Hedeker, D., Gibbons, R. D., & Flay, B. R. (1994). Random-effects regression models for clustered data with an example from smoking prevention research. *Journal of Consulting and Clinical Psychology, 62,* 757–765.

Ickes, W., & Gonzalez, R. (1994). "Social" cognition and social cognition: From the subjective to the intersubjective. *Small Group Research, 25,* 294–315.

Kashy, D. A., & Kenny, D. A. (1990). Analysis of family research designs: A model of interdependence. *Communication Research, 17,* 462–483.

Kashy, D. A., & Snyder, D. K. (1995). Measurement and data analytic issues in couples research. *Psychological Assessment, 7,* 338–348.

Kelley, H. H. (1973). The processes of causal attribution. *American Psychologist, 28,* 107–128.

Kenny, D. A. (1988). The analysis of data from two person relationships. In S. Duck (Ed.), *Handbook of interpersonal relationships* (pp. 57–77). London: Wiley.

Kenny, D. A. (1990). Design issues in dyadic research. In C. Hendrick & M. S. Clark (Eds.), *Review of personality and social psychology: Research methods in personality and social psychology* (pp. 164–184). Newbury Park, CA: Sage.

Kenny, D. A. (1994). *Interpersonal perception: A social relations analysis.* New York: Guilford Press.

Kenny, D. A. (1995). The effect of nonindependence on significance testing in dyadic research. *Personal Relationships, 2,* 67–75.

Kenny, D. A. (1996a). *BLOCKO* [computer program]. Available: http://nw3.nai.net/~dakenny/kenny.htm.

Kenny, D. A. (1996b). The design and analysis of social-interaction research. *Annual Review of Psychology, 47,* 59–86.

Kenny, D. A. (1996c). Models of interdependence in dyadic research. *Journal of Social and Personal Relationships, 13,* 279–294.

Kenny, D. A. (1996d). *SOREMO* [computer program]. Available: http://nw3.nai.net/~dakenny/kenny.htm.

Kenny, D. A., Albright, L., Malloy, T. E., & Kashy, D. A. (1994). Consensus in interpersonal perception: Acquisition and the big five. *Psychological Bulletin, 116,* 245–258.

Kenny, D. A., & Cook, W. (1998). *Partner effects in relationship research: Conceptual issues, analytic difficulties, and illustrations.* Unpublished manuscript, University of Connecticut.

Kenny, D. A., & DePaulo, B. M. (1993). Do people know how others view them? An empirical and theoretical account. *Psychological Bulletin, 114,* 145–161.

Kenny, D. A., Hallmark, B. W., Sullivan, P., & Kashy, D. A. (1993). The analysis of designs in which individuals are in more than one group. *British Journal of Social Psychology, 32,* 173–190.

Kenny, D. A., Horner, C., Kashy, D. A., & Chu, L. (1992). Consensus at zero acquaintance: Replication, behavioral cues, and stability. *Journal of Personality and Social Psychology, 62,* 88–97.

Kenny, D. A., & Judd, C. (1986). Consequences of violating the independence assumption in analysis of variance. *Psychological Bulletin, 99,* 422–431.

Kenny, D. A., Kashy, D. A., & Bolger, N. (1998). Data analysis in social psychology. In D. Gilbert, S. Fiske, & G.

Lindzey (Eds.), *The handbook of social psychology* (4th ed., Vol. 1, pp. 233–265). New York: McGraw-Hill.

Kenny, D. A., & La Voie, L. (1984). The social relations model. In L. Berkowitz (Ed.), *Advances in experimental social psychology* (Vol. 18, pp. 142–182). Orlando, FL: Academic Press.

Levesque, M. J. (1997). Meta-accuracy among acquainted individuals: A social relations analysis of interpersonal perception and metaperception. *Journal of Personality and Social Psychology, 72*, 66–74.

Levesque, M. J., & Kenny, D. A. (1993). Accuracy of behavioral predictions at zero acquaintance: A social relations analysis. *Journal of Personality and Social Psychology, 65*, 1178–1187.

Miller, L. C., & Kenny, D. A. (1986). Reciprocity of self-disclosure at the individual and dyadic levels: A social relations analysis. *Journal of Personality and Social Psychology, 50*, 713–719.

Myers, J. L. (1979). *Fundamentals of experimental design* (3rd ed.). Boston: Allen & Bacon.

Park B., & Judd, C. M. (1989). Agreement on initial impressions: Differences due to perceivers, trait dimensions, and target behaviors. *Journal of Personality and Social Psychology, 56*, 493–505.

Reno, R. R., & Kenny, D. A. (1990). Effects of self-consciousness and social anxiety on self-disclosure among unacquainted individuals: An application of the social relations model. *Journal of Personality, 60*, 79–94.

Snyder, M. (1974). Self-monitoring of expressive behavior. *Journal of Personality and Social Psychology, 30*, 526–537.

Warner, R., Kenny, D. A., & Stoto, M. (1979). A new round robin analysis of variance for social interaction data. *Journal of Personality and Social Psychology, 37*, 1742–1757.

Wasserman S., & Faust K. (1994). *Social network analysis: Methods and applications*. Cambridge, England: Cambridge University Press.

Williams, K. D., & Karau, S. J. (1991). Social loafing and social compensation: The effects of expectations of coworker performance. *Journal of Personality and Social Psychology, 61*, 570–581.

Zaccaro, S. J., Foti, R. J., & Kenny, D. A. (1991). Self-monitoring and trait-based variance in leadership: An investigation of leader flexibility across multiple group situations. *Journal of Applied Psychology, 76*, 308–315.

CHAPTER EIGHTEEN

Modeling Growth and Change Processes

Design, Measurement, and Analysis for Research in Social Psychology

LINDA M. COLLINS AND ALINE G. SAYER

Why is a separate chapter on change issues in social psychological research necessary in this book? Cannot questions about change be answered using the same approaches to design, measurement, and analysis as are used to answer other kinds of research questions? In fact, many straightforward questions about simple pre–post change in experimental designs, such as whether an experimental manipulation produced a mean shift, can be answered effectively using well-known traditional approaches. These kinds of questions are not the focus of this chapter. Instead, we focus on the growing number of questions in social psychology research that must be addressed by modeling change processes measured in complex longitudinal designs. One important example is research on social psychology-based approaches to adolescent substance use prevention. Often a decrease in positive attitudes toward substance use is observed immediately after an intervention. But such a decrease may be due more to compliance than to a lasting change in attitude. In order to develop effective substance use prevention programs, it is important to follow the attitude change process over a longer period of time. If a decrease appearing immediately after an intervention is due to compliance, a nonlinear pattern is expected, where the attitude first becomes negative and then, over time, becomes more positive. In order to determine whether this sort of nonlinear pattern is evident in a sample, it is necessary to have several repeated observations across an appropriate period of time, an attitude measure that is sensitive to change in an individual over time, and the analytic tools to model a growth process.

In this chapter we explain why research questions like this one involving growth and change are best answered using methodological techniques especially suited to this area. We discuss some of the special design, measurement, and analysis issues and concerns facing researchers studying growth and change. In some cases, we will raise issues to which there are not yet good answers, at least to our knowledge.

BACKGROUND

We begin by defining some terms to be used frequently in this chapter. A *latent variable* or *construct* is some quantity that is to be measured. We measure *manifest variables* that we believe are closely related to latent variables and use them as indicators of latent variables. For example, a ruler can be used to measure height, a county recording of a marriage can be used to indicate marital status, and the number of math problems answered correctly can be used to measure math achievement. Often several manifest variables are used as indicators of a single latent variable. If the manifest variables are all closely related to the latent variable, the multiple indicator approach provides more accurate measurement. An important distinction is that between *static* latent variables and *dynamic* latent variables. The term static refers to latent variables involving no systematic change over time, whereas the term dynamic refers to variables involving systematic change.

Another important distinction is that between *interindividual variability* and *intraindividual variability*. Interindividual variability refers to variability among the individuals in a sample. This is what is typically thought

This research was supported in part by a grant from the National Institute on Drug Abuse at the National Institutes of Health (1 P50 DA10075-01). Correspondence should be addressed to Linda M. Collins, The Methodology Center, S-159 Henderson Building, The Pennsylvania State University, University Park, Pennsylvania 16802 (e-mail address: lmc8@psu.edu).

of as variance. Intraindividual variability refers to variability within a person. In this chapter we use the term *intraindividual variability* to refer to variability within an individual across time. Where growth or change is present, there is intraindividual variability. The presence of interindividual variability does not imply the presence of intraindividual variability, nor does the presence of intraindividual variability imply interindividual variability. These are two separate dimensions of variability.

AN INDIVIDUAL-LEVEL PERSPECTIVE ON GROWTH AND CHANGE

Throughout this chapter, we adopt the point of view first advanced by Rogosa and colleagues (Rogosa, Brandt, & Zimowski, 1982; Rogosa & Willett, 1985). According to this point of view, before group or individual differences in change can be modeled, the change itself must be modeled. In other words, modeling intraindividual growth is a logical prerequisite to modeling interindividual variability in growth. One way to demonstrate why we advocate this point of view is to examine the concept of a group-level growth trajectory. Group-level growth trajectories consist of means computed across individuals plotted as a function of time or occasion of measurement. They are used very commonly to represent overall growth trends in a data set. A hypothetical example of a group-level growth trajectory appears in Figure 18.1. The group level growth trajectory suggests that this sample is characterized by linearly increasing growth on this variable. However, a group growth trajectory does not necessarily resemble the growth undergone by any of the individuals making up the sample. Suppose an individual-level approach is taken instead, and growth trajectories are plotted for individual participants. The individual growth trajectories shown in Figure 18.2(a), when averaged, yield the group growth trajectory shown in Figure 18.1. This is not unexpected, as this collection of growth trajectories is generally linearly increasing. But the group growth trajectory shown in Figure 18.1 can also be obtained by averaging the individual growth trajectories shown in Figure 18.2(b), which are not as readily characterized by linearly increasing growth. Whereas the individual growth trajectories in Figure 18.2(a) are represented well by the group growth curve, the individual growth curves in Figure 18.2(b) are not.

Thus, examining mean growth trajectories can be misleading about the nature of individual change. The purpose of means is to represent central tendencies in data, and there is always the possibility that there are individuals whose data are not well represented by the mean. However, there is an important difference between examining group means at a single point in time and examining group growth trajectories. When group means at a single time are examined, it is possible to consider the dispersion of the sample also. This helps the investigator to judge how representative the mean is of the entire sample. In contrast, there is no effective way of conveying variability about a mean growth trajectory. Confidence bands about the mean at each time do not convey the variability in growth over time. For example, confidence bands about the line in Figure 18.1 would not inform the reader about whether the underlying data more closely resembled Figure 18.2(a) or Figure 18.2(b). This makes it difficult for the investigator to judge whether growth at the group level represents any meaningful sort of central tendency with respect to individual growth. (For a thorough discussion of this issue, see Estes, 1956). In this chapter we show that if the individual patterns of growth are modeled, it is possible to examine individual and group differences in growth in a more meaningful way.

This chapter focuses on growth over time at the level of the individual and how variability in growth across individuals and groups can be examined. The design section of this chapter discusses some special considerations relevant to longitudinal studies of individual change, particularly designing studies that can detect individual change if it occurs. The measurement section discusses the shortcomings of traditional instrument development procedures when the objective is to measure individual change in a dynamic latent

Figure 18.1. A group-level growth trajectory.

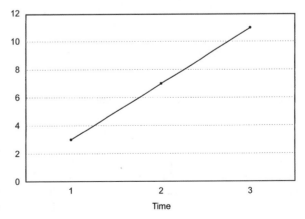

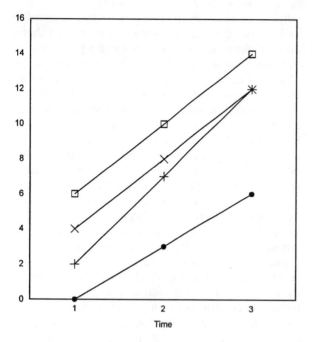

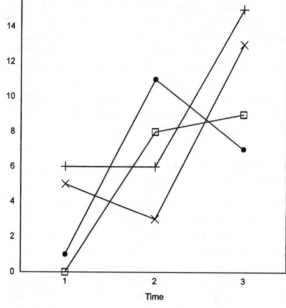

Figure 18.2. Two sets of individual growth trajectories, each of which produces the group growth trajectory in Figure 18.1.

variable. The analysis section reviews some relatively new procedures for addressing questions about individual change, including both continuous and stage-sequential development.

DESIGN

General design issues are covered in other chapters in this volume; the chapter by West et al. is particularly relevant to this one. Here we will discuss only those design issues specific to the study of growth and change.

Designs for studying change fall into two rough categories: cross-sectional and longitudinal. Choosing between these two types of designs is probably the most important single design decision a researcher makes when beginning a study on change. A cross-sectional study compares people at different ages at a single time, whereas a longitudinal study follows people over time, measuring them repeatedly at intervals. A cross-sectional study of how perceptions of peer influence change during the high school years might measure freshmen, sophomores, juniors, and seniors at a single point in time and compare perceptions of peer influence across the four classes. A comparable longitudinal study would obtain a sample of freshmen and follow them for 4 years, taking measures periodically. In the cross-sectional study, the researcher can compare perceptions of peer influence for freshmen vs. sophomores vs. juniors vs. seniors at a particular time, but does not have the data to verify that this is reflective of how individual students' perceptions change across the high school years. In the longitudinal study it is possible for the researcher to follow the change in perceptions of peer influence across the high school years for each person.

Age, Cohort, and Time

In a series of very important articles on design issues for measurement of change, Schaie (1965) pointed out that change in humans can be viewed as a function of three factors: the individual's age, the individual's cohort membership, and time of measurement. Cohort is a shorthand way of identifying a group of individuals subject to similar historical (e.g., the Great Depression, the Vietnam war) and sociological (availability of education, gender role norms) influences. Depending on the study and the part of the lifespan of interest, cohort can be defined variously as year of birth, decade of birth, generation, and so on. Schaie pointed out that although age, cohort, and time are conceptually distinct, they are confounded, because any two perfectly determine the third.

Cross-sectional and longitudinal designs can be evaluated in terms of how they handle age, cohort, and

TABLE 18.1. Illustration of a Cohort-Sequential Design

Cohort	Year of measurement				
	1996	1997	1998	1999	2000
1996	Freshmen	Sophomores	Juniors	Seniors	
1997		Freshmen	Sophomores	Juniors	Seniors
1998			Freshmen	Sophomores	Juniors
1999				Freshmen	Sophomores

time effects. In cross-sectional studies, cohort and age are confounded. When a difference in perceptions of peer influence is observed between freshmen and sophomores in a cross-sectional study, the following three interpretations are possible: (a) perceptions of peer influence change developmentally between the freshman and sophomore years in high school; (b) there are interindividual differences in perceptions of peer influence between the freshman cohort and the sophomore cohort, but no intraindividual differences between freshman year and sophomore year; or (c) there is an interaction between age and cohort, so that there are intraindividual differences between freshman and sophomore year, and these differences vary between the freshman and sophomore cohorts. Cross-sectional data do not contain any information about which of these three possibilities is most likely.

Longitudinal studies have the important advantage of allowing the researcher to observe intraindividual change over time directly. However, in longitudinal studies age and time are confounded. When intraindividual differences in perceptions of peer influence between freshman and sophomore year are observed in a longitudinal study, there are three possible interpretations: (a) perceptions of peer influence change developmentally between the freshman and sophomore years in high school; (b) the observed change in perceptions of peer influence is due to some historical or sociological influence occuring during the study, so that there was an overall change in perceptions of peer influence, not a developmental change; or (c) there is an interaction between age and time, so that the observed effect is unique to this particular cohort at this particular time.

Schaie and Baltes (1975) proposed several alternative designs for attempting to separate age, time, and cohort effects. Table 18.1 illustrates the most widely used of these, the cohort-sequential design. This design involves a series of longitudinal studies, each involving a different cohort of individuals. The longitudinal study depicted in Table 18.1 began in 1996 with that year's freshman class, which is measured periodically until graduation. For each of the next 3 years, longitudinal studies involve the 1997, 1998, and 1999 freshman classes. At the end of the data-collection period, data have been gathered on four successive cohorts of high-school students. With the cohort-sequential design, it is possible to determine whether results obtained in one cohort replicate in the other cohorts. If an effect is not replicated across cohorts, this suggests that the effect is due to some influence specific to one cohort. If the effect is replicated across cohorts but at a specific time rather than at a specific age, this is evidence that the effect is due to historical or sociological factors affecting all cohorts at the same time.

It is important to note the differences in resources required to mount a longitudinal study as opposed to a cross-sectional study. The cohort-sequential longitudinal study described above will take several years to conduct. A cross-sectional study can be finished in a small fraction of the time. Most of the time longitudinal studies are far superior to cross-sectional studies for the investigation of growth and change, but the dramatic increases in time and expense associated with longitudinal studies make it worthwhile to consider very carefully whether a cross-sectional study might be suitable, even with its limitations.

Missing Data and Participant Attrition

Both cross-sectional and longitudinal research are subject to problems caused by missing data. Data can be missing because study participants fail to complete one or more items on a questionnaire, or because participants were unavailable for one or more waves of data in a longitudinal study. If data are missing completely at random, for example, every participant in a study has an equal probability of dropping out, then the only problem is the loss of statistical power associated with a reduced sample size. Unfortunately, a substantial amount of missing data is nonrandom. Poor reading skills, low motivation, and a tendency to avoid questions perceived as unpleasant are all factors that increase the probability of missing data. Longitudinal studies sampling from urban, lower SES, younger, less healthy, and transient populations tend to experience more participant dropout.

Participant dropout, often referred to as *attrition*, can be a serious problem affecting both the internal and external validity of a longitudinal study. Attrition can affect the internal validity of a study if attrition is differential between treatment and control groups. A classic example of differential attrition can occur when an intervention is being given, such as a school-based drug abuse prevention program. Students who become involved with drugs may drop out of the program, or at least make themselves unavailable for data collection. This leaves a higher proportion of students uninvolved with drugs in the treatment condition, which can make the treatment condition look more effective than it really is. External validity is affected whenever some participants have a higher probability of dropping out than others, even if this probability is the same across treatment groups. For example, in the school-age population lower SES students tend to be more transient and therefore tend to move out of the school district and the study. The loss of these participants means that the generalizability of the study to lower SES groups is limited.

Procedural and statistical steps can be used in combination to help the researcher to deal with attrition. Procedurally, it is important to set aside resources for the purpose of minimizing the amount of missing data. Participants should be given enough time to complete any measurement instruments or interviews and strongly encouraged not to omit items carelessly. In longitudinal studies, resources should be devoted to finding and collecting data from people who drop out of a study. Good planning can make this easier; for example, in the first data collection occasion information can be obtained to make it easier to track people if they move, such as place of employment or driver's license number. The recent revolution in statistical procedures for handling missing data (Graham, Hofer, & Piccinin, 1994; Little & Rubin, 1987; Schafer, 1997) has had a big impact on longitudinal research by making it possible to make use of all the data that are present and to eliminate much of the bias associated with nonrandom attrition. Using missing data procedures, the researcher can estimate what the data would have been had there been no participant dropout, based on the data that are available.

Recent work on missing data analysis (Graham et al., 1994) has some important implications for how best to proceed with contacting and collecting data on individuals who drop out of a study. Because statistical missing data procedures can most effectively estimate what the results would have been like in complete data if data from a representative random sample of dropouts are available, obtaining such a sample should be the goal of contacting individuals who have left the study.

Measurement as a Design Consideration

Measurement can present problems in a study of growth and change, for a variety of reasons. First, whenever the same instrument is administered repeatedly, scores can change over time as a result of increased familiarity with the instrument rather than any real change on the latent variable being measured. Or, additional random error can be introduced if bored or overconfident participants rush through a test or questionnaire. Second, the way participants interpret an instrument can change over time. This is particularly dangerous when there is an intervention that causes one group to reevaluate something, whereas the other group does not (Howard, Millham, Slaten, & O'Donnell, 1981). For example, suppose participants are asked to rate their leadership ability, after which a treatment group undergoes leadership training and a control group spends an equal amount of time learning how to make balloon animals. When asked to rate their leadership ability after the intervention, the treatment participants may now have very different ideas about what constitutes good leadership ability and may rate themselves on a different basis both from their earlier ratings and from those of the control group.

Number, Timing, and Temporal Spacing of Observations in a Longitudinal Study

In longitudinal research in social psychology, it is common to collect data in "waves," in other words, to collect data at the same or approximately the same points in time for all participants. The waves are not necessarily evenly spaced. For example, in school-based research, data might be collected on all participants at the beginning and end of each academic year. When designing a longitudinal study, it is important to pay careful attention to the number, timing, and temporal spacing of these data-collection sessions. Every longitudinal study, even those where only the simplest linear model is of interest, should contain more than two waves of data. As will be shown in the analysis section of this chapter, there are now analytic techniques for modeling growth that allow the researcher to make use of multiple waves of data simultaneously. A common problem in otherwise well-designed longitudinal studies is that too few data-collection sessions, spaced too far apart, are planned. Then it becomes difficult or impossible to model growth accurately, because too much of the growth has occured between observations.

For example, suppose a researcher is interested in studying attachment to peers across the elementary school, middle school, junior high, and high school years. Further suppose that attachment to peers is relatively low in elementary school, when attachment to parents is high; then attachment to peers climbs steadily, reaching a peak in ninth grade; then slowly declines as independence increases. The solid line in Figure 18.3 shows the true time course of the variable. This is what would be observed if it were possible to measure attachment to peers continuously. Now suppose the researcher carries out observations in Grades 1, 6, and 11. The dashed line in Figure 18.3 depicts the growth trajectory as it would appear to this researcher. With only three measures spaced years apart, it is impossible for the researcher to obtain an accurate picture of this process unfolding. Measures occurring more frequently would allow a much closer approximation.

Careful planning on the part of the investigator is needed if waves of data collection are to be timed in order to optimize the view of individual growth. In many ways, the decision about the timing of data collection in a longitudinal study is similar to the decisions researchers have to make when doing a power analysis. In a power analysis, the researcher has to make an educated guess about effect size in order to determine the required sample size. This educated guess, even if it is not exactly correct, results in a sample size closer to what is needed than does making no guess. The same is true when timing the waves of a longitudinal study. An educated guess, or better yet a theory-based prediction, about the expected shape and speed of growth provides a solid basis for planning the timing of observations. If the anticipated data analyses will involve procedures that do not require the observations in a longitudinal study to be evenly spaced, it may make the most sense to observe more frequently during periods of expected rapid development and less frequently at other times.

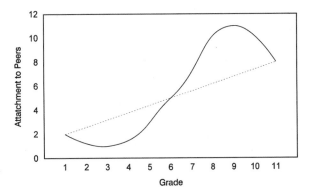

Figure 18.3. A growth trajectory (solid line) and what it looks like if measured in first, sixth, and eleventh grades (dashed).

MEASUREMENT

Validity

The validity of an instrument, the extent to which it measures what it is intended to measure, is a concept that cuts across any and all measurement theories. This is a centrally important idea in measurement of dynamic latent variables, just as it is in all measurement endeavors. In this section we will discuss three major domains of validity: criterion validity, content validity, and construct validity. We will show how these ideas are relevant to the measurement of change, but require some expansion and modification for this context (Collins, 1996).

Dynamic Criterion Validity

With criterion validity, another measure or variable is used as a standard or criterion. If the measure in question is valid, it will show a substantial relation with the criterion. Criterion validity can be assessed as concurrent or as predictive validity. To assess concurrent validity, data on the criterion and data on the measure in question are collected at approximately the same time. To assess predictive validity, data on the criterion are collected at a later time. Both concurrent and predictive validity are assessed by examining the relation between the instrument and the criterion. If a substantial relation is shown, this is evidence for criterion validity. In the case of static latent variables, a correlation is usually used to establish the relation.

Questions about criterion validity should be phrased somewhat differently if the validity of a measure of a dynamic latent variable is being assessed. Because we are measuring a variable that changes over time, the validity question has to do with change. In order to assess concurrent validity, for example, we must investigate whether two variables track along together concurrently over time for each individual. The existence or nonexistence of concurrent change over time cannot be assessed by examining panel correlations over time, that is, by correlating the two variables at Time 1, then correlating them again at Time 2, etc. In fact, Collins (1996) has shown that this approach can be very misleading, because panel correlations between two variables at individual points in time can be large even when the two variables are not undergoing concurrent change. The growth curve modeling techniques discussed in the next section can be used to model the growth trajectory on each variable for each individual and to examine whether there is a relationship between the growth trajectories.

Dynamic predictive validity is the degree to which a measure of interest tracks along with the criterion, but after some time lag. Figure 18.4 shows hypothetical data on a dynamic predictor and a dynamic criterion variable. Although the two variables do not appear to track along together exactly, in fact they are perfectly related: The criterion varies as a function of the predictor one time unit earlier. A lagged relationship between two variables is most readily detected when the research design permits the appropriate temporal lag to be used. In the example in Figure 18.4, such a design would allow the criterion to be measured one time unit later than the predictor. It can be difficult to establish dynamic predictive validity in designs where observations are taken infrequently, because it may not be possible to correlate the variables using the appropriate temporal lag (Cohen, 1991; Collins & Graham, 1991). For example, suppose the validity of a measure

of frustration is being assessed. It is hypothesized that aggressive feelings vary over time as a function of frustration 1 week earlier. If frustration and aggressive feelings can be measured a week apart, this relation can be revealed in a plot like Figure 18.4. But if these variables are measured a month or a year apart, the relation will probably not emerge. In this situation it would be possible to conclude mistakenly that the frustration measure has poor predictive validity, because the study design does not permit measurement to take place at the appropriate temporal lag.

Content Validity

Content validity is the extent to which the items making up a measure cover the entire domain being measured. Content validity can be established without including every possible relevant item – in most cases including all these items would make an instrument prohibitively long. Rather, the idea of content validity is that a representative sample of items is included.

With dynamic latent variables, it is important to consider what constitutes the domain being measured. One aspect of this is the range of skills, abilities, and attitudes of interest. This is what is ordinarily considered in measurement of static variables, and it is important in measurement of dynamic variables as well. But there is an additional aspect of the domain being measured that is important in dynamic variables. Because a dynamic variable is a process changing over time, different items will be relevant to different phases of the process. In other words, the instrument should include some items relevant early, middle, and late in the process. Often items relevant to a single content area but covering a wide range of level of skill required or extremity of attitude will be sufficient to ensure content validity. Other times, depending on the dynamic latent variable being measured, items in different content domains will be needed to measure different phases of the process. For example, different kinds of tasks are used to measure different phases of Piagetian development.

Construct Validity

Construct validity is the sine qua non of measurement. With static latent variables, construct validity is usually demonstrated by making a theoretical prediction and testing it using the instrument in question. For example, if a theory predicts that there are gender differences in emotionally expressive behavior, then

Figure 18.4. A perfect relationship between a dynamic predictor and a dynamic criterion one time unit later.

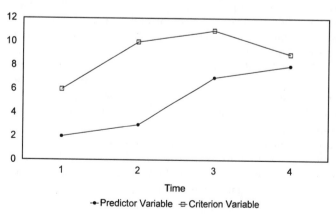

a self-report measure of emotional expression that has construct validity will show statistically significant gender differences.

Theoretical predictions can be used as a way of establishing construct validity of measures of dynamic latent variables in much the same way as they are used to establish construct validity of static latent variables, but here the theoretical prediction is about change over time. For example, if a theory predicts change over time, then a valid instrument will show change. If a theory predicts that change occurs during a certain period and not during other periods, or in a particular form (e.g. linear, exponential), or in a subset of individuals only, then the instrument should reflect this. One way to establish construct validity in this context is to use growth curve modeling (see below) to examine change on the instrument as a function of time for individuals.

Measurement Precision

Much social psychological research is concerned with measuring latent variables. Often a new instrument has to be developed in order to measure a particular latent variable of interest. Measurement theory such as classical test theory has been of tremendous value to researchers in social psychology, by providing guidelines for developing instruments that are precise and that measure what they are intended to measure (see John & Benet-Martínez, this volume, Ch. 13). However, most currently well-known measurement theories were designed to help researchers measure interindividual differences. Because these approaches generally ignore intraindividual differences, which are the essence of change over time, they are of limited usefulness when the objective is to measure growth.

The most widely used definition of measurement precision in use in social psychology is the classical test theory notion of reliability. Reliability is defined as follows:

$$\rho_{XX} = \frac{\sigma_T^2}{\sigma_X^2} = \frac{\sigma_T^2}{\sigma_T^2 + \sigma_E^2}, \tag{1}$$

where σ_X^2 represents total observed score variability, σ_T^2 represents true score variance, and σ_E^2 represents error variability. If an instrument has high reliability, it is considered potentially a good instrument (validity must also be established before final conclusions can be drawn). Classical test theory grew out of research on ability and achievement testing. Therefore, the true score variance referred to in Equation 1 is usually interindividual variance (e.g., Lord & Novick,

1968). (In theory other variances, such as intraindividual variance, could be used to define reliability. However, the details of such an approach, such as how the two variances would be combined, have not been specified.) All of the well-known ways of estimating reliability, such as Cronbach's alpha and test–retest reliability, are based on the idea of interindividual true score variance. It should be emphasized that this definition of measurement precision is excellent for situations where detecting interindividual variability is the primary goal, such as cross-sectional research and testing. But it works much less well where growth and change are to be measured longitudinally. In fact, according to this definition of reliability, an instrument that measures growth with a high degree of precision can be unreliable.

To take an example, suppose a researcher wishes to study the development of altruism in young school children in the kindergarten through third-grade years. Further suppose the researcher has a highly precise measure of intraindividual change in altruism. Wishing to assess the reliability of the instrument, the researcher administers it to a class of kindergarteners and to the same children 1 year later when they are in first grade. There is a considerable amount of change over time in the children, but at each time there is relatively little interindividual variability, because the children are all about the same age. Because the interindividual true score variability, σ_T^2, is small, reliability at each time is very low. Thus, although the instrument is unreliable according to Equation 1, and in fact may be an unreliable measure of interindividual differences, it is a highly precise measure of change over time. The researcher could have pilot tested the instrument on a cross-section of children from kindergarten through third grade in order to assure sufficient interindividual variability to obtain a high reliability, provided that the instrument is a precise measure of interindividual variability. But this would not solve the real problem, which is that the classical test theory definition of measurement precision as it is usually implemented does not apply to the measurement of intraindividual change.

Measuring Dynamic Latent Variables: The Longitudinal Guttman Simplex

We have been arguing that alternatives to traditional definitions of measurement precision and validity are needed for dynamic latent variables. A general strategy is indicated by Coombs' (1964) penetrating observation that "all measurement theory is actually a theory of behavior"(p. 5). This is particularly apropos when discussing measuring change over time in social psychology research and suggests that a useful starting point for measuring dynamic latent variables is a theory of growth or change. One measurement theory based on a model of change is the longitudinal Guttman simplex.

Collins and colleagues (Collins, 1996; Collins & Cliff, 1990; Collins, Cliff, & Dent, 1988) have extended the classic Guttman scale (Guttman, 1950). In three new models, Collins and colleagues have added a third set, times, making the three-set Guttman scale models definitions of human development. One of these models, the longitudinal Guttman simplex (LGS), translates into a model of development where (a) change is characterized by either monotonic increase (increase over time, with no periods of decrease) or monotonic decrease (decrease over time, with no periods of increase), and (b) change is cumulative; in other words, skills or attitudes that are gained are not subsequently lost (or, in the case of decline, skills or attitudes that are lost are not subsequently gained). Because in the LGS model the persons order can vary across items and across times, unlimited heterogeneity in development across persons is allowed. Besides the longitudinal Guttman simplex, there are two other varieties of three-set Guttman simplex models (Collins, 1996). One of these represents a considerably more restrictive model of development where the persons order does not change over time, and the other represents a considerably less restrictive model where growth can be nonmonotonic.

The advantage of the three-set Guttman simplex models is that they are tailor-made to specific kinds of development and can be used to construct instruments uniquely sensitive to certain kinds of change. However, the LGS model is subject to many of the same restrictions as the classic Guttman simplex. The most significant limitation is that the model applies only to dichotomous variables. Furthermore, the model is restricted to cumulative development. A highly promising alternative approach based on item response theory has been developed by Embretson (1991), but this too is primarily for dichotomous variables. More measurement theories for dynamic variables, including guidelines for making up scales consisting of Likert items or other kinds of multicategory items, are needed.

ANALYSIS

Traditionally univariate or multivariate repeated measures analysis of variance (RMANOVA) has represented the primary data analysis strategy for both two-wave and multiwave (i.e., $T > 2$) longitudinal data. When used with polynomial trend analysis, in which the effect of time is reconstructed and analyzed as a collection of $T - 1$ contrast scores that represent the time-dependent trends in the means, RMANOVA can be considered a special case of individual growth modeling. However, this approach has important technical restrictions that limit its applicability. These include

- the inability to model change with a variety of linear and nonlinear growth functions. ANOVA-based methods are restricted to polynomial functions of time, although they can be of any order. This excludes, for example, the broad class of exponential and logistic functions, discontinuous growth functions, or more specialized functions such as Gompertz growth curves (Guire & Kowalski, 1979) or triple-logistic stature curves (Bock & Thissen, 1980).

- the inability to incorporate time-series designs that vary across individuals. A strong assumption of RMANOVA is that the design is balanced on time; that is, the number and spacing of the occasions of measurement are the same for all individuals (although equal interval spacing is not a requirement, the analysis is more straightforward if this condition is also met). Incomplete designs, whereby participants are missing one or more waves of data due to missed appointments or other sources of attrition, cannot be handled under this approach. New advances in missing data imputation may make it possible to restore these participants to the sample (Graham et al., 1994). However, certain kinds of longitudinal designs that involve planned missingness, such as cohort-sequential designs in which several age-staggered cohorts are followed over short periods, are better handled by methods that permit individuals to start their trajectories at different points in time.

- the inability to incorporate predictors (independent variables) measured on a continuous scale. The ability to introduce and control for potentially important predictors of change is forfeited unless the predictors can be converted to a nominal scale without loss of information (we are not advocating reducing the information contained in a continuous scale, via median splits or any other technique, to create a categorical variable). Linked to this restriction is that under RMANOVA, within-group variability in change is treated as error to be ignored rather than as heterogeneity to be explored.

- the inability to incorporate time-varying covariates, or within-person independent variables. Many potentially important predictors of intraindividual change, such as employment status, mood, or stressful life events, fluctuate with time. These time-varying effects cannot be modeled using traditional methods.

The most important shortcoming is conceptual rather than technical, because the RMANOVA approach does not focus explicitly on modeling within-individual change and exploring its heterogeneity across individuals. In contrast, the two analytic approaches discussed in this section focus on specifying a model for intraindividual growth. Individual growth curve modeling is appropriate for addressing questions about growth in continuous variables, whereas latent transition analysis is suitable for estimating and testing models of stage-sequential development.

Individual Growth Curve Modeling

Individual growth curve modeling characterizes the study of growth as a two-phase process. It involves the specification of a hierarchical linear model that enables separate specification of predictors of change measured at the individual and group level. The Level 1 model for intraindividual, or within-person, change describes the underlying growth for each person as a function of time and a set of model growth parameters that define the change function. For example, an investigator interested in correlates of delinquency would fit a Level 1 model to describe and summarize the longitudinal trajectory of deviant behavior for each adolescent in the sample. A researcher hypothesizing that change proceeds at a steady rate might fit a linear growth model. The Level 2 model for interindividual, or between-person, differences in change describes how differences in growth across persons are related systematically to differences in various predictors of growth. The researcher might fit a model to investigate the association between individual differences in linear rates of deviance and differences in (a) individual characteristics such as age, gender, or temperamental dimensions; (b) context characteristics, such as neighborhood cohesiveness or peer attitudes toward deviance; and (c) characteristics of prevention interventions such as program content, duration, or timing. In this subsequent phase, the individual growth parameters from the first phase serve as dependent variables, and relations between these estimated parameters and the predictors are investigated using some form of regression analysis.

An Illustration of Individual Growth Modeling: Trajectories of Ego Development

We illustrate the growth curve approach with data selected from the Health and Illness Project, a longitudinal study of the development of an onset cohort of 61 adolescents with juvenile diabetes and a matched comparison group of healthy participants (Hauser, Jacobson, Wertlieb, Brink, & Wentworth, 1985). A range of individual and family variables were measured on five irregularly spaced occasions: at the onset of the study, annually for the following 3 years, and again at 7 years subsequent to study onset. Here we present growth curve analyses of ego development, an index of psychosocial functioning across the domains of personal relationships, impulse control, moral development, and cognitive style that was assessed at each wave of data collection with the Washington University Sentence Completion Test (Loevinger & Wessler, 1970).

Our general research interest is the description of ego trajectories during adolescence. At Level 1 we describe individual differences in development. Which child grows fastest? Which child exhibits the greatest regression? We are also interested in the pattern of mean growth. For example, do children advance at a constant rate over 7 years, or is there a period of time subsequent to disease onset in which development slows? At Level 2 we describe the extent of heterogeneity in ego trajectories and ask if differences in growth are related to two child characteristics: age at study entry and health status.

INTRAINDIVIDUAL GROWTH: LEVEL 1. The data collected longitudinally for each adolescent is termed the individual time-series or growth record. These empirical growth records can be graphed against the occasions of measurement to enable the researcher to grasp quickly and intuitively the pattern of ego development for each adolescent over the 7-year interval. Figure 18.5 presents the plotted growth records for 2 adolescents drawn at random from the sample of 123, with trend lines that smooth and summarize the records superimposed on each adolescent's set of data points.

An appropriate mathematical model must be selected to represent individual growth in ego development. A stipulation of the growth modeling approach is that the same functional form must be fit to each person's growth record, although the values of the parameters of the function are allowed to vary across participants. The precision with which the chosen function fits each data record will also vary across the sample, and this variation in precision needs to be reflected in the Level 2 analyses. Visual inspection of the individual growth records for the full sample suggested that a straight-line growth model was a reasonable representation for individual changes in ego level over time. Consequently, we modeled each child's set of scores as a linear function of time, using within-subject ordinary least-squares regression analysis to estimate the model parameters. The trend lines displayed in Figure 18.5 are the predicted values from the individual regression fits.

We used the following straight-line growth model to represent each adolescent's longitudinal record:

$$\text{EGO}_{pt} = \pi_{0p} + \pi_{1p}(\text{TIME}_{pt} - 1) + \epsilon_{pt}. \quad (2)$$

In this model, EGO_{pt} represents the ego score for adolescent p at time t (where $p = 1, \ldots, 123$ and $t = 1, 2, 3, 4, 7$ years). π_{0p} is the model y-intercept, an individual growth parameter that describes the expected value of EGO when the predictor TIME is zero. The time metric is typically rescaled to facilitate interpretation of the model intercept and to ensure that it will have a substantively meaningful value as a dependent variable at Level 2. The choice of rescaling is arbitrary and reflects the individual investigator's research interests. In this case, the time metric has been rescaled by subtracting 1 from each time so that times are now 0, 1, 2, 3, and 6. Now, the intercept π_{0p} represents *initial status*, or the value of the ego score at study entry (in year 0). π_{1p} is the model slope, an individual growth parameter that describes the expected difference in EGO for a unit difference in TIME. Because time is measured in years, this can be interpreted as the yearly *growth rate* in ego score, or the constant rate of change in ego level per year for adolescent p. ϵ_{pt} is the deviation of adolescent p's observed score from his or her true growth trajectory at time t. If an appropriate growth model has been fit, this can be interpreted as the measurement error at each timepoint. The estimate of residual variance from each within-subject regression fit can be construed as a measure of precision, or how well the model fits the individual data record. These estimates of within-person residual variance are used to construct weights that enable the investigator to compensate for the variability in precision with which the Level-1 growth parameters are estimated. The ϵ_{pt} are assumed to be mutually independent and normally distributed over children and over time, with mean 0 and variance σ^2. Some methods of fitting growth curves allow the assumption of constant residual variance and zero autocorrelation of the measurement errors to be tested and relaxed, if neces-

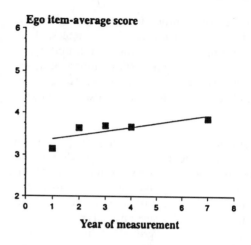

Panel A

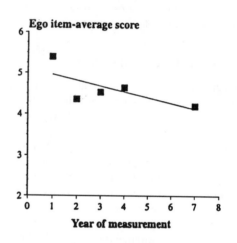

Panel B

Figure 18.5. Fitted linear growth trajectories for two adolescents with diabetes. In each panel, the fitted linear trend is superimposed on ego levels measured at 1, 2, 3, 4, and 7 years subsequent to disease onset.

sary. If the model is correct, each adolescent's growth can be completely summarized by his or her values on the two growth parameters π_{0p} and π_{1p} that, taken together, define the child's underlying growth trajectory. The growth parameters conveniently reduce the information contained in the five individual measurements and can be used to represent the trajectory as dependent variables in subsequent between-person analyses.

INTERINDIVIDUAL DIFFERENCES IN GROWTH: LEVEL 2. An estimate of initial status and growth rate based on fitting a straight-line model is collected for

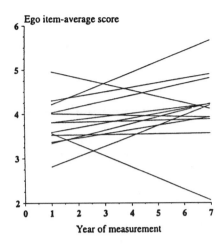

Figure 18.6. A collection of fitted linear growth trajectories for 13 randomly selected diabetic adolescents.

each individual. Then, the first step in the between-child analyses is to examine the empirical distributions of these estimates to assess the extent of heterogeneity in growth in the sample. Figure 18.6 displays the fitted growth trajectories for 13 randomly selected adolescents. This composite plot displays observed variability in both initial status and the yearly rate of change. It suggests that the estimated ego scores at study entry (year 1) are distributed throughout the entire EGO range, suggesting heterogeneity in initial status. There is graphical evidence of both gain and decline in ego level, as well as evidence of little change throughout adolescence, suggesting heterogeneity in ego rate. Finally, note that adolescents with the steepest slopes, either positive or negative, are not concentrated in one section of the ego level distribution but rather are spread throughout the range. This suggests that there is little indication of a relationship between initial status and the rate of change. The correlation of initial status and change is an important quantity to estimate in any growth study, because it indicates if subjects with initially high scores experience the fastest rates of growth.

Inspection of the distributions of the within-person growth parameters, estimated here by ordinary least-squares regression, indicates considerable variability. Estimates of initial status ranged from 2.68 to 4.96, with a mean of 3.7 and a standard deviation of 0.42. The corresponding estimates for rate of change were a range of -0.11 to 0.32, with a mean of 0.09 and a standard deviation of 0.10. These important descriptive statistics enable the researcher to plot the average growth trajectory and to quantify the heterogeneity in growth in ego scores shown in Figure 18.6. Several

computer programs for fitting hierarchical linear models or structural equation models (described later in this chapter) allow the specification of a baseline model that includes no predictors at Level 2. This unconditional or baseline model provides evidence about the amount of variation at each level, including parameter estimates and standard errors to permit a formal test of the hypothesis that the variance of each growth parameter is zero in the population.

Having established that there is heterogeneity in growth to be explained, we procede to investigate selected predictors of change. To answer our research questions – do the growth trajectories of healthy adolescents differ from those with diabetes? Do the growth trajectories of older children differ from younger? – we choose the following between-person model to represent the relationship between growth and the two predictors of interest:

$$\pi_{0p} = \gamma_{00} + \gamma_{01}\,\mathrm{HEALTH}_p + \gamma_{02}\,\mathrm{AGE}_p + u_{0p}, \qquad (3)$$

$$\pi_{1p} = \gamma_{10} + \gamma_{11}\,\mathrm{HEALTH}_p + \gamma_{12}\,\mathrm{AGE}_p + u_{1p}. \qquad (4)$$

The Level 2 model consists of two equations that, taken together, model variation in the overall growth trajectories as a function of health status (a dichotomous variable coded 0 if healthy and 1 if diabetic) and age at study entry. Equation 3 models variation in initial status, and Equation 4 is the corresponding model for rate of growth. γ_{01} (in 3) and γ_{11} (in 4) are regression coefficients that, given the coding of HEALTH, capture the average difference between healthy and ill adolescents in ego level at study entry and in the rate of growth, respectively, net the effects of age. γ_{02} (in 3) and γ_{12} (in 4) capture the relationship between age and initial ego level at study entry and the rate of growth, respectively, net the effects of health. The constants γ_{00} and γ_{10} represent the predicted values of initial status and the mean growth rate, respectively, for the healthy group when AGE is equal to zero. As in the previous example, AGE can be centered on the sample mean to further facilitate interpretation of these intercepts as values for a healthy adolescent of the average sample age.

The Level 2 model can be extended to include interaction terms. For example, if the researcher hypothesized that the effects of age on ego development were different for healthy and ill adolescents, a cross-product term representing the interaction of HEALTH and AGE could be included as a predictor in the model. The associated γ coefficients relate the interaction term to intial status and rate of growth, respectively.

The terms u_{0p} and u_{1p} represent the unique effects of adolescent p on initial status and rate of growth, that is, individual differences in growth not attributable to the adolescent's age or health. The variances of these parameters can be estimated by maximum-likelihood in either dedicated hierarchical model fitting programs (e.g., HLM or ML3) or by structural modeling programs (e.g., LISREL 8); they are not estimated under least-squares estimation procedures. The u_{0p} and u_{1p} are assumed to have a bivariate normal distribution with zero means, variances $\sigma_{u_0}^2$ and $\sigma_{u_1}^2$, and covariance σ_{u0u1}. The interpretation of these important variances and covariances depends on what predictors are in the model. In a model with no predictors, σ_{u0}^2 and σ_{u1}^2 describe the total amount of variance in true initial status and true rate of growth, respectively, and $\sigma_{u_0u_1}$ captures the covariance between true initial status and rate of true growth. As predictors are added to the model that are related to growth, the values of $\sigma_{u_0}^2$ and $\sigma_{u_1}^2$ decline in magnitude, indicating that some of the original variation is being "explained" by the additional predictor(s).

We used the HLM2L program (Bryk, Raudenbush, & Congdon, 1996) to estimate the parameters of the Level 1 and Level 2 models and provide standard errors for testing the null hypothesis that the parameter was zero. The results indicate that a straight-line model provides a good fit, although a polynomial of higher order could have been used as the Level 1 change function if growth proved to be curvilinear. Health status is negatively related to initial status, which, given the coding of HEALTH, indicates that healthy adolescents have higher ego scores on entry ($\gamma_{01} = -.28$, $p < .05$). However, health status is not related to the rate of growth ($\gamma_{11} = .02$, $p > .10$), suggesting that there are no differences in developmental patterns over time for healthy and diabetic adolescents. Age predicts both initial status and the rate of change. Older children have higher levels of ego development at study entry than younger ones ($\gamma_{02} = 43$, $p < .001$). Older children also have flatter slopes ($\gamma_{12} = -.01$, $p < .05$); that is, the differences in ego level between successive ages are greater for younger children than for older. The average growth trajectory suggests that mean initial status for healthy children is mid-range ($\gamma_{00} = 3.91$, $p < .001$) and that they grow at a rate of .23 points per year ($\gamma_{10} = .23$, $p < .01$). The average growth trajectory for diabetic children can also be easily calculated.

This example illustrates the important parameters to be estimated in any study of interindividual differences in growth. To summarize

Level-1

π_{0p}: Status on the dependent variable for participant p at a time point defined by the scaling of time

π_{1p}: Linear rate of growth in the dependent variable for participant p

$\sigma_{\epsilon_p}^2$: Residual variance for participant p

$\sigma_{\epsilon_t}^2$: Measurement error variance across participants at timepoint t

$\sigma_{\epsilon_0\epsilon_1}$: Measurement error autocorrelation across participants for all pairwise timepoints

Level-2

γ_{00}: Predicted initial status when Level 2 predictors are equal to zero

γ_{10}: Predicted growth rate when Level 2 predictors are equal to zero

$\gamma_{01}, \gamma_{02}, \gamma_{11}, \gamma_{12}$: Regression coefficients representing the relations among the predictors of change and the growth parameters

$\sigma_{u_0}^2$: Variance across participants in status

$\sigma_{u_1}^2$: Variance across participants in rate of growth

$\sigma_{u_0u_1}$: Covariance between the growth parameters across participants

Methods for Estimating Growth Curves

Various strategies for estimating the parameters of the Level 1 and Level 2 models in the analysis of change have been proposed. Conceptually, these methods can be organized into two groups: those that estimate the parameters in a univariate context and those that take the hierarchical structure of the data into account (simultaneous estimation). Rogosa and Saner (1995) provided an example of the first strategy, sometimes called *exploratory growth modeling*. They described the use of ordinary least-squares regression-based methods to estimate separately the parameters of the Level 1 and Level 2 models, with reliability-based adjustments to the estimation of the Level 2 coefficients based on the marginal maximum-likelihood methods of Blomqvist (1977). A good application of this method to educational data can be found in Williamson, Appelbaum, and Epanchin (1991).

In an extension of the exploratory approach, Willett (1989) provided weighted least-squares methods that incorporate the varying precision with which the Level 1 model is fit to each growth record. Weights are constructed to be inversely proportional to the magnitude of the standard errors of the growth parameters obtained during the within-person phase of the analysis. Poorly estimated Level 1 slopes and intercepts are downweighted in the estimation of the parameters of the Level 2 model.

Advances in computing algorithms allowing for iterative rather than closed-form solutions brought the second class of methods into being. These methods overcome the flaws of univariate strategies, which include misestimated standard errors and erroneous assessment of explained variance at each level. The work of Bryk and Raudenbush (1987, 1992) is one contemporary example. They conceptualized growth curve modeling as part of a more general class of hierarchical models that model variation at each of two levels as a function of level-specific predictors. They describe strategies for simultaneously estimating the parameters of the Level 1 and Level 2 models using the Expectation-Maximization (EM) algorithm to provide maximum-likelihood estimates of the regression weights and the covariance and variance components. When the levels are combined the result is a mixed linear model with fixed and random effects. These models are termed hierarchical linear models (HLMs). There are many applications of this approach to social psychological data (see Barnett, Marshall, Raudenbush, & Brennan, 1993).

Willett and Sayer (1994) have described strategies for integrating individual growth curve modeling into the framework of covariance structure analysis. Building on the theoretical work of Meredith and Tisak (1990) in formulating a latent growth model, they described how to estimate the parameters of the Level 2 models by modeling the covariance structure directly. They argued that the process of formulating Level 1 and Level 2 models for intraindividual change and for systematic interindividual differences in change is equivalent to postulating a specific structure for the matrix of covariances among the multiple waves of observed data and the predictors of change. By using the general covariance structure model with mean structures to articulate this latter covariance structure explicitly, they obtain maximum-likelihood estimates of the parameters of the between-person model. Other methodologists have proposed latent growth models (McArdle & Epstein, 1987; Muthén, 1991) that are variants on the common factor model but include analysis of the means as well as covariances among the waves of data. Clear examples of this framework are provided by Stoolmiller (1994) and Anderson (1993) for psychological and developmental data.

Advantages and Disadvantages

Each of the methods has its own strengths, and one particular method may offer benefits over another in a specific research setting. To begin, we note the major commonalities among the methods described in this chapter. All methods can accommodate any number of waves of longitudinal data, and additional waves of data lead naturally to higher precision for the estimation of the individual growth trajectory and greater reliability for the measurement of change (Willett, 1989). Univariate strategies depend on least-squares estimation and require a minimum of three waves to estimate a slope; multivariate strategies using empirical-Bayes estimation can include participants with even a single wave of data. All methods can accommodate occasions of measurement that are not equally spaced. Individual change data may be collected at irregular intervals either for convenience (at the beginning and end of each of several school years, perhaps) or because the investigator wishes to estimate certain features of the trajectory more precisely (by clustering data-collection points more closely at times of greater research interest). All methods can represent individual change by either a straight line or a curvilinear trajectory. These approaches can accommodate any type of curvilinear growth model where the Level 1 dependent variable is an additive function of the predictors, including but not limited to polynomial growth of any order. All methods can compare the goodness-of-fits of nested models so the investigator is able to systematically evaluate the adequacy of contrasting models for average growth. All methods can control for covariates measured on a continuous scale in the Level 2 model. An additional advantage of least-squares methods is that they do not require dedicated and expensive software for model-fitting.

There are major differences as well. Most important is the extent to which the method permits unbalanced designs, where the number of waves of data vary across individuals. Both the Ordinary Least-Squares (OLS) approach of Rogosa and Saner (1995) and the HLM approach of Bryk and Raudenbush (1987) can incorporate missing data at Level 1. The methods based on the direct analysis of covariance structures require time-structured data, where all participants are sampled on the same number of occasions. Recent advances in the handling of missing data hold out the promise that incomplete growth records can be incorporated into covariance structure methods (Arbuckle, 1996; McArdle & Hamagami, 1992; Muthén, 1994) but these methods need further refinement and testing in empirical data. At the present time, HLM is the only program that can use all the data available.

There are some distinct features of the covariance structure approach that the other methods have difficulty matching. First, the covariance structure of the occasion-by-occasion measurement errors can be modeled explicitly, and its parameters estimated. Unlike other popular methods for the analysis of longitudinal data, the approach does not restrict the measurement error covariance matrix to a particular shape or pattern. Assumptions of constant variance and zero autocorrelation on the measurement errors – assumptions that are likely to be untenable in the measurement of dynamic processes – can be relaxed. Second, multiple indicators can be used to represent each predictor of change, providing a ready maximum-likelihood adjustment for measurement error. Third, the generality and flexibility of covariance structure analysis permits a wider range of models to be fit. For example, individual change can be modeled simultaneously in more than one domain (Willett & Sayer, 1996). This includes the investigation of (a) interrelationships among the several types of change and (b) the simultaneous and joint association of these several changes and selected predictors of change. Another possibility is the modeling of intervening effects on growth whereby a predictor may not act directly on change, but indirectly via the influence of mediating variables. In contrast to the estimation of mediating effects by HLM or OLS methods, which infer mediation if an effect is reduced to zero when the intervening variable is controlled, the magnitude of indirect effects on growth can be estimated explicitly under the covariance structure approach. Fourth, the method can incorporate time-varying covariates at Level 1, a feature it shares with the HLM approach.

Latent Transition Analysis

Growth-curve modeling is suitable for dynamic variables where growth is continuous. However, in some cases growth can be described as stage-sequential. There are many classic examples of stage-sequential theories in psychology, notably Piaget's theory of intellectual development. In Piaget's theory, growth is qualitative as well as quantitative. Children are increasing in intellectual development, and this increase is taking place in a series of stage transitions. Reasoning ability increases, but this does not tell the whole story. There is also a qualitative change in how the child views the

world. This is a stage transition. Latent transition analysis (LTA) is a procedure for estimating and testing stage-sequential models of growth.

LTA is a variety of latent variable models called a "latent class model." Latent class models involve discrete latent variables. A discrete latent variable divides a population up into groups. For example, a discrete political conservatism latent variable might divide a population up into conservative, moderate, and liberal. LTA extends these ideas to allow movement between classes over time.

To illustrate LTA, we discuss a study by Graham, Collins, Wugalter, Chung, and Hansen (1991) concerning adolescent substance use prevention. Graham et al. conceived of substance use onset as a stage-sequential process consisting of first trying tobacco and alcohol, then having a first experience with drunkenness, then going on to advanced use. Their model consisted of the following six stages: No use; Has tried alcohol only; Has tried tobacco only; Has tried both alcohol and tobacco; Has tried alcohol and tobacco and has been drunk; Has tried alcohol and tobacco, has been drunk, and has engaged in advanced use. Graham et al. used LTA to test the fit of this model in empirical data, and to compare progress through the stages in the model for individuals in two different treatment conditions.

Graham et al.'s (1991) sample were 2,009 junior high school students in the Los Angeles area who were participants in either a program containing a normative education component (norm condition) or a program not containing such a component (no norm condition). Students were measured in seventh grade and again in eighth grade. The data used in the analyses described here consisted of responses to three questionnaire items, recoded for analysis purposes as follows: Have you ever had even one puff on a cigarette? Have you ever had even a sip of alcohol (not for religious purposes)? Have you ever been drunk? Responses of "yes" to each of these items were coded 1, whereas responses of "no" were coded 0. In addition, a composite variable was formed to represent low-level advanced use. Responses indicating any regular tobacco or alcohol use, or any marijuana use at all, were coded 1; any other responses were coded 0.

LTA is a contingency table model, and the goodness-of-fit of LTA models is assessed by means of a chi-square test. In this case the null hypothesis that the model provides a reasonable fit to the data is tested. Graham et al. found that the null hypothesis was not rejected, so they concluded that the model provides a reasonable fit to the data. Thus it made sense to examine group differences in parameter estimates.

TABLE 18.2. Latent Transition Probability Estimates for NORM and NONORM Separately

Time 1 latent status	Time 2 latent status					
	1	2	3	4	5	6
NORM Group						
1. No use	.744	.176	.001	.079	.000	.000
2. Alcohol only	.0	.822	.0	.129	.016	.033
3. Tobacco only	.0	.0	.632	.254	.000	.114
4. Alcohol + tobacco	.0	.0	.0	.836	.000	.164
5. Alcohol + tobacco + drunk	.0	.0	.0	.0	.907	.093
6. Advanced use	.0	.0	.0	.0	.178	.822
NONORM Group						
1. No use	.667	.201	.023	.028	.070	.012
2. Alcohol only	.0	.752	.0	.190	.022	.036
3. Tobacco only	.0	.0	.633	.266	.000	.101
4. Alcohol + tobacco	.0	.0	.0	.759	.000	.241
5. Alcohol + tobacco + drunk	.0	.0	.0	.0	.494	.506
6. Advanced use	.0	.0	.0	.0	.000	1.000

Note. NORM = received normative education curriculum; NONORM = did not receive normative education curriculum. Each value shown is the estimated probability of membership in the "Time 2 latent status" column conditional on membership in the "Time 1 latent status" row. A value of .0 indicates that the parameter was fixed at zero; .000 indicates the value was estimated at zero.

There are several different types of parameters involved in LTA models. The parameter most relevant to the study of change is the transition probability parameter. This parameter represents the probability of membership in a stage at Time 2, conditional on stage membership at Time 1. Table 18.2 shows the transition probability parameters for the norm and no-norm groups. The parameters are arranged into transition probability matrices, where the rows correspond to Time 1 stage membership and the columns correspond to Time 2 stage membership. Graham et al. (1991) noted two particularly interesting points about these matrices. First, overall the norm group is more likely not to transition out of a stage than is the no-norm group. One exception is the advanced use stage, where the norm group is more likely to return to the immediately previous stage than is the no-norm group. Because one purpose of a prevention program is to prevent stage transitions, this suggests that the norm program is more effective than the no-norm program. Second, in both the norm and the no-norm groups, adolescents who started the substance use onset process with tobacco rather than alcohol appeared to be on an accelerated onset trajectory compared with those who started with alcohol.

In many ways, the transition probabilities are conceptually similar to the slope parameters in growth-curve modeling. They represent the amount and direction of change for all individuals who were at a given stage at the immediately previous time. A large diagonal element reflects a slow process where many individuals undergo no change (although note that in some models individuals may undergo change and then end up back in the same stage by the second observation). A large off-diagonal element means there is a lot of movement out of one stage and into another. One important difference is that the transition probabilities in LTA represent change between adjacent times only, whereas the slopes and other parameters in growth-curve models express change across all available times. Examining the LTA transition probabilities separately for treatment groups, as Graham et al. (1991) did, is analogous to incorporating group-level predictors of slope in growth curve models.

SUMMARY

In this chapter we have discussed design, measurement, and analysis issues relevant to the study of growth and change in social psychological research. We began by taking individual growth as a starting point, arguing that the assessment of individual growth is a necessary prerequisite to the assessment of interindividual or group differences in growth. We discussed the age, cohort, and time perspective and its implications for research design. Other design issues were considered, including missing data and participant attrition, and measurement effects. We also demonstrated that the timing of data collection is an important and often neglected design consideration. Some new aspects of measurement validity relevant to measurement of change were discussed. The shortcomings of traditional measurement procedures when applied to the measurement of change were reviewed, and a measurement model that incorporates a model of change was presented. Finally, two frameworks for the statistical analysis of change were discussed. The latent growth curve approach provides a way to model interindividual differences in intraindividual growth. LTA is a method for estimating and testing latent stage-sequential models.

REFERENCES

Anderson, E. R. (1993). Analyzing change in short-term longitudinal research using cohort-sequential designs. *Journal of Consulting and Clinical Psychology, 61,* 929–940.

Arbuckle, J. L. (1996). Full information estimation in the presence of incomplete data. In G. A. Marcoulides & R. E. Schumacker (Eds.), *Advanced structural equation modeling: Issues and techniques* (pp. 243–278). Mahwah, NJ: Erlbaum.

Barnett, R. C., Marshall, N. L., Raudenbush, S. W., & Brennan, R. T. (1993). Gender and the relationship between job experiences and psychological distress: A study of dual-earner couples. *Journal of Personality and Social Psychology, 64,* 794–806.

Blomqvist, N. (1977). On the relation between change and initial value. *Journal of the American Statistical Association, 72,* 746–749.

Bock, R. D., & Thissen, D. (1980). Statistical problems of fitting individual growth curves. In F. E. Johnston, A. F. Roche, & C. Susanne (Eds.), *Human physical growth and maturation: Methodologies and factors* (pp. 265–290). New York: Plenum.

Bryk, A. S., & Raudenbush, S. W. (1987). Application of hierarchical linear models to assessing change. *Psychological Bulletin, 101,* 147–158.

Bryk, A. S., & Raudenbush, S. W. (1992). *Hierarchical linear models: Applications and data analysis methods.* Newbury Park, CA: Sage.

Bryk, A. S., Raudenbush, S. W., & Congdon, R. T. (1996). *Hierarchical linear and nonlinear modeling with the HLM/2L and HLM/3L programs.* Chicago: Scientific Software International.

Cohen, P. (1991). A source of bias in longitudinal investigations of change. In L. M. Collins & J. L. Horn (Eds.), *Best methods for the analysis of change* (pp. 18–25). Washington, DC: American Psychological Association.

Collins, L. M. (1996). The analysis and quantification of change with age. In J. E. Birren & K. W. Schaie (Eds.), *Handbook of the psychology of aging* (4th ed., pp. 38–56). San Diego, CA: Academic Press.

Collins, L. M., & Cliff, N. (1990). Using the Longitudinal Guttman Simplex as a basis for measuring growth. *Psychological Bulletin, 108,* 128–134.

Collins, L. M., Cliff, N., & Dent, C. W. (1988). The Longitudinal Guttman Simplex: A new methodology for measurement of dynamic constructs in longitudinal panel studies. *Applied Psychological Measurement, 12,* 217–230.

Collins, L. M., & Graham, J. W. (1991). Comments on "A source of bias in longitudinal investigations of change." In L. M. Collins & J. L. Horn (Eds.), *Best methods for the analysis of change* (pp. 26–30). Washington, DC: American Psychological Association.

Coombs, C. H. (1964). *A theory of data.* Ann Arbor, MI: Mathesis Press.

Embretson, S. E. (1991). Implications of a multidimensional latent trait model for measuring change. In L. M. Collins & J. L. Horn (Eds.), *Best methods for the analysis of change* (pp. 184–197). Washington, DC: American Psychological Association.

Estes, W. K. (1956). The problem of inference from curves based on group data. *Psychological Bulletin, 53,* 134–140.

Graham, J. W., Collins, L. M., Wugalter, S. E., Chung, N. K., & Hansen, W. B. (1991). Modeling transitions in latent stage-sequential processes: A substance use prevention example. *Journal of Consulting and Clinical Psychology, 59,* 48–57.

Graham, J. W., Hofer, S. M., & Piccinin, A. M. (1994). Analysis with missing data in drug prevention research. In L. M. Collins & L. A. Seitz (Eds.), *Advances in data analysis for prevention intervention research* [NIDA Research Monograph 142; NIH Pub. No. 94-3599] (pp. 13–63). Washington, DC: U.S. Government Printing Office.

Guire, K. E., & Kowalski, C. J. (1979). Mathematical description and representation of developmental change functions on the intra- and interindividual levels. In J. R. Nesselroade & P. B. Baltes (Eds.), *Longitudinal research in the study of behavior and development* (pp. 89–110). New York: Academic Press.

Guttman, L. (1950). The basis for scalogram analysis. In S. A. Stouffer, L. Guttman, E. A. Suchman, P. Lazarsfeld, S. A. Star, & O. A. Clausen (Eds.), *Measurement and production* (pp. 60–90). Princeton, NJ: Princeton University Press.

Hauser, S. T., Jacobson, A. M., Wertlieb, D., Brink, S., & Wentworth, S. (1985). The contribution of family environment to perceived competence and illness adjustment in diabetic and acutely ill adolescents. *Family Relations, 34,* 99–108.

Howard, G. S., Millham, J., Slaten, S., & O'Donnell, L. (1981). Influence of subject response style effects on retrospective measures. *Applied Psychological Measurement, 5,* 89–100.

Little, R. J. A., & Rubin, D. B. (1987). *Statistical analysis with missing data.* New York: Wiley.

Loevinger, J., & Wessler, R. (1970). *Measuring ego development: Volume 1. Construction and use of a sentence completion test.* San Francisco: Jossey-Bass.

Lord, F. M., & Novick, M. R. (1968). *Statistical theories of mental test scores.* Reading, MA: Addison-Wesley.

McArdle, J. J., & Epstein, D. (1987). Latent growth curves within developmental structural equation models. *Child Development, 58,* 110–133.

McArdle, J. J., & Hamagami, F. (1992). Modeling incomplete longitudinal and cross-sectional data using latent growth structural models. *Experimental Aging Research, 18,* 145–166.

Meredith, W., & Tisak, J. (1990). Latent curve analysis. *Psychometrika, 55,* 107–122.

Muthén, B. (1991). Analysis of longitudinal data using latent variable models with varying parameters. In L. M. Collins & J. L. Horn (Eds.), *Best methods for the analysis of change* (pp. 1–17). Washington, DC: American Psychological Association.

Muthén, B. (1994). Multilevel covariance structure analysis. *Sociological Methods Research, 22,* 376–398.

Rogosa, D. R., Brandt, D., & Zimowski, M. (1982). A growth curve approach to the measurement of change. *Psychological Bulletin, 90,* 726–748.

Rogosa, D. R., & Saner, H. (1995). Longitudinal data analysis examples with random coefficient models.

Journal of Educational and Behavioral Statistics, 20, 149–170.

Rogosa, D. R., & Willett, J. B. (1985). Understanding correlates of change by modeling individual differences in growth. *Psychometrika, 50,* 203–228.

Schafer, J. L. (1997). *Analysis of incomplete multivariate data.* New York: Chapman and Hall.

Schaie, K. W. (1965). A general model for the study of developmental research on adulthood and aging. *Psychological Bulletin, 64,* 92–107.

Schaie, K. W., & Baltes, P. B. (1975). On sequential strategies in developmental research and the Schaie-Baltes controversy: Description or explanation? *Human Development, 18,* 384–390.

Stoolmiller, M. (1994). Antisocial behavior, delinquent peer association, and unsupervised wandering for boys: Growth and change from childhood to early adolescence. *Multivariate Behavioral Research, 29,* 263–288.

Willett, J. B. (1989). Some results on reliability for the longitudinal measurement of change: Implications for the design of studies of individual growth. *Educational and Psychological Measurement, 49,* 587–602.

Willett, J. B., & Sayer, A. G. (1994). Using covariance structure analysis to detect correlates and predictors of individual change over time. *Psychological Bulletin, 116,* 363–380.

Willett, J. B., & Sayer, A. G. (1996). Cross-domain analyses of change over time: Combining growth modeling and covariance structure analysis. In G. A. Marcoulides & R. E. Schumacher (Eds.), *Advanced structural equation modeling: Issues and techniques* (pp. 125–157). Mahwah, NJ: Erlbaum.

Williamson, G. L., Appelbaum, M., & Epanchin, A. (1991). Longitudinal analyses of academic achievement. *Journal of Educational Measurement, 28,* 61–76.

CHAPTER NINETEEN

Quantitative Synthesis of Social Psychological Research

BLAIR T. JOHNSON AND ALICE H. EAGLY

As in other scientific fields, the progress of social psychology has always hinged on investigators' abilities to cumulate empirical evidence about phenomena in an orderly and accurate fashion. This empirical evidence, consisting of multiple studies examining a phenomenon, exists as a literature on the topic. Although new studies rarely replicate earlier studies without adding or removing features, many studies are conceptual replications that use different stimulus materials and dependent measures to test the same hypothesis, and still others contain exact replications embedded within a larger design that adds new experimental conditions. In other instances, repeated tests of a relation accrue in a less systematic manner because researchers sometimes include in their studies tests of particular hypotheses in auxiliary or subsidiary analyses.

In order to reach conclusions about empirical support for a phenomenon, it is necessary to compare and contrast the findings of relevant studies. Therefore, accurate comparisons of study outcomes – reviews of

research – are at the very center of the scientific enterprise. Until recently these comparisons were nearly always made using informal methods that are now known as *narrative reviewing*: Scholars drew overall conclusions from their impressions of the overall trend of the studies' findings, sometimes guided by a count of the number of studies that had either produced or failed to produce statistically significant findings in the hypothesized direction. Narrative reviews have appeared in many different contexts and still serve a useful purpose in writing that does not have a comprehensive literature review as its goal. For example, textbooks typically contain narrative reviews of many hypotheses, and introductions to journal articles reporting primary research usually include reviews conducted with narrative methods.

Despite the usefulness of narrative reviewing, the method has often proven to be inadequate for reaching definitive conclusions about the degree of empirical support for a phenomenon or a theory of the phenomenon. One symptom of this inadequacy is that independent narrative reviews of the same literature often reached differing conclusions. For example, two separate reviews (Brubaker & Powers, 1976; Green, 1981) concluded that younger adults are better liked than older adults, but another review (Lutsky, 1981) concluded that there is little difference. In such cases, there are no easy rules for deciding which review has reached the most accurate conclusions about the phenomenon in question.

Critics of the narrative reviewing strategy (e.g., Eagly, 1987; Glass, McGaw, & Smith, 1981; Rosenthal, 1991) have pointed to four general faults in narrative reviewing. Although these faults are not necessarily inherent in narrative reviewing, they typify narrative reviewing as it usually has been practiced.

The preparation of this chapter was facilitated by National Institutes of Health Grants K21 MH01377 and R01 MH58563 to Blair T. Johnson and R01 MH48972 to Alice H. Eagly.

We thank Robert F. Bornstein, Steven J. Karau, Mary E. Kite, Charles M. Judd, David A. Kenny, Kenneth D. Levin, Fulgencio Marín-Martínez, Julio Sánchez-Meca, Charles A. Pierce, Harry T. Reis, M. Blanche Şerban, and Lance S. Weinhardt for their helpful comments on previous drafts of this chapter.

Correspondence should be directed to either Blair T. Johnson, Department of Psychology, University of Connecticut, U-0020, 406 Babbidge Road, Storrs, CT 06269-1020 (e-mail: bjohnson@psych.psy.uconn.edu) or to Alice H. Eagly, Department of Psychology, Northwestern University, Swift Hall, 2029 Sheridan Road, Evanston, IL 60208-2710 (e-mail: eagly@nwu.edu).

1. Narrative reviewing generally involves the use of a convenience sample of studies, perhaps consisting of only those studies that happen to be known to the reviewer. Any criteria that a reviewer may have used to select these studies typically go unstated and may never have been formalized by the reviewer. Because the parameters of the reviewed literature are not explicit, it is not possible to evaluate the adequacy of the definition of the literature or the thoroughness of the search for studies. If the sample of studies was biased, the conclusions reached may also be biased.

2. Narrative reviewers generally do not publicly state the procedures they used for either cataloging studies' characteristics or evaluating the quality of the studies' methods. Moreover, the rules and procedures that are applied are often not applied uniformly to all of the studies in the sample, and checks on the reliability of the reviewers' judgments about studies are generally absent. Therefore, the review's claims about the characteristics of the studies and the quality of their methods are difficult to judge for their accuracy.

3. In cases in which study findings differed, narrative reviewing has difficulty reaching clear conclusions about whether differences in study methods explain differences in results. Because narrative reviewers usually do not systematically code studies' methods, these reviewing procedures are not well suited to accounting for inconsistencies in findings.

4. Narrative reviewing typically relies much more heavily on statistical significance to judge studies' findings than on the magnitude of the findings. Statistical significance is a poor basis for comparing studies that have different sample sizes, because effects of identical magnitude can differ in statistical significance. Because of this problem, narrative reviewers often reach erroneous conclusions about the confirmation of a hypothesis in a series of studies, even in literatures as small as 10 studies (Cooper & Rosenthal, 1980).

Of course, these potential flaws in the review process are aggravated as the number of available studies cumulates. In contemporary psychology, large research literatures are not uncommon: For example, even as early as 1978, there were at least 345 studies examining interpersonal expectancy effects (Rosenthal & Rubin, 1978). Similarly, by 1983, there were over 1,000 studies evaluating whether birth order is related to personality (Ernst & Angst, 1983). As the number of studies grows, the conclusions reached by narrative reviewers become increasingly unreliable because of the informality of the methods they use to draw these conclusions.

Because of the importance of comparing study findings accurately, scholars have dedicated considerable effort to making the review process as reliable and valid as possible and thereby preventing criticisms such as those listed above. The result of these efforts has been the emergence of scientific review techniques known as *quantitative research synthesis*, or *meta-analysis*, which statistically cumulate the results of independent empirical tests of a particular relation between variables. Although scientists have cumulated empirical data from independent studies since the early 1800s (see Stigler, 1986), relatively sophisticated techniques to synthesize study findings emerged only after the advent of such standardized indexes as r-, d-, and p-values (e.g., Birge, 1932; Cochran, 1937; Fisher, 1932; Glass, 1976; Glass et al., 1981; Hunter & Schmidt, 1990; Pearson, 1933; Rosenthal, 1984, 1991; Yates & Cochran, 1938). Reflecting the field's maturation, Hedges and Olkin (1985) presented a sophisticated version of the statistical bases of meta-analysis, and standards for meta-analysis have grown increasingly rigorous.

Social psychologists' first rudimentary applications of quantitative review techniques occurred in the 1960s (e.g., Rosenthal, 1968; Wicker, 1969), but it was not until the late 1970s and early 1980s that these techniques were applied to a wide range of social psychological phenomena (e.g., C. F. Bond & Titus, 1983; Cooper, 1979; Hall, 1978; N. Miller & Cooper, 1991). In many instances these reviews have overturned or enhanced prior narrative reviewers' conclusions. As one example, although Schooler's (1972) and Ernst and Angst's (1983) influential narrative reviews concluded that birth order had little or no relation to personality, Sulloway's (1996, pp. 72–75) subsequent meta-analysis revealed that birth order had significant associations with four of the big five traits (openness to experience, conscientiousness, agreeableness, and emotional instability). Within social psychology, as in many other sciences (Cooper & Hedges, 1994a; Hunt, 1997; Mann, 1994; Thacker, 1988; Wachter & Straf, 1990), quantitative research synthesis is now common and well-accepted because scholars realize that careful application of these techniques will yield the clearest conclusions about a research literature.

In order to provide a general introduction to the techniques of research synthesis, we (a) introduce and detail the steps involved in research synthesis, (b) consider some options that reviewers should consider as they proceed through these steps, (c) discuss appropriate standards for conducting and evaluating quantitative reviews, and (d) evaluate the role of quantitative synthesis relative to primary research and other methods of testing hypotheses.

PROCEDURES FOR QUANTITATIVE SYNTHESES

An Overview of the Process of Quantitative Synthesis

The research process underlying quantitative synthesis can be broken into a number of discrete yet interrelated steps (see Cooper, 1982). Each stage contributes to the attainment of the next stage: Careful work in the early stages of the synthesis makes the later stages easier to accomplish. As a preview to a more detailed exposition, we list the stages and some of the questions that often accompany them:

1. *Conceptual analysis of the literature.* What independent and dependent variables define the phenomenon? How have these variables been operationalized in research? Have scholars debated different explanations for the relation demonstrated between these variables? Can the meta-analysis address these competing explanations? When, how much, and in what pattern should the variables relate? Should the size of the relation be relatively consistent or inconsistent across studies?
2. *Setting boundaries for the sample of studies.* What criteria should be used to select studies into the sample? Should considerations of study quality play a major role? What criteria should be used to *exclude* studies from the sample?
3. *Locating relevant studies.* What strategies will best locate the universe of studies? How can unpublished studies be obtained?
4. *Creating the meta-analytic database.* Which effect size metric should be used? Which study characteristics should be represented, and how can these characteristics be coded or otherwise assessed? How can the quality of studies' methods be assessed?
5. *Estimating effect sizes.* What are the best ways to convert study statistics into effect sizes? How can extraneous influences on effect size magnitude best be controlled?
6. *Analyzing the database.* How should the effect size data be analyzed statistically? Which of the available meta-analytic frameworks for statistical analysis is most appropriate? What sorts of statistical models can be used? How can the tests associated with these

models be interpreted? How can statistical outliers among the effect sizes be located and treated?
7. *Presenting and interpreting the results.* What information about the studies should be presented? Which meta-analytic models should appear? What are the best techniques for displaying the meta-analytic results? What knowledge accrues from the synthesis? How do the meta-analytic results reflect on the theoretical analysis? Has the synthesis uncovered important areas of neglect in the literature that warrant future research?

Conceptual Analysis of the Literature

The initial conceptual exploration of a research literature is critical because ideas formulated at this early point can dramatically affect the methods that follow, such as the criteria the reviewer formulates for including and excluding studies. The first conceptual step leading to a successful meta-analysis is to specify with the greatest possible clarity the phenomenon under review by defining the variables whose relation is the focus of the review. Ordinarily a synthesis evaluates evidence relevant to a single hypothesis that is defined as a relation between two variables, often stated as the influence of an independent variable on a dependent variable (e.g., the influence of group cohesiveness on group performance, synthesized by Mullen & Copper, 1994). Moreover, a synthesis must take study quality into account at an early point to determine the kinds of operations that constitute acceptable operationalizations of these conceptual variables. Typically, studies testing a particular hypothesis differed in the operations used to establish the variables (e.g., different manipulations of the independent variable, different measures of the dependent variable), and it is therefore not surprising that these different operations were often associated with variability in studies' findings. If the differences in studies' operations can be appropriately judged or categorized, it is likely that an analyst can explain some of this variability in effect size magnitude (see sections on *Study characteristics*, and *Testing models of meta-analytic moderators*, below).

Essential to this conceptual analysis is careful study of the history of the research problem and of typical studies in the literature. Theoretical articles, earlier reviews, and empirical articles should be examined for the interpretations they provide of the phenomenon under investigation. Authors' theories or even their more informal and less developed insights may suggest moderators of the effect that could potentially be coded in the studies and examined for their explanatory power. When scholars have debated different explanations for the relation, the synthesis should be designed to address these competing explanations.

The most common way to test competing explanations is to examine how findings pattern across studies. Specifically, a theory might imply that a third variable should influence the relation between the independent and dependent variables: The relation should be larger or smaller with a higher level of this third variable. Treating this third variable as a potential moderator of the effect, the analyst would code all of the studies for their status on the moderator. This meta-analytic strategy, known as the *moderator variable approach*, is analogous to the examination of interactions with primary-level data (see section *Estimating Effect Sizes*). However, instead of testing the interaction within one study's data, the meta-analysis tests whether the moderator affects the examined relation across the studies included in the sample. This moderator variable approach, advancing beyond the simple question of *whether* the independent variable is related to the dependent variable, addresses the question of *when* the magnitude or sign of the relationship varies. Using this strategy, Karau and Williams (1993) found that the tendency for people to expend less effort when working collectively than when working individually (known as *social loafing*) was larger for male participants than for female participants. Similarly, C. F. Bond and Titus's (1983) synthesis showed that the presence of others improves the performance of simple tasks but impairs the performance of complex tasks.

In addition to this moderator variable approach to synthesizing studies' findings, other strategies have proven to be useful. In particular, a theory might suggest that a third variable serves as a mediator of the critical relation because it conveys the causal impact of the independent variable on the dependent variable. If at least some of the primary studies within a literature have evaluated this mediating process, mediator relations can be tested within a meta-analytic framework by performing correlational analyses that are an extension of path analysis with primary-level data. Using such techniques, Driskell and Mullen (1990) reviewed seven studies that correlated status cues, expectations for performance, and performance; their results showed that the influence of status cues on performance was largely mediated by expectations for performance. Shadish (1996) provided a very helpful exposition of this mediator variable approach to analyzing meta-analytic data as well as other approaches.

Setting Boundaries for the Sample of Studies

In beginning a research synthesis, the reviewer should think about how a relation has been tested and consider whether all tests should be included in the synthesis. Decisions about the inclusion of studies are important because the inferential power of any meta-analysis is limited by the methods of the studies that are integrated. To the extent that all (or most) of the reviewed studies share a particular methodological limitation, any synthesis of these studies would be limited in this respect. For example, a synthesis of correlational studies will produce only correlational evidence about the association in question. However, if the critical hypothesis was tested with true experiments, defined by one or more manipulated independent variables and the random assignment of participants to conditions, the synthesis gauges the causal effect of the independent variables on the dependent variable across the studies reviewed. As a general rule, research syntheses profit by focusing on the studies that used stronger methods to test the meta-analytic hypotheses. Nonetheless, it is important to note that studies that have some strengths (e.g., manipulated independent variables) may have other weaknesses (e.g., deficiencies in ecological validity) (see Brewer, this volume, Ch. 1).

Even though research syntheses of experimental studies are better able to draw conclusions about cause-and-effect relations than are syntheses of correlational studies, meta-analyses of experimental studies generally have other limitations. Of particular note, such syntheses produce only correlational evidence concerning the relations of study characteristics to studies' findings when the effect sizes are compared across studies in so-called "between-studies moderator analyses." For example, Wood, Rhodes, and Whelan (1989) found that in studies published after 1978, men reported more positive well-being than women, whereas this pattern reversed in studies published before 1978. As Wood et al. indicated, effects of year of publication are difficult to interpret because they could be confounded with any number of other variables (see discussion by Knight, Fabes, & Higgins, 1996). In contrast, moderator tests can yield stronger causal claims if the moderator dimension reflects within-studies manipulations. In such cases, random assignment of participants in the primary research to levels of the moderator makes it less likely that confounds were associated with the moderator. In this strategy, the results of each study are divided to produce separate effect sizes within levels of the moderator. For example, Karau and Williams (1993) showed that social loafing was more pronounced as groups increased in size, a dimension that was experimentally manipulated in many of the studies. If an analysis were limited to the studies that contained this manipulation, any moderation that would be demonstrated could be attributed to the manipulated variable, and interpretation could proceed with greater certainty. Thus, it may be advantageous for reviewers to pay special attention to those within-study comparisons that are available in the reviewed studies.

In deciding whether some studies may be insufficiently rigorous to include in the meta-analysis, a reviewer should be alert to methodological standards within the area reviewed. Although a large number of potential threats to methodological rigor have been identified (see Brewer, this volume; Campbell & Stanley, 1963; Cook & Campbell, 1979; S. Greenwald & Russell, 1991; Wortman, 1994), there are few absolute standards of study quality, and, in practice, the characteristics considered essential to ensure high study quality vary widely from literature to literature. In some research literatures, it might already be known that a certain method (e.g., a measure or a manipulation) yields seriously flawed results; if so, an analyst might decide to eliminate studies that used this method. Indeed, one possible strategy is to omit obviously flawed studies in order to restrict the synthesis to studies of high quality (S. Greenwald & Russell, 1991). As an alternative, an analyst might attempt to correct the effect sizes for certain methodological biases (e.g., unreliability, restriction of range), a subject that we consider further below (see *Correcting effect sizes for bias*). Retaining potentially flawed studies and representing their quality-relevant features in the coding scheme is another defensible strategy. For example, if an analyst suspects that a given independent variable was not established uniformly across the literature, he or she might be able to code the variable's strength and determine whether it is correlated with effect size magnitude. More generally, when there are questions concerning whether variant methods yield the same results, a meta-analysis can be designed to address this issue. Exemplifying this strategy, Heinsman and Shadish (1996) examined whether randomized and nonrandomized experiments reached the same conclusions within four different research literatures; their results suggested that this dimension of study quality did not dramatically impact results.

In addition to study quality, many other considerations enter into setting the boundaries of the research literature that will be synthesized. Although adequate conceptualization of the phenomenon that is the focus of the synthesis should help to define these boundaries, sometimes boundary-setting is in itself a time-consuming process that forces reviewers to weigh conceptual and practical issues. These issues are particularly acute when a phenomenon has been studied using a variety of methods. Sometimes analysts set boundaries so that the studies included are relatively homogeneous methodologically (e.g., only laboratory studies), and sometimes boundaries encompass different methodologies (e.g., field studies are also included). Surely the boundaries should be wide enough that interesting hypotheses about moderator variables can be tested within the synthesis. Yet, if very diverse methods are included, the reviewer may need to define some moderator variables that can be implemented only within particular methodologies (e.g., participants' organizational status exists only within studies conducted in organizations). Practical considerations sometimes impinge on reviewers' boundary conditions because including a wide range of methods would make the project too large and complex to carry out in a reasonable time frame. In such instances, reviewers may divide a literature into two or more research syntheses, each addressing a different aspect of a broad research question.

If the boundaries of a meta-analysis are too wide, researchers may be the targets of what has become known as the "apples and oranges" critique (Glass et al., 1981). Critics might thus argue that the reviewer has combined in a single analysis studies that use noncomparable methods and thus has mixed apples and oranges. Methodologists have been generally unsympathetic to this line of argument because they regard it as the task of the meta-analyst to show empirically that differences in methods produce consequential differences in study outcomes. This demonstration is achieved by disaggregating studies into various categories, as we discuss in the section on *Analyzing the Meta-Analytic Database*. Of course, analysts who do not perform these analyses that separate studies into various types may be appropriately criticized as having given insufficient attention to the effects that diverse methods may have had on study outcomes.

Analysts often set the boundaries of the synthesis so that the methods of included studies differ dramatically only on critical moderator dimensions. If other, extraneous dimensions are thereby held relatively constant across the reviewed studies, moderator variable analyses can be more clearly interpreted. Nonetheless, an analyst should include in the sample all studies or portions of studies that satisfy the selection criteria. If some studies meeting preliminary criteria established conditions that are judged to be extremely atypical or flawed, the selection criteria may need to be modified to exclude them. Developing selection criteria is to some extent a process that continues as meta-analysts examine more studies and thereby discover the full range of research designs that have been used to investigate a particular hypothesis.

One issue that generally arises when setting the boundaries for the research literature is whether to include unpublished studies. Although these studies are certainly more difficult to access than published studies, the omission of unpublished studies from a review can bias the review's findings, generally in favor of larger effects, a pattern that has been demonstrated in several studies (e.g., Cooper, DeNeve, & Charlton, 1997; Dickersin, 1997; Glass et al., 1981). In a discussion of unpublished studies, Rosenthal (1979) referred to them as producing a file-drawer problem because they may be buried in researchers' file drawers, especially if their results were nonsignificant. In the extreme case of so-called "prejudice against the null hypothesis" (A. G. Greenwald, 1975, p. 1), it might be that the "journals are filled with the 5% of the studies that show Type I errors, while the file drawers back at the lab are filled with the 95% of the studies that show nonsignificant (e.g., $p > .05$) results" (Rosenthal, 1979, p. 638). In partial support of this claim, surveys of researchers suggest that from 15% to 40% of the studies that are conducted are never published (Cooper et al., 1997; Rotton, Foos, Van Meek, & Levitt, 1995; Shadish, Doherty, & Montgomery, 1989; Sommer, 1987). Although it appears common for authors to decide not to pursue the publication of their studies if the results are nonsignificant (A. G. Greenwald, 1975; Rotton et al., 1995), a variety of other factors also affect the publication status of a study (e.g., author productivity; see Sommer, 1987). Moreover, the studies reported in dissertations and master's theses are less likely to be screened for statistical significance than studies reported in journals. Although dissertation and thesis studies are not considered to be published unless they appear in a journal or some other source, they do not languish in file drawers.

These considerations strongly suggest that if it is plausible that studies with stronger findings were more likely to be published (see Begg, 1994), every effort should be made to obtain unpublished studies. Moreover, there are several other reasons that the inclusion of unpublished studies should almost always facilitate the goals of meta-analysis:

1. Because the potential for conducting an informative synthesis increases with a larger number of studies, no source of obtaining studies should be ruled out. As more studies are included, mean effect size estimates stabilize, and the power to detect moderators of effect sizes increases (Johnson, Mullen, & Salas, 1995).

2. It is generally an explicit goal of meta-analysis to describe the *universe* of studies on a topic or at least an unbiased sample of that universe (White, 1994). If a meta-analysis includes all studies in the literature or an appropriate sample of them, the validity of its representation of the research literature is enhanced. The inadequacy of sampling that excludes unpublished studies can be especially acute when research literatures contain large numbers of unpublished studies. In extreme instances, omitting the unpublished studies would eliminate the majority of evidence on the hypothesis (e.g., comparisons of women's and men's leadership styles; Eagly & Johnson, 1990). Ironically, a synthesist would not even learn that this evidence exists unless the unpublished literature were searched. In the section *Locating Relevant Studies*, below, we detail techniques to find such studies.

3. Regardless of whether a study is published, the analyst should judge it against a set of inclusion and exclusion criteria. Uniform implementation of these criteria circumvents the criticism that unpublished studies generally have unacceptable quality due to the absence of peer review. Rather than merely assume (perhaps incorrectly) that unpublished studies have inadequate quality, a meta-analyst should remove all studies, published or unpublished, that do not meet the review's quality criteria and code the remaining studies on quality-relevant study characteristics (e.g., reliability of measures).

Thus, as a general rule, it is advisable to include unpublished studies. To test whether unpublished and published reports differ in their findings, analysts should examine whether this variable moderates the magnitude of the effect sizes.

A further decision that often arises is whether the sample of studies should be restricted to one country or culture. Of course, the reasons that encourage sampling unpublished studies also encourage sampling studies from all countries and cultures. Moreover, including such studies would increase the inclusiveness of the meta-analysis by representing a broader sample of populations of research participants and permitting an analyst to answer questions about the generality of the studied effect across diverse cultures. For example, R. Bond and Smith (1996) found that research participants in collectivistic cultures were more likely to conform in the Asch-style line-judgment experiment than were participants in individualistic cultures, although the conformity effect was significant within both types of cultures. Yet, in many research literatures in which it is reasonable to suspect cross-national variability, it may not be possible to address this issue meta-analytically because only a very small number of studies are available from countries other than the one in which the research paradigm first appeared (e.g., Eagly, Makhijani, & Klonsky, 1992; Kolodziej & Johnson, 1996). Therefore, as a general rule, studies from multiple cultures should be included in the sample if they are available in at least modest numbers. Commercially available computer software often can help to overcome foreign language barriers (e.g., Wood, Lundgren, Ouellette, Busceme, & Blackstone, 1994, used software to translate French documents into English).

A final issue is the completeness with which a research literature is reviewed. Some literatures are so enormous that including all studies would be impractical. In these instances, a practical solution might be to take from the entire literature a reasonably-sized random sample. The most defensible way to accomplish this solution is to list all studies in the pertinent literature, decide how many would make a sufficient sample, and randomly select this number of studies, a procedure that Rosenthal and Rubin (1978) followed in their meta-analysis of the interpersonal expectancy effect literature.

Locating Relevant Studies

Because including a large number of studies generally increases the value of a quantitative synthesis, it is important to locate as many studies as possible that might be suitable for inclusion. When a literature consists at least in part of findings whose presence cannot be discerned from reading studies' titles and abstracts, a reviewer may have to retrieve all studies in the general research area, in order to identify the reports that contain the finding of interest. For example, Eagly and Johnson (1990) screened over 6,000 abstracts of studies on leadership and related topics. They obtained for closer scrutiny those studies that offered the potential, at least, for comparisons of women's and men's leadership styles, and, in the end, 162 studies fit their inclusion criteria. To insure that a sufficient sample of studies is located, reviewers are well advised to err in the direction of being extremely inclusive in their search-

ing procedures. As described elsewhere (e.g., Cooper, 1998; Glass et al., 1981; Mullen, 1989; White, 1994), there are many ways to find relevant studies; ordinarily, analysts should use all of these techniques. Unfortunately, computer searches of databases such as PsycLIT seldom locate all of the available studies, although such searches are extremely useful. The most important retrieval techniques follow:

1. *Computer database searches* are used to find citations of (a) articles whose titles or abstracts contain terms a reviewer has defined or (b) articles that were cataloged in a database under keywords selected by the reviewer. There are many different databases useful for social psychologists, including PsycLIT and PsycINFO (which are made available by the American Psychological Association), *Dissertation Abstracts* (electronic reference products, made available by UMI, contains abstracts for dissertations and some Master's theses), *Social Sciences Citation Index* (compact disc edition, made available by the Institute for Scientific Information), SocioFile, MedLine, and ABI/Inform. ERIC (Educational Resources Information Center) is especially important to psychologists because it contains some entries for papers delivered at meetings of psychological associations as well as unpublished documents such as government reports. ERIC thus provides partial access to the fugitive literature of unpublished studies.

One way for reviewers to generate search terms is to determine whether the studies that they initially have in hand (perhaps identified from prior reviews) are located by preliminary search terms and thus appear on the output from a trial search. This examination as well as an informal process of trial-and-error using various search terms are generally required to shape an appropriate search strategy, and different sets of search terms can be used in multiple passes in databases. It is important to realize that the yield of such searches can vary widely, depending on the terms used. For example, in separate reviews of the literature on attitudes toward homosexuality, Whitley and Kite (1995) obtained 50 more studies than Oliver and Hyde (1993). Such searches can generally obtain more studies if wildcards are used (e.g., *attitud** will match *attitude, attitudes,* and *attitudinal*), because it is often the case that researchers used a variety of related terms to describe the variables they studied. Because the reviewer can interact directly with these databases, preliminary search terms can be quickly tried and adjusted. Reviewers can generate search output easily through the resources available in most university libraries. Therefore, there is little reason not to use inclusive search strategies, even though the yield of suitable studies may be small. Librarians expert on computer-based information searching often can provide helpful advice to novice searchers.

2. The *ancestry approach* involves examining the reference lists of existing reviews and of studies in the targeted literature to find likely candidates for the review. In fact, the reference list of every study that is located should be scrutinized. This method is important for locating studies whose publication dates precede the establishment of databases such as PsycINFO, although the American Psychological Association now provides a database of psychological literature extending to 1887 (PsycINFO Complete) and the dissertation abstracts database begins with 1861.

3. In the *descendancy approach*, a reference to a seminal article is specified in a database, and the articles that have cited it are listed. This type of search can be accomplished in Social SciSearch or (more arduously) in the print copies of the *Social Sciences Citation Index*. These searches are particularly useful in research literatures that were initiated by a particular study that was then typically cited by subsequent investigators.

4. The *invisible college technique* makes use of the network of researchers who work on a given topic. Because these researchers may be in frequent contact with one another, they may know who has new studies on which topics, or in some instances, they may have unpublished data sets that they are willing to make available. The reviewer can contact these individuals and may obtain some of the fugitive literature, even though he or she may not be regarded as a member of the invisible college. Helpful in identifying the invisible college are the programs of recent and upcoming meetings of psychological associations; these programs list titles (and often abstracts) of papers delivered at these events. With the advent of widespread access to the Internet and its discussion groups on various issues, yet another technique is to send electronic mail describing the type of study desired to the various "listservs" to which researchers subscribe. In this way, the need for studies is broadcast to hundreds or even thousands of researchers. Such technology has made the "invisible" college increasingly visible.

5. Hand searches of important journals consist of scrutinizing all articles published in key journals. The abstracts of articles with promising titles are read to determine if the text of the article should be examined. This method may turn up some reports that were overlooked by other techniques, and it certainly provides a good cross-check on the adequacy of searching conducted by the other methods.

Finally, to enable readers to judge the adequacy of search procedures and to enable other reviewers to evaluate and replicate these procedures, the review should describe in detail their methods of locating studies, including the names of databases that were searched, and for each database the time period covered and the keywords used. Reviewers should also describe their inclusion and exclusion criteria and provide a rationale for using these criteria.

Creating the Meta-Analytic Database

Once the sample of studies is in hand, the next step is to code them for their characteristics and to calculate effect sizes that estimate the relation being examined. In other words, the studies must be entered into a data set that includes each study's important characteristics and its effect size information.

STUDY CHARACTERISTICS. In conceptualizing the hypothesis that is under scrutiny and the conditions under which studies' results should vary in magnitude (or direction), reviewers develop ideas about the study characteristics that should be coded. The most important of these characteristics are potential moderator variables, which the analyst expects on an a priori basis to account for variation among the studies' effect sizes. It is also important to consider whether studies that differ along a critical moderator dimension also differ on other dimensions. As Lipsey (1994) suggested, it "is quite unlikely that study characteristics will be randomly and independently distributed over the studies in a given literature" (p. 117). Because such confounds could produce interpretational difficulties, it is important to code these additional characteristics so that their moderating influences can be examined, if only on an exploratory or post hoc basis. Finally, it is also important to code the studies for numerous other characteristics such as their date of publication and participant population, even if these characteristics are not expected to account for variation in studies' outcomes (see Lipsey, 1994). The central tendencies of these characteristics are ordinarily displayed, often in a table, to provide readers of the review with a description of the usual context of studies in the literature.

Study characteristics may be either continuous or *categorical*. Variables on a *categorical* metric consist of a discrete number of values that reflect qualitative differences between those values. For example, among the categorical study characteristics that Bornstein (1989) coded in his synthesis of studies on the mere exposure effect was the type of measure used to assess affect, which had categories such as liking, goodness-of-meaning, and pleasantness. Variables on a *continuous* metric consist of values that exist along ratio, interval, or ordinal scales. For example, among the continuous study characteristics that Bornstein coded was stimulus exposure time. Typically, synthesists code variables by using a coding form that displays the classes comprising each categorical variable and provides blank spaces for entry of the values of continuous variable (see Stock, 1994, for examples of such forms).

Some important features of studies cannot be coded from their method sections but must be assessed from other sources. For example, Eagly and Johnson's (1990) synthesis of differences between men's and women's leadership style retrieved archival data from the U.S. Census in order to estimate the distribution of the sexes in various leadership roles. Similarly, in a review of the effects of tripling in college dormitory rooms, Mullen and Felleman (1989) learned what specific dormitories had been studied and then obtained blueprints from college administrators in order to gauge physical features that were relevant to crowding.

Other techniques may prove useful to gauge study features that are difficult to code accurately. For example, in a meta-analysis on sex-related differences in aggression, Eagly and Steffen (1986) wished to determine whether women and men differed in how unfavorably they perceived the aggressive acts that had been examined in the social psychological literature on aggression. Therefore, they had female and male students rate the extent to which each such act would produce harm to the target of aggression, guilt and anxiety in oneself as the aggressor, and danger to oneself. From these ratings, Eagly and Steffen estimated sex differences in these students' perceptions of the aggressive acts and related these scores to the effect sizes that represented sex differences in aggressive behavior. In other instances, experts' ratings could be obtained based on their reading of the method sections of the reports or of the actual stimulus materials used in the studies (e.g., Johnson & Eagly, 1989; N. Miller & Carlson, 1990). Yet, it is desirable to provide convergent evidence of the validity of the judges' ratings used by these methods, because these judges function only as observers of studies' methods. Observers may be biased, as suggested by the results of studies using

roleplaying participants, which have sometimes deviated from the results of studies using actual participants (e.g., A. G. Miller, 1972). One way to determine the validity of judges' ratings of manipulation effectiveness is to compare them with effect sizes representing the manipulation checks present in the studies. To the extent that these values are highly correlated, the judges' ratings can be trusted (e.g., Bettencourt & Miller, 1996; N. Miller, Lee, & Carlson, 1991).

RELIABILITY OF CODING. Because each study outcome in a meta-analysis represents the data provided by many research participants, coding errors can be very consequential, perhaps even more critical than coding errors made in primary research. These errors are particularly consequential when they pertain to moderator variables. Illustrating this point, Wanous, Sullivan, and Malinak (1989) reviewed four literatures for which two independent meta-analyses had been performed. Their analysis of these syntheses suggested that some of the results differed because moderator variables had been coded differently and perhaps erroneously in some instances. Because accurate coding is crucial to the results of a meta-analysis, the coding of study characteristics should be carried out by two or more coders, and an appropriate index of interrater reliability should be calculated (such as the intraclass correlation and Cohen's, 1960, *kappa*; see Langenbucher, Labouview, & Morgenstern, 1996; Orwin, 1994). In most cases, disagreements between coders can be resolved by discussion, or perhaps by averaging. In order to improve the reliability of the coding of study characteristics, a small subset of the studies can be used as a trial run. If agreement is low on some study characteristics, they should be more carefully defined, and a further trial implemented. Trial runs may also reveal that the preliminary coding scheme is incomplete in its coverage of study attributes.

COMPUTATION OF EFFECT SIZES. To be included in the synthesis, a study must contain a report of a quantitative test of the hypothesis that is under scrutiny. In the best case these reports are quite precise (e.g., means and standard deviations, F-tests), but some reports may be ambiguous (e.g., "the groups did not differ"). Nonetheless, the goal is to convert summary statistics into effect sizes that can be statistically integrated. Most studies precisely report the examined relation by one or more of the following statistics: (a) means (M) and standard deviations (SD); (b) t-tests; (c) F-tests (ANOVAs); (d) r-values (e.g., Pearson, point-biserial, tetrachoric); (e) χ^2 values; (f) proportions or frequencies; and (g) p-values. Ordinarily, each of these statistics can be converted with relative ease into an effect size, although some types of statistical information are more precise than others. In particular, p-values can be quite imprecise if reported only as a p-level (e.g., $p < .05$). Obviously, exact statistics are preferable to inexact statistics for calculating effect sizes. If only an inexact statistic is given, one possibility is to contact the authors of the study for more precise information. If the only information available is imprecise, it should nonetheless be used so that the study outcome can be included in the meta-analysis, as Rosenthal (1991) recommended. Even the information that the relevant finding was nonsignificant should be preserved, in the absence of a more precise statistical report (see *Dealing With Nonreported Results*, below). We list often-used effect size transformations of study information below.

EFFECT SIZE INDEXES. The most commonly used effect size indexes are the standardized difference and the correlation coefficient (see Rosenthal, 1991, 1994). The standardized difference, which expresses the finding in standard deviation units, was first proposed by Cohen (1969) in the following form:

$$g = \frac{M_A - M_B}{SD}, \qquad (1)$$

where M_A and M_B are the sample means of two compared groups, and SD is the pooled standard deviation.[1] Because this formula overestimates population effect sizes to the extent that sample sizes are small, Hedges (1981) produced a correction for this bias, $d = J(m)g$, where d is an unbiased estimator of the population effect size, and $J(m)$ is the correction,

$$J(m) \approx 1 - \frac{3}{4m - 1}, \qquad (2)$$

where m is $n_A + n_B - 2$, the degrees of freedom. To distinguish between corrected and uncorrected effect sizes, we follow Hedges and Olkin's (1985) convention of referring to Cohen's uncorrected effect size as g and Hedges's corrected effect size as d.

---

[1] As a supplement to examining differences between means, it is possible to examine differences in variances between two groups. This procedure is particularly useful when the variances are not homogeneous between the groups that are compared. Procedures that take variance differences as well as mean differences into account appear in articles by Feingold (1995) and Hedges and Friedman (1993)

A common equation for the correlation coefficient, r, is

$$r = \frac{\sum_{i=1}^{N} z_{X_i} z_{Y_i}}{N}, \qquad (3)$$

where z_{X_i} and z_{Y_i} are the standardized forms of X and Y being related for each case i, and N is the number of observations. Like d-values, r-values have a bias, underestimating the population effect size especially for studies with small samples and for r-values near .60. Therefore, it is appropriate to implement the following correction for bias:

$$\tilde{G}_{(r)} \cong r + \frac{r(1 - r^2)}{2(n - 3)}, \qquad (4)$$

where $\tilde{G}_{(r)}$ is the approximation of the population effect size and n is the sample size. Yet, because this bias correction is very small for sample sizes higher than 20, it is often omitted. Because the sampling distribution of a sample correlation coefficient tends to be skewed to the extent that the population correlation is large (see Hays, 1988), it is conventional in meta-analysis to use Fisher's (1921) r-to-Z transform and to perform meta-analytic calculations on the Z-values,

$$Z_r = \frac{1}{2} \log_e \frac{1 + r}{1 - r}, \qquad (5)$$

where $\log_e$ is a natural logarithm operation and r is corrected via Equation 4. Then, following operations on Z_r, Fisher's (1921) Z-to-r transform is used to convert a Z_r-value back into r,

$$r = \frac{e^{(2Z_r)} - 1}{e^{(2Z_r)} + 1}, \qquad (6)$$

where e is the base of the natural logarithm.

Choice of Effect Size Index for Meta-Analysis

Because r can be transformed into d (in its g form),

$$g = \frac{2r}{\sqrt{1 - r^2}}, \qquad (7)$$

and g into r,

$$r = \frac{g}{\sqrt{g^2 + 4}}, \qquad (8)$$

the choice of an effect-size metric for meta-analysis may seem somewhat arbitrary. Some analysts who prefer r argue that it is more immediately interpretable than d (e.g., Mullen, 1989; Rosenthal, 1991, 1994). Others believe that ds are just as interpretable, because they are expressed in units of the standard deviation and are therefore a type of standard score. Despite these considerations of ease of interpretation, the convention is to use r as the effect size if most of the studies that are integrated report correlations between two continuous variables. If most of the studies report ANOVAS, t-tests, and chi-squares for comparisons between two groups (e.g., experimental vs. control; women vs. men), analysts typically use d.

THE SIGN GIVEN TO EFFECT SIZES. The positive or negative sign of the effect sizes computed in a meta-analysis is defined so that studies with opposite outcomes have opposing signs. Ordinarily, in research literatures in which groups are compared, the positive sign is given to outcomes in the expected, hypothesized, or typical direction for the meta-analysis as a whole, and the negative sign is given to outcomes that reverse this direction. Only a relation that is exactly null would have no sign, because the effect size would be 0.00. Illustrating this practice is Kite and Whitley's (1996) meta-analysis of sex-related differences in attitudes toward homosexuals, in which the expected direction of the findings was that women would evaluate homosexuals more positively than do men. Therefore, the positive sign was given to effect sizes indicating that women's evaluations were more positive than men's, and the negative sign was given to effect sizes indicating that men's evaluations were more positive than women's. Alternatively, in research literatures in which experimental groups are compared with control groups, differences in favor of the experimental group might be given a positive sign, and differences in favor of the control group given a negative sign, regardless of the hypothesis or typical direction of the findings. Also, for meta-analyses of correlational studies, the positive sign is generally given to positive associations between the two focal variables, and the negative sign to negative or inverse associations.

MULTIPLE REPORTS FROM INDIVIDUAL STUDIES. When one or both of the variables that are related in the meta-analysis were operationalized in more than one way in a given report, the analyst must decide whether to average the effect sizes that can be computed in order to represent the study with a single effect size estimate. To preserve the independence of the effect sizes in a meta-analysis, they must each come from a different study. That is, the participants whose data contribute to a given effect size must not contribute to any other effect sizes in the analysis. Therefore, the analyst would ordinarily average multiple effect sizes calculated from a single study, especially if the goal of the meta-analysis is to examine uncorrected effect sizes (see *Correcting effect*

sizes for biased methods, below). Alternatively, Rosenthal and Rubin (1986) described a procedure to calculate a combined effect size, $g_{combined}$, for the study such that

$$g_{combined} = \frac{\sum_{i=1}^{N_r} g_i}{\sqrt{r_{dv} N_r^2 + N_r(1 - r_{dv})}}, \tag{9}$$

where N_r is the number of measures, g_i is the effect size for each measure i, and r_{dv} is either the correlation between the two measures or the average correlation between the measures, in the case of three or more measures. This equation relies on the Spearman-Brown prophecy equation, which dictates that augmenting the reliability of variables increases the magnitude of their observed associations (see Cronbach, 1990). Of course, the use of Equation 9 may be precluded in many instances because the requisite correlation or correlations between measures are not reported.[2]

Instead of or in addition to averaging effects within studies, the analyst may wish to investigate whether the results of the studies varied depending on the different operations by which their dependent variables were defined. For this purpose, the analyst should preserve the separate effect size estimates made within individual studies, in order to perform a subsequent analysis examining whether the operations produced differences in the effect sizes. For example, in a meta-analysis of sex differences in leaders' effectiveness, Eagly, Karau, and Makhijani (1995) analyzed effect sizes according to the identity of the raters who provided the effectiveness measure and the basic type of measure (e.g., objective vs. subjective). Although many individual studies contributed several effect sizes to these analyses, each study's effect sizes were subsequently aggregated into a single study-level effect size that was used in additional analyses that did satisfy the assumption that effect sizes are independent. Analyses using multiple effect sizes from single studies can certainly be informative, but they should be interpreted cautiously because they violate the assumption of independence of the effect sizes (see *Consequences of violations of the assumption of effect size independence,* below).

When a study examined the relation of interest within levels of another variable, effect sizes may be calculated within the levels of this variable as well as for the study as a whole. How seriously the use of such within-level effect sizes violates the independence assumption depends on whether these levels were created on a within-subjects basis or a between-subjects

---

[2] In the absence of the relevant correlation, analysts may wish to estimate the correlation from the subset of studies that provide this information.

basis. If the same participants took part at all levels of the variable (i.e., a within-subjects variable), the effect sizes would be highly dependent. The effect sizes would also be dependent if one control group serves as a comparison for more than one treatment group. Even if the participants at the different levels were not the same individuals, the effect sizes would be dependent because they came from the same study, which was carried out under conditions existing in a particular place at a particular point in time (Hedges, 1990). For example, effect sizes might be calculated separately for the male and female participants in experiments in order to examine sex-related differences in the relation (e.g., Eagly, Ashmore, Makhijani, & Longo, 1991; Karau & Williams, 1993), even though these effect sizes would not be independent.

Finally, reports may contain more than one form of statistical information that could be used to calculate a given effect size. For example, a report might contain an F-test as well as means and standard deviations. The analyst should compute the effect size from both such sources, and, as long as the effect sizes are similar, take a simple average of them. Yet, the analyst should keep in mind that more accurate statistics typically have more decimal places and that rounding errors can produce discrepancies in calculated effect sizes. If the effect size estimates are highly dissimilar, there may be errors in the information reported or the analyst's calculations. In the absence of obvious errors, the analyst must judge which value to enter into the data set, if any. Sometimes an inspection of the report's quantitative information for its internal consistency suggests that one form of the information is more accurate. If the discrepancy is serious and not readily resolved, one possibility is to contact the authors of the report. Only as a final resort should the study be discarded as too ambiguous.

Estimating Effect Sizes

A comprehensive treatment of the formulas to convert primary-level statistics to effect sizes is beyond the scope of this chapter (see Cooper & Hedges, 1994b; Glass et al., 1981; Johnson, 1993; Rosenthal, 1991). Here we offer only the most common transforms for deriving g. For producing r from various statistical reports, Glass et al. (1981) provided several useful formulas; alternatively, g may be calculated and transformed to r by Equation 7.

EFFECT SIZES FROM MEANS AND STANDARD DEVIATIONS. Equation 1, which appears in the subsection *Effect size indexes*, transforms two means and a standard deviation into an effect size. However, there are many possible forms for defining the standard deviation that appears in the dominator of the formula. To derive g from means and standard deviations in a between-subjects design, it is conventional to use the pooled standard deviation, SD, computed as follows:

$$SD = \sqrt{\frac{(n_A - 1)(SD_A)^2 + (n_B - 1)(SD_B)^2}{n_A + n_B - 2}}, \quad (10)$$

where n_A and n_B are the number of observations in the two groups being compared, and SD_A and SD_B are their standard deviations (see Glass et al., 1981). Thus, SD represents the square root of a "pooling" of the variances of the two groups and is an identical variability estimate to that obtained when an F- or t-test evaluates the difference between the means of the two groups.

For within-subjects designs, SD can be replaced with SD_d, the standard deviation of the differences between paired observations,

$$SD_d = \sqrt{SD_A^2 + SD_B^2 - 2r_{EC}SD_A SD_B}, \quad (11)$$

where r_{EC} is the correlation between the paired observations (e.g., Dunlap, Cortina, Vaslow, & Burke, 1996). Most often all of the components of this formula are not provided, and a paired-observation t-test or a within-subjects F is given instead. As we indicate in the next subsection, these statistics may be directly converted into the effect size that has the standard deviation of the differences in its dominator.[3]

As a rule, whenever possible, SD should be estimated only from the portion of each study's data entering into the effect size. For example, if the $M_A - M_B$ difference needs to be calculated within a level of another variable, SD should be estimated from the standard deviations given for participants within this level, if this information is available. Often, however, SD is available only pooled across all of the conditions of an experiment. If the SD pooled within the cells of the design is not available, but the report contains a standard deviation for the overall sample, it should be converted to the pooled SD by removing the variance due to the difference between M_A and M_B (e.g., Hedges & Becker, 1986; Johnson, 1993).

---

[3] An alternative is to use the within-groups pooled standard deviation as the denominator. Recommending this strategy, Dunlap et al. (1996) concluded that using the means and the pooled SD provides the least biased effect size estimate. However, this calculation is often not possible because the studies provide only a within-subjects summary statistic such as F or t. Converting such statistics into the pooled SD requires the correlation between the paired observations, which is typically not available in the studies' reports.

EFFECT SIZES FROM t- AND F-VALUES. Calculations of g can also be based on summary statistics. In the case of the t-test for independent groups,

$$t = \frac{M_A - M_B}{\sqrt{\frac{SD_A^2}{n_A} + \frac{SD_B^2}{n_B}}}. \qquad (12)$$

Rearrangement of the terms of this equation produces the following formula for calculating g:

$$g = t\sqrt{\frac{n_A + n_B}{n_A n_B}}. \qquad (13)$$

Or, if $n_A = n_B$,

$$g = t\sqrt{\frac{2}{n}} = \frac{2t}{\sqrt{2n}}. \qquad (14)$$

Because $t = \sqrt{F}$ for a comparison of two groups, when the F results from a between-subjects design with unequal n,

$$g = \sqrt{F\frac{n_A + n_B}{n_A n_B}}. \qquad (15)$$

Or, if $n_A = n_B$,

$$g = \sqrt{\frac{2F}{n}}, \qquad (16)$$

where n is the within-cell n (not the total N). If a within-subjects t (i.e., for paired observations) is reported,

$$g = \frac{t}{\sqrt{n}}. \qquad (17)$$

When a study reports an F for a two-groups within-subjects comparison,

$$g = \sqrt{\frac{F}{n}}. \qquad (18)$$

F-values that derive from designs with three or more conditions require some special consideration. F-values that have more than one degree of freedom in the numerator cannot be directly converted into effect sizes because they do not directly gauge differences between individual means. Rather, a significant omnibus F-value implies that somewhere among the relevant means, one or more significant differences exist (see Judd, this volume, Ch. 14). Thus, for example, a significant F-value from a design that uses low, medium, and high levels of the independent variable must be decomposed in order to permit effect size derivations. If a linear contrast is reported, it will be equivalent to a comparison between the high and low levels. One

could compare the means only for the high and low levels or also compare the medium level with the low and the high levels (e.g., Rhodes & Wood, 1992). Or, if the relation between the independent and dependent variables is expected to be linear, one could compute an F for the linear trend in the means and transform it into g (see Glass et al., 1981; Rosenthal & Rosnow, 1985). Of course, analysts should use the means in a particular study that would produce the most similar comparison to that used to represent the other studies in the sample. Treating studies' results in substantially different ways would introduce noise into the effect sizes in the database.

Similar issues arise in designs with two or more factors. In such instances, in order to make effect size comparisons more similar across the studies in a meta-analytic sample, some methodologists have recommended producing one-way designs by returning the effects of irrelevant factors to the error term of the ANOVA (Glass et al., 1981; Hedges & Becker, 1986; Morris & DeShon, 1997). This procedure should be seriously considered for individual-difference variables that were crossed with the crucial independent variable in only some of the studies, because this source of variability would not have been removed from the error term in studies that did not assess these individual differences. When these irrelevant variables were instead manipulated, the decision is less straightforward, to the extent that researchers have created extreme conditions atypical of natural settings by means of powerful experimental manipulations. Variability due to extreme or atypical conditions would not be in the error term of typical studies. Therefore, adding sums of squares for such manipulated variables to the sum of squares error could greatly inflate these error terms in at least some instances and thus decrease the absolute magnitude of effect sizes based on these error terms. As Morris and DeShon concluded, in deciding whether to return irrelevant factors to the error term, analysts should keep as their goal the production of error terms that are based on the same sources of variability across the studies in the sample.

To illustrate how to return irrelevant factors to the error term, Table 19.1 contains a hypothetical ANOVA for a two-factor design. The top panel contains the ANOVA summary for the two factors. Suppose that Factor A is the focal independent variable, and that Factor B is a meta-analytically irrelevant variable. To represent the impact of Factor A on the dependent variable, the variation due to Factor B can be returned to the error term. This operation is performed by (a) adding the sum-of-squares due to Factor B and its interaction with

Factor A to the error sum-of-squares and (b) adding the degrees of freedom due to Factor B and its interaction to the degrees of freedom for error. Once the sum-of-squares for error has been divided by its new degrees of freedom, the square root of the resulting mean-square for error would be interpretable as the standard deviation pooled within the two levels of A, or $SD = \sqrt{MS_e}$. The result of this reconstitution of the error term appears in Panel b. In this example, g may be derived by converting the F-value that resulted from the reconstitution procedure, or it may be derived by dividing the difference between the means of Factor A by SD. Morris and DeShon (1997) presented other equations and examples of this strategy; Nouri and Greenberg (1995) presented techniques for use with more complex ANOVA designs (e.g., those that mix between- and within-subjects factors).

If the effects of the focal independent variable on the dependent variable are expected to change within the levels of another independent variable, separate effect sizes can be calculated within levels of the second independent variable, as we already mentioned above (see subsection *Multiple reports from individual studies*). Specifically, as an alternative to representing the effect of the focal independent variable aggregated over this other variable (i.e., as a main effect), the analyst can partition each study on this other variable and represent the effect of interest within levels of this variable (i.e., as a simple main effect). When interactions are expected, simple main effects are the desired comparison, and the other, interacting variable can function as a moderator of the relation between the focal variables. As an example, Table 19.2 displays a 2×3 factorial design in which the focal independent variable (IV_{focal}) and a moderator variable ($IV_{moderator}$) serve as the factors. Suppose that we expect the effect of IV_{focal} on the dependent variable to change depending on the level of $IV_{moderator}$. To represent these contrasting expectations, a separate effect size must be derived for each level of $IV_{moderator}$. Thus, the first g would result from a comparison of the means from cells a and b, the second from cells c and d, and the third from cells e and f. In order to perform this calculation, it is necessary to obtain all cell means and either (a) the within-cell standard deviations, (b) the standard deviations for each relevant level of $IV_{moderator}$ (and transformed to SD_{pooled}), or (c) MS_e for the ANOVA. The MS_e can be recovered when

TABLE 19.1. Hypothetical Analysis of Variance Summary Tables (a) Before Reconstitution and (b) After Returning Factor B's Sums of Squares to the Error Term

Source	Sum of Squares	Degrees of Freedom	Mean Squares	F
(a) Before reconstituting				
A	430.33	1	430.33	15.22
B	200.12	1	200.12	7.08
A × B	43.55	1	43.55	1.54
Error	1244.29	44	28.28	
(b) After reconstituting				
A	430.33	1	430.33	13.30
Error	1487.96	46	32.35	

all cells means are reported and at least one F-value is known for the dependent variable, even when the available F is not the most relevant to the analysts' focal comparison (Johnson, 1993; Morris & DeShon, 1997). These calculations are facilitated if the source report contains a complete ANOVA table, but the components of the table can be estimated if the means, cell sizes, and one or more F-values are known (Johnson, 1993). Then, $SD = \sqrt{MS_e}$. Once this value or the standard deviations are known, effect-size derivations continue as though each condition were a separate experiment.

Finally, F-values derived from multivariate analysis of variance (MANOVA), in which one or more independent variables were examined for their simultaneous influence on two or more dependent measures, should not be transformed into effect sizes if the dependent variable of interest was combined with other, irrelevant dependent variables (see Morrison, 1976; Timm,

TABLE 19.1. A Hypothetical Factorial Design in Which a Focal Independent Variable Is Crossed with a Moderator Independent Variable

		IV_{Focal}	
		Level 1	Level 2
$IV_{Moderator}$	Level 1	Cell a	Cell b
	Level 2	Cell c	Cell d
	Level 3	Cell e	Cell f

1975). If several measures of the same conceptual dependent variable were combined in a multivariate analysis, however, the analyst might derive an effect size by taking the square root of the proportion of variance that the independent variable accounts for in the best linear combination of the dependent variables and treating this value as an r (see Tabachnick & Fidell's, 1996, pp. 388–391, discussion of Wilk's Lambda), even if univariate F-values from ANOVAs are not available. However, because such effect sizes would be dependent on the exact set of dependent variables included in the multivariate analysis, some meta-analysts recommend against such procedures (Hunter & Schmidt, 1990).

This section about t- and F-values shows that complex statistical considerations can arise in translating source reports into effect sizes. Because of these potential complexities, a reviewer should never proceed to calculate effect sizes from an ANOVA without thoroughly understanding the design used for the data analysis. The reviewer would be well advised to diagram the design with the relevant ns. Because multiple error terms are common in the designs used in experimental social psychology, it is easy to use the wrong error term for calculating the effect size. To prevent such errors, advanced ANOVA texts are invaluable (e.g., Myers & Well, 1991; Winer, Brown, & Michels, 1991). For reference purposes, meta-analysts may find it convenient to produce a packet of the clearest textbook descriptions of designs that occur often in their literatures.

EFFECT SIZES FROM r-VALUES. Although r can be readily transformed to g by Equation 7, correlational reports often appear in a form other than r (see Carroll, 1961; Cohen & Cohen, 1983; Glass et al., 1981; Rosenthal, 1991, 1994). When r-values other than the product-moment variety are reported (e.g., biserial r, phi coefficient), they can usually be interpreted as product-moment rs, except when they are point-biserial rs. In this case, the meta-analyst would convert the point-biserial r into the biserial r, which approximates the product-moment r. If $n_A = n_B$, or when n_A is approximately n_B, $r_b = 1.253 r_{pb}$, or, if $n_A \neq n_B$,

$$r_b = \frac{r_{pb}\sqrt{n_A n_B}}{\mu N}, \tag{19}$$

where N is the total sample size, and μ is the ordinate of the unit normal distribution (i.e., the height of normal curve with surface equal to 1.0 at the point of division between segments containing n_A and n_B cases). Similarly, if a study reports t calculated based on any r value, the t can be converted to a product-moment

correlation using

$$r_b = \frac{r_{pb}\sqrt{n_A n_B}}{\mu N}. \tag{20}$$

Whereas standardized regression weights (β) deriving from simple linear regressions are r-values and can be so interpreted, βs deriving from regressions with more than one predictor *cannot* be directly interpreted as r-values. The β-value for a given predictor in a multiple regression equation is *adjusted* for the other independent variables present in the equation. In the case of suppressor variables (Cohen & Cohen, 1983), these adjustments can affect not only the value of β but also its sign, which could be reversed from the sign of the correlation between the two variables. Yet another problem with converting β-values to effect sizes is that under some circumstances β-values from multiple regression equations exceed $|1|$, whereas r-values never exceed $|1|$. For example, if Equation 7 is used with a β of 1.1, the denominator of the equation will be the square root of a negative number, -0.21, which is an irrational mathematical operation. Therefore, as a general rule, in meta-analyses for which multiple regression results are the exception and other studies in the sample report statistics unadjusted for the other variables in the equation, multiple regression results should not be converted to effect sizes (see Hunter & Schmidt, 1990). Of course, before discarding a study because its findings were reported in a multiple regression, one should see whether a correlation matrix or comparable statistics appear in the report or could be obtained from its authors.

If many of the studies in a literature contain multiple regression equations that use the same conceptual independent variables to predict the same conceptual dependent variable, syntheses could pursue two strategies. One alternative is to examine how much variance (estimated by multiple R^2) was explained in the criterion variable by the set of predictor variables. For example, an analyst might examine each study to determine how much variance in intentions to perform a behavior was explained by the simultaneous impact of attitudes toward performing the behavior and normative expectations about the behavior (see Sheppard, Hartwick, & Warshaw, 1988). Hedges and Olkin (1985, p. 239) provide an alternative strategy that relies directly on the βs and their sample sizes to produce an aggregate weighted beta-weight.

EFFECT SIZES FROM CHI-SQUARE VALUES. Chi-square (χ^2) values are sometimes used to test for the frequency with which groups meet some criterion or to test for the association between two variables (Hays, 1988). If the χ^2 results from a 2×2 classification table linking a predictor (X) to the outcome (Y),

$$r_\phi = \sqrt{\frac{\chi^2}{n}}, \tag{21}$$

where r_ϕ is a phi coefficient, which approximates the product-moment r and can be converted to g by Equation 7. However, if there is more than 1 degree of freedom in the χ^2 value, it cannot be directly converted into an effect size because the χ^2 may describe a nonlinear pattern. It may be possible to compute χ^2 for an appropriate 2×2 table based on the proportions of the relevant groups that meet a criterion (see next subsection). If the data for these re-computations are not available, the study result cannot be used to derive an effect size.

EFFECT SIZES FROM PROPORTIONS MEETING A CRITERION. In some designs, the proportion of individuals in one group (p_E) who meet a given criterion is compared with the proportion in another group (p_C) who meet it. For example, the proportion of people who help another person in one experimental condition can be compared to the proportion of people who help in another condition (see Eagly & Crowley, 1986). These proportions can be transformed into an effect size by using a probit transformation (Glass et al., 1981) or by treating the proportions as means (Snedecor & Cochran, 1980) such that

$$g = \frac{p_A - p_B}{SD}, \tag{22}$$

where

$$SD = \sqrt{\frac{(n_A - 1)p_A q_A + (n_B - 1)p_B q_B}{n_A + n_B - 2}}, \tag{23}$$

where $q_E = 1 - p_E$ and $q_C = 1 - p_C$. Note that Equations 22 and 23 assume that the proportions are in relation to the study's unit of analysis, which is generally persons. The equations do not apply to proportions that represent values of dependent variables assessed for each unit of analysis. For example, if each participant's helping were assessed a self-report of the proportion of occasions on which he or she helped, these data would produce an effect size by equations that use the variability of these proportions (e.g., Equation 1) rather than Equation 23.

EFFECT SIZES FROM PROBABILITIES ASSOCIATED WITH INFERENTIAL STATISTICS. Source reports sometimes contain only a p-value associated with the critical effect (e.g., $p = .0439$), which can be used to calculate an effect size if the direction of the finding and the sample size (n) are known. To do so, the analyst would use a statistical package's (e.g., SAS, IMSL, SPSS, Stata) inverse probability distribution functions, which provide an exact solution of a test statistic from p. For example, SAS provides BETAINV, which yields F from p and df, after which the F can be converted to g using Equation 15, 16, or 18 (assuming that the F compares the means of only two groups). Obviously, an exact p allows an excellent estimate of a test statistic and therefore of g. However, a level p (e.g., $p < .05$) gives a poorer estimate, because it would ordinarily be treated as exactly the p level given (e.g., $p < .01$ would be understood as $p = .01$). The mere statement that a finding is "significant" can be treated as $p = .05$ in studies that apparently use the conventional $p < .05$ rule for determining significance and indicate the direction of the effect, but the effect sizes estimated on this basis may be quite inaccurate (Ray & Shadish, 1996). Finally, reports often differ in whether a one-tailed or two-tailed probability level is reported; if no information is provided, the convention is that the study authors have used a two-tailed test.

DERIVING EFFECT SIZES FROM STATISTICALLY IMPOVERISHED REPORTS. For many reasons, some source reports will contain less than desirable amounts of information for calculating effect sizes. We have tried to make readers aware of certain "tricks" for deriving effect sizes in such cases, but it is difficult to anticipate all possible problems. Some routes to effect sizes merely require a great deal of effort on the part of the analyst (e.g., reanalyzing raw data found in an appendix of a dissertation). In other instances, deriving an effect size may require the application of several nonroutine techniques in sequence. Each meta-analysis poses different statistical challenges that may call for novel solutions.

Whatever the problems that analysts encounter in trying to calculate effect sizes, we urge them to contact studies' authors, if possible, to acquire any essential information that is not included in a report. In our experience, cordial invitations for authors to provide the requisite information have produced moderate success rates. Obtaining such information allows the report to be represented to fullest advantage in the sample; failing to obtain the needed information renders the meta-analysis less comprehensive and potentially less representative and less valid. Finally, it is important to realize that a lack of statistical detail in reports does not necessarily reflect their authors' oversights, errors, or poor methods. Rather, omissions generally occur because the authors' goals differed from those pursued in a subsequent meta-analysis. For example, to a study's authors, a small sex-of-participant effect on helping behavior might have been incidental and worthy of no more than a footnoted p-value or statement that the effect was nonsignificant; to a meta-analyst pursuing sex-related differences in helping behavior (e.g., Eagly & Crowley, 1986), such findings are crucial.

DEALING WITH NONREPORTED RESULTS. Reports that describe the effect of interest merely as "nonsignificant" are highly problematic in meta-analysis (Bushman & Wang, 1996). It is common to represent such effects by $d = 0.00$, but such estimates are obviously poor. If the N in the study was small, its actual effect size could be quite large and yet not be significant. Introducing such effect sizes into a meta-analysis would yield a mean effect size that underestimates the population value (Schmidt, 1996). Especially if many of these reports exist in a literature, it is advisable to estimate mean effect sizes with and without these 0.00 values. It also may be better to omit these values when attempting to fit models to the effect sizes.

At the synthesis stage of a meta-analysis, one way to incorporate imprecisely reported results, including those described as nonsignificant, is to use so-called "vote-counting procedures" to summarize findings (Bushman, 1994; Bushman & Wang, 1996). In these procedures, rather than using relatively exact effect size estimates to represent the studies' outcomes, an analyst examines how many studies obtained a result in the hypothesized direction or how many obtained a significant result in this direction. Because the strategy relies only on findings' directions or significance levels, it allows an analyst to include even the imprecisely reported nonsignificant results. More formally, calculating what is sometimes called the "sign test," which is based on the binomial distribution, entails determining the exact p of obtaining the observed distribution of positive and negative outcomes (or one more extreme), given that the probability of obtaining a positive result is .5, according to the null hypothesis, which specifies that half of the results should be positive and half negative. This probability can be calculated by standard statistics packages (e.g., SAS's PROBBNML function). An analyst can also use the binomial distribution to calculate a p-value for obtaining the observed distribution of significant positive findings versus other findings (nonsignificant and reversed), given that the probability of obtaining a significant result in one tail of the distribution is .025, according to the null hypothesis and assuming .05 for two-tailed sig-

nificant testing. The p-values associated with the proportion of the studies that have a positive direction or that produced a significant positive result can be used to estimate a mean effect size (e.g., d) for a sample of studies. These estimated effect sizes can then be compared to the exact mean effect size based on the studies that permitted this calculation (see Bushman, 1994; Bushman & Wang, 1996). For example, Wood (1987) used these techniques to estimate the mean effect size for sex-related differences in group performance, because many of the studies did not permit an effect size to be estimated. Of course, it is much better to calculate the mean effect size by averaging effect sizes from individual studies when the majority of studies permit this strategy.

RELIABILITY OF EFFECT SIZE CALCULATIONS. We strongly recommend that at least two analysts compute effect sizes for each of the studies independently and then meet to compare solutions and resolve discrepancies. Given the complexity of many research designs and the ambiguity of some research reports, various errors of effect size estimation do occur. Moreover, sometimes one analyst may discover an indirect route to computing an effect size that is missed by a second analyst. When two or more analysts calculate effect sizes, these errors and omissions can be minimized (see also *Reliability of coding*, above).

CORRECTING EFFECT SIZES FOR BIASED METHODS. In addition to correcting the raw g and r because they are biased estimators of the population effect size (see prior subsection *Effect size indexes*), analysts may correct for many other biases that accrue from the methods used in each study. For example, as already noted, the Spearman-Brown prophecy equation (see Cronbach, 1990) dictates that as the reliability of a measure increases (and its measurement error therefore decreases), its relations with other variables will also increase. Increased measurement error decreases a measure's ability to predict another variable. Corrections for measurement unreliability and other forms of error or bias can be implemented in a meta-analysis, in order to estimate what the strength of a relation would be in the absence of such artifacts. In their presentations of such corrections, Hunter and Schmidt (1990, 1994; Schmidt & Hunter, 1996) explained how to implement corrections in the independent and dependent variables for measurement error, artificial dichotomization of a continuous variable, imperfect construct validity, and range restriction. In theory, correcting for such errors permits a more accurate estimation of the true population effect size – that is, its value had studies not been affected by these biases.

These corrections are quite popular in industrial and organizational psychology, particularly for meta-analyses on the validity generalization question of whether the validity of personnel selection tests varies across organizations (e.g., Hunter, Schmidt, & Hunter, 1979). Such corrections have seldom been used in social psychological meta-analyses because in most research areas relatively few studies include the information that would be required to perform all of the corrections. For example, the majority of the study reports generally do not include information on the reliability or validity of the independent or dependent variables. In research literatures that are more psychometrically developed in the sense that reliabilities and other relevant information are routinely provided, meta-analysts may be able to perform such corrections.

When meta-analysts do implement these corrections, the resultant corrected mean effect size yields an idealized estimate of the magnitude of the population effect rather than an estimate of the relation that would be obtained in a future study in which the corrections were not implemented. Even when it is possible to implement the corrections within a literature, problems may emerge; in particular, Rosenthal (1991) noted that the corrections can result in irrational effect sizes (e.g., correlations larger than 1.00). Therefore, we recommend that analysts consider their goals when deciding whether to use such corrections. If the goal is to estimate the effect size that would exist if there were no contamination by any artifacts of measurement, then the corrections would be desirable. In contrast, if the goal is to show how large a relation is in practice (perhaps the more typical goal for research literatures in which such corrections are seldom implemented), then the corrections would be less useful.

Regardless of whether these corrections are implemented, it is wise for analysts to be aware of potential biases that might enter into their studies' effect sizes. In particular, effect size estimates are a ratio of signal to noise, like all inferential statistics. For example, in a between-groups design, the signal is the difference in means, and the noise is the pooled standard deviation. Methodological factors can influence the effect size through their impact on signal, noise, or both factors. If two identical studies are conducted and one controls for noise that the other study does not (e.g., by statistically controlling for an individual difference characteristic), the first study will have a smaller error term (standard deviation), and the effect size for this study will be larger than that for the second study. To min-

imize this type of variation in effect sizes, our recommendations regarding effect size derivation have emphasized equating as much as possible the comparisons that the studies yield, so that the effect sizes are not impacted by differing statistical operations. For example, one such recommendation was that in meta-analyses of experimental effects, analysts return irrelevant individual difference factors to the error term. Of course, reconstituting the error term in this way would not be necessary if the variable in question were controlled in all of the studies in the review. In such circumstances, the conclusions of the synthesis should take the presence of this controlled factor into account.

Additional problems can arise from the inclusion of studies that used within-subjects designs. For example, a researcher might have implemented a within-subjects design that required each participant to judge two objects along the same dimension. Such multiple assessments can produce many complications, including carryover, priming, and contrast effects (E. Smith, this volume). In analyzing such data, researchers nearly always use a repeated-measures inferential statistic that removes from the error term the variation due to the individual participants (e.g., Equation 11). Consequently, these tests are more statistically powerful than those produced by a comparable between-subjects design (Dunlap et al., 1996). If the meta-analyst uses these within-subjects error terms to calculate effect sizes, it is likely that these effect sizes will be larger than those based on standard deviations pooled from the cells of the design (e.g., Kite & Johnson, 1988; for an exception, see Symons & Johnson, 1997). Therefore, in such circumstances, analysts should use type of design as a moderator variable.

Although it is unrealistic for analysts to take into account all potential sources of bias in a meta-analysis, they should remain aware of biases that may be important within the context of their research literature. Some of these biases can be corrected in the process of computing the effect sizes. Others can be examined empirically for their influence on studies' results. Still others can be eliminated by narrowing the boundaries of the literature under investigation to exclude biased studies. When it is not possible to control a bias in some fashion, analysts should consider what influence a bias might have exerted on their findings and interpret the results accordingly.

Analyzing the Meta-Analytic Database

PRELIMINARY CONSIDERATIONS. The general steps involved in the analysis of effect sizes usually are the following: (a) aggregate effect sizes across the studies to determine the overall strength of the relation between the examined variables; (b) analyze the consistency of the effect sizes across the studies; (c) diagnose statistical outliers among the effect sizes; (d) examine visual displays of the distribution of effect sizes to determine whether any irregularities exist; and (e) perform tests of whether study attributes moderate the magnitude of the effect sizes. The three principal meta-analytic frameworks for analyzing effect sizes that have developed over the past twenty years are those proposed by Hedges and Olkin (e.g., 1985), Rosenthal (e.g., 1991), and Hunter and Schmidt (e.g., 1990). Although each framework encompasses valuable recommendations for the conduct of meta-analysis (for reviews, see Aguinis & Pierce, 1998; Johnson et al., 1995; Sánchez-Meca & Marín-Martínez, 1997), we will focus on the Hedges and Olkin (1985) approach in this section, while occasionally adding elements of the other approaches.

Although our exposition considers only fixed effects models, random effects models or blends of random and fixed effects models may also be useful in some contexts (Hedges & Vevea, 1998; Overton, 1998; Raudenbush, 1994). This fixed versus random distinction may be familiar to readers from discussions of ANOVAs for primary research. In meta-analysis, as in primary research, the model used depends on the type of generalization that the analyst desires to make. Fixed effects models permit an analyst to generalize results only to groups of studies identical (or at least quite similar) to those in the meta-analytic sample, except for the particular participants who appear in the studies. In contrast to fixed effects models, random effects models assume that the studies in the meta-analysis are randomly sampled from some population of studies and permit an analyst to generalize to this population. As Hedges (1994) and Rosenthal (1995) explained, there are pros and cons of treating meta-analytic data by fixed effects or random effects models. Moreover, there are few conventions concerning when to use fixed or random effects models (Cooper, 1998). As a practical matter, nearly all meta-analyses to date have used fixed effects models, and the computational techniques for these models are simpler and have been worked out more completely. Nonetheless, some methodologists argue that, in comparison to random effects models, fixed effects models manifest greater Type I bias in significance tests for the mean effect size and moderator relations and thus are insufficiently conservative (see Hunter & Schmidt, 1997; Overton, 1998). These considerations suggest a greater use of random effects models (Hedges & Vevea, 1998).

The fixed effects model-testing procedures that we present are analogous to techniques used in data analysis in primary research. Categorical models are analogous to fixed effect analyses of variance, and continuous models are analogous to regression procedures. Yet, the procedures used in meta-analysis differ from those used in primary research in two main respects. The first difference pertains to the heterogeneity of the variances ordinarily associated with the individual effect sizes, which would likely violate the homoscedasticity assumption of conventional regressions and ANOVAs – that is, the assumption that the nonsystematic variance associated with every observation is equal. In regressions, this assumption is checked by evaluating the constancy of the residual variance around the regression line for all values of the predictor variable. In ANOVAs, the within-cell variances are checked to determine if they are similar in value across the cells of the design. In contrast, meta-analytic statistics were designed to take advantage of differing variances by calculating the nonsystematic variance of the effect sizes analytically (Hedges & Olkin, 1985). Because this nonsystematic variance of an effect size is inversely proportional to the sample size of the study and sample sizes vary widely across the studies, the error variances of the effect sizes are ordinarily quite heterogeneous. The second difference between the statistical procedures of meta-analysis and primary research is that meta-analytic statistics permit an analysis of the consistency (or homogeneity) of the effect sizes across the studies, a highly informative analysis not produced by conventional statistics. As the homogeneity calculation illustrates, analyzing effect sizes with specialized meta-analytic statistics rather than the ordinary inferential statistics used in primary research allows a reviewer to use a greater amount of the information available from the studies (Rosenthal, 1991, 1995).

COMPUTATION OF A COMPOSITE EFFECT SIZE. As a first step in a quantitative synthesis, the study outcomes are combined by averaging the d-values with each d weighted by the reciprocal of its variance. The weighted mean effect size d_+ is computed as a weighted average of the individual studies' effect sizes,

$$d_+ = \frac{\sum_{i=1}^{k} w_j d_j}{\sum_{j=1}^{k} w_j},$$
(24)

where k is the number of effect sizes. The variance, v_+ of the weighted mean effect size d_+ is

$$v_+ = \frac{1}{\sum_{j=1}^{k} w_j},$$
(25)

where the weights for each effect size j, w_j, are defined

$$w_j = \frac{1}{v_j} = \frac{2\left(n_j^A + n_j^B\right) n_j^A \, n_j^B}{2\left(n_j^A + n_j^B\right)^2 + n_j^A \, n_j^B \, d_j^2}. \quad (26)$$

Note that v is unrelated to the variance of the raw data that entered into the inferential statistics in the first place. Equation 24, which is a simple fixed effects meta-analytic model, gives greater weight to the more reliably estimated study outcomes, which are in general those with the larger sample sizes (Hedges & Olkin, 1985); other frameworks provide for weighting effect sizes on this and other quality-relevant bases (Hunter & Schmidt, 1990; Rosenthal, 1991). As a test for significance of this weighted mean effect size, a confidence interval is computed around this mean, based on its standard deviation, $d_+ \pm 1.96\sqrt{v_+}$, where 1.96 is the unit-normal value for a 95% CI (assuming a nondirectional hypothesis). If the confidence interval (CI) includes zero (0.00), the value indicating exactly no difference, it may be concluded that aggregated across all studies there is no significant association between the independent and dependent variable (X and Y). Alternatively, a unit-normal z-value for a weighted mean effect size can be calculated directly, similar to the convention in the Rosenthal (1991) approach,

$$z_+ = \frac{d_+}{\sqrt{v_+}}, \quad (27)$$

and this z_+ can be evaluated by determining if its exact p-value is less than α or by comparing z_+ against the z equivalent to the chosen significance level (see Becker, 1987; Hedges, Cooper, & Bushman, 1992; Johnson et al., 1995).

When the weighted mean effect size and the CI are computed, the homogeneity of the ds should be examined in order to determine whether the studies can be adequately described by a single effect size (Hedges, 1981; Hunter & Schmidt, 1990; Rosenthal, 1991). If the effect sizes can be so described, they would differ only by unsystematic sampling error. The test statistic, Q, which is known as a test of the homogeneity (or heterogeneity) of the effect sizes, evaluates the hypothesis that the effect sizes are consistent,

$$Q = \sum_{j=1}^{k} w_j \left(d_j - d_+\right)^2, \quad (28)$$

where k is the number of effect sizes in the class. Q has an approximate χ^2 distribution with $k-1$ degrees of freedom. If Q is significant, the hypothesis of the homogeneity (or consistency) of the effect sizes is rejected. In this event, the weighted mean effect size may not adequately describe the outcomes of the set of studies

because it is likely that quite different mean effects exist in different groups of studies. Further explanatory work would be merited, even when the composite effect size is significant. The magnitude of individual study outcomes would differ systematically, and these differences may include differences in the direction (or sign) of the relation. In some studies, X might have had a large positive effect on Y, and in other studies, it might have had a smaller positive effect or even a negative effect on Y. Even if the homogeneity test is nonsignificant, significant moderators could be present, especially when Q is relatively large (for further discussions, see Johnson & Turco, 1992; Rosenthal, 1995). Also, Q could be significant even though the effect sizes are very close in value, especially if the sample sizes are very large. These complexities suggest that Q deserves careful interpretation, in conjunction with inspecting the values of the effect sizes. Nonetheless, in a meta-analysis that attempts to determine X's impact on Y, rejecting the hypothesis of homogeneity could be troublesome, because it implies that the association between these two variables likely is complicated by the presence of interacting conditions. However, because analysts usually anticipate the presence of one or more moderators of effect size magnitude, establishing that effect sizes are not homogeneous is ordinarily neither surprising nor troublesome.

Finally, analysts often present other measures of central tendency in addition to the weighted mean effect size. For example, the unweighted mean effect size shows the typical effect without weighting studies with larger sample sizes more heavily. A substantial difference in the values of the unweighted and weighted mean effect sizes suggests that one or more studies with large sample sizes may deviate from the rest of the sample. Also, the median effect size describes a typical effect size but would be less affected than a mean effect size by outliers and other anomalies of the distribution of effect sizes.

TESTING MODELS OF META-ANALYTIC MODERATORS. To determine the relation between study characteristics and the magnitude of the effect sizes, both categorical models and continuous models can be tested (Hedges, 1982a, 1982b; Hedges & Olkin, 1985; Rosenthal, 1991). In the Hedges and Olkin (1985) approach, *categorical models*, which are analogous to ANOVAs, may show that effect sizes differ in magnitude between the subgroups established by dividing studies into classes based on study characteristics. For example, Stangor and McMillan's (1992) meta-analysis found that studies with expectancy-congruent stimuli increased memory relative to studies with expectancy-incongruent stimuli when the processing goal was to form impressions and that this pattern reversed when the processing goal was to evaluate the presented information. If effect sizes that were found to be heterogeneous become homogeneous within the classes of a categorical model, the relevant study characteristic has accounted for the systematic variability between the effect sizes. Following Hedges and Olkin's (1985) statistical procedures, categorical models provide a between-classes effect (analogous to a main effect in an analysis of variance) and a test of the homogeneity of the effect sizes within each class. The between-classes effect is estimated by Q_B,

$$Q_B = \sum_{i=1}^{p} w_{i+}(d_{i+} - d_{++})^2, \tag{29}$$

where w_{i+} is the reciprocal of variance of d_{i+} for class i, d_{i+} is its weighted mean effect size (using Equation 24 within the class), and d_{++} is the weighted grand mean effect size (Equation 24). Q_B has an approximate χ^2 distribution with $p - 1$ degrees of freedom, where p is the number of classes. To determine the fit of the model, the homogeneity of the effect sizes within each class i around d_{i+} is estimated by Q_{W_i}, which is calculated using Equation 28 with the effect sizes in class i. Q_{W_i} has an approximate χ^2 distribution with $m_i - 1$ degrees of freedom, where m_i is the number of effect sizes in class i. An alternative strategy to examine model specification is to sum the Q_{W_i} values of each class and determine the significance of this total Q value, with $k - p$ degrees of freedom, where k is the number of effect sizes and p is the number of classes. Each Q produced via these strategies is interpreted similarly to the overall Q value, as outlined above. A significant Q value is interpreted as evidence that variability exists in the effect sizes within the class. In other words, the mean effect size provides a poor description of the typical effect size within each class. Also calculated for these models are (a) the weighted mean effect size for each class, calculated with each effect size weighted by the reciprocal of its variance, and (b) a 95% confidence interval for each of these means.

When a categorical model with more than two classes yields a significant Q_B statistic, it is desirable to compute contrasts between the weighted mean effect sizes for these classes (Hedges, 1994; Hedges & Olkin, 1985). For example, Gordon's (1996) meta-analysis found that liking for an ingratiator varied depending on the type of ingratiation tactic used; a contrast showed that studies that used the other-enhancement tactic produced more liking than studies that used the tactic of giving favors. These contrasts, which are analogous to those used in the ANOVA procedure, are approxi-

mated by a χ^2 distribution with 1 degree of freedom for a priori tests. For post hoc tests, the same test is used but with more conservative degrees of freedom or a more conservative α. In the Scheffé method, the degrees of freedom are either $p - 1$, where p is the number of classes, or the number of contrasts, whichever value is smaller. In the Bonferroni method, the degrees of freedom term remains 1, but in order for a contrast to be considered significant at level α in the simultaneous analysis, it must be significant at level α/L, where L is the number of contrasts that could have been conducted, which are typically all pairwise contrasts (see Rosenthal & Rosnow, 1985, and Toothaker, 1991, for discussions of contrasts).

Similarly, *continuous models*, which are analogous to regression models, examine whether study characteristics that are assessed on a continuous scale are related to the effect sizes. As with categorical models, some continuous models may be completely specified in the sense that the systematic variability in the effect sizes is explained by the study characteristic that is used as a predictor. Continuous models are least squares regressions, calculated with each effect size weighted by the reciprocal of its variance (Hedges, 1982b; Hedges & Olkin, 1985; Hedges, 1994). Each such model yields a test of the significance of each moderator as well as a test of model specification, which evaluates whether variation remains unexplained by the moderators. The error sum of squares statistic, Q_E, which provides this test of model specification, has an approximate chi-square distribution with $k - p - 1$ degrees of freedom, where k is the number of effect sizes and p is the number of predictors (not including the intercept). Tests for the significance of the predictor's association with the effect sizes are given by the unstandardized regression (b) weight(s) in the model. For example, Gordon (1996) found that as the transparency of an ingratiation attempt increased, the success of the attempt decreased. Using Hedges and Olkin's (1985) statistical procedures, an analyst can also fit multiple-predictor models to effect sizes, and the predictors for these models can be either continuous or categorical, or both.[4]

---

[4] Regression procedures can represent categorical variables using dummy codes (e.g., Cohen & Cohen, 1983; Hardy, 1993). Although a categorical predictor specified by the regression procedure will explain the same amount of variation among the effect sizes as the corresponding categorical model, it would not be possible by regression procedures to determine which specific sub-classes have significant homogeneity statistics. Therefore, categorical models are usually calculated for categorical variables, which are entered into regression procedure (i.e., continuous models) only along with other predictors in a multiple regression.

Analysts may wish to determine the amount of variation that remains unexplained in the effect sizes after one or more moderators have been modeled. For this purpose, Hedges (1994) described the *Birge ratio*, which represents the amount of unexplained variation as a ratio of unexplained variation to degrees of freedom. Thus, for categorical models, the Birge ratio, R_B, is

$$R_B = \frac{Q_W}{k - p}, \tag{30}$$

where Q_W is the sum of the Q_{W_i} for each class in the model; for continuous models,

$$R_B = \frac{Q_E}{k - p - 1}. \tag{31}$$

In either case, when the model fits exactly, the Birge ratio has an expected value of 1. A Birge ratio of 1.75, in contrast, suggests that, given the amount of within-study sampling variance, there is 75 percent more between-study variation that is unexplained by the model.

OUTLIER DIAGNOSES. As an alternative analysis to predicting effect sizes using categorical and continuous models, an analyst can attain homogeneity by identifying outlying values among the effect sizes and sequentially removing those effect sizes that reduce the homogeneity statistic, Q, by the largest amount. Using such a procedure for several meta-analyses on psychological topics, Hedges (1987) found that the removal of 20% or fewer of the effect sizes from the hetero-

geneous sample included in the synthesis usually produced homogeneity. Studies yielding effect sizes identified as outliers can then be examined to determine if they appear to differ methodologically from the other studies. Also, inspection of the percentage of effect sizes removed to attain homogeneity allows one to determine whether the effect sizes are homogeneous aside from the presence of relatively few aberrant values. Under such circumstances, the mean attained after removal of such outliers may better represent the distribution of effect sizes than the mean based on all of the effect sizes. In general, the diagnosis of outliers should occur prior to calculating moderator analyses; this diagnosis may locate a value or two that are so discrepant from the other effect sizes that they would dramatically alter any models fitted to effect sizes (for e.g., see Stangor & McMillan, 1992; for a more comprehensive treatment of the topic of data outliers, see McClelland, this volume). Under such circumstances, these outliers should be removed from subsequent phases of the data analysis.

VISUAL DISPLAYS. Visual presentations can also assist in the interpretation of meta-analytic results (see Greenhouse & Iyengar, 1994; Light, Singer, & Willett, 1994). Visually examining study outcomes enhances the analyst's potential for finding anomalies in the meta-analytic data. For example, an analyst may determine that effect sizes are related to a continuous

Figure 19.1. Funnel plot when no publication bias is present.

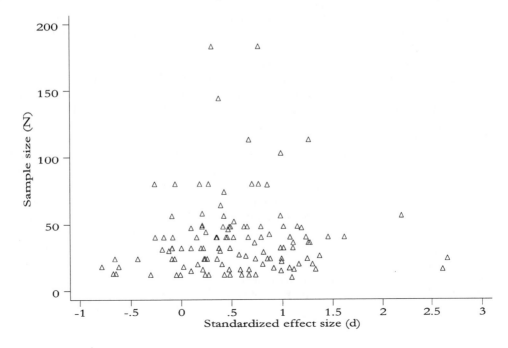

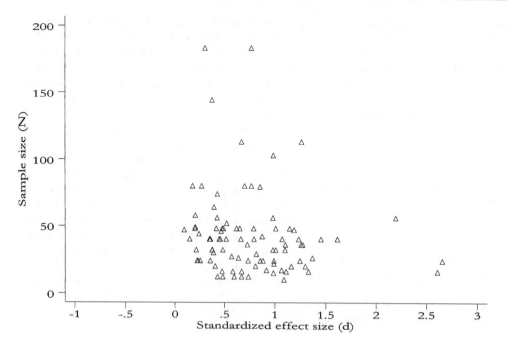

Figure 19.2. Funnel plot that shows a preponderance of significant effect sizes; in such cases, it is possible that there is a publication bias in the literature.

predictor in a nonmonotonic fashion, an outcome that would not be detected by the linear regressions that have been described.[5] Also useful is a *funnel plot* (Light & Pillemer, 1984; Mullen, 1989), which is a scatterplot of sample sizes versus effect sizes. Ordinarily, the scatterplot should take the shape of a funnel sitting on end in the sense that the effect sizes from smaller studies, which are unreliable, would show more scatter than the effect sizes from the larger studies, which would center on the best estimate of the population effect (see Figure 19.1). However, if there is a publication bias in the literature, a funnel plot should reveal few entries in the smaller effect size portion of the graph for smaller sample sizes (see Figure 19.2). Also commonly presented in meta-analytic contexts are some of the exploratory data analysis techniques introduced by Tukey (1977). For example, *stem-and-leaf displays* efficiently plot every effect size in a distribution and are useful for displaying the shape of the distribution. Each effect size appears as a leaf attached to a stem value. The

possible stem values of the effect sizes appear as a scale placed to the left of a line and represent their first digit or first two digits (see Figure 19.3). The next digit is the leaf, which is placed to the right of the line. Because each leaf digit to the right of the line represents a separate effect size, the shape of the distribution is displayed. In addition, *schematic plots*, also known as box-and-whiskers plots, show the maximum and minimum effect sizes, the upper and lower quartile values, and the median.

CONSEQUENCES OF VIOLATING THE ASSUMPTION OF EFFECT SIZE INDEPENDENCE. The section on *Multiple reports from individual studies* introduced the meta-analytic assumption of independence among effect sizes and suggested that as a general rule, it is wise to represent studies' participants only once in effect size calculations. Following this recommendation, analysts should ordinarily combine effect sizes representing conceptually similar measures from any given study. If such effect sizes were not combined, the nonindependence that would result could have several effects on the findings of a meta-analysis, depending on the source of the nonindependence (see Gleser & Olkin, 1994). If the nonindependence results from producing more than one effect size from the same participants on conceptually similar measure, the meta-analysis will be likely to reach a liberal estimate of the significance of the weighted mean effect size: Its CI will grow tighter, and its z_+ larger. Similarly, including more

---

[5] Regression models may include tests of nonlinear associations (see Hedges & Olkin, 1985; Mullen, 1989). However, unless nonmonotonic associations are expected on an a priori basis, they are unlikely to be discovered except by the use of visual displays.

```
1.8 | 19
1.7 |
1.6 | 5
1.5 | 59
1.4 | 13
1.3 |
1.2 | 4
1.1 | 34
1.0 | 22359
0.9 | 0134689
0.8 | 2347
0.7 | 01247788
0.6 | 001111248
0.5 | 02333345799
0.4 | 012233344457889
0.3 | 011122222344455667788999
0.2 | 0122344456677889999
0.1 | 000111122224455689
0.0 | 0000000000000000000000001222344566678889999
-0.0 | 88866443311
-0.1 | 88732
-0.2 | 9540
-0.3 | 421
-0.4 |
-0.5 | 6
-0.6 |
-0.7 |
-0.8 | 9
-0.9 |
-1.0 | 2
```

Figure 19.3. Stem-and-leaf plot of effect sizes rounded to two decimal places. Each effect size is grouped according to its membership in categories defined by the stem, which in this plot is the two digits to the left of the line, ordered from largest at the top to smallest (i.e., largest negative value) at the bottom. Along the stems, each effect size appears as a single leaf digit on the right side of the line, ordered from smallest to largest. In this plot, the first three effect sizes are 1.81, 1.89, and 1.65.

effect sizes from the same groups of participants increases the power of the overall homogeneity test, Q; therefore, the likelihood of rejecting the hypothesis of homogeneity would increase.

Despite these concerns, multiply representing studies may be defensible to address certain meta-analytic questions. For example, an analyst may be interested in whether an effect generalizes across various types of measures of a dependent variable. In such a case, the analyst could examine a model to determine if the effect sizes differed according to the type of measure used. If the synthesis forgoes this analysis to uphold the assumption that effect sizes are independent, potentially valuable information about a moderator would be lost. Therefore, one defensible strategy is to conduct a two-stage meta-analysis that shifts its units of analysis (Cooper, 1998). In the first stage, the meta-analysis would address the study-level effect sizes, which are calculated to represent the information

from each study only once. A second stage would divide study outcomes into the various groupings specified by moderators and would permit information for a group of study participants to appear more than once, in order to examine the differences across the moderator (for examples of this strategy, see Gerrard, Gibbons, & Bushman, 1996; Kite & Johnson, 1988; Kolodziej & Johnson, 1996). This ordering of the stages assumes that analysts are usually interested in learning the overall, more general pattern in the literature first, prior to answering specific questions about moderators. This combination of approaches should help to allay concerns about nonindependence while still yielding the desired information. As yet another alternative, analysts might consider using multivariate procedures for the analysis of multiple effect sizes from each study (see Gleser & Olkin, 1994; Klaian & Raudenbush, 1996; for a general treatment of dependent data, see Kashy & Kenny, this volume, Ch. 17).

INTERPRETATIONS OF MEAN EFFECT SIZE INDEXES. Once a meta-analysis has derived a weighted mean effect size, it must be interpreted. If the mean effect is nonsignificant and the homogeneity statistic is small and nonsignificant, an analyst might conclude that there is no relation between the variables under consideration. However, in such cases, it is wise to consider the amount of statistical power that was available: If the total number of research participants in the studies integrated was small, it is possible that additional data would support the existence of the effect. Even if the mean effect is significant and the homogeneity statistic is small and nonsignificant, concerns about its magnitude arise. To address this issue, Cohen (1969, 1988) proposed some guidelines for judging effect magnitude, based on his informal analysis of the magnitude of effects commonly yielded by psychological research. Cohen intended "that medium represent an effect of a size likely to be visible to the naked eye of a careful observer" (Cohen, 1992, p. 156). He intended that small effect sizes be "noticeably smaller yet not trivial," (p. 156) and that large effect sizes "be the same distance above medium as small is below it" (p. 156). As Table 19.3 shows, a "medium" effect turned out to be about $d = 0.50$ and $r = .30$, equivalent to the difference in intelligence scores between clerical and semiskilled workers. A "small" effect size was about $d = 0.20$ and $r = .10$, equivalent to the difference in height between 15- and 16-year-old girls. Finally, a large effect was about $d = 0.80$ and $r = .50$, equivalent to the difference in intelligence scores between college professors and college freshmen. Although Cohen's guidelines for

TABLE 19.3. Cohen's (1969) Guidelines for Magnitude of d and r.

Size	Effect size metric		
	d	r	r^2
Small	0.20	.10	.01
Medium	0.50	.30	.09
Large	0.80	.50	.25

magnitude of effects are frequently cited, other ways of interpreting the magnitude of effects may prove more useful.

One popular way to interpret mean effect sizes is to derive the equivalent r and square it. This procedure shows how much variability would be explained by an effect of the magnitude of the mean effect size (see Table 19.3). Thus, a mean d of 0.50 produces an R^2 of .09. However, this value must be interpreted carefully because R^2, or variance explained, is a directionless effect size. Therefore, if the individual effect sizes that produced the mean effect size varied in their signs (i.e., the effect sizes were not all negative or all positive), the variance in Y explained by the predictor X, calculated for each study and averaged, would be larger than this simple transform of the mean effect size. Thus, another possible procedure consists of computing R^2 for each individual study and averaging these values, as Hyde (1981) did in a meta-analysis of sex-related differences in cognitive performance.

A number of methodologists have discussed the magnitude of effects and argued that even quantitatively small effects can be quite consequential (e.g., Abelson, 1985; Prentice & Miller, 1992; Rosenthal, 1990, 1994; Ross & Nisbett, 1991). Especially useful in understanding the meaning of small effects is Rosenthal and Rubin's (1982) binomial effect size display (BESD), which is defined as a difference in "success" rates between treatment and control groups. In other words, this index consists of the difference between the proportion of cases (or research participants) who are successful (e.g., pass a test) in the treatment group and the proportion who are successful in the control group.

The BESD can be obtained from r, the correlation between the independent and dependent variables, by computing the success rate in the treatment condition as .50 plus $r/2$ and in the control condition as .50 minus $r/2$. For example, an r of .20 yields a success rate in the treatment group of $.50 + .20/2 = .60$ and a success rate

in the control group of $.50 - .20/2 = .40$. Therefore, if the treatment and control groups each contained 100 individuals, 20 more people would survive in the treatment condition than in the control condition. Researchers who think about associations between variables in terms of the BESD are less likely to trivialize or dismiss small effects by saying, for example, that a correlation of .20 is "small" because it accounts for "only" 4% of the variance in the dependent variable. The BESD shows that, nonetheless, participants' "success rate" would be 20% higher in the treatment group.

The BESD is most easily implemented when researchers use status on a dichotomous independent variable (experimental vs. control group) to predict a dichotomous outcome, such as surviving versus not surviving or helping another person versus not helping. Nonetheless, this calculation can also be performed when the dependent variable is expressed in a continuous metric. In such circumstances, the researcher must dichotomize this variable at the median and thereby categorize participants as "below average" or "above average" on the dependent variable in question. For example, for a sex-related height difference of $d = 2.00$, the point-biserial r between sex and height would be .71. The probability of a man being above the "human" average (or "tall") would be roughly .85, and the probability of a woman being tall would be .14. The BESD would therefore be .61.

Offering another index for interpreting effect magnitude, McGraw and Wong (1992) defined their common language effect size statistic index (CL) as the probability that a score randomly sampled from one distribution will be larger than a score randomly sampled from another distribution. As McGraw and Wong explained, estimation of this index requires computation of the mean and standard deviation of the distribution of difference scores created by randomly comparing cases from the two distributions (e.g., male and female; treatment and control). CL is then the probability of obtaining a difference score greater than 0 in this distribution. This probability can be determined by converting the metric of raw difference scores to one of z-scores and consulting the normal curve (see Dunlap, 1994). For example, for a sex-related difference in height of $d = 2.00$, the CL, which is the probability that the man would be taller in any random pairing of a man and woman, is .92. As another example, the sex-related difference favoring males on the American College Test of math achievement, which can be expressed as a d of 0.48, translates into a CL of .63. That is, 63% of the time, a randomly sampled male will have higher achievement than a randomly sampled female.

In addition to the common language effect size statistic and the binomial effect size display, other helpful indexes for interpreting effect magnitude have been proposed (e.g., Cohen, 1988). These indexes include the *counternull* statistic, which is a nonnull effect size that is as probable as the null value, to which the effect size is ordinarily compared to establish its significance (see Rosenthal & Rubin, 1994).

To answer potential or actual critics' assertions that unpublished or unretrieved studies not present in the meta-analytic sample would invalidate or reverse the review's conclusions, analysts sometimes calculate the number of studies averaging a null effect that would be necessary to bring an overall meta-analytic mean to the point of nonsignificance (Rosenthal, 1979). If this fail safe N (N_{fs}) is large, then the meta-analytic result gains credibility; if it is small, then the result seems less trustworthy. For example, Rosenthal and Rubin (1978) calculated that it would take 65,123 studies averaging a null result in order to invalidate their observed experimenter expectancy effect. To calculate N_{fs},

$$N_{fs} = \frac{\left(\sum_{j=1}^{k} z_j\right)^2}{z_\alpha^2}, \qquad (32)$$

where k is the number of studies, z_j is the unit normal value corresponding to a one-tailed test of significance, and z_α is the critical value (i.e., 1.645 for a one-tailed hypothesis). Orwin (1983) offered a variant of this equation that estimates N_{fs} directly from the mean weighted effect size. Although N_{fs} may have heuristic value in some instances, there are cautions worth noting. The equation for N_{fs} assumes that unretrieved studies would average null when in fact they may have the same pattern as the retrieved studies or even a reversed pattern (Becker, 1994; Begg, 1994). Also, it is difficult to evaluate the magnitude of N_{fs}, because it has no distribution theory (Rosenthal, 1979, 1984).

Another method of interpreting the magnitude of effect sizes is to compare them with effect sizes in similar domains in which magnitude is already known. For example, Eagly (1995) argued that claims that sex-related differences in behavior are necessarily small should be evaluated in relation to the magnitude of other known effects in psychology. Following this strategy, Bettencourt and Miller (1996) compared the magnitude of sex-related differences in aggression to the magnitude of the effect of provocation on aggression; this comparison was especially relevant because the mean effect sizes were derived from the same sample of studies. More generally, meta-analysts ought to compare the magnitude of a newly derived meta-analytic effect size to the magnitude of known effects in related research areas. For example, Lipsey and Wilson (1993) gathered 302 meta-analyses of psychological, educational, and behavioral interventions and determined the typical effect size obtained in such interventions. Similarly, Johnson, Carey, and Muellerleile (1997) gathered meta-analytic tests of the impact of behavioral interventions for behaviors relevant to various public health problems and used fixed and random effects meta-analytic model tests to compare the mean effect sizes obtained in these different literatures. This "meta-meta-analysis" inferentially compared the magnitude of effects across various domains of behavioral interventions. Alliger (1995) described and compared several small-sample techniques for performing these sorts of comparisons.

Many aspects of studies' methods can constrain effect magnitude, as noted above (see *Correcting effect sizes for bias*). Effects are larger or smaller depending on factors such as reliability of measures, heterogeneity of the participant population, and so on. Some of these factors lend themselves to bias corrections, and the magnitude of the effect size that represents a study depends on whether corrections have been applied for such problems. In addition, characteristics of the situation in which experiments are carried out can increase or reduce the impact that experimental manipulations and individual-difference variables have on dependent variables (Prentice & Miller, 1992). Analysts should code the studies in their databases for the presence of a wide range of such factors, in order to account for effect size variance that is produced by studies' nonequivalence on such factors.

CONDUCTING AND EVALUATING QUANTITATIVE SYNTHESES

Our treatment of quantitative synthesis has stressed the importance of high standards in conducting and evaluating these reviews. The hallmarks of a high-quality meta-analysis include success in locating studies, explicitness of criteria for selecting studies, thoroughness and accuracy in coding moderators variables and other study characteristics, accuracy in effect size computations, and adherence to the assumptions of meta-analytic statistics. When research syntheses meet such standards, it is difficult to disagree with Rosenthal's (1994) conclusion that it is "hardly justified to review a quantitative literature in the pre-meta-analytic, pre-quantitative manner" (p. 131). However, even a quantitative review that meets high standards does not necessarily constitute an important scientific contribution.

One factor affecting the scientific contribution is that the conclusions that a research synthesis is able to reach are limited by the quality of the data that are synthesized. Serious methodological faults that are endemic in a research literature may well handicap a synthesis, unless it is designed to shed light on the influence of these faults. Also, to be regarded as important, the review must address an interesting question. Similarly, unless the paper reporting a meta-analysis "tells a good story," its full value may go unappreciated by readers. Although there are many paths to a good story, Sternberg's (1991) recommendations to authors of reviews are instructive: Pick interesting questions, challenge conventional understandings if at all possible, take a unified perspective on the phenomenon, offer a clear take-home message, and write well.

Some reports of research syntheses may fail to tell a good story because they are overly complex. This complexity may arise from the fact that quantitative synthesis forces the reviewer to study the minute details of the studies' methods and findings. Although this close scrutiny can yield valuable insights, it may also foster a review that reflects too many complexities and thereby obscures its major findings. Sharing our concern about excessive complexity, Rosenthal (1995) stated, "I have never seen a meta-analysis that was 'too simple,' but I have often seen meta-analyses that were very fancy and very much in error" (p. 183). In short, even if a synthesis happens to solve a time-honored problem, it will have a poor reception if its message is mired in a forest of distracting minutiae.

Although in practice most critiques of meta-analyses take a narrative form by discussing the methods and findings of a published synthesis, the most informative critiques take a quantitative approach by empirically evaluating the findings and conclusions. A critique that may seem reasonable based on sheer logic may become overwhelming when supported by the data. For example, if a critic reasons that the selection criteria of a meta-analysis are faulty, showing that the presumably superior criteria yield different results makes the argument much more compelling. Similarly, if a critic claims that a particular moderator in a meta-analysis was confounded with another variable that is genuinely causal, he or she should demonstrate that the confound is consequential to the results obtained (e.g., by conducting model tests showing how the findings change when the confound is controlled). In this manner, scientific disputes can be arbitrated by empirical tests. In primary research, the most influential critiques take the form of replications with variations – often showing how an effect disappears once a confound is controlled.

Similarly, criticism of quantitative syntheses proceeds most effectively in an empirical fashion. In our view, replications of meta-analytic reviews should become more frequent, so that faults that may be present in one review are evaluated or improved in later reviews.

With quantitative syntheses becoming commonplace, investigators should redouble their efforts to report the method and results of their primary-level studies as accurately and completely as possible. In particular, for experimental studies, a table of means and standard deviations for each primary dependent variable, reported for all cells of the design, should be conventional. It is very helpful if exact statistics are provided even for auxiliary effects that may be nonsignificant (e.g., the comparison of female and male participants). For correlational studies, a complete matrix of the variables' intercorrelations should be conventional.

ADDITIONAL RESOURCES ON RESEARCH SYNTHESIS

Essential reference works for quantitative synthesis are *The Handbook of Research Synthesis*, edited by Cooper and Hedges (1994b), as well as texts by Hedges and Olkin (1985), Cooper (1998), and Rosenthal (1991). Glass et al.'s (1981) book remains a good source on derivations of effect sizes. Hunt (1997) provides a compelling and highly readable history of the subject of research synthesis. Other works may be particularly valuable for other aspects of meta-analysis. In particular, Hunter and Schmidt's (1990) book provides an extensive treatment of effect size corrections. Mullen (1989) provided a well-rounded treatment of meta-analysis and includes software for many of the analyses he suggests. Schwarzer's (1989) software is in the public domain and contains many useful functions. Johnson's (1993) software is reasonably comprehensive and also includes much practical meta-analytic information (see Normand's, 1995, review of meta-analytic software).

THE FUTURE OF QUANTITATIVE SYNTHESES IN SOCIAL PSYCHOLOGY

The growing numbers of studies on social psychology's central phenomena dictate that, in the future, greater importance will be accorded to high-quality meta-analyses of these knowledge bases. Consumers of research, such as textbook authors, often express enthusiasm about meta-analytic contributions. The information-reduction benefits of quantitative reviews led one author of a social psychology textbook to write,

"I am not so much a critic or connoisseur of meta-analysis as an enthusiastic consumer" (D. G. Myers, 1991, p. 265). Yet, because meta-analysis is relatively new among scholars who practice it, the quality of published syntheses has been quite variable, and some have not been as informative as they might have been. In particular, some meta-analysts have not adequately searched for relevant studies and may have no greater claim to comprehensiveness than typical narrative reviewers. Also, meta-analyses that are confined to aggregating findings over studies fail to examine findings' homogeneity or to account for discrepancies between them. Such reviews inform their readers about the average direction and magnitude of an effect but not about its patterning. However, as the methods of quantitative synthesis have become more sophisticated and widely disseminated, typical published meta-analyses have improved. At their best, meta-analyses advance knowledge about a phenomenon by explicating its typical patterns and showing when it is larger or smaller, negative or positive, and test theories about the phenomenon (see N. Miller & Pollock, 1994).

Meta-analysis should foster a healthy interaction between primary research and research synthesis, at once summarizing old research and suggesting promising directions for new research. One misperception that psychologists sometimes express is that a meta-analysis represents a dead end for a literature, a point beyond which nothing more needs to be known. In contrast, we assert that carefully conducted meta-analyses can often be the best medicine for a literature, by documenting the robustness with which certain associations are attained, resulting in a sturdier foundation on which future theories may rest. In addition, meta-analyses can show where knowledge is at its thinnest, to help plan additional, primary-level research (see Eagly & Wood, 1994). As a consequence of a carefully conducted meta-analysis, primary-level studies can be designed with the complete literature in mind and therefore have a better chance of contributing new knowledge. In this fashion, scientific resources can be directed most efficiently toward gains in knowledge.

The advent of computerized and readily accessible databases of psychological research literatures (e.g., PsycINFO) has meant that less time and financial resources are necessary to conduct meta-analyses. Whereas past reviewers had to spend endless hours examining entries in print volumes of *Psychological Abstracts*, modern meta-analysts are able to quickly generate lists of studies that may be suitable for their reviews. Despite these gains, psychologists face severe limitations in obtaining access to the data underlying completed research. In contrast to some other scientific fields (e.g., sociology, political science), few raw data from primary research are archived in psychology, and this omission greatly limits the opportunity for reviewers to perform the secondary analyses that in some cases are necessary for calculating effect sizes for effects that have not been adequately reported. Primary researchers are often unable or unwilling to provide needed statistical information when they are contacted directly. Routine data archiving in a central location would remedy this unfortunate situation (see Cooper et al., 1997).

As time passes, psychologists and other scientists will rely more on quantitative syntheses to inform them about the knowledge that has accumulated in their research. Although it is possible that meta-analysis will become the purview of an elite class of researchers who specialize in research integration, as Schmidt (1992) argued, we believe that, on the contrary, meta-analysis will become a routine part of graduate training in many fields. With computer programs to aid calculations, most researchers should be able to integrate findings across studies as a normal and routine part of their research activities. Therefore, in the future, a substantial proportion of investigators in many fields will ply the art and science of research synthesis.

REFERENCES

Abelson, R. P. (1985). A variance explanation paradox: When a little is a lot. *Psychological Bulletin, 97*, 129–133.

Aguinis, H., & Pierce, C. A. (1998). Testing moderator variable hypotheses meta-analytically. *Journal of Management, 24*, 577–592.

Alliger, G. M. (1995). The small sample performance of four tests of the difference between pairs of meta-analytically derived effect sizes. *Journal of Management, 21*, 789–799.

Becker, B. J. (1987). Applying tests of combined significance in meta-analysis. *Psychological Bulletin, 102*, 164–171.

Becker, B. J. (1994). Combining significance levels. In H. Cooper & L. V. Hedges (Eds.), *The handbook of research synthesis* (pp. 215–230). New York: Russell Sage.

Begg, C. B. (1994). Publication bias. In H. Cooper & L. V. Hedges (Eds.), *The handbook of research synthesis* (pp. 399–409). New York: Russell Sage.

Bettencourt, B. A., & Miller, N. (1996). Gender differences in aggression as a function of provocation: A meta-analysis. *Psychological Bulletin, 119*, 422–447.

Birge, R. T. (1932). The calculation of errors by the method of least squares. *Physical Review, 40*, 207–227.

Bond, C. F., Jr., & Titus, L. J. (1983). Social facilitation: A meta-analysis of 241 studies. *Psychological Bulletin, 94*, 265–292.

Bond, R., & Smith, P. B. (1996). Culture and conformity: A meta-analysis of studies using Asch's (1952b, 1956) line judgment task. *Psychological Bulletin, 119*, 111–137.

Bornstein, R. F. (1989). Exposure and affect: Overview and meta-analysis of research, 1968–1987. *Psychological Bulletin, 106*, 265–289.

Brubaker, T. H., & Powers, E. A. (1976). The stereotype of "old": A review and alternative approach. *Journal of Gerontology, 31*, 441–447.

Bushman, B. J. (1994). Vote-counting procedures in meta-analysis. In H. Cooper & L. V. Hedges (Eds.), *The handbook of research synthesis* (pp. 193–213). New York: Russell Sage.

Bushman, B. J., & Wang, M. C. (1996). A procedure for combining sample standardized mean differences and vote counts to estimate the population standardized mean difference in fixed effects models. *Psychological Methods, 1*, 66–80.

Campbell D. T., & Stanley, J. T. (1963). *Experimental and quasi-experimental designs for research*. Chicago: Rand-McNally.

Carroll, J. B. (1961). The nature of the data, or how to choose a correlation coefficient. *Psychometrica, 26*, 347–372.

Cochran, W. G. (1937). Problems arising in the analysis of a series of experiments. *Journal of the Royal Statistical Society* (Suppl.), *4*, 102–118.

Cohen, J. (1960). Coefficient of agreement for nominal scales. *Educational and Psychological Measurement, 20*, 37–46.

Cohen, J. (1969). *Statistical power analysis for the behavioral sciences*. New York: Academic Press.

Cohen, J. (1988). *Statistical power analysis for the behavioral sciences* (2nd ed.). Hillsdale, NJ: Erlbaum.

Cohen, J. (1992). A power primer. *Psychological Bulletin, 112*, 155–159.

Cohen, J., & Cohen, P. (1983). *Applied multiple regression/correlation analysis for the behavioral sciences* (2nd ed.). Hillsdale, NJ: Erlbaum.

Cook, T. D., & Campbell, D. T. (1979). *Quasi-experimentation: Design and analysis issues for field settings*. Boston: Houghton Mifflin.

Cooper, H. (1979). Statistically combining independent studies: Meta-analysis of sex differences in conformity research. *Journal of Personality and Social Psychology, 37*, 131–146.

Cooper, H. (1982). Scientific guidelines for conducting integrative research reviews. *Review of Educational Research, 52*, 291–302.

Cooper, H. (1998). *Integrative research: A guide for literature reviews* (3rd ed.). Newbury Park, CA: Sage.

Cooper, H., DeNeve, K., & Charlton, K. (1997). Finding the missing science: The fate of studies submitted for review by a human subjects committee. *Psychological Methods, 2*, 447–452.

Cooper, H., & Hedges, L. V. (Eds.). (1994a). *The handbook of research synthesis*. New York: Russell Sage.

Cooper, H., & Hedges, L. V. (1994b). Research synthesis as a scientific enterprise. In H. Cooper & L. V. Hedges (Eds.), *The handbook of research synthesis* (pp. 3–14). New York: Russell Sage.

Cooper, H., & Rosenthal, R. (1980). Statistical versus traditional procedures for summarizing research findings. *Psychological Bulletin, 87*, 442–449.

Cronbach, L. J. (1990). *Essentials of psychological testing* (5th ed.). New York: Harper Collins.

Dickerson, K. (1997). How important is publication bias? A synthesis of available data. *AIDS Education and Prevention, 9* (Suppl. A), 15–21.

Driskell, J. E., & Mullen, B. (1990). Status, expectations, and behavior: A meta-analytic review and test of the theory. *Personality and Social Psychology Bulletin, 16*, 541–553.

Dunlap, W. P. (1994). Generalizing the common language effect size indicator to bivariate normal correlations. *Psychological Bulletin, 116*, 509–511.

Dunlap, W. P., Cortina, J. M., Vaslow, J. B., & Burke, M. J. (1996). Meta-analysis of experiments with matched groups or repeated measures designs. *Psychological Methods, 1*, 170–177.

Eagly, A. H. (1987). *Sex differences in social behavior: A social-role interpretation*. Hillsdale, NJ: Erlbaum.

Eagly, A. H. (1995). The science and politics of comparing women and men. *American Psychologist, 50*, 145–158.

Eagly, A. H., Ashmore, R. D., Makhijani, M. G., & Longo, L. C. (1991). What is beautiful is good, but . . .: A meta-analytic review of research on the physical attractiveness stereotype. *Psychological Bulletin, 110*, 109–128.

Eagly, A. H., & Crowley, M. (1986). Gender and helping behavior: A meta-analytic review of the social psychological literature. *Psychological Bulletin, 100*, 283–308.

Eagly, A. H., & Johnson, B. T. (1990). Gender and leadership style: A meta-analysis. *Psychological Bulletin, 108*, 233–256.

Eagly, A. H., Karau, S., & Makhijani, M. G. (1995). Gender and the effectiveness of leaders: A meta-analysis. *Psychological Bulletin, 117*, 125–145.

Eagly, A. H., Makhijani, M. G., & Klonsky, B. G. (1992). Gender and the evaluation of leaders: A meta-analysis. *Psychological Bulletin, 111*, 3–22.

Eagly, A. H., & Steffen, V. J. (1986). Gender and aggressive behavior: A meta-analytic review of the social psychological literature. *Psychological Bulletin, 100*, 309–330.

Eagly, A. H., & Wood, W. (1994). Using research syntheses to plan future research. In H. Cooper & L. V. Hedges (Eds.), *The handbook of research synthesis* (pp. 485–500). New York: Russell Sage.

Ernst, C., & Angst, J. (1983). *Birth order: Its influence on personality*. New York: Springer-Verlag.

Feingold, A. (1995). The additive effects of differences in central tendency and variability are important in comparisons between groups. *American Psychologist, 50*, 5–13.

Fisher, R. A. (1921). On the "probable error" of a coefficient of correlation deduced from a small sample. *Metron, 1*, 1–32.

Fisher, R. A. (1932). *Statistical methods for research workers* (4th ed.). London: Oliver and Boyd.

Gerrard, M., Gibbons, F. X., & Bushman, B. J. (1996). Relation between perceived vulnerability to HIV and precautionary sexual behavior. *Psychological Bulletin, 119,* 390–409.

Glass, G. V. (1976). Primary, secondary, and meta-analysis of research. *Educational Researcher, 5,* 3–8.

Glass, G. V., McGaw, B., & Smith, M. L. (1981). *Meta-analysis in social research.* Beverly Hills, CA: Sage.

Gleser, L. J., & Olkin, I. (1994). Stochastically dependent effect sizes. In H. Cooper & L. V. Hedges (Eds.), *The handbook of research synthesis* (pp. 339–355). New York: Russell Sage.

Gordon, R. A. (1996). The impact of ingratiation on judgments and evaluations: A meta-analytic investigation. *Journal of Personality and Social Psychology, 71,* 54–70.

Green, S. K. (1981). Attitudes and perceptions about the elderly: Current and future perspectives. *International Journal of Aging and Human Development, 13,* 99–119.

Greenhouse, J. B., & Iyengar, S. (1994). Sensitivity analysis and diagnostics. In H. Cooper & L. V. Hedges (Eds.), *The handbook of research synthesis* (pp. 383–398). New York: Russell Sage.

Greenwald, A. G. (1975). Consequences of prejudice against the null hypothesis. *Psychological Bulletin, 82,* 1–20.

Greenwald, S., & Russell, R. I. (1991). Assessing rationales for inclusiveness in meta-analytic samples. *Psychotherapy Research, 1,* 17–24.

Hall, J. A. (1978). Gender effects in decoding nonverbal cues. *Psychological Bulletin, 85,* 845–857.

Hardy, M. A. (1993). *Regression with dummy variables.* Newbury Park, CA: Sage.

Hays, W. L. (1988). *Statistics* (4th ed.). Fort Worth, TX: Harcourt Brace Jovanovich.

Hedges, L. V. (1981). Distribution theory for Glass's estimator of effect size and related estimators. *Journal of Educational Statistics, 6,* 107–128.

Hedges, L. V. (1982a). Fitting categorical models to effect sizes from a series of experiments. *Journal of Educational Statistics, 7,* 119–137.

Hedges, L. V. (1982b). Fitting continuous models to effect size data. *Journal of Educational Statistics, 7,* 245–270.

Hedges, L. V. (1987). How hard is hard science, how soft is soft science? The empirical cumulativeness of research. *American Psychologist, 42,* 443–455.

Hedges, L. V. (1990). Directions for future methodology. In K. W. Wachter & M. L. Straf (Eds.), *The future of meta-analysis* (pp. 11–26). New York: Russell Sage.

Hedges, L. V. (1994). Statistical considerations. In H. Cooper & L. V. Hedges (Eds.), *The handbook of research synthesis* (pp. 29–38). New York: Russell Sage.

Hedges, L. V., & Becker, B. J. (1986). Statistical methods in the meta-analysis of research on gender differences. In J. S. Hyde & M. C. Linn (Eds.), *The psychology of gender: Advances through meta-analysis* (pp. 14–50). Baltimore, MD: Johns Hopkins University Press.

Hedges, L. V., Cooper, H., & Bushman, B. J. (1992). Testing the null hypothesis in meta-analysis: A comparison of combined probability and confidence interval procedures. *Psychological Bulletin, 111,* 188–194.

Hedges, L. V., & Friedman, L. (1993). Computing gender differences in the tails of distributions: The consequences of differences in tail size, effect size, and variance ratio. *Review of Educational Research, 63,* 110–112.

Hedges, L. V., & Olkin, I. (1985). *Statistical methods for meta-analysis.* Orlando, FL: Academic Press.

Hedges, L. V., & Vevea, J. L. (1998). Fixed- and random-effects models in meta-analysis. *Psychological Methods, 3,* 486–504.

Heinsman, D. T., & Shadish, W. R. (1996). Assignment methods in experimentation: When do nonrandomized experiments approximate answers from randomized experiments? *Psychological Methods, 1,* 154–169.

Hunt, M. (1997). *How science takes stock: The story of meta-analysis.* New York: Russell Sage.

Hunter, J. E., & Schmidt, F. L. (1990). *Methods of meta-analysis: Correcting error and bias in research findings.* Newbury Park, CA: Sage.

Hunter, J. E., & Schmidt, F. L. (1994). Correcting for sources of artificial variation across studies. In H. Cooper & L. V. Hedges (Eds.), *The handbook of research synthesis* (pp. 323–336). New York: Russell Sage.

Hunter, J. E., & Schmidt, F. L. (1997). *Type I error in the fixed effects formulas for meta-analysis.* Manuscript submitted for publication.

Hunter, J. E., Schmidt, F. L., & Hunter, R. (1979). Differential validity of employment tests by race: A comprehensive review and analysis. *Psychological Bulletin, 31,* 215–232.

Hyde, J. S. (1981). How large are cognitive gender differences? A meta-analysis using ω^2 and d. *American Psychologist, 36,* 892–901.

Johnson, B. T. (1993). *DSTAT 1.10: Software for the meta-analytic review of research literatures.* Hillsdale, NJ: Erlbaum.

Johnson, B. T., Carey, M. P., & Muellerleile, P. A. (1997). Large trials vs meta-analysis of smaller trials [Letter to the editor]. *Journal of the American Medical Association, 277,* 377.

Johnson, B. T., & Eagly, A. H. (1989). Effects of involvement on persuasion: A meta-analysis. *Psychological Bulletin, 104,* 290–314.

Johnson, B. T., Mullen, B., & Salas, E. (1995). Comparison of three major meta-analytic approaches. *Journal of Applied Psychology, 80,* 94–106.

Johnson, B. T., & Turco, R. (1992). The value of goodness-of-fit indices in meta-analysis: A comment on Hall and Rosenthal. *Communication Monographs, 59,* 388–396.

Kalaian, H. A., & Raudenbush, S. W., (1996). A multivariate mixed linear model for meta-analysis. *Psychological Methods, 1,* 227–235.

Karau, S. J., & Williams, K. D. (1993). Social loafing: A meta-analytic review and theoretical integration. *Journal of Personality and Social Psychology, 65,* 681–706.

Kite, M. E., & Johnson, B. T. (1988). Attitudes toward the elderly: A meta-analysis. *Psychology and Aging, 3*, 233–244.

Kite, M. E., & Whitley, B. E. (1996). Sex differences in attitudes toward homosexual persons, behaviors, and civil rights: A meta-analysis. *Personality and Social Psychology Bulletin, 22*, 336–353.

Knight, G. P., Fabes, R. A., & Higgins, D. A. (1996). Concerns about drawing causal inferences from meta-analyses: An example in the study of gender differences in aggression. *Psychological Bulletin, 119*, 410–421.

Kolodziej, M. E., & Johnson, B. T. (1996). Effects of interpersonal contact on acceptance of individuals diagnosed with mentally illness: A research synthesis. *Journal of Consulting and Clinical Psychology, 64*, 1387–1396.

Langenbucher, J., Labouvie, E., & Morgenstern, J. (1996). Measuring diagnostic agreement. *Journal of Consulting and Clinical Psychology, 64*, 1285–1289.

Light, R. J., & Pillemer, D. B. (1984). *Summing up: The science of reviewing research*. Cambridge, MA: Harvard University Press.

Light, R. J., Singer, J. D., & Willett, J. B. (1994). The visual presentation and interpretation of meta-analyses. In H. Cooper & L. V. Hedges (Eds.), *The handbook of research synthesis* (pp. 439–454). New York: Russell Sage.

Lipsey, M. W. (1994). Identifying potentially interesting variables and analysis opportunities. In H. Cooper & L. V. Hedges (Eds.), *The handbook of research synthesis* (pp. 111–138). New York: Russell Sage.

Lipsey, M. W., & Wilson, D. B. (1993) The efficacy of psychological, educational, and behavioral treatment: Confirmation from meta-analysis. *American Psychologist, 48*, 1181–1209.

Lutsky, N. (1981). Attitudes toward old age and elderly persons. In C. Eisdorfer (Ed.), *Annual Review of Gerontology and Geriatrics* (Vol. 1, pp. 287–336). New York: Springer.

Mann, C. C. (1994, November). Can meta-analysis make policy? *Science, 266*, 960–962.

McGraw, K. O., & Wong, S. P. (1992). A common language effect size statistic. *Psychological Bulletin, 111*, 361–365.

Miller, A. G. (1972). Role playing: An alternative to deception? *American Psychologist, 27*, 623–636.

Miller, N., & Carlson, M. (1990). Valid theory-testing meta-analyses further question the negative state relief model of helping. *Psychological Bulletin, 107*, 215–225.

Miller, N., & Cooper, H. M. (Eds.). (1991). Special issue: Meta-analysis in personality and social psychology. *Personality and Social Psychology Bulletin, 17*, 243–349.

Miller, N., Lee, J. Y., & Carlson, M. (1991). The validity of inferential judgment when used in theory-testing meta-analyses. *Personality and Social Psychology Bulletin, 17*, 335–343.

Miller, N., & Pollock, V. E. (1994). Meta-analysis and some science-compromising problems of social psychology. In W. R. Shadish & S. Fuller (Eds.), *The social psychology of science* (pp. 230–261). New York: Guilford Press.

Morris, S. B., & DeShon, R. P. (1997). Correcting effect sizes computed from factorial analysis of variance for use in meta-analysis. *Psychological Methods, 2*, 192–199.

Morrison, D. F. (1976). *Multivariate statistical methods*. New York: McGraw-Hill.

Mullen, B. (1989). *Advanced BASIC meta-analysis: Procedures and programs*. Hillsdale, NJ: Erlbaum.

Mullen, B., & Copper, C. (1994). The relation between group cohesiveness and performance: An integration. *Psychological Bulletin, 115*, 210–227.

Mullen, B., & Felleman, V. (1989). Tripling in the dorms: A meta-analytic integration. *Basic and Applied Social Psychology, 11*, 33–43.

Myers, D. G. (1991). Union is strength: A consumer's view of meta-analysis. *Personality and Social Psychology Bulletin, 17*, 265–266.

Myers, J. L., & Well, A. D. (1991). *Research design and statistical analysis*. New York: Harper Collins.

Normand, S. (1995) Meta-analysis software: A comparative review. *American Statistician, 49*, 298–309.

Nouri, H., & Greenberg, R. H. (1995). Meta-analytic procedures for estimation of effect sizes in experiments using complex analysis of variance. *Journal of Management, 21*, 801–812.

Oliver, M. B., & Hyde, J. S. (1993). Gender differences in sexuality: A meta-analysis. *Psychological Bulletin, 114*, 29–51.

Orwin, R. G. (1983). A fail-safe *N* for effect size in meta-analysis. *Journal of Educational Statistics, 8*, 157–159.

Orwin, R. G. (1994). Evaluating coding decisions. In H. Cooper & L. V. Hedges (Eds.), *The handbook of research synthesis* (pp.139–162). New York: Russell Sage.

Overton, R. C. (1998). A comparison of fixed-effects and mixed (random-effects) models for meta-analysis tests of moderator variable effects. *Psychological Methods, 3*, 354–379.

Pearson, K. (1933). On a method of determining whether a sample size *n* supposed to have been drawn from a parent population having a known probability integral has probably been drawn at random. *Biometrika, 25*, 379–410.

Prentice, D., & Miller, D. T. (1992). When small effects are impressive. *Psychological Bulletin, 112*, 160–164.

Raudenbush, S. W. (1994). Random effects models. In H. Cooper & L. V. Hedges (Eds.), *The handbook of research synthesis* (pp. 301–321). New York: Russell Sage.

Ray, J. W., & Shadish, W. R. (1996). How interchangeable are different estimators of effect size? *Journal of Consulting and Clinical Psychology, 64*, 1316–1325.

Rhodes, N., & Wood, W. (1992). Self-esteem and intelligence affect influenceability: The mediating role of message reception. *Psychological Bulletin, 111*, 156–171.

Rosenthal, R. (1968). Experimenter expectancy and the reassuring nature of the null hypothesis decision procedure. *Psychological Bulletin, 70* (6, Pt. 2), 30–47.

Rosenthal, R. (1979). The "file drawer problem" and tolerance for null results. *Psychological Bulletin, 86*, 638–641.

Rosenthal, R. (1984). *Meta-analytic procedures for social research*. Beverly Hills, CA: Sage.

Rosenthal, R. (1990). How are we doing in soft psychology? *American Psychologist, 45*, 775–777.

Rosenthal, R. (1991). *Meta-analytic procedures for social research* (rev. ed.). Beverly Hills, CA: Sage.

Rosenthal, R. (1994). Parametric measures of effect size. In H. Cooper & L. V. Hedges (Eds.), *The handbook of research synthesis* (pp. 231–244). New York: Russell Sage.

Rosenthal, R. (1995). Writing meta-analytic reviews. *Psychological Bulletin, 118*, 183–192.

Rosenthal, R., & Rosnow, R. L. (1985). *Contrast analysis: Focused comparisons in the analysis of variance*. New York: Cambridge University Press.

Rosenthal, R., & Rubin, D. (1978). Interpersonal expectancy effects: The first 345 studies. *Behavioral and Brain Sciences, 3*, 377–415.

Rosenthal, R., & Rubin, D. B. (1982). Comparing effect sizes of independent studies. *Psychological Bulletin, 92*, 500–504.

Rosenthal, R., & Rubin, D. (1986). Meta-analytic procedures for combining studies with multiple effect sizes. *Psychological Bulletin, 99*, 400–406.

Rosenthal, R., & Rubin, D. B. (1994). The counternull value of an effect size: A new statistic. *Psychological Science, 5*, 329–334.

Ross, L., & Nisbett, R. (1991). *The person and the situation: Perspectives of social psychology*. New York: McGraw-Hill.

Rotton, J., Foos, P. W., Van Meek, L., & Levitt, M. (1995). Publication practices and the file drawer problem: A survey of published authors. *Journal of Social Behavior and Personality, 10*, 1–13.

Sánchez-Meca, J., & Marín-Martínez, F. (1997). Homogeneity tests in meta-analysis: A Monte-Carlo comparison of statistical power and Type I error. *Quality & Quantity, 31*, 385–399.

Schmidt, F. L. (1992). What do data really mean? Research findings, meta-analysis, and cumulative knowledge in psychology. *American Psychologist, 47*, 1173–1181.

Schmidt, F. L. (1996). Statistical significance testing and cumulative knowledge in psychology: Implications for training of researchers. *Psychological Methods, 1*, 115–129.

Schmidt, F. L., & Hunter, J. E. (1996). Measurement error in psychological research: Lessons from 26 research scenarios. *Psychological Methods, 1*, 199–223.

Schooler, C. (1972). Birth order effects: Not here, not now! *Psychological Bulletin, 78*, 161–175.

Schwarzer, R. (1989). *Meta-analysis programs* [Computer software]. Institut für Psychologie (WE 7), Frei Universität Berlin, Berlin, Germany: Author.

Shadish, W. R. (1996). Meta-analysis and the exploration of causal mediating processes: A primer of examples, methods, and issues. *Psychological Methods, 1*, 47–65.

Shadish, W. R., Doherty, M., & Montgomery, L. M. (1989). How many studies are in the file drawer? An estimate from the family/martial psychotherapy literature. *Clinical Psychology Review, 9*, 589–603.

Sheppard, B. H., Hartwick, J., & Warshaw, P. R. (1988). The theory of reasoned action: A meta-analysis of past research with recommendations for modifications and future research. *Journal of Consumer Research, 15*, 325–343.

Snedecor, G. W., & Cochran, W. G. (1980). *Statistical methods* (7th ed.). Ames: Iowa State University Press.

Sommer, B. (1987). The file drawer effect and publication rates in menstrual cycle research. *Psychology of Women Quarterly, 11*, 233–242.

Stangor, C., & McMillan, D. (1992). Memory for expectancy-congruent and expectancy-incongruent information: A review of the social and social developmental literature. *Psychological Bulletin, 111*, 42–61.

Sternberg, R. J. (1991). Editorial. *Psychological Bulletin, 109*, 3–4.

Stigler, S. M. (1986). *History of statistics: The measurement of uncertainty before 1900*. Cambridge, MA: Harvard University Press.

Stock, W. A. (1994). Systematic coding for research synthesis. In H. Cooper & L. V. Hedges (Eds.), *The handbook of research synthesis* (pp. 125–138). New York: Russell Sage.

Sulloway, F. H. (1996). *Born to rebel: Birth order, family dynamics, and creative lives*. New York: Pantheon Books.

Symons, C. S., & Johnson, B. T. (1997). The self-reference effect in memory: A meta-analysis. *Psychological Bulletin, 121*, 371–394.

Tabachnick, B. G., & Fidell, L. S. (1996). *Using multivariate statistics* (3rd ed.). New York: Harper Collins.

Thacker, S. B. (1988). Meta-analysis: A quantitative approach to research integration. *Journal of the American Medical Association, 259*, 1685–1689.

Timm, N. H. (1975). *Multivariate analysis, with applications in education and psychology*. Belmont, CA: Brooks-Cole.

Toothaker, L. E. (1991). *Multiple comparisons for researchers*. Newbury Park, CA: Sage.

Tukey, J. W. (1977). *Exploratory data analysis*. Reading, MA: Addison-Wesley.

Wachter, K. W., & Straf, M. L. (Eds.). (1990). *The future of meta-analysis*. New York: Russell Sage.

Wanous, J. P., Sullivan, S. E., & Malinak, J. (1989). The role of judgment calls in meta-analysis. *Journal of Applied Psychology, 74*, 259–264.

White, H. D. (1994). Scientific communication and literature retrieval. In H. Cooper & L. V. Hedges (Eds.), *The handbook of research synthesis* (pp. 41–55). New York: Russell Sage.

Whitley, B. E., Jr., & Kite, M. E. (1995). Gender differences in attitudes toward homosexuality: A comment on Oliver and Hyde. *Psychological Bulletin, 117*, 146–154.

Wicker, A. W. (1969). Attitude versus actions: The relationship of verbal and overt behavioral responses to attitude objects. *Journal of Social Issues, 25*(4), 41–78.

Winer, B. J., Brown, D. R., & Michels, K. (1991). *Statistical principles in experimental design* (3rd ed.). New York: McGraw-Hill.

Wood, W. (1987). Meta-analytic review of sex differences in group performance. *Psychological Bulletin, 102,* 53–71.

Wood, W., Lundgren, S., Ouellette, J. A., Busceme, S., & Blackstone, T. (1994). Minority influence: A meta-analytic review of social influence processes. *Psychological Bulletin, 115,* 323–345.

Wood, W., Rhodes, N., & Whelan, M. (1989). Sex differences in positive well-being: A consideration of emotional style and marital status. *Psychological Bulletin, 106,* 249–264.

Wortman, P. M. (1994). Judging research quality. In H. Cooper & L. V. Hedges (Eds.), *The handbook of research synthesis* (pp. 97–110). New York: Russell Sage.

Yates, F., & Cochran, W. G. (1938). The analysis of groups of experiments. *Journal of Agricultural Science, 28,* 556–580.

Author Index

Subject Index

negotiation episode, 142, 148, 150, 151–152
NEO-PI-R, 347, 348
nested factors, 22, 28, 30
nested models, 421, 423–424
neural processes, 122
New Look movement, 254, 255, 257, 258
next-in-line effect, 270
nodes, 175
nominal group technique, 181–182, 183
nonadvocacy models, 103, 105, 106–107
nonattitude, 240
noncausal hypotheses, 412, 413–432
nonconscious processes, 256, 267
nondifferentiation, 238–239
non-equivalent control group design, 26
  analysis of covariance, 70
  applications, 68–69
  causal inferences, 75–76
  covariate selection, 69–70
  econometric selection models, 71
  enhancements, 74–75
  equating groups, 69, 71–73
  gain score analysis, 70–71
  history threats, 73, 76–77
  instrumentation, 74, 76–77
  internal validity, 73–74, 75
  matching treatment and control groups, 71–73
  maturation differentials, 73, 76–77
  multiple control groups, 74
  non-equivalent dependent variables, 74
  pattern of results, 75
  pretests, 74–75
  principles, 68
  statistical adjustment techniques, 70–71
  statistical power, 75
  statistical regression threats, 73–74, 75, 76–77
  unreliability corrections, 70
non-experimental design, 17, 26, 412–413, 435
nonhierarchical cluster analysis, 431
nonindependence, 27–28, 29, 49, 382, 396, 452, 453–461
Non-Normed Fit Index, 422
nonparametric statistics, 405
nonresponse error, 225, 233–235
norm adjustment parameter, 103
normal distribution, 393, 394–397, 398, 405
normed fit index, 106
norm-references framework, 153
note-taking, 291, 305
no-treatment control series, 66
novelty effect, 103

NUDIST, 326
null effects, 23–24
null hypothesis significance testing, 45–45, 55, 57, 458–459
null model, 422

O

obedience paradigm, 161, 163
oblique rotations, 415, 417, 418, 432
observations, 356, *see also* Systematic behavioral observation
  adjacent, 65
  independence of, 382
  nonparticipant, 168, 169
  participant, 168, 170
odds ratio, 154, 155
omnibus test, 376–377
operationalization, 6–10, 17
opinion updating, 88
opposition paradigm, 277
optimal design, 34
orbicularis oris EMG, 133, 134
order condition, 420
order effects, 29, 430
ordinal interactions, 24
ordinal scales, 140
ordinary least squares, 212
orthoblique rotations, 417
orthogonal rotations, 417, 432
outcome
  codes, 142–143
  measures, 453–469
  scores, nonindependence in, 453–456
  variables, 73
outliers, 275–276, 393, 396, 397–398, 400, 407–409, 410, 517
oversampling, 231

P

pairwise interjudge correlation, 343
panel surveys, 226–228
paradigms, small-group, 161–162
parafoveal processing, 260–262
parallel analysis, 342, 416, 418, 425
parallel distributed processing connectionist architecture, 91
parallel-form reliability, 343
parameter
  defined, 96
  nesting, 423
  selection processes, 93
parametric experiments, 57
parsimony, model, 415–416, 418, 422, 423, 424, 441
participants, 18; *see also* control participants
  assignment rules, 61, 62, 63
  coded semi-structured interviews, 289
  college students, 11, 40, 224, 246

compliance issues, 50–52, 62, 207, 208
  difficult, 305–306
  dissemination of findings to, 308
  eliminating, 50–51
  event-sampling research issues, 207–209
  exploitation of, 307–308
  external validity and, 10–11
  incentives for, 8, 10
  isolation of, 48
  loss at posttest measurement, 52–53
  multiple groups, 36
  as observers, 168, 170
  as random factor, 10, 19–20
  recordkeeping effects on, 208–209
  selection issues, 61–62
  treatment noncompliers, 50
participation hierarchy, 102–103, 104, 107
partner effect, 462, 463–466, 467, 471, 473
passive contextual effects, 255
passive observational design, 17
path analysis, 204
peak-end rule, 194, 196
Pearson product-moment correlation coefficient, 155, 297, 342, 343, 454
Peer Attachment Interview (PAI), 286, 287, 295, 296, 304, 305
peer ratings, 355
perceptual experience, 254–255
periodicity problem, 231
permutation tests, 153
person memory task, 91
personality of group members, 168, 172
Personality Research Form, 364
personality theory and assessment, 317–318
persuasion, likelihood model of, 32
phi coefficient, 155
photoplethysmograph, 124
physiological response signals, 123
physiological toughness theory, 128
pilot studies, 292, 293, 296
pituitary-adrenocortical activity, 127
plausibility, 415–416
poetic structure, 329
Poisson distribution, 409
polarization effects, 133
polygraph, 117, 124
population, survey, 230, 244
postintervention series, 67–68
power transformations, 406, 409
predictor variables, 4
preference updates, 103
preintervention series, 67–68
pretest–posttest control group design, 125–126

DATE DUE

FEB 1 0 2011	
FEB 1 0 2012	
JAN 0 2 2012	
FEB 1 0 2012	

BRODART, CO.   Cat. No. 23-221